HANDBOOK OF RESEARCH
ON THE EDUCATION OF YOUNG CHILDREN

HANDBOOK OF RESEARCH
ON
THE EDUCATION
OF YOUNG CHILDREN

EDITED BY
Bernard Spodek

MACMILLAN PUBLISHING COMPANY
New York
Maxwell Macmillan Canada
Toronto
Maxwell Macmillan International
New York   Oxford   Singapore   Sydney

Macmillan Publishing Company   Maxwell Macmillan Canada, Inc.
A Division of Macmillan, Inc.   1200 Eglinton Avenue East, Suite 200
866 Third Avenue   Don Mills, Ontario M3C 3N1
New York, NY 10022

Macmillan Publishing Company is part of the Maxwell Communication Group of Companies

Library of Congress Catalog Card Number: 92-21051

Printed in the United States of America

printing number
1   2   3   4   5   6   7   8   9   10

Library of Congress Cataloging-in-Publication Data

Handbook of research on the education of young children/edited by
  Bernard Spodek.
      p.   cm.
    Includes bibliographical references and indexes.
    ISBN 0-02-897405-0
    1. Child development.   2. Early childhood education—Curricula.
  3. Early childhood educaton—Research.   4. Childhood development—
  Research.   I. Spodek, Bernard.
  LB1119.H25   1993
  372.21′072—dc20   92-21051
                                                 CIP

The paper used in this publication meets the minimum requirements of American
National Standard of Information Sciences—Permanence of Paper for Printed Library Materials.
ANSI Z39.48-1984.⊗™

◆

CONTENTS

Part I

CHILD DEVELOPMENT AND EARLY EDUCATION   7

Part II
FOUNDATIONS OF EARLY CHILDHOOD EDUCATIONAL CURRICULUM   89

Part III
FOUNDATIONS OF EARLY CHILDHOOD EDUCATIONAL POLICY   277

Part IV

RESEARCH STRATEGIES FOR EARLY CHILDHOOD EDUCATION 439

PREFACE

Early childhood education is defined in the field as the education of young children from birth through age 8. Seldom does a single program of early childhood education serve children across this entire age range. Nor do programs for all children in this educational range look alike. Programs for infants and toddlers include activities and physical settings that are different form those for children ages 6 through 8. The sponsorship of the programs are also different from one another. Some early childhood programs emphasize the caring function, whereas other programs emphasize the educational function. In addition, there are programs for children within the same age range that differ from one another. They may serve children with different characteristics, for example, children with disabling conditions, gifted children, or children for whom English is not their initial language. Thus, although there is a coherence to the field of early childhood education, programs in the field vary by age, by the characteristics of their clients, by purpose, and by institutional sponsorship.

Although the field of early childhood education has a history of more than 150 years, research specific to early childhood education is more recent. The scientific study of education is only about 100 years old, as is the scientific study of the development of children. Much of the early child development research, from the work of G. Stanley Hall through the studies conducted by the illustrious early childhood research centers funded by the Laura Spellman Rockefeller Foundation, focused primarily on understanding young children. The research attempted to establish patterns of development, the range of individual differences in those patterns, and the influence of various environmental factors on those patterns.

In the 1960s we began to see the creation of a broad range of educational interventions to enhance young children's learning and development. The creation of these models of early childhood education, and the implementation of these models—especially with children who might risk academic failure in their later school careers—led to research on the short- and long-term outcomes of programs for young children. Much of the early research in early childhood education now seems naive. Often the objective of these experimental programs was to increase IQ scores through short periods of attendance in early childhood programs. However, this research led to a realization that early childhood programs can have serious short- and long-term educational consequences for many populations of young children.

Since that time, the field of early childhood education has expanded greatly. Today, the majority of children entering kindergarten have previously been in some early childhood program, and kindergarten education has become almost universal. With this growth has come increased research in the field of early childhood education. One indication of that increase is the creation of two journals in recent years, the *Early Childhood Research Quarterly* and *Early Education and Development,* devoted almost exclusively to reporting research in early childhood education. Not only has the number of studies in the field expanded over the years, but the range of research topics and of research methodologies used has expanded as well.

Research and practice in early childhood education are still closely allied with the field of child development. What children in this age range are capable of learning is determined to a great extent by their level of development. In addition, how children develop at this stage is determined by what they learn. As a result, practice and research in early childhood education are informed by and related to child development research.

Whereas research in the various domains of early child development has generated significant knowledge related to early childhood education, so has research on young children's learning in the various educational content areas. Early childhood research, however, goes well beyond classroom practices. Increasingly, research is being used as a basis for suggesting new social policies as well as for looking at the consequences of established social policies. Setting standards for programs and for personnel requires establishing legal requirements that programs must meet. Such standards are found in state school codes, state licensing regulations for child care centers, and state teacher certification requirements. Standards are also set voluntarily, through the accreditation of early childhood programs and of programs that prepare early childhood personnel. Such standards should not be arbitrary; they should enable the profession to improve the quality of the education offered to young children. Agencies must therefore continually seek knowledge upon which to base these standards. Increasingly in the last several years, research in early childhood education has been policy oriented.

Just as early childhood educational practice changes, so early childhood educational research changes. Understanding the nature of the research process and the new approaches to educational research that are evolving is important to educators who utilize research as well to those who produce research. Thus, a section on methodology is included in this volume.

It is hoped that this *Handbook of Research on the Education of Young Children* will serve the needs of many in the educational community. Scholars seeking the current state of research knowledge in various areas should find this volume useful. Practitioners who are trying to seek knowledge of research and its practical implications should find that this volume serves their needs. Policy markers who shape the early childhood educational enterprise through law and regulation will also find that the volume serves their needs. We have tried to make this *Handbook* both informative and accessible, with individual chapters reviewing relevant research and identifying the implications of this research for practice and policy development.

Bernard Spodek
September 1992

ACKNOWLEDGMENTS

The preparation of this volume involved the work of many people. The contributions of the individual chapter authors are evident, and these authors deserve thanks for their careful attention to the domains they surveyed. A special thanks needs to be given to members of the *Handbook's* Editorial Advisory Board: they have provided excellent advice from the very beginning; they have reviewed and commented on the basic conception of the book; and they also made suggestions about topics to be covered and scholars who might contribute chapters. Individual members of the Editorial Advisory Board also served as chapter reviewers, carefully reading drafts of chapter manuscripts and providing suggestions for their improvement. A special thanks needs to be given to the editor, Lloyd Chilton, now retired from Macmillan Publishing Company, who inspired the development of the book and helped guide its initial progress. Thanks also to Philip Friedman, who continued to guide its development.

ABOUT THE CONTRIBUTORS

James A. Banks is Professor of Education and Director of the Center for Multicultural Education at the University of Washington, Seattle. He has written extensively in multicultural education and in social studies education. His books include *Teaching Strategies for Ethnic Studies* (5th ed.), *Multicultural Education: Issues and Perspectives* (2nd ed.) (with Cherry A. McGee Banks), *Multiethnic Education: Theory and Practice* (2nd ed.), and *Teaching Strategies for the Social Studies* (4th ed.). Dr. Banks is the editor (with Cherry A. McGee Banks) of the *Handbook of Research on Multicultural Education* (Macmillan, in progress).

Arthur J. Baroody is an Associate Professor in the Department of Curriculum and Instruction at the University of Illinois at Urbana-Champaign. He received his doctorate in educational and developmental psychology from Cornell University in 1979. He is interested in the teaching and learning of elementary-level mathematics. His research focuses on the development of a number of arithmetic concepts and skills. His books include *Problem Solving, Reasoning, and Communicating, K–8* (Macmillan, 1993) and *Children's Mathematical Thinking: A Developmental Framework for Preschool, Primary, and Special Education Teachers* (Teachers College Press, 1987).

Brenda Boyd received her Ph.D. in child development from the University of Georgia in 1991. She is currently Assistant Professor of Child Development at the University of Manitoba. Her interests are in the area of play and metacommunication.

Patricia Clark Brown is currently a doctoral candidate in early childhood education at the University of Illinois at Urbana-Champaign, where she also directs a multilingual preschool program. She had previously been a bilingual kindergarten teacher and director of a child care center. Her research interests include curriculum and practice in early childhood education and the education of low-income and minority young children.

Douglas H. Clements is Associate Professor of Early Childhood, Mathematics and Computer Education at the State University of New York at Buffalo. A former kindergarten teacher, he has conducted research and published widely in the areas of computer applications in early childhood and mathematics education. Through a National Science Foundation (NSF) grant, he has co-developed (with Michael T. Battista) an elementary geometry curriculum based on Logo: *Logo Geometry*. He is currently working with colleagues to develop a K–6 mathematics curriculum and is developing computer microworlds for that curriculum. Two of his recent books include *Computers in Early and Primary Education* and *Computers in Elementary Mathematics Education*.

Richard M. Clifford is Associate Director of the Carolina Institute for Child and Family Policy at the Frank Porter Graham Child Development Center at the University of North Carolina at Chapel Hill. He is also Clinical Associate Professor in the School of Education. He has had experience both as a teacher and as a principal in public school. For nearly 20 years, he has been involved in studying public policies and advising local, state, and federal officials and practitioners on policies affecting children and their families. His work has focused on two major themes: public financing of programs for young children, especially children who have disabilities or are at risk, and the provision of appropriate learning environments for preschool and early school-aged children. Dr. Clifford has authored or edited several books and journal issues, as well as numerous published articles. He is co-author of a widely used series of instruments for evaluating learning environments for young children.

Cynthia C. Coleman is currently a graduate student pursuing a master's degree in educational psychology at the University of Illinois at Urbana-Champaign. Ms. Coleman's area of interest is young children's peer relationships and their contributions to early school adjustment. She is currently working on a longitudinal investigation of family, teacher, and peer interaction as predictors of successful versus maladaptive patterns of adjustment to school in kindergarten through grade 3.

Jessica Davis is a cognitive psychologist. As a research associate at Harvard Project Zero, she is the director of Project Co-Arts, a national study of educational effectiveness in community art centers. She is co-principal investigator with Dr. Howard Gardner in a new research initiative—an educational collaboration with the Isabella Stewart Gardner Museum in Boston—which examines issues of access and empowerment for child and adult museum-goers. Her own research addresses the similarities and differences between child and adult art as that comparison informs an observed loss of artistry in middle childhood. She comes to this work with extensive experience as an artist and teacher.

James D. Dempsey is the Senior Vice President of Grounds For Play Inc., a firm in Arlington, Texas, specializing in play environment design and equipment. He received a B.A. in psychology from Texas Tech University and an M.A. and Ph.D. in curriculum and instruction (early childhood) from the University of Texas at Austin. He has served as both teacher and director in child care and preschool settings. He is a board member of the American Association for the Child's Right to Play (IPA/USA) and is currently involved in designing play environments that fully integrate able-bodied children, children with disabilities, and parents. Current research projects include a study of the effects of loose parts construction materials in an outdoor setting on the play of elementary school children.

Anne Haas Dyson is Professor of Education in Language and Literacy at the University of California at Berkeley. A former preschool and primary-grade teacher, she studies how young children use oral and written language as social tools in classroom settings. Among her publications are *Multiple Worlds of Child Writers: Friends Learning to Write* (Teachers College Press, 1989) and, with Celia Genishi, *Language Assessment in the Early Years* (Ablex, 1984). She is especially interested in the developmental interrelationships between young children's use of print and other symbolic media.

Judith Evans is currently working on policy and program development in early childhood care and development. She is currently associated with the Aga Khan Foundation, the consultative Group on Early Childhood Care and Development, UNICEF, and the High/Scope Foundation. She has been involved in international program development in relation to young children, women, and the family for the past 20 years. She was on the faculty at the University of Massachusetts. She then moved to the High/Scope Foundation, where she developed their programs for families. From 1986 to 1992 she was employed as a programme officer with the Aga Khan Foundation. She received her doctorate in developmental psychology from the University of Massachusetts, an M.S. from Stanford University, and a B.A. in education from the University of Minnesota.

Joe Frost received his doctorate in elementary education with a specialty in child development at the University of Arkansas. He is presently Catherine Mae Parker Centennial Professor of Curriculum and Instruction in the program of early childhood education at the University of Texas at Austin. Dr. Frost has written extensively in the field of early childhood education. *The Disadvantaged,* co-edited with Glenn Hawkes, was selected by Pi Lambda Theta as one of the outstanding education books for 1986. *Early Childhood Education Rediscovered* was extensively adopted worldwide. His most recent books are *When Children Play* (Association for Childhood Education International, 1985), *Playground for Young Children* (American Alliance for Physical Education, Recreation and Dance, 1990), and *Play and Playscapes* (Delmar, 1992). Dr. Frost is a past president of the Association of Childhood Education International and was the U.S.A. president and representative to the International Playground Association. His current research interests are children's play and play environments.

David L. Gallahue is Professor of Kinesiology at Indiana University in Bloomington and Senior Director for Youth Development at the National Institute for Fitness and Sport in Indianapolis. He is active in the study of the motor development and movement education of young children. He is the author of several textbooks, journal articles, and book chapters. Dr. Gallahue is a past president of the National Association for Sport and Physical Education (NASPE) and former chair of the Motor Development Academy and the Council of Physical Education for Children (COPEC). Dr. Gallahue is internationally recognizeed as a leader in children's motor development and movement education.

Eugene García is Dean of the Division of Social Sciences and Professor of Education and Psychology at the University of California, Santa Cruz. He received his Ph.D. in human development from the University of Kansas. He has served as a Post-Doctoral Fellow in Human Development at Harvard University and as a National Research Council Fellow. He has been a recipient of a national Kellogg Fellowship and of numerous academic and public honors. He is a faculty member at the University of California, Santa Cruz, where he has served as a research center director and department chair. Dr. García has published extensively in the area of language teaching and bilingual development, holds leadership positions in professional organizations, and continues to serve in an editorial capacity for psychological, linguistic, and educational journals and as proposal panel reviewer for federal, state, and foundation agencies. He is presently Co-Director of the National Center for Research on Cultural Diversity and Second Language Learning and is conducting research in the areas of effective schooling for linguistically and culturally diverse student populations.

Howard Gardner is Professor of Education and Co-Director of Project Zero at the Harvard Graduate School of Education, and Adjunct Professor of Neurology at the Boston University School of Medicine. His research focuses on the development of human cognitive capacities, particularly those central in the arts. He also is engaged in efforts at educational reform, particularly in the areas of assessment, attention to individual differences in learning, and the professional development of teachers. He has published extensively. Among his books are *Quest for Mind* (1973; 2nd ed., 1981); *The Shattered Mind* (1975); *Developmental Psychology* (1978; 2nd ed., 1982); *Art, Mind, and Brain* (1982); *The Mind's New Science* (1985); *To Open Minds: Chinese Clues to the Dilemma of Contemporary Education* (1989); and *Art Education and Human Development* (1990). His newest book is *The Unschooled Mind: How Children Think, How Schools Should Teach* (Basic Books, 1991). He is in the process of completing "The Creators of the Modern Era," a collection of case studies of 7 highly creative individuals who lived around the turn of the century.

Celia Genishi, a former preschool and secondary Spanish teacher, is a member of the Early Childhood Education Faculty at Teachers College, Columbia University. She is the editor of *Ways of Assessing Children and Curriculum: Stories of Early Childhood Practice,* co-author (with Anne Haas Dyson) of *Language Assessment in the Early Years,* and co-author (with Millie Almy) of *Ways of Studying Children.* Her interests include observational research in classrooms, children's language development, and the role of story in teaching, learning, and assessing.

Laura D. Goodwin received her Ph.D. in research methodology, evaluation, and measurement through the Laboratory of Educational Research at the University of Colorado, Boulder (1977). After several years at the University's Health Sciences Center teaching and evaluating projects for the School of Nursing, she moved to the Denver Campus of the University of Colorado, where she is now Professor and Associate Dean of the School of Education. Also a President's Teaching Scholar for the University of Colorado system, she teaches courses in statistics, measurement, and research design. She has published extensively, often on methodological issues in measurement and research, and particularly in education and nursing journals.

William L. Goodwin received his Ph.D. in educational psychology at the University of Wisconsin, Madison (1965). He was an AERA-USOE postdoctoral fellow in early childhood education at Harvard University's Laboratory of Human Development (1969–1970) and also was a fellow in the USOE Leadership Training Institute for Early Childhood Education. He has been at the Denver Campus of the University of Colorado since 1970 and is now Professor and Coordinator of the Educational Psychology and Special Education Division. He teaches courses in early childhood education, educational psychology, measurement, and research methodology. His previous publications include books in both educational psychology and early childhood education, as well as numerous articles.

Elizabeth Graue is Assistant Professor of Early Childhood Education in the Department of Curriculum and Instruction at the University of Wisconsin, Madison. She received her Ph.D. in research methodology at the University of Colorado at Boulder. Her research interests include early childhood policy, research methodology (particularly qualitative methods), and assessment.

Stanley I. Greenspan is a founder and former president of the National Center for Clinical Infant Programs. He is Clinical Professor of Psychiatry and Pediatrics at George Washington University Medical School, a Supervising Child Psychoanalyst at the Washington Psychoanalytic Institute, and Director of the ABC Initiative. A former director of the National Institute of Mental Health's Clinical Infant Development Program and Mental Health Study Center, Dr. Greenspan is the author or editor of more than 15 books and 90 articles. For his work in infancy and early childhood, Dr. Greenspan has received a number of national awards, including the American Psychiatric Association's Ittelson Prize for Outstanding Contributions to Child Psychiatry Research and the Edward A. Strecker Award for Outstanding Contributions to American Psychiatry.

Claire Hamilton is currently completing her doctoral studies in education at the University of California at Los Angeles. She is interested in how children enrolled in child care develop relationships with their teachers and their peers, and how issues of quality may influence such relationships. On a broader level, her research also examines the continuity and discontinuity of attachment relationships.

Thelma Harms is Director of Curriculum Development at the Frank Porter Graham Child Development Center and an adjunct Associate Professor in the School of Education at the University of North Carolina at Chapel Hill. She earned a doctorate in early childhood education at the University of California, Berkeley. Prior to her present position, Dr. Harms was Head Teacher at the Harold E. Jones Child Study Center Preschool Program, University of California, Berkeley. Dr. Harms is first author of 3 widely used program assessment instruments, the *Early Childhood Environment Rating Scale* (Teachers College Press, 1980), the *Family Day Care Rating Scale* (Teachers College Press, 1989), and the *Infant/Toddler Environment Rating Scale* (Teachers College Press, 1990), and is co-author of other publications and video programs. Her work on environment and curriculum has been translated and is used in many countries.

Ruth A. Hough is Associate Professor of Early Childhood Education at Georgia State University. Dr. Hough is a former primary-grade teacher and is now a university teacher, educator, and researcher in the fields of early childhood education and English as a second language. Her teaching and publications have focused on language and literacy acquisition and instruction for students learning English as a native language and as an additional language.

Ann C. Howe is Professor of Science Education and Chair of the Department of Curriculum and Instruction at the University of Maryland at College Park. She received her Ph.D.

from the University of Texas in Austin and has been on the faculties of Syracuse University and North Carolina State University. Her research has focused on how children and adolescents learn science. She is currently in the classroom application of research in science education and is co-author of the recently published *Engaging Children is Science*.

Carollee Howes completed her Ph.D. in developmental psychology at Boston University and postdoctoral work in social psychiatry at Harvard University. She is currently Professor of Education in the Graduate School of Education of the University of California at Los Angeles. Her program of research concerns the development of social communication and social relationships with peers and adults, within child care settings, and within families.

Sharon Lynn Kagan is a Senior Associate at Yale's Bush Center in Child Development and Social Policy. She is a Governing Board member of the National Association for the Education of Young Children, the President-Elect of the Family Resource Coalition, and Vice President of the Institute for Responsive Education. Dr. Kagan's scholarship focuses on improving schools and other institutions that serve young children. She edited the 90th Yearbook of the prestigious National Society for the Study of Education on *Early Care and Education: Obstacles and Opportunities* and the Phi Delta Kappan special edition on Early Childhood Education. She has written a volume on collaboration, *United We Stand: Improving Services to Young Children and their Families,* and has co-edited a special edition of the *Early Childhood Research Quarterly* on educating culturally and linguistically diverse preschoolers. Dr. Kagan has also co-edited three volumes: *Children; Families and Government: America's Family Support Programs;* and *Early Schooling: The National Debate.*

Nancy Karweit is currently a principal research scientist at the Johns Hopkins University's Center for Study of Disadvantaged Students. She received her Ph.D. in sociology from the Johns Hopkins University in 1976. Her work has focused on school organization, time and learning, disadvantaged students, and the development of integrated curriculum for prekindergarten and kindergarten classes.

Gary W. Ladd received his doctorate at the University of Rochester and is currently Professor of Educational Psychology at the University of Illinois at Urbana-Champaign. Dr. Ladd has been a school psychologist and serves as a consultant to several early childhood and elementary schools. He has published numerous empirical studies, theoretical articles, and reviews of research in the area of children's social development. Included in his recent work are the books *Peer Relationships in Child Development,* co-authored with Dr. Thomas R. Berndt, and *Family-Peer Relationships: Modes of Linkage,* co-authored with Dr. Ross D. Parke. Professor Ladd is Associate Editor for the journal *Child Development* and was previously the associate editor for the *Journal of Social and Personal Relationships.* He has also served on the

editorial boards of several other journals including *Developmental Psychology* and the *Journal of Consulting and Clinical Psychology.* He is currently conducting research on the contributions of families, peers, and teachers to children's early school adjustment, and on the linkages between children's family and peer relations.

Shinying Lee received her undergraduate degree from the National Taiwan University and her Ph.D. degree in psychology from the University of Michigan. Since completing her doctoral dissertation she has been interested in the motivational patterns in Chinese and American students, especially as they are related to children's academic achievement. She is currently conducting a detailed analysis of the teaching practices of Chinese, Japanese, and American elementary school teachers.

Jana M. Mason is Professor of Educational Psychology at the University of Illinois at Urbana-Champaign. She has written extensively about young children's reading development. With K. Au she published a reading instruction textbook, *Reading Instruction for Today* (HarperCollins, 1990), and she has edited two books: *Reading and Writing Connections* (Allyn & Bacon, 1989) and *Risk Makers, Risk Takers, Risk Breakers* (Heinemann, 1989), co-edited with J. Allen. She is also the co-author of *Little Books* (Goodyear Press), low-cost original stories for young children to read before they begin formal reading instruction in school. Dr. Mason's extensive research on children's early literacy development has led her to apply the social cognition framework of Vygotsky to learning and teaching.

Susan Maude is an Evaluator at the Allegheny-Singer Research Center in Pittsburgh, PA, where she is working on statewide issues related to early intervention. Dr. Maude completed her doctorate in early childhood special education at the University of Illinois at Urbana-Champaign following several years as a classroom and home-based teacher in Oregon, Connecticut, and Illinois. During her doctoral work, she coordinated a federally funded personnel preparation project and completed a dissertation designed to identify the views of faculty and practitioners with regard to the competencies in multiple disciplines needed by early intervention personnel. She continues to pursue her interests in personnel issues as part of her current position.

Jeannette McCollum is Professor of Early Childhood Special Education at the University of Illinois at Urbana-Champaign. After teaching for 4 years in south Texas, she received her Ph.D. in early childhood special education from the University of Texas at Austin in 1976. During her doctoral program, she worked on the Special Education Supervisor Training Project and at the Texas Regional Resource Center, leaving there to become an Assistant Professor at Murray State University in Kentucky. Since 1976 she has coordinated the program in Early Childhood Special Education at Illinois, pursuing her interests in personnel preparation and parent-infant interaction.

Samuel J. Meisels serves as Professor and Associate Dean for Research in the School of Education at the University of Michigan. He is also a Research Scientist in the Center for Human Growth and Development. Dr. Meisels has published extensively in the fields of early childhood development, assessment, and special education, and he is co-editor for the *Handbook of Early Childhood Intervention.* His research focuses on the impact of standardized tests on young children, the development of alternative assessment strategies in early childhood and elementary years, developmental screening, and the developmental consequences of high-risk birth.

Bonnie K. Nastasi is an Assistant Professor in the School Psychology Program at University of Connecticut. She is past president of the Louisiana School Psychological Association and worked as a school psychologist in the New Orleans Public Schools for several years. Her research and applied interests include the role of school and family environments in the development of children's social and cognitive skills. She has published several articles and conducted numerous presentations regarding the influence of educational computer environments on children's social interaction and motivation and the link between social interactions and cognitive outcomes.

Joanne R. Nurss is Professor of Early Childhood Education and Director of the Center for the Study of Adult Literacy at Georgia State University. She has been a primary-grade teacher and has worked extensively with early childhood professionals and administrators throughout the United States as well as abroad. Her research, teaching, and service projects have focused on language and literacy development, instruction and assessment with young children, and the roles that adults may play in these critical areas. Dr. Nurss is the primary author of the *Metropolitan Readiness Tests Assessment Program,* and she has authored numerous publications in the areas of language and literacy development with children and adults in various early childhood settings, primary-grade classrooms, and intergenerational groups.

J. Craig Peery received his B.A. in psychology and his M.A. and Ph.D. in developmental psychology with a minor in clinical psychology from Columbia University. He was a Congressional Science Fellow sponsored by the American Association for the Advancement of Science and by the Society for Research in Child Development. He worked subsequently as Special Assistant to the Chairman of the United States Senate Committee on Labor and Human Resources, and on the staff of the Senate Family and Human Services Subcommittee. He is currently Professor of Human Development in the Department of Family Sciences at Brigham Young University.

Anthony D. Pellegrini received his Ph.D. in early childhood education from Ohio State University. He is Professor of Early Childhood Education and a Research Fellow of the Institute for Behavioral Research at the University of Georgia. His research interests are in children's play, social behavior, and early language-literacy relations.

Donald L. Peters received his Ph.D. in educational psychology from Stanford University. He is currently Amy Rextrew Professor of Individual and Family Studies at the University of Delaware. From 1968 to 1985 he was on the Faculty of Human Development and Family Studies at the Pennsylvania State University. He has done research and evaluation studies on Head Start, day care, and early intervention programs for young children with developmental disabilities and their families since 1966. He is the author or editor of numerous publications in the field of early childhood education. His most recent books include *Professionalism and the Early Childhood Practitioner* and *Continuity and Discontinuity of Experience in Child Care.*

Kathleen Quinn-Leering is a doctoral student in the Combined Program in Education and Psychology at the University of Michigan. An experienced child care teacher, she is interested in cultural issues affecting early childhood programs. Her research has focused on early literacy, the home-school connection, and early childhood developmental screening tests.

Olivia N. Saracho is Professor of Education in the Department of Curriculum and Instruction at the University of Maryland. She received her Ph.D. in early childhood education from the University of Illinois. Prior to that, she taught Head Start, preschool, kindergarten, and elementary classes in Brownsville, Texas, and was director of the Child Development Associate Program at Pan American University. Her current research and writing are in the areas of cognitive style, academic learning, and teacher education in relation to early childhood education. Dr. Saracho's most recent books are *Professionalism and the Early Childhood Practitioner* (Teachers College Press, 1988), edited with Bernard Spodek and Donald J. Peters, and *Foundations of Early Childhood Education* (Prentice Hall, 1987, 1991), with Bernard Spodek and Michael J. Davis. Dr. Saracho is co-editor of the *Yearbook in Early Childhood Education,* an annual series published by Teachers College Press. The first volume of that series, published in 1990, is *Early Childhood Teacher Education;* the second, published in 1991, is *Issues in Early Childhood Curriculum;* and the third, published in 1992, is *Issues of Child Care.* She is also editor, with Roy Evans, of the forthcoming *Early Childhood Teacher Education: An International Perspective,* to be published by Gordon & Breach.

Kelvin Seifert is Professor and Chairperson of the Department of Educational Psychology at the University of Manitoba, where he specializes in child development and early childhood education. He completed his Ph.D. in the Combined Program in Education and Psychology from the University of Michigan in 1973. His research interests include, and have led to publications about, gender issues related to early childhood education and informal theorizing about children. His most recent major publications include (with Robert Hoffnung) a third edition of *Child and Adolescent Development* and a second edition of *Educational Psychology*.

Lorrie A. Shepard is Professor of Education at the University of Colorado at Boulder. She earned her doctorate in research and evaluation methodology at the University of Colorado. Her work in educational policy research has focused on the uses of tests for special school placement and on the effects of testing on teaching and student learning. Her recent book, with Mary Lee Smith, is entitled *Flunking Grades: Research and Policy on Retention*. She has served as president of the National Council on Measurement in Education, vice president for Division D of the American Educational Research Association, editor of the *Journal of Educational Measurement*, and editor of the *American Educational Research Journal*.

Shobha Sinha is a Ph.D. student at the University of Illinois at Urbana-Champaign. She has worked with Dr. Jana Mason on an early intervention program at the Center for the Study of Reading. Her interests include literacy in the classroom context and sociocultural aspects of literacy. She is currently working on her dissertation.

Bernard Spodek (editor) is Professor of Early Childhood Education at the University of Illinois at Urbana-Champaign. He received his doctorate in early childhood education from Teachers College, Columbia University, then joined the faculty of the University of Wisconsin, Milwaukee. He has also taught nursery, kindergarten, and elementary classes in New York City. Dr. Spodek's research and scholarly interests are in the areas of curriculum, teaching, and teacher education in early childhood education. From 1976 to 1978 he was President of the National Association for the Education of Young Children, and from 1981 through 1983 he chaired the Early Education and Child Development Special Interest Group of the American Educational Research Association. He is widely published in the field of early childhood education.

Bernard Spodek's most recent books are *Professionalism and the Early Childhood Practitioner* (Teachers College Press, 1988), edited with Olivia N. Saracho and Donald J. Peters; *Foundations of Early Childhood Education* (Prentice Hall, 1987, 1991), with Olivia N. Saracho and Michael J. Davis; and *Today's Kindergarten: Exploring Its Knowledge Base, Expanding Its Curriculum* (Teachers College Press, 1986). He is co-editor of the *Yearbook in Early Childhood Education,* an annual series published by Teachers College Press. The first volume of that series, published in 1990, is *Early Childhood Teacher Education;* the second, published in 1991, is *Issues in Early Childhood Curriculum;* and the third, published in 1992, is *Issues of Child Care.* He is also editor of the forthcoming *Handbook of Research on the Education of Young Children,* to be published by Macmillan.

Dorothy M. Steele is a research assistant at the University of Michigan as well as a Social Science Research Assistant at Stanford University. She has been an early childhood educator and program director for more than 20 years. Ms. Steele is a member of the advisory panel for the National Academy of Early Childhood Programs of the National Association for the Education of Young Children and has published a monograph on establishing child care programs in churches and synagogues.

Joseph R. Stevens, Jr., was a professor of early childhood education at Georgia State University until his death in September 1991. A prolific researcher, he was the recipient of 7 grants to investigate early childhood education and parenting, and he produced over 25 publications and 30 unpublished papers. His scholarly work focused on the impact of social support networks on parents, especially low-income teen parents. In addition, Dr. Stevens served the editorial boards of 5 professional journals, was a member of the Board of Directors of the Family Resource Coalition, and consulted with many family support research projects.

Harold W. Stevenson is Professor of Psychology at the University of Michigan. A Stanford Ph.D., he has been interested in children's learning in both laboratory and school settings throughout his academic career. He has been president of the Division of Developmental Psychology of the American Psychological Association, the Society for Research in Child Development, and the International Society for the Study of Behavioral Development. His current research is focused on comparative studies of East Asian and American students' academic achievement.

Cynthia Szymanski Sunal is Professor of Curriculum and Instruction at the University of Alabama. Her research interests have a strong focus on social studies for young children and on international education. She is the author of *Early Childhood Social Studies* and *Social Studies for the Elementary/Middle School Student.* Her research has been conducted in the United States, Nigeria, and Latin America. She has published widely in journals, including *Social Studies for the Young Learner, Journal of Research in Childhood Education,* and *Theory and Research in Social Education.* She has served as chair of the Early Childhood Advisory Committee for the National Council for the Social Studies and as a member of the Board of its College and Faculty Assembly.

Joseph Tobin is Associate Professor in the Department of Curriculum and Instruction and The Center for Youth Research at the University of Hawaii, Manoa. Dr. Tobin received his Ph.D. in 1982 from the Committee on Human Development at the University of Chicago. His current scholarly interests center on ethnographic research methods applied to educational settings and questions, on Japanese preschool and elementary education, and on cultural critiques of American early childhood education. He is currently engaged in a comparative study of attitudes towards preschool children's sexuality in Japan, Ireland, and the United States.

Daniel Walsh is Associate Professor of Early Childhood Education at the University of Illinois at Urbana-Champaign. He received his Ph.D. from the University of Wisconsin, Madison, in 1985. An active interpretive researcher, he is most interested in issues of policy as they affect early public schooling and in how public school teachers of young children make sense of their lives as teachers. He has published in various journals, including *Early Childhood Research Quarterly, Early Education and Development, Teachers College Record,* and *Educational Evaluation and Policy Analysis.*

Serena Wieder is a graduate of the Clinical Psychology Program at the City University of New York. She has worked with infants and their families in a variety of settings for the last 20 years. She is Clinical Director of the Infant Diagnostic Classification Task Force Study for the National Center for Clinical Infant Programs, and she is the Educational Director for the ABC Initiative. As clinical director of the Clinical Infant Development Program, a 6-year longitudinal MIMH research study, she developed assessment and early intervention methods for infants in multiproblem families. As founding director of the Reginald Lourie Center for Infants and Young Children, she established integrated services for infants and their families, including the Parenting Psychotherapy Program and the Therapeutic Special Education Preschool. Dr. Wieder also served on the Maryland Interagency Coordinating Council, consults and provides training for numerous programs, and has published and presented extensively nationwide. Currently she is in private practice and consultation, specializing in infants with complex developmental problems.

Dennie Palmer Wolf is Senior Research Associate at Harvard Graduate School of Education. Currently, Dr. Wolf is the Director of PACE (Performance Assessment Collaboratives for Education), a multi-year project in diversified approaches to assessment funded by the Rockefeller Foundation. For 5 years she was co-director of ARTS PROPEL, an innovative approach to integrated curriculum and assessment based on practices native to the arts and humanities. Dr. Wolf has maintained an active career as a basic researcher, working on studies of narrative and life history. She is widely published in the fields of developmental psychology, linguistics, and education.

◆ 1 ◆

INTRODUCTION

Bernard Spodek

UNIVERSITY OF ILLINOIS AT URBANA-CHAMPAIGN

The practice of educating young children is built upon a range of different kinds of knowledge. This includes the practical knowledge that teachers develop from working directly in early childhood programs. Such knowledge, often implicit, is seldom set down in formal ways. It is communicated through demonstration and verbal description in meetings and in modeling as novice teachers gain understanding working alongside more experienced teachers, some of whom serve as their mentors. Early childhood educational practice is also based upon ethical considerations. It has been said that educating another person is essentially an ethical act. If the education is effective, that person will be changed in some significant way. Early childhood education programs are based upon a vision of what children are like and what children ought to be like. Not only should the outcomes of programs reflect an ethical view of children, but the program practices—the experiences we provide children—should be judged as worthy in their own right.

In addition to these forms of knowledge, a body of research knowledge has evolved over the years that informs the practice of early childhood education. Research in the field has been increasing at a significantly higher rate over the last quarter century. This reflects (1) the increase in size of the field of early childhood education in this period, (2) the increasing importance of the field of early childhood education in our society, and (3) the increased importance attributed to the education of young children.

A HISTORICAL PERSPECTIVE

The pioneers of early childhood education—Robert Owen, who developed the Infant School, and Friedrich Froebel, who created the kindergarten—both based their programs on philosophical speculation. Owen was concerned about the development of character in those individuals who would inhabit his ideal society. Froebel, basing his work on philosophic idealism,

used his symbolic kindergarten materials to help young children come to know the basic relationship among man, God, and the universe. Both of these forms of early childhood education were developed in the first half of the nineteenth century.

When Charles Darwin presented his theory on the origin of the human species, the modern era of research on human beings began. If the human race did indeed descend from other species, rather than from God, then it could be studied like other species—that is, scientifically. The growth of research led to significant changes in many aspects of human life, including education.

The research tradition in early childhood education can probably be traced back to the work of G. Stanley Hall. After studying scientific psychology in Germany, Hall returned to America to begin studying children. In 1880 he conducted a survey of "The Contents of Children's Minds Upon Entering School," using kindergarten teachers as his questioners (Ross, 1976). He maintained close relations with kindergarten educators, despite the early rejection of his work by some members of that field. The research tradition in the kindergarten environment continued at Teachers College, Columbia University. Work at this institution was conducted both by Patty Smith Hill, a leader in kindergarten education, and by Edward L. Thorndike, an educational psychologist (Weber, 1984).

As nursery education evolved in the United States, it became closely intertwined with the field of child development. Laboratory nursery schools were established in many child development departments and institutes in colleges and universities. Nursery schools, which offered programs for young children before they entered public elementary schools, provided available subjects for childhood researchers. The knowledge gained from such studies was often informative for early childhood practitioners.

Another beginning for research in early childhood education came with the establishment of the Bureau of Educational Experiments in 1916. This research bureau, which functioned for 15 years, led to the creation of the Bank Street College of Education (Antler, 1987). The research at both Bank Street College and the Bureau was, like the work at Teachers College, driven by the philosophy of the progressive education movement.

The Montessori method was developed out of what might be considered scientific inquiry—the careful observation and codification of use of children's materials adapted from Froebel and Edward Sequin, a nineteenth-century educator of mentally handicapped children. Montessori used her materials, first with handicapped children and later for normal children. However, this method was never actually subjected to any scientific inquiry during the life of Maria Montessori (Kramer, 1988).

The contemporary research tradition in early childhood education stems from the work of the 1960s. Such work began when new views of child development challenged the belief in fixed intelligence and suggested that children could learn more than was expected of them. Psychologists and educators began to test educational programs for young children in relation to their short- and long-term effects on learning and development. New models of early childhood education were generated and tested. Competition among the many different approaches to early education led to a greater need for research.

The research enterprise on the education of young children has been thriving in recent years. Journals reporting research on the education of young children, such as *Early Child Development and Care, Early Education and Development,* and *Early Childhood Research Quarterly,* have been established to report research related to the education of young children. Research studies on various topics of interest to the early childhood educator can be found in other journals in child development and education. Reports of research on the education of young children have also become increasingly available in the programs of conferences of such associations as the American Educational Research Association.

The reporting of research on the education of young children is so diffuse that it is difficult to get a comprehensive look at what we know from research about specific topics in early childhood education. There is a need to take a thorough look at this research. Just as important is the need to organize the developing body of knowledge into some coherent units, allowing more convenient access to those seeking this research information. This volume is designed to serve those purposes.

The *Handbook of Research on the Education of Young Children* presents critical reviews of research in important areas of early childhood education. Although these chapters are broadly conceived, they do not represent everything we know about the education of young children; no one volume can present all the information available. Each chapter is selective in its focus, presenting a review of research in an area as seen from a particular author's point of view. Some authors survey an area of the field broadly, whereas others view only a narrow portion of that area, but in greater depth. Some offer an inclusive survey, whereas others take a critical view. This book attempts to offer reviews that are as comprehensive as possible in areas of early childhood education that are considered important to the field.

ORGANIZATION

This volume is organized into 4 parts: (I) Child Development and Early Education, (II) Foundations of Early Childhood Educational Curriculum, (III) Foundations of Early Childhood Educational Policy, and (IV) Research Strategies for Early Childhood Education. The chapters contain summaries of particular aspects of research knowledge related to topics about the education of young children. They also provide a discussion of the significance of this knowledge for practice. Part IV focuses more on knowledge of research strategies that can be used to extend the research base of early childhood education.

Part I, which presents research from child development, contains chapters that inform early childhood education about research knowledge in several domains of human development. The ways children learn to think, to move, to use language, to interact with their peers, and to deal with their emotions provides a basis for the way we can design activities to help them achieve significant goals in these areas.

In chapter 2 Kelvin L. Seifert identifies the key views and recent research on young children's thinking. He presents research on information processing in young children, offering both a serial-processing model and a parallel-processing model. He also discusses structural theories of development, focusing especially on the neo-Piagetian positions. Within this position he presents the sociocultural view of development, as exemplified by the work of L. S. Vygotsky. (Although Vygotsky was a contemporary of Piaget, his work is considered to fit into the post-Piagetian framework.) Seifert also suggests ways to stimulate young children's thinking within the theoretical models presented. These views of development are currently being applied to studies of early childhood curriculum processes and their outcomes.

David L. Gallahue, in chapter 3, explains the stages of movement skill acquisition in young children along with the conditions that affect movement skill acquisition. He also discusses individual differences in movement acquisition. This chapter presents a framework for the development of programs of movement education for young children.

In chapter 4 Dennie Palmer Wolf focuses on the development of narrative in young children's discourse, the language of "there and then." These narrative skills provide the basis for much of later academic learning as young children learn the rules of such discourse. The skills of both oral and written language evolve from such discourse. Children are able to recollect events, share them with others, and make plans for future activities through narrative.

Gary W. Ladd and Cynthia C. Coleman discuss young children's peer relations in chapter 5. Given the large amount of time that children in our society spend with their peers, the increase in enrollments in early childhood programs, and the time that many young children spend in these programs each day, this topic is taking on increasing importance. The research reviewed in this chapter demonstrates that children can form peer relations at an early age. Some of the strategies that young children use in developing these relations are identified. Children's personal characteristics are also seen as important in their development of social competence. There is a need for research in the continued relationships of children with their peers in different social settings as well as the consequences of both positive and negative experiences with peers on children's later lives. Some of this research, which is becoming available today, could become the basis for providing opportunities to learn social competence in the early childhood classroom.

Chapter 6 discusses the emotional basis of learning. Serena Wieder and Stanley I. Greenspan present a model of learning based upon children's relationships and emotional understanding, beginning at birth and continuing throughout the early years of life. Stages in children's emotional development are reviewed, and children's learning strategies, including shared attention, interaction, communication, and symbolic thinking, are presented. Wieder and Greenspan stress the need for broadly based evaluation of children's learning capabilities in planning for each child's educational program.

Part II presents research on the foundations of the early childhood educational curriculum. It informs early childhood educators about the basis for classroom activities and the possible consequences of these activities. In chapter 7 Bernard Spodek and Patricia Clark Brown present a historical perspective on the curriculum alternatives in early childhood education. The nature of the educational programs and the educational goals established for young children have changed over the past 2 centuries. These changes have resulted from (1) changing needs of societies and nations in relation to the education of their citizens, (2) changes in the ways that societies have organized themselves to meet the needs of their people, (3) technological changes in societies, and (4) changes in social values and a move toward democratization. Some of the contemporary approaches to early childhood education are also discussed in the current social context.

In chapter 8 Anthony D. Pellegrini and Brenda Boyd discuss the role of play in early education and development. They analyze the functional and structural dimensions of play, along with the multiple criteria used to identify play in young children. Pellegrini and Boyd analyze play as manifested in young children, including exploratory play, fantasy play, and rough-and-tumble play. They describe the consequences of play and the use of play for purposes of evaluation.

Chapter 9 presents a vision of young children as language users and discusses research on language and language education in early childhood. Anne Haas Dyson and Celia Genishi discuss how Jerome Bruner has influenced recent research with his concept of children making knowledge of language their own as a member of a community. Their emphasis is on how children learn oral and written language as a result of their use of language to interact with people—adults as well as other children—in purposive activity. Both the language arts curriculum and the ways in which we assess language learning are seen as needing to be embedded within the community of the classroom.

In chapter 10 Jana M. Mason and Shobha Sinha discuss the research and theory underlying approaches to emergent literacy. They construct a model of literacy learning based on the work of L. S. Vygotsky (see chapter 2). This Vygotskian perspective is first contrasted with the "reading readiness" perspective in early literacy development. Then the authors apply that perspective to an emergent literacy program, demonstrating how children develop concepts of the written language that enable them to learn to read and write. Theory and practice become intertwined in this discussion.

In chapter 11 Arthur J. Baroody reviews the nature of mathematics learning in young children. He presents relevant research related to both prearithmetic and arithmetic instruction and learning as it relates to young children. He also identifies research related to special populations of young children, including gifted young children, young children with mental handicaps, and young children with learning disabilities. This research is critically reviewed and implications for the education for young children are presented.

Cynthia Szymanski Sunal's chapter on social studies in early childhood education, chapter 12, traces the development of four types of social understandings in young children: social competence and morality, a sense of history, geographic learning, and economic understandings. Sunal presents a critical review of research in each of these areas and in the area of political socialization. Implications for teaching young children are also drawn.

In chapter 13, which deals with the arts in early childhood education, Jessica Davis and Howard Gardner draw a cognitive-developmental portrait of the young child as an artist. They describe the gift of artistic expression that young children have and how that gift develops. They present the different kinds of knowledge that young children master and integrate in developing their ability to express themselves in the arts: intuitive knowledge, first-order symbolic knowledge, knowledge of notational systems, formal bodies of knowledge, and skilled knowledge. Davis and Gardner draw implications for a cognitive approach to the arts in early childhood education and for the influence that this approach would have on the learning of young children.

Chapter 14, by J. Craig Peery, discusses the role of music in the education of young children. This chapter reviews the research on the development of music understanding, appreciation, aptitude, skill, and ability in young children. It covers such topics as children's musical preferences, children's musical perception, and the development of performance skills in young children. Cultural issues related to music are also raised. An important area of research covered here is the influence of musical development on other areas of children's competence, including their cognitive ability, motor skills, language and literacy, and personality and social skill. A discussion of music education for young children is also provided.

Anne C. Howe reviews the research on science in early childhood education in chapter 15. She provides a historical perspective, focusing on the work on early childhood science education during the curriculum reform movement of the 1960s and on the programs that have been developed since that movement. She also discusses the impact of the research of cognitive psychologists, especially of Jean Piaget's theories, on science teaching in early childhood education. Research on science teaching with young handicapped children is also reviewed. Finally, Howe looks to the future, discussing the continued influence of Piaget on this area of the field, as well as the development of increasingly sophisticated points of view relating to constructivist psychology. A discussion of appropriate science instruction for young children is also provided.

In chapter 16 James A. Banks discusses research on multicultural education for young children. He critically analyzes research on racial and ethnic attitudes of young children, presenting the classical studies of the Clarks as well as other research done within the Clarks' paradigm. Banks then discusses some of the methodological problems in the Clarks' paradigm and the challenges that have been raised to it. Next, he describes research studies on the modification of young children's racial attitudes. Implications of these studies for research and early childhood education practice are also presented.

In chapter 17 Douglas H. Clements and Bonnie K. Nastasi review the research on electronic media and early childhood education. This chapter covers research on children's use of television, both instructional and commercial, and the influence of television on children's cognitive, social, and emotional development. This chapter also deals with children's use of computers. Computers are being used increasingly with children at younger ages. Research is presented on computers' influence on cognition and academic achievement in young children. Special attention is given to the areas of language arts and mathematics, as well as to creativity and higher-order thinking. Implications for the uses of television and computers in early childhood education programs are also presented.

Part III of this *Handbook* deals with policy issues. Early childhood educators are becoming increasingly aware that legislation and regulation established at the local, state, and national levels influence all facets of early childhood programs. Whether programs for young children are available to some, all, or no young children is determined by policy decisions. Policy decisions determine what the content of the programs will be, who will teach in these programs, what populations of young children will be served, and how young children and their programs will be evaluated. Educators have begun to see the importance of research in informing such policies; executives, legislators, and administrators should be making decisions based on the best available information. Knowledge of the consequences of policy decisions is also increasingly the focus of policy research. In addition, policy research enables educators and citizens to identify the values upon which these decision are made.

The testing and evaluation of young children is becoming more important in the field of early childhood education. Although testing of young children was deliberately avoided in years past, standardized and nonstandardized forms of evaluation are increasingly being used with young children. In chapter 18 Samuel J. Meisels, Dorothy M. Steele, and Kathleen Quinn-Leering identify the background issues relating to the use of standardized and nonstandardized tests. They suggest why schools have moved toward an acceptance of tests for young children. They discuss the prevalence of "high-stakes testing" with young children—that is, testing used as the basis

for making significant decisions about young children's education and, ultimately, their future. They especially focus on the impact of tests on minority children. The authors also identify the kinds of tests that should be used with young children and some alternatives to testing.

Lorrie A. Shepard and M. Elizabeth Grau continue the discussion of testing as they review the research on school readiness screening. In chapter 19 they focus especially on test use and test validity. They review the uses of screening and readiness tests before and during young children's school careers. They also discuss the current standards for validity evidence. Shepard and Grau analyze different types of readiness measures, including individual intelligence tests, developmental screening measures, the Gesell School Readiness Screening Test, and academic readiness tests. They discuss the validity of readiness tests for specific purposes, such as identifying children as handicapped, selecting children for school entry, placing children in 2-year kindergarten programs or in at-risk kindergartens, and instructional planning.

Play has been considered a key element in early childhood education since programs for young children have been specially designed. The settings in which play takes place have a significant influence on what and how young children play. In chapter 20 James D. Dempsey and Joe L. Frost discuss research on play environments for early childhood education. They analyze the ecology of play from the point of view of child development. They also discuss the variables in indoor and outdoor play settings, including density, space arrangement, materials and equipment, the effects of social variables on play, and temporal aspects of play settings. They also look at the effects of nationality, culture, and socioeconomic status on the uses of play settings. Finally, they provide a model for designing a good play environment for young children.

With changes in the work force, in families, and in the role of women in American society, child care has been the fastest-growing sector in early childhood education in the past generation. Carollee Howes and Claire E. Hamilton review the research on child care for young children in chapter 21. They describe the child care clientele and the forms of child care available in America. They then present research on the quality of child care in centers and family day care homes. Likewise, Howes and Hamilton discuss research on differences in children's development in different forms of child care and in relation to regulatory quality and process quality. They also describe the effects of child care in relation to children's family characteristics and age of entry. At the end of the chapter, Howes and Hamilton draw conclusions from the available research on the quality and effects of different child care arrangements on young children.

Parents are the first teachers of their children. In addition, parental involvement has been seen as a major component of high-quality early childhood programs. Joseph H. Stevens, Jr., Ruth A. Hough, and Joanne R. Nurss review research on the influence of parents on children's development and education in chapter 22. This review covers parents' knowledge and beliefs about development and child-rearing practices. It deals with parent-support systems and programs related to these systems.

It also deals with research relating to intervention programs to train parents to educate their children in a variety of contexts.

In chapter 23 Jeanette A. McCollum and Susan P. Maude present the changing policies and practices that have evolved in early childhood special education. They review the development over time of special legislation in support of early intervention for children with handicapping conditions. They also discuss the characteristics of early childhood special education programs. An important element of current programs is a family-centered approach to early intervention; this element, which is becoming an increasingly common theme of contemporary programs, is also discussed.

Over the past few years special early childhood education programs have been developed for linguistically and culturally diverse children. Eugene E. García discusses research related to the education of these children in chapter 24. He discusses research on language and cognition as well as on bilingualism/multilingualism. García reviews research related to such cultural issues as Americanization and cultural differences within education programs for diverse young children. He critically reviews research on the care and education of linguistically and culturally diverse infants, toddlers, and young children, suggesting the need for a responsive pedagogy.

Other groups for whom special early childhood education programs have been developed are those students identified as being at risk of future educational failure. This is a diverse population that has to be defined differently in different situations. Some children are identified as "at-risk" because of developmental delays. Others are thus identified using demographic characteristics (e.g., poverty, migrant families, families who use languages other than English, teenage parents). In chapter 25 Nancy Karweit reviews research on preschool and kindergarten programs for these children. She analyzes special preschool programs and their effects on at-risk children. She also analyzes how kindergarten practices such as retention, full-day kindergarten, and special instruction affect these children. This analysis presents a profile of programs that are presently available and the outcomes of such programs.

Olivia N. Saracho, in chapter 26, reviews research on the preparation of early childhood teachers in the United States. Her review is organized around the specific elements of a teacher education program, including recruitment and selection, general education, professional foundations, instructional knowledge, practice, and program modification. Because the quality of early childhood programs is closely related to the quality of the staff teaching in such programs, knowledge of teacher preparation serves an important function in the field.

Early childhood education is an international field. Institutions and curricula for young children that have developed in one country have been introduced and modified in others. In chapter 27 Judith A. Evans analyzes early childhood care and development issues from the perspective of developing nations. She analyzes the accomplishments and attendant challenges within these nations. She also analyzes the changes in policy within these nations, the models of programs that are available for the education and care of young children, and the

evidence that provides support for integrated programs. Her argument for early intervention reflects the needs and interests of women and children in these nations. Finally, Evans calls for collaboration to make good models of early education and care internationally available.

Many different research methods are used to expand the body of knowledge in early childhood education, and many different topics are studied. Each of the previous chapters addresses a topic that has been considered worthy of study. Part IV of the *Handbook* presents many of the research methodologies and strategies that are used in studying early childhood education.

In the first chapter of Part IV, chapter 28, William L. Goodwin and Laura D. Goodwin describe the array of standardized and nonstandardized instruments that can be used for measuring the skills and aptitude of young children. They discuss issues related to the value of educational and developmental measurement in American society, the fairness of instruments used to measure young children, the influence of measuring devices on the field of early childhood education, and the different needs for measurement that researchers and practitioners have. They then present a review of different kinds of educational and psychological tests, including cognitive and psychomotor measures. They conclude their chapter with comments on the appropriateness of different measurement devices for young children.

The different forms of measurement used in education provide quantitative data on children and setting. Increasingly, the field of early childhood education is also using techniques that provide qualitative data—information that is descriptive and that cannot be quantified. In chapter 29 Daniel J. Walsh, Joseph J. Tobin, and M. Elizabeth Grau discuss qualitative research methodologies used in early childhood education. They characterize these approaches to research as interpretive research. Such interpretive studies include ethnography and case studies. The authors critique such studies from a constructivist position, offering a wide range of studies as examples. They also raise questions about studying young children in this manner, discussing ways of judging interpretive research and concluding with a section on the politics of interpretive research.

Whereas the first 2 chapters in part IV focus on studying children, in chapter 30 Thelma Harms and Richard M. Clifford discuss the value of studying educational settings. They provide a theoretical framework for studying such settings and use this framework to identify the key components of educational settings. Harms and Clifford then describe the instruments that can be used to assess the quality of early childhood setting, discussing the advantages and disadvantages of each.

In chapter 31 Donald L. Peters discusses trends in demographic and behavioral research on teaching in early childhood settings. He identifies the questions addressed by such research, including demographic questions, status/characteristic questions, historical/contextual questions, process questions, and developmental questions. Peters also discusses the role of theory in such research as well as the qualitative and quantitative methodologies used. Finally, he addresses the future directions that such research should take.

As noted earlier, the relationship between research and policy is becoming increasingly important in the education of young children. In chapter 32 Sharon Lynn Kagan discusses the apparent schism between research and policy. She also discusses the various challenges to policy research, including those related to the lack of definitional clarity, those associated with process and context, and those associated with measuring outcomes relevant to policy. Policy research is interpreted in relationship to children's rights, which include their rights to optimal development; physical health; a healthy, safe environment; enduring love and support from parents and family; support from other individuals and institutions; continuity; and developmentally appropriate care and education. Kagan also discusses the function of policy in providing quality early childhood care and education that is cost-effective, accessible, and affordable, and in coordinating and integrating that care with other child- and family-development services.

The final chapter in the *Handbook* is devoted to cross-national research methodology. Using a case study of Chinese and Japanese kindergartens, Harold Stevenson, Shinying Lee, and Theresa Graham discuss cross-cultural research on kindergarten education. They first present the historical and philosophical background on Asian early childhood education, focusing specifically on kindergartens in Japan, China, and Taiwan. They also discuss ways of devising their observational method. The authors then present comparative data for kindergartens in Japan, Taiwan, and the United States, including data on academic achievement and cognitive ability, kindergarten teachers' beliefs, and mothers' attitudes and beliefs. The authors also discuss quantitative studies of cross-cultural phenomena, and means of making cross-cultural comparisons.

A FINAL NOTE

A book such as this is often seen as more theoretical than practical. Although research studies educational practice, it seldom directly leads to the creation of educational practice. Yet research informs practice. By helping practitioners reflect on practice and assess their ideas about their work, the *Handbook* can suggest new visions of early childhood education. In this way it may be among the most practical of all educational endeavors.

References

Antler, J. (1987). *Lucy Sprague Mitchell: The making of a modern woman*. New Haven, CT: Yale University Press.

Kramer, R. (1988). *Maria Montessori: A biography*. Reading, MA: Addison-Wesley.

Ross, E. D. (1976). *The kindergarten crusade*. Athens, OH: Ohio University Press.

Weber, E. (1984). *Ideas influencing early childhood education*. New York: Teachers College Press.

CHILD DEVELOPMENT AND EARLY EDUCATION

COGNITIVE DEVELOPMENT AND EARLY CHILDHOOD EDUCATION

Kelvin L. Seifert

UNIVERSITY OF MANITOBA

Assessing cognition in young children is like the old story of the blind feeling the elephant: What the animal "is" depends on which part you touch, and for what purpose. Although cognitive theorists are not cognitively blind, they do examine different parts of children's thinking, highlight different cognitive processes and structures, and present different metaphors for cognition. The multiple meanings that result are not always consistent. But they are desirable for early educators, provided that they stimulate broader, more flexible practices in teaching young children, rather than prompting theoretical evangelisms determined to promote only a "one true" perspective on cognition.

In writing this chapter, therefore, I hope to promote flexibility and breadth of perspective. The chapter will organize key views and research about children's thinking and use the views where possible to suggest desirable teaching practices for young children. The rest of the chapter is divided into 3 main sections. First comes a discussion of human information processing, especially as it relates to preschool and young school-age children. The discussion includes work inspired both by the dominant serial-processing models of thinking and by the newer parallel-processing, or "connectionist," model. Second, the chapter discusses structural views of cognitive development. Note, though, that this section does *not* focus on the most famous exemplar of this structural theory, Jean Piaget, since so much research during the past 2 decades has demonstrated a substantial need to revise and qualify Piaget's version of structuralism. Instead the section will focus on Piaget's intellectual descendants, the "neo-Piagetians." The third part of the chapter presents sociocultural views of cognitive development, such as exemplified by Vygotsky, and as elaborated by other culturally oriented developmental psychologists. All 3 sections will comment in passing on the relevance of theoretical concepts and models to developmentally appropriate practices that stimulate young children's thinking. The emphasis, however, will be on theories, models, and the research they generate.

There are obviously many more developmental themes and variations than the ones covered in this chapter, but the selection herein reflects the major perspectives for understanding children developmentally, as identified by philosophers and historians of developmental psychology (Kuhn & Meacham, 1983; Overton, 1988). Philosophically, and in spite of intermittent "rationalist" overtones, information-processing theory belongs to the tradition of British empiricism of Locke and Hume, in which the mind begins with few features and gains structure and knowledge directly from experience. Structural theories of development come from the more truly rationalist tradition of Kant and Descartes, in which dimensions of thought emerge on the basis of rational reflection about experiences, and new knowledge is fitted to the emerging dimensions. The Vygotskian perspective comes from the sociohistorical tradition originating with Hegel and continued by Marx, in which the give-and-take of social circumstances provides a framework within which individuals learn to think in culturally meaningful and appropriate ways. As the following comments will indicate, however, these characterizations are approximate rather than exact.

The author wishes to thank Robbie Case and Raphael Diaz, for their helpful comments on earlier versions of this chapter. Research for this chapter was completed at the Center for Educational Research at Stanford University.

INFORMATION PROCESSING
IN YOUNG CHILDREN

Information-processing theory models human thinking after the workings of a computer. The approach has gained considerable support among psychologists during the past 2 decades (Siegler, 1983). Its popularity probably reflects 2 events: the enormous growth of computer technology in society, and the failure of numerous research studies during the 1970s and 1980s to support Piaget's theory of broad cognitive stages (Gelman & Baillargeon, 1983). Although information-processing theorists began by studying adult thinking, the field has expanded both to investigate children's thinking and to include a wider range of processing models. These changes have led to major shifts in certain research questions and consequent findings, some of which are discussed below (Klahr, 1989).

Whether applied to children or to adults, information-processing theory focuses on the precise, detailed steps of thinking. In this regard it differs noticeably from broad-scale theories of development, such as Piaget's or Freud's. Similar to a computer, the mind is viewed as having distinct parts that make distinct contributions to thinking in a distinct order. In one common version of the theory, environmental stimuli enter through a *sensory register* or buffer, which preserves stimuli exactly as it receives them, though only briefly. Within a fraction of a second, the input fades unless transferred to *short-term memory* for further processing. Short-term memory corresponds approximately to what people regard as momentary awareness: the feeling of attending to an idea or experience for a few seconds, and then forgetting about it. Unless further processing occurs in short-term memory, in fact, memories and stimuli located there will spontaneously deteriorate or disappear after about 2 to 20 seconds (Ellis, 1987). By using various mental strategies, however, a person can transfer the contents of short-term memory to *long-term memory*, where they can be preserved for very long periods, and perhaps even indefinitely.

The model just described has a serial or linear organization, with just one or a few steps occurring at a time. As noted later in this section, however, other cognitive architecture for information processing is possible—especially architecture that assumes parallel or simultaneous steps during thinking. The nature of this cognitive architecture has important consequences, both theoretical and practical. For the moment, though, consider only the serially organized model of thinking—roughly, attention/short-term memory/long-term memory. This is still the model most often associated with information processing theory.

When this serial view of thinking has been applied to children, it has led to specific questions not originally asked in information-processing theory applied to adults (Kail, 1984; Siegler & Jenkins, 1989; Bjorklund, 1990). Do younger children, for example, have the same memory capacity as older children, either short-term or long-term? Do they use the same memory strategies as older children and adults, or simpler ones, or none at all? Can cognitive strategies be taught, or (a subtle distinction) must they simply be learned?

As it turns out, research on children's thinking offers no final answers to questions like these. But the research does suggest important possibilities about children's thinking, including hypotheses that promise to help in planning educational programs for young children. To understand some of these, consider four areas of research on information processing in young children. The first concerns the nature of children's short-term memory; the second, the development and effectiveness of preschoolers' thinking strategies; the third, the origins and nature of long-term memory in the preschool years; and the fourth, the nature of basic mental architecture for processing information. These are by no means the only areas relevant to early education, but they suggest the range of the implications and some of the differences among information-processing theorists themselves.

Short-Term Memory in Young Children

Once children pass infancy, age seems to make little difference in how well they register information in their senses (Rovee-Collier, 1987). Preschool children can notice a simple familiar object or shape (like a triangle or a face) just about as quickly as do older children when the object is flashed on the screen for a fraction of a second. What does change during the preschool years is *how much* information can be processed at once. Three-year-olds can repeat fewer random digits immediately after hearing them than can 6- or 8-year-olds. And compared to older children, younger children find it very hard to perform a secondary task, such as tapping a finger on the table, while performing a primary task, such as counting a set of objects (Bjorklund & Harnishfeger, 1987). The majority of information-processing psychologists (but not all) have taken these findings to mean that short-term memory develops with age, making older, school-age children able to deal with more simultaneous information than preschool children (Case, Kurland, & Goldberg, 1982). With greater age, children need not just tap *or* count; they can do both.

What do changes in short-term memory imply for teachers and other professionals working with young children? For one thing, the changes confirm the importance of a long-standing practice of good teachers: that they should make the classroom as free of unnecessary or distracting stimuli as possible. As the study by Bjorklund and Harnishfeger suggests, distractions interfere with thinking in young children more than in older children. (Unfortunately, however, the research about short-term memory does *not* help teachers distinguish between true distractions and unexpected positive opportunities to shift attention. If one child has only partly finished a painting when another child begins talking with her, is this a distraction from painting or a social opportunity?)

Less obviously, perhaps, the evidence for increases in short-term memory suggests that many preschool tasks could profit from detailed analysis into constituent tasks that require handling less information at any one moment. Tying shoelaces, for example, requires attending to 2 strings, a half-hitch knot, and 2 bows, all in a specific coordinated sequence. However well a preschool child may be able to perform each element separately, he or she may be overwhelmed by doing them as an integrated, continuous series. Analyzing and practicing the elements separately, and later in controlled combinations, may therefore meet the challenge of shoelaces consistent with the child's short-term memory limitations (see also Reid, 1992).

Cognitive Strategies in Young Children

Cognitive strategies are deliberate methods for organizing and remembering information. In learning the identities of baseball players, for example, a young baseball fan might deliberately classify the players according to which team each belonged to, or according to which position (e.g., pitcher, first base) that a player held. Many cognitive strategies are more sophisticated than this, but whatever their exact nature, they are a primary way for transferring information from short-term memory (seeing the ball player on TV for the first time) to long-term memory (recalling the player's identity later).

Production Deficiencies. Early studies suggest that preschool and early school-age children do not spontaneously use cognitive strategies, but that they can do so when specifically instructed (Harnishfeger & Bjorklund, 1990). In a typical memory study, a child might be given a collection of pictures depicting animals, vehicles, and furniture, and told to learn the pictures well enough to remember them later. Given this task, older children (third grade and up) engage in a variety of strategies: They may classify the pictures as an aid to memory, study the more unfamiliar pictures longer, or rehearse names for the pictures vocally. Younger children tend not to use these methods of their own accord. They will use them when coached to do so; but typically they still fail to use the strategies spontaneously on further, related memory tasks.

Cognitive psychologists at first dubbed this problem a *production deficiency* (Flavell, 1970), because young children showed capacity for cognitive strategies, but merely failed to "produce" them. More recent research, however, suggests a more complex picture of how preschoolers use (or fail to use) strategies. In many situations, it seems, young children actually do use cognitive strategies, but the strategies are overly simple or vulnerable to mistakes. A 3-year-old may deliberately remember where he or she hides a stuffed animal, for example, by pointing at the hiding place continuously, or by staring at the location (Wellman, 1988). These behaviors qualify as cognitive strategies because they are deliberate efforts to remember a piece of information. Unfortunately they do not work reliably if the child has to leave the room temporarily or must turn to carry out some other action; after these interruptions, the child may fail to find the right place to stare or point at.

Utilization Deficiencies. Even when a preschool child uses a strategy suited to the task, the strategy does not seem to help learning and memory as effectively as when it is used by an older child (Miller, 1990). In one series of studies, for example, 4-year-olds were asked to learn the names of pictures hidden under 12 small trapdoors (DeMarie-Dreblow & Miller, 1988; Woody-Ramsy & Miller, 1988). Six of the doors had a picture of a cage on them, indicating that they concealed a picture of an animal; the other 6 had a picture

of a house, indicating that they concealed a picture of a household object. The child's job was to learn the names of only one kind of object—either the animals or the household objects—by lifting the appropriate doors and studying their contents.

In this situation, only the youngest children showed no sign of strategic learning: Toddlers (2-year-olds) lifted the doors at random. Older preschool children used a deliberate strategy, namely spending more time opening the doors of the relevant category. By age 4, in fact, many children were devoting nearly all of their study time to the relevant doors—presumably the most effective strategy of all. Unfortunately the strategy did not seem to make any difference: The recall of the 4-year-old strategy users was no better than the recall of children the same age who failed to use the strategy.

In this and other situations requiring deliberate learning, the benefits of cognitive strategies do not seem to occur until a child has practiced using them for a while. A transitional period occurs, marked not so much by a production deficiency as by a *utilization deficiency:* a failure not to produce, but to use the results of what is produced (Miller, 1990). The problem seems to come from mental effort needed to use new, unfamiliar strategies: Initially, a strategy must be carried out self-consciously and deliberately, leaving little attention or short-term memory space for processing the results of the strategy. As a child practices the strategy, however, it becomes more automatic, requires less attention, and allows more attention to the cognitive results. Similar patterns of development occur for school-age children (Bjorklund & Harnishfeger, 1987).

Connectionism: Do Children Develop General Strategies at All? In recent years, some psychologists have begun questioning whether rule-like strategies are really an important part of information processing at all, either for children or adults (Smolensky, 1988; Rummelhart, 1989). Instead they propose *connectionism:* the view that regularities in thinking appear rule-governed because of the simultaneous interplay of countless connections between specific neurons or neural networks in the brain. Unlike the traditional associationist view of learning favored in earlier times, the new connectionists see human knowledge as contained entirely in the specific relations or connections *between* nodes, rather than somehow "in" the nodes themselves (Bereiter, 1991).

This view leads to a very different architecture of human information processing than described earlier: Instead of short-term and long-term memory functions governed by rule-like constraints, the mind has literally millions of nodes and connections, each able to activate or inhibit neighboring nodes slightly each time they are used. What is important is that the connections operate simultaneously rather than sequentially, as computers usually do, and as conventional models of information processing have assumed. A multitude of nodes and connections operating in parallel, it seems, can create organized, stable patterns even without a central processor or "executive" function, which the serial models have required.

The connectionist view has had notable, counterintuitive successes in explaining children's cognitive development. Children's acquisition of past tense verb forms, for example, can be explained very accurately—not as children's search for implicit rules of grammar, as previously thought, but as the gradual development of a vast network of associations be tween specific verbs and their past tense forms (Rummelhart & McClelland, 1987). As children acquire these associations, the associations influence each other so as to make rule-like use of past tenses increasingly likely on any one occasion, though never completely certain. Computer simulations of this process have even demonstrated that temporary overgeneralizations of verb tenses are inevitable, given connectionist assumptions, and that overgeneralizations are followed by later, more accurate use of regular forms combined with selected irregularities.

Connectionist processes may also coexist with rule-using strategies. Research by Siegler and his associates (Siegler & Jenkins, 1989; Siegler, in press) suggests this possibility. They have found that first-grade children use rule-like algorithms as fall-back strategies to solve unfamiliar problems (23 + 56; or sounding out the word "locomotive") where they cannot re trieve an answer directly from memory. With familiar problems (2 + 2; "cat"), they tend to use simple retrieval or association, even though it leads to more errors and even though they are capable of the longer, but less error-prone accurate algorithm. Children's simple retrieval, furthermore, shows connectionist patterns: Selecting a particular answer from memory depends on the strength of its association with other, competing answers, as well as with the original problem.

Implications for Early Educators. For early childhood edu cators, this research suggests several useful ideas for teaching young children to use cognitive strategies. First and most obvi ously, teachers should be aware of the limitations in children's abilities to use cognitive strategies. Most young children cannot use strategies widely, effectively, or consciously. Yet a teacher can reasonably encourage many young children to use the sim plest strategies (like grouping objects for later recall), provided the teacher does not assume that a child's learning will benefit immediately.

In encouraging young children to think strategically, fur thermore, it is important to remember that failure to benefit immediately from a cognitive strategy may not signify failure to think. Instead it may signify an initial step toward making the strategy more automatic, and therefore eventually effective. Classroom situations illustrating this initial step are common place. A 4-year-old child may, for example, deliberately leave a day's paintings or craft work where he or she will remember them "easily" at the end of the day; yet in spite of deliberate effort, the child cannot remember the chosen spot later. In at least some such cases, the child may be so busy being delib erate that the to-be-remembered materials themselves escape notice.

Connectionist views of information processing provide more controversial implications for teachers of young children. They seem to suggest a need for direct teaching of specific knowledge to young children (Bereiter, 1991)—an idea that has not often been well received by leaders in early education, who more often highlight children's right to choose their own learning (Bredekamp, 1987). However, if connectionism con tinues to prove fruitful in explaining children's learning and de velopment, early educators may need to rethink their frequent, pervasive commitment to curricular self-choice.

Consider, for example, ways of introducing children to read ing. Advocates of "whole-language" approaches object, at times strenuously, to teaching relationships between written letters and spoken sounds. Although some of their reasons may be sound (Teale & Sulzby, 1986), others may stem from miscon struing this task as one of teaching hard-and-fast, but ineffec tive rules about letter-sound correspondences (Adams, 1990). Connectionists would argue, in contrast, that learning the corre spondences is more like a form of perceptual learning—seeing and recognizing numerous specific patterns in specific cases. If phonics is approached in this spirit, then the connectionist architecture of the brain presumably organizes the letter-sound correspondences on its own, sooner or later.

Long-Term Memory in Young Children

The term "long-term memory in young children" may seem like an oxymoron, given how frequently children forget signifi cant events in everyday life. As older children and adults, most people cannot recall much that happened before the age of 5 or 6, and usually nothing at all before the age of about 3 or 4 (Wetzler & Sweeney, 1986). Determining whether long-term memory actually exists therefore presents a challenging test of whether information-processing views have relevance to early childhood.

In spite of everyday forgetfulness and early childhood am nesia, it turns out that certain kinds of long-term memory do occur even in early childhood. An assortment of studies shows that preschoolers can recall events that happened many months earlier (Nelson, 1989). Two-year-olds can often remember the locations of novel objects seen only once, many months earlier—for example, the drawer where a rarely-visited grand parent kept a deck of cards on a previous visit (Hudson & Nel son, 1986). Four-year-olds can remember and verbally recount many details of unusual experiences (like a museum visit) ex perienced a full year earlier (Hudson, 1984). When the expe rience is a repeated one, such as a meal or bedtime routine, however, the particulars of specific occasions quickly become clouded with a general memory of the routine—in this exam ple, a meal or bedtime "script."

Kinds of Long-Term Memory. Memory researchers sort out these findings by distinguishing among different kinds of mem ories, and attempting to study each kind separately (Solomon, Goethals, Kelley, & Stephens, 1989). One kind, for example, is *semantic memory,* which is a recollection of enduring mean ings and recurring events; another is *episodic memory,* which is a recollection of specific events or objects experienced on a specific occasion. Preschool children develop both kinds simultaneously, whether or not they attend any educational pro gram, such as preschool or kindergarten, where skillful mem ory is helpful.

Katherine Nelson has proposed several steps by which mem ory develops in the preschool years, based on reviewing the research in this area (1989). During the first and second year of life, infants and toddlers have primarily episodic memories— recollections of specifics. As certain events begin to repeat themselves (such as feeding), however, young children be gin developing semantic or generalized memories for them, though the "scripts" for such events still remain cognitively isolated and fragmented from each other.

As individual scripts develop, they cause children to expect certain events and behaviors in the future (such as how an adult *ought* to act when reading a storybook). They also allow children to differentiate specific occasions of a script (how father told that story on occasion X) from the script itself (how fathers tell stories). Conscious distinctions between episodes and scripts eventually create a budding awareness of "history," a sense that events unfold in some larger framework of meanings. This sense of historical process develops and generalizes to many of the events and scripts that children experience, finally creating a sense of personal life history—one expressed through autobiographical memory (or the "story of my life"). This last development does not usually occur until early school age; but when it finally does, it brings an end to childhood amnesia. From them on, personal episodic memories can be placed into a comprehensive, ongoing script that describes the child's particular life story.

Factors Influencing Long-Term Memory. Information-processing researchers have identified a number of factors affecting the speed and completeness of memory: (1) how knowledge is represented, (2) knowledge base, (3) children's informal theories, and (4) parents' styles of interactions. These are not mutually exclusive, even though the discussion that follows considers them one at a time.

FORMS OF KNOWLEDGE REPRESENTATION. The first factor is *how knowledge is represented:* the congruence between how a child commits an experience to memory, compared to how the child tries to recall it later. One study found, for example, that first-grade children recall the names of their classmates much better in sequences based on children's seating arrangements in the classroom than in sequences based on alphabetical order or gender category (Chi, 1988). Presumably, sequencing by table arrangements reflected how children experienced and organized the information when learning it. Requiring the children to use conventional adult categories for organizing recall made the children seem less cognitively capable. Asking for "all the girls" or "all the boys" led to a cumbersome strategy of mapping the seating arrangement onto the more abstract category. All the girls (or boys) at one table were recalled first, followed by all the girls (or boys) at the next, until all tables were reviewed.

KNOWLEDGE BASE. A second factor affecting memory development is the extent of children's *knowledge base:* how much they know that is related to a topic or experience. Lack of background knowledge contributes to apparent inconsistencies in children's thinking, as well as to less reliable memory. Preschool children's concepts of *animism* (whether or not something is alive) shows the problem clearly. Decades ago, Piaget found that preschool-age children often claim that many nonliving objects are in fact animate (Piaget, 1951). Clouds and automobiles, for example, may both be seen as alive because they "sometimes move." These particular responses have been confirmed repeatedly over the years in various studies, student theses, and informal conversations with preschoolers.

Piaget interpreted such responses as showing egocentrism in young children, but more recent research has questioned this interpretation. Gelman, Spelke, and Meck (1983) found that children have very accurate knowledge about certain aspects of animism when the objects in question are highly familiar. A stuffed doll, for example, is *not* alive because "it's legs can't grow." But a pet dog *is* in fact alive because "you can go running with it," even though children also know that you cannot go running with a stuffed doll.

One way to reconcile Piaget's observations with Gelman's is to view preschoolers' knowledge as existing in isolated pieces or pockets (Chi & Ceci, 1987). A young child may have bits of knowledge about dolls, dogs, clouds, and the concept of *being alive*, but those bits of knowledge are not coordinated with each other. The child may therefore contradict himself or herself without being aware of the contradiction. As additional knowledge develops about the superordinate concept (in this case, animism), the bits become coordinated and the child's responses become more consistent. Children's knowledge therefore becomes more fully organized as they get older.

CHILDREN'S INFORMAL THEORIES. In contrast to the somewhat bottom-up mechanism proposed by Chi and Ceci, some developmental psychologists view cognitive changes as based on the development of broad, informal theories believed by children implicitly. The informal theories concern basic realms of knowledge, and children restructure or change them as they grow older.

The inconsistencies about animism between Piaget and Gelman, for example, have been interpreted by Susan Carey (1985) as signifying a change in children's informal theories about biological life. Drawing on both her own and others' research on animism, she notes several ways that younger preschoolers do not differentiate at first between psychological functions and biological functions. When asked, for example, which animals have a (fictitious) internal organ called an "omentum," given that either a human or a dog has one, individuals usually grant an omentum to other creatures in spite of ignorance about the nature of an omentum. But a developmental trend occurs: Adults and older children generalize more strongly from one animal to another animal, whereas preschoolers generalize more strongly from humans to other animals (Carey, 1988a).

To Carey, results of this and related experiments suggest that young children have an informal theory of "life" that undergoes change from about age 4 to 10. For several reasons, the revision does not represent an increase in knowledge, but a radical restructuring of children's thinking, akin to a paradigm shift in formal scientific research (Carey, 1988b). One reason is that early in this period, children seem to regard psychology and biology as part of the "same" domain of knowledge. A function like eating, for example, is treated at first as psychological. Eating is relevant to whether you can eat candy, what your favorite food is, and the like. Only later do biological functions like nutrition and survival become identified and differentiated as a separate realm of discourse. Along with the differentiation come changes in what constitutes a biologically satisfactory explanation ("You brush your teeth to kill the germs on them" instead of "You brush your teeth to make your breath smell better"). Throughout this change, core biological concepts take on new meanings ("life" is no longer equivalent to consciousness, for example).

Another informal theory, one that may be even more basic is children's "theory of mind," which is made up of preschoolers' guiding assumptions about how desires and beliefs influence human action (Astington, Harris, & Olson, 1988; Wellman, 1990). A theory of mind develops in toddlerhood even before young children begin distinguishing biology from psychology. It becomes relatively sophisticated even before children enter school, and influences how children represent and remember knowledge about people.

Much of the evidence for preschoolers' theory of mind comes from research about children's capacity for false beliefs (Flavell, 1988; Wimmer & Penner, 1983). In a typical false-belief task, a preschool child watches a story reenacted with dolls or puppets in which one of the characters is deceived because an object has been moved; one character moves a piece of candy from one hiding place to another, for example, without telling the other character. Will a child watching this story understand that the misled character will look in the original hiding place, and presumably therefore have a false belief about where the candy is hiding? In the basic form of this experiment, just described, children 3 and under fail to understand; but children 4 and over tend to succeed—that is, they "understand false belief." Varying the conditions of the task, however, can sometimes make even the younger preschoolers seem to understand false belief (Hala, Chandler, & Fritz, 1991).

This line of research, along with other related work, suggests that preschool children do indeed have a theory of mind for understanding the everyday actions of individuals. Wellman (1990) proposes, for example, that a "belief-desire psychology" guides children starting around the age of 3. In this theory of mind, other peoples' action simply reflect their beliefs and desires, with no further mental processing modifying outward, visible actions. Individuals also learn directly from experience, by passively copying or registering experiences that come their way.

During the years 3 to 6, however, children add to their theory of mind complications that include the influence of perceptions, emotions, physical states, and psychological traits. These additional factors account for why a person's actions do not always match their beliefs and desires. Children develop from a simple "copy" theory of learning to an "interpretative" theory of learning. Instead of passively registering input, children now believe that the mind construes, filters, or interprets input. As a result, the same experience may now produce different learnings in different individuals, and actions may sometimes mask or modify beliefs and desires. These changes in theory of mind make substantial differences in what young children can learn about persons' motives, thoughts, and feelings, as well as what they can therefore recall of them. A copy theory of mind, for example, makes a child prone to confusion about another person's true intentions whenever the person expresses tactfulness.

PARENT INTERACTION. A fourth factor influencing the development of memory is *parent interaction styles,* some of which encourage particular ways of organizing knowledge. One study examined parental influence by observing conversations between mothers and their preschool children during visits to a museum. Mothers varied in their conversational styles: Some engaged in narrative reminiscences ("Do you remember when we went to the zoo and saw a bear like this?"), whereas others made more factual and conceptual comments ("There's another example of a reptile"). Interviews with the preschoolers afterwards showed two important results: first, that the children only remembered the particular museum displays where *both* mother and child had actually conversed (versus only the mother speaking, or only silence); and second, that children with reminiscing parents recalled much more of the museum visit than children with conceptualizing parents (Nelson, 1989).

Why did reminiscing help? One possibility is that reminiscing places knowledge in a narrative context, a form that may be especially basic or powerful in human learning and development. In distinguishing between narrative knowing and "paradigmatic" or analytic knowing, for example, Bruner has argued that narrative is far more fundamental psychologically (Bruner, 1986, 1990). Consistent with Nelson's findings described above, he argues that narrative forms of knowing develop very early—perhaps even before language is established. Throughout the life span, narrative knowledge gets its power because it combines episodic memory with semantic memory (Bruner, 1989). By nature, narrative interprets unique events—a plot—in terms of typical or "canonical" knowledge of background culture or circumstances.

Implications for Early Educators. The research on memory described in the previous sections has a number of implications for early education. First, research on knowledge representation (e.g., Chi's) suggests that teachers should attend to how children prefer to organize new knowledge. Young children may learn more about animals if they sort them not by official biological taxonomy, for example, but by "petability," softness, or size. They may learn to zipper jackets more easily if the task is represented as a story ("A bird flying out of its nest"), rather than as expository instructions. Leading children toward adult, categorical representations of knowledge remains an important goal for the long term, but getting to that goal may first require recognizing and accepting children's idiosyncratic, childlike representations and building from them.

Second, the research shows the importance of broadening young children's knowledge base, but it also suggests that children can only do this with adult support. In practical teaching terms, this means continually offering children new domains of activity and information—and more controversially, it means not always tolerating self-choice of activities when they are offered. The child who chooses crafts to the exclusion of other activities can learn little about other activities; perhaps therefore such a child should be encouraged to try an unfamiliar activity some of the time. Of course, research about memory also shows the comparative difficulty and slowness of learning in knowledge-poor areas (see Chi, in press). So deliberately broadening students' experiences carries a responsibility to support their experiences, once begun, and to relate knowledge-poor with knowledge-rich areas. For example, a child who always paints and never reads can make paintings about books; and a child who always reads and never paints can read books about painting.

Third, teachers should recognize that informal theories of knowledge may guide the actions of even the youngest preschoolers. The likelihood that 3-year-olds have a "copy theory" of learning, for example, may prevent them from using metacognitive strategies, which generally involve interpretation and modification of knowledge (see Wellman, 1988). Likewise, there may be little point in correcting very young children for making what look to adults like falsehoods. But there may be some point in helping older children (kindergarten age and up) to understand developmental differences about deception: showing them that falsehoods may mean something different to them, with their awareness of false belief, than to a playmate or sibling a few years younger.

Fourth, teachers should recognize that accumulating knowledge piecemeal or bit by bit may still lead to organized outcomes, even without efforts by adults to teach explicit rules for organizing it (see Bereiter, 1991). This is the connectionist legacy. Ironically, after decades of serving as an exemplar of rule-oriented learning, language acquisition may provide the most dramatic example of bottom-up, piecemeal learning in early childhood (see Rummelhart & McClelland, 1987). But other rule-like skills may also develop that are actually learned better by the acquisition of interplay of numerous connections than by explicit rule learning. As already mentioned, reading may be one such skill; and complex thinking and problem-solving skills may even be another (Thagard, 1989).

Note, though, that where bottom-up learning does occur, children need ample practice at recognizing specific connections or associations. To be effective, furthermore, the practice must occur in context where the connections normally occur. Toddlers need to hear conversational dialogue, not isolated samples of language. Preschoolers need to learn phoneme-grapheme connections by hearing print connected to speech in natural stories, not by hearing explicit statements about the rules governing phonics.

STRUCTURAL THEORIES OF COGNITIVE DEVELOPMENT

As the preceding section shows, information-processing theories have stimulated research about specific cognitive functions, and some of the research has implications for developmentally appropriate practice. Teachers can use the research on short-term memory, cognitive strategies, and long-term memory development to guide classroom activities for young children.

At the same time, though, the highly focused quality of processing theories obscures the broader cognitive organization that unfolds in children over time, as well as many of the relationships among diverse, everyday cognitive tasks. These are serious limitations for early childhood educators, who normally work with children in diverse, everyday settings, and who often do so for months or even years at a time. In such settings, it makes more sense to speak of children developing, rather than of strategies developing, or of a function like short-term or long-term memory developing. Early childhood teachers usually see their work as assisting "whole children," rather than selected cognitive aspects of a child.

The persistence of issues like these has kept information-processing theories from dominating early childhood education as much as they have dominated the fields of cognitive and developmental psychology. In early education, instead, an important place has remained for *structural theories* of thinking—those that emphasize broad relationships among cognitive skills, as well as comparatively long-term changes (Levin, 1986; Case, 1986, 1991). Structural theories are often also called "neo-Piagetian," because most show the influence of Piaget's classic stage theory, while modifying or elaborating on key assumptions of that theory.

Two Basic Assumptions of Structural Theories

In addition to emphasizing broad relationships and long-term changes, structural theories have borrowed 2 other ideas from Piaget. First, they propose universal sequences among cognitive structures. Ability A must come before ability B, and (in most structural theories) a child cannot skip ability B and go directly to ability C. In classic Piagetian theory, for example, sensorimotor thinking must come before preoperational thinking, which in turn must come before concrete operational thinking. The various neo-Piagetian theorists propose analogous cognitive landmarks; and just as Piaget did, they also propose minor substages within each major stage (Demetriou, 1988). The names and timing of stages vary with the theory, but bear a family resemblance to each other.

The lockstep in sequencing stages results from their logically hierarchical relationship: Each later stage is thought to include, by its nature, the features of the stage preceding it. In classic Piagetian theory, for example, the symbolic thought of preschoolers supposedly entails (or grows logically out of) what Piaget called "object permanence," created by infants out of earlier, purely sensorimotor skills.

Second, structural theories borrow Piaget's emphasis on self-construction of thinking. Many cognitive skills do not originate directly from experiences, it is argued, but indirectly by mentally organized experiences to fit with prior knowledge and cognitive strategies. The conservation skills made famous by Piaget supposedly originate through such indirect organization (Piaget, 1936/1963): Adults do not normally teach children explicitly that 2 clay balls retain the same volume even if one ball is squashed; instead, children surmise this invariance from numerous experiences with changeable objects, and from pondering those experiences repeatedly.

Given these key assumptions, it is actually surprising that early childhood educators have found one classic structural theory—the one developed by Piaget—so appealing (Elkind, 1976, 1981). As both proponents and critics have pointed out, structural theories such as Piaget's emphasize stages or levels of cognitive development rather than the bread-and-butter concerns of teaching, which are transitions between stages and levels (Sternberg, 1984; Case, 1991). Most of the time, teachers are less concerned about where children belong developmentally, than about what children can become next.

At first look, therefore, structural approaches often imply that teachers have little work to do. Stages seem to emerge inevitably, thanks to children organizing thinking on their own. They also are inevitable because the inherent logic of later stages is more compelling than the logic of earlier stages, and therefore impossible to give up once in place. Three-year-olds do not adopt symbolic representations of objects (like words, make-believe gestures), for example, because someone teaches symbolic representations to them directly. Instead they make this cognitive change because they independently construct sensory and motoric representations of objects, and because they find symbolic representations to be convenient and powerful, once developed. The early childhood educator's role therefore appears to be passive, consisting of making sure that children have opportunity to teach themselves important cognitive skills. In the reality of classroom practice, few early educators probably behave so passively, but many do seem to believe in "watching and waiting" as an ideology (Lay-Dopyera & Dopyera, 1990; Kohlberg & DeVries, 1987a, 1987b).

Revised Assumptions in Structural Theories

Actually, the comments above apply only to the most classic version of the structural approach—the stage theory of cognition developed by Piaget earlier in this century. More recent versions of the structural approach have extended and modified the basic assumptions to give more emphasis to the actual processes of thinking. Even committed Piagetians, it seems, have elaborated on Piaget's originally limited comments about cognitive processes and given less attention to his assertions about cognitive landmarks and stages (Beilin, 1989). The newer structural theories have also concentrated on how specific or "local" cognitive structures are built, rather than on comprehensive cognitive abilities that supposedly operate in all areas of thinking. This pair of changes has made structural theories more directly useful to teachers helping young children to learn.

Examples of Structural Theory-in-Use

To understand these revisions and their effect on teaching practices, consider 2 examples of structural theory—one published by an early childhood educator (Kamii, 1985, 1989) and the other by a developmental psychologist (Case, 1992). As it turns out, the 2 examples have complementary strengths. What the educational theory gains in classroom usefulness, it loses in theoretical coherence—and vice versa.

(Neo-)Piagetian Theory Applied. A number of educators and psychologists have made direct, explicit efforts to relate Piaget to early childhood education (e.g., Elkind, 1987; Hohmann, Banet, & Weikart, 1979; Weikart, 1989; Kamii & DeVries, 1977; Kamii, 1985). The last of these—the work by Kamii and her associates—illustrates how such efforts lead to changes and elaborations in classical structural theory, even though the changes are not always acknowledged as such.

In their most recent work, Kamii and her associates suggest numerous activities for stimulating children's thinking about arithmetic, or what Piaget would have called "number" (Kamii & DeVries, 1977; Kamii, 1985, 1989). None of the activities rely on direct, didactic teaching by the teacher. Instead they emphasize games among children or capitalize on normal classroom routines. One game activity, for example, involves variations

on the Las Vegas card game "blackjack": Children reveal cards from a deck one at a time, keeping a running total and trying to make the total reach as close to 21 as possible. In another activity, children play a variation of the card game "war." In the classic version, children match cards one at a time, and the higher card wins the pair. In Kamii's variation, children show 2 cards at a time, and compare the *sums* of the 2 pairs. Both the blackjack and the war games require additive composition—thinking about and comparing the different ways that addends create a particular sum.

Kamii and associates also describe classroom routines that involve numerical thinking. In one routine, for example, children vote on which of 2 class activities to do, and compare the 2 resulting number sets: the total votes for one activity and the total votes for the other. In another routine activity, one child takes responsibility for photocopying enough weekly newsletters to send home with each child, plus enough extras for other school staff (like the principal) who should receive a copy. These 2 activities call for a working knowledge of numerical equality, and they stimulate children to devise their own procedures for addition, such as the "counting on" often observed among older grade-school students.

Although Kamii considers herself Piagetian rather than neo-Piagetian, her educational applications in fact embody the revised assumptions of the newer structural theories discussed earlier. The neo-Piagetian influence shows up in 2 ways. First is the emphasis on processes of thinking—in this case, on what young children do when they deal with number. Complementing this emphasis is a focus on relatively specific cognitive achievements—in this case, on knowledge of cardinality and ordinality as expressed in specific classroom activities. The curriculum itself makes no claim to be developing broad "structures of the whole," in the sense described by Piaget in his earlier work; it only presents an assortment of number skills that seem logically related to each other.

Nonetheless, Kamii's curriculum shows important commitments to the classic structural tradition of cognitive developmental theory. Curriculum activities are presented together with many informal experiments, reminiscent of Genevan writings and designed to diagnose naturally occurring, minor stages of development for specific thinking skills. Underlying the experiments seems to be a key structuralist message: that children build their own knowledge in an orderly way, at least in the areas illustrated by Kamii's informal experiments.

Underlying the curriculum activities themselves is a different message that is in fact specifically Piagetian: that the process of stage transition is facilitated by social interactions, especially among peers. Kamii does not, however, explicitly discuss whether certain kinds of interactions facilitate cognitive development better than others. Do peers' opinions prove more challenging, for example, when they seem to be about "facts," compared to when they seem to be about "beliefs"? This sort of question has been investigated in recent studies, and with complex results (Goodnow, 1990; Flavell, Flavell, Green, & Moses, 1990; Tudge, 1990). Given the importance of social interaction in early childhood classrooms, the question deserves fuller attention than the structural tradition has given it. Fortunately (for teachers), another theoretical tradition—the sociohistorical one—has attended carefully to the impact of social interaction on cognitive development. That tradition is discussed more fully later in this chapter.

Structural Theory Kept Coherent. Unlike Kamii, who emphasizes curricular aspects, some psychologists have concentrated on building structural theories that are coherent and logical, and that nonetheless take into account the revised structural assumptions described earlier (e.g., Levin, 1986; Demetriou, 1988). Their efforts have led to relatively clear portraits of cognitive development, especially in infancy and early childhood. At the price of clarity, however, applications to early education have been left more implicit than explicit.

The work of Robbie Case, for example, illustrates these qualities (Case, 1985, 1992). After carefully reviewing other neo-Piagetian theories, and after making numerous studies of cognitive development, Case has presented a coherent model of how thinking evolves from birth through adolescence, though with emphasis on infancy and early childhood. In the model, children are continually learning to coordinate cognitive structures that they have learned previously. During early childhood most of these structures are rather specific and concrete, such as drawing with a pencil, throwing a ball, or counting a set of objects. As the structures guiding these actions become coordinated with each other, however, they form new, superordinate cognitive structures, which in turn become coordinated with other superordinate structures. As development unfolds, children gradually acquire abilities to use ever more general cognitive structures. Put in everyday terms, they begin thinking more abstractly and broadly.

To understand this model, consider how children learn to draw—one of many examples described by Case in his publications. During infancy, the child develops 2 cognitive structures of special importance for drawing. One of these allows the child to track interesting objects, such as a crayon, and a second allows him to reach for interesting objects. With practice and cognitive effort, the child gradually becomes able to coordinate these 2 structures into a single superordinate structure: reaching-and-grasping. This new superordinate structure, in turn, gradually becomes coordinated with other newly emerging structures, such as visually monitoring the appearance of the paper while at the same time monitoring the movement of a crayon across the paper. When these superordinate structures finally become coordinated, the child can make marks intentionally, though still randomly. In the dialect of parenting, the child becomes able to "scribble."

These developments take most of the first 2 years to unfold. By the time a child becomes a preschooler, he or she faces new challenges in coordinating cognitive structures. Scribbling continues, but the 2- or 3-year-old child also begins coordinating previous structures that controlled the relationship between crayon and paper, with evolving structures for tracking the relationship between drawn lines and the edge of the paper. The new, higher-order relationship allows the child to draw particular kinds of lines on request—an "up and down" line or a "curve," for example.

Eventually these coordinated structures become cognitive structures in their own right, while at the same time becoming coordinated with each other at still higher levels of generality and flexibility. Around age 5, therefore, most preschoolers

can draw a series of lines and curves with a coordinated visual goal in mind. Stated in more everyday terms, they begin making representational drawings: a sun with rays emanating, or a flower with petals, or a person that looks like a stick figure.

This account of the development of drawing skills is consistent with specific research on children's spatial understandings (Goodnow, 1977; Dennis, 1992; Reid, 1992), as well as with general reviews and informal observations of that development (Winner, 1982; Gardner, 1980, 1983). Its power comes from the 4 qualities of the newer structural theories discussed earlier: (1) the account proposes a series of unpredictable stages that all children normally experience; (2) it assumes that children propel themselves, so to speak, through the stages via their ongoing cognitive constructions; (3) it focuses not on cognitive changes as a whole, but on a relatively discrete area of development (in this case, drawing); and (4) it comments on *how* cognitive development occurs—about its processes rather than only its stages or landmarks.

Implications for Early Education. The most obvious implication of structural approaches like Kamii's and Case's is that they help teachers to match activities to children's current levels of development. Children who cannot yet coordinate lines and curves, for example, can be encouraged to scribble rather than immediately make representational drawings. This "diagnostic placement" function is also the essential legacy of Piagetian theory: Stated in Piagetian terms, children who show limited readiness for symbolic representation (Piaget's preoperational period) supposedly could be stimulated with sensorimotor activities instead, or at least with less abstract forms of symbolic representations.

The new structural theories also have an additional implication: They promise to identify key dimensions of cognitive change that are somewhat general, and in this way promise to make curriculum planning more efficient. It is here that the Piagetian tradition promised too much, by claiming that stages and stage changes were more general than they really are (Gelman & Baillargeon, 1983). The newer structural theories have hopefully corrected this limitation of classic Piagetian theory by focusing squarely on factors that make children's cognitive performances variable, while still searching for central conceptual structures and processes (Case, 1992).

How do neo-Piagetian theories accomplish this goal? First, by distinguishing between cognitive changes that happen quickly through specific learning experiences and those that unfold very slowly, they allow teachers to set priorities among educational goals. In learning to draw, for example, a young preschooler may need months or even years to begin coordinating scribbles into realistic presentations. But the child can profit immediately from practicing the skills he or she currently does have—skills such as manipulating a pencil or crayon, and observing its still-random visual effects on the paper. The changes resulting from the latter activities are variously called *assimilation, focusing, differentiation,* or *automatization of cognitive structures,* depending on the theorist (Sternberg, 1984). Teachers, it would seem, have important responsibilities in fostering both long- and short-term changes; but by understanding both types of changes, they can plan an educational program more effectively.

In addition, the newer structural theories generally agree on the major mechanisms of cognitive change (Fischer & Pipp, 1984; Case, 1985; Pascual-Leone, 1988). They agree in particular that children need (1) to observe others' demonstrating or using thinking skills effectively, (2) to practice newly observed skills themselves, and (3) to set themselves appropriate cognitive goals. In the example of development described earlier, a preschooler must see others draw, practice drawing, and *want* to draw at a level appropriate to his or her current development.

What remains unclear from the revised structural theories is exactly how teachers should translate these uncontroversial conclusions into daily teaching strategies. A number of structural approaches, such as Kamii's discussed earlier, have tried giving such advice about general curriculum planning (e.g., Hohmann et al., 1979). Others have confined their curricular advice to selected tasks or reasoning skills (e.g., Case & Griffin, 1991). Either way they tend to give good teaching advice. As illustrated by Kamii's program earlier, though, the broader the range of advice is, the more the structural theoretical integrity of the advice tends to be compromised.

At the bottom, though, the trade-off between theoretical coherence and educational usefulness may really be a problem belonging primarily to the structuralists, who by definition make rational coherence a hallmark of their approach. The apparent dilemma reduces significantly when viewed from theoretical perspectives that highlight, rather than merely acknowledge, the situational influences on children's thinking. The next section describes such a perspective, and assesses its particular educational usefulness.

SOCIOHISTORICAL PERSPECTIVES ON COGNITIVE DEVELOPMENT

Although cognitive psychology has traditionally emphasized the study of single individuals, some psychologists have deliberately expanded that focus to include the relationship between individuals and the social situations in which individuals do their thinking. This is the *sociohistorical* perspective, one in which thinking is socially and historically situated, and in which thinking cannot even be understood without reference to its social context. As noted earlier, structural theories also acknowledge the importance of social context when they name observation and modeling as important mechanisms of cognitive development. But only sociohistorical theory gives the social context a central place in children's cognitive development. And only it spells out how that context is internalized meaningfully by the child.

The most well-known version of the sociohistorical perspective originated with the Soviet psychologist Lev Vygotsky (1978; Wertsch, 1985, 1989). Vygotsky's ideas grew out of the following questions: How could complex thinking develop in children out of simpler thinking, if the complex forms were not somehow "present" in the first place? Vygotsky's answer was that cognition originates as a shared experience: Knowledge and skills exist at first between an adult and a developing child, or between an older peer and the child. Only gradually do knowledge and skills get internalized by the child. The transfer

happens through a combination of observation, imitation, and internal assimilation of the knowledge and skills. Adults and peers assist this process by transferring greater responsibility for cognitive tasks as they judge the child ready to perform them.

This developmental process contrasts markedly with the one envisioned by the structuralists, including Piaget. In Vygotsky's view, the child begins cognitive life socially, only gradually moving toward cognitive autonomy. The classic structuralist (or Piagetian) view reverses this sequence: Cognitively, a young child begins life alone, gradually becoming more social and less egocentric in perspective. This theoretical difference parallels a common philosophical difference that may exist between certain early childhood curricula: Some (e.g., Montessori) assume that children solve problems best when working independently, but others favor adult involvement during a wide range of problem-solving situations (see Simons & Simons, 1986).

The Zone of Proximal Development

For early childhood educators, a key concept in the sociohistorical tradition is what Vygotsky called the *zone of proximal development* (ZPD), the level at which a child finds a problem too difficult to solve alone, but at which the child can solve it with support from an adult or from a more competent peer (Rogoff & Wertsch, 1984). At a certain point in development, for example, tying a shoelace may frustrate a preschooler who tries this task alone. But at the same point in development, the child may succeed if given a bit of help at crucial points, such as in forming one of the loops.

Research has documented numerous examples of the ZPD in action, beginning in infancy and extending throughout childhood (Rogoff, 1989, 1990; Trevarthen & Logotheti, 1989). All of the situations have an apprenticeship quality: The child observes an adult (the "master craftsperson") perform a relatively complex skill, but the child actually carries out selected parts of it as well, to the extent he or she is able. In engaging in dialogue or conversation, for example, parents of 3- and 4-year-olds frequently extend, elaborate on and recast the preschool child's comments and questions (Nelson, 1985; Tizard & Hughes, 1984). The following (fictitious) example shows the process:

Child: More milk.
Father: You want more milk, do you?
Child: Ummm. [takes a drink] Good.
Father: Tastes good, doesn't it? Especially after playing outside for awhile.

In this exchange, the father provides support for a more elaborate dialogue than the child alone could sustain, and thereby creates a ZPD. Bruner and others have called this process cognitive "scaffolding" (Bruner, 1984; Wood, Bruner, & Ross, 1976).

Similar scaffolding occurs in children's problem solving. In one study Saxe, Guberman, and Gearhart (1987) observed mothers teaching several number tasks (e.g., counting thirteen dots) to their own preschool children. Most mothers adjusted their guidance to the skill level of the child shown at the outset of the task, and they further adjusted the level during the course of the task if the child showed changes in understanding. Yet whatever level of skill a child in fact showed, all mothers ensured eventual "success" for the child by taking over aspects of the task that the child could not do.

Diaz and his associates have observed similar dynamics using 2 other problem-solving tasks (Diaz, Neal, & Amaya-Williams, 1990; Diaz, Neal, & Vachio, 1991). In the first of these, 3-year-olds identified pictures of objects that were alike either in shape or in size; in a second task, they made story-sequences from sets of pictures. As in Saxe's study, mothers assisted the preschoolers to various degrees on both tasks, depending on the skills shown by the children as the tasks unfolded. To a greater degree than in Saxe's study, though, Diaz found evidence suggesting that gradually *withdrawing* or relinquishing support also benefited the children's problem solving. Withdrawing support presumably forced the child to take greater responsibility for the task—provided, of course, that the mother has timed the withdrawal strategically. The ZPD appeared in these studies, but also showed itself as dynamic and changing, not as static.

Implications of the ZPD and the Sociohistorical Perspective

For teachers of young children, the sociohistorical approach offers both good, useful news and bad, overwhelming news. The good, useful news is that the concept of the ZPD has proved helpful in planning teaching strategies. It suggests the importance of active, sensitive involvement with the classroom tasks that children undertake, and reminds teachers of their role in making children's initial activities meaningful to children themselves. "Watching and waiting" for children to teach themselves makes little sense developmentally, in spite of its popularity as an ideology among practitioners (Weikart, 1986). Young children need adults, or at least other individuals more competent than themselves, to create zones of proximal development as the children develop and learn.

This idea has formed a theoretical basis—though not the only basis—for a number of well-publicized educational programs for school-age children (e.g., Palincsar & Brown, 1984; Cole, 1990; King, Griffin, Diaz, & Cole, in press). Some successful kindergarten and primary-grade programs (e.g., Gallimore & Tharp, 1990; Newman, Griffin, & Cole, 1989) also explicitly favor creating zones of proximal development for young children. Still others, especially in early education, do so only implicitly, by favoring close child observation, modeling of competent performance, and cooperative group work in their detailed curriculum descriptions (see Consortium for Longitudinal Studies, 1983; or Lay-Dopydera and Dopydera, 1987, 1990).

The bad, or at least overwhelming news about the sociohistorical approach is the ease with which this perspective leads to theoretically-based critiques of the larger social context of teaching (Bruner, 1984), and in doing so highlights some of the limitations under which teachers normally work. Whatever early education programs they serve, all teachers work within certain social, political, and economic constraints, only some of which favor learning and development (Kagan, 1991). Gallimore and Tharp (1990) have pointed out the constraints for early education teachers working in public schools, including large class size, little time with individual children, and isolation from peers. Others have pointed out constraints in other settings (Johnson, 1990; Kidder, 1989). Part-time nurseries, for example, tend to have better ratios of children to teachers, more contact with parents, and more team teaching; but frequently they have little financial support or professional contacts with which to generate innovative programs.

In grounding learning in culture, the sociohistorical perspective highlights the impact of teachers' working conditions on children's daily learning, and it implies that teachers and other educational leaders must therefore work to improve them (Tharp & Gallimore, 1988). The approach makes little distinction between the learning needs of children and those of their teachers: Both need proper scaffolding, or their own version of the zone of proximal development. In this way the sociohistorical perspective is distinct from the other major approaches discussed in this chapter, which tend to regard the conditions of teaching as outside their official domain of theoretical interest (though advocates of other positions also, no doubt, favor better working conditions as a practical matter). Just as children need cognitive assistance to learn, so do teachers need assistance to provide this assistance. Neither learning nor teaching should be solitary activity in the sense of being motivated and supported entirely from "in" one individual.

Ironically, the socially determined constraints of modern schooling may limit the appeal of the sociohistorical approach by leading teachers to foster learning that is predictable and cognitively *un*challenging across a wide range of situations (Goodlad, 1984). Yet the ZPD and the sociohistorical traditions are not primarily about consistency. They are about why children behave *differently* on different occasions, given changes in the social context; and about how that context should change so that learning is eventually regulated by the child independently. From a teacher's point of view, therefore, the sociohistorical has laudable goals, but the approach seems to call for close observation of children as individuals—closer than some teachers may feel they have time for.

In fairness, the information-processing and structural theories may suffer from their own problems related to the social context of schooling. In their cases, though, the problem centers on comparative *in*attentiveness to the broad social context of learning. Because these theories focus on specific cognitive activities "in" the developing child, they may promise teachers more consistency in children's everyday behavior than really exists. The notion of "context" certainly exists in structural and information-processing theories, but it tends to concern detailed variations in task demands and conditions, rather than the large, complex effects of the culture of schooling (Feiman-Nemser & Floden, 1986).

What Next for the Sociohistorical Perspective?

It remains to be seen whether early educators as a community will ever pick up the social change agenda of the sociohistorical tradition; if they do, they will certainly receive a lot of support from research leaders in the field (Elkind, 1991; Zigler, 1991). Until that day comes, much remains to be learned about when and under what conditions notions like scaffolding, ZPDs, and the like actually promote the learning and development of individual children.

Consistent with its dynamic nature, the ZPD does not always happen where it might be expected (Goodnow & Wharton, 1991). In studying preschoolers' drawings of human beings, for example, drawings made on request (a ZPD-like situation) do indeed differ from drawings made spontaneously (Goodnow, Wilkins, & Dawes, 1986). But the significance of the difference is ambiguous: On request, children depict more complex body parts, but they also portray less bodily action. Do these differences show advancement under conditions of support, or regression? The answer depends on the artistic standards for judging the drawings.

Another study has documented parents' frequent failure to teach children household tasks (Goodnow, 1988), even though the situation has all the essential qualities of a supportive ZPD. The supportive adult (a parent) is willing to share knowledge of culturally important knowledge and skills (housekeeping tasks) to the extent that the apprentice (a child) is able to learn it. The adult takes ample time with the child, and does so in the actual learning context (i.e., at home). Yet learning does not necessarily occur; in Goodnow's research, as in the experience of many parents, children often resisted household learning openly and vehemently.

Just having a mentor and a learner to work together, then, does not necessarily create a ZPD. Observations of mothers (Valsiner, 1984), elementary teachers (Good & Brophy, 1987), and peer-mentors (Tudge, 1990) show that well-meaning peers and adults frequently reinforce preexisting, *less* developed knowledge and skills in tutee-children, rather than new, more developed forms. Perhaps they do so, Valsiner suggests, because supporting the more developed forms can be inconvenient, because doing so can threaten preexisting social and power relations, or because the adults or peer-mentors may not believe a child capable of more development. Tutorial learning situations are not necessarily serene and helpful, a fact that the research on the ZPD has yet to address fully.

Until that research agenda can be completed, the most sensible implication of the sociohistorical perspective, when applied to classroom learning, is this: that classroom teaching methods "distributing" tasks and knowledge among individuals hold considerable promise, provided that the individuals share common interest and goals in solving the tasks at hand. It is one thing for a teacher to assist a 4-year-old to dress warmly when the child and teacher are both anxious to get out in the snow. It is another thing for the teacher to attempt the same goal when the child would rather stay indoors to play.

Current research about the ZPD suggests a need for teachers to scrutinize their motives when in direct, individual interactions with children and to observe the effects of those encounters honestly. When a child is busily drawing a picture, does talking about it really help the child learn more and produce a better drawing? Hopefully it does; but there may be times when choosing *not* to talk is really more supportive than holding a conversation. Sometimes—though certainly not always—what may work best is combining the classic Piagetian stance with the situational bias of the sociohistorical tradition: Let the child construct his or her own knowledge at this particular time, in this particular place.

CONCLUSIONS

Not long ago, my youngest child asked which of my children I loved the best. Was it she, her brother, or her sister? Even without having read parental-advice manuals, I knew the answer: "I love you each in your own ways." This answer seemed to satisfy her, but it did not fully satisfy me. I realized that I could only give it if I actually knew each of my children in some detail—knew each well enough to understand their similarities and differences accurately and honestly.

Evaluating the major theories of cognitive development reminds me of my daughter's question. As with children, the correct assessment of theories is this: to love each theory in its own way, for the strengths and unique ideas it brings to early childhood education. Finding strengths and ideas in one approach need not preclude finding other, different strengths and ideas in other approaches. Responding ecumenically, however, means understanding each theory thoroughly, rather than superficially, so that evaluations grow from real knowledge of each research tradition, rather than from stereotypes or distortions of the tradition.

This chapter is therefore an effort to stimulate a broad, ecumenical assessment of the major theoretical approaches to children's cognitive development as those approaches might be viewed by teachers and other educators of young children. The 3 major approaches discussed—information-processing theory, structuralism, and the sociohistorical perspective—each have unique advantages. Research on information processing has succeeded especially well in highlighting specific cognitive changes in young children, such as their use of cognitive strategies and their short- and long-term memories. Research in the structural tradition has helped to identify key conceptual landmarks, while beginning to describe mechanisms by which structures gradually (or sometimes quickly) change. Research in the sociohistorical tradition has begun detailing the active role that adults and peers play in promoting cognitive development.

In building these theoretical strengths, of course, each tradition has also acquired certain theoretical blind spots. This chapter has also pointed out some of these, many of which are embodied in various research studies about children's thinking. Information-processing theories, for example, explain important cognitive functions and changes, but sometimes leave unclear how or why these functions change and get coordinated in real, live children. Structural theories recognize the importance of key conceptual structures, but often do not say enough about social influences. And sociohistorical research identifies helpful social influences on cognitive change, only to discover situational and societal limitations to those influences at the same time under current conditions of teaching.

Yet none of these theoretical limitations keeps theories of cognitive development from contributing significantly to practical knowledge of children's thinking—a knowledge that is keyed to life in classrooms and to the work of early childhood teachers and educators. Given this conclusion, the job of the early childhood profession is not to judge which theory it "likes best," but to get to know them all well and learn what each, in its own way, can do.

References

Adams, M. (1990). *Beginning to read: Thinking and learning about print.* Cambridge, MA: MIT Press.

Astington, J., Harris, P., & Olson, D. (1988). *Developing theories of mind.* New York: Cambridge University Press.

Beilin, H. (1989). Piagetian theory. In R. Vasta (Ed.), *Annals of child development: Six theories of child development* (pp. 61–84). Greenwich, CT: JAI Press.

Bereiter, C. (1991). Implications of connectionism for thinking about rules. *Educational Researcher, 20*(3), 10–16.

Bjorklund, D. (Ed.). (1990). Children's strategies: Contemporary views of cognitive development. Hillsdale, NJ: Erlbaum.

Bjorklund, D., & Harnishfeger, D. (1987). Developmental differences in the mental effort requirements for the use of an organizational strategy in free recall. *Journal of Experimental Child Psychology, 44,* 109–125.

Bredekamp, S. (1987). *Developmentally appropriate practice in early childhood programs.* Washington, DC: National Association for the Education of Young Children.

Bruner, J. (1984). Vygotsky and the ZPD: The hidden agenda. In B. Rogoff & J. Wertsch (Eds.), *Children's learning in the zone of proximal development* (pp. 93–98). San Francisco: Jossey-Bass.

Bruner, J. (1986). *Actual minds, possible worlds.* Cambridge, MA: Harvard University Press.

Bruner, J. (1989, April). *Culture and human development.* Paper presented at the biennial meeting of the Society for Research on Child Development, Kansas City, MO.

Bruner, J. (1990). *Acts of meaning.* Cambridge, MA: Harvard University Press.

Carey, S. (1985). *Conceptual change in childhood.* Cambridge, MA: MIT Press.

Carey, S. (1988a). Reorganization of knowledge in the course of acquisition. In S. Strauss (Ed.), *Ontogeny, phylogeny, and historical development* (pp. 1–27). New York: Ablex.

Carey, S. (1988b). Conceptual differences between children and adults. *Mind and Language, 3,* 167–181.

Case, R. (1985). *Intellectual development: Birth to adulthood.* Orlando, FL: Academic Press.

Case, R. (1986). The new stage theories in intellectual development: Why we need them; what they assert. In M. Perlmutter (Ed.), *Perspectives on intellectual development: Minnesota Symposia on child psychology* (Vol. 19, pp. 57–96). Hillsdale, NJ: Erlbaum.

Case, R. (1991). Potential contributions of research in the Piagetian tradition in the planning of curriculum and instruction. Stanford, CA: Center for Educational Research, Stanford University.

Case, R. (1992). General and specific views of the mind, its structure and development. In R. Case (Ed.), *The mind's staircase* (pp. 3–15). Hillsdale, NJ: Erlbaum.

Case, R., & Griffin, S. (1991). *Rightstart: An early intervention program for insuring that children's first formal learning of arithmetic is grounded in their intuitive knowledge of number.* Stanford, CA: Center for Educational Research, Stanford University.

Case, R., Kurland, M., & Goldberg, J. (1982). Operational efficiency and the growth of short-term memory span. *Journal of Experimental Child Psychology, 33,* 386–404.

Chi, M. (1988). Children's lack of access and knowledge reorganization: An example from the concept of animism. In F. Weinert & M. Perlmutter (Eds.), *Memory development: Universal changes and individual differences* (pp. 169–184). Hillsdale, NJ: Erlbaum.

Chi, M. (in press). Conceptual change within and across ontological categories. In M. Giere (Ed.), *Cognitive models of science.* Minneapolis, MN: University of Minnesota Press.

Chi, M., & Ceci, S. (1987). Content knowledge: Its role, representation, and restructuring in memory development. *Advances in Child Development and Behavior, 20,* 91–177.

Cole, M. (1990). Cultural psychology. In J. Berman (Ed.), *Nebraska Symposium on Motivation, 1989: Cross-cultural psychology* (pp. 279–336). Lincoln, NB: University of Nebraska Press.

Consortium for Longitudinal Studies. (1983). *As the twig is bent: Lasting effects of preschool programs.* Hillsdale, NJ: Erlbaum.

DeMarie-Dreblow, D., & Miller, P. (1988). The development of children's strategies for selective attention: Evidence for a transitional period. *Child Development, 59,* 1504–1513.

Demetriou, A. (Ed.). (1988). *The neo-Piagetian theories of intelligence: Toward an integration.* Amsterdam: North Holland.

Dennis, S. (1992). Stage and structure in the development of children's spatial representations. In R. Case (Ed.), *The mind's staircase* (pp. 229–245). Hillsdale, NJ: Erlbaum.

Diaz, R., Neal, C., & Amaya-Williams, M. (1990). The social origins of self-regulation. In L. Moll (Ed.), *Vygotsky and education* (pp. 127–154). New York: Cambridge University Press.

Diaz, R., Neal, C., & Vachio, C. (1991). Maternal teaching in the zone of proximal development. *Merrill-Palmer Quarterly, 37*(1), 87–108.

Elkind, D. (1976). *Child development and education.* New York: Oxford University Press.

Elkind, D. (1981). *Children and adolescents: Essays in honor of Jean Piaget,* 3rd edition. New York: Oxford University Press.

Elkind, D. (1987). *Miseducation: Preschoolers at risk.* New York: Knopf.

Elkind, D. (1991). Developmentally appropriate practice: A case study of education inertia. In S. Kagan (Ed.), *The care and education of America's young children: Obstacles and opportunities* (pp. 1–16). Chicago: University of Chicago Press.

Ellis, H. (1987). Recent developments in human memory. In V. Makosky (Ed.), *G. Stanley Hall Lecture Series* (Vol. 7, pp. 159–206). Washington, DC: American Psychological Association.

Feiman-Nemser, S., & Floden, R. (1986). The cultures of teaching. In M. Wittrock (Ed.), *Handbook of research on teaching* (3rd ed., pp. 505–526). New York: Macmillan.

Fischer, K., & Pipp, S. (1984). Processes of cognitive development: Optimal level and skill acquisition. In R. Sternberg (Ed.), *Mechanisms of cognitive development* (pp. 45–80). New York: Freeman.

Flavell, J. (1970). Developmental studies of mediated memory. In H. Reese & L. Lipsitt (Eds.), *Advances in child development and child behavior* (Vol. 5, pp. 181–211). New York: Academic Press.

Flavell, J. (1988). From cognitive connections to mental representations. In J. Astington, P. Harris, & D. Olson (Eds.), *Developing theories of mind* (pp. 244–267). New York: Cambridge University Press.

Flavell, J., Flavell, E., Green, F., & Moses, L. (1990). Young children's understanding of fact-beliefs versus value-beliefs. *Child Development, 61,* 915–928.

Gallimore, R., & Tharp, R. (1990). Teaching mind in society: Teaching, schooling, and literate discourse. In L. Moll (Ed.), *Vygotsky and education: Implications and applications of socio-historical psychology* (pp. 175–205). New York: Cambridge University Press.

Gardner, H. (1980). *Artful scribbles.* New York: Basic Books.

Gardner, H. (1983). **Frames of mind.** New York: Basic Books.

Gelman, R., & Baillargeon, R. (1983). A review of some Piagetian concepts. In P. Mussen (Ed.), *Handbook of child psychology* (Vol. 3, pp. 167–230). New York: Wiley.

Gelman, R., Spelke, E., & Meck, E. (1983). What preschoolers know about animate and inanimate objects. In D. Rogers & J. Sloboda (Eds.), *The acquisition of symbolic skills* (pp. 297–326). New York: Plenum Press.

Good, T., & Brophy, J. (1987). *Looking in classrooms* (4th ed.). New York: Harper and Row.

Goodlad, J. (1984). *A place called school.* New York: McGraw-Hill.

Goodnow, J. (1977). *Children's drawing.* Cambridge, MA: Harvard University Press.

Goodnow, J. (1988). Children's household labor: Its nature and functions. *Psychological Bulletin, 103,* 5–26.

Goodnow, J. (1990). The socialization of cognition: What's involved? In J. Stigler, R. Shweder, & G. Herdt (Eds.), *Cultural psychology: Essays on comparative human development* (pp. 259–286). New York: Cambridge University Press.

Goodnow, J., & Wharton, P. (1991). Social bases of social cognition. *Merrill-Palmer Quarterly, 37*(1), 27–58.

Goodnow, J., Wilkins, P., & Dawes, L. (1986). Acquiring cultural forms: Cognitive aspects of socialization illustrated by children's drawings and judgments of drawings. *International Journal of Behavioral Development, 9,* 485–505.

Hala, S., Chandler, M., & Fritz, A. (1991). Fledgling theories of mind: Deception as a marker of three-year-olds' understanding of false belief. *Child Development, 61*(1), 83–97.

Harnishfeger, K., & Bjorklund, D. (1990). Children's strategies: A brief history. In Bjorklund, D. (Ed.), *Children's strategies* (pp. 1–22). Hillsdale, NJ: Erlbaum.

Hohmann, M., Banet, B., & Weikart, D. (1979). *Young children in action: A manual for preschool educators.* Ypsilanti, MI: High/Scope Educational Research Foundation.

Hudson, J. (1984). Recollection and reconstruction in children's autobiographical memory. Unpublished doctoral dissertation, City University of New York, New York.

Hudson, J., & Nelson, K. (1986). Repeated encounters of a similar kind: Effects of familiarity on children's autobiographic memory. *Cognitive Development, 1,* 253–271.

Johnson, S. (1990). *Teachers at work.* New York: Basic Books.

Kagan, S. (Ed.). (1991). *The care and education of America's young children: Obstacles and opportunities.* Chicago: University of Chicago Press.

Kail, R. (1984). *The development of memory in children* (2nd ed.). New York: Freeman.

Kamii, C. (1985). *Young children reinvent arithmetic: Implications of Piaget's theory.* New York: Teachers College Press.

Kamii, C. (1989). *Young children continue to reinvent arithmetic: Second-grade.* New York: Teachers College Press.

Kamii, C., & DeVries, R. (1977). Piaget for early education. In M. Day & R. Parker (Eds.), *The preschool in action* (2nd ed., pp. 363–420). Boston: Allyn & Bacon.

Kidder, T. (1989). *Among school children.* New York: Avon Books.

King, C., Griffin, P., Diaz, E., & Cole, M. (in press). A model systems approach to reading instruction and the diagnosis of reading disabilities. In R. Glaser (Ed.), *Advances in instructional psychology.* Greenwich, CT: JAI Press.

Klahr, D. (1989). Information processing approaches. In R. Vasta (Ed.), *Annals of child development: Six theories of child development* (pp. 133–187). Greenwich, CT: JAI Press.

Kohlberg, L., & DeVries, R. (1987a). *Child psychology and childhood education: A cognitive-developmental view.* New York: Longman.

Kohlberg, L., & DeVries, R. (1987b). *Programs in early education: A constructivist view.* New York: Longman.

Kuhn, D., & Meecham, W. (Eds.). (1983). *The development of developmental psychology.* Basel, Switzerland: S. Karger.

Lay-Dopydera, M., & Dopydera, J. (1987). Strategies for teaching. In C. Seefeldt (Ed.), *The early childhood curriculum: A review of current research* (pp. 13–34). New York: Teachers College Press.

Lay-Dopydera, M., & Dopydera, J. (1990). The child-centered curriculum. In C. Seefeldt, (Ed.). *Continuing issues in early childhood education* (pp. 207–222). New York: Teachers College Press.

Levin, I. (Ed.). (1986). *Stage and structure: Reopening the debate.* Norwood, NJ: Ablex.

Miller, P. (1990). The development of strategies of selective attention. In D. Bjorklund (Ed.), *Children's strategies* (pp. 157–184). Hillsdale, NJ: Erlbaum.

Nelson, K. (1985). *Making sense: The acquisition of shared meaning.* New York: Academic Press.

Nelson, K. (1989). Remembering: A functional-developmental perspective. In P. Solomon, G. Goethals, C. Kelley, & B. Stephens (Eds.), *Memory: Interdisciplinary approaches* (pp. 127–150). New York: Springer-Verlag.

Newman, D., Griffin, P., & Cole, M. (1989). *The construction zone: Working for cognitive change in school.* New York: Cambridge University Press.

Overton, W. (1988). The structure of developmental theory. In P. Van Gleert & L. Mos (Eds.), *Annals of Theoretical Psychology* (Vol. 6, pp. 191–226). New York: Plenum.

Palincsar, A., & Brown, A. (1984). Reciprocal teaching of comprehension-fostering and monitoring activities. *Cognition and Instruction, 1,* 117–175.

Pascual-Leone, J. (1988). Organismic processes for neo-Piagetian theories: A dialectical causal account of cognitive development. In A. Demetriou (Ed.), *The Neo-Piagetian theories of cognitive development: Toward an integration* (pp. 25–65). Amsterdam: North Holland.

Piaget, J. (1936/1963). *The origins of intelligence in children.* New York: Norton.

Piaget, J. (1951). *The child's conception of the world.* London: Routledge and Kegan Paul.

Reid, D. (1992). Horizontal and vertical structure: Stages and substages in children's motor development. In R. Case (Ed.), *The mind's staircase.* (pp. 247–266). Hillsdale, NJ: Erlbaum.

Rogoff, B. (1989). The joint socialization of development by young children and adults. In A. Gellatly, D. Rogers, & J. Sloboda (Eds.), *Cognition and social worlds* (pp. 57–82). Oxford, UK: Oxford University Press.

Rogoff, B. (1990). *Apprenticeship in thinking.* New York: Oxford University Press.

Rogoff, B., & Wertsch, J. (Eds.). (1984). *Children's learning in the zone of proximal development.* San Francisco: Jossey-Bass.

Rovee-Collier, C. (1987). Learning and memory in infancy. In J. Osofsky (Ed.), *Handbook of infancy* (2nd ed., pp. 98–148). New York: Wiley.

Rummelhart, D. (1989). The architecture of mind: A connectionist approach. In M. Posner (Ed.), *Foundations of cognitive science* (pp. 133–159). Cambridge, MA: MIT Press.

Rummelhart, D., & McClelland, J. (1987). Learning the past tenses of English verbs: Implicit rules or parallel distributed processing? In B. MacWhinney (Ed.), *Mechanisms of language acquisition* (pp. 195–248). Hillsdale, NJ: Erlbaum.

Saxe, G., Guberman, S., & Gearhart, M. (1987). Social processes in early number development. *Monographs of the Society for Research on Child Development, 52* (2, No. 216).

Siegler, R. (1983). Information processing approaches to child development. In P. Mussen (Ed.), *Handbook of child psychology* (Vol. 1, pp. 129–211). New York: Wiley.

Siegler, R. (in press). Individual differences in strategy choices: Good students, not-so-good students, and perfectionists. *Child Development.*

Siegler, R., & Jenkins, E. (1989). *How children discover new strategies.* Hillsdale, NJ: Erlbaum.

Simons, J., & Simons, F. (1986). Montessori and regular preschools: A comparison. In L. Katz (Ed.), *Current topics in early childhood education* (Vol. 6, pp. 195–223). Norwood, NJ: Ablex.

Smolensky, P. (1988). On the proper treatment of connectionism. *Behavioral and Brain Sciences, 11*(1), 1–74.

Solomon, P., Goethals, G., Kelley, C., & Stephens, B. (Eds.). (1989). *Memory: Interdisciplinary approaches*. New York: Springer-Verlag.

Sternberg, R. (Ed.). (1984). *Mechanisms of cognitive development*. San Francisco: Freeman.

Teale, W., & Sulzby, E. (Eds.). (1986). *Emergent literacy: Writing and reading*. Norwood, NJ: Ablex.

Thagard, P. (1989). Explanatory coherence. *Brain and Behavioral Science, 12*(3), 435–502.

Tharp, R., & Gallimore, R. (1988). *Rousing minds to life*. New York: Cambridge University Press.

Tizard, B., & Hughes, M. (1984). *Young children learning*. Cambridge, MA: Harvard University Press.

Trevarthen, C., & Logotheti, K. (1989). Child and culture: Genesis of cooperative knowing. In A. Gellatly, D. Rogers, & J. Sloboda (Eds.), *Cognition and social worlds* (pp. 37–56). Oxford, UK: Oxford University Press.

Tudge, J. (1990). Vygotsky, the zone of proximal development, and peer collaboration: Implications for classroom practice. In L. Moll (Ed.), *Vygotsky and education* (pp. 1–24). Cambridge, UK Cambridge University Press.

Valsiner, J. (1984). Construction in the zone of proximal development in adult-child joint action. In B. Rogoff & J. Wertsch (Eds.), *Children's learning in the zone of proximal development* (pp. 65–76). San Francisco: Jossey-Bass.

Vygotsky, L. (1978). *Mind in society*. Cambridge, MA: Harvard University Press.

Weikart, D. (1986). What do we know so far? *High/Scope ReSource*. Winter. Ypsilanti, MI: High/Scope Educational Research Foundation.

Weikart, D. (1989). Quality preschool programs: A long-term social investment. New York: Ford Foundation.

Wellman, H. (1988). The early development of memory strategies. In F. Weinert & M. Perlmutter (Eds.), *Memory development: Universal changes and individual differences* (pp. 3–30). Hillsdale, NJ: Erlbaum.

Wellman, H. (1990). *The child's theory of mind*. Cambridge, MA: MIT Press.

Wertsch, J. (1985). *Vygotsky and the social formation of mind*. Cambridge, MA: Harvard University Press.

Wertsch, J. (1989). A socio-cultural approach to mind. In W. Damon (Ed.), *Child development today and tomorrow* (pp. 14–33). San Francisco: Jossey-Bass.

Wetzler, S., & Sweeney, J. (1986). Childhood amnesia: An empirical demonstration. In D. Rubin (Ed.), *Autobiographical memory* (pp. 91–201). New York: Cambridge University Press.

Wimmer, H., & Penner, J. (1983). Beliefs about beliefs: Representation and constraining function of wrong beliefs in young children's understanding of deception. *Cognition, 13*, 103–128.

Winner, E. (1982). *Invented worlds: The psychology of the arts*. Cambridge, MA: Harvard University Press.

Wood, D., Bruner, J., & Ross, G. (1976). The role of tutoring in problem-solving. *Journal of Child Psychology and Psychiatry, 17*, 89–100.

Woody-Ramsey, J., & Miller, P. (1988). The facilitation of selective attention in preschoolers. *Child Development, 59*, 1497–1503.

Zigler, E. (1991). Using research to inform policy: The case of early intervention. In S. Kagan (Ed.), *The care and education of young children: Obstacles and opportunities* (pp. 154–172). Chicago: University of Chicago Press.

·3·

MOTOR DEVELOPMENT AND MOVEMENT SKILL ACQUISITION IN EARLY CHILDHOOD EDUCATION

David L. Gallahue

INDIANA UNIVERSITY

Movement is at the very center of young children's lives. It is an important facet of all aspects of their development, whether in the motor, cognitive, or affective domains of human behavior. To deny children the opportunity to reap the many benefits of regular, vigorous physical activity is to deny them the opportunity to experience the joy of efficient movement, the health effects of movement, and a lifetime as confident, competent movers.

The motor and perceptual development of young children should not be left to chance. Children follow a developmental progression in the acquisition of their movement skills that is not unlike the developmental progressions found in their cognitive and affective development. Children's failure to develop and refine fundamental movement skills frequently leads to frustration and failure in games, sports, and recreational activities. Failure to develop mature patterns in throwing, catching, and striking, for example, make it quite difficult to experience success and enjoyment in even a recreational game of softball. No matter what the activity, a child cannot participate successfully if the essential fundamental movement skills contained within that activity have not been sufficiently learned.

This does not mean that the fundamental movement skills not learned in early childhood cannot be learned later in life. The individual is, however, often beyond the sensitive period during which it is easiest to master these skills; as a result, the skills frequently do remain unlearned. Several factors contribute to this situation. One is the accumulation of bad habits from improper learning. Learned behaviors, whether they take the form of correct or incorrect performances, are difficult to erase. It is much more difficult to "unlearn" faulty movement patterns than to learn them correctly in the first place. Self-consciousness and personal embarrassment make up the second factor. "I have 2 left feet," "I'm all thumbs," or "What a klutz" are all self-deprecating statements frequently used to describe poor performance. A third factor causing many move-

ment skills to remain unlearned is fear. Fear of injury and fear of peer ridicule and rejection are very real anxieties that contribute markedly to difficulty in learning movement skills later in life.

Young children have the potential for mature skill development in most fundamental movement skills. This chapter addresses the topics of early childhood motor and perceptual development from the standpoint of their impact on fundamental movement skill acquisition. Knowing more about these interrelated processes enables educators to design and implement curricula that are not only age-appropriate, but also individually appropriate and geared to the developmental level of those being taught.

MOVEMENT AND THE YOUNG CHILD

As children approach their second birthdays, a marked change can be observed in how they relate to their environment. Most have mastered the characteristic rudimentary movement tasks of infancy. These motor milestones are universal in their sequence of appearance but vary from child to child in the rate of acquisition. Milestones such as learning how to reach, grasp, and release objects; sitting without support; pulling up to a standing position; and achieving an independent upright gait are among the major rudimentary movement tasks of infancy. Rudimentary movements form the basis upon which children develop and refine the fundamental movement patterns of early childhood and the specialized movement skills of later childhood and beyond. Figure 3–1 depicts the phases and stages of motor development associated with the ever-expanding world of the young child.

At the fundamental movement phase of development, children no longer need to maintain a relentless struggle against the force of gravity; rather, they gain increased control over their musculature in opposition to it (stability). Children are no

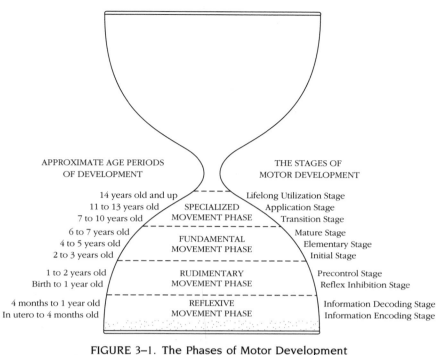

FIGURE 3–1. The Phases of Motor Development
From David L. Gallahue, *Motor Development: Infants, Children, Adolescents*, 2d. ed. Copyright © 1989, by Benchmark Press, Inc. Reprinted by permission of Wm. C. Brown Communications, Inc., Dubuque, Iowa. All rights reserved.

longer immobilized by a basic inability to move about freely. They are now able to explore the movement potential of their bodies as they move through space (locomotion). Children no longer have to be content with the crude and ineffective reaching, grasping, and releasing of objects characteristic of infancy. They now rapidly develop the ability to make controlled and precise contact with objects in their environment (object manipulation). Young children are involved in the process of developing and refining fundamental movement skills in a wide variety of stability, locomotor, and manipulative movements. As such, they need to be involved in a series of coordinated and developmentally appropriate movement experiences designed to enhance these basic movement abilities.

Unlike at the rudimentary phase, maturation is insufficient in accounting for mature movement skill acquisition at the fundamental movement phase of development. A variety of environmental factors play essential roles in the mature development of these important basic movement skills. Fundamental movement skill acquisition is not so much concerned with the development of high degrees of skill in a limited number of movement situations as it is with the development of proper body mechanics in a wide variety of basic movement tasks such as running, jumping, throwing, and catching. The body mechanics of fundamental movements are essentially the same for all children, unless there is a particular limiting condition or developmental disability. Additionally, a fundamental movement involves the basic elements of that particular movement only and does not include such factors as the individual's personal style or peculiarities in performance. Fundamental movement skills are first learned as discrete skills in relative isolation from one another. Only as they are

mastered can they be linked successfully with others to form the specialized movement skills that are so closely associated with sport performances, such as the lay-up shot in basketball or base running in baseball. The fundamental locomotor movements of running, jumping, and leaping, or the manipulative movements of throwing, catching, and striking are examples of fundamental movements that must be learned prior to being combined with other skills to become specialized movement skills.

The development of mature fundamental movement skills is basic to the motor development and movement education of young children. A wide variety of movement experiences provide them with a wealth of information on which to base their perceptions of themselves and the world around them.

THE DEVELOPMENT OF FUNDAMENTAL MOVEMENT ABILITIES

With the renewed interest in the study of motor development that began in the 1960s, several scales appeared that illustrated a relationship between age and motor performance. Johnson (1962), using a large sample of boys and girls from grades 1 through 6, found that the mean scores on a variety of motor performance items showed a definite upward trend until the fifth grade. Cratty and Martin (1969) presented age-related sequences of acquisition for a variety of locomotor, manipulative, and perceptual abilities of 365 children ranging in age from 4 to 12 years. Williams's (1970) summary of the movement abilities of children between 3 and 6 years old revealed more advanced forms of movement with increases in age.

Sinclair (1973) studied the motor development of 2- to 6-year-old children. The results of her longitudinal film analysis of 25 movement tasks at 6-month intervals lent further support to the basic assumption that movement skill acquisition is a developmental process during the early childhood years. Tables 3–1 through 3–3 provide a visual reference for appreciation of the sequence of the development of selected fundamental locomotor, manipulative, and stability movements, respectively.

These normative studies provide quantitative information about the outcome of movement in that they answer questions about "how far," "how fast," and "how many." They fail, however, to provide important information about qualitative changes that occur as children progress toward more mature form.

The study of qualitative change in children's movement deals with changes in the mechanics or process of the movement itself. A number of investigators, all using film and computer techniques, have analyzed the intraskill aspects of

TABLE 3–1. Sequence of Emergence of Selected Locomotor Abilities

Movement Pattern	Selected Abilities	Approximate Age of Onset
Walking		
Walking involves placing one foot in front of the other while maintaining contact with the supporting surface	Rudimentary upright unaided gait	13 months
	Walks sideways	16 months
	Walks backward	17 months
	Walks upstairs with help	20 months
	Walks upstairs alone—follow step	24 months
	Walks downstairs alone—follow step	25 months
Running		
Running involves a brief period of no contact with the supporting surface	Hurried walk (maintains contact)	18 months
	First true run (nonsupport phase)	2–3 years
	Efficient and refined run	4–5 years
	Speed of run increases, mature run*	5 years
Jumping		
Jumping takes three forms: (1) jumping for distance, (2) jumping for height, and (3) jumping from a height. It involves a one- or two-foot takeoff with a landing on both feet	Steps down from low objects	18 months
	Jumps down from object with one foot lead	2 years
	Jumps off floor with both feet	28 months
	Jumps for distance (about 3 feet)	5 years
	Jumps for height (about 1 foot)	5 years
	Mature jumping pattern*	6 years
Hopping		
Hopping involves a one-foot takeoff with a landing on the same foot	Hops up to three times on preferred foot	3 years
	Hops from four to six times on same foot	4 years
	Hops from eight to ten times on same foot	5 years
	Hops distance of 50 feet in about 11 seconds	5 years
	Hops skillfully with rhythmical alteration, mature pattern*	6 years
Galloping		
The gallop combines a walk and a leap with the same foot leading throughout	Basic but inefficient gallop	4 years
	Gallops skillfully, mature pattern*	6 years
Skipping		
Skipping combines a step and a hop in rhythmic alteration	One-footed skip	4 years
	Skillful skipping (about 20 percent)	5 years
	Skillful skipping for most*	6 years

*The child has the developmental "potential" to be at the mature stage. Actual attainment will depend on environmental factors.

From David L. Gallahue, *Motor Development: Infants, Children, Adolescents*, 2d ed. Copyright © 1989, by Benchmark Press, Inc. Reprinted by permission of Wm. C. Brown Communications, Inc., Dubuque, Iowa. All rights reserved.

TABLE 3–2. Sequence of Emergence of Selected Manipulative Abilities

Movement Pattern	Selected Abilities	Approximate Age of Onset
Reach, Grasp, Release		
Reaching, grasping, and releasing involves making successful contact with an object, retaining it in one's grasp and releasing it at will	Primitive reaching behaviors	2–4 months
	Corralling of objects	2–4 months
	Palmar grasp	3–5 months
	Pincer grasp	8–10 months
	Controlled grasp	12–14 months
	Controlled releasing	14–18 months
Throwing		
Throwing involves imparting force to an object in the general direction of intent	Body faces target, feet remain stationary, ball thrown with forearm extension only	2–3 years
	Same as above but with body rotation added	3.6–5 years
	Steps forward with leg on same side as the throwing arm	4–5 years
	Boys exhibit more mature pattern than girls	5 years and over
	Mature throwing pattern*	6 years
Catching		
Catching involves receiving force from an object with the hands, moving from large to progressively smaller balls	Chases ball; does not respond to aerial ball	2 years
	Responds to aerial ball with delayed arm movements	2–3 years
	Needs to be told how to position arms	2–3 years
	Fear reaction (turns head away)	3–4 years
	Basket catch using the body	3 years
	Catches using the hands only with a small ball	5 years
	Mature catching pattern*	6 years
Kicking		
Kicking involves imparting force to an object with the foot	Pushes against ball. Does not actually kick it.	18 months
	Kicks with leg straight and little body movement (kicks *at* the ball)	2–3 years
	Flexes lower leg on backward lift.	3–4 years
	Greater backward and forward swing with definite arm opposition.	4–5 years
	Mature pattern (kicks *through* the ball)*	5–6 years
Striking		
Striking involves sudden contact to objects in an overarm, sidearm, or underhand pattern	Faces object and swings in a vertical plane	2–3 years
	Swings in a horizontal plane and stands to the side of the object.	4–5 years
	Rotates the trunk and hips and shifts body weight forward.	5 years
	Mature horizontal pattern with stationary ball	6–7 years

*The child has the developmental "potential" to be at the mature stage. Actual attainment will depend on environmental factors.

From David L. Gallahue, *Motor Development: Infants, Children, Adolescents*, 2d ed. Copyright © 1989, by Benchmark Press, Inc. Reprinted by permission of Wm. C. Brown Communications, Inc., Dubuque, Iowa. All rights reserved.

TABLE 3–3. Sequence of Emergence of Selected Stability Abilities

Movement Pattern	Selected Abilities	Approximate Age of Onset
Dynamic Balance		
Dynamic balance involves maintaining one's equilibrium as the center of gravity shifts	Walks 1-inch straight line	3 years
	Walks 1-inch circular line	4 years
	Stands on low balance beam	2 years
	Walks on 4-inch wide beam for a short distance	3 years
	Walks on same beam, alternating feet	3–4 years
	Walks on 2- and 3-inch beam	4 years
	Performs basic forward roll	3–4 years
	Performs mature forward roll*	6–7 years
Static Balance		
Static balance involves maintaining one's equilibrium while the center of gravity remains stationary	Pulls to a standing position	10 months
	Stands without handholds	11 months
	Stands alone	12 months
	Balances on one foot 3–5 seconds	5 years
	Supports body in basic 3-point inverted positions	6 years
Axial Movements		
Axial movements are postures that involve bending, stretching, twisting, turning, and the like	Axial movement abilities begin to develop early in infancy and are progressively refined to a point where they are included in the emerging manipulative patterns of throwing, catching, kicking, striking, trapping, and other activities	2 months– 6 years

*The child has the developmental "potential" to be at the mature stage. Actual attainment will depend on environmental factors.

From David L. Gallahue, *Motor Development: Infants, Children, Adolescents*, 2d ed. Copyright © 1989, by Benchmark Press, Inc. Reprinted by permission of Wm. C. Brown Communications, Inc., Dubuque, Iowa. All rights reserved.

a variety of fundamental movement patterns. This work has led to the current stage concept of movement skill acquisition during early childhood (Halverson, 1966; Seefeldt, 1972; McClenaghan & Gallahue, 1978a; Roberton, 1982; Roberton & Halverson, 1984; Haubenstricker & Seefeldt, 1986). These researchers conducted important investigations in the intraskill sequences of a variety of fundamental movement tasks. Out of these investigations have come 4 popular methods of charting the stage classification of children in actual observational settings.

The systems devised by Roberton (1978), Seefeldt and Haubenstricker (1976), and McClenaghan and Gallahue (1978b), and later expanded by Gallahue (1989, 1993) and Ulrich (1985) have been used successfully in observational assessment with young children. The Roberton method expands stage theory to an analysis of the separate components of movement within a given pattern, and is commonly referred to as a *segmental analysis approach*. The Seefeldt method assigns an overall stage classification score (stage 1 through stage 5), and is referred to as a total body configuration approach. The McClenaghan-Gallahue method provides opportunities for both segmental analyses and total body assessment, depending on the needs, interests, and abilities of the observer. Their method recognizes the differential rates of development within fundamental movement patterns as well as the need for an easy-to-apply tool for daily teaching situations. The Ulrich approach is unique in

that it permits both qualitative and quantitative assessment of 10 fundamental movement skills.

McClenaghan and Gallahue (1978a) identified 3 characteristic stages within the fundamental movement phase of development (Table 3–4). Termed the *initial, elementary,* and *mature*

TABLE 3–4. The Three Stages Within the Fundamental Movement Phase

Initial Stage:
Characterized by the child's first observable attempts at the movement pattern. Many of the components of a refined pattern, such as the preparatory action and follow-through, are missing.
Elementary Stage:
A transitional stage in the child's movement development. Coordination and performance improve, and the child gains more control over his movements. More components of the mature pattern are integrated into the movement, although they are performed incorrectly.
Mature Stage:
The integration of all the component movements into a well-coordinated, purposeful act. The movement resembles the motor pattern of a skilled adult [in terms of control and mechanics, but it is lacking in terms of movement performance as measured quantitatively*].

*Author's Addition.

From: McClenaghan and Gallahue, 1978a, p. 78. Used with permission.

stages, each described typical observable patterns of movement behavior for 5 fundamental movement tasks. Since then, this approach has been further expanded to include over 20 fundamental movement skills (Gallahue, 1989, 1993).

Not all movement patterns fit precisely into an arbitrary 3-stage progression. The developmental aspects of some movements may be more completely described in a 4- or 5-stage sequence, depending on the specific movement pattern and the level of sophistication of the observer. The 3-stage approach

is advocated here because it accurately and adequately fits the developmental sequence of most fundamental movement patterns, and provides the basis for a reliable, easy-to-use observational assessment instrument. Tables 3–5 through 3–14 and Figures 3–2 through 3–11 provide verbal and visual descriptions of 10 fundamental movements common to children during the period of early childhood. Common developmental difficulties that children encounter as they move toward the mature stage are also included for each movement task.

TABLE 3–5. Developmental Sequence for Walking

I. Walking:
  A. Initial stage.
    1. Difficulty maintaining upright posture.
    2. Unpredictable loss of balance.
    3. Rigid, halting leg action.
    4. Short steps.
    5. Flat-footed contact.
    6. Toes turn outward.
    7. Wide base of support.
    8. Flexed knee at contact followed by quick leg extension.
  B. Elementary stage.
    1. Gradual smoothing out of pattern.
    2. Step length increased.
    3. Heel-toe contact.
    4. Arms down to sides with limited swing.
    5. Base of support within the lateral dimensions of trunk.
    6. Out-toeing reduced or eliminated.
    7. Increased pelvic tilt.
    8. Apparent vertical lift.
  C. Mature stage.
    1. Reflexive arm swing.
    2. Narrow base of support.
    3. Relaxed, elongated gait.
    4. Minimal vertical lift.
    5. Definite heel-toe contact.
II. Common problems:
  A. Inhibited or exaggerated arm swing.
  B. Arms crossing midline of body.
  C. Improper foot placement.
  D. Exaggerated forward trunk lean.
  E. Arms flopping at sides or held out for balance.
  F. Twisting of trunk.
  G. Poor rhythmical action.
  H. Landing flat-footed.
  I. Flipping foot or lower leg in or out.

INITIAL

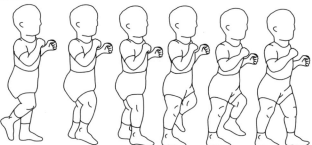

ELEMENTARY

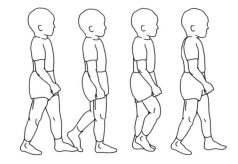

MATURE

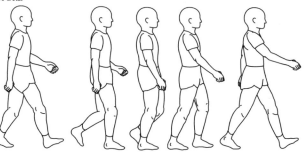

FIGURE 3–2. Stages of the Walking Pattern

TABLE 3–6. Developmental Sequence for Running

I. Running:
  A. Initial stage.
    1. Short, limited leg swing.
    2. Stiff, uneven stride.
    3. No observable flight phase.
    4. Incomplete extension of support leg.
    5. Stiff, short swing with varying degrees of elbow flexion.
    6. Arms tend to swing outward horizontally.
    7. Swinging leg rotates outward from hip.
    8. Swinging foot toes outward.
    9. Wide base of support.
  B. Elementary stage.
    1. Increase in length of stride, arm swing, and speed.
    2. Limited but observable flight phase.
    3. More complete extension of support leg at takeoff.
    4. Arm swing increases.
    5. Horizontal arm swing reduced on backswing.
    6. Swinging foot crosses midline at height of recovery to rear.
  C. Mature stage.
    1. Stride length at maximum; Stride speed fast.
    2. Definite flight phase.
    3. Complete extension of support leg.
    4. Recovery thigh parallel to ground.
    5. Arms swing vertically in opposition to legs.
    6. Arms bent at approximate right angles.
    7. Minimal rotary action of recovery leg and foot.
II. Common problems:
  A. Inhibited or exaggerated arm swing.
  B. Arms crossing the midline of the body.
  C. Improper foot placement.
  D. Exaggerated forward trunk lean.
  E. Arms flopping at the sides or held out for balance.
  F. Twisting of the trunk.
  G. Poor rhythmical action.
  H. Landing flat-footed.
  I. Flipping the foot or lower leg in or out.

INITIAL

ELEMENTARY

MATURE

FIGURE 3–3. Stages of the Running Pattern

TABLE 3–7. Developmental Sequence
for Horizontal Jumping

I. Horizontal jumping:
  A. Initial stage.
    1. Limited swing; arms do not initiate jumping action.
    2. During flight, arms move sideward-downward or rearward-upward to maintain balance.
    3. Trunk moves in vertical direction; little emphasis on length of jump.
    4. Preparatory crouch inconsistent in terms of leg flexion.
    5. Difficulty in using both feet.
    6. Limited extension of the ankles, knees, and hips at takeoff.
    7. Body weight falls backward at landing.
  B. Elementary stage.
    1. Arms initiate jumping action.
    2. Arms remain toward front of body during preparatory crouch.
    3. Arms move out to side to maintain balance during flight.
    4. Preparatory crouch deeper and more consistent.
    5. Knee and hip extension more complete at takeoff.
    6. Hips flexed during flight; thighs held in flexed position.
  C. Mature stage.
    1. Arms move high and to rear during preparatory crouch.
    2. During takeoff, arms swing forward with force and reach high.
    3. Arms held high throughout jumping action.
    4. Trunk propelled at approximately 45-degree angle.
    5. Major emphasis on horizontal distance.
    6. Preparatory crouch deep, consistent.
    7. Complete extension of ankles, knees, and hips at takeoff.
    8. Thighs held parallel to ground during flight; lower leg hangs vertically.
    9. Body weight forward at landing.
II. Common problems:
  A. Improper use of arms (that is, failure to use arm opposite the propelling leg in a down-up-down swing as leg flexes, extends, and flexes again).
  B. Twisting or jerking of body.
  C. Inability to perform either a one-foot or a two-foot takeoff.
  D. Poor preliminary crouch.
  E. Restricted movements of arms or legs.
  F. Poor angle of takeoff.
  G. Failure to extend fully on takeoff.
  H. Failure to extend legs forward on landing.
  I. Falling backward on landing.

INITIAL

ELEMENTARY

MATURE

FIGURE 3–4. Stages of the Horizontal Jumping Pattern

TABLE 3–8. Developmental Sequence
for Jumping from a Height

I. Jumping from a height:
  A. Initial stage.
    1. One foot leads on takeoff.
    2. No flight phase.
    3. Lead foot contacts lower surface prior to trailing foot leaving upper surface.
    4. Exaggerated use of arms for balance.
  B. Elementary stage.
    1. Two-foot takeoff with one-foot lead.
    2. Flight phase, but lacks control.
    3. Arms used ineffectively for balance.
    4. One-foot landing followed by immediate landing of trailing foot.
    5. Inhibited or exaggerated flexion at knees and hip upon landing.
  C. Mature stage.
    1. Two-foot takeoff.
    2. Controlled flight phase.
    3. Both arms used efficiently out to sides to control balance as needed.
    4. Feet contact lower surface simultaneously with toes touching first.
    5. Feet land shoulder-width apart.
    6. Flexion at knees and hip congruent with height of jump.
II. Common problems:
  A. Inability to take off with both feet.
  B. Twisting body to one side on takeoff.
  C. Exaggerated or inhibited body lean.
  D. Failure to coordinate use of both arms in the air.
  E. Tying one arm to side while using the other.
  F. Failure to land simultaneously on both feet.
  G. Landing flat-footed.
  H. Failure to flex knees sufficiently to absorb impact of landing.
  I. Landing out of control.

INITIAL

ELEMENTARY

MATURE

FIGURE 3–5. Stages of the Jump from a Height

TABLE 3–9. Developmental Sequence for Hopping

I. Hopping:
  A. Initial stage.
    1. Nonsupporting leg flexed 90 degrees or less.
    2. Nonsupporting thigh roughly parallel to contact surface.
    3. Body upright.
    4. Arms flexed at elbows and held slightly to side.
    5. Little height or distance generated in single hop.
    6. Balance lost easily.
    7. Limited to one or two hops.
  B. Elementary stage.
    1. Nonsupporting leg flexed.
    2. Nonsupporting thigh at 45-degree angle to contact surface.
    3. Slight forward lean, with trunk flexed at hip.
    4. Nonsupporting thigh flexed and extended at hip to produce greater force.
    5. Force absorbed on landing by flexing at hip and by supporting knee.
    6. Arms move up and down vigorously and bilaterally.
    7. Balance poorly controlled.
    8. Generally limited in number of consecutive hops that can be performed.
  C. Mature stage.
    1. Nonsupporting leg flexed at 90 degrees or less.
    2. Nonsupporting thigh lifts with vertical thrust of supporting foot.
    3. Greater body lean.
    4. Rhythmical action of nonsupporting leg (pendulum swing aiding in force production).
    5. Arms move together rhythmically lifting as the supporting foot leaves the contact surface.
    6. Arms not needed for balance but used for greater force production.
II. Common problems:
  A. Hopping flat-footed.
  B. Exaggerated movements of arms.
  C. Exaggerated movement of nonsupporting leg.
  D. Exaggerated forward lean.
  E. Inability to maintain balance for five or more consecutive hops.
  F. Lack of rhythmical fluidity of movement.
  G. Inability to hop effectively on both left foot and right foot.
  H. Inability to alternate hopping feet in a smooth, continuous manner.
  I. Tying one arm to side of body.

INITIAL

ELEMENTARY

MATURE

FIGURE 3–6. Stages of the Hopping Pattern

TABLE 3–10. Developmental Sequence
for Overhand Throwing

I. Throwing:
  A. Initial stage.
    1. Action is mainly from elbow.
    2. Elbow of throwing arm remains in front of body;
       action resembles a push.
    3. Fingers spread at release.
    4. Follow-through is forward and downward.
    5. Trunk remains perpendicular to target.
    6. Little rotary action during throw.
    7. Body weight shifts slightly rearward to maintain
       balance.
    8. Feet remain stationary.
    9. There is often purposeless shifting of feet during
       preparation for throw.
  B. Elementary stage.
    1. In preparation, arm is swung upward, sideward,
       and backward to a position of elbow flexion.
    2. Ball is held behind head.
    3. Arm is swung forward, high over shoulder.
    4. Trunk rotates toward throwing side during
       preparatory action.
    5. Shoulders rotate toward throwing side.
    6. Trunk flexes forward with forward motion of arm.
    7. Definite forward shift of body weight.
    8. Steps forward with leg on same side as throwing
       arm.
  C. Mature stage.
    1. Arm is swung backward in preparation.
    2. Opposite elbow is raised for balance as a
       preparatory action in the throwing arm.
    3. Throwing elbow moves forward horizontally as it
       extends.
    4. Forearm rotates and thumb points downward.
    5. Trunk markedly rotates to throwing side during
       preparatory action.
    6. Throwing shoulder drops slightly.
    7. Definite rotation through hips, legs, spine, and
       shoulders during throw.
    8. Weight during preparatory movement is on rear
       foot.
    9. As weight is shifted, there is a step with opposite
       foot.
II. Common problems:
  A. Forward movement of foot on same side as throwing
    arm.
  B. Inhibited backswing.
  C. Failure to rotate hips as throwing arm is brought
    forward.
  D. Failure to step out on leg opposite the throwing arm.
  E. Poor rhythmical coordination of arm movement with
    body movement.
  F. Inability to release ball at desired trajectory.
  G. Loss of balance while throwing.
  H. Upward rotation of arm.

INITIAL

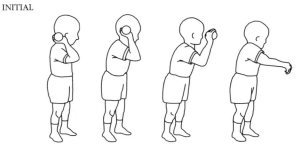

ELEMENTARY

MATURE

FIGURE 3–7. Stages of the Overhand Throwing Pattern

TABLE 3–11. Developmental Sequence for Catching

I. Catching:
  A. Initial stage.
    1. There is often an avoidance reaction of turning the face away or protecting the face with arms (avoidance reaction is learned and therefore may not be present).
    2. Arms are extended and held in front of body.
    3. Body movement is limited until contact.
    4. Catch resembles a scooping action.
    5. Use of body to trap ball.
    6. Palms are held upward.
    7. Fingers are extended and held tense.
    8. Hands are not utilized in catching action.
  B. Elementary stage.
    1. Avoidance reaction is limited to eyes closing at contact with ball.
    2. Elbows are held at sides with an approximately 90-degree bend.
    3. Since initial attempt at contact with child's hands is often unsuccessful, arms trap the ball.
    4. Hands are held in opposition to each other; thumbs are held upward.
    5. At contact, the hands attempt to squeeze ball in a poorly timed and uneven motion.
  C. Mature stage.
    1. No avoidance reaction.
    2. Eyes follow ball into hands.
    3. Arms are held relaxed at sides, and forearms are held in front of body.
    4. Arms give on contact to absorb force of the ball.
    5. Arms adjust to flight of ball.
    6. Thumbs are held in opposition to each other.
    7. Hands grasp ball in a well-timed, simultaneous motion.
    8. Fingers grasp more effectively.
II. Common problems:
  A. Failure to maintain control of object.
  B. Failure to "give" with the catch.
  C. Keeping fingers rigid and straight in the direction of object.
  D. Failure to adjust hand position to the height and trajectory of object.
  E. Inability to vary the catching pattern for objects of different weight and force.
  F. Taking eyes off object.
  G. Closing the eyes.
  H. Inability to focus on, or track the ball.
  I. Improper stance, causing loss of balance when catching a fast-moving object.
  J. Closing hands either too early or too late.
  K. Failure to keep body in line with the ball.

INITIAL

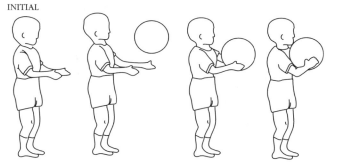

ELEMENTARY

MATURE

FIGURE 3–8. Stages of the Catching Pattern

TABLE 3–12. Developmental Sequence for Kicking

I. Kicking:
  A. Initial stage.
    1. Movements are restricted during kicking action.
    2. Trunk remains erect.
    3. Arms are used to maintain balance.
    4. Movement of kicking leg is limited in backswing.
    5. Forward swing is short: there is little follow-through.
    6. Child kicks *at* ball rather than kicking it squarely and following through.
    7. A pushing rather than a striking action is predominant.
  B. Elementary stage.
    1. Preparatory backswing is centered at the knee.
    2. Kicking leg tends to remain bent throughout the kick.
    3. Follow-through is limited to forward movement of the knee.
    4. One or more deliberate steps are taken toward the ball.
  C. Mature stage.
    1. Arms swing in opposition to each other during kicking action.
    2. Trunk bends at waist during follow-through.
    3. Movement of kicking leg is initiated at the hip.
    4. Support leg bends slightly on contact.
    5. Length of leg swing increases.
    6. Follow-through is high; support foot rises to toes or leaves surface entirely.
    7. Approach to the ball is from either a run or leap.
II. Common problems:
  A. Restricted or absent backswing.
  B. Failure to step forward with nonkicking leg.
  C. Tendency to lose balance.
  D. Inability to kick with either foot.
  E. Inability to alter speed of kicked ball.
  F. Jabbing at ball without follow-through.
  G. Poor opposition of arms and legs.
  H. Failure to use a summation of forces by the body to contribute to force of the kick.
  I. Failure to contact ball squarely, or missing it completely (eyes not focused on ball).
  J. Failure to get adequate distance (lack of follow-through and force production).

INITIAL

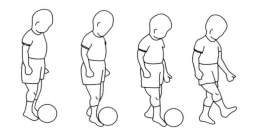

ELEMENTARY

MATURE

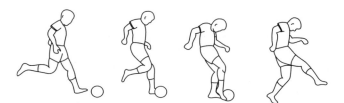

FIGURE 3–9. Stages of the Kicking Pattern

TABLE 3–13. Developmental Sequence for Striking

I. Striking:
  A. Initial stage.
    1. Motion is from back to front.
    2. Feet are stationary.
    3. Trunk faces direction of tossed ball.
    4. Elbow(s) fully flexed.
    5. No trunk rotation.
    6. Force comes from extension of flexed joints in a downward plane.
  B. Elementary stage.
    1. Trunk turned to side in anticipation of tossed ball.
    2. Weight shifts to forward foot prior to ball contact.
    3. Combined trunk and hip rotation.
    4. Elbow(s) flexed at less acute angle.
    5. Force comes from extension of flexed joints. Trunk rotation and forward movement are in an oblique plane.
  C. Mature stage.
    1. Trunk turns to side in anticipation of tossed ball.
    2. Weight shifts to back foot.
    3. Hips rotate.
    4. Transfer of weight is in a contralateral pattern.
    5. Weight shift to forward foot occurs while object is still moving backward.
    6. Striking occurs in a long, full arc in a horizontal pattern.
    7. Weight shifts to forward foot at contact.
II. Common problems:
  A. Failure to focus on and track the ball.
  B. Improper grip.
  C. Failure to turn side of the body in direction of intended flight.
  D. Inability to sequence movements in rapid succession in a coordinated manner.
  E. Poor backswing.
  F. "Chopping" swing.

INITIAL

ELEMENTARY

MATURE

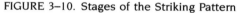

FIGURE 3–10. Stages of the Striking Pattern

TABLE 3–14. Developmental Sequence
for One-Foot Balance

I. One-foot balance:
  A. Initial stage.
    1. Raises nonsupporting leg several inches so that thigh is nearly parallel with contact surface.
    2. Either in or out of balance (no in-between).
    3. Overcompensates ("windmill" arms).
    4. Inconsistent leg preference.
    5. Balances with outside support.
    6. Only momentary balance without support.
    7. Eyes directed at feet.
  B. Elementary stage.
    1. May lift nonsupporting leg to a tied-in position on support leg.
    2. Cannot balance with eyes closed.
    3. Uses arms for balance but may tie one arm to side of body.
    4. Performs better on dominant leg.
  C. Mature stage.
    1. Can balance with eyes closed.
    2. Uses arms and trunk as needed to maintain balance.
    3. Lifts nonsupporting leg.
    4. Focuses on external object while balancing.
    5. Changes to nondominant leg without loss of balance.
II. Common problems:
  A. Tying one arm to side.
  B. No compensating movements.
  C. Inappropriate compensation of arms.
  D. Inability to use either leg.
  E. Inability to vary body position with control.
  F. Inability to balance while holding objects.
  G. Visually monitoring support leg.
  H. Overdependence on outside support.

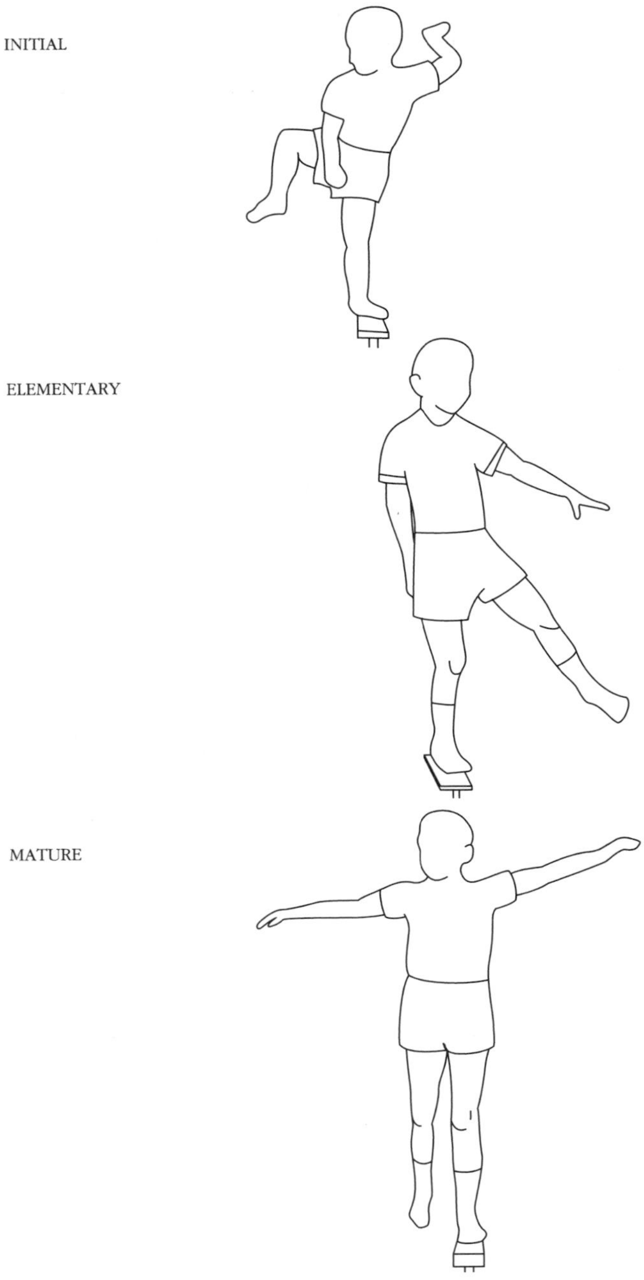

INITIAL

ELEMENTARY

MATURE

FIGURE 3–11. Stages of the One-Foot Balance

CONDITIONS AFFECTING FUNDAMENTAL MOVEMENT SKILL ACQUISITION

The fundamental movement phase of development has been extensively studied over the past several years. Most agree that this phase follows a sequential progression that may be subdivided into stages. The cognitive and physically intact child progresses sequentially in a segmental manner from one stage to another through the interaction of maturation, experience, and the goal of the task itself. Children cannot rely solely on maturation to attain the mature stage in their fundamental movement abilities. Environmental conditions that include such factors as opportunities for practice, encouragement, and instruction are crucial to the development of mature patterns of fundamental movement.

Miller (1978) investigated the facilitation of fundamental movement skill learning in children 3 to 5 years of age. She found that programs of instruction can increase fundamental movement skill development beyond the level attained solely through maturation. She also found that an instructional program in skill development was more effective than a free-play program and that parents working under the direction of a trained specialist can be as effective as physical education teachers in developing fundamental movement skills. Luedke (1980) found similar results with boys and girls by utilizing 2 different methods of instruction designed to attain the mature stage of throwing. Both instructional groups were more proficient in terms of form (qualitative movement) and performance (quantitative movement) than a noninstructed control group.

The mover's interaction with environmental conditions and the goal of the task may have a dramatic impact on the observed developmental maturity of a fundamental movement task. Natural conditions within the environment such as temperature, lighting, surface area, and gravity may have an influence on the quantitative as well as the qualitative aspects of a movement task (Keogh & Sugden, 1985). Similarly, artificial conditions such as the size, shape, color, and texture of objects may dramatically influence performance (Payne & Isaacs, 1991). Furthermore, whether the task is underinhabited or overinhabited in terms of other children present affects the ecology of the environment and the displayed developmental maturity of a movement task (Heston, 1989).

The goal of the task itself is a third important influencing factor on the observed developmental status of a fundamental movement task. If, for example, the focus in a throwing task is on accuracy—such as with the game of darts—then it is reasonable to assume that the pattern of movement will be different than if the goal were distance. To this end, Langendorfer (1988) observed 2 groups of subjects (children and adults) performing an overhand throwing pattern under 2 different goal conditions (force and accuracy). The results of his investigation indicated that fundamental motor patterns are not completely robust to all environmental conditions. Some movers can accommodate their movements to shifting environmental constraints, but others encounter difficulty. In other words, the degree to which a mover is able to make adjustments to an altered goal is influenced by several factors within the mover as well as by the degree to which the task demands have changed. For example, the individual with limited ability to increase the velocity of a thrown ball (whether due to faulty body mechanics or lack of strength) will be limited in the adjustments he or she can make when switching from an accuracy throwing task to a distance throwing task.

The link between the mover, the conditions of the environment, and the demands of the task itself is not completely understood. It is interesting to note, however, that many of the developmental descriptions of fundamental movement abilities are laboratory generated. That is, they are hypothesized developmental sequences that are the product of research in a laboratory setting—a setting quite unlike the real world in which children move. Little is known, as yet, about the changing ecology of the environment and its influence on the observed developmental status of children's movement. As we turn to methods of analyzing children's movement in more natural settings, we may find these hypothesized stages of development to be somewhat different from the actual stages.

This point is echoed by Roberton (1988), who indicated that researchers have frequently been so concerned with describing changes in the movement characteristics of their subjects that they have failed to consider the powerful influence of the movement conditions (i.e., conditions of the environment and goal of the task) on the resulting observed developmental status of the fundamental movement pattern itself.

DEVELOPMENTAL DIFFERENCES IN FUNDAMENTAL MOVEMENTS

When observing and analyzing the fundamental movement abilities of young children, it becomes apparent that there are various stages of development for each pattern of movement. It should also be obvious that differences in abilities exist between children, between patterns, and within patterns.

Between-Child Differences

Between-child differences should remind us of the principle of individuality in all learning. The sequence of progression through the initial, elementary, and mature stages is the same for most children. The rate, however, tends to vary, depending on both environmental and hereditary factors. Whether or not a child reaches the mature stage depends primarily on environmental, task, and ecological factors.

Between-Pattern Differences

Between-pattern differences are seen in all children. A child may be at the initial stage in some, the elementary in others, and the mature in still others. Children do not progress at an even rate in the development of their fundamental movement abilities. Development, therefore, should be viewed as a discontinuous process occurring at various rates between patterns as well as within patterns.

Within-Pattern Differences

Within-pattern differences are an interesting and often curious phenomenon. Within a given pattern, a child may exhibit a combination of initial, elementary, and mature elements. In the throw, for example, the arm action may be at the elementary stage while the leg action is at the mature stage and the trunk action at the initial stage. Developmental differences within patterns are common and usually the result of one of the following: (1) incomplete modeling of the movement of others, (2) initial success with the inappropriate action, (3) failure to require an all-out effort, (4) inappropriate or restricted learning opportunities, or (5) incomplete sensorimotor integration. Children exhibiting within-pattern differences should be assessed utilizing a segmental analysis approach. This permits the observer to accurately determine the stage of development of each body segment. With this knowledge, appropriate intervention strategies can be mapped out.

Creative, diagnostic teaching can do much to aid the young child in the balanced development of fundamental movement abilities. Observational assessment of children's fundamental movement enables planning for movement experiences and instructional strategies that can help them attain mature patterns of movement. Once movement control has been established, these mature patterns may be further refined in terms of force production and accuracy at the specialized movement phase of development. Failure to achieve proficiency in a wide variety of fundamental movement skills is a barrier to the development of specialized movement skills that may be applied to the game, sport, and dance activities characteristic of our culture.

VISUAL PERCEPTION DURING EARLY CHILDHOOD

By the time children reach 2 years of age, the ocular apparatus is mature. The eyeball is nearly adult size and weight. All anatomical and physiological aspects of the eye are complete, but the perceptual abilities of young children are still incomplete. Although the child is able to fixate on objects, track them, and make accurate judgments of size and shape, numerous refinements still need to be made. Young children are unable to intercept a tossed ball with any degree of control (Payne, 1981; Isaacs, 1984). Their perception of moving objects is poorly developed (Williams, 1983; Payne & Isaacs, 1991), as are their figure-ground perceptual abilities (Gallahue, 1968; Williams 1983) and perception of depth (Williams, 1983; Sage, 1984; Payne & Isaacs, 1991). The extent to which movement plays a role in visual perceptual development is speculative, but the extent to which visual perception influences movement cannot be denied. Fundamental movement tasks such as catching, striking, kicking, and trapping a ball all require considerable visual perceptual input. This input must be sufficiently accurate to permit successful performance of the movement task. It is important, therefore, that we become familiar with children's developing perceptual abilities and the vital impact of visual perception on movement skill acquisition. Visual acuity, figure-ground perception, depth perception, and visual-motor coordination are important qualities that are developmentally based and that significantly influence movement performance. Table 3–15 provides a synthesis of findings for each of these abilities.

IMPLICATIONS FOR THE DEVELOPMENTAL MOVEMENT PROGRAM

Fundamental movement skill acquisition is dependent in large measure upon environmental factors such as opportunities for practice, encouragement, and instruction, as well as the goals of the task itself. Knowledge of this fact has vital implications for the movement education of young children. For the vast majority of children, personalized, developmentally appropriate instruction is essential if they are to attain mature skill levels in a variety of fundamental movement tasks. This instruction must be coupled with sufficient time for practice in movement skill learning and the use of positive reinforcement techniques to continually encourage the learner.

The process of movement skill development is age related but not age dependent. Movement skill acquisition is highly individualized because of the unique hereditary and experiential background of each child. Therefore, it is inappropriate to classify movement activities solely by age or by grade level. Care should be taken to select movement experiences based on the ability levels of the "real" children being taught, not the mythical "average" children of textbooks.

TABLE 3–15. Selected Developmental Aspects of Children's Visual Perception

Visual Quality	Selected Abilities	Approximate Age
Visual acuity	Rapid improvement	5–7
The ability to distin-	Plateau	7–8
guish detail in static	Rapid improvement	9–10
and dynamic settings	Mature (static)	10–11
	Plateau (dynamic)	10–11
	Mature (dynamic)	11–12
Figure-ground perception	Slow improvement	3–4
The ability to separate	Rapid improvement	4–6
an object from its	Slight spurt	7–8
surroundings	Mature	8–12
Depth perception	Frequent judgement	3–4
The ability to judge	errors	5–6
distance relative to	Few judgement	7–11
oneself	errors	By age 12
	Rapid improvement	
	Mature	
Visual-motor coordination	Rapid improvement	3–7
The ability to integrate	Slow slight improve-	7–9
use of eyes and	ment	
hands in terms of	Mature	10–12
object tracking and		
interruption		

Developmental movement programs are those that emphasize sequential movement skill acquisition and increased physical competency based on the unique developmental level of the individual. Developmental movement programs encourage the uniqueness of the individual, and are based on the fundamental proposition that teacher decisions must be centered around the concept of individual appropriateness, and only secondarily on the concept of age-group appropriateness (Bredekamp, 1987; Gallahue, 1993).

Individual appropriateness is the cornerstone of developmentally appropriate education. It is based on the central proposition that each child has his or her unique timing and pattern of development. Therefore, the movement activities engaged in by children are geared to their individual level of motor and perceptual development. Age-group appropriateness is of only secondary importance in the developmentally based movement program. Although the developmental program is not based on age or grade level, it is influenced by both. The process of development is universally accepted as hierarchal and predictable; preceding from simple to complex and from general to specific in the universal quest for increased movement competence. As a result, patterns of behavior emerge that may be used to provide a framework for guiding the selection of movement experiences that are typically appropriate for specific age groups.

The developmental movement education program should be part of the daily life experience of all children. To be of maximum benefit it should be developmentally based. Only when we understand the processes of motor and perceptual development are we equipped to make curricular decisions in the best interest of the children that we serve.

References

Bredekamp, S. (Ed.). (1987). *Developmentally appropriate practice in early childhood programs serving children from birth through age 8.* Washington, DC: National Association for the Education of Young Children.

Cratty, B. J., & Martin, M. (1969). *Perceptual-motor efficiency in children.* Philadelphia: Lea and Febiger.

Gallahue, D. L. (1968). The relationship between perceptual and motor abilities. *Research Quarterly, 39,* 948–952.

Gallahue, D. L. (1989). *Understanding motor development: Infants, children, adolescents.* Dubuque, IA: Wm. C. Brown and Benchmark.

Gallahue, D. L. (1993). *Developmental physical education for today's children.* Dubuque, IA: Wm. C. Brown and Benchmark.

Halverson, L. (1966). Development of motor patterns in young children. *Quest, 6,* 44–50.

Haubenstricker, J., & Seefeldt, V. (1986). Acquisition of motor skills during childhood. In V. Seefeldt (Ed.), *Physical activity and well-being* (pp. 41–92). Reston, VA: American Alliance for Health, Physical Education, Recreation and Dance.

Heston, M. L. (1989). *Influence of inhabiting level and skill proficiency on satisfaction, and affective expression in eight-, nine-, and ten-year-old boys on a sport game setting.* Unpublished doctoral dissertation, Indiana University.

Isaacs, L. D. (1984). Players' success in T-baseball. *Perceptual and Motor Skills, 59,* 852–854.

Johnson, R. (1962). Measurement of achievement in fundamental skills of elementary school children. *Research Quarterly, 33,* 94–103.

Keogh, J., & Sugden, D. (1985). *Movement skill development.* New York: Macmillan.

Langendorfer, S. (1988). Goal of a motor task as a constraint on developmental status. In J. E. Clark & J. H. Humphrey (Eds.), *Advances in motor development research.* New York: AMS Press.

Luedke, G. C. (1980). *Range of motion as the focus of teaching the overhand throwing pattern to children.* Unpublished doctoral dissertation, Indiana University.

McClenaghan, B. A., & Gallahue, D. L. (1978a). *Fundamental movement: A developmental and remedial approach.* Philadelphia: W. B. Saunders.

McClenaghan, B. A., & Gallahue, D. L. (1978b). *Fundamental movement: Observation and assessment.* Philadelphia: W. B. Saunders.

Miller, S. (1978). *The facilitation of fundamental motor skill learning in young children.* Unpublished doctoral dissertation, Michigan State University.

Payne, V. G. (1981). Effects of object size and experimental design on object reception by children in the first grade. *Journal of Human Movement Studies, 11,* 1–9.

Payne, V. G., & Isaacs, L. D. (1991). *Human motor development: A lifespan approach.* Mountain View, CA: Mayfield.

Roberton, M. A. (1978). Stages in motor development. In M. Ridenour (Ed.), *Motor development: Issues and application.* Princeton, NJ: Princeton University Press.

Roberton, M. A. (1982). Describing stages within and across motor tasks. In J. A. S. Kelso & J. Clark (Eds.), *The development of movement control and coordination.* New York: Wiley.

Roberton, M. A. (1988). Developmental level as a function of the immediate environment. In J. E. Clark & J. H. Humphrey (Eds.), *Advances in motor development research.* New York: AMS Press.

Roberton, M. A., & Halverson, L. E. (1984). *Developing children: Their changing movement.* Philadelphia: Lea and Febiger.

Sage, G. H. (1984). *Motor learning and control: A neuropsychological approach.* Dubuque, IA: Wm. C. Brown.

Seefeldt, V. (1972). *Discussion of walking and running.* Unpublished research, Michigan State University.

Seefeldt, V., & Haubenstricker, J. (1976). *Developmental sequences of fundamental motor skills.* Unpublished research, Michigan State University.

Sinclair, C. (1973). *Movement of the young child.* Columbus, OH: Merrill.

Ulrich, D. A. (1985). *Test of gross motor development.* Austin, TX: Pro-Ed.

Williams, H. (1970). *A study of perceptual-motor characteristics of children in kindergarten through sixth grade.* Unpublished paper, University of Toledo.

Williams, H. (1983). *Perceptual and motor development.* Philadelphia: Lea and Febiger.

·4·

THERE AND THEN, INTANGIBLE AND INTERNAL: NARRATIVES IN EARLY CHILDHOOD

Dennie Palmer Wolf

PROJECTS IN LANGUAGE DEVELOPMENT

HARVARD GRADUATE SCHOOL OF EDUCATION

INTRODUCTION: THE LANGUAGE OF THERE AND THEN

One of the stunning aspects of early speech is how effectively children recognize what must be spelled out and what can be inferred from context. A 2-year-old can say "Give it me," and be understood because of the careful, intuitive way in which she combines words, gesture, gaze, and the immediate, close-to-hand contents of the here-and-now world. Out of that combinatorial sleight-of-hand, and helped by her listener's willingness, it is clear that "it" is a sandwich in the making and "me" is none other than the child herself. These intuitions about message making built from every available raw material are elegant—so much so that they have, for almost a century of child study, kept our attention trained on the pragmatics and the grammar of language uttered in an immediate context. But "here-and-now" speech is only half of language use. Equally important and developing just as quickly is what could be called "there-and-then" language—the structures and intuitions that make extended discourse about the past, the internal, the imagined, and the hypothetical possible. It is this set of skills that permits children to engage in making and sharing their autobiographies and the histories of their families, to inquire into and reflect on the psychological aspects of human experience, to enter into the literary worlds authors invent, and finally, to probe the workings of the social and natural worlds via hypothetical explorations of the "what-if" variety.

The powerful, even the necessary, role of narrative in allowing young children to make meaning of the flow and flux of experience is captured in the following:

Ms. Miller has read a story about a young Indian boy and looks up to talk about it with her class of 4- and 5-year-olds:
Ms. Miller: And his mother and his baby sister and his grandmother . . . bows and shield made of buffalo skin.
    Didi: Where's his grandfather?
Ms. Miller: Maybe his grandfather has gone to hunt buffalo.
    Didi: Maybe his grandfather died.
Ms. Miller: It could be his grandfather died. When they get old, they do. Everybody dies when they get old.
    Didi: But not me! I'm never gonna die!
    Bart: Yes, you are—sometime.
(Ms. Miller returns to talking about the story. Linda and Didi have a conversation of their own.)

(A little later):
    Linda: Teacher, Didi says she's never gonna die, and she is when she gets old.
Bart (*to Didi*): You're gonna die.
    Ms. Miller: Linda, Didi and her mother have talked about that a lot at home. We'll let them talk about it. (*Didi's grandfather had, in fact, died, occasioning much discussion at her home about death and who dies.*)
(Genishi & Dyson, 1984, p. 117)

Didi, Bart, and Ms. Miller make several vital points about narrative. First, as indicated, narrative encompasses much more

This work was supported through grants from the Carnegie Corporation, the John T. and Catherine D. MacArthur Foundation, the National Institutes of Health, and the School Reform Program of the Rockefeller Foundation.

than stories. It takes in a large family of activities where several characteristics are present: a remove from immediate circumstances, events sequenced in time, and a perspective taken on those events. Thus, the focus of the paper will be on a deliberately wide spectrum of children's linguistic activity: including personal anecdotes about recent, actual experience; imaginative play that portrays much about inventing both plausible and fantastic experiences; as well as children's efforts to hypothesize, plan, and build models through talking over what might or could happen.

Second, much of our talk, particularly talk directed to making meaning of daily events, is narrative in impulse, even when it is not fully realized as a story with a beginning, a middle, and an end. Little of what Didi, Bart and Ms. Miller do is continuously narrative, but narrative crops up continuously wherever background and explanation are at issue. Thus, narrative is quite a varied category. The teacher and the children use the temporal flexibility and the sequencing characteristic of narrative to work their way from the safe story-world discussion of death to the frightening actual death of a real grandfather, and from there to the tense hypothetical discussion of future death. Their teacher uses a short account of what she knows has happened at Didi's house to help Bart stop insisting that Didi, too, will die.

Third, Didi, Bart, and Ms. Miller make it plain that we cannot view narrative skill as simply linguistic. Although there is no question about the importance of the acquisition of a pronoun or a tense system, other ingredients matter: Children have to grasp the social and affective functions of narrative—why bother telling, after all? They have to have the social understandings that will help them design their telling for particular listeners, using the forms and materials that will make their accounts meaningful in their family or community. They need to grasp narrative as not just story time, but "life time"—a way of portraying not just particulate events, but causes and origins, explanations, and long-term consequences.

Fourth, we too often take written text as the model for narratives. Narratives are performances that bring together face, gesture, posture, and intonation in ways that particular cultures have designated these channels as meaning bearing—a fact that, unfortunately, a written survey text such as this one cannot adequately capture. We also too often think of narratives as monologues told by *a* teller. But as the children's account of death shows, this is rarely so. Tellers depend on listeners to supply details, to ask questions, and to be amazed. The onset and continued development of children's narrative skills is a social affair. It is in the hands of many: peers, parents, grandparents, and increasingly, the day care workers and preschool teachers who work with and care for young children (Genishi & Dyson, 1984; Paley, 1988; Vygotsky, 1962).

Finally, this example points out the very important difference between chronicling and narrating. No one—not the book author, not Didi or Bart, nor Ms. Miller—creates a faithful chronicle of what happened in the story world or the actual world. What they do is much more constructive than that. Any narrative is full of a radical selection and shaping to create a story world and demands inference from listeners (Polanyi, 1985; White, 1980). For example, it is not clear where the Indian grandfather went or what exactly occurred at Didi's house. Narratives aren't

faithful; they bear the imprint of a teller who means to make a point to a listener—so they are selected, weighted, and shaped tellings. To learn to narrate is, in effect, to learn to select, to shape, and to evaluate.

Even though Didi and Bart are only in preschool, they already move fluently across multiple forms of narration—finding a theme, developing it, weaving in the turns of several speakers. Although it may be true that children do not tell coherent, formal stories until middle childhood, it is clear that narrative skill is not that late arriving. Rather, narrative understanding, like syntax, pragmatics, and vocabulary, develops—or is stunted—from very early on.

In what follows, I want to take up the question of why we need to make narrative a part of the study of child language. Then I will look, in close detail, at the several processes that contribute to children becoming effective narrators. Finally, I will turn to teachers and classrooms, asking what it is that can be done to acknowledge and nurture children's narrative capacities. Throughout, I have drawn on transcripts from my own observational studies of early play and narrative in 9 middle-class American children and also from a larger study of 52 middle class American children. I have supplemented that work with examples drawn from other researchers' work with a broader spectrum of North American and European children in order to suggest what may be some general contours of narrative growth. The major point here is not that all children tell narratives in the same way. Their gender, culture, class, and neighborhood leave, of course, a deep imprint on what is narrated and how that narration is presented. Instead, the point is that all but those children with the most severe impairments arrive at school with the capacity to form and perform nuanced accounts of what they observe and feel. This is a point from which much growth can begin—if children's narrative capacities were to be acknowledged and built upon.

Why Study the There-and-Then Language of Narratives?

Acquiring the language in which to talk about past, imagined, and plausible experiences is one of the broadest avenues we have out of living a life restricted to the literal and the immediate. What Middleton describes certainly applies to Didi and Bart as much as to adult narrators:

The properties of a culture, embodied in its artifacts, tools, social customs and institutions, language and terms of reference, provide a historical dimension to everyday living that enables knowledge of what has already happened or been achieved to be used in the service of present and future activity. Our modes of being and doing are cultural products that constitute a guiding constraint concerning what form our present and future actions should or could take. (Middleton, 1987, p. 2)

Being able to speak about times other than the present is a basic tool for creating a coherent autobiography (Kihlstrom, 1982; McAdams & Ochberg, 1986). Without the ability to describe sequences of events, their connections, and meanings, it would be impossible to build up an understanding of one's history or to convey it to someone else. To be able to do this is vital: It forms the texture of the kinds of everyday exchanges that make for close relationships. In much more serious circumstances, narrative is what allows outsiders—teachers, clinicians, and social workers—to understand what may be troubling or even abusive in young children's lives (Wolf, in press).

Narrative is also a passport into reading and writing (Sulzby & Otto, 1982; Teale, 1982; Wells, 1982; Wells & Raban, 1978). Frequently, it is through having cereal boxes or addresses read aloud, through recitation of folktales, through being read to, and even through pretending to read stories that young children come to understand that print carries messages, and more broadly what the features of formal language are in a given community. Often, children's most constant and significant encounters with the core of literacy—the stepping back to select and reflect on experience—come not just from books, but from pausing to talk over experience.

A very different kind of narrative, the hypothetical or what-if account, also figures in children's lives much as it does in the thought and work of adult scientists and philosophers. When children ask or explain about how dreams appear and disappear, when they wonder aloud about what happens when you get very, very old, or when they ask what would happen if the world ran out of air, they are using their narrative capacities to probe the future and the possible (Piaget, 1962).

Finally, narrating is complex work that brings together often disparate aspects of being alive: the affective work of realizing what we feel, the cognitive work of making sense, the social work of sharing experience, and the cultural work of taking up the tools and forms we inherit for composing personal, familial, or community histories. But to grasp this, we need to understand the much larger work of **narrativizing**—that is, how narrators create out of their experience narratives, rather than running commentaries, reports, or plain records (White, 1980).

FROM EXPERIENCE TO NARRATIVE

If we listen to the narratives of children of different ages, we see that learning to narrate experience includes at least three processes: becoming a narrator, becoming an author, and making texts.

Becoming a Narrator

Narrators aren't born; they become. The first steps of this process, however, are so fundamental that we often forget to think of them as acquisitions or something to be learned. Sketched out, these steps include the following: entering the community of narrators, developing memories, acquiring the language markers for recollection, and finally, becoming a narratable self.

Entering a Community of Narrators. The capacity to say what happened to oneself, in some other place, or 10 minutes ago, becomes particularly important from the second year on, when the advent of walking and other forms of autonomy mean that young children spend portions of their days apart from the immediate presence of care givers. Attachment that was

once carried out largely in terms of glance, touching, and face-to-face exchanges of sound and gesture is now complemented by talk and the exchange of experience. The fine-tuning between parents, other care givers, and children gains a verbal and narrative dimension (Wolf, 1982) as the following example of a middle-class mother and her daughter shows:

(Naomi, age 32 months, and her parents are at home together.)
Child: I had those dancing people. (*No referent in sight.*)
Adult: What dancing people, Naomi?
Child: Happy people.
Adult: What happy people, Naomi?
Child: Happy people.
Adult: What happy people? Do you mean puppets?
Child: Uh huh.
Adult: Clowns?
Child: Uh huh.
Adult: On television? People on television?
Child: I need that book about dancing people.
Adult: You need that book about dancing people. You mean the Fantasia book: The book about dancing hippopotamuses?
Child: (*shouting*) I need dancing book. I need it.
Adult: Well, where is it, Naomi? Do you know where it is?
Child: No, I don't know.
Adult: Well, we're trying to figure out which one you want so we can get it. (*Naomi has been growing more and more frantic and is now crying.*)
Adult: Hey, hey, calm down. Tell us more about the book so maybe we'll be able to figure out which one it is.
Child: (*crying*) I need the dancing people.
(Sachs, 1983, p. 14)

At this juncture, competent and engaged narration means that care givers and children can keep in touch with what happened earlier that morning, 3 miles away at school, or in the otherwise secret and wholly internal worlds of the mind and heart. To exchange narratives of personal experience is, in effect, one way to preserve emotional attachment—the mutual following and mirroring of one another's states and experiences. But also at this time, many children begin to spend significant hours outside their homes—at preschool, at a babysitter's, or at a day care center. Each of these worlds carries its own rules about how obedient children have to be, how bad behavior is noticed and punished, and whether children are to react to pain or loss in other children to when they are not related. It is a time, consequently, when children, young as they are, may begin to reflect on rules and conduct and want or need to talk out the contradictions or injustices they feel they see.

As a young student father walks home in the dark with his 2-year-old in a backpack, they talk about their days:

F: You're getting heavy, you know, not like when you were a baby.
J: Baby?
F: Not any more. I saw a real baby today. Baby Jake. He came 'cause his dad came to work at our house....Jake played with your busy box.

J: My baby Marta.
F: Marta was at Nonnie's today?
J: Mmmm. She cried.
F: Why'd she cry?
J: Nonnie said, "No, no, no. Don't touch."

These are also years when children's social worlds virtually explode. During these years, children's formerly simple one-to-one relations (child-mother, child-father) give way to much more complex family interactions. New forms of competitions arise: Children may have younger siblings to contend with or may realize that they compete for their parents' attention with spouses, other children, and work. Many 3-year-olds face a new and more demanding, even troubling, understanding of human relationships that requires talking over (Dunn, 1988; Emde & Sorce, 1983).

In this flux and demand, narrative provides one way of staying attached. In learning how to select, present, and comment on stories of their own experience, children learn how to claim and hold adult attention, whether from the back of the car or at a crowded dinner table. In learning to tell narratives in their family or their community, young children learn how to signal where they "belong." They learn a subtle network of rules for public presentation: how close you stick to the truth, how much you can brag, and what kinds of tales girls and women tell (Heath, 1983, 1985; Miller, 1982, 1988a, 1988b; Miller & Moore, 1991; Miller & Sperry, 1987). In this light, narratives are one of the great socializers and the persistent carriers of the effects of community and family values (Feagans, 1982; Gee, 1991; Heath, 1983; Michaels, 1981; Scollon & Scollon, 1981; Wolf, in press). So it is that when the children of some black working-class communities are scolded, they can listen obediently or retort so cleverly that their offenses are forgotten. For instance, one mother scolded her son, age 3 years and 9 months, as follows: "What'd you do with that shoe? You want me to tie you up, put you on the railroad track?" He retorted:

> Railroad track
> Train all big 'n black
> On dat track, on dat track.
> Ain't no way I can't get back.
> Back from dat train,
> Big 'n black, I be back. (Heath, 1983, p. 118)

Delighted with her son's display of the kind of narrative play so prized in their community, this mother quit scolding.

In this way, as children move out of late infancy, they often investigate the separations made possible by walking, the arrival of other children, the return of their mothers to work, and care outside of home. Narrative provides at least 2 ways of staying close: (1) it offers an envelope for sharing what happened while apart, and (2) as children take up its forms and practices, they adopt (a) ways of remembering and telling that mark them as belonging to the particular histories of their families and (b) ways of recall, sharing, and performing that signal their membership in a social community.

A Memory System for Narrative. Having the urge to tell is not sufficient condition for narrative. Any narrative also requires memory not just for the literal recall of events, but for remembering plausible details for fiction, or information to include in a plan or exploration of what might be. Much of what we know about the organization of children's early memory comes, in fact, from their first narratives. What we know suggests that long-term memory for experience develops in 2 stages. In an initial stage, children focus considerable attention on coming to understand the regularities of their lives: The common sequences or scripts for events, which will eventually form the background against which other, outstanding, or high-pitched events become the materials for stories (Mandler, 1984; Nelson, 1988; Nelson & Gruendel, 1986). For example, as a part of daytime discussions or crib monologues, children use their emerging narrative skills to describe the expected patterns of their lives (Nelson, 1986, 1988; Sachs, 1983). Thus, preschoolers as young as 3 can verbally report what happens in events they are familiar with, such as going to a restaurant or having a birthday party. They have a temporally sequenced, general knowledge about events that they can put into words (Fivush, 1984; Hudson, 1990; Nelson & Hudson, 1986; Slackman & Hudson, 1984).

In addition, numerous studies show that, between 2 and 3 years, children can verbally recall details of past events, almost as far back as their first birthdays (Eisenberg, 1983, 1985; Hudson, 1990; Sachs, 1983). At this point, children have developed the skill to report the specific events of a personal history: for example, *crying* at one's own birthday party; riding in the back of an open truck with a big dog; or seeing costumed children arrive for Halloween. It is from this point onward that most older children and adults begin to have reliable memories of their own distinctive pasts (Kihlstrom, 1981; Nelson, 1988; Snow, 1990).

This working out of the commonplace versus the extraordinary is much more than rehearsal or play. Recent work on the formation of a coherent autobiography and sense of self suggests that it is the interplay between grasping what is commonplace and normative (e.g., that parents sometimes get angry with their children) and what is odd or extreme (e.g., that your parent was abusive) is a central element in life-span adaptation.

Acquiring the Linguistic Tools for Narrative. Even before 3, young children begin to have the bare bones of narrative language. They form whole and even coordinated sentences ("Mommy came and I went with her."). They can make appropriate and contrastive use of simple present, past, and future tenses. For example, Roger Brown's data indicates that the highly noticeable forms of the irregular past appear in his 3 subjects between 2:3 and 2:11, and the regular past morpheme (-ed) comes to be used reliably between the ages of 2:2 and 4:0 (1973). In addition, during their second year, young children elaborate a pronominal system that allows them to distinguish between several agents in a scene and the basic elements of subject-verb agreement ("He goes; they go") so that their narratives can make it plain who is doing what to whom (Bates, 1990). In addition, they begin to understand the simplest kinds of conjunctions and adverbs, which they are capable of using to indicate the relationships between events: words like "and," "then," and "so" (McCabe & Peterson, 1991). Moreover, they know some of the most basic narrative strategies: They can use the order of mentioning events to suggest the sequence and cause of events. ("He came up and I said, "Go back."") For example, Nicolich (1978) found that object transformations and short episodes of play do occur early in the second year. Moreover, as children advance toward their second birthdays, they are increasingly likely to gather needed objects and make arrangements prior to launching into a sequence of make-believe.

A Narratable Self. If we want someone else to grasp what it is that has happened to us, we must become narrators capable of reflecting on our own experience and translating it into words. This demands stepping outside of immediate experience and choosing what to say. To become a narratable self is, in effect, to regard one's own self and life from without, as if the individual is the observing storyteller, not the poor subject trudging through events. During this same period, as many observers have remarked, children begin to treat mirror images and photographs as representations of themselves (Amsterdam, 1972; Kaye, 1982; Lewis & Brooks-Gunn, 1979). It is in the context of a sharply differentiating sense of self that children acquire a set of linguistic markers that may either partake of or amplify their shifting notions of self. In the months around the second birthday, children acquire a network of terms for the self—both proper names and nominals as well as personal pronouns and the possessive morpheme. In addition, they gain mastery of the dyadic complexities of personal pronouns that permit them to talk about "mine and yours," "you and me" (Bates, 1990; Brown, 1973; Kagan, 1981; Leopold, 1939; Sully, 1896). But more important for the development of narrative skills, these skills also make it possible for children to speak either from the vantage point of a subject ("I want big pants") or the point of view of an observer of their own or of someone else's experience (e.g., looking at self in the mirror, saying, "J.'s got big pants"). Thus, during the second year, children give us verbal evidence that they know something of "me" that acts and "I" who anticipates, compares, remembers, and judges. The self becomes an observing entity as well as a subjective state (Kagan, 1981; Mead, 1934; Stern, 1985).

One of the results of these combined linguistic, social, and affective events is the advent of "memory talk" between children and adults, in which the 2 partners move between comments made in the present tense and recollections couched as historically distant. In this talk, children take an increasingly prominent role not just as subjects, but as **narrators**. In effect, they come to stand in 3 places in the conversation: They are the person who identifies with the younger, distant person (the object of the memory), the person who engages in recollection (the subject who currently has the memory), and the narrator who tells. Consider J., at 2:6, who returns from child care at the end of the day. He talks with his mother about a drawing he has brought home with him. It becomes the occasion for comparing his younger and his current selves—for his acting as a narrator:

Mo: Did you make that? Such a big one.
  J: At school. With big marker(s).
Mo: By yourself? Or did the teachers help?
  J: No, J. See (*points to where an adult has written his name*).
Mo: I like it. I didn't know you could make people.

  J: Not people. A man with gray pants. See (*he points to gray scrawl on top of what may be a tadpole-like figure*).
Mo: Is it Daddy going to work in his gray pants?
  J: Yeah, a Daddy man. Put it on a 'frigerator. Take that one down. It's old.
Mo: I like it. You just did it when you were little.
  J: I was little. Not now. Do the new one. Do the daddy-man one up there. It's a big daddy-man one now.

Even though his command of temporal markers is just beginning and his vocabulary is borrowed in part from his mother, J., acting as a narrator, draws an effective contrast between "then" when he "was little" and made "yuck" drawings, and "now," which is cast in the present tense, when he makes "new" and "big" drawings.

It is in the period beginning with their third birthdays that children increasingly take charge of forming the public record of their histories, bringing up episodes they remember as they recall them (Eisenberg, 1983, 1985; Sachs, 1983). For instance, at 2:10, J. is playing in the middle of his bedroom floor, entirely engrossed in the here and now, when he looks up at his father and refers to an episode of their joint play when he (J.) battered one of his trucks.

Need to make a garage for my big dump truck...we need to make a big garage for this truck. Let's not crash into the garage because they still need fixing, the garage man's, ya, this is broken (*examines front of the truck*) this one has a broken muffler. 'Member the other time, when a man, he crashed in, and he had a broken muffler, a broken muffler, the other day?

In a particularly sharp example, J., at 3:0, is struggling to build some stairs out of blocks. He has tried this several times before, growing frustrated and simply scattering the blocks. On this occasion, when he fails, he uses the voice of a fictional character to mock his own performance, acknowledging what he observes, but displacing it.

J. struggles to place a block so that he gets a jagged outline, but instead, he produces a rectangular, wall-like structure.
J: I can't do it. I don't know how.
J. goes on and turns the wall-like structure into a building. As he continues to play, he comes upon a bag of marbles. Taking several out, he jokes at trying to stack them up, hamming it up when they tumble and roll away.
J: These stairs are too hard to make.
J. makes a little figure hop up to the top of a stack of blocks. He makes that figure call down to another one to join him.
J: (*for Figure 1*) Hey, come on up here.
J. makes the second figure struggle up (as there is only a stack with no toe-holds). When the stack topples, he makes that second figure complain.
J: (*for Figure 2*) Hey you dummy, that didn't work, you make dumb stairs.

Using all these tools, and sensitized to their use by other people, children become narrators who can engage in the formation of an autobiography (Hudson, 1990; Snow, 1990), in which they begin to select, narrate, and evaluate the events of their lives.

Becoming an Author

Between the ages of 2 and 4, children (with the help of their families) construct an aspect of narrative skill that goes beyond being a narrator who is able to give simple accounts of what usually happens or what happened last night at Tia Marta's. This second cluster of developments yields what might be called *authorship*. An author is, in essence, someone who makes experience, not someone who reports it. To make experience certainly demands word choices and kinds of sentences, but perhaps even more than these, authorship includes **invention, emphasis, performance,** and **rendition.**

Invention. Between the ages of 2 and 4, two abilities appear that make this separation possible. The first is the ability to "uncouple" various lines of experience. This can take many forms: simulation and pretense (when a person transforms the actual situation through thought or fantasy); and deceit or joking (when a person deliberately distorts or denies what they feel or know). In each of these situations children rearrange, edit, or change the "facts" to suit themselves. As early as the second year, children exhibit a capacity for uncoupling language from literal reference and recoupling it either to a transforming reference (when a cookie with a bite out of it becomes a "moon") or to fantasy (when language can be used to summon up purely imagined events and states). At this point the world that is donated by physical fact or convention is no longer given, no longer the only possible reality. So it is that Heather, at 14 months, can use the word "horsie" to refer to a book illustration, as well as to one at the children's zoo. But she can also yell it out when she sees her mother's sewing machine silhouetted against a window. Josh, at 2:6 can see "rabbit ears" when a wave breaks on the rocks, or line his shoes up in a discarded aluminum foil box and announce, "peas in a pod." This capacity means that even young narrators are more than strict historians—they can imagine innumerable alternatives to the present situation. With it comes the first break with the language of the "here and now." (Scarlett & Wolf, 1979; Winner, 1988).

Emphasis. Effective and powerful narratives are more than well-formed accounts of what has happened. Strong narratives combine events with evaluation—explicit or implicit evaluations that let a listener know how the narrator views or relates to the events being recounted. Studies of internal state language show that as early as their second and third years children acquire an interest in and the terms for describing their own and others' interior lives (Bretherton & Beeghly, 1982; Hood & Bloom, 1979; Johnson & Maratsos, 1977; Johnson & Wellman, 1980; Wolf, Goldfield, & Beeghly, 1984; Wolf, Rygh, & Altshuler, 1984). The result is that children produce at least simple narratives that combine the two major elements of stories: chains of events and evaluations of events. Consider, for instance, the narrative offered by Amanda, age five:

See, we went out on the playground. And we were doing the seesaw, you know, walking down it. So then Lissa fell and she was shouting ouch and there was blood all over her knee...both knees...Ugh!

Of the two events here, we understand the drama of the fall—not just because of its danger—but because Amanda highlights it for us, using a combination of evaluative elements: the background information about shouting and blood, the repair to say it is both knees, and the exclamation. Without such evaluative elements we might take the fall as a passing incident, rather than a disaster.

Lines of Talk and the Work of Performing a Narrative. During the later preschool years, children develop a theory of mind. That is, they come to understand two crucial aspects of human experience: First, people are more than their observable behaviors—they also have minds; and second, any two minds may have quite different takes on events, depending on what individuals experience, believe, or witness. (Imagine that you leave your coat on a bench, then leave the room. While you are out, I hang it up for you in the closet. When you return, you are upset, thinking that someone has stolen it. I am calm, knowing it is safe. In order to set things to rights, I will explain—but only if I have a theory of mind that alerts me to the fact that we will have differing interpretations.) Thus, between 3 and 5, another major function for narrative appears: Children tell because they understand the possibility of different understandings arising in different minds (Johnson & Maratsos, 1977; Johnson & Wellman, 1980; Wellman & Estes, 1986).

Through the acquisition of a much richer syntax, as well as a set of discourse-level understandings, children come to perform their narratives in a way that is quite aptly tuned to reaching another mind. Nowhere is this so visible as in their use of different lines of talk. **Lines of talk** are the different kinds of speaking a narrator has to engage in in order to protect, monitor, repair, and nurture the narrative in the presence of listeners (Goffman, 1986). The following example of Jonathan, age four, illustrates accordingly:

I was going and then Stanton comed to play...you know Stanton?... so Stanton said, "Get out, you can't be playing with us."

To form and perform even that short bit of narrative, the young speaker uses three lines of talk: **narration** ("I was going..."); **conversation with the listener** ("you know Stanton?"); and **character dialogue** ("Get out, you can't be playing with us.") to signal the several perspectives they can take on experience (Wolf, Moreton, & Camp, in press; Wolf & Hicks, 1989).

In their simplest forms, these lines of talk are distinguishable in everyday conversations or narratives when the child momentarily drops the frame of the ongoing talk, makes a comment, and then returns to the original topic (Schegloff, 1971; Schriffrin, 1982). Or, using the contrasts between past and present, the child may talk about different chapters or moments in his evolving autobiography. So it is that J., at the age of 2:2, is taking off his sweater, hat, mittens, and boots in the hallway after returning home from child care:

Mo: Here give me the mittens.
J. holds out his hands, and his mother tugs off the mittens.
Mo: Those are wet. Did you play in the snow this afternoon?
J: We made a snowman. A big one.

Mo: Yeah? Did you give him a face?

    J: Rocks...eyes.

(Outside the late afternoon train rolls by.)

    J: Train's coming. (*He listens for a minute and then looks back to his mother.*)...And sticks for his arms.

Mo: No wonder these mittens are sopping.

J. and his mother are talking about a snowman when the train hurtles by, distracting him. For a moment he focuses on its roar, but then he comes back to the snowman, signaling his return to the earlier topic with "and" and "his." Already, he can juggle the roles of the present-tense observer (the one who listens to the train) and the backward-looking reciter of an anecdote.

Children's play with small objects offers some of the most elaborate examples of this interplay of voices. In play, children freely enter and exit the world of a narrative, sometimes speaking as the teller, imitating the voices of distinct characters; and other times dropping out to ask for information or help remembering, then returning to the tale exactly where they left off. In this kind of talk, children make use of many of the voices they have developed elsewhere: the direct discourse of the speaking subject, the voice of a narrator, and the outsider voice of a critic or commentator. Here children achieve considerable **intratextuality**, juggling several lines of information within their discourse without destroying the overall coherence or cohesion of their talk. Earlier studies (Wolf, Goldfield, & Beeghly, 1984) showed that many 3-year-olds could move between at least 3 prominent voices: stage managing, character dialogue, and narrative.

Additional studies (Wolf & Hicks, 1989) have shown how children use their emerging knowledge of grammar and discourse to distinguish further between the several voices. For instance, children make differential use of pronouns in each voice: Stage managing and character dialogue are marked with first and second persons, whereas narrative utterances are marked with the third person. Children also employ various forms of utterance to signal the perspective from which they are speaking. Narrative segments are normally recounted through use of declarative utterances, since what is being encoded in the narrative voice is "what happened." Dialogue and stage managing, however, reflect a more interactive stance, so that questions and commands may be used as well as declarative utterances. Early on, these different lines of talk are marked chiefly in performance (e.g., with different ways of talking, patterns of gaze, and object handling). However, with practice, and as their linguistic systems develop, children begin to use increasingly complex networks of linguistic features within each line of talk. Stage-managing utterances become distinctive in that they are a forum for interactions with the experimenter about the nature of the fictional world being created. In this sense, these utterances represent an excursion from the story world itself, not unlike the asides or departures that adult speakers index with changes of tone, markers like "excuse me" and "as I was saying" or shifts in topic (Polanyi, 1985; Schriffrin, 1982). Stage-managing utterances are linguistically distinguished from narrative and dialogue by the frequent use of a collaborative second person pronoun ("we're," "let's," etc.) and use of the future to forecast what will happen in the play ("...and then

he's gonna go in the tree"). The narrative line comes to be marked with the past tense and to carry clear markers for temporal sequencing ("and," "then," "while"). Dialogue lines are marked with the present tense, a high frequency of first- and second-person pronouns, deictic speech ("come here," "take this," etc.) and conversational conventions ("hi," "bye," "how ya doing").

The following passage shows a 4-year-old child playing with a puppet theater and a set of small figures, including the members of a family, a cat, and a pirate. (The transcript is marked to indicate which roles the child is taking at each point when he speaks.)

(The child knocks down some of the trees in the theater.)

    (Narrator): And all the trees fell down.

    (Cat character, to clown): Put your legs down.

    (Pirate character, stalking in, threatening voice): I am the pirate.

    (Speaking as himself to the observer): See his sword? Is he really a pirate?

    (Observer): Yeah.

    (Speaking as himself to the observer): Are you telling the truth?

    (Observer): Yeah.

    (Speaking as himself): Not really. Just in here.

    (Cat character, scratching pirate): Scratch, scratch, scratch.

    (Pirate character): Don't you dare.

He has the figures continue to fight.

    (Man character): Don't kill me, don't kill me...and don't kill any of my friends either.

This episode of play lasts not more than 10 or 15 seconds, but within it the child is by turns the organizing, framing narrator; the scrappy, aggressive character; and a young boy candidly mapping out the reality status of a plastic pirate. It is possible that the child uses the interplay among those several lines of talk to explore the power and the limits of the pirate. First, he uses the character voices to portray how mean the pirate is, then he uses his own voice (the stage-managing line) to check on the limits of that power. Once he has established for himself just where the pirate is powerful, he resumes his aggressive play. Potentially then, these lines of talk are not merely a part of the conventional way to play. They may be one way of talking around a question and raising its several sides, or even a way of talking one's way toward resolution of that question. Certainly these lines of talk fashion a fine tool with which to etch out the tricky boundaries between fantasy and reality that absorb many 4- and 5-year-olds, as they do this child (Flavell, 1986; Flavell, Green, & Flavell, 1986).

Rendition Using Genres. Moreover, children begin to experiment with different **versions** or genres for portraying their experience. **Genres** are the distinctive envelopes a culture offers its speakers and writers for framing experience. Each suggests a particular kind of world, a different kind of narrator, and a particular relation between speaker and listener. Thus, when we give testimony ("It was a little after six on Tuesday, March 6. I was waiting for the M104 as I usually do . . . "), write a short story ("It was gray and early at the bus stop that evening. . . . ") or explain how to take the M104 bus to the terminal ("You wait at the corner of 40th and First. The buses come about every 15 minutes at that time of night . . . ") we create very particular kinds of worlds, perspectives, and relationships (Bakhtin, 1981; Dore, 1989; Fowler, 1982). Genres can be as formal and recognizable as a fairy tale or as informal and private as the pattern of talk a particular child and parent develop during a bedtime ritual (Dore, 1989). They are recognizable along any number of channels. Each version has its own distinctive content: Consider the princes and caskets of fairy tales or the talk about sleep, waking, and tomorrow characteristic of bedtime conversations. Versions can also be picked out based on formal linguistic markers: Think about the past tenses of a fairy tale as compared to the future-oriented chat of bedtime rituals (tomorrow, when you wake up, we'll . . .). We also cue listeners about which version of telling we are in through performance qualities: A tale is often given a dramatic rendition with different character voices and a lilting delivery for the voice-over narrative portions, whereas a bedtime sequence frequently is marked by hushed tones, which give way to whispering, singing, and cuddling.

By the age of 4, many children can render the "same" experience in a variety of formats. For instance, they can tell about going to bed in general, recall a particular and personal bedtime anecdote, or make up a story where the very specific emotional contours of their own nighttime rituals are projected onto someone else, in some other time and place. Often, in their spontaneous talk, these forms intermingle, conveying the fluctuating point of view of a self who lives in, knows about, or is concerned with what is customary, actual, or fictional at different moments.

Each of those channels is marked in quite elaborate ways. Take, for example, the case of linguistic marking. We signal that we are outlining the generalized script for an event, not giving a report or telling a tale, with at least three levels of features. At the level of the individual clause, we use the second person and the historical present (first you get in the car) to signal that this is a general, not a specific, past time narrative. At the level of rhetorical features (e.g., the texture of the telling), we tell a script very plainly. There is little detail or evaluative language. We use chiefly a narrative voice, omitting dialogue or many side comments. At the level of structure, a script moves steadily forward in time (there may be branches, but no forecasts or flashbacks) and lacks any kind of high point or resolution—quite unlike what we expect of a story.

As sophisticated as these abilities may seem, there is now considerable research in child language and discourse analysis showing that children as young as 3 and 4 make rather clear distinctions between genres, particularly narrative ones. Thus, when telling highly-scripted narratives, even 3-year-olds typically mark their accounts by use of the present tense, second-person pronouns, simple sequencing connectives in a matrix of rather spare language, and a steady, forward temporal organization (Mandler, 1984; Nelson & Hudson, 1986; Nelson, 1986). By

contrast, when engaged in storytelling, children typically mark their utterances with patterns of first- or third-person pronouns, predominance of the past tense, more specific sequential connectives, richer language, and more complex temporal organizations (Applebee, 1978; Eisenberg, 1985; Peterson & McCabe, 1983; Wolf, in press). When children provide running commentary on ongoing events they may also make use of first- or third-person pronouns and sequential connectives, but in those "on-line replays" they combine these features with distinctive patterns of temporal features, such as the predominant use of the English progressive form (Gee, 1986; Heath, 1983, 1985).

In order to illustrate these points about lines of talk and genres, here is a sample of script (generalized account) and then a much more evaluated narrative from a 5-year-old girl:

Experimenter: Tell me about what happens when you go out on the playground?
Child: About my school? Where I go? The Harrington?
Experimenter: Yeah, about your school.
Child: Okay . . . when you're all done with recess you go outside to the playground and you can play in the field or on the swings or the jungle gym.
Experimenter: What? The what?
Child: You know, the climbing thing, the jungle gym.
Experimenter: Oh, okay, the jungle gym.
Child: Yeah then you stay out there until B . . . your teacher . . . rings the bell and says, "Everyone to come in."
Child: But one time something happened there.
Experimenter: Yeah?
Child: My friend Alyssa was going out to recess and she said to meet her on the jungle gym so I did. I started climbing and doing this trick. See like this with my hands (*demonstrates hand-over-hand climbing*).
Experimenter: Yeah.
Child: So I was doing that trick only I missed with one hand and so then I fell and conked my head and it was bleeding and Alyssa went to get the nurse saying like "Hurry, hurry." There was blood all over the cement what a mess.

In response to the initial question, the speaker sketches the general, or characteristic, events that typify a visit to the playground. For this purpose, she uses the genre of a script, employing several devices that operate at different levels of discourse. Thus, she indicates the generality of her account with regular use of the historical present, the second person, and simple connectives like "and" and "and then." In this script, the speaker provides her listener with a chronological, evenly paced rendition of events, in which no particular incident stands out above others. Thus there is little use of either durative-descriptive information or evaluative comment to underscore any particular event as central or especially significant.

But once the discourse warms up, the child moves on to tell what happened to her once when she had a playground accident. Then she tells a sharply focused personal anecdote where the features of individual clauses, as well as the overarching structure of the whole, are starkly different. The units of this narrative (e.g., clauses) are marked with past tense and the first and third person. The whole has what is often referred to as a high-point structure, with the cardinal event standing out from the prologue and the conclusion. By contrast, the child uses these kinds of narrative constituents effectively in her story to underscore its surprise and upset ("conked," "all over the cement," "what a mess"), as well as added features of the performance (such as miming the actions of climbing). Thus, as was suggested above, narrative genres do not occur in talk as they do in literary anthology: as self-contained chapters, or unified texts. Rather, speakers move across and between genres in order to convey different aspects of or contrasts within their experience.

Moreover, in naturally occurring discourse, many **lines of talk** are under construction simultaneously. Both versions of the playground narratives are broken up by asides in which the speaker and listener clarify meaning, thus juggling moments of real-world conversation and moments of the narration of typical or past experiences. Within the story account of the playground accident, the teller juggles 2 different lines of talk: the main-line events in which she tells what happened next, and the comments in which she adds durative-descriptive information about those events (e.g., "What a mess.").

It is this mutual movement across the worlds and stances carried by genres and lines of talk that makes it possible for a speaker to evoke and a listener to understand what is meant by the narrative. It is in this kind of joint activity that participants achieve what might be called **narrative attunement**. This is the mutual ability to share not only "what happened" but "what sense" is to be made of it.

Making Texts

Children also work on a third process (of those taken up here) as young narrators. This third process involves *text making*. This is the work of making the separate elements of a narrative cohere into a larger whole. This work is carried out in many ways, from the microscopic work of word choice (e.g., in a jungle story, "giraffe," "palm," "lion," and "vine" would occur and make the narrative cohere) to the much broader understandings about the structure of different genres (e.g., the presence of an orientation, a climax, a resolution, and a coda help a given story to appear whole).

Text making thus refers, not to writing, but to all those forms of connected discourse where the teller refers not to the here-and-now world but to the world created by the spoken or written text itself, thereby producing running language that is coherent, cohesive, functional, and interesting without either the sustained intervention of another conversationalist or the support of the immediate pragmatic demands of a task.

In the period between 4 and 7, children have shown the ability to go from constructing their narratives in a highly local, bit-by-bit manner to treating their narratives as systems in which all, or at least many, of the parts are carefully connected. This is evidence in their ability to create both thematic and referential strategies that connect earlier and later portions of their narratives. So, for instance, in telling about a bad frog, a 5-year-old begins and sets off on her story laying the groundwork for how very bad that frog is:

One time there was a **very bad** big frog who **frowned and bit and did bad things**. One time when his boy, the boy who owned him, got a birthday present of another little frog, he **hated** the poor little frog and **wanted to lose** that little frog.

In this same example, it is possible to observe the child carefully establishing and maintaining a system for referring to the complex cast of characters. First she introduces the central figure of the bad frog. Thereafter, she uses pronominal forms to track that central character ("his boy," "owned him," "he hated"), and names other contrasting characters, like the little frog, using noun phrases ("the poor little frog," "that little frog"). This is a systematic strategy that she can pursue throughout a story in highly organized ways (Bamberg, 1986; Karmiloff-Smith, 1980). Also, children begin to create stories with highly integrated time lines in which there is a coherent anchor tense ("there was a very bad frog who frowned and bit and did bad things") and forecasts and flashbacks that contrast to it ("wanted to lose that little frog") (Hemphill, Wolf, & Camp, 1990; Wolf & Grollman, 1982). In this same period, young narrators cease telling loose collections of events and begin, instead, to include the expected parts of stories (orientations, climaxes, resolutions) in the expected order (Applebee, 1978; Botvin & Sutton-Smith, 1977; Peterson & McCabe, 1983; Stein & Glenn, 1979).

These changes in children's narratives signify much more than conventionality or good housekeeping. Once a child can treat a narrative as an integrated whole, it becomes possible to portray a dense network of motivations, results, implications, and long-term consequences for human actions, as this 5-year-old's narrative shows:

See, this was the day my brother, Mikey was born. I woke up in the morning, and I could tell something was different because my mother's bathrobe wasn't on the back of the door, the red one, like it usually is. So I went in to find my father and he wasn't there either. Right there in my parents' bed was 2 friends of theirs who they knew when they were growing up. So then I remembered what my mother said when it was the other week. That one day something like this might happen. So I went into the room for the baby and no one was there. And then I knew that they must still be waiting or maybe at the hospital. I went to school but all day when someone was at the door I was thinking it would be my father. So that's why my head was jumpy all day long and I couldn't write when Ms. B. told it was time for stories. But then later, after Mikey was home and my head wasn't jumping I wrote a very big story about the day he was born. Just like this one.

The story is effectively a closely woven text. The child uses the language of surprise and relief throughout to make her theme and the quality of her experience clear. It is a narrative in which the past, the moment of the telling, and what happened thereafter are systematically organized and ordered via a careful use of tenses. There are hints of events to come, and reflections of earlier events. The teller borrows from the canonical form of stories to structure her personal experience, building to the climax of discovering her parents gone, and then working out immediate and longer-term consequences. The effect is more than orderliness. With these kinds of tools in hand, she can, as a narrator, evoke in her listeners her own sense of surprise and anticipation, then relief.

This emerging system for stories clearly shows itself, and all its delicate workings, when children *repair* their tellings—revising and changing the original text of their narratives until they get something close to the effect they want. For instance, consider 5-year-old Lizzie, who tells the story of her brother being scolded at school. She tells the entire story three separate times and carefully reworks her choice of words and her patterns of evaluation in several places until she emerges with a telling in which, even though he is the culprit, her brother is, at the very least, honest and brave.

Version 1

Mom: Can you tell me the story of what happened when T drew on the um…book at school? Mrs. R and Mrs. N were telling me about that.

    L: Okay, well, well…but…first we saw some…some marker…some craypas on the table and then on the wall and then on the…and then on her library book and then on a stuffed animal and we didn't know who it was and at group time T…telled…V…um…said, "It was T." and then T said, "Well, yes it was me." And then the teacher was proud of him because he didn't lie.

Mom: Oh, so that's why Mrs. R wasn't very mad at T.

Version 2

    L: Well…I'll tell you…Can you erase um…um…a part of it because I made a mistake? (*L. knows that her mother is recording their bed-time conversations.*)

Mom: Sure. You tell it to me the right way now.

    L: Okay…well…T…well…we found some on the table and on the wall and on the stuffed animal…well…a couple times after on the stuffed animal…and um…then…um…when it was time for group time, T told it was him and then…Oops, I made a mistake again.

Version 3

Mom: Oh, try again.

    L: Okay…well…once when T was having a craypas in his hand, the teacher didn't notice and they found some on the wall and on the table and on the stuffed thing [?] and…and…and once at group…at group time V said T did it and because the craypas was in T's hand…blue craypas and then V said, "It was T did it." and then T stepped up and he said, "It was me." and then he said, "Mrs. R, it was me." and then she was very very proud of him because he told the truth.

(Wolf and Polanyi, 1991)

What such a telling also makes clear is that the very early processes of narrating, like those involved in becoming a member of a community of narrators, continue to develop. Lizzie is not a solo narrator, she is one half of an intensely mutual performance in which her mother's questions, patience, and listening provide an extensive scaffolding (Wolf & Polanyi, 1991).

CLASSROOMS AND NARRATIVE GROWTH FOR YOUNG CHILDREN

Suppose that we want for all children, not just a chosen and lucky few, the kinds of narrative control and expression that 5-year-old Lizzie has. What can we do?

Narratives as Sustained Investigation

Preschool children have much on their minds. Didi, Bart, and Linda, the children mentioned at the opening of this chapter, moved between a storybook and narrative-like conversation to approach the topic of death. At other times and places, 4-year-olds want to know about fairness, evil, babies, and dreams. Narratives, both literal and fanciful, are among their chief tools for entering and sustaining these kinds of investigations. Vivian Paley, a preschool teacher, has provided vivid records of this process (Paley, 1988). Thus, throughout nearly an entire year, her 4-year-olds explored the consequences of being bad. They wrote stories about bad guys, they played being Skeletor and He-Man; and around the edges of this growing narrative, they often paused to comment and discuss:

Fredrick: You don't see bad guys on your birthday.
    Paley: Hmmm. I wonder if bad guys see other bad guys on their birthdays.
Fredrick: Bad guys don't have birthdays.
    Paley: Aren't they born on a certain day?
Fredrick: Bad guys don't have names so they can't have birthdays.
(Paley, 1988, p. 5)

Because Paley understood the importance of the children's making an extended, many-legged inquiry through their play, stories and talk, she permits that play and often engages them in talking about its rules and their implications. She discusses what she notices—such as the conflict between the boys wanting to prolong and invent bad-guy play, and the girls wanting to do away with the shooting and chasing that is involved:

    Paley: Why did Mollie leave the ship, Barney?
Barney: You can't have a baby if there's bad guys.
    Paley: Then why have bad guys?
Barney: They already saw the cannon. We have to shoot at them. Then take them to jail. That's the whole real way. You can't say no bad guys if you already said bad guys.
(Paley, 1988, p. 20)

Likewise, Paley discusses with the children the rules for what makes a bad guy and when they can appear:

"How did you decide who could be a Boy Scout?" I ask as we walk upstairs to the music room.
"Someone that doesn't wear a cape," Fredrick says pointedly.
"I can take it off it I want," Christopher assures him.
"Do you want?" Mollie asks.
"No, in case of bad guys."
"Not in music, Christopher," I murmur hastily.
"He means he's thinking in his mind what if there's bad guys," Barney explains.
(Paley, 1988, p. 20)

This conversation has wide implications. If we care about young children being able to use their narrative abilities to model and explore what they imagine to be the patterns of life, the point may not be to teach the vocabulary of "because," "so," and "maybe." Nor is it to teach the manners of raising hands and taking turns. Rather, the point may be to make room for the kinds of fierce issues that children bring with them and to be willing to climb into, scaffold, and sustain *that* conversation through all its forms and across many speakers, for as long as it will last.

There is a second lesson also. Children's narrative competence is widespread. Only impaired, depressed, and frightened children cannot, with the support of an intimate adult, tell a narrative that exhibits the features described so far. That is not to say that all children tell the *same* kinds of narratives. Precisely as was indicated earlier, narration inevitably bears the imprint of gender, culture, and class—in content, in conduct, and in form. Compare the examples of 2 young girls each telling the "same" narrative based on a short silent film they have watched. In that film a young boy finds a yellow hat with silver wings on the grass of a neighborhood park—only to have it stolen away by other boys who gang up on him (Wolf, 1985).

Consider René, a 7-year-old African American from a working-class family, telling her version. For her it is a highly evaluated story, bordering on a dramatization. It is carried out, in large part, in the immediate present through the voices of different characters—voices that carry all the pauses and melodies of delight or frustration. In this sense, René, only in primary school, draws on the oral narrative traditions of her community (Gee, 1986, 1991; Heath, 1983; Michaels, 1981).

So those two guys in the bushes, I mean, the house, they are eating some pie, some grape pie. And the other…and there's a boy comes and throws a yellow hat and hides behind the bushes. And then the oth…the boy goes, saw it and picked it up and put it on and said, "Look what I found over there?" And his friend said, "That's a nice bright yellow hat." And then, "Are you gonna keep it?" And he said, "Yeah, but I'm gonna comb my hair a little." And so his friend put it right down. Then the other one started eating and the *other* one was combing his hair, then they—the boys—took the hat away. And the friend said, "Where's my hat? Where's my hat? It was right over there!" And then the other guy said, "Do you, Are you hiding it from me?" And the other guy said, "No, I'm not." And the guy said, "I believe you." And they started looking in the bushes….(Wolf & Hicks, 1989)

Now consider Malka, a 7-year-old white girl from a middle-class family, offering her version. Malka chooses to focus on the careful sequencing of events, rarely going beyond the clearly observable events in the film and taking the point of view of an outside narrator. In so doing, she is taking on the conventions her culture lends her for telling—conventions that require even spoken language to have the cadences and the markers typical of printed stories (e.g., "one day,"…"he said," use of the past tense, etc.).

One day two boys were hiding in the park with a hat. "Let's surprise the boy who always walks through," one whispered to the other. This boy walked into the park. He looked around and then one of the boys threw the hat in. He picked it up and put it on. Then he started twirling around. One of the boys ran out and grabbed the hat, pulling it back in. The boy dove into the bushes after his hat. He probably had a headache afterwards cause he dove in headfirst….(Wolf & Hicks, 1989, pp. 346–348)

Generous Literacy

Both René and Malka came to first grade as capable narrators. They, like virtually all children who have been narrating since their third year, have the raw materials for becoming readers and writers: They can take the reflective stance of narrators on their own experience; they can make the articulate choices of authors; and they can form carefully connected texts. Yet many studies underscore that, although there is little difference in children's expressive abilities at home, there is a strong correlation between class and race and how well or poorly children do in school at the tasks of early literacy (Feagans, 1982; Heath, 1983; Wells, 1982). If early schooling is to break down, rather than replicate and amplify inequalities, early childhood educators must ask how such a change might be effected. How might early literacy training honor both René's dramatization and Malka's near-text?

Health (1983) and Wells (1981) argue that school literacy depends from the very outset, not on children's considerable narrative abilities, but rather on their fluency in particular types of interactions. Wells argues that early literacy lessons focus largely on moments of **display**, rather than on instances of meaning making. Displays are those occasions when teachers know something and want to get children to offer that particular answer displayed in a particular way. In classrooms, teachers often teach from a framework that demands the naming of objects, actions, and attributes in isolation from the particular experience in which they are rooted in the children's lives. Information is elicited for its own sake rather than for its relevance to some immediate practical activity. (The teacher holds up an illustration of a camel and asks, "What's this?" It's considered poor to answer, "I have a picture of one of them camels at my house.", but better to answer, "That is a camel.") Further, being able to recognize and participate in these forms of display is often the prerequisite to learning to read and write. Failure to engage, or failure to engage smoothly and quickly, results in miscommunication and misevaluation (Heath, 1983). The result can be unequal access to the more demanding forms of literacy: Those without control of the display mode are tracked into work sheets and drills rather than reading and writing.

A second issue occurs when teachers focus—or are told to focus—on the mechanics of reading and writing, the recognition and naming of letters, the decoding of words, and the motor skills of handwriting as gates to literacy, rather than as embedded components in early reading and writing.

One way of reworking the preface to literacy in early childhood education is to determine how classroom experiences and instances of teaching might help *all* young children to translate their very considerable narrative skills into oral forms that communicate widely and textual forms rich enough to hold onto substantial personal meaning. In this context there is every reason to help children bring together their own spontaneous forms of narrative into conversation with those expected by or useful in school (Wolf & Pusch, 1985). Consider the following example of a child being offered a fundamental example of the differences between conversation and reading, at only 15 months:

Maja: (*Turns to a rabbit picture in a book and sniffs.*)
Adult: That's right, who sniffs like that?
Maja: (*Points to her own nose.*)
Adult: Right, Maja sniffs. Who sniffs in the picture? (*She points at the book illustration.*)
Maja: (*Points to the rabbit as she sniffs again.*)
Adult: Yes, the bunny is sniffing his nose.
(Wolf & Pusch, 1985)

The adult reader certainly recognizes the connection between Maja's nose and the rabbit's, but she also encourages Maja to relate her comments to the world **within the text**. This kind of teaching implicitly teaches children to understand the complex ways in which books refer to the world.

In the following example, even though the reader is only three, the adult models the important skills of thinking about and reflecting on what is being read:

J: (*Points to a figure in a complicated illustration, full of little pigs.*) Dat's the baby sister pig.
Adult: No, I don't think so. (*He pages through the book and finds an illustration of the pig family all in a line.*) See the baby sister pig has a blue dress. (*He turns back to the original illustration and points to the pig J. had shown him.*) See this one has a pink dress. I think she is the **big** sister pig. See, look here. (*He shows J. the pig in the pink dress in the family picture.*)

This is in many ways a very elementary literacy interaction. It is about little more than picture identification or labeling, yet the adult makes the effort to ruminate about it, to solve the problem aloud, and in implicit ways to model the kind of gradual text building and remembering that any sophisticated reader working on a novel or a science article has to engage in.

Finally, consider an example from a primary school classroom. A group of children were writing stories based on the same silent film that Malka and René narrated out loud. Left on her own, Lisa Marie simply drew the figures of a boy and a hat. When asked what she wanted the book to say, she interpreted the question as "What does the boy say?" With that she simply inscribed "O boy" under her figures. If her paper had been collected at that moment, Lisa Marie would have looked at least disinterested, if not unaware of how to write a narrative. However, when she was asked to "tell the story of the movie" out loud, she could narrate the adventures from the film quite fully. When she was asked how to make that into a book, she replied, "I don't know how to make big books, just some words." However, when she was reminded about the "chapter books" that had been read aloud in class, she asked, "You mean do it like they do?" She went to work, borrowing like any author, and produced a text with the following title, prologue, and narration:

THE BOY

THIS IS THE BOY WHO HIS A YELLO HAT HERE GOES THE STOY

THE BOY HAS A HAT HE WAS PLAYING WITH IT

Having forged that much connection between her own memory of the film, her own writing, and what she knew about the workings of books, she reframed her original label "O boy": "Now, that's for what he said" (meaning that the label had become character dialogue) (Wolf, Davidson, Davis, Walters, Hodges, & Scripp, 1988).

Simple as these examples are, they are suggestive. They indicate how children's own narrative abilities offer bridges to the conventional forms of text. But they can only do so if they become moments in a sustained series of interactions in which the relationships between memory, narrative, print, and the acceptable forms of literacy are examined. This must include talk about language per se, the linking of one book to other books, rumination on the way books work, and opportunities to produce, not just to listen to, the language of literacy. For instance, there is every reason to ask René: "You know how you make the boys sound surprised or happy to find the hat—how could you make the words in your book do what you do with your voice? That way, when people read, they could really tell what is happening to those boys."

Encouraging Wide Autobiographies

Many children live at distances from grandparents, experience the divorce and separation of their parents, and move numerous times before they reach school age. They lead lives in which the formation of an organized and certain autobiography is unlikely—no matter how sustaining it is. In such a world, the role of supplementary care givers and institutions that care for young children becomes crucial. These people and places, though never so intended, can become the holders of autobiographies, if they so choose. Examples from a set of remarkable preschools illustrate this fact (Rinaldi, 1991).

Reggio Emilia is a small city in Italy. It is remarkable not only for its art and architecture, but also for the traditions it has built up around children as the single most important resource of the community—a resource deserving long and deep investment. It is also remarkable because of its long history of women working and so needing to share the responsibility for children with wise and nurturant others. Today in Reggio, 75% of women work outside of the home—20% more than in the rest of Italy. The teachers insist that they work in a community, more than a school. Consequently, they explain that the schools are not "for children" but "of children." Learning cannot be for the self alone, it must be shared in order to be full. In this context, teachers believe that one of the most substantial projects is to help children to build life stories—as individuals who are members of a community. They want these stories to integrate current events and memory, the life of home and school. Toward this end, they have developed a network of practices that engage adults and children jointly in telling life stories. For example, each child, on the first day of school, receives a bag that is his or her very own. The child learns that the purpose of the bag is to carry messages and memories between the two contexts in which he or she now lives: the familiar world of home and the new world of school. Each child also has an album. In that album, the child, his or her parents, and teachers keep the documents that tell that child's story: photographs, notes, and souvenirs from memorable events. The album stays at school so that, at any time, on any day, a child can find an image for a drawing he or she wants to make, the name of the beach visited over the summer, or some other footprint of the past that matters suddenly. In addition, each child has a box, labeled with a photograph, to keep the bulkier forms of memory and current life: a favorite rock, a big drawing to keep working on, or a tree ornament from Christmas.

Life in these schools is not purely individual, and so history cannot be solitary. The children also create documents that record their joint past. Throughout the school there are exhibitions of past projects and outings. Children can revisit their writing and drawings about a trip to see the lion in the town square months, or even years, after it first took place. They are able to revisit, not just their own records, but the insights and recollections of the entire group of children who went. The older children often make books for children new to the school. In these books they explain what is important about the life of the school, what the different areas are, and what projects can be like. They also pass on the "lore" of the school—how to play tricks, how to fool teachers, and funny events that are a part of the school's recent history.

Children also prepare a yearly event in which *they* present their work of the year for their parents. First, they discuss which work belongs in this public history. Their teachers join in and make suggestions. Then children collaborate on who will say what and how they will arrange the room so that all present can hear and see. Parents are invited with a note announcing that it will be "Children, not teachers, who speak." At the meeting, children take turns presenting and parents interview them about, "What and how and why it matters." In this context everyone contributes to a rich, coherent, and well-documented autobiography—a substantial foundation for recollection and discussion, a reason to be pleased with having grown older, and an equal reason to consider planning a future.

CONCLUSION

Our conceptions of young children's language development have often revolved around their ability to capture the "here and now." But that kind of immediate commentary is, at best, only half of what they learn to do with words. In addition, they pick up the reasons and the rules that inform recollection, literacy, modeling the possible, and planning the future. If these narrative skills are recognized, they contain the resources for beginning to master some of the most basic challenges of later schooling. Moreover, incipient in these skills are the resources for being able to discuss and probe the events life deals out and to stay in touch with the lives of others. Because these skills matter throughout life, not just for children, they deserve our fierce and constant notice.

References

Amsterdam, B. K. (1972). Mirror self-image reactions before age two. *Developmental Psychology, 5,* 297–305.

Applebee, A. (1978). *The child's concept of story.* Chicago: University of Chicago Press.

Bakhtin, M. (1981). *The dialogic imagination: Four essays.* Austin, TX: University of Texas Press.

Bamberg, M. (1986). A functional relationship to the acquisition of anaphoric relationships. *Linguistics, 24,* 227–284.

Bates, E. (1990). Language about you and me: Pronominal reference and the emerging concept of self. In D. Cicchetti & M. Beeghly (Eds.), *The self in transition: Infancy to childhood* (pp. 165–182). Chicago: University of Chicago Press.

Botvin, G., & Sutton-Smith, B. (1977). The development of complexity in children's fantasy narratives. *Developmental Psychology, 13,* 377–388.

Bretherton, I., & Beeghly, M. (1982). Talking about internal states. The acquisition of an explicit theory of mind. *Developmental Psychology, 18,* 906–921.

Brown, R. (1973). *A first language.* Cambridge, MA: Harvard University Press.

Dore, J. (1989). How monologue re-envoices dialogue. In K. Nelson (Ed.), *Narratives from the crib* (pp. 42–57). Cambridge, MA: Harvard University Press.

Dunn, J. (1988). *The beginnings of social understanding.* Cambridge, MA: Harvard University Press.

Eisenberg, N. (1983). *Early descriptions of past experiences: Scripts as structure.* Princeton, NJ: E.T.S.

Eisenberg, N. (1985). Learning to describe past experiences in conversation. *Discourse Processes, 8,* 177–204.

Emde, R. N., & Sorce, J. E. (1983). The rewards of infancy: Emotional availability and social referencing. In J. D. Call, E. Galenson, & R. Tyson (Eds.), *Frontiers of infant psychiatry, Vol. 2.* New York: Basic Books.

Feagans, L. (1982). The development and importance of narratives for school adaptation. *The language of children reared in poverty: Implications for evaluation and intervention* (pp. 95–116). New York: Academic Press.

Fivush, R. (1984). Learning about school: The development of kindergarten school scripts. *Child Development, 55,* 1697–1709.

Flavell, J. H. (1986). The development of children's knowledge about the appearance-reality distinction. *American Psychologist, 41,* 418–425.

Flavell, J. H., Green, F. L., & Flavell, E. R. (1986). The development of knowledge about the reality-appearance distinction. *Monographs of the Society for Research in Child Development, 51*(1, Serial No. 1).

Fowler, A. (1982). *Kinds of literature: An introduction to the theory of genres and modes.* Cambridge, MA: Harvard University Press.

Gee, J. (1986). *Beyond semantics: A discourse analysis of the verb inflectional system in distinct narrative-like and communicative formats in the speech of a two-year-old.* Paper presented at the Symposium on the Acquisition of Temporal Structures in Discourse, Chicago Linguistics Society Meetings, Chicago.

Gee, J. (in press). Memory and myth: A perspective on narrative. In A. McCabe & C. Peterson (Eds.), *Developing narrative structure*. Hillsdale, NJ: Erlbaum.

Genishi, C., & Dyson, A. H. (1984). *Language assessment in the early years*. Norwood, NJ: Ablex.

Goffman, E. (1986). *Frame analysis*. Boston: Northeastern Universities Press.

Heath, S. B. (1983). *Ways with words: Language, life and work in communities and classrooms*. Cambridge, MA: Cambridge University Press.

Heath, S. B. (1985). *The cross-cultural study of language acquisition*. Keynote address, Stanford Child Language Research Forum, Stanford, CA.

Hemphill, L., Wolf, D., & Camp, L. (1991). *Narrative abilities of children with normal and mildly retarded developmental patterns*. Paper presented at the Gatlinburg Conference on Mental Retardation, Coral Gables, FL.

Hood, L., & Bloom, L. (1979). What, when, and how about why: A longitudinal study of early expressions of causality. *Monographs of the Society for Research in Child Development, 44* (6, Serial No. 181).

Hudson, J. A. (1990). The emergence of autobiographic memory in mother-child conversation. In R. Fivush & J. A. Hudson (Eds.), *Knowing and remembering in young children* (pp. 166–196). New York: Cambridge University Press.

Johnson, C. N., & Maratsos, M. (1977). Early comprehension of mental verbs: Think and know. *Child Development, 48,* 1743–1747.

Johnson, C. N., & Wellman, H. M. (1980). Children's developing understanding of mental verbs: Remember, know, and guess. *Child Development, 51,* 1095–1102.

Kagan, J. (1981). *The second year: The emergence of self-awareness*. Cambridge, MA: Harvard University Press.

Karmiloff-Smith, A. (1980). Psychological processes underlying the pronominalisation and non-pronominalisation in children's connected discourse. In J. Kreiman & A. E. Ojeda (Eds.), *Papers from the parasession on pronouns and anaphora*. Chicago: Chicago Linguistics Society.

Kaye, K. (1982). *The mental and social life of babies*. Chicago: University of Chicago Press.

Kihlstrom, J. (1981). On personality and memory. In N. Cantor & J. Kihlstrom (Eds.), *Personality, cognition, and social interaction*. Hillsdale, NJ: Erlbaum.

Leopold, W. F. (1939). *Speech development of a bilingual child, Vol. 1.* Evanston: Northwestern University Press.

Lewis, M., & Brooks-Gunn, J. (1979). *Social cognition and the acquisition of self*. New York: Plenum Press.

Mandler, J. (1984). *Stories, scripts, and scenes*. Hillsdale, NJ: Erlbaum.

McAdams, D. P., & Ochberg, R.L. (Eds.). (1986). Psychobiography and life narratives. *Journal of Personality, 56,* 1.

McCabe, A., & Peterson, C. (1991). Linking children's connective use and narrative macrostructure. In A. McCabe & C. Peterson (Eds.), *Developing narrative structure* (pp. 29–54). Hillsdale, NJ: Erlbaum.

Mead, G. H. (1934). *Mind, self, and society*. Chicago: University of Chicago Press.

Michaels, S. (1981). Sharing time: Children's narrative styles and differential access to literacy. *Language and Society, 10,* 423–442.

Middleton, D. (1987). Collective memory and remembering: Some issues and approaches. *The Quarterly Newsletter of the Laboratory of Comparative Human Cognition, 9,* 1.

Miller, P. J. (1982). *Wendy, Amy, and Beth: Learning language in South Baltimore*. Austin, TX: University of Texas Press.

Miller, P. J. (1988a). Early talk about the past: The origins of conversational stories of personal experience. *Journal of Child Language,* 293–315.

Miller, P. J. (1988b). The socialization and acquisition of emotional meanings with special reference to language: A reply to Saarni. *Merrill-Palmer Quarterly, 34,* 217–222.

Miller, P. J., & Moore, B. B. (1991). Narrative conjunction of caregiver and child: A comparative perspective on socialization through stories. *Ethos,* 293–315.

Miller, P. J., & Sperry, L. L. (1987). The socialization of anger and aggression. *Merrill-Palmer Quarterly, 33,* 1–31.

Nelson, K. (1986). *Event knowledge: Structure and function in development*. Hillsdale, NJ: Erlbaum.

Nelson, K. (Ed.). (1988). *Narratives from the crib*. Cambridge, MA: Harvard University Press.

Nelson, K., & Gruendel, J. M. (1986). Children's scripts. In K. Nelson (Ed.), *Event knowledge: Structure and function in development* (pp. 21–46). Hillsdale, NJ: Erlbaum.

Nelson, K., & Hudson, J. (1986). Repeated encounters of a similar kind: Effects of familiarity on children's autobiographic memory. *Cognitive Development, 1,* 253–271.

Nicolich, L. M. (1978). Beyond sensorimotor intelligence: Assessment of symbolic maturity through analysis of pretend play. *Merrill-Palmer Quarterly, 23,* 89–101.

Paley, V. (1988). *Bad guys don't have birthdays: Fantasy play at four*. Chicago: University of Chicago Press.

Peterson, C., & McCabe, A. (1983). *Developmental psycholinguistics: Three ways of looking at a child's narrative*. New York: Plenum Press.

Piaget, J. (1962). *Play, dreams, and imitation*. London: Kegan-Paul.

Polanyi, L. (1985). *Telling the American story: A cultural and structural analysis*. Norwood, NJ: Ablex.

Rinaldi, C. (1991). *The schools of Reggio Emilia*. Address Paper given at Skidmore College, Summer Institute on Assessment in the Arts, Saratoga Springs, NY.

Sachs, J. (1983). Talking about there and then: The emergence of displaced reference in parent-child discourse. In K. E. Nelson (Ed.), *Children's language, Vol. 4* (pp. 1–28). Hillsdale, NJ: Erlbaum.

Scarlett, W. G., & Wolf, D. (1979). When it's only make-believe: The construction of a boundary between fantasy and reality. *Early Symbolization, New Directions for Child Development, 3,* 29–40.

Schegloff, E. A. (1971). Notes on conversational practice formulating place. In P. P. Giglioli (Ed.), *Language and social context*. Hammondsworth: Penguin Books.

Schriffrin, D. (1982). *Discourse markers: Semantic resource for the construction of conversation*. Unpublished doctoral thesis, University of Pennsylvania, Philadelphia.

Scollon, R., & Scollon, S. B. K. (1981). *Narrative, literacy, and face in interethnic communication*. Norwood, NJ: Ablex.

Slackman, E. A., & Hudson, J. A. (1984, October). *Filling in the gaps: Inferential processes in children's comprehension of oral discourse*. Paper presented at the Boston University Conference on Language Development.

Snow, C. (1990). Building memories: The ontogeny of autobiography. In D. Cicchetti & M. Beeghly (Eds.), *The self in transition: Infancy to childhood* (pp. 213–242). Chicago: University of Chicago Press.

Stein, N., & Glenn, C. (1979). Analysis of story comprehension in elementary school children. In R. Freedle (Ed.), *Advances in discourse processes: New directions in discourse processing (Vol. 2)* (pp. 53–120). Norwood, NJ: Ablex.

Stern, D. (1985). *The psychological world of the human infant*. New York: Basic Books.

Sully, J. (1986). *Studies in childhood.* New York: D. Appleton.

Sulzby, E., & Otto, B. (1982). Text as an object of metalinguistic awareness: A study in literacy development. *First Language, 3,* 181–199.

Teale, W. (1982). Reading to young children: Its significance for literacy development. In H. Goelman, A. Oberg, & F. Smith (Eds.), *Awakening to literacy* (pp. 110–122). Exeter, NH: Heinemann Educational Books.

Vygofsky, L. (1962). *Thought and language.* Cambridge, MA: MIT Press.

Wellman, H., & Estes, D. (1986). Early understanding of mental entities: A reexamination of childhood realism. *Child Development, 57,* 910–923.

Wells, G. (Ed.). (1981). *Learning through interaction: The study of language development.* Cambridge, England: Cambridge University Press.

Wells, G., & Raban, B. (1978). *Children learning to read.* Final report to the Social Science Research Council, University of Bristol.

White, H. (1980). The value of narrativity in the representation of reality. In W. J. T. Mitchell (Ed.), *On narrative* (pp. 1–49). Chicago: University of Chicago Press.

Winner, E. (1988). *The point of words.* Cambridge, MA: Harvard University Press.

Wolf, D. (1982). Understanding others: The origins of an independent agent concept. In G. Forman (Ed.), *Action and thought: From sensorimotor schemes to symbol use* (pp. 297–328). New York: Academic Press.

Wolf, D. (1985). Ways of telling: Text repertoires in elementary school children. *Journal of Education, 167*(1), 71–87.

Wolf, D. (in press). Narrative attunement: The process of sharing experience. In A. Slade & D. Wolf (Eds.), *Modes of meaning: Clinical and developmental approaches to symbolic play.* New York: Oxford University Press.

Wolf, D., Davidson, L., Davis, M., Walters, J., Hodges, M., & Scripp, L. (1988). Beyond A, B, C: A broader and deeper literacy. In A. Pellegrini (Ed.), *The psychological bases for early education* (pp. 123–152). Cichester, UK: Wiley.

Wolf, D., Goldfield, B., & Beeghly, M. (1984, October). *"There's not enough room," the baby said.* Paper presented at the Boston University Language Conference, Boston.

Wolf, D., & Grollman, S. (1982). Ways of playing: Individual differences in imaginative play. In K. Rubin and D. Pepler (Eds.), *The play of children: Current theory and research* (pp. 46–63). New York: Karger.

Wolf, D., & Hicks, D. (1989). Voices within narratives: The development of intertextuality in young children's stories. *Discourse Processes, 12*(3), 329–351.

Wolf, D., Moreton, J., & Camp, L. (in press). Early discourse development: The case of narrative. In J. Sokoloff & C. Snow (Eds.), *CHILDES and children's language development.* Hillsdale, NJ: Erlbaum.

Wolf, D., & Polanyi, L. (1991). *Repair and recontextualization in children's narratives.* A paper presented at the Boston University Child Language Conference, Boston.

Wolf, D., & Pusch, J. (1985). The origins of autonomous texts in play boundaries. In L. Galda & A. Pellegrini (Eds.), *Play, language, and stories: The development of children's literate behavior* (pp. 63–78). Norwood, NJ: Ablex.

Wolf, D., Rygh, J., & Altshuler, J. (1984). Agency and experience: Actions and states in play narratives. In I. Bretherton (Ed.), *Symbolic play: The development of social understanding* (pp. 195–218). Orlando, FL: Academic Press.

· 5 ·

YOUNG CHILDREN'S PEER RELATIONSHIPS:
FORMS, FEATURES, AND FUNCTIONS

Gary W. Ladd and Cynthia C. Coleman
UNIVERSITY OF ILLINOIS AT URBANA-CHAMPAIGN

Early experiences in a child's development have taken on a special significance in our culture. As Kessen (1979) has observed, our cultural roots, philosophical perspectives, history, and scientific theories have encouraged us to become believers in the critical role of early experience. Within the social sciences, this view of the child has fostered an enduring interest in early relationships and their potential contributions to growth and development. Much of this interest has been translated into investigations of early caretaking, attachment, and stimulation, and the consequences of these experiences for the child. Within this tradition, scientific scrutiny has been focused primarily on mothers and mothering, although fathers and siblings have received more attention in recent years.

However, recent changes in our society have begun to raise questions about the influence of other forms of early rearing environments and agents. It is not uncommon today for children to enter day care or preschool environments at an early age and spend large amounts of time in the company of peers. Anecdotal evidence suggests that in contemporary society peer contact is beginning at earlier ages than ever before. According to Vandell and Mueller (1980), about 60% of American infants under 1 year of age come into contact with other infants at least once a week, and 40% are exposed to other babies 3 or 4 times a week.

A major reason for the shift toward earlier exposure to peers is the rising tendency for women, in particular mothers of young children, to be employed outside the home. In the United States, the rate of mothers' participation in the work force tripled between 1950 and 1981. While the most dramatic increase in the 1940s and 1950s occurred among mothers with school-age children, since the early 1960s the pattern has reversed, with the largest increase in the labor force being among mothers of children under 6 years of age (U.S. Department of Labor, 1983). In fact, U.S. Department of Labor statistics (1986,

1991) show that the percentage of children under 6 with employed mothers increased from 30.3% in 1970 to 53.7% in 1985. From 1985 to 1990, labor force participation rates for women with children under 6 years of age stabilized, remaining between 53 and 54%. As this trend suggests, the number of preschool children with employed mothers has nearly doubled since 1970, and remains at its highest point in recent history.

With more mothers and fathers involved in the labor force, the demand for child care services has been rising steadily. According to the U.S. Department of Labor (1983), in 1980 there were 2.0 million children enrolled in day care centers or preschools, compared to 1.1 million enrolled in 1970. These figures demonstrate an increase of over 80%, which occurred despite a 15% drop in the overall number of 3- and 4-year-olds. Moreover, the percentage of children 4 years old and under enrolled in child care or preschool programs has been increasing steadily. Whereas only 21% of all prekindergarten choldren were enrolled in child care programs in 1970, 39% of this population attended some form of center care by 1986 (Bureau of the Census, 1989).

As Edwards (1992) has observed, "The increasing use of preschools, organized playgroups, and child care arrangements has bought the age of access to peer relations down near the beginning of life." Edwards also notes that this trend is widespread among the industrialized nations of the world. For example, among the middle-class populations of North America, Europe and Asia, families are becoming increasingly isolated within the community and separated from their larger kin networks. Furthermore, parents who value achievement and economic success enroll their children in preschool and day care programs at early ages so they can be exposed to agemates and develop the skills needed for success in grade school (Edwards, 1992).

Given this trend, it has become increasingly important for parents and child-oriented professionals to understand the nature and value of children's early experience with peers. Toward this end, researchers have begun to explore children's early social capacities and the types of peer relationships children form throughout the early childhood period. The purpose of this chapter is to survey the accumulating evidence in these domains and explore the role that early peer relationships play in children's social and emotional development.

NATURE OF CHILDREN'S EARLY PEER EXPERIENCE AND RELATIONSHIPS

Rudimentary forms of peer sociability emerge during infancy. Infants as young as 2 months of age orient toward peers (Vincze, 1971), and by 3 or 4 months, early social gestures emerge (Hartup, 1970). By 6 months of age, peer-directed smiles and vocalizations emerge (Vincze, 1971). During the first year, infants perform a variety of social behaviors and engage in sequential actions with peers. Throughout the second and third years, toddlers become capable of coordinating social actions with their partners (e.g., imitating a peer's nonverbal actions), which, in turn, allow them to engage in more sophisticated forms of "games" and reciprocal play (see Eckerman, Davis, & Didow, 1989; Vandell & Mueller, 1980).

There is also evidence to suggest that young children are capable of forming relationships with peers. Vandell and Mueller (1980) have shown that, as early as age 2, children begin to develop preferences for particular peers and seek them out as play partners. Over time, early playmate interactions and preferences may lead to other, more complex forms of relationships. In fact, research suggests that at least 2 types of peer relationships emerge during the preschool years: *friendship* and *peer acceptance*. Whereas friendship refers to a *dyadic* relationship, peer acceptance is defined as the degree to which an individual child is liked and/or disliked by all the members of his or her social *group* (Ladd, 1988).

Thus, it is important to recognize that friendship and peer acceptance refer to different forms of relationship. This is illustrated by the fact that many researchers have found that measures of friendship and peer acceptance are only moderately related (Masters & Furman, 1981; Howes, 1988). For example, it is possible for a child to have low peer acceptance in the classroom, and still be nominated by one or more classmates as a best friend (Masters & Furman, 1981; Parker & Asher, 1989).

It is also important to recognize that friendship and peer acceptance are theoretical constructs and that researchers have differing views about how each of these forms of relationships are best defined and measured. Moreover, the meaning of these relationships and their defining features or referents may change as children grow older. For these reasons, it is essential to consider how researchers have defined and measured friendship and peer status at different age levels.

Infants' and Toddlers' Friendships

Some investigators have argued that young children do not form friendships because "true" friendships do not emerge until children reach middle childhood and early adolescence (see Price & Ladd, 1986). However, recent research on the nature of young children's peer relationships contradicts this premise.

"Friendship" among infants and toddlers has often been operationalized in terms of peer familiarity, consistency of social interaction between the partners, and/or the presence of particular behaviors within the dyad, such as mutual display of positive affect, sharing, and play (Howes, 1988; Ladd, 1988; Price & Ladd, 1986; Vandell & Mueller, 1980). Moreover, it has increasingly become clear that early friendships may have a strong emotional component, making them similar to the attachment relationship young children form with parents (Howes, 1983, 1988).

The most common means of identifying early friendships include reports from parents and child care professionals, and/or direct observations of social interaction between pairs of children (see Ladd, 1988; Price & Ladd, 1986). For example, Howes (1983) defined friendship as an "affective tie" between 2 children with 3 key features: "mutual preference, mutual enjoyment, and the ability to engage in skillful interaction" (p. 1042). Dyads were classified as friends if they achieved all of the following criteria: (a) at least 50% of their social initiations resulted in social interaction (mutual preference); (b) at least one exchange of positive affect occurred between the partners (mutual enjoyment); and (c) at least one episode of reciprocal and complementary play occurred between the partners (skillful interaction).

More recently, Ross and Lollis (1989) have shown that toddlers' peer relationships are unique, in the sense that both partners tend to adjust the interactions they conduct with each other, and interact in ways that are different from the ways they treat other children. Moreover, there is evidence that some toddler friendship choices and relationships are stable over time (Vandell & Mueller, 1980; Howes, 1983). Howes (1983) classified dyads as "maintained friends" if they had met the criteria for friendship in one of 3 observation periods and continued to achieve the criteria in subsequent time periods. Two other categories were created in Howes' (1983) study: "sporadic friends," or pairs that had inconsistently met the friendship criteria, and "nonfriends," that is, dyads that had never been classified as friends. Of the friendship dyads formed by infants, 100% were classified as maintained (i.e., were maintained for the duration of the study). Furthermore, 60% of the toddler pairs were classified as maintained friends, indicating that early friendships are relatively stable over time (Howes, 1983).

Preschoolers' Friendships

Many of the assessment methods that have been utilized to identify friendships among infants and toddlers are also used with preschoolers. However, developmental gains in children's social and symbolic abilities pave the way for new ways of interacting and, thus, new bases for friendships. These emergent characteristics not only transform the meaning of friendship, but also have important implications for methods used to identify preschoolers' friendships.

Identifying Preschoolers' Friendships: Mapping Forms and Features. Preschoolers are better able to conceptualize, reflect on, and describe their friendships because of advances in their cognitive and language abilities. As a result, researchers have been able to obtain information about peer relationships directly from the child (Price & Ladd, 1986). For example, Hayes (1978) found that preschool children are able to name their best friends and also articulate their reasons for liking them (e.g., common activities, general play).

Mutual friendships among preschool-age children are often defined on the basis of reciprocal nominations given in the context of a sociometric interview (Howes, 1988). Investigators typically ask children to nominate 3 or more classmates whom they like, 3 or more whom they dislike, and/or 3 or more classmates with whom they are best friends. Pairs of friends are identified as children who mutually nominate each other as a liked peer or a best friend (Masters & Furman, 1981; Howes, 1988). Although the nomination criteria "liking" and "best friend" appear to be based upon the same definition of friendship (i.e., mutual liking), they may not assess the same relationship dimension (Price & Ladd, 1986).

The task of nominating "liked" peers requires that children differentiate between classmates on the basis of liking or interpersonal attraction. Conversely, the nomination of "best friends" requires that children identify peers with whom they have a particular form of relationship. Presumably, it is possible for children to like each other without being friends. Moreover, the rationales children articulate as the basis for friendship change with age (Bigelow, 1977; Bigelow & La-Gaipa, 1975; Furman & Bierman, 1983). Thus, although liking or interpersonal attraction may be a necessary element of friendship, this single attribute may not be sufficient to define friendship.

Affective factors are also emphasized as a defining feature of friendship during the preschool period and are often utilized in addition to mutual liking as a means of defining friendship. Howes (1983), for example, argues that a defining feature of preschoolers' friendships is the mutual exchange of positive affect. In fact, some investigators argue that preschoolers achieve a level of emotional maturity that enables them to form close, affective relationships with peers (Howes, 1983, 1988).

Other characteristics have been used to define and identify friendship in the preschool years. For example, Hayes, Gershman, and Bolin (1980) developed a definition of preschoolers' friendships based on the *amount* of available time children spent in interaction. According to Hayes et al. (1980), play partners could not be considered "friends" unless they spent at least 50% of their available time interacting with each other in either parallel or cooperative play. Similarly, Hinde, Titmus, Easton, and Tamplin (1985) suggested that "strong associates" could be identified when preschoolers were observed to be in each other's company at least 30% of the time sampled.

The *quality* of the interaction between a pair of preschoolers is another dimension along which many researchers differentiate friends from nonfriends. One component of Howes' (1983) definition of friendship is the partners' ability to participate in skillful interaction. In research by Howes (1983), dyads were classified as friends only if they were able to interact in a skillful manner (i.e., if at least 50% of the initiations of either

partner resulted in social interaction between the pair). Alternatively, Masters and Furman (1981) describe preschool friends as children who display more positive than negative behavior toward each other.

Friendships among preschoolers may also be identified and characterized on the basis of the level, or *complexity* of interaction that occurs between members of the dyad. Howes (1983, 1988) includes the occurrence of at least one instance of complementary and reciprocal play (levels 4 and 5 on her scale of complexity) as a criterion for friendship. Complementary and reciprocal play are defined as activities in which "each child's action reverses the other's, demonstrating awareness of the role of the other" (Howes, 1983, p. 1043). Furthermore, Parker and Gottman (1989) describe preschoolers' play with friends as differing from both acquaintances and strangers in terms of the level of coordination or interdependence achieved by the partners.

According to Parker and Gottman (1989), the putative goal of preschool children's play is to maximize enjoyment, entertainment and satisfaction within the ongoing play activity. Achievement of this goal depends upon the partners' coordination of play. At the lowest level of coordination, children play in parallel—performing the same activity, perhaps side by side—but with little or no social interaction (i.e., "peaceful companionship," Parker & Gottman, 1989, p. 105). At a higher level of coordination between peers is joint activity, which offers greater potential for conflict as well as for solidarity and amusement. Fantasy play is the most complex form of joint activity, and it typically occurs between friends. In this type of play, the partners immerse themselves in mutually defined symbolic and make-believe activities, and thus reach the highest level of coordination and presumably the highest level of enjoyment (Parker & Gottman, 1989).

As with toddlers, another defining feature of friendship in the preschool years is *stability*. Evidence from several studies suggests that preschoolers' friendships are stable over relatively long periods of time. Using parents' reports, Park and Waters (1989) identified a number of preschool-age dyads who had been best friends for over 7 months, and about half of these had been best friends for as long as 18 months. Gershman and Hayes (1983) found that of the reciprocal friendship dyads in their sample, two-thirds maintained a stable relationship across an academic year. More recently, Ladd (1990) found that many of the friendships formed in preschool were maintained not only across the transition into kindergarten but also throughout the kindergarten year.

Further evidence for the stability of preschool friendships can be found in a longitudinal study conducted by Howes (1988). Howes found that preschoolers tended to maintain their mutual friendships when both dyad members remained in the same day care program for an extended period of time. Specifically, 50 to 70% of the reciprocal friendships in the sample were maintained from year to year, while approximately 10% were maintained for as long as 2 years (Howes, 1988). These findings were especially impressive because the stability estimates reported by Howes (1988) were much longer than might have been predicted from previous literature.

Preschoolers' Peer Acceptance

Many researchers define the concept of peer acceptance or status as the degree to which individuals are liked or disliked by members of their peer group (Hymel, 1983; Ladd, 1988). Children's peer acceptance is typically assessed by asking all group members (e.g., preschool classmates) to rate and/or nominate individuals with whom they most or least like to associate (Ladd, 1988).

Identifying Children Who Differ in Peer Status. Although most researchers who employ sociometric techniques with preschoolers utilize a combination of both rating and nomination methods, some investigators rely on only one form of assessment. The most commonly used sociometric *rating* method is a technique developed by Asher, Singleton, Tinsley, and Hymel (1979) in which children are asked to rate classmates in terms of how much they like to play with them. Children rate each peer on a scale from 1 to 3 by placing a photograph of the classmate into one of 3 boxes, each of which is marked so as to signify differing levels of liking. An acceptance score is calculated for each child by averaging and standardizing the rating he/she receives from each group member. Children who have high standardized rating scores are generally considered to be more liked or accepted, while those with low standardized rating scores are referred to as disliked or less accepted.

The peer *nomination* method is also used to identify children who differ in peer status, and is most useful when investigators wish to classify children into sociometric groups or "status" categories. When this procedure is employed, children are asked to nominate a specific number of classmates (typically up to 3 or 4) according to given sociometric criteria (e.g., best friend, liked playmate, disliked playmate; Asher & Hymel, 1981). In most cases, researchers employ both positive and negative nomination criteria when assessing peer status (Asher et al., 1979). Negative sociometric criteria (e.g., asking children to nominate peers with whom they do not like to play) are needed in order to· determine a child's level of rejection as well as acceptance by peers (Asher & Hymel, 1981).

Over the past decade or so, several investigators have developed schemes for classifying children into distinct sociometric groups based on nomination data. Peery (1979) suggested that positive and negative nomination scores could be combined to create 2 additional peer status dimensions: "social impact" (i.e., the sum of a child's positive nominations plus his/her negative nominations) and "social preference" (i.e., the number of positive nominations minus the number of negative nominations). A modified version of this scheme was developed by Coie, Dodge, and Coppotelli (1982) and is now used by most researchers.

In the Coie et al. classification scheme (Coie et al., 1982; Cole & Dodge, 1983), the absolute numbers of nominations a child receives for the "liked most" and "liked least" categories are summed, standardized, and converted into social impact and social preference scores. These preference and impact scores are then standardized within age- or grade-level and used to classify children into one of 5 peer status categories. "Popular" children are those who receive a social preference score greater

than 1 standard deviation above the mean, a "like most" score (total number of positive nominations) greater than the mean, and a "like least" score (total number of negative nominations) below the mean. In other words, these children tend to receive a large number of positive nominations and few negative nominations. Children classified as "rejected" receive a social preference score more than 1 standard deviation unit below the mean, a "like least" score above the mean, and a "like most" score below the mean (Coie et al., 1982). These children tend to receive few positive nominations and many negative nominations from peers.

Children who have a social impact score more than 1 standard deviation below the mean, and "like most" and "like least" standardized scores less than zero are defined as the "neglected" status group. Neglected status, therefore, is assigned to children who receive few positive or negative nominations from peers and implies that these children are overlooked by peers. Children classified as "controversial" in peer status are above the mean for positive and negative nominations, and have a social impact score greater than 1 standard deviation above the mean. Thus, these children are considered controversial because they receive many positive and many negative nominations from peers, or are well liked by some and very disliked by others. Finally, the members of the "average" peer status group are those who receive a social preference score that is less than one-half of a standard deviation unit above or below the class mean (Coie et al., 1982).

Although the Coie et al. (1982) classification scheme was originally developed for use with school-age children, it is commonly utilized in research with younger children (e.g., see Hazen & Black, 1989; Mize & Ladd, 1990). As an illustration, Mize and Ladd (1990) modified this classification method in order to identity 4- and 5-year-old children who were either average, liked, mildly rejected, or mildly neglected by peers. Less stringent criteria were used as a means of identifying children who were at risk for more extreme forms of status-related difficulties (e.g., rejection) in later school years.

Although the use of sociometrics to assess preschool children's social status is widespread, researchers are not agreed on the utility, value, or appropriateness of differing sociometric measures with young children. Many researchers report superior test-retest reliability of peer-ratings over nominations (see Asher & Hymel, 1981; Hymel, 1983). For example, Asher et al. (1979) compared the 4-week stability of positive nominations, negative nominations, and ratings for children with an average age of 4 years, 4 months. Only moderate reliability was found for the positive and negative nomination measures, with correlation coefficients of .56 and .42, respectively. However, the test-retest correlation obtained for the rating scale measure ($r = .81$) was impressive.

It has been suggested that the stability of nomination scores, especially for young children, may be underestimated when investigators obtain small numbers of nominations (typically 3) from each nominator. Data obtained in this manner may be biased by short-term fluctuations in preschool children's friendship choices (Hymel, 1983). In an attempt to improve the reliability of preschoolers' peer-nominations, Alain and Begin (1987) devised a procedure that allowed for more than the usual 3 peer choices. They found that a 4-choice format produced the highest level of reliability for kindergarten-age children. Specifically, the social preference scores derived from this method were found to be relatively reliable over a 2-month interval ($r = .70$) with kindergarten-age children. However, the social impact measures created from differing numbers of nominations were not found to be reliable with kindergarten- or younger preschool-age children.

Conversely, results of a study by Poteat, Ironsmith, and Bullock (1986) indicated that peer-nomination and rating scale measures of peer status were equally reliable over an interval of approximately seven weeks (r's ranging from .64 to .68 for peer nominations, and from .55 to .66 for ratings). Thus, in contrast to conclusions drawn by Hymel (1983), Poteat et al. (1986) argue that nomination techniques can be used reliably to assess the peer status of preschool-age children.

The choice between nominations and rating scale sociometric measures for preschool children is often dictated by the investigator's particular research interest or goal (see Asher & Hymel, 1981). For example, positive nomination measures may be useful for determining the number of peers who consider an individual child as a best friend or a preferred playmate (depending on the nomination criterion employed), while rating scales can provide an index of a child's overall level of acceptance by peers. Moreover, the use of negative sociometric nominations along with positive nominations allows researchers to distinguish children who are *neglected* from those who are *rejected* by their peers.

Children's Peer Status and Their Peer Group Relations. When used with children, sociometry is intended to index the structure and organization of the peer group. The term group may be defined as a collection of interacting individuals who possess common goals and/or shared interests (Hartup, 1970). According to Gronlund (1959), the pattern of sociometric choices given and received by each individual in the group reveals the network of interpersonal relations among group members (i.e., the group structure).

Researchers who study preschoolers have identified various forms of social organization, including "dominance hierarchies", "attention structures" (Strayer, 1980; Vaughn & Waters, 1981), and "networks" (Ladd, Price, & Hart, 1990). For the purposes of play and social interaction, young children's peer groups are often organized into multiple subgroups (e.g., cliques), containing individuals who prefer each other's company (see Ladd, 1983, 1988). Moreover, children's peer contact patterns often change during the course of a school year. Typically, children become more selective and interact with fewer playmates as the school year progresses (Ladd et al., 1990).

Research on peer group dynamics also indicates that children's experience in the peer group varies as a function of their peer status (Ladd, 1983). Masters and Furman (1981) found that young children interacted in a nonpunitive manner more frequently with liked peers than with other classmates. In addition, Ladd et al. (1990) found that, as the school year progressed, preschoolers at all levels of social status interacted with popular classmates most often; thus, the popular children appeared to become the focus of the entire peer group's interactions (Ladd et al., 1990). Similarly, the "high status" children in the

Mize and Ladd (1990) study interacted with peers significantly more often than did "low-status" children.

There is also evidence to suggest that once children are rejected by the peer group, they change the nature of their play and contact patterns with peers. Ladd et al. (1990) found that, whereas popular children appeared to become more selective over time and focused their interactions upon a relatively small number of consistent play partners, rejected children appeared to maintain an extensive pattern of play contacts, and often "bounced" from one playmate to another. Thus, the patterns of peer contact that emerge after children become rejected may be a consequence of their prior, negative reputations among peers. Once children become disliked, they may be increasingly avoided by peers, and thus, forced to search out playmates among a broad range of peers (Ladd et al., 1990).

The plight of peer-rejected children is especially problematic in light of the relative stability of peer status classifications over time and across peer groups (Ladd & Price, 1987). In Howes' (1988) study, 60% of the popular-, 60% of the rejected-, 65% of the average-, 33% of the neglected-, and 80% of the controversial-status preschoolers were assigned to the same status classifications one year later. Furthermore, Ladd et al. (1987) found that group acceptance scores (i.e., mean sociometric ratings received from all peer group members) were relatively stable from preschool to the beginning of kindergarten ($r = .48$), and from preschool to the end of kindergarten ($r = .47$). Moreover, peer rejection appears to become increasingly stable and difficult to change as children get older (Coie & Dodge, 1983; Poteat et al., 1986). For example, Coie and Dodge (1983) found that nearly one-third of the children identified as rejected by peers in third grade had the same status classification in early junior high school.

In the next section, evidence pertaining to the formation of young children's peer relationships, particularly their friendships and peer acceptance, will be considered. Of particular interest are studies that shed light on the processes by which young children form peer relationships, and the potential contributions of caretakers (e.g., parents) and child care settings.

ANTECEDENTS OF RELATIONSHIP FORMATION

We will begin our discussion of the formation of young children's peer relationships by exploring the means through which children gain *access* to peers. There are many different social contexts and agents that foster preschool children's contact with peers. Parents and child care settings are among the most important of these resources, and both will be examined in detail in the following sections.

Early Parental Involvement and Management of Children's Peer Relations

Many researchers agree that the parent-child and the child-peer social systems are closely related. Moreover, some have proposed theories concerning possible linkages between parent-child and child-child relations (Hartup, 1979, in press; Parke & Ladd, 1992). These theories may be divided into two groups: "stage setting" and "intervention" theories which propose "indirect" and "direct" pathways of family influence, respectively (Hartup, in press; Parke, MacDonald, Beitel, & Bhavnagri, 1988).

In the case of *indirect* influences, parents do not have the explicit goal of modifying their children's relationships with peers. Instead, much of the parent's behavior is directed at the goal of maintaining a harmonious relationship with their child (Ladd, Profilet, & Hart, 1992). Any changes that occur in a child's peer relations may be regarded as unintended effects of indirect parental influence. "Stage setting" theories refer to this type of parental activity as "setting the stage" for the development of their child's social relationships (Hartup, in press). Parents may "set the stage" or indirectly influence their children's peer relationships by (a) providing "working models" of relationships which may be transferred to encounters with peers (Sroufe & Fleeson, 1986); (b) providing their children with an emotionally secure base from which to explore the social environment, thereby increasing the likelihood of contact with peers (Hartup, 1979); or (c) interacting with them in ways that establish cognitive and behavioral skills that transfer to encounters with peers (Parke, MacDonald, Beitel, & Bhavnagri, 1988).

Direct pathways, on the other hand, are those through which parents purposely seek to influence or "manage" their children's peer relations or social competence (Ladd et al., 1992; Parke & Bhavnagri, 1988). Examples of direct influences include parents' attempts to design or control features of children's social environment, mediate or regulate children's access to particular playmates, and supervise children's interactions with peers (Ladd et al., 1992).

Parents can be viewed as "designers" when they select environments for children that provide opportunities for interaction with peers. They may, for example, choose safe neighborhoods with large populations of children, or enroll their children in child care settings or other organized activities involving peers (Rubin & Sloman, 1984). Parents can be viewed as "mediators" when they initiate or arrange peer contacts for their child, choose or regulate play partners, and so on. As "supervisors" parents may directly monitor and supervise their children's peer interactions with the goal of promoting or modifying the development of their children's social skills (see Ladd et al., 1992; Lollis et al., 1992). For example, parents may oversee children's peer interactions in the home and intervene from time to time to offer instructions or guidance (e.g., suggesting ways to resolve conflicts; see Lollis et al., 1992). In the following sections further consideration will be devoted to the role parents play as "designers" and "mediators"—that is, persons who create opportunities for children to meet and form relationships with peers.

Informal Contexts: Parents' Enhancement of Children's Peer Relations in the Home and Neighborhood

A large proportion of parents' efforts to manage children's peer relations occur within the home and neighborhood (Ladd et al., 1992). In these informal settings, parents may utilize a variety of techniques to create opportunities for their children to meet and interact with peers.

Choice of Neighborhood. As "designers" of the interpersonal environment, parents may exert substantial impact upon children's opportunities for peer interaction through their choice of neighborhoods (Parke & Bhavnagri, 1988). From the perspective of a child, the neighborhood is something more than a geographical location; it is a "social universe" (Medrich, Roizen, Rubin, & Buckley, 1982). Since young children have minimal freedom and capacity for mobility, their daily activities and social encounters are, in part, dictated by physical characteristics of the neighborhood environment (Medrich et al., 1982).

The location of the family's home may influence children's patterns of social interaction in a number of ways. The neighborhood makes a substantial impact for example, on children's access to peers. Children's exposure to peers may be greatly restricted by a neighborhood that is remote, dangerous, or difficult to access (Ladd et al., 1992). Research by Medrich et al. (1982), conducted with a sample of sixth-graders, indicates that children who grow up in residential neighborhoods with dense child populations, relatively flat landscapes, and public amenities, such as sidewalks, parks, and school playgrounds have greater opportunities to meet peers. In contrast, children are less likely to be exposed to peers and potential playmates when they reside in "hilly" areas, locations with fewer agemates, or communities where safety considerations limit the distances children can travel from home.

Medrich et al. (1982) also discovered that, in neighborhoods where houses are closely-spaced and have few barriers between them, children tend to have greater numbers of friends and more spontaneous and informal patterns of play contacts. In contrast, children living in neighborhoods with widely-separated houses and few sidewalks tended to have fewer friends due, in part, to transportation problems (Medrich, et al., 1982).

Arrangement of Peer Contacts. One way in which parents may "mediate" the development of their children's relationships with peers is by initiating and arranging peer contacts for their children. Some parents may encourage or initiate informal contacts with peers as a means of helping their young children build a transition from the family to the peer social system (Ladd et al., 1992). The extent to which parents engage in this form of peer management may vary depending on their perceptions of the child or the peer group. For example, whereas parents of shy or withdrawn children may be more likely to initiate peer contacts in order to compensate for their children's potential rejection by peers, parents whose children are very sociable may be less likely to do so (Ladd et al., 1992). Parents may also employ this type of management as a means of controlling the types of playmates their children meet or to encourage friendships with specific peers (e.g., neighborhood children, future classmates).

Researchers have found that many, but not all, parents attempt to manage their preschool children's peer contacts. Ladd and Golter (1988) utilized a series of telephone interviews to assess parents' efforts to organize play contacts for their preschool children, and found that slightly more than half of the parents interviewed (51%) had not initiated any of their children's informal peer contacts during a 2-month period.

Although the remaining 49% of parents in the sample did initiate some of their preschool children's peer contacts, there was considerable variation in this activity, with some parents arranging only 6% and others initiating all (100%) of their children's recorded contacts with peers.

There is also evidence to indicate that parents' attempts to arrange play opportunities and peer contacts tend to vary as a function of the child's age. Research by Bhavnagri (1987) has shown that parents are more likely to plan and initiate play contacts for younger (as opposed to older) children. Bhavnagri interviewed mothers of children age 2 through 6, and found that parent-initiated peer contacts were more common among toddlers than among $3\frac{1}{2}$- to 6-year-olds. The older children in the sample tended to initiate many of their own contacts with peers.

Current evidence also points to a relationship between parental initiation of young children's peer contacts and their children's social competence. Ladd and Golter (1988), for example, found that parental initiation was positively related to the quality of children's peer relationships. Specifically, children whose parents initiated and arranged peer contacts were likely to have a larger network of playmates and more consistent play partners than the other children in the sample. Moreover, boys with parents who initiated peer contacts in preschool tended to become better accepted by classmates in kindergarten.

Playgroups. Another way that parents may mediate children's early peer relationships is by arranging larger, more consistent peer activities, such as playgroups. Within the group context, children may acquire the communicative and other social skills that are needed for success in school and other "group-oriented" environments (Ladd et al., 1992).

In a study conducted by Lieberman (1977), children with prior experience with peers, both in dyadic play and in playgroups, were found to be more responsive to playmates and to engage in more verbal exchanges with peers. Evidence of a link between children's experience in playgroups and their social adjustment and competence was also reported in a recent study conducted by Ladd, Hart, Wadsworth, and Golter (1988). In this study, the number of playgroups (groups of 3 or more children) children participated in on a regular basis was used to predict subsequent adjustment in preschool. Results indicated that the number of playgroups was positively correlated with classroom adjustment for older preschoolers (ages 41 to 55 months), but negatively correlated for younger preschoolers (ages 23 to 40 months). It would appear that the experiences children have in peer playgroups, which may closely parallel those that occur in child care settings, may be more adaptive or beneficial for older as opposed to younger preschoolers.

Formal Contexts: Parents' Influence on Children's Peer Relations in the Community and School

Many of the formal social systems that exist outside the immediate family and neighborhood can also serve as settings for children to meet, interact, and form relationships with peers (Ladd et al., 1992). In this section, we will explore 2 such contexts—the community and the school (e.g., preschool or child care)—and highlight some of the ways in which parents may affect their children's participation in these contexts.

Community Settings. Researchers have found that participation in adult-sponsored, community-based activities varies as a function of a child's age and family's social class. For example, older children appear to have greater levels of participation in these activities than do younger children. In a recent study, Bryant (1985) found that 10-year-olds were involved in organized community settings to a greater extent than were 7-year-olds. Moreover, after analyzing data obtained from interviews of 59 families with children 5 to 14 years of age, O'Donnell and Stueve (1983) concluded that middle-class children were the primary consumers of organized community activities. Specifically, they found that middle-class parents are more likely than working-class parents to enroll their children in relatively costly programs, such as private music lessons, as well as publicly sponsored and low-cost services, such as after-school programs and scouting. Working-class children were less likely than their middle-class counterparts to participate in formal, community-based programs and activities, regardless of the monetary investment required.

Although we know something about the type of children who participate in formal community social settings, little information has been gathered on the impact of these programs. However, data gathered by Bryant (1985) begin to shed some light on this question. Bryant distinguishes between community settings in terms of the types of activities that occur within them (i.e., structured versus unstructured).

One type of community setting offers *structured* activities for children, often requiring direct interaction with peers. Examples of this type of community setting include formal organizations, such as the Brownies, Cub Scouts, and Little League (Bryant, 1985). However, Byrant's research reveals little evidence to indicate that children's participation in these settings contributes significantly to their ties with peers or to their social and emotional development.

Community settings may also be *unstructured* (Bryant, 1985). These settings, which include parks, public libraries, and neighborhood pools, offer children primarily unstructured opportunities to meet and interact with peers. For example, children may accompany their parents on visits to the local library or community recreational area and be allowed to interact freely with nearby peers.

Although there is little direct evidence to indicate that these settings foster children's friendships or peer competence, Bryant's (1985) research indicates that participation in unstructured community social activities is associated with some aspects of children's social-emotional development. For example, among the older children (10- versus 7-year olds) in her sample, involvement in unstructured community settings was associated with more advanced forms of perspective taking. Similarly, Ladd and Price (1987) discovered that preschool children's experience in unstructured community settings predicted lower levels of school avoidance during both the beginning and end of kindergarten. It would appear that regular exposure to peers in unstructured community contexts fosters adaptation to novel situations, such as those encountered during school entrance.

The Early School Setting. Another important way in which parents may influence children's early exposure to peers is by placing them in child care or preschool programs. Although many parents choose to enroll their children in some form of early child care or schooling, the motivations behind these decisions often vary and thus, reflect differing "management" or socialization objectives (Ladd et al., 1992). For many parents, economic and employment considerations may determine whether young children are placed in child care or preschool programs. For example, parents who work long hours may view these programs as sources of custodial care and may be more likely to utilize full-day child care arrangements. Other parents may perceive full- or half-day preschool programs as contexts in which their children may enhance their cognitive skills and prepare for the academic tasks of kindergarten and grade school. Still other parents may send their children to preschool or child care settings with the goal of exposing them to a variety of peers and fostering early social development. Parents with this type of objective may see preschool as a setting in which children can meet peers and learn to interact in contexts (e.g., group-based activities) where they are not the "center of attention" (Rubin & Sloman, 1984). Moreover, these parents may select specific preschool programs because they are designed to teach children how to get along and form relationships with peers and, thus promote independence from the family (Belsky, 1984; Rubin & Sloman, 1984).

In fact, recent research suggests that many parents send their children to preschool for the latter reason. Research conducted by Bhavnagri (1987) reveals that most parents view social development as a "top priority" when selecting a preschool. Although the fathers interviewed in this study rated the social benefits of preschool significantly lower than did mothers, they still rated peer interaction and social skills more highly than other possible objectives.

Parents also control, to some degree, the timing of children's preschool experience. Parents determine not only the age at which their child enters preschool or child care, but also the length of time he or she will remain in a particular program. Decisions concerning time of entry and program duration may affect children's social experience within the child care setting. For example, parents who maintain their child's child care arrangements, rather than changing them frequently, help to preserve the stability of the child's peer group. Moreover, as will be discussed in subsequent sections, stable peer groups affect the quality of children's relationships with peers.

Role of Early Schooling and Child Care Programs

Although parents may utilize child care or preschool programs for many different reasons, a general result is that children are given the opportunity to interact with agemates at an early age. Ladd et al. (1992) have argued that, regardless of parents' motives, early child care or schooling is beneficial for most young children, because it fosters early friendships and social skills. It is also likely that children who are enrolled in larger preschool programs, as compared to those who attend family child care or are reared at home, are exposed to a greater number of unfamiliar peers. Results from several studies comparing children reared in child care centers to children raised at home tend to support this claim. Research has shown, for example, that children who attend child care centers have earlier and increased opportunities for peer interaction (see Belsky, 1984; Rubenstein & Howes, 1983).

Research also shows that children in child care settings form relationships with peers. Howes (1983) found that "friendships" were common within infant, toddler, and preschool-age child care groups. Using behavioral and affective criteria, Howes (1983) identified one or more friendships for the majority of children in the sample. More recently, Howes (1988) found that although 30% of her sample of 3- to $4\frac{1}{2}$-year-olds were classified as having no friends in their preschool classrooms, 42% had one friend, and 28% had many friends. Moreover, children not only form peer relationships in early child care settings, but they also maintain these relationships over substantial periods of time. In fact, Howes (1988) found that between 50% and 70% of the friendships identified among children enrolled in full-time child care remained stable over a 1-year period, and 10% of the friendships were maintained as long as 2 years.

BEYOND ACCESS: HOW CHILDREN MAKE FRIENDS AND BECOME ACCEPTED BY PEERS

Investigators have also begun to explore the *origins* of young children's peer relationships and, in particular, factors that may be responsible for the development of early friendships and peer status. Most of this research has been focused on characteristics associated with the child (e.g., personal characteristics, such as behavior or physical appearance), the child's play partners and peer group, and the social environment (i.e., the preschool or child care setting). Unfortunately, past efforts to investigate the bases of early peer relationships have produced many correlational studies and a focus on the concomitants rather than the causes of early friendship and peer status. Recently, however, investigators have begun to employ longitudinal designs and to explore the antecedents or processes that foreshadow relationship formation and maintenance. In the sections that follow, the contribution of recent longitudinal investigations will be emphasized.

Personal and Interpersonal Factors that Affect Relationship Formation

Children's personal characteristics and behavior occupy a position of central importance in research on the development of early friendships and peer group status. Because friendship and peer status constitute different forms of relationship, they are reviewed separately.

Friendship. In order for young children to form friendships, they must first have the opportunity to meet and interact with peers. In fact, as we have discussed in previous sections, both the availability and accessibility of peers may affect the size of a child's friendship network (see also Lewis & Feiring, 1989). When children do have the opportunity to interact with a variety of peers, they are selective about the persons they choose as friends. Typically, they prefer children who are similar to themselves in age (Hartup, 1970), gender (Masters & Furman, 1981; see Gottman, 1986), and race (Asher, Oden, & Gottman, 1977). Less observable characteristics may also affect children's friendship choices, but research findings on these factors are mixed. For example, some researchers have found that childhood friends are similar in intellectual ability, whereas others have not, and conclude that implicit personality traits, such as intelligence, "carry less weight" in children's attraction to particular peers (Parker, 1986).

Moreover, some aspects of similarity may vary with children's developmental stage or may be "created" out of children's interests and interactions. Also, children may not need to be similar in all ways to become friends. Rather only those characteristics or interests that are salient or important to the two partners may matter (Furman, 1982). For example, among toddlers, shared interest in a particular toy could provide the foundation for sustained interaction and, eventually, "friendship."

While research on similarity speaks to the question of how children are attracted to specific peers, it has little to say about the friendship formation process (Parker, 1986). Although there is evidence indicating that children are attracted to peers with whom they share essential similarities, it is also clear that children do not develop friendships with all of the children to whom they are attracted (Parker, 1986). In fact, the friendship formation process entails much more than the initial screening of potential play partners. As the two children interact and become acquainted, they become aware of each other's social behaviors, skills, and other personality characteristics. A child's interest in another may wax or wane as they become better acquainted and consistent interaction patterns begin to emerge (Furman, 1982).

Some researchers have studied the acquaintanceship process by documenting changes in the patterns of interaction among unacquainted children over time. Gottman and Parkhurst (1980), for example, observed preschool children's interactions with an unfamiliar peer and proposed an 8-level hierarchy of interactional events and processes. According to this view, dyads must successfully progress through the lower levels of interaction (e.g., arousing the partner's interest in an object or activity; participating in social comparison activities) to higher-level events (e.g., complex, extended fantasy play), in order to achieve higher levels of acquaintanceship and, ultimately, closeness or intimacy.

More recently, Furman (1982) proposed that findings from several studies, including those conducted by Gottman and Parkhurst (1980) and Furman and Childs (1981), could be integrated into a theory of acquaintanceship which emphasizes 4 central processes: (a) disclosure of personal information and discovery of similarities; (b) establishment of a common activity based on similarities; (c) "individualization" of the relationship into a form that is desirable to both children; and (d) development of an affective bond. The first 3 processes are thought to emerge in hierarchical order with (a) preceding (b) and (c). The affective bond may develop through the formation of a relationship, but its strongest form is thought to emerge as the relationship becomes "individuated" (Furman, 1982).

Like attraction, however, research on the acquaintanceship process may not fully explain how children become friends. Parker (1986) has argued that, even with repeated contact

and interaction, children may not become friends with every child with whom they are acquainted. Because of this, Gottman (1983) has urged investigators to study processes that may account for differences in children's success at making friends. Toward this end, Gottman (1983) conducted 2 studies on the role of conversational processes in the formation of preschoolers' friendships. A primary aim of these studies was to determine whether variations in specific conversational processes predicted the extent to which pairs of unacquainted children "hit it off" and progressed toward friendship.

In the first, cross-sectional study, 26 pairs of preschool-aged children were audiotaped while playing in their homes for 1 session, with either a stranger or a best friend. In a second, longitudinal study, 18 pairs of unacquainted children were audiotaped while playing in 1 child's home for 3 consecutive sessions. Two months after the third play session, mothers in the longitudinal sample completed a questionnaire intended to measure the extent to which the pairs of children had progressed toward friendship (e.g., whether the 2 children had made positive remarks about one another, asked to see each other again, telephoned, visited, etc.).

Gottman's first aim was to develop, from recorded transcripts of the interaction obtained in the cross-sectional data, a coding scheme that could reveal how pairs of friends differed in their interactions from pairs of strangers (Study 1). Once developed, these codes were applied to the longitudinal data to determine how pairs of unacquainted children hit it off and advanced toward friendship (Study 2). In the longitudinal study, the factor which proved to be the most reliable and valid indicator of potential friendship was the proportion of agreements expressed by the "guest" child in interactions with the "host" (i.e., the child who was playing in his or her own home). The proportion of guest agreement was significantly correlated with mothers' estimates of "hitting it off."

A second objective, addressed with the longitudinal data, was to select, operationalize, and validate a small number of salient conversational processes and evaluate their ability to predict friendship formation. Results indicated that 6 conversational processes could account for 80% of the variance in the dyads' progress toward friendship: (1) connectedness and clarity of communication, (2) information exchange, (3) establishment of common ground, (4) conflict resolution, (5) positive reciprocity, and (6) self-disclosure.

Gottman's (1983) study also revealed that children who were successful at making friends were likely to use information exchange as a "home base," or safe interaction strategy when conversation went astray, and were able to adeptly escalate and de-escalate levels of play as necessary. Moreover, there is evidence to suggest that children differ in their ability to successfully execute many of these conversational processes. Taken together, these findings suggest that some or all of these 6 conversational processes are instrumental in the development of children's friendships.

Building upon this work, Parker (1986) designed a novel study in which the same 6 conversational processes identified by Gottman (1983) were manipulated in order to determine whether they were causally related to friendship formation. Parker's objective was to control the important conversational processes while preserving as much of the spontaneity of children's naturally occurring interactions as possible. To accomplish this task, he constructed a "surrogate" preschool child called "Panduit" to act as an experimental confederate. Panduit, a 2-foot-tall green doll, was dressed in silver clothing and contained a hidden electronic receiver/speaker that enabled it to carry on age-appropriate conversations with the preschool subjects.

To manipulate systematically the nature of the conversation between the child and Panduit, examples of skilled and unskilled behavior were identified for each of the conversational processes. A female and a male assistant were trained to speak as Panduit in a child-like voice while systematically varying the skillfulness of their conversation. Thus, 2 experimental conditions were created, 1 in which Panduit was skilled and 1 in which Panduit was unskilled. It was expected that children who interacted with Panduit in the skilled condition would be more likely than those in the unskilled condition to "hit it off" and progress toward friendship. Results from this study indicated that children who interacted with the skilled Panduit were many times more likely to hit it off than children who were paired with the unskilled Panduit.

The findings from this study, and from Gottman's (1983) longitudinal investigation, also illustrate the relative importance of particular conversational processes at different points during the development of friendship. Specifically, as children become acquainted, the clarity and connectedness of communication, information exchange, establishment of common-ground activities, and conflict resolution became increasingly important as determinants of friendship or "hitting it off." Similarly, although self-disclosure processes were of little predictive value during initial encounters, they did forecast progress toward friendship by the second and third sessions. On the other hand, the predictive power of reciprocity decreased across play sessions.

The significance of these findings is further illustrated by the fact that Gottman (1983) found that these processes could account for more than 80% of the variance in children's progress toward friendship. Thus, these investigators have constructed studies that yield considerable insight into the means by which young children form friendships.

Peer Status. Research suggests that the origins of young children's reputations among peers, particularly their popularity or status in peer groups (e.g., classrooms), are diverse. Although some researchers view peer status as a condition imposed upon children by others (Hymel, Wagner, & Butler, 1990; Moreno, 1934), others think that children's characteristics and behavior play an important role in the development of their peer reputations (see Coie, Dodge, & Kupersmidt, 1990). Most of the research conducted to date has been based on the latter perspective.

Consistent with this view, there is evidence to suggest that children's personal characteristics are related to their level of acceptance or rejection by the peer group. For example, several investigators have found that the attractiveness of children's facial appearance is correlated with their peer status (e.g., Vaughn & Langlois, 1983; Young & Cooper, 1944). Other investigators (e.g., McDavid & Harari, 1966) have shown that popularity in the peer group is positively related to the desirability of children's first names (see Asher et al., 1977, for a review).

Researchers have also studied the relation between children's social cognitions (i.e., how they think about and interpret interactions with peers) and their status among peers. Recent studies suggest that several social-cognitive variables are related to children's peer status, including the types of goals that children devise for peer interactions (Renshaw & Asher, 1983), the content or quality of the strategies they construct (Asher & Renshaw, 1981; Ladd & Oden, 1979; Mize & Ladd, 1988), and the outcomes they expect for these strategies (Crick & Ladd, 1990; Perry, Perry, & Rasmussen, 1986). These cognitive processes are thought to be the means by which children understand, interpret, and construct responses to their social environment, thereby influencing their social adjustment and behavior with peers (see Ladd & Crick, 1989).

Most of the research on the origins of peer status has been designed to illuminate the role that children's behavior plays in the formation of peer reputations (see Coie et al., 1990). For more than two decades, researchers have known that positive social behaviors are related to peer acceptance, and negative, antisocial behaviors are related to peer rejection. For example, Hartup, Glazer, and Charlesworth (1967) found that giving positive reinforcement (e.g., attention, approval, or affection) to peers was related to social acceptance, and giving negative reinforcement (e.g., noncompliance, interference, or attack) was associated with social rejection. Similarly, Moore (1967) discovered that social preference (i.e., positive nomination score minus negative nomination score) was positively correlated with friendly approach behavior and negatively related to aggressive and rule-violating behavior.

However, as Moore (1967) first recognized, studies of the correlates of peer status are of limited value because they do not permit strong inferences about the direction of effect. In recent years, researchers have begun to design studies that shed greater light on linkages between children's social behavior and their peer status. Exemplary studies include those conducted with gradeschoolers by Coie and Kupersmidt (1983) and Dodge (1983), both of which utilized short-term longitudinal designs to investigate the emergence of social status in newly formed peer groups. Dodge (1983) created small playgroups of unacquainted boys and observed their interactions during 8 play sessions conducted over a 2-week period. Following the final play session, children completed sociometric interviews, and those who had become popular, average, rejected, or controversial with their play partners were identified. Analyses were then conducted to determine how children behaved before they developed their status or reputations with play partners.

Dodge found that different patterns of behavior emerged over time for children in each status group. For example, boys who became well-accepted by playgroup companions had engaged in high rates of social conversation and cooperative play, and seldom acted aggressively. Rejected boys, on the other hand, were prone to display more inappropriate, disruptive play behaviors and made more hostile verbalizations than the boys who were later identified as average in status. Compared to children in the other status groups, rejected boys also hit peers more often.

Using a similar methodology, Coie and Kupersmidt (1983) identified boys who were classified as popular, average, rejected, or neglected by their peer groups at school, and then observed them in either unfamiliar or familiar playgroups over a 6-week period. Four boys, 1 from each of the 4 sociometric categories, were assigned to each group. Videotaped observations and sociometric interviews were used to chart the boys' behavior and their evolving peer status in each type of playgroup.

These data yielded findings that were similar to those published by Dodge (1983). In both types of playgroups (i.e., familiar and unfamiliar partners), popular boys rarely engaged in aggressive behavior, often reminded others of the rules, and established group norms. Rejected boys, in contrast, were viewed by playmates as troublemakers (e.g., as persons who start fights) and tended to be more hostile and aggressive in their interactions with peers.

The results of the Coie and Kupersmidt (1983) study extend the work by Dodge (1983) and are important because they illustrate the stability of children's peer status and help to illuminate its potential causes. These investigators found that boys who were rejected by their classmates in school quickly formed the same reputations in unfamiliar playgroups. In fact, after only 3 play sessions the correlation between children's classroom peer status and the reputations they acquired in their playgroups was as high in the unfamiliar condition as it was in groups of familiar peers. Based on these findings, Coie and Kupersmidt concluded that rejected peer status can be quite stable across peer groups, because boys who are rejected by peers tend to bring aversive behavior patterns with them into new situations.

Similar findings have been reported with samples of preschool children in naturalistic contexts (e.g., classrooms and playgrounds). In a short-term longitudinal investigation of children's entrance into preschool, Ladd, Price, and Hart (1988, 1990) found that children's playground behaviors at the outset of school predicted changes in their status among classmates by the middle and end of the school year. Children with higher levels of cooperative play tended to become better liked by classmates over time, whereas children who frequently argued and engaged in physical aggression tended to become disliked and rejected by peers. Findings from this study also shed light on the consequences of peer rejection. Specifically, preschoolers who were eventually rejected by peers had greater difficulty finding consistent play partners than did well-accepted children. Thus, these studies suggest that children's success at forming supportive peer relationships in preschool is determined, in part, by the quality of their interactions during the early week of the school year. Interactions that lead to peer rejection appear to prevent children from developing stable play partners and relationships.

In a related study, Ladd and Price (1987) investigated the antecedents and maintenance of children's peer status across early school transitions (i.e., from preschool into kindergarten). They found that children who utilized prosocial behaviors with a broad range of peers in preschool tended to become more liked and less rejected by their new classmates in kindergarten. In contrast, preschoolers who tended to coerce many of their classmates in preschool (i.e., they often employed antisocial and aggressive behaviors) were often rejected by peers and perceived by teachers as hostile toward classmates as they entered kindergarten.

In addition to early prosocial and antisocial behaviors, other aspects of children's social interactions and skills may play a role in the development of peer status. As is the case with friendship (cf. Gottman, 1983), recent studies suggest that children's communication skills, particularly those contributing to the connectedness and coherence of their discourse with peers, are related to the emergence and maintenance of social status. Hazen and Black (1989) found that well-liked (i.e., high-status) children were more skilled than disliked children at clearly directing verbal and nonverbal communications toward specific peers, and at responding to peers' communications in a contingent and relevant way. High-status children were also more likely to offer a rationale or alternative idea when rejecting peer's initiations.

In a second study, Black and Hazen (1990) identified high- and low-status preschoolers and then observed their communications with acquainted and unacquainted peers. In both the acquainted and unacquainted groups, low-status children were less likely than their high-status counterparts to respond contingently to the questions and initiations of others. They also initiated more irrelevant turns in the conversation than did more accepted peers. Because these response patterns were demonstrated by disliked children with acquainted and unacquainted peers, the investigators concluded that communication clarity and connectedness may contribute to both the formation and maintenance of peer status (Black & Hazen, 1990).

In sum, findings from research with preschool and grade-school samples illustrate the importance of children's behavior (i.e., interaction patterns) as a determinant of their status among peers. Moreover, we may also infer from these data that there is substantial continuity in children's social status across school settings and peer groups. Clearly, these findings support the conclusion that children's behaviors are partly responsible for the form of status they develop among peers. However, 1 important qualification should be noted. Wright, Giammarino, and Parad (1986) have argued that the reputational outcomes of specific social behaviors may vary depending on the social context in which they are employed. In fact, these investigators found that aggressive grade-school children tended to be more disliked in peer groups composed of nonaggressive peers, and that withdrawn children tended to be more disliked in groups containing more aggressive peers. Perhaps, as these investigators suggest, the effect of children's behavior (or other characteristics) on their peer status is mediated by their similarity to the peer group.

Schooling and School-Related Processes that Affect Relationship Formation

In addition to children's behavior and personal characteristics, factors associated with the early school environment may have an impact on the development of children's peer relationships. Both the physical and interpersonal features of preschool classrooms (e.g., center-based care) may influence the extent to which children interact and form relationships with peers.

Physical Organization of Classrooms. The question of whether classrooms "affect" children's social interactions and peer relationships have been the impetus for a number of empirical investigations. Although largely correlational in nature, the findings from many of these studies suggest that the physical environment of the preschool, including the design of the classroom and the school, the arrangement of play areas, and the provision of play materials, is related to the quality of children's social interactions and early peer relationships.

Classroom spatial density, or the amount of physical space available per child, has received some attention from researchers during the last 2 decades (for reviews, see Phyfe-Perkins, 1980; Smith & Connolly, 1980). Campbell and Dill (1985) varied the levels of spatial density in 2 day care classrooms (i.e., increasing vs. constant density) and then assessed changes in children's classroom behaviors. Data from teacher interviews (but not classroom observations) indicated that, as density increased, behavior problems became more common in the classroom. Under higher levels of density, children tended to become less focused and more agonistic in their interactions with peers, and displayed higher levels of irritation and frustration.

Two studies conducted by Smith and Connolly (1980) further illuminate the potential effects of spatial density. In one study, the investigators monitored children's behavior within each of 3 density conditions (25, 50, and 75 sq. ft. per child). Children's social behaviors did not vary greatly by setting, except that group play was less common in the higher density conditions. However, larger differences in children's behavior were found in a second study, where more extreme levels of density (15 to 60 sq. ft.) were employed. Compared to their counterparts in the less dense settings, children in the highest density condition (only 15 sq. ft. per child) displayed lower levels of social interaction and positive affect, and higher levels of aggression. Based on these findings, Smith and Connolly (1980) and others (see Phyfe-Perkins, 1980) recommend that preschool administrators provide a minimum of 25 sq. ft. of space per child.

In addition to spatial density, researchers interested in children's social development have investigated factors such as the design and organization of classrooms and indoor play areas. Howes and Rubenstein (1981) investigated children's play patterns in family day care settings and found that the structure of the physical environment was related to the types of play activities children pursued with peers. They found that more sophisticated forms of play developed when children "used the spatial arrangement of the home to structure their play" (e.g., chasing each other along a path created by intersecting rooms, p. 392). Other investigators have found that children's peer interactions are enhanced by the provision of small, enclosed spaces in preschool classrooms (Phyfe-Perkins, 1980; Smith & Connolly, 1980). There is also evidence to suggest that higher levels of peer interaction, including cooperative play and positive talk, tend to occur when child care centers are arranged into individual learning centers (Field, Masi, Goldstein, Perry, & Parl, 1988).

For young children, outdoor playgrounds are also an important context for peer interaction and relationships (see Ladd & Price, in press). Indeed, some researchers have found that outdoor playgrounds can stimulate as much or more social play as indoor environments (Frost, 1986), and may be especially beneficial for some types of children (Henniger, 1985). Playground

environments have typically been classified into 4 types (see Campbell & Frost, 1985; Frost, 1986; Pederson, 1985), including traditional (e.g., flat surface with swings, slides, etc.), designer (e.g., architect-designed structures with wood, stone, and timber terracing), adventure (e.g., space with scrap materials for children to build their own structures), and creative (e.g., a combination of the above types).

Several investigators have compared children's play and interactive behaviors within differing playground environments and obtained mixed results (for a review, see Hartle & Johnson, in press). Although Campbell and Frost (1985) observed similar levels of cooperative play on both traditional and creative playgrounds, they found that children engaged in higher levels of solitary play on creative playgrounds and higher levels of parallel play on traditional playgrounds. Hart and Sheehan (1986) conducted a similar study in which they compared children's peer-play behaviors on both traditional and designer playgrounds. Higher levels of unoccupied and solitary play behaviors were found on the designer as opposed to the traditional playground, but the observed differences were not large. In a study conducted by Bruya (1985), large wooden play structures were moved together or apart in order to compare children's play in simulated traditional and designer playgrounds. The designer arrangements, in which the structures were linked together, appeared to produce the highest levels of peer contact among 3- to 5-year old children.

The amount or availability of toys and play materials in the preschool environment may also have a significant impact on preschoolers' peer interactions and relationships. Smith and Connolly (1980) examined the nature of children's play when the quantity of toys was varied, and found that children were more likely to fight or engage in parallel play when fewer as opposed to many toys were available, and they tended to play alone when many toys were provided.

In addition to availability, the nature or type of play equipment found in preschool environments may have an impact on the quality of children's peer interactions and behavior. Some types of play materials, including Play-Doh, sand, and water appear to elicit primarily nonsocial behavior (Rubin, Fein, & Vandenberg, 1983). For example, Rubin's (1977) observational studies show that when children use Play-Doh, sand, water, crayons, or paint most of their behavior (65% to 85% of observed time) can be classified as solitary or parallel play. Other activities, such as house play, vehicle play, and reading or number activities are primarily social in nature, and seem to elicit high levels of associative and cooperative play.

Similar findings have been obtained in research on the effects of large- versus small-motor activities on the quality of children's play and social interactions. Smith (1974) examined children's play in each of three contexts, including a large-apparatus condition (e.g., climber, play house), small toy condition (e.g., puzzles, dolls, tea set), and a control condition (i.e., containing both large- and small-motor equipment). Relative to the control condition, significantly more peer interaction (talking and physical contact) occurred in the large-apparatus condition. Interestingly, this condition also appeared to elicit higher levels of cooperative play from children who typically played alone or in parallel. In contrast, onlooking and adult-oriented interaction was more common in the small-toy condition.

Other studies have produced similar results. Vandenberg (1981), for example, compared preschoolers' play in rooms containing "big-muscle" equipment (e.g., tumbling mats, jungle gym) and "fine-motor" equipment (e.g., paper, crayons, scissors), and found that peer interaction was more common in the large-motor context. Also, Pellegrini and Perlmutter (1989) observed preschoolers in various classroom contexts, including art, block, and replica (dress-up or pretend play) areas, and found that social interaction was much more common in the replica as compared to the art or block areas.

There is also some evidence to suggest that features of the play environment influence the *valence* of children's interactions with peers. Higher levels of prosocial behaviors have been found in preschools where large play objects (such as climbers, which can accommodate more than one child at a time) are provided (Doyle, 1975, as cited in Gump, 1978). In contrast, lower levels of positive social interaction are found in preschool settings where play is focused on "one-person" activities (e.g., puzzles) or parallel play objects (e.g., rocking horses, tricycles). Some types of play materials, including blocks and other small toys (e.g., doll houses, toy cars, and standing figures) appear to produce higher levels of conflict and negative peer interaction (Doyle, 1975, as cited in Gump, 1978). Houseman (1972, as cited in Gump, 1978), for example, found that conflicts were common in the block area, because many children used the area at once and often "needed" peers' blocks. Moreover, features of the materials themselves (i.e., the interchangeability of the blocks) may have made conflicts more likely.

Studies conducted with grade school children suggest that organizational characteristics of classrooms may also affect the development of children's peer relationships. According to Hallinan (1976), the organizational properties of classrooms impose restrictions on students' behavior and determine, to a large degree, qualities of their peer interaction and friendship patterns. Based on this hypothesis, Hallinan (1976) compared students' peer interactions and relationships in "open" and "traditional" classrooms. Using a classification scheme devised by Walberg and Thomas (1972), Hallinan defined "open" classrooms as those that enable students to move about and interact with peers and to make decisions regarding texts, materials, and classroom activities. By contrast, "traditional" classrooms were those characterized as highly structured, teacher-centered, and teacher-controlled. Her findings indicated that popularity was more uniformly distributed in open as opposed to traditional classrooms and that open classrooms had fewer social "stars" and "isolates." Furthermore, distressed relationships (e.g., asymmetric or unbalanced dyadic, and intransitive triadic relationships) were resolved more quickly in open classrooms.

Similar findings have been reported in studies conducted with young adolescents. Epstein (1983), for example, compared friendship patterns in open classrooms (i.e., those in which students were allowed to choose their own seats and to move freely around the room to discuss schoolwork with classmates) to those in more traditional classrooms. Data from this study showed that students in open classrooms, as compared to those in traditional classrooms, were less isolated, and had a wider variety of friends.

Because the Hallinan (1976) and Epstein (1983) investigations were conducted with grade schoolers and adolescents, respectively, the findings may not readily generalize to preschoolers. However, preschool classrooms are often "open" environments, and these findings support the conclusion that "open" classrooms create greater opportunities for children to become known and liked by peers and to participate in common tasks or activities that may further the processes of friendship formation.

In sum, most of the findings reviewed in this section are consistent with the hypothesis that physical and organizational features of the classroom affect children's social interactions and behaviors with peers. However, most of this evidence is correlational in nature, and carefully controlled experimental studies (e.g., systematic testing of planned variations on classroom designs) are the exception rather than the rule. Considerable work is needed to determine whether the observed variation in children's interaction and relationships with peers should be attributed to classroom features, the child (e.g., characteristics such as children's abilities, interests, and maturity levels), or both.

Interpersonal Features of the School Environment. In addition to the physical milieu, the interpersonal features of the early school environment may play an important role in the development of children's peer interactions and relationships. Interpersonal factors, such as care giver- or teacher-child ratio, teacher/care giver training and experience, and classroom size have been investigated in recent research on the quality of child care (e.g., Field et al., 1988; Howes, 1990; Vandell, Henderson & Wilson, 1988).

The results of these studies show a consistent relation between the general quality of child care programs and the social interaction and development of the children who attend them. Children who attend high-quality child care programs, such as those found in Sweden (Andersson,1989), appear to develop higher levels of social competence than do children who experience early, extensive care in low-quality settings (Vandell and Corasaniti, 1989). Moreover, even within the same culture, variations in child care quality appear to be associated with children's social competence. In a study conducted with U.S. samples, Vandell, Henderson, and Wilson (1988) found that children in high-quality day care settings, as compared to their counterparts in low-quality centers, tended to have more friendly interactions with peers and were perceived as happier, less shy, and more socially competent. Furthermore, Howes (1990) found that children in high-quality child care settings displayed more positive affect and less anger and distress during play with peers than did their counterparts in low-quality programs (who tended to have more peer difficulties).

Research on specific features of the classroom interpersonal environment is also revealing. Among the factors that have been studied are teacher qualities, such as level of experience and amount of child development training, the care giver- or teacher-child ratio, and patterns of teacher-child interaction (see Clarke-Stewart, 1989 and Clarke-Stewart & Gruber, 1984).

Linkages have also been found among care giver qualities and children's social interactions in the classroom or child care setting. For example, care givers who engage children in higher levels of verbal interaction (Phillips, McCartney, & Scarr, 1987) and who are responsive, nurturant, and positive in their interactions with children (see Clarke-Stewart, 1989) appear to enhance children's social development. Higher (i.e., "better") care giver/child ratios have been moderately associated with children's ability to be considerate of peers (Phillips et al., 1987).

In contrast, there is also some evidence to suggest that characteristics of the teacher may discourage children's peer interactions. A study by Innocenti and colleagues revealed that lower levels of peer interaction tended to occur when teachers were present (rather than absent) and directing the children's social behaviors (Innocenti, Stowitschek, Rule, Killoran, Striefel, & Boswell, 1986). Moreover, at least one study shows that the teacher's academic training is negatively related to children's social competence with peers (Clarke-Stewart & Gruber, 1984). One possible explanation for this relationship is that teachers who train in programs that emphasize children's cognitive development may tend to neglect children's social skills (see Clarke-Stewart, 1989; Clarke-Stewart & Gruber, 1984).

Interpersonal factors such as the size and age composition of the peer group may also be related to the development of social competence and peer relationships. Mueller and Vandell, (1979), based on a review of this literature, found that both the amount of time spent in social interaction and the complexity of social behaviors increased over time for young toddlers in dyads, whereas no change was observed for children in larger group settings. Mueller and Vandell concluded that very small groups may promote social interaction among infants and young toddlers by helping them focus their social behavior on a partner. In a group setting, larger numbers of peers may distract young children, and make it difficult for them to focus on specific interaction partners and maintain interactions.

Recent studies with toddlers tend to corroborate this view. Howes and Rubenstein (1981) found that among family day care toddlers vocalizations to peers were more frequent as the size of the group decreased and the age heterogeneity increased. Similarly, Brownell (1990) observed that 18-month-old toddlers were more socially active, affectively enthusiastic, and advanced in their use of social behaviors when paired with older, rather than same-aged, playmates.

Research on mixed-age effects, however, produces somewhat inconsistent results with late-toddler and preschool-age groups. According to Howes (1987), larger and more heterogeneous (i.e., mixed-age) peer groups may support competent peer interaction at these age levels. Moreover, older children may model more mature social behaviors, thereby stimulating the younger children to adopt, through imitation, new and slightly more advanced social skills (Brownell, 1990; Howes, 1987). On the other hand, Clarke-Stewart and Gruber (1984) found that mixed-age composition and large class size were both related to lower levels of social competence with peers.

Although not systematically studied with preschool children, research on methods of grouping children during the school day has been conducted with grade-school samples, and data from these studies may have important implications for early social development. Ability grouping, for example, has been found to encourage friendship formation by promoting social interaction within ability groups and limiting inter-

action across groups (Hallinan & Sorensen, 1985). Similarly, numerous studies show that participation in cooperative learning groups is associated with improvements in children's peer relations (e.g., Johnson, Johnson, & Scott, 1978; Slavin & Karweit, 1981; Slavin, 1983). In a recent review, Furman and Gavin (1989) point out the potential value of cooperative learning techniques as a means of promoting positive peer relations in the classroom. However, they also emphasize the fact that we still understand very little about the *processes* that are responsible for the effects of cooperative learning groups on children's peer interaction and friendship formation.

In sum, with the exception of the formation of cooperative learning groups, we are aware of no studies in which classroom features have been systematically manipulated as a means of understanding their effects on children's social relations with peers. Further research is needed to shed light on the direction of effect between interpersonal features of the early school setting and children's peer relationships.

CONSEQUENCES OF EARLY PEER RELATIONSHIPS

Much of the research on the correlates and antecedents of children's group-oriented peer relationships and dyadic friendships has been motivated by the hypothesis that these early relationships have an impact on children's social development and competence. Findings from several studies provide support for this proposition and shed light on the possible effects of early peer relationships. However, the evidence gathered thus far is not extensive, and few studies permit direct causal inferences (cf. Berndt & Ladd, 1989). Available evidence suggests that peers may contribute to several areas of children's development, including their emotional well-being, classroom performance and school adjustment, and social skills and competencies.

Emotional Well-Being

Research findings indicate that young children display less distress and tend to engage in more exploratory behavior in novel surroundings when accompanied by a friend or acquaintance (i.e., familiar peer). Schwarz (1972), for example, found that, when placed into an unfamiliar environment in the presence of a friend, 4-year-olds displayed more positive affect than when alone or paired with an unfamiliar peer. Children accompanied by a friend conversed with their partner more often and were more motile, exploring the environment to a greater extent than either pairs of unfamiliar peers or children alone. Schwarz interprets these findings as support for the hypothesis that friends serve a supportive or distress-reducing function for preschoolers in novel or strange environments.

Similar findings were obtained by Ipsa (1981) with a sample of very young children (i.e., $1\frac{1}{2}$- to 3-year-olds). Toddlers were encouraged to enter a novel situation (i.e., an unfamiliar playroom with a unknown adult observer) in 1 of 3 conditions: with a familiar peer, an unfamiliar peer, or alone. Children in the company of a familiar peer adjusted to the strange situation more successfully than those with an unfamiliar peer, who, in turn, fared better than those with no peer partner. The children paired with familiar agemates vocalized more often and displayed less negative affect than children in the unfamiliar peer or alone conditions. The most striking differences among the three experimental groups emerged when the strange adult left the playroom for a brief period of time. The adult's departure had much less of an impact on the children in the familiar peer condition, which led Ispa to conclude that familiar agemates provide emotional support and security, and enable young children to feel more comfortable in novel settings.

School Adjustment

Support for the premise that early peer relationships affect children's social development and competence can also be found in investigations of children's adjustment following early school transitions. Ladd and Price (1987), for example, found that the presence of familiar peers was positively correlated with children's social and school adjustment following the transition from preschool to new kindergarten classrooms. Data from this study revealed that children who entered kindergarten with familiar peers became more accepted and less rejected by classmates over the course of the school year. These children also tended to develop positive attitudes toward school and exhibited lower levels of school avoidance (e.g., absences, requests to see the school nurse) at the beginning of the school year.

As an extension of the Ladd and Price (1987) investigation, Ladd (1990) further explored the relation between children's peer relationships in new kindergarten classrooms and their school adjustment. Measures included the number of friends and acquaintances (i.e., familiar peers) that were enrolled in children's kindergarten classrooms at the beginning of the school year, and the number of friendships that were maintained, and established (i.e., new friendships) during the first 2 months of school. Results showed that children with more classroom friends at school entrance developed more favorable perceptions of school by the second month, and children who maintained these relationships tended to like school better as the year progressed. Children who made more new friends in the classroom increased in school readiness over the school year.

In addition to friendships, Ladd (1990) also explored linkages between children's classroom peer acceptance and their adjustment to kindergarten over the school year. These findings were even stronger than those obtained for friendship, and indicated that rejection by one's classmates early in the school year forecasted less favorable school perceptions, higher levels of school avoidance, and lower levels of scholastic readiness by the end of the school year.

These findings suggest that prior friendships may serve an important familiarization function as children enter new classrooms. The presence of prior friends may make the new school environment seem less "strange" and more accommodating to a young child. Moreover, if these friendships are maintained and if new friendships are formed, they may provide emotional support as children must cope with ever-increasing school demands. In contrast, rejection by classmates early in the year appears to function as a stressor in the new school context and may impair many aspects of children's school adjustment (Ladd, 1990).

Social Skills and Competence

There is also evidence to suggest that children's early peer experience and relationships may contribute to the development of social skills and competencies. Several investigators have found that the familiarity of children's peer partners affects the skillfulness of their social interactions (e.g., Field & Roopnarine, 1982; Mueller, 1979; Mueller & Vandell, 1979). Doyle, Connolly, and Rivest (1980), for example, found that children were more socially active (i.e., made more social overtures toward peers) and more socially competent (i.e., engaged in more complex forms of play) when they were in the presence of familiar, as opposed to unfamiliar peers. Moreover, infants as young as 12 months of age have been found to display higher levels of proximal behaviors (e.g., body contact, touching) and social interactions when they are with familiar as opposed to unfamiliar agemates, and they also are more inclined to imitate the behaviors of familiar playmates (Lewis, Young, Brooks, & Michalson, 1975).

In a similar vein, observations of male toddlers in playgroups conducted by Mueller and Brenner (1977) reveal that boys with more playgroup experience developed more sophisticated and coordinated forms of play and social interaction than did boys with less playgroup experience. Moreover, in a recent investigation, Howes (1988) found that toddlers who had been in child care with the same group of peers for an extended period of time (e.g., a year or more) tended to develop more skillful forms of social interaction, and were viewed by teachers as having less difficulty with peers.

Although the amount of children's experience with a group of peers has been correlated with skillful social behavior, Ladd et al. (1992) suggest that it is more the *quality* of children's early social experiences (e.g., formation and maintenance of friendships) than the sheer amount of time they spend with peers that predicts later social competence. Howes (1983), for example, found that toddlers and preschoolers who experienced stable or "maintained" friendships in the child care setting tended to develop more complex and sophisticated forms of social interaction. This finding indicates that the skills required for complex social interaction may develop in the context of stable dyads and that social skills may emerge within the context of a friendship (Howes, 1983). Together, the findings reported in this section suggest that there may be important social benefits of children's participation in early relationships with peers.

CONCLUSIONS AND IMPLICATIONS

Recent trends in our society have produced important changes in the way we socialize young children. Within this chapter, we have tried to highlight one such transformation—specifically, the expanded role that peers play in young children's development. Increasingly, peers have become important socialization agents for young children, and early childhood programs have become one of the primary settings in which children meet peers, learn social skills, and form peer relationships.

In light of these developments, a primary aim for this chapter was to survey relevant research on early peer relations, and present information that might be useful to persons interested in the education and development of young children. Having done this, we think it may be instructive to look back over the empirical "landscape" found in this review, and consider its implications for future research and practice. But what may we infer from the findings reviewed in this chapter? Clearly, the state of the art in this domain is immature and, therefore, not conducive to strong inferences, firm policy statements, or definitive conclusions. We do think, however, that the literature is advanced enough to warrant some preliminary observations and tentative conclusions. These are offered below for your consideration.

1. *Children are capable of forming peer relationships at early ages.* There is still much more to learn about the forms and features of young children's peer relationships, and the specific processes that characterize them. However, it does appear that very young children (e.g., toddlers) are capable of forming "friendships" with peers—that is, dyadic relationships that contain important affective and/or affiliative features (e.g., the partners prefer each other's company and mutually adjust their interactions for each other; see Ross & Lollis, 1989; Howes, 1983, 1988). Furthermore, there is growing evidence to suggest that differing forms of peer status, or group reputations, emerge and are maintained at early ages. Moreover, there is reason to suspect that preschoolers' experiences in peer groups differ depending on their social status and that low-accepted preschoolers have more difficult or negative experiences than do well-liked children.

2. *There are important pathways to friendship and peer acceptance for young children.* Children's success in forming friendships and becoming accepted by group members probably depends on many factors, only some of which have been studied systematically. However, factors such as *access* and *interaction* consistently emerge in recent studies with young children as important precursors of friendship and peer acceptance. Access to peers can be viewed as a necessary condition for interaction which, in turn, is an important building block for relationship formation. As we have noted, parents and care givers are in a position to control children's access to peers, and they may do this in a variety of ways (e.g., creating opportunities for interaction, such as playgroups, engineering features of the child care setting, choosing particular play partners, etc.).

Convincing evidence has also been gathered to suggest that, once children achieve sufficient access to peers, their characteristics and interactions (behavior) may have a direct bearing on relationship outcomes. The most recent and compelling studies of early friendship formation (e.g., Gottman, 1983; Parker, 1986) point to the importance of children's communicative exchanges. Indeed, it would appear that even the earliest friendships hinge, to a great extent, on the child's ability to communicate and share a common frame of reference with their partner. A similar conclusion

can be inferred from recent research on the emergence of children's social status in peer groups. Children's peer reputations, or the perceptions that group members form about individuals, seem to be greatly influenced by their use of prosocial and antisocial behaviors. Even at early ages, antisocial behaviors such as physical aggression and arguing appear to precipitate rejection and other negative social consequences for children in the classroom and other peer groups.

3. *Peer relationships are significant in children's lives and may make important contributions to their development and well-being.* Clearly the empirical foundation needed to understand how children's peer relationships contribute to their development and well-being is the least developed of all the areas we have examined. At present, we know more about when and how children form peer relationships than we do about their effects on the child. However, the evidence that is available on the functions of early peer relationships is intriguing, and much of it is consistent with the premise that peers affect children's social development.

What we know so far seems to suggest that children's peer relationships serve both support and socialization functions. The support value or emotional significance of early peer relationships is illustrated by evidence indicating that young children are less distressed in the presence of friends or familiar peers, and are seemingly "liberated" by this type of companionship in novel situations. The fact that children feel distressed and tend to become less competent when they lose friends, and have more difficulty adjusting to school when they lack friends or are rejected by their classmates (see Howes, 1988; Ladd, 1990) further attests to this function.

It is also likely that children learn important lessons from their relationships with peers. The idea that peers serve important socialization functions is not new (see Hartup, 1970, 1989), but systematic efforts to understand how peer relationships impact young children's social skills and competence remain at an early stage. Several recent studies, however, suggest that peer relationships provide a context for skill learning and development, and in the absence of such relationships, young children fall behind or become less competent.

Unfortunately, further research is needed before we can achieve a better understanding of peers' contributions to children's development. Several key issues occur to us as potential directions for this work (see also Berndt, 1989). These include investigations of (a) the potential *negative* as well as positive effects of peers; (b) the specific contributions of differing types of peer relationships; and (c) variations in relationship quality and processes. For example, in addition to being a source of learning and support, it is possible that children's peer relationships produce emotional distress and contribute to long-term adjustment problems. Studies conducted by Asher, Hymel, and Renshaw (1984) and Asher and Wheeler (1985) have shown that children's feelings of loneliness and dissatisfaction are related to their acceptance by peers. Generally, low-status children report higher levels of loneliness and dissatisfaction than do well-liked peers. There is also a growing body of evidence to suggest that, once established, poor peer relationships (i.e., low peer acceptance) may be maintained and perpetuated by biased social cognitive processing and prejudicial behavior of peer group members toward rejected children (Hymel et al., 1990; Price & Dodge, 1989). For example, peers may prefer to view low-accepted or aggressive children negatively even when they change their behavior or act in positive ways (see Ladd, Price, & Hart, 1988).

Moreover, poor peer relationships in childhood have been linked to adjustment difficulties in adolescence and adulthood (see Kupersmidt, Coie, & Dodge, 1990; Parker & Asher, 1987). Research shows that childhood social difficulties, such as peer rejection and aggression, forecast many types of adjustment problems in later life, including juvenile delinquency, school failure, mental health problems, criminality, and suicide.

Knowledge about the functions of early peer relationships also requires a more complete examination of different forms of relationship (e.g., dyadic friendship versus peer group acceptance). In recent years, researchers have begun to recognize that children's friendships and peer acceptance may represent different social domains, and that each form of relationship may make different contributions to their social development and adjustment (e.g., Asher & Hymel, 1981; Bukowski & Hoza, 1989; Furman & Robbins, 1985, Parker, 1986). Bukowski and Hoza (1989) have argued that having a friend and being liked or accepted by the members of one's peer group have distinct influences on children's feelings of self-worth. In one study with grade schoolers, Bukowski and Newcomb (1987) found

that, even after controlling for children's peer acceptance, their feelings of self-worth were predicted by the presence of at least one mutual friend in the classroom. Having at least one friend at school may partially counteract feelings of loneliness among children who are rejected by the peer group (Parker & Asher, 1989).

Evidence of the differential contributions of friendship and peer acceptance can also be found in research on early school adjustment (Ladd, 1990). In this recent investigation, although both children's classroom friendships and peer acceptance predicted changes in their adjustment to kindergarten, the 2 types of relationships were associated with different types of outcomes. Whereas friendships were primarily associated with gains in school perceptions and scholastic performance, acceptance by classmates also forecasted lower levels of school avoidance.

Finally, even within the same type of relationship, variations in quality or interactional processes may lead to different developmental outcomes. Howes (1983), for example, found that children in "maintained" friendships were more successful at initiating interaction and spent more time in complex reciprocal play than did "sporadic" friends. The fact that more skillful behaviors and complex forms of play occurred within maintained friendships suggest that interpersonal skills may best be learned in the context of *stable* as opposed to less enduring relationships (Howes, 1983, 1988).

References

Alain, M., & Begin, G. (1987). Improving reliability of peer-nomination with young children. *Perceptual and Motor Skills, 64,* 1263–1273.

Anderson, B. E. (1989). Effects of public day care: A longitudinal study. *Child Development, 60,* 857–866.

Asher, S. R., & Hymel, S. (1981). Children's social competence in peer relations: Sociometric and behavioral assessment. In J. D. Wine & M. D. Smye (Eds.), *Social competence* (pp. 125–157). New York: Guilford Press.

Asher, S. R., Hymel, S., & Renshaw, P. D. (1984). Loneliness in children. *Child Development, 55,* 1456–1464.

Asher, S. R., Oden, S. L., & Gottman, J. M. (1977). Children's friendships in school settings. In L. G. Katz (Ed.), *Current topics in early childhood education* (Vol. 1, pp. 33–61). Norwood, NJ: Ablex.

Asher, S. R., & Renshaw, P. D. (1981). Children without friends: Social knowledge and social skill training. In S. R. Asher & J. M. Gottman (Eds.), *The development of children's friendships* (pp. 273–296). New York: Cambridge University Press.

Asher, S. R., Singleton, L. C., Tinsley, B. R., & Hymel, S. (1979). A reliable sociometric measure for preschool children. An extended version of a brief report in *Developmental Psychology, 15,* 443–444.

Asher, S. R., & Wheeler, V. A. (1985). Children's loneliness: A comparison of rejected and neglected peer status. *Journal of Consulting and Clinical Psychology, 53,* 500–505.

Belsky, J. (1984). Two waves of day care research: Developmental effects and conditions of quality. In R. C. Ainslie (Ed.), *The child and the day care setting: Qualitative variations and development* (pp. 37–53). New York: Praeger.

Berndt, T. J. (1989). Contributions of peer relationships to children's development. In T. J. Berndt & G. W. Ladd (Eds.), *Peer relationships in child development* (pp. 407–416). New York: Wiley.

Berndt, T. J., & Ladd, G. W. (Eds.). (1989). *Peer relationships in child development* (pp. 407–416). New York: Wiley.

Bhavnagri, N. (1987). *Parents as facilitators of preschool children's peer relationships.* Unpublished doctoral dissertation, University of Illinois at Urbana-Champaign.

Bigelow, B. J. (1977). Children's friendship expectations: A cognitive-development study. *Child Development, 48,* 246–253.

Bigelow, B. J., & LaGaipa, J. J. (1975). Children's written descriptions of friendship: A multidimensional analysis. *Developmental Psychology, 11,* 857–858.

Black, B., & Hazen, N. L. (1990). Social status and patterns of communication in acquainted and unacquainted preschool children. *Developmental Psychology, 26,* 379–387.

Brownell, C. A. (1990). Peer social skills in toddlers: Competencies and constraints illustrated by same-age and mixed-age interaction. *Child Development, 61,* 838–848.

Bruya, L. D. (1985). The effect of play structure format differences on play behavior of preschool children. In J. L. Frost & S. Sunderlin (Eds.), *When children play* (pp. 115–120). Wheaton, MD: Association for Childhood Education International.

Bryant, B. (1985). The neighborhood walk: Sources of support in middle childhood. *Monographs of the Society for Research in Child Development, 50*(3, Serial No. 210).

Bukowski, W. M., & Hoza, B. (1989). Popularity and friendship: Issues in theory, measurement, and outcome. In T. J. Berndt & G. W. Ladd (Eds.), *Peer relationships in child development* (pp. 15–45). New York: Wiley.

Bukowski, W. M., & Newcomb, A. F. (1987). *Friendship quality and the "self" during early adolescence.* Paper presented at the biennial meeting of the Society for Research in Child Development, Baltimore, MD.

Campbell, S. D., & Dill, N. (1985). The impact of changes in spatial density on children's behaviors in a day care setting. In J. L. Frost & S. Sunderlin (Eds.), *When children play* (pp. 255–264). Wheaton, MD: Association for Childhood Education International.

Campbell, S. D., & Frost, J. L. (1985). The effects of playground type on the cognitive and social play behaviors of grade two children. In J. L. Frost & S. Sunderlin (Eds.), *When children play* (pp. 81–88). Wheaton, MD: Association for Childhood Education International.

Clarke-Stewart, K. A. (1989). Infant day care: Maligned or malignant? *American Psychologist, 44,* 266–273.

Clarke-Stewart, K. A., & Gruber, C. P. (1984). Day care forms and features. In R. C. Ainslie (Ed.), *The child and the day care setting* (pp. 35–62). New York: Praeger.

Coie, J. D., & Dodge, K. A. (1983). Continuities and changes in children's social status: A five-year longitudinal study. *Merrill-Palmer Quarterly, 29,* 261–282.

Coie, J. D., Dodge, K. A., & Coppotelli, H. (1982). Dimensions and types of social status: A cross-age perspective. *Developmental Psychology, 18,* 557–570.

Coie, J. D., Dodge, K. A., & Kupersmidt, J. B. (1990). Peer group behavior and social status. In S. R. Asher & J. D. Coie (Eds.), *Peer rejection in childhood* (pp. 17–59). New York: Cambridge University Press.

Coie, J. D., & Kupersmidt, J. B. (1983). A behavioral analysis of emerging social status in boys' groups. *Child Development, 54,* 1400–1416.

Crick, N. R., & Ladd, G. W. (1990). Children's perceptions of the outcomes of social strategies: Do the ends justify being mean? *Developmental Psychology, 26,* 612–620.

Dodge, K. A. (1983). Behavioral antecedents of peer social status. *Child Development, 54,* 1386–1399.

Doyle, A. B., Connolly, J., & Rivest, L. P. (1980). The effect of playmate familiarity on the social interactions of young children. *Child Development, 51,* 217–223.

Eckerman, C., Davis, C., & Didow, S. (1989). Toddler's emerging ways of achieving social coordination with a peer. *Child Development, 60,* 440–453.

Edwards, C. P. (1992). Cross-cultural perspectives on family-peer relations. In R. D. Parke & G. W. Ladd (Eds.), *Family- peer relationships: Modes of Linkage* (pp. 285–316). Hillsdale, NJ: Erlbaum.

Epstein, J. L. (1983). Selection of friends in differently organized schools classrooms. In J. L. Epstein & N. Karweit (Eds.), *Friends in school: Patterns of selection and influence in secondary schools* (pp. 73–92). New York: Academic Press.

Field, T., Masi, W., Goldstein, S., Perry, S., & Parl, S. (1988). Infant day care facilitates preschool social behavior. *Early Childhood Research Quarterly, 3,* 341–359.

Field, T. M., & Roopnarine, J. L. (1982). Infant-peer interactions. In T. M. Field, A. Huston, H. C. Quay, L. Troll, & G. E. Finley (Eds.), *Review of human development* (pp. 164–179). New York: Wiley.

Frost, J. L. (1986). Children's playgrounds: Research and practice. In G. Fein & M. Rivikin (Eds.), *The young child at play* (pp. 195–211). Washington, DC: National Association for the Education of Young Children.

Furman, W. (1982). Children's friendships. In T. M. Field, A. Huston, H. C. Quay, L. Troll, & G. E. Finley (Eds.), *Review of human development* (pp. 327–339). New York: Wiley.

Furman, W., & Bierman, K. L. (1983). Developmental changes in young children's conceptions of friendship. *Child Development, 54,* 549–556.

Furman, W., & Childs, M. K. (1981, April). *A temporal perspective on children's friendships.* Paper presented at the biennial meeting of the Society for Research in Child Development, Boston.

Furman, W., & Gavin, L. A. (1989). Peers' influence on adjustment and development: A view from the intervention literature. In T. J. Berndt & G. W. Ladd (Eds.), *Peer relationships in child development* (pp. 319–340). New York: Wiley.

Furman, W., & Robbins, P. (1985). What's the point? Issues in the selection of treatment objectives. In B. H. Schneider, K. H. Rubin, & J. E. Ledingham (Eds.), *Children's peer relations: Issues in assessment and intervention* (pp. 41–56). New York: Springer-Verlag.

Gershman, E. S., & Hayes, D. S. (1983). Differential stability of reciprocal friendships and unilateral relationships among preschool children. *Merrill-Palmer Quarterly, 29,* 169–177.

Gottman, J. M. (1983). How children become friends. *Monographs of the Society for Research in Child Development. 48*(3, Serial No. 201).

Gottman, J. M. (1986). The world of coordinated play: Same- and cross-sex friendship in young children. In J. M. Gottman & J. G. Parker (Eds.), *Conversations of friends* (pp. 197–253). New York: Cambridge.

Gottman, J. M., & Parkhurst, J. T. (1980). A developmental theory of friendship and acquaintanceship processes. In W. A. Collins (Ed.), *Development of cognition, affect, and social relations: The Minnesota symposia on child psychology* (Vol. 13). Hillsdale, NJ: Erlbaum.

Gronlund, N. E. (1959). *Sociometry in the classroom.* New York: Harper.

Gump, P. V. (1978). School environments. In I. Altman & J. F. Wohlwill (Eds.), *Children and the environment.* New York: Plenum.

Hallinan, M. T. (1976). Friendship patterns in open and traditional classrooms. *Sociology of Education, 49,* 245–265.

Hallinan, M. T., & Sorensen, A. B. (1985). Ability grouping and student friendships. *American Educational Research Journal, 22,* 485–499.

Hart, C., & Sheehan, R. (1986). Preschoolers' play behavior in outdoor environments: Effects of traditional and contemporary playgrounds. *American Educational Research Journal, 23,* 668–678.

Hartle, L., & Johnson, J. E. (in press). Developmental influences of outdoor play environments. In C. H. Hart (Ed). *Children on playgrounds: Research perspectives and applications.* Albany, NY: State University of New York Press.

Hartup, W. W. (1970). Peer interaction and social organization. In P. Mussen (Ed.), *Carmichael's manual of child psychology* (pp. 361–456). New York: Wiley.

Hartup, W. W. (1979). The social worlds of childhood. *American Psychologist, 34,* 944–950.

Hartup, W. W. (1989). Behavioral manifestations of children's friendship. In T. J. Berndt & G. W. Ladd (Eds.), *Peer relationships in child development* (pp. 46–70). New York: Wiley.

Hartup, W. W. (in press). Peer relations in early and middle childhood. In V. B. Van Hasselt & M. Hersen (Eds.), *Handbook of social development: A lifespan perspective.* New York: Plenum.

Hartup, W. W., Glazer, J. A., & Charlesworth, R. (1967). Peer reinforcement and sociometric status. *Child Development, 38,* 1017–1024.

Hayes, D. S. (1978), Cognitive bases for liking and disliking among preschool children. *Child Development, 49,* 906–909.

Hayes, D. S., Gershman, E., & Bolin, L. J. (1980). Friends and enemies: Cognitive bases for preschool children's unilateral and reciprocal relationships. *Child Development, 51,* 1276–1279.

Hazen, N. L., & Black, B. (1989). Preschool peer communication skills: The role of social status and interaction context. *Child Development, 60,* 867–876.

Henniger, M. L. (1985). Preschool children's play behaviors in an indoor and outdoor environment. In J. L. Frost & S. Sunderlin (Eds.), *When children play* (pp. 145–149). Wheaton, MD: Association for Childhood Education International.

Hinde, R. S., Titmus G., Easton, D., & Tamplin, A. (1985). Incidence of "friendship" and behavior toward strong associates versus nonassociates in preschoolers. *Child Development, 56,* 234–245.

Howes, C. (1983). Patterns of friendship. *Child Development, 54,* 1041–1053.

Howes, C. (1987). Social competency with peers: Contributions from child care. *Early Childhood Research Quarterly, 2,* 155–167.

Howes, C. (1988). Peer interaction of young children. *Monographs of the Society for Research in Child Development, 53*(1, Serial No. 217).

Howes, C. (1990). Can the age of entry into child care and the quality of child care predict adjustment in kindergarten? *Developmental Psychology, 26*, 292–303.

Howes, C., & Rubenstein, J. L. (1981). Toddler peer behavior in two types of day care. *Infant Behavior and Development, 4*, 387–393.

Hymel, S. (1983). Preschool children's peer relations: Issues in sociometric assessment. *Merrill-Palmer Quarterly, 29*, 237–260.

Hymel, S., Wagner, E., & Butler, L. J. (1990). Reputational bias: View from the peer group. In S. R. Asher & J. D. Coie (Eds.), *Peer rejection in childhood* (pp. 156–188). New York: Cambridge University Press.

Innocenti, M. S., Stowitschek, J. J., Rule, S., Killoran, J., Striefel, S., & Boswell, C. (1986). A naturalistic study of the relation between preschool setting events and peer interaction in four activity contexts. *Early Childhood Research Quarterly, 1*, 141–153.

Ipsa, J. (1981). Peer support among Soviet day care toddlers. *International Journal of Behavioral Development, 4*, 255–269.

Johnson, D. W., Johnson, R. T., & Scott, L. (1978). The effects of cooperative and individualized instruction on student attitudes and achievement. *Journal of Social Psychology, 104*, 207–216.

Kessen, W. (1979). The American child as a cultural invention. *American Psychologist, 34*, 815–820.

Kupersmidt, J. B., Coie, J. D., & Dodge, K.A. (1990). The role of poor peer relationships in the development of disorder. In S. R. Asher & J. D. Coie (Eds.), *Peer rejection in childhood* (pp. 274–308). New York: Cambridge.

Ladd, G. W. (1983). Social networks of popular, average, and rejected children in school settings. *Merrill-Palmer Quarterly, 29*, 283–307.

Ladd, G. W. (1988). Friendship patterns and peer status during early and middle childhood. *Journal of Developmental and Behavioral Pediatrics, 9*, 229–238.

Ladd, G. W. (1990). Having friends, keeping friends, making friends, and being liked by peers in the classroom: Predictors of children's early school adjustment? *Child Development, 61*, 1081–1100.

Ladd, G. W., & Crick, N. R. (1989). Probing the psychological environment: Children's cognitions, perceptions, and feelings in the peer culture. In M. Maehr & C. Ames (Eds.), *Advances in motivation and achievement: Motivation enhancing environments* (Vol. 6, pp. 1–44). Greenwich, CT: JAI Press.

Ladd, G. W., & Golter, B. S. (1988). Parents' management of preschoolers' peer relations: Is it related to children's social competence? *Developmental Psychology, 24*, 109–117.

Ladd, G. W., Hart, C. H., Wadsworth, E. M., & Golter, B. S. (1988). Preschoolers' peer networks in nonschool settings: Relationship to family characteristics and school adjustment. In S. Salzinger, J. Antrobus, & M. Hammer (Eds.), *Social networks of children, adolescents, and college students* (pp. 61–92). Hillsdale, NJ: Erlbaum.

Ladd, G. W., & Oden, S. (1979). The relationship between peer acceptance and children's ideas about helpfulness. *Child Development, 50*, 402–408.

Ladd, G. W., & Price, J. M. (1987). Predicting children's social and school adjustment following the transition from preschool to kindergarten. *Child Development, 58*, 1168–1189.

Ladd, G. W., & Price, J. M. (in press). Play styles of peer-accepted and peer-rejected children on the playground. In C. H. Hart (Ed.), *Children on playgrounds: Research perspectives and applications.* Albany, NY: SUNY Press.

Ladd, G. W., Price, J. M., & Hart, C. H. (1988). Predicting preschooler's peer status from their playground behaviors. *Child Development, 59*, 986–992.

Ladd, G. W., Price, J. M., & Hart, C. H. (1990) Preschoolers' behavioral orientations and patterns of peer contact: Predictive of social status?

In S. R. Asher & J. D. Coie (Eds.), *Peer rejection in childhood* (pp. 90–118). New York: Cambridge.

Ladd, G. W., Profilet, S., & Hart, C. H. (1992). Parents' management of children's peer relations: Facilitating and supervising children's activities in the peer culture. In R. D. Parke & G. W. Ladd (Eds.), *Family-peer relationships: Modes of linkage* (pp. 215–254). Hillsdale, NJ: Erlbaum.

Lewis, M., & Feiring, C. (1989). Early predictors of childhood friendship. In T. J. Berndt & G. W. Ladd (Eds.), *Peer relationships in child development.* New York: Wiley.

Lewis, M., Young, G., Brooks, J., & Michalson, L. (1975). The beginning of friendship. In M. Lewis & L. A. Rosenblum (Eds.), *Friendship and peer relations* (pp. 27–66). New York: Wiley.

Lieberman, A. F. (1977). Preschoolers' competence with a peer: Relations with attachment and peer experience. *Child Development, 48*, 1277–1287.

Lollis, S. P., Ross, H. S., & Tate, E. (1992). Parents' regulation of children's peer interactions: Direct influences. In R. D. Parke & G. W. Ladd (Eds.), *Family-peer relations: Modes of Linkage* (pp. 255–284). Hillsdale, NJ: Erlbaum.

Masters, J. C., & Furman, W. (1981). Popularity, individual friendship selection, and specific peer interaction among children. *Developmental Psychology, 17*, 344–350.

McDavid, J. W., & Harari, H. (1966). Stereotyping of names and popularity in grade-school children. *Child Development, 37*, 453–459.

Medrich, E. A., Roizen, J., Rubin, V., & Buckley, S. (1982). *The serious business of growing up: A study of children's lives outside of school.* Berkeley: University of California Press.

Mize, J., & Ladd, G. W. (1988). Predicting preschoolers' peer behavior and status from their interpersonal strategies: A comparison of verbal and enactive responses to hypothetical social dilemmas. *Developmental Psychology, 24*, 782–788.

Mize, J., & Ladd, G. W. (1990). A cognitive-social learning approach to social skill training with low status preschool children. *Developmental Psychology, 26*, 388–397.

Moore, S. G. (1967). Correlates of peer acceptance in nursery school children. In W. W. Hartup & N. L. Smothergill (Eds.), *The young child* (pp. 229–247). Washington, DC: National Association for the Education of Young Children.

Moreno, J. L. (1934). *Who shall survive?: A new approach to the problem of human interrelations.* Washington, DC: Nervous and Mental Disease Publishing.

Mueller, E. (1979). (Toddlers + Toys) = (An autonomous social system). In M. Lewis and L. A. Rosenblum (Eds.), *The child and its family* (pp. 169–194). New York: Plenum.

Mueller, E., & Brenner, J. (1977). The origins of social skills and interaction among playgroup toddlers. *Child Development, 48*, 854–861.

Mueller, E., & Vandell, D. L. (1979). Infant-infant interaction: A review. In J. D. Osofsky (Ed.), *Handbook of infant development* (pp. 591–622). New York: Wiley-Interscience.

O'Donnell, L., & Stueve, A. (1983). Mothers as social agents: Structuring the community activities of school aged children. In H. Z. Lopata & J. H. Pleck (Eds.), *Research in the interweave of social roles: Families and jobs* (pp. 113–129). Greenwich, CT: JAI Press.

Park, K. A., & Waters, E. (1989). Security of attachment and preschool friendships. *Child Development, 60*, 1076–1081.

Parke, R. D., & Bhavnagri, N. P. (1988). Parents as managers of children's peer relationships. In D. Belle (Ed.), *Children's social networks and social supports* (pp. 241–259). New York: Wiley.

Parke, R. D., & Ladd, G. W. (Eds.). (1992). *Family-peer relations: Modes of Linkage.* Hillsdale, NJ: Erlbaum.

Parke, R. D., MacDonald, K. B., Beitel, A., & Bhavnagri, N. (1988). The role of the family in the development of peer relationships. In

R. Peters & R. J. McMahon (Eds.), *Social learning systems approaches to marriage and the family* (pp. 17–44). New York: Brunner Mazel.

Parker, J. G. (1986). Becoming friends: Conversational skills for friendship formation in young children. In J. M. Gottman & J. G. Parker (Eds.), *Conversations of friends* (pp. 103–138). New York: Cambridge.

Parker, J. G., & Asher, S. R. (1987). Peer relations and later personal adjustments: Are low-accepted children at risk? *Psychological Bulletin, 102,* 357–389.

Parker, J. G., & Asher, S. R. (1989, April). Peer relations and social adjustments: Are friendship and group acceptance distinct domains? In W. Bukowski (Chair), *Properties, Processes, and Effects of Friendship Relations During Childhood and Adolescence.* Symposium conducted at the biennial meeting of the Society for Research in Child Development, Kansas City, KS.

Parker, J. G., & Gottman, J. M. (1989). Social and emotional development in a relational context: Friendship interaction from early childhood to adolescence. In T. J. Berndt & G. W. Ladd (Eds.), *Peer relationships in child development* (pp. 95–131). New York: Wiley.

Pederson, J. (1985). The adventure playground of Denmark. In J. L. Frost & S. Sunderlin (Eds.), *When children play* (pp. 201–207). Wheaton, MD: Association for Childhood Education International.

Peery, J. C. (1979). Popular, amiable, isolated, rejected: A reconceptualization of sociometric status in preschool children. *Child Development, 50,* 1231–1234.

Pellegrini, A. D., & Perlmutter, J. C. (1989). Classroom contextual effects on children's play. *Developmental Psychology, 25,* 289–296.

Perry, D. G., Perry, L. C., & Rasmussen, P. (1986). Cognitive social learning mediators of aggression. *Child Development, 57,* 700–711.

Phillips, D., McCartney, K., & Scarr, S. (1987). Child care quality and children's social development. *Developmental Psychology, 23,* 537–543.

Phyfe-Perkins, E. (1980). Children's behavior in preschool settings: A review of research concerning the influence of physical environment. In L. G. Katz (Ed.), *Current topics in early childhood education* (Vol. 3, pp. 91–125), Norwood, NJ: Ablex.

Poteat, G. M., Ironsmith, M., & Bullock, J. (1986). The classification of preschool children's sociometric status. *Early Childhood Research Quarterly, 1,* 349–360.

Price, J. M., & Dodge, K. A. (1989). Peers' contributions to children's social maladjustment: Description and intervention. In T. J. Berndt & G. W. Ladd (Eds.), *Peer relationships in child development* (pp. 341–370). New York: Wiley.

Price, J. M., & Ladd, G. W. (1986). Assessment of children's friendships: Implications for social competence and social adjustment. In R. J. Prinz (Ed.), *Advances in behavioral assessment of children and families, Vol. 2* (pp. 121–149). Greenwich, CT: JAI Press.

Renshaw, P. D., & Asher, S. R. (1983). Children's goals and strategies for social interaction. *Merrill-Palmer Quarterly, 29,* 353–374.

Ross, H. S., & Lollis, S. P. (1989). A social relations analysis of toddler peer relationships. *Child Development, 60,* 1082–1091.

Rubenstein, J. L., & Howes, C. (1983). Social-emotional development of toddlers in day care: The role of peers and of individual differences. In S. Kilmer (Ed.), *Advances in early education and child care, Vol. 3* (pp. 13–45). Greenwich, CT: JAI Press.

Rubin, K. H. (1977). Play behaviors of young children. *Young Children, 32,* 16–24.

Rubin, K. H., Fein, G., & Vandenberg, B. (1983). Play. In E. M. Hetherington (Ed.), Paul H. Mussen (Series Editor), *Handbook of child psychology: Social development* (pp. 693–774). New York: Wiley.

Rubin, Z., & Sloman, J. (1984). How parents influence their children's friendships. In M. Lewis (Ed.), *Beyond the dyad* (pp. 223–250). New York: Plenum.

Schwarz, J. C. (1972). Effects of peer familiarity on the behavior of preschoolers in a novel situation. *Journal of Personality and Social Psychology, 24,* 276–284.

Slavin, R. E. (1983). *Cooperative learning.* New York: Longman.

Slavin, R. E., & Karweit, N. (1981). Cognitive and affective outcomes of an intensive student team learning experience. *Journal of Experimental Education, 50,* 29–35.

Smith, P. K. (1974). Aspects of the playgroup environment. In D. Carter & T. Lee (Eds), *Psychology and the built environment.* New York: Halsted.

Smith, P. K., & Connolly, K. J. (1980). *The ecology of preschool behavior.* Cambridge, UK: Cambridge University Press.

Sroufe, L. A., & Fleeson, J. (1986). Attachment and the construction of relationships. In W. W. Hartup & Z. Rubin (Eds.), *Relationships and development* (pp. 51–71). Hillsdale, NJ: Erlbaum.

Strayer, F. F. (1980). An ethological analysis of preschool social ecology. In W. A. Collins (Ed.), *Development of cognition, affect, and social relations: The Minnesota symposia on child psychology* (Vol. 13). Hillsdale, NJ: Erlbaum.

U.S. Bureau of the Census. (1989). Current population reports, Series P-23, No. 159, *Population Profile of the United States: 1989.* Washington, DC: U.S. Government Printing Office.

U.S. Department of Labor, Women's Bureau. (1983). The labor market activity of women. *Time of change: 1983 handbook of women workers* (Bulletin No. 298). Washington, DC: U.S. Government Printing Office.

U.S. Department of Labor, Bureau of Labor Statistics. (1986). Rise in mother's labor force activity includes those with infants. *Monthly Labor Review,* Washington, DC: U.S. Government Printing Office.

U.S. Department of Labor, Bureau of Labor Statistics. (1991). Employment and earnings characteristics of families. *News* (2-7-91). Washington, DC: U.S. Government Printing Office.

Vandell, D. L., & Corasaniti, M. A. (1989). Variations in early child care: Do they predict subsequent social, emotional, and cognitive differences? *Early Childhood Research Quarterly, 5,* 555–572.

Vandell, D. L., Henderson, V. K., & Wilson, K. S. (1988). A longitudinal study of children with day care experiences of varying quality. *Child Development, 59,* 1286–1292.

Vandell, D. L., & Mueller, E. C. (1980). Peer play and friendships during the first two years. In H. C. Foot, A. J. Chapman, & J. R. Smith (Eds.), *Friendship and social relations in children* (pp. 181–208). Chichester, England: Wiley.

Vandenberg, B. (1981). Environmental and cognitive factors in social play. *Journal of Experimental Child Psychology, 31,* 169–175.

Vaughn, B. E., & Langlois, J. H. (1983). Physical attractiveness as a correlate of peer status and social competence in preschool children. *Developmental Psychology, 19,* 561–567.

Vaughn, B. E., & Waters, E. (1981). Attention structure, sociometric status, and dominance: Interrelations, behavioral correlates, and relationships to social competence. *Developmental Psychology, 17,* 275–288.

Vincze, M. (1971). The social contacts of infants and young children reared together. *Early Child Development and Care, 1,* 99–109.

Walberg, H. J., & Thomas, S. C. (1972). Open education: An operational definition and validation in Great Britain and the United States. *American Educational Research Journal, 9,* 197–208.

Wright, J. C., Giammarino, M., & Parad, H. W. (1986). Social status in small groups: Individual-group similarity and the social "misfit." *Journal of Personality and Social Psychology, 50,* 523–536.

Young, L. L., & Cooper, D. H. (1944). Some factors associated with popularity. *Journal of Educational Psychology, 35,* 513–535.

·6·

THE EMOTIONAL BASIS OF LEARNING

Serena Wieder and Stanley I. Greenspan

GEORGE WASHINGTON UNIVERSITY

Although educational models have had to consider the developmental capacities of the child, they have given little attention to integrating emotional development into early childhood educational curriculum and experience. The child's abilities to walk, climb, handle materials, and use language are immediately evident and all programs encourage the continuing development of these areas. Cognition is also addressed, primarily through instruction and acquisition. But two tendencies occur with respect to emotional goals. They are either incidental or assumed, for example, the child will enjoy the activities they are doing, or will learn to get along with others in the group while they do other tasks. Or, they are addressed only in the absence or deficit of certain emotional abilities which interfere with other educational goals, that is, the child is inattentive or aggressive, gets frustrated easily, or disrupts the routine and therefore is not learning. Whether it is assumed or deficient, the important emotional goals of development and affective processes central to learning may be left to chance.

This chapter will present an educational model based on the process of learning through relationships and emotional understanding. It will also consider the implications of individual differences in self-regulation, sensory reactivity and behavioral organization on learning. The process of emotional learning begins at birth when an infant and parent connect through their own unique form of communication and the parent learns to recognize their infant's individual capacities to relate and adapt to experience. By focusing on the process of learning, rather than the content, it becomes possible to establish the foundations for successful learning in the future.

Healthy relationships throughout childhood are critical for emotional development, which in turn creates the basis for learning in several important areas. These include the ability to communicate and use language, problem solving, and the development of self-esteem. Few would argue that all learning requires the development of these abilities. This means that parents, teachers, and other care givers play a major role in a child's healthy emotional development and, therefore, in his ability to learn.

In the first 4 to 5 years of life, critical ideas or perceptions of life are learned as part of relationships. In these relationships, basic emotional stages are mastered (or not), and these very first milestones become the child's very first cognitive lessons. These combined emotional-cognitive lessons become the basis for all subsequent learning. Therefore, to determine how to help children become capable of formal learning later on, we must pay attention to these early processes or stages.

There are 6 general emotional stages of early development, each building upon the other. Mastering these stages enables the child to grow socially and cognitively as well. Ultimately, the ability to think, that is, to connect ideas and see relationships, is the result of this 6-stage process. Because children are born with individual differences in their ability to process information, to relate, and to learn, it is important to identify and consider these differences from the start if we hope to support each child's ability to learn successfully.

STUDIES OF EMOTIONAL DEVELOPMENT

It is worth briefly reviewing how we first learned about children and emotional development. Our earliest developmental theories emerged from clinical case studies and naturalistic observations of infants and young children in normal and stressful situations. The descriptions of hospitalized infants (Spitz, 1945), war babies (Freud & Burlingham, 1945; Freud, 1965), and attachment difficulties (Bowlby, 1952, 1969) left vivid impressions on everyone concerned with early development, especially regarding the importance of early relationships and the complexity of early problems when these are unavailable. Several developmental frameworks followed which provided understanding of individual lines of development in normal children, including those of Erikson (1959), Piaget (1962), Anna Freud (1965), and Mahler, Pine, and Bergman (1975). Further knowledge was derived from clinical intervention studies which not only observed infants in various environments but tried to work with infants and their families to support healthy development

(Fraiberg, 1980; Provence, 1983; Greenspan, Wieder, Lieberman, Nover, Lourie, & Robinson, 1984).

For the last three decades understanding of infant development also expanded tremendously through numerous empirical studies which identified the remarkable capacities of infants at birth beginning with the pioneering work of Escalona (1968) on individual differences. This brought everyone's attention back to how individual each child was and following studies tried to define these differences with respect to adaptation and learning. It was found infants could even organize cycles and rhythms such as sleep-wake and alertness states (Sander, 1962), and that the infant's organization of experience broadens during the early months of life to reflect increases in the capacity to experience and tolerate a range of stimuli, including responding to social interactions and stable and personal configurations during the subsequent early years (Brazelton, Koslowski, & Main, 1974; Sroufe, Waters, & Matas, 1974; Stern, 1974; Murphy & Moriarity, 1976; Emde, Gaensbauer, & Harmon, 1976). Further studies looked at complex emotional responses such as surprise and affiliation, wariness, fear, exploration, and refueling patterns, as well as differential emotional expressions (Bowlby, 1969; Ainsworth, Bell, & Stayton, 1974; Sroufe & Waters, 1977; Izard & Malatesta, 1987). It was Ayres (1966), an occupational therapist, who first described specific sensory processing capacities in relation to the specific behavioral patterns noted by others.

This body of research on emotional development evolved quite separately from the work on the impact of the social world on cognitive development. Employing a different set of concepts and theories, studies on the socialization of cognition were concerned with how children talking and acting with others affects learning. On the whole these studies separated cognitive processes from emotional processes. Even though Vygotsky's early theory of the zone of proximal development (ZPD) identified how an adult guides the child's learning through directives, feedback and demonstrations until the child learns to take over or regulate his or her own activity (i.e., attention, communication, memory, problem solving, action, or manipulation of objects), his emphasis on affect as the motivating force in thinking did not get integrated into later studies (Vygotsky, 1987). Recent studies, however, indicate affective-motivational variables within the ZPD are more predictive of young children's cognitive learning (Diaz, Neal, & Amaya-Williams, 1992).

Feuerstein's theory of structural cognitive modifiability proposed the concept of mediated learning experience (MLE) to enhance cognitive functions by focusing on the relationship between the mediator and learner where the mediator can foster changes in the ways the learner constructs his or her experience (Feuerstein & Jensen, 1980; Feuerstein, Rand, Hoffman, & Miller, 1980). While the interaction between the child and the adult guide is essential for the acquisition of higher cognitive functions and the role of affect in motivating learning is central, these theories were not directly concerned with emotional development and the role of internalized relationships. It has only recently become apparent that the separation of thinking and feeling distorts understanding of both processes and an integrated perspective is necessary (Ratner & Stettner, 1991).

The absence of an integrated perspective in both theory and research of early emotional and cognitive development is notable throughout the literature. Furthermore, individual differences in infants have not been readily integrated into either one. Most everyone claims to recognize differences and knows children develop and learn in different ways or at different rates, yet few models apply these considerations with the exception of the Greenspan (1989) developmental-structuralist framework. This framework considers the implications of sensory reactivity, self-regulation and behavioral organization on emotional development and learning. First the framework will be presented, then the specific learning goals will be identified, and last educational strategies will be presented which address individual differences.

THE GREENSPAN DEVELOPMENTAL-STRUCTURALIST THEORY

Greenspan (1979, 1981, 1989, 1991) proposed an integrated approach encompassing the multiple lines of development and individual differences in a model which focuses on "emotional experience." This model of 6 stages of ego development includes consideration of the infant's underlying physical or biological capacities (e.g., sensory-affect reactivity and processing, motor tone, and motor planning), the interactive underpinnings or early relationship patterns, and the progressive stages or levels the ego uses to organize experience. These are the mental functions that perceive, organize, elaborate, differentiate, integrate, and transform experience.

Central to this approach is the assumption that each child is born with the capacity to organize experience and this capacity progresses to higher levels as the child matures. A second assumption is that for each phase of development there are also certain characteristic types of experience or dramas (e.g., interests or wishes, fears and curiosities) that play themselves out within this organizational structure. Here one looks at emotional and behavioral patterns, or thoughts, concerns, inclinations, wishes, fears, and so forth. These expectable dramas or themes are characterized by their complexity, richness, depth, and content.

The development-structuralist approach alerts the clinician to look not only for what the infant or toddler is doing, but for what he or she is not evidencing. For example, the 8-month-old who is calm, alert, and enjoyable, but who has no capacity for discrimination or reciprocal social interchanges, may be of far greater concern than an irritable, negativistic, food-refusing, night-awakening 8-month-old with age appropriate capacities for differentiation and reciprocal social interchanges.

The interplay between age-appropriate experience and maturation of the central nervous system (CNS) ultimately determines the characteristics of this organizational capacity at each phase. The active and experiencing child uses his maturational capacities to engage the world in ever changing and more complex ways. The organizational level of experience may be delineated along a number of parameters, including age or phase appropriateness, range and depth (i.e., animate and inanimate, full range of affect and themes), stability (i.e., response to stress), and personal uniqueness.

In this theory, developed from observations of infants and young children, there is a sequence of psychological stages from interest in the world to forming a human attachment, to cause and effect interactions, to engaging in complex organized behavioral and affective patterns, to constructing and differentiating representations. It is important to realize the stages overlap, beginning at birth and becoming the predominant task of development at the interval they are identified for. The stages are presented here.

Homeostasis: Self-Regulation and Interest in the World

The infant's first task is to simultaneously take an interest in the world and regulate himself by establishing smooth sleep-wake cycles and self-calming abilities. In order to compare the ability of certain infants who can do so with those who cannot, it is clinically useful to examine each sensory pathway individually, as well as the range of sensory modalities available for phase-specific challenges.

Each sensory pathway—whether it is visual, tactile, movement, or auditory—may be hyperarousable, for example, the infant who overreacts to normal levels of sound, touch, or brightness; or hypo arousable, for example, the baby who hears and sees but evidences no behavioral or observable affective response to routine sights and sounds, appearing to not register the stimuli provided through the senses. The latter infant is often described as "the floppy baby" with poor muscle tone who is unresponsive and seemingly looks inward.

Some infants are neither hypo- nor hyperarousable but have a subtle type of early processing disorder that falls in between these 2 types. A processing disorder may presumably involve perception, modulation, and processing of the stimulus and/or integration of the stimulus with other sensory experiences (cross-sensory integration), with stored experience (action patterns or representations) or with motor proclivities.

If an individual sensory pathway is not functioning optimally, then the range of sensory experience available to the infant is limited. This limitation, in part, determines the options or strategies the infant can employ and the type of sensory experience that will be organized. Some babies can employ the full range of sensory capacities such as babies who look at mother's face or an interesting object and follow it. When such a baby is upset, the opportunity to look at mother helps the baby to become calm and happy. Similarly, a soothing voice, a gentle touch, rhythmic rocking, or a shift in position (offering vestibular and proprioceptive stimulation) can also help such a baby to relax, organize, and self-regulate.

There are babies who only functionally use 1 or 2 sensory modalities. We have observed babies who brighten up, become alert, and calm to visual experiences, but who are either relatively unresponsive, become hyperexcitable, or appear to become "confused" when someone speaks and gestures to them. They can become alert to a sound or visual clue but are not able to turn and look at a stimulus that offers visual and auditory information at the same time. When confronted with both they may even have active gaze aversion or go into a pattern of extensor rigidity and avoidance. Or, they may become irritable even with gentle stroking and are calm only when held horizontally, becoming hyperaroused when held upright. Some

are acutely sensitive to certain sounds and get alarmed by vacuum cleaners, hair dryers, sirens, or unexpected noises. Still others only calm down when rocked to their own heart rate, respiratory rate, or mother's heart rate.

At the first stage it is expected that the baby be able to convey interest in the world by a posture or glance, letting her primary care giver know she is ready for interesting visual, auditory, and tactile sensations. The sensory pathways are usually observed in the context of sensory motor patterns, e.g., turning toward the stimulus or brightening and alerting involve motor "outputs." At the same time the baby who needs to calm down is learning the means for getting the need to be comfortable met. Dependency is the first thematic-affective organizing inclination or proclivity. Babies who are uncomfortable with dependency, either because of specific sensory hypersensitivities or higher-level integrating problems, often evidence a severe compromise of the regulatory part of this equation (Greenspan, 1981). Babies born with a tendency toward hyper- or hypoarousal may not be able to later organize the affective-thematic domains of joy, pleasure, and exploration. Instead, they may evidence apathy and withdrawal or a total disregard for certain sensory realms while over-focusing on others (e.g., babies who stare at an inanimate object while ignoring the human world).

Excessive irritability, hypersensitivities, tendencies toward withdrawal, apathy, and gaze aversion illustrate some of the dramatic, maladaptive patterns in this first stage of development. If there are maladaptive environmental accommodations, these early patterns may form the basis for later disorders, including avoidance of the human world, and defects in such basic personality functions as perception, integration, regulations, and motility.

During this stage ego organization, differentiation and integration are characterized by a lack of differentiation between the physical world, self, and object worlds. Ego functions include global reactivity, sensory affective processing, and regulation, or sensory-hypo-reactivity and disregulation.

Attachment (2–7 months)

The second stage involves forming a special emotional interest in the primary care givers. There is still a relative lack of differentiation between self and object but there is differentiation of the physical world and the human-object world which allows the child to form specific attachments and therefore this stage follows homeostasis, although attachment too starts at birth. Here the ability to use all the senses allows a rich affective relationship with the human world to develop through touching, looking, listening, and movement seen in the smiling and cooing infant who kicks and moves his arms and mouth in synchrony with mother's voice and gaze.

If one or more sensory pathways is hyper- or hyposensitive, the infant may only be able to respond to looks and movement, or listening and not looking, already compromised in the range and depth of sensory experience. As a result, certain affects characteristic of this stage, including dependency, pleasure, assertiveness, and protest may become compromised. Such infants will appear flat or shallow in their affective responses and are hard to reengage with their care givers if distracted by the environment. It is during this stage the functioning of the ego is characterized by intentional object seeking, differentiation of the physical world and human world, and global patterns of reactivity to the human world through pleasure, protest, withdrawal, and diffuse discharge of affects.

Somatopsychological Differentiation: Purposeful Communication (3–10 months)

During this stage the differential use of the senses is most evident. The infant is developing the capacity for cause and effect communication observable through reciprocal interaction patterns. When an infant does not respond in turn to the parent's look or smile, either by gaze averting or random movements, they may be having difficulty taking in or processing the communication, or organizing a response to the parent in return, because of some compromises in sensory processing in one or more of the senses. Parents may begin reacting to the lack of reciprocity by withdrawal and only engage the infant through earlier forms of relatedness which are more symbiotic or synchronous. As the infant misses the appropriate interaction or is only responded to in certain domains that are acceptable to the parent, for example, dependency but not anger, uneven or delayed development occurs.

At this stage the infant seems capable of almost the full range of emotions, from dependency to curiosity to anger and protest, but needs the differential reciprocal signaling from the parent to learn these emotions are different. When the parent can read and respond to the infant's emotional signals, the infant learns to differentiate and to feel emotions can be treated equally. When parents are more conflicted around some areas than others, there will be more anxiety without cause and effect feedback, and the infant learns that different affects have different consequences. It is here that pre-representational causality is established, the first step in reality testing. The symptoms during this stage include developmental delay in sensorimotor functioning, apathy, fear, clinging, lack of curiosity and exploration, irritability, and sleep and eating difficulties. The intentional reaching out or rejecting modes of the infant suggests a behavioral comprehension of "self" influencing the "other", that is, if "I" do this it causes that. The ego is now able to differentiate aspects of emotional experience but not in a representational form.

Behavioral Organization, Initiative, and Internalization: A Complex Sense of Self (9–18 months)

At this stage the infant is able to sequence together many cause and effect units into a chain or an organized behavioral pattern. Such organized behavior requires coordinated and orchestrated use of the senses where the infant or early toddler perceives various vocal and facial gestures, postural cues, and complex affect signals and figures out how to get what he wants. The mobile toddler can feel secure using distal modes of communication to remain in contact with the care giver. Between 12 and 18 months children are able to integrate many behavioral units but not intense emotions, so when angry they lose sight of the fact that this is the same person they love.

As they approach 18 months they relate to the object world in a more functional way seen in semi-realistic play with an understanding of how the world works through purposeful use of objects. They also begin to see the emotional proclivities of their parents, noting when they are warm and nurturing, or controlling and intrusive. Just as they sense their parents' feelings, they are also abstracting their own patterns of feelings and behaviors. Using gestural communication, through facial expressions, movement, body postures, and vocal patterns, they make their own intentions and learn to comprehend the intentions of others by which they will determine whether they are safe, accepted, and approved of. Gestures provide an early warning system, and help define and express feelings. This provides the critical foundation for representational communication.

By the end of this stage the toddler reads the signals of others and is able to modify her behavior, responding to looks, words, and other gestures of approval and disapproval. The signal function of affect is in the process of being developed as part of a more conceptual attitude toward the world. During this stage ego structure formation is undergoing rapid progress and deficits of experience as well as conflicts between behavioral affective tendencies may undermine structure formation. A lack of empathy and intrusive overcontrol leads to humiliation, rage, and fear of object loss as well as deficits in self-object experiences and poor regulation of self-esteem. Conflict leads to deficits and deficits lead to unresolvable conflicts.

Representational Capacity (18–30 months)

This stage of ego organization is characterized by the capacity to elevate experience to the representational level. The earlier patterns of somatic sensations and simple and complex chains of behavior and interaction are now interpreted through mental representation. The ego will represent some areas of experience better than others depending on the early patterns, abstracting ability and the emerging dynamic character of the ego. Lags in sensory processing can compromise abstracting abilities because sensory information may not be interpreted accurately and interferes with organizing early representations. If the care giver's interactive experience available to the infant at this time is concrete or ignores or distorts certain representational themes, the child may remain concrete, constricted, develop encapsulations around certain representational areas, or become exaggerated or labile in thought, affects, and behaviors around certain dynamic areas. The capacity to now represent experience in pretend play and words, and therefore go beyond behavioral discharge, helps the toddler diminish anger and aggression without a sense of inhibition in order to still feel satisfied and gratified.

Representational Differentiation (24–48 months)

Representational elaboration and differentiation creates the basis for internal life to be symbolized and categorized along dimensions of self and nonself, affective meanings, time, and space. The categorization of experience in turn becomes the basis for basic ego functions, new relationship patterns, more differentiated and internalized conflicts, higher-level defenses, and psycho-social advances. The child broadens the range of representational themes including closeness and dependency, pleasure and excitement, assertiveness, curiosity, aggression, self-limit setting, and the beginnings of empathy and consistent love. In pretend play dramas, language becomes more complex and ideas more causally and logically connected. It is during this stage the child learns to shift gears between make-believe and the real world.

With more representational elaboration, the ego abstracts representations into groupings leading to increased differentiation. Self-representations are differentiated from the other, nonself, or object representations and each affective-thematic domain becomes a basis for further interactions and refined meanings. Anxiety and conflict can already be observed between self-object representations at the level of ideas (e.g., the good me and you, versus the angry me and you, or between the greedy me and the strict you).

Now more than ever sensory processing is critical. The young child must understand what he hears, sees, touches, and feels, not only in terms of ideas, but in terms of what is me and not-me, what is past, present, and future, and what is close and far. Learning depends on the ability to sequence and categorize information. If, for example, sounds are confused, words will not be easily understood, or if spatial references are confused, visual-spatial symbolic abstracting capacities may be compromised.

THE EMOTIONAL STAGES IN RELATIONSHIP TO LEARNING

At each stage abilities are developed which allow the child to learn. The child who is calm and alert begins to attend to the parent's face and voice (homeostasis) and begins to show joyful smiles and cooing as she moves her arms and kicks in rhythm with the parents voice (attachment). Attention grows as the child follows the parent, maintains eye contact for longer periods, and begins to reach out. The parent is learning too. The parent learns to coo and sing, dance, or make funny faces to keep the child engaged. By following the baby's lead, the parent helps the child develop a sense that she can communicate to the parent who will understand her needs, and thus learns to trust, love, and feel emotionally close to the parent. Respecting a baby's need tells her that feelings are important, that she is important, and that the human world is more interesting and rewarding than things.

The next steps in learning coincide with the baby's increasing motor abilities. When the baby can grasp and hold objects, he can reach out and take or give a toy to the parent. As he turns or sits, he begins to point to what he wants, or bangs and throws in displeasure indicating what he feels through these important gestures rather than just crying. It is at this time the baby begins to look expectantly for the care giver's response and waits to be admired for her accomplishments. As he stands and walks new interactions emerge such as chase games, hide and seek, or building tall towers. Thus, between 6 and 18 months purposeful 2-way communication is being learned as the infant becomes capable of initiating and organizing behavior (stages of somatopsychological differentiation and behavioral organization, initiative, and internalization).

Two-way communication is also the child's first lesson in logic and reality. Even before language, the baby can express and respond to a wide range of gestures and emotions. When the parent responds to something the child has initiated, he or she is opening the circle of communication. When the child responds to what the parent has said or gestured, he or she closes the circle of communication. Warm and accepting looks are associated with feelings of trust and safety. Through menacing looks and gestures the child learns about danger. It is how children learn to be prepared for later encounters in the real world.

In the second and third years of life children learn through symbolic or pretend play. Every parent notices just how much the child has learned when they see their child acting just like them. At first pretend play involves pretending real life as the child experiences it. This is when children are busy feeding and caring for their baby dolls, or going places in their little cars and trucks. Early themes involve nurturing and closeness, followed by dramas of assertiveness such as cars crashing or monsters. Imaginative play allows the child to create dramas and express ideas and feelings through gestures and emerging language. Through it (representational capacity) children learn to reason about feelings and solve certain emotional issues and problems, such as separation and fear. The capacity to represent experience in pretend play and words, in interaction with the parent, helps the child develop a meaningful inner world where they can safely experience and express all feelings, including anger and aggression, without behavioral discharge and fear of retaliation.

During the last few years of early childhood the child begins to distinguish reality from fantasy and begins to think logically (representational differentiation). Themes broaden to include curiosity, aggression, self-limit setting, and the beginnings of empathy. Through play and conversations the child learns to reason about strong feelings and connects them to behaviors. They learn to negotiate and compromise, able to follow rules but also feel confident and self-assured. Knowing how to reason about cause and effect, differentiating fantasy and reality, and enjoying a whole range of emotional experiences is essential for relating to peers and success in school.

The emotional learning of these stages is the most complex and important learning occurring during the preschool years. Through relationships with parents and teachers children interact with the world in ever-increasing ways and learn how to learn. As we respond to their gestures, initiative, curiosity, and assertiveness through play and conversation, life takes on meanings which get organized in thoughts, feelings, and self-concept. The children learn whether they can learn successfully.

INDIVIDUAL DIFFERENCES: INFANCY TO PRESCHOOL

Until now the focus has been on children with relatively intact developmental abilities who can organize experience and learn successfully because they interpret information about the world accurately and can also respond appropriately. When children are not born with (or suffer some insult that impedes) the abilities to learn, early assessment, diagnoses, and intervention are necessary to help the child learn. While all children are of course individuals and different from each other, there are certain organizational and sensory processing differences that may have greater impact on development and learning. These individual differences are observable even in the earliest months of life. For example, consider these 2 infants.

At 5 months Matthew sleeps quietly in a darkened room. The phone is turned off. His parents do not vacuum, play the stereo, or talk loudly. During infancy several months of crying, fussiness, endless rocking, and disrupted sleep led to this. Every effort is taken to make sure Matthew never missed his nap in his own crib. He cringes when his diaper is changed and arches away. Although he likes to look around, he is slow to turn over and follow sounds or movement. Matthew also startles at unexpected loud sounds and cries when the hair dryer or blender is on. His parents notice he does not reach for things. When he finally sits on his own, he stretches his legs and stiffens his upper body for stability. His parents often feel exhausted and puzzled, trying hard to hide their feelings of disappointment and self-doubt, even from each other.

In contrast, there is Mark, who is also 5 months old. His mother is about to whisk him off to meet a friend although it is his nap time. He can always nap there, the noise and lights and commotion of the cafe do not bother him. He loves to look around and follow people and sounds, turning eagerly in every direction. He calmed himself quickly as an infant sucking on his fist and now quiets just looking at mother's face and hearing her voice. In fact, last night he stayed up for dinner with friends, joyfully entertaining everyone with coos and smiles as he went hand to hand beaming at his glowing parents.

Why are these infants so different? The knowledge gained through clinical and empirical studies and the developmental structuralist framework now provides better understanding of the differences between Matthew and Mark. Mark could use vision, hearing, touch, and movement to self-regulate and learn about the world. When upset, just looking at his mother helped him become calm and happy, and so did her soothing voice and touch. In fact, he would brighten and take in the world around him with great confidence and security, able to organize the various sensations and information coming at him at the same time. He had already learned to engage and relate to others, enjoying the interaction, and expected more as he reached out to the world. The pleasure he derived helped him develop a sense of security and intimacy, enhanced motor and language development, as well as his attitude about learning.

In contrast, little Matthew needed to shut out sounds and vision as he was calmed more by the slow steady rocking movements of his mother in the quiet darkened room. When alert he could take in his parents by looking or listening to one at a time, but too many people or too much stimulation in the environment overwhelmed him, and he would become disorganized and fussy. Matthew had difficulty because of specific sensory hypersensitivities as well as problems in integrating different sensory experiences with motor output seen in motor delays. As a result, he was not showing pleasure and joy or exploration, and was unable to experience dependency comfortably. In the absence of trusting, positive expectations, distrust,

suspiciousness, or apathy take their place and do not support learning.

These 2 infants illustrate how differently 2 children begin life and how differently they may be prepared to learn later on. The examples isolated the constitutional characteristics from other psychodynamic or reality stress factors not to oversimplify, but to highlight, particular sensory, sensory-motor, and organizational processing difficulties. Children with sensory processing difficulties may develop relatively intact ego and learning capacities when not overwhelmed by the anxiety triggered by their sensory reactivity or behavioral patterns. They may have good cognition, relate to others warmly and can function more or less appropriately in the outside world as their sense of reality, self, and other continue to grow. Care givers and educators who can observe and work with the child's unique patterns are important in helping the child overcome special challenges and develop in adaptive and competent ways.

Sometimes, however, the impact of sensory processing difficulties is far more detrimental with pervasive effects on development. As these children grow, some become highly anxious, highly aggressive, withdrawn, or pervasively delayed. This often occurs when the environment is unable to respond to individual differences and instead reacts to the child in maladaptive ways. In all cases, particular sensory processing difficulties can be identified along with particular behavioral patterns and learning difficulties.

What happens as these infants reach preschool age? For example, little Michael loves to play with his little cars, up and down the ramps, sirens wailing as the ambulances arrive at numerous accidents on his roads. He loves making noise but reacts anxiously to someone else doing the same. He never seems to lack energy no matter when he goes to sleep, but his parents report he can rarely fall asleep before 11 or 12 each night. Nighttime rituals and quiet do not seem sufficient to help him unwind. During the day, Michael no longer goes to fast food restaurants, supermarkets, or crowded playgrounds. Previous trips resulted in wild and aggressive outbursts as he could not contain his reactions to the noise, proximity, or unexpected actions of others. At school he yells articulately and dashes for his toys before anyone gets near them. He attacks before he may be attacked, acutely sensitive to "danger," and already insists he only wants to play the "bad guy."

Or take Ben who is oblivious to the children around him and prefers to do his puzzles over and over again except for running around excitedly when the room gets too noisy. At home he watches videotapes hour after hour. At two and a half he is adept at getting the tapes in and out, as well as finding favorite episodes. To leave him, his parents put on the video to avoid a scene. To visit friends, the parents take a video to keep him busy. TV is rejected outright since he never knows what will happen next and has no control over the timing, unable to replay or skip the parts he does not like. At school he overfocuses on one or two toys, visibly cringing at loud or unexpected sounds. He does not seem to follow group directions until he sees the other children move. But he knows all his letters and numbers, which never change, and feels comfortable with the ritualized routines at school.

Andrew plays in the corner, making his little car clang and spin on the cabinet. He does not respond to his teacher's asking him to come over and play. When the teacher joins him, he prefers to take his little car and roll it back and forth across his belly. If the teacher is too persistent, he walks to the other side of the room and picks up a motorcycle which he again rolls without even a glimmer of a smile. The teacher asks if he could have a turn, Andrew looks up and hands him the toy, but goes on looking for something else. Andrew has no difficulty with separation, barely acknowledging someone's departure.

These children present complex developmental challenges. Since birth they have had difficulties with self-regulation, initially evidenced by difficulties calming themselves or even being calmed down, being highly reactive or underreactive to the stimulation in their environments, showing hypersensitivities to touch, sounds, or movement, and invariably, having difficulties going to sleep. A variety of explanations were offered to these parents regarding these difficulties. These varied from blaming the baby in such comments as, "You have a fussy baby. He will grow out of it." To blaming the parent with such "thoughtful" suggestions as, "Let him cry it out. Don't let this baby control your life."

Teachers recognize the developmental delays or behavioral difficulties quickly, especially difficulties communicating and interacting in school, but it is not always clear which specific processes are involved or what to do about them. The children described above had difficulties with auditory, visual, and tactile processing, as well as motor planning and motor tone difficulties. By two to three years of age, when they had to go out into the world, they were evidencing poor adaptation and emotional stress. Without the security of being able to interpret the world accurately or being able to count on their bodies to do what has to be done, they are less able to develop a differentiated sense of self and others. They are much more dependent on parents and care givers to help them function and regulate their reactivity. Furthermore, young children cannot tolerate anxiety well and tend to "dump" their anxiety by disorganizing in frustration or rage, leaving it to the teacher or parent to resolve the situation. Because they tend to overfocus, overreact, or tune out the outside world which so effects them, it may be more difficult to develop their inner world and to learn to differentiate fantasy and reality.

APPROACHES TO LEARNING

The challenge in early childhood education is to find ways to generate the important processes for learning, including shared attention, interaction and communication, and symbolic thinking within a highly interactive and emotionally expressive relationship. The examples come from children with developmental challenges to highlight the interaction between emotional and cognitive processes and suggest approaches to working with them.

Shared Attention and Meaning

The most important process needed for learning is that of attention. It is often the first observation made of a child. For example, Suzie's attention wanders, Billy is so overfocused, Judy attends so easily, or Alec seems lost in his own world. When

a child has good attention it is not necessary to think about it because it is a given; it works. When a child's attention is very fleeting and shifts from moment to moment, or at the opposite end of the continuum, is so overfocused that it is difficult to enter his or her world in any manner, the development of this process is crucial.

Structure has often been used as a solution to poor attention and organization. It is provided by the teacher who organizes the sequence of activities, duration, and content to be learned. It often consists of small tasks or splinter skills to be mastered according to a prescribed curriculum which outlines the goals, methods, and outcomes. Highly structured classrooms do not usually provide opportunities to learn more spontaneously by letting the child explore, discover, and pursue their individual curiosity. By selecting what is to be learned, the child may be denied the opportunity to learn how to learn, and the teacher may miss the opportunity to develop the underlying processes needed to learn successfully.

The capacity for *shared attention* through interaction can be learned. Start by paying attention to whatever the child attends to, looks at, touches, moves toward, that is, anything the child shows interest in. Shared attention begins with the teacher or the parent following a child's lead and showing interest in whatever the child is prepared to attend to. It really does *not* matter what the child is doing. It matters that the child will in time become *aware* that someone is pursuing and showing interest in what they are showing interest in. By doing so, the care giver gives the child's choice *meaning,* that is, helps him become aware that what he is doing is meaningful. The next thing the care giver does or organizes will also be meaningful.

This approach is in some ways similar to one of the characteristics of Klein and Feuerstein's (1985) mediated learning experience (MLE) which also encourages the child to discover meaning in the world, but allows the child to take the lead. The mediator arouses in the child curiosity in order to achieve a change in the child's perception and processing, evident when the child responds to the adult's intentions (Klein, 1985).

Initially, children with poor attention will typically go from object to object wandering around aimlessly, or may get overfocused, or will actually become more flighty when someone pays attention to them. Since it is so characteristic for adults to get the child's attention by calling them, asking them to look, putting something in front of them, and so on, it is usually a surprise to the child to have someone follow their lead. Since it does not matter what the child is doing, it is only necessary to enter the child's experience so that whatever he does, there is a response to it. One can imitate what the child is doing by doing it too, watch carefully, or just say the obvious. For example, "Oh, you're looking out the window." "Hmm, what do you see there?" "Oh, I see, a tree, a car, oh, there's a bicycle." If the child is picking up an object and manipulating it, it is sufficient to simply comment, for example, "Ah, this looks very interesting, you're turning it round and round, we can see what it does." These words may be more for the teacher, but also open the door to the actions that follow. You might then turn it too or pick up something similar and turn it the same way the child is. As the child moves, it is important to follow the child at a comfortable distance. It is also useful to note transitions in order to build awareness, for example, "Oh, we're finished with this. Let's see what's next!" The teacher's emotional tone can capture and prolong the child's interest.

By paying attention to what the child is doing, you convey to the child that what he does is important, and that he can choose what he is interested in, and that he can determine how long he wants to stay with it. In this way the child learns to organize experience and learns to learn. Allowing the very first choice, that is, figuring out what to do, is the crucial first step in organizing experience. By lending your attention to the child's attention, he will begin to recognize this important step. By investing in whatever the child wishes to do, by closing and opening circles, the next step for engagement begins. Again, since it does not matter what the child does, but how he learns, show interest in it and give meaning to the behavior. Once it has meaning, that is, deserving of attention and effort, it can also become interactive.

For example, little Joey liked to line up his cars in a perfectly straight row. He did this for so long and so often that at the very sight of doing so was causing great distress to his parents. Yet any attempt to distract him, to use the cars to go somewhere, to get people into the cars, or to offer other more interesting toys, never worked. Joey's parents were urged to simply join him in this behavior and, in fact, to help him do what he wanted to do, which was to simply line up all the cars in the particular order he wanted them. They could predict which car would follow which having seen this so often before. And so, by joining him, instead of trying to interrupt, or distract or take away something which was of interest and purpose to Joey, they had a chance to learn to understand Joey a little better and try to see what was meaningful to him.

At first mom would simply watch and observe, putting into words what Joey was doing, identifying the color of the car and the position it was in. Joey learned to just accept his parents' interest at his side, probably somewhat surprised by the change in their approach. Next, mom would offer Joey the car she thought he would want and help him put it in place, with Joey beginning to accept the car although he would not look or acknowledge that he had taken the car from his mother. Soon Joey was expecting his mom to have the cars ready for him and waited for her to hand him the next car. Before long, Joey even allowed his mother to put the car down exactly where he wanted it while he then put the following car down.

In this way they slowly began to take turns at putting down the cars in alternating fashion. In fact, they had already begun to close circles earlier when Joey began to expect his parents' interest and began to show some indication that he knew mom would be handing him a car which he would then put down. As mom continued to "play" with Joey and his cars, he allowed her into his world and soon even let her put the car down where she wanted to. At first he would protest and fuss and she would indicate, "Oh Joey, you don't want me to put it there; oh, well I better put it here, it looks like you want it here where you always have it." And thus, as she could empathize and show Joey she understood what had meaning to him, he could allow her to be more engaged and interactive with him.

This scenario could be played out in many ways. As parents and teachers begin to show interest in what their children do, they slowly become engaged in learning together as they share attention and begin to interact with each other. While studies have shown that an adult's enthusiasm and interest will increase a child's attention and support learning (Azmitia & Perlmutter, 1989), concern was still with performance outcomes. This approach is more concerned with the specific processes underlying learning such as promoting shared understanding within interaction where facial expressions, tone of voice, and other gestures (with and without language) begin to signal important functions. It is both very simple and very difficult to do. It is simple in that the objective is just to first share attention and become engaged interactively. It is difficult because it is the child who must be in the lead.

Interaction and Communication

Certain strategies encourage interaction. These include not responding automatically because you know what the child wants and thereby making it unnecessary for the child to communicate to you. It is often useful to "play dumb" or get in the way so that the child works harder to convey what they want. For example, you might open the door to the playhouse when the child wants to close it, or you might use the wrong size block or puzzle piece, or you might put little people in the bus when the child really wants the bus empty, thereby requiring some attention or negotiating. The process of negotiating is critical for it keeps the child engaged in opening and closing circles.

Another approach to children who overfocus or play repetitively is to encourage the child to do whatever they are doing and help them do it too, even if they are doing it for the hundredth time, in order to get in on the act and even be allowed to try it. If children expect interference all the time they will defend their territory and shut you out, but joining them in this way reduces their defensiveness.

It is important to realize that if a child's attention is quickly changing or a child moves away, it is not necessarily a rejection of the parent or teacher, but often just part of the problem they have organizing their attention and engaging in purposeful activity. In some cases a child keeps moving or tuning out because she does not quite know what to make of the teacher's interest and change in behavior. It is crucial that parents or teachers not give up or misinterpret the meaning of the child's behavior. It is also important that the parent not worry for how long the child is paying attention, but simply follow the child and show interest in what they are doing for as long as possible. As interaction improves, so will attention.

In some cases a child's intensity or anger can be so disarming and distressing, that distraction or "giving in" is resorted to avoid the sense of helplessness the child and adult both feel. But other times, it is the adult's boredom or lack of focus that results in the adult going onto another circle or task, before the child has had a chance to finish the first one. A delayed or lack of response on the part of the child may lead to the parent to change the subject. Instead of finding ways to encourage the child to respond, the adult assumes the child did not understand or was not interested in what was said, and finds it easier to go on. This is a signal to teachers or parents to examine their own reactions and feelings about working with the child.

Sometimes children respond with protest or anger when they do not welcome the pursual as they try to do things themselves the way they usually do. This response is a very important response indicating the child is now aware of what you are doing and able to express some feelings about it, as well as take some action to try to get you to change. In this way the child is certainly closing the circle and communicating that they object and do not like what is going on. This type of protest and anger should be welcomed and will lead the way to further communication through new negotiations where the child can protest or argue for what they want. Let the child win when possible, to show that negotiations are worthwhile.

But when the child cannot win, or is very upset or angry at the parent who has just set limits, it is helpful to express the child's feeling with him, using the same tone of voice he is for protesting. For example, Joey is about to lose it as his mother insists it is time to stop playing, but he cannot hear her empathy when she calmly reflects his feelings and reassures Joey he will play again tomorrow. Joey is getting overwhelmed by the intensity of his own emotions and cannot yet process the emotion with words. As soon as she joins him by imitating his intensity and tone of voice, they get on the same wavelength and he begins to calm down feeling she does know how he feels as she says, "Oh Joey, you want to play with your cars more than anything else in the world, you love those cars, you're so angry you can't play all night. I wish you could play with those cars too." And then calmly adds, when she observes some visceral signs of Joey calming down, "But we have to stop now." This way even if he does not understand all her words, he feels understood through her tone and gestures. He also has a chance to calm down on his own without being told to calm down and develops a greater sense of security through self-regulation.

Some parents or teachers worry about frustrating a child, or they get impatient and tend to take over and tell the child what to do. This does not help the child as much as his or her trying to figure something out, experimenting, or doing it his own way. Instead, work side by side with the child as you mediate different ways to solve the problem and praise specific aspects of the effort so they know how they are learning. For example, "Suzy, you're looking at all the pieces to see which has an edge," or "Bobby, you figured out which went on top first," or "David, that door was stuck, but you had Big Bird climb through the window," and so on. Again, it does not really matter if the solution succeeds, as much as encouraging the child to develop strategies to solve a problem. Also, it is as important to interact with the child emotionally and cognitively around failure and frustration as with success.

It is emotional understanding of the interaction which opens the door to further learning. This understanding is conveyed through gestures even before language. It might be the look of bewilderment conveying, "Don't you know what I want," or "Get out of my way." It might be the look of alarm or tears when someone gets hurt or leaves, even when it is just a toy. It might be turning red with anger or throwing in protest. It might even be a great big smile showing a sense of accomplishment or a clever grin indicating, "I got you this time." Such gestures convey important emotional understanding of a situation at hand and the interaction between the engaged parties. They convey the idea that the child knows what's up and is reading the signals being communicated. They represent the kind of "smarts" it is not possible to assess through concrete tests but are very indicative of the child's true potential.

Symbolic Play

Symbolic play and representational thinking is the other critical process to encourage. As noted above, it is through pretend or symbolic play the child conveys her understanding of how the world functions. At first, the child will pretend what she experiences in real life, reflecting the functional use of objects and the different roles she perceives. Dependency themes are typical when toddlers imitate feeding, affection, taking care of "boo boos" and other life events. The more elaborate the productions, the more complex the child's thinking and ability to organize ideas and feelings and actions. While everyone feels comfortable with dependency themes, it is important to encourage the child to work on "negative" themes such as jealousy, competition, being the boss, fear, and aggression in play. Let the child choose the roles and tell the teacher what to do. It is only in play that it is safe to be the "bad guy" or the controlling "boss" without fear of retaliation. The ability to represent these feelings and impulses and still experience safety, acceptance, and approval from the teacher or care giver supports the process of abstract thinking and problem solving without having to resort to acting out behavior.

In the classroom a few points have been selected to highlight ways to promote a more process-oriented approach to learning:

1. Provide an environment that encourages exploration and choices. Every curriculum provides for free play where small group interaction, sharing and symbolic play is encouraged. It is important to provide enough choices for children to make so they have more of an opportunity to learn to choose for themselves. Too often shelves are covered or toys are kept behind doors so children will not get too distracted or have too many things to choose from. Keeping toys at a minimum does not help the child learn to choose and focus, even when there are other things around. It is important to have more rather than less materials around so that interest can be piqued and exploration encouraged. The child's choice indicates what motivates him and motivation is essential for taking the next steps, for example, relating to the next choice and building sequences.

2. Provide enough time to pursue a child's lead. It takes time to follow a child's lead, especially in the beginning of this process. Free play is often the shortest activity period of the day when in fact it requires the most amount of time proportionate to other activities. To get things "cooking" may take twenty or more minutes as the child wanders around or moves from thing to thing. All too often playtime is over just as the child begins to get into something.

3. Consider play as the opportunity to integrate all learning processes and skills. This includes fine and gross motor skills, visual and spatial discrimination, sensory integration input, as well as language and conceptual thinking. In the process of both preplay and symbolic play, language and actions are continuously identifying categories, concerning what fits, which way to go, who to involve, feelings, and ideas. Of all educational activities, play is the most complex and requires integration of all the child's abilities in a final

common pathway. It is in play that learning occurs in its most natural and spontaneous way and where it has particular meaning to the child.

4. The most motivating force in all learning for children and adults alike is pleasure. It is important that learning be fun and children do things they enjoy. To find out, it is again important to follow their lead and to understand why certain activities or behaviors are repetitive. Young children may do the same thing over and over again because they enjoy it, as part of mastery, because it is safely familiar or provides certain sensory input, or to tune out the rest of the world to name just a few reasons. Often several of these reasons may be operative. Whatever the reasons, the goal should be to make it interactive and fun so that a relationship develop and provide the basis for further learning.

5. Consider the specific tasks of each stage of emotional development and make these the goals because they address the processes children need to learn on their own.

A PHILOSOPHY OF EDUCATIONAL ASSESSMENT

In conclusion, to implement an educational approach based on emotional learning and individual differences, it is also necessary to be able to assess children's learning capacities. The tasks of each stage provide a road map of functions to check for as development unfolds in lieu of structured isolated tasks presented on most standardized tests.

Development can be very uneven as strengths and weaknesses become apparent and need to be supported. The emotional tasks require integrating all developmental processes such as looking, listening, speaking, moving, thinking, relating, and interacting. When a child is not accomplishing emotional learning, it is necessary to learn more about the child. This should be done in multiple contexts, observing and interacting with the child in school, home, outdoors, and in the community. As these observations and interactions with the child proceed, the assessor tries to determine the degree to which constitutional factors, interactive difficulties, and relatedness contribute to the child's level of functioning. This in turn will help determine which formal assessments are indicated.

Not only should a child be evaluated for overall health, hearing, and vision, but for all sensory processing. This should include auditory processing by speech and language therapists, and sensory integration evaluations by occupational therapists. Developmental and educational testing should be undertaken only once the child's capacity for interaction and reciprocity has been established if the results are to be interpreted meaningfully and not just reflect the child's difficulty taking the test. The environment and people should also be familiar to reduce initial anxiety.

Most important, it is necessary to observe the child in free unstructured play sessions with each of the parents and the evaluator, to assess the basic emotional and learning processes of attention, engagement, organization, initiative, interaction, and symbolic capacities.

References

Ainsworth, M., Bell, S. M., & Stayton, D. (1974). Infant-mother attachment and social development. In M. Richards (Ed.), *The integration of the child into a social world* (pp. 99–136). Cambridge, England: Cambridge University Press.

Ayres, A. J. (1966). *Sensory integration and the child.* Torrance: Sensory Integration International.

Azmitia, M., & Perlmutter, M. (1989). Social influences on children's cognition: State of the art and future directions. In H. Reese (Ed.), *Advances in child development and behavior* (pp. 89–144). San Diego: Academic Press.

Bowlby, J. (1952). *Maternal care and mental health.* WHO Monograph Series No. 2. Geneva: World Health Organization.

Bowlby, J. (1969). *Attachment and loss* (Vol. 1). New York: Basic Books.

Brazelton, T., Koslowski, B., & Main, N. (1974). The origins of reciprocity: The early mother-infant interaction. In M. Lewis & L. Rosenblum (Eds.), *The effect of the infant on its caregiver* (pp. 49–76). New York: Wiley.

Diaz, R. M., Neal, C. J., & Amaya-Williams, M. (1992). The social origins of self-regulation. In L. Moll (Ed.), *Vygotsky and education.* New York: Cambridge University Press.

Emde, R. N., Gaensbauer, T. J., & Harmon, R. J. (1976). Emotional expressions in infancy: A biobehavioral study. *Psychological Issues,* Monograph No. 37. New York: International Universities Press.

Erikson, E. H. (1959). Identity and the life cycle. *Psychological Issues,* Monograph Series No. 1. New York: International Universities Press.

Escalona, S. (1968). *The roots of individuality.* Chicago: Aldine.

Feuerstein, R., Rand, Y., Hoffman, M., & Miller, R. (1980). *Instrumental enrichment.* New York: University Park Press.

Feuerstein, R., & Jensen, M. R. (1980). Instrumental enrichment: Theoretical basis, goals, and instruments. *The Educational Forum,* 44(4), 401–423.

Fraiberg, S. (1980). *Clinical studies in infant mental health.* New York: Basic Books.

Freud, A. (1965). Normality and pathology in childhood. In *The Writings of Anna Freud* (Vol. 6). New York: International Universities Press.

Freud, A., & Burlingham, D. (1945). *Infants without families.* New York: International Universities Press.

Greenspan, S. I. (1979). Intelligence and adaptation: An integration of psychoanalytic and Piageten developmental psychology. *Psychological Issues,* Monograph 47/48. New York: International Universities Press.

Greenspan, S. I. (1981). *Psychopathology and adaptation in infancy and early childhood.* New York: International Universities Press.

Greenspan, S. I. (1989). *The development of the ego.* Madison, CT: International Universities Press.

Greenspan, S. I. (1991). *Infancy and early childhood: The practice of clinical assessment and intervention with emotional and developmental challenges.* Madison, CT: International Universities Press.

Greenspan, S. I., Wieder, S., Lieberman, A., Nover, R., Lourie, R., & Robinson, M. (1984). *Infants in multirisk families: Case studies in preventive intervention.* Clinical Infant Reports, No. 3. New York: International Universities Press.

Izard, C. E., & Malatesta, C. (1987). Perspectives on emotional development: Differential emotions theory of early emotional development. In J. Osofsky (Ed.), *Handbook of infant development* (pp. 555–578). New York: Wiley.

Klein, P. (1985). *Developing intelligence in infancy and early childhood: Promoting flexibility of mind.* Ramat Gan, Israel: Bar Ilan University Press.

Klein, P. S., & Feuerstein, R. (1985). Environmental variables and cognitive development: Identification of potent factors in adult child interaction. In S. Harel & W. W. Anastasio (Eds.), *The at-risk infant: Psycho-socio-medical aspects* (pp. 369–378). Baltimore: Paul H. Booker.

Mahler, M. S., Pine, F., & Bergman, A. (1975). *The psychological birth of the human infant.* New York: Basic Books.

Murphy, L. B., & Moriarty, A. (1976). *Vulnerability, coping and growth.* New Haven: Yale University Press.

Piaget, J. (1962). The stages of the intellectual development of the child. In S. Harrison & J. McDermott (Eds.), *Childhood psychopathology.* New York: International Universities Press.

Provence, S. (1983). *Infants and parents: Clinical case reports.* Clinical Infant Reports, No. 2. New York: International Universities Press.

Ratner, H. H., & Stettner, L. J. (1991). Thinking and feeling: Putting Humpty Dumpty together again. *Merrill-Palmer Quarterly, 37,* 1–26.

Sander, L. (1962). Issues in early mother-child interaction. *Journal American Academy Child Psychiatry, 1,* 141–166.

Spitz, R. A. (1945). Hospitalism: An inquiry into the genesis of psychiatric conditions in early childhood. *The Psychoanalytic Study of the Child, 1,* 53–74. New York: New York University Press.

Sroufe, L. A., & Waters, E. (1977). Attachment as an organizational construct. *Child Development, 48,* 1184–1199.

Sroufe, L. A., Waters, E., & Matas, L. (1974). Contextual determinants of infant affective response. In M. Lewis & L. Rosenblum (Eds.), *The origins of fear.* New York: Wiley.

Stern, D. (1974). The goal and structure of mother-infant play. *Journal American Academy Child Psychiatry, 13,* 402–421.

Vygotsky, L. S. (1987). The problem and the method of investigation. In R. Rieber & A. Carton (Eds.), *The collected works of L. S. Vygotsky: Vol. I. Problems of general psychology.* New York: Plenum.

Part

·II·

FOUNDATIONS OF EARLY CHILDHOOD EDUCATIONAL CURRICULUM

· 7 ·

CURRICULUM ALTERNATIVES IN
EARLY CHILDHOOD EDUCATION:
A HISTORICAL PERSPECTIVE

Bernard Spodek and Patricia Clark Brown
UNIVERSITY OF ILLINOIS AT URBANA-CHAMPAIGN

Although early childhood education as a separate field of education emerged slowly during the nineteenth century, a number of factors contributed to the development of the field. The emergence of new states and their need for an educated citizenry contributed to the development of education at all levels. Added to that was the improvement in child survival, which made it worthwhile to invest in children. Other factors included increased industrialization and urbanization, which led to changes in western society's organization for the production of goods as well as changes in family organization and structures.

One of the earliest approaches to the education of young children was merely to enroll these children in the "common school" along with their older brothers and sisters. While common schools did not serve young children exclusively, the program needs to be acknowledged as the first approach to educating young children in America. Essentially, the common school predated early childhood education programs. This approach to educating their children was used by many parents in America. These schools, at least through the mid-nineteenth century, were concerned with teaching the basic skills of reading, writing and arithmetic, and their atmosphere was characterized by a strict concern for discipline (Finkelstein, 1979). Since the basic assumption for enrolling young children in these schools was that these children were not different in any significant ways from their older counterparts, there was no need for a specific early childhood curriculum.

The development of the field of early childhood education as a separate entity has been based on the premise that young children are in some ways different from older children. Because of this difference it was felt that the education of young children should be different from the education of older children and youth. While the pioneers of early childhood education had an intuitive sense of the nature of early childhood, they were unclear as to the process of development from the early years through adulthood. There was a belief, however, that the experiences provided to young children would influence the emerging adult. To that aim, they established unique programs for young children, though they were not necessarily built upon theories of child development. Each of the programs developed by these pioneers was unique, based upon a particular view of childhood and of the processes of education. Thus each program represented a particular curriculum model.

CURRICULUM MODELS IN
EARLY CHILDHOOD EDUCATION

A curriculum model is an ideal representation of the theoretical premises, administrative policies, and pedagogical components of a program aimed at obtaining a particular educational outcome. It is derived from theories about how children develop and learn, notions about how best to organize learning resources and opportunities for children, and value statements about what is worthwhile and important for children to know (Biber, 1984; Schubert, 1986; Spodek, 1973). Curriculum models can be examined in terms of their theoretical foundations, administrative policies, curriculum content, and method of instruction (Evans, 1982). While most current models of early childhood education are related to particular theories of learning and/or development, this was not true of earlier models. The field of child development began to emerge only in the

91

1890s. Curriculum models designed before that time, and even some that developed at that time, were little influenced by this emerging field. Other theoretical sources were often used, however.

EARLY HISTORICAL MODELS

A number of historical models of early childhood education exist that differ significantly from more recent models. Early childhood education programs that evolved in the eighteenth and nineteenth centuries were designed before the creation of the scientific study of human development. Knowledge of children's characteristics were intuitive and programs were based more on philosophic conceptions of knowledge than on psychological conceptions of the impact of experiences on children's development (Spodek, 1991). Some of these models are discussed below.

Knitting School

Perhaps the earliest program designed specifically for young children was the "knitting school," founded by Jean Frederick Oberlin in Alsace, France around 1767. Children as young as two would gather in a circle around the "teacher" who would talk to them as she knitted. The program included exercise, play, and learning handicrafts, as well as learning about nature and history through pictures. The children would first learn the names of objects in the pictures in their regional dialect and later in standard French (Deasey, 1978). This knitting school expanded to five other French villages before Oberlin's death in 1826, but was never adopted elsewhere in France or in other countries in Europe. The French Revolution and the anticlerical attitude of the emerging nation was probably one of the reasons for this lack of influence. Although Oberlin did not suffer the fate of many other clerics during that revolution, church-related activities were severely limited or curtailed.

Oberlin's model of education was different from other contemporary schools. While his school shared the oral tradition of other contemporary schools (though without recitations), play and handicraft activities were included. An additional difference was that reading and writing were not stressed. Teaching, however, was done by direct instruction and, aside from pictures, without instructional materials.

The Infant School

An institution that had much more widespread influence, the "infant school," was established in 1816 by Robert Owen in a mill town in Scotland. Owen was concerned about the living and working conditions of his mill employees, some of whom were as young as six. He initiated several social reforms, including raising the minimum working age to 10 years, providing goods at less than prevailing prices, and providing better housing for employees. He also established the Institute for the Formation of Character to train children "in good practical habits" (Owen, 1857). Students age 3 to 20 attended the Institute, which was organized into 3 levels. The infant school,

the first level, was set aside for the children age 3 to 6. The second level was for children 6 to 10 years old, and the third level, which consisted of evening classes, was designed for students 10 to 20. Children in the Institute learned reading, writing, arithmetic, geography, history, sewing, dance, and music. Children went on many field trips, and the youngest children spent a lot of time outside (Spodek, 1973).

The purpose of this school was to prepare children for a new type of society that Owen envisioned. Owen's writings about a new society and the education that would support that society were read throughout Europe and the United States. A number of U.S. infant schools were established in the 1820s. However, the movement was short-lived, and by the mid-1830s most of the infant schools in the United States no longer existed (Harrison, 1968). This was partly the result of the attitudes of the public school establishment toward the education of young children, the radical infant school activities of Bronson Alcott, and the influence of the emerging parent education movement called "fireside education" (Strickland, 1982).

While Owen had a philosophy of education that influenced the methods and goals of the infant school, it was not based on any developmental theory. The goals of education were broader than for the common school. While children were taught the basic skills of reading, writing and arithmetic, they were also taught various aspects of the physical world, handicrafts, singing and dancing, and practical moral principles. There was a belief that school should be a happy place and that children should not be physically punished or coerced into learning or behaving properly. There was also the belief that learning should be based on reason (Spodek, 1973).

Froebel's Kindergarten

In 1837 the kindergarten was created in Germany by Friedrich Froebel. Conceiving of his program well before there was any scientific study of child development, Froebel had a unique view of the nature of childhood, the nature of knowledge, and the purposes to which education should be put that allowed him to make a major contribution to the field that is still felt today.

Froebel's ideas about education reflected a belief that school should encourage the natural development of the young child. He viewed children as flowers in a garden who would flourish if properly cared for. Froebel's ideas also reflected his belief in the unity of the individual, God, and nature. He felt it was important for children to come to understand this concept of unity. Froebel designed materials (called "gifts") and activities (called "occupations") which were to symbolically represent these ideas. The gifts included ten sets of materials such as woolen balls; wooden balls, cubes and cylinders; wooden blocks segmented in different ways; and other materials, including wax pellets with sharpened sticks or straws, wooden squares and circles, and circles and circle segments made of wood or paper. All of these materials were to be used to make specific constructions as directed by the teacher. The occupations included work with clay, paper cutting, paper folding, bead stringing, drawing, weaving, and embroidery. While engaging in these activities the children were also to follow specific directions. The program also included nature study, work in language and arithmetic, and games and songs (Lilley, 1967). Froebel's kindergarten program was taught to the children in the morning; the mothers were trained to bring the program into the home in the afternoon.

Froebel's kindergarten became popular in Germany and soon spread to other European countries and to the United States. The first American kindergarten was opened in Wisconsin in 1856 by Margarethe Schurz, whose sister opened the first English kindergarten. This first kindergarten, which enrolled Margarethe Schurz's own children and her nieces and nephews, was taught in German. In 1860 the first English-speaking kindergarten in America was established in Boston by Elizabeth Peabody. By 1873 the first public school kindergarten was started in St. Louis with Susan Blow as its teacher. During the late 1800s kindergartens were also sponsored by churches, factories, trade unions, and settlement houses. Kindergartens were seen as especially important for children of immigrants and of the poor (Weber, 1969).

Although kindergartens were sponsored by various agencies and institutions during this period, they all basically followed the curriculum model designed by Froebel. The gifts, occupations, and mother songs and games were central to the curriculum. Nature study and the use of children's literature, including fairy tales and poems, augmented these materials. The teacher was seen as a follower of children's leads, and direct instruction was shunned. The program was a highly prescriptive one, however, since the children were expected to use the gifts and occupations in a manner specified by the teacher (Spodek, 1973).

TWENTIETH-CENTURY CURRICULUM MODELS

Just prior to the beginning of the twentieth century the child study movement was established. With increasing knowledge of how children learn and develop, new influences came to bear on the early childhood curriculum. Influences from progressive education and psychoanalytic theory impacted the emerging curriculum. One of the programs developed at this time that had a significant impact on early childhood education was conceived of by Maria Montessori. While Montessori's conceptions of development were more influenced by anthropology than developmental psychology, the model of early education she created had a strong developmental component and fits within this framework.

Montessori Schools

Maria Montessori was a physician who first worked with mentally handicapped children. She later applied what she had learned working with these children to the education of normal children in her school, the *Casa dei Bambini,* in a working-class neighborhood in Rome. While Montessori created a unique approach to early childhood education, it was rooted in the work of earlier philosophers and educators, including Rousseau, Pestalozzi, Froebel, Itard, and Seguin. Her curriculum model rested most heavily on the work of Seguin,

who devised a system of education for handicapped children (Kramer, 1988).

Like Froebel, Montessori believed that children's development unfolded naturally. However, rather than seeing children's knowledge as coming from manipulating objects that represent abstract symbols, she saw knowledge as being based in children's perceptions of the world. Because of this, she felt that children's senses must be trained. Montessori developed numerous materials and activities to train the senses. Each material was to be used in a specific way, and most of the materials were self-correcting and could be used by children without teacher supervision. Montessori's program also included "exercises in practical life"—such as washing, getting dressed, and cleaning tables—that were meant to help children function independently. Montessori also included reading and writing, nature study, gardening, arithmetic, and geography in her program (Montessori, 1964).

Montessori held young children in reverence, believing that children had the capacity to influence their own development, which unfolded from within. Her curriculum model allowed the environment to modify that development. As children moved through various stages of development, or sensitive periods, the teacher would prepare the environment so that the child could seek those new experiences that would nurture this development. Children would seek out these experiences within a free environment that would allow the children to manifest their developing abilities. The educational program began with materials that appealed to children's senses, enabling them to gather and order sensory information as the basis of their developing knowledge. More symbolic information was used later, after the child had the opportunity to develop this sensory training. Exercises in practical life allowed children to cope more effectively with their own needs and become more independent (Spodek, 1973).

As codified by Maria Montessori, the Montessori curriculum included sensory training, exercises in practical life, muscular education, and the teaching of basic academic skills. Her belief in the primacy of children's self-education led to an indirect teaching role for the Montessori directress, who prepared the environment and demonstrated the use of the apparatus. Children were free to select the learning material they desired and could use it as long as they wished, as long as they used it in the proper manner. No system of rewards and punishments was used, with children's liberty to be tempered by their love of order.

This curriculum has remained intact in contemporary Montessori education, although additional educational activities have been included in many Montessori programs in the last two decades.

Nursery Schools

Another early childhood program that was developed in the early 20th century was the nursery school. Margaret McMillan, along with her sister Rachel, founded the first nursery school in a London slum in 1911. Margaret, who had served on the school board in Bradford, England, before coming to London, was concerned with the unhealthy conditions under which children were living. She had helped pass legislation to raise the minimum age for children to go to work, and she fought to get the schools to provide lunches, baths, and medical examinations for children.

After leaving Bradford in 1902, Margaret joined her sister Rachel in London, where they opened a medical clinic for poor school children. As time passed, Margaret McMillan came to realize that medical treatment was not enough to influence the lives of these children. The children returned to unhealthy living conditions and were soon ill again. In 1911 the McMillans set up an open-air night camp where children could sleep out in the fresh air. Soon after, they opened the daytime nursery where very young children could get an appropriate education, as well as the benefits of fresh air and good food.

Margaret McMillan compared her nursery school to nurseries for wealthy children. She envisioned a place where poor children would have the same kind of nurturing environment that well-to-do children had—a kind of "private nursery enlarged" (McMillan, 1919). In addition to meeting the children's physical needs for adequate nutrition, exercise, fresh air, cleanliness, and medical examinations, the nursery school provided an educational program. Sensory learning was important, and although some sensory-training apparatus were available (similar to Seguin's boards or Montessori materials), McMillan believed that the garden and everyday experiences were more appropriate for sensory learning. The garden was an important part of the open-air nursery; it was located in the center of the facility, with classrooms all around it. It contained vegetables, herbs, flowers, and trees; pools, ponds, and fountains; paths, apparatus for the children, and animals. Children were encouraged to help with the gardening and to play in the water. The garden served a practical purpose in these children's education but also stood for a more ideal life outside the confines of the inner city (Steedman, 1990).

Creativity, the development of the imagination, and play were valued in the nursery. McMillan felt that it was important to teach poor children to solve problems and come up with creative solutions so that one day they could become leaders. The nursery school program also included the teaching of reading, writing, and arithmetic to older children (5-year-olds) in the school (McMillan, 1919). McMillan viewed the nursery school as supporting both the physical and mental development of poor children by providing, in a collective form, the qualities of the child-rearing environment of more affluent families. Central to the program were its *caring* aspects: eating, sleeping, and outdoor activities. Perceptual-motor learning activities were also provided, as McMillan was also influenced by Seguin. But, unlike Montessori, McMillan provided many activities for self-expression, including handicrafts, clay work, block building, and dramatic play. Stories, songs and discussions were also important parts of the program. The role of the teacher was that of a teacher-nurse (Spodek, 1973).

The open-air nursery school became internationally known, and many came to visit the school. In 1922 the first nursery schools were opened in the United States. During the next 10 years nursery schools were established at many colleges and universities throughout the country; private and philanthropic nursery schools were also established at this time.

Owen's infant school, Froebels' kindergarten, Montessori's Casa dei Bambini, and the McMillans' nursery school each had a major impact on the field of early childhood education. All of these programs, except Froebel's kindergarten, were initiated to improve the lives of young children living in poverty. Each program valued the period of early childhood as central to the intellectual and moral development of the individual. Each curriculum expressed a unique view of how experiences and interactions with materials and people would influence that development. Montessori's curriculum model has been maintained with probably the least change. McMillan's nursery school was reconstructed as it became a middle class institution, though it was revived more nearly in its original form as part of the Head Start program of the 1960s. While Owen's infant school withered away in America, Froebel's kindergarten ideal was to undergo significant change but continue to be a part of the American educational scene.

Progressive Reform Kindergarten

In the early 1900s in the United States, many educators began to question the relevance of the formal and symbolic aspects of Froebelian kindergarten education. The "gifts" were seen as too abstract for children and as unrelated to children's lives; the occupations were seen as too tedious. Influenced by the growing child study movement of the early twentieth century, and by John Dewey's writings on education, these practitioners effected a change in the goals and practices of American kindergarten education. Different arts-and-crafts activities supplanted Froebel's occupations, and building blocks and dramatic play replaced the gifts. American songs and games became a part of the kindergarten program (Spodek, 1991). Many of the activities and materials used in public school kindergartens in the United States today are identical to those used in the 1920s.

Leaders of the reform movement emphasized the need for kindergarten education to draw on children's real-life experiences, and for children to come to new understandings as they explored their immediate environment. Rather than focus on structured activities designed to enable children to understand abstract ideas (as in the Froebelian kindergarten), the new kindergarten was to provide children with concrete, personally meaningful experiences from which they would achieve understanding about the world.

Following Dewey, the reformers saw the social life of the community as the basis of children's education. The kindergarten offered children experiences in the community, then provided activities that allowed children to reconstruct their experiences through play and other forms of expression that allowed children to create meaning from these experiences (Spodek, 1991).

The reformers emphasized the importance of subject-matter learning. In a report to the International Kindergarten Union, Patty Smith Hill (1913) stressed that the kindergarten curriculum should grow out of the subject matter of the school. She felt that school subjects were aspects of the total social experience, reflections of human achievement that were separated out for purposes of study (Spodek, 1973). Knowledge was seen as growing out of social life, and as having meaning only in a social context. It was also felt that children's personal experiences would help them understand ideas about the past, present, and future.

Another reformer, Caroline Pratt, who established the City and Country School in New York City, stressed the importance of play in young children's learning. She felt that children's play was an organizing experience, and that it helped to "raise new inquiries" and "offer opportunities for new [intellectual] relationships" (Pratt, 1924, pp. 3–4). Lucy Sprague Mitchell, who was a strong supporter of the City and Country School, developed a "here-and-now" approach to selecting experiences for young children (Mitchell, 1921). She argued that children can best understand concepts and relationships that are part of familiar events and objects. She felt that children could learn many concepts in the social sciences from studying their own neighborhoods.

The new kindergartens retained some aspects of the Froebelian kindergarten, such as the emphasis on self-activity and the importance of art and music. Some of Montessori's ideas and activities, too, were included and adapted to the new curriculum. Blocks and dramatic play became an important part of the reformed kindergarten. Most important was the idea that children would learn from the world around them and that teachers would help children better understand that world.

The Influence of Child Development on Models of Early Education

One of the major influences on early childhood curriculum in the 20th century has been the field of child development. As new theories of child development were promulgated, they influenced the way in which early childhood educators conceived of developmentally appropriate programs.

Certainly the first child developmentalist to influence early childhood programs was G. Stanley Hall, the father of the child study movement. His influence, along with that of John Dewey, led to the progressive reform of kindergarten education noted in the preceeding section, "Progressive Reform Kindergarten." The belief developed that kindergarten programs should be consistent with the levels of development of the children being served. Hall and his student, Arnold Gesell, were concerned with establishing the basis for the scientific study of young children. Many of their activities were concerned with finding "norms" or average levels of development for children of various ages. Their developmental theory was a maturational one. Children were seen as developing through a process of unfolding. Education should follow development, providing educational experiences that would fit the developing competencies of young children. The concept of *readiness* evolved from this point of view. Children's capabilities could be assessed, and this assessment would help teachers determine what these children were capable of learning. This view of development influenced nursery school education with its "child development point of view," as well as the kindergarten.

Over the years, early childhood curriculum was influenced by other theories of psychological development as well. Thorndike's theories of learning, with his emphasis on habit

training, became the basis of an exemplary kindergarten curriculum that was developed at the laboratory school of Teachers College, Columbia University, which was under the direction of Patty Smith Hill, one of the leaders of the progressive kindergarten movement (Burke, 1923). Psychoanalytic theory also influenced early childhood education. Forms of expression, such as art and dramatic play, were viewed as important in the lives of young children. These activities provided a catharsis for young children so they could rid themselves of fears, anxieties, and hostilities. If these feelings were not given expression, they would be repressed and could negatively influence the adult lives of these children. Later, the theories of Piaget and Skinner also influenced early childhood curriculum (Spodek, 1991).

Early childhood education curriculum development remained dormant from the 1930s to the 1960s in the United States. Economic conditions led Montessori education to fade from the scene. Nursery schools served as a form of work relief for teachers during the depression. Child care, which became an important national service in support of defense industries, lost its support at the close of World War II. Kindergartens were a part of the public schools in only a minority of states. Early childhood education served a small portion of the community. While the public schools were being dared to build a new social order during this period (Counts, 1932), early childhood programs merely served to sustain children's healthy development.

Curriculum Models of the 1960s and 1970s

A number of factors—social, political, economic, and ideological—brought about some profound changes in early childhood education in the 1960s. One of these was a renewed interest by the scientific community in the role of the environment on human development. One of the most influential works to appear at this time was J. McVicker Hunt's *Intelligence and Experience* (1961). In this book, Hunt argues that intelligence is the product of environmental factors, and he stresses the importance of early experience. Shortly after Hunt's work, Bloom (1964) also emphasized the importance of experience in development. Bloom argued that a greater proportion of development occurs during the early years of life and that an organism is most sensitive to environmental influences during periods of rapid growth. Both of these works figured importantly in the thinking of early childhood researchers in the 1960s. A number of early childhood programs were initiated by these researchers for the purpose of studying the effects of experimental early intervention programs on children from low-income families. These programs served both urban and rural populations and utilized diverse curriculum approaches.

At the same time, an increased social awareness was developing in the United States. The civil rights movement, which began in the late 1950s, was gaining attention and support by the early 1960s. An evolving conception of government during the early 1960s considered it the government's responsibility to help disadvantaged groups to compensate for inequality in social or economic conditions. Additionally, there was a new awareness of poverty in the United States. Michael Harrington's book, *The Other America: Poverty in the United States,* reawakened readers to the extent of poverty by proclaiming that one in four Americans lived in poverty, without adequate food, shelter, or health care (Ross, 1979).

The concern for poverty in the United States, the belief in the government's responsibility to reduce social and economic inequalities, and the increased theoretical importance of early experience on human development combined in a social reform movement that culminated in the War on Poverty, as the programs under the Economic Opportunity Act were labeled. Initiated in 1964 by the Johnson administration, the War on Poverty included (1) the Job Corps, to provide training and education for employment; (2) VISTA, a domestic Peace Corps; and (3) Community Action Programs to help communities plan and implement their own programs to aid the poor. One of the most important and long-lasting of these programs was Head Start. Head Start emerged from the Community Action Program component and opened its doors to children the summer of 1965.

Contemporary Models

At the beginning of Head Start, little attention was paid to what type of preschool program was likely to be most effective, so traditional nursery school programs were promulgated. The curriculum document *Daily Program I for the Child Development Center* (Project Head Start, n.d.) was promulgated as part of the "Rainbow Series" of Head Start pamphlets. This document defined curriculum as "all the experiences which the [Child Development] Center makes possible for its children" (p. 12). It suggested that teachers start where the children are, that is, support "learning through living … all the time" (p. 14) and be sensitive to children's immediate interests. It emphasized the importance of materials and schedules and focused on four aspects of teaching: language, curiosity, self-image, and discipline. The readings suggested in the document's appendix were standard early childhood and child development texts.

It was soon clear that there were a number of different approaches available, many of these having been developed in the 1960s with the support of private foundations. These approaches could be classified into four general categories: (1) Montessori programs, (2) behavioral programs, (3) open education programs, and (4) constructivist approaches.

These models differed in a number of ways. The behavioral and constructivist models differed in the developmental theory underlying their programs. Beyond these differences were differences in program goals: Behavioral programs focused on academic skills, among other things, while constructivist programs focused on developing cognitive processes. The open-education models generally had broad educational goals and held expressive skills and personal autonomy to be as important as cognitive processes and academic preparation. All of the models that were part of the Head Start and Follow Through Planned Variations approaches also had some elements in common, as prescribed by the federal requirements. For example, they all had to include a strong parent-involvement component.

The Montessori program was different from the others in that it represented an extension of a model developed much earlier (see section "Montessori Schools" in this chapter). There was a renewed interest in Montessori education in the late 1950s, which continued through the 1960s and early 1970s. Montessori programs were generally established in private schools and were not part of Head Start. A number of public school systems — Cincinnati and Milwaukee, for example — have operated Montessori programs as alternative preschool programs for a limited number of children.

Currently, there are two distinct approaches to Montessori education. The Association Montessori Internationale (AMI) tries to maintain the program as originally conceived by Maria Montessori. The American Montessori Society (AMS), on the other hand, feels that Montessori schools should incorporate new knowledge about how children learn. AMS schools often adapt the Montessori curriculum to include activities not present in the original Montessori classroom, including play and arts programs.

The behavioral programs developed in the 1960s and 1970s included the Bereiter-Englemann-Becker program (Bereiter & Englemann, 1966; Englemann & Osborn, 1976); DARCEE (Gray, Klaus, Miller, & Forrester, 1966); and the Behavior Analysis program (Bushell, 1973). Each of these programs is distinct in its adherence to behavioral principles, as well as in its goals. Goals are considered value judgements, and a variety of goals can be achieved within a behavioral program (Bijou, 1977). Each program states its goals in behavioral terms, organizes learning in small, sequenced steps, and consistently uses some form of reinforcement. The teacher controls children's activities during instructional time.

One of the models, the Bereiter-Englemann program, developed as a program of direct instruction outside the theoretical framework of behaviorism, but with the exit of Carl Bereiter from the team of developers and the entrance of Wesley Becker, the program became more behaviorally oriented. The Bereiter-Englemann-Becker program was developed in the 1960s to help "disadvantaged" children learn the skills necessary to succeed in school. It later evolved into DISTAR, a commercially published program to teach language, arithmetic, and reading. The program is highly structured and demanding of children. It uses a fast-paced, focused, direct-instruction approach. Children are grouped by ability and receive small-group instruction in which they are required to provide a verbal group response to teacher queries. Teachers praise children frequently and are encouraged to use a wide variety of rewards.

Another category of programs could be called *open education* approaches. Identifying the common characteristics of open education has been considered an elusive task partly because it has been a grass-roots movement characterized by individuality, partly because of the use of slogans rather than theories to justify it, and partly because many of its practitioners fear codification (Spodek, 1975). While the theory of open education as an open system is continually changing, there are nevertheless some elements common to all open education programs. In open education programs, the total development of the child is the most important goal, and children's interests provide the basis for learning in school. Different instructional methods are used, but the emphasis is on active learning and "discovering," rather than on teacher telling.

A major source of open-education strategies was the informal education that characterized many English infant schools in the 1960s and 1970s. Programs sponsored by the Educational Development Center in Boston reflected this approach (Rivlin & Timpane, 1975). Other approaches, such as the Tucson Early Education Model, developed at the University of Arizona, explicitly sought education that would be responsive to children of minority backgrounds in America (Hughes, Wetzel, & Henderson, 1973).

One open-education approach, the Bank Street Approach (Biber, Shapiro, & Wikens, 1971), has a history of more than 50 years, and is rooted in the progressive education movement (see section, "Progressive Reform Kindergarten"). This approach originated in the Bureau of Educational Experiments under the direction of Lucy Sprague Mitchell in the 1920s and 1930s. It was influenced by the works of John Dewey and by psychodynamic theory. Initially, the Bank Street Approach was designed to serve children from families whose values, beliefs, and expectations were similar to those of the leaders of this approach. However, during the 1960s an attempt was made to adapt the model for use with minority and low-income children.

The Bank Street Approach focuses on engaging children in meaningful learning and on helping them to feel able and competent. It stresses helping children to understand more fully what is important to them, rather than focusing on achievement of specific academic objectives to prepare children for something that will come later. This approach is child centered; it is geared to serve the needs and interests of the children in the program. The classroom is organized into centers, and active learning is encouraged (Biber, Shapiro, & Wickens, 1971).

The final category of programs comprises constructivist approaches, such as the High/Scope model (Hohmann, Banet, & Weikart, 1979) and programs developed by Copple, Sigel, and Saunders (1979); Forman and Kuschner (1984); Furth and Wachs (1974); and Kamii and DeVries (1977). These approaches use the work of Jean Piaget as a basis for developing programs for young children. Piaget did not intend for his work to be directly translatable into curriculum for young children; as a result, approaches derived from his work often differ in significant ways. These differences result from the way in which Piaget's work has been interpreted by the curriculum developer, the specific elements of Piaget's theory that are central to the curriculum, and the elements other than developmental theory that are included in the curriculum conception. Forman and Fosnot (1982) have compared several Piagetian programs, including Forman's own, in relation to four propositions of constructivism: (1) action, not logic, is the source of deductive thinking; (2) understanding results from self-regulated activities; (3) meaningful learning results from conflict resolution; and (4) correspondences and transformations should be coordinated.

Probably the best-known constructivist approach is the High/Scope Cognitively Oriented Curriculum (Hohmann, Banet, & Weikart, 1979). The bases of this curriculum are that children must be actively involved in learning and that they con-struct knowledge from interaction with the world around them. The role of the teacher is to supply children with experiences and help them think about these experiences through the use of thought-provoking questions. Teachers are expected to monitor children's development and work to challenge them. The daily routine in a High/Scope classroom involves both teacher and children in planning what the children will do, carrying out the activities, and then reviewing what they have done (Hohmann, Banet, & Weikart, 1979).

Research on Early Childhood Curriculum

Although no research was conducted on early childhood education curriculum models before the 1960s, a great deal of research was conducted during the 1960s and 1970s on early childhood programs, both through the Office of Child Development's Head Start Planned Variation project, and at universities and research and development centers throughout the country. When Head Start began, the research emphasis was on whether preschool programs have positive effects on the children enrolled. There was great interest in the influence of the environment on intelligence in the 1960s and a belief that early childhood intervention could affect children's developing intelligence. Partly for this reason and partly because IQ tests were easy to obtain and administer, most of the initial research on early childhood programs used children's IQ scores as the outcome variable. The results from these first research projects indicated that children's IQs did increase following participation in an early childhood program. However, later studies found that these increases were not sustained over time. Enthusiasm for early childhood programs was further dampened by the publication of the Westinghouse-Ohio University Report in 1969, the first large-scale study to evaluate the impact of Head Start on later academic achievement. This study found that any results of higher achievement tended to fade out 2 to 3 years after the preschool program was completed. According to the study, Head Start did not produce lasting effects (Cicarelli et al., 1969).

In 1975, partly in response to the Westinghouse-Ohio University report, a number of researchers who had been studying the effects of early childhood programs since the 1960s formed the Consortium for Longitudinal Studies. The purpose of the Consortium was to assess the long-term effects of early childhood education across different programs. Sponsors of early intervention studies that focused on low-income children, utilized a specific curriculum, had an original sample of over 100 subjects, and were completed by 1969 were invited to join the Consortium; all but one agreed. Thus, the Consortium included not just a sample of early childhood programs, but the whole population of large-scale early childhood intervention studies conducted in the 1960s (Consortium for Longitudinal Studies, 1983). Eleven early intervention studies were included in the long-term study (see Table 7–1). Most of these projects had not been collecting longitudinal data on participants, but through the Consortium follow-up data were gathered, original data from each of the programs were reanalyzed, and results were statistically pooled. Since by 1975 the children who had originally participated in the studies were 8 to 18 years old,

TABLE 7–1. Programs Involved in the Consortium for Longitudinal Studies

1. The Early Training Project, Peabody College
2. The Perry Preschool Program, High/Scope Educational Research Foundation
3. The Gordon Parent Education Infant and Toddler Program, University of Florida
4. A comparative study of five preschool programs, University of Illinois
5. The Louisville Experiment, University of Louisville
6. The Harlem Study
7. The Verbal Interaction Project, Adelphi University
8. The Micro-Social Learning Environment, Institute of Educational Research
9. The New Haven Project, Yale University
10. The Philadelphia Study
11. The Institute for Developmental Studies Program, New York University

it was possible to look at long-term effects of early childhood programs.

Results from the pooled data and from follow-up studies showed lasting effects of preschool in 4 areas: (1) school competence, as evidenced by retention rates and rate of placement in special education programs; (2) developed abilities, as evidenced by achievement test scores and IQ scores; (3) children's attitudes and values; and (4) impact on the family. The Consortium found that children who had participated in preschool programs had lower rates of retention and of placement in special education programs than did those who did not attend preschool. Participation in a preschool program was related to an increase in IQ test scores that lasted 2 to 4 years. During most of elementary school, arithmetic and reading achievement scores were higher for preschool participants than for nonparticipants. Program participants were more likely to graduate from high school and had higher occupational aspirations and expectations. In addition, parents of preschool participants had higher occupational aspirations for their children (Consortium for Longitudinal Studies, 1983).

The purpose of the Consortium's efforts was to determine whether early childhood programs produced positive results for children, not to determine which early childhood program best served young children. Many different types of programs were included in the Consortium's study, and all were found to be effective with respect to school competence and completion. The researchers involved in the Consortium concluded that "any well-designed, professionally supervised program to stimulate and socialize infants and young children from poor minority families will be efficacious" (Consortium for Longitudinal Studies, 1983, p. 462).

There were a number of studies, however, that did attempt to compare the effectiveness of different program models. The Head Start Planned Variation study, begun in 1969, was an effort to compare the effectiveness of a variety of early childhood programs. This study continued through 1970 and 1971 and included twelve program models operating at 44 different sites. In addition to looking at the short-term effects of Head Start on children, the Planned Variation Study attempted to address the question whether the various models differed in their effects on children. The instruments used to measure the success of the programs included 4 cognitive tests, an 8-Block Sort Task, the California Preschool Social Competency Scale, and the Stanford-Binet IQ test. Child demographic information was also collected, as well as background information on the teachers and teacher aides. Classrooms were observed by outside evaluators, and parents were interviewed.

The study found that children who participated in Head Start programs scored higher on the IQ test and all cognitive measures than children who did not participate in the program, but there were few differences in effectiveness among the models. Two strong differences did appear, however: (1) children in the academically oriented behavior analysis approach and Engelmann-Becker approach scored better on a test of letters and numbers; and (2) children in the High/Scope program had higher scores on the Stanford-Binet IQ test. It was also found that children who were younger, more passive, and generally "less ready" did better in the directive models, while children who were identified as more competent and less passive were more successful in the less directive models (Smith, 1975).

The main conclusion from the study was that Head Start did make a difference, but that no one program could be determined to be more successful than any other in producing cognitive growth. However, the study did show that there were some differences in effects for different types of programs. Children in programs that emphasized cognitive learning and achievement showed stronger gains in these areas, even though all programs demonstrated some gains.

The Louisville Experiment (Miller & Dyer, 1975) was also designed to compare the effects of different early childhood programs. Four approaches were selected for this study: (1) the Bereiter-Engelmann approach, (2) Montessori, (3) DARCEE, and (4) a "traditional" nursery school program. A number of standardized tests were used to measure IQ, achievement, motivation and attitudes, perceptual development, and behavior in prekindergarten through grade 2. A follow-up study was done when the children were in sixth through eighth grades. Different effects were found for different programs, mainly for boys. For example, boys who had been in the Montessori early childhood program performed better on achievement tests in middle school than those who had been in other programs.

In another comparative study, Schweinhart, Weikart, and Larner (1986) discuss results of a longitudinal study of children who attended three preschools using different curriculum models: DISTAR, High/Scope, and a traditional nursery school model. They found that all three models achieved positive results with regard to academic achievement and school success, when compared with a control group that received no preschool education. However, they also found that the DISTAR group had significantly higher levels of self-reported juvenile delinquency and other problems (family relations, employment, financial affairs, and mental health) than did either the High/Scope group or the traditional nursery school group.

Research on early childhood programs has been criticized on the basis of a distinction between what is being and what should be assessed, as well as questions about how it is being assessed. A significant problem with the early research, such as that noted above, was the emphasis on IQ scores as a measure of the success of a program. These early studies did little to assess gains in other areas—such as social development, child health, impact on the family—which reflected the goals of some of the programs. In Head Start programs, for example, cognitive development was only one of the goals of the programs. In general, Head Start was concerned with all aspects of a child's development—physical, emotional, social, and intellectual. In addition, health and nutrition services were an important aspect of Head Start programs. These services were often overlooked in evaluations of Head Start. However, Head Start provided millions of children with health care services that they would not otherwise have received (North, 1979). In addition, the health and nutrition policies of Head Start programs have influenced other day care and preschool programs. Moreover, Zigler and Berman (1983) note that the increase in IQ scores commonly found following intervention may reflect changes in motivational factors rather than an actual increase in intelligence.

Zigler and Berman (1983) also criticize evaluations of intervention programs that only consider the target child. They stress the need to look at effects on families and communities as well. Additionally, the benefits to children's current lives that occur when children are enrolled in a preschool program are often overlooked. While politicians and educators are concerned with long-term benefits and cost-effectiveness, parents are satisfied to see their children healthier and happier (Zigler & Berman, 1983).

There has also been debate over when assessment should take place. Initial studies immediately following intervention often showed gains that did not hold up over time. On the other hand, some results, such as those found by Schweinhart, Weikart, and Larner (1986), do not appear until much later.

One of the major comparative evaluations of early childhood programs was the evaluation of the Follow Through program. Designed as an extension of Head Start into kindergarten and primary grades, Follow Through used the *Planned Variations* philosophy, allowing programs from different curriculum models with different goals and methods to be implemented in different parts of the country, in the belief that by comparing program outcomes one could determine which are the best programs. The evaluation found that programs focusing on academic skills did better on the outcome measures used in the program evaluation. They also found site effects, that is, much variation among different classrooms implementing the same program (Abt Associates, 1977).

The Follow Through evaluation, however, has been criticized as unfair (House, Glass, McLean, & Walker, 1978). It was felt that outcome measures were too narrow and favored some models over others. There was also criticism of the methods of data analysis. In addition, the variation between sites raised serious question about the efficacy of program models.

Concern over the validity of instruments used to evaluate early childhood education programs has been raised recently by Powell and Sigal (1991). They see advances in the validity of evaluations for early childhood programs with the movement away from IQ as an indicator of program outcomes. They raise

concerns, though, about the continued use of readiness tests in spite of their questionable validity. They feel that further work needs to be done in designing evaluations for early childhood programs. This is important because of the link between social policy and evaluation. Shepard (1991) also raises serious concerns about the influence of evaluation on curriculum. The current concerns for reform of the curriculum have led to a situation where the evaluation drives the curriculum. Unfortunately, that leads to a situation in which what is taught is determined by what is evaluated rather than by the values of the community, with evaluation used to determine the degree to which those goals are achieved.

CURRENT CURRICULUM INITIATIVES

In the 1980s, federal funds for programs became scarcer and the issue of whether a program was in place supplanted concern for the content of early childhood programs (Spodek, 1991). While there seem to have been few new approaches developed in the 1980s, some of the approaches developed earlier have survived and continue to influence curriculum in early childhood education (Roopnarine & Johnson, 1987; Warger, 1988).

Programs based on Maria Montessori's principles are still popular. While there are differences in specific programs, they are all guided by general principles concerning learning and teaching that were central to Montessori's approach to working with young children. As noted earlier, some of the Montessori programs have changed very little from the program implemented in Montessori's Casa dei Bambini. Others have incorporated ideas from other approaches, while still retaining the basis of a Montessori program.

Behaviorist approaches to early childhood education—highly structured, direct instruction—continue to receive support, particularly for use with children who live in poverty (McNamara, 1987). Behavioral approaches to early childhood education can also be seen in programs designed for children with handicapping conditions (Spodek, Saracho, & Lee, 1984).

Few programs currently call themselves "open education" programs. However, the Bank Street College of Education approach is still used. Additionally, there are many early childhood programs that do not define themselves as having a particular approach but that incorporate many of the ideas and goals for young children that fit open-education approaches.

Probably the most consistently popular approach to early childhood curriculum from the initiatives of the 1960s is the High/Scope model. In particular, many prekindergarten programs for children considered to be educationally "at risk" have adopted this approach. Perhaps the continued popularity of this approach is due to the rapid expansion of prekindergarten programs in the public schools, with new teachers finding that they need to implement programs without school district guidelines. In addition, the availability of written materials and training provided by High/Scope educators makes adoption of this curriculum viable.

There are other early childhood approaches based on recently formulated developmental principles, but none that have been broadly used. An example of one of these is the experimental preschool at the University of Wisconsin laboratory nursery school that is based in part on an Ausubelian approach to learning (Lawton, 1987). This program, which also draws on the work of Piaget and of Bruner, was started in the late 1970s. In this program, teachers identify basic concepts that are introduced in a series of lessons called "advance organizers." The advance organizers are followed by related learning activities that exemplify the basic concepts and require children to go beyond the information given in the advance organizer lesson. For example, the teacher might provide the children with a lesson on the concept that some animals are mammals. Related activities would provide examples of this concept through books, films, pictures, real-life objects, toy objects, and field trips.

Programs to Serve Particular Goals

Early childhood curriculum models have also been developed recently to achieve specific goals or to meet the needs of a particular population of students. One such model is the peace education curriculum. The purpose of this approach is not only to help young children understand ideas concerning peace and war, but also to help young children learn to resolve conflicts in peaceful ways. The focus of this approach is on including messages about peaceful coexistence in all areas of the curriculum. Carlsson-Paige and Levin (1985) believe that the best way to teach children about war and peace is "in the *context of values, skills and classroom competencies*" (p. 24; italics in the original). For these authors, peace education affects almost every area of teaching and learning. They emphasize that peace education involves learning about cooperation and respect, and developing an appreciation of cultural similarities and differences. They also suggest that a peace education curriculum should teach skills in negotiating, conflict resolution, and problem-solving (see also Boston Area Educators for Social Responsibility, 1983; Center for Peace & Conflict Studies, 1988; Grenier, 1984; Marion & Stremmel, 1983; Myers-Walls & Fry-Miller, 1984).

The *Anti-Bias Curriculum* (1989) developed by Louise Derman-Sparks and her associates and published by the National Association for the Education of Young Children is also designed to achieve specific goals. This curriculum suggests ways to combat and eliminate bias related to gender, race, disabilities, and culture. It provides suggestions for materials and activities to achieve these goals, and discusses ways in which teachers can help children learn about differences among human beings in a positive way. The authors note that children notice differences and begin to develop attitudes at a very early age. For this reason, they believe that educators must take the initiative in helping children form positive attitudes, rather than ignoring issues of bias and stereotyping.

The authors of the *Anti-Bias Curriculum* emphasize that their curriculum is meant to be integrated into all aspects of teaching and learning. This curriculum, like the peace curriculum, stresses the values being taught to young children. Derman-Sparks and her colleagues include a chapter in their publication that deals with holiday activities in the classroom and encourages teachers to think about why teachers include such activities and what children might learn from these activities. It also urges teachers to help children find ways to work together to change things they think are unfair. In addition, the curriculum discusses working with parents, particularly those who might disagree with the values and beliefs that the curriculum promotes.

Programs Designed to Serve Particular Populations

Early childhood programs have also been developed to meet the needs of particular populations, including bilingual children, migrant children, minority children, children with special developmental needs, and (more recently) programs for children identified as at risk for school failure.

Bilingual early childhood programs serve children who speak languages other than English. Sometimes these programs use an already-developed model of early childhood education and adapt instruction to meet the needs of children whose home language is not English. There are also some early childhood programs that have been specifically developed for children who speak a language other than English.

The Tucson Early Education Model (TEEM), mentioned earlier, was not originally designed to be a bilingual program, however it was felt that the model could be easily adapted for use with children whose home language was not English (Arizona Center for Educational Research and Development, 1983). TEEM emphasizes using each child's experiences as the basis for school learning. The children's language and culture are incorporated into classroom activities, and skills and concepts are taught in the children's first language, as they develop oral skills in English. TEEM was developed with a cognitive-developmental framework and stresses active learning by the children.

Project P.I.A.G.E.T. is a Title VII bilingual education program specifically designed to develop cognitive and English language capabilities in 5-year-old children whose dominant language is not English. It includes both a classroom component and a home component. The classroom program emphasizes English language and cognitive development, and uses *The Kindergarten Keys* (1980) curricular materials. For the home component, the classroom aide visits the home and instructs parents in the home language on how to work with their children at home on academic as well as social tasks, routines, and assignments (Yawkey, 1987). Other bilingual early childhood program models exist as well (Saracho & Spodek, 1983).

Hale-Benson (1982, 1986) describes a preschool program for African American children designed to teach cognitive skills while strengthening African American children's self-esteem and identity. The program uses mixed-age and mixed-ability grouping, a high adult-child ratio, small-group learning, and peer tutoring to provide a high level of affective support for children. Opportunities are provided for various forms of creative expression, and children's self-confidence is fostered through frequent praise, displaying children's work, and performances. African and African American cultures are emphasized in the curriculum.

Recently there has been an increased interest in programs serving children who have been identified as at risk for school failure. As in the 1960s, there is some feeling that it is important to reach these children before the age they would normally start school. A number of states are now funding prekindergarten programs for this particular population. Some of these programs are designed to serve a similar population of children as those described as "disadvantaged" in the 1960s, that is, children from low-income families, as well as children from bilingual backgrounds, children of migrant workers, of teenage or single parents or from a variety of backgrounds associated with school failure. Children with developmental delays may also be served by these programs.

There is no one curriculum model being used in these programs. Many of them are adopting the High/Scope model, as noted above. Others use eclectic models developed locally. There also seems to be an emphasis on ensuring that these public school programs are "developmentally appropriate."

While programs such as the ones described above can be found currently in the United States, most early childhood programs probably are not based in any one model. In fact, most early childhood programs consist of a collection of loosely related activities organized around a theme for the week, usually related to a holiday or season. While most programs claim they are providing for the social, emotional, physical, and cognitive development of the child, few pay much attention to the content of the curriculum or to individual children's development in each of these areas. In many cases these programs have been influenced by the demands of the primary grades concerned with improving academic achievement by starting instruction early and by the uses of standardized tests of achievement and readiness. This influence has led early childhood educators to seek ways of ensuring that programs offered young children are appropriate to their developmental levels.

Developmentally Appropriate Practices

While the 1980s saw reductions in federal funding for social programs such as early childhood programs, state and local governments increasingly included early childhood programs in the public schools. Kindergarten education has become essentially universal throughout the United States, with the vast majority of these kindergarten children enrolled in public schools. In addition, many of these kindergartens are all-day rather than part-day programs. This is very different from 1965, the year Head Start began, when less than half of the 5-year-olds being enrolled in kindergartens, both public and private. In addition, 27 states presently support prekindergarten programs in the public schools (Mitchell, Seligson, & Marx, 1989).

Professionals in the field of early childhood education became concerned that, with this push for public school programs for 3- and 4-year-olds, control over the early childhood programs would no longer be in the hands of early childhood professionals. In 1986 the National Association for the Education of Young Children (NAEYC), the major national group representing the field of early childhood education, published a position statement, *Developmentally Appropriate Practice in Early Childhood Programs Serving Children from Birth through Age 8* (Bredekamp, 1986). This document includes position papers on developmentally appropriate practices for children of different age levels as well as additional material. The publication establishes guidelines for programs in early childhood education. It also contains examples of appropriate and inappropriate practices.

NAEYC's position statements have been widely disseminated. The term "developmentally appropriate" has become the one and only standard by which early childhood programs are judged. The basic statements within the first part of the document are validated through references to various publications on early childhood education. References to the professional literature are included in subsequent parts as well, but not to the same extent. The references, however, are not limited to studies of child development, but rather to the professional literature of early childhood eduction more broadly. Thus, one might question the validity of the *developmental* basis for these practices.

There have been criticisms of the guidelines established by NAEYC, as well as the use of developmental appropriateness as the sole criterion for judging educational programs for young children. Spodek (1991) suggests that the developmental dimension of a program is only one of three dimensions that need to be looked at. The other two include the cultural dimension and the knowledge dimension. The cultural dimension takes into consideration society's values and is ultimately a reflection of what we want children to be and become (Biber, 1984). The knowledge dimension relates to what we believe children need to know to get along in their present lives, as well as to function successfully in the future. While it is important to consider theories of child development in terms of the methods we use to teach young children, developmental theory alone does not provide guidance as to *what* should be taught.

Many educators are also concerned that the NAEYC position paper is further limiting diversity in early childhood education. By assuming consensus and focusing on a narrow definition of acceptable practice, the NAEYC document tends to inhibit discussion concerning approaches to early childhood education, rather than to promote it. Jipson (1991) suggests that issues regarding cultural aspects of early childhood curriculum are being ignored. *Developmentally Appropriate Practice* considers only one cultural view and orientation, without regard to cultural issues and other ways of knowing. Kessler (1991) finds that by focusing on child development theory, the NAEYC document obscures the political and philosophical issues involved in curriculum decisions. Finally, Walsh (1991) argues that the one view of development and learning presented in the position paper limits discussion of other recent ideas about how young children learn.

While matching educational programs to the developmental levels of children is certainly important, a concern voiced by Hunt (1961) three decades ago, there are other equally important concerns about programs. For example, the availability of programs that teach young children to combat various kinds of bias or to live in a peaceful society suggests that evaluating the goals of early childhood programs is as important as matching programs to developmental levels. Both of these elements need to be assessed in early childhood education, as does the effectiveness of each of these programs, with judgments made on the basis of the outcome data collected. Future development in early childhood education curriculum development and evaluation must consider all of these assessment areas.

CONCLUSIONS

The development of early childhood curriculum models has gone through several distinct phases. The first phase included the initial development of curriculum models. These models, including those developed by Owen and Froebel, were based on an intuitive view of the nature of childhood and children. They were also based on explicit assumptions about the nature of knowledge and how knowledge could be acquired by children.

The second phase can be characterized by the influence of the scientific knowledge about children's development and learning on early childhood education. Montessori drew her knowledge from anthropological studies of child development. McMillan was heavily influenced by physiological studies of development as well as by psychoanalysis. The reform kindergarten movement and the evolution of the nursery school model in America was influenced by a range of developmental theories, most prominent of which was the maturationist theories of Gesell and his followers.

In the third phase, evident in the creation of alternative early childhood curriculum models in the 1960s and 1970s, early childhood programs reflected a variety of developmental theories and programs goals. This phase might best be characterized by the idea of planned variations where a variety of different program models were conceived based on different assumptions about the nature of learning and development and different views of what knowledge is most worthwhile for children to acquire.

We might consider the current scene in early childhood education as representing a fourth phase. While curriculum development initiatives continue, there are no new curriculum models being developed. This change in curriculum development patterns may be the result of earlier assessments of models that indicated greater variation within a model than among models. Teachers tend not to remain consistent with a theory in their practice. They are influenced by elements within the school context that lead them to diverge from the theoretical position of any curriculum model. These influences include the management needs of classrooms and the requirements imposed by school systems that often establish goals and evaluate learning outside the model. Teachers are also prone to adopt practices that work in their classrooms regardless whether these practices are consistent with any accepted model.

There also seems to be less willingness in the field to accept alternative views of the nature of learning and development. Views of what knowledge is most worth knowing is generally held implicitly and is seldom evaluated. Rather, there seems to be an acceptance of a norm regarding the form and content of education for young children. This is most often articulated as "developmentally appropriate practices."

This approach is, however, being critcized. In addition, specific programs aimed at teaching particular content to young children or designed to educate particular populations of young children are being developed, and these programs are often considerably different than the norm.

It would seem likely that curriculum development will continue in the field of early childhood education, but that this development would serve to reform existing curriculum models and practices rather than replace them. It is hard to determine at this time exactly what these reforms will be. Certainly, the current critics will have their influences. The demands of public education on the field as it increasingly incorporates it into the public schools will influence curriculum development, as well. As early childhood teachers become better prepared, it is possible that they, too, will exercise greater influence, with reform coming from early childhood classrooms rather than from the work of educators and psychologists in universities. All this should make for a fertile field of early childhood curriculum development in the future.

References

Abt Associates. (1977). *Education as experimentation: A planned variation model.* Cambridge, MA.

Arizona Center for Educational Research and Development. (1983). *Tucson Early Education Model (TEEM).* Tucson, AZ.

Bereiter, C., & Englemann, S. (1966). *Teaching disadvantaged children in the preschool.* Englewood Cliffs, NJ: Prentice Hall.

Biber, B. (1984). *Early education and psychological development.* New Haven: Yale University Press.

Biber, B., Shapiro, E., & Wickens, D. (1971). *Promoting cognitive growth: A developmental-interactionist point of view.* Washington, DC: National Association for the Education of Young Children.

Bijou, S. W. (1977). Behavior analysis applied to early childhood education. In B. Spodek & H. J. Walberg (Eds.), *Early childhood education: Issues and insights* (pp. 138–156). Berkeley, CA: McCutcheon.

Bloom, B. (1964). *Stability and change in human characteristics.* New York: Wiley.

Boston Area Educators for Social Responsibility. (1983). *Perspectives: A teaching guide to concepts of peace.* Cambridge, MA: National Educators for Social Responsibility.

Bredekamp, S. (1986). *Developmentally appropriate practice in early childhood programs service children from birth through age 8.* Washington, DC: National Association for the Education of Young Children.

Burke, A. (1923). *A conduct curriculum for kindergarten and first grade.* New York: Scribner's.

Bushell, D. (1973). The behavior analysis classroom. In B. Spodek (ed.), *Early Childhood Education.* Englewood Cliffs, NJ: Prentice Hall.

Carlsson-Paige, N., & Levin, D. E. (1985). *Helping young children understand peace, war, and the nuclear threat.* Washington, DC: National Association for the Education of Young Children.

Center for Peace and Conflict Studies. (1988). *World order values bibliography: Books and audiovisual materials for children and youth.* ERIC Document Reproduction Service No. ED 266 922.

Cicarelli, V., et al. (1969). *The impact of Head Start: An evaluation of the effects of Head Start on children's cognitive and affective development.* Athens, OH: Westinghouse Learning Corp., Ohio University.

Consortium for Longitudinal Studies. (1983). *As the twig is bent.* Hillsdale, NJ: Erlbaum.

Copple, C., Sigel, I., & Saunders, R. (1979). *Educating the young thinker: Classroom strategies for cognitive growth.* New York: Van Nostrand.

Counts, G. S. (1932). *Dare the schools build a new social order.* New York: John Day.

Deasey, D. (1978). *Education under six.* New York: St. Martin's Press.

Derman-Sparks, L. (1989). *The Anti-Bias Curriculum.* Washington, DC: National Association for the Education of Young Children.

Englemann, S., & Osborn, J. (1976). *Distar language I: An instructional system.* Chicago: Science Research Associates.

Evans, E. (1982). Curriculum models and early childhood education. In B. Spodek (Ed.), *Handbook of research in early childhood education* (pp. 107–134). New York: Free Press.

Finkelstein, B. (Ed.). (1979). *Regulated children/liberated children: Education in psychohistoric perspective.* New York: Psychohistory Press.

Forman, G. E., & Fosnot, C. T. (1982). The use of Piaget's constructivism in early childhood education. In B. Spodek (Ed.), *Handbook of research in early childhood education* (pp. 185–211). New York: Free Press.

Forman, G. E., & Kuschner, D. (1984). *The child's construction of knowledge: Piaget for teaching children.* Washington, DC: National Association for the Education of Young Children.

Furth, H., & Wachs, H. (1974). *Thinking goes to school.* New York: Oxford University Press.

Gray, S., Klaus, R., Miller, J., & Forrester, B. (1966). *Before first grade.* New York: Teachers College Press.

Grenier, R. (1984). Peace education: A bibliography focusing on young children (2nd ed.). ERIC Document Reproduction Service No. ED 244 868.

Hale-Benson, J. (1982). *Black children: Their roots, culture, and learning styles.* Baltimore: Johns Hopkins University Press.

Hale-Benson, J. (1986). *Visions for children: African American early childhood education program.* ERIC Document Reproduction Service No. ED 303 269.

Harrington, M. (1962). *The other America: Poverty in the United States.* New York: Macmillan.

Harrison, J. (1968). *Utopianism and education: Robert Owen and the Owenites.* New York: Teachers College Press.

Hill, P. S. (1913). Second Report. *The kindergarten: Reports of the Committee of Nineteen on the theory and practice of the kindergarten.* New York: Houghton Mifflin.

Hohmann, M., Banet, B., & Weikart, D. P. (1979). *Young children in action: A manual for preschool educators.* Ypsilanti, MI: High/Scope Press.

House, E. R., Glass, G. V., McLean, L. D., & Walker, D. F. (1978). No simple answer: Critique of the Follow Through evaluation. *Harvard Educational Review, 48,* 128–160.

Hughes, M. M., Wetzel, R. J., & Henderson, R. W. (1973). The Tucson Educational Model. In B. Spodek (Ed.), *Early Childhood Education* (pp. 230–247). Englewood Cliffs, NJ: Prentice Hall.

Hunt, J. M. (1961). *Intelligence and experience.* New York: Ronald Press.

Jipson, J. (1991). Developmentally appropriate practice: Culture, curriculum, connections. *Early Education and Development, 2,* 120–136.

Kamii, C., & DeVries, R. (1977). Piaget for early education. In M. Day & R. Parker (Eds.), *The preschool in action: Exploring early childhood programs* (2nd ed., pp. 363–420). Boston: Allyn & Bacon.

Kessler, S. (1991). Early childhood education as development: Critique of the metaphor. *Early Education and Development, 2,* 137–157.

The kindergarten keys. (1980). Oklahoma City, OK: The Economy Company.

Kramer, R. (1988). *Maria Montessori: A biography.* Reading, MA: Addison-Wesley.

Lawton, J. (1987). The Ausubelian preschool classroom. In J. Roopnarine & J. Johnson (Eds.), *Approaches to early childhood eduction.* Columbus, OH: Merrill.

Lilley, I. (1967). *Friedrich Froebel: A selection from his writing.* Cambridge, England: Cambridge University Press.

Marion, M., & Stremmel, A. (1983). Teaching peace in the classroom. *Day Care and Early Education, 10*(3), 6–10.

McMillan, M. (1907). *Labour and childhood.* London: Swan, Sonnenschein.

McMillan, M. (1919). *The nursery school.* London: J. M. Dent.

McNamara, T. (1987). *A large school district's perspective on the structure controversy.* ERIC Document Reproduction Service, No. ED 281 289.

Miller, L., & Dyer, J. (1975). Four preschool programs: Their dimensions and effects. *Monographs of the Society for Research in Child Development, 40,* (5–6, Serial No. 162).

Mitchell, A., Seligson, M., & Marx, F. (1989). *Early childhood programs and the public schools: Beyond promise and practice.* Dover, MA: Auburn House.

Mitchell, L. S. (1921). *Here and now storybook.* New York: Dutton.

Montessori, M. (1964). *The Montessori method.* New York: Schocken.

Myers-Walls, J., & Fry-Miller, K. (1984). Nuclear war: Helping children overcome fears. *Young Children, 39*(4), 27–32.

North, A. (1979). Health services in Head Start. In Zigler & Valentine (Eds.), *Project Head Start: A legacy of the War on Poverty* (pp. 131–158). New York: Free Press.

Owen, R. (1857). *The life of Robert Owen, written by himself, Vol. 1.* London: Effingham Wilson.

Powell, D. R., & Sigal, I. E. (1991). Searches for validity in evaluating young children and early childhood programs. In B. Spodek & O. N. Saracho (Eds.), *Issues in early childhood curriculum: Yearbook in early childhood education, Vol. 2* (pp. 190–212). New York: Teachers College Press.

Pratt, C. (1924). *Experimental practice in city and country schools.* New York: Dutton.

Project Head Start. (n.d.) *Daily program I for a child development center.* Washington, DC: Office of Economic Opportunity.

Rivlin, A. M., & Timpane, P. M. (1975). *Planned variation in education.* Washington, DC: Brookings Institute.

Roopnarine, J., & Johnson, J. (1987). *Approaches to early childhood education.* Columbus, OH: Merrill.

Ross, C. (1979). Early skirmishes with poverty: The historical roots of Head Start. In Zigler & Valentine (Eds.), *Project Head Start: A legacy of the War on Poverty.* New York: Free Press.

Saracho, O. N., & Spodek, B. (1983). *Understanding the multicultural experience in childhood education.* Washington, DC: National Association for the Education of Young Children.

Schubert, W. (1986). *Curriculum: Perspective, paradigm, and possibility.* New York: Macmillan.

Schweinhart, L., Weikart, D., & Larner, M. (1986). Consequences of three preschool curriculum models through age 15. *Early Childhood Research Quarterly, 2*(3), 15–45.

Shepard, L. A. (1991). The influence of standardized tests on the early childhood curriculum, teachers, and children. In B. Spodek & O. N. Saracho (Eds.), *Issues in early childhood curriculum: Yearbook in early childhood education, Vol. 2* (pp. 166–169). New York: Teachers College Press.

Smith, M. S. (1975). Evaluation findings in Head Start Planned Variation. In A. Rivlin & P. M. Timpane (Eds.), *Planned variation in education* (pp. 101–112). Washington, DC: Brookings Institute.

Spodek, B. (1973). *Early childhood education*. Englewood Cliffs, NJ: Prentice-Hall.

Spodek, B. (1975). Open education: Romance or liberation. In B. Spodek & H. J. Walberg (Eds.), *Studies in open education* (pp. 3–12). New York: Agathon Press.

Spodek, B. (1991). Early childhood curriculum and cultural definitions of knowledge. In B. Spodek & O. N. Saracho (Eds.), *Issues in early childhood curriculum: Yearbook in early childhood education, Vol. 2* (pp. 1–20). New York: Teachers College Press.

Spodek, B., Saracho, O. N., & Lee, R. C. (1984). *Mainstreaming young children*. Belmont, CA: Wadsworth.

Steedman, C. (1990). *Childhood, culture and class in Britain: Margaret McMillan, 1860–1931*. London: Virago Press.

Strickland, C. E. (1982). Paths not taken: Seminal models of early childhood education in Jacksonian America. In B. Spodek (Ed.), *Handbook of research in early childhood education* (pp. 321–340). New York: Free Press.

Walsh, D. (1991). Extending the discourse on developmental appropriateness: A developmental perspective. *Early education and development, 2,* 109–119.

Warger, C. (Ed.). (1988). *A resource guide to public school early childhood programs*. Alexandria, VA: Association for Supervision and Curriculum Development.

Weber, E. (1969). *The kindergarten: Its encounter with educational thought in America*. New York: Teachers College Press.

Yawkey, T. D. (1987). Project P.I.A.G.E.T.—a holistic approach to early childhood bilingual education. In J. Roopnarine & J. Johnson (Eds.), *Approaches to early childhood education* (pp. 197–212). Columbus, OH: Merrill.

Zigler, E., & Berman, W. (1983). Discerning the future of early childhood intervention. *American Psychologist, 38,* 894–906.

·8·

THE ROLE OF PLAY IN EARLY CHILDHOOD DEVELOPMENT AND EDUCATION: ISSUES IN DEFINITION AND FUNCTION

A. D. *Pellegrini and Brenda Boyd*
UNIVERSITY OF GEORGIA

The role of children's play in their development and education is a topic of considerable interest, indications of which can be found at many levels. For example, its prominent role in academic research is evidenced by the inclusion of an outstanding chapter in the latest *Handbook of Child Psychology* (Rubin, Fein, & Vandenberg, 1983). Play is an almost hallowed concept for teachers of young children. More recently, however, a few scholars, notably P. K. Smith (1982, 1988) and Brian Sutton-Smith (1988), have raised serious questions concerning the definition of play and what role it plays in education and development.

Because of these equivocal conclusions, we think it is time to evaluate critically the meaning of play and its role in early development and education. In this chapter we will address definitional and functional aspects of play as they pertain to children from infancy through the primary grades. Because an excellent review of play already exists (Rubin et al., 1983) and because of the passage of nearly 10 years since its publication, we will try to minimize our overlap with it. Instead, we will try to supplement that paper, paying specific attention to research published after its publication and to educational implications of play research.

WHAT IS PLAY?

This may seem like a simple enough question, answerable by lay people and students of play alike (Smith & Vollstedt, 1985). Indeed, at a gross level most people can reliably differ-entiate certain forms of children's play from nonplay. Partially for this reason, some think that a formal definition of play is not necessary. However, the need for such a definition becomes more understandable when observers try to explicate what they mean by play and the fit between these attributes and examples of play and nonplay. Further, the need for detailed definitions is important in examinations of the developmental and educational functions of play (Martin & Caro, 1985; Smith & Cowie, 1988). In such ventures one must ask what, specifically, about play is responsible for educational and developmental effects. To document developmental and educational functions of play we must pair specific aspects of play, such as reciprocal role taking or nonliterality, with theoretically related outcome measures, such as perspective taking and writing, respectively. After all, different forms of play have many dimensions; these dimensions are often shared with other types of behavior not typically considered play. For example, social-dramatic play, considered to be the paradigm case of play for preschoolers (McCune-Nicholich & Fenson, 1984; Smith & Vollstedt, 1985), includes the following dimensions: verbalization, social interaction, conceptual conflict, and nonliterality. Teacher-led discussions often share the first 3, as well. Now, if these 3 dimensions (not the last dimension) turn out to be important mediators of developmental and educational status, that tells us something about play per se and about ways in which we should plan educational experiences for young children.

In trying to define play in this section, we will first examine its functional and structural dimensions, following the advice of Martin and Caro (1985) and Smith and Cowie (1988). Briefly,

A. D. Pellegrini acknowledges the support of the H. F. Guggenheim Foundation for supporting the work on this chapter.

functional definitions of behavior examine both proximal and distal consequences; for example, rough-and-tumble play (R & T) leads immediately into games for some elementary-school children (proximal consequence), whereas preschoolers' levels of object transformations predict writing in kindergarten (distal consequence). Structural definitions address the specific behaviors that are considered playful, for example, chase and "play face."

Although functional and structural definitions are commonplace in ethological studies of play (see especially Martin & Caro, 1985, and Fagen, 1981), none were proffered by Rubin et al. (1983), who defined play according to dispositional, contextual, and observable behavior dimensions. Further, the behavioral dimension of the Rubin et al. definition might be termed "behaviors by consequence," or a specific behavior or set of behaviors that have a specific consequence, such as functional or symbolic play. We will use the term *behavior* (differently than Rubin et al., 1983) to describe physical events, such as running, laughing, and hitting. We will, however, address each of Rubin et al.'s types of "play as observable behavior" in our discussion of play during the infancy, preschool, and primary-school periods, because they each represent the most common forms of play for each period.

Rubin et al.'s dispositional criteria will be examined as part of our attempt to define play from a multiple-criteria perspective. Lastly in this section, play will be defined in relation to exploration, a set of behaviors with which it is often confused.

Functional Dimensions

The function of a behavior and its definition are inextricably linked. This point has been repeatedly made by linguists (e.g., Sapir, 1925), anthropologists (e.g., Hymes & Cazden, 1980), and ethologists (e.g., Hinde, 1982). An example inspired by Sapir's work on phonemes conveys this point. In English the phoneme /1/ has 2 distinct phones, but is considered 1 functional unit. In Russian, on the other hand, each of the phones in /1/ has a distinct function. In short, definition, in this case of phonemes, is determined by function.

In this chapter *function* will be used to mean a beneficial consequence, rather than the stricter biological sense of adaptation (see Hinde, 1983, for a discussion of the meaning of *function*). Beneficial consequences of behavior can be established by 3 means: (1) through proximal and distal consequences of a behavior, (2) through a design-features argument, and (3) through experimental manipulation.

As noted above, consequences of play can be either proximal, as in the case of R & T leading directly into games for some children (Pellegrini, 1988), or distal, as in the case of symbolic play at year 1 predicting writing status at year 2 (Galda, Pellegrini, & Cox, 1989). These consequences are typically observed as part of naturally occurring behavior, not as results of experimental manipulation. To further complicate the picture, play can have either continuous or discontinuous consequences. The former case simply involves examining the relation between an aspect of play, such as reciprocal role taking, and a consequence, such as perspective taking. Identifying discontinuous consequences, which can be much more difficult, involves looking for relations between one aspect of play,

such as reciprocal role taking in preschool, and a dissimilar consequence, such as the ability to write persuasive text in third grade. (Both of these aspects involve perspective taking.)

Interestingly, the ethological literature has been concerned with the distal consequences of play—those consequences that play in childhood has for adulthood. Conversely, the child development and early childhood literature has been concerned, for the most part, with play's proximal consequences, though not in the pursuit of a definition of play per se. We will, however, examine those studies and attempt to derive a definition from them.

In order to establish proximal consequence, observations of *sequences* of behavior must be observed to determine the probability of specific consequences of play. (See Bakeman & Gottman, 1986, for an excellent discussion of the forms of sequential analysis necessary for this type of work.) Contemporaneous correlations between play and various outcome measures will not be considered under consequential criteria for the obvious reason that such work cannot differentiate antecedents from consequences. The most general examinations of this sort are typically embedded in the exploration/play literature (to be discussed in greater detail later). This research suggests that the play of preschoolers is followed by diverse exploration, or searching the environment for stimuli that are arousing. Research in this tradition defines play as a rather stable set of responses to stimuli, such as casual and easily distracted attention to objects and stereotyped actions, whereas exploration is seen as more deliberate and often stereotyped (Voss, 1987a, 1987b; Wohlwill, 1984). That children in these studies are often observed alone in laboratory settings, suggests that play has a solitary dimension. The transition from play to diverse exploration is continuous, rather than discontinuous. Indeed, some scholars (e.g., Hutt, 1966) have considered them to be one and the same.

Proximal consequences of 2 aspects of social play, parallel and R & T play, have also been examined. Parallel play is a situation where 2 children play in spatial proximity to but not with each other. Parten (1932) originally posited that parallel interaction was a stage in children's movement toward cooperative social play (a distal consequence). Bakeman and Brownlee (1980) tested the sequential probability of preschool children's parallel play being followed by group play (a proximal consequence), and found that parallel play led to group play at a probability greater than chance. This result suggests that parallel play may function, proximally, to give children opportunity to "size up" a group before entering it (Bakeman & Brownlee, 1980); thus, play can be observed either in groups or in individuals relative to groups. The parallel-to-group transition is likewise continuous in that parallel and group behaviors are both affiliative.

Children's R & T has provided reasonable sequential data for both elementary- and middle-school children. With American elementary-school children, Pellegrini (1988) found that the R & T of children sociometrically defined as popular (not rejected) lead to cooperative games, such as chase leading into tag. Conversely, the R & T of rejected children lead to aggression. Such observations suggest that popular children treat R & T as affiliative and cooperative behavior, whereas rejected children understand it as aggression. When differences in sociometric status are not considered—that is, when all children are pooled—we likewise find that R & T generally leads to games, not aggression (Pellegrini, 1989a). The middle-school data comes from Boulton and Smith (1989) in Sheffield, England. They, like Pellegrini (1989a), found that R & T did not lead to aggression. The only other consequence they examined, however, was non–R & T. They found that R & T led to non–R & T most frequently. Definitionally, we can still say that R & T is not a form of aggression for most children. The R & T–to–games transition is continuous to the extent that similar behaviors are used in both R & T and games.

Distal consequences can be inferred only from longitudinal studies. Interestingly, there is a paucity of longitudinal play research; this is an interesting oversight considering the "hallowed" status bestowed on play. Some of the longitudinal work is related to the proximal measures discussed above, specifically parallel play and R & T. Parten (1932) suggested that parallel play is a stage traveled by children en route to cooperative interaction. Smith (1978) examined the progression of preschoolers' play from solitary and parallel to group play across a 9-month period and found that children generally moved from solitary to group play, not from parallel to group. Consequently, parallel play does not seem to be a stage, but a strategy, as pointed out above.

Distal consequences of parallel play, as well as other forms of play, was also examined longitudinally by Rubin and Daniels-Beirness (1983). Using the nested play matrices of Smilansky (1968) and Parten (1932), these researchers found that kindergarten children's parallel-dramatic play, as well as solitary-functional, solitary-exploratory, and R & T play, were *negative* predictors of sociometric status in first grade. Definitionally, these results suggest that certain forms of nonsocial play have negative consequences for popularity. These relations, with the exception of the R & T data, suggest a continuous developmental function to the extent that both antecedent and outcome measures are not affiliative. The inconsistency between these R & T findings and those reviewed earlier could be due to a number of factors, such as age differences in samples, non-differentiation of children's sociometric status or the confounding of R & T and aggression.

Distal consequences of preschool children's symbolic play have also been examined by Pellegrini and colleagues (Galda et al., 1989; Pellegrini & Galda, 1991). In this 2-year longitudinal study, the researchers considered consequences of preschoolers' object-dependent play transformations (i.e., object transformations) and transformations independent of objects (i.e., ideational transformations) for early reading and writing. Analyses, in which children's receptive vocabulary was controlled, indicated that both object and ideational transformations had a positive consequence for early writing, though not for reading. This is a case, unlike the consequences reported earlier, of discontinuous development whereby a set of play behaviors predicts conventional writing status. It is probably the case that the facility with symbolization gained/practiced in play was transformed into a socially agreed-upon symbol system, writing.

Play does seem to have both proximal and distal consequences. Most of these consequences, however, seem to be continuous rather than discontinuous. These relations are represented in Table 8–1.

TABLE 8–1. Continuous Consequences of Play

Proximal
    Diverse exploration
    Social play and games
    Social problem solving
Distal
    Perspective taking
    Writing
    Low *and* high social affiliation

Function Can Also Be Deduced from Design Features. Design-features arguments explicate similarities between specific aspects of play and related outcome measures, such as reciprocal role taking and perspective taking. Design-features arguments, as will be discussed in the next section, are most convincing when they are combined with experimentation.

Function Can Also Be Deduced from Experimentation. Experimentation and longitudinal designs are obviously the most convincing avenues to establish causality. This approach was originally used in the animal literature whereby animals were *deprived* of opportunities to play either through social isolation or opportunities to play with toys (e.g., Harlow & Harlow, 1962; Caro, 1980, respectively) or through drugs (Einon, Morgan, & Kibbler, 1978). An interesting "deprivation experiment" with children, however, was carried out by Smith and Hagan (1980), in which preschool children were "deprived" of the opportunity for exercise play. In this innovative experiment, children were observed on the playground of their preschool for incidence of exercise play after periods of either short (i.e., 30 minutes of nonvigorous activity in their regular preschool classrooms) or long (i.e., 90 minutes in their regular preschool classrooms) confinement. Results revealed that exercise play increases as a function of previous confinement and that exercise play on the playground decreased as function of time. These results were replicated with primary-school children (Pellegrini & Huberty, in press). These results, which have important implications for the role of recess in our schools (see Pellegrini, 1989c), seemingly support a surplus energy theory (i.e., children play to blow off steam). However, it seems more reasonable and current to consider these findings in the context of arousal theory. Children may have played in the described ways for arousal. Their need for novelty increased with confinement in the classroom and with time on the playground.

The more typical experimental effects of play on children usually involve the manipulation of provision to play, not deprivation. This is most convincingly done, we think, when specific design features of play are manipulated so as to determine specific correspondent effects. The seminal, and often cited, experiments of Smilansky (1968) and Saltz, Dixon, and Johnson (1977) are excellent examples of this genre of research design, despite the confounding effects of tuition (Pellegrini, 1984; Rubin et al., 1983; Silvern, Taylor, Williamson, Surbeck, & Kelley, 1986; Smith & Syddall, 1978; Williamson & Silvern, 1990). When such confounds are controlled there are questionable effects of fantasy play per se on various dimensions of preschool and primary-school children's cognitive status. That is, children's use of language to reconstruct play stories and conceptual conflict with peers seems to contribute to children's story comprehension, whereas "play" makes a minimal contribution (Pellegrini, 1984; Williamson & Silvern, 1991).

Convincing experimental data also come from examinations of the effects of play on preschool children's perspective-taking status (Burns & Brainerd, 1979; Smith & Syddall, 1978). The reciprocal role taking and conceptual conflict dimensions of play are probably responsible for these relations. So, it may be that aspects of peer interaction typifying play (e.g., reciprocal role taking, verbal encoding, conceptual conflict resolution) have important implications for children's perspective taking.

In summary, experimental consequences of play are most strongly documented in the case of social competence, not in more traditional areas of cognition. Indeed, experimental, design-features, and consequential studies all point in this direction. However, these 2 literatures may converge. It may be, for example, that the social processes responsible for the gains in social competence also play an important role in the cognitive area. What is needed to provide a more definitive answer, however, is research that combines approaches by experimentally manipulating relevant design features on proximal and distal measures of cognition and social competence. For example, what is the effect of increased opportunities for preschoolers to engage in symbolic play on their third-grade reading and writing status? Further, how would increased opportunities to engage in R & T affect perspective taking? It may be that the social skills gained in play translate into measures of cognition. In other words, cognition may be rooted in social interaction.

Structural Dimensions

Structural definitions of play, like design-feature definitions, use physical appearances and features of behavior (Martin & Caro, 1985). Structural definitions, however, attempt to differentiate play from nonplay; they do not relate play behaviors to other outcome measures. Common structural dimensions of play include: play face (e.g., laughing), exaggerated movements (e.g., giant steps), exaggerated voice (e.g., deep, adult-like voice), and reciprocal roles (e.g., alternating between bully and victim).

Pretend play has been defined structurally, based on Piaget's (1962) components, in Fein (1981) and Rubin et al. (1983) to include (1) decontextualized behavior (i.e., taking a familiar behavior, such as eating movements, out of context, such as eating invisible food; (2) self-other relationships (i.e., children treat themselves, first, and then other objects as fantastic, such as enacting mother-child roles with a doll); (3) substitute objects (children invest realistic objects, such as dolls, first, with fantasy characteristics, and then do not rely on objects to make transformations, such as declaring a space to be a doctor's office); and (4) sequential combinations (i.e., where play episodes move from a single enactment, such as feeding a doll, into embedded themes, such as feeding a doll, then, bathing it, reclothing it, and putting it to bed). Research into these components of pretense documents the progression toward greater differentiation of the components (see Rubin et al., 1983), but has not addressed the definitional aspects of these components.

Although such structural definitions have intuitive appeal, in that a list of observable behaviors exist, they are problematic. First and foremost, structural aspects of play may also exist in nonplay categories; for example, play face can be observed in many nonplay areas, such as an adult reading a ridiculous claim of scientific fact; exaggerated movements are often observed in real aggression, without play face. Second, and relatedly, no one structural dimension distinguishes play from nonplay. Consequently, a polythetic definition of play, or defining play according to numerous criteria, seems most plausible. Although even this is problematic, it may be a useful way in which observers can agree, among themselves, on what "play" is.

Multiple Criteria of Play

Defining play according to multiple criteria assumes that behaviors containing more of the hypothesized components should be considered more playful than those with fewer components. Further, certain components may be more important than others in discriminating play from nonplay. Krasnor and Pepler (1980) have recently conceptualized a definition of play utilizing multiple criteria. The original model of play contained the following 4 criteria: flexibility, positive affect, intrinsic motivation, and nonliterality. The newer definition includes the following criteria: nonliterality, intrinsic motivation, attention to means, "What can I do with it?" vs. "What can it do?", freedom from external rules, and active engagement. Rubin et al. (1983) argued that behaviors should be considered more or less play, not as play or nonplay, according to the number of criteria met. The assumptions behind this definition for *preschool* children's play were tested and supported by Smith and Vollstedt (1985). In this study nonliterality was the most potent criterion, especially when combined with either positive affect or flexibility, whereas intrinsic motivation was not associated with play, and the means/end distinction was minimally associated. The importance of nonliterality in defining play in this study was probably an artifact of the age of the sample: The paradigm case of play among preschool children is fantasy play, in which nonliterality is crucial. Further research, utilizing methods similar to those of Smith and Vollstedt, should be directed at other periods of childhood.

This method has been applied to preschool (Smith & Boulton, 1990), elementary-school (Pellegrini, 1988), and middle-school (Aston & Smith, 1987) children's R & T and the ways in which it differs from aggression. In viewing videotapes of R & T and aggressive behaviors, preschool children can reliably differentiate between the two (Smith & Lewis, 1985); popular elementary-school children differentiate better than do rejected children (Pellegrini, 1988). Further, when asked to generate criteria for each form of behavior, children generally describe presence or absence of physical characteristics of actions, such as making physical contact with a blow and not making contact, respectively. Immediate consequence of the behaviors was also important in their discrimination; children stay together after an R & T bout but separate after aggression. Like criteria for fantasy, positive affect differentiated R & T from aggression, which was marked by negative affect. Like other forms of play, R & T can be most reliably defined and differentiated from other behaviors when it is defined along many dimensions; any 1 aspect, like positive affect or affiliation, is also characteristic of other, nonplay, behaviors.

To conclude this section, it seems, first, that explicit definitions of play would greatly benefit the research effort. Second, simple definitions of play should be avoided, because they usually do not exclude other forms of behavior. For these reasons, the multiple-criteria approach to defining play may be most useful for observers trying to reliably differentiate between behaviors that are more or less playful. Further research is needed, particularly on distal and discontinuous consequences of play. This research should go beyond the fertile and well-cultivated ground of the preschool period.

Exploration and Play

A discussion of exploration and play is a logical extension of definitional issues: For conscious or less-than-conscious reasons, exploration and play are often not differentiated. Further, as will be explicated in this section, exploration precedes play both microgenetically and ontogenetically. Briefly, exploration is a set of deliberate, information-gathering behaviors, whereas play is more casual and diverse (Wohlwill, 1984). Differentiation between play and exploration is particularly difficult with infants (see Wohlwill, 1984, for a discussion).

Wohlwill (1984) has proffered a useful model to differentiate play and exploration along 3 dimensions: stereotypy, deployment of attention, and affective state. Exploration is characterized by stereotyped behaviors, or behaviors that do not vary markedly across situations, such as visual and tactile inspection. Play, on the other hand, involves numerous behavioral forms that are often exaggerated and recombined in novel ways. Second, and based on the important work of Corrine Hutt (1966), deployment of attention is more deliberate in exploration than in play. After all, information is gathered in the former; therefore, children are less easily distracted than in play. Children do not look at props as much or as intently in play as in exploration; consequently, they are more easily distracted from objects in play than in exploration. The higher attention rate is also evidenced by the more variable heart rate in exploration, compared to play (Hughes & Hutt, 1979). Lastly, exploration is characterized by neutral or slightly negative affect, whereas play is positive. These distinctions are summarized in Table 8–2.

These differences between exploration and play are not meant to imply that the two are unrelated. Indeed, they are closely interrelated microgenetically and ontogenetically (Voss, 1987a, 1987b; Wohlwill, 1984). At the microgenetic level, or as individual events unfold temporally, when children are presented with a novel stimulus, they first explore it, then play with it. Thus, exploration temporally precedes play. In Wohlwill's study (1984), exploration led to play or affective exploration. After children became bored with playing, or with affective exploration, they then moved into diverse exploration. In this form of exploration, children explored the larger environment, that is, beyond the single stimulus level, because they sought arousal.

Ontogenetically, or as individuals develop across the life span, exploration also precedes play, in terms of the amount of time spent exploring or playing with an object (Belsky & Most, 1981; Voss, 1987a, 1987b). Exploration is dominant in infancy, strikes a balance with play in toddlerhood, and is replaced by play during the preschool period.

In conclusion, exploration involves gaining information, whereas play involves practicing and recombining that information. Children's behavior can be reliably categorized as play or exploration. There are mediating effects due to the age of the child and the stimuli with which they interact. Although this dichotomy between play and exploration may be too simplistic (they are, after all, highly interrelated) we should differentiate between the 2 behaviors. If our future research shows that such a distinction is unwarranted, then the distinction can be eliminated. To date, we have not paid close enough attention to the 2 behaviors to make that decision. The mediating variables may be particularly important in educational and assessment contexts, as pointed out by Rubin et al. (1983). Children's responses are affected, not only by their levels of competence, but also by the props with which they interact. For example, when we assess kindergarten children's cognitive or social status by observing the level of their play, they appear to be more competent (e.g., ideational transformations) with familiar than with unfamiliar props. This issue is of particular concern when assessing culturally different children, who have limited experience with props typically used in playroom assessment. Their seemingly low-level fantasy play could reflect a familiarization period with the stimuli.

PLAY THROUGH CHILDHOOD

In this section we will describe the forms of play enacted from infancy through the primary-school period. Such normative information is necessary if play-oriented curricula are to be developmentally appropriate. More specifically, common forms of play for each period of childhood should be the starting point for a corresponding play curriculum. This assumption is based on the notion that a direct positive relation should exist between resources allocated to an activity, in this case, time and energy, and any potential outcome: The more time and energy expended, the larger the benefits (Martin & Caro, 1985). For example, fantasy play is most commonly observed during the preschool period and declines during the primary-school years. It seems, then, that fantasy play may be a more appropriate instructional strategy for preschoolers than for fourth-graders (see Williamson & Silvern, 1990, for an interesting counter-case to this argument). That is not to say that different forms of play do not co-occur within periods. Indeed they do, and children should be given opportunities to engage in those forms of play as well. It may be that the most common form of play for a period is also the most effective instructional strategy for that period. This is an empirical question, of educational and developmental importance, that begs to be answered.

TABLE 8–2. Distinctions Between Exploration and Play

	Exploration	Play
Stereotypy	Stereotyped behavior	Variable behavior
Attention	Deliberate	Casual
Affect	Neutral or negative	Positive

The organization of this section is such that the *most common forms of play* of infancy, preschool, and primary-school children will be described. Additionally, *antecedent factors* for these forms of play, such as infants' attachment status or preschoolers' gender, will be outlined, as will the *consequences* of these behaviors. For example, a consequence of primary-school children's R & T is social affiliation. Children's constructive activities will not be reviewed in this chapter because they do not constitute play in the sense used here. From a Piagetian perspective, construction is more accommodative than assimilative and it, generally, does not vary with the age of the preschool child (see Smith, Takhvar, Gore, & Volstedt, 1986).

Infancy: Exploration

Infants—that is, children from birth to approximately 2 years of age—commonly engage in exploration behaviors. Although not play as defined earlier, exploration is an important precursor to play. In the literature, however, it is often not distinguished from play. In an attempt to integrate the play and exploration literatures, exploration will be examined here. Infants spend most of their time exploring their environment (Belsky & Most, 1981; O'Connell & Bretherton, 1984; Voss, 1987a, 1987b). Exploration initially involves single objects, until children are about 9 months old, and then multiple objects, until about 18 months old. Combinations of 2 objects, that is, putting 2 objects together, is rather uncommon during this period (Rubin et al., 1983). Where combinatory acts are observed, they tend to follow, within the same observation period, children's exploration of single objects (O'Connell & Bretherton, 1984).

Exploration can be solitary or social, with the latter typically involving a parent or other adult. Infants' exploration is more complex in the adult context than in the solitary context, to the extent that they exhibit more diverse and combinatorial behaviors in the former (O'Connell & Bretherton, 1984). These results are consistent with Vygotsky's (1978) notion of the social origins of cognition, whereby children's thought is a result of their interaction with a more competent other. Adults structure, or *scaffold* (Bruner, 1975), children's interactions so as to facilitate their competence at a higher level than is possible alone. Infants, it seems, attend to those parental suggestions relevant to tasks that they are in the process of mastering and ignore comments relevant to skills already mastered or beyond their capabilities (O'Connell & Bretherton, 1984).

The extent to which adults serve this scaffolding function for infants should of course vary in relation to the quality of their relationship, *an antecedent factor affecting exploration.* A common, as well as a valid, indicator of parent-child relations is attachment status, as defined by interactions in the Ainsworth Strange Situation (Ainsworth, Blehar, Waters, & Wall, 1978) or in the correlated Q-sort methodology (Waters & Deane, 1985). Coordinated interaction around objects between adult and infant should reflect a relationship in which the participants' interactions are also coordinated. Securely attached infants, compared to anxiously attached infants, are more successful at *initiating* certain types of interaction around toys, such as toy exchanges, because their mothers are responsive to them

(Roggman & Langlois, 1987). Further, the tenor of the interactions of securely attached infants is more positive, involving, for example, more positive tone and less distressed infant vocalizations (Roggman & Langlois, 1987). The nature of the attachment relationship, then, is an important antecedent of infant exploration. Securely attached children are more likely than anxiously attached children to explore and gather information in their environments because they have a safe base from which to explore their world. This secure base further results in securely attached children engaging in longer and more complex forms of fantasy (Slade, 1987a, 1987b). This latter point will be explicated in the section, "Childhood: Fantasy."

Other factors also affect the ways in which infants explore objects. These include the temperament of the infant (e.g., Wohlwill, 1984); the fit between the infant's temperament and that of the playmate (e.g., Thomas & Chess, 1977); gender of child and playmate (Power & Parke, 1982); and the props around which they interact (e.g., Wohlwill, 1984). Of course, these mediators of play may have independent effects, but it is more likely that they have interactive effects; for example, fathers play with their sons differently around blocks than they do with their daughters around the same props.

Consequences of infants' exploration, as noted above, are increased knowledge of the objects being explored (Hutt, 1966), boredom with one object and corresponding motivation to play with that object (Belsky & Most, 1981), and then to search the larger environment for other objects to explore (Wohlwill, 1984). In short, exploration results in infants coming to know their environment, mastering the methods used in exploration, and practicing novel recombinations of that knowledge and those methods.

Social learning may be another consequence of prop-related exploration for young children. It is well documented that parents provide male and female infants with gender-appropriate toys (Rheingold & Cook, 1975). Further, fathers tend to use toys less when interacting with infant sons than with infant daughters; the interaction between fathers and sons is likewise more physically vigorous than between fathers and daughters (Power & Parke, 1982). These antecedent conditions, it is argued, result in children developing gender-stereotyped toy and play preferences. These preferences then, the argument goes, predispose children to play in gender-segregated groups. Play with peers in these groups then further reinforces gender-stereotyped behavior (see Maccoby & Jacklin, 1987, and Maccoby, 1986, for evidence on this line of reasoning).

Childhood: Fantasy

Children begin to engage in fantasy during the second year of life. Like other forms of play, fantasy play follows an inverted-U developmental function, increasing in frequency of occurrence for the next 3 to 4 years and then declining (Fein, 1981). Interestingly, the frequency of occurrence of fantasy, relative to other forms of play, is rather limited: 10 to 17% for preschoolers and 33% for kindergarten children (Fein, 1981). This statistic is interesting for at least 2 reasons. First, it suggests that different forms of play co-occur within developmental periods. Second, the relatively low frequency of fantasy should raise questions about its function. That is, as teachers of young children and researchers, we could ask why it is that fantasy play is considered so important in children's education and development when it accounts for such a limited portion of their behavior. Of course, it may be that the research contexts giving rise to these statistics do not encourage fantasy play, but the question is still worth consideration.

Fantasy play can generally be defined as nonliteral activity, or activity where one thing represents something else. Further, fantasy can be social (with an adult or peer) or solitary. Earlier in this chapter, in the section, "Structural Dimensions," we noted that fantasy had the following structural components: self-other relations, decontextualized behavior, substitute objects, and sequential combinations (Fein, 1981; Rubin et al., 1983). These components are thoroughly treated by Fein (1981) and by Rubin et al. (1983); the interested reader is referred to those sources. Suffice it to say here that self-other relations move from self-referenced (e.g., a 1-year-old child drinks an imaginary cup of milk) to other referenced (a $1\frac{1}{2}$-year-old child gives his doll an imaginary drink), and that these acts develop from initially independent forms to integrated themes (Wolf & Grollman, 1980). Decontextualized behavior relates directly to the nonliteral dimension of play. A behavior is decontextualized when it is removed from its appropriate context—for example, a child might construct a nonliteral reenactment of a tea party.

Children frequently use substitute objects (one thing substituted for another) in fantasy play. When children are between $1\frac{1}{2}$ and 2 years of age, substitutions are dependent upon realistic props, for example, a doll. Children progress from such transformations to using less realistic props (both cases of object transformations) and then to using no props at all, for example, rocking an invisible baby and proclaiming, "She's tired." Within this most abstract level of substitutions (i.e., ideational transformations) are included role and situation transformations, in which children, mainly through the use of language, transform their roles and those of their peers and situations from the real to the fantastic (Garvey, 1984, 1990; McLoyd, 1980; Pellegrini, 1987; Wolf & Grollman, 1980). Although 3-year-olds are very capable of making ideational transformations (McLoyd, 1980; Pellegrini, 1987), we have argued that children must use explicit language in order to convey the meaning of ideational transformations to their peers. Because of the lack of correspondence between the symbol and its referent, meaning cannot be conveyed without such explication. For example, how is a child to know that his friend's grimacing and walking in long strides signifies a transformation into a soldier unless the "soldier" conveys it verbally?

Sequential combinations involve moving from single, unrelated acts of fantasy to interrelated series of acts. Wolf and Grollman (1980) have developed a continuum outlining this process. Their research suggests that children's play episodes move from single, unrelated schemes to well-integrated, narrative-like themes. As in the case of object substitutions, the ability to generate an integrated play theme is dependent upon children's ability to use language to encode the theme.

Children's ability to engage in fantasy play is *affected* by a number of contextual factors, such as socioeconomic status, gender, and group composition. The cultural-ecological theory of Bronfenbrenner (1979) is useful in describing these rela-

tions. According to this model, children's play, like other dimensions of their behavior, is affected at the microsystem level by toys or play partners; these microsystems are further affected by the more general macro- and exosystems in which they are embedded. Our discussion will begin with the exosystem and move to the microsystem.

The effects of 2 dimensions of the exosystem (school and public policy toward play and socioeconomic effects) on play will be discussed. First, the attitudes of the public at large and school personnel, specifically, have an important impact on children's fantasy play. At the level of preschool policy, the role of fantasy play for preschoolers seems, for the moment at least, well established. Slogans such as "Play is children's work," the NAEYC (National Association for the Education of Young Children, 1988) guidelines for developmentally appropriate curricula, and the general "play ethos" (Smith, 1988) suggests that play, generally, and fantasy, specifically, is important for preschoolers. Consequently, home and school settings try to encourage, or at least give lip service to the importance of, fantasy play for preschool children's education and development. This encouragement may come in the form of providing time, materials, and space for fantasy, as well as allowing children to engage in the fantasy themes of their choice. The recent debate over the "appropriateness" of children's fantasy with war toys and play guns is relevant to this issue regarding choice of fantasy theme (see Connor, 1989; Smith & Costablie, in press; Watson, in press; Sutton-Smith, 1988, for provocative discussions).

The play ethos seems more in line with preschool education than with kindergarten and primary-school education. Kindergarten classrooms generally are more similar to primary schools than they are to preschools. For example, retention exists in kindergarten, but not in preschool; there is probably less time per day allocated for free play in kindergarten than in preschool; likewise, the role of outdoor play is not often questioned by preschool educators or parents of preschoolers, but the legitimacy of recess in public kindergartens is seriously debated (Pellegrini, 1989b; Pellegrini & Huberty, in press). In short, children's opportunities to play and the forms of play (when it is permitted) differ according to school policy.

Socioeconomic status (SES), an aspect of the *exosystem,* has a long and interesting history of affecting preschool and kindergarten children's fantasy play. Indeed, the seminal studies of children's fantasy are studies of SES and fantasy (Smilansky, 1968; Saltz et al., 1977). The impetus for studies in this genre came from Smilansky (1968) who suggested, without the presentation of quantitative evidence, that the fantasy of lower-SES Israeli children was less frequent and less diverse than that of their middle-class counterparts. This suggestion stimulated numerous studies examining class differences in play, as well as other aspects of child development and educational attainment (see McLoyd, 1982, and Ogbu, 1981, 1988, for interesting discussions of this type of research). These studies, discussed in Rubin et al. (1983), generally concluded, like Smilansky, that the fantasy play of lower-SES preschool and kindergarten children was less complex, frequent, and varied than that of middle-class children.

McLoyd's (1982) concise critique of these studies, however, raises serious questions regarding their results. She points out first, and most importantly, that economic class and race are typically confounded. The ethnographic work of Heath (1983), among others, illustrates the different ways in which low-SES black and white children interact with parents and peers; thus, there is a definite need to separate race and economic status.

A second problem with the extant play literature concerns the failure to control classroom and school variables. As will be explained later in this section, children's play, both verbal and nonverbal, is extremely sensitive to classroom variables, such as teacher presence, type of peer-group configuration, types of toys, and so so. According to McLoyd (1982), most of the studies in the literature have been observations of children's free play in classrooms. Consequently, observed differences may have been due to either class or classroom variables. Relatedly, experimental studies that manipulate children's play with toys do not always circumvent this problem. As Rubin et al. (1983) have suggested, the toys in these experimental playrooms, and indeed the playrooms themselves, are more familiar to mainstream-culture children than to non-mainstream children. As a consequence, non–mainstream culture children, compared to their mainstream counterparts, may spend *more time* exploring toys and the environment and *less time* engaging in symbolic play. Researchers, then, have often drawn the spurious conclusion that the fantasy play of these children is deficient.

To conclude this discussion of exosystem antecedents of fantasy, we can say that the findings of class differences are fraught with methodological problems that must be adequately addressed. Further, the basic assumption driving most of the race comparisons is that black children are cognitively deficient and need remediation. We should assume no difference—that is, the null hypothesis—until differences are clearly illustrated. To date these differences have not been unequivocally presented.

Microsystem-level variables are also related to children's play. In this section we will outline ways in which mother-child relationships and specific aspects of classrooms and playgrounds relate to and affect children's fantasy play. An important consideration here is the way in which different levels of contexts are embedded in other levels. Similarly, the microsystem is embedded in larger macro- and exosystems. An example of this embeddedness was provided in the discussion of SES: Non–mainstream culture children play with props differentially, depending on familiarity. The larger influences should be kept in mind when reading this discussion, in that the research reported here was conducted, for the most part, in university lab school classrooms and experimental playrooms.

In the previous section, "Infancy: Exploration," we noted that the quality of the child's attachment to his/her mother relates to the ways in which the child explores the environment. There are also relations between attachment status and toddlers' symbolic play, in that, at 20 months, securely attached children engage in longer and more complex symbolic play bouts than do anxiously attached children (Slade, 1987a). These results are consistent with a number of theories. First, like the explanation given earlier for exploration, securely attached children may be better able to engage in symbolic play because they are less concerned with mother's emotional and physical availability (Belsky, Garduque, & Hrncir, 1984; Main, 1983;

Slade, 1987a, 1987b). Second, following Werner and Kaplan (1952) and Vygotsky (1978), the origins of symbolization may lie in the dyadic interaction of mothers and young children. Consistent with Vygotsky (1978), mothers' actual involvement in children's play episodes seems to be a particularly important dimension of the interactive process (Slade, 1987a).

Regarding studies at another microsystem level, the preschool classroom, research strategies might involve (1) observing children in their classrooms and describing variation in children's play with different toys and with different social-group compositions; or (2) taking children into an experimental playroom and manipulating exposure to props and peers. We will discuss 2 sets of studies. In a study of 3- and 4-year-olds' play in their university preschool classrooms, Pellegrini (1984d) found that props and group composition were related to children's fantasy. Specifically, in art areas, 3-year-olds engaged in fantasy, whereas 4-year-olds were exploratory with the materials. In both the dramatic and block-play areas, children engaged in fantasy play, especially when they had peers in the latter area. Of course, this latter finding could be due to the fact that children's fantasy in group contexts is easier to observe in that language is used; in solitary contexts, fantasy may be occurring though not readily observable, because children talk less frequently in nonsocial than in social settings (Vygotsky, 1962).

Adult presence in play areas was also related to fantasy for each group. For both groups, adult presence was *negatively* related to fantasy, whereas peer presence was positively related. Although these results were not replicated with a group of similar children (Pellegrini & Perlmutter, 1989), the results are important in that they illustrate the relationship between social groupings and play. Indeed, this is one reason for experimentally manipulating or controlling group composition. That is, in naturalistic studies, researchers measure not only the relations between props and play behavior, but also the relations among props, group composition, and self-selection into different contexts.

All problems are not solved, however, by moving from the classroom into the laboratory. Experiments should be ecologically valid in that similar, or the same, children used in classroom observations should also be used in experimental analogues of classrooms; further, the demand characteristics of the experiment should be the same as those in the classroom (Bronfenbrenner, 1979). In conducting a study that met the criteria for ecological validity, Pellegrini and Perlmutter (1989) found, not surprisingly, that more fantasy was observed when preschoolers played with doctor props than when they played with blocks. More interesting, however, was the interaction among age, props, and gender composition of the groups. Pellegrini and Perlmutter found that, with age (i.e., 3-, 4-, and 5-years of age), children's play conformed to gender-role stereotypes. For example, in mixed-gender dyads, boys were more dominant than girls in terms of initiating fantasy topics and issuing commands, with both male-preferred and gender-neutral props. Gender socialization can certainly be considered an exosystem variable that affects play at the microsystem level. An interesting outcome of these findings (i.e., children's play behaviors vary according to age, gender, props, and group composition) is that context seems to be defined differently by children at different periods. For example, a block's context for girls would have different meaning, in terms of demand characteristics, at 3 years of age than at 5 years of age. Context, then, is not a unidirectional force of the environment on children; it is a transaction between children and their environment.

Whereas the previously described studies examined fantasy at a gross level, in terms of its being dramatic, constructive, or functional, other research has examined the extent to which play props affect specific aspects of verbalized fantasy, object substitution, and sequential combinations. Regarding object substitution, it seems that, by 4 years of age, children are quite capable of making ideational transformations; indeed, almost half of their transformations take this form (Fein, 1981; McLoyd, 1980; Pellegrini, 1987). This may explain why functionally ambiguous (e.g., blocks and Styrofoam shapes) and functionally explicit (e.g., doctor kits) have been equally successful in eliciting ideational transformation.

When we look at children's ability to weave these individual transformations into a theme (i.e., the ability to make sequential combinations) we also find prop effects during the preschool period. Generally, thematically related sequences become more integrated across the preschool period, but they are still rather fragmented and short (Pellegrini, 1985a; Wolf & Grollman, 1980). Children also seem to have a more difficult time generating integrated themes around functionally ambiguous props than they do around explicit props (Pellegrini, 1987). It may be that children at this age expend most of their cognitive resources on verbally encoding individual transformations and, consequently, have fewer resources left to verbally integrate these transformations.

Children also engage in fantasy on the playground (see Frost & Sanderlin, 1985, for a collection of articles on this topic). Boys generally choose to play outdoors more than girls do and, correspondingly, exhibit more complex behavior while outdoors (Campbell & Frost, 1985; Harper & Sanders, 1975; Henninger, 1985; Lever, 1975–1976). So the "effects" of playground variables may be mediated by gender. That aside, 7-year-old children engage in more fantasy play on creative playgrounds (e.g., climbing structures, swings, and a houselike structure) than on traditional playgrounds (e.g., seesaws, swings, slides) (Campbell & Frost, 1985).

To conclude, we have seen the ways in which different levels of context affect the type and frequency of children's fantasy play. Context is conceptualized as a transaction between children and their environments. These findings are important in designing preschool environments and in evaluating the play research literature.

In this final discussion regarding children's fantasy play, we will address some of the *consequences* of fantasy play. Some of the consequences of fantasy were discussed above in our definition of fantasy. Consequence, as noted above, can be deduced by specific temporal relations between fantasy and outcome measures. That is, play is antecedent to some consequence. Longitudinal or experimental manipulations are necessary, then, to make causal inferences. In this discussion we will review selected longitudinal and experimental studies that have been conducted after Rubin et al. (1983). In the first series of studies to be reviewed, we will discuss relations between fantasy

and language and literacy (see Pellegrini, 1985b, for a critical review of the play, language, and literacy issue.) Next, studies that make causal attributions about fantasy in relation to creativity and problem solving will be presented.

As noted earlier, there is a paucity of longitudinal research in children's play. Again, this is very surprising in light of the high interest in the study of play. The longitudinal work of Bates and colleagues (e.g., Bates, 1979; Shore, O'Connell, & Bates, 1986), Heath (1985), Galda et al. (1989), and Pellegrini and Galda (1991) are exceptions. The work of Bates and colleagues follows a Piagetian and Wernerian tradition that was empirically explored initially by Nicholich (1977): Structural dimensions of symbolic play were thought to provide the basis for the production of similar linguistic structure. The longitudinal work of Shore et al. (1986) further suggests that symbolic play and language production co-occur at 20 months, but not at 28 months. As Fein (1979) suggests, it may be more fruitful to examine relations between fantasy and language comprehension, because Piagetian and Vygotskiian theories stress the meaning or control functions of language, rather than the production function. Although there is contemporaneous correlation support for the relation between fantasy and language comprehension, not production (Fein, 1979), longitudinal research is needed in this area.

In another short-term longitudinal study (6 weeks) examining relations between play and language production, Heath (1985) examined the ways in which a 3-year-old Korean girl (SooJong) used a specific form of fantasy, role playing, to help her learn a second language, English. SooJong initially used English narrative discourse in solitary fantasy play. In these play episodes she practiced school-relevant dialogues, symbolically transformed toys, and played roles and situations. She then used English in social play to set goals and transform settings and roles. Like her monolingual playmates, SooJong was motivated to comprehend and produce stretches of discourse because she enjoyed playing. When she experienced difficulty in cooperative play, she would go back to solitary doll play in Korean and, with the help of her mother, practice her English while "reading" to her doll. In short, play provided a safe environment in which to learn and practice a new language.

The short-term longitudinal work of Galda and Pellegrini, as discussed earlier, also shows a relation between aspects of symbolic play and early literacy. Briefly, Galda and Pellegrini (Galda et al., 1989; Pellegrini & Galda, 1991) showed that the level of transformations used in the fantasy of $4\frac{1}{2}$- and $3\frac{1}{2}$-year-olds predicted writing status, not reading status, 6 months and 2 years later, respectively. This data fits Vygotsky's (1978) notion that writing moves from symbolic play, to drawing, to conventional writing. Further, children in both of these studies used linguistic verbs (e.g., *say, talk, read, write*) during fantasy at $3\frac{1}{2}$ years but not at $4\frac{1}{2}$ years, even though the frequency of occurrence of these verbs increased during this time. It seems that the children used the fantasy context to practice this complex set of verbs, which they were probably exposed to during joint reading with parents (Pellegrini, Perlmutter, Galda, & Brody, 1990), and then, later, generalized usage to more realistic peer interaction contexts. This finding is clearly in keeping with the "play as practice" notion.

Consequence can be inferred from *experimental manipulation* of play treatments, as well as longitudinal research. In 2 experimental studies Pellegrini (Pellegrini & Galda, 1982; Pellegrini, 1984c) examined the extent to which training in thematic fantasy play facilitated children's (kindergarten, first-, and second-grade children in the first study; kindergarten and second-grade children in the second study) story comprehension and production. In these training studies the concern was with identifying specific aspects of thematic fantasy that might be responsible for corresponding narrative competence. The researchers were not concerned with using a training regimen with a group of children because they did not consider the children deficient in any way (see McLoyd, 1982, for a discussion of deficit assumptions behind play training models). The first aspect of the thematic play paradigm that must be considered as having a possible impact on development and learning is what Peter K. Smith (Smith & Syddall, 1978) calls *play tutoring,* or the extent to which adults' coaching of children's play is responsible for observed gains. Indeed, as Smith and Syddall (1978) point out, most play-training studies confound play with play tuition. In the Pellegrini (1984c) and the Silvern et al. (1986) studies, no between group differences were observed for tutored and nontutored thematic play groups. Consistent with observational research (e.g., Eiferman, 1971; Fein & Stork, 1981), these findings suggest that 5-year-old children are very capable of sustaining fantasy play without adult support. This finding has obvious educational implications: Kindergartners are capable of sustaining their own play. Indeed, the evidence from the classroom ecological studies cited earlier (e.g., Pellegrini, 1984d) suggests that adults actually inhibit children's fantasy.

The second interesting finding in 1 of these 2 studies (Pellegrini & Galda, 1982) was the treatment X grade interaction, whereby play was more effective for kindergarten children than for older children. Williamson and Silvern (1990), however, found play training with third-graders was effective. Their results suggest that play training can be useful in facilitating the story comprehension of children identified as poor comprehenders. Like the original work of Saltz et al. (1977) suggests, play training seems to interact with children's level of competence. Clearly, more research examining such interactive effects is necessary.

The third interesting finding of Pellegrini and Galda (1982) relates to the "unpacking" of the thematic play paradigm. As noted earlier, tutoring was not an important component for this age group, though it may be important for 2- and 3-year-olds (Pellegrini, 1984c; Silvern et al., 1986). Additionally, the researchers were interested in the following components: verbal interactions around the play theme, conceptual conflict, resolution of the play theme, and fantasy. For *immediate* measures (i.e., measurers given immediately after the training) of story comprehension and production, conditions that had all of these components were more effective than those with only verbal interactions and conceptual conflict; in other words, thematic fantasy play was more effective than discussion and conceptual conflict production and resolution. This speaks to the importance of fantasy, in addition to these other components. For *maintained* measures (i.e., measures given 1 week after the training), the conditions of conceptual conflict and verbal interaction were as effective as the play conditions. Consistent with the findings of Williamson and Silvern, fantasy does not add anything to the other components. As in all training studies that do not show the predicted effects, it may be the case that the training sessions were neither long nor frequent enough. Alternatively, it may be that fantasy is not an important causal element in thematic fantasy play, whereas verbal interaction and conceptual conflict are. More optimistically put, thematic fantasy is as good as verbal interaction and conceptual conflict. Certainly, more research on this issue is needed. With the importance assigned to fantasy in early education it is surprising that we do not have the types of longitudinal research that would allow us to answer this question more clearly. Longitudinal, rather than training studies, would be the preferred method to addressing this question.

The next series of studies that will be discussed are those that examine the effects of play on associative fluency (an aspect of creativity) and problem solving. The theoretical orientation of most of these studies is that the assimilative nature of unstructured fantasy is responsible for the novel uses assigned to conventional stimuli (Dansky, 1980; Sutton-Smith, 1966). Specifically, the assumption is made that play facilitates creativity, both in terms of novel uses for objects and in novel problem solutions, because preschool children are concerned with the means of activities and not ends. Further the suspension of reality allows children to recombine behavioral routines in novel ways (see Bruner, 1972, for a discussion of this orientation). The empirical support for the effects of preschoolers' play on associative fluency and problem solving has been reported in the widely cited works of Dansky (Dansky, 1980; Dansky & Silverman, 1973, 1975) for associative fluency and Sylva, Bruner, and Genova (1976) for problem solving. It is important to note, however, that these studies did not demonstrate empirically that children actually engaged in fantasy during play sessions. As noted above, it is important for research to first explicate specific dimensions of play and then examine empirical relations between these dimensions and outcomes measures.

More recently, however, these claims have been questioned, primarily by J. A. Cheyne (1982), Peter K. Smith and colleagues (Smith, 1988; Smith & Whitney, 1987; Simon & Smith, 1983, 1985), and Vandenberg (1980). Because the Vandenberg work is discussed in Rubin et al. (1983) and the Smith work is not, we will only discuss the latter body of research. Though both associative fluency and problem solving will be discussed, the results favoring play conditions in the earlier experiments in both genres, according to Smith, may have been affected by experimenter bias. First, regarding associative fluency, Smith and Whitney suggest that the effects attributed to play may have been due to experimenter bias (i.e., experimenters in earlier studies apparently knew the hypotheses and administered the treatments and the tests of associative fluency). When experimenter bias was eliminated, differences favoring play groups were not found by Smith and Whitney. Other data relevant to this question also suggests that free play with objects is no more effective than a control condition on preschoolers' associative fluency (Pellegrini, 1984b).

The reasons for these *noneffects,* we think, are simple enough. First, experimenter bias is a real problem that influences results. Second, the play treatments were incredibly short, usually a *maximum* of 10 minutes. Obviously, if we want to change well-established behaviors and attitudes, we need more than one 10-minute treatment.

The problem-solving tasks are based on the seminal work of Wolfgang Kohler (1925) involving the problem solving of chimpanzees. In the play experiments, children are given sticks and clamps and exposed to play, modeling, or, in some cases, control conditions. Criterion measures included the number of hints needed from a tester and the duration needed to solve a lure-retrieval task (Simon & Smith, 1983, 1985; Sylva et al., 1976; Vandenberg, 1980). Once again, most of these studies, with the exception of the Simon and Smith work, were tainted by experimenter bias and lack of an adequate control group. Again, when these precautions are taken, play groups perform no better or worse than other treatment or control groups (Simon & Smith, 1985).

The results of these experimental studies are important for a number of reasons. First, the short training periods employed in this work suggest a need for research using longer periods. Second, play seems to be as good as other ways of training children to do specific tasks. If this is the case, particularly in light of the short duration of these periods, then play does have an important part in the preschool curriculum. It may be, of course, that the other treatments, too, were too short to adequately address their impact. Third, these results should lead us to be aware of the "play ethos." It is not the unequivocal royal road to preschoolers' developmental competence, at least if we are to believe the research. Part of the problem, obviously, has been the ways in which researchers have chosen to examine these questions. The use of 10-minute training sessions as well as biased testers and experimenters limits our understanding. Following Simon and Smith (1985), the use of short, repetitious, and frequent play periods may be a better approach as long as such a strategy is used in natural settings.

Early Primary School: Rough-and-Tumble Play

When children move from preschool to primary school they enter an institution that places little value on play. As noted earlier, elementary schools, compared to preschools, give children little opportunity to engage in self-directed play. Where such opportunities exist, they are often reserved for the playground at recess. The implications of such policy for the study of play is clear. We have fewer opportunities to study primary children's play. When we choose to study it, we are often relegated to the playground. The study of play on the playground is a skewed view of play in that it is a male-preferred setting and the play behaviors observed there are typically male. In this section we will discuss a well-researched form of play that boys exhibit on the playground and in other spacious areas: rough-and-tumble play (R & T). Indeed, as the frequency of fantasy play decreases, at the beginning of the school years, the frequency of R & T increases. R & T seems to represent an intermediary between fantasy and games-with-rules. R & T and games (e.g., tag) share design features, such as chase, hit-at, alternating roles, and

strategies (Parker, 1984). Further, the gender differences observed in R & T are also observed in games-with-rules. Games-with-rules will not be discussed in this chapter because they constitute a form of play more typical of concrete-operational children (Piaget, 1962) and not often observed in primary-school children's spontaneous play (Garvey, 1990; Parker, 1984; Rubin, et al., 1983).

In studies of preschool children's social behavior (Blurton-Jones, 1972; Smith & Connolly, 1972) R & T was found to be a distinct empirical factor composed of the following behaviors: play face, run, chase, flee, wrestle, and open-hand beat. Structurally, R & T is typified by reciprocal role taking (Fagen, 1981; Humphreys & Smith, 1984); for example, children often alternate between victim and victimizer. Like other forms of play, R & T follows an inverted-U developmental function, whereby it accounts for about 5% of the free play of preschoolers, increases to about 10 to 17% in early elementary school, and declines to 5% again in middle childhood (Humphreys & Smith, 1984; Pellegrini, 1989a, 1989d).

R & T, unlike fantasy play, is not uniformly accepted as being beneficial for children. The reason for this, we think, lies in its apparent similarity to aggression. Brian Sutton-Smith (1988) has suggested that adults, including child psychologists, teachers, and playground supervisors, often confuse R & T and aggression. Close behavioral and structural examinations, however, show that the 2 behaviors are distinct for most children. Behaviorally, aggression is empirically distinct from R & T (Blurton-Jones, 1972; Pellegrini, 1989c; Smith & Connolly, 1972) and composed of the following behaviors; fixate, frown, hit with closed hand, push, take, and grab. Aggression, unlike play, is stable throughout childhood (Olweus, 1979). Structurally, too, they are different to the extent that aggression is characterized by unilateral, not reciprocal roles; in aggression children do not voluntarily change roles.

There are cases, however, when R & T and aggression seem to co-occur (Coie & Kupersmidt, 1983; Pellegrini, 1988, 1989c). Such cases involve the R & T of sociometrically rejected children. Sociometric status, generally, refers to the extent to which children are liked (i.e., popular), disliked (i.e., rejected), or ignored (i.e., neglected) by their peers. In short, the R & T of popular children is playful while the R & T of rejected children is aggressive (Pellegrini, 1988, 1989c). Further, popular elementary-school children, compared to rejected children, more accurately discriminate between filmed R & T and aggressive bouts. When taken together, the behavioral observations and the film data suggest that the rejected children may have a deficit for interpreting ambiguous social events, such as R & T (Dodge & Frame, 1982).

Contextual Effects on R & T at Exosystem and Microsystem Levels. The exosystem variable that will be considered is, again, school policy. The aspect of school policy that is relevant to R & T is the role given to recess in the school curriculum. An important policy variable that affects R & T is the amount of time that children are "confined," or kept in their classrooms with little physical activity, before recess. Experimental research with preschool and primary-school children suggests that the longer children are confined, the more vigorous is their outdoor play (Pellegrini & Huberty, in press; Smith & Hagan, 1980). Clearly, more research with older elementary school children is necessary to address the important policy implications of this question.

Microsystem Level Variables that Affect R & T. Boys, more than girls, engage in R & T (Humphreys & Smith, 1984). This finding is incredibly robust in that it seems to be a cross-cultural truth (Whiting & Edwards, 1973). That gender is a microsystem variable is questionable, however. It may be an exosystem variable to the extent that males and females are socialized differently. On the other hand, gender may not be a contextual variable at all; the male bias in R & T may be biologically determined. Our conception of gender, however, is that it has both biological *and* social components. We will consider the effects of both on children's R & T.

First we will discuss the effects of hormones on children's R & T. The dominant theory in this area, *androgen theory,* suggests that sufficient amounts of androgen sex hormones are necessary if the child is to develop male-typical behavior, like R & T. Low levels of androgens are associated with less-active behavior (Meyer-Bahlburg, Feldman, Cohen, & Ehrhardt, 1988; Meaney, Stewart, & Beatty, 1985). In natural experiments in which mothers experiencing pregnancy difficulties are given androgens, their female offspring are more active and engage in more R & T than other female controls (Meyer-Bahlburg et al., 1988). These data, in conjunction with animal data (see Fagen, 1981, Meaney et al., 1985, and Smith, 1982 for excellent reviews of animal play), suggest that males have a biological predisposition to engage in R & T.

Boys also seem to be socialized to engage in R & T more than girls. Fathers, more than mothers, engage in physical play with their children, especially boys, from infancy through early childhood (MacDonald & Parke, 1986). Parents also provide children with gender-stereotyped toys that, in turn, elicit different levels of activity (O'Brien & Huston, 1986). Children, from the toddler period onward, prefer to play with such gender-appropriate toys. The male-preferred toys seem to elicit more active play than the female-preferred toys.

The preference for active play may also be related to the peer groups in which R & T occurs (Maccoby, 1986; Maccoby & Jacklin, 1987). Specifically, boys' preference for R & T results in their playing with other boys, not girls. Correspondingly, girls' dislike for this type of play results in their playing together and not with boys. The result of all this is that boys tend to engage in R & T with other boys who are of similar dominance and sociometric status (Humphreys & Smith, 1987).

The last microsystem variable affecting R & T that will be discussed is the playground. Not surprisingly, we find that R & T is more likely to occur on soft, grassy areas than on hard surfaces (Pellegrini, 1989a). Further, children need space to engage in R & T. Consequently, more-spacious areas, compared to less-spacious areas, tend to elicit R & T (Smith & Connolly, 1980).

R & T's Consequences for Children's Development. R & T's effects on child development may be aspects of the microsystem, children's sociometric status, and their R & T playmates. When boys engage in R & T with other popular or rejected boys, they have different opportunities to observe, imitate, and practice prosocial and antisocial behaviors and social strategies. Indeed, we find that popular elementary-school children engaging in R & T typically move into games-with-rules (e.g., chase turns into tag) (Pellegrini, 1988). Additionally, our longitudinal work shows that popular children's R & T in year 1 predicts games-with-rules in year 2 (Pellegrini, 1989d). For rejected children, on the other hand, R & T moves into aggression and does not relate to prosocial behavior either contemporaneously or longitudinally (Pellegrini, 1988, 1989d).

To conclude this section, R & T seems to be a playful category for popular children and an aggressive category for rejected children. Socialization and hormonal events lead to its status as a male-preferred activity that is not valued in school settings. The variation in the peer groups in which R & T is observed is probably responsible for its differential consequences.

PLAY AS EVALUATION

The research that we have discussed suggests that play has an important place in the education of young children. As noted, we recommend that the modal forms of play for specific periods of childhood be used as the corresponding forms of play used in curriculum at those periods. Further, the contextual effects outlined for each of the 3 forms of play discussed provide guidance for the design of classrooms, recess periods, and playgrounds. The consequences of the forms of play provide information on the specific outcomes we can expect. The specific design features of different forms of play should match the specific features of the outcome measures. In this section we will discuss the use of play as an evaluation construct.

The term *evaluation* may seem antithetical to play as we have discussed it; after all, evaluation brings to mind such nonplayful images as testing, the transmission of discrete bits of information from teacher to student, and convergent thought. In this section we will discuss play as evaluation, but evaluation considered in a broader context than test orientation. Evaluation is defined in this section as a process by which we can measure change in children. Change can be the result of innovative or traditional educational programs. The evaluative data could be summative, as in the case of measuring impact, or formative, as in cases when it is used to improve instruction.

Play is a particularly useful evaluation construct in early childhood education. In play children seem to exhibit levels of competence that are often higher than those exhibited in other contexts (Vygotsky, 1978). Indeed, Vygotsky (1978) considered play to be a prime example of children's operation in the zone of proximal development: In play children exhibit levels higher than they are ordinarily capable of exhibiting. Other examples of the zone of proximal development, of course, include children interacting with a more competent other. Consequently, play provides a context where children exhibit maximum competence. This is in stark contrast to the traditional testing and experimental environments, which, because they involve strange and anxiety-producing situations, often suppress children's exhibition of competence (Bronfenbrenner, 1979; Dunn, 1988; Messick, 1983).

A related reason for considering play an important and appropriate evaluation tool in early childhood education is the belief that we gain insight into children's cognitive, emotional, and social competence through play; in other words, it is a window into children's minds. The method presented in this section for evaluating children's play is appropriate through the preschool years. This method is the well-known and extensively used play matrix developed by Rubin (see Rubin, et al., 1983, for an extensive description), which combines the cognitive dimensions of play outlined by Smilansky in 1968, (i.e., functional, constructive, and dramatic), with an adaptation of Parten's (1932) social participation categories, (i.e., solitary, parallel, and cooperative). This method is most appropriate at the preschool level, in that the forms of behavior contained in it are most commonly observed during that period. It should be noted that this scheme has been criticized by Takhvar and Smith (1990). The inclusion of constructive activity as play is an important component of their critique. They argue that neither Piaget nor other scholars cited by Smilansky considered construction as play because of its accommodative nature. Takhvar and Smith also take issue with the noninclusive nature of the model (e.g., where does R & T fit in the model). A great deal of research, however, has been generated by the use of the Smilansky-Parten matrix. This matrix is useful for teachers of young children in that it provides (1) established relations between specific aspects of behavior, some of which are play, and (2) traditional outcome measures often used in schools.

We advocate using this matrix because it processes high psychometric qualities. For example, high interrater reliability can be easily attained; the matrix possesses predictive and concurrent validity and, simultaneously, is relatively easy to use in classroom settings. Teachers do not have to undergo extensive training to use the instrument or interpret the results. We have trained pre- and in-service teachers to use the matrix reliably in a 2-hour training session. This is accomplished by first discussing the definitions of the categories listed on a prepared observation sheet, then observing and discussing videotaped play episodes, and, lastly, observing "real" children.

The use of prepared observation sheets makes for systematic recording and storing of data. Figure 8–1 shows an example of such a sheet.

These coding sheets should be duplicated *en masse* so that teachers can use a separate sheet for each observation of each child. Children should be observed during free play, when they are free to interact with peers and activities of their own choice. The observer should decide in advance on a specific time interval by which play behavior will be sampled; for example, one child's play may be categorized in sequence at 10-second intervals for 5 minutes (see Bakeman & Gottman, 1986; Martin & Bateson, 1986, for systematic observation procedures). At each interval the observer should record a number (corresponding to first, second, third, etc., in the sequence of observation) in the appropriate box in the matrix. In the interest of accurate record keeping, only 1 child's play should be recorded on each sheet. The context of the play behavior and the number of participants in the area is obviously important to record (as noted in the discussion of microsystem effects on fantasy) because they systematically relate to the form of play that children exhibit. As such, context, in addition to developmental status or program, may affect children's play behavior.

Teachers should sample children's behavior frequently so as to collect a representative sample of behaviors in different contexts. In general, the more observations recorded, the more reliable is the data.

Children's status on this matrix provides valid information about their levels of competence. In terms of construct validity, the cognitive dimensions of the matrix seem to be hierarchic (if we exclude construction) in that functional play decreases across the preschool period, whereas dramatic play increases; construction does not vary significantly across the period (see Rubin et al., 1983; and, for a counterargument, Takhvar & Smith, 1990). Further, preschool children who engage primarily in functional play perform poorly, compared to their peers who

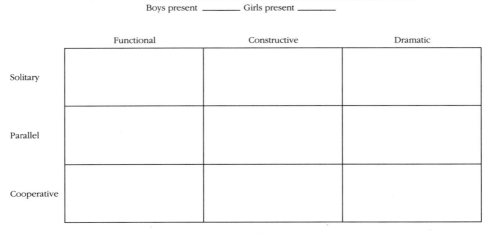

FIGURE 8–1. Play Matrix

engage in dramatic play, on classification and spatial tasks (Rubin, Maioni, & Hornung, 1976).

The power of the matrix, however, lies in its combining cognitive and social aspects of play, not in isolating them. For example, preschoolers who engage primarily in solitary-functional and solitary-dramatic play are also unpopular with peers. Such children are rated as hyperactive and anxious/fearful, respectively, by their peers. Numerous other relations between aspects of play, as measured on this matrix, can be found in Rubin et al. (1983). The point to be made here is that the matrix provides a reliable and valid means for assessment. It should be noted, however, that factors other than children's developmental status (e.g., classroom contextual variables) relate to their play behavior. Observers should beware of these relations and maximize the situations in which children are observed.

CONCLUSION

In this chapter we have tried to provide a review of the recent (i.e., after Rubin et al., 1983) research on children's play. We have stated that clear definitions of play are necessary if we hope to explicate relations between play and various outcome measures. The reasoning here is straightforward: Play behavior has numerous dimensions, some of which co-occur with other nonplay behaviors. To identify the extent to which play per se is responsible for specific consequences, we must explicate empirical relations between theoretically related design features.

We have also described commonly observed forms of play for three periods of childhood: exploration in infancy; fantasy in preschool; and R & T in primary school. The intent here was twofold: first, to provide normative information, and second, to provide a basis for curricular decisions. These curricular decisions can further be derived from our description of contextual effects on play (i.e., ways in which specific aspects of context relate to specific aspects of play) and from discussions of the consequences of play (i.e., what consequences does play have for children).

Throughout the chapter we have kept in mind the notion of the "play ethos." Although some research questions the causal role of play in spurring development, the extent to which play provides opportunities to practice a skill has not been questioned. Indeed, the often-reported correlations between play and various outcome measures can be interpreted as supporting the argument for the causal or practice value of play. From an educational perspective, both are valuable.

Children's play offers numerous implications for research as well as for practice and policy. As mentioned throughout the chapter, research should strive to explicate theoretically important dimensions of play as a first step in any examination. Next, relations between these dimensions and specific outcome measures should be tested. Such a strategy is necessary because play is a broad and sometimes ambiguous construct. Other important research implications relate specifically to research methodology. There is a real need for longitudinal research. In reviewing the research literature, we were amazed by the paucity of longitudinal designs. If educators are to truly understand the ways in which children develop, longitudinal research is the most appropriate strategy.

Another methodological issue involves the locus of studies on play. The time has come to study children in the laboratory, in the classroom, and in the home. Such a strategy is necessary if we are to understand the ways in which children develop. As McCall (1977) noted, studies restricted to the laboratory often tell us what children are capable of doing, whereas studies of children in their natural ecologies tell us what they actually do. An excellent study of children's fantasy play by Haight and Miller (in press), which includes both the longitudinal design and home observations, is a model for this type of research.

The practice and policy implications of this chapter are too numerous to list. We will highlight some important ones. First, we think it is necessary to match play-oriented curricula with children's developmental status. As noted above, specific forms of play may be more or less effective with specific age groups of children. Relatedly, we know that specific aspects of play during the preschool period (e.g., children's use of transformations and use of linguistic verbs) are good predictors of early writing and reading, respectively. Such findings have important curricular implications in that they provide guidance for developmentally appropriate practice. For example, social fantasy play seems to be a good strategy for teaching early literacy because the former develops into the latter.

More specific to the policy level, this review has provided empirical evidence for the role of certain forms of play in school. Such evidence should be a basis for making policy decisions. Preschool policymakers less often need to be convinced of this than do primary-school administrators. The work of Williamson and Silvern (1990), among others, attests to the value of play for such traditional school measures as reading achievement. Relatedly, empirical research reviewed in this chapter provides guidance for other aspects of primary-school policy. The legitimacy of the school recess period is increasingly being questioned by school boards around the country; evidence of the national level of concern is reflected in a recent *New York Times* (8 January, 1989) article on the subject. Children need recess just as adults need breaks from their work. Further, what children do at recess is "educational" in that they learn to take different perspectives, cooperate, and communicate with peers.

The last policy implication that we have addressed relates to evaluation. American schools have become increasingly concerned with evaluation. Further, the role of evaluation in schools seems to be expanding. The value placed on "high-stakes testing" is one distressing dimension of the sometimes undue concern with evaluation. Play, however, provides an excellent medium through which to evaluate children. The fact that play is enjoyable and motivating suggests that children might exhibit high levels of competence in a play-oriented assessment procedure. Young children fail to exhibit high levels of competence in many formalized assessment contexts because they simply don't find those contexts interesting.

At a basic level, children enjoy play. For some individuals that may be enough justification for its inclusion in schools. But as an added benefit, play seems to be instrumental in children's social and cognitive development.

References

Ainsworth, M., Blehar, M., Waters, E., & Wall, S. (1978). *Patterns of attachment.* Hillsdale, NJ: Erlbaum.

Aston, J., & Smith, P. K. (1987). Rough-and-tumble play in middle school children. Paper presented at annual meeting of the Developmental Section of the British Psychological Society, Lancaster, UK.

Bakeman, R., & Brownlee, J. (1980). The strategic uses of parallel play: A sequential analysis. *Child Development, 51,* 873–878.

Bakeman, R., & Gottman, J. (1986). *Observing interaction: An introduction to sequential analysis.* New York: Cambridge University Press.

Bates, E. (1979). *The emergence of symbols.* New York: Academic Press.

Belsky, J., Garduque, L., & Hrncir, E. (1984). Assessing performance, competence, and executive capacity in infant play. *Developmental Psychology, 20,* 406–417.

Belsky, J., & Most, R. (1981). From exploration to play: A cross-sectional study of infant free-play behavior. *Developmental Psychology, 17,* 630–639.

Blurton-Jones, N. (1972). Categories of child interaction. In N. Blurton-Jones (Ed.), *Ethological studies of child behavior* (pp. 97–129). London: Cambridge University Press.

Boulton, M., & Smith, P. K. (1989). Issues in the study of children's rough-and-tumble play. In M. Bloch & A. Pellegrini (Eds.), *The ecological context of children's play* (pp. 57–83). Norwood, NJ: Ablex.

Bronfenbrenner, U. (1979). *The ecology of human development.* Cambridge, MA: Harvard University Press.

Bruner, J. (1972). The nature and uses of immaturity. *American Psychologist, 27,* 687–708.

Bruner, J. (1975). From communication to language—A psychological perspective. *Cognition, 3,* 255–287.

Burns, S., & Brainerd, C. (1979). Effects of constructive and dramatic play on perspective taking in very young children. *Developmental Psychology, 15,* 512–521.

Campbell, S., & Frost, J. (1985). The effects of playground type on the cognitive and social play behaviors of grade two children. In J. Frost & S. Sunderlin (Eds.), *When children play* (pp. 81–88). Wheaton, MD: ACEI.

Caro, T. (1980). The effects of experience on the predatory patterns of cats. *Behavioral and Neural Biology, 29,* 1–28.

Cheyne, J. (1982). Object play and problem solving. In D. Pepler & K. Rubin (Eds.), *The play of children* (pp. 79–96). Basel, Switzerland: Karger.

Coie, J., & Kupersmidt, J. (1983). A behavioral analysis of emerging social status in boys' groups. *Child Development, 54,* 1400–1416.

Connor, K. (1989). Aggression: Is it in the eye of the beholder? *Play and Culture, 2,* 213–217.

Dansky, J. (1980). Make-believe: A mediator of the relationship between play and associative fluency. *Child Development, 51,* 576–579.

Dansky, J., & Silverman, I. (1973). Effects of play on associative fluency in preschool-age children. *Developmental Psychology, 9,* 38–43.

Dansky, J., & Silverman, I. (1975). Play: A general facilitator of associative fluency. *Developmental Psychology, 11,* 104.

Dodge, K., & Frame, C. (1982). Social cognitive biases and deficits in aggressive boys. *Child Development, 53,* 620–635.

Dunn, J. (1988). *The beginnings of social understanding.* Cambridge, MA: Harvard University Press.

Eiferman, R. (1971). Social play in childhood. In R. Herron & B. Sutton-Smith (Eds.), *Child's play* (pp. 156–171). New York: Wiley.

Einon, D., Morgan, M., & Kibbler, C. (1978). Brief periods of socialization and later behavior in the rat. *Developmental Psychobiology, 11,* 213–225.

Fagen, R. (1981). *Animal play behavior.* New York: Oxford University Press.

Fein, G. (1979). Echoes from the nursery: Piaget, Vygotsky and the relationship between languages and play. In E. Winner & H. Gardner (Eds.), *Fact, fiction, and fantasy in childhood* (pp. 1–14). San Francisco: Jossey-Bass.

Fein, G. (1981). Pretend play: An integrative review. *Child Development, 52,* 1095–1118.

Fein, G., & Stork, L. (1981). Social class effects in integrated preschool classrooms. *Journal of Applied Developmental Psychology, 2,* 267–279.

Frost, J., & Sanderlin, S. (Eds.). (1985). *Children's play and playgrounds.* Wheaton, MD: Association for Childhood Education International.

Galda, L., Pellegrini, A. D., & Cox, S. (1989). A short-term longitudinal study of preschooler's emergent literacy. *Research in the Teaching of English, 23,* 292–309.

Garvey, C. (1984). *Children's talk.* Cambridge, MA: Harvard University Press.

Garvey, C. (1990). *Play* (2nd ed.). Cambridge, MA: Harvard University Press.

Haight, W., & Miller, P. (in press). *Ecology and development of pretend.* Albany, NY: State University of New York Press.

Harlow, H., & Harlow, M. (1962). Social deprivation in monkeys. *Scientific American, 207,* 136.

Harper, L., & Sanders, K. (1975). Preschool children's use of space: Sex differences in outdoor play. *Developmental Psychology, 11,* 119.

Heath, S. B. (1983). *Ways with words.* New York: Cambridge University Press.

Heath, S. B. (1985). Narrative play in second language learning. In L. Galda & A. D. Pellegrini (Eds.), *Play, language, and stories: The development of children's literate behavior* (pp. 147–166). Norwood, NJ: Ablex.

Henninger, M. (1985). Preschool children's play behavior in indoor and outdoor environments. In J. Frost & S. Sunderlin (Eds.), *When children play* (pp. 145–149). Wheaton, MD: ACEI.

Hinde, R. (1982). *Ethology.* London: Fontana.

Hinde, R. (1983). Ethology and child development. In J. J. Campos & M. H. Haith (Eds.), *Handbook of child psychology: Infancy and developmental psychobiology, Vol. 11* (pp. 27–94). New York: Wiley.

Hughes, M., & Hutt, C. (1979). Heart-rate correlates of childhood activities: Play exploration, problem solving and day dreaming. *Biological Psychology, 8,* 253–263.

Humphreys, A., & Smith, P. K. (1984). Rough-and-tumble in preschool and playground. In P. Smith (Ed.), *Play in animals and humans* (pp. 241–270). London: Blackwell.

Humphreys, A., & Smith, P. K. (1987). Rough-and-tumble play, friendship and dominance in school children: Evidence for continuity and change with age. *Child Development, 58,* 201–212.

Hutt, C. (1966). Exploration and play in children. *Symposia of the Zoological Society of London, 18,* 61–81.

Hymes, D., & Cazden, C. (1980). Narrative thinking and story-telling rights: Folklorists' clue to a critique of education. In D. Hymes (Ed.), *Language in education: Ethnolinguistic essays* (pp. 126–138). Washington, DC: Center for Applied Linguistics.

Kohler, W. (1925). *The mentality of apes.* New York: Harcourt Brace.

Krasnor, L., & Pepler, D. (1980). The study of children's play. In K. Rubin (Ed.), *Children's play* (pp. 85–95). San Francisco: Jossey-Bass.

Lever, J. (1975–1976). Sex differences in the games children play. *Social Problems, 23,* 478–487.

Maccoby, R. (1986). Social groupings in childhood: Their relationship to prosocial and antisocial behavior in boys and girls. In D. Olweus, J. Block, & M. Radkye-Yarrow (Eds.), *Development of antisocial and prosocial behavior: Research, theory, and issues* (pp. 263–284). New York: Academic Press.

Maccoby, E., & Jacklin, C. (1987). Gender segregation in childhood. In H. Reese (Ed.), *Advances in child development, Vol. 20* (pp. 239–287). New York: Academic Press.

MacDonald, K., & Parke, R. (1986). Parent-child physical play. *Sex Roles, 15,* 367–378.

Main, M. (1983). Exploration, play, and cognitive functioning related to infant-mother attachment. *Infant Behavior and Development, 6,* 167–174.

Martin, P., & Bateson, P. (1986). *Measuring behaviour.* London: Cambridge University Press.

Martin, P., & Caro, T. (1985). On the functions of play and its role in behavioral development. In J. Rosenblatt, C. Beer, M. C. Busnel, & P. Slater (Eds.), *Advances in the study of behavior, Vol. 15* (pp. 59–103). New York: Academic Press.

McCall, R. (1977). Challenges to a science of developmental psychology. *Child Development, 48,* 333–394.

McCune-Nicolich, L., & Fenson, L. (1984). Methodological issues in studying early pretend play. In T. Yawkey & A. D. Pellegrini (Eds.), *Child's play* (pp. 81–104). Hillsdale, NJ: Erlbaum.

McLoyd, V. (1980). Verbally expressed modes of transformation in the fantasy and play of black preschool children. *Child Development, 51,* 1133–1139.

McLoyd, V. (1982). Social class differences in sociodramatic play. A critical review. *Developmental Review, 2,* 1–30.

Meaney, M., Stewart, J., & Beatty, W. (1985). Sex differences in social play: The socialization of sex roles. In J. Rosenblatt, C. Beer, M. C. Busnel, & P. Slater (Eds.), *Advances in the study of behavior, Vol. 15* (pp. 2–58). New York: Academic Press.

Messick, S. (1983). Assessment of children. In W. Kessen (Ed.), *Handbook of child psychology, Vol. 1, History, theory, and methods* (pp. 477–526). New York: Wiley.

Meyer-Bahlburg, H., Feldman, J., Cohen, P., & Ehrhardt, A. (1988). *Psychiatry, 51,* 260–271.

National Association for the Education of Young Children. (1988). Position statement on standardized testing of young children three through eight years of age. *Young Children, 43,* 42–47.

Nicholich, L. (1977). Beyond sensori-motor intelligence. *Merrill-Palmer Quarterly, 22,* 89–99.

O'Brien, M., & Huston, A. (1986). Activity level and sex-stereotyped toy choice in toddler boys and girls. *Journal of Genetic Psychology, 146,* 527–533.

O'Connell, B., & Bretherton, I. (1984). Toddler's play, alone and with mother. The role of maternal guidance. In I. Bretherton (Ed.), *Symbolic play* (pp. 337–368). New York: Academic Press.

Ogbu, J. (1981). Origins of human competence. A cultural-ecological perspective. *Child Development, 52,* 413–429.

Ogbu, J. (1988). Culture, development, and education. In A. D. Pellegrini (Ed.), *Psychological basis for early education* (pp. 245–276). Chichester, UK: Wiley.

Olweus, D. (1979). Stability and aggressive reaction patterns in males: A review. *Psychological Bulletin, 86,* 852–875.

Parker, S. (1984). Playing for keeps: An evolutionary perspective on human games. In P. K. Smith (Ed.), *Play in animals and humans* (pp. 271–294). London: Basil Blackwell.

Parten, M. (1932). Social participation among preschool children. *Journal of Abnormal and Social Psychology, 27,* 243–269.

Pellegrini, A. D. (1984a). The effect of dramatic play on children's generation of cohesive text. *Discourse Processes, 7,* 57–67.

Pellegrini, A. D. (1984b). The effects of exploration and play on young children's associative fluency: A review and extension of training studies. In T. Yawkey & A. D. Pellegrini (Eds.), *Child's play: Applied and developmental* (pp. 237–253). Hillsdale, NJ: Erlbaum.

Pellegrini, A. D. (1984c). Identifying causal elements in the thematic-fantasy play paradigm. *American Educational Research Journal, 21,* 691–703.

Pellegrini, A. D. (1984d). The effects of classroom ecology on preschoolers' functional uses of language. In A. D. Pellegrini & T. Yawkey (Eds.), *The development of oral and written language in social contexts* (pp. 129–144). Norwood, NJ: Ablex.

Pellegrini, A. D. (1985a). The narrative organization of children's play. *Educational Psychology, 5,* 17–25.

Pellegrini, A. D. (1985b). Relations between symbolic play and literate behavior. In L. Galda & A. D. Pellegrini (Eds.), *Play, language, and story: The development of children's literate behavior* (pp. 79–97). Norwood, NJ: Ablex.

Pellegrini, A. (1986). Play centers and the production of imaginative language. *Discourse Processes, 9,* 115–125.

Pellegrini, A. D. (1987). The effects of play contexts and the development of children's verbalized fantasy. *Semiotica, 65,* 285–293.

Pellegrini, A. D. (1988). Elementary school children's rough-and-tumble play and social competence. *Developmental Psychology, 24,* 802–806.

Pellegrini, A. D. (1989a). Elementary school children's rough-and-tumble play. *Early Childhood Research Quarterly, 4,* 245–260.

Pellegrini, A. D. (1989b). So what about recess, really? *Play and Culture, 2,* 354–356.

Pellegrini, A. D. (1989c). What is a category? The case of rough-and-tumble play. *Ethology and Sociobiology, 10,* 331–341.

Pellegrini, A. D. (1989d). A longitudinal study of popular and rejected boys' rough-and-tumble play. *Early Education and Development, 2,* 205–213.

Pellegrini, A. D., & Galda, L. (1982). The effects of thematic-fantasy training on the development of children's story comprehension. *American Educational Research Journal, 19,* 443–452.

Pellegrini, A. D., & Galda, L. (1991). Longitudinal relations among preschoolers' symbolic play, linguistic verbs, and emergent literacy. In J. Christie (Ed.), *Play and early literacy* (pp. 47–68). Albany, NY: State University of New York Press.

Pellegrini, A. D., & Huberty, P. D. (in press). Confinement effects on children's recess and classroom behavior. *British Journal of Educational Psychology.*

Pellegrini, A. D., & Perlmutter, J. (1989). Classroom contextual effects on children's play. *Developmental Psychology, 25,* 289–296.

Pellegrini, A. D., Perlmutter, J., Galda, L., & Brody, G. (1990). Joint book reading between black Head Start children and their mothers. *Child Development, 61,* 443–453.

Piaget, J. (1962). *Play, dreams, and imitation.* New York: Norton.

Power, T. G., & Parke, R. D. (1982). Play as a context for early learning: Lab and home analysis. In L. M. Laosa & I. E. Sigel (Eds.), *Families as learning environments for children* (pp. 147–178). New York: Plenum.

Rheingold, H., & Cook, K. (1975). The contents of boys' and girls' rooms as an index of parents' behavior. *Child Development, 46,* 459–463.

Roggman, L., & Langlois, J. (1987). Mothers, infants, and toys: Social play correlates of attachment. *Infant Behavior and Development, 10,* 233–237.

Rubin, K., & Daniels-Beirness, T. (1983). Concurrent and predictive correlates of sociometric status in kindergarten and grade-school children. *Merrill-Palmer Quarterly, 29,* 337–351.

Rubin, K., Fein, G., & Vandenberg, B. (1983). Play. In E. M. Hetherington (Ed.), *Handbook of child psychology: Socialization, personality and social development, Vol. IV* (pp. 693–774). New York: Wiley.

Rubin, K., Maioni, T., & Hornung, M. (1976). Free play in middle and lower class preschoolers: Parten and Piaget revisited. *Child Development, 47,* 414–419.

Saltz, E., Dixon, D., & Johnson, J. (1977). Training disadvantaged preschoolers on various fantasy activities: Effects on cognitive functioning and impulse control. *Child Development, 48,* 367–380.

Sapir, E. (1925). Sound patterns in language. *Language, 1,* 37–51.

Shore, C., O'Connell, B., & Bates, E. (1986). First sentences in language and symbolic play. *Developmental Psychology, 20,* 872–880.

Silvern, S., Taylor, J., Williamson, P., Surbeck, E., & Kelley, M. (1986). Young children's story recall as a product of play, story familiarity, and adult intervention. *Merrill-Palmer Quarterly, 32,* 73–86.

Simon, T., & Smith, P. K. (1983). The study of play and problem solving in preschool children. *British Journal of Developmental Psychology, 1,* 289–297.

Simon, T., & Smith, P. K. (1985). Play and problem solving: A paradigm questioned. *Merrill-Palmer Quarterly, 31,* 265–277.

Slade, A. (1987a). A longitudinal study of maternal involvement and symbolic play during the toddler period. *Child Development, 58,* 367–375.

Slade, A. (1987b). Quality of attachment and early symbolic play. *Developmental Psychology, 23,* 78–85.

Smilansky, S. (1968). *The effects of sociodramatic play on disadvantaged preschool children.* New York: Wiley.

Smith, P. K. (1978). A longitudinal study of social participation in preschool children: Solitary and parallel play reexamined. *Developmental Psychology, 14,* 517–523.

Smith, P. K. (1982). Does play matter? Functional and evolutionary aspects of animal and human play. *Behavioral and Brain Sciences, 5,* 139–184.

Smith, P. K. (1988). Children's play and its role in early development: A re-evaluation of the "play ethos". In A. D. Pellegrini (Ed.), *Psychological bases for early education* (pp. 207–226). Chichester, UK: Wiley.

Smith, P. K., & Boulton, M. (1990). Rough-and-tumble play, aggression, and dominance: Perception and behavior in children's encounters. *Human Development, 33,* 271–282.

Smith, P. K., & Connolly, K. (1972). Patterns of play and social interaction in preschool children. In N. Blurton-Jones (Ed.), *Ethological studies in child behavior* (pp. 65–96). New York: Cambridge University Press.

Smith, P. K., & Connolly, K. (1980). *The ecology of preschool behaviour.* London: Cambridge University Press.

Smith, P. K., & Costablie, A. (in press). War toys and children's play. *Early Education and Development.*

Smith, P. K., & Cowie, H. (1988). *Understanding children's development.* London: Blackwell.

Smith, P. K., & Hagan, T. (1980). Effects of deprivation on exercise play in nursery school children. *Animal Behavior, 28,* 922–928.

Smith, P. K., & Lewis, K. (1985). Rough-and-tumble play, fighting, and chasing in nursery school children. *Ethology and Sociobiology, 6,* 175–181.

Smith, P. K., & Syddall, S. (1978). Play and group play tutoring in preschool children. Is it play or tutoring which matters? *British Journal of Educational Psychology, 48,* 315–325.

Smith, P. K., Takhvar, M., Gore, N., & Volstedt, R. (1986). Play in young children: Problems of definition, categorization, and measurement. In P. K. Smith (Ed.), *Children's play* (pp. 39–55). London: Gordon and Breach.

Smith, P. K., & Vollstedt, R. (1985). On defining play. *Child Development, 56,* 1042–1050.

Smith, P. K., & Whitney, S. (1987). Play and associative fluency: Experimenter effects may be responsible for previous positive findings. *Developmental Psychology, 23,* 49–53.

Sutton-Smith, B. (1966). Piaget on play: A critique. *Psychological Review, 73,* 109–110.

Sutton-Smith, B. (1988). War toys and childhood aggression. *Play and Culture, 1,* 57–69.

Sylva, K., Bruner, J., & Genova, P. (1976). The role of play in the problem-solving behavior of children 3–5 years old. In J. Bruner, A. Jolly, & K. Sylva (Eds.), *Play—its role in development and evolution* (pp. 244–261). New York: Basic Books.

Takhvar, M., & Smith, P. K. (1990). A review and critique of Smilansky's classification scheme and the "nested hierarchy" of play categories. *Journal of Research in Early Childhood, 4,* 112–122.

Thomas, A., & Chess, S. (1977). *Temperament and development.* New York: Brunner/Mazel.

Vandenberg, B. (1980). Play, problem solving, and creativity. In K. Rubin (Ed.), *Children's play* (pp. 49–68). San Francisco: Jossey-Bass.

Voss, H. G. (1987a). Exploration and play. In D. Gorlitz & J. Wohlwill (Eds.), *Curiosity, imagination, and play* (pp. 43–58). Hillsdale, NJ: Erlbaum.

Voss, H. G. (1987b). An empirical study of exploration-play sequences in early childhood. In D. Goorlitz & J. Wohlwill (Eds.), *Curiosity, imagination, and play* (pp. 151–178). Hillsdale, NJ: Erlbaum.

Vygotsky, L. (1962). *Thought and language.* Cambridge, MA: MIT Press.

Vygotsky, L. (1978). *Mind in society.* Cambridge, MA: Harvard University Press.

Waters, E., & Deane, K. (1985). Defining and assessing individual differences in attachment relationships: Q-methodology and the organization of behavior in infancy and early childhood. *Monographs of the Society for Research in Child Development, 50,* (1, Serial No. 209), 41–65.

Watson, M. (in press). War toys and aggression. *Early Education and Development.*

Werner, H., & Kaplan, E. (1952). The acquisition of word meanings: A developmental study. *Monographs of the Society for Research in Child Development, 15,* (1, Serial No. 51).

Whiting, B., & Edwards, C. (1973). A cross-cultural analysis of sex-differences in the behavior of children age three through eleven. *Journal of Social Psychology, 91,* 171–188.

Williamson, P., & Silvern, S. (1990). The effects of play training on the story comprehension of upper primary children. *Journal of Research in Childhood Education, 4,* 130–134.

Williamson, P., & Silvern, S. (1991). Thematic fantasy play and story comprehension. In J. Christie (Ed.), *Play and early literacy development* (pp. 69–90). Albany, NY: SUNY Press.

Wohlwill, J. (1984). Relationships between exploration and play. In T. Yawkey & A. D. Pellegrini (Eds.), *Child's play* (pp. 143–170). Hillsdale, NJ: Erlbaum.

Wolf, D., & Grollman, S. (1980). Ways of playing. In D. Pepler & K. Rubin (Eds.), *The play of children* (pp. 46–63). Basel, Switzerland: Karger.

·9·

VISIONS OF CHILDREN AS LANGUAGE USERS: LANGUAGE AND LANGUAGE EDUCATION IN EARLY CHILDHOOD

Anne Haas Dyson

UNIVERSITY OF CALIFORNIA, BERKELEY

Celia Genishi

TEACHERS COLLEGE, COLUMBIA UNIVERSITY

During the latter part of this century, developmentalists have portrayed children as constructors—inventors—of their own gradually evolving understandings of the world. While children are becoming speakers, writers, and readers, they are also becoming meaning makers—making sense of what surrounds them (Piaget, 1954; Smith, 1975; Wells, 1986). The meanings children create for themselves are interwoven with the social history each child brings to educational settings (Vygotsky, 1978). Thus the child is not a lone scientist, but an active participant in a community, a culture. In Bruner's words:

I have come increasingly to recognize that most learning in most settings is a communal activity, a sharing of the culture. It is not just that the child must make his knowledge his own, but that he must make it his own in a community of those who share his sense of belonging to a culture. It is this that leads me to emphasize not only discovery and invention but the importance of negotiating and sharing—in a word, of joint culture creating as an object of schooling and as an appropriate step enroute to becoming a member of the adult society in which one lives out one's life. (1986, p. 127)

In this chapter we discuss how this vision of the child as a member of a community has been reflected in and has helped shape recent research in language arts education in early childhood. To introduce our review, we present a slice of classroom life in an urban K–1 classroom. The talk among the first graders and their teacher, Genevive, foreshadows the research themes and issues we explore.

Genevive's first graders have just finished taking a standardized test and are eager to voice their opinions about their initiation into this school ritual. Genevive explains to the children that the test is required by the school board.

Shawnda: But why would the school board give us such a hard test? We never gave them a hard test.

Genevive: That's a good question for you to ask them. . . . What else might you want to ask them?

Monique: Why did you just give us a hard test? Because some of us don't really think it's good, cause me and Maya started to cry. And it was hard for some of us.

Many other children express similar sentiments. Edward J., however, begins to get silly:

Edward J: I would write [to the school board], "Scram, beat it, get lost."

Genevive: But would they know what you meant?

Eugenie: They would get mad.

Genevive: Would that help? . . .

Eugenie: They'd mark it wrong.

And Edward offers a more appropriate sentence:

Edward: That test is hard.

Genevive suggests that the children act on their concerns and write to the school board. She talks to them about how letters are written, and they begin writing their own letters to the school board—in their own handwriting, using their own ways of spelling. Mollie offers Genevive a suggestion:

Mollie: I think that what you should do is when we're done, you should read them cause they might not be able to understand them.

Genevive: After I read them, I'll see if they need editing.

Through dialogue, Genevive and her children become a group of people whose lives are socially bound together—they become a community. As members of this community, Genevive's children are eager to articulate their ideas about a significant experience. With Genevive's guidance, they participate in a complex activity in which oral and written language are both necessary. In this way, their activity reflects the emphasis in recent language arts research on how children learn language, oral and written, as they use language in *interaction with other people in purposeful activities*.

Further, undergirding much recent research is an assumption that the goal of the language arts curriculum is to help children gain control over the use of oral and written language for a range of purposes in a variety of situations—That is, that children become more *communicatively competent* as a community and, more broadly, as society members. In Genevive's activity, both Genevive herself and one of her children, Eugenie, call Edward's attention to the situational consequences of his way of expressing his opinion. Genevive offers all the children specific information to help them better accomplish their communicative end.

As we will discuss, researchers in language and language education have focused on a range of *genres,* or socially defined language events: among them, how children use oral and written language to construct or respond to narratives or stories, to explore and gain information about the world, and to offer information to others. They have also focused on *individual and sociocultural variation* in children's language use, emphasizing differences in the kinds of genres with which children are familiar. This vision of language learning as occurring in the context of meaningful, interaction-rich activities has raised many pedagogical issues. Indeed, Genevive's children themselves raise these questions. The children—active talkers, writers, and readers—have performed poorly on the state standardized achievement test, and they know that they have (not because Genevive tells them so, but because they are intelligent children aware of their own difficulties). In such measures of skills, the competence of the children—many of whom come from minority and/or low-income homes—is not always evident. What is to be made of this? Are the children not learning their "skills"? Or, are the tests not testing the children's skillfulness?

In the following sections, the themes of dialogue, of genres, and of individual and sociocultural variation are woven throughout our discussion of research on young children's language use, including their talking, writing, and responding to literature. Although written and oral language use are intertwined, we highlight first oral, then written, language. Then we consider some of the curricular and assessment issues raised by Genevive and her children and, finally, the implications of the reviewed research for teachers and children.

THE BEGINNINGS OF COMMUNICATIVE COMPETENCE

The Interactive Infant

The story of children's communicative development is embedded in their individual histories and so begins well before first contacts with schooling. Most theorists agree that human beings are born to become language users. For example, the linguist Chomsky believed that only an innate ability could enable children to acquire language so early in life (1965). This inborn mechanism was called the *language acquisition device,* or *LAD* (Chomsky, 1965; McNeill, 1966). Current theorists and researchers assume such a mechanism exists, but they highlight the interaction that must occur between a LAD and aspects of the learner's social world. As thinkers and rule formulators, children play the key role in learning the complex system of rules that make up a language. They build upon innate abilities as they actively learn from people and objects around them, their *language acquisition support system,* or *LASS* which care givers and others provide from birth onward (Bruner, 1983).

Although many people consider the first months of life to be a time of sleeping, nursing, and crying, the careful observer realizes that this is a time of rapid growth. Infants who seem to "just lie there" are from birth in a periodic state of "alert inactivity" when they take in what goes on around them (Wolff, 1966). During these times they are impressively perceptive, as if they are preparing for full participation in a community dialogue. For example, newborns (who demonstrate greater attention by more frequent sucking on a pacifier) prefer to listen to human speech rather than music or other rhythmic sounds (Butterfield & Siperstein, 1974); by 6 weeks they prefer to look more closely at faces that speak, rather than those that don't (Haith, 1980); and between 3 and 4 months they can notice when something is "out of sync" or when a speaker's words are not synchronized with mouth movements (Dodd, 1979). These studies show that infants are born not only to learn language, but also to perceive the distinct aspects of communication: listening, as well as watching and coordinating what they see with what they hear.

In short, the current portrait of the developing infant is a much more interactive one than that of 20 years ago. Thus, parents and out-of-home care givers feel a responsibility to provide a safe environment that also allows for broad exploration and for the development and orchestration of perceptual, motoric, social, and linguistic abilities.

The Development of Symbol Making: The Young Child as Oral Communicator

Children as communicators come to the foreground as soon as they are able to mesh with others, for example, through eye contact or smiling. These nonverbal behaviors develop within the first 3 months of life as child and adult begin the "dance" that is the basis for their interactive life together (Stern, 1977). The first uses of gesture add to the communicative repertoire. As Vygotsky explained, children's initial attempts to grasp objects are interpreted by their adult care givers as communicative; thus the care givers respond to children accordingly, and children's grasping movements become communicative acts of pointing (1978).

This first use of a cultural tool—a gesture—to symbolize for others inner wants and desires initiates the entire developmental history of symbol use in the child, including the use of symbols in literacy development. During the early childhood period, children become fluent and inventive users of many kinds of symbols (Vygotsky, 1978; Gardner, 1982; Nelson, 1985). Like the adults around them, children invest certain kinds of forms (e.g., movement, lines, sounds) with meaning, and thus they begin to use the movements of play, the lines of drawing, and the sounds of language to represent or symbolize the people, objects, and events that compose their world. This ability to organize and express inner feelings and experiences through shared gestural, visual, and verbal symbols is a part of children's human heritage; meaning making, like eating and sleeping, is an inherent part of being alive (Langer, 1967; Winner, 1989).

Children are viewed as meaning makers who are also *language users* when several related capacities emerge: "the capacity to make the self the object of reflection, the capacity to engage in symbolic action such as play, and the acquisition of language" (Stern, 1985, p. 165). Stern refers to this landmark as the emergence of the "verbal self," the self who will eventually be able to manipulate verbal symbols (i.e., language) to tell her or his own life story. For many developmentalists, language is the primary enabler of interpersonal relationships. So from the beginning the child acts to become a participant in a community dialogue, toward the "acquisition of shared meaning" through the use of gestures and sounds (Nelson, 1985).

Usually between their first and second birthdays, children combine sounds meaningfully to utter their first words. Although folk wisdom would say that children learn these by imitating what adults say, researchers demonstrate repeatedly that the words young children learn are always embedded in their own meaningful experiences. Nelson, for instance, found that children's first 50 words include mainly nouns that, in addition to being present in the environment, name objects acted upon or manipulated by children (1973). Nelson theorized that, once the child is able to represent experiences mentally, he or she develops "event representations" of recurring events like feeding or bathing (1985). Concepts, such as "milk," that are part of the events develop concurrently and are later labeled. This conceptual view of language development highlights the child's own point of view and need to experience events, conceptualize them, and use language to refer to them.

The acquisition of syntax, the component of language that many call *grammar* and that refers to relationships among morphemes or words in sentences, follows the 1-word stage. The multiple meanings children weave using 2-word combinations have been the subject of numerous studies, which have aimed to describe children's early grammars (Brown, 1973; Braine, 1963; Ervin & Miller, 1966). These combinations, the children's first "sentences," convey certain basic meanings about who performs actions (referred to as agent + action), where they occur (action + locative), what objects are like (attribution), and so on. Researchers have also described the development of later

utterances, such as complex sentences and those including conventional verb forms (Bloom, Lahey, Hood, Lifter, & Fiess, 1980; Gerhardt, 1989) as they add to what is known about the child as a learner of syntax or grammar explorer (Bellugi, 1988, p. 155). Further, such studies extend to include acquisition processes in languages other than English (Hakuta, 1985; McLaughlin, 1984; Slobin, 1985; Wong Fillmore, 1979). Whether children are learning one or more languages, they are consistently portrayed as resourceful and active thinkers and symbol weavers.

At the same time, researchers continue to investigate the ways in which preschoolers use language to participate in the life of their communities. As Garvey and Hogan noted, young children often appear to be *sociocentric*, rather than egocentric (1973). They show awareness of the interests and feelings of others well before age 7 or 8, the stage of concrete operations (Piaget & Inhelder, 1969). Some 2-year-olds, for example, can contribute to conversations about feelings (Dunn, 1987); and preschoolers can take the perspective of others and demonstrate the beginnings of logical inference when features of a task are familiar and sensible to them (Donaldson, 1978, 1987; Tizard & Hughes, 1984).

EARLY LANGUAGE SOCIALIZATION: THE CHILD AS SOCIAL EXPLORER

For the past 20 years, researchers have studied children not only as "grammar explorers," but also as "social explorers" (Cazden, John, & Hymes, 1972; Corsaro, 1985) and, during the past decade, as "literacy explorers" (Bissex, 1980; Dyson, 1989; Ferreiro & Teberosky, 1982; Harste, Woodward, & Burke, 1984). The fundamental work of investigators interested in the social aspects of language—sociolinguistics—called educators' attention to *language variation*. The person with communicative competence is one who can vary or adjust genres or styles of speaking to fit particular social situations (Cazden, 1970; Ervin-Tripp & Mitchell-Kernan, 1977; Gumperz & Hymes, 1972; Halliday, 1977; Labov, 1970). How these genres develop in early childhood has been the focus primarily of cross-cultural researchers who document the ways that members of a family or community socialize children into what Heath calls the group's "ways with words," (1983b). These researchers have demonstrated the notable differences between groups around the world (Schieffelin & Ochs, 1986; Snow & Ferguson, 1977). A recent example (Toda, Fogel, & Kawai, 1990) contrasts mothers of 3-month-old infants in the United States with mothers of 3-month-olds in Japan. American mothers presented more information in speech to their children than did their affect-oriented Japanese counterparts, who used more baby talk and playful sounds.

Such culture-specific ways of talking continue as children become speakers themselves. As Miller observed family interactions in the white working-class community of South Baltimore (1982), she concluded that the early grammar of the three girls she studied was similar to those of middle-class children studied earlier (Bloom, Lightbown, & Hood, 1975). The interactions, however, contained more examples of "direct instruction" than middle-class interactions do. For example, the mother of one subject, 23-month-old Amy, would say things like, "Tell her [your cousin], say "keep off"; and Amy would respond with, "Keep off. Keep off." (Miller, 1982, p. 75.)

Heath found similar patterns of interaction in a white working-class community in the Piedmont Carolinas (1983b). Her data reflected the adults' belief that they tell children what to say and that they teach appropriate ways of interacting. In contrast, Heath also recorded examples like the following in a nearby African American working-class community:

At 18 months, Lem was playing on the porch with a toy truck while his mother [Lillie Mae] and neighbor [Mattie] discussed Miss Lula's recent trip to the doctor.
Lillie Mae: Miz Lula done went to de doctor.
   Mattie: Her leg botherin' her?
      Lem: Went to *(rolling his truck and banging it against the board that separates the two halves of the porch)* de doctor, doctor leg, Miz Lu Lu Lu, Rah Rah Rah
(Heath, 1983b, p. 92)

In this community, in which children also successfully learned to talk, adults did not believe that they taught children to talk but rather that children learned by attending to the conversations of others, much as Lem does here.

On the other side of the world, Schieffelin found examples of "direction instruction," when the Kaluli of Papua New Guinea enacted routines (predictably patterned interactions) in which adults told beginning speakers (about age 2 years) exactly what to say (1986). As in other cultures, the children did not always comply, but adults persisted with their customary ways of interacting. Schieffelin also observed other routines, such as teasing, which had specific functions within the Kaluli culture. Adults tease even prelinguistic children, although they reserve provocative forms of teasing for children over 2 years of age. For example, one mother repeatedly told her 30-month-old daughter that her baby brother had died. When the daughter began to cry, the teasing mother quickly distracted and calmed her. According to Schieffelin, such interactions prepare the Kaluli children for culturally appropriate responses to grief as adults.

Dore analyzed the speech of an upper-middle-class girl named Emily, whose talk was recorded with her parents and without them (1989). The child as conversationalist is evident in this dialogue, in which Emily and her father have been talking about a trip to Childworld; the father has already described it twice:

Emily: Say again.
Father: One more time . . . and then we go to bed. On Saturday . . . we're gonna go to Childworld and we're gonna buy diapers for Emily and diapers for Stephen [her younger brother] and an intercom system so we can hear Stephen in different parts of the house . . . Good night . . . Hon. I love you.
Emily: I sleep in here.
Father: I love you, Sweety.
(Dore, 1989, p. 257)

Emily, aged 23.5 months, appears to have no trouble sustaining this conversation, perhaps so she can delay the time when she is alone. Shortly afterwards, in response to her crying, her father reminds her that babies like Stephen cry but that "big kids" don't. Thus Emily is socialized into her family's world of a house large enough for an intercom, verbal expressions of love, trips to the store, and norms for the behavior of big kids.

These examples of "ways with words" demonstrate not only that socialization through language occurs differently in different groups and cultures, but also that these "ways" are at the heart of each culture and so are taken for granted within it. Outside observers need to remind themselves that the *meaning* of events varies from culture to culture. So for middle-class parents in the United States, Schieffelin's example of the Kaluli's teasing might be interpreted as cruel; but for the Kaluli it is a necessary part of learning to be a competent member of the community. Similarly, varied ways of socializing children across cultures within the United States have purpose and meaning within the cultures.

SOCIALIZATION THROUGH TALK

The Child as Story Teller

Where Do Stories Come From?

Daddy said buy diapers for Stephen and Emmy and buy sokething [sic] for 'tephen . . . plug in . . . and say ahhh . . . and put . . . the . . . in . . . on Saturday go Childworld . . . buy diapers for Emmy and diapers for the baby . . . (deleted data)
   And the (unclear: next over?) the next people that came. Then . . . babies can cry but—big kids like Emmy don't cry . . . they go sleep but the babies cry . . . (?) everybody—the big kids like Emmy don't cry. The big kids at Tanta's cry and (say dah) but the big kids don't cry.
(Dore, 1989, p. 259)

This is a bit of 2-year-old Emily's monologue, recorded after her father left the room. Is it an early example of Emily's ability to tell her own stories? Dore suggests that it is. Although Emily is verbally precocious, the researcher proposes that all children begin to use contrasting language *functions* very early in order to accomplish their own personal and social goals. Dore uses the term *genre* (after Bakhtin, 1986) to refer to a way of organizing linguistic content, style, and structure—what others might call a *register* (Ferguson, 1977) or *code* (Berko Gleason, 1973; Gumperz, 1982). The way that adults talk to young children, sometimes called "baby talk," is a vivid example that incorporates both content and syntactic structures appropriate for children. It is also distinct from other ways of speaking—that is, it has a recognizable style.

Emily seems to *play with* the genres she hears and uses in the special social-interactive "envelope" she shares with her parents, just as Lem played with the words adults around him wove as he played with his toy truck (Heath, 1983b). A parallel situation is explored by Miller, Nemoianu, and DeJong (1986). Drawing on Miller's study of language acquisition in South Baltimore (1982), they point out that the observed working-class mothers and children contrasted with middle-class families, who often develop fictional stories based on book-reading routines. Miller's families instead engaged chiefly in factual storytelling throughout the day. This rich experience with stories would seem a good foundation for literacy learning in school (see also Miller, Potts, & Fung, 1989). Because the supposedly single genre of "storytelling" is woven differently in different families and communities, we would expect Lem, Emily, and Miller's subjects (Amy, Wendy, and Beth) to tell distinctive stories in school. *All* children learn a range of complex genres that they weave according to the ways of their families and communities.

Stories Told in School. Children tell their own stories in a range of situations. The most familiar one in early childhood settings may be that of sociodramatic play, where children assign roles and enact scenes based on actual or imagined experience. Play of this kind blends a number of abilities and skills, for example, the ability (1) to symbolize, (2) to make one object or person stand for another, and (3) to use language as a means of initiating and negotiating play, as well as a means for carrying it out (Garvey, 1977; Genishi & DiPaolo, 1982; Genishi & Galvan, 1985; Paley, 1981). Children capture what they know about physical reality and rules for living together—in other words, what they know about the world. This interaction illustrates how play provides the setting for negotiation that is child-, not teacher-, directed:

> Tessa: I'm the mother!
> Lee: Uh unh, I'm the mother! I'm the mother. She said I'm the mother.
> Teacher: You can have two mothers.
> Lee: No, we have to have one mother.
> Tessa: Two.
> Lee: One.
> Tessa: Two.
> Teacher: Lee, in our house we can have two mothers.
> Tessa: I can be the grandmother.
> Lee: No, we don't need a grandmother.
> Tessa: Yes!! You and me can be a sister, you and me can be sisters, and Lee's the mother, OK?
> (Genishi & DiPaolo, 1982, pp. 60–61)

In centers and classrooms, many adults naturally and unconsciously make judgments about play and stories that don't sound like the pretend worlds they remember or published "storybooks" with a clear beginning, middle, and end. Cazden gives a striking demonstration of such judgments, based on 12 (5 black and 7 white) graduate students' responses to the following contribution to sharing time (1988):

At Grandmother's

> Leona: On George Washington's birthday I'm goin' ice my grandmother we never haven't seen her since a long time and and she lives right near us and she's and she's gonna I'm gonna spend the night over her house and every weekend she comes to take me like on Saturdays and Sundays away from home and I spend the night over her house and one day I spoiled her dinner and we were having we were she paid ten dollars and I got eggs and stuff and I didn't even eat anything.
> (Cazden, 1988, pp. 17–18)

The students' responses to first-grader Leona's story varied; white raters judged it negatively, some suggesting it was "a terrible story" and that the child would have problems with schoolwork. In contrast, the black respondents viewed it positively; they said it was easy to understand and full of detail and interest. In fact, 3 of the black raters thought it was the best of the 5 stories they'd heard. Such divergent responses show that stories, like other ways of communicating, embody the social and linguistic styles and values of particular cultures. Thus, stories are similar to other culturally derived genres and dialects: There is nothing inherently "better" about one style of storytelling over another, just as there is nothing inherently better about one dialect over another. The stories in most children's books and textbooks reflect only a single middle-class style, which can be appreciated along with other less school-like styles and which can be learned in the classroom through exposure and interaction (Heath, 1983a).

The Child as Student

"At first it did not occur to me I was supposed to talk or to pass kindergarten.... It was when I found out I had to talk that school became a misery, that the silence became a misery" (Kingston, 1976, p. 193). This is how novelist Maxine Hong Kingston recalls her silent kindergarten year in a California public school. As a Chinese speaker, she "flunked" kindergarten because she was unaware of the demands of her classroom. Through poignant stories like hers, we discover what classroom researchers also tell us: The classroom is a communicative setting full of rules that are mysteries to some young children. The unstated rules vary, "answer when asked a question," "speak when you have 'free choice' time," "don't speak when you're working," "speak English at all times," or even "speak whenever you want." Each classroom or teacher has complex rules, depending on the teacher's, center's, or school's social and linguistic values.

One of the most common rules for child-teacher talk is, "answer when asked a question even if the teacher already knows the answer" (Labov, 1970; Mehan, 1979). This test-like situation, the "school-talk" genre, is one that many middle-class children are familiar with because their parents have asked such questions during countless comfortable interactions at home, for example, games like peek-a-boo or book reading (Cazden, 1983; Ninio & Bruner, 1978). However, in the African American working-class community that Heath studied, parents did not ask children test-like questions about things present or visible (1983b). Instead they asked for analogic comparisons ("What's that like?"); such questions were genuine since the adult did not already know the answers. So, although working-class parents may talk about topics that appeal to their children in engaging ways, they may not include "test-like" questions to which adults already know the answers (Tizard & Hughes, 1984). One point of such observations is not to judge the different ways of speaking as better or worse, but to alert educators to differences that may affect how children learn in school. This research highlights the need for early childhood teachers' to acquire greater general knowledge about differences, sensitivity, and nonjudgmental attitudes toward the genres they hear.

SOCIALIZATION THROUGH TALK ABOUT PRINT: CHILDHOOD LITERACY BEGINS

Recent research on young children's literacy development has documented how children make use of and acquire knowledge about written language, just as they do oral language, through interaction with others. Just as Genevive introduced her young students into a genre of literacy use, so too do parents and other care givers initiate children into a range of literacy genres in homes and communities. They do not do so through planned lessons, but by demonstrating and engaging children in everyday literacy activities.

Indeed, even in communities where literacy assumes a relatively minor role, children are not isolated from written language (Heath, 1983b). In our society, children are surrounded by traffic signs; dotted lines for signatures; and labeled cans, boxes, and even clothes. Even children who do not conventionally read and write may take to pen and paper. Accordingly, they may participate in literacy activities with more skilled others and explore print's functions and features—thus using it as a means of social connection, self-expression, and individual and joint exploration of a basic cultural tool (Bissex, 1980; Clay, 1975; Gundlach, McLane, Stott, & McNamee, 1985; McLane & McNamee, 1990; Tizard & Hughes, 1984). In Nelson's terms, print is part of the scripts of children's everyday lives (1985).

Studies of children's initiation into literacy in the home highlight qualities of environments that help literacy become an interesting and valued part of children's lives. The most extensive of such studies is that of Heath, who, as discussed above, documented language use in 2 working-class communities and in the homes of middle-class teachers in the Piedmont Carolinas (1983b). Individuals in all 3 settings were literate, in that all made use of written language. For example, in all communities, people made lists and wrote notes. However, only children in the middle-class homes were involved in a kind of literacy activity particularly valued in early childhood classrooms—elaborate talk about fictional storybooks.

Children in the middle-class classrooms, both African American and white, were socialized to become members of a society in which books and information gained from books play a significant and ongoing role in helping one learn about the world. With children as young as 6 months old, parents interacted during book-reading events in ways that paralleled the school-talk genre, including that of primary-grade reading lessons.

Children from the observed white working-class community were also involved in book-reading events, but these events centered on alphabet and number books, "real-life" stories, Bible stories, and nursery rhymes. In both conversations about such books and children's and adults' oral stories, the focus was on factual reporting of events. Similarly, children from the observed African American community had much experience with story and with the print in their environment but not with story-reading events. Instead children heard and told a kind of story that was, in some ways, unique to their cultural heritage. The stories, which could be performed rather than simply told, were fictionalized versions of true events that put those familiar events into new contexts.

Heath's work thus highlights the variation in the kinds of experiences with literacy that children bring to school. More broadly, it highlights variation in the nature of stories—oral, written, factual, and fictional—and in how stories or experience in general is talked about. A story's elements may be labeled, its events recounted, and its nature linked to other experiences in other places, including in other books. Further, as also emphasized by Schieffelin and Cochran-Smith, these variations in literacy use come about because of how literacy figures into ongoing human purposes and relationships (1984).

Schieffelin and Cochran-Smith compare literacy experiences as revealed in three distinctive studies of community and family life: Cochran-Smith's (1984) study of preschool children from a Philadelphia suburb attending a nursery school; Schieffelin's study of immigrant Chinese families from Vietnam, also in Philadelphia, and Schieffelin's study of families in traditionally nonliterate Papua New Guinea.

The children in Cochran-Smith's study were not, as she comments, "so much surrounded by print as by adults who routinely chose to use print" in a variety of ways. For example, adults labeled children's belongings, used books and other printed materials to introduce or verify new information and experiences, acted as scribes to record children's ideas and feelings for self-expression and for communication, and relaxed and entertained the children through storybooks. At first, adults initiated the use of print in response to children's perceived needs, but, eventually, the children themselves did so.

Although the Chinese children Schieffelin studied were not from "literate" family environments, they were from a tradition that has long valued literacy and, in addition, were faced with many literacy demands in their new U.S. environment. The school-aged children helped their parents cope with these demands and found for themselves social networks for literacy learning in school. On the other hand, a Papuan mother, at her 2-year-old's request, interacted with the child about books obtained for literacy lessons at a mission. However, the book-reading activity was "to no purpose," in the mother's words. Becoming literate was a part of gaining access to mission life, to life outside the village; it was not a way of becoming a more powerful member of the village itself or of the family. Thus, the activity would seem to have no enduring function in the life of the child.

As Schieffelin and Cochran-Smith note, "one theme that emerges from all of our study examples is that, for an individual to become literate, literacy must be functional, relevant, and meaningful for individuals and the society in which they live" (1984, p. 22). And, as the Chinese children suggest, socialization into particular kinds of literacy use does not need to occur in the home.

LITERACY SOCIALIZATION AT SCHOOL: THE CLASSROOM AS LITERACY COMMUNITY

The general qualities of environments for literacy learning at home have influenced researchers' efforts to study how these qualities would be realized in the early childhood classroom.

First, a number of researchers have, in varied ways, studied *literacy's embeddedness in the daily life of the classroom*. For example, Taylor, Blum, and Logsdon collaborated with preschool teachers in developing classroom environments for literacy learning (1986). They then studied the nature of the environments that the teachers created and how differences in the richness of those environments were related to children's awareness of written language and to vocabulary growth. They thus provided evidence that simple activities integrating print into children's daily classroom life—activities like having children sign in every morning, making child-level labels and written displays, and providing ample opportunities to explore written materials—can indeed help children learn of the functional as well as the technical aspects of print (letters, sounds, words).

Many of the functions that children experience in adult-guided situations may be explored by them when literacy becomes a part of their daily dramatic play. Thus, researchers and educators have been interested in how adults might encourage this activity through the arrangement of play centers (Hall, 1987). For example, Neuman and Roskos (1990) demonstrated that clearly defined play centers stocked with appropriate literacy props (e.g., "the post office," "the office") can support play with the social roles and functions of print. On the other hand, some researchers suggest that open-ended "writing centers" may promote valuable exploratory play with print; children explore its visual and orthographic qualities just as they play with qualities of line and shape in drawing and with the malleable nature of clay in sculpting (Clay, 1975; Cochran-Smith, 1984; Dyson, 1983).

Well-designed classroom libraries also help literacy to become an important part of children's daily routines (Morrow, 1982, 1987; Morrow & Weinstein 1982, 1986). From nursery school through the elementary grades, a cozy corner filled with a variety of kinds of books, some of which beckon to children from open-faced shelving, is a fine place for 5 or 6 children to read alone or with a friend or, perhaps, to listen to a taped story.

Whereas the above studies have detailed the qualities of environments, a second critical aspect of literacy *communities* is *the nature of the talk accompanying literacy activities*. It is talk that reveals the social function and the semantic sense of text to children. Much research focused on qualities of teacher-child dialogue has centered on particularly valued school literacy activities, especially talk about story.

As part of Cochran-Smith's study of the Philadelphia preschool, she closely examined the interactional process through which the teacher helped the children enter into the worlds of storybooks (1984). During story reading teacher and children negotiated the meaning of books together. The teacher paid attention to what the children noticed, understood, or were confused by in the text and pictures. Moreover, through her own responses, the teacher guided the children through different kinds of texts, helping them to experience and respond to different genres in different ways: Some books are filled with information, some make us laugh, others make us sad in a gentle way.

Any introduction of story into a classroom community can be assumed to affect the life of the children there in some way. Feitelson has provided illustrations of this influence in Israeli classrooms for children who, unlike Cochran-Smith's children, come from homes with few books (Feitelson, 1988; Feitelson & Goldstein, 1986; Feitelson & Iraqi, 1990). Some children of the studies spoke a local Arabic dialect differing from the literary Arabic dialect used in school texts. Compared to children in control classrooms, children in classrooms with daily story times improved significantly on tests of reading comprehension and other language skills; moreover, the children began to use literary language themselves in the play corner. Indeed, for children from a diversity of sociocultural backgrounds, a daily time for reading and talking about books has been consistently shown to influence strongly children's interest in, knowledge of, and ability to engage with books (for a thorough review, see Galda & Cullinan, 1991).

In one project teachers read children serial books about the pranks of a monkey named Kofiko, a set of books not particularly valued as quality literature by teachers but generally liked by children (Feitelson & Goldstein, 1986). The children became fond of the character and even requested Kofiko books as holiday presents. The power of children themselves to bring books into the home in culturally appropriate ways has also been studied by Kawakami (1990).

Another valued classroom activity involving much teacher-child dialogue is story dictation. Vivian Paley has written extensively about the kind of community building that occurs in her own classroom as drama is used to bring children's dictated stories into the classroom community (1990). McNamee, McLane, Cooper, and Kerwin (1985; see also McLane & McNamee, 1990) introduced variations of Paley's story by using dictating and dramatization activities in 10 preschool, kindergarten, and day care center classrooms serving approximately 200 3- to 5-year-olds. Although children in the 5 control classrooms dictated stories, only the children in the 5 experimental classrooms dramatized their narratives at a teacher-directed group time. These children dramatized classic fairy tales, picture book stories, and poems. As McNamee and colleagues suggest, their characters and themes (which dealt with their wishes and dreams) became a part of the community, and thus the children had a reason to become more active controllers of their stories.

Similarly, in primary-grade classrooms influenced by Graves's work on young children's writing in classroom "workshops," children's skills as written language users are supported by teacher-child dialogue about their written pieces and through much sharing in the classroom community (1983). Teachers confer with children about their work, including their writing processes and products and their evaluations of their own work.

As explained by Sowers, this approach was influenced by Donald Murray's work on writing and teaching writing to older students (1985). To provide developmental underpinnings for conferencing, Sowers turns to Vygotskian theory (Vygotsky, 1978). Teacher-student interaction during conferences may be internalized by children, so that they begin to ask themselves and each other questions that are similar to those asked them by their teachers. Moreover, the social energy of the classroom community itself—the children's interest in and involvement with each other's texts—may fuel their individual efforts, much as in Paley's classroom (Dyson, 1987).

A third key characteristic of literacy learning is *the existence of sociocultural diversity in ways of using oral and written language.* Researchers and educators have studied how this diversity manifests itself in the classroom. Kamehameha Elementary Education Program (KEEP) is an exemplary research and development organization that aims to support teachers' efforts to respond to cultural diversity, particularly for native Hawaiian children (Au & Jordan, 1981; Vogt, Jordan, & Tharp, 1987). Among its most significant aspects have been its emphasis, during reading instruction, on children's comprehension of text and, particularly, on their relating story content to their own personal experiences. This talk about story takes place in comfortable, culturally compatible ways. Rather than teachers calling on children individually to respond to text questions, teacher and children jointly reconstruct the story, voluntarily taking turns in offering comments, overlapping one another's talk.

In addition to allowing this "talk story" (this cultural style of co–narration of stories), KEEP also encourages teachers to allow children to help each other so that support for language activities is not dependent only on teacher intervention. When the KEEP program was initiated at a Navajo reservation, the Navajo children engaged in much less spontaneous interaction than the Hawaiian children had. In order to support peer interaction and help, the teachers organized the students so that they were in small groups (2 or 3 students of the same sex), a grouping format more comfortable for them.

Sociocultural differences also manifest themselves in children's ways of writing. Dyson analyzed the classroom literacy behaviors of a first grader, Jameel, who had a performative, rather than a simply communicative, style of writing stories (1992). He used school story-writing events to perform, often exploiting the musical aspects (e.g., the rhythm and rhyme) of language. For example, following is Jameel's story about cat and his ill-fated friend hat:

> Sat on Cat Sat on Hat
> Hat Sat on CAT
> CAt GoN [gone.] 911 for CAt

Jameel's stories were not always "sensible" to others who expected literal and explicit sense in stories, even though such demands were not necessarily made of trade books in his classroom, which tended to by rhythmic and repetitive. However, Jameel would use explicit, analytic prose when he viewed himself as a teacher of someone needing information (Chafe, 1982). Studies of nonmainstream children's stories and word definition tasks have suggested that students are unable to control expository or explicit, analytic prose (Dickinson & Snow, 1987; Michaels & Collins, 1984). Jameel's case thus suggests the importance of looking across social situations before making judgments about a child's language repertoire (Cazden & Mehan, 1989; Labov, 1970).

Jameel's case also emphasizes the importance of *children's* perspectives on literacy events in the classroom, rather than those of adults in the classroom community. In the next section, we examine more closely children's ways with written words.

THE DEVELOPMENT OF SYMBOL MAKING: THE CHILD AS WRITTEN COMMUNICATOR

To understand how children make sense of written language, researchers have had to consider children's use of a range of symbolic media. For young children may participate in "literacy" activities by using other, earlier-controlled symbolic tools. For example, pictures may be used in ways that foreshadow the use of written language (Dyson, 1982; Gundlach, 1982; Halliday, 1977; Werner & Kaplan, 1963). Children often send letters made up of drawing to grandparents or teachers.

Researchers must also consider children's behavior in a range of literacy situations. Children's initial use of any symbolic tool, including written language, is very fluid and flexible, so that they can freely explore its nature and gain some comfort, some familiarity, with its functions, forms, and processes (Nelson & Nelson, 1978; Vygotsky, 1962; Werner, 1948). For example, when children play waiter or reporter, they may use cursive-like script, trying out writing's functional possibilities without attempting to precisely encode; at other times, they may use scribble or "cursive" writing to encode long stories or letters (Dyson, 1983; Sulzby, 1985a). They may even manipulate the graphic forms themselves without any particular intended message (Clay, 1975). Thus, very young children's style of writing varies with purpose.

As children explore the written system in a variety of social situations, they begin to discover its inner workings—how meaning and print connect. In their earliest writing, young children do not precisely encode meaning. Rather, as in their first drawings, it is the act itself—the gesture and any accompanying talk—that makes the writing meaningful (Dyson, 1983, 1989; Luria, 1983). Children make lines and letter-like marks that approximate the writing of those around them. They may read their own writing or ask others to read it (Clay, 1975). As discussed above, they may incorporate writing into dramatic play, making grocery lists, taking phone messages, and generally carrying on daily business (Schickedanz, 1978; Jacob, 1984). They may offer their graphics to others and thereby confer upon such works the status of "gifts" or "presents" (Bissex, 1980; Dyson, 1982; Taylor, 1983).

When young children begin to realize that forming letters is not enough to produce something readable, they may continue to "just write" letters or to use cursive-like writing for longer discourse, like stories, but attempt particular letters for shorter units, like their names. Indeed, most children have an intense interest in the letters of their own names (see Baghban, 1984, and Ferreiro, 1986, for detailed analyses of young children's explorations of the letters of their names).

Researchers have examined children's construction of the spelling system, documenting early efforts like a 3-year-old's string of circles and curvy lines, to more sophisticated forms like a 6-year-old's ILVBS ("I love 'basghetti") (Ferreiro &

Teberosky, 1982; Read, 1986). Initially, children may use a certain number of letters or letter-like marks to represent their meaning, hypothesizing a direct and concrete relationship between features of those letters and their intended meaning. Children seem particularly sensitive to the size and age of the referent. For example, one 4-year-old, Marianna, asked for a small number of letters to write her own name and as much as a thousand to write her father's name, which had only 2 syllables (Ferreiro, 1980).

Such hypotheses introduce many puzzling circumstances for children. For example, the names of fathers and mothers may well have fewer letters than the names of babies. As children resolve such puzzles, their encoding behavior may gradually reflect an understanding that there must be differences in the selection and/or arrangement of letters if there are to be differences in the meanings found there. They begin to search for some sort of reliable one-to-one correspondence between selected letters and referents. Children often assume that, in carefully pronouncing the referent's name, they will articulate the names of the necessary letters themselves. Thus they write words like *KD* ("candy") and, of course, *TV*. Eventually, as Read has documented, children may begin to use characteristics of the sound of the word itself to invent spellings, evidence that children are beginning to use written language as a second order or notational system: using letters to represent sounds, rather than letters being themselves the sounds (1971, 1986; Beers & Henderson, 1977).

Young children often "weave" their written words with talk and drawing to create their early stories and reports (Dyson, 1986, 1989; Newkirk, 1987, 1989). Typically, the writing itself labels an important object or figure or it may represent the actual words spoken by a drawn character. In time, children must differentiate between all the symbol systems they use as authors. An important resource for this differentiation between symbol systems is the talk children themselves engage in about their efforts. To understand the contribution of peer talk, we must first consider how shared symbol making comes to play a role in peer social life in the classroom community.

Creating Imaginary Worlds in the Classroom Community

As earlier discussed, Paley has described how opportunities to dictate stories allow her young students opportunities to organize their responses to daily experiences—their thoughts, feelings, and dreams (1981, 1986, 1990). Moreover, articulating those experiences in stories that are then acted out brings each child's themes and scripts into the classroom community, thereby allowing children together to make the world more reasonable and more controlled than any child could alone.

In classrooms, the organization and sharing of experience can happen through the use of varied media. For example, children use play, like storytelling, to transform emotionally significant experiences in order to express and interpret them, to give outer form to their inner worlds. To use Fein's image, play is a "canvas" in which young children can symbolize ideas and feelings through gestures and speech (1987). As children grow

as symbolic players and social beings, they paint the canvas collaboratively with their friends.

In centers and classrooms, children's skill as collaborative storytellers and players may infuse their drawing, as the blank page can also become a canvas for children's shared dramas. For example, two kindergarten boys, Nate and Chiel, playfully enacted Nate's drawing of a person jumping off a diving board:

Nate: Boing, boing, boing *(bouncing in his chair)*. Boing, boing, boing…Chiel, I made a picture of somebody diving off the diving board. And there's no water in the swimming pool. Hah hah hah hah.

Chiel: Oh! I have no head. *(feeling above his head and playing along with Nate)*

The written words of kindergarten and early primary grade children often do not capture the stories enacted through talk and drawing. Dyson observed 4- to 8-year old children's symbol making and social interactions during a daily composing period (1989, 1991). The observed children initially relied on drawing and talking to carry much of their story meaning and, also, to engage their peers' attention, just as Nate did. Their writing and dictating served primarily to describe their pictures. In time, though, the children began to attend to each other's reading and planning of their texts, evidencing the curiosity children have about what their peers are doing. Their playful and critical talk thus engulfed their writing and helped it become a legitimate object of attention, separate from their pictures.

In Dyson's study, children began to consider critically the relationship between their pictures and their texts as they assumed more deliberate control over the kind of information they would include in each medium. Gradually, their written stories contained more narrative action, their pictures more illustrations of key ideas. Moreover, they began to use writing to playfully engage their friends. They used friends as characters in their stories, and they also began to deliberately plan to include certain words or actions to amuse or tease them. Thus, the children came to understand that writers and readers interact within words, and that, as authors, they were in charge of the interaction.

Responding to Imaginary Worlds in the Classroom Community

The use of multiple media and peer talk is also a theme of research on children's ways of reading and responding to literature. In rereading favorite storybooks, very young children may depend upon the pictures, labeling what they see there, whereas older children may come increasingly to depend upon print and their knowledge of the specific register of storybooks as well as of the demands of the orthographic system (Bussis, Chittenden, Amarel, & Klausner, 1985; Sulzby, 1985b). In an insightful analysis of picture books, Meek details the layers of meaning—the foreshadowing, the ironic twists, the subtleties of theme and metaphor, even the complementary but different genres—that exist in the illustrations of picture books (1988).

The "lessons" that children learn from books are not solely about print but about the power of different media.

Moreover, children's own interpretations of text—their understandings of the basic characters, plot, and theme, as well as the connections they see to their own lives—are often revealed in children's use of play, drawing, or writing (Hickman, 1981, 1983). Young children's *verbal* understandings of book themes may be expressed in terms close to those of the book. Hickman offers this example: After hearing "The Little Red Hen," a first grader proclaimed that its lesson was that "when someone already baked the cake and you haven't helped, they're probably just gonna say no" (1980, p. 101). The replaying of the tale's themes of cooperation and laziness may occur, not in explicit verbal discussion, but in the child's actual play, as characters, actions, and the very words of the text are recast in new child-constructed contexts. In such ways, children's voices, drawn pictures, and expressive movements help them fill the words on the page with their own memories and images, just as may happen when they draw and write their own stories (Rosenblatt, 1978).

Further, the language, images, characters, and plots of literature can become interwoven into the life of the classroom, just as can those of children's own stories—each infusing the other, and passing from child to child in complex ways (Feitelson, 1986; Hickman, 1983). Paley's description of children at play seems, in a metaphoric sense, to capture how children take over stories and infuse them into their own ongoing story as class members:

The children sounded like groups of actors, rehearsing spontaneous skits on a moving stage, blending into one another's plots, carrying on philosophical debates while borrowing freely from the fragments of dialogue that floated by. Themes from fairy tales and television cartoons mixed easily with social commentary and private fantasies, so that what to me often sounded random and erratic formed a familiar and comfortable world for the children. (1986, p. 124)

CURRENT ISSUES: SUPPORTING AND ASSESSING CHILD LANGUAGE IN THE CLASSROOM COMMUNITY

What Is an Appropriate Curriculum?

As we have shown, research on oral and written language development depicts children as impressively healthy communicators who are born to make sense of the situations around them, often through the use of spoken and written language. The situations to which they're accustomed are lifelike and meaningful—that is, they contain people and things that are familiar and sensible. By the time children enter an educational setting, all normal children are developing or have developed appropriate ways of learning and communicating within their own families and communities. And once they are in out-of-home settings, teachers need to allow children to *continue* to make sense of situations in light of previous experience.

Because children come to educational settings with varied histories, early childhood educators work to provide curricula that are responsive to diverse groups of children. In other words, the main challenge for educators is to provide a *range* of developmentally appropriate settings (Bredekamp, 1987), not a single type of setting appropriate for all children.

Once children attend preschool or primary school, choices among types of curriculum may vary sharply. The most widely debated contrast between types is the *developmentally appropriate* versus the academic. Broad studies of classrooms that are either developmentally appropriate or inappropriate provide preliminary evidence that less academically oriented programs are associated with children demonstrating fewer stress behaviors (Burts, Hart, Charlesworth, & Kirk, 1990). Hirsh-Pasek, Hyson, and Rescorla, measuring such variables as academic skills, anxiety, attitude toward school, and creativity, found no academic advantages for middle-class prekindergarten and kindergarten children who attended highly academic (teacher-directed) schools (1990). Further, they reported possible disadvantages in creativity and emotional well-being. A controversial older study, based on a retrospective look at 54 subjects, also supported less structure or less teacher direction (Schweinhart, Weikart, & Larner, 1986). According to their self-reports at age 15, the former Head Start pupils who experienced the highly structured Distar curriculum more often led socially dysfunctional lives (with stays in reform school or prison) than did pupils in less structured programs.

In terms of curricula for language and literacy education, *whole language* (holistic) versus *phonics* (sequenced and skills-oriented) instruction are as controversial as those studies contrasting highly-structured versus less-structured early childhood classrooms. There is controversy partly because the boundaries between terms like *whole language* and *phonics* are fuzzy, especially when one observes the complex and varied activities that occur in actual classrooms. Further, these approaches are associated most often with ways of teaching beginning reading in the primary grades; there's little research available on how these approaches vary at the preschool level. For example, Stahl and Miller reported that whole language or language experience approaches to language arts and reading instruction are more effective in kindergarten than in first grade (1989). In a critique of this study, Schickedanz pointed out that the greatest number of programs studied showed no significant differences between the approaches; thus Stahl and Miller's analysis was misleading (1990). Further, she stated that longitudinal data following the students beyond third grade was not available, making Stahl and Miller's conclusions less definitive. Other proponents of whole language highlight the narrowness of research methods that purport to contrast different types of instruction. McGee and Lomax (1990) and Edelsky (1990) argue that critics of whole language often fail to understand the nature of a "whole-language classroom," which focuses not narrowly on learning to read, but broadly on learning all subject matter through meaningful, holistic uses of language. The point on which whole language advocates and researchers (e.g., Stahl, 1990; McKenna, Robinson, & Miller, 1990) who are not identified with whole language agree is that more in-depth research is needed comparing different approaches to instruction.

In practice, whole language classrooms are not in the majority. Many studies, including Smith's (1986) of over 400 kindergartens in California, Durkin's (1987, 1990) of kindergartens in Illinois, and Strickland and Ogle's (1990) study of 5 kindergartens in various areas of the country, suggest that workbooks and work sheets oriented toward phonics teaching are dominant in kindergarten and primary-grade classrooms. At the same time, there are teachers who favor a flexible child-centered curriculum and combine holistic, language-based activities with occasional purposeful teaching of skills, including letter naming and sound-to-symbol correspondences (see chapter 3 in Perl & Wilson, 1986; Schickedanz, 1989). The controversies that polarize researchers need not prevent classroom teachers from making their own eclectic and sensible choices.

What Is Appropriate Assessment?

Closely linked to the issue of appropriate curricula is the issue of *how best to assess* children as they engage in language arts activities. At the early childhood level, studies of more broadly based issues are more common than those related only to language. As the number of programs available for young children grows (for example, public-school programs for 4-year-olds, full-day kindergarten, bilingual programs), the number of standardized measures increases. Thus, children take tests before entering preschool or kindergarten and then before entering first grade, that often "sort" them into specially funded or transitional kindergarten classes versus regular first grades. Such practices seem to be increasing despite the results of research showing that transitional classes and kindergarten retention do little to improve children's school achievement in later years (Smith & Shepard, 1988; Sternberg, 1991).

With respect to language arts education, recent research has focused on assessment of beginning reading. Like other measures of reading achievement, most reading tests are traditional paper-and-pencil ("bubble-sheet") tests. The young children in Genevive's class, introduced as this chapter opened, already knew about such tests and the issues of fairness they raised. Standardized tests function less to provide information about individuals than to provide information about groups of children to people outside the classroom, such as principals and boards of education. Test scores have the advantage of being "comparable" from school to school and state to state. They are well designed to measure and compare *products,* children's performances on specific questions or tasks (Clay, 1990). Thus, they effectively assess a curriculum built upon uniform and specific objectives for all children.

Curricula that are intended to respond to diverse needs (developmentally appropriate or child-oriented curricula) avoid a narrow band of objectives and so are difficult to assess within the traditional framework of testing. So, many proponents of whole language resist this framework, as well as the term *assessment* because of its association with standardized testing. Likewise, they reject conventional research methods, which incorporate test scores and numerical outcome measures. These proponents recommend qualitative methods that focus on the processes of teaching and learning in particular classrooms (Edelsky, 1990; Goodman, Goodman, & Hood, 1989). Teachers' own observations and documentations are seen as most appropriate for following progress and learning. This "grass-roots" approach is based on a belief that ways of following (assessing, in our view) what children do and know is intimately linked with the curriculum, that is, what is taught and learned. A major purpose of assessing is to guide next steps in teachers' work with individual children. Thus, child-oriented assessment has a clear function in daily classroom life; it becomes part of the ongoing dialogue between children and teachers and helps establish the direction that dialogue takes in language arts activities and across the curriculum.

The opposition between these two world views of assessment parallels that between a skills-oriented and holistic approach to language arts. Researchers and practitioners articulate their support of alternatives to traditional testing from varied viewpoints (Barr, Ellis, Hester, & Thomas, 1988; Carini, 1982; Chittenden & Courtney, 1989; Genishi, 1992; Genishi & Dyson, 1989; Kamii, 1990; Meisels, 1987; National Association for the Education of Young Children, 1991; Teale, Hiebert, & Chittenden, 1987; Wexler-Sherman, Gardner, & Feldman, 1988). Common themes in their writing are that assessment should be conceived of broadly to reflect the abilities of children in a number of domains (artistic and motoric, as well as verbal and mathematical) and that it should reflect the judgments and knowledge of those closest to children, including teachers and parents. Observation of processes of learning, as in early writing, along with means for documenting the processes, are also emphasized. Alternative means include portfolios and focused discussion of content in areas such as science and math (Chittenden, 1990; Moxley, Kenny, & Hunt, 1990).

For teachers with children whose dialect or language is different from middle-class English speakers, assessment is especially troublesome. Standardized tests for children who know English may penalize the linguistically different, and even tests for bilingual children may be inappropriate for those who are strangers to the school-talk genre and the demands of paper-and-pencil tests (Wong Fillmore, 1991). So it is for the children who find dialogue in the typical classroom difficult that alternative ways of assessing language and literacy are most essential. As school children become increasingly diverse, responsive teachers recognize that what is appropriate socially and linguistically in their own communities may not be in their children's. Thus, reserving judgment about children's abilities is a first step in teachers' assessments of what linguistically different children can do or want to do. Careful observation of what children do is a second step (Genishi, 1992; Genishi & Dyson, 1984; Jaggar & Smith-Burke, 1985). A concurrent step is to initiate and maintain dialogues with parents: what do families want for their children? And what are their goals and expectations as children become part of a wider "school culture"? (Delpit, 1988; Wong Fillmore, 1989).

CONCLUSION

Curricula and assessment for all children needs to be developed from within classroom communities that acknowledge the uniqueness of each child. All children have learned to use symbolic tools—the gestures, sounds, and movements of drawing, play, and dance—to represent the world for themselves and others. They thus gain an understanding of themselves as active agents in a social world—as successful learners who can learn to act on and in their worlds.

In classrooms, teachers like Genevive work to expand children's senses of themselves as competent, skillful people who can use language to take action as well as to play and to reflect. Teachers do so by creating safe, affirming, and challenging environments for children, particularly by creating an interactive "envelope"—networks of relationships, a community—within which children can continue to learn. For, in order to learn new ways with oral and written words, all learners must have trust in their teachers—trust that their efforts will be rewarded, their basic human competence respected (Erickson, 1987). Trust in the community can be threatened if children's resources are not recognized.

In the community of the classroom, children are often expected to act through spoken and written language, although curricula that are truly child-oriented leave spaces for expression through movement, the arts, spatial or mathematical manipulation, and so on. As Stern noted, language is a double-edged sword that can at once join us to a community and distance us from our own deeply felt nonverbal responses and actions (1985). The kind of classroom supported by much of the research reviewed here values language as just one critical tool that children and teachers use to make sense of experience. Understanding children's social networks in and out of the classroom, their symbolic tools, and their memories and images as carried through those tools may help us transform early childhood classrooms into places where all children can build on the resources they bring.

References

Au, K. H., & Jordan, C. (1981). Teaching reading to Hawaiian children: Finding a culturally appropriate solution. In H. T. Trueba, G. Guthrie, & K. H. Au (Eds.), *Culture and the bilingual classroom: Studies in classroom ethnography* (pp. 139–152). Rowley, MA: Newbury House.

Baghban, M. (1984). *Our daughter learns to read and write: A case study from birth to three.* Newark, DE: International Reading Association.

Bakhtin, M. (1986). *Speech genres and other late essays.* Austin, TX: University of Texas Press.

Barr, M., Ellis, S., Hester, H., & Thomas, A. (1988). *The primary language record: Handbook for teachers.* Portsmouth, NH: Heinemann.

Beers, J. W., & Henderson, E. H. (1977). A study of developing orthographic concepts among first graders. *Research in the Teaching of English, 11*(2), 133–148.

Bellugi, U. (1988). The acquisition of spatial language. In F. Kessel (Ed.), *The development of language and language researchers* (pp. 153–186). Hillsdale, NJ: Erlbaum.

Berko Gleason, J. (1973). Code switching in children's language. In T. E. More (Ed.), *Cognitive development and the acquisition of language* (pp. 159–168). New York: Academic Press.

Bissex, G. (1980). *Gnys at wrk: A child learns to read and write.* Cambridge, MA: Harvard University Press.

Bloom, L., Lahey, J., Hood, L., Lifter, K., & Fiess, K. (1980). Complex sentences: Acquisition of syntactic connectives and the semantic relations they encode. *Journal of Child Language, 7,* 235–261.

Bloom, L., Lightbown, P., & Hood, L. (1975). Structure and variation in child language. *Monographs of the Society for Research in Child Development, 40* (2, Serial No. 160).

Braine, M. D. S. (1963). The ontogeny of English phrase structure: The first phase. *Language, 39,* 1–13.

Bredekamp, S. (Ed.). (1987). *Developmentally appropriate practice in early childhood programs serving children from birth through age 8.* Washington, DC: National Association for the Education of Young Children.

Brown, R. (1973). *A first language.* Cambridge, MA: Harvard University Press.

Bruner, J. (1983). *Child's talk.* New York: W. W. Norton.

Bruner, J. (1986). *Actual minds, possible worlds.* Cambridge, MA: Harvard University Press.

Burts, D. C., Hart, C. H., Charlesworth, R., & Kirk, L. (1990). A comparison of frequencies of stress behaviors observed in kindergarten children in classrooms with developmentally appropriate vs.

developmentally inappropriate practices. *Early Childhood Research Quarterly, 5,* 407–424.

Bussis, A. M., Chittenden, E. A., Amarel, M., & Klausner E. (1985). *Inquiry into meaning: An investigation of learning to read.* Hillsdale, NJ: Erlbaum.

Butterfield, E. C., & Siperstein, G. N. (1974). Influence of contingent auditory stimulation upon non-nutritional suckle. In *Proceedings of Third Symposium on Oral Sensation and Perception: The mouth of the infant* (pp. 123–126). Springfield, IL: Charles C. Thomas.

Carini, P. (1982). *The school lives of seven children.* Grand Forks, ND: University of North Dakota Press.

Cazden, C. B. (1970). The neglected situation in child language research. In F. Williams (Ed.), *Language and poverty: Perspectives on a theme.* Chicago: Markham.

Cazden, C. B. (1983). Peekaboo as an instructional model: Discourse development at school and at home. In B. Bain (Ed.), *The sociogenesis of language and human conduct: A multidisciplinary book of readings* (pp. 257–277). New York: Plenum.

Cazden, C. B. (1988). *Classroom discourse: The language of teaching and learning.* Portsmouth, NH: Heinemann.

Cazden, C. B., John, V., & Hymes, D. (Eds.). (1972). *Functions of language in the classroom.* New York: Teachers College Press.

Cazden, C. B., & Mehan, H. (1989). Principles from sociology and anthropology: Context, code, classroom, and culture. In M. C. Reynolds (Ed.), *Knowledge base for the beginning teacher* (pp. 163–172). New York: Pergamon.

Chafe, W. (1982). Integration and involvement in speaking, writing, and oral literature. In D. Tannen (Ed.), *Spoken and written language: Exploring orality and literacy* (pp. 35–53). Norwood, NJ: Ablex.

Chittenden, E. (1990). Young children's discussions of science topics. In G. Hein (Ed.), *The assessment of hands-on elementary science programs.* Monograph of the North Dakota Study Group on Evaluation. Grand Forks, ND: University of North Dakota Press.

Chittenden, E., & Courtney, R. (1989). Assessment of young children's reading: Documentation as an alternative to testing. In D. S. Strickland & L. M. Morrow (Eds.), *Emerging literacy: Young children learn to read and write* (pp. 107–120). Newark, DE: International Reading Association.

Chomsky, N. (1965). *Aspects of a theory of syntax.* Cambridge, MA: M.I.T. Press.

Clay, M. (1975). *What did I write?* Auckland, New Zealand: Heinemann.

Clay, M. M. (1990). Research currents: What is and what might be in evaluation. *Language Arts, 67,* 288–298.

Cochran-Smith, M. (1984). *The making of a reader.* Norwood, NJ: Ablex.

Corsaro, W. A. (1985). *Friendship and peer culture in the early years.* Norwood, NJ: Ablex.

Delpit, L. (1988). The silenced dialogue: Power and pedagogy in educating other peoples' children. *Harvard Educational Review, 58,* 280–298.

Dickinson, D. K., & Snow, C. E. (1987). Interrelationships between pre-reading and oral language skills in kindergartners from two social classes. *Early Childhood Research Quarterly, 2*(1), 1–25.

Dodd, B. (1979). Lip reading in infants: Attention to speech presented in- and out-of synchrony. *Cognitive Psychology 11,* 478–484.

Donaldson, M. (1978). *Children's minds.* New York: Norton.

Donaldson, M. (1987). The origins of inference. In J. Bruner & H. Haste (Eds.), *Making sense: The child's construction of the world* (pp. 97–107). New York: Methuen.

Dore, J. (1989). Monologue as reenvoicement of dialogue. In K. Nelson (Ed.), *Narratives from the crib* (pp. 231–260). Cambridge, MA: Harvard.

Dunn, J. (1987). Understanding feelings: The early stages. In J. Bruner & H. Haste (Eds.), *Making sense: The child's construction of the world.* New York: Methuen.

Durkin, D. (1987). A classroom observation study of reading instruction in kindergarten. *Early Childhood Research Quarterly, 2,* 275–300.

Durkin, D. (1990). Reading instruction in kindergarten: A look at some issues through the lens of new basal reader materials. *Early Childhood Research Quarterly, 5,* 299–316.

Dyson, A. Haas. (1982). The emergence of visible language: Interrelationships between drawing and early writing. *Visible Language, 6*(4), 360–381.

Dyson, A. Hass. (1983). The role of oral language in early writing processes. *Research in the Teaching of English, 17,* 1–30.

Dyson, A. Haas. (1986). Transitions and tensions: Interrelationships between the drawing, talking and dictating of young children. *Research in the Teaching of English, 20*(4), 379–409.

Dyson, A. Haas. (1987). The value of "time off task": Young children's spontaneous talk and deliberate text. *Harvard Educational Review, 57,* 396–420.

Dyson, A. Haas. (1989). *Multiple worlds of child writers: Friends learning to write.* New York: Teachers College Press.

Dyson, A. Haas, (1991). The word and the world: Reconceptualizing written language development, or, do rainbows mean a lot to little girls? *Research in the Teaching of English, 25,* 97–123.

Dyson, A. Haas. (1992). The case of the singing scientist: A performance perspective on the "stages" of school literacy. *Written Communication, 9,* 3–47.

Edelsky, C. (1990). Whose agenda is this anyway? A response to McKenna, Robinson, and Miller. *Educational Researcher 19*(8), 7–11.

Erickson, F. (1987). Transformation and school success: The politics and culture of educational achievement. *Anthropology and Education Quarterly, 18*(4), 335–356.

Ervin, S. M., & Miller, W. (1966). The development of grammar in child language. In U. Bellugi & R. Brown (Eds.), *The acquisition of language. Monographs of the Society for Research in Child Development, 29* (1, Serial No. 92).

Ervin-Tripp, S., & Mitchell-Kernan, C. (Eds.). (1977). *Child discourse.* New York: Academic Press.

Fein, G. G. (1987). Pretend play: Creativity and consciousness. In D. Gorlitz and J. F. Wohlwill (Eds.), *Curiosity, imagination, and play: On the development of spontaneous cognitive and motivational processes* (pp. 281–304). Hillsdale, NJ: Erlbaum.

Feitelson, D. (1986). Effects of listening to series and stories on first-graders composition and use of language. *Research in the Teaching of English, 20*(4), 339–356.

Feitelson, D. (1988). *Facts and fads in beginning reading: A cross language perspective.* Norwood, NJ: Ablex.

Feitelson, D., & Goldstein, Z. (1986). Patterns of book ownership and reading to young children in Israeli-oriented and non-school oriented families. *The Reading Teacher, 39,* 924–930.

Feitelson, D., & Iraqi, J. (1990). Storybook reading: A bridge to literary language. *The Reading Teacher, 44,* 262–265.

Ferguson, C. A. (1977). Baby talk as a simplified register. In C. E. Snow & C. A. Ferguson (Eds.), *Talking to children: Language input and acquisition.* New York: Cambridge University Press.

Ferreiro, E. (1980). The relationship between oral and written language: The children's viewpoints. In Y. Goodman, M. Haussler, & D. Strickland (Eds.), *Oral and written language development research: Impact on the schools.* Newark, DE: International Reading Association and National Council of Teachers of English.

Ferreiro, E. (1986). The interplay between information and assimilation in beginning literacy. In W. Teale & E. Sulzby (Eds.), *Emergent literacy: Writing and reading* (pp. 15–49). Norwood, NJ: Ablex.

Ferreiro, E., & Teberosky, A. (1982). *Literacy before schooling.* Exeter, NH: Heinemann.

Galda, L., & Cullinan, B. (1991). Literature for literacy: What research says about the benefits of using trade books in the classroom. In J. Jensen, J. Flood, D. Lapp, & J. R. Squire (Eds.), *Handbook of research on teaching the English language arts* (pp. 397–403). Sponsored by the National Council of Teachers of English and the International Reading Association. New York: Macmillan.

Gardner, H. (1982). *Developmental psychology* (2nd ed.). Boston: Little, Brown.

Garvey, C. (1977). *Play.* Cambridge, MA: Harvard University Press.

Garvey, C., & Hogan, R. (1973). Social speech and social interaction: Egocentrism revisited. *Child Development 44,* 562–568.

Genishi, C. (Ed.). (1992). *Ways of assessing children and curriculum: Voices from the classroom.* New York: Teachers College Press.

Genishi, C., & DiPaolo, M. (1982). Learning through argument in a preschool. In L. C. Wilkinson (Ed.), *Communicating in the classroom* (pp. 49–68). New York: Academic Press.

Genishi, C., & Dyson, A. Haas. (1984). *Language assessment in the early years.* Norwood, NJ: Ablex.

Genishi, C., & Dyson, A. Haas. (1989). *Making assessment functional: Fighting what comes naturally.* Paper presented at the annual convention of the American Educational Research Association, San Francisco.

Genishi, C., & Galvan, J. (1985). Getting started: Mexican-American preschoolers initiating dramatic play. In J. L. Frost & S. Sunderlin (Eds.), *When children play* (pp. 23–30). Washington, DC: Association for Childhood Education International.

Gerhardt, J. (1989). Monologue as a speech genre. In K. Nelson (Ed.), *Narratives from the crib* (pp. 171–230). Cambridge, MA: Harvard University Press.

Goodman, K. S., Goodman, Y. M., & Hood, W. J. (Eds.). (1989). *The whole language evaluation book.* Portsmouth, NH: Heinemann.

Graves, D. H. (1983). *Writing: Teachers and children at work.* Portsmouth, NH: Heinemann.

Gumperz, J. J. (1982). *Discourse strategies.* New York: Cambridge University Press.

Gumperz, J. J., & Hymes, D. (1972). *Directions in sociolinguistics: The ethnography of communication.* New York: Holt, Rinehart, & Winston.

Gundlach, R. (1982). Children as writers: The beginnings of learning to write. In M. Nystrand (Ed.), *What writers know* (pp. 129–147). New York: Academic Press.

Gundlach, R., McLane, J. B., Stott, F. M., & McNamee, G. D. (1985). The social foundations of children's early writing development. In M. Farr (Ed.), *Advances in writing: Vol. 1. Children's early writing development* (pp. 1–58). Norwood, NJ: Ablex.

Haith, M. M. (1980). *Rules that babies look by.* Hillsdale, NJ: Erlbaum.

Hakuta, K. (1985). *Mirror of language: The debate on bilingualism.* New York: Basic Books.

Hall, N. (1987). *The emergence of literacy.* Portsmouth, NH: Heinemann.

Halliday, M. A. K. (1977). *Learning how to mean.* London: Edward Arnold.

Harste, J., Woodward, V., & Burke, C. (1984). *Language stories and literacy lessons.* Portsmouth, NH: Heinemann.

Heath, S. B. (1983a). Research currents: A lot of talk about nothing. *Language Arts, 60,* 999–1007.

Heath, S. B. (1983b). *Ways with words: Language, life, and work in communities and classrooms.* New York: Cambridge University Press.

Hickman, J. (1980). Response to literature in a school environment. In Y. Goodman, M. Haussler, & D. Strickland (Eds.), *Oral and written language development research: Impact on the schools* (pp. 95–104). Newark, DE: International Reading Association and National Council of Teachers of English.

Hickman, J. (1981). A new perspective on response to literature: Research in an elementary school setting. *Research in the Teaching of English, 15,* 343–354.

Hickman, J. (1983). Everything considered: Response to literature in an elementary school setting. *Journal of Research and Development in Education, 16*(3), 8–13.

Hirsh-Pasek, K., Hyson, M. C., & Rescorla, L. (1990). Academic environments in preschool: Do they pressure or challenge young children? *Early Education and Development 1,* 401–423.

Jacob, E. (1984). Learning literacy through play: Puerto Rican kindergarten children. In H. Goelman, A. Oberg, & F. Smith (Eds.), *Awakening to literacy* (pp. 73–86). Exeter, NH: Heinemann.

Jaggar, A., & Smith-Burke, T. (Eds.). (1985). *Observing the language learner.* Newark, DE: International Reading Association.

Kamii, C. (Ed.). (1990). *Achievement testing in the early grades: The games grown-ups play.* Washington, DC: National Association for the Education of Young Children.

Kawakami, A. J. (1990). Ho'olulu i ka heluhelu: Fitting book reading into the lives of Hawaiian children and their families. In M. Foster (Ed.), *Readings on equal education: Vol. 11* (pp. 151–166). New York: AMP Press.

Kingston, M. Hong. (1976). *The woman warrior: Memoirs of a girlhood among ghosts.* New York: Vintage International.

Labov, W. (1970). The logic of nonstandard English. In J. E. Alatis (Ed.), *Linguistics and the teaching of standard English to speakers of other languages or dialects* (pp. 1–44). Washington, DC: Georgetown University Press.

Langer, S. K. (1967). *Philosophy in a new key.* Palo Alto, CA: National Press Books.

Luria, A. (1983). The development of writing in the child. In M. Martlew (Ed.), *The psychology of written language* (pp. 237–277). New York: Wiley.

McGee, L. M., & Lomax, R. G. (1990). On combining apples and oranges: A response to Stahl and Miller. *Review of Educational Research, 60,* 133–140.

McKenna, M. C., Robinson, R. D., & Miller, J. W. (1990). Whole language: A research agenda for the nineties. *Educational Researcher, 19*(8), 3–6.

McLane, J., & McNamee, G. (1990). *Early literacy.* Cambridge, MA: Harvard University Press.

McLaughlin, B. (1984). *Second-language acquisition in childhood: Preschool children* (rev. ed.). Hillsdale, NJ: Erlbaum.

McNamee, G. E., McLane, J. G., Cooper, P. M., & Kerwin, S. (1985). Cognition and affect in early literacy development. *Early Child Development and Care, 20,* 229–244.

McNeill, D. (1966). Developmental psycholinguistics. In F. Smith & G. Miller (Eds.), *The genesis of language* (pp. 32–55). Cambridge, MA: MIT Press.

Meek, M. (1988). *How texts teach what readers learn.* Lockwood, Gloucestershire: The Thimble Press.

Mehan, H. (1979). *Learning lessons.* Cambridge, MA: Harvard University Press.

Meisels, S. J. (1987). Uses and abuses of developmental screening and school readiness testing. *Young Children, 42*(2), 4–6, 68–73.

Michaels, S., & Collins. J. (1984). Oral discourse styles: Classroom interaction and the acquisition of literacy. In D. Tannen (Ed.), *Coherence in spoken and written discourse* (pp. 219–244). Norwood, NJ: Ablex.

Miller, P. J. (1982). *Amy, Wendy, and Beth: Learning language in South Baltimore.* Austin, TX: University of Texas Press.

Miller, P., Nemoianu, A., & DeJong, J. (1986). Early reading at home: Its practice and meanings in a working-class community. In B. Schieffelin & P. Gilmore (Eds.), *The acquisition of literacy: Ethnographic perspectives* (pp. 3–15). Norwood, NJ: Ablex.

Miller, P. J., Potts, R., & Fung, H. (1989, March). *Minority perspectives on narrative development.* Paper presented at the Annual Meeting of the American Educational Research Association, San Francisco.

Morrow, L. M. (1982). Relationships between literature programs, library corner designs, and children's use of literature. *Journal of Educational Research, 76,* 221–230.

Morrow, L. M. (1987). Promoting inner-city children's recreational reading. *The Reading Teacher, 41*(3), 266–274.

Morrow, L. M., & Weinstein, C. S. (1982). Increasing children's use of literature through program and physical design changes. *Elementary School Journal, 83*(2), 131–137.

Morrow, L. M., & Weinstein, C. S. (1986). Encouraging voluntary reading: The impact of a literature program on children's use of library centers. *Reading Research Quarterly, 21*(3), 330–346.

Moxley, R. A., Kenny, K. A., & Hunt, M. K. (1990). Improving the instruction of young children with self-recording and discussion. *Early Childhood Research Quarterly, 5,* 233–250.

National Association for the Education of Young Children and the National Association of Early Childhood Specialists in State Departments of Education. (1991). Guidelines for appropriate curriculum content and assessment in programs serving children ages three through eight. *Young Children, 46*(3), 21–38.

Nelson, K. (1973). Structure and strategy in learning to talk. *Monographs of the Society for Research in Child Development, 38* (1–2, Serial No. 149).

Nelson, K. (1985). *Making sense: The acquisition of shared meaning.* Orlando, FL: Academic Press.

Nelson, K. E., & Nelson, K. (1978). Cognitive pendulums and their linguistic realizations. In K. E. Nelson (Ed.), *Children's language: Vol. 2* (pp. 233–285). New York: Gardner.

Neuman, S., & Roskos, K. (1990). Play, print, and purpose: Enriching play environments for literacy development. *The Reading Teacher, 44,* 214–221.

Newkirk, T. (1987). The non-narrative writing of young children. *Research in the Teaching of English, 21,* 121–145.

Newkirk, T. (1989). *More than stories: The range of children's writing.* Portsmouth, NH: Heinemann.

Ninio, A., & Bruner, J. (1978). The achievement and antecedents of labeling. *Journal of Child Language, 5,* 1–15.

Paley, V. G. (1981). *Wally's stories.* Cambridge, MA: Harvard University Press.

Paley, V. G. (1986). On listening to what the children say. *Harvard Educational Review, 56,* 122–130.

Paley, V. G. (1990). *The boy who would be a helicopter: The uses of storytelling in the classroom.* Cambridge, MA: Harvard University Press.

Perl, S., & Wilson, N. (1986). *Through teachers' eyes: Portraits of writing teachers at work.* Portsmouth, NH: Heinemann.

Piaget, J. (1954). *The construction of reality in the child.* New York: Basic Books.

Piaget, J., & Inhelder, B. (1969). *The psychology of the child.* New York: Basic Books.

Read, C. (1971). Pre-school children's knowledge of English phonology. *Harvard Educational Review, 41,* 1–34.

Read, C. (1986). *Children's creative spelling.* London: Routledge & Kegan Paul.

Rosenblatt, L. (1978). *The reader, the text, the poem: The transactional theory of the literary work.* Carbondale: Southern Illinois University Press.

Schickedanz, J. A. (1978). "You be the doctor and I'll be sick." *Language Arts, 55,* 713–718.

Schickedanz, J. A. (1989). The place of specific skills in preschool and kindergarten. In D. S. Strickland & L. M. Morrow (Eds.), *Emerging literacy: Young children learn to read and write* (pp. 96–106). Newark, DE: International Reading Association.

Schickedanz, J. A. (1990). The jury is still out on the effect of whole language and language experience approaches for beginning reading: A critique of Stahl and Miller's study. *Review of Educational Research, 60,* 127–132.

Schieffelin, B. B. (1986). Teasing and shaming in Kaluli children's interactions. In B. B. Schieffelin & E. Ochs (Eds.), *Language socialization across cultures* (pp. 165–181). New York: Cambridge University Press.

Schieffelin, B. B., & Cochran-Smith, M. (1984). Learning to read culturally: Literacy before schooling. In H. Goelman, A. A. Oberg, & F. Smith (Eds.), *Awakening to literacy* (pp. 3–23). Exeter, NH: Heinemann.

Schieffelin, B. B., & Ochs, E. (Eds.). (1986). *Language socialization across cultures.* New York: Cambridge University Press.

Schweinhart, L. J., Weikart, D. P., & Larner, M. B. (1986). Consequences of three preschool curriculum models through age 15. *Early Childhood Research Quarterly, 1,* 15–45.

Slobin, D. I. (Ed.). (1985). *The crosslinguistic study of language acquisition.* Hillsdale, NJ: Erlbaum.

Smith, D. (1986). *California kindergarten survey.* Fresno, CA: California State University, School of Education.

Smith, F. (1975). *Comprehension and learning: A conceptual framework for teachers.* New York: Holt, Rinehart, & Winston.

Smith, M. L., & Shepard, L. A. (1988). Kindergarten readiness and retention: A qualitative study of teachers' beliefs and practices. *American Educational Research Journal, 25,* 307–333.

Snow, C. E., & Ferguson, C. A. (Eds.). (1977). *Talking to children: Language input and acquisition.* New York: Cambridge University Press.

Sowers, S. (1985). Learning to write in a classroom workshop: A study in grades one through four. In M. F. Whiteman (Ed.), *Advances in writing research: Vol 1. Children's early writing development* (pp. 297–342). Norwood, NJ: Ablex.

Stahl, S. A. (1990). Riding the pendulum: A rejoinder to Schickedanz and McGee and Lomax. *Review of Educational Research, 60,* 141–151.

Stahl, S. A., & Miller, P. D. (1989). Whole language and language experience approaches for beginning reading: A quantitative research synthesis. *Review of Educational Research, 59,* 87–116.

Stern, D. N. (1977). *The first relationship: Infant and mother.* Cambridge, MA: Harvard University Press.

Stern, D. N. (1985). *The interpersonal world of the infant: A view from psychoanalysis and developmental psychology.* New York: Basic Books.

Sternberg, D. (1991). *The efficacy of an early primary transitional program as an alternative strategy within a pupil-placement policy.* Unpublished doctoral dissertation, Teachers College, Columbia University.

Strickland, D., & Ogle, D. (1990). Teachers coping with change: Assessing the early literacy curriculum. In L. Morrow & J. Smith (Eds.), *Assessment for instruction in early literacy* (pp. 205–218). Englewood Cliffs, NJ: Prentice Hall.

Sulzby, E. (1985a). Kindergartners as writers and readers. In M. Farr (Ed.), *Advances in writing research: Vol 1. Children's early writing development* (pp. 127–200). Norwood, NJ: Ablex.

Sulzby, E. (1985b). Children's emergent reading of favorite storybooks: A developmental study. *Reading Research Quarterly, 20*(4), 458–481.

Taylor, D. (1983). *Family literacy: Young children learning to read and write.* Exeter, NH: Heinemann.

Taylor, N., Blum, I., & Logsdon, D. M. (1986). The development of written language awareness: Environmental aspects and program characteristics. *Reading Research Quarterly, 21,* 132–149.

Teale, W. H., Hiebert, E., & Chittenden, E. (1987). Assessing young children's literacy development. *The Reading Teacher, 40,* 772–777.

Tizard, B., & Hughes, M. (1984). *Young children learning.* Cambridge, MA: Harvard University Press.

Toda, S., Fogel, A., & Kawai, M. (1990). Maternal speech to 3-month-old infants in the United States and Japan. *Journal of Child Language, 17,* 279–294.

Vogt, L., Jordan, C., & Tharp, G. (1987). Explaining school failure, producing school success: Two cases. *Anthropology & Education Quarterly, 18,* 276–286.

Vygotsky, L. S. (1962). *Thought and language.* Cambridge, MA: M.I.T. Press.

Vygotsky, L. S. (1978). *Mind in society.* Cambridge, MA: Harvard University Press.

Wells, G. (1986). *The meaning-makers: Children learning language and using language to learn.* Portsmouth, NH: Heinemann.

Werner, H. (1948). *Comparative psychology of mental development.* New York: International University Press.

Werner, H., & Kaplan, B. (1963). *Symbol formation: An organismic-developmental approach to language and the expression of thought.* New York: Wiley.

Wexler-Sherman, C., Gardner, H., & Feldman, D. H. (1988). A pluralistic view of early assessment: The Project Spectrum approach. *Theory Into Practice, 27*(1), 77–83.

Winner, E. (1989). Development in the visual arts. In W. Damon (Ed.), *Child development today and tomorrow* (pp. 199–221). San Francisco: Jossey-Bass.

Wolff, P. (1966). The causes, controls and organization of behavior in the neonate. *Psychological Issues, 5,* 17.

Wong Fillmore, L. (1979). Individual differences in second-language acquisition. In C. Fillmore, D. Kempler, & W. Wang (Eds.), *Individual differences in language development and language behavior* (pp. 203–228). Orlando, FL: Academic Press.

Wong Fillmore, L. (1989). *Latino families and the schools.* Paper prepared for the Seminar on California's Changing Face of Race Relations: New Ethics in the 1990s. California Senate Office of Research, Sacramento, CA.

Wong Fillmore, L. (1991). Language and cultural issues in early education. In S. L. Kagan (Ed.), *The care and education of America's young children: Obstacles and opportunities, The 90th yearbook of the National Society for the Study of Education* (pp. 30-49). Chicago: University of Chicago Press.

·10·

EMERGING LITERACY IN THE EARLY CHILDHOOD YEARS: APPLYING A VYGOTSKIAN MODEL OF LEARNING AND DEVELOPMENT

Jana M. Mason and Shobha Sinha

CENTER FOR THE STUDY OF READING

UNIVERSITY OF ILLINOIS AT URBANA-CHAMPAIGN

Research in education has focused in the last decade on the process of learning: metacognition, strategies for learning and remembering, planning, questioning, and problem solving. Most of this research centers on what children do to learn and how teachers can guide children's educational experiences. An entire issue of the *Elementary School Journal* (1988) has been devoted to these aspects of learning and teaching. These areas likewise have been discussed by Brown, Collins, and Duguid (1989), who propose the term *situated cognition* to describe them. Similarly, Rogoff (1990) has explained the use of *mediated learning* approaches. Either explicitly or implicitly, most of this research draws on the theoretical perspective of Lev Vygotsky and includes the role of the teacher or tutor and the cultural milieu for learning.

Vygotsky's theory entails social constructs of development and provides an explanation of how changing social interactions between learner and tutor—where the tutor could be a parent, teacher, or more knowledgeable child—lead the learner toward proficiency. The theory is articulated in his book *Thought and Language* (1934/1986) and to a lesser extent in the book compiled after his death, *Mind in Society* (1978); it is also discussed by Kozulin (1990).

Recent educational applications of Vygotsky's work, found in Moll (1990) and Rogoff (1990), explain learning and instruction principles: for example, (1) adult modeling and coaching processes, or how to learn something; (2) *scaffolding* the learning environment, or setting up instructional situations that allow learners to succeed as they advance toward higher levels of understanding; and (3) working within the student's "zone of proximal development," which means to provide instruction that spans the region in which a learner can advance both with and without help. Moreover, settings for learning and instruction are considered in terms of social interactions to support realistic or "authentic" settings and in terms of student opportunities to explore, direct their own learning, and work in collaboration with one another under the support and guidance of the teacher. These constructs seem to be replacing the traditional emphasis on teacher-directed learning, which features incremental steps to learning, as well as drill-and-practice routines. In many respects, then, time-honored early childhood educational principles that have featured child-directed exploration, adult-guided learning, and cooperative learning through peer interactions are coming into fashion for the education of older children.

Unfortunately, at this same time, greater numbers of kindergarten teachers are turning back toward traditional, teacher-directed instruction (Kliebard, 1986). Such a development may be a result of research suggesting that more academic kindergarten programs can be beneficial, particularly for educationally disadvantaged students (Pallas, Natriello, & McDill, 1989), and could lead to a palliative or "quick educational fix" using traditional instructional techniques (Walsh, 1989). Misunderstandings arise about how to foster effective, informal educational approaches when questions are raised about the effectiveness of socially based early childhood programs, such as Head Start (Datta, 1986) and whole-language kindergarten programs (Evans & Carr, 1985; Stahl & Miller, 1989). Ironically, the urgent need for early education could turn kindergarten teachers away from the very principles that the educational research community has begun to appreciate and apply to older children's instruction.

This chapter articulates the view that emergent literacy constructs ought to be framed by a Vygotskian model of learning and development. In the preschool and kindergarten years, children acquire literacy principally through exploration and adult support, which does not preclude adults from fostering children's interest but also does not lead to direct instruction. Our aim is to show how emergent literacy constructs could be embedded within the rubric of a literacy-rich early childhood program.

A major problem regarding emergent literacy is its inadequate tie to theory. As Clay (1979b) concludes, "If teachers are to generate individual programs to meet particular needs, and if the matter of strategies for processing information is critical for some learners, then this must be written down in a way that enables teachers to go easily from behavior signals, through theoretical constructs, to program" (p. 170). Constructs of emergent literacy—some aspects of which have been termed *beginning reading, reading readiness, prereading,* or *early reading*—have long been atheoretical. Authors in the 3 volumes edited by Resnick and Weaver (1979) began to articulate connections to a cognitive-learning perspective, but most research has focused on descriptions of the constructs. For example, Mason and Allen's (1986) review of emergent literacy only briefly touches on theory; Sampson's (1986) work describes only the occurrence of literacy; and the Sulzby and Teale (1991) review, although embedding a Vygotskian perspective in the descriptions, devotes only one separate paragraph to it.

We would argue, with others (e.g., Coltheart, 1979; Durkin, 1987a; Mason, 1984; Teale & Sulzby, 1986), that the acquisition of reading ability has, for most of this century, been misunderstood and has led to extreme positions regarding educational support for literacy. For example, believing that children might be pressed by adults to learn at too early an age (Elkind, 1981) has led some educators to reject all support for literacy before the first grade. Unfortunately, this belief builds on the erroneous assumption that children cannot develop reading concepts until a certain maturational level is reached. This belief, which Walsh (1989) argues is mythical and sentimental, was given credence in 1940 by an influential physician, Arnold Gesell, who wrote the following:

Reading is a complex achievement, which came late in the cultural history of the race. Why should it not come with difficulty and delay for countless children who for reasons of maturity and inheritance have insufficient command of basic coordination of eyes, hands, speech perception, and comprehension at the age of 6 years?...It is most significant that many of the early reading difficulties would vanish if the natural processes of maturation were given a chance to assert themselves. (pp. 312–313)

Gesell's conclusion was directly countered by Clay (1979a) who devised Reading Recovery, a successful program devel-oped in New Zealand that provides intensive tutoring for first-grade children who would otherwise become poor readers. Clay asked the following:

Do we have any evidence of accelerated progress in late starters? There may be isolated examples which support this hope, but correlations from a follow-up study of 100 children two and three years after school entry lead me to state rather dogmatically that where a child stood in relation to his age-mates at the end of his first year at school was roughly where one could expect to find him at 7:0 or 8:0. This is what one would expect if learning to read is dependent on the acquisition and practice of a complex set of learned behaviors, and not the product of sudden insights. (p. 13)

In the United States, Juel (1988) and Mason, Dunning, Stewart, and Peterman (1991) reached the same dismal conclusion—poor readers in first grade remain at the bottom of the class in later grades. Thus, waiting for low-performing children to mature denies them the opportunity to learn about literacy concepts before they are too far behind their peers. Indeed, recently constructed instructional interventions in kindergarten and first grade have improved children's later reading (e.g., Bradley & Bryant, 1983; Cunningham, 1989; Lundberg, Frost, & Petersen, 1988; Mason, Kerr, Sinha, & McCormick, 1990; McCormick & Mason, 1989; Phillips, Norris, Mason, & Kerr, 1990; Pinnell, 1989).

We believe that a way out of this theoretical conflict is for educators to learn about and apply a Vygotskian model to literacy development. Before explaining how it can be applied, we contrast the traditional perspective, reading readiness, with emergent literacy, the perspective that is gaining influence on early reading instruction in the United States. We then present Vygotsky's general model and apply it to basic constructs of literacy development. We complete the chapter by suggesting how early childhood educational principles and the roles that teachers play can be modified through application of the Vygotskian model to foster literacy for young children.

A READING READINESS PERSPECTIVE

Although we are primarily interested in the new theoretical position of emergent literacy, we would like to discuss briefly the earlier position of reading readiness. Reading readiness theory, though undergoing several changes in its application, has remained a most influential theory in the United States. However, the reason for our interest in the theory is not merely historical: Reading readiness continues to play an important role among educational practitioners.

In this section we will review its present status, its historical development and influence, and the problems with this theory that necessitated a shift to a different perspective.

Present Status

Although some school districts are adopting different philosophies of early reading and some are including literacy in the program as early as preschool, there is no reason to believe that reading readiness is a theory of the past, at least not in terms of educational practices in schools. Durkin (1987b) has found that the concept of reading readiness and related instructional practice persists in most kindergarten classrooms. She notes the influence of "Gesell-like" philosophy in the schools (p. 289). This philosophy was reflected in the developmental tests being used that emphasize the more general cognitive, social, and motor skills while excluding literacy skills, and also in the interview data obtained from the teachers. Walsh (1989) found that Gesell's philosophy was also influential among kindergarten teachers in determining the placement of children. Apart from these studies, we have reason to believe that even in school districts where emergent literacy programs have been espoused, teachers follow readiness programs, not having totally assimilated the ideas of the emergent literacy theory. They use the labels of emergent literacy, but not the constructs.

Reading readiness, with its emphasis on "waiting" until the child is ready to learn to read, also appears to be attractive to scholars concerned with childhood stress. Elkind (1981) states that "learning to read is not a spontaneous or simple skill." However, in the very next paragraph he says that "the majority of children can . . . learn to read with ease if they are not hurried into it" (p. 32). It is difficult to see how this conclusion about educational practice follows from his earlier statement about the nature of reading. He gives an example of a teacher who made her students do long hours of drills and exercises to teach them to read at ages 4 and 5. Elkind noticed that although the children could read fluently, they seemed to experience no pleasure in reading. Hence, he advocates waiting before giving reading instruction. However, it would seem that if reading is a difficult skill to acquire, then instruction should begin early and not late.

Elkind also assumes that there is only one way of teaching reading and that way is based on his observation of one teacher. There are many ways of teaching reading. It can be done, for instance, in an enjoyable manner, taking the nature of the child into account. The teaching of reading need not be done in the manner Elkind observed. Formal instruction with reading readiness lessons includes rote memorization, sequential drills, and repetitive practices and could thus be more stressful.

Outline of the Theory

Reading readiness theory has existed since the beginning of this century, but it has undergone several transformations. To outline the theory, we present a brief account of how it originally appeared and in what form it exists today.

According to Coltheart (1979), the term *readiness* was first used by Patrick in 1899. Patrick viewed cognitive development as a function of "ripening" and stated that "a child's powers, whether physical or mental, ripen in a certain rather definite order . . . at the age of 7, there is a certain mental readiness for some things and an unreadiness for others" (cited in Coltheart, p. 3).

When reading readiness was first introduced in the 1900s (Coltheart, 1979), it was generally agreed that maturation was the precondition of reading readiness. Gesell, who was very influential in development studies and early educational practices in the United States during the period ranging from the 1920s to the 1950s (Teale & Sulzby, 1986), advocated a naturalist position and believed that development was the result of maturation. Gesell was especially influential in propagating the theory of neural ripening and intrinsic growth (Durkin, 1987a). Neural ripening, Gesell claimed, determined growth not only in motor skills but also in cognitive skills. The direct outcome of this kind of position was the philosophy of "wait and see" until the child was ready for instruction. Applied to reading instructions, this theory translated into the reading readiness approach. Accordingly, educators delayed reading instruction until a child was "ready" to read, that is, until the child possessed some prerequisite skills.

Although Gesell's biological model was widely accepted, there was controversy from the beginning about the educational implications of such a theory. Proponents of a maturational view might say, "Time is the answer—not special drills or special practice" (Coltheart, 1979, p. 4), whereas opponents recognize that merely waiting for such development is not sufficient. Coltheart provides an excellent critique of this position. Stating that a child has not learned to read because he is not ready is a circular argument. The failure to learn to read can be the evidence for not being ready.

From an instructional viewpoint too, Coltheart saw several problems with a reading readiness theory. If one believes that readiness can be influenced by instruction, then the maturational concept must be rejected. On the other hand, if instruction does influence reading readiness, then prereading instruction will help a child to read, and research has shown that prereading instruction for children who are lagging behind their classmates helps. Another problem with the theory is its assumption that the age when formal reading instruction begins should matter. In some countries instruction begins at age 5, in others at age 6, and in still others at age 7. If the maturational viewpoint were correct, then the countries that began instruction at 5 would have numerous cases of reading failure, and those that began at 7 would have few failures. This prediction has not been borne out.

In the last several decades, reading readiness concepts have undergone another change of emphasis (Durkin, 1987a; Teale & Sulzby, 1986). According to Durkin, the changes were due to the concern felt about the quality of American education after the launching of Sputnik and the concern for the performance of children from low socioeconomic backgrounds. According to Teale and Sulzby, changes were also driven by the shift in the discipline of psychology. Research and writings in the 1950s and 1960s by cognitive psychologists such as Bruner (1960, 1966) and Bruner, Goodnow, and Austin (1956) provided evidence that early childhood was crucial in the cognitive development of an individual. This conclusion called into question the notion of waiting for children to mature. Readiness programs now began to include activities to develop auditory discrimination and memory and visual discrimination and memory. Later, letter names and sounds, word recognition, and some general skills were added (Teale & Sulzby, 1986).

Critique of the Theory

When trying to understand the influences of different psychological movements on reading readiness, note how very divergent movements have influenced its instructional practices. In the earlier phase of the movement the major influence was of a maturational viewpoint; later it adopted the behavioristic model of instruction while retaining some beliefs of the earlier theory. It is amazing how these contrasting models of psychology were assimilated within reading readiness practices and the contradictions were not even noted. It seems that reading readiness programs have played the role of an attic where all the models could be kept without the need for finding any relationships among them.

The one thing that has been resistant to change is the belief that reading instruction has to be delayed until the child is ready for it. Although, superficially, there was still "wait" time required prior to direct involvement with reading, the time was filled with rigorous instruction in supposedly related or prerequisite skills.

Assumptions About the Nature of Reading and Cognition

Reading has long been viewed in a dichotomous manner, with an "all-or-none" belief about its nature (Mason & Allen, 1986). Either children can read or they cannot. One reason for this belief could be the understanding about the nature of reading itself. Gough (1972) noted, "The Reader is a decoder; the child must become one" (p. 526). Thus, reading itself was narrowly defined in terms of an ability to decode. By this definition, a child who knows about other aspects of reading but can't decode is viewed as a nonreader, or a "Stage 0" reader, according to Chall (1983). Second, transfer was assumed between skills without necessarily any scientific basis. For instance, even skills like crawl, hop, and skip were supposed to indicate readiness in reading. This suggests that maturation in sensorimotor skills is assumed to transfer to reading skills. Third, it was assumed that general cognitive skills transfer to reading skills: If children were trained in the general cognitive skills, they would acquire reading readiness constructs. There is little evidence, however, that children develop reading skills from general cognitive and motor skills, although there is much evidence that children who experience reading, even informally, do develop reading skills (Mason, 1980, 1984). That is, they learn to read in part through involvement in the act of reading.

Although Vygotsky's influence on developmental psychology in the United States is relatively recent, Piaget has been a familiar figure here for several decades. Superficially, the wait-and-see aspect of reading readiness theory might seem to be compatible with Piaget's theory, at least his earlier and better-known theory, which viewed the child as being impervious to experience (Vygotsky, 1934/1986). Yet the research methodology and later the instruction in reading readiness has almost nothing in common with his work. Piaget demonstrated that the child is an active constructor of knowledge and is capable of observing and theorizing about his environment. His research methodology tried to uncover the thinking processes of children. Had this view been applied in early reading, then the dichotomous nature of reading would have been questioned. It would have been evident that a child can form ideas about reading very early in life.

From the Vygotskian perspective, too, the reading readiness theory contains several flaws. First of all, Vygotsky has criticized the biological model of development because it did not do justice to the "uniquely human" (sociocultural) forms of behavior. He believed that development occurred in 2 interactive but qualitatively different lines: elementary processes that were biological in origin and higher psychological functions that were sociocultural in origin. The latter was not "biologically given" but culturally acquired (Vygotsky, 1978). So, from this perspective, it would seem that Gesell was viewing development in its more elementary form by seeing it as a function of neural ripening. Basing reading development on Gesell's model forces one to follow a simplistic model of development for reading, which in reality is a very sophisticated and culturally acquired skill.

The second critique from a Vygotskian perspective concerns the idea of waiting until a child reaches a certain developmental level. Such an idea entails the inherent assumption that learning and development are independent of each other. According to Vygotsky (1978), learning, rather than development per se, sets in motion a variety of developmental processes. So, by waiting, the adults do not take advantage of the child's possible development capacities and hence might delay development.

AN EMERGENT LITERACY PERSPECTIVE

Although there have been objections to the reading readiness concept from the beginning, they have become more apparent in research and theory building in the last 15 years. A principal reason has been the perspective termed *emergent literacy*. In this section, we outline the present status of emergent literacy research and practice, the historical context in which it was formed, and its major characteristics as a theory.

Most researchers studying literacy acquisition now accept this paradigm. This is reflected in the vast numbers of papers written on this topic as well as some major reviews (e.g., Mason & Allen, 1986; Sulzby & Teale, 1991). Publishers and researchers have noted enthusiastic responses for this perspective from teachers and school administrators. Mason, Kerr, Sinha, and McCormick (1990), for example, were invited to participate in research in a school district that was implementing an emergent literacy program at preschool level (Early Start) and at kindergarten level. However, so far there is no clear cut pattern of change in our schools, or if there is, it has not been documented. If we review Durkin's (1987b) or Walsh's (1989) studies, then, indeed, it seems that much of the classroom practice is based on reading readiness philosophy, often in a very warped form.

Although reading readiness was accepted more or less uncritically from the beginning of this century, it was not until the 1970s that readiness was really presented with a "unified challenge" (Teale & Sulzby, 1986, p. xiv). Then there appeared a proliferation of studies challenging both behaviorist theory and the notion of neural ripening. Notable examples of early research and application to classroom programs have been published on the subject (e.g., Allen & Mason, 1989; Clay, 1979a; Mason, 1989; Sampson, 1986; Schieffelin & Gilmore, 1986; Teale & Sulzby, 1986). Other significant books are based on single pieces of research (Bissex, 1980; Ferreiro & Teberosky, 1979; Heath, 1983; Soderbergh, 1977). All these studies shared the following shifting perspective:

- Literacy emerges before children are formally taught to read.
- Literacy is defined to encompass the whole act of reading, not merely decoding.
- The child's point of view and active involvement with emerging literacy constructs is featured.
- The social setting for literacy learning is not ignored.

The term applied to this type of research is *emergent literacy*. Coined by Clay (1979a), the term gives legitimacy to children's literacy behaviors but still indicates a difference from conventional reading behavior (Teale & Sulzby, 1986) and provides a way to broaden its focus and to integrate reading and writing (Mason & Allen, 1986). For example, although decoding is a necessary component of learning to read, it should not be the only measure of beginning reading. Knowledge about directionality, reading print in context, the ability to distinguish print from other graphic forms, understanding the function of print and that the print has meaning, pretend or invented reading and writing, and shared reading and writing all constitute aspects of early literacy development of children that need to be considered as well.

Another noticeable effect of the shift in perspective about literacy acquisition was the adoption of an active-constructive role of the child. Clay (1975) and Harste, Woodward, and Burke (1984) collected the scribblings of children to study their changing knowledge about representing print. Mason (1980) studied young children's attempts to read, spell, and remember printed words to understand the strategies they could use. Read's (1971) research in invented spelling led to studies about developmental changes in children's phonological awareness and knowledge about letter-sound correspondences. This approach of studying children's responses to discover the kinds of mental strategies they understand and can apply is central to both Piaget's and Vygotsky's perspectives about child development. Piaget studied the child's attempts and mistakes in order to assess stages of development and reasoning. Vygotsky described children as active constructors of their language and literacy; they do not develop in a vacuum. Although several researchers emphasized the natural way in which children learn to read (e.g., Goodman & Goodman, 1974), a close inspection of the so-called "natural" reading would reveal that a plethora of activities—informal interactions that use literacy concepts, involvement in reading and writing, and staged opportunities for exploration of literacy materials—go on at home under the tutelage of a parent or older sibling.

Emergent literacy researchers have also used the concept of interaction implicitly in their research, for instance, while discussing story reading to children or in shared reading (Mason, Peterman, & Kerr, 1989; Sulzby & Teale, 1991). These studies have been descriptive in nature, focusing on the literacy construct itself and on the role played by the adult; accordingly, these studies often use terms like *scaffolding* and the *interactive nature of learning*.

Vygotskian theory offers a very important framework for studying and applying adult–young child interactions in shared literacy activities. The zone of proximal development focuses not only on the completed level of development (the stage of development where the child can solve the problem independently) but also on the expected level of development where the child solves a problem with the help of an expert. The difference between the completed and expected level is the zone of proximal development. According to Vygotsky (1978), "Learning awakens a variety of internal developmental processes that are able to operate only when the child is interacting with people in his environment and in cooperation with his peers. Once these processes are internalized they become part of the child's independent developmental achievement" (p. 90).

Most emergent literacy research is compatible with this viewpoint. For instance, an adult reading a story to the child would be functioning in the child's zone of proximal development. In the process, there are things that the child may already know (e.g., the concept of a story, pictures and their relation to the story, or picture-print connections). Teaching to the level for which the child is "ready" would be, according to Vygotsky, "teaching to yesterday's development" (p. 89). But there are areas where the child would soon reach developmentally but has not reached yet (e.g., being able to predict, relating experiences to the text, and so on). The adult acts as a "mediator" between the child and the text in the areas where the child cannot function alone.

A VYGOTSKIAN PERSPECTIVE

In 1929 Vygotsky proposed a model of development that matched the basic principles of early childhood education and suggested an appropriate way for teachers to guide and support children's learning and development. He distinguished two kinds of development, natural and cultural. Natural development "is closely bound up with the processes of general organic growth and the maturation of the child." Cultural development allows mastery not only of "the items of cultural experience, but the habits and forms of cultural behavior, the cultural methods of reasoning" (p. 415). Cultural development, under which literacy learning and development are explained, arises from the use of symbols to solve problems, that is, through the use of speech and actions involving more abstract representations. Vygotsky considered this concept analogous to the invention and use of tools.

When the child uses symbols, the structures that govern the child's reasoning process become more complex, though still evolving in harmony with natural development. Structural change originates with the child. Although it can't be forced on the child, as Bruner (1985) has pointed out, opportunities for the child to solve problems in the context of appropriate props and adult support can influence development.

One of the central tenets of Vygotsky's theory is that children practice skills unconsciously and spontaneously before they have conscious control over a concept. At first, that idea seems impossible. As Bruner (1985) phrased it, "How could 'good learning' be that which is in advance of development and, as it were, bound initially to be unconscious since unmastered?" (p. 4). Bruner's answer was that the teacher or other tutor

> serves the learner as a vicarious form of consciousness until such a time as the learner is able to master his own action through his own consciousness and control. When the child achieves that conscious control over a new function or conceptual system, it is then that he is able to use it as a tool. Up to that point, the tutor in effect performs the critical function of "scaffolding" the learning task to make it possible for the child, in Vygotsky's words, to internalize external knowledge and convert it into a tool for conscious control. (pp. 24–25)

Vygotsky (1929) proposed 4 stages in cultural development. These can be applied to the development of reading and writing as well as to other aspects of reasoning. This nonintuitive construct of action occurring before understanding is evident in the first 2 stages. The first stage is the natural developmental level in which the child creates "associative or conditional reflexive connections between the stimuli and reactions" (p. 419). At this point, the child is limited by attention, interest, and memory. Movement into the second stage can occur after a more or less protracted search or, if beyond the memory resources of the child, with the assistance of an adult. In this stage, the child makes some use of symbols. The adult operates within the child's range of understanding, providing connecting links or concrete representations of concepts, maintaining the child's interest, and easing memory demands. At the same time the adult leads the child to new understandings. The third stage is marked by the child figuring out how to make effective use of symbols or tools and then practicing that discovery. Then, in the fourth stage the child is freed from external signs or symbols; the process becomes internalized. That is, its physical presence is no longer needed as the child "starts to use the inner schemes, tries to use as signs his remembrances, the knowledge he formerly acquired" (p. 427).

Vygotsky (1929) provided examples of these stages of development using arithmetical reasoning and verbal reasoning. With respect to arithmetical reasoning, he said that at first, children have a natural knowledge of quantity, comparison, distribution into single objects, and so forth. Next, they imitate adults by counting, but without knowledge of purpose for counting or how to count with figures. Third, they count with aid of fingers. Fourth, they can count in their mind with no props.

Vygotsky proposed that the first stage of verbal reasoning is expressive-communicative speech. Williams (1989), in a review of Wertsch's (1985) book about Vygotsky, distinguishes the first stage from the next 2 in this way: "Words are extensions of the needs, interests, and desires of the child. In this early use of language, the word and the object are fused. Word meaning is not separable from the particular object indicated by the word" (p. 113). In the second stage, adults help the child expand word use and support the child's referential use. However, the child's understanding of meanings of words is not yet well developed. In the third stage, the child realizes that words have instrumental functions, discovering that "each thing has its own name." Vygotsky (1929) refers to this insight as a crisis in development, which is demonstrated by the child widening his or her vocabulary in an active manner, asking what everything is called. Finally, the fourth stage is marked by a transition from external to internal speech. The child begins to use "egocentric" speech, that is, private speech of planning, monitoring, and commenting on one's own actions, a construct that is now referred to as metacognition, or thinking about one's thoughts.

APPLICATION OF VYGOTSKY'S MODEL OF CULTURAL DEVELOPMENT OF EMERGENT LITERACY

In a 1983 paper, Vygotsky argues that the "psychic functions" required for learning the basic school subjects are not mature at the beginning of schooling. As a result, teachers cannot expect children to draw exclusively on what they already know in order to progress. Reading instruction need not be delayed, but it does need to be supported; that is, because of its complexity, reading cannot be expected to develop without assistance from others. However, the nature of assistance does not follow a reading readiness or direct instruction model. As suggested in the earlier quote from Bruner (1985), we can say that the tutor/teacher provides "vicarious forms of consciousness" until children have experienced various aspects of the concepts. That is, the tutor organizes (scaffolds) learning tasks, making it possible for children to try them out and, in applying concepts to practical and increasingly more complex tasks, learn to understand how to use them *for their own purposes*.

In the following analysis, we apply Vygotsky's model to 3 major constructs of literacy acquisition: concepts about texts, concepts about words, and concepts about letters. Couching the emergent literacy research in terms of Vygotskian framework is our interpretation because most of the research was carried out without reference to that model, and we have had to make conjectures about some constructs to show the full set of stages of development. By interweaving Vygotsky's 1929 developmental model with researchers' descriptions of children's acquisition of emergent literacy constructs, we can explain how children's first constructs about literacy can be interpreted and then extended to early childhood instruction.

CONCEPTS ABOUT TEXT

Young children acquire an understanding of various aspects of literature by listening to, telling, and acting out stories; by reciting texts that have been reread to them; and eventually by independent reading and writing (Chomsky, 1979; Holdaway, 1979; Strickland & Morrow, 1989; Sulzby, 1985; Yaden, Smolkin, & Coulon, 1989). Children also acquire concepts about the nature of literature, how one listens and remembers, reads, and writes. Thus, preschool and kindergarten activities with stories and expository texts are framed by storybook reading to children, shared writing, shared reading, story dictation, repeated reading, and story dramatization (Bissex, 1980; Dobson, 1989; Dyson, 1985, 1986, 1988, 1990; Paley, 1981; Wolf, 1989).

Vygotsky's stages can be applied to concepts about texts. The first stage of development is seen in children's spontaneous use of text. Wolf (1989) observed her daughter borrowing story language in her conversations and language play, using literature concepts spontaneously. Language play was evident, for example, in the child's mimicry of storybook words and phrases such as "cheeks like roses," hair "as dark as the night," and "you shall have no pie." When helping her mother clean a shed, the child borrowed a story question when she noticed a small frog in a pot, saying, "Will you get my golden ball?" Smilansky (1990) also describes preschool children's spontaneous story construction through dramatic play: "I am the daddy, you are the mommy, and the doll is our baby." Another play activity began, "Let's pretend that this is a hospital and there are a lot of sick children here" (p. 19).

At the second stage, adults often encourage children to view their language play in new ways. Paley (1981) presents many examples of the support she provided as a kindergarten teacher in an inner-city school. Here is an example of story dictation, which Paley followed by having the child act out the story so that he could move to a new level of understanding (p. 12):

Wally's story: The dinosaur smashed down the city and the people got mad and put him in jail.
Paley: Is that the end? Did he get out?
Wally's prompted
continuation: He promised he would be good so they let him go home and his mother was waiting.

Wolf (1989) offers examples from her own family to explain how parents' story enactment and elaboration extends children's understanding of literature. In reading her daughter the story *Little Red Riding Hood,* Wolf (coincidentally named) took on the role of the wolf and encouraged her child, Lindsey, to take on the role of Little Red Riding Hood. Then they acted out some of the story conversations (until the child stopped the enactment, exclaiming, "You're not the wolf!"). Elaborating on the child's literature play, both parents would follow Lindsey's lead, yet introduce subtle changes.

At a tea party of Lindsey and her girlfriends, I played the part of the butler according to Lindsey's instructions. Yet, I changed the action by serving tea with a haughty British accent which the girls rapidly took up and incorporated into their own conversation. Kenny changed the object by introducing an element of reality. He brewed a pot of herbal tea, which then prompted the girls to request real sugar and cream. (p. 9)

Sulzby and Teale (1991) suggest in their review that storybook reading is a socially created and interactive activity. Because it is typically routinized in the sense that adults repeat many of the same ways of talking about a book, children can gradually take over major portions of the book talk. The routines "provide predictable, but not rigid, formats that help children learn how to participate in the activity, . . . thus helping the children complete a task that is beyond their individual capacity" (p. 732). Adults organize and control those elements of the task that at first are too difficult for the child, permitting the child to focus on those elements that are within his or her range of competency. Subsequent readings of books, as children take over more of the interactions, are not merely repetitions but are variations that provide flexibility within a framework.

Thus, there is change in the nature of storybook reading. As children become more knowledgeable about the meaning of stories, adults provide fewer explanations and interpretations of story events. However, differences in the nature of the interactions, which depend on the type and difficulty of the book, also affect interactions (Mason, Peterman, & Kerr, 1989). With very easy and predictable books, teachers may lead children to take over the reading itself. With difficult texts, they may do all the reading and ask many questions to make sure children understand the underlying concepts and vocabulary.

At the third stage of development, a child independently uses props to reconstruct aspects of the text. Wolf's (1989) examples of the child's use of props and body movement show how the child has learned to express, coordinate, and extend her understanding of literature.

For Lindsey, dramatic play meant action. At the beginning of each production, she began an active search through her reality and imagination for the props to create an appropriate visual image. Certain movements were ascribed to individual scenes, releasing the motions and emotions of a story through pantomime. Lindsey used gestures and facial expressions to signify worlds that would ordinarily be limited by words. Ultimately, the purpose of her play was the expression of theme. She made a careful selection of the roles she wished to play and enacted them again and again. In her mind and movement, she dressed like the character, moved through the character's emotions, and evoked the character's theme. . . . In Lindsey's play, story and life met, combined, and recombined. And out of past and present, her play created possibilities for the future. (pp. 6–7)

Wolf offers the following examples of prop-invention. After listening to a story about a child who became an arrow to the sun, Lindsey became that story child, pointing her arms into the shape of an arrow and projecting herself forward. Similarly, when building a tower with blocks that had no doors, Lindsey explained that she and her mother could climb up using her Rapunzel-like long hair.

In the fourth stage, children are released from the use of props and pictured representations of story information.

Through book reading, they gradually replace picture-directed understandings with text-directed understandings, thus acquiring more abstract representations of story ideas. The first stories that children memorize and recite, and then learn to read, are replete with helpful pictures to augment the text and replenish the imagination. They serve as props. Gradually, though, children can read a text alone and use their imagination to picture the ideas and their reasoning processes to interpret and criticize and analyze and synthesize. As Sulzby and Teale (1991) describe the process, "The endpoint of the process is internalization of the interaction, an ability to conduct the task independently" (p. 734).

Lartz and Mason (1988) collected data on a 4-year-old child, Jamie, who seemed to be reaching toward the fourth stage. Jamie heard the story *Danny and the Dinosaur,* by Syd Hoff, and after repeated retellings of the story, she began reaching toward text reading, trying to break her dependence on the pictures. Jamie applied her knowledge of how stories are organized, how characters talk to one another and confront and solve problems, and how picture and text information can be used to read words. She then began to take on the additional burden of using letter information, and in so doing was turning from a dependence on pictures as concrete representations of the story to the print itself.

An example from 1 page of the text depicts her attempts over the 8 sessions to retell the story. At first, Jamie relied simply on the picture, and then, with support from Lartz, she began to integrate text and picture with her text memory. Eventually, she came quite close to the text itself in telling the story. In the last 2 sessions, Jamie apparently felt confident enough about the story line to read some of the printed words, though, as she conceded to Lartz in the last session, "This is a hard way to read!" The following responses of her successive retellings of page 1 are from the original transcript and were not published in the 1988 article.

Text of page 1: *One day Danny went to the museum. He wanted to see what was inside* (picture shows a little boy climbing upstairs to a large building).
Session 1. Jamie: One time Danny went to the zoo.
Session 2. Jamie: One time Danny went to the zoo. He wished he could have an animal but he didn't know if his mom would let him.
Session 3. Jamie: One time Danny went to the zoo.
Session 4. Jamie: One time Danny went to the zoo.
Session 5. Jamie: One time I went to the museum. We saw lots of things there.
Session 6. Jamie: One day Danny went to the m-m-museum.
Session 7. Jamie: One day Dan went to the museum. He (long pause) s-start? [Lartz: What did you say here? You said wan-wanted. He wanted-] Jamie: He wanted a animal.
Session 8. Jamie: One day—Danny—went—to—the—museum. He wished . . . [Lartz: to]. Jamie: to–have–my–[Lartz: What's that letter?] Jamie: My own animal a-n-i-m-a-l [spells the word animal].

Pappas and Brown (1987) obtained similar results in a study analyzing a kindergarten child's 3 retellings of a story. They concluded that "the approximation observed in reading-like behavior cannot be explained simply in terms of rote memory.

The ontogenesis of the register of written language, instead, appears to be just as much a constructive process as we have seen in other areas of cognitive development" (pp. 174–175).

Thus, as Teale (1987) proposes,

a child's independent reenactments of books play a significant role in the ontogeny of literacy. They provide opportunities of the child to practice what was experienced in interactive storybook reading events. Also important, however, is that independent reenactments provide opportunities for the child to develop new understandings about reading in general and about the individual book in particular. (p. 62)

Text writing can be similarly framed in terms of Vygotsky's developmental stages. Dyson (1988) presents a 2-year case study of 8 children's writing, 4 from kindergarten to Grade 1, and 4 from Grade 1 to Grade 2. She argues that learning to write is difficult because children must learn to "differentiate the boundaries between the written, drawn, and spoken symbol systems. . . . And, if it is to be a fictional world, they must distinguish as well between the imaginary world they are creating, the experienced world they are transforming, and the ongoing social world in which they are acting" (pp. 357–358).

Dyson (1988) found that changes in children's writing over 2 years depict movements across stages, although she does not discuss stages or roles played by teachers to foster movement. She found that children became

less governed by drawing and any accompanying talk; to oversimplify, as authors of imaginary worlds, the group moved from a tendency to comment on pictures, to a tendency to observe scenes and, finally, to act within dynamic worlds. . . . [The] young authors wrestled with and, at times, got caught on the borders between differing symbolic and social space/time structures, differing worlds. To help resolve these tensions, the children found new ways to use the resources offered by these worlds (e.g., sequencing pictures to capture narrative movement; incorporating talk—dialogue—into their text; fictionalizing self, peers, and experiences to meld the ongoing social, the wider experienced, and the evolving symbolic world in new ways. (p. 384)

Bissex (1980) demonstrated the conjoint development of reading and writing, from letter naming to text reading and writing, in the analysis of her son's literacy development. At age 5, he nudged his mother with his spontaneous note "R U DF" ("Are you deaf?") to elicit her attention. As he moved into the second stage, he began trying to read labels on food packages, signs, and his own name, picking up information from his environment with help from parents. His attempts to write were encouraged, and he began to look at and try to read more words. Before he was 6, he had moved into the third stage by extending his reading and writing, noticing and commenting on letter sound patterns and trying to read new words using letter cues as well as context. At the fourth stage, which happened toward the end of first grade, he stopped asking parents to read to him. He was now reading novels, comics, dictionaries, almanacs, and an encyclopedia. He also began writing for his own purposes—to tabulate possessions and keep track of personal activities. He even wrote a song book and set up his own spelling list of harder words than those given at school. In the next 2 years, he read factual materials to inform himself, he kept a personal diary, and with friends he set up a newspaper and made quiz booklets. Thus, from this wide range of activities and guided instruction and practice, he became able to utilize reading and writing concepts for his own purposes.

CONCEPTS ABOUT WORDS

Before they read, children form concepts, not just about texts, but also about words and letters. Mason (1980) suggested 3 levels of word reading development based on changes in understandings about printed words from learning letters and from attempts to read, write, and remember words. Akin to Vygotsky's first stage, children's first attempts are fanciful—1 child said the first word in a list he was asked to read was "Once," the next was "upon," then "atime." When given magnetic letters and asked to spell words, some place all the letters into a long line—they know that words are strings of letters, but have no idea about which letters to select. With guidance from adults, however, children soon move into a second stage as they recognize favorite words, such as their own name, and begin to write words using initial sounds they hear in words, expanding these concepts with invented spellings of word- and sentence-like segments [e.g., Bissex (1980) reports a sign her son made: DO.NAT.KM.IN.ANE.MORE.JST.LETL.KES]. Eventually, they operate using conventional spelling, and on their own begin to realize the more complex morphemic structures of words.

In the first stage of word concept development, then, children usually treat print no differently than objects. Print is meaningful within the context that children see it, and each printed word is connected uniquely with something that is meaningful. From studying young children's word concept development, Ferreiro (1978) reported that in an early stage of development, children believe that only names of things are represented in texts, and that each printed word is a complete utterance. Sulzby (1986) captured this understanding when she described a child who said he could read only 1 word at a time, who told her, "The first word is: 'He did it in space'" (p. 226). Harste, Burke, and Woodward (1982) asked young children to "read" printed labels in and out of context. Their answers revealed an expectation that written language would make sense. For example, 1 child read *Crest* on a toothpaste package as *Brush teeth.* Another child read "Wendy's Hamburgers" on a plastic cup as "Wendy's cup."

Also in the first stage, children's writing begins as a part of their drawings, continuing the symbolic function of representing things (e.g., scribble writing can represent writing). Children may not be attempting to encode speech; they might not realize that writing can be used to characterize speech. Harste, Burke, and Woodward (1982), however, showed that younger children were good observers of the form of print. Four-year-old children from the United States, Saudi Arabia, and Israel, when asked to write everything they could write, produced scribbles that resembled the writing from their country.

In the second stage, when guided by parents and teachers to notice and make use of printed labels, children memorize words, and whole texts in books, on signs, and on labels.

They realize that content words (particularly object names) are represented in written form. In so doing, they acquire requisite concepts about words in print and begin to separate the stream of speech into word units (Sulzby, 1986). They hear and separate out the beginning (alliterative) and ending (rhyming) patterns in words (Treiman, 1992). They also hear connections made between letters and words in alphabet books, they learn to recognize their own name, and they ask to have names of signs and labels identified. These informal and indirect lessons help children to recognize printed words as separate spoken words and lead them to formulate connections between letters and sounds in words.

Soderbergh (1977), who began teaching her 30-month-old daughter to read using word cards, frequently adjusted her planned lessons according to her child's responses. For example, she found that the child had no difficulty learning concrete nouns and verbs "To her the written words were the things, and the cards with *mormor* (grandmother), *morfar* (grandfather), *kuddle* (pillow), etc. immediately became favorites" (p. 19). However, she had great difficulty when given function words, that is, words that lack concrete referents: "So I decided to give up the book with too many functors and to write a special book myself, taking care: 1) that there were as few functors as possible; 2) that the sentences were short; 3) that the vocabulary was suited to a child of two and a half; and 4) that the story appealed to her" (p. 23). This approach, of constructing books for preschool children that are simple and meaningful, has been successfully adapted in research by McCormick and Mason (1989) for introducing written texts to at-risk children.

Children's activity at this second stage was described by Dobson (1989) in her observation of children in kindergarten classrooms. One child "finger-tracked the print so that the beginning and end of his spoken sentence coincided with the print" (p. 88). With the text *Go, Go, Go*, one child said, "I know that one is G. and 'That's the first name of Graham.' I have Leslie Graham" (p. 88). But without teachers' help, few could yet integrate the letters, words, and picture cues to produce a meaningful reading.

Movement into the third stage was also observed by Dobson (1989) as she followed the children's progress in first grade. Children began building words and phrases from consonant sounds to words using sounds and words they knew, extending concepts they understood, and moving toward the use of new print concepts. Here are 2 of her examples:

After 10 months at this level, on November 20 of the first grade year [Zelko] produced a message that indicated a new level of development. He printed RABO HOS and read it as 'rainbow house.' Four months later he made his first attempt to read the print in a storybook word by word.... Once Shirley began to match letters and sounds, she continued to do so. Successive samples of her writing in the fall of first grade indicate rapid progress:

1. TWATN [There was a tornado.]
2. TW—AMSLD [There was a magical land.]
3. TR WZ A BTA FL HS [There was a beautiful house.]
4. TR WZA BTAFL PESTD [There was a beautiful present.]
(Dobson, 1989, p. 90)

The fourth stage of word concept development is seldom discussed by emergent literacy researchers because most do not follow children's development after conventional word writing is established. Ehri (1989), however, does explain this later stage in terms of spelling:

Spellers begin recognizing and using word-based spelling patterns when these are seen as more appropriate than phonetic spelling—for example, spelling past-tense verbs consistently with -ed rather than according to their sounds (woched rather than wocht for watched). This stage is thought to emerge after children learn the conventional spellings of several specific words and begin recognizing spelling patterns that recur across words. (p. 78)

CONCEPTS ABOUT LETTERS AND LETTER SOUNDS

The first stage of letter concept development could begin when babies spontaneously make sounds—they play with the sound and feel of their own noises (e.g., bubbling, squealing, and sneezing) and are delighted when adults repeat sounds that they make. Later, toddlers are particularly attuned to sound patterns of their language and then of words when they begin to speak, which is why Soderbergh (1977) investigated the possibility that her daughter could easily learn to read at this stage. Preschool children spontaneously produce rhymes, such as the examples offered by Wolf (1989) of language sound games borrowed from texts. One time her child stomped through the house reciting, "Ducky, Lucky, Goosey Loosey, Cocky Locky, Lindsey Mindsey." She also revised rhymes to fit the occasion with, "I'm in the milk and the milk's in me. Beat it, bake it, shake it, take it."

Toddlers and preschoolers also play with ABC books, blocks, and magnetic letters and learn to name the letters just as they learn to name objects. When they are given paper and drawing implements, they may draw letters along with other objects from their world and identify words in terms of one letter. McGee and Richgels (1989) describe a child saying *K* for *Special K* cereal and *M* for *K-Mart* and *McDonalds* at age 2. They also tell about a child making a G shape (and no more) when she said that she was writing *Gitti, Grandma,* and *Grandpa.*

Ferreiro (1986) depicted children's first understandings of letters by focusing upon the constructive aspects rather than the forms of letters. Santiago, at age 2, used a "belonging-to rule" about letters and people's names (e.g., *R* is *Rubin, M* is *mommy*). But his rule was inconsistent (e.g., he used *U* for *fingernail*), and conflicts arose (he had a problem when two different people had names beginning with the same initial letter). His first solution was to accept that words in context stand for objects (e.g., word cards with pictures, labels on cars and fruit). He then made up some letters to stand for names. A whole year passed before Santiago finally asked who else a letter belonged to.

The second stage of letter and letter sound development overlaps with the first because parents often begin assisting their child's letter learning at a very young age. Snow (1983), for example, describes reading an alphabet book with her son,

aged 32 months (p. 178, part of Table 4). The portion of the transcript reveals an effective balance between informing the child while keeping him on task and letting him make comments about the task:

Child	Mother
4. read dis dat book	
5.	This is a Christmas book
6. ABC book	
7.	that's an ABC book
	how did you know that?
8. dat's a present	
9.	where's it say ABC?
10. dis eh A	
11. dat's a present	
12.	yeah, it was a present a long time ago
13. as a present day	
14.	this says A is for angel
15.	B is for bell
16.	C is for candle and carol as well
17.	D is for
18. donkey	

From: Snow, Catherine E., "Literacy and Language: Relationships during the Preschool Years," *Harvard Educational Review,* 53:2, pp. 165–189. Copyright ©1983 by the President and Fellows of Harvard College. All rights reserved.

Because letters and letter sounds are often directly taught in preschool and kindergarten, there is much research evaluating the effectiveness of letter and letter-sound instruction. Bradley and Bryant (1983) showed that letter-name instruction can be effective if children learn to hear sounds in words along with the names of the letters. Mason, Kerr, Sinha, and McCormick (1990) showed that providing predictable books that preschool children learn to read (recite) through repeated readings with their teachers enhances letter name knowledge and later improves their reading. Also, Lundberg, Frost, and Petersen (1988) showed that introducing phonological awareness, that is, the sounds of the language, can be an effective first step. They "started with easy listening games that included nonverbal as well as verbal sounds. A period of rhyming games followed, using nursery rhymes, rhymed stories, and games for rhyme production. Sentences and words were introduced a couple of weeks later by means of games and exercises focusing on segmentation of sentences and investigation of word length. In the second month, syllables were carefully introduced by clapping hands, first to the syllables in the children's own names, and then to other multisyllabic words in the immediate environment. Dancing, marching, and walking in place with various syllabic intonation patterns were other exercises that were common during this period" (p. 268). Thus, there may not be one "best" method for introducing children to letters and sounds, except that it needs to be supported after children have experienced an exploratory stage.

At the third stage of letter development, children read and write, but they use props and receive some help. Letter concept understanding at this stage is best seen in children's writing, which they usually carry out in order to form words. Their attempts begin as preconventional forms—scribbling, drawing, nonphonetic letterings, phonetic spelling and copying—before they are able to write conventionally (e.g., Allen et al., 1989; Clay, 1975, 1979a; Sulzby, Barnhart, & Hieshima, 1989). In the review by Sulzby and Teale (1991), it is apparent that young children vary in their understandings of how to write depending in part on the task, but by the beginning of first grade, most are writing conventionally. The third stage of letter development also becomes linked with the third stage of word and text concept building, as children's constructions are directed to goals of producing meaningful and communicative messages.

The fourth stage of letter construction is completely encompassed by word and text concept development. Letter knowledge per se has no separate, conscious function, except perhaps for spelling (see Ehri, 1989, 1991; Ehri & Wilce, 1987). Letter pattern structures in words, for example, are not usually thought about consciously, though some patterns might remind readers of rules that were learned to aid spelling.

APPLICATION OF CULTURAL DEVELOPMENT TO EARLY CHILDHOOD PROGRAMS AND INSTRUCTION

Rounding out the theory, Vygotsky (1983) expounded on the role of the adult in assisting development.

[It is not true that] imitation is a mechanical activity and that anyone can imitate almost anything if shown how. To imitate, it is necessary to possess the means of stepping from something one knows to something new. With assistance, every child can do more than he can by himself—though only within the limitations . . . of his development. . . . [Imitation and instruction] bring out the specifically human qualities of the mind and lead the child to new developmental levels. . . . What the child can do in cooperation today he can do alone tomorrow. Therefore the only good kind of instruction is that which marches ahead of development and leads it; it must be aimed not so much at the ripe as at the ripening functions. . . . For a time our schools favoured the "complex" system of instruction, which was believed to be adapted to the child's way of thinking. In offering the child problems he was able to handle without help, this method failed to utilize the zone of proximal development and to lead the child to what he could not yet do. Instruction was oriented to the child's weakness rather than his strength, thus encouraging him to remain at the preschool stage of development. (p. 268)

Dyson (1990), however, cautions educators not to conceive of scaffolding in too narrow a manner, recommending replacing the notion of *scaffolding* with a *weaving* metaphor:

To accommodate the rich diversity of children's ways of exploring and using written language, the classroom itself should allow diverse kinds of experiences, including space for children to follow their own agendas and for teachers to guide them toward new possibilities. But despite the importance of a range of language and literacy-rich opportunities, providing opportunities is not enough to support children's literacy development, nor is helping children within the context of each activity. For it is through weaving together experiences in and out of school that children create comfortable learning places for more skillful literacy efforts. Thus, a rich diversity of experiences—composing, dictating, exploring, labeling, storytelling, and playing—enriches our own decision-making, as well as the children's literacy learning. Observing children across a range of learning spaces allows us to discover the texture of individual children's resources and to help them make connections among them. (pp. 211–212)

Keeping Dyson's caution in mind, we draw on Vygotsky's stages in our proposal for four instructional steps for the acquisition of literacy concepts. The four steps weave together home and classroom language, literacy, and play activities through mediation by the teacher who understands how to accompany observation of children's entering and changing levels of competency with support and guidance toward new learning and cultural development.

We call the first step *natural involvement*, in which teachers provide opportunities for students to explore literacy activities and events. Although the settings for learning can vary in their authenticity—that is, in their similarity to real-world tasks—the more realistic they are, the more likely students are to become effective learners. Thus the term *situated learning*, or learning in which tasks are embedded in everyday activities, should be part of this step. When a task has a realistic setting, it is more meaningful to students and a teacher can more easily observe how students are exploring, what they are interested in, and how proficient they are naturally. Teachers will then have better ideas about how to encourage movement to the second step, what to model, and how an activity could be introduced or organized.

Our second step is *mediated learning*, in which there is support or assistance by an adult. To move children into and through this step, teachers guide students' participation in new activities. They establish learning environments in which students try out the skills under their tutelage, and they help them become self-directed learners by using instructional approaches that encourage students to operate on their own. Two approaches, *modeling* and *coaching*, are effective. As new topics or procedures are introduced, teachers model the process to be learned and then coach students as they try out the techniques of thinking about and monitoring the processes.

To help children focus on their own mental operations so they can figure out how to think through the steps on their own, teachers assist children in identifying problems and using effective strategies. For example, memorizing a list of printed words may not entail strategies for recognizing the same words in a story or new, related words, so is not as important as knowing how to choose what words to remember, what they mean, and how to use the words in other settings. Thus, strategies for learning, remembering, and solving problems and techniques for carrying out self-directed learning are the instructional goals, even for beginning readers.

The third step is *external activity*, or child-directed learning and practice with the aid of props and occasional coaching by an adult. As children practice and realize how to use varying strategies they gain self-confidence and independent control of the concepts, and teachers can arrange varied opportunities for working independently and in collaboration with peers.

Internal or independent activity, the fourth step, occurs when students can link learned concepts to other, related concepts, test out general principles, and operate without help or signs or expert others and so begin to have an internalized process of thinking, reasoning, and solving problems. Eventually, then, students carry out tasks unaided and, through thinking and talking about the concepts, achieve a more general understanding of the procedures and underlying concepts.

GENERAL IMPLICATIONS FOR EARLY CHILDHOOD EDUCATION

Considerable disagreement remains among researchers working within the emergent literacy framework about the need to instruct children. Part of the problem may be with the term *instruction* and the images it conjures up. Those who object to *instruction* and advocate natural literacy learning would not object to *shared reading and writing, choral reading*, and

so on. In this report, we have relied on the terms *scaffolding, mediation*, and *assisted learning* instead of *instruction* because they suggest joint activity and support rather than directing. The mediating role notion is also compatible with Vygotskian theory and allows us to recommend a range of adult-child interactions. We believe that classroom practices ought to include informal learning opportunities, exploration by children, interactive and shared events, and opportunities for children to weave together various aspects of tasks, concepts, and their own background knowledge and interests.

Classroom activities should vary in their structure, purpose, and focus. They should be functional (useful to children), realistic (meaningful to children), and flexible (able to meet needs at various levels of development), shared (able to provide optimal opportunities for children to help and learn from one another), and holistic (involving the initiation, process and completion of an event). Finally, effective communication patterns should be developed and maintained between teachers and parents so that key care givers at school and home have a coordinated program for each child.

References

Allen, J., Clark, W., Cook, M., Crane, P., Fallon, I., Hoffman, L., Jennings, K., & Sours, M. (1989). Reading and writing development in whole-language kindergartens. In J. Mason (Ed.), *Reading and writing connections* (pp. 121–146). Boston: Allyn & Bacon.

Allen, J., & Mason, J. (1989). *Risk makers, risk takers, risk breakers*. Exeter, NH: Heinemann.

Bissex, G. (1980). *GYNS AT WRK: A child learns to write and read*. Cambridge, MA: Harvard University Press.

Bradley, L., & Bryant, P. (1983). Categorizing sounds and learning to read: A causal connection. *Nature, 301,* 419–421.

Brown, J., Collins, A., & Duguid, P. (1989). Situated cognition and the culture of learning. *Educational Researcher, 18,* 32–42.

Bruner, J. (1960). *The process of education*. Cambridge, MA: Harvard University Press.

Bruner, J. (1966). *Toward a theory of instruction*. New York: Norton.

Bruner, J. (1985). Vygotsky: A historical and conceptual perspective. In J. Wertsch (Ed.), *Culture, communication, and cognition: Vygotskian perspectives* (pp. 21-34). New York: Cambridge University Press.

Bruner, J., Goodnow, J., & Austin, G. (1956). *A study of thinking*. New York: Wiley.

Chall, J. (1983). *Stages of reading development*. New York: McGraw-Hill.

Chomsky, C. (1979). Approaching reading through invented spelling. In L. B. Resnick & P. A. Weaver (Eds.), *Theory and practice of early reading* (Vol. 2, pp. 43–46). Hillsdale, NJ: Erlbaum.

Clay, M. (1975). *What did I write?* Auckland, New Zealand: Heinemann.

Clay, M. (1979a). *Reading: The patterning of complex behavior*. Portsmouth, NH: Heinemann.

Clay, M. (1979b). Theoretical research and instructional change: A case study. In L. Resnick & P. Weaver (Eds.), *Theory and practice of early reading*. (Vol. 2, pp. 149–171). Hillsdale, NJ: Erlbaum.

Coltheart, M. (1979). When can children learn to read—and when should they be taught? In T. G. Waller & G. E. Mackinnon (Eds.), *Reading research: Advances in theory and practice* (Vol. 1, pp. 1–30). New York: Academic Press.

Cunningham, A. (1989). Phonemic awareness: The development of early reading competency. *Reading Research Quarterly, 24,* 471–472.

Datta, L. (1986). Benefits without gains: The paradox of the cognition effects of early childhood programs and implications for policy. In M. Schwebel & C. Maher (Eds.), *Facilitating cognitive development: International perspectives, programs, and practices* (pp. 103–126). New York: Haworth Press.

Dobson, L. (1989). Connections in learning to write and read: A study of children's development through kindergarten and first grade. In J. Mason (Ed.), *Reading and writing without connections* (pp. 83–104). Boston: Allyn & Bacon.

Durkin, D. (1987a). *Teaching young children to read*. Boston: Allyn & Bacon.

Durkin, D. (1987b). A classroom-observation study of reading instruction in kindergarten. *Early Childhood Research Quarterly, 2,* 275–300.

Dyson, A. (1985). Individual differences in emerging writing. In M. Farr (Ed.), *Advances in writing research, Vol 1: Children's early writing development* (pp. 59–126). Norwood NJ: Ablex.

Dyson, A. (1986). Children's early interpretations of writing: Expanding research perspectives. In D. B. Yaden & S. Templeton (Eds.), *Metalinguistic awareness and beginning literacy* (pp. 201–218). Portsmouth, NH: Heinemann.

Dyson, A. (1988). Negotiating among multiple worlds: The space-time dimensions of young children's composing. *Research in the Teaching of English, 22,* 355–390.

Dyson, A. (1990). Weaving possibilities: Rethinking metaphors for early literacy development. *The Reading Teacher, 44,* 202–213.

Ehri, L. (1989). Movement into word reading and spelling: How spelling contributes to reading. In J. Mason (Ed.), *Reading and writing connections* (pp. 83–104). Boston: Allyn & Bacon.

Ehri, L. (1991). Development of the ability to read words. In R. Barr, M. Kamil, P. Mosenthal, & P. D. Pearson (Eds.), *Handbook of reading research* (Vol. 2, pp. 383–417). New York: Longman.

Ehri, L., & Wilce, L. (1987). Does learning to spell help beginners learn to read words? *Reading Research Quarterly, 22,* 47–65.

Elementary School Journal. (1988), *90,* 111–250. Whole language.

Elkind, D. (1981). *The hurried child: Growing up too fast and too soon*. Reading, MA: Addison-Wesley.

Evans, M., & Carr, T. (1985). Cognitive abilities, conditions of learning, and the early development of reading skill. *Reading Research Quarterly, 20,* 327–340.

Ferreiro, E. (1978). What is written in a written sentence? A developmental answer. *Journal of Education, 160,* 25–39.

Ferreiro, E. (1986). The interplay between information and assimilation in beginning literacy. In W. Teale & E. Sulzby (Eds.), *Emergent literacy: Writing and reading* (pp. 15–49). Portsmouth, NH: Heinemann.

Ferreiro, E., & Teberosky, A. (1979). *Literacy before schooling.* Exeter, NH: Heinemann.

Gesell, A. (1940). *The first five years of life: A guide to the study of the preschool child.* New York: Harper.

Goodman, K., & Goodman, Y. (1974). Learning to read is natural. In L. Resnick & P. Weaver (Eds.), *Theory and practice of early reading* (Vol. 1, pp. 137–154). Hillsdale, NJ: Erlbaum.

Gough, P. (1972). One second of reading. In J. Kavanough & I. Mattingly (Eds.), *Language by ear and by eye* (pp. 331–358). Cambridge, MA: MIT Press.

Harste, J., Burke, C., & Woodward, V. (1982). Children's language and world: Initial encounters with print. In J. Langer & M. Smith-Burke (Eds.), *Reader meets author: Bridging the gap* (pp. 105–131). Newark, DE: International Reading Association.

Harste, J., Woodward, V., & Burke, C. (1984). *Language stories and literacy lessons.* Exeter, NH: Heinemann.

Heath, S. B. (1983). *Ways with words: Language, life, and work in communities and classrooms.* New York: Cambridge University Press.

Holdaway, D. (1979). *The foundations of literacy.* Sydney: Ashton Scholastic.

Juel, C. (1988). Learning to read and write: A longitudinal study of fifty-four children from first through fourth grades. *Journal of Educational Psychology, 80,* 437–447.

Kliebard, H. (1986). *The struggle for the American curriculum, 1893–1980.* Boston: Routledge & Kegan Paul.

Kozulin. A. (1990). *Vygotsky's psychology.* Cambridge, MA: Harvard University Press.

Lartz, M., & Mason, J. (1988). Jamie: One child's journey from oral to written language. *Early Childhood Research Quarterly, 3,* 193–208.

Lundberg, I., Frost, J., & Petersen, O. (1988). Effects of an extensive program for stimulating phonological awareness in preschool children. *Reading Research Quarterly, 23,* 263–284.

Mason, J. (1980). When do children begin to read: An exploration of four-year-old children's letter- and word-reading competencies. *Reading Research Quarterly, 15,* 203–227.

Mason, J. (1984). Early reading from a developmental perspective. In P. D. Pearson (Ed.), *Handbook of reading research* (pp. 505–543). New York: Longman.

Mason, J. (1989). *Reading and writing connections.* Boston, MA: Allyn & Bacon.

Mason, J. M., & Allen, J. (1986). A review of emergent literacy with implications for research and practice in reading. In E. Z. Rothkopf (Ed.), *Review of research in education* (Vol. 13, pp. 3–47). Washington, DC: American Educational Research Association.

Mason, J., Dunning, D., Stewart, J., & Peterman, C. (1991). *Measuring effects on later reading ability of language, home characteristics, and emerging knowledge about reading.* Unpublished manuscript, Urbana-Champaign, IL, Center for the Study of Reading.

Mason, J., Kerr, B., Sinha, S., & McCormick, C. (1990). Shared book reading in an Early Start program for at-risk children. In J. Zutell & S. McCormick (Eds.), *Literacy theory and research: Analysis from multiple paradigms* (pp. 189–198). Chicago: National Reading Conference.

Mason, J., Peterman, C., & Kerr, B. (1989). Reading to kindergarten children. In D. Strickland & L. Morrow (Eds.), *Emerging literacy:* *Young children learn to read and write* (pp. 52–62). Newark, DE: International Reading Association.

McCormick, C., & Mason, J. (1989). Fostering reading for Head Start children with little books. In J. Allen & J. Mason (Eds.), *Risk makers, risk takers, risk breakers: Reducing the risks for young learners.* (pp. 154–177). Portsmouth, NH: Heinemann.

McGee, L., & Richgels, D. (1989). "K is Kristen's": Learning the alphabet from a child's perspective. *The Reading Teacher, 43,* 216–225.

Moll, L. (1990). *Vygotsky and education.* New York: Cambridge University Press.

Paley, V. (1981). *Wally's stories: Conversations in the kindergarten.* Cambridge, MA: Harvard University Press.

Pallas, A., Natriello, G., & McDill, E. (1989). The changing nature of the disadvantaged population: Current dimensions and future trends. *Educational Researcher, 18,* 16–22.

Pappas, C., & Brown, E. (1987). Learning to read by reading: Learning how to extend the functional potential of language. *Research in the Teaching of English, 21,* 160–184.

Phillips, L., Norris, S., Mason, J., & Kerr, B. (1990). In J. Zutell & S. McCormick (Eds.), *Literacy theory and research: Analysis from multiple paradigms: 39th yearbook of the National Reading Conference* (pp. 199–208). Chicago: National Reading Conference.

Pinnell, G. (1989). Success of at-risk children in a program that combines writing and reading. In J. Mason (Ed.), *Reading and writing connections* (pp. 83–104). Boston: Allyn & Bacon.

Read, C. (1971). Pre-school children's knowledge of English phonology. *Harvard Educational Review, 41,* 1–34.

Resnick, L., & Weaver, P. (Eds.). (1979). *Theory and practice of early reading.* Hillsdale, NJ: Erlbaum.

Rogoff, B. (1990). *Apprenticeship in thinking: Cognitive development in social context.* New York: Oxford University Press.

Sampson, M. (Ed.). (1986). *The pursuit of literacy: Early reading and writing.* Dubuque, IA: Kendall/Hunt.

Schieffelin, B., & Gilmore, P. (1986). *The acquisition of literacy: Ethnographic perspectives.* Norwood, NJ: Ablex.

Smilansky, S. (1990). Sociodramatic play: Its relevance to behavior and achievement in school. In E. Klugman & S. Smilansky (Eds.), *Children's play and learning: Perspectives and policy implications* (pp. 18–42). New York: Teachers College, Columbia.

Snow, C. (1983). Literacy and language: Relationships during the preschool years. *Harvard Educational Review, 53,* 165–189.

Soderbergh, R. (1977). *Reading in early childhood: A linguistic study of a preschool child's gradual acquisition of reading ability.* Washington, DC: Georgetown University Press.

Stahl, S., & Miller, P. (1989). Whole language and language experience approaches for beginning reading: A quantitative research synthesis. *Review of Educational Research, 59,* 87–116.

Strickland, D. S., & Morrow, L. M. (Eds.). (1989). *Emerging literacy: Young children learn to read and write.* Newark, DE: International Reading Association.

Sulzby, E. (1985). Children's emergent reading of favorite storybooks: A developmental study. *Reading Research Quarterly, 20,* 458–481.

Sulzby, E. (1986). Children's elicitation and use of metalinguistic knowledge about Word during literacy interactions. In D. B. Yaden & S. Templeton (Eds.), *Metalinguistic awareness and beginning literacy* (pp. 219–233). Portsmouth, NH: Heinemann.

Sulzby, E., Barnhart, J., & Hieshima, J. (1989). Forms of writing and rereading from writing: A preliminary report. In J. Mason (Ed.), *Reading and writing connections* (pp. 31–64). Boston: Allyn & Bacon.

Sulzby, E., & Teale, W. (1991). Emergent literacy. In R. Barr, M. Kamil, P. Mosenthal, & P. D. Pearson (Eds.), *Handbook of reading research* (Vol. 2, pp. 727–757). New York: Longman.

Teale, W. (1987). Emergent literacy: Reading and writing development in early childhood. In J. Readence, & R. Baldwin (Eds.), *Research in literacy: Merging perspectives 36th Yearbook of the National Reading Conference* (pp. 45–74). Rochester, NY: National Reading Conference.

Teale, W., & Sulzby, E. (1986). Introduction: Emergent literacy as a perspective for examining how young children become writers and readers. In W. Teale & E. Sulzby (Eds.), *Emergent literacy: Writing and reading* (pp. vii-xxv). Norwood, NJ: Ablex.

Treiman, R. (1992). Role of intersyllabic units in learning to read and spell. In P. Gough, L. Ehri, & R. Treiman (Eds.), *Reading acquisition* (pp. 65–106). Hillsdale, NJ: Erlbaum.

Vygotsky, L. (1929). The problem of the cultural development of the child. *Journal of Genetic Psychology, 26,* 415–434.

Vygotsky, L. (1934/1986). *Thought and language.* Cambridge, MA: MIT Press.

Vygotsky, L. (1978). *Mind in society: The development of higher psychological processes.* Cambridge, MA: Harvard University Press.

Vygotsky, L. (1983). School instruction and mental development. In M. Donaldson, R. Grieve, & C. Pratt (Eds.), *Early childhood development and education: Readings in psychology* (pp. 263-269). New York: Guilford Press.

Walsh, D. (1989). Changes in kindergarten: Why here? Why now? *Early Childhood Research Quarterly, 4,* 377–391.

Wertsch, J. (Ed.). (1985). *Culture, communication, and cognition: Vygotskian perspectives.* New York: Cambridge University Press.

Williams, M. (1989). Vygotsky's social theory of mind. *Harvard Educational Review, 59,* 108–126.

Wolf, S. (1989). *Thinking in play: A young child's response to literature.* Paper presented at the annual meeting of the National Reading Conference, Austin, Texas.

Yaden, D., Smolkin, L., & Coulon, A. (1989). Preschoolers' questions about pictures, print conventions, and story text during reading aloud at home. *Reading Research Quarterly, 24,* 188–214.

·11·

FOSTERING THE MATHEMATICAL
LEARNING OF YOUNG CHILDREN

Arthur J. Baroody
UNIVERSITY OF ILLINOIS AT URBANA-CHAMPAIGN

There is considerable concern these days about widespread mathematical illiteracy, or *innumeracy* (see, e.g., Cockcroft, 1982; Paulos, 1988). Many students—particularly female students—feel inadequate, helpless, and even anxious about mathematics (see Wigfield & Meece, 1988. See Fennema & Leder, 1990, for a detailed discussion of gender differences). Frequently, such students avoid advanced mathematics, which limits their choice of jobs (Fox, Fennema, & Sherman, 1977; Ware & Lee, 1988). Many who become teachers feel so insecure about mathematics that they worry about teaching it to children (Civil, 1990).

The roots of innumeracy frequently begin in early childhood (e.g., Price, 1989). It is in the primary grades that beliefs about mathematics and one's mathematical ability are forged (e.g., Baroody, 1987; Cobb, 1985). It is in these early grades that one's predisposition toward learning and using mathematics is first shaped and, in many cases, forever fixed.

Various reports have decried the state of mathematics education in the United States and called for reform (e.g., Carnegie Forum on Education and the Economy, 1986; Holmes Group, 1986; National Commission on Excellence in Education, 1983). New visions of the nature of mathematics education—including early childhood mathematics education—have been offered in such publications as the *Curriculum and Evaluation Standards for School Mathematics* (National Council of Teachers of Mathematics, 1989), *Everybody Counts* (National Research Council, 1989), *New Directions for Elementary School Mathematics: 1989 National Council of Teachers of Mathematics Yearbook* (Trafton & Shulte, 1989), *On the Shoulders of Giants* (Steen, 1990a), *Reshaping School Mathematics: A Philosophy and Framework for Curriculum* (Mathematical Science Education Board of the National Research Council, 1990), and *Teaching and Learning Mathematics in the 1990's* (Cooney & Hirsch, 1990).

SUBJECT MATTER, CHILDREN, AND TEACHING

Those who attempt to reform and to teach early childhood mathematics need to be informed about the nature of mathematics, of children's learning, and of developmentally appropriate instructional methods. This chapter only touches upon the first. (For a more thorough discussion of the nature of mathematics see, for example, Davis & Hersh, 1981; Jacobs, 1970.) The chapter focuses on what we have learned about the development of young children's mathematics and how to foster it.

Mathematics

The way mathematics is commonly taught fosters many inaccurate conceptions or beliefs about it (see review by Underhill, 1988). A few of these are discussed below.

Mathematics as Arithmetic. Many children and adults equate mathematics with arithmetic (a set of arithmetic facts, rules, and procedures) and, perhaps, geometry. Indeed, mathematics is sometimes described as the science of numbers and shapes. Many people view mathematicians as exceptionally good calculators. In fact, mathematics is a way of thinking about the world and organizing our experiences. It entails reasoning about and solving problems. Mathematics is, at heart, an effort to find and define order and has been described as "the language and science of patterns" (Steen, 1990a, p. iii). "Seeing and revealing patterns are what mathematicians do best" (Steen, 1990b, p. 1).

It is important that young children not only learn mathematical content but that they engage in the *processes* of mathematics: searching for patterns, reasoning about data, solving problems, and communicating their ideas and results (e.g., Lappan & Schram, 1989; National Council of Teachers of Mathematics, 1989; Silver, Kilpatrick, & Schlesinger, 1990). In this way they develop the critical thinking and communication skills vital in today's workplace.

In this regard it is worth considering how the Japanese teach mathematics (see Easley, 1983). Recent research finds that Japanese children outperform U.S. children on word problems and real-world applications of mathematics over all topics in the curriculum—as well as on computational skills (see Fuson, 1992a). Unlike the typical U.S. classroom where much class time is spent on individual seatwork consisting of numerous routine computations, the Japanese classroom spends considerable time working on and discussing 1 or 2 *difficult* problems.

Mathematics as a Static Body of Knowledge.

For many children and adults, mathematical knowledge is an unchanging body of information passed down by ancient geniuses. In fact, as an open-ended search for patterns, mathematics is growing at a tremendous rate (Steen, 1990b). With the advent of computers, some predict that our mathematical knowledge may double in 5 years (Lindquist, 1989a). Although the new mathematical theories and applications are, for the most part, inappropriate for primary instruction, it is important to teach mathematics in such a way that young children see it as an evolving body of knowledge, which frequently grows out of an attempt to solve a practical problem. Such an approach may help children develop a sense of mathematical power: They might grow to see mathematical knowledge as a tool they can construct, control, and shape to help solve the problems that confront them. At the very least, instruction should give children a better understanding of the nature of knowledge, in general, and mathematics, in particular.

Mathematics: For Geniuses Only.

Many children and adults believe that mathematical ability is essentially innate—something you are either born with or without. Whereas U.S. teachers, parents, and children attribute mathematical success to ability, their Japanese counterparts attribute it to effort (Fuson, 1992b). Whether or not mathematical genius is determined largely by genetics, the fact remains that many people do not realize their potential because they believe there is little point in trying to understand mathematics. It is important to encourage the belief that everyone is capable of developing significant mathematical competence (e.g., National Council of Teachers of Mathematics, 1989).

Children's Mathematical Thinking

In the past 25 years, cognitive psychology has greatly expanded our understanding of children's mathematical thinking (see, e.g., Carpenter, Moser, & Romberg, 1982; Davis, 1984; Fuson, 1988; Gelman & Gallistel, 1978; Ginsburg, 1983, 1989; Grouws, 1992; Hiebert, 1986; Leinhardt, Putnam, & Hattrup, 1992; Nesher, 1986; Nesher & Kilpatrick, 1990; Resnick & Ford, 1981; Saxe, 1990; Shuell, 1986; Skemp, 1987; Steffe, von Glasersfeld, Richards, & Cobb, 1983). See, for example, Baroody

(1987, 1989, 1993), Hughes (1986), Kamii (1985, 1989), Peck and Jencks (1987), Price (1989), Thomas (1991), and Van de Walle (1990) for instructional implications of this research for early childhood education.

Active Construction of Knowledge.

Research suggests that children actively construct mathematical understandings by interacting with their physical and social environments and by reflecting on these experiences (Kamii, 1985; Wood, Cobb, & Yackel, 1990). Cognitive theory distinguishes between learning by rote and meaningful learning (see, e.g., Resnick & Ford, 1981). The former involves memorizing isolated pieces of information, which are often quickly forgotten or poorly applied to new tasks. Meaningful learning involves seeing or making connections. Unlike rotely learned knowledge, meaningful knowledge cannot be imposed from without but must be constructed from within. Meaningful learning, then, is not simply a matter of passively absorbing information but entails actively making sense of the world.

Viewing Errors in a New Light.

Cognitive theory suggests that errors are a natural part of learning and provide a window to children's thinking. The construction of meaningful knowledge is necessarily a gradual process. Typically, it is not possible for children to construct an entirely complete and accurate understanding all at once—even when instruction is highly effective (Resnick & Ford, 1981). The natural results of children's partially successful efforts to construct knowledge are systematic errors. For example, children make such counting errors as fourteen, *fiveteen*; nineteen, *ten-teen;* or twenty-nine, *twenty-ten* because of an overgeneralized rule or pattern they have discerned (e.g., Ginsburg, 1989). Because incomplete understandings and the systematic errors that result are the natural products of instruction (Resnick, Nesher, Leonard, Magone, Omanson, & Peled, 1989), errors should be viewed as *incomplete* responses rather than "wrong" responses (e.g., DeRuiter & Wansart, 1982).

Components of Mathematical Learning.

Maximizing mathematical learning involves fostering conceptual knowledge as well as procedural knowledge, encouraging the development of strategies and metacognitive knowledge, and promoting a positive disposition.

Procedural knowledge is *how-to* knowledge. It includes the algorithms (step-by-step procedures) for writing numerals or for adding 2 multidigit numbers such as 37 + 28. Conceptual knowledge entails mathematical understandings: the idea behind a symbol, the connection between 2 facts, or *why* a procedure is done the way it is. See Hiebert (1986) for an in-depth review concerning the distinction between procedural knowledge and conceptual knowledge.

Mathematical knowledge also includes strategies for applying existing knowledge and making sense of new situations (problem-solving skills). Strategies can be task-specific (e.g., arithmetic "thinking strategies" that use known facts like 5 + 5 = 10 to reason out unknown facts like 5 + 6) or broadly applied ("cognitive-learning strategies" such as labeling and rehearsing information or using mnemonics to memorize factual information) (see reviews by Pressley, Goodchild, Fleet, Zajchowski, & Evans, 1989; and Scheid, 1989).

Conceptual knowledge and strategies alone cannot ensure their effective use in completing assignments, learning new material, solving problems, and so forth. There must be an awareness of what resources a task requires and oversight or regulation of resource use (e.g., Reeve & Brown, 1985). Knowledge about one's own knowledge (concepts, learning strategies, or thinking processes) and the active monitoring and regulation of learning and cognitive processes has been called metacognition (e.g., Brown & Deloache, 1978). In brief, metacognitive knowledge permits self-regulated learning and problem solving (see review by Garofalo & Lester, 1985; Scheid, 1989).

Piaget and Inhelder (1969) noted that cognition and affect are complementary aspects of behavior. Affective factors such as needs, feelings, and interests energize or motivate action and thus exert a tremendous influence on learning (Reyes, 1984). Affective factors like drive, which involves interest, self-confidence, and perseverance, are important for problem-solving success (Lester, 1980; Silver & Thompson, 1984). Beliefs link cognition and affect in that they are assumptions about the self or world that prompt certain actions including attentive or avoidance behaviors (Baroody, 1987). In brief, affective factors and beliefs shape an individual's disposition to learn and to use knowledge (see reviews by McLeod, 1992; Reyes, 1984; Schoenfeld, 1985).

Processes of Change. Conceptual knowledge and strategies are actively constructed by relating (assimilating) new experiences to what is already known or by combining (integrating) existing pieces of knowledge (Ginsburg, 1989; Hiebert, 1986). Both processes involve making a *connection* (insight), and both are mechanisms for making understanding more complete and accurate (see, e.g., Lawler, 1981). Understanding and thinking grow when children must reorganize existing knowledge to deal with real problems, surprises, or conflicts.

Learners filter and interpret new information in terms of what they already know (Piaget, 1964). During the process of assimilation, a child may encounter aspects of a new experience that do not fit existing mental representations or structures exactly. This creates a disequilibrium, which requires an adjustment (accommodation). As a result of the complementary processes of assimilation and accommodation, knowledge structures become complex and more responsive to the environment. Learning, then, is not merely a process of adding information, it is a process of transforming mental structures (DeRuiter & Wansart, 1982).

By reflecting on experiences, a child may see a connection between existing but previously isolated aspects of knowledge. For example, a child may recognize that the symbolic expression 5 + 5 can represent how many fingers she has altogether on both hands, which may help the child learn the basic number fact 5 + 5 = 10. Integration can also result from the disequilibrium caused by 2 conflicting schemata. For example, by viewing a square as a special kind of rectangle, a child can resolve the conflict between viewing squares as different from rectangles and the fact that squares share the same critical (defining) attributes of rectangles: both are 4-sided enclosed figures with parallel opposite sides (parallelograms) in which two adjacent sides meet at a right angle.

Informal and Formal Mathematical Knowledge. Research shows that the development of mathematical knowledge begins well before children enter school (see, e.g., Baroody, 1987; Cooper, 1984; Fuson, 1988, Fuson & Hall, 1983; Gelman & Gallistel, 1978; Ginsburg, 1989; Ginsburg & Russell, 1981; Saxe, Guberman, & Gearhart, 1987; Starkey & Gelman, 1982; Strauss & Curtis, 1984; Wagner & Walters, 1982). This *informal* knowledge is based, in large part, on everyday experiences and counting. For example, by the time they enter kindergarten, children typically understand that the counting sequence represents increasingly large quantities (Schaeffer, Eggleston, & Scott, 1974). Such informal knowledge provides an important basis for understanding numbers, arithmetic, and other aspects of formal (school-taught, largely written or symbolic) mathematics (e.g., Hughes, 1986; Resnick, 1989; Young-Loveridge, 1987).

Even after children begin school, they often continue to rely on their informal mathematics instead of doing mathematics the way it is taught (e.g., Ginsburg, 1989; Resnick & Ford, 1981). For example, despite the emphasis in many schools on memorizing the number facts, many children persist in computing sums, differences, and products (see, e.g., Baroody, 1987; Carpenter & Moser, 1984; Ginsburg, Posner, & Russell, 1981; Ginsburg & Russell, 1981)— often surreptitiously—because they trust their self-invented computing procedures.

Informal mathematics enables children to exhibit surprising strengths. For example, research (e.g., Carpenter & Moser, 1983) indicates that young children have previously unsuspected problem-solving skill (Carpenter, 1986; Riley, Greeno, & Heller, 1983). Even kindergartners and first-graders can solve simple addition, subtraction, multiplication, and division word problems by using counting strategies that model the meaning of a problem (see, e.g., Kouba, 1989). On the other hand, informal mathematical knowledge may not be complete, coherent, or logical (see, e.g., Baroody & Ginsburg, 1986; Piaget, 1965). A significant inconsistency, for example, is that, even though young children can deal effectively with quantitative questions involving small numbers, they cannot always do so with large numbers (e.g., Gelman, 1972; Ginsburg, 1989).

The formal (symbolic) mathematics taught in school can greatly extend children's ability to deal with quantitative issues. Indeed, the mathematical skills and concepts taught in the primary grades are not only the foundation for learning more advanced mathematics later in school, but also basic "survival skills" in our technologically oriented society. However, the extent to which children benefit from formal instruction depends on how well it connects with their existing knowledge.

Mathematics Instruction

Mathematical literacy and, hence, the goals of mathematical instruction can be defined in different ways. Mathematics instruction can focus on (1) promoting *mastery of basic skills;* (2) fostering an *understanding* of mathematical facts, rules, and procedures; or (3) encouraging the development of *critical thinking* (problem solving and reasoning) (e.g., Labinowicz, 1985; Resnick & Ford, 1981).

Different Perspectives of Mathematics Education. Traditional textbook-based approaches have typically focused on fostering skill mastery. The primary aim of a *skills approach* is to have children *memorize* facts, rules, and procedures. (In the past, this was deemed important because computational skill, for instance, was necessary to do higher mathematics or for everyday life.) Instruction concentrates on *how* to do mathematics. A skills approach is based on the assumption that direct instruction is the most effective means of fostering skill mastery. It entails breaking a subject matter into small steps, explaining and demonstrating each step, providing guided practice, and assigning large amounts of practice to ensure mastery of each step. Such an approach often largely involves working with (abstract) symbols and doing paper-and-pencil tasks.

The second approach focuses on understanding: helping children see the relationships among facts and the underlying reasons for rules and procedures. A *conceptual approach* concentrates on *why*. It often uses manipulatives or pictorial representations to make instruction more concrete and frequently emphasizes student involvement. An effectively implemented conceptual approach takes into account students' readiness to learn and their interest, needs, and feelings.

The third approach focuses on the critical-thinking skills necessary to solve new problems. A *problem-solving approach* concentrates on solving and reasoning out problems. It may entail learning about and practicing Polya's (1973) 4-phase method for solving problems: (1) understand the problem (e.g., define the unknown and decide what information is relevant), (2) devise a plan (generate possible solution strategies and choose the most appropriate one), (3) carry out the plan, and (4) check the results. Children may also learn and practice heuristics: problem-solving aids such as drawing a picture, organizing data into a list or table, considering a simpler version of a problem, or determining whether a problem is similar to familiar problems. See, for example, Charles and Silver (1989), Curcio (1987), Lester and Garofalo (1982), Schoenfeld (1992), and Silver (1985) for reviews of the problem-solving literature. Particularly good references for incorporating problem solving in the primary grades include Burns (1992), Burns and Tank (1988), Krulik and Reys (1980), and Nelson and Worth (1983).

Major Trends in Mathematics Education. Historically, U.S. schools have featured a skills approach with its narrow focus on written arithmetic and rote memorization (e.g., Romberg, 1982). There has been a long-standing effort to change the nature of mathematics instruction in the United States (see, e.g., Brownell, 1935). After the Soviets launched Sputnik in the late 1950s, there was a renewed cry to reform mathematics and science education in the United States. The idea behind the "new math" was to help children understand and reason through mathematics, eliminating the need to memorize mathematics by rote. Although much was learned from the effort, the new math was not successful for a variety of reasons (Kline, 1974), including the fact that it did not adequately take into account the psychology of children (Baroody, 1987).

The "back-to-basics" movement evolved, in part, as a reaction to the perception that modern approaches such as the new math did not adequately emphasize skill mastery. This movement essentially advocates a return to the traditional skills approach.

The *teacher-effectiveness movement* represents one important, recent, research-based effort to improve instruction. Dissatisfied with laboratory-based research and theories of instruction and learning, process-product researchers have tried to develop a model of effective instruction by observing the behaviors of classroom teachers (process variables) and gauging their impact on student achievement and attitudes (product variables) (Brophy & Good, 1986; Putnam, Lampert, & Peterson, 1990). A basic premise of this approach is that student achievement is low because mathematics, for instance, is not taught in an efficient and effective manner. It follows that teachers should be trained on successful methods for delivering instruction. Thus, process-product researchers have attempted to identify the teaching techniques used by effective teachers—teachers whose classes have yielded relatively high achievement scores (see, e.g., Brophy, 1986a; Brophy & Good, 1986; Good, Grouws, & Ebmeier, 1983 for summaries of the process-product or teacher-effectiveness research effort).

The main recommendation of this approach is that instruction should be systematic (see Easley, Taylor, & Taylor, 1990, for a different view). More specifically, class should begin with a *review* (e.g., reexamine the last content covered, address questions raised by the homework, and reinforce the previous content with mental computation exercises). The main portion of the class time should be spent on *development* (e.g., review prerequisite skills and concepts, promote understanding by using interesting explanations and demonstrations, evaluate student understanding via questions and controlled practice, and reinforce understanding by repeating or elaborating on the content as necessary). The last phase of class should focus on *seatwork* (e.g., provide uninterrupted practice, ensure all are involved and successful, and follow up by checking students' work). Another critical component is *homework*, which should be assigned regularly and which should entail about 15 minutes work.

Clearly there are some important lessons to be learned from the teacher-effectiveness research. It makes sense, for example, that instruction should focus on promoting an understanding of mathematical content. Research indicates, not surprisingly, that achievement increases dramatically when teachers spend more time on development (Good et al., 1983).

Nonetheless, the teacher-effectiveness movement has led to a lively debate (see, e.g., Brophy 1986a, 1986b, versus Confrey, 1986) and drawn considerable criticism (see. e.g., Putnam et al., 1990; Romberg & Carpenter, 1986). One criticism is that it defines mathematical achievement narrowly as success on standardized tests—tests that tend to measure skills but not understanding and critical thinking (problem solving and reasoning). Another related criticism is that it views mathematics teaching and learning in relatively narrow terms. Although teacher-effectiveness proponents do advocate more emphasis on lesson development (understanding), they basically propose a teacher-centered instructional approach.

In contrast, constructivists argue that instruction should be child-centered. In this view, teaching is a process of helping students to construct their own mathematical knowledge. A teacher's responsibility is not to transmit information but to create classroom activities that provide children with opportunities to construct understandings and strategies (e.g., Putnam et al., 1990; Resnick, 1983b). See, for instance, Davis, Mahr, and Noddings (1990) and Steffe and Wood (1990) for more complete descriptions of a constructivist approach to teaching.

In conclusion, although a teacher-effectiveness approach is a move toward a conceptual approach, critics might argue that it does not move far enough in this direction. Moreover, it does not adequately address the need to cultivate critical thinking. Although the teaching strategies identified by the process-product researchers can be used to significantly improve student achievement, they do not represent the fundamental change that is needed to improve mathematics instruction. As Romberg and Carpenter (1986) have noted, the recommendations of the teacher-effectiveness approach "can only make current teaching more efficient or effective, but they cannot make it radically different" (p. 865).

In recent years a new reform movement has gained considerable momentum (see, e.g., Lindquist, 1989a). Its key points are outlined in the *Curriculum and Evaluation Standards for School Mathematics* recently issued by the National Council of Teachers of Mathematics (1989). This visionary document calls for fundamental changes in the way mathematics is taught, recommending that instruction focus on fostering problem solving and understanding, rather than the memorization of facts and procedures.

For grades K–4, the *Curriculum Standards* recommend using problem solving as a means of teaching mathematical content (see, e.g., Cobb & Merkel, 1989; Schroeder & Lester, 1989). It suggests also promoting problem-solving competence by encouraging children to solve a wide variety of problems and to formulate their own problems (see, e.g., Bebout & Carpenter, 1989; Irons & Irons, 1989; Rathmell & Huinker, 1989). (The term "problem" here refers to puzzling situations for which a child does not have an immediate solution strategy. In contrast, an exercise entails answering questions by using an existing strategy. Textbook publishers sometimes label as problems work sheet pages that serve to practice facts or computational procedures; such work sheets really constitute little more than an exercise.) The *Curriculum Standards* recommend giving children numerous opportunities to interact and to communicate their ideas and strategies (see, e.g., Johnson & Johnson, 1989; Lappan & Schram, 1989). In particular, children should discuss the relationship between everyday experiences, manipulative models or pictorial representations, and mathematical ideas or symbols. It is especially important that children regularly justify their strategies and answers to others (e.g., Lampert, 1986). Writing, which has traditionally been overlooked in mathematics education, can be an invaluable learning tool (see, e.g., Azzolino, 1987; Connolly & Vilardi, 1989). The *Curriculum Standards* also underscore the importance of reasoning. Children should be given opportunities to reason inductively (analyze examples to discover a rule) and deductively (use given information or rules to draw a conclusion).

Sources such as Baratta-Lorton (1976) and Baroody (1989) describe numerous activities and games that involve the induction of a rule. Games like Clue, Mastermind, Battleship, and 20 Questions all entail deductive reasoning.

The *Curriculum Standards* recommend giving children the opportunity to make connections between personal experiences and school-taught mathematics, among various representations (models, examples, symbolic expressions, and so forth) of concepts and procedures, and between concepts and procedures. Instruction and practice should be meaningful and purposeful—in a context that is real and interesting to children (see Burns, 1992; Kamii, 1985; Kilpatrick, 1985). Mathematics games are one way this can be accomplished (e.g., Bright, Harvey, & Wheeler, 1985).

A primary mathematics curriculum should emphasize the development of a number sense including estimation of quantities, measurement, and computations (see, e.g., Bright, 1976; Reys, 1984; Schoen & Zweng, 1986). It should include work on 2- and 3-dimensional geometry, a spatial sense, and measurement. (For some instructional ideas, see Banchoff, 1990; Bezuska, Kenney, & Silvey, 1977; Hill, 1987; Lindquist & Shulte, 1987; Senechal, 1990; Schultz, Colarusso, & Strawderman, 1989.) The *Curriculum Standards* also recommend including an *informal* introduction to such topics as probability (e.g., collecting data to answer genuine questions) and statistics (see Shaughnessy, 1992, for a review of the literature). For some instructional ideas regarding statistics and probability, see Curcio (1989), Moore (1990), and Shulte and Smart (1981).

Forces of Change. Four factors drive the current reform movement.

1. *Changes in technology have changed how mathematics is done and what is needed to do mathematics.* With the advent of computers and calculators, understanding and problem solving are more important, while memorizing computational facts and procedures are less important (e.g., Coburn, 1989). With the arrival of inexpensive calculators and computers, proficiency with arithmetic skills is no longer necessary for the effective use of mathematics (Fey, 1990). What is now important is the ability to know what to do with data, how to use technology to process the data, and to gauge whether or not the results are reasonable.

2. *Changes in society have greatly extended the applications of mathematics and what constitutes basic survival skills.* The essential mathematical competences for an information-based, technologically oriented society are different than those required by an industrial society (e.g., Davis, 1984; Fuson, 1992b; Lindquist, 1989a). Quantitative methods are now needed in nearly all aspects of our personal and professional lives. Mastery of arithmetic skills is inadequate for many contemporary problems, which "require the ability to organize, manipulate, and interpret quantitative information.... Quantitatively literate young people need a flexible ability to identify critical relations in novel situations, to express these relations in effective symbolic form, to use computing tools to process information, and to interpret the results of those calculations" (Fey, 1990, p. 65).

3. *Evidence of educational shortcomings indicates that traditional approaches to mathematics instruction are inadequate for preparing children for the future.* The "disaster studies" clearly indicated the shortcomings of the traditional skill approach (see review by Davis, 1984). Both national-level research like the National Assessment of Educational Progress (see, e.g., Lindquist, 1989b) and cross-cultural research (e.g., McKnight et al., 1987; Stevenson, Lee, & Stigler, 1986) indicate low levels of mathematical achievement by U.S. children (see Fuson 1992a, for a more complete review)—even in the primary grades (Price, 1989). Research (e.g., Erlwanger, 1973) has found that even apparently successful students (students who had successfully memorized skills and were average or above average in mathematical achievement) do not understand why computational procedures work, cannot apply their knowledge to even slightly new situations, and have little ability to solve problems (Davis, 1984).

4. *Cognitive research indicates that traditional approaches to instruction do not adequately foster the construction of mathematical knowledge.* Research by cognitive researchers (e.g., Vygotsky, 1978) indicates that teachers must consider issues of developmental readiness and what constitutes developmentally appropriate instruction. Research suggests that a gap between formal instruction and informal knowledge is a primary cause of learning difficulties (Allardice & Ginsburg, 1983; Ginsburg, 1989; Hiebert, 1984). When symbolic representations are introduced too quickly and not related to children's existing informal knowledge, students do not have the opportunity to construct an understanding of school mathematics and, thus, must memorize it by rote. As a result, many children cannot apply their school-learned arithmetic (e.g., deciding what operation to use when solving a problem). Many others forget all or critical parts of what they have memorized. For example, in the situation below, a child could not remember all the steps of the renaming algorithm (step-by-step procedure): The child borrowed but did not reduce the tens digit.

$$
\begin{array}{r} 136 \\ -28 \\ \hline 118 \end{array} \qquad
\begin{array}{r} 147 \\ -49 \\ \hline 108 \end{array} \qquad
\begin{array}{r} 124 \\ -56 \\ \hline 178 \end{array}
$$

Some children do not see any point in memorizing information that does not seem important or make sense to them. Others stop trying to memorize facts and procedures because they become fearful of failing.

A skills approach frequently undermines the construction of understanding, the development of problem-solving strategies, autonomy (metacognitive skills), and a positive disposition toward mathematics (e.g., Baroody, 1987; Kamii, 1985; Eccles et al., 1983; Schoenfeld, 1985; Tobias, 1978). For example, emphasis on memorizing *the* correct (teacher-taught) algorithm undercuts children's efforts to invent their own strategies and fosters the belief that there is only one way to solve a given mathematical problem. Such an approach essentially encourages children to depend on external authorities, not themselves. One result is that children

learn to do mathematics mechanically, without thinking. For instance, the child who subtracted 56 from 124 and got 178 was not bothered by the fact that the answer was actually *larger* than the minuend (starting amount), because she did not bother to reflect on her work.

A Developmental Approach. To promote meaningful learning and thoughtful applications of knowledge, a teacher must ensure that mathematics instruction is developmentally appropriate for each student. That is, a teacher must decide whether or not instructional materials or methods suit a child's thinking.

To implement a developmentally appropriate approach, teachers must understand a child's current level of understanding or thinking and pose problems and questions just beyond it. They should give children the opportunity to use their existing knowledge to puzzle through a problem or question. Teachers should listen carefully to children as they explain their ideas and solutions (Carpenter, Fennema, Peterson, Chiang, & Loef, 1989). Even confused or incorrect answers can be informative because these reflect a child's current level of understanding. Moreover, it is important to encourage children to share their ideas and strategies with others (Carpenter et al., 1989; Johnson & Johnson, 1989; Kamii, 1985; Silver et al., 1990; Wood et al., 1990). When adults and other students listen to them, it "tells" children their ideas and strategies are important, which helps build confidence. It also helps them understand that the most important part of mathematics is thinking and communicating. Additionally, sharing strategies helps children to see that there can be more than one way to solve problems. Moreover, it can create the cognitive conflict that encourages children to reorganize their thinking and to construct more complete understandings (e.g., Cobb, Wood, & Yackel, 1990). Getting students into the habit of justifying their answers further helps them to see that mathematics is something they are supposed to think about and comprehend.

PREARITHMETIC INSTRUCTION AND LEARNING

This section summarizes some of the research on the development of a number sense and its implications for early childhood education.

Psychological Origins of a Number Sense

Informal knowledge provides the basis for a number sense, which entails a well-organized network of understandings about number magnitude, the effects of adding and subtracting, and part-whole relationships (see Resnick, 1989; Sowder, 1992; Sowder & Schapple, 1989). A well-developed number sense allows for flexible problem solving and a sense of control or power over numbers.

Prequantitative Knowledge. From their everyday experiences, children learn much about quantities and their behavior. This prequantitative knowledge permits children to reason about quantitative situations—sometimes quite effectively and other times ineffectively. Their knowledge is prequantitative, because it does not entail measuring or numbering (e.g., counting).

Preschoolers can make comparisons of "the same," "more," "bigger," and "longer" on the basis of appearances (direct perception). For example, offered a choice between 2 rows of candies, even 2-year-olds choose the longer row. However, sometimes appearances can be deceiving and mislead children. The classic illustration of this point is Piaget's (1965) number-conservation experiment, where 2 rows are matched up in one-to-one correspondence and then 1 row is lengthened or shortened. Even after initially agreeing that both rows originally had the same number, young children claim that the longer row has more in its final form.

By playing with collections of 1, 2, and 3, preschoolers recognize that adding something to a collection makes it larger and taking away something makes it smaller. This provides an informal conceptual basis for understanding addition as an incrementing process and subtraction as a decrementing process.

Preschoolers know that a whole is larger than its parts (e.g., a cake is bigger than a piece of it). Kindergarten-age children even have a prequantative basis for understanding division and fractions. Given a collection of 12 cookies and asked to share them fairly between 2 or 3 puppets, many children will use a dealing-out strategy. They will give each puppet a cookie until the collection is exhausted (e.g., Hiebert & Tonnessen, 1978; Hunting & Sharpley, 1988; Miller, 1984). This process does not guarantee, however, that children know how many each puppet got or even that the puppets got the same number (Davis & Pitkethly, 1990).

Informal Quantitative Knowledge. Considerable debate surrounds the question of what role counting plays in the development of number and arithmetic understanding (see, e.g., Brainerd, 1973). Piaget (1965) argued that counting was not an important basis for number and arithmetic concepts. In his view, children could not achieve an understanding of number and arithmetic until they achieved what he called the concrete operational stage—the stage at which they develop prerequisite logical concepts and reasoning ability. Before they obtained the age of reason, children might learn to count by imitating others, but they could not use this rotely learned skill in meaningful fashion—that is, to reason about quantitative problems.

Success on Piaget's number-conservation task has been taken as key evidence that a child has attained the concrete operational stage and hence is ready for meaningful number and arithmetic instruction (see, e.g., Hendrickson, 1983). However, it is clear that children can construct much meaningful knowledge about these domains before they conserve (e.g., Mpiangu & Gentile, 1970). (See Hiebert and Carpenter, 1982, and Young-Loveridge,1987, for reviews on Piagetian tasks as measures of readiness.) Although neo-Piagetians such as Case (1982) have attempted to refine Piaget's stage model, there is now considerable skepticism about Piaget's proposition that children's thinking proceeds through 4 across-the-board qualitatively different stages of thinking (see, e.g., reviews by Ashton, 1975; Brainerd, 1978; Flavell, 1963; Fodor, 1972; Phillips & Kelly, 1975; Starkey & Gelman, 1982).

There is evidence, though, that children's concepts and reasoning within a *specific domain* evolve in a qualitative fashion. That is, for a particular topic, children can have an insight that gives them a new perspective and allows them to think about a problem in new ways. Most post-Piagetian research has focused on describing and explaining development within specific domains, without trying to ascribe it to general intellectual changes. Groen and Kieran (1983) noted this shift in emphasis by saying:

A few years ago, research on children's mathematics was dominated by Piaget [even though] the priority seemed to frequently lie in "disproving" Piaget....[Recent] research...relegates Piaget to the background. Information-processing theory, broadly conceived, has replaced the Piagetian framework as a broad explanatory model (pp. 351–2).

One type of information-processing model is the skills-integration model (see, e.g., Klahr & Wallace, 1973; Schaeffer et al., 1974). In this view, as basic skills become automatic, they put less demand on working memory. As a result, children can coordinate and combine these skills to form more complex skills, thus forming a hierarchy of skills. In this view number conservation is the result of integrating more basic number skills, including counting skills (Young-Loveridge, 1987).

Similarly, others (see, e.g., Baroody, 1987; Fuson, 1988; Gelman & Gallistel, 1978) have argued that counting experiences are the key to the development of children's understanding of number and arithmetic. In this view, children gradually construct basic number and arithmetic concepts from real experiences that largely involve counting. In recent years some Piagetians (e.g., Sinclair & Sinclair, 1986) have concluded that an analysis of number development would be psychologically incomplete without considering the contribution of counting experiences.

Gelman and Gallistel (1978) concluded that preschoolers implicitly understood key principles governing counting. (They adduced 5 basic counting principles: [a] the stable-order principle [tags must be generated in the same sequence on every count]; [b] the one-to-one principle [every item in a collection must be tagged with 1 and only 1 unique tag]; [c] the cardinality principle [the tag of the last item in a collection represents the total number of items in the collection]; [d] the abstraction principle [various kinds of items may be collected together for the purpose of counting]; [e] the order-irrelevance principle [the order in which the items of a collection are tagged does not affect the outcome of counting as long as the one-to-one principle is observed].) This seminal work has sparked a debate over the relationship between the development of counting skills and counting principles (concepts). Three views about this issue are summarized below.

1. In the *counting-skills-first view* (Briars & Siegler, 1984), children acquire counting skills through imitation and reinforcement, without really understanding their underlying rationale. Variable performance across counting tasks is attributed to the absence of principles. Children abstract counting principles by noticing commonalities across different tasks.

2. In the *counting-principles-first view* (e.g., Gallistel & Gelman, 1992; Gelman & Meck, 1986, 1992) the development of counting skills is principle driven. That is, a set of innate counting principles directs the development of counting procedures. In this view, variable performance across tasks can be explained by distinguishing among conceptual, procedural, and utilization competence (e.g. Greeno, Riley, & Gelman, 1984). In brief, understanding can be masked, because children may not know how to implement the principles (procedural competence) or because they do not understand the requirements of a task (utilization competence). Evidence supporting the counting-principles-first view is equivocal (Baroody, 1992).

3. According to a *mutual-development view* (Baroody, 1992; Fuson, 1988; Sophian, 1992), the development of counting principles and skills are intertwined. In this view, innate organizing tendencies may facilitate the acquisition of counting-skill components. Initially, children may acquire and use counting skills or their components without understanding. Purposeful or principled counting develops gradually (see also Baroody & Ginsburg, 1986; Fuson & Hall, 1983; von Glasersfeld, 1982; Wagner & Walters, 1982). The construction of understanding leads to further skill acquisition, which in turn leads to further conceptual insights, and so forth. Performance variability across tasks is, thus, partly attributed to incomplete understanding.

One notable model of number development has been adduced by Steffe and his colleagues (see Steffe & Cobb, 1988; Steffe et al., 1983). They have proposed that children construct an increasingly complex and abstract concept (understanding) of number ("counting types"). See Fuson (1988, 1992b) for a summary of and an elaboration on the counting-types model and Carpenter (1985) for a critique of the model.

As counting skill and understanding progress, children acquire an exact and useful tool for making quantitative comparisons (see the section on number skills that follows). Counting-based knowledge provides a key basis for children's informal reasoning about arithmetic and for the elaboration of a part-whole concept (see the section on arithmetic instruction and learning later in the chapter).

Number Skills

Oral Counting. To count to 100, a child needs to know: (a) the single-digit sequence one to nine; (b) that a nine signals a transition (e.g., nineteen signals the end of the teens and the beginning of a new series); (c) the transition terms for the new series (e.g., twenty follows nineteen); (d) the rules for generating the new series (e.g., the twenties and all subsequent series are generated by combining the transition term with, in turn, each term in the single-digit sequence; and (e) the exceptions to the rules (Baroody, 1989). (See Hurford, 1975, for a discussion of the rules for forming the teen and decade terms.) Children beginning school typically can count to 9, if not 19 (Fuson, 1988). Many kindergartners, though, have not acquired the second component mentioned in the list and, as a result,

tend to overextend their counting rules—that is, make rule-governed errors such as "...nineteen, *ten-teen, eleven-teen,...*" or "...twenty-nine, *twenty-ten, twenty-eleven,...*"). (Although some suggest that children learn the teens in a rule-governed fashion [e.g., Ginsburg, 1989; Hurford, 1975], others suggest the teens are rotely learned [Fuson, 1988; Siegler & Robinson, 1982]. Rule-governed errors like "five-teen" and "ten-teen" seem to support the first view.) Likewise, most kindergartners do not know the decade term to begin the new series (e.g., they count to 29 and stop because they do not know that 30 is next). Indeed, it is not until first grade that many children recognize that the decade series parallels the single-digit sequence (e.g., six + ty, seven + ty, eight + y) and master the decades (e.g., "twenty" is followed by "twenty + one, twenty + two,...twenty + nine"). Finally, exceptions to counting patterns often cause difficulties. For example, 15 is the most commonly missed teen (e.g., Fuson, 1988). The highly regular nature of the Chinese counting sequence (e.g., "fifteen" is literally "ten and five") no doubt helps to account for the fact that Chinese children have significantly less difficulty learning to count than do U.S. children (Miller & Stigler, 1987). (Similarly, Beilin [1975] found that 5-year-olds performed poorly on ordinal-number tasks. He attributed this difficulty, in part, to the irregular nature of English ordinal terms [see also Fuson, 1988]. In Chinese, ordinal terms are formed by using the prefix *di* before the cardinal [counting-sequence] term. The highly regular nature of the ordinal sequence should facilitate learning this sequence by Chinese children [Kevin Miller, personal communication, November 14, 1990].)

By the time they enter kindergarten, children typically have learned to use their mental representation of the number sequences in some elaborate and flexible ways (e.g., Fuson, Richards, & Briars, 1982). Asked what comes after a number up to 9, most children no longer have to count from 1 to determine the successor but can automatically state it. Stating the number before a given number is more difficult, because children have to operate on the number-sequence representation in the "opposite" direction the sequence was learned. Moreover, the term "before" may be relatively unfamiliar to children and interpreted as "after" (cf. Donaldson & Balfour, 1968). Because it may serve as a prerequisite for counting backwards, a deficiency in number-before knowledge can impede the development of this counting skill. Difficulty in counting backward can, in turn, hinder the development of counting down, an informal subtraction strategy.

Object Counting. To enumerate sets of objects correctly, a child must know (a) the count sequence, (b) that each object in a set is labeled with 1 counting word (one-for-one tagging), and (c) how to keep track of counted and uncounted objects so that each object is tagged once and only once (Gelman & Gallistel, 1978). Kindergartners typically have mastered the first 2 components, but many have not devised effective keeping-track strategies (e.g., Fuson, 1988). This may result in skipping an item or items or counting an item or items more than once, particularly when the set is large and/or haphazardly arranged.

Numerical Relationships. Most children entering school can use their representation of the number sequence to determine which of 2 adjacent numbers indicates the larger quantity (e.g., which is more, 7 or 8?). From their experiences with small sets and numbers, they construct a number-ordering rule: A number that comes after another in the number sequence is more than its predecessor (Schaeffer et al., 1974). As children master the number-after relationships for more and more of the number sequence, they can apply the ordering rule to larger and larger numbers. However, children with relatively little informal mathematical experience or those with learning difficulties may not develop this number-comparison ability (see Baroody, 1986, 1988b). Unfortunately, this important skill is often overlooked or not adequately emphasized in the evaluation and the teaching of kindergartners. Gauging which term is "less" is even more difficult because, in part, children rarely hear or apply the term (e.g., Donaldson & Balfour, 1968; Weiner, 1974).

Reading and Writing Single-Digit Numerals. Reading numerals entails distinguishing among these symbols. This requires constructing a mental image of each numeral: knowing its component parts and how the parts fit together to form the whole. For example, a 6 consists of 2 parts, a curved line and a loop, that distinguish it from all other numerals except 9. The relationship between these parts (the loop of a 6 joins the lower right-hand side of the curved line) distinguishes it from a 9 (in which the loop joins the *upper left-hand* side of the curved line). Although an inability to distinguish among numerals is often attributed to a perceptual disability, cognitive research indicates that such problems stem from an incomplete or inaccurate mental image (Baroody, 1987). In particular, children frequently confuse numerals that share familiar characteristics (2 and 5 or 6 and 9). The numerals 6 and 9 are particularly difficult to distinguish, because the numerals have the same parts and differ only in orientation: where the curve joins the loop.

Although a mental image is necessary for accurate numeral writing, it is not a sufficient condition. The child must also have a preplanned course of action for translating this mental image into motor actions. A motor plan specifies where to start (e.g., at the top of a line or just below it), in what direction to head (left, right, up, down, diagonally), what needs to be drawn (e.g., a straight line, an arc), when to stop a given step, how to change directions, how to begin the next step, and where to stop (Goodnow & Levine, 1973). Although writing difficulties such as reversals are frequently attributed to perceptual-motor deficiencies (Mann & Suiter, 1974; Sears, 1986), cognitive research suggests that these difficulties stem from an incomplete or inaccurate mental image or motor plan (Baroody, 1989, Baroody & Cohn, in press). Children without an accurate motor plan may, for example, repeatedly start in the wrong place and head in the wrong direction—and, as a result, consistently reverse the numeral—even with a model numeral in front of them.

Estimation. Traditionally, this topic has not been introduced until third grade and then is only given slight attention (e.g., Driscoll, 1981). Instruction has usually focused narrowly on multidigit computation estimation and only one strategy (rounding) at that (Trafton, 1978). Moreover, it typically has fostered rote memorization because little or no effort was made to connect an estimation procedure to other topics and students did not understand its purpose or use (e.g., Reys, 1984). Not surprisingly, many children are uncomfortable making estimates (Trafton, 1986) and respond inflexibly and poorly on estimation tasks (e.g., Carpenter, Coburn, Reys, & Wilson, 1976).

It is now recognized that estimation instruction should be initiated in the primary years in order to provide a solid basis for training (Carter, 1986; Carlow, 1986). Moreover, it should be broadened to include estimation of quantities, measurement, and single-digit computation (e.g., Bright, 1976; National Council of Teachers of Mathematics, 1989; Siegel, Goldsmith, & Madson, 1982). Unfortunately, little research has been done with children in the early primary years (e.g., Carter, 1986; Fuson & Hall, 1983; Sowder, 1988). Siegel et al. (1982) found that children as early as second grade could estimate quantities by using perceptual anchors—mental images of landmark collections, such as 10 or 50. Fuson and Hall (1983) hypothesized that younger children, however, may have difficulty estimating the size of collections larger than 5 because they have not constructed perceptual anchors. Baroody and Gatzke (1991) found, in fact, that many kindergartners in a program for the potentially gifted could not accurately estimate set sizes ranging from 15 to 35, and some even had difficulty estimating sets of 8 items. The children appeared to have an exaggerated mental image of 10 and 20. Some even had an exaggerated view of 5 (see also Siegler & Robinson, 1982).

ARITHMETIC INSTRUCTION AND LEARNING

Traditionally, the mainstay of the primary mathematics curriculum has been the mastery of arithmetic facts, rules, and procedures. Addition, subtraction, and multiplication will continue to be a central focus of instruction (Coburn, 1989). This section focuses on research on teaching and learning of single- and multidigit addition and subtraction. For information on multiplication see, for example, chapters in Heibert and Behr (1988) and articles by Kouba (1989) and Quintero (1985).

Single-Digit Addition and Subtraction

Research indicates that teachers and publishers often overlook children's informal strengths and the need to build on these strengths.

Informal Arithmetic Concepts and Problem Solving. It is often assumed that solving word problems is a relatively difficult task and that word problems should be introduced after formal addition and subtraction skills—or at least after more concrete experiences (see Baratta-Lorton, 1976; Garland, 1988). However, children can often solve simple word problems before they comprehend formal expressions such as $5 + 2 = ?$ or $5 - 2 = ?$ (Ginsburg, 1989; Fuson, 1992b). Indeed, research indicates that many children can use their informal arithmetic knowledge to analyze and solve simple addition and subtraction word problems before they receive any formal arithmetic instruction (Carpenter, 1986).

A variety of addition and subtraction situations exist in the real world. Table 11–1 summarizes one way of classifying these situations as word problems. For a more complete taxonomy, see Fuson (1992b).

The first, second, and fourth sections in Table 11–1 indicate situations that involve action (active-type problems); the third and fifth sections indicate situations that do not (static-type problems). Change problems involve beginning with a *single* collection and changing this initial amount by adding something to make it larger (change add-to problems) or removing something to make it smaller (change take-away problems). All other problems involve beginning with *2* numbers, which are either added or subtracted to the find the whole or one of the parts. For each of the 5 main types of problems, the unknown can vary. The first column of problems involves a missing outcome or whole; the second and third columns involve a missing addend.

As noted earlier, a fundamental understanding of addition and subtraction evolves from children's early counting experiences (Gelman & Gallistel, 1978; Ginsburg, 1989). Preschoolers have numerous experiences that involve adding something to an existing collection to make it larger or removing items from a collection to make it smaller. Preschoolers are also sensi-

tive to differences between 2 collections (e.g., "Brother got more candies than me.") and often try to dispel those differences. Children can use their change add-to view of addition, take-away view of subtraction, and even their understanding of differences to comprehend and to solve simple word problems.

If allowed to use objects (e.g., blocks or fingers) or drawings (e.g., pictures or tally marks), most first graders and many kindergartners can—with little or no help—solve problems in which the outcome, whole, or difference is unknown (Riley et al., 1983). Children initially model the meaning of such problems directly (e.g., Carpenter & Moser, 1984; DeCorte & Verschaffel, 1987). Thus, their solution strategy typically varies from one type of problem to another (see Table 11–2).

Modeling a problem in which the outcome, whole, or difference is unknown is relatively easy. Within this category, *equalize and compare* problems may be more difficult to model than change and part-part-whole problems (Carpenter & Moser, 1984; Fuson, 1992b; Kamii, 1985; Suydam & Weaver, 1975). Because of their change add-to and change take-away views, it is even more difficult for children to model a problem in which the change or a part is unknown. Unknown start or first part problems may be especially confusing because such problems do not parallel children's informal arithmetic experience.

TABLE 11–1. A Taxonomy of Addition and Subtraction Word Problems

Change Add-To with …	Unknown Outcome	Unknown Change	Unknown Start
	Alex had 5 candies. Barb gave him 3 more. How many candies does he have altogether now?	Alex had 5 candies. Barb gave him some more. Now he has 8 altogether. How many candies did Barb give him?	Alex had some candies. Barb gave him 3 more. Now he has 8 altogether. How many candies did he start with?
Change Take-Away with …	Unknown Outcome	Unknown Change	Unknown Start
	Alex had 8 candies. He gave 5 to Barb. How many candies does he have left?	Alex had 8 candies. He gave some to Barb. Now he has 3 left. How many candies did he give to Barb?	Alex had some candies. He gave 5 to Barb. Now he has 3 left. How many candies did he start with?
Part-Part-Whole with …	Unknown Whole	Unknown Part	
	Alex had 5 fireballs and 3 lollipops. How much candy did he have altogether?	Alex had 5 fireballs and some lollipops. He had 8 candies altogether. How many were lollipops?	
Equalize with …	Difference Unknown	Second Part Unknown	First Part Unknown
	Alex had 8 candies. Barb had 5. How many more does Barb have to buy to have as many as Alex?	Alex had 8 candies. Barb had to get 3 more candies to have the same number as Alex. How many candies did Barb start with?	Alex had some candies. Barb, who had 5 candies, had to get 3 more to have the same number as Alex. How many candies did Alex have?
Compare with …	Difference Unknown	Second Part Unknown	First Part Unknown
	Alex had 8 candies. Barb had 5. How many more candies did Alex have than Barb?	Alex had 8 candies. He had 3 more than Barb. How many candies did Barb have?	Alex had some candies. He had 3 more than Barb who had 5. How many candies did Alex have?

TABLE 11–2. Concrete Strategies for Directly Modeling Various
Types of Addition and Subtraction Word Problems

Type of Word Problem	Direct Modeling (Concrete Strategies)
Change Add-To and Part-Part-Whole: Outcome or Whole Unknown	Concrete counting all: 1. Count out objects to represent the starting amount (one part). 2. Produce objects to represent the amount added (the second part). 3. Count all the objects put out to determine the outcome (the whole).
Change Take-Away: Unknown Outcome	Concrete taking away: 1. Count out objects to represent the starting amount. 2. Remove the number that the problem specifies were taken away. 3. Count the remaining objects to determine the amount left.
Equalize: Difference Unknown	Adding on: 1. Create two parallel rows of objects to represent each set. 2. Add objects to the smaller row until it is equal to the other row. 3. Count the number of objects added to the smaller row.
Compare: Difference Unknown	Matching: 1. Create two parallel rows of objects to represent each set. 2. Count the number of unmatched objects in the larger row.

The wording of story problems can have a profound effect on children's performance. Consider the following: There were 6 birds and 4 worms. How many more birds than worms are there? Hudson (1983) found that changing the wording of such a compare problem to what Fuson (1992a) called a "won't-get-compare" problem (Each bird wants a worm. How many birds won't get a worm?) significantly improved performance. In a similar vein DeCorte, Verschaffel, and DeWin (1985) found that the wording of part-part-whole missing-part problems significantly affected young children's problem-solving success. Kindergartners and first-graders do better when wording that clarifies the relationship between the parts and the whole (the phrase in brackets in the problem below) is included (see Fuson, 1992a for additional examples).

Six children helped the teacher clean up. Four were boys [and the rest were girls].
How many girls helped the teacher?

Textbooks and teachers typically expose children to just a few problem situations, namely change add-to and take-away unknown-outcome and part-part-whole unknown-whole problems (e.g., Fuson, 1992a, 1992b; Rathmell & Huinker, 1989). Research suggests that exposure to a wide range of problem types from the beginning of school—as is done in Russia—could significantly improve children's performance, even with more difficult problem types (Stigler, Fuson, Ham, & Kim, 1986). Children can learn to distinguish among different types of addition and subtraction word problems and can learn to solve them (Fuson, 1992b). For example, teachers who participated in the Cognitively Guided Instruction (CGI) in-service program were introduced to a relatively broad range of problem types and how children informally solve them (see, e.g., Carpenter et al., 1989). After a year, the students of these teachers significantly outperformed control students in traditional classrooms on relatively difficult types of word problems. Moreover, they exhibited significantly greater understanding and confidence.

The role of part-whole understanding in children's comprehension and solution of word problems is unclear (Fuson, 1992b). Some researchers have suggested that such an understanding underpins competence with all or at least the more difficult types of problems (e.g., Resnick, 1983a; Riley et al., 1983). The use of part-whole schematic drawings (see, e.g., Rathmell & Huinker, 1989) has resulted in improved performance on all types of word problems in at least one study, but not others (Fuson, 1992b). Moreover, currently there is no evidence that improved problem-solving competence is actually due to part-whole understanding.

Basic Formal Concepts and Skills. Research suggests that instruction frequently overlooks children's need for a prolonged period of informal exploration (e.g., Carpenter & Moser, 1984). Physical models are often used only briefly, if at all, to introduce addition and subtraction (Fuson, 1992b). Frequently, instruction jumps quickly to drilling number combinations. Moreover, it is commonly assumed that, with sufficient practice, children can memorize the single-digit addition combinations like $9 + 6 = 15$ and their subtractive counterparts such as $15 - 9 = 6$ quickly—by the end of first grade (e.g., Chicago Public Schools, 1988; University of the State of New York & New York State Education Department, 1980).

Informal arithmetic knowledge is a key basis for making sense of symbolic arithmetic (e.g., Ginsburg, 1989; Hiebert, 1984). More specifically, children interpret formal addition expressions like $4 + 2 = ?$ in terms of their informal change add-to view of addition: How much are 4 things and 2 more altogether? Moreover, children tend to interpret symbolic subtraction expressions such as $6 - 4 = ?$ in terms of their informal change take-away view of subtraction: Six things take away 4 leaves what? If children do not see the connection between the formal symbolism and their informal concepts and strategies, they may not comprehend formal expressions like $5 + 3 = ?$ or $8 - 3 = ?$ and perform poorly on written arithmetic assignments. (Given verbally presented word problems with the identical terms, these same children may well compute the correct answer to these problems.)

Research indicates that memorizing the single-digit addition and subtraction combinations is a prolonged process, not a quick one. Children proceed through 3 phases of development: (1) counting, (2) reasoning, and (3) recall (e.g., Steinberg, 1985). (This is a gross characterization of development. Although children may initially compute the sums or differences for all problems, they soon begin to reason out and recall the sums of at least some problems. Moreover, although some older children [and adults] may recall all the sums and differences, many continue to use fairly efficient reasoning processings to determine the answers for some combinations. Siegler and Jenkins [1989] have adduced a distribution-of-associations model to account for strategy choice—why a child might use a strategy with one problem but a different strategy with another problem. See Baroody [in press] for an evaluation of the evidence on the model's account of how the representation of number combination evolves. For other reviews of mental-arithmetic development see Ashcraft [1982, 1992]; Baroody and Ginsburg [1986]; Kaye [1986]; McCloskey, Harley, and Sokol [1991]; McCloskey and Sokol [1992]; and Pellegrino and Goldman [1989].) Initially, children rely on counting strategies to compute sums and differences (see Baroody & Ginsburg, 1986; Fuson, 1988, for summaries). During this phase, children invent increasingly sophisticated and efficient counting strategies (see, e.g., Fuson, 1992b; Fuson & Willis, 1988; Resnick & Ford, 1981). They also discover important patterns and relationships and incorporate these discoveries into "thinking strategies," that can be used to reason out unpracticed or unknown combinations. For example, children who know the addition doubles like $6 + 6$ may reason out near doubles like $7 + 6$ (e.g., if $6 + 6$ is 12 and 7 is one more than 6, then $7 + 6$ must be 1 more than 12, or 13). Unfortunately, U.S. textbooks have generally done little to support children's informal arithmetic (see Fuson, 1992a).

Research suggests that introducing drill before children understand symbolic arithmetic or before they devise their own ways to compute or reason out answers can hinder mastery (Suydam & Weaver, 1975). Moreover, instruction that helps children to focus on patterns and relationships appears to be more effective than drill alone in fostering retention and transfer to unpracticed problems (Suydam & Weaver, 1975; Thorton & Smith, 1988). Practice, then, appears most effective after a period of informal exploration.

Furthermore, research indicates that a problem-solving approach can provide children purposeful practice and actually facilitate number-combination mastery. Although teachers on the CGI program spent significantly more time on problem solving and significantly less time on drilling the basic combinations than did teachers in a control group, students of CGI teachers recalled significantly more combinations than those trained in more traditional ways (Carpenter et al., 1989). Apparently, a problem-solving approach to arithmetic instruction can also have a positive effect on disposition at no cost to achievement (Fuson, 1992a). Cobb (e.g., Cobb, Wood, & Yackel, 1991; Cobb, Yackel, Wood, Wheatley, & Merkel, 1988) had children work in small groups and required them to reach a consensus about problem solutions. Teachers encouraged acceptance of everyone's thinking and viewing errors as a natural outcome of learning. The result appeared to be students who were more confident, autonomous, and persistent.

Extending Arithmetic Understanding. Although children's informal arithmetic allows them to solve simple word problems and to assign meaning to basic symbols, it is incomplete in some important ways. Children's informal knowledge typically does not include a quantitative understanding of part-whole relationships (e.g., Fuson, 1992b; Resnick, 1983a). They do not recognize that a whole such as 7 can be created by or decomposed into its component parts in various ways. Because of their informal change add-to view of addition, many children do not realize the operation is commutative: that the order of the addends does not affect the sum. For example, because they interpret $5 + 2$ as 5 and *2 more* and $2 + 5$ as 2 and *5 more* (as different situations), children naturally assume that these expressions will have different sums (Baroody, 1987). Moreover, they may assume that different-looking expressions like $5 + 2$, $6 + 1$, and $4 + 3$ also have different sums. Resnick (1983a) has concluded that the elaboration of a part-whole concept is one of the most important developments during the elementary years.

Because of their informal take-away concept of subtraction meaning, many primary-age children do not realize that a symbolic subtraction expression like $5 - 3 = ?$ can represent difference (equalize and compare) situations as well as take-away situations. Moreover, instruction often introduces subtraction from a single (change take-away) perspective which further reinforces a narrow conception of their operation (Rathmell & Huinker, 1989). Recognizing that symbolic subtraction can have an equalize meaning may help children figure out differences and master basic subtraction combinations. For example, the difference of $5 - 3$ can be determined by thinking 3 plus what is 5 ($3 + ? = 5$) and recalling that $3 + 2 = 5$ (Kamii, 1985). This insight, then, allows children to use known addition combinations to determine the answers for subtraction combinations. (Interestingly, even before school, children have some sense that addition and subtraction are related. Specifically, they realize that adding 1 to a set can be undone by taking 1 away or vice versa [Gelman & Gallistel, 1978]. That is, they have some understanding that addition and subtraction are *inverse* operations— that they undo each other. During the primary years, they construct a *general* inverse principle: Adding any number can be undone by subtracting that number [Bisanz, Lefevre, Scott, & Champion, 1984].)

When the symbolism is not connected to real situations, children often have difficulty understanding nontypical formats, such as $5 + ? = 8$. Indeed, Kamii (1985) concluded that missing-addend expressions are so difficult for first-graders that there is little point introducing them to young children. However, Carpenter, Moser, and Bebout (1988) found that children could understand and use symbolic expressions like $5 + ? = 8$, if they were related to word problems.

Other nontypical formats that represent mathematical concepts may also be perplexing to children, partly because they do not have an accurate understanding of the $=$ sign. Formally, the equals sign has a relational meaning: the same number as. However, most children interpret = as meaning "adds up to" or "produces" (e.g., Behr, Erlwanger & Nichols, 1980). This operator meaning stems from their informal knowledge of mathematics and from the fact that schooling often reinforces this view and does not adequately foster a relational view (Baroody, 1987). Because of their operator view of equals, children view an expression such as $7 + 3 = 3 + 7$, which illustrates the principle of commutativity, as incorrect. (How can $7 + 3$ "add up to" $3 + 7$?) Expressions like $10 = 3 + 7$, $7 + 3 = 5 + 5$, and $3 + 7 = 12 - 2$, which illustrate the more general other-names-for-a-number concept, are also confusing to children who have an operator view of equals. The confusion about such expressions is compounded because they commonly associate just 10 with the number ten. (The numeral 10 is but one name for this number that can also be named $3 + 7$, $5 + 5$, $12 - 2$, and so forth.) See, for example, Baroody (1989) and Wynroth (1986) for teaching suggestions on fostering a part-whole concept, extending subtraction meanings, and encouraging a relational view of equals.

Multidigit Addition and Subtraction

Children typically have little difficulty mastering multidigit arithmetic procedures without renaming (carrying or borrowing). For a variety of reasons, though, many have considerable difficulty mastering procedures involving renaming.

Systematic Errors. Because children generally do not understand the underlying rationale for algorithms (step-by-step procedures) that involve renaming (e.g., see Fuson, 1992b), they often fail to remember all the steps of an algorithm, and many resort to inventing their own steps. Partially or incorrectly learned algorithms often manifest themselves as systematic errors (Brown & Burton, 1978; VanLehn, 1983). Sample 1 below illustrates a partially learned procedure: A child carried but placed the carried digit(s) on the far left. Sample 2 illustrates a self-invented procedure: A child could not recall what to do with the digit that should be carried and so simply "vanished" it (Fuson, 1990a). A variety of systematic errors are described in sources such as Ashlock (1982), Baroody (1989), Brown and Burton (1978), Brown and VanLehn (1982), Ginsburg (1989), and Labinowicz (1985).

Sample 1:	47 +19 66	138 +45 273	138 +275 593
Sample: 2	47 +19 56	138 +45 173	138 +275 303

The Task Confronting Children. To understand the underlying rationale for the written renaming algorithms, children must construct a new view of number (a grouping or base-ten concept) and an understanding of place value (the value of a digit is determined by its position in a multidigit numeral). Children first interpret multidigit numbers in terms of a *unit*

concept of number (e.g., they view 24 as 24 things or units). A *base-ten concept* (e.g., interpreting 24 as 2 tens and 4 ones) is a difficult concept for many U.S. children. A relatively sophisticated base-ten concept, moreover, entails viewing 10 *simultaneously* as a single group and as 10 units (Cobb & Wheatley, 1988; Steffe, 1983). That is, children need to view 10 as a special unit entitled to distinctive treatment *and* as something that can be "unpacked" into 10 units. Meaningful learning of multidigit arithmetic procedures also entails relating base-ten concepts to a concept of place value: Each position in a multidigit numeral increases tenfold as we move to the next position to the left.

Sources of Difficulty. Several factors appear to interfere with the development of base-ten, place-value concepts. Recent cross-cultural research indicates that U.S. children have more difficulty constructing such concepts than do Oriental children because of differences in their respective languages (see, e.g., Miura, 1987). Oriental languages have a structure that clearly highlights grouping by tens (e.g., see Table 11-3). The structure of the English count does not explicitly underscore its

TABLE 11–3. A Comparison of Two Oral Count Systems

Hindu-Arabic Numeral	English Count	Korean Count*
1	one	eel
2	two	ee
3	three	sahm
4	four	sah
5	five	oh
6	six	yook
7	seven	chil
8	eight	pal
9	nine	goo
10	ten	sip
11	eleven	sip-eel
12	twelve	sip-ee
13	thirteen	sip-sahm
14	fourteen	sip-sah
15	fifteen	sip-oh
.		
.		
19	nineteen	sip-goo
20	twenty	ee-sip
21	twenty-one	ee-sip-eel
.		
.		
30	thirty	sahm-sip
40	forty	sah-sip
50	fifty	oh-sip
.		
.		
90	ninety	goo-sip

*According to Song and Ginsburg (1988), Koreans have two count systems. The one delineated above is highly regular and the main system employed in formal mathematics instruction. A second system is more irregular and usually learned informally during the preschool years and, in some cases, kindergarten and first grade.

base-ten structure (e.g., 40, is "four + ty," not "four tens"), and some terms hide this structure altogether (e.g., "twelve" does not even hint at a group of 10 and 2 units).

Instructional factors appear to be another impediment in constructing base-ten, place-value concepts by U.S. children. Children are frequently taught how to read and write multidigit numerals before they receive base-ten, place-value instruction or at least before they have a chance to construct an understanding of it. Manipulatives, if used at all, are often used too briefly to be effective (Fuson, 1990b). Moreover, existing textbook treatments of base-ten and place-value do not adequately help children construct these concepts (see, e.g., Baroody, 1987; Cobb & Wheatley, 1988; Fuson, 1990a; 1992b). Introducing children to written multidigit numbers before they understand the underlying rationale for this symbolic system may reinforce and entrench a child's unit concept of number, making it more difficult to construct base-ten, place-value concepts later (Baroody, 1990). In brief, symbolic instruction may be introduced too quickly, not giving children the opportunity to construct the base-ten, place-value concepts necessary to understand the renaming algorithms.

Instructional Questions. It remains unclear when base-ten, place-value concepts and the multidigit algorithms should be introduced. Constance Kamii (1985, 1989) has argued that her research indicates that it is undesirable to introduce place value and written multidigit arithmetic in first grade. Fuson (1990b) similarly concluded from her research (Fuson, 1986; Fuson & Briars, 1990) that such instruction for most children should be postponed until second grade. Some have even advocated delaying the introduction of the written arithmetic algorithms until third or fourth grade (Coburn, 1989). However, existing evidence does not clearly indicate what learning is possible by young children, *if* effective instructional approaches can be found (Baroody, 1990).

Research suggests that the use of manipulative aids can significantly improve the meaningful learning of base-ten, place-value concepts and the multidigit algorithms (Fuson, 1992a, 1992b). Less clear, though, is (a) what manipulatives should be used and (b) when they should be introduced into the curriculum (Baroody, 1990). (These same points apply to other primary topics as well. See, for example, Beishuizer, 1985; Post, 1988; Resnick & Ford, 1981; and Suydam & Weaver, 1975. See Sowell, 1989, for a review of the literature regarding the effectiveness of manipulatives on mathematics instruction.)

Many mathematics educators (e.g., Dienes, 1960) have argued that prolonged work with concrete models before the introduction of the written renaming algorithms may give children the opportunity to construct a solid understanding of the base-ten, place-value concepts underlying the algorithm. Fuson (1990b) has noted that her research (Fuson, 1986; Fuson & Briars, 1990) indicates that substantial improvement over traditional textbook-based instruction could be made possible by introducing concrete models and the written renaming algorithms *simultaneously.* However, existing research does not demonstrate that Fuson's integrated approach is more effective than introducing concrete models in first grade or even kindergarten well before the written algorithm, as is done in

the *Mathematics Their Way* Program (Baratta-Lorton, 1976) or the *Wynroth* (1986) *Math Program* (Baroody, 1990).

It is even unclear whether manipulatives are a necessary or a sufficient condition for meaningful learning of the written algorithms. For example, Kamii (1989) adduced evidence that children can construct base-ten, place-value concepts primarily through *mental-arithmetic* activities. Nevertheless, further evidence is needed to determine whether such an approach fosters a solid understanding of these concepts. Other research (e.g., Ross, 1989) shows that the use of manipulatives like base-ten blocks does not guarantee understanding. Children frequently do not see the connection between a concrete model and written procedures (Resnick, 1982). Instruction that links each step in a written algorithm to each step in a concrete procedure using base-ten blocks can apparently improve learning (e.g., Fuson & Briars, 1990) but does not ensure success (see Resnick & Omanson, 1987). It may be that some primary children lack the readiness to benefit from conceptually (manipulative) based instructions.

MATHEMATICS INVOLVING CONTINUOUS QUANTITIES

Counting and introductory arithmetic involve discrete quantities—collections of discrete things. Some mathematical topics involve continuous quantities—quantities that can be divided into parts and that must be measured rather than counted. The number of people in a family is an example of a discrete quantity: The individuals can be counted but not subdivided (e.g., a family of $2\frac{1}{2}$ is not possible). The width of a sheet of paper is an example of a continuous quantity: A width must be measured and can include a fractional part of a unit (e.g., an $8\frac{1}{2}$-inch × 11-inch sheet of paper).

Fractions

Fractions can represent situations involving either discrete *or* continuous quantities. Moreover, they can represent various meanings. Fractions are commonly used to represent a part-of-a-whole situation (e.g., 2 parts of a pizza divided into 5 equal parts were eaten). One of several other meanings a fraction such as $\frac{2}{5}$ can represent is division (e.g., 2 things shared fairly among 5 people).

Informal Partitioning Strategies. As noted earlier, many young children invent a dealing-out strategy for dividing up (partitioning) collections (discrete quantities). For continuous quantities, though, they must use a different partitioning strategy—a subdividing procedure (Hiebert & Tonnesen, 1978; Hunting & Sharpley, 1988; Miller, 1984). To divide a clay snake in half, for example, children need to gauge the midpoint, subdivide the snake at its midpoint and check the resulting portions to ensure they are equal. Unlike the dealing-out procedure, there is no single way to subdivide continuous quantities (e.g., subdividing a clay snake into thirds requires a different procedure than subdividing it into halves). Other than halving, subdividing procedures can be difficult for children to implement (see Pothier & Sawada, 1983, for a description of levels of subdividing skill).

Common Difficulties. Fractions are notoriously difficult for children (see, e.g., the review by Post, Behr, & Lesh, 1986). Even when children can use dealing-out and subdividing procedures successfully to solve division word problems, they do not relate such informal strategies to verbal fraction labels like "one-half" (e.g., Clements & Campo, 1987) or written symbols such as $\frac{1}{2}$. This may be due to the fact that instruction typically introduces fractions exclusively in terms of a part-of-a-whole meaning.

Furthermore, fraction tasks involving discrete quantities appear more difficult than those involving continuous quantities (Behr, Wachsmuth, & Post, 1988; Novillis, 1976; Payne, 1976). Indeed, many children do seem to understand that it is possible to have a fractional part of discrete quantities. For example, Clements and Campo (1987) asked children to give them one-half of a set of blocks. One fourth-grader responded: "There are 12 blocks here, so how can you get half? What do you mean? Half a block?" (p. 103). The relative difficulty of discrete-quantity tasks has been attributed to their psychological complexity (e.g., Behr et al., 1988; Novillis, 1976). A factor that surely contributes to the relative difficulty of discrete-quantity tasks is the fact that children seldom see fraction models involving such quantities (e.g., Kerslake, 1986). Examples of fractions typically involve a continuous quantity and one type of continuous quantity at that: circles (pie or pizza diagrams) (Ball, 1990; Burns, 1984; Silver, 1983). Children need to see a wide variety of fraction models, including discrete-quantity models (Behr, et al., 1988).

Children initially base their judgments regarding fractions on appearances. For example, shown a pie divided into 5 pieces with 2 pieces colored in, some children will indicate that the fraction of colored pieces is $\frac{2}{5}$. Such children do not realize that a fraction represents a relationship between a part and a whole. Young children commonly do not realize that a fraction involves a part of so many *equal-sized* parts. They also have difficulty comprehending equivalent fractions (e.g., that $\frac{2}{4}$ is equivalent to $\frac{1}{2}$) or comparing fractions (e.g., judging whether $\frac{1}{2}$ or $\frac{1}{3}$ is larger). For the latter, many children incorrectly apply their whole-number knowledge—for example, because 3 is bigger than 2, than $\frac{1}{3}$ must be bigger than $\frac{1}{2}$ (e.g., Post, Wachsmuth, Lesh, & Behr, 1985).

For an in-depth analysis of informal fraction knowledge and learning difficulties with fractions, see Behr, Harel, Post, and Lesh (1992); Carpenter, Fennema, and Romberg (1992), and Kieren (1988). These references also discuss implications from recent research for teaching fractions (see also Behr & Post, 1988; Bezuk & Cramer, 1989).

Geometry

The van Hiele model suggests that knowledge of geometry proceeds gradually through a series of stages (Crowley, 1987; Hoffer, 1983). At the intuitive level (level 0) children learn to recognize geometric figures such as squares and circles by their physical appearance. At level 1 children begin to learn isolated characteristics or attributes of the forms. At level 2 they establish *relationships* between the attributes of a form (e.g., in a quadrilateral, parallel opposite sides necessitates equal opposite angles) and between figures (e.g., a square is a rectangle because it has all the properties of this figure). At more advanced levels, a person can construct geometric proofs and see geometry in the abstract (e.g., compare different axiometric systems). See Clements and Battista (1992) for a thorough discussion of the development of geometric thinking.

Elementary instruction typically focuses on the first 2 levels: memorizing the names and the attributes of forms (Dana, 1987). As a result, children develop partial and even incorrect concepts. For example, many children fail to identify a square as a rectangle because instruction does not help them understand that a form is defined by its critical attributes (e.g., square has all the critical attributes of a rectangle) and how the critical attributes are related (e.g., a square is a special class of rectangles, because it is a rectangle with an additional critical attribute: equal opposite sides) (Hershkowitz, Bruckheimer, & Vinner, 1987). See, for example, Baratta-Lorton (1976), DeGuire (1987), and Schultz et al. (1989) for instructional activities that focus on helping children analyze patterns and forms or discern relationships among forms.

SPECIAL CHILDREN

Gifted

Evaluation. Methods for identifying young gifted and mathematically precocious children require further development. In particular, methods are needed to identify such children who come from disadvantaged environments and who frequently are not identified by standardized tests. Furthermore, the evaluation of mathematical knowledge must advance beyond the stage of assessing basic skills (memorized facts and procedures) and must gauge levels of understanding and thinking (National Council of Teachers of Mathematics, 1989).

Although there is a growing body of research on the mathematical thinking of gifted children, the vast majority of it has focused on children beyond the primary grades. The work of Krutetskii (1976) and his Soviet colleagues, for instance, included children as young as 6-years-old (second grade) but—for the most part—involved children beyond the third grade. Moreover, with few exceptions (e.g., Baroody & Gatzke, 1991; Buchanan, 1987; Krutetskii, 1976), research on young gifted children (e.g., Bowie, 1980; Morgan, 1983; Renfrow, 1987) has focused on general intellectual characteristics, not specific knowledge of subject matter. Even less has been done to investigate their *potential* for learning particular aspects of mathematics. In brief, there is much to learn about the mathematical knowledge and learning potential of young gifted children—particularly those in preschool to first grade.

Instruction. Although considerable effort has been expended over the last few decades to develop programs to meet the learning needs of young children with learning difficulties (see, e.g., Baratta-Lorton, 1976; Cawley, Fitzmaurice-Hayes, & Shaw, 1988; Wynroth, 1986), little has been done to meet the learning needs of young gifted children (Vance, 1983). Research (Maryland, 1972) indicates that nonstructured, independent study—a prevalent practice in gifted education—too often does not work (Kurtz, 1983). Moreover, though some important contributions have been made (see, e.g., Grossnickle, 1956; House, 1987; National Council of Teachers of Mathematics, 1981; Weaver & Brawley, 1959), relatively little has been written specifically addressing how to challenge gifted students with mathematics (Kurtz, 1983). Some efforts have been made to develop or adopt primary mathematics programs for young gifted children. Yet, further systematic efforts are needed to develop and to evaluate curricula for such children. This is particularly important to do in light of the standards recently announced by the National Council of Teachers of Mathematics (1989).

Learning Disabled

Evaluation. The label *learning disability* frequently connotes an organically based cognitive dysfunction (see Kosc, 1974). If a neurological impairment is not apparent, then the dysfunction is often attributed to "minimal brain damage." Children are sometimes classified as learning disabled or minimally brain damaged on the basis of soft signs of neurological dysfunction. In contrast to hard signs (e.g., an abnormal electroencephalogram or brain-wave pattern), soft signs (developmental disabilities such as short attention span and difficulties in fine-motor coordination are *not* clear indicators of brain damage or learning difficulties (see Coles's 1978 review of the literature). Many children are labeled learning disabled simply because they score 2 or more years below grade level on an achievement test. Although there are many reasons for low achievement, once children are labeled learning disabled, it is often assumed by teachers, parents, and the children themselves that a brain dysfunction is the source of the learning difficulties. Many children, then, are unnecessarily stigmatized by the label of learning disabled on the basis of questionable evidence (e.g., Algozzine & Ysseldyke, 1986; Cawley, 1985). Although there are children who experience difficulties learning mathematics because of a neurological impairment (e.g., see Deloche & Seron, 1987), many—perhaps most—children labeled learning disabled are not really cognitively disabled. That is, most such children are simply—as David Elkind put it— "curriculum disabled," the victims of poor instruction (e.g., Hendrickson, 1983).

The testing of children with learning difficulties should focus first on undercovering specific difficulties, the causes of difficulties, strengths on which to build remedial instruction, and *potential* for learning (Baroody & Ginsburg, 1991). Assessment should focus on how to adjust instruction so that it is developmentally appropriate for a child rather than generating labels that essentially blame the child for the learning difficulty (Glaser, 1981; Wallace & Larsen, 1978).

Instruction. Meeting the needs of children with real handicaps (hard signs of neurological dysfunction) may well require special instructional methods. However, a large proportion of children labeled as learning disabled basically need meaningful and purposeful instruction (Baroody, 1991). When a skills approach has been unsuccessful with special children, the traditional remedial approach has been to foster "overlearning." Unfortunately, simply assigning 2 or 3 times the normal amount of practice usually has limited and disappointing results (Moyer & Moyer, 1985). Moreover, because ineffective instruction probably compounds the learning difficulties of those with genuine neurological involvement (e.g., Fitzmaurice-Hayes, 1985; Kosc, 1974), it is important to devise developmentally appropriate instruction for all those with learning difficulties. Mathematics programs for children classified as learning disabled should not be limited to computation but should be comprehensive, including topics such as geometry, fractions, and decimals (e.g., Cawley, 1985; Wilmot & Thornton, 1989). In addition, it is important to remedy difficulties early—before a child is caught in a vicious cycle of defeat, fear, and anxiety. For suggestions, see Baroody (1987, 1989, 1991); Cawley (1984, 1985); Cawley, Fitzmaurice-Hayes, and Shaw (1988); Scheid (1989); Pellegrino and Goldman (1987); Thornton and Bley (1982); and Thornton and Toohey (1985).

Mentally Handicapped

Evaluation. Research suggests that children classified as moderately mentally handicapped (IQ between 25 and 50) can learn to count, recognize small sets, or memorize sums and differences by *rote* (e.g., Warren, 1963) but are incapable of acquiring functional academic skills (e.g., Burton, 1974; Hirshoren & Burton, 1979). Baroody and Snyder (1983), for example, found that children classified as moderately mentally handicapped were not able to use their counting-sequence knowledge to determine the larger of 2 numbers up to 10 or even 5. Many such children may also have difficulty counting out a specified number of objects (see also Spradlin, Cotter, Stevens, & Friedman, 1974).

A common view is that children classified as mildly mentally handicapped (IQ between 50 and 75) are capable of acquiring functional academic skills by rote memorization but are incapable of understanding the rationale for these skills. For example, research has found that such children can acquire basic computational skills but are severely limited in terms of concepts, reasoning, and problem solving (e.g., Cornwall, 1974; Cruickshank, 1948; Gelman & Cohen, 1988; Kirk, 1964; Noffsinger & Dobbs, 1970; Quay, 1963).

Traditional assumptions about children labeled as mentally handicapped may have the effect of a self-fulfilling prophecy. If educators assume such children are not capable of understanding, they may devote little or no time to concept development, and *this* may cause or exacerbate cognitive deficiencies (Cawley & Vitello, 1972; Iano, 1971). Failure to benefit from existing problems does not necessarily mean that children classified as mentally handicapped are incapable of learning; it may be that effective teaching methods have not yet been developed.

Recent developmental research and training studies have been more optimistic about the abilities of children classified as mentally handicapped (see Vitello, 1976). (Baroody and Snyder

[1983] found that some children classified as mildly mentally handicapped could engage in rule-governed counting and a few demonstrated a basic form of problem solving—using the commutativity principle to shortcut computational effort. Piagetian researchers have found that children classified as mildly mentally handicapped progress through the same stages of number development as normal-IQ children, though at a slower rate [e.g., Inhelder, 1968; Robinson & Robinson, 1965]. Training studies have been successful in inducing number conservation and improvement on other number-related Piagetian tasks [Bulgarella, 1971; Lister, 1974]. Some research [e.g., Cawley & Goodman, 1969] indicates that introducing conceptual material into a mathematics curriculum can result in significant achievement [e.g., Iano, 1971]. Lancioni [1982], for example, found that peer tutoring by normal third- and fourth-graders had a positive impact on mildly handicapped children's performance in solving addition, subtraction, multiplication, and division word problems.) For example, in controlled training studies, Baroody (1988a, 1988b) found that mentally handicapped children can learn a counting-based, number-comparison rule and induce simple arithmetic patterns (e.g., the answer to addition expressions involving 1 is simply the number after the larger addend).

Unfortunately, much research on the topic suffers from important limitations (see Mastropieri, Bakken, & Scruggs, 1991, for a thorough review of intervention studies). For example, using reinforcement procedures, children classified as moderately mentally handicapped have learned counting procedures, children classified as moderately mentally handicapped have learned counting procedures for calculating sums and differences (Bellamy, Greiner, & Buttars, 1974; Brown & Bellamy, 1972), counting money (Bellamy & Buttars, 1975), and making change (Cuvo, Veitch, Trace, & Konke, 1978). However, rote learning of skills probably does not contribute to the development of real mathematical understanding; it may not be retained, and it may not be applied (transferred) to other school or real-life situations (see, e.g., Belmont, 1966; Brown & Deloache, 1978). Methodological problems afflicting many interventions studies include no or inadequate measures of retention or transfer, small sample size (which limits generalizeability), and lack of control groups.

Research does reveal considerable variation in individual performance and learning ability among children classified as mildly or even moderately mentally handicapped (e.g., Baroody, 1986). This underscores the need to evaluate individual strengths and weaknesses and to take individual differences into account even for the supposedly "homogeneous" groups of special children.

Instruction. Recently, researchers have taken a renewed interest in defining what is appropriate mathematics instruction for children classified as mentally handicapped (Cawley, Miller, & Carr, 1989). A focus on understanding, reasoning, and problem solving rather than rote memorization of facts and procedures may be helpful for such children. There are indications, for example, that early, intensive intervention enables Down syndrome children to obtain normal or near-normal achievement.

Providing special children with experiences per se may be insufficient. Feuerstein (1980) argued that many cognitive de-ficiencies are due to a lack of "mediated experiences": instruction that helps children organize their experiences and make sense of them. He concluded that merely providing factual knowledge (e.g., solutions) is of little help. Special children need instruction that provides insight into *how* problems are solved, which should help children to think more deeply about the skill or strategy being taught.

SOME INSTRUCTIONAL IMPLICATIONS

Like other "consequential knowledge" (Sternberg, 1984), mathematics is not simply a collection of isolated facts and procedures to be memorized through repeated practice. It entails a highly structured body of information replete with relationships. Recent cognitive research indicates that the meaningful learning of mathematics involves actively constructing an understanding of these relationships. It also indicates that fostering such learning entails building on children's existing knowledge, including their informal counting-based knowledge.

One key implication of recent research, then, is that preschool and primary educators need to consider the informal mathematical strengths of young children—including those in preschool or just beginning kindergarten. Primary curricula typically underestimate young children's competence and spend considerable time having them "learn" and practice already-learned skills and concepts (Fuson, 1992a). Such instruction is often boring to children and a potentially destructive way to introduce children to mathematics. Furthermore, by overlooking informal strengths, instruction sometimes needlessly puts off introducing important ideas, including division. By ignoring informal strengths, instruction may also miss opportunities to introduce mathematical ideas in a meaningful fashion. Research-based programs such as the University of Chicago School Mathematics Project and the Wynroth Math Program (Wynroth, 1986) take into account children's informal knowledge better than traditional textbook series. A premise of the University of Chicago project is that children are capable of doing much more mathematics if it is done in a way that makes sense to them (see Fuson, 1992a, for overview). Finding ways to do this remains an important challenge to early childhood educators.

A second key implication is that teachers need to identify and remedy weaknesses in informal knowledge so that children have a solid basis for learning formal mathematics. Children from disadvantaged homes, for example, may not have the opportunities to develop a wide array of informal knowledge (Baroody, 1987). Ginsburg and Russell (1981) found that, though lower-class children had many counting and number skills, they did significantly poorer than middle-class children in solving simple addition and subtraction word problems. It is essential that preschool and primary teachers detect and remedy deficiencies in informal counting skills early. Teachers should be particularly alert for children who do not have basic counting skills when they begin kindergarten. Such children should be given ample, supervised, and purposeful counting experiences. Moreover, kindergarten should extend the counting skills (foster, for example, counting backwards and counting by 2s and

5s) of all children so that they have a strong informal basis for arithmetic.

A third key implication is that teachers need to consider individual differences, even when children are at an early age. This is important so that children of all abilities realize their mathematical potential. Mathematically gifted children from all parts of society need to be identified and challenged. For children with learning difficulties, educators must look beyond labels and consider each child's unique set of strengths and weaknesses.

In conclusion, if mathematics instruction is approached developmentally, mathematics can engage and excite even young children. Only then will each of them have a chance of making the most of their often surprising mathematical potential.

References

Algozzine, B., & Ysseldyke, M. E. (1986). The future of the LD field: Screening and diagnosis. *Journal of Learning Disabilities, 19,* 394–398.

Allardice, B. S., & Ginsburg, H. P. (1983). Children's learning problems in mathematics. In H. P. Ginsburg (Ed.), *The development of mathematical thinking* (pp. 319–375). New York: Academic Press.

Ashcraft, M. H. (1982). The development of mental arithmetic: A chronometric approach. *Developmental Review, 2,* 213–236.

Ashcraft, M. H. (1992). Cognitive arithmetic. A review of data and theory. *Cognition.*

Ashlock, R. B. (1982). *Error patterns in computation* (3rd ed.). Columbus, OH: Merrill.

Ashton, P. (1975). Cross-cultural Piagetian research: An experimental perspective. *Harvard Educational Review, 45,* 475–506.

Azzolino, A. (1987). *How to use writing to teach mathematics.* Keyport, NJ: Mathematical Concepts.

Ball, D. L. (1990). The mathematical understandings that prospective teachers bring to teacher education. *The Elementary School Journal, 90,* 449–466.

Banchoff, T. F. (1990). Dimensions. In L. A. Steen (Ed.), *On the shoulders of giants* (pp. 11–59). Washington, DC: National Academy Press.

Baratta-Lorton, M. (1976). *Mathematics their way.* Menlo Park, CA: Addison-Wesley.

Baroody, A. J. (1986). Counting ability of moderately and mildly mentally handicapped children. *Education and Training of the Mentally Retarded, 21*(4), 289–300.

Baroody, A. J. (1987). *Children's mathematical thinking: A developmental framework for preschool, primary, and special education teachers.* New York: Teachers College Press.

Baroody, A. J. (1988a). Mental-addition development of children classified as mentally handicapped. *Educational Studies in Mathematics, 19,* 369–388.

Baroody, A. J. (1988b). Number-comparison learning by children classified as mentally handicapped. *American Journal of Mental Deficiency, 92,* 461–471.

Baroody, A. J. (1989). *A guide to teaching mathematics in the primary grades.* Boston: Allyn & Bacon.

Baroody, A. J. (1990). How and when should place-value concepts and skills be taught? *Journal for Research in Mathematics Education 21,* 281–286.

Baroody, A. J. (1991). Teaching mathematics developmentally to children labeled learning disabled. In D. K. Reid, W. P. Hresko, & H. L. Swanson (Eds.), *A cognitive approach to learning disabilities* (2nd ed., pp. 375–429). Austin, TX: Pro-Ed.

Baroody, A. J. (1992). The development of preschoolers' counting skills and principles. In J. Bideaud, C. Meljac, & J. P. Fischer (Eds.), *Pathways to number* (pp. 99–126). Hillsdale, NJ: Erlbaum.

Baroody, A. J. (1993). *Problem solving, reasoning, and communicating, grades K–8.* New York: Macmillan.

Baroody, A. J. (in press). An evaluation of evidence supporting fact-retrieval models. *Learning and Individual Differences.*

Baroody, A. J., & Cohn, L. (in press). The case of Lee: Assessing and remedying a numeral-writing difficulty. *Teaching Exceptional Children.*

Baroody, A. J., & Gatzke, M. S. (1991). The estimation of set size by potentially gifted kindergarten-age children. *Journal for Research in Mathematics Education, 22*(1), 59–68.

Baroody, A. J., & Ginsburg, H. P. (1986). The relationship between initial meaningful and mechanical knowledge of arithmetic. In J. Hiebert (Ed.), *Conceptual and procedural knowledge: The case of mathematics* (pp. 75–112). Hillsdale, NJ: Erlbaum.

Baroody, A. J., & Ginsburg, H. P. (1991). A cognitive approach to assessing the mathematical difficulties of children labeled learning disabled. In H. L. Swanson (Ed.), *Handbook on the assessment of learning disabilities: Theory, research and practice* (pp. 177–227). Boston: College-Hill Press.

Baroody, A. J., & Snyder, P. M. (1983). A cognitive analysis of basic arithmetic abilities of TMR children. *Education and Training of the Mentally Retarded, 18*(4), 253–259.

Bebout, H. C., & Carpenter, T. P. (1989). Assessing and building thinking strategies: Necessary bases for instruction. In P. R. Trafton & A. P. Shulte (Eds.), *New directions for elementary school mathematics* (pp. 59–69). Reston, VA: National Council of Teachers of Mathematics.

Behr, M. J., Erlwanger, S., & Nichols, E. (1980). How children view the equals sign. *Mathematics teaching, 22,* 13–15.

Behr, M. J., Harel, G., Post, T., & Lesh, R. (1992). Rational number, ratio, and proportion. In D. A. Grouws (Ed.), *Handbook of research on mathematics teaching and learning* (pp. 296–333). New York: Macmillan.

Behr, M. J., & Post, T. R. (1988). Teaching rational number and decimal concepts. In T. R. Post (Ed.), *Teaching Mathematics in Grades K–8* (pp. 190–231). Boston: Allyn & Bacon.

Behr, M. J., Wachsmuth, I., & Post, J. (1988). Rational number learning aids: Transfer from continuous models to discrete models. *Focus on Learning Problems in Mathematics, 10*(4), 1–18.

Beilin, H. (1975). *Studies in the cognitive basis of language development.* New York: Academic Press.

Beishuizer, M. (1985). Evaluation of the use of structured materials in the teaching of primary mathematics. In B. S. Alloway, G. M. Mills, & A. J. Trott (Eds.), *Aspects of educational technology, Volume 18: New directions in education and training technology* (pp. 246–258). New York: Nichols.

Bellamy, T., & Buttars, K. L. (1975). Teaching trainable level retarded students to count money: Toward personal independence through academic instruction. *Education and Training of the Mentally Retarded, 10,* 18–26.

Bellamy, G. T., Greiner, C., & Buttars, K. L. (1974). Arithmetic computation for trainable retarded students: Continuing a sequential instructional program. *Training School Bulletin, 70,* 230–240.

Belmont, J. M. (1966). Long-term memory in mental retardation. In N. R. Ellis (Ed.), *International review of research in mental retardation* (Vol. 1, p. 219–255).

Bezuk, N., & Cramer, K. (1989). Teaching about fractions: What, when, and how? In P. R. Trafton & A. P. Shulte (Eds.), *New directions for elementary school mathematics* (pp. 156–167). Reston, VA: National Council of Teachers of Mathematics.

Bezuska, S., Kenney, M., & Silvey, L. (1977). *Tessellations: The geometry of patterns*. Palo Alto, CA: Creative Publications.

Bisanz, J., Lefevre, J., Scott, C., & Champion, M. A. (1984, April). *Developmental changes in the use of heuristics in simple arithmetic problems*. Paper presented at the annual meeting of the American Educational Research Association, New Orleans, LA.

Bowie, E. L. (1980). The utility of Piagetian tasks for the assessment of arithmetic reasoning ability in intellectually gifted first and second grade students. (Doctoral dissertation, University of Washington, 1979). *Dissertation Abstracts International, 40,* 02A–0723.

Brainerd, C. J. (1973). The origins of number concepts. *Scientific American,* March, 101–9.

Brainerd, C. J. (1978). *Piaget's theory of intelligence*. Englewood Cliffs, NJ: Prentice Hall.

Briars, D. J., & Siegler, R. S. (1984). A featural analysis of preschoolers' counting knowledge. *Developmental Psychology, 20,* 607–618.

Bright, G. W. (1976). Estimation as part of learning to measure. In D. Nelson (Ed.), *Measurement in school mathematics*. Reston, VA: National Council of Teachers of Mathematics.

Bright, G. W., Harvey, J. G., & Wheeler, M. M. (1985). Learning and mathematics games. *Journal for Research in Mathematics Education, Monograph No.1.* Reston, VA: National Council of Teachers of Mathematics.

Brophy, J. (1986a). Teaching and learning mathematics: Where research should be going. *Journal for Research in Mathematics Education, 17,* 323–346.

Brophy, J. (1986b). Where are the data?: A reply to Confrey. *Journal for Research in Mathematics Education, 17,* 361–368.

Brophy, J., & Good, T. L. (1986). Teacher behavior and student achievement. In M. C. Wittrock (Ed.), *Handbook of research on teaching* (3rd ed., pp. 328–375). New York: Macmillan.

Brown, A. L., & Deloache, J. S. (1978). Skills, plans, self-regulation. In R. S. Siegler (Ed.), *Children's thinking: What develops?* (pp. 3–35). Hillsdale, NJ: Erlbaum.

Brown, J. S., & Burton, R. R. (1978). Diagnostic models for procedural bugs in basic mathematical skills. *Cognitive Science, 2,* 155–192.

Brown, J. S., & VanLehn, K. (1982). Towards a generative theory of bugs. In T. P. Carpenter, J. M. Moser, & T. A. Romberg (Eds.), *Addition and subtraction: A cognitive perspective* (pp. 117–135). Hillsdale, NJ: Erlbaum.

Brown, L., & Bellamy, T. (1972). A sequential procedure for teaching addition to trainable mentally retarded students. *The Training School Bulletin, 69,* 31–44.

Brownell, W. A. (1935). Psychological considerations in the learning and the teaching of arithmetic. In *The teaching of arithmetic* (10th Yearbook of the National Council of Teachers of Mathematics, pp. 1–31). New York: Bureau of Publications, Teachers College, Columbia University.

Buchanan, N. K. (1987). Factors contributing to mathematical problem-solving performance: An exploratory study. *Educational Studies in Mathematics, 18,* 399–415.

Bulgarella, R. A. (1971). *Facilitation of cognitive development among children with learning deficits*. Final Report. Washington, DC: Office of Education.

Burns, M. (1992). *About teaching mathematics: A K–8 resource*. Sausalito, CA: Marilyn Burns Education Associates.

Burns, M., & Tank, B. (1988). *A collection of math lessons for grades 1 though 3*. Sausalito, CA: Marilyn Burns Education Associates.

Burton, T. A. (1974). Education for trainables: An impossible dream? *Mental Retardation, 12,* 46.

Carlow, C. D. (1986). Critical balances and payoffs of an estimation program. In H. L. Schoen & M. J. Zweng (Eds.), *Estimation and mental computation* (pp. 93–102). Reston, VA: National Council of Teachers of Mathematics.

Carnegie Forum of Education and the Economy. (1986). *A nation prepared: Teachers for the 21st century*. New York: Carnegie Corporation.

Carpenter, T. P. (1985). Toward a theory of construction. *Journal for Research in Mathematics Education, 16,* 70–76.

Carpenter, T. P. (1986). Conceptual knowledge as a foundation for procedural knowledge. Implications from research on the initial learning of arithmetic. In J. Hiebert (Ed.), *Conceptual procedural knowledge: The case of mathematics* (pp. 113–132). Hillsdale, NJ: Erlbaum.

Carpenter, T. P., Coburn, T. G., Reys, R. E., & Wilson, J. W. (1976). Notes from national assessment: Estimation. *Arithmetic Teacher, 23*(4), 297–302.

Carpenter, T. P., Fennema, E., Peterson, P. L., Chiang, C. P., & Loef, M. (1989). Using knowledge of children's mathematics thinking in classroom teaching: An experimental study. *American Educational Research Journal, 26,* 499–532.

Carpenter, T. P., Fennema, E., & Romberg, T. A. (Eds.). (1992). *Rational numbers: An integration of research*. Hillsdale, NJ: Erlbaum.

Carpenter, T. P., & Moser, J. M. (1983). The acquisition of addition and subtraction concepts. In R. Lesh & M. Landau (Eds.), *Acquisition of mathematical concepts and processes* (pp. 7–44). New York: Academic Press.

Carpenter, T. P., & Moser, J. M. (1984). The acquisition of addition and subtraction concepts in grades one through three. *Journal for Research in Mathematics Education, 15,* 179–202.

Carpenter, T. P., Moser, J. M., & Bebout, H. C. (1988). Representation of addition and subtraction word problems. *Journal for Research in Mathematics Education, 19,* 345–357.

Carpenter, T. P., Moser, J. M., & Romberg, T. A. (Eds.). (1982). *Addition and subtraction: A cognitive perspective*. Hillsdale, NJ: Erlbaum.

Carter, H. L. (1986). Linking estimation to psychological variables in the early years. In H. L. Schoen & M. J. Zweng (Eds.), *Estimation and mental computation* (pp. 74–81). Reston, VA: National Council of Teachers of Mathematics.

Case, R. (1982). General developmental influences on the acquisition of elementary concepts and algorithms in arithmetic. In T. Carpenter, J. Moser, & T. Romberg (Eds.), *Addition and subtraction: A cognitive perspective* (pp. 156–170). Hillsdale, NJ: Erlbaum.

Cawley, J. F. (Ed.). (1984). *Developmental teaching of mathematics for the learning disabled*. Rockville, MD: Aspen.

Cawley, J. F. (1985). Cognition and the learning disabled. In J. F. Cawley (Ed.), *Cognitive strategies and mathematics for the learning disabled* (pp. 1–32). Rockville, MD: Aspen.

Cawley, J. F., Fitzmaurice-Hayes, A., & Shaw, R. (1988). *Mathematics for the mildly handicapped: A guide to curriculum and instruction*. Boston: Allyn & Bacon.

Cawley, J. F., & Goodman, J. O. (1969). Arithmetic problem solving: A program demonstrated by teachers of the mentally retarded. *Exceptional Children, 36,* 83–88.

Cawley, J., Miller, J., & Carr, S. (1989). *Arithmetic*. In G. A. Robinson, J. R. Patton, E. A. Polloway, & L. R. Sargent (Eds.), *Best practices in mild mental disabilities* (pp. 67–86). Reston, VA: Division of Mental Retardation of the Council for Exceptional Children.

Cawley, J. F., & Vitello, S. J. (1972). Model for arithmetical programming for handicapped children. *Exceptional Children, 39,* 101–110.

Charles, R. I., & Silver, E. A. (Eds.). (1989). *The teaching and assessing of mathematical problem solving*. Hillsdale, NJ: Erlbaum. Reston, VA: National Council of Teachers of Mathematics.

Chicago Public Schools. (1988). *A measure of mathematics success: The comprehensive mathematics program—A ready reference for parents.* Chicago: Board of Education of the City of Chicago.

Civil, M. (1990). *Doing and talking about mathematics: A study of preservice elementary teachers.* Doctoral thesis, University of Illinois, Urbana-Champaign.

Clements, D. H., & Battista, M. T. (1992). Geometry and spatial reasoning. In D. A. Grouws (Ed.), *Handbook of research on mathematics teaching and learning* (pp. 420–464). New York: Macmillan.

Clements, M. A., & Campo, G. D. (1987). Fractional understanding of fractions: Variations in children's understanding of fractional concepts, across embodiments (Grades 2 through 5). In J. D. Novak (Ed.), *Proceedings of the second international seminar on misconceptions and educational strategies in science and mathematics.* (Vol. 3, pp. 98–110). Ithaca, NY: Cornell University.

Cobb, P. (1985). A reaction to three early number papers. *Journal for Research in Mathematics Education, 16,* 141–145.

Cobb, P., & Merkel, G. (1989). Thinking strategies: Teaching arithmetic through problem solving. In P. R. Trafton & A. P. Shulte (Eds.), *New directions for elementary school mathematics* (pp. 70–84). Reston, VA: National Council of Teachers of Mathematics.

Cobb, P., & Wheatley, G. (1988). Children's initial understanding of ten. *Focus on Learning Problems in Mathematics, 10*(3), 1–28.

Cobb, P., Wood, T., & Yackel, E. (1990). Classrooms as learning environments for teachers and researchers. In R. B. Davis, C. A. Maher, & N. Noddings (Eds.), Constructivist views on the teaching and learning of mathematics (pp. 125–146). *Journal for Research in Mathematics Education, Monograph No. 4.* Reston, VA: National Council of Teachers of Mathematics.

Cobb, P., Wood, T., & Yackel, E. (1991). A constructivist approach to second grade mathematics. In E. von Glasersfeld (Ed.), *Constructivism in mathematics education* (pp. 157–176). Dordrecht, Holland: Kluwer.

Cobb, P., Yackel, E., Wood, T., Wheatley, G., & Merkel, G. (1988). Creating a problem-solving atmosphere. *Arithmetic Teacher, 36*(1), 46–47.

Coburn, T. G. (1989). The role of computation in the changing mathematics curriculum. In P. R. Trafton & A. P. Shulte (Eds.), *New directions for elementary school mathematics* (pp. 43–58). Reston, VA: National Council of Teachers of Mathematics.

Cockcroft, W. H. (Chair). (1982). *Mathematics counts.* London: HMSO.

Coles, G. S. (1978). The learning disability test battery: Empirical and social issues. *Harvard Educational Review, 48,* 313–340.

Confrey, J. (1986). A critique on teacher effectiveness research in mathematics education. *Journal for Research in Mathematics Education, 17,* 347–360.

Connolly, P., & Vilardi, T. (Eds.). (1989). *Writing to learn mathematics and science.* New York: Teachers College Press.

Cooney, T. J., & Hirsch, C. R. (Eds.). (1990). *Teaching and learning mathematics in the 1990's.* Reston, VA: National Council of Teachers of Mathematics.

Cooper, R. G. (1984). Early number development: Discovering number space with addition and subtraction. In C. Sophian (Ed.), *Origins of cognitive skills* (pp. 157–192). Hillsdale, NJ: Erlbaum.

Cornwall, A. C. (1974). Development of language, abstraction and numerical concept formation in Down's syndrome children. *American Journal of Mental Deficiency, 79*(2), 179–190.

Crowley, M. L. (1987). The van Hiele model of the development of geometric thought. In M. M. Lindquist & A. P. Shulte (Eds.), *Learning and teaching geometry, K–12* (pp. 1–16). Reston, VA: National Council of Teachers of Mathematics.

Cruickshank, W. M. (1948). Arithmetic work habits of mentally retarded boys. *American Journal of Mental Deficiency, 52,* 318–330.

Curcio, F. R. (Ed.). (1987). *Teaching and learning: A problem-solving focus.* Reston, VA: National Council of Teachers of Mathematics.

Curcio, F. R. (1989). *Developing graph comprehension: Elementary and middle school activities.* Reston, VA: National Council of Teachers of Mathematics.

Cuvo, A. J., Veitch, V. D., Trace, M. W., & Konke, J. L. (1978). Teaching change computation to the M. R. *Behavior Modification, 2,* 531–548.

Dana, M. E. (1987). Geometry: A square deal for elementary school. In M. M. Lindquist & A. P. Shulte, *Learning and teaching geometry, K–12* (pp. 113–125). Reston, VA: National Council of Teachers of Mathematics.

Davis, G. E., & Pitkethly, A. (1990). Cognitive aspects of sharing. *Journal for Research in Mathematics Education, 21,* 145–153.

Davis, P. J., & Hersh, R. (1981). *The mathematical experience.* Boston: Houghton-Mifflin.

Davis, R. B. (1984). *Learning mathematics: The cognitive science approach to mathematics education.* Norwood, NJ: Ablex.

Davis, R. B., Maher, C. A., & Noddings, N. (Eds.). (1990). Constructivist views on the teaching and learning of mathematics, *Journal for Research in Mathematics Education, Monograph No. 4.* Reston, VA: National Council of Teachers of Mathematics.

DeCorte, E., & Verschaffel, L. (1987). The effects of semantic structure on first graders' strategies for solving addition and subtraction word problems. *Journal for Research in Mathematics Education, 18,* 363–381.

DeCorte, E., Verschaffel, L., & DeWin, L. (1985). The influence of rewording verbal problems on children's problem representations and solutions. *Journal of Educational Psychology, 77,* 460–470.

DeGuire, L. J. (1987). Geometry: An avenue for teaching problem solving in grades K–9. In M. M. Lindquist & A. P. Shulte (Eds.), *Learning and teaching geometry, K–12* (pp. 59–68). Reston, VA: National Council of Teachers of Mathematics.

Deloche, G., & Seron, X. (Eds.). (1987). *Mathematical disabilities: A cognitive neuropsychological perspective.* Hillsdale, NJ: Erlbaum.

DeRuiter, J. A., & Wansart, W. L. (1982). *Psychology of learning disabilities.* Rockville, MD: Aspen.

Dienes, Z. P. (1960). *Building up mathematics.* New York: Hutchinson.

Donaldson, M., & Balfour, G. (1968). Less is more. *British Journal of Psychology, 59,* 461–471.

Driscoll, M. J. (1981). *Research within reach: Elementary school mathematics.* Reston, VA: National Council of Teachers of Mathematics.

Easley, J. A. (1983). A Japanese approach to arithmetic. *For the Learning of Mathematics, 3*(3), 8–14.

Easley, J., Taylor, H. A., & Taylor, J. (1990). Dialogue and conceptual splatter in mathematics classes. *Arithmetic Teacher, 37*(7), 34–37.

Eccles, J., Adler, J. F., Futterman, R., Goff, S. B., Kaczala, C. M., Meece, J. L., & Midgley, C. (1983). Expectancies, values, and academic behavior. In J. Spence (Ed.), *Achievement and achievement motivation* (pp. 75–146). San Francisco: W. H. Freeman.

Erlwanger, M. (1973). Benny's concept of rules and answers in IPI mathematics. *Journal of Children's Mathematical Behavior, 1,* 7–26.

Fennema, E., & Leder, G. H. (1990). *Mathematics and gender.* New York: Teachers College Press.

Feuerstein, R. (1980). *Instrumental enrichment.* Baltimore, MD: University Park Press.

Fey, J. T. (1990). Quantity. In L. A. Steen (Ed.), *On the shoulders of giants* (pp. 61–94). Washington, DC: National Research Council.

Fitzmaurice-Hayes, A. M. (1985). Assessment of the severely impaired mathematics student. In J. F. Cawley (Ed.), *Practical mathematics: Appraisal of the learning disabled* (pp. 249–277). Rockville, MD: Aspen.

Flavell, J. (1963). *The developmental psychology of Jean Piaget.* New York: Van Nostrand.

Fodor, J. (1970). Some reflections of L. S. Vygotsky's *Thought and Language. Cognitive Psychology, 1,* 324–340.

Fox, L. H., Fennema, E., & Sherman, J. (1977). *Women and mathematics: Research perspectives for change (NIE papers in education and work: Number eight)*. Washington, DC: National Institute of Education.

Fuson, K. C. (1986). Roles of representation and verbalization in the teaching of multi-digit addition and subtraction. *European Journal of Psychology of Education, 1*(2), 35–36.

Fuson, K. C. (1988). *Children's counting and concepts of number*. New York: Springer-Verlag.

Fuson, K. C. (1990a). Conceptual structures for multiunit members: Implications for learning and teaching multidigit addition, subtraction, and place value. *Cognition and Instruction, 7,* 343–403.

Fuson, K. C. (1990b). Issues in place-value and multidigit addition and subtraction learning and teaching. *Journal for Research in Mathematics Education, 21,* 273–286.

Fuson, K. C. (1992a). Research on learning and teaching addition and subtraction of whole numbers. In G. Leinhardt, R. T. Putnam, & R. A. Hattrup (Eds.), *The analysis of arithmetic for mathematics teaching* (pp. 53–187). Hillsdale, NJ: Erlbaum.

Fuson, K. C. (1992b). Research on whole number addition and subtraction. In D. Grouws (Ed.), *Handbook of research on mathematics teaching and learning* (pp. 243–275). New York: Macmillan.

Fuson, K. C., & Briars, D. J. (1990). Using a base-ten blocks learning/teaching approach for first- and second-grade place-value and multidigit addition and subtraction and place-value concepts. *Journal for Research in Mathematics Education, 3,* 180–206.

Fuson, K. C., & Hall, J. W. (1983). The acquisition of early number word meanings: A conceptual analysis and review. In H. P. Ginsburg (Ed.), *The development of mathematical thinking* (pp. 49–107). New York: Academic Press.

Fuson, K. C., Richards, J., & Briars, D. J. (1982). The acquisition and elaboration of the number word sequence. In C. Brainerd (Ed.), *Children's logical and mathematical cognition: Progress in cognitive development* (pp. 33–92). New York: Springer-Verlag.

Fuson, K. C., & Willis, G. B. (1988). Subtracting by counting up: More evidence. *Journal for Research in Mathematics Education, 19,* 402–420.

Gallistel, C. R., & Gelman, R. (1992). Preverbal and verbal counting and computation. *Cognition, 44,* 43–74.

Garland, C. (1988). *Mathematics their way summary newsletter*. Saratoga, CA: Center for the Innovation in Education.

Garofalo, J., & Lester, F. K., Jr. (1985). Metacognition, cognitive monitoring, and mathematical performance. *Journal for Research in Mathematics Education, 16,* 163–176.

Gelman, R. (1972). The nature and development of early number concepts. In H. Reese (Ed.), *Advances in child development and behavior* (Vol. 7, pp. 115–167), New York: Academic Press.

Gelman, R., & Cohen, M. (1988). Qualitative differences in the way Down Syndrome and normal children solve a novel counting problem. In L. Nadel (Ed.), *The psychobiology of Down Syndrome* (pp. 51–99). Cambridge, MA: MIT Press.

Gelman, R., & Gallistel, C. (1978). *Young children's understanding of number*. Cambridge: Harvard University Press.

Gelman, R., & Meck, E. (1986). Counting principles. In J. Hiebert (Ed.), *Conceptual and procedural knowledge: The case of mathematics* (pp. 45–49). Hillsdale, NJ: Erlbaum.

Gelman, R. & Meck, E. (1992). Early principles and concepts of number. In J. Bideaud, C. Meljac, & J. P. Fischer (Eds.), *Pathways to number*. (pp. 171–189, 385–386). Hillsdale, NJ: Erlbaum.

Ginsburg, H. P. (Ed.). (1983). *The development of mathematical thinking*. New York: Academic Press.

Ginsburg, H. P. (1989). *Children's arithmetic* (2nd ed.). Austin, TX: Pro-Ed.

Ginsburg, H. P., Posner, J. K., & Russell, R. L. (1981). The development of mental addition as a function of schooling. *Journal of Cross-Cultural Psychology, 12,* 163–178.

Ginsburg, H. P., & Russell, R. L. (1981). Social class and racial influences on early mathematical thinking. *Monographs of the Society for Research in Child Development, 46* (16, Serial No. 193).

Glaser, R. (1981). The future of testing: A research agenda for cognitive psychology and psychometrics. *American Psychologist, 36,* 923–936.

Good, T. L., Grouws, D. A., & Ebmeier, H. (1983). *Active mathematics teaching*. New York: Longman.

Goodnow, J., & Levine, R. A. (1973). "The grammar of action": Sequence and syntax in children's copying. *Cognitive Psychology, 4,* 82–98.

Greeno, J. G., Riley, M. S., & Gelman, R. (1984). Conceptual competence and children's counting. *Cognitive Psychology, 16,* 94–143.

Groen, G., & Kieran, C. (1983). In search of Piagetian mathematics. In H. P. Ginsburg (Ed.), *The development of mathematical thinking* (pp. 351–375). New York: Academic Press.

Grossnickle, F. C. (1956). Arithmetic for those who excel. *Arithmetic Teacher, 3,* 41–48.

Grouws, D. A. (Ed.). (1992). *Handbook of research on mathematics teaching and learning*. New York: Macmillan.

Hendrickson, A. D. (1983). Prevention or cure? Another look at mathematics learning problems. In D. Carnine, D. Elkind, A. D. Hendrickson, D. Meichenbaum, R. L. Sieben, & F. Smith (Eds.), *Interdisciplinary voices in learning disabilities and remedial education* (pp. 93–107). Austin, TX: Pro-Ed.

Hershkowitz, R., Bruckheimer, M., & Vinner, S. (1987). Activities with teachers based on cognitive research. In M. M. Lindquist & A. P. Shulte (Eds.), *Learning and teaching geometry, K–12* (pp. 59–68). Reston, VA: National Council of Teachers of Mathematics.

Hiebert, J. (1984). Children's mathematics learning: The struggle to link form and understanding. *Elementary School Journal, 84,* 497–513.

Hiebert, J. (1986). *Conceptual and procedural knowledge: The case of mathematics*. Hillsdale, NJ: Erlbaum.

Hiebert, J., & Behr, M. (Eds.). (1988). *Number concepts and operations in the middle grades*. Reston, VA: National Council of Teachers of Mathematics.

Hiebert. J., & Carpenter, T. P. (1982). Piagetian tasks as readiness measures in mathematics instruction: A critical review. *Educational Studies in Mathematics, 13,* 329–345.

Hiebert, J., & Tonnessen, L. H. (1978). Development of the fraction concept in two physical contexts: An exploratory investigation. *Journal for Research in Mathematics Education, 9,* 374–378.

Hill, J. M. (Ed.). (1987). *Geometry for grades K–6: Readings from the Arithmetic Teacher*. Reston, VA: National Council of Teachers of Mathematics.

Hirshoren, A., & Burton, T. A. (1979). Teaching academic skills to trainable mentally retarded children: A study in tautology. *Mental Retardation, 17*(4), 177–179.

Hoffer, A. (1983). Van Hiele–based research. In R. Lesh & M. Landau (Eds.), *Acquisition of mathematics concepts and processes* (pp. 205–227). New York: Academic Press.

Holmes Group. (1986). *Tomorrow's teachers*. East Lansing, MI: Author.

House, P. A. (Ed.). (1987). *Providing opportunities for the mathematically gifted K–12*. Reston, VA: National Council of Teachers of Mathematics.

Hudson, T. (1983). Correspondences and numerical differences between disjoint sets. *Child Development, 54,* 84–90.

Hughes, M. (1986). *Children and number: Difficulties in learning mathematics*. New York: Basil Blackwell.

Hunting, R. P., & Sharpley, C. F. (1988). Fraction knowledge in preschool children. *Journal for Research in Mathematics Education, 19,* 175–180.

Hurford, J. R. (1975). *The linguistic theory of numerals*. Cambridge, England: Cambridge University Press.

Iano, R. D. (1971). Learning deficiency versus developmental conceptions of mental retardation. *Exceptional Children, 38*(4), 301–310.

Inhelder, B. (1968). *The diagnosis of reasoning in the mentally retarded*. New York: John Day.

Irons, R. R., & Irons, C. J. (1989). Language experiences: A base for problem solving. In P. R. Trafton & A. P. Shulte (Eds.), *New directions for elementary school mathematics* (pp. 85–98). Reston, VA: National Council of Teachers of Mathematics.

Jacobs, H. R. (1970). *Mathematics: A human endeavor*. San Francisco: W. H. Freeman.

Johnson, D. W., & Johnson, R. T. (1989). Cooperative learning in mathematics. In P. R. Trafton & A. P. Schulte (Eds.), *New directions for elementary school mathematics* (pp. 234–245). Reston, VA: National Council of Teachers of Mathematics.

Kamii, C. (1985). *Young children reinvent arithmetic: Implication of Piaget's theory*. New York: Teachers College Press.

Kamii, C. (1989). *Young children continue to reinvent arithmetic—2nd grade*. New York: Teachers College Press.

Kaye, D. (1986). The development of mathematical cognition. *Cognitive Development, 1*, 157–170.

Kerslake, D. (1986). *Fractions: Children's strategies and errors*. Windsor, Ontario: NFER-Nelson.

Kieren, T. E. (1988). Personal knowledge of rational numbers: Its intuitive and formal development. In J. Hiebert & M. Behr (Eds.), *Number concepts and operations in the middle grades* (pp. 162–181). Reston, VA: National Council of Teachers of Mathematics.

Kilpatrick, J. (1985). Doing mathematics without understanding it: A commentary on Higbee and Kunihira. *Educational Psychologists, 20*, 65–68.

Kirk, S. A. (1964). Research in education. In H. A. Stevens & R. Heber (Eds.), *Mental retardation: A review of research* (pp. 57–99). Chicago: University of Chicago Press.

Klahr, D., & Wallace, J. G. (1973). The role of quantification operators in the development of conservation of quantity. *Cognitive Psychology, 4*, 301–327.

Kline, M. (1974). *Why Johnny can't add*. New York: Vintage.

Kosc, L. (1974). Developmental dyscalculia. *Journal of Learning Disabilities, 7*, 164–177.

Kouba, V. L. (1989). Children's solution strategies for equivalent set multiplication and division word problems. *Journal for Research in Mathematics Education, 20*, 147–158.

Krulik, S., & Reys, R. E. (Eds.). (1980). *Problem solving in school mathematics*. Reston, VA: National Council of Teachers of Mathematics.

Krutetskii, V. A. (1976). *The psychology of mathematical abilities in school children*. Chicago: University of Chicago Press. (Translated from the Russian by J. Teller and edited by J. Kilpatrick & I. Wirszup).

Kurtz, R. (1983). Mathematics for elementary and middle school gifted students. *School Science and Mathematics, 83*, 576–586.

Labinowicz, E. (1985). *Learning from children: New beginnings for teaching numerical thinking*. Menlo Park, CA: Addison-Wesley.

Lampert, M. (1986). Knowing, doing, and teaching multiplication. *Cognition and Instruction, 3*, 305–342.

Lancioni, G. E. (1982). Employment of normal third and fourth graders for training retarded children to solve problems dealing with quantity. *Education and Training of the Mentally Retarded, 17*(2), 93–102.

Lappan, G., & Schram, P. W. (1989). Communication and reasoning: Critical dimensions of sense making in mathematics. In P. R. Trafton & A. P. Shulte (Eds.), *New directions for elementary school mathematics* (pp. 14–30). Reston, VA: National Council of Teachers of Mathematics.

Lawler, R. W. (1981). The progressive construction of mind. *Cognitive Science, 5*, 1–30.

Leinhardt, G., Putnam, R. T., & Hattrup, R. A. (Eds.). (1992). *Analysis of arithmetic for mathematics teaching*. Hillsdale, NJ: Erlbaum.

Lester, F. K., Jr., (1980). Research on mathematical problem solving. In R. J. Shumway (Ed.), *Research in mathematics education* (pp. 286–323). Reston, VA: National Council of Teachers of Mathematics.

Lester, F. K., Jr., & Garofalo, J. (Eds.). (1982). *Mathematical problem solving: Issues in research*. Philadelphia: Franklin Institute.

Lindquist, M. M. (1989a). It's time for change. In P. R. Trafton & A. P. Shulte (Eds.), *New directions for elementary school mathematics* (pp. 1–13). Reston, VA: National Council of Teachers of Mathematics.

Lindquist, M. M. (Ed.). (1989b). *Results from the Fourth Mathematical Assessment of the National Assessment of Educational Progress*. Reston, VA: National Council of Teachers of Mathematics.

Lindquist, M. M., & Shulte, A. P. (Eds.). (1987). *Learning and teaching geometry, K–12*. Reston, VA: National Council of Teachers of Mathematics.

Lister, C. M. (1974). Teaching number conservation. *Special Education: Forward Trends, 1*(2), 13–15.

Mann, P. H., & Suiter, P. (1974). *Handbook in diagnostic teaching: A learning disabilities approach*. Boston: Allyn & Bacon.

Maryland, S. P. (1972). *Education of the gifted and talented: Report to the Congress of the United States*. Washington, DC: U.S. Government Printing Office.

Mastropieri, M. A., Bakken, J. P., & Scruggs, T. E. (1991). Mathematics instruction for individuals with mental retardation: A perspective and research synthesis. *Education and Training of the Mentally Retarded, 26*, 115–129.

Mathematical Science Education Board of the National Research Council. (1990). *Reshaping school mathematics: A philosophy and framework for curriculum*. Washington, DC: National Academy Press.

McCloskey, M. (1992). Cognitive mechanisms in numerical processing: Evidence from acquired dyscalculia. *Cognition, 44*, 107–157.

McCloskey, M., Harley, W., & Sokol, S. M. (1991). Models of arithmetic fact retrieval: An evaluation in light of findings from normal and brain-damaged subjects. *Journal of Experimental Psychology: Learning, Memory and Cognition, 17*, 377–397.

McKnight, C. C., Crosswhite, F. J., Dossey, J. A., Kifer, E., Swafford, J. O., Travers, K. J., & Cooney, T. J. (1987). *The underachieving curriculum: Assessing U.S. school mathematics from an international perspective*. Champaign, IL: Stipes.

McLeod, D. B. (1992). Research on affect in mathematics education: A reconceptualization. In D. Grouws (Ed.), *Handbook of research on mathematics teaching and learning* (pp. 575–596). New York: Macmillan.

Miller, K. F. (1984). Child as the measures of all things: Measurement procedures and the development of quantitative concepts. In C. Sophian (Ed.), *Origins of cognitive skills* (pp. 193–288). Hillsdale, NJ: Erlbaum.

Miller, K. F., & Stigler, J. (1987). Counting in Chinese: Cultural variation in a basic cognitive skill. *Cognitive Development, 2*, 279–305.

Miura, I. (1987). Mathematics achievement as a function of language. *Journal of Educational Psychology, 79*, 79–82.

Moore, D. S. (1990). Uncertainty. In L. A. Steen (Ed.), *On the shoulders of giants* (pp. 95–137). Washington, DC: National Academy Press.

Morgan, H. L. (1983). Learning styles: The relation between need for structure and preferred mode of instruction for gifted elementary students. (Doctoral dissertation, University of Pittsburgh, 1981). *Dissertation Abstracts International, 43*, 07A-2223.

Moyer, M. B., & Moyer, J. C. (1985). Ensuring that practice makes perfect: Implications for children with learning difficulties. *Arithmetic Teacher, 33*(1), 40–42.

Mpiangu, B., & Gentile, J. R. (1970). Is conservation of number a necessary condition for mathematical understanding? *Journal for Research in Mathematics Education, 1,* 179–192.

National Commission on Excellence in Education. (1983). *A nation at risk.* Washington, DC: U.S. Government Printing Office.

National Council of Teachers of Mathematics (1981). *Arithmetic Teacher, 28* (special issue entitled Challenge: The Mathematically Able Student).

National Council of Teachers of Mathematics. (1989). *Curriculum and evaluation standards for school mathematics.* Reston, VA: Author.

National Research Council (1989). *Everybody counts: A report to the nation on the future of mathematics education.* Washington, DC: National Academy Press.

Nelson, D., & Worth, J. (1983). *How to choose and create good problems for primary children.* Reston, VA: National Council of Teachers of Mathematics.

Nesher, P. (1986). Learning mathematics: A cognitive perspective. *American Psychologist, 41,* 1114–1122.

Nesher, P., & Kilpatrick, J. (Eds.). (1990). *Mathematics and cognition: A research synthesis by the International Group for the Psychology of Mathematics Education.* Cambridge, England: Cambridge University.

Noffsinger, T., & Dobbs, V. (1970). Teaching arithmetic to educable mentally retarded children. *Journal of Educational Research, 64*(4), 177–184.

Novillis, C. G. (1976). An analysis of the fraction concept into a hierarchy of selected subconcepts and the testing of the hierarchical dependencies. *Journal for Research in Mathematics Education, 7,* 131–144.

Paulos, J. A. (1988). *Innumeracy: Mathematical illiteracy and its consequences.* New York: Hill and Wang.

Payne, J. N. (1976). Review of research on fractions. In R. A. Lesh & D. A. Bradbard (Eds.), *Number and measurement: Papers from a research workshop* (pp. 145–187). Columbus, OH: ERIC/SMEAC.

Peck, D. F., & Jencks, S. M. (1987). *Beneath rules.* Menlo Park, CA: Benjamin Cummings.

Pellegrino, J. W., & Goldman, S. R. (1987). Information processing and elementary mathematics. *Journal of Learning Disabilities, 20,* 23–32, 57.

Pellegrino, J. W., & Goldman, S. R. (1989). Mental chronometry and individual differences in cognitive processes: Common pitfalls and their solutions. *Learning and Individual Differences, 1,* 203–225.

Phillips, D. C., & Kelly, M. E. (1975). Hierarchial theories of development in education and psychology. *Harvard Educational Review, 45,* 351–375.

Piaget, J. (1964). Development and learning. In R. E. Ripple & V. N. Rockcastle (Eds.), *Piaget rediscovered* (pp. 7–20). Ithaca, NY: Cornell University.

Piaget, J. (1965). *The child's conception of number.* New York: Norton.

Piaget, J., & Inhelder, B. (1969). *The psychology of the child.* New York: Basic Books.

Polya, G. (1973). *How to solve it* (39th ed.). Princeton, NJ: Princeton University Press.

Post, T. R. (1988). Some notes on the nature of mathematics learning. In T. R. Post (Ed.), *Teaching mathematics in grades K–8: Research based methods* (pp. 1–19). Boston: Allyn & Bacon.

Post, T. R., Behr, M. J., & Lesh, R. (1986). Research-based observations about children's learning of rational number concepts. *Focus on Learning Problems in Mathematics, 8*(1), 39–47.

Post, T. R., Wachsmuth, I., Lesh, R., & Behr, M. J. (1985). Order and equivalence of rationale numbers: A cognitive analysis. *Journal for Research in Mathematics Education, 16,* 18–36.

Pothier, Y., & Sawada, D. (1983). Partitioning: The emergence of rational number ideas in young children. *Journal for Research in Mathematics Education, 14,* 307–317.

Pressley, M., Goodchild, F., Fleet, J., Zajchowski, R., & Evans, E. D. (1989). The challenges of classroom strategy instruction. *Elementary School Journal, 89,* 301–342.

Price, G. G. (1989). Research in review: Mathematics in early childhood. *Young Children, 44*(4), 53–58.

Putnam, R. T., Lampert, M., & Peterson, L. P. (1990). Alternative perspectives on knowing mathematics in elementary schools. In C. B. Cazden (Ed.), *Review of research in education* (Vol. 16, pp. 57–150). Washington, D.C.: American Educational Research Association.

Quay, L. C. (1963). Academic skills. In N. R. Ellis (Ed.), *Handbook of mental deficiency* (pp. 664–690). New York: McGraw-Hill.

Quintero, A. H. (1985). Conceptual understanding of multiplication: Problems involving combination. *Arithmetic Teacher, 33*(3), 36–39.

Rathmell, E. C., & Huinker, D. M. (1989). Using "part-whole" language to help children represent and solve word problems. In P. R. Trafton & A. P. Shulte (Eds.), *New directions for elementary school mathematics* (pp. 99–110). Reston, VA: National Council of Teachers of Mathematics.

Reeve, R. A., & Brown, A. L. (1985). Metacognition reconsidered. Implications for intervention research. *Abnormal Child Psychology, 13,* 343–356.

Renfrow, M. J. (1987). A descriptive study of problem solving in young children with above average and superior abilities. (Doctoral dissertation, University of Washington, 1986). *Dissertation Abstracts International, 47,* 04A–1256.

Resnick, L. B. (1982). Syntax and semantics in learning to subtract. In T. P. Carpenter, J. M. Moser, & T. A. Romberg (Eds.), *Addition and subtraction: A cognitive perspective* (pp. 136–155). Hillsdale, NJ: Erlbaum.

Resnick, L. B. (1983a). A developmental theory of number understanding. In H. P. Ginsburg (Ed.), *The development of mathematical thinking* (pp. 109–151). New York: Academic Press.

Resnick, L. B. (1983b). Toward a cognitive theory of instruction. In S. G. Paris, G. M. Olson, & H. W. Stevenson (Eds.), *Learning and motivation in the classroom* (pp. 5–38). Hillsdale, NJ: Erlbaum.

Resnick, L. B. (1989). Developing mathematical knowledge. *American Psychologist, 44*(2), 162–169.

Resnick, L. B., & Ford, W. W. (1981). *The psychology of mathematics for instruction.* Hillsdale, NJ: Erlbaum.

Resnick, L. B., Nesher, P., Leonard, F., Magone, M., Omanson, S., & Peled, I. (1989). Conceptual bases for arithmetic errors: The case of decimal fractions. *Journal for Research in Mathematics Education, 20,* 8–27.

Resnick, L. B., & Omanson, S. F. (1987). Learning to understand arithmetic. In R. Glaser (Ed.), *Advances in instructional psychology* (Vol. 3, pp. 41–95). Hillsdale, NJ: Erlbaum.

Reyes, L. H. (1984). Affective variables and mathematics education. *Elementary School Journal, 84,* 558–581.

Reys, R. E. (1984). Mental computation and estimation: Past, present, and future. *The Elementary School Journal, 84,* 547–557.

Riley, M. S., Greeno, J. G., & Heller, J. I. (1983). Development of children's problem-solving ability in arithmetic. In H. P. Ginsburg (Ed.), *The development of mathematical thinking* (pp. 153–196). New York: Academic Press.

Robinson, H. B., & Robinson, N. M. (1965). *The mentally retarded child: A psychological approach.* New York: McGraw-Hill.

Romberg, T. A. (1982). An emerging paradigm for research on addition and subtraction skills. In T. P. Carpenter, J. M. Moser, and T. A. Romberg (Eds.), *Addition and subtraction: A cognitive perspective* (pp. 1–7). Hillsdale, NJ: Erlbaum.

Romberg, T. A., & Carpenter, T. C. (1986). Research on teaching and learning mathematics: Two disciplines of scientific inquiry. In M. C. Wittrock (Ed.), *Handbook of research on teaching* (3rd ed., pp. 850–873). New York: Macmillan.

Ross, S. H. (1989). Parts, wholes, and place value: A developmental review. *Arithmetic Teacher, 36*(6), 47–51.

Saxe, G. B. (1990). *Culture and cognition development: Studies in mathematical understanding.* Hillsdale, NJ: Erlbaum.

Saxe, G. B., Guberman, S. R., & Gearhart, M. (1987). Social processes in early number development. *Monographs of the Society for Research in Child Development, 52* (2, Serial No. 216).

Schaeffer, B., Eggleston, V., & Scott, J. (1974). Number development in young children. *Cognitive Psychology, 6,* 357– 379.

Scheid, K. (1989). *Cognitive and metacognitive learning strategies: Their role in the instruction of special education students.* Columbus, OH: LINC Resources.

Schoen, H. L., & Zweng, M. J. (Eds.). (1986). *Estimation and mental computation.* Reston, VA: National Council of Teachers of Mathematics.

Schoenfeld, A. H. (1985). *Mathematics problem solving.* New York: Academic Press.

Schoenfeld, A. H. (1992). Learning to think mathematically: Problem solving, metacognition, and sense making in mathematics. In D. Grouws (Ed.), *Handbook of research on mathematics teaching and learning* (pp. 334–370). New York: Macmillan.

Schroeder, T. L., & Lester, F. K., Jr. (1989). Developing understanding in mathematics problem solving. In P. R. Trafton & A. P. Shulte (Eds.), *New directions for elementary school mathematics* (pp. 31–42). Reston, VA: National Council of Teachers of Mathematics.

Schultz, K. A., Colarusso, R. P., & Strawderman, V. W. (1989). *Mathematics for every young child.* Columbus, OH: Merrill.

Sears, C. J. (1986). Mathematics for the learning disabled child in the regular classroom. *Arithmetic Teacher, 33*(5), 5–11.

Senechal, M. (1990). Shape. In L. A. Steen (Ed.), *On the shoulders of giants* (pp. 139–181). Washington, DC: National Academy Press.

Shaughnessy, J. M. (1992). Research in probability and statistics: Reflections and directions. In D. A. Grouws (Ed.), *Handbook of research on mathematics teaching and learning* (pp. 465–494). New York: Macmillan.

Shuell, T. J. (1986). Cognitive conceptions of learning. *Review of Educational Research, 56,* 411–436.

Shulte, A. P., & Smart, J. R. (Eds.). (1981). *Teaching statistics and probability.* Reston, VA: National Council of Teachers of Mathematics.

Siegel, A. W., Goldsmith, L. T., & Madson, C. R. (1982). Skill in estimation problems of extent and numerosity. *Journal for Research in Mathematics Education, 13,* 211–232.

Siegler, R. S., & Jenkins, E. (1989). *How children discover new strategies.* Hillsdale, NJ: Erlbaum.

Siegler, R. S., & Robinson, M. (1982). The development of numerical understandings. In H. W. Reese & L. P. Lipsitt (Eds.), *Advances in child development and behavior* (Vol. 1, pp. 241– 312). New York: Academic Press.

Silver, E. A. (1983). Probing young adults' thinking about rational numbers. *Focus on Learning Problems in Mathematics, 5,* 105–117.

Silver, E. A. (Ed.). (1985). *Teaching and learning mathematical problem solving: Multiple research perspectives.* Hillsdale, NJ: Erlbaum.

Silver, E. A., Kilpatrick, J., & Schlesinger, B. (1990). *Thinking through mathematics: Fostering inquiry and communication in mathematics classrooms.* New York: College Entrance Examination Board.

Silver, E. A., & Thompson, A. G. (1984). Research perspective on problem solving in elementary school mathematics. *Elementary School Journal, 84,* 529–545.

Skemp, R. S. (1987). *The psychology of learning mathematics.* Hillsdale, NJ: Erlbaum.

Song, M. J., & Ginsburg, H. P. (1988). The effect of the Korean number system on young children's counting: A natural experiment in numerical bilingualism. *International Journal of Psychology, 23,* 319–332.

Sophian, C. (1992). Learning about numbers: Lesson for mathematics education from preschool number development. In J. Bideaud, C. Meljac, & J. P. Fischer (Eds.), *Pathways to number.* Hillsdale, NJ: Erlbaum.

Sowder, J. T. (1988). Mental computation and number comparison: Their roles in the development of number sense and computational estimation. In J. Hiebert & M. Behr (Eds.), *Number concepts and operations in the middle grades* (pp. 182–197). Reston, VA: National Council of Teachers of Mathematics.

Sowder, J. (1992). Estimation and number sense. In D. A. Grouws (Ed.), *Handbook of research on mathematics teaching and learning* (pp. 371–389). New York: Macmillan.

Sowder, J. T., & Schapple, B. P. (Eds.) (1989). *Establishing foundations for research on number sense and related topics: Report of a conference.* San Diego, CA: San Diego State University, Center for Research in Mathematics and Science Education.

Sowell, E. J. (1989). Effects of manipulative materials in mathematics instruction. *Journal for Research in Mathematics Education, 20,* 498–505.

Spradlin, J. E., Cotter, V. M., Stevens, C., & Friedman, M. (1974). Performance of mentally retarded children on pre-arithmetic tasks. *American Journal of Mental Deficiency, 78,* 397–403.

Starkey, P., & Gelman, R. (1982). The development of addition and subtraction abilities prior to formal schooling in arithmetic. In T. P. Carpenter, J. M. Moser, & T. A. Romberg (Eds.), *Addition and subtraction: A cognitive perspective* (pp. 99–116). Hillsdale, NJ: Erlbaum.

Steen, L. A. (Ed.). (1990a). *On the shoulders of giants: New approaches to numeracy.* Washington, D.C.: National Academy Press.

Steen, L. A. (1990b). Pattern. In L. A. Steen (Ed.), *On the shoulders of giants: New approaches to numeracy* (pp. 1–10). Washington, DC: National Academy Press.

Steffe, L. P. (1983). Children's algorithms as schemes. *Educational Studies in Mathematics, 14,* 233–249.

Steffe, L. P., & Cobb, P. (1988). *Construction of arithmetical meanings and strategies.* New York: Springer-Verlag.

Steffe, L. P., von Glasersfeld, E., Richards, J., & Cobb, P. (1983). *Children's counting types: Philosophy, theory, and application.* New York: Praeger Scientific.

Steffe, L. P., & Wood, T. (Eds.). (1990). *Transforming children's mathematics education.* Hillsdale, NJ: Erlbaum.

Steinberg, R. M. (1985). Instruction on derived fact strategies in addition and subtraction. *Journal for Research in Mathematics Education, 16,* 337–355.

Sternberg, R. J. (1984). *Mechanisms of cognitive development.* New York: W. H. Freeman.

Stevenson, H. W., Lee, S. Y., & Stigler, J. W. (1986). Mathematics achievement of Chinese, Japanese, and American children. *Science, 231,* 693–699.

Stigler, J. W., Fuson, K. C., Ham, M., & Kim, M. S. (1986). An analysis of addition and subtraction word problems in American and Soviet elementary mathematics textbooks. *Cognition and Instruction, 3,* 153–171.

Strauss, M. S., & Curtis, L. E. (1984). Development of numerical concepts in infancy. In C. Sophian (Ed.), *Origins of cognitive skills* (pp. 131–155). Hillsdale, NJ: Erlbaum.

Suydam, M., & Weaver, J. F. (1975). Research on mathematics learning. In J. N. Payne (Ed.), *Mathematics learning in early childhood:* 37th Yearbook of the National Council of Teachers of Mathematics (pp. 43–67). Reston, VA: National Council of Teachers of Mathematics.

Thomas, D. A. (1991). *Children, teachers, and mathematics.* Boston: Allyn & Bacon.

Thornton, C. A., & Bley, N. S. (1982). Problem solving: Help in the right direction for LD students. *Arithmetic Teacher, 29*(6), 26–41.

Thornton, C. A., & Smith, P. J. (1988). Action research: Strategies for learning subtraction facts. *Arithmetic Teacher, 35*(8), 8–12.

Thornton, C. A., & Toohey, M. A. (1985). Basic math facts: Guidelines for teaching and learning. *Learning Disabilities Focus, 1*(1), 44–57.

Tobias, S. (1978). *Overcoming math anxiety.* New York: Norton.

Trafton, P. R. (1978). Estimation and mental arithmetic: Important components of computation. In M. N. Suydam & R. E. Reys (Eds.), *Developing computational skills* (pp. 196–213). Reston, VA: National Council of Teachers of Mathematics.

Trafton, P. R. (1986). Teaching computational estimation: Establishing an estimation mindset. In H. L. Schoen & M. J. Zweng (Eds.), *Estimation and mental computation* (pp. 16–30). Reston, VA: National Council of Teachers of Mathematics.

Trafton, P. R., & Shulte, A. P. (Eds.). (1989). *New directions for elementary school mathematics.* Reston, VA: National Council of Teachers of Mathematics.

Underhill, R. (1988). Mathematics learners' beliefs: A review. *Focus on Learning Problems in Mathematics, 10,* 55–69.

University of the State of New York & New York State Education Department. (1980). *Mathematics K–6: A recommended program for elementary schools.* Albany: New York State Education Department, Bureau of General Education Curriculum Development.

Vance, J. H. (1983). The mathematically talented student revisited. *Arithmetic Teacher, 31*(1), 22–25.

Van de Walle, J. A. (1990). *Elementary school mathematics: Teaching developmentally.* White Plains, NY: Longman.

VanLehn, K. (1983). On the representation of procedures in repair theory. In H. P. Ginsburg (Ed.), *The development of mathematical thinking* (pp. 197–252). New York: Academic Press.

Vitello, S. J. (1976). Quantitative abilities of mentally retarded children. *Education and Training of the Mentally Retarded, 11,* 125–129.

von Glasersfeld, E. (1982). Subitizing: The role of figural patterns in the development of numerical concepts. *Archives de Psychologie, 50,* 191–218.

Vygotsky, L. S. (1978). *Mind in society: The development of higher psychological processes.* Cambridge, MA: Harvard University Press.

Wagner, S., & Walters, J. (1982). A longitudinal analysis of early number concepts: From numbers to numbers. In G. Forman (Ed.), *Action and thought* (pp. 137–161). New York: Academic Press.

Wallace, G., & Larsen, S. C. (1978). *Educational assessment of learning problems: Testing for teaching.* Boston: Allyn & Bacon.

Ware, N. C., & Lee V. E. (1988). Sex differences in choice of college science majors. *American Educational Research Journal, 25,* 593–614.

Warren, S. A. (1963). Academic achievement of trainable pupils with five or more years of schooling. *Training School Bulletin, 60,* 75–86.

Weaver, J. F., & Brawley, C. F. (1959). Enriching the elementary school mathematics program for more capable children. *Journal of Education, 142,* 1–40.

Weiner, S. L. (1974). On the development of more and less. *Journal of Experimental Child Psychology, 17,* 271–287.

Wigfield, A., & Meece, J. L. (1988). Math anxiety in elementary and secondary school students. *Journal of Educational Psychology, 80,* 210–216.

Wilmot, B., & Thornton, C. A. (1989). Mathematics teaching and learning: Meeting the needs of special learners. In P. R. Trafton & A. P. Shulte (Eds.), *New directions for elementary school mathematics* (pp. 212–222). Reston, VA: National Council of Teachers of Mathematics.

Wood, T., Cobb, P., & Yackel E. (1990). The contextual nature of teaching: Mathematics and reading instruction in one second-grade classroom. *Elementary School Journal, 90*(5), 497–513.

Wynroth, L. (1986). *Wynroth Math Program—The natural numbers sequence.* Ithaca, NY: Wynroth Math Program.

Young-Loveridge, J. M. (1987). Learning mathematics. *British Journal of Developmental Psychology, 5,* 155–167.

·12·

SOCIAL STUDIES IN EARLY CHILDHOOD EDUCATION

Cynthia Szymanski Sunal

THE UNIVERSITY OF ALABAMA

The social studies are "social" because they deal with our social lives, with how we live in our social world. There are many definitions of social studies, all reflecting our roles as member-citizens of our society (Barr, Barth, & Shermis, 1977, p. 69; Engle, 1976, p. 234; Kenworthy, 1980, p. 6; Michaelis, 1985, p. 2). In 1983 the National Council for the Social Studies developed the following definition.

The social studies may be defined as an area of the curriculum that derives goals from the nature of citizenship in a democratic society and links to other societies, draws content from the social sciences and other disciplines, and reflects personal, social, and cultural experiences of students (p. 1).

This definition highlights the development of children's understanding of the society in which they live as the focus of the social studies.

The social studies have the following characteristics:

- They involve a search for patterns in our lives.
- They are a daily part of human activity.
- They involve both content and processes of learning.
- They are based on information.
- They require information processing.
- They require decision making and problem solving.
- They are concerned with the development and analysis of one's own values. (Sunal, 1990)

Social studies content to be explored and discussed during the early childhood years is extensive. It is derived from a group of social sciences, including anthropology, economics, geography, history, political science, psychology, and sociology. All of these sciences focus on understanding and explaining human behavior and relationships, but each closely examines a different aspect. Social studies content is also derived from the humanities and from the integration of various social sciences and humanities. Some content enters social studies from the natural sciences, particularly in relation to geographic learning.

This chapter will discuss research related to the teaching of social studies in early childhood education. The child's development of social competence and morality will be discussed first. This is followed by a discussion of children's development of a sense of history. Then geographic learning in young children is considered. Next, the development of economic understanding is described. Finally, children's political socialization is discussed. As each topic is considered, implications of the research in the area are outlined.

DEVELOPMENT OF SOCIAL COMPETENCE AND MORALITY

Developing competence in social relationships is an important part of living in the social world. Sociability develops about age 2, and appears to remain relatively stable thereafter. Bronson (1978) found that measures of sociability at age 2 were correlated with sociability at age $3\frac{1}{2}$. Videotaped observations of 38 toddlers from middle-income families in play groups were examined to determine commonalities between individual behaviors in the first versus the third trimester of their second year. Additional observation of the same children at age $3\frac{1}{2}$ indicated more consistent behaviors, as well as behaviors to those observed earlier. It also indicated a wider range of play behaviors. Predictions of the children's behavior based on earlier observations were substantiated in the later observations.

Bronson's work supported Bayley and Schaefer's (1960) earlier finding that sociability remains fairly stable over time. In their work, Bayley and Schaefer examined extensive data from the Berkeley Growth Study on a sample of 27 boys and 27 girls. They also used child behavior ratings to collect additional data on these children when they were placed in a situation where they could interact with other children. Mothers remaining in the study were interviewed between 9 and 14 years later. Schaefer and Bayley used evidence of patterns of high correlations to conclude that a friendly and outgoing preschooler is likely to be a friendly and outgoing adolescent. The research of Bayley and Schaefer and Bronson suggests that children who are overly shy, uncomfortable, or aggressive with peers may need intervention, since these characteristics of sociability tend to be stable over time. Such intervention should primarily involve modeling by the teacher or by a peer of appropriate behaviors. Modeled behaviors can include smiling at a peer, sharing materials, and suggesting activities that might be cooperatively carried out—such as building a sand castle together and thanking others for help they have given. Teachers can model such behaviors when working individually with the child. When the child is interacting with a peer, teachers can give the child cues for appropriate behavior. This might include asking the child whether he or she can suggest an activity that could be carried out cooperatively with the peer.

Social interactions often require children to consider their concepts of right and wrong, regulate their own behavior, and decide whether to conform to socially accepted standards. A socially competent individual is not necessarily a highly moral individual, but social interaction does affect moral development. Social interaction often requires one to accept restrictions imposed by society while trying to satisfy personal needs and desires. Society sets requirements for children's appropriate behavior, which includes exercising self-control, working toward exemplary conduct, feeling guilty over transgressions, and rewarding themselves only when they attain the highest standards set. In order to attain these standards, children must often delay their own gratification.

Three Aspects of Morality

Shaffer (1988) describes morality as having 3 aspects. The cognitive aspect is moral reasoning—understanding the difference between right and wrong. The affective aspect is moral self-evaluation, which typically results in pride following doing what one thinks is right and guilt following transgressions. The behavioral aspect of morality is resistance to deviation when a situation tempts a person to behave in an incorrect manner. Each of these is an aspect of morality not easily separated from the other.

In 1969 Kohlberg formulated a theory of moral development in which moral reasoning was the focus. He tested individuals from a variety of cultures and economic levels and found similarities in moral development. As a result of his research, he outlined the following ideas:

1. Cognitive development is the major factor in social behavior. As cognitive development occurs, understanding of morally appropriate behavior and the reasons for that behavior also occur.
2. Cognitive and social development occur in stages, each qualitatively different from the one that precedes it.
3. Maturational factors and the continuing restructuring of behavior through experience and maturation result in the requirement that no new stage may be achieved until all preceding ones have been attained.

Kohlberg developed a *moral judgment scale* that was used to determine which of 6 stages a person was in. This scale was based on an evaluation of people's responses to a problem with many possible solutions. Each solution was different and represented the moral basis that a person used to resolve the problem.

Kohlberg's theory has implications for teaching. Young children cannot understand adult explanations of right and wrong because they do not have the cognitive ability to do so. They are likely to be motivated by whether or not an action is rewarded rather than whether it is right or wrong. If explanations of moral behavior are given, students begin to mature and understand why a behavior is right or wrong. Eventually they will develop their own set of moral standards and values. To make logical and moral decisions, children need experience in situations that require reflection and decision making.

Beyer (1974) has suggested 5 guidelines for teaching in a way that stimulates children's movement to higher stages in moral development. First, genuine moral issues, real dilemmas, must be considered by children. Second, moral and social conflict must be experienced during the discussion of a dilemma. Third, children need practice in applying their limited moral guidelines to new problems. Fourth, children need to be exposed to peers who are in the next highest stage of development. Fifth, children need to be confronted with their own inconsistencies over time. Teachers should supply the basic information needed in a dilemma, remain neutral, and facilitate discussion of that dilemma in an open, nonthreatening atmosphere.

Kurtines and Greif (1974) suggest that Kohlberg's scale has several shortcomings. These include the fact that many of the details of the administration of the scale are left to the examiner, the use of intuitive scoring methods, and uncertain reliability, because a person's score may fluctuate widely over a short period of time. They note some issues that have been raised related to Kohlberg's theory. These include indications that moral conduct often does not match a person's stage of moral development and evidence suggesting that children's development may skip around and not clearly follow the hierarchy of stages Kohlberg identified. They suggest that the problems noted might be caused by inherent flaws in the scale. Kurtines and Greif do not dispute the idea that cognitive development is the major factor in moral development. Instead, they are concerned with the means by which moral development is assessed.

Moral reasoning is an important factor in moral development. Several researchers have indicated that moral reasoning is fostered in a child through the use of inductive reasoning.

In using inductive reasoning, adults give explanations or reasons for requiring that a behavior be maintained or changed (Hoffman, 1970). Moral reasoning is also fostered when the consequences of a child's behavior are pointed out, for example, when one child taunts another child and causes her to become sad. Hoffman (1970) also suggests that appealing to the child's desire to be "grown up" and thought of as mature can be a productive strategy. Parpal and Maccoby (1985) have found that the children of parents who use reasoning and stress concern for other's needs and emotions have the highest levels of moral development. In a study of 39 lower-middle-class children, ranging in age from 3.2 to 4.6 years, mothers were observed asking their children to perform a series of tasks. Parpal and Maccoby found that mothers who preferred to discipline by using explanations combined with voiced displeasure were likely to have children who resisted deviation, exhibited self-control, and tried to comply with rules.

Hoffman (1970) explains the effectiveness of reasoning in raising morally mature children. Through inductive reasoning, adults provide cognitive rationales that children can use in self-evaluation of their own behavior and activities. In providing the rationale, adults generally ask children to consider others' feelings in a situation involving that child and another. Such consideration encourages children to be empathetic and to put themselves in the other's place, and thereby contributes to the development of moral reasoning—the cognitive aspect of morality. The use of inductive reasoning also involves the affective aspect of morality, as adults talk with children about self-evaluation and the emotions related to it, such as pride or shame. Adults address the behavioral aspect of morality by explaining what behaviors can help children resist deviation and what the child can do to make up for deviations. Reasoning, which involves all 3 aspects of morality, may help the individual child integrate those aspects (Hoffman, 1970).

Kuczynski (1984) suggests that parents are more likely to use inductive reasoning when they want long-term compliance from their children, rather than when trying to stop a behavior that is occurring. When children are about age 4 or 5, parents typically begin to prefer inductive reasoning as a means of preventing children from engaging in a behavior. These parents recognize that children at this age are beginning to understand such reasoning. Children at this time also begin to use negotiation, a form of reasoning, instead of noncompliance or defiance (Kuczynski, Kochanska, Radke-Yarrow, & Girnius-Brown, 1987).

One hundred children, age 4 through 18, were asked to evaluate mothers' disciplinary techniques used in a range of situations where a child had transgressed (Siegal & Cowan, 1984). Maternal strategies included inductive reasoning, physical punishment, love withdrawal, and permissiveness. The children evaluated inductive reasoning as the most appropriate form of discipline, with physical punishment receiving mild approval. Further research involving other significant adults in the young child's life is needed. Future research should also investigate very subtle reasoning techniques. Other techniques of power assertion besides physical punishment might also be examined.

Perspective Taking

Learning to take the perspective of others increases children's ability to make mature moral judgments (Selman, 1971, 1976). Among children of the same age and general level of intelligence, Selman found that children who had reached the higher levels of perspective taking on his scale were more likely to have reached the higher levels of moral reasoning when discussing Kohlberg's (1989) dilemmas. Being a skillful perspective taker—that is, knowing what others want, feel, and believe—is not enough to make individuals behave considerately and in a prosocial way. Adults who frequently call attention to and explain other people's perspectives help children learn to be sensitive to these perspectives.

Implications

Social Competence. Sociability develops early and is central in the development of social competence. Social competence is affected by the strategies adults use in working with children, particularly in situations where inappropriate behavior may be expressed. There has been little research investigating the relative importance of the roles of home and school in the development of social competence. Longitudinal research, perhaps ethnographic in methodology, focusing on a small sample of children studied in depth, might begin to reveal the impact of school factors on children's social competence.

Morality. Morality has 3 facets—cognitive, affective, and behavioral—that social studies programs should work to develop. Researchers have found that developmental changes occur in children's ability to make moral judgments. Moral behavior, however, does not always match the level of ability to make logical moral judgments.

Research has indicated that parents' use of inductive reasoning with children fosters moral maturity, enabling children to develop a sensitivity to the perspectives of others. Perspective taking appears to be related to moral development: Research suggests that cognitive developmental level influences children's ability to understand reasons for moral actions and for rules.

Children need adult guidance. Such guidance should include logical, prosocial reasons for acting in a particular way in a given situation. In social studies, teachers should utilize inductive reasoning and foster perspective taking as means for promoting moral development in their children. Children should not be punished when they cannot understand that an action is wrong or inappropriate. Explanations and inductive reasoning accomplish more, as do the adult's understanding and appreciation of children's development.

Researchers should investigate the effects of both parents' and teachers' use of inductive reasoning with children. Does a lack of congruity between parent and teacher approaches create confusion in students? How do students from homes where inductive reasoning is used respond to classrooms where it is not used, and vice versa? To what extent do parents adapt their strategies as children mature? What differences are found between teachers of different ages of children? Do parent and teacher strategies change (and if so, to what extent) according to the various crises in which a student might be involved?

DEVELOPMENT OF A SENSE OF HISTORY

History examines both change and continuity in human affairs over time. Historical reasoning, then, requires a structure that likewise incorporates time (Thornton & Vukelich, 1988, p. 69).

Children's Understanding of Time

Many preschool and primary-grade children are fascinated to learn about their own unremembered past. It is unremembered because children begin forgetting their past right after experiencing it. They do not move it into their long-term memory (Ghiray, Altkin, Vaught, & Roodin, 1976). What is remembered is a fair number of isolated facts and events, mostly as eidetic images (Ghiray et al., 1976). Eidetic images are vivid recollections of past visual, auditory, or tactual experiences that may result from centration. *Centration* is the centering of attention on one feature of a situation, to the exclusion of all others (Piaget, 1964). When centering, children focus on part of an event, on a particular slice of time. Therefore, young children are seldom capable of imposing a structured time sequence on their experiences. When preoperational children do try to link experiences together, transductive thinking occurs. In *transductive thinking*, children link experiences together as they are, with no time sequence logically imposed. The result is a stream of events that the child understands as connected, but that may not actually consist of cause-and-effect relationships (Ginsburg & Opper, 1988).

Reversibility involves understanding that something that has been changed can be mentally, and sometimes physically, returned to its original state by reversing the process of change. For example, a ball of clay that has been rolled out into a long, thin rope can be rolled back into a ball, a physical reversal (Stassen Berger, 1980, p. 552). Young children can observe such a reversal and carry it out following someone's directions, but still may be fooled by the way the clay looks. When stretched out, the rope looks longer and therefore seems to have more clay. Young children can't reverse the process—that is, they can't mentally follow the rolled-out clay back to its start, the clay ball. Older children in the concrete operational stage can quickly reverse the process in their minds. Reversibility is essential to an understanding of time. Centering, however, interferes with reversibility. When children devote all attention to one point in time and ignore other points along the way, they do not capture mental steps to retrace (Piaget, 1970).

Children have a hard time realizing that their parents and familiar adults were once little. They seem, in fact, to entertain 2 contradictory ideas. On the one hand, children believe that an adult's past stretches far into the past. On the other hand, children find it almost unthinkable that the world was ever very different from the way it is now. Many children expect to catch up with their parents. Chukowsky (1963) quotes a child who asks, "Mother, who was born first, you or I?" These contradictory views and the comments that express them suggest that children do not understand time concepts appropriately and that they may have difficulty with historical reasoning.

Few researchers have examined how historical reasoning relates to structures incorporating time. Little research has been carried out to examine whether and how children can learn history when their understanding of time and their thinking structures incorporating time are immature. Young children make what adults consider to be errors in working with time. Children's exploration of history does appear to be affected by their conception of time. Because there is only limited research on this subject, it is difficult to develop a consensus as to how much emphasis should be placed on history in the social studies curriculum for young children though age 8. Peel (1965) suggests that history has little place in the social studies curriculum for young children since they are not capable of historical reasoning. An opposing view is expressed by Levstik and Pappas (1987), Muir (1985), Diem (1982), and Spieseke (1963), who view children as capable of understanding history when it is simplified or carefully presented. In a review of the psychological literature, Zaccaria (1978) hypothesized that children's difficulty in learning to "think historically" might be due to a limited ability to deal with time. In his review, Zaccaria found that first-grade children's time span for thinking about events is around 1 week. In third grade it is about 1 month and in sixth grade about 1 year. In adolescence many students become capable of dealing with the time periods often used in a chronological account of history.

Thornton and Vukelich (1988) have divided the research literature pertaining to this subject into 2 parts. One portion of the literature describes how children perceive the duration and speed of time (Piaget, 1970). The second portion describes children's development of clock, calendar, and historical time concepts. Clock time divides time into small equivalent numerical pieces that can be displayed on a device such as a watch. Calendar time involves larger blocks of time displayed on calendars, such as days, weeks, seasons, and years. It also includes specified days such as holidays. Historical time involves the largest block of time and is usually involved with assigning a calendar time to a person, object, place, or event. In historical time President John F. Kennedy can be associated with the twentieth century, with the year 1961, or with a corresponding time in one's own experience, such as, "when I was in college." Friedman (1982) has suggested an integration of both portions of the literature, which would encourage researchers to investigate underlying cognitive structures common to the 3 types of time concepts.

Personal Time. In addition to the time concepts based on how time is divided up, a conception of personal time and an ability to sequence daily events develop throughout childhood. Thornton and Vukelich (1988) describe an awareness of personal time as emerging between the ages of 4 and 7. At this point children begin using terms such as "before," "now," and "then" in relation to things they have done and things occurring around them (Harner, 1982). Children gradually differentiate personal time and begin using terms and tenses appropriate to their language, such as the past progressive tense in English. The full range of terminology related to personal time, including terms such as "already" and "next week," is mastered around age 10 or 11 (Harner, 1982, p. 163).

The Cycle of Daily Events. Another concept that young children develop between the ages of 4 and 6 involves analyzing daily events cyclically. The child is able at this age to describe regular daily activities in an appropriate sequence (Thornton & Vukelich, 1988). An example might be a description of daily activities in school, such as, "first, we put away our sweaters in our cubby, then we have circle time, then we work at centers, then we play outside." By describing daily activities in the sequence that they occur, teachers create a time line for children. A daily time line can be constructed by children when they draw pictures of 3 or more activities of the day and then arrange them in sequence. The sequenced pictures can be placed on a line that has been divided into the hours of the school day. This type of activity helps the child build the concept of a time line and to understand that different activities take different amounts of time. For example, the child may find that several activities cluster around one time slot, whereas another activity, such as nap time, stands alone because it takes up a large block of time. As the child matures, this concept can be extended to cover 2 days, a week, a month, a year, and so on. The sequencing of daily events is a first step towards understanding historical time.

Clock and Calendar Skills. Clock and calendar skills appear somewhat later, by 6 or 7 years of age (Thornton & Vukelich, 1988). Clock time appears to develop from larger to smaller units—hour to minute to second. Conversely, calendar time develops from smaller to larger units—days to weeks to months. Aptitude with historical time seems to require an understanding of personal, clock, and calendar time and is, therefore, late in developing.

Much development related to understanding time and historical concepts occurs around ages 8 and 9. Children accurately employ the terms "past," "present," and "future," correctly associating people and events with these terms. Harner (1982) suggests that understanding of the future is the last to develop, probably because it is the most abstract of the 3 terms. Children also begin to master historical dates and associate dates with particular people and events. Jahoda (1963) found that children at this age begin to appropriately sequence family members such as parents and grandparents. Children order dates such as 1970, 1980, and 1990 but have difficulty in matching a year to a person or event (Oakden & Sturt, 1922; Friedman, 1944). Thornton and Vukelich (1988) suggest that some of the more abstract time terms may be learned by children during the early childhood years only with appropriate instruction.

The Relationship Between Understanding Time Concepts and History

The research literature on the development of specific time concepts is larger than the literature investigating the relationship between understanding time concepts and understanding history. Hallam (1970) considered the understanding of time and history to be a part of cognitive development. He hypothesized that some kinds of historical reasoning are dependent upon formal operations because time and historical concepts are sometimes interwoven in a complex and abstract manner. To investigate his hypothesis, Hallam asked students of various ages questions such as, "Can you tell me some people who lived in ancient Greece?" and, "Why aren't the boys in your class trained like Spartan boys?" (Hallam, 1979, pp. 18–19). Preoperational children's answers were inadequate according to Hallam because of an incomplete understanding of time concepts. Hallam noted a lack of reversibility in these children's answers to the first question; the children responded to the questions as if they related to events occurring today (p. 19). In response to the second question, many children gave responses similar to the one in the following exchange:

"Why aren't boys in your class trained like the Spartan boys?"
"Too young."

Responses to follow-up comments were similar to the one in this exchange:

"The Spartan boys were young as well."
"We don't battle anybody in fights."
"Would the boys today be trained like the Spartans if we did fight?"
"Now-a-days you have different things to learn, shooting and all sorts of different things." (Hallam, 1979, p. 19)

These responses also suggest egocentrism: The respondent viewed the questions from his own current time frame, not from one reflecting a different time frame (Hallam, 1979, p. 19). Hallam (1979, p. 21) did, however, find evidence that children in the concrete operational stage are less egocentric and usually do not frame their responses in relation to their personal time frame.

Hallam's research indicates that an understanding of time is related to the development of logical reasoning and that historical reasoning is dependent upon logical reasoning. The implication is that children's understanding of time and history is related to their cognitive development. Therefore, depending on their developmental level, children are able to understand certain kinds of historical concepts but are not able to understand others (Hallam, 1970; Sleeper, 1975). However, neither Hallam, Sleeper, nor any other researcher has specified which concepts children of different developmental levels can understand. Spieseke (1963) suggests that time and historical concepts should be taught in the context of meaningful social problems but does not present empirical data supporting her suggestion.

Based on their review of the research literature, Thornton and Vukelich (1988) suggest several implications for early childhood education. They acknowledge historical time as a major component in historical reasoning. Learning time appears to be tied to an individual's current developmental structure. Concepts of history and historical time that are within the limits of children age 6 and older should be taught systematically and sequentially. Such teaching should recognize that dates and some time terms are not well understood by young children. Although children may use more abstract time terms, they do not necessarily understand them and use them appropriately.

Another implication is that time understandings should be a major consideration when deciding how historical topics are introduced (Vukelich, 1984). Time language that matches the child's development should be used. Thornton and Vukelich (1988) suggest that the past-present dichotomy be introduced after 4 years of age, that the cyclical and sequential nature of events starting with those in their immediate life be introduced by age 5 or 6, and that persons or events of the past be introduced and discussed without dates prior to age 9.

A third implication is that historical time concepts be taught in conjunction with history. Diem (1982) suggests that time concepts are often haphazardly introduced with time concepts. The lack of an organized approach is therefore likely to engender confusion in children. As a result, history is often overly complex for young children (Diem, 1982).

Fourth, educators should recognize that time and historical concepts develop throughout childhood. Hallam (1970) and Sleeper (1975) suggest that the teaching of history should be delayed until formal operational thinking has begun. It appears, however, that learning can occur earlier. Levstik and Pappas (1987) and Egan (1982), for example, contend that elementary school children are capable of much more complex reasoning than Hallam suggests. In their study, Levstik and Pappas introduced a piece of historical fiction, *Thunder at Gettysburg,* to second, fourth, and sixth graders (1987). After the story was read, the children were asked to retell the story and answer a series of questions about the book. Next, they responded to questions about their conceptions of history and the past. Levstik and Pappas identified 2 concurrent patterns distinguishing development of historical understanding across the grade levels studied. These patterns entailed differences in kind and differences of degree. Qualitative differences in the features of the book appeared in the retelling of the story by younger and older children. Children gradually refined the chronology used in defining history and determining when the past becomes history. The prevalent pattern of historical understanding appeared to be one of degree; children gradually come to understand more aspects of a situation. However, more research is needed to substantiate this pattern. This study, which contained 24 subjects, needs to be done with a larger population and with different populations.

Levstik and Pappas conclude that elementary children as young as second grade know something about time and history. Their subjects were able to deal with history both as an abstraction and in particular. In dealing with history as an abstraction, the children were able to consider under what conditions might some events become history. In dealing with particular instances in history they were able to describe the nature and causes of conflicts in the stories. Levstik and Pappas believe that their study can be better understood in the light of Donaldson's (1978) findings regarding the effect of context on successful completion of Piagetian tasks. Donaldson (1978) found that careful presentation of a task, with appropriate directions, resulted in children's successful completion of it. Levstik and Pappas (1987) think it is the context in which history

is presented, examined, and discussed that may be the crucial factor in whether elementary children come to understand and engage in history. They suggest that, by second grade, children should have increased exposure to history and that a good vehicle for such exposure would be the use of historical fiction. Current history curricula are narrow in scope, according to Levstik and Pappas, and could be easily widened through the use of historical fiction.

Implications

Thornton and Vukelich (1988) find there is a need for a better understanding of how children learn history. We presently know little about how children come to understand history. There is evidence, though, that young children can learn some history if they are involved with it in a concrete manner. Historical fiction can provide some of the concreteness young children need. Historical nonfiction may also do this, although research has not been carried out using it. This is an area that requires in-depth research. Further research is also needed to determine what contributions history makes to children's cognitive development and how it affects appropriate curriculum and instruction. Much of the existing research on the development of concepts of time does not directly relate this development to understanding history.

THE DEVELOPMENT OF GEOGRAPHIC LEARNING

Young children physically explore their environment in all sorts of ways—by climbing in it, crawling through it, hopping across it, and so on. This physical exploration is the beginning of geography (Sunal, 1990; Sunal & Sunal, 1978; Sauvy & Sauvy, 1972). Through geography people describe, explain, and structure the interactions that occur between objects physically existing in space (Sunal, 1990, p. 169). Borchert (1983) has described geography as a description of the physical and cultural features of human settlements and their natural settings. The study of geography involves considering data in terms of geographic patterns and the changes in those patterns. Geographic concepts are rooted in space concepts that the young child develops as he or she explores the environment (Sunal, 1990).

Understanding Space

Children's exploration of the environment begins early. By the third month, infants coordinate eyes with hand and foot movement, an ability that enables them to investigate space (Piaget & Inhelder, 1967). Early understandings of space provide information from which the child develops a representational mapping of space, beginning around age 2 (Laurendeau & Pinard, 1968).

Concepts related to an understanding of topological space develop first (Piaget & Inhelder, 1967). These concepts include the spatial relationships formed by neighborhood, or proximity (or "nearby-ness"); enclosure (in 2 dimensions); envelopment (in 3 dimensions); continuity; separation; and order. Children come to understand their relationship in space to the things around them. They also begin to understand the relationship of things to other things in space. The child may understand, for example, that she is enveloped by a room. The walls of the room enclose a space used for certain activities, perhaps a kitchen. If she is nearby (has proximity to) the refrigerator when she is in the kitchen, then she is not nearby the sink. When she goes outside the child understands that a curb is continuous until it is broken by a driveway. The driveway separates one stretch of curb from another stretch of curb. She also understands that there is an order to things outside, so that when she leaves her house her friend's house is closer than is her cousin's house. These topological relationships are examined in detail but at first do not allow children to understand space in terms of euclidean geometry. An object is not seen as being composed of points at invariant distances from each other. Children do not at first understand placing an object precisely in a frame of reference. Very young children can be introduced to topological space because it requires neither reference to straight lines nor measurement (Sauvy & Sauvy, 1972).

Around age 4 or 5, projective space and euclidean space begin to be sketched in against a background of topological space. At first, a child can distinguish his right from his left hand, but only later can he distinguish the right and left hands of a child facing him. Laurendeau and Pinard (1968) suggest that this occurs because the child's thought is still centered and is not yet integrating the parts of the whole situation or incorporating reversibility. Projective relations, which involve straight lines and perspective, begin to develop but are not thoroughly accomplished before age 7. Euclidean geometric relationships are present only in the form of a rough sketch in young children. As children come to understand projective space, they begin to see that items appear differently from various distances and angles. They begin to develop the idea that locations are related to other places. This leads to a better understanding of distance and direction. As a result, their maps become roughly accurate (Catling, 1978). Maps, graphs, and diagrams incorporate and depend on topological, euclidean, and projective concepts to provide a variety of information.

Children's understanding of euclidean space develops as they become formal operational. Such an understanding enables them to relate locations correctly to one another simultaneously (Holloway, 1967). Knowledge of direction and distance becomes accurate and can be measured in relationship to such abstract coordinates as the prime meridian, equator, and poles.

Because topological space concepts are grasped first by young children, they should serve as the starting point for geographic activities. Activity can progress from work with children's self-image outward. Children need to understand concepts such as "up" and "back" in relation to their own body before trying to apply them to the space they live in (Piaget & Inhelder, 1967; Barsch, 1967). As children progress outward, they need ample opportunities to experience their surroundings concretely. Spatial relationships are the beginning point for geographic education. What does research tell us about teaching specific geographic skills and concepts?

Children's Geographic Learning

Two important reviews of the research relating to children's geographic learning were done, 10 years apart, in 1968 and in 1978. These provide a useful overview of the kind and level of research conducted over a long period of time and offer points from which later research can be considered. Rushdoony (1968) reviewed research specifically relating to map skills. He found that studies were generally not longitudinal, not systematically investigated, and involved only a small number of students. As a result, he found that he could draw few conclusions from a review of the research. Rushdoony found that most map skill research prior to 1960 consisted of status studies. Only in the later years of his study did he find concern about what children learn as a result of systematic instruction. These studies, however, were affected by the limitations cited earlier.

Rice and Cobb (1978) reviewed research in a somewhat broader context, relating to geographic education in general rather than to map skills specifically. They found that few studies had been done relating to the geographic concepts children could learn. As a result, the review focused on studies relating to map skills and children's conceptual and analytic processes. A number of the studies reviewed reported that children in primary grades, if given systematic instructions, could perform at a higher map skill and conceptual level than had been previously noted. In 2 studies, Crabtree (1968, 1974) examined the effects of systematic instruction of geographic skills and concepts on children in grades 1 through 3. In the first study, 2 curricula were used to teach area association. Significant gains were found at all grades at various levels of symbolic abstraction. The second study investigated the sequencing of geographic skills. In his review of the research, Rushdoony found that Crabtree's 2 studies provided the most systematic, valid evidence of young children's potential for learning geographic concepts, map interpretation skills, and analytic processes. Rice and Cobb concluded that young children can learn complex analytic processes and concepts of geography when they are active participants in a highly structured and sequential series of geographic inquiries. This conclusion was supported by the studies of Hart (1971); Imperatore (1968); Savage and Bacon (1969); and Stoltman and Goolsby (1973). These other studies also found evidence that systematic map activities improved map skills of students in primary grades.

Systematic presentation of map skills appears to be important. If this is the case, then, in what order should map skills be presented? Rice and Cobb examined a group of studies (Balchin & Coleman, 1973; Klett & Alpaugh, 1976; Neperud, 1977) investigating this question. These studies provided conflicting views about the order of presentation of map skills. Some found evidence for a progression in graphic presentation and spatial development supporting Piaget's developmental stages, whereas others found there was no definite progression. Cox (1977) found mixed results in his study. He tried to identify a sequence in which map skills are learned and to match it to information related to Piaget's stages of cognitive development. Some parts of Piaget's developmental sequence were supported, but Cox's evidence was not clear enough to be conclusive. Cox indicated that research in geographic education needed to examine the effects of instruction on performance.

One means of identifying the sequence in which map skills are best taught is to determine the age at which children learn a geographic concept or skill. Several studies have attempted to do this. Blaut, McCleary, and Blaut (1970) found that first-graders can read some maps. In a later study, Blaut and Stea (1974) found that 3-year-olds can understand some kinds of simple maps. Cardinal directions are important to the understanding of mapping and of maps. Lanegran, Snowfield, and Laurent (1970) found that children can learn cardinal directions in kindergarten. These studies indicated that young children can work with maps to some extent; however, the researchers have provided limited information regarding what is best taught at a given age.

In their review of the research, Rice and Cobb (1978) found the studies available to them to indicate that systematic geographic education can begin in the primary grades. They identified a number of limitations in the studies reviewed: In general the studies were not systematic; not longitudinal, not comprehensive considering only a few areas of map skills and concepts; and not concerned with instructional quality. Despite these limitations and a lack of conclusiveness, the studies did indicate where further research was needed and when geographic education could begin.

In a later study, Atkins (1981) examined the effects of instruction on young children's understanding of map and globe skills. Atkins studied 22 4- and 5-year-old preschoolers in 2 intact groups. One group received an experimental treatment; the other was a control group. No differences were found between the groups on a pretest. The experimental group was systematically taught map and globe skills for a month. The lessons included instruction in the earth's shape, the globe as a model of the earth, directions, orienting a map, distance, scale, map symbols, location, the earth-sun relationship, and abstract location. The experimental group did significantly better on all parts of the posttest, with the exception of the part covering abstract location. Neither group demonstrated an understanding of abstract location. A year later, the experimental group outperformed the control group on a follow-up test. Atkins concluded that young children learn when map and globe skills are presented systematically.

In order to discover how lessons should be structured, Buggey (1971) examined the relationship between classroom questions and map skill achievement. She investigated the use of 2 instructional strategies over a 3-week period with 108 second-graders in 3 groups—2 experimental and 1 control. The first experimental instructional strategy used 70% knowledge-level questions and 30% higher-level questions. The second used 30% knowledge-level questions and 70% higher-level questions (Bloom, 1956). The groups were not significantly different on a pretest. During the study, the control group received no instruction, whereas the 2 experimental groups received daily instruction. Instruction focused on the concept of location. The questioning strategies were used with visual materials presenting the concept. Students whose instruction included most higher-level questions performed better on the posttest than did those whose instruction used mostly knowledge-level questions. The control group

performed rather poorly in comparison to the experimental groups. Similar results were found by Tyler (1971) in a parallel study.

During the 1970s geographic education made use of a new technology, mapping the earth from space using Landsat satellites. Kirman studied the use of Landsat map in 1977, finding that third-graders could use infrared false-color Landsat images. In a 1981 study Kirman investigated whether children could use black-and-white Landsat images. His results with 70 third- through fifth-graders, although not conclusive, suggested that these children could use the black-and-white images. In 1984 Kirman studied a class of third-graders, providing them with 18 hours of instruction. This group correctly interpreted "Band 5" black-and-white Landsat images on an achievement test. Although further research is needed, Kirman's work suggests that, as early as the third grade, children can use the false-color Landsat images, and with systematic and intensive instruction may be able to use the black-and-white Landsat images.

Geography Content and Teaching

Systematic instruction by a well-prepared teacher appears to be important in children's learning of geography. However, the appropriate sequence for the teaching of map and globe skills is still uncertain. Herman (1983) used a nonempirical approach to address this question. He asked academicians and educators to identify map and globe skills and their appropriate grade placement. The results of his study indicate that, in kindergarten through grade 3, geography instruction should help children describe and appreciate the relationship between the physical and cultural worlds with a focus on human-land relationships. Children should also be involved in explaining how people and places (regions) differ from one another at various scales—local, national, and world—and should describe how areas are different from each other. Finally, children should identify problems resulting from physical and economic factors, including population distribution and density.

In 1984 the *Guidelines for Geographic Education* were published by the Association of American Geographers. The guidelines identify 5 fundamental themes of geography and describe them so that they can be used by teachers. These themes are

1. *Location.* Position on the Earth's surface
2. *Place.* Natural and cultural characteristics
3. *Relationships within places.* Humans and environments
4. *Movement.* Humans interacting on the Earth
5. *Regions.* How they form and change

Five geographic skills were also identified in the guidelines:

1. Asking geographic questions
2. Acquiring geographic information
3. Presenting geographic information
4. Interpreting geographic information
5. Developing and testing geographic information

Geographic literacy involves these themes and skills (Backer & Stoltman, 1986). The *Guidelines for Geographic Education* provide general guidance for organizing geographic concepts and skills.

Teachers often rely on textbooks in their teaching. Haas (1988) used content analysis to examine what geographic concepts appear in elementary social studies textbooks for grades 1 through 4. She found that geographic instruction is introduced in grades 1 and 2 and is emphasized in textbooks in grades 3 and 4. Throughout the 4 grades, the following are emphasized in textbooks: identification of map and globe terms; use of the compass to find directions; computation of distance; collection of information; making of inferences and predictions; and drawing conclusions. First- and second-graders are typically introduced to map skills with a picture of the Earth. They are asked to distinguish the Earth's shape and the differences between land and water. The first textbook maps are of classrooms and familiar locations, such as shopping centers. Children learn map skills related to the uses of symbols, the legend, and cardinal directions. In the third grade, children begin studying scale. Small-scale political maps appear in textbooks as early as the second grade. Location and place receive the most emphasis in elementary textbooks. Such an emphasis often results in students trying to memorize information in isolation rather than trying to analyze relationships (Haas, 1989).

Problems exist in the teaching of geography to some extent because it is often associated only with the study of maps (Haas, 1989). Teachers often feel a shortage of time available to teach all that they must and, instead of working toward comprehension, tend to teach geography as material to be covered in textbooks (Thornton & Wenger, 1989). Most elementary textbook series lack the organization and practice necessary to assist students in learning and retaining key ideas (Haas, 1989).

Although research results do not clearly support any specific sequence of skills, Sunal and Haas (1993) draw some implications for teaching young children. One activity important to geographic learning is children's construction of their own maps. In such activities, children encounter and solve the same kinds of problems as professional mapmakers. They may also be encouraged to examine professionally made maps in order to see how others dealt with the same problems. Teachers should provide children with opportunities to look at a wide variety of maps.

Globe-related activities should be introduced before formal maps are used. The globe is a more realistic and concrete representation of the Earth. Children are familiar with other models because of their toys and can understand a globe as a model more easily than a map. Also, the globe presents information more accurately than does a map.

The first maps and globes used should be simple. Maps should be of familiar locations and use few symbols. Topographic, raised-relief maps are especially appropriate for young children.

Most globes and maps make extensive use of symbols. Symbols are usually understood between ages 5 and 7 as things that stand for other things. Young children need to work with maps and globes that use just a few symbols.

Direction is another important component of maps and globes. Some beginning directional activities should include pointing to and describing where things are in relationship to the self, other people, and other objects. Specific directions such as "north" and "south" should be taught after children can differentiate left from right. At that time they should be taken outside to learn the directions. First, teachers should indicate which direction is north. Then the children should face north and locate east and west by raising their arms and turning around to locate south. East can be located as 90 degrees right of north and west as 90 degrees left of north.

Distance is another important factor in reading globes and maps. Relative distances can be introduced to young children. Terms used in discussing relative distance include "near," "farther away," and "farthest." Pieces of string can be stretched between points on a globe and compared to see which is longest.

The final important facet in working with globes and maps involves the use of grid systems. This is the most complex of the four facets. In the grid system a vertical line and a horizontal line intersect in only 1 place. Young children can begin working toward an understanding of grid systems by tracing roads on maps with their fingers, by examining maps of small communities that have roads intersecting at right angles in a checkerboard fashion, and by using blocks to build roads that cross each other and then drawing a map of the roads.

Implications

The research is not clear on what geographic concepts should be taught; however, it is clear that whatever is taught needs to be done systematically with well-prepared teachers. There is a strong need for research studies examining when children are ready to learn geographic concepts and skills. It is also not clear whether a specific sequence can be determined in the acquisition of geographic concepts and skills. Studies need to follow geographic skills and concepts over several years, investigating how and when they develop. Qualitative studies should be used along with quantitative studies in order to provide information from different viewpoints. Such studies would strengthen our knowledge of the development of geographic skills and concepts.

THE DEVELOPMENT OF ECONOMIC UNDERSTANDING

Economics is the study of how people balance unlimited wants with limited resources (Sunal, 1990; Senesh, 1963). In practice, economics involves a complex network of decisions. The tension between wants and resources means that an economic system must resolve 5 basic concerns: what to produce, how to produce, how much to produce in the short run, how much to produce in the long run, and how to distribute output (Hartoonian, 1981). As each economic system works to answer these questions, a wide range of economic concepts are utilized. Which economic concepts can children in early childhood understand? Kourilsky and Hirshleifer (1976) identified 9 concepts as comprehensible to children in kindergarten and the primary grades: scarcity; decision making; opportunity cost and cost-benefit analysis; production; specialization;

distribution, consumption, and savings; demand and supply; business organization and business venture; and money and barter. Kourilsky (1985) introduced these concepts to young children through concrete experiences, learning centers, simulations, and other strategies.

Stages in Economic Development

Four stages in the development of economic thought were postulated by Danziger (1958) after interviewing 41 Australian children, ages 5 through 8. Danziger found the youngest children demonstrated little or no understanding of money, exchange, or poverty. Somewhat older children used functional, ritualistic, or moralistic explanation for exchange and the use of money. As they matured, children described reciprocity between people and saw money more as a medium of exchange than as one item traded for another. The most mature and oldest students, around age 8, understood and described relationships between a range of economic concepts.

Money

Money is a medium of exchange found in most societies and is evident in settled cultures, particularly as larger populations develop. It is a basic economic concept. Furth (1980) and Fox (1978) studied 4- to 6-year-old children's understanding of the concept of money. They found that young children had little or no understanding of the reciprocal nature of transactions between buyers and sellers in stores. Their subjects viewed money, instead, as part of a ritual occurring in stores. The youngest children did not relate money to buying and selling but were interested in it as a set of concrete objects to be physically investigated. Feldman (1981) concluded that simply being involved in economic experiences does not result in an understanding of money as a medium of exchange.

Furth's Stages of Social Understanding and Economic Concepts

Furth's 1980 study examined additional economic concepts as part of a broader study of social concepts. He interviewed 195 English children, ages 5 through 11, and proposed a 4-stage theory describing the development of all social understanding including economic concepts. In the first stage, children ages 5 through 6 represent their social world in terms of their own personal views and desires. Furth found that children of these ages were highly imaginative and playful in their representations. Although imaginative, they were unable to distinguish between personal and societal roles. They were also unable to see beyond superficial aspects of particular events.

In the second stage, children ages 6 through 8 understood first-order societal functions, including the basic function of money as a means of exchange, but were unable to see beyond this level. They recognized the role of money in an exchange and could describe what occurred therein, but could not place the transaction within a broader scheme.

In the third stage, children ages 8 through 10 went beyond a superficial explanation of economic concepts but were limited to "part-systems." They could not coordinate multiple reasons for an economic event nor adequately relate causes and effects.

In the fourth stage, children ages 9 through 11 had developed a concrete and systematic framework for social concepts, including economic concepts. Their descriptions of economic concepts were more logical and reflective than those of children in earlier stages. However, their descriptions were highly concrete. They understood the role of money in exchange and could explain production costs and profit. They demonstrated limited understanding of the role of government in the economy or of the economy in a broad sense.

Children's Ability to Learn Economic Concepts

Research by Armento and Flores (1986), Schug (1981, 1983), and Schug and Birkey (1985) lent support to Furth's (1980) theory and to Danziger's (1958) view that there are developmental differences in children's learning of economics. These studies also provided information regarding children's ability to learn various economic concepts. Schug (1983) and Schug and Birkey (1985) interviewed preschool and first- and third-grade children about the concepts of scarcity, choice, opportunity cost, and monetary value. Younger children's responses demonstrated reasoning that was concrete and at times moralistic. As suggested by Danziger (1958), and evident in Furth's (1980) and Fox's (1978) research with specific concepts, these younger children did not understand relationships between concepts and were unable to define or explain particular economic concepts. More mature children (the older subjects) and younger children who had been involved in the greatest range of personal economic experiences relating to specific concepts were able to describe relationships between economic concepts and generally demonstrated more flexible reasoning patterns. This result supported earlier research by Sutton (1962), in which 85 children, ages 6 through 13, were interviewed. The children generally demonstrated greater verbal facility with those economic concepts with which they had some experience.

Armento and Flores (1986) identified the period between ages 5 and 7 as a time of developmental change in understanding microeconomic concepts such as work, wants, and decision making with one's own money. Armento interviewed with 355 children ages 3 through 16. Armento and Flores found certain consistencies in the responses of children younger than age 5. They tended to respond by naming specific concrete examples of the concept. They also used tautological examples, such as, "Yes, people have everything they want because they always do." A third characteristic was egocentrism; children viewed economic processes only from their own perspectives. The fourth characteristic involved responding with inaccurate and moralistic responses, such as, "No, people do not have everything they want, because Jesus don't want them to." Between 5 and 7 years of age, children's responses indicated accurate conceptions of work, wants, and scarcity and a method for making decisions.

With macroeconomic concepts, such as taxes and international trade, no developmental change was evident until ages 10 through 12. Armento and Flores suggested that children have fewer direct experiences of macroeconomic concepts and that the experiences they have are neither systematic nor focused.

The child therefore has no adequate basis for forming these concepts.

Armento and Flores (1986) found significant age-related, developmental change in children's responses to queries related to micro- and macroeconomic concepts. However, they also occasionally found that some very young children's responses were much more mature than was typical in the group and that some older children's responses were far more immature than was typical. These findings suggest that systematic exposure to direct activities with economic concepts may be important in children's development of those concepts.

Leahy (1981, 1983) studied children's development of the concept of economic inequality. (Economic inequalities exist in all but some of the most rudimentary economic systems.) This series of studies dealt with how children come to describe, explain, and usually justify economic inequalities in their society. Children ages 6 through 18 were asked to describe rich and poor people, to describe similarities and differences between them, and to discuss whether economic inequalities are appropriate and how the poor could become rich.

Leahy identified cognitive developmental differences among the subjects, as well as trends toward socialization into society's explanations for economic inequalities. Both found that the youngest children, through age 8, were able to describe differences between the rich and the poor and to offer reasons for the economic inequalities they described. Their descriptions focused on surface qualities such as differences in clothing much more than did those of older children.

In an analysis of existing research, Armento and Flores (1986) suggested that the economic content of the curriculum for young children should be contained in the ordinary transactions, relationships, and events in the child's life and community. Children should examine buying, selling, and trading transactions; the process of making goods and services; and the origin of materials and products in their everyday lives (p. 95). The curriculum should provide experiences illustrating economic concepts and thereby help students to question and organize their spontaneously generated experiences (p. 96).

Teaching Economic Concepts

How are economic concepts best taught to young children? In 2 studies, Laney (1988, 1989) investigated the effects of experience and type of concept label on first-graders' learning and retaining of economic concepts. In his 1989 study Laney used 8 intact first-grade classrooms with a total of 129 students. Four instructional treatments were used, each with 2 classrooms. An immediate posttest and a 6-week delayed posttest were used. Laney concluded that real-life experiences and invented concept labels enhance first-graders' learning and retaining of the economic concept of opportunity cost. Laney encourages teachers to introduce an economic concept by providing real-life experiences with the concept, as opposed to activities that provide only vicarious experiences. Kourilsky (1985) has reported research supporting Laney's contention that real-life experiences are more likely to result in learning than are vicarious experiences.

Hansen (1985) summarized the research relating to economic education in early childhood. He concluded that children enter kindergarten possessing an experience-based economic literacy and are therefore capable of acquiring economic concepts. He also found that economic education programs show greater student gains when teachers are well versed in economics (p. 220). Hansen has indicated that a variety of economic materials and teaching approaches are both available and effective. Evaluation procedures are also available, and new ones are being established even though they need continued refinement.

Implications

There is evidence that children as young as 5 years old can learn economic concepts and make decisions using them (Kourilsky, 1985). It is also evident that children best learn economic concepts through real-life experiences. As with some other areas in social studies education, it is not yet clear when children are developmentally ready to learn specific economic concepts or what limitations cognitive development places on their learning of economic concepts. Even if children are ready to learn a specific concept, Kourilsky (1985) suggests that this does not necessarily mean they should be taught it. She suggests, instead, that a concept should be taught if the individual is personally benefited by being able to use the concept in personal decision making or if society is benefited by the individual's ability to contribute usefully to social decision making. Further research should explore those areas, related to economic concepts and their teaching, that are not yet well understood.

POLITICAL SOCIALIZATION

Political socialization involves children's gradual development of an ability to understand their culture's political system and compare it to political systems in other cultures. The socialization process involves developing a rationale for the appropriateness of the political system in one's culture and often for the appropriateness of the political system for all cultures. The socialization of the child is important because the culture must develop responsible citizens to function in its political system.

A child who has been socialized to the culture's political system understands that certain types of behavior on the part of citizens are evaluated as deviant, whereas others are accepted. The child learns to evaluate his or her own personal behavior partly in terms of the political culture. As the child reaches higher levels of moral reasoning, the categories of acceptable and unacceptable behavior in the political system are evaluated. Such evaluation may eventually place the individual in conflict with the culture's political system or it may reaffirm the culture's evaluations of behaviors.

Considering the available body of research, Easton and Dennis (1969) concluded that the formative years in political socialization are between ages 3 and 13. Though research in this area is limited, studies involving children in preschool and the primary grades substantiate Easton and Hall's conclusion. Many more studies have been carried out with adolescents than with younger children through the elementary years. This imbalance is explained in part by the fact that researchers often use written questionnaires inappropriate for younger children.

Political Development Studies

In a 1967 study Hess and Torney surveyed approximately 12,000 children, in grades 2 through 8, in 8 U.S. cities. This study investigated children's political beliefs. Young children were found to have strong, emotional ties to their country, to governmental institutions, and to political figures in major roles, especially the president. (Children consider political figures, and particularly the president, to be people who respond personally to a citizen's requests. Younger children think, for example, that they can pick up a telephone and talk directly to the president.) Hess and Torney found that, among local political figures, the police officer was considered more important by children than the mayor. The police officer was viewed as someone who will help when the child or any member of the society needs help. Children perceived the political system as one that they could depend on and that would help them. A good citizen in such a system was identified as a good, helpful person.

Older children defined the role of the citizen in greater detail, saying that the good citizen should vote and be interested in political issues. Older children expressed the belief that citizens have power and can effect change, especially through voting.

Hess and Torney's (1967) study and those of others indicate that political development continues throughout childhood and into adolescence (Easton & Dennis, 1969; Schwartz, 1975; Allen, Freeman, & Osbourne, 1985). Children develop highly positive basic attachments to and identifications with political figures and political roles. Children's views are concrete and personal. Parker and Kaltsounis (1986) have suggested that young children have feelings about the nation and the president, and that these feelings are usually positive. Such feelings are established long before children have much understanding of the functions of president and nation.

Later studies have investigated early development in political socialization. Schwartz (1975) investigated preschool children's ability to identify political and nonpolitical authority figures and their understanding of the role of each. A group of 79 children ages 3 to 5 years responded to questions and pictures in the study. Most of the children correctly identified pictures of a police officer (90%), a mail carrier (89%), and a milk deliverer (84%). However, the president (Nixon) was not as frequently identified, although 60% said they had heard of him. Other familiar figures were George Washington (72%), Abraham Lincoln (53%), and God (84%). The children were generally less capable of appropriately describing what each of the figures discussed did. They were more capable of describing the functions of those figures they had greater experience with. Schwartz found the children (75%) were most likely to correctly describe at least 1 function of a policeman.

Allen, Freeman, and Osborne (1985) investigated children's understanding of the police. About 50% of their subjects identified the police as part of the government. In another study, a part of which investigated children's perceptions and understandings of the police, Easton and Dennis (1969) found that, around age 8, children began to describe the police less positively. Both Schwartz (1975) and Easton and Dennis (1969) concluded that children's concept of the police officer as an authoritative political figure is an important indicator of children's developing knowledge and attitude about the government.

Children's identification and understanding of the functions of the president were also investigated by Allen, Freeman, and Osborne (1985). They talked with 30 3- to 5-year-old children 5 months after the 1984 presidential election. Many of the children (60%) correctly identified Ronald Reagan as president. More children (75%) correctly identified a task associated with the presidential role. When asked, "How does somebody get to be president?" 20% of the children mentioned voting. Most of the children evaluated the president positively; their evaluation, however, was not overwhelmingly positive, as had been found in earlier studies.

Other studies have examined children's perceptions and understandings of political issues, particularly conflict. Escalona (1975, 1982) found that children were, by age 3, fearful and pessimistic about international politics and global conflicts. In an earlier study Cooper (1965) investigated 300 English children's concepts of war. He found that children can, by 7 years of age, describe war and peace, including objects associated with war, such as guns, soldiers, tanks, and planes. Generally, they were less able to respond to questions about peace. Prior to age 10, most children associated peace with friendship or positive social activity. Cooper suggested that children develop a "schema of conflict." His subjects perceived linkages between their own "play-fighting," media reports of wars, parental teachings about war, and social/interpersonal conflicts. Children may use such perceived linkages to construct a schema for reasoning about conflict.

In their 1985 study Allen, Freeman, and Osborne also investigated preschoolers' perceptions and understanding of conflict. When asked how countries resolve their disagreements, 40% mentioned violence; 40% mentioned nonviolent means such as talking and forgiving; and 10% mentioned law, social order, or appeals to authority figures such as calling the police. When asked how they solve their own disagreements, 80% mentioned nonviolent methods such as talking about the problems. Usually these children did not mention violence as a way of solving their own disagreements. Allen, Freeman, and Osborne concluded that these children accepted violence as a means to resolve conflicts on a global scale but not on an interpersonal scale.

A longitudinal study was conducted by Moore, Lare, and Wagner (1985) to investigate political socialization among young children. In 1974 they interviewed kindergartners in 5 suburban California school districts. These children were interviewed again at the end of each school year through the fourth grade. The sample included 119 lower- or middle-class boys and 124 girls, who were 81.5% Anglo and 18.5% non-Anglo. Comments of family members, especially parents, concerning candidates, issues, and governmental processes seemed to have the greatest influence on political interest and information during the first years of elementary school. Parents passed their political consciousness on to their children, but usually avoided discussion of political tensions and conflicts. Moore, Lare, and Wagner (1985) postulated that the role of the home is to promote order and unity. Accordingly, parents may delay introducing discussion of divisions in policymaking responsibility and the sources of political tension or conflict. The researchers saw this postponement as detrimental to the proper functioning of a participatory democracy (p. 221).

Three major theories have been used to explain how children become politically socialized: psychodynamic theory, social-learning theory, and cognitive developmental theory. Moore (1987) has suggested that not just 1 theory but a combination of the 3 may be more useful.

One theory used in earlier research was a psychodynamic theory, which suggests that children generalize their beliefs about authority figures from their emotional responses in regard to close authority figures, such as a parent. Therefore, children view the president very positively because of their need to believe that authority figures are benevolent (Hess & Torney, 1967). A second theory, social-learning theory, suggests that children observe and model political behaviors and attitudes of significant adults (Bandura, 1969). The third theory is a cognitive developmental theory (Piaget, 1923/1926, 1937/1954). According to this perspective, children organize and interpret their own experiences and perspectives to construct an understanding of the social and physical world (Allen, 1988). They use their personal social experiences and knowledge to interpret and understand global political events. None of the 3 theories has been used extensively in formulating research questions and hypotheses. They have been utilized more often in explaining the findings of studies regarding children's political socialization.

Implications

The research on political socialization suggests that social studies programs might best foster children's development through discussion of political personages, issues, and concerns. Because the home may actually delay children's awareness of political conflict, teachers may have to make additional efforts to introduce discussion of conflict. Researchers have noted the importance of nonpolitical experiences, such as social interaction with peers, parents, and teachers, that help children learn and generalize understanding of the political world (Schwartz, 1975). In both research and naturalistic settings, young children have been found to be intuitive political thinkers (Connell, 1971) who "not only show evidence of political socialization, but of surprisingly outspoken, idiosyncratic, blunt, and imaginative political opinions" (Coles, 1986, p. 27).

Much of the research on political socialization has not involved the use of interview methodology. Multiple interviews with students and their families, both longitudinally and with cross-sectional samples, could yield much valuable information.

SUMMARY

There is a diverse body of research literature relating to early childhood social studies. This literature has many gaps; some areas are studied more thoroughly than others. It is evident that social studies are important to the full development of children during the early childhood years. This is an area that needs to become an important part of early childhood programs. To fully address the needs of young children, however, much more research needs to be carried out in all areas of the social studies.

References

Allen, J. (1988). Children's cognition of stressful events. *Day Care and Early Education, 16*(2), 12–14.

Allen, J., Freeman, P., & Osborne, S. (1985). *Preschool political socialization.* Paper presented at the meeting of the National Association for the Education of Young Children, New Orleans, LA.

Armento, B., & Flores, S. (1986). Learning about the economic world. In V. Atwood (Ed.), *Elementary school social studies: Research as a guide to practice* (pp. 85–101). Bulletin No. 79. Washington, DC: National Council for the Social Studies.

Atkins, C. (1981). Introducing basic map and globe concepts to young children. *Journal of Geography, 80,* 228–233.

Backer, A., & Stoltman, J. (1984). The nature of geographic literacy. *ERIC Digest, 35,* 1–2. Bloomington, IN: Clearinghouse for Social Studies/Social Science Education.

Balchin, W., & Coleman, A. (1973). Progress in graphicacy. *Times Educational Supplement, 44,* 3024.

Bandura, A. (1969). Social learning theory of identificatory processes. In D. A. Gosine (Ed.), *Handbook of socialization theory and research* (pp. 213–262). Chicago: Rand McNally.

Barr, R., Barth, J., & Shermis, S. (1977). *Defining the social studies.* Washington, DC: National Council for the Social Studies.

Barsch, R. (1967). Introducing basic map and globe concepts to young children. *Journal of Geography, 80,* 228–233.

Bayley, H., & Schaefer, E. (1960). Relationships between socioeconomic variables and the behavior of mothers toward young children. *Journal of Genetic Psychology, 96,* 61–77.

Beyer, B. (1974). *Ethnicity in America.* Pittsburgh, PA: Social Studies Curriculum Center, Carnegie Mellon University.

Blaut, J., McCleary, G., Jr., & Blaut, A. (1970). Environmental mapping in young children. *Environment and Behavior, 2,* 335–349.

Blaut, J., & Stea, D. (1974). Mapping at the age of three. *Journal of Geography, 73,* 5–9.

Bloom, B. (Ed.). (1956). *Taxonomy of educational objectives. Handbook I: Cognitive domain.* New York: David McKay.

Borchert, J. (1983). Questions students ask. *Journal of Geography, 82,* 43.

Bronson, G. (1978). Aversive reactions to strangers: Adval process interpretation. *Child Development, 49,* 495–499.

Buggey, L. (1971). *A study of the relationship of classroom questions and social studies achievement of second-grade students.* Unpublished doctoral dissertation, University of Washington, Seattle.

Catling, S. (1978). The child's spatial conception and geographic education. *Journal of Geography, 77,* 24–28.

Chukowsky, K. (1963). *From two to five.* Berkeley, CA: University of California Press.

Coles, R. (1986). *The political life of children.* Boston: Atlantic Monthly Press.

Connell, R. (1971). *The child's construction of politics.* Carlton, Australia: Melbourne University Press.

Cooper, P. (1965). The development of the concept of war. *Journal of Peace Research, 21*(1), 1–17.

Cox, W. (1977). *Children's map reading abilities with large scale urban maps.* Doctoral dissertation, University of Wisconsin at Madison. Duplicated as Publication No. 78–4, Geography Curriculum Project, University of Georgia, 1978.

Crabtree, C. (1968). *Teaching geography in grades one through three: Effects of instruction in the core concept of geographic theory* (Project No. 5–1037). Washington, DC: Department of Health, Education, and Welfare, Office of Education.

Crabtree, C. (1974). *Children's thinking in the social studies, Part 1: Some factors of sequence and transfer in learning the skills of geographic analysis.* Los Angeles: University of California.

Danziger, K. (1958). Children's earliest conceptions of economic relationships. *Journal of Social Psychology, 47,* 231–240.

Diem, R. (1982). Developing chronological skills in a world history course. *Social Education, 46,* 191–194.

Donaldson, M. (1978). *Children's minds.* New York: Norton.

Easton, D., & Dennis, J. (1969). *Children in the political system: Origins of political legitimacy.* New York: McGraw-Hill.

Egan, K. (1982). Teaching history to young children. *Phi Delta Kappan, 63,* 439–441.

Engle, A. (1976). Exploring the meaning of the social studies. In P. Martorella (Ed.), *Social studies strategies: Theory into practice* (pp. 230–231). New York: Harper & Row.

Escalona, S. (1975). Children in a warring world. *American Journal of Orthopsychology, 45,* 765–772.

Escalona, S. (1982). Growing up with the threat of a nuclear war: Some indirect effects on personality development. *American Journal of Orthopsychiatry, 52,* 396–412.

Feldman, H. (1981). Beyond universals: Toward a developmental psychology of education. *Educational Researcher, 10*(9), 21–32.

Fox, K. (1978). What children bring to school: The beginnings of economic education. *Social Education, 42*(6), 478–481.

Friedman, K. (1944). Time concepts of elementary school children. *Elementary School Journal, 44,* 337–342.

Friedman, W. (1982). *The developmental psychology of time.* New York: Academic Press.

Furth, H. (1980). *The world of grown-ups: Children's conceptions of society.* New York: Elsevier North Holland.

Ghiray, E. F., Altkin, W., Vaught, G. M., & Roodin, P. A. (1976). The incidence of eidetic imagery as a function of age. *Child Development, 47,* 1207–1210.

Ginsburg, H., & Opper, S. (1988). *Piaget's theory of intellectual development* (3rd ed.). Englewood Cliffs, NJ: Prentice Hall.

Haas, M. (1988). An analysis of geographic concepts and locations in elementary social studies textbooks: Grades one through four. ERIC Document Reproduction Service No. ED 305 309.

Haas, M. (1989). Teaching geography in the elementary school. Bloomington, IN: Clearinghouse for Social Studies/Social Science Education. ERIC Digest EDO-50-89-6.

Hallam, R. (1970). Piaget and thinking in history. In M. Ballard (Ed.), *New movements in the study and teaching of history* (pp. 236–249). Bloomington, IN: Indiana University Press.

Hallam, R. (1979). Attempting to improve logical thinking in school history. *Research in Education, 21,* 1–24.

Hansen, J. (1985). The economics of early childhood education in Minnesota. *Journal of Economic Education, 24,* 219–224.

Harner, L. (1982). Talking about the past and the future. In W. Friedman (Ed.), *The developmental psychology of time* (pp. 201–234). New York: Academic Press.

Hart, R. (1971). *Aerial geography: An experiment in elementary geography.* Master's thesis, Clark University, Worcester, MA. Duplicated for distribution by Environmental Research Group, Chicago, Peace Perception Report No. 6.

Hartoonian, M. (1981). Development of decision-making ability through the use of economic content. In S. Symmes (Ed.), *Economic education: Links to the social studies* (pp. 9–27). Washington, DC: National Council for the Social Studies.

Herman, W., Jr. (1983). What should be taught where? *Social Education, 47,* 96.

Hess, R., & Torney, J. (1967). *The development of political attitudes in children.* Chicago: Aldine.

Hoffman, M. (1970). Moral development. In P. H. Mussen (Ed.), *Carmichael's manual of child psychology* (pp. 90–126). New York: Wiley.

Holloway, G. (1967). *An introduction to the child's conception of space.* New York: Humanities Press.

Imperatore, W. (1968). *Earth, man's home: A beginning geography unit.* Athens, GA: Geography Curriculum Project.

Jahoda, G. (1963). Children's concepts of time and history. *Educational Review, 15,* 87–107.

Joint Committee on Geographic Education of the National Council for Geographic Education and Association of American Geographers. (1984). *Guidelines for geographic education: Elementary and secondary schools.* Washington, DC: The Association of American Geographers. (ERIC/CHESS Document Reproduction Service No. ED 252 453).

Kenworthy, L. (1980). *Social studies for the eighties in elementary and middle schools* (3rd ed.). New York: Wiley.

Kirman, J. (1977). The use of infrared color satellite images by grades 3, 4, and 5 pupils and teachers. *Alberta Journal of Educational Research, 23,* 52–64.

Kirman, J. (1981). Use of "band 5" black-and-white Landsat images in the elementary grades. *Journal of Geography, 80,* 224–228.

Kirman, J. (1984). A new elementary level map skill: Landsat "band 5" satellite images. *Social Education, 48,* 191–195.

Klett, F., & Alpaugh, D. (1976). Environmental learning and large-scale environments. In G. Moore and R. Coledge (Eds.), *Environmental Knowing: Theories, research, and methods* (pp. 121–130). Stroudsburg, PA: Dowden, Hutchinson and Ross.

Kohlberg, L. (1969). Stage and sequence: The cognitive developmental approach to socialization. In D. Goslin (Ed.), *Handbook of socialization theory and research* (pp. 118–140). Chicago: Rand McNally.

Kourilsky, M. (1985). *Children's use of cost-benefit analysis: Developmental or non-existent.* Paper presented at the annual meeting of the American Educational Research Association, Chicago. (ERIC Document Reproduction Service No. ED 261 948.)

Kourilsky, M., & Hirshleifer, J. (1976). Mini-society vs. token economy: An experimental comparison of the effects on learning and autonomy of socially emergent and imposed behavior modification. *Journal of Educational Research, 69,* 376–389.

Kuczynski, L. (1984). Socialization goals and mother-child interaction: Strategies for long-term and short-term compliance. *Developmental Psychology, 20,* 1061–1073.

Kuczynski, L., Kochanska, G., Radke-Yarrow, M., & Girnius-Brown, O. (1987). A developmental interpretation of children's noncompliance. *Developmental Psychology, 23,* 799–806.

Kurtines, W., & Greif, E. (1974). The development of moral thought: Review and evaluation of Kohlberg's approach. *Psychological Bulletin, 81,* 453–470.

Lanegran, D., Snowfield, J., & Laurent, A. (1970). Retarded children and the concepts of distance and direction. *Journal of Geography, 69,* 157–160.

Laney, J. (1988). Can economic concepts be learned and remembered? A pilot comparison of elementary school students at three grade levels. *Journal of Educational Research, 82,* 99–105.

Laney, J. (1989). Experience- and concept-label-type effects on first-graders' learning, retention of economic concepts. *Journal of Educational Research, 83,* 231–236.

Laurendeau, M., & Pinard, A. (1968). *Les premières notions spatiales de l'enfant* [The first spatial understandings in the child]. Montreal: Delachaux & Niestle.

Leahy, R. (1981). The development of the conception of economic inequality, I. Descriptions and comparisons of rich and poor people. *Child Development, 52,* 523–532.

Leahy, R. (1983). Development of the conception of economic inequality: II. Explanations, justifications, and concepts of social mobility and change. *Child Development, 111*–125.

Levstik, L., & Pappas, C. (1987). Exploring the development of historical understanding. *Journal of Research and Development in Education, 21,* 1–14.

Michaelis, J. (1985). *Social studies for children: A guide to basic instruction.* Englewood Cliffs, NJ: Prentice Hall.

Moore, S. (1987, April). *Piaget and Bandura: The need for a unified theory of learning.* Paper presented at the meeting of the Society for Research in Child Development, Baltimore, MD.

Moore, S., Lare, J., & Wagner, K. (1985). *The child's political world: A longitudinal perspective.* New York: Praeger.

Muir, S. (1985). *Teaching time concepts to young children.* Paper presented at the annual meeting of the National Council for the Social Studies, Chicago.

National Council for the Social Studies. (1983). Definition of the social studies. Washington, DC: National Council for the Social Studies.

Neperud, R. (1977). The development of children's graphic representations for the large-scale environment. *Journal of Environmental Education, 8,* 57–65.

Oakden, E., & Sturt, M. (1922). The development of the knowledge of time in children. *British Journal of Psychology, 12,* 309–336.

Parker, W., & Kaltsounis, T. (1986). Citizenship and law-related development. In V. Atwood (Ed.), *Elementary school social studies: Research as a guide to practice* (pp. 59–71). Bulletin No. 79. Washington, DC: National Council for the Social Studies.

Parpal, M., & Maccoby, E. (1985). Maternal responsiveness and subsequent child compliance. *Child Development, 56,* 1326–1334.

Peel, E. (1965). Intellectual growth during adolescence. *Educational Review, 17,* 165–180.

Piaget, J. (1923/1926). *The language and thought of the child.* (M. Gabain, Trans.). New York: Harcourt, Brace & World.

Piaget, J. (1937/1954). *The moral judgment of the child.* (M. Gabain, Trans.). New York: Basic Books.

Piaget, J. (1964). *The early growth of logic in the child.* (E. A. Lunzer & D. Papert, Trans.). London: Routledge & Kegan Paul.

Piaget, J. (1970). *The child's conception of time.* (A. Pomerans, Trans.). New York: Basic Books.

Piaget, J., & Inhelder, B. (1967). *The child's conception of space.* New York: Norton.

Rice, M., & Cobb, R. (1978). *What can children learn in geography?: A review of the research.* Boulder, CO: Social Science Education Consortium.

Rushdoony, H. (1968). A child's ability to read maps: Summary of the research. *Journal of Geography, 67,* 213–222.

Sauvy, J., & Sauvy, S. (1972). *The child's discovery of space.* Baltimore, MD: Penguin.

Savage, T., Jr., & Bacon, P. (1969). Teaching symbolic map skills with primary-grade children. *Journal of Geography, 68,* 326–332.

Schug, M. (1981). What educational research says about the development of economic thinking. *Theory and Research in Social Education, 45*(3), 25–36.

Schug, M. (1983). The development of economic thinking in children and adolescents. *Social Education, 47*(2), 141–145.

Schug, M., & Birkey, J. (1985). The development of children's economic reasoning. *Theory and Research in Social Education, 49,* 231–244.

Schwartz, S. (1975). Preschoolers and politics. In D. Schwartz & S. Schwartz (Eds.), *New directions in political socialization* (pp. 229–253). New York: Free Press.

Selman, R. (1971). The relation of role-taking to the development of moral judgment in children. *Child Development, 42,* 79–92.

Selman, R. (1976). Social-cognitive understanding: A guide to educational and clinical practice. In T. Lickona (Ed.), *Moral development and behavior* (pp. 115–140). New York: Holt, Rinehart & Winston.

Senesh, L. (1963). *Our working world: Families at work.* Chicago: Science Research Associates.

Shaffer, D. (1988). *Social and personality development.* Pacific Grove, CA: Brooks/Cole.

Siegal, M., & Cowan, J. (1984). Appraisals of intervention: The mother's versus the culprit's behavior as determinants of children's evaluations of discipline techniques. *Child Development, 55,* 1760–1766.

Sleeper, M. (1975). A developmental framework for history education in adolescence. *School Review, 84,* 91–107.

Spieseke, A. (1963). Developing a sense of time and chronology. In H. Carpenter (Ed.), *Skill development in social studies, 33rd yearbook* (pp. 61–86). Washington, DC: National Council for the Social Studies.

Stassen Berger, K. (1980). *The developing person.* New York: Worth.

Stoltman, J., & Goolsby, T. (1973). Developing map skills through reading instruction. *Journal of Geography, 72,* 32–36.

Sunal, C. (1990). *Early childhood social studies.* Columbus, OH: Merrill.

Sunal, C., & Haas, M. (1993). *Social studies for the elementary and middle school student.* Fort Worth, TX: Holt, Rinehart & Winston.

Sunal, C., & Sunal, D. (1978). Space concepts for young children. *Day Care and Early Education, 5*(4), 33–41.

Sutton, R. (1962). Behavior in the attainment of economic concepts. *Journal of Psychology, 53,* 37–46.

Thornton, S., & Vukelich, R. (1988). Effects of children's understanding of time concepts on historical understanding. *Theory and Research in Social Education, 16*(1), 69–82.

Thornton, S., & Wenger, N. (1989). *Geographic education in the elementary school: Current practices and the prospects for reform.* Paper presented at the American Educational Research Association, San Francisco, March 27–31.

Tyler, J. (1971). *A study of the relationship of two methods of question presentation, sex, and school location to the social studies achievement of second-grade children.* Unpublished doctoral dissertation, University of Washington, Seattle.

Vukelich, R. (1984). Time language for interpreting history collections to children. *Museum Studies Journal, 4*(1), 43–50.

Zaccaria, M. (1978). The development of historical thinking: Implications for the teaching of history. *History Teacher, 11,* 323–340.

·13·

THE ARTS AND EARLY CHILDHOOD EDUCATION: A COGNITIVE DEVELOPMENTAL PORTRAIT OF THE YOUNG CHILD AS ARTIST

Jessica Davis and Howard Gardner

HARVARD GRADUATE SCHOOL OF EDUCATION

A BRIEF AND FAMILIAR STORY: THE "GIFT" IN ACTION

It's September, and all the kindergarten children are seated at tables in their classroom. They are engrossed in the process of drawing with crayons on 10 × 12–inch sheets of newsprint. The teacher has asked them to draw pictures of their families; and as she walks from table to table, she is both warmed and amused by the drawings. The figures have a generic quality to them: Except for a circle of curls around the face, Lucy's mother is presented in much the same way as her father (Figure 13–1). The representations are spare, economical, and effective. Indeed, as simple and primitive as the drawings appear, there is a human quality about all of them, a poignancy in the tilt of one figure's head or the solidity of presentation of 4 stalwart family members comfortably filling and weighting the page. The teacher is momentarily transported; hadn't she had a similar sensation of being wrapped in feeling and form when she passed through the modern wing of her local art museum last weekend?

Lucy has drawn a large version of her mother to the extreme left of the page, a similar version of her father next to the mother, a similar shape and size for herself; but squeezed into the extreme right of the page, a tiny version of her brother who in real life is 4 years older and 2 heads taller than Lucy. There is a vitality about the drawing, a nice sense of the whole. Indeed Lucy adds some tall scribbly lines squeezed in next to the extreme left of the page near her presentation of her mother, as if to balance the tiny tilted version of her brother on the extreme right. Aware of the teacher's inquisitive gaze over her shoulder, Lucy stares at the twisted lines and considers them for a moment—almost as if they had been drawn by someone else. Adding a few circles to the lines, she looks up at her teacher and explains, "My mother likes flowers."

"What a lovely drawing!" the teacher exclaims, "Can you tell me about it?" "Well this is my mother," Lucy begins, and as she speaks, the teacher prints on top of each figure in that perfect script that only teachers of very young children can produce: "My mother. My father. Me. My brother." And finally in the space that is left, the teacher writes in bold letters across the top of the page: "Lucy's family." Gently touching Lucy's little shoulder, the teacher whispers in her ear: "Nice work."

DRAWING AS A FRAGILE GIFT

Preschool children display such a fluid and constructive rapport with the world of ideas, feelings, and symbols that they may aptly be described as flourishing in a "golden age of

Research efforts described in this manuscript have been generously supported by the Rockefeller Brothers Fund, the Rockefeller Foundation, and the Lilly Endowment. We gratefully acknowledge the support and useful feedback provided by Bernard Spodek.

191

FIGURE 13–1.

creativity" (Gardner, 1982). In the symbolic domain of language, they make verbal associations that are reminiscent of poetry; in the symbolic domain of play, they display an ability to "suspend disbelief" evocative of real theater; and in the symbolic domain of drawing, their work bears at least a surface resemblance to museum-quality modern art. As the school years progress, however, "the incidence of spontaneous metaphoric speech appears to decline" (Winner, 1988, p. 103); dramatic play gives way to rule-governed games (Piaget, 1962); and the expressive drawings of the preschooler are replaced by convention-bound representations that apparently disappoint both the child who draws them (Rosenstiel & Gardner, 1977) and the adult who hopes to appreciate them (Rosenblatt & Winner, 1988). For most children, the constrained and conventionalized drawings of middle childhood are their last real attempts at graphic representation (Gardner, 1982); by adolescence, they have forever abandoned the activity of drawing (Winner, 1982). In short, Lucy and the other 5-year-old children in our story display a glowing facility with graphic symbols that can and has been regarded as a kind of gift—a gift that appears to be quite fragile. For the majority of children, this gift has been lost by the time they have completed elementary school.

The designation of this facility as a "gift" derives from the serious comparisons that have been made between the art of the young child and that of the professional artist by scholars, researchers, and art educators (e.g., Arnheim, 1969; Gardner, 1973, 1979, 1980, 1982; Gardner & Winner, 1982; Gardner, Wolf, & Phelps, 1990; Lowenfeld, 1939; Read, 1943; Schaefer-Simmern, 1948; Winner, 1982). This nascent ability has been revered by artists as well (see e.g., the Expressionists in Leeds, 1989).

"Once I drew like Raphael," Pablo Picasso exclaimed, "but it has taken me a whole lifetime to learn to draw like children" (quoted in Gardner, 1980, p. 8). At first glance, one might think that Picasso was actually referring to those of his adult drawings that look as if they had been created by a young child (see, for example, Arnheim, 1962, p. 36). However, it is more likely that Picasso was referring to the attitude young children have toward their drawing, an attitude that many artists seek to recapture. It has been described as a kind of courage and freedom of expression (Davis, 1989); a gleeful lack of regard for the comments of others (Gardner, 1982); a directness of approach and "plasticity of mind" (Leeds, 1989); and even as a level of engagement characteristic of optimal experience or *flow* (Csikszentmihalyi, 1990).

As surely as involvement is hailed as common ground, intention is most often cited as the demarcation between the drawings of artists and children. Equipped with the ability to achieve a range of effects in graphic representation, artists are able to make intentional choices that children seem unable to make (Gardner, 1973, 1980, 1982; Winner, 1982). The child, drawing spontaneously, violates (or fails to achieve) those mandates of representational form that the artist may consciously choose to ignore. The differences, of course, are less surprising than the similarities. We expect there to be differences between the work of novices and experts, especially those separated by such a large span of development and training. The fact that there are real similarities, however, is compelling: It places in a new light what might otherwise be thought of as the romantic notion of the child as artist, or of the preschool child arriving on the scene of school as a bearer of gifts.

The similarities have been deemphasized in traditional approaches that consider the youngest child's drawings to be crude and inadequate (see, e.g., Stern, 1924). Such approaches are guided by the notion that "aesthetic aim" reflects a conscious attempt to represent objects in the physical world on paper as they actually appear to the human eye. From this vantage point, the freely expressive drawings of young children are far less comparable to the work of artists than are the more constrained and clearly representational efforts of older children. From our perspective, the convention-bound drawings of middle childhood are distanced from the work of artists and young children whose convention-free drawings merit real comparison (Rosenblatt & Winner, 1988).

The place of honor assigned to the young child in our comparison challenges the traditional view of the preschool child as an empty slate ready to receive the imprints of early education. To be sure, such recent didactic approaches as "active" or "independent" learning have encouraged teachers to foster ways of empowering young children to engrave their own slates in their own manner. Still, the preschool child is most often regarded as deficient—lacking the crucial competences, which school will impart. This "deficit" view contrasts with our portrait of the preschool child as glittering in a golden age of creativity too soon to turn lackluster.

We maintain that young children come to school exhibiting a certain form of mastery in symbolic expression that is all too frequently lost throughout the early years of schooling. In sharp contrast to the usual picture of development from absence to achievement of a competence, we propose that the challenge in graphic activity is to maintain and sustain an early proclivity. Regardless of whether our claim is accepted, the fact that most children do indeed stop drawing sometime in middle childhood is not debatable. The abandonment or loss of this facility may reflect a natural course of development—that is, few of us were meant to grow up to be artists anyway. More fearfully, the acquisition of "school" knowledge or the school's reflection of the culture's lack of regard for the domain may account for the child's growing disenchantment with graphic symbolization.

Why should the early childhood educator care whether children lose interest in such a specialized activity as drawing? Traditionally, art educators have valued drawing because it provides an open release for sensibilities and emotions—an outlet for expression of inner being (Lowenfeld & Brittain, 1964). Classroom teachers dedicated to more "intellectual" goals may have devalued it for the same reason. The last 30 years, however, have seen a change in a way researchers and educators regard this activity; a change brought about by what is known as the cognitive revolution. This is a revolution in the way that scholars and researchers think about human thought and action. One very important and relevant reconceptualization that has resulted from this major change in thought concerns the strong lines that have been traditionally drawn between emotion and intellect. A cognitive approach demands a redrawing of these lines and a consequent change in approach toward drawing on the part of both art educators and classroom teachers (Burton, Lederman, & London, 1988; Smith, 1989).

From a cognitive perspective, the loss of the ability to employ graphic symbols freely is not so easily dismissed as the loss of an outlet for energy or emotion. This loss must instead be reconsidered as the loss of an ability to construct understanding or knowledge—an ability to participate through production and perception in the trafficking of expressive symbols that represent and define human culture.

In this chapter we review research into children's drawing undertaken from a cognitive perspective. We begin by arming our reader with a basic understanding of a cognitive approach to children's drawing: specifically, the origins of that perspective and some relevant contemporary variations. Next, we address the questions of where the young child's gift comes from and where it goes. In other words, we apply a cognitive lens to the young child's development in graphic symbolization from preschool scribbling to the apparent disappearance of the behavior. We consider the role that the acquisition of school knowledge plays in this disappearance. Application of a cognitive approach to the concept of the child as artist reviews the theories we have discussed and lays the groundwork for our conclusion: a discussion of the educational implications of the proposed view of early graphic symbolization.

A COGNITIVE APPROACH

In the mid-1950s the behaviorist approach to learning was already stagnant, if not on the decline. At the same time, interest in the digital electronic computer as a model of human thought was on the rise. Where behaviorism had focused on visible external behavior, interest was turning to processes of thought that transpired out of sight, inside the confines of the human brain or the electronic computer. At this juncture, a view of children's learning known as the *cognitive approach* began to take hold (see Gardner, 1985).

Origins of the Approach

Two founding figures of the cognitive approach to human development were the Genevan genetic epistemologist Jean Piaget (see, e.g., Piaget, 1962, and Piaget & Inhelder, 1948) and the Soviet psychologist Lev Vygotsky (see, e.g., 1978, 1987). Both of these influential figures were interested in the effects of the child's interaction with external realities and the internal conceptualizations that the child forms and constructs. For both of these cognitivists, these internal conceptualizations change predictably with development.

Piaget saw this change progressing in hierarchical levels or stages, with each new understanding facilitated by the last. According to Piaget, the child progresses from physical actions upon physical objects (a form of early intelligence he identified as "sensorimotor") to mental actions upon abstract concepts (an advanced stage of knowledge which he identified as "formal operations"). His concern was primarily with the internal structures that the child constructs: internal versions (*mental representations*) of reality that inform and are informed by external reality. Piaget's interest in drawing, therefore, was as an external indicator of the state of the child's internal understanding (see, e.g., Piaget & Inhelder, 1948).

Accordingly, in considering Lucy's drawing of her family, Piaget might have attended to her attempts to balance her view of each part of the drawing (i.e., each person) with her understanding of the whole (i.e., the whole family). For Piaget the developing child struggles to balance and maintain knowledge of each part with a simultaneous and larger understanding of the whole; and clearly Lucy is as yet unable to see objects in proper relation to one another. Indeed, Piaget would say that Lucy drew herself as large as the other members of the family because, like all young children, she is basically "egocentric"—not selfish, but unable to differentiate self and personal viewpoint from the rest of the world.

Vygotsky's interest centered on the social context through which children inform and operationalize their internal conceptualizations. Social context provides symbolic tools (such as spoken or written language), which the child internalizes and employs to give form to thought. Through symbols, the child can also make private thought public, that is, known to others. According to Vygotsky, children's drawings are "first-order symbols"; that is to say they directly denote objects or actions. Second-order symbols such as written words, on the other hand, stand for the spoken symbols for objects or actions. Children learn to write by appreciating that the marks they put on paper can refer not only to objects, but also to spoken words. In this way the activity of drawing becomes a form of "written speech" (1978, p. 115).

Vygotsky would have noted Lucy's reaction to the scribbles she added to the extreme left of her drawing ("she considers them for a moment—almost as if they had been drawn by someone else"). The "naming of presentations" after they are drawn was of interest to Vygotsky. He considered that phenomenon a step in the child's development of the ability to *plan*, a most important feature in problem solving (see 1987). Given his emphasis on social context, he would certainly call attention to Lucy's awareness of her teacher's interest in and attempt to understand what was happening in Lucy's drawing. A developing awareness of one's self as a part of a larger social and cultural whole propels a developing desire to communicate through the symbols of one's culture.

These early theorists redirected psychological thought from its former preoccupation with overt actions in the world (behaviorism) or with underlying unconscious motivation (Freudian theory). The behaviorist approach's focus on visible external action had overlooked the internal human facilities of conceptualizing and problem solving. Piaget awakened interest in the internal structures that constituted knowledge.

Vygotsky awakened interest in the ability of externally encountered symbols to mediate and communicate the child's processes of thought.

In a Freudian approach, symbols were regarded from outside in, as unintended external "clues" to hidden inner feelings. The cognitive approach readjusted the lens to a view from inside out: Symbols were regarded as carefully chosen building blocks in the construction of a world view (Bruner, 1986). Our understanding of expression through visual images was hereby transformed from a view of unconscious release of emotion to one of conscious construction of meaning.

Contemporary Variations

While Jean Piaget and Lev Vygotsky are traditionally regarded as the founders of the cognitive view in developmental psychology, that view has recently been adopted and expanded by a number of contemporary theorists. Here we review 2 principal approaches.

Information Processing. Embracing the notion that the electronic computer is a model of human thought, cognitivists of the information-processing disposition take a mechanistic view of cognition as, broadly speaking, the receipt, storage, manipulation, and issuing of information. Contemporary information processors have described the "software" with which the human child is equipped at birth, and developed theories sufficiently detailed to be tested by means of computer simulation (see Case, 1985; Siegler, 1986).

Information-processing theories illustrate a contemporary focus on the cognitive strategies children employ to solve the problems before them. In drawing, the problem at hand is seen as the mapping, articulation, and organization of spatial relationships perceived in the physical world and transferred onto paper. These issues have guided much of the research into children's drawing undertaken by such cognitive developmentalists as Freeman (1980), Goodnow (1977), Golomb (1983, 1992), and Willats (1977). These researchers investigate children's strategies for planning, sequencing, and deciding upon acceptable equivalences in the representation of a 3-dimensional world on a 2-dimensional plane.

Cognitivist Jacqueline Goodnow (1977) applies an information-processing approach to children's drawings that appear to be drawn with an "aerial perspective"—for example, a portrayal of a train drawn with 2 wheels on the top, and 2 wheels on the bottom. Although one might be tempted to view this drawing as manifestation of a sophisticated use of perspective, Goodnow suspected it was a result of an error in planning. In one study she and Roslyn Dawes presented children with the task of completing a drawing of a train that had 2 big wheels already filling the space on the bottom. They found that the addition of 2 wheels to the empty space on the top was indeed one solution to the problem presented by a lack of space on the bottom (1977, pp. 45–6).

Consider again the spatial organization of Lucy's drawing in which she has drawn a large portrayal of all but her older brother, who is squeezed into the space to the right. One interpretation of this arrangement might be that the child has drawn largest the figures she cares most about; or smallest the figure who represents the person with whom she has most difficulty dealing (see Edwards, 1979; Lowenfeld & Brittain, 1964; also see Coles, 1967, for a discussion of an important variation on this approach). Information-processing theorists, however, would no doubt be more likely to attribute the composition to an error in planning; that is, there wasn't enough space left for Lucy to render the brother the same size as the other members of her family.

Reflecting its Piagetian origins as well as its information-processing overtones, Case's theory (1985) posits 4 general stages of cognitive development. Each stage is marked by changes in an executive control strategy that is constrained by the increasing capacity of the young child's short-term memory storage space (1985, p. 415). In the tradition of Piaget, research into children's drawing deriving from Case's theory considers the extent to which drawing reflects the more general cognitive development described in his theory—for example, the relationship between capacity of working memory and performance on drawing tasks (Dennis, 1984).

Accordingly, in one study the drawing tasks involved the request for increasingly more numerous and complex elements to be interrelated in a drawing (Dennis, 1991). For example, the first task was to draw a human figure; the second, a girl and a tree; and so forth up until the fifth and most complex task. The successful completion of a task indicated the extent to which the subject was able to legislate the various components of the elicitation. In assessing the child's ability to differentiate and integrate these various components, the emphasis in this work is on the "what" of the drawing—that is, the number of specific elements of content differentiated and integrated into a structural whole. These researchers have found that working memory accounts for "some of the variance in drawing performance within an age group" (Dennis, 1991, p. 235). This research exemplifies a recent information-processing approach to drawing: The view of the child is of a draftsman coordinating more general cognitive skills in the service of spatial organization.

Symbol Systems. The symbol systems approach is a variety of cognitive theory that pays special attention to the arts. Rather than situating drawing within the larger sphere of cognitive development, as information processors do, symbol systems researchers isolate the behavior and consider the unique cognitive strategies that control it.

At the heart of the symbol systems approach is the distinction between *presentational* symbols (e.g., the lines used in drawing or the gestures used in dance) in which constitutive properties of the symbol itself are important and conspire with reference to embody meaning; and *discursive* or notational symbols (e.g., words or musical notation) whose construction is typically arbitrary and which "refer to" rather than "embody" meaning (after Langer, 1957). Presentational symbols need to be appreciated in their entirety and invite multiple interpretations; discursive forms of symbolization can be discretely ordered and precisely analyzed.

Lucy's graphic representations of the members of her family are examples of nondiscursive symbols; the words the teacher adds to the page are discursive symbols. Lucy's graphic representations embody joy and animation; the teacher's words indicate which figure represents which family member. Where presentational or nondiscursive symbols *may* be more expressive, discursive or notational symbols *may* be more exact. Both discursive and nondiscursive symbols interact with other symbols of their kind to define the distinct systems of symbols from which the various symbolic productions of our culture emerge.

Symbol systems researchers explore the development of symbolic competences, especially in the arts. Their research considers the different symbolic domains outlined by philosopher Nelson Goodman (1976), including language, gesture, music, and visual art; the aesthetic dimensions described by the gestalt psychologist of art, Rudolf Arnheim (1974); and the precepts of stage-like development launched by Jean Piaget (Piaget & Inhelder, 1969). Much of the research that is guided by a symbol systems approach has been carried out at Harvard's Project Zero. Founded by Goodman in 1967, the Zero in the title was meant to represent the state of knowledge about an arts education that would view the arts as a cognitive domain and aesthetics as criteria for symbolic functioning (Gardner & Perkins, 1989).

Developmentalists who consider performance in specific symbolic domains as reflective of more general cognitive processes (as Piaget and Case regard drawing) disregard differences in media and materials and assume that these processes obtain irrespective of such differences. Symbol systems researchers, however, have sought to discover the extent to which "knowledge how" in one symbolic domain does or does not predict performance in any other. From early longitudinal studies of the development of symbolic functioning (e.g., Gardner & Wolf, 1983), it was discovered that different symbol systems offer problems to the symbol user that are *system-specific* and require *system-specific solutions*. The problem of working out the basic relations to pitch that obtain in a musical scale is one example of a system-specific problem. Such problems and solutions were identified as "streams." Certain other symbolic capacities, such as the ability to vest symbols with analogic resemblance to their referents (analogical mapping), have implications across symbolic domains and were designated as "waves" (Gardner & Wolf, 1983). A brief review of symbol systems theory with relation to the domain of the visual arts facilitates further discussion of the cognitive development of the child as artist.

In his seminal work *Languages of Art* (1976), Goodman proposes that aesthetic symbols are not necessarily different from any other symbols; rather they are ordinary symbols exploited by the symbol user in such a way that their aesthetic properties demand the perceiver's attention (1976, p. 229). A willow tree is perceived in one way when it is being inspected for disease and in quite another when the passive hanging of its branches is perceived as sorrowful. Just as Goodman maintains that "the properties a symbol expresses are its own property" (1976, p. 86), the gestalt psychologist Rudolf Arnheim attributes the sorrowfulness of the willow to the shape of its branches— "the phenomenon in question is actually present in the object of perception" (1966, p. 64).

From this perspective, children as artists are confronted with the problem of exploiting the aesthetic potential of the symbols they are using to construct meaning. In order for the drawing being created to be expressive, according to Goodman, it must "metaphorically exemplify" that expression. In other words, in order for a drawing, for example, to express sadness, it must both refer to sadness as well as exemplify sadness or BE (like the sad willow) itself a sad drawing—but only metaphorically; a drawing, like a tree, cannot literally be sad.

How might the child achieve expression? Like the artist, the child may do so by employing line and composition in the construction of this effect. The notion that expression results from such construction helps resolve the conflict between emotion and cognition that is inherent in a cognitive approach to the arts (see Scheffler, 1986). Expression has traditionally marked the demarcation between emotion and cognition in art; in this context, expression of emotion emerges as a cognitive construct.

Two means for "constructing" expression may be distinguished as *repleteness of line* and *balance of composition*. A line will always have properties such as shape, direction, and width, but they will not always be of concern to the perceiver of that line. When these qualities have inextricable attachment to the meaning expressed (e.g., as in presentational symbols above), Goodman considers the line to be relatively "replete" (1976, p. 229). Compare the direction of the lines Lucy has employed to describe the lower appendages of her drawings of her mother and father. The resultant difference in the presentation of these 2 figures would be of little importance to the geometry student who is counting Lucy's "ankles" as acute angles. However, that difference completely transforms the feeling of movement derived from the figures by a perceiver who is experiencing the whole drawing. What is insignificant in the description of 4 acute angles is "replete" when it determines the expressive stance of the figures.

Balance in composition also achieves expressive effects (Arnheim, 1974; for example, remember Lucy's teacher's reaction, "the solidity of presentation"). All drawings have composition; composition is the drawing's structure or organizing system. The frame around the drawing (even as the edges of the piece of paper on which it is drawn) defines a space removed from ordinary space, an "aesthetic space" (Maquet, 1986, p. 129) that is governed by visual order (Arnheim, 1971). When this ordering is unified, the drawing is considered to be balanced and its expressive statement, intelligible (Arnheim, 1974; Lowenfeld & Brittain, 1964; Nicolaides, 1969).

Balance can be achieved either symmetrically, where shapes of equal size are perceived as balanced from side to side or top to bottom (Lucy's drawing is an example of symmetrical balance); or asymmetrically, where, for example, a large dense shape in a lower-right quadrant is balanced by a smaller shape in the higher-left quadrant. Just as differences in replete lines achieve different perceptual experiences, the different sorts of balance achieve different sorts of responses from the audience. Without balance, however, "the artistic statement becomes incomprehensible" (Arnheim, 1974, p. 20).

Theories created with special attention to the arts are concerned less with the "what" of the drawing (e.g., enumeration of elements represented on the page) and more with the "how" of the drawing (e.g., the ways in which whatever is being presented is accomplished and its effects upon the perceiver). In order to appreciate this distinction, consider the drawing that is made in response to Task 5 in Dennis's study described above: "In this task, children were asked to depict the two scenes (a "mother in house" scene and a "son in park" scene) such that the mother (in scene 1) can see the face of her son (depicted in scene 2) but not his body, because the body is hidden behind a tree" (Dennis, 1991; p. 231). From an information-processing perspective, the child as problem solver facing this task has many elements to consider, including the content details of scene as well as the spatial structure (the coordination of 2 3-dimensional scenes interrelating to one another).

In contrast, symbol systems researchers might consider whether the expression portrayed on the face of the mother reveals concern for the whereabouts of the child; whether the line quality of the drawing embodies distress or playfulness; whether the composition reflects considerations of the balancing of forms in an aesthetic space. In short, contemporary theories that have been created with attention to the arts attend specifically to the aesthetic aspects of the symbols (e.g., expression) as unique achievements of cognitive development, and less to the components in drawing that may reflect more general cognitive skills (e.g., the capacity of working memory). The symbols themselves and the problems inherent therein comprise the object of attention, not their processing as bits of information.

DEVELOPMENT OF THE "GIFT": APPLYING THE COGNITIVE APPROACH

With some basic theories, vocabulary, and criteria at hand, we can now consider the developmental trajectory of the child's "gift" in graphic symbolization through a cognitive lens.

An Overview: U-Shaped Development

The development we describe has been labeled "U-shaped." This U-shaped behavioral growth in "the ways one represents one's world" is usually marked by 3 phases in which (1) the behavior appears—one high point in the U; (2) it disappears— the floor of the U; and (3) it apparently reappears—the other high point of the U (Strauss, 1982, p. 2). For the majority, the U-shaped development in drawing is not completed. As most individuals do not ascend to the other high point in the U, their development converts the U into a simpler downward slope. Only those who go on to become amateur or professional artists experience the third phase and exemplify the reappearance and/or full development of the behavior. For the majority, phase 2, or the "disappearance" of the behavior, marks its permanent cessation (Davis, 1991; Gardner & Winner, 1982). In the portrait of development that follows, we document the appearance and disappearance (phases 1 and 2) of this development.

Through the cognitive lens we apply, drawing is regarded as *meaning making*, that is, the construction and communication of understanding through graphic symbols. Indeed, our developmental portrait of the child as artist can be clarified as a portrait of the attainment of symbolic literacy in the cognitive domain of the visual arts. Becoming "literate" in a symbolic code involves the ability to "write" (in the visual arts, "produce") the "language" (in the visual arts, the "language of forms"), and "read" (in the visual arts, "perceive" and "conceptualize"). We can therefore frame our discussion of this development within the parameters of *production* and *perception*.

Symbolic Literacy: Production

We begin our discussion of production with a description of early development in the visual arts from early marks to stereotypical schemes (see also Chapman, 1978; May, 1989; and Wilson & Wilson, 1981 for a skeptical view of the "stage approach"). The discussion of production is further informed by symbols systems research into the child's control of the aesthetic properties of expression and composition, and is offset by a review of research into the perception or "reading" of graphic symbolization.

The Early Stages. The first stage of graphic symbolization to which most researchers attend is the scribbling that children 2 or 3 years of age seem to enjoy. From a cognitive approach, this early scribbling may be considered either as outward manifestation of Piaget's sensorimotor stage or as a form of early symbolization. John Matthews (1989) holds with the first interpretation and has isolated 3 basic forms of "mark making" (the "vertical arc," the "horizontal arc," and "push-pull" action) as physical explorations that he claims are necessary precursors for later drawing activity.

As symbolic representations, however, these sensorimotor explorations of form might seem to be "purposeless pencilings." Dennie Wolf has defended scribbling from that charge, challenging the scope of a concept of symbolization that would consider these earliest drawings as meaningless scratches when they are produced by the same 2-years-olds who are rampant symbolizers in pretend play, block building, and the articulation of metaphoric connections (1983; 1988, p. 236). Wolf claims that children as young as 2 have acquired the more general ability to negotiate what Vygotsky has called a "transfer of meaning" (1978, p. 98), that is, to separate meaning and assign it to an object of choice (Biber, 1967, 1984; Kellogg, 1969; Piaget, 1962; Smith, 1979). The child may demonstrate this acquisition by using a hairbrush as a telephone in pretend play; by identifying certain piles of blocks as garages; or by calling a playful friend a "monkey." It seems unlikely that, once achieved, this cognitive developmental prerequisite to the employment of first-order symbols would not be manifest in some way in drawing as well as in these other symbolic domains.

Indeed, Claire Golomb has demonstrated that the same young children who scribble when they engage in free drawing are able to assign meanings to their drawings when they "draw on dictation." Specifically, they represent and properly place the parts of the body on elicited drawings of human figures if they are instructed to do so by a researcher (Golomb,

1974). We would not mean to suggest that these findings indicate that young children's scribbling is (at this stage) a choice made among many options for graphic symbolization. However, these findings indicate that it is shortsighted to dismiss scribbling merely as an output of physical energy when it is more reasonably some sort of agent of meaning employed by budding symbolizers.

The activity of "naming presentations" (see Vygotsky, 1978, p. 28; Stern, 1924), "romancing" (Gardner, 1980; Winner, 1982), or "fortuitous realism" (Luquet in Piaget & Inhelder, 1969, p. 64) also invites contrasting interpretations. When children 3 or 4 years of age announce the object of representation in their drawings after their drawings have been completed, they may be "romancing," or only acting "as if" they had a meaning in mind when they began. However, they may just as possibly be exhibiting a working knowledge of symbolic functioning—that is, they already apprehend that symbols represent referents that are determined by the symbolizer (consider again Lucy's post hoc decision that her scribbles were flowers, and see Davis & Gardner, 1992).

If one follows the "reverse in direction" we describe from outside-in to inside-out, the child's "scribbling" is no longer seen as chaotic physical exercise or inadequate representation of physical form; similarly, the declaration of representation is no longer viewed as the pretense of intention. Rather, both activities may be regarded as successful externalization of the child's current internal understanding of the requirements for symbolization (Arnheim, 1974; Read, 1966).

Although it is undetermined whether scribbling is a *necessary* precursor of later drawing development (see Golomb, 1992), development is usually described as proceeding therefrom. Kellogg (1966, 1969) identified 20 basic categories of scribbles and tracked the development of scribbling into the construction of a circle, an upright cross, diagonal crossings of line, and ultimately the combination of these forms into a mandala (a "gestalt" made by all normal 3- or 4-year-olds). The mandala is refined into a sun and ultimately into the more representational form of a human being. The child's earliest depictions of human form are so clearly variations of the mandala, that they have been called *mandaloids* (Gardner & Wolf, 1979; Kellogg, 1969; Kellogg with O'Dell, 1967). These representations are organized around a generalized example that can be seen as standing for any human being (Gardner & Wolf, 1979). The "human quality" Lucy's teacher sensed in all the children's drawings exemplifies this phenomenon. Accordingly, the mandaloid more aptly describes "humanness" than it does a particular human, and fulfills what gestalt psychologists Rudolf Arnheim has launched as a criterion for symbolic meaning: "the sensing of the universal in the particular" (1974, p. 454).

Ives and Gardner (1984) have combined Piagetian and Vygotskian perspectives on the developing of graphic competence. They propose a stage view of development in drawing as it is influenced by culture:

I. *The dominance of universal patterns* (ages 1 to 5)
II. *The flowering of drawing* (ages 5 to 7)
III. *The height of cultural influences* (ages 7 to 12)

In stages I and II the universal scribblings evolve into the rich expressive statements that have invited the comparison between child and artist (Arnheim, 1969; Gardner, 1973, 1979, 1980; Schaefer-Simmern, 1948; Winner, 1982). At stage III children attend to the details of photographic reality in recreating perceived physical form or stereotypical equivalences thereof (Gardner & Wolf, 1979, p. 80). Children's art at this stage reflects the growing internalization of the surrounding culture that was of interest to Vygotsky. It employs such conventional culture-specific symbols as the rainbow for happiness (Golomb, 1989) and explores the realm of visual narrative through media-inspired comic book serials (Hoff, 1982; Wilson, 1974; Wilson & Wilson, 1976).

Expression. The expressivity of the 5-year-old's drawing which we extol is often cited as the common ground shared by young children and mature artists (Davis, 1989, 1991; Davis & Gardner, 1992; Gardner, 1979, 1980, 1982; Gardner & Winner, 1982; Kellogg, 1969). However, the results of a 1979 study by Carothers and Gardner challenge this affirmation. Indeed, their findings suggest that both production and perception of expression are rather late acquisitions in the child's aesthetic repertoire (specifically, appearing in the sixth grade). Though widely accepted (e.g., Golomb, 1992; Ives, 1984; Rosenblatt & Winner, 1988; Wolf & Perry, 1988), the Carothers and Gardner finding may be challenged on the grounds that the methodology in their study relied on children's completion of stimulus drawings rather than on drawings created entirely on their own—a potential flaw in terms of eliciting children's engagement. It is possible that the problem-solving demands of completing another person's drawing differ from those of constructing one's own, or that young children do not attend to the same aesthetic properties in the work of others that concern them in their own (Davis, 1989; Davis & Gardner, 1992).

Carothers and Gardner's claim for increase in perceptual sensitivity in preadolescence is well documented (Gardner, 1982; Gardner & Wolf, 1979; Parsons, 1987), but the observation of an increase in production of expressive drawings at that age is controversial. Indeed, although there are those who extol this period as a time of acquisition of new artistic skills (Smith, 1983; Wolf, 1987), others share our view of the sixth-grade child as in the heart of what has been called the "literal stage." This is the stage that hugs the floor of U-shaped development. It is a time when children's drawing loses much of its flavorfulness and its artistry (Gardner, 1980, 1982; Ives, Silverman, Kelly, & Gardner, 1981; Rosenblatt & Winner, 1988; Winner, Blank, Massey, & Gardner, 1983; Winner & Gardner, 1981; and see Bamberger, 1978, 1982; Hargreaves, 1986; Pollio & Pollio, 1974, for decline in flavorfulness in other art forms).

Golomb has documented an increase in "literalism" in expression of emotion in children's drawing. In a study of expressivity in which children drew happy, sad, and angry children, Golomb noted the use of tears as a "literal indication of sadness" in 10% of the drawings of first-graders, 90% of the drawings of third-graders, and 50% of the drawings of sixth-graders (1989, p. 208). The ability to employ these literal signs or outward manifestations of emotion may be a symptom of the developing differentiation that is attributed to children of this age. Where the preschool child may begin a drawing of a sad person by wrinkling his or her own face into a sad configuration, the more-distanced older child will consciously add teardrops to an otherwise undefined drawing of a face. The preschool child's instinctive behavior is reminiscent of the conscious activity of adult artists who themselves assume the position of the model as they reproduce gesture in life drawing (Nicolaides, 1969, pp. 14–20).

The older child's activity, which reflects a more distanced or differentiated self, stands at the opposite pole from the example of the gestural representation (Smith, 1983; Wolf, 1983; Wolf & Perry, 1988) of the 18-month-old drawing a rabbit, as observed by Wolf. The child took the marker and "hopped it around on the page, leaving a mark with each imprint and explaining as she drew, 'Rabbit goes hop-hop'" (Winner, 1986, p. 26). One is reminded by this behavior of the performance artists of the adult world. A slightly more differentiated perspective is found in the charming example Winner and Gardner give of the preschooler who responds to the directive to make a "scary house" by drawing a standard house "simultaneously growling at the experimenter in order to scare him" (1981, p. 16). They attribute this sort of early solution to the task to the fact that very young egocentric children do not respect the boundary between themselves and their drawings. Here again we are reminded of adult artists and the lack of respect for boundaries that is often attributed to their creativity.

The aesthetician E. H. Gombrich says that artists have long been interested in that form of boundary breaking known as *synaesthesia* or the "splashing over of impressions from one sense modality to another" (1984, p. 366). In S. W. Ives's 1984 study into expressivity, he found that children as young as 4 could depict expressive qualities in a meaningful way using abstract forms. Their use of such abstract linear forms as angularity and largeness could be correctly (with 84% reliability) identified by adults (1984, p. 157). Across ages, he found that the Werner and Kaplan (1963) observations from work with adult line drawing were confirmed; that is, lines were up and curved for positive, down and angular for negative (1984, p. 158). Ives attributes these contrasts to conscious or inborn "cross-modal links." Synaesthesia is equivalent to the cross-modal comparisons Ives cites in his study and to Gardner's observation that even 5-year-old children can match the brightness of a light with the loudness of a sound in the same manner as adults (1973, p. 171). Accordingly, research into expressivity (Arnheim, 1966; Edwards, 1986; Ives, 1984; Lundholm, 1921) supports the view that the preschool child's drawing shares aspects of the expressive content of the work of artists. No wonder Lucy's teacher recognizes a similarity between her response to her kindergartner's expressive familial portrayals and her experience in a museum.

Composition. Many traditional studies into children's control of composition revolve around the achievement of a consensual view of the framed physical space, involving a baseline interpreted by the child as the ground and an horizon line interpreted as the sky (Goodnow, 1977; Lowenfeld, 1964; Mendelowitz, 1963). Using Arnheim's criteria, more recent research into composition has attended to whether and at what ages children's drawings are balanced (Golomb, 1983, 1992; Winner & Gardner, 1981; Winner, Mendelsohn, Garfunkel, Arangio, & Stevens, 1981). Attention has also been given to the question of whether children employ different compositional strategies to express different emotions or themes (Davis, 1989, 1991; Edwards, 1979; Golomb & Farmer, 1983).

Examples of the use of compositional strategies for expressing emotions or themes can be found in the distribution of size among forms and in the use of asymmetrical or symmetrical balance to articulate different meanings. The distribution of size among family members described in Lucy's drawing may be an example of such a compositional strategy; that is, the decision (conscious or not) to allot a small space for the brother in order to express her current regard for him (see Edwards, 1979, p. 67). The "sad" drawing of the 5-year-old who placed the crying face of the sun in the upper left corner of a vast empty page ("the sun is crying because there are no clouds or stars in the sky") illustrates the compositional control of asymmetrical balance as an expressive strategy (Davis, 1989, p. 51). The child, whose other drawings were centrally balanced, used this composition aptly to express the "off-center" feeling of sadness, the "asymmetry" of the theme. In a 1983 study, Golomb and Farmer documented the young child's ability to use different compositional strategies to express different themes. They found that different thematic tasks elicited different compositional strategies for all but their oldest (here, 7-year-old) subjects (1983, p. 92).

The claim for children's intentional use of asymmetrical balance might be challenged by the notion that asymmetrical balance is *harder* to achieve (Dondis, 1973; Golomb, 1983); young children might not have the requisite cognitive skills for the more complex task of achieving asymmetrical balance. However, it has not been proven that asymmetrical balance (which occurs in nature at least as frequently as symmetrical balance) is any more difficult to achieve than symmetrical balance. In fact, Winner and Gardner found in one of their studies that about a quarter of the drawings of subjects of all ages were asymmetrically or dynamically balanced (1981, p. 18; and see Golomb & Farmer, 1983, for an information-processing approach to the use of asymmetrical balance that renders apparently challenging data).

Winner has found that children of all ages seem to prefer balanced drawings to unbalanced drawings, but preschoolers' tendency toward balance seems to be as strong or stronger than that of older children (Winner et al., 1981, p. 4). The prevalence of balance (symmetrical or asymmetrical) or unity in young children's drawing has been attributed to young children's lack of differentiation. As Smith describes it: "Their images do convey emotions and do strive for unity. In fact, their capacity to integrate the narrative, emotional, and compositional aspects... surpasses that of most adults since these strands have not yet become separated for them" (1983, p. 11; see also Schaefer-Simmern, 1966). The decline in the occurrence of balance or unity in older children's drawing (D'Amico, 1966; Edwards, 1979, p. 99) may represent the cost of the acquisition of differentiation. The conscious attention to the details of part which differentiation affords threatens to obscure the initial intuitive balanced sense of the whole.

Taking into account the different perspectives and criteria that guide and inform different methodological approaches to research in composition, a simple claim seems documented by the research. Young children display an intuitive sense of balance in composition that seems to get lost in the course of subsequent development. Research into composition further supports the "feeling" Lucy's teacher enjoys—the clarity of expressive statement that unified or balanced composition affords.

Symbolic Literacy: Perception

The question that considerations of perception frame can be reduced to, "What does the young child see in a work of art?" This question is important not only in terms of how young children will react to works of art they will encounter on field trips to museums, but also in terms of how they will respond to their own productions as works in progress or to the productions of peers around them.

In terms of perception, young children responding to a picture may first attend to subject matter—that is, they may ask the question Lucy's teacher was veiling when she asked Lucy to "tell her about" her drawing. That question is "What is this a picture of?" However, research has shown that if the element of subject is controlled or if the child is asked to sort works according to style, young children can display sensitivity to stylistic features (Gardner, 1972, 1973). Researchers have demonstrated that even preschoolers can recognize the work of other child artists in their class on the basis of style (Hartley & Somerville, 1982; Nolan & Kagan, 1980, 1981). Although left on their own they show little interest in these attributes, young children have been shown to attend to such aesthetic aspects as expression, composition, and texture when provided with the proper scaffolding (Gardner & Winner, 1982; see also MacGregor, 1974; Seefeldt, 1979).

In terms of conceptualizations, however, young children have very limited understandings of art, thinking, for example, that works of art might be made by machines or increase in value according to size (Gardner, Winner, & Kircher, 1975). By middle childhood, children seem to adopt the rigid view that photographic reality is the goal of art: "Any 2-year-old can make an abstract picture!" the 11-year-old art critic will dismissively declare (Gardner, 1980, p. 198). Adolescents, like many adults, are inclined to abandon these stringent expectations for a more relativistic view (Gardner, 1990).

Reflecting the same Piagetian stage-like considerations that have guided research in other areas (e.g., Kohlberg for moral reasoning, 1981; Kegan for evolution of self, 1982), Parsons (1987) and Housen (1983) have conducted research that has resulted in descriptions of stage-like development in aesthetic response. Although differences obtain between the 5-stage sequences each researcher describes (see Mockros, 1989), the similarities attest to the viability of the claim for stage-like development in this domain. An important difference in the methodologies of Parsons and Housen should be noted. Where Parsons interviewed his subjects in "semistructured" interviews that included a list of standard topic questions (see Parsons, 1987, p. 19), Housen elicited "stream of consciousness" responses. We can summarize broadly and synthesize their findings as follows.

At the first stage, viewers rely upon the most obvious stimuli in their responses; either they attend to the subject in the work that may trigger personal associations or narratives, or they delight in the sensuous appeal of such salient aesthetic dimensions as color, texture, and line. At the next stage, viewers consider what happens "behind the canvas" in terms of the way a work is made and the difficulties the artist may face in attaining the prevailing stage 2 "aesthetic" of realism. Stages 3 and 4 include an appreciation for the expressivity of the work and the personal encounter it affords the viewer, or the understanding that the work "fits" in a larger historic scheme of cultural context and tradition. For Housen, history precedes expression; for Parsons, it is the reverse. For both, stage 5, reached by few viewers, is a stage at which viewers "reconstruct" meaning for themselves and synthesize it with autonomous judgment that is rooted in emotional experience and personal values.

Clearly some development in aesthetic perception can or will occur without tutelage. As we have mentioned, the naturally unfolding developmental process of differentiation invites different orientations on the part of the child either as perceiver or producer of art. However, other advancements require instruction: for example, the attainment of conceptualizations based on the knowledge of how paintings are constructed or where they "fit" in stylistic schools. In other words, some understandings, such as those that emanate from the physical realities that concerned Piaget, may be gained independently of instruction; but others, such as the culturally mediated symbol systems that concerned Vygotsky, are only available through instruction by experienced citizens of the particular symbolic domains (see Feldman, 1980; Gardner, 1991). Accordingly, our portrait of the attainment of symbolic literacy in the domain of the visual arts is everywhere tinted by the fact that the development we describe is unfolding in children who are attending school, that haven for instruction in culturally mediated domains.

DIFFERENT KINDS OF KNOWLEDGE: THE CHALLENGE OF INTEGRATION

The research and theory summarized in this chapter suggest that there are at least 5 different kinds of knowledge that individuals who grow up in schooled environments must attempt to master and integrate (Gardner, 1990, 1991). Significant to our purposes is the recognition that the arts feature many kinds of knowledge, and it is important to keep them straight in education— both in terms of the uniqueness of understandings they access and the developmental appropriateness of the instruction they require.

The first can be labeled *intuitive* knowledge. This is the sort of knowledge attained in Piaget's sensorimotor stage through sensory perceptions and motor interactions with physical objects and with other persons. Acquired in the very first years of life, this knowledge persists throughout human development. *First-order symbolic* knowledge, knowledge of the first-order symbols Vygotsky describes (see also Olson & Campbell, 1989;

Werner & Kaplan, 1963), occurs at the latest in the second year of life and is easy to integrate with intuitive knowledge: Reference is direct from word or picture to those referents that have become familiar to the child throughout the early acquisition of intuitive knowledge.

Around ages 5 to 7, children begin to employ the more formal symbolic codes that are known as *notational system* (Olson, 1977; Vygotsky, 1978). Unlike first-order symbols that refer directly to referents, notational symbols refer to first-order symbols. Written words refer to spoken words; musical notes refer to features of the music; and so on. Knowledge of notational systems relies on instruction, as does the fourth form of knowledge: *formal bodies of knowledge*. The formal bodies of knowledge comprise the information the culture preserves and shares with literate members of the culture—for example, its science, history, literature. Although the 4 knowledges seem to fit in a developmental scheme, the fifth form of knowledge, *skilled knowledge*, does not fit so easily in the pattern. Skills are acquired from the start and infuse and enrich every level of knowledge. Therefore skilled knowledge may best be conceived as weaving throughout the developmental pattern. It manifests its development from novice to expert in whatever type of knowledge it develops, or in the integration of different kinds of knowledge that are relevant and available to its purposes (Gardner, 1990).

The integration of these 5 different kinds of knowledge is not as straightforward an enterprise as one might imagine. Indeed, considerable research (Gardner, 1990, 1991) indicates that these various ways of knowing may be inconsistent with one another, either clashing or proceeding in independent tracks. Bamberger (1978, 1982) has demonstrated a tension between intuitive knowledge and notational knowledge in the domain of music. Children are able to enjoy music quite readily through their sensorimotor exploration of the sounds. Their intuitive knowledge may lead them to think, for example, that certain pitches belong together because of their pleasant sound, whereas musical notation requires that temporal value be the criterion for grouping pitches. When this notational knowledge is attained, its incompatibility with intuitive knowledge threatens to silence the former.

In a study of artistic development across symbolic media (Ives et al., 1981), school-age children were found to prefer "real language" (here, written stories) to drawing and to modeling clay, presumably because it proved a more robust vehicle of communication. Considering the tension among ways of knowing, this disenchantment may be another example of a lack of integration of one kind of knowledge with another, with that dissonance squelching the former way of making meaning. From their acquisition of notational knowledge, children have gained a new way of seeing; and they vainly try to process former knowledge through that lens. When they apply the criteria of notational knowledge to drawing, drawing seems inadequate. Unable to reconcile the tension between these 2 ways of knowing, the activity of drawing is rejected.

The precision afforded by notational knowledge appeals to the child who is herself attempting to delineate the rules and boundaries that govern differentiation. Winner (1988) has noted a lessening of interest among schoolchildren in the category violation that intrigues preschool children and is manifest in their delightful early metaphors (see Mendelsohn, Robinson, Gardner, & Winner, 1984). She attributes the developing resistance to metaphor to the same concern with convention that saps the flavorfulness from school-age children's drawing (Winner, 1988, p. 104; see also Gardner, 1980; Gardner & Winner, 1982; and see Pollio & Pollio, 1974). Concern with convention, like precision in communication, is a marker of the impact of the culture of school that has afforded newly acquired notational knowledge. In these examples, this new acquisition may be supplanting former kinds of knowledge.

In the domain of music, Bamberger fears this lack of integration precisely because it threatens fruitful exchange between the different kinds of knowledge, or worse, because newly acquired knowledge may silence earlier ways of knowing. Accordingly, she considers the integration of intuitive with notational knowledge to be the challenge in music education (see Gardner, 1990, p. 65). Our sense is that the same challenge may await the early childhood educator devising curricula in the visual arts.

THE VIEW OF THE YOUNG CHILD AS ARTIST: APPLYING THE COGNITIVE APPROACH

Setting the stage for a discussion of the educational implications of a view of the child as artist, we review the cognitive approach as it informs that controversial perspective. The perspective dates back to the mid-nineteenth century and, depending largely on shifts in values in aesthetics and psychology, has run the gamut of receptive descriptors from "romantic" to "ridiculous" to "instructive" (see Korzenik, 1981; Leeds, 1989). We align ourselves with the last characterization.

Critics of the perspective may contend that the "child as artist" is a potentially artificial claim (D. Pariser, personal communication, January 24, 1990), that is, that modern artists consciously emulating the drawings of young children have produced works of art that naturally bear a resemblance to their models. But what are the reasons that modern artists would emulate the work of children? Is it pure *tour de force* or the recognition that these earliest symbolizations reflect universal understandings of form that transcend the limitations of cultural bias? The cognitive approach shapes our response.

A cognitive approach to graphic symbolization redefines the domain of drawing as a medium through which understanding is constructed and/or communicated. Although this "redefinition" does not exclude the construction and communication of emotion, it enlarges the scope of graphic symbolization's potential. The notion of mental representation extends the province of graphic symbolization from representation on paper to representation of understanding. This is a negotiated understanding—negotiated between 2 active constructors of meaning, the producer and the perceiver, who are often (as in the process of constructing a drawing) the same individual. The notion of perception as active construction of meaning has important educational implications. Not only does the child who will develop into a maker of art require the symbolic tools of literacy in the visual arts, but also in need is the child who will

develop into a maker of meaning through literate "reading" of the aesthetic symbols of her culture.

The notion of "first-order symbols" and the persistence of the knowledge that perceives and produces them (*first-order symbolic knowledge,* which is acquired at an early age) enlarges our understanding of children's drawings. These concepts explain the power of these childhood products: They communicate meaning above and beyond the separate codes of notational symbol systems. Young children, like professional artists, employ symbols that have primary and universal meaning. Development in drawing reflects the values of the culture informing the work of the child. The work of professional artists is similarly informed. Individual artists' work may be enlarged by the vocabulary of forms the surrounding culture of artists provides (Gombrich, 1984). However, young children's artistic productions may be correlatively diminished by the examples, expectations, and criticisms of the surrounding culture of peers and teachers (see Rosenstiel & Gardner, 1977).

Indeed, the child in middle childhood who exhibits artistic behavior in school may not find support for that behavior. The child who sits so totally absorbed in the exploration of charcoal on paper that the sound of the school bell goes unheard may be chastised; the child who has perfected the latest greatest quick sketch of Mickey Mouse is more likely to receive the praise of her schoolmates and teacher. The move to stereotypical symbols in middle childhood is therefore not only a manifestation of the child's mandates for photographic literalism (see also Eisner, 1976), but also of the mandates of the peers and teachers that comprise the culture of school and reinforce these values (Gardner, 1989; May, 1989; Rosario & Collazo, 1981; Zurmuehlen, 1977).

An information-processing approach to children's drawing emphasizes the many elements involved in graphic symbolization and the cognitive skills that are balanced and coordinated in the service of constructing meaning. The child, like the artist, coordinates available knowledge with the problems to be solved in the work at hand. The process for both is compelling and all engrossing (see Gardner, 1980).

A symbol systems approach contributes to a view of the child, like the artist, exploiting the aesthetic potential of ordinary symbols, manipulating line so that it will contain expression and interrelating forms into balanced coherent compositions. In a view of literate symbolic functioning, children, like artists, coordinate their perceptions and conceptualizations of art with their productions. And of course, herein lie the seeds of their difference.

Adult artists have command of a vocabulary of forms that most children will never acquire. Artists have an awareness of artistic conventions that makes their deviations from the norm conscious decisions; while young children's deviations may be uninformed or even accidental explorations. There is significant difference between innocent boundary breaking and the breaking of boundaries that are known. However, research into drawing as a cognitive process suggests that, in spite of the differences, young children share a prize that artists work to achieve; and further, that somewhere in the middle years of schooling they lose hold of that prize (Davis, 1991) and, perhaps like the dominant surrounding culture (see Harris, 1966) that lets their grip loosen, they really don't seem to care.

IMPLICATIONS FOR EDUCATION

The "not caring" may reflect a cultural perspective that is changing. Enthusiasm for the appreciation of children's art is demonstrated by such serious ventures as Oslo's International Museum of Children's Art (see Shenker, 1990), a museum entirely devoted to the artwork of children of all ages. Further, the cognitive approach has manifested itself in the Getty-Trust–sponsored art educational reform movement known as DBAE (Discipline Based Art Education). DBAE proposes attention to 4 content areas in art instruction that foster understanding in art and that clearly emerge from the considerations of a cognitive approach to the arts: (1) art production, (2) art history, (3) art criticism, and (4) aesthetics (see *Beyond Creating*, 1985; Eisner, 1987; Smith, 1989).

Perhaps the most dramatic shift in emphasis in DBAE—specifically, the move from an art education that primarily consisted of the making of art (e.g., Lowenfeld & Brittain, 1964) to a curriculum in which production is only one part of a larger scheme (Broudy, 1972; *Towards Civilization*, 1988)—proved to be the most controversial (Burton et al., 1988). Least disputed and most inspirational to the field of research and education was the new gauntlet that the cognitive revolution had fashioned and proponents of DBAE had taken up: the notion that every child is entitled to, no, indeed *requires*, the sort of art education that had heretofore been reserved only for the future artists or artistic connoisseurs in our society.

Another approach to art education that champions this cause results from a joint effort involving Harvard Project Zero, the Educational Testing Service, and the Pittsburgh Public schools. Initially conceived to facilitate developmentally informed assessment in the arts, ARTS PROPEL has developed curricula and modules for the arts that seek to synthesize the 5 kinds of knowledge we have described: Symbolic literacy is to be attained through involvement in numerous rich activities and projects entailing production, perception, and reflection. This triad is not evenly weighted, in that production is considered the point of entry, that is, the central activity in PROPEL's process approach to cognitively informed arts curricula (see Gardner, 1988, 1989, 1990; Zessoules, Wolf, & Gardner, 1988). Although the cognitive approach is often offered as the antidote for an art education that has focused on free expression through production with little, if any, "talk about art," PROPEL demonstrates that production need not be denigrated in reform.

Recent research into the arts through a cognitive lens (specifically the symbol systems approach) might suggest to educators and researchers alike that they revise their approach to the activity of graphic symbolization. The tendency has been to regard it as an element in, an agent to, or a reflection of other cognitive domains. Consequently, drawing may not have been appreciated as a domain of value in its own right. Researchers "use" drawing as a means to determine the child's inner state of knowledge or emotional well-being. Educators "use" drawing to help children acquire the "more important" graphic skills of written language.

For example, perhaps nowhere is the devaluation of a child's drawing more apparent than in the early educator's unfettered imposition of written words on a child's visual composition. "Tell me about your drawing," Lucy's well-meaning teacher asks (already implying that the drawing "says" nothing on its own), and when the child responds, the teacher manifests a whole network of values in the simple action of writing the words the child has spoken across the page. Let us consider that action through the lens of a symbol systems approach.

Assuming this approach, the teacher regards Lucy's drawing as a symbolic statement that may only in part be translated into the notational system of words. The lines, shapes, and balance of form that the child employs articulate a unique symbolic statement not susceptible to translation into another symbolic system. And although the use of line and composition may be specific to the domain of drawing, the child's sense of herself as a competent symbolizer has implications across symbolic domains.

When the teacher writes the "about" of a child's drawing on the page, there is a perhaps unconsidered hidden agenda to her action. First, her act of writing tells the child that drawings do not indeed convey specific meaning without the aid of words—that is, words are a better, more competent symbol system than drawings. Second, her placement of her writing on the child's drawing suggests to the child that the composition of those forms on that page are of little consequence; the teacher's written words can be added without violating compositional integrity. Finally, and perhaps this is the most salient message that pervades all aspects of this well-meaning action on the part of the teacher, the child as symbolizer does not own her symbolic statement; the teacher can add her splendid written code to that page without fear of trespassing.

How different would a response from a teacher to a young child's drawing be if, informed by the fruits of a cognitive perspective on drawing, she could help the child attend to the aesthetic accomplishments she is achieving in graphic symbolization? Rather than asking the child to "tell," the teacher can, on her own, perceive and, through her demonstrated perception, instruct: "Look at the action in this line; this figure is indeed scribbling around on this page." "This is a nicely balanced drawing; see how you have placed these large figures over here; it makes your drawing very strong."

Lucy's teacher might have complimented Lucy on the addition of the "flowers" to the extreme left of her drawing. Instead of the unspoken (in this case) "product" question of "What are these scribbly lines?" Lucy's teacher might as easily have attended to Lucy's aesthetic process: "What a good idea it was to place these lines here. They balance your drawing so well!" This comment instructively acknowledges that lines themselves have power above or beyond any representational meaning they may contain.

By attending to what *is* happening in the child's drawing, the teacher can express her appreciation for the intuitive knowledge the child has externalized in her drawing. Further, she can begin to introduce a vocabulary of forms that the child can bring to the productions of artists and other children that she will encounter. One can only imagine how such changes in practice might effect future measures of the development of aesthetic perception.

The artwork that is hung in the child's classroom reflects the values of the culture of school. Consider the impact of surrounding children with the very works of art that have contributed to the comparison between child and artist: to prints of Picasso, Miró, Klee, Chagall, and others who capture the indirection in representation that children naturally enjoy. Through the appreciation of these works, and the recognition that they are valued, children can learn to respect their own work and to conceive of their own artistic productions as articulated through the same language as venerable masters. How different from the realistic illustrations that so often decorate children's classrooms are the children's drawings that are dutifully hung beside them!

Perhaps by appreciating the various kinds of knowledge the child has and is acquiring, teachers can ward off their future disassociation. By separating materials—for example, leaving certain specific materials for writing words and others for drawing—the teacher can alert the child to the fact that different symbolic domains require different tools to solve their different problems. Most importantly, different symbolic domains are both separate and equal in terms of the respect that they merit.

WHAT HAPPENS TO THE GIFT?

Where does the "gift" go? As long as our schools allot progressively fewer minutes and hours to the activity of drawing as children get older, we will not be free to attribute the loss of ability in graphic symbolization to the natural course of development. Early instruction in graphic symbolization seems inappropriate; the intuitive and first-order symbolic knowledge that govern the process do not rely for development on school instruction. However, as children enter middle childhood and bring new mandates for symbolic expression to their drawing, teachers can offer guidance in, for example, the technicalities of perspective. Research has shown that great artists like Picasso, Toulouse-Lautrec, and Klee survived and may even have enjoyed the literal stage (Pariser, 1989). Like many adolescent artists of today (see Wilson, 1974; Wilson & Wilson, 1976), they copied from comic books and incorporated the culture's visual schemes into their repertoire. As is the tradition in DBAE, educators can look to the examples of experts in the field to frame curricula. Respect for the genres children naturally embrace and implementation of the tools they need to achieve them are the sorts of efforts that may help to keep the "gift" alive.

Educators are in a position to set an example for the sort of integration of knowledge that we expect children to accomplish. Every educational decision reflects the values of a culture and a time. If indeed we value aesthetic expression, which research has reconstrued as a cognitive accomplishment, we can express that value in our education of the facility to make and find meaning in the symbols of our culture. The recognition that children are artists does not mean that they come to school already formed and sufficiently accomplished in artistic domains. On the contrary, it is the recognition that children bring a "gift" with them that in size and shape has tangible likeness to the artistry of experts in the field (Davis, 1991). Our decision to cultivate rather than eradicate the promise that gift holds may anticipate lessons that have educational implications across the board (see Eisner, 1972; Moody, 1990).

Adolescents are not just deciding they are not artists; they are deciding they are not students. If school is a place that diminishes or erases rather than develops early gifts, is there any reason for children not to become disenchanted with the arena? A cognitive approach to aesthetic education expands the notion of literacy to include the vocabulary of many children who have traditionally not been able to find voice in the notational symbols that schools often embrace exclusively. Attention to developmental sequences requires that educators revise their reception of the child's early knowledge from one of deficiency to one of promise. The recognition and incorporation of the earliest understandings in each new way of knowing not only legitimizes the young child's unique perspective; it also enlarges each subsequent understanding. It may be vainglorious to propose that such reform might succeed in keeping children in school longer, or in identifying more artists among us, or in enriching the society with more literate producers and perceivers of the best that culture can construct. But these possibilities are well articulated if they serve to inspire or even to intrigue the early childhood educator, whose choice it is to receive and develop, or to ignore and diminish, the facility in graphic symbolization which the young child brings to school.

References

Arnheim, R. (1962). *Genesis of a painting: Guernica.* Berkeley, CA: University of California Press.

Arnheim, R. (1966). *Toward a psychology of art.* Berkeley, CA: University of California Press.

Arnheim, R. (1969). *Visual thinking.* London: Fabar and Fabar.

Arnheim, R. (1971). *Entropby and art.* Berkeley, CA: University of California Press.

Arnheim, R. (1974). *Art and visual perception, a psychology of the creative eye.* Berkeley, CA: University of California Press. (Original work published 1954).

Bamberger, J. (1978). Intuitive and formal musical knowing. In S. Madeja (Ed.), *The arts, cognition, and basic skills* (pp. 173–209). St. Louis: Cemrel.

Bamberger, J. (1982). Revisiting children's descriptions of simple rhythms. In S. Strauss (Ed.), U-*shaped behavioral growth* (pp. 191–226). New York: Academic Press.

Beyond creating: The place for art in American schools. (1985). Los Angeles: Getty Center for Education in the Arts.

Biber, B. (1967). *Children's drawings from lines to pictures.* New York: Bank Street College of Education. (Original work published 1934.)

Biber, B. (1984). Drawing as expression of thinking and feeling. In B. Biber (Ed.), *Early education and psychological development* (pp. 155–186). New Haven, CT: Yale University Press.

Broudy, H. (1972). *Enlightened cherishing: An essay on aesthetic education.* Champaign, IL: University of Illinois Press.

Bruner, J. (1986). *Actual minds, possible worlds.* Cambridge, MA: Harvard University Press.

Burton, J., Lederman, A., & London, P. (Eds.). (1988). *Beyond DBAE: The case for multiple visions of art education.* Sponsored by the University Council on Art Education.

Carothers, T., & Gardner, H. (1979). When children's drawings become art, the emergence of aesthetic production and perception. *Developmental Psychology, 15,* 570–580.

Case, R. (1985). *Intellectual development: Birth to adulthood.* New York: Academic Press.

Case, R. (Ed.). (1991). *The mind's staircase: Exploring the conceptual underpinnings of children's thought and knowledge.* Hillsdale, NJ: Erlbaum.

Chapman, L. (1978). *Approaches to art in education.* New York: Harcourt, Brace, Jovanovich.

Coles, R. (1967). *Children of crisis. Vol. 1: A study of courage and fear* (Chap. 5, pp. 37–71). Boston: Little Brown.

Csikszentmihalyi, M. (1990). *Flow: The psychology of optimal experience.* New York: Harper & Row.

D'Amico, V. (1966). The child as painter. In E. Eisner & D. Ecker (Eds.), *Readings in art education* (pp. 232–237). Waltham, MA: Blaisdell.

Davis, J. H. (1989). *The artist in the child: A literature review of criteria for assessing aesthetic dimensions.* Qualifying paper, Harvard Graduate School of Education, Cambridge, MA.

Davis, J. H. (1991). Artistry lost: U-shaped development in graphic symbolization. Doctoral dissertation, Harvard Graduate School of Education, Cambridge, MA.

Davis, J. H., & Gardner, H. (1992). The cognitive revolution: Its consequences for the understanding and education of the child as artist. In B. Reimer & R. A. Smith (Eds.), The arts, education, and aesthetic knowing. *Ninety-first Yearbook of the National Society for the Study of Education,* Part II (pp. 92–123). Chicago: University of Chicago Press.

Dennis, S. (1984, April). *Stages in the development of children's drawing.* Paper presented at the 68th meeting of the American Educational Research Association, New Orleans, LA.

Dennis, S. (1991). Stage and structure in the development of children's spatial representations. In R. Case (Ed.), *The mind's staircase: Exploring the conceptual underpinnings of children's thought and knowledge.* Hillsdale, NJ: Erlbaum.

Dondis, D. A. (1973). *A primer of visual literacy.* Cambridge, MA: MIT Press.

Edwards, B. (1979). *Drawing on the right side of the brain.* Los Angeles: J. P. Tarcher.

Edwards, B. (1986). *Drawing on the artist within.* New York: Simon & Schuster.

Eisner, E. (1972). *Educating artistic vision.* New York: Macmillan.

Eisner, E. (1976). What we know about children's art and what we need to know. In E. Eisner (Ed.), *The arts, human development, and education* (pp. 5–18). Berkeley, CA: McCutchan.

Eisner, E. (1987). *The role of discipline-based art education in America's schools.* Los Angeles: Getty Center for Education in the Arts.

Feldman, D. H. (1980). *Beyond universals in cognitive development.* Norwood, NJ: Ablex.

Freeman, N. (1980). *Strategies of representation in young children.* New York: Academic Press.

Gardner, H. (1972). Style sensitivity in children. *Human Development, 15,* 325–338.

Gardner, H. (1973). *The arts and human development.* New York: Wiley.

Gardner, H. (1979). Entering the world of the arts: The child as artist. *Journal of Communication, 29*(4), 146–156.

Gardner, H. (1980). *Artful scribbles.* New York: Basic Books.

Gardner, H. (1982). *Art, mind, and brain.* New York: Basic Books.

Gardner, H. (1983). *Frames of mind: The theory of multiple intelligences.* New York: Basic Books.

Gardner, H. (1985). *The mind's new science: A history of the cognitive revolution.* New York: Basic Books.

Gardner, H. (1988). Towards more effective arts education. In R. A. Smith (Ed.), *Journal of Aesthetic Education, 22*(1), 157–167.

Gardner, H. (1989). Zero-based arts education: An introduction to ARTS PROPEL. *Studies in Art Education, 30*(2), 71–83.

Gardner, H. (1990). *Art education and human development.* Los Angeles: Getty Center for Education in the Arts.

Gardner, H. (1991). *The unschooled mind.* New York: Basic Books.

Gardner, H., & Perkins, D. (1989). *Art, mind and education: Research from Project Zero.* Champaign, IL: University of Illinois Press.

Gardner, H., & Winner, E. (1982). First intimations of artistry. In S. Strauss (Ed.), *U-shaped development* (pp. 147–167). New York: Academic Press.

Gardner, H., Winner, E., & Kircher, M. (1975). Children's conceptions of the arts. *Journal of Aesthetic Education, 9,* 60–77.

Gardner, H., & Wolf, D. (1979). First drawings: Notes on the relationships between perception and production in the visual arts. In C. Nodine & D. Fisher (Eds.), *Perception and pictorial representation* (pp. 361–387). New York: Praeger.

Gardner, H., & Wolf, D. (1983). Waves and streams of symbolization: Notes on the development of symbolic capacities in young children. In R. R. Rogers & J. A. Sloboda (Eds.), *The acquisition of symbolic skills* (pp. 19–42). London: Plenum.

Gardner, H., Wolf, D., & Phelps, E. (1990). The roots of creativity in children's symbolic products. In C. Alexander & E. Langer (Eds.), *Higher stages of human development* (pp. 79–96). New York: Oxford University Press.

Golomb, C. (1974). *Young children's sculpture and drawing: A study in representational development.* Cambridge, MA: Harvard University Press.

Golomb, C. (1983). Young children's planning strategies and early principles of spatial organization in drawing. In R. R. Rogers & J. A. Sloboda (Eds.), *The acquisition of symbolic skills* (pp. 81–87). London: Plenum.

Golomb, C. (1992). *The child's creation of a pictorial world: Studies in the psychology of art.* Berkeley, CA: University of California Press.

Golomb, C., & Farmer, D. (1983). Children's graphic planning strategies and early principles of spatial organization in drawing. *Studies in Art Education, 24*(2), 87–100.

Gombrich, E. (1984). Art and illusion, a study in the psychology of pictorial representation. *The A. W. Mellon Lectures in the Fine Arts, 1956.* Princeton: Princeton University Press.

Goodman, N. (1976). *Languages of art.* Indianapolis: Hackett.

Goodnow, J. (1977). *Children drawing.* Cambridge, MA: Harvard University Press.

Hargreaves, D. J. (1986). *The developmental psychology of music.* New York: Cambridge University Press.

Harris, N. (1966). *The artist in American society: The formative years.* New York: Braziller.

Hartley, J. L., & Somerville, S. (1982). Abstraction of individual styles from the drawings of five-year old children. *Child Development, 53,* 1193–1214.

Hoff, G. R. (1982, March). The visual narrative: Kids, comic books, and creativity [Special issue]. *Art Education,* 20–23.

Housen, A. (1983). *The eye of the beholder: Measuring aesthetic development.* Unpublished doctoral dissertation, Harvard Graduate School of Education, Cambridge, MA.

Ives, S. W. (1984). The development of expressivity in drawing. *British Journal of Educational Psychology, 54,* 152–159.

Ives, S. W., & Gardner, H. (1984). Cultural influences on children's drawings: A developmental perspective. In R. Ott & A. Hurwitz (Eds.), *Art education: An international perspective.* University Park, PA: Penn State University Press.

Ives, S. W., Silverman, J., Kelly, H., & Gardner, H. (1981). Artistic development in the early school years: A cross-media study of storytelling, drawing, and clay modelling. *Journal of Research and Development in Education, 14*(3), 91–105.

Kegan, R. (1982). *The evolving self, problem and process in human development.* Cambridge, MA: Harvard University Press.

Kellogg, R. (1966). Stages of development in preschool art. In H. P. Lewis (Ed.), *Child art, the beginnings of self-affirmation* (pp. 37–43). Berkeley, CA: Diablo Press.

Kellogg, R. (1969). *Analyzing children's art.* Palo Alto, CA: Mayfield.

Kellogg, R., with O'Dell, S. (1967). *The psychology of children's art.* New York: Random House CRM.

Kohlberg, L. (1981). *Essays on moral development.* (Vols. I & II). San Francisco: Harper & Row.

Korzenik, D. (1981, September). Is children's work art? Some historical views. *Art Education,* 20–24.

Langer, S. K. (1957). *Philosophy in a new key. A study in the symbolism of reason, rite, and art.* Cambridge, MA: Harvard University Press.

Leeds, J. A. (1989). The history of attitudes toward children's art. *Studies in Art Education, 30*(2), 93–103.

Lowenfeld, V. (1939). *The nature of creativity.* New York: Harcourt Brace.

Lowenfeld, V., & Brittain, W. L. (1964). *Creative and mental growth.* New York: Macmillan.

Lundholm, H. (1921). The affective tone of lines. *Psychological Review, 28,* 43–60.

Luquet, G. (1927). *Le dessin enfantin* [Children's art]. Paris: Alcan. In J. Piaget & B. Inhelder (1969), *The psychology of the child.* New York: Basic Books.

MacGregor, R. (1974). Response strategies adopted by elementary school children to items in a perceptual index: An exploratory study. *Studies in Art Education, 16*(3), 54–61.

Maquet, J. (1986). *The aesthetic experience: An anthropologist looks at the visual arts.* New Haven, CT: Yale University Press.

Matthews, J. (1983). Children drawing: Are young children really scribbling? Paper presented at the British Psychological Conference on Psychology and the Arts, Cardiff, UK.

May, W. (1989). *Understanding and critical thinking in elementary art and music.* East Lansing, MI: Michigan State University, Center for the Learning and Teaching of Elementary Subjects.

Mendelowitz, D. (1963). *Children are artists.* Stanford, CA: Stanford University Press.

Mendelsohn, E., Robinson, S., Gardner, H., & Winner, E. (1984). Are preschooler's renamings intentional category violations? *Development Psychology, 20*(2), 187–192.

Mockros, C. (1989). *Aesthetic judgment: An empirical comparison of two stage developmental theories.* Unpublished master's thesis, Tufts University Eliot-Pearson Child Study Center, Medford, MA.

Moody, W. J. (Ed.). (1990). *Artistic intelligences: Implications for education.* New York: Teachers College Press.

Nicolaides, K. (1969). *The natural way to draw.* Boston: Houghton Mifflin.

Nolan, E., & Kagan, J. (1980). Recognition of self and self's products in preschool children. *Journal of Genetic Psychology, 137,* 285–294.

Nolan, E., & Kagan, J. (1981). Memory for products in preschool children. *Journal of Genetic Psychology, 1*(38), 15–26.

Olson, D. (1977). From utterance to text: The bias of language in speech and writing. *Harvard Educational Review, 47,* 257–282.

Olson, D., & Campbell, R. (1989). *Representations and misrepresentations: On the beginnings of symbolization in young children.* Unpublished manuscript.

Pariser, D. (1989). Normal and unusual aspects of artistic development in the juvenalia of Klee, Toulouse-Lautrec, and Picasso. *Visual Arts Research, 13*(2:26), 53–67.

Parsons, M. J. (1987). *How we understand art. A cognitive developmental account of aesthetic experience.* Cambridge, UK: Cambridge University Press.

Piaget, J. (1962). *Play, dreams, and imitation in childhood.* New York: Norton.

Piaget, J., & Inhelder, B. (1948). *The child's construction of space.* New York: Norton.

Piaget, J., & Inhelder, B. (1969). *The psychology of the child.* New York: Basic Books.

Pollio, M., & Pollio, H. (1974). The development of figurative language in school children. *Journal of Psycholinguistic Research, 3,* 185–201.

Read, H. (1943). *Education through art.* New York: Pantheon.

Read, H. (1966). Art as a unifying principle in education. In H. P. Lewis (Ed.), *Child art, the beginnings of self-affirmation* (pp. 17–35). Berkeley, CA: Diablo Press.

Rosario J., & Collazo, E. (1981). Aesthetic codes in context: An exploration in two preschool classrooms. *Journal of Aesthetic Education, 15*(1), 71–82.

Rosenblatt, E., & Winner, E. (1988). The art of children's drawing. *Journal of Aesthetic Education, 22*(1).

Rosensteil, A. K., & Gardner, H. (1977). The effect of critical comparisons upon children's drawing. *Studies in Art Education, 19,* 36–44.

Schaefer-Simmern, H. (1948). *The unfolding of artistic activity.* Berkeley, CA: University of California Press.

Schaefer-Simmern, H. (1966). The mental foundation of art education in childhood. In H. P. Lewis (Ed.), *Child art, the beginnings of self-affirmation* (pp. 47–68). Berkeley, CA: Diablo Press.

Scheffler, I. (1986). In praise of the cognitive emotions. In I. Scheffler (Ed.), *Inquiries* (pp. 347–362). Indianapolis: Hackett.

Seefeldt, C. (1979). The effects of a program designed to increase young children's perception of texture. *Studies in Art Education, 20*(2), 40–44.

Shenker, I. (1990, October). The Louvre of children's art. *Smithsonian, 21*(7), 148–157.

Siegler, R. S. (1986). *Children's thinking.* Englewood Cliffs, NJ: Prentice Hall.

Smith, N. R. (1979). How a picture means. In H. Gardner & D. Wolf (Eds.), *Early Symbolization* (pp. 59–72). San Francisco: Jossey-Bass.

Smith, N. R. (1983). *Experience and art.* New York: Teachers College Press.

Smith, R. A. (Ed.). (1989). *Discipline-based art education: Origins, meaning, and development.* Champaign, IL: University of Illinois Press.

Stern, W. (1924). *Psychology of early childhood up to the sixth year of age.* New York: Henry Holt.

Strauss, S. (Ed.). (1982). *U-shaped behavioral growth.* New York: Academic Press.

Towards civilization: A report on arts education. (1988). Washington, DC: National Endowment for the Arts.

Vygotsky, L. S. (1978). *Mind in society: The development of higher psychological processes* (M. Cole, V. John-Steiner, S. Scribner, & E. Souberman, Eds.). Cambridge, MA: Harvard University Press.

Vygotsky, L. S. (1987). *Thought and language.* (A. Kozulin, Ed.). Cambridge, MA: MIT Press.

Werner, H., & Kaplan, B. (1963). *Symbolic formation.* New York: Wiley.

Willats, J. (1977). How children learn to represent three-dimensional space in drawings. In G. Butterworth (Ed.), *The child's representation of the world.* New York: Plenum.

Wilson, B. (1974, November). The super heroes of J. C. Holz and a theory of child art. *Art Education, 27*(8), 209.

Wilson, B., & Wilson, M. (1976). Visual narrative and the artistically gifted. *Gifted Child Quarterly, 20*(4), 432–447.

Wilson, B., & Wilson, M. (1981). The use and uselessness of developmental stages. *Studies in Art Education, 34*(5), 4–5.

Winner, E. (1982). *Invented worlds, the psychology of the arts*. Cambridge, MA: Harvard University Press.

Winner, E. (1986, August). Where pelicans kiss seals. *Psychology Today*, pp. 25–35.

Winner, E. (1988). *The point of words, children's understanding of metaphor and irony*. Cambridge, MA: Harvard University Press.

Winner, E., Blank, P., Massey, C., & Gardner, H. (1983). Children's sensitivity to aesthetic properties of line drawings. In D. R. Rogers & J. A. Sloboda (Eds.), *The acquisition of symbolic skills* (pp. 97–104). London: Plenum.

Winner, E., & Gardner, H. (1981). The art in children's drawings. *Review of Research in Visual Arts Education, 14,* 18–31.

Winner, E., Mendelsohn, E., Garfunkel, G., Arangio, S., & Stevens, G. (1981). *Are children's drawings balanced? A new look at drawing: Aesthetic aspects*. Unpublished symposium presentation at the Society for Research in Child Development, Boston.

Wolf, D. (1983, September). *Representation before picturing*. Transcript of symposium presentation, the Annual Meeting of the British Psychological Association, Cardiff, UK.

Wolf, D. (1987). Drawing conclusions: Insights into the nature of art from children's drawings. In J. G. P. von Hohenzollern & M. Liedtke (Eds.), *Vom Kritzeln Zur Kunst* (pp. 186–198). Bad Heibrunn/ Obb, Germany: Verlag Julius Kinkhardt.

Wolf, D. (1988). Drawing the boundary: The development of distinct systems for spatial representation in young children. In D. Stiles-Davis & U. Belugi (Eds.), *The development of spatial representation*. Chicago: University of Chicago Press.

Wolf, D., & Perry, M. D. (1988). From endpoints to repertoires: Some new conclusions about drawing development. *Journal of Aesthetic Education, 22*(1), 17–34.

Zessoules, R., Wolf, D., & Gardner, H. (1988). A better balance: ARTS PROPEL as an alternative to discipline based art education. In J. Burton, A. Lederman, & P. London (Eds.), *Beyond DBAE: The case for multiple visions of art education* (pp. 117–130). Sponsored by the University Council on Art Education.

Zurmuehlen, M. (1977). Teachers' preferences in children's drawings. *Studies in Art Education, 19*(1), 52–65.

MUSIC IN EARLY CHILDHOOD EDUCATION

J. Craig Peery

BRIGHAM YOUNG UNIVERSITY

Music is among the child's first social experiences. In fact children are sensitive to music before birth (Shetler, 1989). Fast music elicits a fast fetal heartbeat, slow quiet music yields a more relaxed fetal heartbeat (Olds, 1986). The emotional reactions to intrauterine musical experience, however, may not be completely positive (see Feldman, 1986, p. 200, for an account of a youngster who reported not liking his mother's singing when he was still in the womb, and see Verny & Kelly, 1981, for an account of a mother whose fetus kicked so vigorously while the mother was attending a rock concert, that it broke one of the mother's ribs). First feedings are likely to be accompanied by lullabies. Music becomes part of a child's life from experiences in the family, from the media, as a part of religious worship, in the school curriculum, and in play and organized recreation.

Music education and the psychology of music have a long and venerable history. In the more recent past, music research has come of age with the emergence of several journals, handbooks, and texts. Educators began to organize material about music, primarily within an education context. The grandfather of music research is the *Music Educators Journal,* which began publication in 1914, and has maintained a primarily pedagogical focus. The *Journal of Research in Music Education,* first published in 1952, followed in the education tradition but has also published basic research dealing with musical issues beyond those related strictly to education. The *Journal of Music Therapy* began publication in 1963 and includes basic research in addition to research that applies to music therapy. Also in 1963, the *Bulletin of the Council for Research in Music Education* began publishing refereed articles and reviews of doctoral dissertations. More recently two more focused journals have emerged to pursue specific interest in investigating human musical mechanisms: *Psychology of Music,* which began

publication in 1972, was the first research journal devoted exclusively to human musical experience, and *Psychomusicology* was first published in 1981 in an attempt to integrate a number of very disparate approaches ranging from audiology to music education into a broader understanding of human musical experience. Deutsch's (1982) book, *Psychology of Music,* and Dowling and Harwood's (1986) book, *Music Cognition,* contributed to the broad interface of music and psychological concerns. Each of these sources contains research related to early childhood, but there is no specific conceptual or editorial method or approach that separates early childhood material from the broader context.

While music educators have been interested in the psychology of music and music education, developmental psychologists and early childhood educators have not demonstrated the same interest in music as a phenomenon of childhood. One notable exception is David Hargreaves (1986a, 1986b), who has made the most comprehensive and clearest attempts to bring the worlds of music and child development together. During the 1980s several conferences, especially the Music Educators National Conference, and several books, particularly *The Developmental Psychology of Music* (Hargreaves, 1986b), and *Music and Child Development* (Peery, Peery, & Draper, 1987), sought to draw attention specifically to interfacing the study of music in the lives of children. This chapter is written primarily from the perspective of developmental psychology with a focus on the role music can play in the lives of children. Consequently, the emphasis in this chapter is more on understanding basic psychological principles than on applying them to the "how to's" of music education. The rubric of research is another filter used to select material for this chapter. Since this volume is a handbook of research, we have focused almost exclusively on reporting research findings. As the section on

---

An earlier version of this chapter, "The Role of Music in Child Development" (Peery & Peery, 1987), appeared in Peery, J. C., Peery, I. W. & Draper, T. D. *Music and Child Development,* New York: Springer-Verlag.

music education for young children (below) points out, a number of professional interests have music and children as part of their domains, and there is some dynamic and probably healthy tension among these different approaches. With a focus on research, however, music education per se has been given less attention here, not because it has, by implication, less value, but merely because some delimitations have been necessary.

Though this chapter does not deal directly with the reason for music in society per se, we believe that the elements of music reflect the organization of the human central nervous system. We also believe that in music and musical experience we reproduce in an emphasized and stereotypical way many of the behaviors and experiences necessary for human social communication. In her pioneering work on the emergence of musical gestures, Cohen's (1980) conceptual model hypothesized inborn traits that are directly manifest by body movement and responses to sound. By including music so naturally as an integral part of a child's world, educators, too, may be unconsciously assuming fundamental parallels between music, normal neurological functioning, and normal social communication. So basic is music to human society that Margaret Mead has said it is a fundamental human *need* that bridges cultural diversity (Mead, 1972).

Given the universal involvement of music in children's lives, surprisingly little attention has been paid to developing a systematic view of the role and significance of music in childhood. This chapter is structured around a model for considering the ways music can have significance for children. It examines currently available research findings encompassed by the model.

Two major divisions for conceptualizing the influence of music on children are suggested. First, and perhaps most significant, music is important because it has inherent merit in itself. Many see value in exposing, training, and enculturating children with regard to music because music is a good and desirable part of life and one of the beauties of human culture. Second, developing music skills may have attendant benefits that generalize to other categories of personal and social competence. By developing performance, listening, and appreciation abilities in music, music educators, child development experts, and parents demonstrate a belief that children may also be developing or enhancing cognitive, physical, and social development. These distinct approaches are illustrated in Figure 14–1. The following material gives an overview of the state of the art in each approach. The interrelationships between them (represented by the broken lines in Figure 14–1) promise fruitful areas for further understanding the role of music in children's lives.

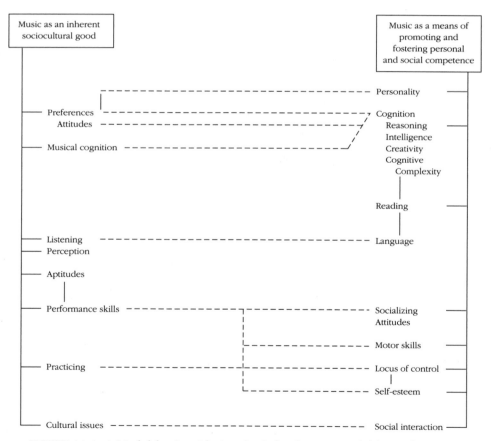

FIGURE 14–1. A Model for Considering the Role of Music in Child Development.
From: Peery, Peery, & Draper, 1987, p. 4. Reprinted with permission.

MUSIC AS MUSIC: DEVELOPING UNDERSTANDING, APPRECIATION, APTITUDES, SKILLS, AND ABILITIES

Many parents feel musical exposure and training is an enriching and positive part of human experience. Available research on music-for-its-own-sake can be divided into 8 topics: preferences, musical cognition, listening, perception, musical aptitude, performance skills, practicing, and cultural issues.

Musical Preferences

LeBlanc (1987) discusses the history of research in musical preferences, presents a comprehensive theory of the development of musical preferences, and discusses its implications in detail. There are three frequently occurring hypotheses regarding the formation of musical preference. First, music training (Geringer, 1982; Geringer & McManus, 1979; Gordon, 1971) or repeated exposure to particular music (either a specific piece or a particular style) increases taste for that music; that is, what you hear is what you like. Second, musical preference is influenced by salient variables identified in social learning theory; that is, children tend to model their musical preferences after the preferences of important people in their lives, such as authority figures (Radocy, 1976), adults, and teachers. Third, certain qualities inherent in the music influence preference (Kalanidhi, 1970; Kulka, 1981; McMullen, 1974), particularly style (LeBlanc, 1979), "popular is preferred to classical"; tempo (LeBlanc & McCrary, 1983), "faster is better"; complexity (Dowling & Harwood, 1986; Heyduk, 1975); and performing medium (LeBlanc, 1981; LeBlanc & Cote, 1983), "instruments are (slightly) preferred to voice." Some of this research has focused exclusively on preschool children. Peery and Peery (1986) found that at age 4 children have eclectic musical tastes. The processes of exposure, modeling, and enculturation probably cause a shift in preferences most frequently away from classical music toward popular music, beginning about age 5 or 6.

Repetition. Repetition increases the taste for classical music in older students from fourth grade through college (Getz, 1966; Heingartner & Hall, 1974; Bradley, 1971, 1972; Mull, 1957). It is certainly reasonable to assume that repeated exposure in early childhood will also enhance enjoyment of a variety of music.

Social Influences. While peers have a significant influence on adolescents' music preference (Inglefield, 1972), we would speculate this is much less true in early childhood. Approval and support by adults and teachers have a positive influence on music selection for grade-school children (Greer, Dorow, Wachhaus, & White, 1973; Greer, Dorow, & Hanser, 1973; Dorow, 1977).

Style. Preschool children seem to like most musical styles. Greer, Dorow, and Randall (1974) found no differences between preschoolers and first-graders in their preference for popular over classical music, but even at preschool and first-

grade ages Greer (1974) reported a tendency to prefer rock to non-rock music.

Schuckert and McDonald (1968) were not able to influence preschoolers' musical preference significantly solely by exposure to less-preferred music. Peery and Peery (1986) found that at age 4 children have eclectic musical tastes and like classical and popular music equally well. They found evidence that sometime during the fifth or sixth year there is a shift away from liking classical music. However, they also found this shift away from preferring classical music can be avoided by exposing children to classical music and to music appreciation training in a preschool classroom setting. Geringer (1977) found that preschool children play most frequently with timpani, piano, step bells, ukulele, metallophone, and slide whistle in that order during nondirected free-play activities; other orchestral instruments were not available to the children in his study, however.

In studies with grade-school children, there is a consistent finding that musical style is the most salient variable influencing musical preference. Popular music is increasingly preferred to classical music as children get older (Rogers, 1957; Greer, Dorow, & Randall, 1974; LeBlanc, 1979). LeBlanc, in studies of fifth- and sixth-grade children, has found that musical style affects preference significantly independent of tempo and medium, with popular (but not necessarily rock) music generally preferred to classical. He has developed an elaborate theory of musical preference that identifies personal characteristics of the listener, characteristics of the music, and cultural environment as the key variables (LeBlanc, 1987). In his theory of the development of musical preference, LeBlanc is one of the few attempting to relate musical issues to other characteristics of personal and social competence, as the model in Figure 14–1 suggests should be done.

Musical Cognition

Dowling (1982) discusses a developmental sequence for melodic information processing. He notes that infants can detect changes in temporal presentation, rhythm, and pitch intervals of melody (Melson & McCall, 1970; Kinney & Kagan, 1976; Chang & Trehub, 1977a, 1977b). In older children the ability to remember melodies is dependent on at least three subskills; (a) remembering melodic contour, (b) remembering pitch intervals, and (c) identifying tonality (and distinguishing between tonal and atonal music). Training enhances these skills for adults (reviewed in Bartlett & Dowling, 1980); in children these abilities develop with age (and therefore presumably with musical experience).

Ability to recognize pitch direction in 3-, 4-, and 5-year-olds was studied by Webster and Schlentrich (1982). They found some children of each age could make pitch-direction discriminations accurately, although the skill improved with age. But about one-third of the children they tested could not perform this discrimination well, even when performance-based modes of responding were used instead of verbal responses.

Bartlett and Dowling (1980) discovered that it is easier to distinguish between melodies from harmonically distant keys than from harmonically similar keys. They also found that adults were generally better at remembering melodies than children, and that older children (grades 1 and 2) were better than kindergartners in these memory tasks. Their results suggest harmonic "key" becomes a part of the cognitive-cultural structure that humans use to understand music at an early age.

Billingsley and Rotenberg (1982) tested the ability to remember sequences of random musical intervals in first-, fourth- and seventh-grade children. The seventh-graders did significantly better than the first-graders, and there was evidence of consistent improvement as children got older. For tonal aspects of melody, an understanding of diatonic scale characteristics seems to develop first, followed by an understanding of pitch relationships in the tonic triad as children reach third to fifth grade (Krumhansl & Keil, 1982). Children 4 to 9 years old do not identify the octave as sounding like test pitches (Sergeant, 1983). Sergeant concludes that the octave is a learned concept, not an innate perceptual characteristic of human hearing. Similarly, Krumhansl and Keil's (1982) data indicate that octave relations are preferred to other notes in the tonic triad more by adults than by first graders, and the fact that this preference seems to develop over time indicates cognitive rather than strictly perceptual influences at work.

Children 5 to 7 years can remember musical phrases well enough to distinguish actual repetitions from variations (Abel-Struth, 1982). Abel-Struth (1982) also found that children's recognition of musical phrases was better for complex rather than simple musical phrases and that girls were slightly better at recognition tasks than boys.

Children can understand the emotional, or affective, meaning of music (Terwogt & Grinsven, 1988). Cunningham and Sterling (1988) found developmental changes in children's understanding of the affect communicated by musical passages. Preschoolers have considerable ability to understand the affective meaning of music (happy, sad, angry, afraid), in ways similar to adults. This finding is contrary to some Piagetian predictions about young children's egocentrism, but parallel to other findings related to social cognition (e.g., Borke, 1971).

The idea that musical cognition parallels the development of other cognitive abilities has a venerable history. Zimmerman (Pflederer, 1964) first posited the notion of music conservation, and she has been active in pursuing research evidence of a music conservation construct (Pflederer, 1967; Zimmerman & Sechrest, 1970; Webster & Zimmerman, 1983). Because music is temporal, there have been doubts expressed about parallels with transformations of pairs of concrete objects (Hargreaves, 1986a; Gardner, 1973). Hildebrandt (1987) has found that children display a growing capacity to recognize variances and invariances in musical elements (melody, rhythm, etc.) and relations across musical contexts. She feels that there are two types of musical cognition: logical and grammatical. Musically logical reasoning is involved in tasks that require discrimination and classification of pitches, durations, timbres, themes, and larger musical forms. These classifications involve the ability to identify similarities and differences. Musical logic also involves seriation and representation tasks that involve the measurement of time and rhythm. Musically grammatical reasoning, by contrast, involves understanding of the form and meaning of music within given styles and traditions.

The ability to perform cognitive operations (in the Piagetian sense) on musical tasks is related to other cognitive skills. Preschool children who were incapable of performing concrete operational tasks involving number were also incapable of combining musical sounds in memory. Children who exhibited concrete operations were more successful at the tasks requiring musical cognition (Serafine, 1981). Children's understanding of the concept of meter in music becomes increasingly sophisticated as their cognitive development proceeds through the stages outlined by Piaget (Jones, 1976). Starting at about 9.5 years of age it is easier for children to understand and talk about concepts of meter (Jones, 1976). Though Upitis (1987) found 7-year-olds could frequently respond meaningfully to meter in music, the ability to conceptualize about meter and to verbalize those concepts clearly increases with age and cognitive development (Davidson & Colley, 1987). Once again, training can improve a child's ability to use Piagetian conservation skills on tonal and rhythmic patterns (Foley, 1975). There is also evidence that training in conservation of musical concepts facilitates development of conservation with nonmusical concepts (Botvin, 1974). McDonald (1974) found a relationship between intelligence and musical concept formation for middle-class subjects, but not for lower-class subjects.

There is evidence that some children as young as first grade have abilities in all these areas, while most children do not develop facility with musical cognition until approaching adolescence. Just why there are some early bloomers and others take longer to develop skill at musical cognition is not clear. Neither prodigious musical talent nor general intelligence seem to account for the early appearance of these abilities. One finding does emerge, however. The results consistently point to the importance of experience with and exposure to music in order to enhance pitch, melodic, and metrical abilities of musical cognition. Few of the skills in musical cognition are innate. The more exposure to music children have both through direct training and by indirect experience, the more readily their abilities to grasp musical ideas seem to progress.

Listening

Very young infants can listen attentively to music (Kelley & Sutton-Smith, 1987). Music listening skills are positively influenced by age and experience in the first three school grades; there is a greater improvement between first and second grade, than between second and third grade in listening and performing ability (Simons, 1976). Age, experience, and intelligence all combine to increase ability to discriminate rhythmic patterns, pitch and tonal sequences, though even 6-year-olds can be quite skilled in rhythm duplication (Gardner, 1971). Hickman (1970) found that children perceive the octave, minor seventh, and perfect fifth as intervals that are more "unitary" than other intervals. Hickman also found that perception of rhythm was influenced by pitch, intelligence, and practice and that the perception of timbre was influenced by experience. Both McDonald's and Hickman's work support the utility of our model proposing relationships between musical skills and other areas of social and personal competence.

Davidson (1985) discovered that children from 1 to 7 years grasp tonal materials in what might be characterized as a set of increasingly prominent tonal structures and contour schemes. These contour schemes are characterized by the interval between the top and bottom note of the tonal phrase, the ways the boundary notes are connected, and the direction of the contour. Davidson found that the expected space for these contour schemes increased progressively with age during the first 7 years from the interval of a third to nearly an octave by age 7.

Krumhansl and Keil (1982) describe what they identify as an acquisition of the hierarchy of tonal functions in music. Students from first to sixth grade and college students expressed their preference for tonal sequences; ratings show a pattern of increasing differentiation of scale tones, tonic triad tones, and other scale components with age. The ability to discriminate similar interpretations of melodic passages from dissimilar interpretations also improves significantly from first to third, but only modestly from third grade to fifth grade (Heller, Campbell, & Gibson, 1982).

Both age and experience have an important impact on listening and discrimination skills. Development psychologists believe both maturation and experience can influence individual changes, and that maturation and experience can interact to produce changes that are different from what either factor might produce separately. A major difficulty with most research in music and child development, however, has been a failure to consider both of these variables in planning and in evaluating research studies.

Perception

Infants are sensitive to changes in melodic contour and changes in rhythm (Trehub, 1987). Not only do infants show a preference for correctly segmented speech (Kemler-Nelson, Hirsh-Pasek, Jusczyk, & Wright-Cassidy, 1989), 6-month-olds can perceive segmental organization in musical passages, and they prefer musical passages that are interrupted at phrase boundaries, not in the middle of phrases (Krumhansl & Jusczyk, 1990). Here indeed is evidence that music may reflect the natural perceptual structures in the human central nervous system.

Buckton (1977) stated that pitch discrimination and tonal memory, but not melodic abilities, could be improved by training programs for 6- to 8-year-olds. Children as young as first grade can perceive and identify ascending and descending sequences of tone presentation (Hair, 1982); understanding the relationship between cross-modal aural and visual representations of the concepts of "ascending" and "descending" is more difficult, with fourth-graders performing better than first-graders on cross-modal tasks (Hair, 1982). The relationship between pitch discrimination and pitch matching is not strong, and indeed these may be separate abilities. Fourth-grade children are better at pitch matching than preschool children, but this could be due to vocal and muscle maturation (Geringer, 1983). Pick, Palmer, Hennessy, Unze, Jones, & Richardson (1988) found that young children can perceive key changes in the transposition of melodies, but they can also detect melodic similarities over key transpositions.

They can also distinguish between melodies with the same contour but different intervals. Infants and young children can perceive differences in pitch as small as a semitone, and by age 4 to 6, children use a diatonic structure in preference to a non-diatonic (Trehub, Cohen, Thorpe, & Morrongiello, 1986). Sensitivity to melodic contour, intervals, and key is present in young children but increases with age (Trehub, Morrongiello, & Thorpe, 1985).

Musical Aptitude

Considerable attention over many years has been given to developing measures of musical aptitude. The distinction between musical aptitude and musical achievement should be noted (Shuter-Dyson, 1982). Musical aptitudes are thought to remain relatively stable over time (Gordon, 1971) and are not improved by drills or exercises (Colwell, 1972). Musical achievement concerns the actual abilities that an individual can demonstrate, and these should improve with practice, experience, and training. Children with musical aptitude will demonstrate achievement in response to training and experience. Identifying aptitude is important so that decisions about musical training can be guided intelligently.

Bloom and his colleagues (Bloom, 1985a) did an extensive study of developing talent in young people. Learning to be a concert pianist was one of the aspects of talent development on which they focused (Sosniak, 1985).

To identify superior performers, panels (or juries) of teacher-performers are used (Peery, Nyboer, & Peery, 1987). While teacher-performers' opinions are necessary in judging musical competitions, the purpose of these activities is focused more on recognizing achievement among individuals who have musical aptitude than on identifying aptitude per se.

If parents are seeking an answer to the question, "Is my child musically talented enough that he should be given music lessons?" an audition with a competent teacher may provide sufficient information. However, it is possible for an individual child to have understanding and insight into sound, but lack the psychomotor ability necessary for performance. Such a child might benefit greatly from exposure to music and training in music appreciation. Some, however, believe that teachers' opinions may not be completely accurate in assessing aptitude (Rubenger, 1979). This may be particularly true when considering musical aptitudes that are not linked with the psychomotor skills necessary for success in performance training.

Freeman (1976) reports that the difference between musically and artistically talented children lies not in differences between innate abilities (which were approximately equal between the two groups in his study) but in differences of opportunity and encouragement provided by parents in the home environment. Specifically, families of musically talented children provided many musical instruments, support for orchestra playing, support for extra lessons, incentive to practice music, a high regard for music education, others in the family who played music, and good quality music in the home. The time to begin such family support is in early childhood, and it is appropriate to begin music lessons at age 4 or 5. These findings are consonant with the theory that exceptional talent can be developed by "the earliness, intensity, persistence, regularity, family concentration, tutorial approach, and the presence of dominant family intellectual cultural value orientations" in the child's life (Fowler, 1969). In fact, Fowler (1962) has shown music to be one of the specialized abilities that can be fostered by the kind of family environment that focuses on music attitudes and abilities.

Bloom and his colleagues (Bloom, 1985b) discovered a number of factors involved in the development of exceptionally talented children. Home and family support were paramount. According to Bloom (1985b) parents of individuals who developed into world-class performers in any area, including music, came from a variety of backgrounds and economic levels. These parents were *child oriented* and shared a commitment to devoting their time and resources to promoting optimal conditions for their children's development. The home atmosphere stressed achievement. Working hard and spending one's time wisely were continuously emphasized, with parents serving as role models and children learning early on to work hard over long periods for distant goals. In the early years, participation is seen as a form of recreation and play that parent and child share. Next comes a long sequence of specialized teachers, hard work, and long hours where skills are acquired and honed. Bloom (1985b) reports that parents of exceptional performers value one particular area of talent (e.g., music), to the exclusion of others (e.g., sports). Teachers for young performers make the learning process fun and are able to maintain motivation through age-appropriate encouragement and support. The work with the teacher is buttressed by follow-up in the home, where routines of practice are developed, usually with the mother's support in the case of young musicians.

Musical aptitude probably includes a number of perceptual and motor skills in constellation. Barrett and Barker (1973) found a significant relationship between musical aptitude and 3 of 5 separate perceptual tasks supporting a multifaceted approach to musical aptitude. The child's ability to understand the concept of meter in music is related to age and development of the concept of time, as Piaget outlines (Jones, 1976). Buckton (1977) found that pitch discrimination and tonal memory, but not melodic abilities, could be improved by training programs for 6- to 8-year-olds.

Dorhout (1982) and Shuter-Dyson (1982) review the many methods currently available for assessing musical aptitude and remind us that information from multiple sources (e.g., tests, teachers' opinions, parental feedback) may be helpful. "A coordinated effort should be undertaken to pool the information derived from all available sources," Dorhout suggests (p. 57). There are a number of tests of musical aptitude. Most of these would be relevant to teachers trying to devise and organize a musical curriculum in a school setting.

Attempts to measure musical aptitude by examining music audition have been made by Gordon (1979) in order to illuminate musical aptitudes of children 5 to 8 years old. It is important to continue work on identifying aptitudes of younger children. Children seem to respond to music in potent ways (Zimny & Weidenfeller, 1962) and clearly enjoy music before they can conceptualize about it verbally.

Absolute pitch (or perfect pitch) is one of the most highly regarded musical abilities. Individuals who posses absolute pitch (AP) are able to state the name of a pitch upon hearing it and frequently can sing a given pitch on command. The etiology of absolute pitch has received attention (Crozier, Robinson, & Ewing, 1976–77). Some believe AP is hereditary, while most have argued that AP is learned either as a result of rigorous training, or as a combination of experience and maturation. In their excellent and comprehensive discussion of AP, Ward and Burns (1982) conclude that neither the hereditary nor the training-imprinting models for explaining AP have demonstrated conclusive proof of their validity. Some young children demonstrate the ability with matter-of-fact ease, while others struggle to develop AP with limited or no success. Stories like the 4-year-old girl who was told the names of the notes on the piano keyboard one day, only to be able to match the name of the notes with the pitches the next day, "Because you said so yesterday, Mommy," seem incredible to someone who does not have AP, but are quite common among those who have this ability. The earlier the ability is manifest, the more accurate it is likely to be (Wellek, 1938; Sergeant, 1969). Apparently, early exposure and experience is important, but the child must have the innate "gift" for the experience or training to be effective.

Performance Skills

In contrast to research on the mental aspects of music and child development, work on performance skills and children is much harder to find. This is unexpected since much of the intensity of the experience of studying a musical instrument is involved with practicing, which is a motor performance concern. The relative paucity of research on performance skills suggests that parents and teachers feel that studying and practicing a musical instrument falls into the category of activities that are desirable for their own sake and do not need ancillary improvement in other areas to justify them.

Gilbert (1979) has developed a Motoric Music Skills Test (MMST) to provide information on the development of motoric music skills. The test measures motor pattern coordination, eye-hand coordination, speed of movement, range of movement, and compound factors. Her preliminary findings with the test indicated that these motor skills improve with age and that girls perform better than boys on three of the subtests: motor pattern coordination, eye-hand coordination, and compound factors. Longitudinal research with the MMST (Gilbert, 1981), with two data points taken a year apart from the same children, revealed that individuals did improve consistently from year 1 to year 2. Gilbert also found significant predictive relationships between scores taken a year apart on the speed-of-movement, the motor-pattern-coordination, and the range-of-movement subtests. There was an overall positive correlation from year 1 to year 2 on all subtests except eye-hand coordination. These findings indicate that skills at one time are good predictors of skills in later development. Gilbert did not find any difference between boys and girls in the improvement of motor skills, but she did find that 4-year-olds improved significantly more than 6- or 7-year-olds in the year that elapsed between testing.

For Gilbert, the finding that young children seem more plastic and susceptible to improvement has several implications. First, it is consistent with research findings in other domains (e.g., Rarick, 1961) that "most fundamental motor patterns emerge before the age of 5, and that skills are merely stabilized beyond that point" (Gilbert, 1981). For example, training 4-year-olds in motor skills related to gymnastics has demonstrated levels of improvement substantially greater than would be predicted by observations of motor development in children without such training (Leithwood & Fowler, 1971). Second, since the 4-year-olds showed the greatest score gains in every subtest of the MMST, greater attention should be given to helping preschoolers develop the motor skills required for musical performance, and practice with motor skills might well be integrated into the preschool curriculum. Additionally, these observations about improvement in motor skills between age 4 and 5 reinforce the practical experience of many piano teachers that the best time to start a young child on piano lessons is late in the fourth or early in the fifth year.

The link between performance skills and the concept of using music as a means of promoting intellectual, social, and personal competence is perhaps the strongest of any in the model in Figure 14–1. The pianists interviewed by Sosniak (1985) who were world caliber in their young adulthood usually began taking piano lessons in their early childhood; with the combination of good teaching and supportive parents, these individuals were the best pianists in their neighborhood, if not in their town, at an early age. Peery, Nyboer, and Peery (1987) report a similar pattern for young pianists who are not necessarily destined to world-class status, but who have begun to participate in local piano competitions at an early age. Children in the 4-to-7-year age range seem particularly susceptible to improvement in motor performance skills with training. Many of these skills are likely to have carryover to other large and small motor tasks from game playing to penmanship.

Practicing

Learning to play a musical instrument consists of regular lessons sandwiched between hours of potentially lonely and demanding practice. Practicing is seldom the motivation for musical study and it is frequently the reason lessons are terminated. The rigor of practice yields amazing results in the lives of millions of children every year; they actually learn to play instruments and make music. Yet despite millions of children practicing tens of millions of hours, little research has focused on practicing a musical instrument. Sosniak (1985) did inquire about the childhood practice habits of the exceptional pianists in their research. According to Sosniak, these individuals lived in homes where music was constantly heard. As young children they had no choice about whether to take music lessons; they began because their parents felt that musical training was appropriate for all children. As young children these future concert pianists enjoyed their early lessons and soon developed a routine of daily practice *before* they had a chance to engage in a lot of other competing activities. Sosniak also notes that as young children these future pianists spent more time playing and practicing the piano than their peers spent on any other single activity except, possibly, *watching television*. One cannot help but wonder what the large-scale effect would be of putting children to practice music instead of watching so much television in their early years, but there is no additional research. What children do most when learning to play a musical instrument is not well studied at all; to date we have been unable to find a single study related to practicing. Yet research on the motivations and methods for encouraging practice, and on the musical and nonmusical results of practice, would seem logically to be among the most important studies for enhancing our understanding of the role of music in children's lives.

Cultural Issues

Gordon (1967) attempted to identify musically talented students in culturally disadvantaged environments; he found that disadvantaged environments generally depress musical sensitivity but that some children from disadvantaged environments showed considerable musical talent. Freeman (1976) and Shuter-Dyson (1979) showed that music in the home environment was a significant factor in children displaying musical aptitudes.

Further inquiries about the relationship between cultural influences in childrearing and musical development seem appropriate and needed. One interesting phenomenon is the relatively high proportion of children with an Asian heritage who perform successfully in music competitions (Peery, Nyboer, & Peery, 1987). We have guessed that cultural differences in childrearing practices may be influential, but the nature of the salient variables is not obvious.

In the broader view, substantial cultural and social enrichment results from involving children with music. Parents seem to understand such enrichment from both a practical and an aesthetic perspective. Once again, however, we are confronted with a domain of child development that is being driven in the real world by parents' intuitive understanding but on which virtually no research has been focused. Perhaps substantial face validity is a contraindication for research scrutiny.

MUSIC AS A MEANS OF PROMOTING AND FOSTERING PERSONAL AND SOCIAL COMPETENCE

In this section we turn attention to the second reason our model proposes for exposing children to music: Developing musical skills may have attendant benefits that generalize to other categories of personal and social competence. Our purpose here is not so much to provide evidence that confirms music as a means of fostering development in other areas of personal and social competence, as to explore the possibilities that music can enhance competence suggested by the existing research. Relationships and proposed relationships between music and personal and social competence have long been part of the music education scene. As Draper and Gayle (1987) have pointed out, we have an extensive tradition of justifying development of children's music performance, listening, and appreciation abilities in terms of contingent gains in cognitive, physical, and social development. Early childhood education has been particularly infected with the tendency to justify involvement in music by claiming such involvement will enhance whichever social or cognitive skill is currently in vogue in the early childhood curriculum.

It is not clear from much of the research cited in this section whether involvement with music is the salient influence or if other confounding variables associated with music study may be the critical force. Possibly music is a contextual catalyst for many developmental outcomes, doing little by itself but enlarging the effect of certain kinds of activities. It is also possible, however, that music and musical tasks do indeed promote specific developmental outcomes. In most cases, precisely what causes which effects is not clearly explicated in the studies below. And, as is often the case in science, one is left with more intriguing questions than clear answers.

We have divided this section on music as a means of promoting and fostering personal and social competence into nine areas: personality, cognition (including reasoning, intelligence, and creativity), reading, language skills, socialization of attitudes, motor skills, locus of control, self-esteem, and social interaction.

Personality

One long-standing hypothesis is that musical preferences are an indication of personality style. Cattell and Anderson (1953) first developed a musical preference test as part of the Institute for Personality Ability and Testing (IPAT) protocol. Cattell and Saunders (1954) sought to discover factors for musical preferences on the IPAT and related these to personality diagnosis. They were only moderately successful in identifying music-preference factor structures that correlated with personality factor structures. It is by no means clear that relationships between music preference and personality factors are discernable in early childhood.

Cognition

Gardner, Winner, and Kircher (1975) found that children conceptualize the arts in increasingly sophisticated ways as they grow older. This work points to an interface between cognitive development and art appreciation. Castell (1982) found children between ages 8 and 11 are remarkably sensitive to musical style and use instrument cues to identify classical music and tempo cues to identify popular music.

Several attempts have been made to bridge the gap between the notions of involving children in music as a good in itself and involving them in music to stimulate mental abilities. Neufeld (1986), for example, has found that a formal Kodaly program can increase a preschooler's understanding of prenumber concepts of comparison, order, classification, and pattern—but only for girls. Some other tantalizing indications of an important link between musical performance skill training and other cognitive abilities have emerged.

Field Dependence, Spatial Ability, Social Adjustment, Analytic Ability. Field-dependent individuals appear to benefit from musically based movement instruction (Schmidt & Lewis, 1987). Parente and O'Malley (1975) found that training in the

performance of musical rhythms significantly improved the performance on the rod-and-frame task in 6- to 9-year-old children. Their evidence parallels research indicating that field independence improves with perceptual-motor training. Even though the motor-music training in their study was much less sophisticated and much less structured than the gymnastics training, Leithwood and Fowler (1971) did find that 4-year-olds who received either gymnastic performance training or motor-music training also improved their analytic ability, social adjustment with peers, and relationships with adults.

Karma (1982) has found that verbal-analytic skills are correlated with musical ability in younger subjects and that spatial abilities correlate with musical ability in adolescents and adults. Wagley (1978) discovered that preschool children enjoyed learning cognitive skills more when training was accompanied with musical experiences.

Cognitive skills of classification, seriation, spatial understanding, and temporal relations can also be improved in preschool children through guided music listening (Parker, 1973). Hurwitz, Wolff, Bortnick, and Kokas (1975) found that grade-school boys improved on tests of spatial cognition after they had training in a Kodaly Music Curriculum. Botvin (1974) found that training sixth-graders to perform Piagetian-type conservation tasks with melody also improves their performance with nonmusical concepts of mass, weight, and number. Nelson (1980) found that third-graders are able to conserve meter both verbally and behaviorally, and that kindergartners demonstrate some, but much less, ability on meter conservation tasks. Musical ability is related to auditory conservation, but visual conservation skills and auditory conservation skills may not be related in kindergartners (Norton, 1978).

Intelligence. After reviewing the research of Getz (1966), Keston and Pinto (1955), and Rubin-Rabson (1940), Wapnick (1976) concludes there is no likely relation between intelligence and music preference. Musical aptitude and intelligence are more likely to be related. Young (1982) found intelligence related both to music-reading ability and to developing musical performance skills.

Gordon (1968) notes that several studies have shown low but consistently positive correlations between musical aptitude scores and scores on intelligence tests, and Gordon's (1968) study replicates this finding. Research in the early part of this century suggested that high ratings of musical performance correlate with intelligence. Both Gordon (1968) and Moore (1966) note the traditional conclusion that intelligent people are not necessarily musical, but that musical people are necessarily intelligent.

Phillips (1976) studied relationships between the Wing battery of musical aptitude tests and several measures of intelligence. Phillips concludes that there is considerable relationship between musical aptitude and intelligence. However, Phillips believes family and social influence play a major role in influencing ability to score well on all his tests. Most psychologists believe the kind of ability measured on standard IQ tests is largely genetic in character; consequently, Phillips' (1976) work may be confounding intelligence and other kinds of information variables. Wingert (1972) found an increase in intelligence manifested by retarded children after exposure to a music enrichment program.

Gardner (1983) has proposed a theory of multiple intelligences, with music as one of the specific intelligence types. Gardner (1983) believes that musical abilities, aptitudes, and talents result from physiological and personality differences in individuals that may not be detectable using a standard intelligence test. He cites evidence, for example, that verbal skills seem to be produced in the left hemisphere of the brain, while musical perception and skills seem to function in the right hemisphere. Neal's (1983) research comparing children with high musical aptitude to children of normal musical aptitude accords with Gardner's suggestion. Neal found that right-ear (therefore left cerebral hemisphere) dependent scores distinguished high-aptitude from normal-aptitude children. Neal suggests that children with high musical aptitude learn to analyze musical concepts with their left-brain (verbal/analytic) functions, in addition to exercising the right-brain abilities found in children with normal musical aptitude.

Creativity. Webster (1987) discusses children's musical creativity within the broad context of a theory of creative thought. He believes that creative behavior is a normal human activity, and he has developed an instrument, the Measures of Creative Thinking in Music (MCTM) for measuring creative musical thought children 7 to 10 years old. Cleall (1981) believes that cognition is promoted by creative activity. Burns (1986) suggests that musically creative learning may foster problem-solving skills. Musical play fosters positive creative experiences as children try different instruments, modes, melodies, and the like. Young children improvise not to make shaped, symmetrical tunes, but to generate patterns and shapes from rhythmic figures and note intervals (Pillsbury Foundation Studies, 1978). Younger than age 4, children are interested in the different sounds musical instruments make and improvise with instruments to experience new sounds (Flohr, 1981), by age 4, more complex patterns are added, and by age 8 improvisations reflect the concept of musical form (Flohr, 1985).

Plummeridge (1980) acknowledges the frequent call for curriculum activities that foster creativity and notes that musical training or activities are often proposed as vehicles for stimulating creativity. However, Plummeridge (1980) believes one must distinguish between creative *productivity* and creative (or imaginative) *thinking* styles; he also indicates that substantial differences in perspective may lead discussions of music and creativity to focus on very different matters. Cleall (1981) believes children should be allowed to "play" with musical elements to foster creativity.

Lowery (1982) tested three curricula designed to increase creativity in children. Two of these curricula were nonmusical, one (Music and Imagery or MI) was musical in orientation. Lowery reports significantly higher creativity scores in verbal fluency, verbal originality, figural originality, total verbal, and grand total creativity for the children who had the MI curriculum.

Cognitive Complexity. Heyduk (1975) theorized that personal preference for psychological complexity and the complexity of the music combine to predict preference in many individuals.

Heyduk argues that the preference perception of a musical excerpt is also a function of the individual's usual level of psychological complexity. Several researchers have postulated that complexity, and therefore psychological arousal, is positively correlated with preference (Fiske & Maddi, 1961; Berlyne, 1971; Zajonc, 1968). According to this line of reasoning, expanded in Heyduk's (1975) research, individuals who are accustomed to higher levels of psychological complexity will prefer more complex music than individuals who are accustomed to lower levels of psychological complexity. Logically then, one might expect preschool children to prefer less-complex music. However, some inferences are possible in terms of guiding musical experiences in early childhood. In terms of musical preference, exposure and instruction in the characteristics of classical music seem likely to render the relative cognitive complexities of classical music more familiar and therefore less psychologically complex and more preferred. If this is the case, one might argue that training in classical music decreases the likelihood that an individual will be "satisfied" with stimulation by relatively less complex musical forms, and increases the probability of preferring classical music. Unfortunately, many live performances of classical music explicitly exclude children under 6 (they can become restless and sometimes noisy). Such a policy may actually be contributing to the extinction of the audience for classical music. Opportunities for young children to be exposed to the musicians, instruments, and performances (young people's concerts, for example) ought to be built into our approach to classical music and young children.

An analysis of the correlation between musical style and psychological complexity has not yet been undertaken. It seems likely that both classical and popular music might be conceptualized accurately on a continuum of psychological complexity. It is, however, tempting to speculate that, overall, classical music has a greater range of variation on a complexity continuum. If Heyduk is correct, it would be logical that a naive listener would prefer the simpler pieces regardless of style. Given the relatively greater amount of study usually required to compose classical music successfully, study leading to a cognitive grasp of the music may be required in order to reduce the psychological complexity of classical music to an acceptable level for enjoyment and appreciation. One might therefore expect individuals who spend a good deal of their time in psychologically complex tasks (mathematicians, for example) to prefer classical music and, conversely, that individuals who come to appreciate classical music in its more complex forms prefer to be engaged in psychologically complex tasks.

If the development of preferences for complex thinking and for classical music are mutually interactive, a parent who encourages his child to appreciate classical music (and/or relatively more complex popular music) may be fostering a preference for cognitive-reinforcing complexity in other areas. This kind of theorizing suggests numerous avenues of research both in musical preference and in development domains.

Reading

Music has been found to be a potential distraction when used as a background for other tasks (Fogelson, 1973). If the music is familiar, however, the distracting effect on reading ability is decreased (Etaugh & Michals, 1975), and easy-listening background may actually facilitate on-task performance in fifth-graders (Davidson & Powell, 1986). The notion that access to music is reinforcing or, more generally, that music can be a pleasant accompaniment and can strengthen learning in other domains has been discussed but not widely researched or practiced. Integrating music with other academic pursuits is an intriguing idea deserving further attention.

Cohen (1974) suggests music and song as a vehicle for facilitating children's development of interest in reading, but (as Draper and Gale, 1987, suggest is frequently the case) he presents no data demonstrating the efficacy of this approach. Hurwitz et al. (1975) report an improvement in reading skills for grade-school children who have been involved in Kodaly Music Curriculum training. This improvement in reading ability was measured on standard reading tests that were a part of the school's student evaluation and had nothing to do with music. Children with 2 years of Kodaly training (through second grade) continued to have higher reading scores than a matched control group, indicating a potential long-range improvement over increasingly complex reading skills (Hurwitz et al., 1975). Weeden (1971) found no improvement on reading or math skills in black children who had been involved in one semester of Suzuki violin training. However, Weeden himself suggests that one semester may be too short a time to generate appreciable differences in other skills.

Montessori developed a program for early childhood education that has had a major impact on the early childhood education curricula (see Chattin-McNichols, 1981). Montessori planned and discussed an approach to music education requiring student experience for learning (Montessori, 1965). While aspects of children's perceptual, motor, and intellectual functioning in relation to the Montessori classroom approach have been examined, little is known about the effect of the Montessori music curriculum (McDonald, 1983). Montessori clearly saw parallels between music learning and other kinds of learning, but research integrating the Montessori methods of music education with other educational issues has yet to appear.

Language

Papousek and Papousek (1981) point out the paucity of information relating to infant vocalization, music, and language. They suggest that important relationships may indeed exist. Kokas (1969) has conducted preliminary studies indicating that participation in a Kodaly Music Curriculum can improve a child's ability with language development.

Jalongo and Bromley (1984) suggest that picture song books help children develop linguistic competence. They believe that bilingual children and children with learning difficulties benefit from the added exposure to vocabulary, syntax, semantics, and rhythm. Gifted children also benefit linguistically from exposure to picture books, according to Jalongo and Bromley (1984), because the songs add extra dimensions of comprehension and encourage teaching/learning activities that prompt divergent thinking. Information about the song's history, social context, or cultural context can also lead to expanded abilities to deal with the song from a more meaningful linguistic base.

Similarly, Kuhmerker (1969) advocates learning songs to facilitate adoption of beginning-reading vocabulary. She believes that the rhythm and phrasing of the words, as well as the actions and kinesthetic experiences associated with the song, help the child associate words with a wider variety of linguistic experience. McCarthy (1985) believes that special musical qualities can promote language development and reading skills, but although he provides some detailed suggestions about implementing music in a handicapped reading curriculum, he offers no evidence that his approach is effective.

Motor Skills

Although practicing an instrument is a specific case of motor skill training, little is known about the interrelationships of these issues in normal human development. Lewis (1988) found that movement training had a moderately positive effect on some listening skills of first- and third-graders. Such a finding still fits within our model, but the direction of influence is in reverse from motoric competence to musical ability. Sims (1986) discovered that cognitive abilities mediated motor responses to musical phrases; preschool children respond less precisely than grade-school or college students on hopping-to-music tasks. Groves (1966) found no relationship between training or home musical background and children's ability to synchronize body movements to rhythmic stimuli. Groves did find that overall motor ability and age were correlated with rhythmic movement ability, as did Christianson (1938). Hurwitz et al. (1975) found significantly better scores on tests of sensorimotor rhythmic behavior for first-grade children who had been involved with Kodaly training.

Socialization of Attitudes

Several researchers (Greer et al., 1973; Peery & Peery, 1986) who have studied the development of musical preferences agree that exposure to a particular kind of music (especially at young ages) influences musical taste. There is substantial reason to believe that cognitive and listening skills required to understand a particular musical style are enhanced by exposure and, further, that social attitudes resulting from being able to understand and appreciate a particular musical style are also influenced as preferences develop.

Research in aesthetic education is relatively new. Piaget (1962) posited that stages in affectivity corresponded exactly with stages of development of intellectual structures. There has, therefore, been a widespread presumption of a strong correlation between conceptual development and aesthetic sophistication. Nelson (1985) substantiated this view when he found that age was the primary factor in determining aesthetic responsiveness. While it is true that younger children tend to be more egocentric in their aesthetic judgments, it is also true that 5-year-olds are capable of aesthetic experiences (see Gardner, Winner & Kircher, 1975, for example). A consensus is emerging that music may be one medium that can help children understand how art "works" (Saffle, 1983). Saffle (1983) also believes music can be a vehicle for communicating information about culture and aesthetics from different cultures. In fact, Stone

(1983) suggests that including elements from the pop music culture into a music education curriculum may help children develop a variety of skills necessary for general music appreciation. If the hypothesized generalization of learning is true, music's ability to spread an appreciation for aesthetics and additional aspects of other cultures may be one of the most potent reasons for teaching a variety of music to children.

The development of attitudes about music parallels the "cultural capital" concept. If one wants to associate on a highbrow level, one needs to have an understanding of highbrow attitudes and tastes. We suspect that many children have been taken involuntarily to orchestral concerts by parents who want them to be able to appreciate the finer things.

In Japan a mandatory, progressive system of music education is incorporated into elementary and secondary school curricula. Every child in Japan must take 6 years of elementary music, plus additional exposure in junior high school. Such a broad national commitment means that "almost every person who graduates from junior high school [in Japan] can read music and has the basic historical and theoretical tools to appreciate and enjoy it" (Abdoo, 1984, p. 53). In what was until recently called the Soviet Union there are more than 10,000 specialized music schools that emphasize performance but also teach the history and theory of music. These exist outside the regular day-school system and are attended in the afternoon and evenings after regular school has dismissed. The United States lacks the commitment and will at present to devote such energy to music training. Yet the data presented in this chapter point to the possibility of enhancing cognitive and motor skills, as well as music appreciation, by a blanket approach such as the Japanese adopted.

Self-Esteem

Of the teacher education and early childhood education textbooks studied by Draper and Gayle (1987), 11% state that music can be used to enhance self-esteem. Though self-esteem enhancement is a frequently stated goal of early childhood education programs, we have been unable to find any research actually relating music to self-esteem. However, personal experience suggests that young children who can demonstrate performance competence, especially at an advanced level (children who can compete in a performance competition in a state fair, for example) frequently receive considerable positive feedback from close family, extended family, teachers, and peers. These positive reactions seem to enhance the child's sense of accomplishment and capacity, and they help supply both instrumentality and understanding of how to match one's abilities to tasks at hand in order to be successful.

Social Interaction

Music is frequently used in the classroom as a mechanism of social interaction. Music education may facilitate social cognition. Kalliopuska and Ruokonen (1986) report that listening to music is similar to emotional empathy in that the listener must temporarily try to experience feelings stimulated by the music, while simultaneously maintaining his own individuality. They further found that a holistic musical education program, including elements of feelings and movement to feelings, facilitated the development of empathy in preschoolers. Musical performance is inherently social from several aspects, but little is known about the interplay of these issues in child development. Chertock (1974) reports a statistically nonsignificant but intriguing finding that social cooperation was higher under conditions of background art and mood music than with background noise of adult reading, or silence. Facilitating social interaction is one of the major functions of music, from pep bands at football games to dance bands at dances. The relationship between social encounters and music deserves much more scrutiny.

Locus of Control

Locus of control is a psychological construct for describing whether individuals see themselves as basically in charge of their lives (internal locus of control) or as controlled primarily by people and events outside themselves (external locus of control). Internality is positively correlated with many socially desirable skills and social characteristics (e.g., better school performance, low incidence of delinquency), but the relation between locus of control and musical skill development has not been examined. Lawrence and Dachinger (1967) found that self-taught child pianists continued to be involved with music as adults, while children who had formal piano training frequently were not involved with music as adults. This suggests that an internal locus of control may be helpful in maintaining interest in music across the life span. Lawrence and Dachinger (1967) also report that studying another instrument as well as the piano as a child increased the individual's involvement with music as an adult.

MUSIC EDUCATION FOR YOUNG CHILDREN

Music educators have long struggled to justify their function. Draper and Gayle (1987) discovered that early childhood textbook writers stated a number of reasons for involving children with music. These claims fall into several categories, of which the most common are: provides self-expression and creative pleasure (70% of the tests make this claim); fosters motor and rhythmic development (67%)—as reviewed above, there is some solid research evidence to confirm this idea; develops an aesthetic sense (46%); teaches vocal and language development (31%); promotes cultural heritage (26%); promotes cognitive development and abstract thought (25%); and teaches social and group skills (20%). However, Draper and Gayle note that *Child Development Abstracts and Bibliography* between the years 1927 and 1983 revealed almost no empirical research on any of these proposed relations. We have seen earlier in the chapter that a broader literature search does reveal some research linking music and other desirable developmental outcomes, but though the record is promising, the evidence is frequently scanty.

In a broader historical context, according to Elliott (1983), the music education profession has vacillated between adopting two views (similar to those proposed in our model) for justifying its existence and labor. One of these approaches, the "intrinsic value" perspective declares that music has innate value for its own sake, that reading music is as noteworthy a human skill as reading language, for example. The other is the "utilitarian" view that music facilitates other abilities. In addition to the list developed by Draper and Gayle (1987), claims have been made from time to time that music facilitates democratic living, patriotism, racial understanding, and academic skill. Elliott believes,

The root of our problems is that regardless of the philosophy we adopt, we rarely offer evidence to support it. Music educators are chronic bandwagon jumpers and more often than not the arguments we offer to justify public school music are based on expediency and wishful thinking. (Elliott, 1983, p. 37)

There is a growing body of evidence that music is a native part of human development and that music can enhance and possibly be a catalyst for other developmental tasks. It would, however, be a mistake to foreclose on including music in the lives of young children while waiting for more evidence to accumulate. It is also imprudent to jump on a current bandwagon and make claims for the benefits of music education that are ultimately not true.

The major motivation driving music education for children of all ages is being able to perform. As noted in the next subsection, "Performance Instruction," parents and children understand this fact better than music teachers and administrators. Children like to be able to perform and parents like to see them do it. Parents probably spend more on private music performance education than on any other educational agenda.

Here there is a necessary parting of the professional ways. Early childhood educators are not trained to provide music lessons in performance, and music teachers know little about early childhood education in a classroom setting. Yet each kind of professional who works with young children may benefit by learning something from the other. In particular, music teachers need to understand the cognitive and social characteristics of young children if their teaching is to be most effective. And early childhood educators who desire to include some musical structure would do well to include some kind of performance as one of the outcomes.

Performance Instruction

The overwhelming majority of effort that is put into integrating music into children's lives comes through individual instruction in playing a specific music instrument. Though no hard data exist to back up this assertion, a visit to most public and private schools would make it clear that performance instruction is the locus of musical activity in the schools, although this instruction does not usually include the younger grades. In addition, many millions of young people have private music lessons, during which they learn to perform vocally or with a musical instrument.

Although performance is a multimillion dollar industry and every community has educators whose primary career emphasis is performance training, there is almost no research on the outcomes of this training. Parents attend recitals and are univer-

sally pleased, so the training goes on, grounded in face validity. However, it is the author's subjective impression that learning to be able to do something, possibly almost anything, really well during early childhood lays a positive groundwork for developing other skills later. Developing self-mastery, understanding that long hours of effort are necessary if one is to accomplish tasks, and comprehending the complexities of music seem to be among the benefits of performance study. This is one of the areas that might well justify music education most poignantly. For children studying solo instruments who may not have the opportunity to perform in an ensemble regularly, music competitions can provide support, evaluation, and recognition for the long hours of hard work (Peery, Nyboer, & Peery, 1987). Parental support and involvement is a natural outcome of performance education, as parents promote practicing, attend performances, and pay for lessons. If one is to develop superior performance abilities, early childhood is the time to begin performance training, and training must continue over a number of years in order to take advantage of emerging cognitive and motoric abilities.

Classroom Instruction

Even though music research has influenced music curricula to some extent since the turn of the century or before, music educators have tended to focus on pedagogy and method rather than on research regarding child development. Humphreys (1985) observes,

Perhaps music teachers were unaware of the work of others that related to their field; perhaps they lacked the training to interpret the results or to conduct their own research; perhaps they believed, as did William James, that the new experimental approaches to psychology produced, 'a string of raw facts; a little gossip and a wrangle about opinions.' It is more likely that they were simply too preoccupied with other more pressing matters. (p. 85)

Managing a classroom full of young people is a more pressing matter. Yet those who have the greatest opportunity to take advantage of the research findings regarding children and music are the classroom teachers. One might hope that the merger of research and application will proceed in that arena.

Kalekin-Fishman (1986) found that kindergarten teachers created musical situations from instrumental pieces and songs that were relevant in content and suitable for kindergarten use. She found kindergarten songs about a variety of topics: nature, day and night, rain, wind, trees, flowers, animals, home, and family. Children would sing spontaneously—when playing with dolls, for example—or when being led by the teacher, with the majority of songs performed in a group setting. Kindergartners pay only low to moderate amounts of attention during music activities, even when teacher affect and enthusiasm are high (Sims, 1986).

Integrating Performance Skills into the Classroom

Each of the several approaches discussed in the next section, "Music Curricula," could allow individual children to demonstrate performance abilities in a classroom setting. Performance need not be limited to typical performer-audience modalities, but could include child performers playing while other children move, dance, sing, or tell stories. When individual children develop some advanced performing abilities, they can receive considerable recognition and support from peers as a result of performing before them in groups. And seeing such skill development tends to inspire peers, sometimes to enhance their own talents and abilities. Once again, here is an area where systematic empirical research might well provide justification for performance training, as well as direction in how performance training could be systematically integrated into the classroom setting even at the earliest ages.

Music Curricula

Brown (1987) outlines the four major approaches for teaching music to children: Orff, Kodály, Dalcroze, and Comprehensive Musicianship. These are probably the most widely accepted and adopted models for music education in a classroom setting.

The Orff Approach, named after the German composer Carl Orff (1895–1982), comes from his efforts outlined in the *Orff Schulwerk*. Orff, who was an avid nature lover, believed that, given the opportunity, children would express their natural musical ideas and development. He endorsed the experimental use of instruments, the combination of music productivity with movement and dancing, and the gradual introduction of melody and harmony. Orff developed wooden and metal xylophones (called metallophones) with removable bars, drums, claves, rattles, and blocks, which can be easily played by children to develop their sense of rhythm. More advanced ensembles include recorders, guitars, a cello, and a bass. Later Orff added singing as part of his curricular approach. In 1948 Orff conducted a series of radio programs in which musically untrained children performed on his instruments. The success of these programs led to considerable interest in music education. *Music für Kinder* (in five volumes) is the standard Orff work for music education. Orff classrooms combine rhythm, movement, speech, and singing to foster music growth from simple to more complex musical forms.

The Kodály (pronounced Ko-die-ee) approach was developed by the Hungarian composer and musicologist Zoltán Kodály (1882–1967), and is based upon singing indigenous folk songs. Working with Béla Bartók, Kodály collected Hungarian folk songs and began to study their structure and style. From this work came a program to enrich the lives of young children by teaching them to sing, read, and write music in a process that Kodály viewed as parallel to the development of speaking, reading, and writing language. In contrast to Orff, the Kodály approach emphasizes singing as the first natural musical expression. Children learn solfege (singing notes assigned specific names: do, re, mi, etc.) and develop the ability to recognize intervals, transpose, and compose from this base. For younger children childhood chants and singing games begin the learning sequence, folk songs are added as appropriate, and finally classical music is introduced. American adaptations of the Kodály concepts can be found in the works of Chosky (1974) and Szonyi (1973), for example.

The basis of the Dalcroze approach is eurythmics, studying music through movement and rhythm. Dalcroze (1865–1950)

combined movement, solfege (sight singing using the syllables), and improvisation in his curriculum. Moving to the feeling that music invokes, singing according to "inner hearing," and performing musical improvisation lead to personal insight and enhanced self-knowledge, according to the Dalcroze theoretical view. These benefits transfer to other areas of life. Training begins with relaxed listening in preschool and expands to singing games and accompanying stories.

Comprehensive Musicianship is the name given an approach to musical education that originated in the United States. Based on thinking developed in a 1965 Northwestern University "Seminar in Comprehensive Musicianship—the Foundation for College Education," this approach seeks to bring continuity and coherence to what had been a fragmented method of music education. Emphasizing the skills of listening, creating, and thinking, the comprehensive approach guides children through the concepts of pitch, duration, and musical texture. Children experiment with sound; act out ideas, such as duration by walking or clapping; and gain knowledge of other musical elements, such as tempo and dynamics, by performing and playing in a variety of musical settings. Musical performance is seen as a means of enhancing musical thinking, not an end. *Comprehensive Musicianship Through Classroom Music* (Thompson, 1974) is perhaps the best-known work for teachers interested in this approach.

Montessori developed ideas about music education in conjunction with her broader theories of general education for young children. Working with Maria Maccheroni, her music consultant, Montessori published 35 or so booklets on music education, though these are little known (Rubin, 1983). The booklets suggested a number of musical activities appropriate for young children, including such intriguing titles as "Let Us Walk with the Melody," "Long Notes in Short Melodies," "Families of the Scales," "Graphics of Sound," and "Library Concerts." These approaches advocated the use of Gregorian chant for early singing activities; the use of 21 dolls to represent letter names of musical notes in their sharp, flat, and natural versions; and the use of listening exercises that consisted of very brief classical excerpts. They also discuss the use of the Montessori bells and tone bars, which allow children to focus on one aspect of musical instruments and to compose their own musical experiences.

Greer (1980) presents a behaviorally oriented approach to music learning designed to teach specific skills in a step-by-step sequence. By identifying specific learning tasks and composing these into hierarchical sequences, Greer presents a program for guiding the teacher and then the student through the music-learning tasks.

The Manhattanville Music Curriculum Project was developed and implemented in the United States during the late 1960s and early 1970s. The Manhattanville Project (MMCP) is less a curriculum than an approach to music education. According to Walker (1984), the emphasis is on exploring and experiencing rather than implanting fact and knowledge. Singing, listening, dancing, painting, and theater are all encouraged as part of early childhood music learning. The child experiences different ways to produce different sounds and becomes absorbed in activities aimed at developing an understanding of music, not skill in musical performance. There is a very detailed set of instructions for teachers leading them through each phase of the process: simple encounters, principal ideas, objectives, procedures, and evaluations.

Music as a Part of the Classroom Curriculum

In the summer of 1967 the Music Educators National Conference participated in the Tanglewood Symposium, whose aim was to deliberate on music in American society. One of the outcomes of this deliberation was a firming up of musical education goals. Among their conclusions:

We believe that education must have as major goals the art of living, the building of personal identity, and nurturing creativity. Since the study of music can contribute much to these ends we now call for music to be placed in the core of the school curriculum. (Choate, 1968, p. 39)

The utilitarian idea that music can foster attendant benefits in many domains of child development is the framework of this argument, and we have seen some promise that music may facilitate other developmental competencies.

However, it is probably an error for those who promote music education to rely too heavily on hopes for which there are little supporting data. Plummeridge (1985) describes a trend toward a desire for more theoretical elegance and sophistication in curriculum development in music education. He notes that a drive toward a firmer theoretical footing may lead to outlining specific skills, knowledge, attitudes, and values by opting into what Elliott (1983) calls the utilitarian model. But at the current state of the art, the utilitarian view makes more promises than it can keep. Plummeridge urges that the proper development of teachers, who are on the firing line and who must make judgments from moment to moment about both the practice and evaluation, must be one of the central aims of curriculum development. He urges that we may need to study what teachers do, both in private lessons and in the classroom, in order to promote curriculum development that is directly related to real-world teaching. That knowledge can then provide a framework for research, teacher development, and music curriculum planning.

Teachers need to understand that musical development follows the same cognitive milestones as other aspects of social and cognitive skill development (Warrener, 1985). For young children in particular, most music curricula point to the importance of emphasizing intuitive and creative aspects of music before concentrating on the cognitive formal aspects, and this is probably the best approach (Hargreaves, 1986a).

There is growing enthusiasm for including music education in the lives of preschool children and even toddlers (Brand, 1985). In fact, some speculate that the ages from birth to age 9 may be a critical period for children's musical growth (Sims, 1986). Though, as we have seen above with the broader rationales for music education, this enthusiasm is based more on common sense validity and intuition than on a broad body of research findings. Teachers, parents, and students may each have different objectives for studying music in the classroom (Phillips, 1970; Wessler, 1976). Children and parents tend to want to produce a musical performance, while teachers may prefer developing related cognitive and motor skills (Murphy & Brown, 1986). This observation about older children should not be lost on the preschool teacher. Listening activities, moving to music (Herkowitz, 1977), and even some performance will probably all be preferred to activities that focus on cognitive skills, like music notation reading. The learning must be part of the doing. Many advocate that musical creativity ought to be a part of the classroom experience, but it is frequently bypassed for other musical tasks (see Burns, 1986).

SUMMARY AND CONCLUSIONS

This chapter has reviewed much of the past research relating music and early childhood development. A model for considering the role of music in child development was presented that divides motivations and research problems into 2 major subheadings: Music as an inherent good in itself and music as a means of promoting and fostering personal and social competence. The 2-part model is helpful in conceptualizing music research related to children. There are some research findings on almost every topic outlined in our model (Figure 14–1). It should be said, however, that little attempt has been made to demonstrate that musical experiences themselves cause changes in children. Just because music is associated with certain child characteristics does not mean that music causes the development of those characteristics. In statistical jargon, correlation is not causality. Studies that carefully control for potentially confounding variables will be necessary before it is possible to detail exactly which kind of musical experience influences which developmental characteristic; or whether music is a catalyst or conjunct medium for other causes of change.

Gaps in research findings are an invitation to scholars from many disciplines to expand and refine our knowledge of the influence of music on childhood. The dotted lines between the two conceptual columns in our model (Figure 14–1) represent areas where there might be a logical relationship between issues in studying music as music and in studying music to facilitate other development. We did not find any research with a specific focus on making such a bridge. Relationships between these domains seem logical: Is there a relationship between listening-perception skills in music and abilities in language development, for example? But questions of this order await future research.

Three general themes run through the music and child development research. First, there is considerable evidence supporting the importance of the role music can play in a child's life, both as he comes to enjoy and appreciate music for itself, and because music involvement can enhance other aspects of cognitive, physical, and social development. Second, the processes of maturation in normal child development are an important part of a child's developing music-related abilities. Parents, teachers, researchers, and curriculum developers need to take into consideration a child's age-appropriate skills and developing capacities when planning how to integrate music into the child's life. Finally, the data point again and again to experience that encourages and refines musical aptitudes and abilities being even more important than innate musical gifts.

Musical experiences need to be planned and monitored. Developing a taste for classical music, for example, is not a likely outcome for a child left strictly to the public school system and the network TV and radio producers.

Finally we have reviewed music education approaches for young children. As the research would suggest they should, most curricula for young children encourage musical activities and involvement rather than formal instruction in the logic of music cognition. Having carefully designed musical experiences in the classroom, however, can make an important difference in the way children appreciate music. And we have seen that there is some promising research suggesting that early

involvement in musical activities and experiences can pay off in several aspects of the child's development.

Some of the research findings and much common sense suggest that the place where music appreciation and involvement must begin and be sustained is in the home. Parents are particularly influential in encouraging music involvement. Starting children's musical life very early and devoting time and resources to music pays dividends as children become musically enculturated. Neither the schools nor private lessons alone are likely to be as effective as parental influence and a family environment that consistently synthesizes these outside educational experiences with a musically supportive home atmosphere.

References

Abdoo, F. H. (1984). Music education in Japan. *Music Educators Journal, 70*(6), 52–56.

Abel-Struth, S. (1982). Experiment on music recognition. *Psychology of Music,* 1982 [Special Issue] 7–10.

Barrett, H. C., & Barker, H. R. (1973). Cognitive pattern perception and musical performance. *Perceptual and Motor Skills, 36,* 1187–1193.

Bartlett, J. C. & Dowling, W. J. (1980). Recognition of transposed melodies: A key-distance effect in developmental perspective. *Journal of Experimental Psychology, 6,* 501–515.

Berlyne, D. E. (1971). *Aesthetics and psychobiology.* New York: Appleton.

Billingsley, R., & Rotenberg, K. J. (1982). Children's interval processing in music. *Psychomusicology, 2*(1), 38–43.

Bloom, B. S., (1985a). *Developing talent in young people.* New York: Ballantine.

Bloom, B. S., (1985b). Generalizations about talent development. In B. S. Bloom (Ed.), *Developing talent in young people* (pp. 507–549). New York: Ballantine.

Borke, H. (1971). Interpersonal perception of young children. *Developmental Psychology, 5,* 263–269.

Botvin, G. J. (1974). Acquiring conservation of melody and cross-modal transfer through successive approximation. *Journal of Research in Music Education, 22*(3), 226–233.

Bradley, I. (1972). Effect on student musical preference of a listening program in contemporary art music. *Journal of Research in Music Education, 20*(3), 344–353.

Bradley, I. L. (1971). Repetition as a factor in the development of musical preference. *Journal of Research in Music Education, 19,* 295–298.

Brand, M. (1985). Lullabies that awaken musicality in infants. *Music Educators Journal, 71*(7), 28–31.

Brown, A. (1987). Approaches to classroom music for children. In J. C. Peery, I. W. Peery, & T. W. Draper (Eds.), *Music and Child Development* (pp. 184–193). New York: Springer-Verlag.

Buckton, R. (1977). A comparison of the effects of vocal and instrumental instruction on the development of melodic and vocal abilities in young children. *Psychology of Music, 5,* 36–47.

Burns, M. T. (1986). Musical creative learning and problem solving. *The Creative Child and Adult Quarterly, 11,* 234–241.

Castell, K. C. (1982). Children's sensitivity to stylistic differences in "classical" and "popular" music. *Psychology of Music,* [Special Issue] 22–25.

Cattell, R. B., & Anderson, J. C. (1953). The measurement of personality and behavior disorders by the IPAT MPT. *Journal of Applied Psychology, 37,* 446.

Cattell, R. B., & Saunders, D. R. (1954). Musical preferences and personality diagnosis: I. A factorization of one hundred and twenty themes. *Journal of Social Psychology, 39,* 3–24.

Chang, H-W, & Trehub, S. (1977a). Auditory processing of relational information by young infants. *Journal of Experimental Child Psychology, 24,* 324–331.

Chang, H-W, & Trehub, S. (1977b). Infants' perception of temporal grouping in auditory patterns. *Child Development, 48,* 1666–1670.

Chattin-McNichols, J. P. (1981). The effects of Montessori school experience. *Young Children, 11,* 49–66.

Chertock, S. L. (1974). Effect of music on cooperative problem solving by children. *Perceptual and Motor Skills, 39*(2), 986.

Choate, R. A. (Ed.) (1968). *Documentary report of the Tanglewood symposium* (p. 39). Washington, DC: Music Educators National Conference.

Chosky, L. (1974). *The Kodaly Method.* Englewood Cliffs, NJ: Prentice Hall.

Christianson, H. (1938). *Bodily rhythmic movements of young children in relation to rhythm in music.* New York: Bureau of Publications, Teachers College, Columbia University.

Cleall, C. (1981). Notes toward the clarification of creativity in music education. *Psychology of Music, 9*(1), 44–47.

Cohen, M. (1974, February). Move him into reading with music. *Instructor,* pp. 60–62.

Cohen, V. W. (1980). The emergence of musical gestures in kindergarten children. Ann Arbor, MI: *University Microfilms International.*

Colwell, R. (1972). Review of *Measures of Musical Abilities.* In O.K. Buros, *The seventh mental measurements yearbook (Vol. 1).* Highland Park, NJ: Bryphon.

Crozier, J., Robinson, E., & Ewing, V. (1976–77). Etiology of absolute pitch. *Bulletin de Psychologie, 30,* 792–803.

Cunningham, J. G., & Sterling, R. S. (1988). Developmental change in the understanding of affective meaning in music. *Motivation and Emotion, 12*(4), 399–413.

Davidson, C. W., & Powell, L. A. (1986). The effects of easy-listening background music on the on-task performance of fifth-grade children. *Journal of Educational Research, 80*(1), 29–33.

Davidson, L. (1985). Tonal structures of children's early songs. *Music Perception, 2*(3), 361–373.

Davidson, L., & Colley, B. (1987). Children's rhythmic development from age 5 to 7: Performance, notation, and reading of rhythmic patterns. In J.C. Peery, I. W. Peery, & T. W. Draper (Eds.), *Music and child development* (pp. 107–136). New York: Springer-Verlag.

Deutsch, D. (1982). *The Psychology of Music.* New York: Academic Press.

Dorhout, A. (1982). Identifying musically gifted children. *Journal for the Education of the Gifted, 5*(1), 56–66.

Dorow, L. G. (1977). The effect of teacher approval/disapproval ratios on student music selection and concert attentiveness. *Journal of Research in Music Education, 25,* 32–40.

Dowling, J. W. (1982). Melodic information processing and its development. In D. Deutsch (Ed.), *The psychology of music.* New York: Academic Press.

Dowling, J. W., & Harwood, D. L. (1986). *Music cognition.* Orlando: Academic Press.

Draper, T. D., & Gayle, C. (1987). An analysis of historical reasons for teaching music to young children: Is it the same old song? In J. C. Peery, I. W. Peery, & T. W. Draper (Eds.), *Music and Child Development* (pp. 195–205). New York: Springer-Verlag.

Elliott, C. A. (1983). Behind the budget crisis, a crisis of philosophy. *Music Educators Journal, 70*(2), 36–37.

Etaugh, C., & Michals, D. (1975). Effects on reading comprehension of preferred music and frequency of studying to music. *Perceptual and Motor Skills, 41,* 553–554.

Feldman, D. H. (1986) *Nature's gambit: Child prodigies and the development of human potential.* New York: Basic Books.

Fiske, D. W., & Maddi, S. R. (1961). A conceptual framework. In D. W. Fiske & S. R. Maddi (Eds.), *The functions of varied experience.* Homewood, IL: Dorsey.

Flohr, J. W. (1981). *Musical improvisation behavior of young children.* Music Educators 47th National Conference. (ERIC Document Reproduction Service No. ED 210 408.)

Flohr, J. W. (1985). Young children's improvisations: Emerging creative thought. *The Creative Child and Adult Quarterly, 10,* 79–85.

Fogelson, S. (1973). Music as a distractor on reading test performance of eighth-grade students. *Perceptual and Motor Skills, 36,* 1265–1266.

Foley, E. A. (1975). Effects of training in conservation of tonal and rhythmic patterns on second-grade children. *Journal of Research in Music Education, 23*(4), 240–248.

Fowler, W. (1962). Cognitive learning in infancy and early childhood. *Psychological Bulletin, 59,* 116–152.

Fowler, W. (1969). The effect of early stimulation: The problem of focus in developmental stimulation. *Merrill-Palmer Quarterly, 15*(2), 157–170.

Freeman, J. (1976). Developmental influences on children's perception. *Educational Research, 19*(1), 69–75.

Gardner, H. (1971). Children's duplication of rhythmic patterns. *Journals of Research in Music Education, 19,* 295–298.

Gardner, H. (1973). *The arts and human development.* New York: Wiley.

Gardner, H. (1983). *Frames of mind.* New York: Basic Books.

Gardner, H., Winner, E., & Kircher, J. (1975). Children's conceptions of the arts. *Journal of Aesthetic Education, 9*(3), 60–77.

Geringer, J. M. (1977). An assessment of children's musical instrument preferences. *Journal of Music Therapy, 14,* 172–179.

Geringer, J. M. (1982). Verbal and operant music listening preferences in relationship to age and musical training. *Psychology of Music,* [Special Issue] 47–50.

Geringer, J. M. (1983). The relationship of pitch-matching and pitch-discrimination abilities of preschool and fourth-grade students. *Journal of Research in Musical Education, 31*(2), 93–99.

Geringer, J. M., & McManus, D. (1979). A survey of musical taste in relationship to age and musical training. *College Music Symposium, 19,* 69–76.

Getz, R. P. (1966). The influence of familiarity through repetition in determining music preference. *Research in Music Education, 14,* 179.

Gilbert, J. P. (1979). Assessment of motoric music skill development in young children: Test construction and evaluation procedures. *Psychology of Music, 7*(2), 3–12.

Gilbert, J. P. (1981). Motoric music skill development in young children: A longitudinal investigation. *Psychology of Music, 9*(1), 21–25.

Gordon, E. (1967). A comparison of the performance of culturally disadvantaged students with that of culturally heterogenous students on musical aptitude profile. *Psychology in the Schools, 4*(3), 260–262.

Gordon, E. (1968). A study of the efficacy of general intelligence and musical aptitude tests in predicting achievement in music. *Council for Research in Music Education, 13,* 40–45.

Gordon, E. (1971). *The psychology of music teaching.* Englewood Cliffs, NJ: Prentice-Hall, 1971.

Gordon, E. (1979). Developmental music aptitude as measured by the Primary Measures of Music Audition. *Psychology of Music, 7*(1), 42–49.

Greer, R. D. (1980). *Design for Music Learning.* New York: Teachers College Press.

Greer, R. D., Dorow, L. S., & Hanser, S. (1973). Music discrimination training and the music selection behavior of nursery and primary level children. *Council for Research in Music Education, 35*(4), 30–43.

Greer, R. D., Dorow, L. G., & Randall, A. (1974). Music listening preferences of elementary school children. *Journal of Research in Music Education, 22,* 284–291.

Greer, R. D., Dorow, L. G., Wachhaus, G., & White, E. R. (1973). Adult approval and students' music selection behavior. *Journal of Research in Music Education, 21,* 345–354.

Groves, W. C. (1966). Rhythmic training and its relationship to the synchronization of motor-rhythmic responses. *Dissertation Abstracts International, 27,* 3A, 702–703.

Hair, H. I. (1982). Microcomputer tests of aural and visual directional patterns. *Psychology of Music, 10*(2), 26–31.

Hargreaves, D. J. (1986a). Developmental psychology and music education. *Psychology of Music, 14,* 83–96.

Hargreaves, D. J. (1986b). *The developmental psychology of music.* New York: Cambridge University Press.

Heingartner, A., & Hall, J. V. (1974). Affective consequences in adults and children of repeated exposure to auditory stimuli. *Journal of Personality and Social Psychology, 19,* 719–723.

Heller, J., Campbell, W., & Gibson, B. (1982). The development of music listening skills in children. *Psychology of Music,* [Special Issue] 55–58.

Herkowitz, J. (1977). Movement experiences for preschool children. *Journal of Physical Education and Recreation, 48,* 15–16.

Heyduk, R. G. (1975). Rated preference for musical compositions as it relates to complexity and exposure frequency. *Perception and Psychophysics, 17*(1), 84–91.

Hickman, A. (1970). Experiments with children involving pitch, rhythm and timbre. *Research in Education, 3,* 73–86.

Hildebrandt, C. (1987). Structural-developmental research in music: Conservation and representation. In J. C. Peery, I. W. Peery, & T. W. Draper (Eds.), *Music and child development* (pp. 80–95). New York: Springer-Verlag.

Humphreys, J. T. (1985). The child-study movement and public school music education. *Journal of Research in Music Education, 33*(2), 79–86.

Hurwitz, I., Wolff, P. H., Bortnick, B. D., & Kokas, K. (1975). Nonmusical effects of the Kodaly music curriculum in primary grade children. *Journal of Learning Disabilities, 8*(3), 167–174.

Inglefield, H. G. (1972). Conformity behavior reflected in the musical preference of adolescents. *Contributions to Music Education, 1,* 56–65.

Jalongo, M. R., & Bromley, K. D. (1984). Developing linguistic competence through song picture books. *Reading Teacher, 37*(9), 840–845.

Jones, R. L. (1976). The development of the child's conception of meter in music. *Journal of Research in Music Education, 24,* 142–154.

Kalanidhi, M. S. (1970). Preference for concordant and discordant intervals: A study among school children. *Manas, 17,* 111–118.

Kalekin-Fishman, D. (1986). Music and not-music in kindergarten. *Journal of Research in Music Education, 34*(1), 54–68.

Kalliopuska, M., & Ruokonen, I. (1986). Effects of music education on development of holistic empathy. *Perceptual and Motor Skills, 62,* 187–191.

Karma, K. (1982). Musical, spatial and verbal abilities: A progress report. *Psychology of Music* [Special Issue], 69–71.

Kelley, L., & Sutton-Smith, B. (1987). A study of infant musical productivity. In J. C. Peery, I. W. Peery, & T. W. Draper (Eds.), *Music and Child Development* (pp. 35–53). New York: Springer-Verlag.

Kemler-Nelson, D. G., Hirsh-Pasek, K., Jusczyk, P. W., & Wright-Cassidy, K. (1989). How the prosodic cues in motherese might assist language learning. *Journal of Child Language, 16,* 53–68.

Keston, M. J., & Pinto, I. M. (1955). Possible factors influencing musical preference. *Journal of Genetic Psychology, 87,* 101–113.

Kokas, K. (1969). Psychological tests in connection with music education in Hungary. *Journal of Research in Music Education, 8*(3), 102–114.

Kinney, K. D., & Kagan, J. (1976). Infant attention to auditory discrepancy. *Child Development, 47,* 155–164.

Krumhansl, C., & Keil, F. C. (1982). Acquisition of the hierarchy of tonal functions in music. *Memory and Cognition, 10,* 243, 251.

Krumhansl, C. L., & Jusczyk, P. W. (1990). Infants' perception of phrase structure in music. *American Psychological Society, 1,* 70–73.

Kuhmerker, L. (1969, January). Music in the beginning reading program. *Young Children,* 157–163.

Kulka, J. (1981). Preference choice and identification of simple musical structures by children. *Studia Psychologica, 23*(1), 85–92.

Lawrence, S. J., & Dachinger, N. (1967). Factors relating to carryover of music training into adult life. *Journal of Research in Music Education, 15*(1), 23–31.

LeBlanc, A. (1979). Generic style music preferences of fifth-grade students. *Journal of Research in Music Education, 27,* 255–270.

LeBlanc, A. (1981). Effects of style, tempo, and performing medium on children's music preference. *Journal of Research in Music Education, 29,* 143–156.

LeBlanc, A. (1987). The development of music preference in children. In J. C. Peery, I. W. Peery, & T. W. Draper (Eds.), *Music and Child Development* (pp. 137–157). New York: Springer-Verlag.

LeBlanc, A., & Cote, R. (1983). Effects of tempo and performing medium on children's music preference. *Journal of Research in Music Education, 31,* 57–66.

LeBlanc, A., & McCrary, J. (1983). Effect of tempo on children's music preference. *Journal of Research in Music Education, 31,* 283–294.

Leithwood, K. A., & Fowler, W. (1971). Complex motor learning in four-year-olds. *Child Development, 42* (3), 781–792.

Lewis, B. E. (1988). The effect of movement-based instruction on first- and third-graders' achievement in selected music listening skills. *Psychology of Music, 16,* 128–142.

Lowery, J. (1982). Developing creativity in gifted children. *Gifted Child Quarterly, 26*(3), 133–139.

McCarthy, W. G. (1985). Promoting language development through music. *Academic Therapy, 21*(2), 237–242.

McDonald, D. (1974). Environment: A factor in conceptual listening skills of elementary school children. *Journal of Research in Music Education, 22*(3), 205–214.

McDonald, D. T. (1983). Montessori's music for young children. *Young Children, 39*(1), 58–63.

McMullen, P. T. (1974). Influence of number of different pitches and melodic redundancy on preference responses. *Journal of Research in Music Education, 22*(3), 198–204.

Mead, M. (1972, October). Music is a human need. *Music Educators Journal,* 24–29.

Melson, W. H., & McCall, R. B. (1970). Attentional responses of five-month girls to discrepant auditory stimuli. *Child Development, 41,* 1159–1171.

Montessori, M. A. (1965). *A Montessori handbook: Dr. Montessori's own handbook.* R. C. Orem, (Ed.). New York: Putnam.

Moore, R. (1966). The relationship of intelligence to creativity. *Journal of Research in Music Education, 14,* 243–253.

Mull, H. K. (1957). The effect of repetition upon the enjoyment of modern music. *Journal of Psychology, 43,* 155–162.

Murphy, M. K., & Brown, T. S. (1986). A comparison of preferences for instructional objectives between teachers and students. *Journal of Research in Music Education, 34*(2), 134–139.

Neal, C. (1983). Dichotically stimulated cerebral hemisphere asymmetries in children with high music aptitude and normal music aptitude. Ann Arbor Michigan: *University Microfilms International.*

Nelson, D. J. (1980). The conservation of metre in beginning violin students. *Psychology of Music, 8*(1), 25–33.

Nelson, D. J. (1985). Trends in the aesthetic responses of children to the musical experience. *Journal of Research in Music Education, 33*(3), 193–203.

Neufeld, K. A. (1986). Understanding of selected pre-number concepts: Relationships to a formal music program. *The Alberta Journal of Educational Research, 32,* 134–139.

Norton, D. (1978). Relationship of music ability and intelligence to auditory and visual conservation of the kindergarten child. *Journal of Research in Music Education, 27*(1), 3–13.

Olds, C. (1986). A sound start in life. *Pre- and Peri-Natal Psychology, 1,* 82–85.

Papousek, M., & Papousek, H. (1981). Musical elements in the infant's vocalization: Their significance for communication, cognition, and creativity. *Advances in Infancy Research, 1,* 163–224.

Parente, J., & O'Malley, J. (1975). Training in musical rhythm and field dependence of children. *Perceptual and Motor Skills, 40,* 392–394.

Parker, J. J. (1973). Discriminative listening as a basis for problem solving among four year olds. *Dissertation Abstracts International, 33*(8A), 4460–4461A. (University Microfilms 73-2979).

Peery, I. W., Nyboer, D., & Peery, J. C. (1987). The virtue and vice of musical performance competitions for children. In J. C. Peery, I. W. Peery, & T. W. Draper (Eds.), *Music and child development* (pp. 225–236). New York: Springer-Verlag.

Peery, J. C., & Peery, I. W. (1986). Effects of exposure to classical music on the musical preferences of preschool children. *Journal of Research in Music Education, 34*(1), 24–33.

Peery, J. C., Peery, I. W., & Draper, T. W. (1987). *Music and child development.* New York: Springer-Verlag.

Pflederer, M. (1964). The responses of children to musical tasks embodying Piaget's principle of conservation. *Journal of Research in Music Education, 12,* 251–268.

Pflederer, M. (1967). Conservation laws applied to the development of musical intelligence. *Journal of Research in Music Education, 15,* 215–223.

Phillips, D. (1976). An investigation of the relationship between musicality and intelligence. *Psychology of Music, 4*(2), 16–31.

Phillips, R. W. (1970). Attitudes: A comparison of senior high school music students and music instructors toward public school music in St. Louis County, Missouri. *Dissertation Abstracts International, 31,* 5255A. (University Microfilms No. 71–10, 046).

Piaget, J. (1962). The relation of affectivity to intelligence in the mental development of the child. *Bulletin of the Menninger Clinic, 26,* 129–136.

Pick, A. D., Palmer, D. F., Hennessy, B. L., Unze, M. G., Jones, R. K., & Richardson, R. M. (1988). Children's perception of certain musical properties: Scale and contour. *Journal of Experimental Child Psychology, 45,* 28–51.

Pillsbury Foundation Studies (1978). *Music of young children,* Santa Barbara, CA: Pillsbury Foundation for Advancement of Music Education.

Plummeridge, C. (1980). Creativity and music education—the need for further clarification. *Psychology of Music, 8*(1), 34–40.

Plummeridge, C. (1985). Curriculum development in music education: The limitation of theory. *Psychology of Music, 13*(1), 49–57.

Radocy, R. D. (1976). Effects of authority figure biases on changing judgments of musical events. *Journal of Research in Music Education, 24,* 119–128.

Rarick, G. L. (1961). *Motor development during infancy and childhood.* Madison, WI: College Printing and Typing Co.

Rogers, V. R. (1957). Children's musical preferences as related to grade level and other factors. *Elementary School Journal, 57*(8), 433–435.

Rubenzer, R. (1979, Summer). Identification and evaluation procedures for gifted and talented programs. *The Gifted Child Quarterly, 23,* 304–316.

Rubin, J. S. (1983). Montessorian music method: Unpublished works. *Journal of Research in Music Education, 31*(3), 215–226.

Rubin-Rabson, G. (1940). The influence of age, intelligence, and training on reactions to classic and modern music. *Journal of General Psychology, 22,* 413–429.

Saffle, M. (1983). Aesthetic education in theory and practice: A review of recent research. *Bulletin of the Council for Research in Music Education, 74,* 22–38.

Schmidt, C. P., & Lewis, B. E. (1987). Field dependence/independence, movement-based instruction and fourth graders' achievement in selected musical tasks. *Psychology of Music, 15,* 117–127.

Schuckert, R. F., & McDonald, R. L. (1968). An attempt to modify the music preferences of preschool children. *Journal of Research in Music Education, 16*(1), 39–44.

Serafine, M. L. (1981). Musical timbre imagery in young children. *Journal of Genetic Psychology, 139*(1), 97–108.

Sergeant, D. (1969). Experimental investigation of absolute pitch. *Journal of Research of Music Education, 17,* 135–143.

Sergeant, D. (1983). The octave: Percept or concept. *Psychology of Music, 11*(1), 3–18.

Shetler, D. J. (1989). The inquiry into prenatal musical experience: A report of the Eastman Project 1980–1987. *Pre- and Peri-Natal Psychology, 3,* 171–189.

Shuter-Dyson, R. (1979). Music in the environment: Effects on the musical development of the child. *International Review of Applied Psychology, 28*(2), 127–133.

Shuter-Dyson, R. (1982). Musical ability. In D. Deutsch (Ed.), *The Psychology of Music.* New York: Academic Press.

Sims, W. L. (1986). The effect of high versus low teacher affect and passive versus active student activity during music listening on preschool children's attention, piece preference, time spent listening, and piece recognition. *Journal of Research in Music Education, 34*(3), 173–191.

Simons, G. M. (1976). A criterion-referenced test of fundamental music listening skills. *Child Study Journal, 6*(4), 233–234.

Sosniak, L. A., (1985). Learning to be a concert pianist. In B. S. Bloom (Ed.), *Developing talent in young people,* (pp. 19–67). New York: Ballantine.

Stone, M. (1983). Some antecedents of music appreciation. *Psychology of Music, 11*(1), 26–31.

Szonyi, E. (1973). *Kodaly's Principles in Practice.* New York: Boosey & Hawkes.

Terwogt, M. M., & Grinsven, F. V. (1988). Recognition of emotions in music by children and adults. *Perceptual and Motor Skills, 67,* 697–698.

Thompson, W. (1974). *Comprehensive musicianship through classroom music.* Belmont, CA: Addison-Wesley.

Trehub, S. E. (1987). Infants' perception of musical patterns. *Perception & Psychophysics, 41,* 635–641.

Trehub, S. E., Cohen, A. J., Thorpe, L. A., & Morrongiello, B. A. (1986). Development of the perception of musical relations: Semitone and Diatonic Structure. *Journal of Experimental Psychology: Human Perception and Performance, 12*(3), 295–301.

Trehub, S. E., Mortrongiello, B. A., & Thorpe, L. A. (1985). Children's perception of familiar melodies: The role of intervals, contour, and key. *Psychomusicology, 5*(1–2), 39–56.

Upitis, R. (1987). Toward a model for rhythm development. *Psychology of Music, 11*(1), 26–31.

Verny, T., & Kelly, J. (1981). *The secret life of the unborn child.* New York: Summit Books.

Wagley, M. W. (1978). The effects of music on affective and cognitive development of sound-symbol recognition among preschool children. *Dissertation Abstracts International, 29*(3A), 1316. (University Microfilms 78-15605).

Walker, R. (1984). Innovation in the music classroom. II. The Manhattanville Music Curriculum Project. *Psychology of Music, 12*(1), 25–33.

Wapnick, J. (1976). A review of research on attitude and preference. *Bulletin of the Council for Research in Music Education, 48,* 1–20.

Ward, W. D. & Burns, E. M. (1982). Absolute pitch. In D. Deutsch (Ed.), *The Psychology of Music* (pp. 431–451). New York: Academic Press.

Warrener, J. J. (1985). Applying learning theory to musical development: Piaget and beyond. *Music Educators Journal, 72*(3), 22–27.

Webster, P. R. (1987). Conceptual bases for creative thinking. In J. C. Peery, I. W. Peery, & T. W. Draper (Eds.), *Music and Child Development* (pp. 159–174). New York: Springer-Verlag.

Webster, P. R., & Schlentrick, K. (1982). Discrimination of pitch direction by preschool children with verbal and nonverbal tasks. *Journal of Research in Music Education, 30*(3), 151–161.

Webster, P. R., & Zimmerman, M. P. (1983). Conservation of rhythmic and tonal patterns of second through sixth grade children. *Bulletin of the Council for Research in Music Education, 73,* 28–49.

Weeden, R. E. (1971). A comparison of the academic achievement in reading and mathematics of negro children whose parents are interested, not interested, or involved in a program of Suzuki violin. *Dissertation Abstracts International, 32,* 3582A.

Wellek, A. (1938). Das absolute Gehor. *Seitschrift für Angewandte Psychologie & Charakterkunde-Beihefte, 83,* 1–368.

Wessler, R. A. (1976). An assessment of achievement and attitudes toward music among fourth, fifth and sixth grade students in Corozal, Puerto Rico. *Dissertation Abstracts International, 37,* 6336A–6337A (University Microfilms No. 77–9239).

Wingert, M. L. (1972). Effects of a music enrichment program in the education of the mentally retarded. *Journal of Music Therapy, 9,* 13–22.

Young, L. P. (1982). An investigation of young children's music concept development using nonverbal and manipulative techniques. *Dissertation Abstracts International, 43,* 1345A.

Zajonc, R. B. (1968). Attitudinal effects of mere exposure [monograph]. *Journal of Personality and Social Psychology, 9* (Suppl. 2, Part 2).

Zimmerman, M. P., & Sechrest, L. (1970). Brief focused instruction and musical concepts. *Journal of Research in Music Education, 18*(1), 25–35.

Zimny, G., & Weidenfeller, E. (1962). Effects of music upon GSR of children. *Child Development, 33,* 891–896.

·15·

SCIENCE IN EARLY CHILDHOOD EDUCATION

Ann C. Howe

UNIVERSITY OF MARYLAND AT COLLEGE PARK

This century's most famous scientist said that science "is not just a collection of laws, a catalogue of unrelated facts. It is a creation of the human mind, with its freely invented ideas and concepts" (Einstein & Infield, 1938). Children, perhaps even more than adults, freely invent ideas and concepts in their continuing effort to make sense of their world. This is the beginning of scientific thinking, but in the beginning the ideas are unconnected, often contradictory, inchoate, and unarticulated. The purpose of science education is to provide the learning environment, the experiences, and the opportunities for discussion and reflection that will lead to interconnected, coherent, and articulated frameworks for understanding natural phenomena.

HISTORICAL PERSPECTIVE

Since colonial times, American educators have believed that science should be a part of children's education (Underhill, 1941; Hurd & Gallagher, 1968); science was, however, seldom included in the school curriculum before the end of the last century. At that time the best known proponent of science as an integral part of the elementary school curriculum was John Dewey (1956). What he proposed was not a rigid adherence to a set of topics, but the direction of children's natural interest in aspects of everyday life that would lead them to knowledge of science at their own level of understanding.

While Dewey was active in promoting his ideas of progressive education, another movement that would have an impact on science education for children was initiated at Cornell University by a professor of horticulture, Liberty Bailey (1903). The work that he began was continued by Comstock and others, particularly in the Cornell Rural School Leaflets, a series of suggested nature-study lessons that were sent regularly to rural elementary teachers in the state of New York. The work of the Cornell group had wide influence in elementary schools in New York and beyond from the 1890s until well into the 1940s

(Champagne & Klopfer, 1979). The nature-study movement, of which the activity centered at Cornell was a part, was criticized for a tendency toward anthropomorphism and sentimentality. However, it had much in common with what we now call environmental education in that it focused on local plants and animals, it advocated observation and experience as the basis for learning, and it had a strong affective component.

Another center of science education for children was the Laboratory School of the University of Chicago, founded by Dewey in 1896. Dewey soon moved on to Teachers College in New York, leaving advocacy of science instruction for children to Jackman, whose ideas prefigured current views of appropriate methods and expected outcomes of science instruction for children. In 1891 he wrote "the very essence of science work, upon whatever plan conducted, must be direct, individual observation." He went on to say "true science work does not stop with mere seeing, hearing or feeling; it not only furnishes a mental picture as a basis for reasoning, but it includes an interpretation of what has been received through the senses" (Jackman, 1891, p. 2). Although Jackman was trained in biology and often used the term "nature study" in his writing, his curriculum for children at the Laboratory School included topics in physics, chemistry, meteorology, astronomy, geology, and mineralogy as well as botany and zoology.

The interest and energy directed toward science education for children gradually declined, and, by the 1940s, very little science was being taught in the primary grades. It was not until the 1960s that attention turned again to science education for children. A period of intense curriculum development, but little research in science education for young children, followed. The next decade saw the growth of Piagetian research, much of it devoted to the stage theory of development and questions about the relation of cognitive development to concept development. More recently, interest has turned to children's naive concepts of natural phenomena and how these concepts can best be elaborated or restructured.

CURRICULUM DEVELOPMENT AND EVALUATION

The general revival of interest in science education in the early 1960s brought renewed energy and resources to elementary science education, culminating in several well-funded projects that produced articulated curriculum materials for schoolchildren from kindergarten through sixth grade. The best known and most widely used were *Elementary Science Study* (or *ESS*, developed by Educational Development Center, Newton, MA; now distributed by Delta Education, Inc., Nashua, NH), the *Science Curriculum Improvement Study* (or *SCIS*, developed by Science Curriculum Improvement Study, University of California, Berkeley), and *Science-A Process Approach* (or *SAPA*, developed by American Association for the Advancement of Science, Washington, DC; now distributed by Xerox Education Division, Stamford, CT), all of which were supported by the National Science Foundation and were widely reported and discussed (for a summary see Hurd and Gallagher, 1968). By 1971 almost 7 million children were enrolled in classes where these materials were used (Welch, 1976). Topics from both the physical sciences and life sciences were included in series of lessons that emphasized the development of logical thinking, of scientific modes of thought, and of science concepts. Whereas earlier materials had been based on what was thought to be of intrinsic interest to children, the new curricula were based on theories of cognitive development or learning derived directly from the work of Piaget (ESS and SCIS), Bruner (ESS), and Gagne (SAPA). Opportunities for elementary teachers to study these programs were offered at many sites across the country with the support of the National Science Foundation. None of the programs used student textbooks; written materials were addressed to teachers with detailed explanation of activities for children and appropriate teaching methods for each activity.

Curriculum Projects of the 1960s

The first of the projects, Elementary Science Study, which owed much to Bruner (1960), sought to incorporate both the spirit and the substance of science in a collection of units that brought children into direct contact with materials. Conventional ideas of curriculum and teaching were abandoned in favor of allowing children to "mess around in science" at their own developmental levels, following their own interests and asking their own questions. Successful implementation required skill and knowledge on the part of teachers, who had to sequence the lessons, forgo directing and controlling children's activities, and exercise restraint "born of self-confidence and supported by confidence in and respect for children" (Educational Development Center, 1969). That was a difficult assignment for teachers who were accustomed to teaching from a textbook and who had scant confidence in their science background; few were able to use the materials successfully without special training. The program was never widely adopted for use in schools but it had a profound influence on science educators' thinking about teaching, as evidenced by the incorporation of ESS activities and materials in many subsequent programs and textbooks. Of the major projects of the time, ESS was the

most child-centered and used methods with which preschool teachers felt most comfortable. ESS embodied a spirit of playfulness and creativity and a delight in childhood that is still rare in science teaching materials and that is seldom captured in ESS-derived activities now found in textbooks.

Science Curriculum Improvement Study, also designed for use in kindergarten through third grade, was an articulated, coherent, developmentally sequenced series of units in both physical and life sciences that was designed with the express purpose of translating Piaget's work on cognitive development into classroom practice. To this end, each unit was based on a "learning cycle" that began with exploration of materials by children, followed by the teacher's use of children's findings to "invent" a concept and culminating in children's "discovery" of how the concept could be used in predicting the outcomes of their actions on materials. The teacher's role was delineated in more detail in SCIS that in ESS, and children's activities were more controlled. However, SCIS still offered a great deal of freedom for children to be actively engaged with materials, to interact with each other, and to express ideas.

Science-A Process Approach was guided by Gagne's (1965) hierarchical learning theory and his definition of processes of science. SAPA was, in the original version, a series of structured lessons arranged in ascending order of difficulty of process application—rather than by topic or concept—and driven by behavioral objectives. The developers of these lessons assumed that mental development is a consequence of learning rather than the reverse; thus, a child's inability to perform a given task was not thought to be related to the child's cognitive developmental level but to lack of experience or prior knowledge. Each lesson included detailed directions for the teacher that were meant to make it possible for any teacher to lead pupils through the exercises and achieve the desired ends. SAPA's most enduring influence has been in the wide adoption of "processes of science" as a component of almost all commercial programs and textbooks up to and including the present.

At the same time, a movement in Great Britain also sought to emphasize the teaching of science to children. Materials were developed for use in schools there, of which the most widely known in the United States is *Science 5/13* (sponsored by the Schools Council, the Nuffield Foundation, and the Scottish Education Department; published by Macdonald Educational, London). A series of booklets, each devoted to a broad topic, provided help for teachers and suggested activities for children that allowed them to carry out investigations related to such topics as trees, colored things, working with wood, and "minibeasts". The aim of the program was to help the child develop an inquiring mind and a scientific approach to problems rather than to teach science; the emphasis was on choosing developmentally appropriate activities to accomplish broad aims. A detailed set of objectives was mapped onto Piagetian levels to give teachers a theoretical basis for using the program.

Analysis and Evaluation of the Curriculum Projects

These planned curricula had certain elements in common: reliance on experience rather than the authority of the teacher or a text as the basis for learning, the focus on the learner's interaction with and action on materials, emphasis on discussion of results, and the use of charts and graphs. All recognized the need for teacher training and all produced interesting sets of equipment and apparatus for children's use. The major differences among the programs were in the degree to which children's activities were preplanned and outcomes were specified. In ESS, for example, children were allowed to interact with materials, ask questions, and try things out on their own, whereas in SAPA all activities were planned in advance and behavioral objectives were specified at the beginning and assessed at the end of each lesson. The objective of ESS and SCIS for primary children included experiences related to a limited number of specific concepts; SAPA was organized completely around processes, making science content incidental.

The programs are described in the past tense because all of them have undergone extensive revision and are not generally available in original form. A large sum of money and a great deal of time and intellectual energy were devoted to the development of these curricula and to encouraging and promoting the teaching of science in the elementary school, but little was allocated for evaluation. Evaluation of the programs at the time of development was limited and unsystematic. Since that time there have been many small studies but no overall, large-scale, planned assessments. Bredderman (1984) synthesized the results of 11 carefully selected studies of the effects of ESS, SCIS, and SAPA on teachers' classroom practices. He found that there was more pupil activity and less time spent by the teachers in telling pupils about science when teachers with appropriate training used these curricula. A study of attitudes toward science among pupils who had had 6 years' experience in SCIS found that the program had a positive impact on attitudes, with boys having more positive attitudes than girls by the time they reached sixth grade (Lowery, Bowyer, & Padilla, 1980). The latest meta-analysis, based on all available research meeting the authors' standards, shows that the programs had a positive impact on achievement and process-skill development of children in kindergarten through third grade (Shymansky, Hedges, & Woodworth, 1990).

The impact of the elementary science projects supported by the National Science Foundation was far greater than the limited results of formal evaluations would indicate. For the first time, theoretically based, sequential, systematic science programs were available for students from kindergarten through sixth grade. As a result of the workshops and institutes associated with the programs, many teachers changed the way they taught science. Virtually all elementary science methods textbooks are now designed to prepare prospective teachers to use more active, process-oriented teaching methods (for examples see Cain & Evans, 1990; Carin & Sund, 1989). Science is now included everywhere in curricula for the primary grades. However, it is fair to say that science teaching in the primary school was not revolutionized as some had hoped; these projects did not address science for prekindergarten children at all. Although the influence of these programs remains, their use has declined, leaving science teaching in the primary grades to be dominated by textbooks. Analyses have shown that textbooks now in use require a reasoning level beyond that attained by most of the children in the primary grades (Staver & Bay, 1989),

and that they use vocabulary far outside the experience and beyond the comprehension of primary-grade children (Myerson, Ford, Jones, & Ward, 1991).

Constructivist Approach to Curriculum Development

Two of the curriculum projects mentioned above, *Science Improvement Curriculum Study* and *Science 5/13,* used Piaget's work as the theoretical basis for the content and sequence of the materials. However, the most thoroughgoing Piagetians have been Kamii and DeVries, who for more than 2 decades have explored the meaning of Piagetian theory for the education of prekindergarten children (Kamii & DeVries, 1977; Kamii & DeVries, 1978; DeVries & Kohlberg, 1987). Although they draw a strong distinction between their work and the science they find in textbooks for children, their methods and goals are compatible with what many science educators of today would advocate for young children. Their constructivist approach to building physical knowledge through acting freely on objects is based directly on an interpretation of Piagetian theory and is more explicitly theoretical than any of the programs described above. In drawing the distinction between the empiricist assumption that knowledge of the world is derived directly from observation through use of the senses and the constructivist belief that knowledge is created by the child through actions on objects, they have drawn attention to the fallacy of the notion that observation and manipulation of objects alone, popularly known as "hands-on science," is enough to ensure learning.

Others in the Piagetian tradition who have made important contributions to knowledge of teaching and learning through their years of work with young children and teachers are Duckworth (1987) in the United States and Harlen (1985) in Great Britain. Unlike Kamii and DeVries, they assume that the goals of constructivism are compatible with, if not the same as, the goals of science education and take a constructive approach to science education.

This approach to science education is ably presented by Chaillé and Britain (1991) in a volume that seeks to show teachers how to create a learning environment in which children can be actively involved in constructing knowledge about the physical world and the forms of life around them. The approach to children's learning that is described in this volume is very similar to the one taken in the original ESS materials, but the approach proposed for teachers' learning is different. The focus of the ESS materials was on children's activities; Chaillé and Britain focus, instead, on providing a theoretical framework, specific examples, and detailed explanations that allow a teacher to construct the knowledge needed to use the constructivist approach. Their purpose is not to produce a science curriculum or even science activities but to help the teacher learn how to choose and carry out appropriate activities; the specific activities described are used only as examples.

It is important to note that those who come from a background in developmental or early childhood education tend to take a different approach to early science education from those who come from a background in science or elementary education. The former group focuses more on the child and the teacher, extending the methods and ideas of preschool education upward into primary school. The latter group focuses more on the processes and content of science, extending the methods and ideas of the upper grades downward into the primary grades and kindergarten. For the former any developmentally appropriate activity is acceptable and useful; for the latter there are specific ideas and activities that are thought to be a necessary part of children's education.

RESEARCH ON DEVELOPMENT OF SCIENCE CONCEPTS

The developers of the elementary science curriculum projects assumed that a curriculum based on major science themes and concepts and taught by teachers who followed prescribed methods would almost automatically lead to pupil learning. Difficulties remained, however, and researchers sought to identify sources of learning problems.

Relation of Science Concept Development to Piaget's Cognitive Stages of Development

Although Piaget's work had long been known to psychologists and early childhood specialists, it first came to the attention of science educators in the late 1960s, partly as a result of the work in curriculum development. Interest was intense, first in replication studies and later in efforts to teach children how to perform what came to be called "Piaget tasks." This initial interest came from the belief, or the hope, that the development of science concepts could be mapped onto cognitive development in a rather direct way. It was proposed that Piaget's theory of stages in development of logical thinking was the key to understanding learning difficulties in science. If one knew, for example, that a child was at the preoperational level, one would have an indication of what the child could learn and, therefore, what to teach.

The following examples illustrate the general thrust of this line of research. Preschool, kindergarten, and first-grade children participated in a study in which the investigators used clinical interviews to elicit responses to Piaget tasks and to questions about electromagnetism and gravity (Selman, Krupa, Stone, & Jaquette, 1982). They found only moderate correlations between Piagetian cognitive level and level of concept development, and concluded that "general cognitive development promotes development of specific science concepts and those promote the child's general cognitive development," but neither acts in isolation (p. 193). Another study sought to determine the association between conservation of length and the ability to learn how to make linear measurements. The investigators were successful in teaching kindergarten and primary children the desired skill but found no difference between conservers and nonconservers in skill attainment; that is, the ability to make linear measurements did not appear to be associated with operational level (Smith, Trueblood, & Szabo, 1981).

The evidence from a decade or more of research indicates that operational level is not as decisive in learning science concepts and processes as it was once thought to be. In retrospect, it is clear that this research was simplistic, if not misguided,

in ignoring language, prior knowledge, motivation, and other factors and seeing cognitive level as the only relevant variable in science learning. The question of the relative importance of domain-specific knowledge and general knowledge in learning science is still open.

Children's Science Concepts and Misconceptions

The study of children's naive ideas, concepts, and misconceptions has become the most active area of research in science education during the last decade. Although educators never overtly express the view that children's minds are blank slates, science is often taught as if that were the case. One looks in vain in primary science curriculum materials, including those described above, for serious attention to what children think or believe before instruction begins. Most programs do not recognize that children, even as toddlers, form their own ideas and explanations about events. By the time they enter school, children have had experiences and have developed concepts or naive theories about many of the things that make up the traditional science curriculum.

Although the study of science concept learning has been carried forward for years by Novak (1977) and the current interest in this line of research owes much to him, the clinical method used by most researchers and many of the tasks they employ are derived from Piaget's work. The tasks Piaget devised to explore children's explanations for natural phenomena, which he used in building his theory of genetic epistemology, are now being used as vehicles for work on concept development. In this work it is the tasks and explanations themselves, rather than what they represent, that are of interest.

A great number of studies of concepts related to a wide range of topics in the science curriculum have now been reported, reviewed, and summarized (Eylon & Linn, 1988; Osborne & Freyberg, 1985; Children's Learning in Science Research Group, 1991; Confrey, 1990; Driver, Guesne, & Tiberghein, 1985). In some cases the studies are purely descriptive; others have a theoretical basis; and a few report the results of interventions. The majority report findings related to concepts held by older elementary children, adolescents, or college students. Most of the works reviewed or cited here focus on young children, although a few cross-age studies are included in which only the youngest subjects fall within the age group.

A wide range of concepts drawn from physical and biological sciences have been the subject of study. Energy concepts have been a frequent focus. Erickson (1979), in a study of 6- to 12-year-olds, showed that the younger children do not differentiate between heat and temperature and think of heat and cold as substances that flow in and out of bodies. Wiser and Carey (1983) showed that young children have a single thermal concept that includes both heat and temperature and resembles the caloric theory once held by scientists. In a third example a hierarchy of energy concepts was found in a study of concept attainment of elementary children in Nigeria (Urevbu, 1984).

Children's ideas about light and shadows have been another area of interest (Piaget, 1930; Siegler, 1981; Guesne, 1985; DeVries, 1986; Feher & Rice, 1987). Young children think of a shadow as an object or a substance and light as an agent that causes an object to form a shadow or that allows people to see a shadow that is present even in the darkness. Other science topics that have been the subject of recent studies, all of which have used tasks and questions derived from Piaget, include conservation of momentum and dynamic equilibrium (Kaiser & Proffitt, 1984), size, weight, and density of objects (Smith, Carey, & Wiser, 1985); judgments of the size of objects (Gelman & Ebeling, 1989); gravitation, floating, and sinking (Rodrigues, 1980); magnetism and gravity (Selman, Krupa, Stone, & Jaquette, 1982); and the material composition of objects (Dickinson, 1987). Some of these take a developmental cross-age perspective and others are simply descriptive of children's ideas at one age or grade level.

The implications for science teaching that might be derived from these research reports are not always clear and are seldom given. The reason for this lack of clarity may be a lack of differentiation between these concepts drawn from everyday experience and those that are not. Three examples of concepts, taken from different domains of science, are examined below to illustrate the point that there are important differences among concepts and that these differences should be taken into account in making instructional decisions.

Origin of Concepts and Misconceptions

Consider, as the first example, concepts of speed and movement involving time and space relationships. Piaget (1970) studied these concepts using tasks based on small cars traveling at various speeds, with starting and stopping points that were sometimes visible and sometimes not. Piaget found that the perception of the vehicles' starting points was the salient feature for young children, overwhelming other perceptions or considerations. The tasks Piaget used were modified for use in a study of Japanese kindergarten children (Mori, Kojima, & Deno, 1976), in which a series of demonstrations followed by questions was used as an instructional treatment. The authors concluded that the earliest intuition of speed is not necessarily based on the notion of one car or object overtaking another; they suggested, rather, that it may be based on observation of objects traveling with different velocities. This finding was challenged by others (Siegler & Richards, 1979; Acredolo & Schmid, 1981; Cross & Mehegan, 1988) who found, instead, that the idea of one object overtaking another was primary. The most detailed findings are those of Perry & Obenauf (1987) who developed elaborate versions of Piaget's tasks and used them to conduct individual interviews with first-, third-, and fifth-grade children. They found an age-related hierarchy of an expanded group of tasks and presented a diagram of the order of acquisition of subordinate concepts that supported Piaget's views.

A second example involves concepts of living and nonliving. Children's explanations of what it means to be alive, involving underlying assumptions of animism and dynamism, were the subject of an early work by Piaget (1965) and a major replication effort by Laurendeau and Pinard (1962). At an early age, children believe that all things are alive. Later, they tend to believe that moving objects—for example, a bicycle or a cloud—are alive in contrast to a tree, which stays in one place. The literature on this subject is extensive (Brumby, 1982; Dolgin & Behrend, 1984; Gelman, Spelke, & Meck, 1983; Mayr, 1982; Russell & Dennis, 1940); it has been significantly augmented by Carey's (1985) series of studies investigating 4-, 6-, and 10-year-olds' understandings of "living things," "animals," and "human body functions." In Carey's study the younger children were found to have intuitive theories of human behavior and human needs that differed, as expected, from those of the 10-year-olds', whose ideas had presumably undergone restructuring to become similar to those generally held by adults. Carey suggests that this restructuring is based on changes in causal explanation, similar to that posited for changes in concepts of the physical world. However, she does not propose an explanation or mechanism for the conceptual change that usually takes place by age 10.

The third example is the concept of the Earth as an object moving through space with a gravitational pull of its own. This is a basic component of the modern scientific worldview, but the main proposition, that the earth is spherical, is counterintuitive and not accessible to observation. Research on children's ideas about the earth was initiated by Nussbaum and Novak (1976), who used an interview technique to evaluate a series of lessons for second-graders. In contrast to the studies on speed, cited above, Nussbaum and Novak's work was not based on Piagetian theory and used tasks developed by themselves. The instructional program they devised did not produce the hoped-for results, but the authors were able to classify children's responses into a series of 5 progressively more advanced concepts. They interpreted the results as consistent with Ausubel's (1968) theory of progressive differentiation. This study was repeated in Israel (Nussbaum, 1979) and in Nepal (Mali & Howe, 1979) with generally similar results and was used as the basis for a tutorial intervention with second-graders (Nussbaum & Sharoni-Dagan, 1981) and for a cross-cultural study in Minnesota (Klein, 1982). Probably the most interesting finding was that children were able to say that the earth is "round," but when pressed they gave answers indicating a strong belief in a flat earth. Children who have come to believe in the spherical earth still think that an object on the other side of the world would fall off into space. The most comprehensive study on this topic, building on the previous work, was conducted by Sneider and Pulos (1983), who presented slightly modified versions of Nussbaum and Novak's tasks to California children in grades 3 through 8. Their results confirmed and extended earlier findings.

These examples suggest 3 possible sources from which children's concepts may originate. Piaget's account of his experiments and subsequent reports suggest that children's notions of speed and movement are at first perceptually based and are later modified or expanded by reasoning. Because the source is perceptual and based on observation of tasks directly presented, and because the child can manipulate objects and come to some conclusions, suitable activities can be designed for use with young children. It seems unlikely that children's concepts of speed and movement form and continue to develop without opportunities to engage in suitable activities. In contrast, ideas about what it means to be alive are derived principally from everyday experience, including the child's own spontaneous questions. These ideas become gradually restructured through continued experience and questioning. School activities involving plants and animals may add something to outside experience, but children develop a concept of living and nonliving by about the age of 10, regardless of school experience.

The final example is different from either of the others. The idea that the Earth is not flat as it seems but is, rather, a sphere rotating in space is counterintuitive; nothing in the child's everyday experience and no activity presented in school can lead to that conclusion. The child can observe day and night, regularities in the rising and setting of the moon and the sun, perhaps even an eclipse, but none of those will lead spontaneously to the concept of the Earth as a sphere. This is an example of social knowledge: It is a concept that, when presented and explained, is usually resisted, since its acceptance requires a major conceptual change based on logical thinking separated from the child's own experience. It is inappropriate and, in fact, futile to present concepts of this nature to children in preschool or the primary grades.

RESEARCH ON INSTRUCTIONAL METHODS

What Piaget called "the American question"—how to accelerate cognitive development—has taken on a new form as the question of how to accelerate concept development. This is derived from and consistent with the neo-Piagetian perspective that knowledge is domain-specific and that concept acquisition depends more on prior knowledge than on cognitive level (e.g., Case, 1978). There is general agreement among scientists that there are certain basic and important complex concepts in science that are eventual goals of instruction for all students (American Association for the Advancement of Science, 1989). Some examples of these concepts are force and motion, evolution, the unity and diversity of forms of life, and the atomic molecular theory. Cognitive scientists and science educators are coming to believe that these complex concepts can only be developed over a long period of time by a process of structuring and restructuring the concepts and misconceptions that children develop as they mature (Carey, 1986).

Teaching for Conceptual Change

Several studies have explored the effects of specific teaching strategies designed to persuade pupils to change their spontaneous or naive concepts about natural phenomena. The strategies in these studies, which go beyond provision of opportunities for exploration and discussion, have as objectives the construction of specific concepts.

An illustrative example is a study of the effects of teaching strategies designed to change the concepts held by primary children (K–3) about light and shadows (Neale, Smith, & Weir, 1991). Drawing on previous work on light and shadows and on teaching strategies designed to effect conceptual change (Smith & Neale, 1989; Neale, Smith, & Johnson, 1990), the investigators first taught teachers, over an extended period, the science concepts involved and the teaching strategies to be used. Close contact was maintained with teachers throughout the entire study, including careful monitoring of classroom activities during the

instructional sequence of 10 lessons. The principal findings, based on interviews of children before and after instruction, were that there was a substantial increase in children's use of scientific reasoning about light and shadows but little change in their misconceptions. The children had new knowledge of the subject but had not assimilated it into a coherent conceptual framework that excluded the previously held concepts. The investigators were not able to say whether the changes occurred as a result of instruction or whether the interviews themselves had an effect.

In another experiment Piaget's (1930) descriptions of 2 forms of physical causality, animism and dynamism, were invoked in an attempt to determine the effects of teaching on children's concepts of living and of floating and sinking (Wolfinger, 1982). Children ages 4 to 7 participated in small groups in a series of activity-based lessons while control groups participated in lessons unrelated to science. Experimental groups learned the concept of "living," but their ideas of why an object floats or sinks were not influenced by teaching. This result could have been anticipated by recognition of the essential differences in the concepts.

Nonspecific Teaching Methods

There is little evidence, so far, to indicate that the use of specific teaching strategies promotes the desired conceptual change in young children. Rather, there is some evidence that explicit strategy instruction is not as effective as less directive teacher intervention: Padilla and Ollila (1980), for example, studied first-grade children's responses to different levels of teacher intervention in learning to perform a seriation task. Retention scores were found to be highest for children who were forced to find their own solutions to the tasks presented. This result should not be interpreted as suggesting that children do not profit from a teacher's planning and guidance. The positive effect of teachers' asking questions and suggesting things for children to do is illustrated in Heath and Heath's (1982) study of the effects of verbal and physical intervention by preschool and kindergarten teachers. In the experimental groups, teachers invited the children to handle the objects and to think of things to do with them; children in the control groups were left on their own. The authors reported a significant relationship between teacher intervention and both the extent and cognitive level of young children's manipulation of magnets and other objects. When teachers encouraged children to handle the objects and asked what they might do with them, children responded by being more active and thoughtful. A similar finding is reported by Iatridis (1984).

A series of play-based centers were used to teach chemistry to children in a preschool. The outcomes were reported to be "generally positive" in terms of cognitive, socioemotional, and language goals (Norman & Taddonio, 1990). Although these authors found that their materials were developmentally appropriate, there has been some controversy among educators over the appropriateness of using chemistry in early childhood programs. Although the American Chemical Society has promoted the teaching of chemistry to children, one well-known chemist and science educator has advised his colleagues to "keep chemistry out of kindergarten" (Bent, 1985).

RELATION OF OTHER FACTORS TO LEARNING IN SCIENCE

Some researchers have shown interest in several other factors that may have an impact on children's learning in science. The four factors discussed in the following sections represent areas that have been studied extensively in other contexts but have not been investigated as broadly in relation to science education.

Gender

Girls' lower achievement, interest, and motivation in science has been well documented and publicized. A comprehensive synthesis of findings of major national surveys, international surveys, and other research on gender differences in science (Steinkamp & Maehr, 1984) shows that there are consistent but small gender-related differences in achievement and motivation, favoring boys. However, the age at which this difference appears is not yet clear, since many of Steinkamp and Maehr's chief data sources, including the National Assessment of Educational Progress, do not include children below the age of 9. In addition, children in all grades of the elementary school were combined into one category for purposes of data analysis. A recent study (Tracy, 1990) found that no overall difference in science achievement between girls and boys had emerged by grade 5. However, girls with a strong feminine orientation tended to have low science achievement scores, suggesting that adult approval of traditional feminine behavior may have an intellectually stifling effect on girls.

Although no available research focuses specifically on gender-related differences in science among young children, several studies include gender as an incidental variable. In such studies, gender differences were found to be very small or absent at the preschool or primary level (Rodriguez & Bethel, 1983; Heath & Heath, 1982; Wolfinger, 1982; Neale, Smith, & Weir, 1991). Research now indicates that gender differences in interest and achievement in science are not present during early childhood, suggesting that differences found in older children are the result of socialization rather than innate factors.

Children with Special Needs

Several curricula have been modified or developed for children with handicapping conditions. A SCIS adaptation for blind or visually impaired children was reported to have produced gains in content and process objectives (Linn & Peterson, 1973; Linn & Thier, 1975). In an experimental study using adaptations of SCIS, ESS, and SAPA, researchers compared the outcomes of teaching deaf children in special classes with the outcomes of teaching in mainstreamed classrooms (Linn, Hadary, Rosenberg, & Haushalter, 1979). The mainstreamed children showed improved self-images from finding acceptance among nonhandicapped peers. However, no differences in knowledge gains were found between the 2 groups. The authors argue for placing children in mainstreamed classrooms, provided that resources are available for teachers. Bybee and Hendricks (1972) were able to improve language development in deaf preschool children by

using SCIS activities as the basis for teaching language. It is clear that activity-based science programs can be adapted for handicapped children.

Language

Another group that is in one sense handicapped in this country comprises children whose native language is not English. One approach to the problems caused by this circumstance has been to use science as a vehicle for teaching English. Rodriguez and Bethel (1983) used science as a framework for the development of language in a program for third-grade Mexican American children whose native language was Spanish. After using manipulative materials, a high level of interaction with the teacher, children's action on objects, and both independent and group work, the researchers reported improved performance in both language and science. A comparison study (Mori, Kajima, & Tadang, 1976) of Japanese and Thai kindergarten children showed that Japanese children's confusion between 2 words with similar pronunciations prevented them from acquiring the related concept. The authors interpreted the result to be evidence of the importance of language in concept acquisition, a consideration that is important in teaching nonnative speakers.

Attitude

One of the persistent goals of science teaching has been to help children develop a positive attitude toward the subject. As noted earlier, some evidence has shown that the SCIS program succeeded in this objective. A meta-analysis of the relationship between science achievement and attitude, which included data from children in primary grades and elementary school, found that correlations between achievement and attitude toward science were low up to grade 6 (Wilson, 1983). The data produced more evidence for achievement preceding attitude than vice-versa; the author suggests that positive affect follows achievement—and that attention should be focused on improving achievement rather than on improving attitude.

ISSUES AND FUTURE DIRECTIONS

Science educators have approached research on children's learning with the assumption that there is a body of scientific knowledge that should be learned by all students. They have been concerned with the content and sequence of the curriculum, instructional strategies to facilitate the development of specific concepts, and the age at which instruction may begin. The prevailing research perspective has been empirical and has been informed, whether recognized or not, by a behaviorist-positivist model of learning in which learning is equated with a change in behavior and science is equated with reality. Science educators have placed high value on tests with known characteristics, controlled experiments, and generalizability of results. This perspective has separated science educators from early childhood educators, whose research has most often been naturalistic and descriptive. Without drawing sharp distinctions between curriculum development and research, early childhood educators have held to the Piagetian view that knowledge is constructed by the individual on the basis of intentional action, experience, and thought.

There are indications that the gap, both theoretical and practical, that has separated these two groups has begun to be bridged. Science educators are increasingly embracing a constructivist model (Clemenson, 1990) and early childhood educators are recognizing that science begins with exploration of the natural world (Chaillé & Britain, 1991). Scientists themselves have shown that they recognize science education goals that are broader than the accumulation of knowledge. In a recent set of science curriculum recommendations from a group of distinguished scientists, one of the criteria for content selection was, "Will the proposed content enhance childhood (a time of life that is important in its own right and not solely for what it may lead to in later life)?" (American Association for the Advancement of Science, 1989, p. 21). The convergence around a constructivist framework does not settle all the issues, but it may open the way for dialogue on issues that have not previously been addressed.

Continuing Influence of Piaget

One of the interesting aspects of recent research is that cognitive scientists and science educators have come to the realization that almost every "misconception" or "alternative framework" that they have found was already described and analyzed by Piaget. Cognitive scientists could almost be said to have reinvented, rather than rediscovered, Piaget in their search for misconceptions about natural phenomena. Piaget's interpretation of the data, which led to the formulation of a cognitive stage theory with concomitant limitations on knowledge development, has long been questioned. Nonetheless, Piaget's descriptions of children's responses to the tasks from the Genevan interviews remain an overwhelmingly rich source of data on children's understanding of natural phenomena.

Restructuring of Naive Concepts

The existence of explanations of natural phenomena among even very young children is not in doubt, but questions remain about the restructuring of these ideas or concepts. What is the mechanism for conceptual change? Why do some concepts persist in spite of years of schooling, whereas others disappear seemingly of their own accord? Two kinds of restructuring of knowledge have been posited: (1) *weak restructuring* that gradually replaces old ideas and explanations with new, more adequate conceptions and (2) *radical restructuring* that replaces core concepts with new, often radically different ones. These conceptualizations of knowledge restructuring, in addition to the one proposed by Piaget, are summarized by Carey (1986) and Vosniadou and Brewer (1987). The latter study cites as an example of radical restructuring the conceptual change that takes place as children give up their geocentric view of a flat earth (with its self-determining moon and sun) and accept the heliocentric view of a spherical, rotating earth.

The problem could also be cast in a framework suggested by Vygotsky (1962), who credited Piaget with dividing scientific concepts into (1) those that are spontaneous, which are developed mainly through the child's own mental efforts, and (2) those that are nonspontaneous, which are developed only through the influence or guidance of adults. Spontaneous concepts change through gradual assimilation of unplanned experiences and ideas encountered in the environment. This is the case, for example, with concepts of life and with conservation. Nonspontaneous concepts change only as the result of adult intervention; without appropriate experiences and instruction the naive concepts remain essentially unchanged.

Appropriate Science Instruction for Young Children

A question for education is whether instruction in nonspontaneous concepts, or those that require radical restructuring, is appropriate in early childhood. Both practical and theoretical considerations argue that such instruction is not appropriate. On practical grounds, it has not been found to be feasible or even possible to change concepts through direct intervention, as shown by some of the experiments reviewed earlier. Here again we return to Vygotsky, who wrote: "Practical experience also shows that direct teaching of concepts is impossible and fruitless. A teacher who tries to do this usually accomplishes nothing but empty verbalism, a parrotlike repetition of words" (1962, p. 83). From a theoretical perspective, one might accept either the Piagetian position that knowledge restructuring requires representational and logical structures not yet present in young children, or the alternative position that restructuring requires domain-specific prior knowledge that children have not yet acquired (Carey, 1986). Regardless of which position is taken, the effort to teach concepts that are not accessible to children through their own experience and thinking is inappropriate in preschool and the primary grades. Children can make their own observations and draw their own conclusions about the changes that take place in the life of a butterfly, for example, but it is not possible for them to observe that matter is composed of particles or that the flat Earth of their experience is not actually flat.

The same thing can be said for teaching vocabulary, a common goal in elementary science textbooks. Vocabulary should follow experience, not the reverse. Learning vocabulary that cannot be applied leads children to believe that some words have no real meaning. For the child, too many vocabulary words have no meaning related to personal experience or everyday life (Flick, 1991). Children may come to believe, then, that there are 2 kinds of words—words to be understood and used and words to be memorized.

A challenge for researchers is to differentiate among children's science concepts that become restructured through everyday experience, those that can become restructured through appropriate guided experiences, and those that must be learned through analogies, models, mathematical expressions, or other representations inaccessible to young children. Research in this area could provide a theoretical basis and a practical guide for developing science activities for young children.

Exploration of children's representation of knowledge is another area that holds promise. How children structure concepts, make or assume interconnections, and overlook salient features may be aspects that are better represented graphically than through language. Such representations may help children understand their own thinking. A related area for exploration and study is young children's metacognition. At what age do children begin spontaneously to think about their own mental processes, and how does this intersect with the school science program?

SUMMARY

Significant accomplishments have occurred in the past decade, more in a change of direction than in specific research findings. Science educators have returned to an interest in children's ideas and explanations, recognizing that children cannot be taught new concepts without attention to what they already know or believe. Constructivism is now widely accepted, though it is often vaguely defined and is in danger of becoming a catchword rather than a way of thinking about teaching and learning. Naturalistic research methods and classroom action research have come into broader use in science education and we can expect this trend to extend to research with young children. The differences of viewpoint and practice between science educators and early childhood educators are declining; this may signal the beginning of a period when productive collaboration will be possible and the gap between preschool and primary school can be bridged.

References

Acredolo, C., & Schmid, J. (1981). The understanding of relative speeds, distances and durations of movement. *Developmental Psychology, 17* (4), 490–493.

American Association for the Advancement of Science. (1989). *Project 2061: Science for all Americans.* Washington, DC: Author.

Ausubel, D. (1968). *Educational psychology—A cognitive view.* New York: Holt, Rinehart & Winston.

Bailey, L. (1903). *The nature-study idea.* New York: Doubleday Page.

Bent, H. (1985). Let's keep chemistry out of kindergarten. *Journal of Chemical Education, 62*(12), 1071.

Bredderman, T. (1984). The influence of activity-based elementary science programs on classroom practices: A quantitative synthesis. *Journal of Research in Science Teaching, 21*(3), 289–303.

Brumby, M. (1982). Students' perceptions of the concept of life. *Science Education, 66*(4), 613–622

Bruner, J. C. (1960). *The process of education.* Cambridge, MA: Harvard University Press.

Bybee, R., & Hendricks, P. (1972). Teaching science concepts to preschool deaf children to aid language development. *Science Education, 56,* 303–310.

Cain, S., & Evans, J. (1990). *Sciencing: An involvement approach to elementary science methods.* (3rd ed.). Columbus, OH: Merrill.

Carin, A., & Sund, R. (1989). *Teaching science through discovery.* Columbus, OH: Merrill.

Case, R. (1978). A developmentally based theory and technology of instruction. *Review of Educational Research, 48*(3), 439–463.

Carey, S. (1985). *Conceptual change in childhood.* Cambridge, MA: MIT Press.

Carey, S. (1986). Cognitive science and science education. *American Psychologist, 41*(10), 1123–1130.

Chaillé, C., & Britain, L. (1991). *The young child as scientist. A constructivist approach to early childhood education.* New York: HarperCollins.

Champagne, A., & Klopfer, L. (1979). Pioneers of elementary school science. *Science Education, 63*(3), 299–322.

Children's Learning in Science Research Group. (1991). *Research on children's concepts in science. A bibliography.* Leeds, UK: University of Leeds.

Clemenson, A. (1990). Establishing an epistemological base for science teaching in the light of contemporary notions of the nature of science and how children learn science. *Journal of Research in Science Education, 27*(5), 429–445.

Confrey, J. (1990). A review of the research on student conceptions in mathematics, science and programming. In C. Cazden (Ed.), *Review of research in education* (pp. 3–56). Washington, DC: American Educational Research Association.

Cross, R., & Mehegan, J. (1988). Young children's conception of speed: Possible implications for pedestrian safety. *International Journal of Science Education, 10*(3), 253–265.

DeVries, R. (1986). Children's conceptions of shadow phenomena. *Genetic, Social & General Psychology Monographs, 112*(4), 479–530.

DeVries, R., & Kohlberg, L. (1987). *Programs of early education. The constructivist view.* New York: Longman.

Dewey, J. (1956). *The child and the curriculum. The school and society.* Chicago: University of Chicago Press. (Original editions published in 1902 and 1900, respectively)

Dickinson, D. (1987). The development of a concept of material kind. *Science Education, 71*(4), 615–628.

Dolgin, K., & Behrend, R. (1984). Children's knowledge about animates and inanimates. *Child Development, 55,* 1646–1650.

Driver, R., Guesne, E., & Tiberghein, A. (Eds.). (1985). *Children's ideas in science.* Philadelphia: Open University Press.

Duckworth, E. (1987). *"The having of wonderful ideas" and other essays of teaching and learning.* New York: Teachers College, Columbia University.

Educational Development Center. (1969). *Introduction to elementary science study.* New York: Webster Division, McGraw-Hill.

Einstein, A., & Enfield, L. (1938). *The evolution of physics.* Cambridge, UK: Cambridge University Press.

Erickson, G. (1979). Children's conception of heat and temperature. *Science Education, 63*(2), 221–230.

Eylon, B. S., & Linn, M. (1988). Learning and Instruction: An examination of four research perspectives in science education. *Review of Educational Research, 58*(3), 251–301.

Feher, E., & Rice, K. (1987) Shadows and anti-images. *Science Education, 72*(5), 637–649.

Flick, L. (1991). Where concepts meet percepts: Stimulating analogical thought in children. *Science Education, 72*(2), 215–230.

Gagne, R. (1965). *The conditions of learning.* New York: Holt, Rinehart & Winston.

Gelman, S., & Ebeling, K. (1989). Children's use of nonegocentric standards in judgments of functional size. *Child Development, 60,* 920–932.

Gelman, S., Spelke, E., & Meck, E. (1983). What preschoolers know about animate and inanimate objects. In D. Rogers & J. Sloboda (Eds.), *The acquisition of symbolic skills.* New York: Plenum.

Guesne, E. (1985). Light. In R. Driver, E. Guesne, & A. Tiberghein (Eds.), *Children's ideas in science* (pp. 10–31). Philadelphia: Open University Press.

Harlen, W. (1985). *Teaching and learning primary science.* Washington, DC: National Science Teachers Association.

Heath, P., & Heath, P. (1982). The effect of teacher intervention on object manipulation in young children. *Journal of Research in Science Teaching, 19*(7), 577–585.

Hurd, P., & Gallagher, J. (1968). *New directions in elementary science teaching* (pp. 21–23). Belmont, CA: Wadsworth.

Iatridis, M. (1984). Teaching science to preschoolers. In M. McIntyre (Ed.), *Early childhood and science.* Washington, DC: National Science Teachers Association.

Jackman, W. S. (1891). *Nature study for the common schools.* New York: H. Holt.

Kaiser, M., & Proffitt, D. (1984). The development of sensitivity to causally relevant dynamic information. *Child Development, 55,* 1614–1624.

Kamii, C., & DeVries, R. (1977). In M. C. Day & R. K. Parker (Eds.), *The preschool in action. Exploring early childhood programs. (2nd ed.).* Boston: Allyn & Bacon.

Kamii, C., & DeVries, R. (1978). *Physical knowledge in preschool education: Implications of Piaget's theory.* Englewood Cliffs, NJ: Prentice Hall.

Klein, C. (1982). Children's concepts of the earth and sun: A cross cultural study. *Science Education, 65* (1), 95–107.

Laurendeau, M., & Pinard, A. (1962). *Causal thinking in the child.* New York: International Universities Press.

Linn, M., Hadary, D., Rosenberg, R., & Haushalter, R. (1979). Science education for the deaf: Comparison of ideal resource and mainstream setting. *Journal of Research in Science Teaching, 16*(4), 305–316.

Linn, M., & Peterson, R. (1973). The effect of direct experience with objects on middle class, culturally diverse and visually impaired young children. *Journal of Research in Science Teaching, 10,* 83–99.

Linn, M., & Thier, H. (1975). Adapting science materials for the blind. (ASMD) Expectations for student outcomes. *Science Education, 59,* 237–246.

Lowery, L., Bowyer, J., & Padilla, M. (1980). The science curriculum improvement study and student attitudes. *Journal of Research in Science Teaching, 17*(4), 327–355.

Mali, G., & Howe, A. (1979). Development of earth and gravity concepts among Nepali children. *Science Education, 63*(5), 685–691.

Mayr, E. (1982). *The growth of biological thought.* Cambridge, MA: Harvard University Press.

Mori, I., Kojima, M., & Deno, T. (1976). A child's forming the concept of speed. *Science Education, 60*(4), 521–529.

Mori, I., Kojima, M., & Tadang, N. (1976). The effect of language on a child's conception of speed: A comparative study on Japanese and Thai children. *Science Education, 60*(4), 531–534.

Myerson, M., Ford, M., Jones, W., & Ward, M. (1991). Science vocabulary knowledge of third and fifth grade students. *Science Education, 75,*(4), 419–428.

Neale, D., Smith, D., & Johnson, V. (1990). Implementing conceptual change teaching in primary science. *Elementary School Journal, 91* (2), 110–129.

Neale, D., Smith, D., & Weir, E. (1991). *Effects of conceptual change teaching on children's thinking about light and shadows.* Paper presented at the Annual Meeting of the American Educational Research Association, Chicago.

Norman, J., & Toddonio. (1990, April). *An exploratory study of the effectiveness of a play-based center approach for learning chemistry in an early childhood program.* Paper presented at the Annual Meeting of the Association for Research in Science Teaching, Atlanta.

Novak, J. (1977). *A theory of education.* Ithaca, NY: Cornell University Press.

Nussbaum, J. (1979). Israeli children's conception of the earth. *Science Education, 63*(1), 83–93.

Nussbaum, J., & Novak, J. (1976). An assessment of children's concepts of the earth utilizing structured interviews. *Science Education, 60*(4), 535–550.

Nussbaum, J., & Sharoni-Dagan, N. (1981). *Changes in children's perceptions and alternative frameworks about the earth as a cosmic body resulting from a short series of auto-tutorial lessons.* Jerusalem: Science Teaching Center, Hebrew University.

Osborne, R., & Freyberg, P. (1985). *Learning in science. The implications of children's science.* Auckland, New Zealand: Heineman.

Padilla, M., & Ollila, L. (1980). Effect of small-group teaching on acquisition and transfer of nonvisual seriation abilities. *Science Education, 64*(3), 357–366.

Perry, B., & Obenauf, P. (1987). The acquisition of notions of qualitative speed: The importance of spatial and temporal alignment. *Journal of Research in Science Teaching, 24*(6), 553–565.

Piaget, J. (1930). *The child's conception of physical causality.* Totowa, NJ: Littlefield, Adams.

Piaget, J. (1965). *The child's conception of the world.* Totowa, NJ: Littlefield, Adams.

Piaget, J. (1970) *The child's conception of movement and speed.* New York: Basic Books.

Rodrigues, D. N. (1980). Notions of physical laws in childhood. *Science Education, 64*(1), 59–84.

Rodriguez, I., & Bethel, L. (1983). An inquiry approach to science and language teaching. *Journal of Research in Science Teaching, 20*(4), 291–296.

Russell, R., & Dennis, W. (1940). Studies in animism II. Development of animism. *Journal of Genetic Psychology, 46,* 353–356.

Selman, R., Krupa, M., Stone, C. M., & Jaquette, D. (1982). Concrete operational thought and the emergence of the concept of unseen force in children's theories of electromagnetism and gravity. *Science Education, 66*(2), 181–194.

Siegler, R. (1981). Developmental sequences within and between concepts. *Monographs of the Society for Research in Child Development, 46* (2, Serial No. 189).

Siegler, R., & Richards, D. (1979). The development of time, speed and distance concepts. *Developmental Psychology, 15,* 288–298.

Shymansky, J., Hedges, L., & Woodworth, G. (1990). A reassessment of the effects of inquiry-based science curricula of the 60's on student performance. *Journal of Research in Science Teaching, 27*(2), 127–144.

Smith, C., Carey, S., & Wiser, M. (1985). On differentiation: A case study of the development of size, weight and density. *Cognition, 21,* 177–237.

Smith, D., & Neale, D. (1989). The construction of subject matter knowledge in primary science teaching. *Teaching and Teacher Education, 5*(1), 1–20.

Smith, S., Trueblood, C., & Szabo, M. (1981). Conservation of length and instruction in linear measurement in young children. *Journal of Research in Science Teaching, 18*(1), 61–68.

Sneider, C., & Pulos, S. (1983). Children's cosmologies: Understanding the earth's shape and gravity. *Science Education, 67*(2), 205–221.

Staver, J., & Bay, M. (1989). Analysis of the conceptual structure and reasoning demands of elementary science texts at the primary (K–3) level. *Journal of Research in Science Teaching, 26*(4), 329–350.

Steinkamp, M., & Maehr, M. (1984). Gender differences in motivational orientations toward achievement in school science: A quantitative synthesis. *American Educational Research Journal, 21*(1), 39–59.

Tracy, D. (1990). Toy-playing behavior, sex-role orientation, spatial ability and science achievement. *Journal of Research in Science Teaching, 27*(7), 637–650.

Underhill, O. E. (1941). *The origins of development of elementary school science.* Chicago: Scott, Foresman.

Urevbu, A. (1984). Teaching concepts of energy to Nigerian children in the 7–11 year-old age range. *Journal of Research in Science Teaching, 21*(3), 255–267.

Vosniadou, S., & Brewer, W. (1987). Theories of knowledge restructuring in development. *Review of Educational Research, 57*(10), 51–67.

Vygotsky, L. (1962). *Thought and language.* Cambridge: MIT Press.

Welch, W. (1976). Evaluating the impact of national curriculum projects. *Science Education, 60*(4), 475–483.

Wilson, V. (1983). A meta-analysis of the relationship between science achievement and science attitude from kindergarten through college. *Journal of Research in Science Teaching, 20*(9), 839–850.

Wiser, M., & Carey, S. (1983). When heat and temperature were one. In D. Gentner & A. Stevens (Eds.), *Mental models.* Hillside, NH: Erlbaum.

Wolfinger, D. (1982). Effect of science teaching on the young child's concept of Piagetian physical causality: Animism and dynamism. *Journal of Research in Science Teaching, 19*(7), 595–602.

MULTICULTURAL EDUCATION FOR YOUNG CHILDREN: RACIAL AND ETHNIC ATTITUDES AND THEIR MODIFICATION

James A. Banks

UNIVERSITY OF WASHINGTON, SEATTLE

THE NATURE AND BOUNDARIES OF MULTICULTURAL EDUCATION

Multicultural education is a process whose major aims are to help students from diverse cultural, ethnic, gender, and social-class groups attain equal educational opportunities, and to help all students develop positive cross-cultural attitudes, perceptions, and behaviors (Banks & Banks, 1989). Multicultural education in the United States consists of a wide variety of approaches, paradigms, concepts, and strategies. In another publication (Banks, 1992), the author describes 3 major approaches to multicultural education: *content approaches, achievement approaches*, and *intergroup education approaches*.

Content approaches conceptualize multicultural education as an educational process that involves additions to or changes within the curriculum in the various content areas. Achievement approaches conceptualize multicultural education as a set of goals, theories, and strategies designed to increase the academic achievement of lower-class students, students of color, students from both gender groups, and students from diverse cultural groups. Intergroup education approaches have as a major aim helping all students to develop positive attitudes toward people from various racial, gender, and cultural groups.

Although these major approaches to multicultural education can be distinguished conceptually, they are often blended and interrelated in practice. For example, the major goal of intergroup education approaches is to help students attain more positive attitudes toward racial, gender, and cultural groups, yet diverse curricular interventions, techniques, and approaches are often used to modify those children's attitudes.

INTERGROUP EDUCATION AND CHILDREN'S RACIAL ATTITUDES

It is not possible within one research review to discuss each of the 3 major approaches to multicultural education identified in the preceding section. Consequently, the scope of this chapter is limited in several ways. It is limited primarily to the intergroup education approach and will focus on the characteristics and modification of young children's attitudes. The research on ways in which curriculum and other kinds of interventions can modify young children's attitudes will be discussed.

The scope of this chapter is limited in the kind of attitudes discussed. It describes the characteristics and modification of racial and ethnic attitudes. Gender attitudes and attitudes toward individuals and groups with disabilities are not discussed because a comprehensive review and discussion of research related to these variables—and ways to modify them through curriculum interventions—cannot be adequately treated within one chapter. However, the research and theory on the characteristics and modification of racial and ethnic attitudes may be related in some significant ways to the characteristics and modification of other kinds of attitudes and beliefs held by young children.

The Racial and Ethnic Attitudes of Young Children

Many teachers with whom the author has interacted in university classes and school district workshops have stated that young children are unaware of racial and ethnic differences—that they don't "see" the colors of various racial and ethnic groups. Such teachers are reluctant to teach young children about racial and ethnic differences because they may destroy the children's racial and ethnic innocence. Teachers who express these feelings believe that our goal as a society and as teachers should be to make children color-blind on issues related to race and ethnicity.

There are a number of problems with a "color-blind" approach to race and ethnic issues in early childhood education. One major problem with this approach is that it is inconsistent with how children actually develop racial views. Research has rather consistently established, during a period extending over 50 years, that young children are not only aware of racial and ethnic differences, but have internalized the dominant society's norms regarding the social status of different racial and ethnic groups (Goodman, 1946; Horowitz, 1939; Katz, 1987; Lasker, 1929; Minard, 1931; Ramsey & Myers, 1990; Spencer, 1982).

Lasker's (1929) pioneering research on children's racial attitudes indicated that young children are aware of racial differences. Lasker also described some of the emotional components that accompany racial prejudice. A study by Minard (1931) indicated that children's racial attitudes are formed during the earliest years of life.

Since the seminal research by Lasker and Minard, many other researchers have studied race awareness, preference, and identification in young children (Cross, 1991; Phinney & Rotheram, 1987; Ramsey & Myers, 1990). This body of research is extensive and comprehensive. Several thorough and helpful reviews have been published since 1970, including those by Brand, Ruiz, and Padilla (1974), Katz (1982), and the book-length reviews by Milner (1983) and Cross (1991). A comprehensive review of this research is beyond the scope of this chapter; however, the chapter does provide a discussion of selected intervention studies, describing implications for further research, policy, and practice. Consequently, the reader is provided with an overview of the major findings of the research on children's racial attitudes, the important paradigms and issues in the field, the different interpretations of the research, the major debates regarding methodology, and unresolved research questions.

The Studies by the Clarks and the Establishment of a Paradigm

In a series of landmark studies with African Americans ages 3 to 7, Kenneth and Mamie Clark (1939a, 1939b, 1940, 1947, 1950) established a paradigm in racial attitude research that is still highly influential. Although the findings by the Clarks have not been disconfirmed, Spencer (1982, 1984, 1987, 1988) and Cross (1985, 1987, 1991) have developed fresh and innovative interpretations of the negative self-concept hypothesis. This hypothesis is a significant component of the Clarks' paradigm. A few studies have contradicted the Clarks' findings (e.g., Gregor & McPherson, 1966a; Hraba & Grant, 1970; Ogletree, 1969). The findings of other studies have indicated that the issues of racial attitude are more complex than the Clarks stated (e.g., Banks & Rompf, 1973). W. C. Banks (1976) has described what he considers the serious methodological weaknesses in the Clarks' paradigm and the subsequent research that supports it. The

new interpretations of and challenges to the Clarks' paradigm will be discussed later in this chapter.

In his book-length review of the research on the racial attitudes of children, Cross (1991) states that the research paradigm for which the Clarks are credited was actually formulated by Eugene and Ruth Horowitz. Eugene Horowitz (1936) studied the racial attitudes of children using photographs that constituted a "show-me" test. The African American children showed a slight but statistically significant preference for photographs of white individuals on this test. Ruth Horowitz (1939) examined the racial self-identification of black and white nursery school children in a pioneering study. She concluded that the black children made out-group racial preferences indicating self-rejection.

Cross concludes that Eugene and Ruth Horowitz, rather than the Clarks, originated the hypothesis of self-hatred among blacks. This hypothesis is referred to as the Clarks' paradigm in this chapter because their research was highly influential in popularizing this paradigm in social science research and among students of psychology and education.

The major postulates and findings of the early research by the Horowitzs and the subsequent research by the Clarks have not been disconfirmed, despite the new interpretations of and the challenges to the methodology of this research. Consequently, it is essential that we consider the Clarks' research when discussing the racial and ethnic attitudes of young children today. Details of only one of the Clarks' studies will be described. It typifies the paradigm that has become associated with their work.

The Clarks (1947) studied *racial preference, racial differences,* and *racial self-identification* by using brown and white dolls with a sample of 253 African American children. The children's ages ranged from 3 to 7. The sample was drawn from nursery schools in Arkansas and Massachusetts.

The Clarks found that the children had an accurate knowledge of racial differences. Ninety-four percent of the children chose the white doll when asked to give the researcher the white doll; 93% of them chose the brown doll when asked to give the researcher the colored doll. Most of the children (66%) identified with the colored doll, but 33% of them identified with the white doll.

The majority of the children in the study preferred the white doll and rejected the colored doll. About two-thirds of the children indicated that they liked the white doll best, and that they preferred to play with the white rather than the colored doll. Fifty-nine percent of the children indicated that the colored doll looked bad, while only 17% described the white doll this way. Although a majority of the children expressed a preference for the white doll, the preference for white decreased as children grew older. In other words, the older children were, the less likely they were to favor the white over the brown doll. The Clarks also found that the southern children, who attended segregated nursery schools, were less pronounced in their preference for the white dolls than were the northern children, who attended racially mixed schools.

The most salient findings of all the Clarks' studies are exemplified in the study described above. These findings constitute the essence of the paradigm used by Kenneth and Mamie

Clark in their research. Collectively, the Clarks' studies indicated that young children have an accurate knowledge about racial differences and that African American children often make incorrect racial self-identifications, frequently expressing a preference for white dolls, drawings, or other stimuli when asked to choose a white or brown stimulus. The Clarks interpreted the tendency of African American children to make incorrect racial self-identifications and to prefer white to brown images as an indication that the children were aware of and had internalized the dominant society's attitudes, perceptions, and evaluations of blacks and whites (Clark, 1963).

Other Research in the Clarks' Paradigm

During the 1950s, 1960s, and 1970s, a number of researchers studied the racial attitudes of black and white children using stimuli such as dolls, pictures, puppets, and other images to elicit children's responses related to racial awareness, preference, and identification. These studies include those conducted by Radke and Trager (1950), Goodman (1952), Trager and Yarrow (1952), Morland (1958), Porter (1971), Williams, Boswell, and Best (1975), and a series of studies reported by Williams and Morland (1976). Most of these researchers included both black and white children in their samples. In general, their findings confirmed those made by the Clarks, although a number of these researchers crafted more complex designs, especially Radke and Trager (1950), Trager and Yarrow (1952), and Porter (1971). Several of these researchers described more of the complexity involved in the development of racial attitudes than did the Clarks (Porter, 1971; Radke & Trager, 1950; Williams et al., 1975). Several of these studies will be discussed to give the reader an idea of their implications.

Children's perceptions of the social roles of blacks and whites were examined by Radke and Trager (1950). Their sample consisted of 242 kindergarten, first-, and second-grade children in the Philadelphia public schools. The subjects consisted of 90 blacks and 152 whites. The schools ranged from predominantly white to predominantly black.

The investigators used cut-out figures of men and women, plywood clothes to fit the figures, and plywood forms of a house to elicit the children's social and racial attitudes. The children were asked to dress the black and white dolls and to place them in houses. Thirty-eight percent of the white children and 16% of the black children ascribed inferior roles to the black dolls. A majority of both the black and white children gave the poor house to the black doll and the good house to the white doll. The white doll was preferred by 89% of the white children and 57% of the black children. However, the researchers provided no discussion of the 43% of black children who did not prefer the white doll or of the white and black children who did not ascribe inferior roles to the black dolls. This type of omission is frequent in research in this paradigm.

Trager and Yarrow (1952) reported another study using the same children that were used in the study by Radke and Trager (1950) described above (Yarrow of the 1952 study had the surname Radke in the 1950 study). In this study children were shown a picture of several white children playing and a black child in the foreground who could be interpreted as part of the play group or as isolated. The researchers concluded: "more than two-thirds of the white children and a quarter of the Negro children, for whom is involved some measure of 'self-hate,' verbalize hostility or rejection of the Negro child in the picture or of Negroes in general. Unqualified positive and accepting attitudes are verbalized by only 11% of the Negro children" (p. 140). Trager and Yarrow also concluded that the children showed an "overwhelming preference for white group membership. Not only do white children like being white (88%), but Negro children, too, rarely say that the white child does not like being white (10%)" (p. 141). The researchers also noted that they found much conflict in the responses of the black children.

Morland (1958, 1966) has conducted a number of studies of the racial attitudes of nursery school children, many of whom lived in the South. His studies have, in general, confirmed the findings by the Clarks and by Trager and Yarrow. In a study of 454 children attending 6 nursery schools in Lynchburg, Virginia, he used a set of 8 pictures to determine the racial attitudes and preferences of black and white children (Morland, 1958).

Most of the white children (99.5%) and about half of the black children (52.0%) correctly identified their racial group when asked, "Are you white or are you colored?" Morland wrote that the significant proportion of black children who incorrectly identified their racial group may be explained by the possibility that they were "unconsciously identifying themselves with the dominant, privileged race" (p. 137). He stated that this possibility was supported by the fact that, when many of the black children stated they were colored, they "did so reluctantly and with emotional strain" (p. 137). Morland found that the ability to recognize racial differences increased with age but was not related to sex.

Morland's findings were confirmed by Miel (Miel with Kiester, 1967) in a study of the racial attitudes of first-, second-, and third-grade students attending school in a predominantly white suburban community near New York City. The investigator showed 235 children a picture of a black boy and a white boy walking together and asked them, "Which boy would you choose to play with?" Most of the children (187) chose the white boy, 31 chose the black boy, and 15 chose both boys. Two children stated that they did not want to play with either boy. The researchers stated that the children showed great anxiety when they tried to respond to the question. The investigators also asked the children, "Which boy would most children choose to play with?" The children responded to this question more freely. Each of the 13 African American children who responded to the latter question said that most children would choose to play with the white boy.

In a series of studies Williams and his colleagues have examined bias toward the colors white and black in preschool children using instruments they have developed, such as Preschool Racial Attitude Measures and the Color Meaning Test (Williams & Edwards, 1969; Williams, Best, Wood, & Fuller, 1973; Williams et al., 1975). Most of their subjects have been black and white children in the United States. However, they have conducted some of their research in other nations, such as Germany (Williams & Carter, 1967).

In one study (Williams et al., 1975) where the color meaning test was used, children were given stimuli such as 2 horses (1 white and 1 black), told a brief story, and asked, "Which is the good horse?" The students were also shown other identical animals colored black and white and asked to evaluate them. Williams and his colleagues found in this study (Williams et al., 1975)—as they have in others—that most of the Euro-American and African American children showed a white bias and a tendency to evaluate the color white more positively than black (see Williams & Morland, 1976). However, although the white bias was evident among both black and white preschoolers, it was less pronounced among the black children. Williams and his colleagues (1975) concluded, "Theoretically, it is proposed that pro-white/anti-black color bias may be related to the child's status as a diurnal animal, and hence, to his experiences with the light of day and dark of night" (p. 501).

Most researchers who have examined racial awareness, preference, and identification in young children have used white and African American children as subjects (Katz, 1982; Milner, 1983). Only a few studies have been conducted with Mexican Americans or other children of color. Two exceptions are studies by Werner and Evans (1968) and Rice, Ruiz, and Padilla (1974). Werner and Evans examined the racial attitudes of Mexican American children. Their findings confirmed those of the Clarks. Mexican American children described the black doll more negatively than they did the white doll. The results of this study must be interpreted with caution, because a black doll does not accurately represent the range of skin colors among Mexican Americans.

Racial awareness and preferences among preschool and third-grade Anglo, African American, and Chicano children were examined by Rice et al. (1974). They used photographs of young adult males from these ethnic groups as stimuli. Although most of the children were able to correctly identify the black male, many of them had trouble differentiating the Chicano and Anglo males. These investigators concluded that only the Chicano preschool children showed a clear preference for their own ethnic group and that black and Anglo children made out-group preferences.

The Quest for New Interpretations

Since the research by the Horowitzs and the Clarks and the other researchers who have confirmed their findings and perpetuated their paradigm, many social scientists have assumed that African American children have low self-esteem, negative self-concepts, and harbor self-hate because they internalize Eurocentric racial attitudes. The *self-hate hypothesis* was widespread in the literature from the 1940s through most of the 1970s (e.g., Kardiner & Ovesey, 1962; Pettigrew, 1964; Trager & Yarrow, 1952).

During the 1980s, researchers such as Spencer (1982, 1984, 1985, 1988) and Cross (1985, 1987, 1991) developed concepts, theories, and research strongly challenging the notion that young black children who express Eurocentric racial preferences have negative self-esteem, self-hate, and dysfunctional personalities. These researchers have made a useful conceptual distinction between *personal identity* (self-concept, self-esteem) and *group identity* or reference-group orientation.

In a series of pioneering studies, Spencer (1982, 1984) has marshalled significant support for these postulates: (1) that young African American children are able to distinguish their personal identity from their group identity, (2) that they can have high self-esteem and yet express a white bias, and (3) that the expression of a white bias results from a cognitive process that enables young children to accurately perceive the norms and attitudes toward whites and blacks in American society.

In a study of the relationship between social cognition, cultural cognition, and racial preference of 130 black preschool children in Chicago, Spencer (1982) found that the racial stereotyping of black children during the preoperational period was not necessarily internalized as part of their personal identity or self-esteem. She stated, "Racial stereotypes in these children must be viewed as objectively held information about the environment and not as reflections of personal identity" (p. 285). The relationship among race awareness, racial attitudes, and self-concept was further clarified in a study published later by Spencer (1984). This study used the same subjects as the 1982 study. Spencer found that most (80%) of the children obtained high self-concept scores, yet expressed racial attitudes and preferences favoring whites. Spencer concluded that preschool black children successfully compartmentalize "personal identity (i.e., self-concept) from knowledge of racial evaluations" (p. 440).

Banks (1984) found results supporting those of Spencer in a study of the racial attitudes and self-concepts of older African American children (mean age 12.8 years) who lived in predominantly white suburban communities. He found that self-concept of ability was not significantly related to ethnocentrism (pro-blackness) on either of 2 different measures, and that pro-blackness on 1 of the 2 measures was moderately but negatively related to self-esteem. This finding indicates that children who evaluated blacks more positively on one of the racial attitude scales administered tended to score slightly lower on the Rosenberg self-esteem scale.

Other Challenges to the Clarks' Paradigm

The challenges to the Clarks' paradigm have taken several forms, including (1) different explanations of the pro-white bias that is exemplified by preschool African American children (Cross, 1985, 1987; Spencer, 1987, 1988), (2) a few studies that disconfirm the pro-white bias among young children, and (3) arguments that describe the methodological weaknesses of the studies by the Clarks and their followers. The search for alternative explanations was discussed in the preceding section. The studies that contradict the Clarks' findings and the observations concerning methodological weaknesses will now be considered.

In their comprehensive review of studies of children's racial attitudes, Brand et al. (1974) reported 4 studies that disconfirmed the findings by the Clarks. Two of the studies they reported will be discussed in this chapter (Gregor & McPherson,

1966a; Hraba & Grant, 1970) as will 2 that they did not discuss (Banks & Rompf, 1973; Ogletree, 1969). As is the case in each section of this chapter, no attempt is made to describe each study that contradicts the Clarks' findings. Rather, the goal is to give the reader a sampling of such studies in order to convey salient characteristics.

In Gregor and McPherson's (1966a) study of 6- and 7-year-old children in the segregated South, both White and African American students made own-group preferences. The researchers used a variant of the Clarks' doll test to solicit responses from the children. The magnitude of own-group preference was greater among white than among black children. White own-group choices attained or exceeded 79% of all preference requests. Own-group choices by African American children attained or exceeded 50%. Gregor and McPherson hypothesized that the more minority group children are integrated into racially mixed settings, the more likely they are to express out-group preferences. They cited research that they conducted in Hawaii and South Africa to support this explanation (Gregor, 1963; Gregor & McPherson, 1966b). Gregor and McPherson believed that the African American children in their study made own-group preferences because they lived in racially segregated communities and attended racially segregated schools.

In a skin color preference test administered by Ogletree (1969), most of the African American children (72%) colored 2 human figures brown, and 75% of the white children painted them white. The sample was from a Detroit elementary school, and consisted of children ages 3, 4, and 5.

In a replication of the Clarks' doll study, Hraba and Grant (1970) found that both white and black children made own-group preferences. The children were between the ages of 4 and 8 and attended interracial schools in Lincoln, Nebraska. The investigators found that a majority of the black children of all ages preferred the black doll, and that own-group preference increased with age. Their finding that own-group preference increases with age is consistent with the findings of most other studies. This study is an interesting one because 70% of the black children had white friends and 59% of the white children had black friends. The researchers also found that black children who had both white and black friends were more likely to make own-group preferences than black children who had only black friends.

W. C. Banks and Rompf (1973) examined the self-rejection hypothesis by asking 6- to 8-year-old children to view a black and a white player in a ball-tossing game. The white children showed a preference for the white player. They more often chose him as the winner and rewarded him more for his performance. The responses of the African American children were more complex. They rewarded the white player more, suggesting a white preference. However, they also showed a preference for the black player by choosing him more often as the winner. The authors stated, "No consistent white preference in blacks was found to support an interpretation of global 'self-rejection.' Instead, black children showed preference for whites and blacks as a function of the expressive task within which they were asked to make evaluations" (p. 776).

Methodological Problems in the Clarks' Paradigm

A number of researchers, including W. C. Banks (1976) and Abound (1987), have described methodological problems and limitations of the Clarks' paradigm. Abound believes that 4 aspects of the typical designs used in this paradigm are problematic, including "the use of a doll to represent an ethnic group, appearance as the basis of similarity, forced choices, and reliability and validity" (p. 38).

W. C. Banks (1976) contends that issues related to methodology and to validity and reliability are moot because white preference among African Americans has not been demonstrated by existing research. He examined 21 studies conducted between 1947 and 1971 and concluded that the pattern of black choice responses had been at the chance level. He found that 69% of the studies he reviewed showed nonpreference, 25% indicated black preference, and only 6% showed white preference in blacks. W. C. Banks concluded that these findings are difficult to interpret. However, Williams and Morland (1979), 2 of the leading proponents of the Clarks' paradigm, disagreed strongly with the W. C. Banks critique. W. C. Banks, McQuater, and Ross (1979) rejoined. The debate continues among scholars and researchers over the extent to which African American children make out-group racial preferences.

Summary

There is still considerably debate among scholars and researchers about young children's racial preferences, attitudes, and identifications. However, many researchers agree that (1) preschool and kindergarten African Americans often make out-group preferences on a variety of measures and (2) these out-group preferences decrease with age, but increase within interracial settings and situations. Current research and theory cast considerable doubt on the postulate, popular from the 1940s through the 1970s, that African American children who express a bias toward whites have self-concept problems, low self-esteem and harbor self-hate. Recent research and theory indicates that personal identity and group identity are separate phenomena, and that young African American children can express a bias toward whiteness and white people and yet have high self-esteem and positive self-concepts.

Most early childhood educators would agree that it is important to help young children of color develop more in-group racial preferences. However, educators should not misinterpret what their expression of white bias means cognitively and emotionally. Most educators in a multicultural society do not want children of color to develop ethnocentric attitudes such as those held by most preschool white children. Most white children make own-group racial preferences, as well as express negative attitudes toward other racial and ethnic groups from age 4 onward (Williams & Morland, 1976).

Harrison (1985) has pointed out an important problem and, at the same time, described a dilemma. She states that social scientists assume that high own-group racial preference is normal and desirable because this is a characteristic of most white children. Yet most educators would agree that they want to help reduce racism and to help white children develop more positive racial attitudes and interracial contacts. Young children who express strong in-group preferences also tend to reject and to express negative attitudes toward out-groups (Abound, 1987; Williams & Morland, 1976).

Harrison's perceptive observation suggests that an important goal of education in a pluralistic society should be to help students from all racial and cultural groups to develop *bicultural* racial attitudes and behavior rather than high in-group racial preferences. Banks's study of African American suburban youth (1984a), as well as many of the studies reviewed earlier, supports the postulate that African American children tend to be bicultural in their racial attitudes and behaviors. However, almost none of the studies reviewed by the author reports or discusses findings related to the bicultural attitudes of African American children. The students in Banks's study (1984a) had biracial attitudes. They liked both their white and black friends, but wished that they had more black friends. They lived in predominantly white suburban communities and attended predominantly white suburban schools. More attention needs to be focused on the extent to which children make choices from different racial groups and less on the extent to which they make own-group racial preferences. Researchers need to examine the extent to which parents of color, such as African American and Hispanic parents, socialize their children to be bicultural so that they can function effectively in both their ethnic communities and in the larger civic community.

THE MODIFICATION OF YOUNG CHILDREN'S RACIAL ATTITUDES

The research and literature that describe the racial awareness, attitudes, and self-identification of young children is much richer than the research that describes ways in which their intergroup attitudes can be modified. Only a few research reviews in recent years have described the ways in which children's intergroup attitudes can be modified (e.g., Banks, 1991a; Katz, 1976; Stephan, 1985). The Stephan review includes studies with both adults and children as subjects.

No interventions are reported by the Clarks that were designed to modify the racial preferences that children made in their famous doll studies of the 1930s and 1940s. A few intervention studies were conducted in the 1940s (Agnes, 1947; Jackson, 1944). However, most of these were conducted using adolescent youths as subjects. The number of intervention studies did not increase substantially until the intergroup education movement reached its peak in the 1950s (Cook & Cook, 1954). Most of the intervention studies conducted during the intergroup education movement of the 1940s and 1950s also used older children as subjects. One exception was the important study by Trager and Yarrow (1952) that was conducted using children between the ages of 5 and 8 in kindergarten, first grade, and second grade. A cumulative body of research and theory on the modification of young children's racial attitudes did not develop until studies were conducted by Williams and his colleagues at Wake Forest University in the 1960s and 1970s

(Best, Smith, Graves, & Williams, 1975; Williams & Edwards, 1969).

Several types of studies have been conducted to help children develop more democratic racial attitudes and behaviors. These include the *reinforcement studies* conducted by Williams and his colleagues (e.g., Best et al., 1975; Williams & Edwards, 1969; Williams & Morland, 1976), *perceptual differentiation studies* conducted by Katz and her colleagues (e.g., Katz, 1973, 1976, 1982; Katz & Zalk, 1978), *curricular intervention studies* (e.g., Litcher & Johnson, 1969; Trager & Yarrow, 1952; Yawkey & Blackwell, 1974); and studies that use *cooperative activities* and *contact situations* to help children develop more democratic attitudes and values (e.g., Aronson & Bridgeman, 1979; DeVries, Edwards, & Slavin, 1978; Slavin, 1979, 1983, 1985). Most intervention studies conducted using preschool and primary-grade children as subjects have been reinforcement studies. Only a few perceptual differentiation studies have been reported. Most curriculum intervention studies have used older students as subjects (Banks, 1991a). All of the cooperative learning intervention studies reviewed by the author used elementary and high-school students as subjects; none used kindergarten and primary-grade children. However, these studies do have implications for educating young children.

Each of the 4 categories of studies identified above is discussed in the next section of this chapter.

Reinforcement Studies

In the late 1960s, Williams and his colleagues (Williams & Edwards, 1969; Williams & Morland, 1976) began a series of reinforcement studies to modify preschool children's attitudes toward the colors black and white, and to determine whether a reduction of white bias toward objects and animals would generalize to white and black people. One of the first in a series of laboratory experiments was conducted by Williams and Edwards (1969). The sample consisted of 84 white preschool children in Winston-Salem, North Carolina, who ranged in age from 5:0 to 5:11 when the intervention began.

Two kinds of assessments were used to determine the children's color concepts and racial attitudes: (a) a picture-story procedure for assessing connotative meanings of black and white, and (b) a picture-story technique that measured attitudes toward black and white persons. In the first procedure the experimenter showed the child, for example, a white horse and a black horse and asked: "Which is the good horse? Which is the ugly horse? Which is the clean horse? Which is the stupid horse?" In the second procedure the child was shown drawings of 2 identical figures, one pinkish-tan with light yellow hair (an Anglo American) and the other medium-brown with black hair (an African American). The experimenter said: "Here are 2 girls. Everyone says that one is pretty. Which is the pretty girl?"

In the experimental groups the children received positive reinforcement for choosing black animals in response to story sentences that contained positive adjectives, or for choosing white animals when responding to story sentences that contained negative adjectives. The subjects were divided into 3 experimental groups and 1 control group. The 3 experimental groups were (a) positive reinforcement only, (b) negative reinforcement only, and (c) positive and negative reinforcement. The control group received no reinforcement.

The picture-story procedure with animals was administered twice at 2-week intervals. The procedure with human figures was administered 2 weeks after the administration of the second session of the color-meaning procedure. During the administration of the color-meaning procedure, a child in the positive-reinforcement group was given candy when he or she made a "correct" response. In the negative-reinforcement group, children would lose 2 of the 30 pennies that they had been given every time they gave an incorrect response. In the positive-reinforcement/negative-reinforcement group, the children received candy when they gave correct responses and lost 2 pennies when they gave incorrect responses. In the control group, no mention was made of right and wrong answers and no reinforcement was given. When the racial attitude procedure was administered, no reinforcement was given in any of the groups.

Williams and Edwards (1969) found that their reinforcement procedures reduced white bias in the children and that children whose white bias had been weakened generalized their attitude to people. They showed less of a tendency to describe blacks negatively and whites positively. The investigators pointed out, however, that though the change effected in racial attitudes was statistically significant, it was not substantial. Williams and Edwards emphasized that, even though the reinforcement procedure reduced white bias, it did not remove the children's color connotations for black and white. They wrote, "In the typical case, the procedure merely weakened the customary connotations of white as good and black as bad, and left the child with no consistent evaluative response to the colors" (p. 748).

The Williams and Edwards (1969) findings were confirmed in a study reported later (Edwards & Williams, 1970). Most reinforcement interventions by other researchers have, in the main, confirmed these major findings by Williams and his colleagues (Hohn, 1973; Parish & Fleetwood, 1975; Parish, Shirazi, & Lambert, 1976): (a) that preschool children tend to evaluate the color black negatively and white positively, (b) that reinforcement procedures can reduce bias toward white, and (c) that children can generalize their reduced white bias to African American people.

Using procedures adapted from Renninger and Williams (1966), Spencer and Horowitz (1973) examined the color perception of 24 African American and white children and designed a reinforcement procedure to modify their color connotations and racial attitudes. They found (a) that the black preschool children were as negative about the color black as were the white preschoolers, (b) that the children generalized color concepts to racial concepts, (c) that social and token reinforcement reduced white bias, and (d) that the effects of the experiment were evident over a 2-week period and for some children over a 4-week period.

Perceptual Differentiation Studies

In a series of interesting and innovative studies, Katz and her colleagues (Katz, 1973; Katz, Sohn, & Zalk, 1975; Katz & Zalk, 1978) examined the perceptual concomitants of racial attitudes in young children. Katz (1973) predicted that preschool children would have more difficulty differentiating the faces of out-group individuals than the faces of individuals who were members of their own racial groups. She tested this prediction using a sample of 192 African American and white preschool children who lived in New York City. Katz's prediction was confirmed; she concluded that "racial labels may increase the perceptual similarity of faces of another group" (p. 298).

Katz reasoned that, if children could be taught to differentiate perceptually the faces of minority individuals, racial prejudice would be reduced. In an important study Katz and Zalk (1978) investigated the effect of teaching children to differentiate minority-group faces. In the same study they also examined the effects of 3 other interventions: increased positive racial contact, vicarious interracial contact, and reinforcement of the color black. The researchers examined the effects of these interventions on second- and fifth-grade white students who were high in prejudice. The children were randomly assigned to 1 of the 4 experimental treatment groups.

In the racial contact situation, 2 black and 2 white children worked together to complete a jigsaw puzzle as fast as they could in order to win a prize. Each of the experimental interventions lasted for 15 minutes in order to control for time. The children in the vicarious contact situation listened to a story with slides that described an African American boy (for the males) or girl (for the females) who was heroic. In one of the experimental conditions for the stimulus predifferentiation groups, the children were shown 4 slides of the same model that varied along several dimensions. In the other condition, they observed black faces. This intervention taught the children to differentiate minority-group faces. The children participated in several tasks in the reinforcement condition. In one of them, they were shown 10 black and 10 white animal pictures. When they chose a black animal, they were reinforced with marbles that could be exchanged for prizes.

The investigators found that each of the interventions resulted in a short-term reduction of prejudice on the combined attitude measures used in the study. The most effective interventions for reducing prejudice were the vicarious contact and the perceptual differentiation conditions. The children's racial attitudes were measured 2 weeks after the experiment and again 4 to 6 months later. The experimental gains were reduced over time, but some were maintained. The vicarious contact and perceptual differentiation groups were the most effective interventions for inducing long-term effects.

Curriculum Interventions

Since the 1940s a number of curriculum intervention studies have been conducted to determine how the racial attitudes and perceptions of young children are affected by (1) teaching units and lessons, (2) multiethnic materials, (3) role playing, and (4) other kinds of simulated experiences.

One of the earliest studies was conducted by Trager and Yarrow (1952). They examined the effects of a curriculum intervention on the racial attitudes of children in the first and second grades. In one experimental condition the children experienced a democratic curriculum; in the other nondemocratic values were taught and perpetuated. No experimental condition was created in the control group. The democratic curriculum had a positive effect on the attitudes of both the students and teachers.

In a study conducted by Litcher and Johnson (1969), white second-grade children developed more positive racial attitudes after using multiethnic readers. However, when Litcher, Johnson, and Ryan (1973) replicated this study using photographs instead of readers, the children's racial attitudes were not significantly changed. The investigators stated that the shorter length of the later study (1 month compared to 4) and the different racial compositions of the 2 communities in which the studies were conducted may explain why no significant effects were produced on the children's racial attitudes in the second study. The community in which the second study was conducted had a much higher percentage of black residents than did the community in which the first was conducted.

Bogatz and Ball's (1971) longitudinal evaluation of the television program "Sesame Street" supports the postulate that multiethnic simulated materials and interventions can have a positive effect on the racial attitudes of young children. These investigators found that children who had watched the program for long periods had more positive racial attitudes toward outgroups than did children who had watched the show for shorter periods.

Weiner and Wright (1973) examined the effects of a simulation on the racial attitudes of third-grade children. They divided a class into "orange" and "green" people. The children wore colored armbands designating their group status. On one day of the intervention the students who wore orange armbands experienced discrimination. On the second day the children who wore green armbands were the victims. On the third day and again 2 weeks later, the children expressed less prejudiced beliefs and attitudes.

Yawkey and Blackwell (1974) examined the effects of multiethnic social studies materials and related experiences on the racial attitudes of 4-year-old black children. The children were divided into 3 groups. The students in the first group read and discussed the materials. The students in the second group read and discussed the materials, and took a related field trip. The students in the third group experienced the traditional preschool curriculum. The interventions in the first and second groups had a significant positive effect on the students' racial attitudes toward blacks and whites.

Cooperative Learning and Interracial Contact

Since 1970 a group of investigators has accumulated an impressive body of research on the effects of cooperative-learning groups and activities on students' racial attitudes, friendship choices, and achievement. Much of this research has been conducted as well as reviewed by investigators such as Aronson and his colleagues (Aronson & Bridgeman, 1979; Aronson & Gonzalez, 1988), Cohen (Cohen, 1972, 1986; Cohen & Roper, 1972), Johnson and Johnson (1981, 1991), and Slavin (1979, 1983, 1985). Most of this research has been conducted using elementary and high-school students as subjects, rather than kindergarten and primary-grade students (Slavin, 1983, 1985). Nevertheless, research on cooperative-learning methods has important implications for the education of young children.

Many of the lessons and group activities in the preschool and primary grades can be structured in ways that are consistent with cooperative-learning theory and instructional methods (Cohen, 1986; Johnson & Johnson, 1991, Ramsey, 1987; Slavin, 1983).

The research that has been conducted on cooperative learning and interracial contact since 1970 has been based on the theory of intergroup relations developed by Allport (1954). Allport stated that prejudice can be reduced if:

1. The intergroup situation is cooperative rather than competitive.
2. Group members pursue common goals.
3. Group members have equal status.
4. Group members get to know each other as individuals.
5. The contact has institutional support and is sanctioned by authorities.

The research accumulated since 1970 lends considerable support to the postulate that cooperative interracial contact situations in schools have positive effects on both student interracial behavior and student academic achievement, provided that the conditions stated by Allport are present (Aronson, 1988; Slavin, 1979, 1983). In his review of 19 studies of the effects of cooperative-learning methods, Slavin (1985) found that 16 had positive effects on interracial friendships.

Most of this research supports the following postulates: (a) that students of color and white students have a greater tendency to make cross-racial friendship choices after they have participated in interracial learning teams such as the jigsaw teams (Aronson & Bridgeman, 1979) and the Student Teams-Achievement Divisions (Slavin, 1979); (b) that the academic achievement of students of color, such as African Americans and Mexican Americans, increases when cooperative-learning activities are used; and (c) that the academic achievement of white students remains about the same in both cooperative- and competitive-learning situations (Aronson & Gonzalez, 1988; Slavin, 1985). Investigators have also found that cooperative-learning methods increase student motivation and self-esteem (Slavin, 1985), and help students develop empathy (Aronson & Bridgeman, 1979).

An essential characteristic of effective cooperative-learning groups and methods is that the students experience equal-status contact (Allport, 1954). Cohen (1972) has pointed out that both African American and white students may expect and attribute higher status to whites in an initial interracial contact situation that may perpetuate white dominance. Cohen and Roper (1972) designed an intervention to change this expectation. They taught African American children to build transistor radios and to teach this skill to others. The black children taught the white children to build the radios after the children watched a videotape showing the black children building radios. When interracial work groups were structured, only those in which the African American children had taught the white students to build radios experienced equal status. The white children dominated in the other groups. The research by Cohen and Roper (1972) indicates that equal status between groups in interracial situations may have to be constructed rather than assumed.

Summary

The 4 types of intervention studies reviewed lend considerable support to the postulate that the racial attitudes and interracial behavior of young children can be changed by well-conceptualized and -planned interventions. As Katz (1976) has pointed out, the intervention research on children is much more hopeful than the intervention research on adults. The intervention research on adults indicates that it is much more difficult to change their racial attitudes and behavior, because their attitudes are crystallized and held tenaciously (Stephan, 1985). This research indicates that early childhood educators have the best opportunity to positively influence the racial and ethnic attitudes of children. It becomes increasingly difficult to influence the attitudes of children as they grow older and move through the grades.

Reinforcement studies indicate that young children's bias toward the color white can be changed by interventions that reinforce the color black. Furthermore, when white bias in young children is reduced, this reduction of bias is generalized to people. Katz (1973, 1982) and her colleagues (Katz & Zalk, 1978) have established the fact that it is more difficult for children to differentiate the faces of out-group individuals than it is for them to differentiate the faces of individuals who are members of their own racial groups. Interventions can help children to differentiate the faces of out-group individuals. These interventions also reduce prejudice toward out-groups.

A variety of curricular interventions can be used to help young children develop more positive racial attitudes and perceptions. Such interventions include multicultural materials, vicarious experiences, role playing, and simulations. The most famous race-related curriculum intervention is the one undertaken by Jane Elliott, a third-grade teacher in Riceville, Iowa, who discriminated against brown-eyed children the first day and blue-eyed children the next. Elliott's intervention is described in a book (Peters, 1987) and in 2 video presentations, *The Eye of the Storm* and *A Class Divided*. Research also indicates that cooperative-learning activities and experiences, if they have the characteristics identified by Allport (1954), can help students develop more friendships across racial groups. Cooperative-learning activities can also help students of color, such as African Americans and Mexican Americans, to increase their academic achievement. Research indicates that cooperative learning activities do not have a measurable effect on the academic achievement of mainstream Anglo American students (Aronson & Gonzalez, 1988).

IMPLICATIONS FOR RESEARCH AND PRACTICE

Research Implications: The Need for a Bicultural Paradigm

Kuhn (1970) defines a *paradigm* as a set of beliefs, values, techniques, and research assumptions shared by the members of a specific scientific community. An interrelated set of postulates, principles, explanations, and theories constitutes a paradigm. Kuhn states new paradigms arise throughout the history of a science to replace older ones. He calls such phenomena *scientific revolutions*. When a scientific revolution occurs, new paradigms replace older ones, effecting a paradigmatic transformation. Rarely does one paradigm completely replace another. Instead, the usual progression is that new paradigms emerge to challenge, compete with, and coexist with older, established paradigms.

The most important research implication of the studies reviewed in this chapter is that there is a need for a new paradigm that can provide an adequate explanation of the complex factors interacting in the development and expression of the racial attitudes, preferences, and self-identification of young children. The research paradigm established by the pioneering empirical and theoretical work of the Horowitzes (1936, 1939) and the Clarks (1939a) is not adequate to explain the complex findings by Spencer (1982, 1984), Cross (1985, 1987, 1991), and Banks (Banks & Banks, 1983; Banks, 1984a).

The paradigm established by the Horowitzes and the Clarks (which can be called the *self-rejection hypothesis*) dominated the research on young children's racial attitudes and preferences for over 30 years, from the late 1930s to the 1970s. When analyzing the data from their own experiments, researchers looked for evidence to confirm the major hypotheses and postulates of this paradigm, often ignoring evidence to the contrary. In the study by Radke and Trager (1950) discussed earlier in this chapter, for example, they reported that 38% of the white children and 16% of the black children ascribed inferior roles to black dolls in the dollhouse activity. Although these percentages did not constitute majorities of either the white or black children, the researchers offered no interpretation of the 62% of white children and 84% of black children who did not assign the black doll to an inferior house.

Researchers who have worked within the self-rejection paradigm have not only tended to ignore evidence not supporting its major tenets, but have also assumed that a high rate of own-group preference was both desirable and normative because most young white children evidenced high own-group preferences (Harrison, 1985). A new paradigm needs to be developed that assumes that bi-group or biracial choices are both healthy and needed within a pluralistic society. This new paradigm can be called *biculturalism*.

There is some evidence that many African American families socialize their children in ways that result in them expressing preference for both blacks and whites and developing biracial attitudes and behaviors. In a study of 64 African American families living in the predominantly white communities of Seattle, Washington, Banks (1984b) found that the parents were *bicultural* in their beliefs, attitudes, and behaviors. Many had positive attitudes toward both black and whites, voluntarily interacted with both black and whites frequently, and valued their interactions with both racial groups. Although most of the parents valued their interactions with whites and had positive attitudes toward whites as a group, they maintained contact with the black community, felt that their children needed to interact with African Americans frequently in order to have good mental health, considered most of their close friends to be black, and attended a black or racially integrated church.

In an investigation of the racial attitudes, preferences, and identification of the 23 preschool and kindergarten children of these parents, Banks and Banks (1983) found that the parents had successfully conveyed biracial attitudes to their children. The Morland Picture Inventory was used to measure the children's racial attitudes, preferences, and identifications (Williams & Morland, 1976). The children were positive toward both blacks and whites. When asked why they chose a black or white child in a picture, they responded with statements about how the child seemed to be friendly or nice. These children looked beyond race and expressed preferences for playmates that seemed by the pictures to have positive human characteristics. Most of the children believed that blacks and whites were equally good looking, good students, and nice. However, they were slightly biased toward African Americans. The older siblings of these children were also biracial in their attitudes and bicultural in their behavior (Banks, 1984a).

A paradigm needs to be constructed that focuses on the bicultural and biracial choices that children make, that interprets the important differences within ethnic groups, and

that assumes that bi-group preferences—rather than own-group preferences—are healthy and desirable within a multicultural society. The *stages of ethnicity* theory developed by Banks (1988) has these characteristics, is the basis for a needed paradigm, and can be used to interpret racial attitudes and self-concept findings (Banks, 1982).

This theory consists of a typology illustrated in Figure 16–1. It conceptualizes 6 stages of ethnicity, emphasizes the differences within ethnic groups, and views biracial and multiracial choices more positively than exclusive own-group preferences (Banks, 1988). In *Stage 1, Cultural psychological captivity*, the individual internalizes the negative attitudes and beliefs about his or her ethnic or racial group that are institutionalized within the dominant society. *Stage 2, Cultural encapsulation*, is characterized by ethnic exclusiveness, strong in-group preferences, the rejection of out-groups, and ethnocentric beliefs and behaviors. In *Stage 3, Cultural identity clarification*, the individual is able to clarify his or her attitudes and ethnic identity, and to develop clarified positive attitudes toward his or her ethnic group. The individual learns to accept self, thus developing

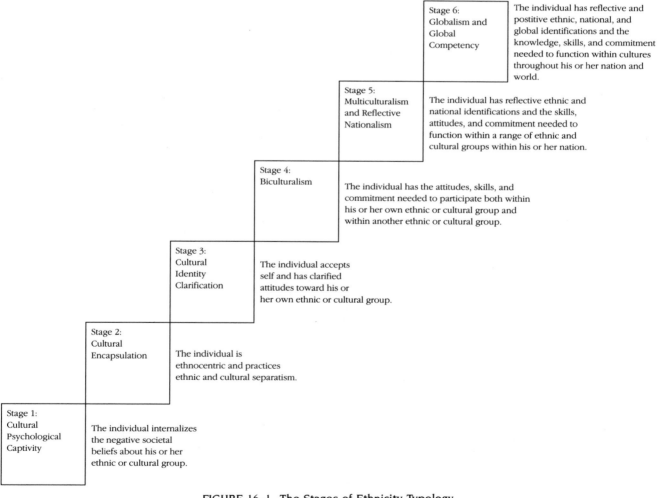

FIGURE 16–1. The Stages of Ethnicity Typology

From: Banks, 1988, p. 50. Reprinted with permission.

the characteristics needed to accept and to respond more positively to outside ethnic groups. During this stage, ethnic pride is genuine rather than contrived.

Individuals in *Stage 4, Biculturalism or biethnicity*, have a healthy sense of ethnic identity and the psychological characteristics and skills needed to participate successfully within their own ethnic culture, as well as within another ethnic culture. The individual has a strong desire and the knowledge, attitudes, and skills needed to function within two cultures — his or her own and one other. The individual in *Stage 5, Multiculturalism and reflective nationalism*, has clarified, reflective, and positive personal, ethnic, and national identifications, has positive attitudes toward other ethnic and racial groups, and is self-actualized. The individual is able to function, at least beyond superficial levels, within several ethnic cultures in his or her nation. Individuals in this stage have a strong commitment to their ethnic groups, an empathy and concern for other ethnic groups, and a strong but reflective commitment and allegiance to the nation state and its idealized values, such as human dignity and justice.

The final stage of this typology is *Stage 6, Globalism and global competency*. The individual in this stage has (1) clarified, reflective, and positive ethnic, national, and global identifications and (2) the knowledge, skills, attitudes, and abilities needed to function within ethnic cultures in his or her own nation as well as within cultures outside his or her nation in other parts of the world. The individual in Stage 6 has the ideal delicate balance of ethnic, national, and global identifications, commitments, literacy, and behaviors.

Implications for Practice: The Need for Total School Reform

Research within the last 60 years has established the fact that young children have accurate knowledge about racial differences and the evaluations that society makes of different racial and ethnic groups. Researchers have also established that by the age of 4 most white children have developed strong in-group preferences and negative attitudes toward other racial groups. Research is less clear about the extent to which African American and Mexican American children make in-group preferences. What is clear, however, is that many of them make more out-group than in-group preferences and that others make biracial choices because of the ways they are socialized.

The research reviewed in this chapter indicates that educators can help young children to develop more positive racial attitudes and behaviors (defined here as biracial choices) by implementing well-planned and well-conceptualized curricular interventions. Major goals of these interventions should be to help children of all racial, ethnic, and cultural groups (1) to develop more positive connotations for brown and other non-white colors; (2) to have positive vicarious experiences with people from a variety of racial and ethnic groups; (3) to learn to differentiate the faces of individuals from different racial and ethnic groups; and, where possible, (4) to have positive cross-racial interactions with children from different ethnic groups that are characterized by cooperation, equal status, and shared goals, and that are sanctioned by the teacher and the school culture.

To teach the principles derived from the research reviewed in this chapter, *multicultural education* must be implemented. Multicultural education requires that the total school environment be restructured and transformed to reflect the racial and cultural diversity within American society and to help children from diverse groups experience educational equality (Banks, 1988, 1991b; Banks & Banks, 1989). To implement multicultural education successfully, the total school must be conceptualized as a unit (see Figure 16–2), and significant changes must be made in each of its major variables — such as the values and attitudes of the school staff, the curriculum and teaching materials, assessment and testing procedures, teaching and motivational styles, and the values and norms sanctioned and perpetuated by the school. A number of useful resources are available to help early childhood educators implement multicultural education (Banks, 1991b; Derman-Sparks & the A.B.C. Task Force, 1989; Kendall, 1983; Ramsey, 1987; Saracho & Spodek, 1983).

Curriculum Reform Approaches. Although all of the variables described in Figure 16–2 must be reformed in order to successfully implement multicultural education for young children, it is reasonable and practical to begin school reform by focusing on the curriculum. Banks has identified 4 major approaches to multicultural curriculum reform (1991b). The *contributions approach* is frequently used by early childhood and kindergarten teachers to infuse ethnic content into the curriculum. This approach is characterized by the addition to the curriculum of ethnic heroes. Ethnic heroes are selected using criteria similar to those used to select mainstream heroes for curriculum inclusion. Despite the "good intentions" of the contributions approach, it leaves the mainstream curriculum unchanged in terms of its basic assumptions, goals, and salient characteristics.

The *heroes and holidays approach* is a variant of the contributions approach. In this approach, ethnic content is limited primarily to special days, weeks, and months related to ethnic events and celebrations. Cinco de Mayo, Martin Luther King's Birthday, and African American History month are examples of ethnic days and months that are celebrated in the schools. When this approach is used, students study little or nothing about ethnic groups before or after the special event or occasion.

The contributions approach is an easy one for teachers to use to integrate ethnic content into the curriculum. However, it has several serious limitations. It does not enable students to view ethnic groups as an integral part of U.S. society and culture. Rather, such an approach encourages students to view an introduction of ethnic groups primarily as an addition to the curriculum and consequently as an appendage to the main story of the development of the nation. The contributions approach, especially in the early childhood curriculum, tends to focus on the material aspects of the cultures of ethnic groups, such as foods and dances, rather than on the cultural meanings of material objects and artifacts within an ethnic culture. By focusing on material objects and artifacts, ethnic groups are often stereotyped as static and unchanging.

The *additive approach* is characterized by the addition of ethnic content, concepts, themes, and perspectives to the curriculum without changing its basic structure, purposes, and

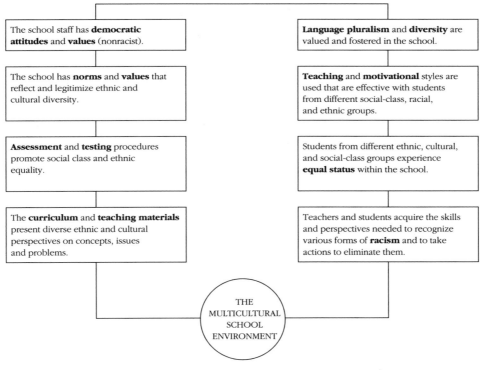

FIGURE 16–2. The Multicultural School Environment

This figure describes the characteristics of a multicultural school environment that has been restructured and transformed. The total school environment is conceptualized as a system that consists of a number of identifiable factors, such as the staff attitudes and values; assessment and testing procedures; and the curriculum and teaching materials. In the restructured multicultural school, each of these variables has been changed and reflects ethnic, cultural, and social-class equality. Although any one of these factors may be the focus of initial school reform, changes must take place in each of them to create and sustain a school environment in which students from diverse racial, ethnic, and cultural groups experience equality.

From: Banks & Lynch, 1986, p. 23. Reprinted with permission.

characteristics. Such an approach often involves the addition of a book or unit to the existing curriculum. The additive approach can be the first phase of a more substantial curriculum reform effort. However, it shares several problems with the contributions approach. Its most important shortcoming is that it usually results in the teaching of ethnic content from the perspectives of mainstream writers, artists, storytellers, and historians. An example of the additive approach can be seen in the way that kindergarten children study Thanksgiving—that is, by viewing Native Americans primarily from the point of view of the Pilgrims. Native Americans are added to the curriculum but they are viewed through the eyes of the Pilgrims.

The *transformation approach* differs fundamentally from the contribution and additive approaches. This approach changes the basic assumptions of the curriculum and enables students to view events, concepts, themes, issues, and problems from several ethnic perspectives. When kindergarten children study Thanksgiving using the transformative approach, the teacher presents the views of the Pilgrims as well as those of the Native Americans. The teacher reads the children stories about Thanksgiving from the perspectives of the Pilgrims, as well as stories and documents explaining how the Native Americans perceived the occupation of their lands by the British colonists. Thus, what was a thanksgiving for one group was in many ways

a day of mourning for another. The teacher may also ask the students to assume the roles of both the Pilgrims and the Indians in role-play situations.

The *personal-, social-, and civic-action approach* includes all of the elements of the transformation approach but adds components that require students to make decisions and to take actions related to the concept, issue, or problem they have studied in a lesson or unit. Preschool and kindergarten children are limited in the actions they can take related to racial and ethnic issues. However, there are meaningful actions they can take to help create a school culture that is more accepting of diverse ethnic groups. Young children can make a commitment to stop laughing at racist jokes and to stop using ethnic slurs. Instead, they can ask their parents to read them books that deal with children from other cultures and ethnic groups, and seek friendships with children from other racial, ethnic, or religious groups. Teachers can also help young children become more sensitive to and critical of television's depictions of people of color.

To implement multicultural education effectively, early childhood educators should make infrequent use of the contributions approach to ethnic content integration and move gradually toward the full implementation of the transformative and social-action approaches. These 4 approaches are mixed and blended in actual classroom practice. For a variety of reasons, a teacher may begin integrating her curriculum with ethnic content using the contributions approach. However, the goal should be to move toward a transformative and action-oriented curriculum so that young children can understand the complex nature of ethnic groups in U.S. society and develop the knowledge, skills, and attitudes needed to become effective citizens in the pluralistic society of the next century.

The Importance of the Teacher

The teacher is a key variable in successfully implementing multicultural education and in helping young children develop democratic racial attitudes and behaviors. Teachers are human beings who bring their cultural perspectives, values, hopes, and dreams to the classroom. The teacher's values and behaviors strongly influence the views, conceptions, and behaviors of young children. The teacher's values and perspectives also mediate and interact with what they teach and influence the ways that messages are communicated and perceived by students. A teacher who makes strong in-group preferences and believes that white is more beautiful than brown or that whites have been the main contributors to American culture and civilization will, whether intending to or not, convey these attitudes and beliefs to young children. Consequently, teacher education

is essential for implementing an effective program of multicultural education for young children. Most American teachers have, after all, internalized many of the same Eurocentric values and attitudes exemplified by young children in the research reviewed in this chapter (Gay, 1986).

Teacher educators should help classroom teachers attain the knowledge, attitudes, and skills they will need to function effectively in the multicultural classroom of the twenty-first century (Banks, 1988, 1991b; Gay, 1986). Such a step should be undertaken because of a need to create a more caring nation, and because of the demographic changes that are taking place in U.S. society. By 2020, about 46% of the nation's school-age youth will be students of color (Pallas, Natriello, & McDill, 1989). The increasing racial, ethnic, and cultural diversity in the nation presents new challenges as well as opportunities. If the United States does not become a more culturally sensitive society in which citizens from different racial and cultural groups can live and work in harmony, its survival as a strong and democratic nation will be endangered. The research described in this chapter provides early childhood educators hope as well as specific guidelines for the decisive action needed to transform the total school culture. Transformation of the total school is essential in order to create citizens who have the multicultural literacy, perspectives, and competencies needed to function effectively in the twenty-first century.

References

Abound, F. E. (1987). The development of ethnic self-identification and attitudes. In J. S. Phinney & M. J. Rotheram (Eds.), *Children's ethnic socialization: Pluralism and development* (pp. 32–55). Beverly Hills, CA: Sage Publications.

Agnes, M. (1947). Influences of reading on the racial attitudes of adolescent girls. *Catholic Educational Review, 45,* 415–420.

Allport, G. W. (1954). *The nature of prejudice.* Cambridge, MA: Addison-Wesley.

Aronson, E., & Bridgeman, D. (1979). Jigsaw groups and the desegregated classroom: In pursuit of common goals. *Personality and Social Psychology Bulletin, 5,* 438–446.

Aronson, E., & Gonzalez, A. (1988). Desegregation, jigsaw, and the Mexican-American experience. In P. A. Katz & D. A. Taylor (Eds.), *Eliminating racism: Profiles in controversy* (pp. 301–314). New York: Plenum.

Banks, J. A. (1982, March). *A study of black suburban youths: Implications of the major findings for the stages of ethnicity typology.* Paper presented at the Annual Meeting of the American Educational Research Association, New York.

Banks, J. A. (1984a). Black youths in predominantly white suburbs: An exploratory study of their attitudes and self-concepts. *The Journal of Negro Education, 53,* 3–17.

Banks, J. A. (1984b, April). *An exploratory study of assimilation, pluralism, and marginality: Black families in predominantly white suburbs.* Paper presented at the Annual Meeting of the American Educational Research Association, New Orleans.

Banks, J. A. (1988). *Multiethnic education: Theory and practice* (2nd ed.). Boston: Allyn & Bacon.

Banks, J. A. (1991a). Multicultural education: Its effects on students' racial and gender role attitudes. In J. P. Shaver (Ed.), *Handbook of research on social studies teaching and learning* (pp. 459–469). New York: Macmillan.

Banks, J. A. (1991b). *Teaching strategies for ethnic studies* (5th ed.). Boston: Allyn & Bacon.

Banks, J. A. (1992). Multicultural education, history of. In M. C. Alkin (Ed.), *Encyclopedia of educational research* (6th ed.). Vol. 3. pp. 870–874. New York: Macmillan.

Banks, J. A., & Banks, C. A. M. (1983). *The self-concept, locus of control, and racial attitudes of preschool and primary grade black children who live in predominantly white suburban communities.* Unpublished paper, University of Washington, Seattle.

Banks, J. A., & Banks, C. A. M. (Eds.). (1989). *Multicultural education: Issues and perspectives.* Boston: Allyn & Bacon.

Banks, J. A., & Lynch, J. (Eds.). (1986). *Multicultural education in Western societies.* London: Holt, Rinehart & Winston.

Banks, W. C. (1976). White preference in blacks: A paradigm in search of a phenomenon. *Psychological Bulletin, 83,* 1170–1186.

Banks, W. C., McQuater, G. V., & Ross, J. A. (1979). On the importance of white preference and the comparative difference of blacks and others: Reply to Williams and Morland. *Psychological Bulletin, 86,* 33–36.

Banks, W. C., & Rompf, W. J. (1973). Evaluative bias and preference behavior in black and white children. *Child Development, 44,* 776–783.

Best, D. L., Smith, S. C., Graves, D. J., & Williams, J. E. (1975). The modification of racial bias in preschool children. *Journal of Experimental Child Psychology, 20,* 193–205.

Bogatz, G. A., & Ball, S. (1971). *The second year of Sesame Street: A continuing evaluation.* Princeton, NJ: Educational Testing Service.

Brand, E. S., Ruiz, R. A., & Padilla, A. M. (1974). Ethnic identification and preference: A review. *Psychological Bulletin, 81,* 860–890.

Clark, K. B. (1963). *Prejudice and your child.* Boston: Beacon Press. Reissued: (1988). Middletown, CT: Wesleyan University Press.

Clark, K. B., & Clark, M. P. (1939a). The development of consciousness of self and the emergence of racial identification in Negro preschool children. *Journal of Social Psychology, 10,* 591–599.

Clark, K. B., & Clark, M. P. (1939b). Segregation as a factor in the racial identification of Negro preschool children. *Journal of Experimental Education, 8,* 161–163.

Clark, K. B., & Clark, M. P. (1940). Skin color as a factor in racial identification and preference in Negro children. *Journal of Negro Education, 19,* 341–358.

Clark, K. B., & Clark, M. P. (1947). Racial identification and preference in Negro children. In T. M. Newcomb & E. L. Hartley (Eds.), *Readings in social psychology* (pp. 169–178). New York: Holt, Rinehart & Winston.

Clark, K. B., & Clark, M. P. (1950). Emotional factors in racial identification and preference in Negro children. *Journal of Negro Education, 19,* 341–350.

Cohen, E. G. (1972). Interracial interaction disability. *Human Relations, 25,* 9–24.

Cohen, E. G. (1986). *Designing groupwork: Strategies for the heterogeneous classroom.* New York: Teachers College Press.

Cohen, E. G., & Roper, S. S. (1972). Modification of interracial interaction disability: An application of status characteristic theory. *American Sociological Review, 37,* 643–657.

Cook, L., & Cook, E. (1954). *Intergroup education.* New York: McGraw-Hill.

Cross, W. E., Jr. (1985). Black identity: Rediscovering the distinction between personal identity and reference group orientation. In M. B. Spencer, G. K. Brookins, & W. R. Allen (Eds.), *Beginnings: The social and affective development of black children* (pp. 155–171). Hillsdale, NJ: Erlbaum.

Cross, W. E., Jr. (1987). A two-factor theory of black identity formation: Implications for the study of identity development in minority children. In J. S. Phinney & M. J. Rotheram (Eds.), *Children's ethnic socialization: Pluralism and development* (pp. 117–133). Beverly Hills, CA: Sage Publications.

Cross, W. E., Jr. (1991). *Shades of Black: Diversity in African-American identity.* Philadelphia: Temple University Press.

Derman-Sparks, L., & the A.B.C. Task Force. (1989). *Anti-bias curriculum: Tools for empowering young children.* Washington, DC: National Association for the Education of Young Children.

DeVries, D. L., Edwards, K. J., & Slavin, R. E. (1978). Biracial learning teams and race relations in the classroom: Four field experiments on Teams-Games-Tournament. *Journal of Educational Psychology, 70,* 356–362.

Edwards, C. D., & Williams, J. E. (1970). Generalization between evaluative words associated with racial figures in preschool children. *Journal of Experimental Research in Personality, 4,* 144–155.

Gay, G. (1986). Multicultural teacher education. In J. A. Banks & J. Lynch (Eds.), *Multicultural education in Western societies* (pp. 154–177). London: Holt, Rinehart & Winston.

Goodman, M. E. (1946). Evidence concerning the genesis of interracial attitudes. *American Anthropologist, 48,* 624–630.

Goodman, M. E. *Race awareness in young children.* (1952). New York: Collier Books.

Gregor, A. J. (1963). Ethnocentrism among the Australian Aborigines: Some preliminary notes. *Sociology Quarterly, 4,* 162–167.

Gregor, A. J., & McPherson, D. A. (1966a). Racial attitudes among white and Negro children in a deep-South standard metropolitan area. *Journal of Social Psychology, 68,* 95–106.

Gregor, A. J., & McPherson, D. A. (1966b). A racial preference and ego identity among white and Bantu children in the Republic of South Africa. *Genetic Psychology Monographs, 73,* 217–253.

Harrison, A. O. (1985). The black family's socializing environment: Self-esteem and ethnic attitudes among black children. In H. P. McAdoo & J. L. McAdoo (Eds.), *Black children: Social, educational, and parental environments* (pp. 174–193). Beverly Hills, CA: Sage Publications.

Hohn, R. L. (1973). Perceptual training and its effect on racial preference of kindergarten children. *Psychological Reports, 32,* 435–441.

Horowitz, E. L. (1936). The development of attitude toward the Negro. *Archives of Psychology.* No. 104. Columbia University.

Horowitz, R. E. (1939). Racial aspects of self-identification in nursery school children. *Journal of Psychology, 7,* 91–99.

Hraba, J., & Grant, G. (1970). Black is beautiful: A reexamination of racial preference and identification. *Journal of Personality and Social Psychology, 16,* 398–402.

Jackson, E. P. (1944). Effects of reading upon the attitudes toward the Negro race. *Library Quarterly, 14,* 47–54.

Johnson, D. W., & Johnson, R. T. (1981). Effects of cooperative and individualistic learning experiences on interethnic interaction. *Journal of Educational Psychology, 73,* 444–449.

Johnson, D. W., & Johnson, R. T. (1991). *Learning together and alone* (3rd ed.). Englewood Cliffs, NJ: Prentice Hall.

Kardiner, A., & Ovesey, A. (1962). *The mark of oppression.* New York: World.

Katz, P. A. (1973). Perception of racial cues in preschool children: A new look. *Developmental Psychology, 8,* 295–299.

Katz, P. A. (1976). Attitude change in children: Can the twig be straightened? In P. A. Katz (Ed.), *Towards the elimination of racism.* New York: Pergamon.

Katz, P. A. (1982). A review of recent research in children's attitude acquisition. In L. Katz (Ed.), *Current topics in early childhood education* (Vol. 4, pp. 17–54). Norwood, NJ: Ablex.

Katz, P. A. (1987). Developmental and social processes in ethnic attitudes and self-identification. In J. S. Phinney & M. J. Rotheram (Eds.), *Children's ethnic socialization: Pluralism and development* (pp. 92–99). Beverly Hills, CA: Sage Publications.

Katz, P., Sohn, M., & Zalk, S. (1975). Perceptual concomitants of racial attitudes in urban grade-school children. *Developmental Psychology, 11,* 135–144.

Katz, P. A., & Zalk, S. R. (1978). Modification of children's racial attitudes. *Developmental Psychology, 14,* 447–461.

Kendall, F. E. (1983). *Diversity in the classroom: A multicultural approach to the education of young children.* New York: Teachers College Press.

Kuhn, T. S. (1970). *The structure of scientific revolutions* (2nd ed., enlarged). Chicago: University of Chicago Press.

Lasker, B. (1929). *Race attitudes in children.* New York: Holt, Rhinehart & Winston.

Litcher, J. H., & Johnson, D. W. (1969). Changes in attitudes toward Negroes of white elementary school students after use of multiethnic readers. *Journal of Educational Psychology, 60,* 148–152.

Litcher, J. H., Johnson, D. W., & Ryan, F. L. (1973). Use of pictures of multiethnic interaction to change attitudes of White elementary school students toward Blacks. *Psychological Reports, 33,* 367–372.

Miel, A., with Kiester, E., Jr. (1967). *The shortchanged children of suburbia: What schools don't teach about human differences and what can be done about it.* New York: Institute of Human Relations Press, the American Jewish Committee.

Milner, D. (1983). *Children and Race.* Beverly Hills, CA: Sage Publications.

Minard, R. D. (1931). *Race attitudes of Iowa children.* (University of Iowa) *Studies in Character, 4*(2).

Morland, J. K. (1958). Racial recognition by nursery school children in Lynchburg, Virginia. *Social Forces, 37,* 132–137.

Morland, J. K. (1966). A comparison of race awareness in northern and southern children. *American Journal of Orthopsychiatry, 36,* 22–31.

Ogletree, E. (1969). Skin color preference of the Negro child. *Journal of Social Psychology, 79,* 143–144.

Pallas, A. M., Natriello,.G., & McDill, E. L. (1989). The changing nature of the disadvantaged population: Current dimensions and future trends. *Educational Researcher, 18,* 16–22.

Parish, T. S., & Fleetwood, R. S. (1975). Amount of conditioning and subsequent change in racial attitudes of children. *Perceptual and Motor Skills, 40,* 79–86.

Parish, T. S., Shirazi, A., & Lambert, F. (1976). Conditioning away prejudicial attitudes in children. *Perceptual and Motor Skills, 43,* 907–912.

Peters, W. (1987). *A class divided: Then and now* (Expanded ed.). New Haven, CT: Yale University Press.

Pettigrew, T. F. (1964). *A profile of the Negro American.* Princeton, NJ: Van Nostrand.

Phinney, J. S., & Rotheram, M. J. (Eds.). (1987). *Children's ethnic socialization: Pluralism and development.* Beverly Hills, CA: Sage Publications.

Porter, J. D. R. (1971). *Black child, white child: The development of racial attitudes.* Cambridge, MA: Harvard University Press.

Radke, M. J., & Trager, H. G. (1950). Children's perceptions of the social roles of Negroes and whites. *Journal of Psychology, 29,* 3–33.

Ramsey, P. G. (1987). *Teaching and learning in a diverse world: Multicultural education for young children.* New York: Teachers College Press.

Ramsey, P. G., & Myers, L. C. (1990). Salience of race in young children's cognitive, affective, and behavioral responses to social environments. *Journal of Applied Behavioral Psychology, 11,* 49–67.

Renninger, C. A., & Williams, J. E. (1966). Black-white color connotations and race awareness in children. *Perceptual and Motor Skills, 22,* 771–785.

Rice, A. S., Ruiz, R. A., & Padilla, A. M. (1974). Person perception, self-identity, and ethnic group preference in Anglo, black, and Chicano preschool children. *Journal of Cross-Cultural Psychology, 5,* 100–108.

Saracho, O. N., & Spodek, B. (Eds.). (1983). *Understanding the multicultural experience in early childhood education.* Washington, DC: National Association for the Education of Young Children.

Slavin, R. E. (1979). Effects of biracial learning teams on cross-racial friendships. *Journal of Educational Psychology, 71,* 381–387.

Slavin, R. E. (1983). *Cooperative learning.* New York: Longman.

Slavin, R. E. (1985). Cooperative learning: Applying contact theory in desegregated schools. *Journal of Social Issues, 41,* 45–62.

Spencer, M. B. (1982). Personal and group identity of black children: An alternative synthesis. *Genetic Psychology Monographs, 106,* 59–84.

Spencer, M. B. (1984). Black children's race awareness, racial attitudes, and self-concept: A reinterpretation. *Journal of Child Psychology and Psychiatry, 25,* 433–441.

Spencer, M. B. (1985). Cultural cognition and social cognition as identity correlates of black children's personal-social development. In M. B. Spencer, G. K. Brookins, & W. R. Allen (Eds.), *Beginnings: The social and affective development of black children* (pp. 215–234). Hillsdale, NJ: Erlbaum.

Spencer, M. B. (1987). Black children's ethnic identity formation: Risk and resilience of castelike minorities. In J. S. Phinney & M. J. Rotheram (Eds.), *Children's ethnic socialization: Pluralism and development* (pp. 103–116). Beverly Hills, CA: Sage Publications.

Spencer, M. B. (1988). Self-concept development. In D. T. Slaughter (Ed.), *Black children and poverty: A developmental perspective* (pp. 103–116). San Francisco: Jossey-Bass.

Spencer, M. B., & Horowitz, F. D. (1973). Effects of systematic social and token reinforcement on the modification of racial and color concept attitudes in black and in white preschool children. *Developmental Psychology, 9,* 246–254.

Stephen, W. G. (1985). Intergroup relations. In G. Lindzey & E. Aronson (Eds.), *The handbook of social psychology* (3rd ed., pp. 599–658). New York: Random House.

Trager, H. G., & Yarrow, M. R. (1952). *They learn what they live: Prejudice in young children.* New York: Harper & Brothers.

Weiner, M. J., & Wright, F. E. (1973). Effects of undergoing arbitrary discrimination upon subsequent attitudes toward a minority group. *Journal of Applied Social Psychology, 3,* 94–102.

Werner, N. E., & Evans, I. M. (1968). Perception of prejudice in Mexican-American preschool children. *Perceptual and Motor Skills, 27,* 1039–1046.

Williams, J. E., Best, D. L., Wood, F. B., & Filler, J. W. (1973). Changes in the connotations of racial concepts and color names: 1963–1970. *Psychological Reports, 33,* 983–996.

Williams, J. E., Boswell, D. A., & Best, B. L. (1975). Evaluative responses of preschool children to the colors white and black. *Child Development, 46,* 501–508.

Williams, J. E., & Carter, D. J. (1967). Connotations of racial concepts and color names in Germany. *Journal of Social Psychology, 72,* 19–26.

Williams, J. E., & Edwards, C. D. (1969). An exploratory study of the modification of color and racial concept attitudes in preschool children. *Child Development, 40,* 737–750.

Williams, J. E., & Morland, J. K. (1976). *Race, color and the young child.* Chapel Hill, NC: University of North Carolina.

Williams, J. E., & Morland, J. K. (1979). Comment on Banks' "White preference in Blacks: A paradigm in search of a phenomenon." *Psychological Bulletin, 86,* 28–32.

Yawkey, T. D., & Blackwell, J. (1974). Attitudes of 4-year old urban black children toward themselves and whites based upon multi-ethnic social studies materials and experiences. *Journal of Educational Research, 67,* 373–377.

·17·

ELECTRONIC MEDIA AND EARLY
CHILDHOOD EDUCATION

Douglas H. Clements
STATE UNIVERSITY OF NEW YORK AT BUFFALO

Bonnie K. Nastasi
UNIVERSITY OF CONNECTICUT

YOUNG CHILDREN AND ELECTRONIC MEDIA

Historical Perspectives: The More Things Change, the More They Remain the Same

Books will be obsolete. Scholars will soon be instructed through the eye. It is possible to teach every branch of human knowledge with [this new technology]. Our school system will be completely changed in ten years.

Though sounding quite modern, the statement about technology was made in 1913, by Thomas Edison, about motion pictures (Griffin, 1983, p. 96). Nearly 50 years later, similar pronouncements were made about television. Recently, advocates of the educational potential of computer technology predict another impending revolution. What has been the effect of existing technologies on young children's development? What might we see in the future? Does the school system's resistance to fundamental technological change disclose Luddites or concerned educators aware of the limitations of electronic media?

History offers us an initial perspective on such issues. For each new technology, research progresses through three phases (Wartella & Reeves, 1983). As the medium is being developed, researchers initially address concerns about how much and in what manner children use it. Researchers usually confirm that innovation displaces previous activities, including earlier media. Attention then shifts to the quality of this time, for example, are there deleterious physical and emotional effects of

viewing films in dark (possibly unsanitary) movie houses, listening to too much radio, or watching and being too close to TV screens? Research indicates that these concerns are generally unwarranted, and concern finally turns to the content of the media, for example, what are effects on emotional, moral, and cognitive development of "gangsterism" on radio, sex and violence on films, and banal programming on TV and computers?

In this chapter, we will review research on 2 critical technologies, television and computers. All three phases of research will be synthesized, with an emphasis on children's development. Because simple answers have proven unsatisfactory, we take an ecological perspective, considering the mediating and moderating effects of the myriad individual and environmental factors (Bronfenbrenner, 1989). This represents a recent, fourth phase of research (Desmond, Singer, Singer, Calam, & Colimore, 1985).

Children's Use of Television

Viewing. Children spend more time engaged in TV watching than in any other waking activity. By the time they leave high school, most will have spent 11,000 hours in the classroom compared to at least 22,000 hours viewing TV. The greatest consumers are preschoolers, who average 25 to 35 hours per week (Clements, 1985; Singer & Singer, 1981). During that week, they may view over 2,000 violent incidents, storing more than 500 in memory (Braithwaite & Holman, 1981; Comstock, Chaffee, Katzman, McCombs, & Roberts, 1978). How early does such viewing begin? Some children are already viewing TV $1\frac{1}{2}$ hours a day before their first birthday. Most children, however, become systematic viewers in the preschool years; by the age of three, viewing habits are well established (Clements, 1985; Singer & Singer, 1981).

The notion of children's TV viewing, however, is not as straightforward as it first appears. Research by Anderson and his colleagues indicates that preschoolers actually *watch* TV only 1.3 hours per day; using video cameras in volunteers' homes, they found that data from parents was unreliable and inflated. In addition, children do not necessarily just stare at the set. Instead, TV can be a backdrop for toy play and other activities. If peers are present, they influence each other in synchronous fashion; when one child looks at the television or displays overt involvement, others tend to do the same. So, viewing television is a transactional process among the viewer, the TV, and the TV viewing environment (Anderson, Lorch, Smith, Bradford, & Levin, 1981; Clements, 1985).

What do children view? Like most people, they decide first to watch television, then choose a specific program (Comstock et al., 1978). As soon as they begin viewing, however, children have definite preferences. Many watch child-oriented shows, especially cartoons and situation comedies (Comstock et al., 1978). They also view every other type of programming, however, including a sizable proportion of adult fare such as "soaps" and prime-time programming that contain violence and sexuality (Singer & Singer, in press; Singer & Singer, 1981). Children, especially boys, of parents with dysfunctional parenting attitudes, such as lack of empathy and sensitivity, are even heavier viewers of TV. They prefer violent, fantasy-oriented content; possible detrimental effects of such viewing patterns must be considered. In addition, parents' own viewing choices also influence the patterns of children's TV viewing. In sum, TV plays a substantive role in the acculturation of our young children (Singer & Singer, in press). Possible detrimental effects of viewing adult-oriented programming must be considered. Parents and teachers should play an active role in monitoring and mediating children's choices of TV fare.

Although they view much TV, young children, when asked, say they prefer to play outside or with Play-Doh. TV is one of their least favored activities, maybe because it is less active. TV may sometimes be viewed because other activities are not available, or the visual and auditory stimulation of television distracts children from other activities (Slavenas, 1987). Adults can thus influence the amount of TV watching by controlling or monitoring availability of TV and alternative activities.

Attention and Comprehension. Even the very young respond to TV. For example, 6-month-old infants alter their vocalization pattern after listening to a televised model (Hollenbeck & Slaby, 1982). Similarly, 14- to 24-month-old infants imitate TV actions, even after a full day's delay (Meltzoff, 1988). Unfortunately, the TV does not understand and respond to the infants' reactions. Such early response leads to the question: What do children of different ages attend to and comprehend of TV?

The results of several investigations have disproved the popular notion that television viewing is passive. Comprehensibility, promoted by such features as understandable dialogue, is crucial in maintaining children's attention (Anderson, Lorch, Field, & Sanders, 1981). So, children are not mesmerized by screen action regardless of their understanding of its contents, in contrast to early claims.

Children learn to select important content; integrate events; and infer conditions, motives, and events not shown (Wright & Huston, 1983). They use fairly sophisticated strategies to determine which segments require visual and auditory attention and which do not (Pezdek & Hartman, 1983). Note that this implies that looking is not an adequate measure of attention. The question arises, how do children know where and when to look? The answer is that they learn to use TV's formal features (Wright & Huston, 1983).

Formal features of television include auditory and visual production and editing techniques. Features such as animation, character or adult female voices, and sound effects elicit and maintain young children's attention to TV. The reason for this, however, is not just the stimulation these features provide. Rather, they signal to children that the content of the program segment is going to be comprehensible and interesting to them (Wright & Huston, 1983). For example, they may call attention to child dialogue. Children who attend to child dialogue and ignore adult dialogue are more likely to understand television content (Clements, 1985). This is especially true if the linguistic features are similar to adjustments parents make in their live interactions with young children, as they are in some children's programming (Rice, 1984).

Even sophisticated features such as pans, zooms, and cuts do not interfere with young children's comprehension; children 4 to 7 years old can reconstruct televised segments with or without these features with about equal accuracy. Further, even preschool children understand these features and grasp information about the story that the features convey, although this ability does increase with age (Smith, Anderson, & Fischer, 1985). Development of this ability is facilitated by television content that is related to children's knowledge, and that demands cognitive skills just above children's present level of functioning. Also helpful is commentary made in an informal way by an adult. In sum, research findings contradict the popular notion that superficial production features alone capture and maintain young children's attention (Clements, 1985).

Supporting this conclusion is evidence that children are schema-guided viewers. For example, 4- and especially 6-year-olds recalled important information better than less-important information. These effects were not attributable to associated factors such as presentation mode or formal features (Lorch, Bellack, & Augsbach, 1987). So, children attend to content that makes sense in the context of what they know about the world. This fact, which serves as an important guide to classroom use, will be discussed in a subsequent section.

Nevertheless, a strict passive-versus-active dichotomy is probably inaccurate. Certain features of TV may capture attention; however, some attention is directed by conscious, or at least strategic, control (Pingree, 1986). Children actively allocate attention in at least 2 ways. First, even young children actively assimilate what they view into their existing knowledge structures, as we have seen. Primary-grade children recall content better when presented in a story format than in a magazine format with successive independent bits. Slow pacing also enhances recall. All young children stop attending to TV programs that fall below a minimum threshold of comprehension (Pingree, 1986). Second, older children are strategic in allocating attention and processing information. Children in grades 3 and 4 attend to story programs in synchrony with the story's pace, giving longer looks to slow-paced and shorter looks to fast-paced programs. Older children try harder to understand difficult segments than do younger children (Pingree, 1986). So, there is evidence for active, schema-based (e.g., based on knowledge of story scripts) processing of television by children and for strategic attending by older children, based on perceived processing demands (Wright et al., 1984).

Evidence of active viewing by young children does not, of course, imply ease of comprehension. For example, 5-year-olds have more mature reality perceptions of both cartoons and human fantasies than do 4-year-olds, but all young children may confuse reality and fantasy, especially regarding shows with live actors (Skeen, Brown, & Osborn, 1982). Kindergartners, more so than second-graders, believe that victims of aggression are really hurt, and that the aggression acts portrayed on TV happen frequently in everyday life (Watkins, Sprafkin, Gadow, & Sadetsky, 1988). Preoperational children may gain only a vague idea of what programs are about (Choat & Griffin, 1986a).

Programs with certain characteristics are better understood. Apparent difficulty should not be extremely high or low. The material must be at least minimally appealing, as signaled by its format; for example, child-oriented formats facilitate attention and comprehension. Attention must not be manipulated by extrinsic factors (e.g., the presence of toys as a distracter), but controlled by intrinsic factors, such as signals of the level of interest, comprehensibility, and entertainment (Campbell, Wright, & Huston, 1987). The material should be communicated using a story format with slow pacing (Wright et al., 1984), especially for lower achievers.

Other factors also mediate young children's comprehension. Children comprehend better when they have direct and rich real-world experience and a participatory style of viewing. Adult mediation enhances children's comprehension; for example, discussing program content before, during, and after viewing and giving feedback (Choat & Griffin, 1986b; Desmond et al., 1985; Field & Anderson, 1985; Reiser, Tessmer, & Phelps, 1984). This may be especially important for young boys (Desmond, Hirsch, Singer, & Singer, 1987). Parents, however, do *not* usually view television with their children, much less provide mediation (Lawrence & Wozniak, 1989). Finally, the child's family background must be considered. For example, when parents' viewing is high, children's comprehension is low. Children may not understand characters' emotions and motivations due to lack of interpersonal communication within the family (Corcoran & Schneider, 1985). In sum, from an ecological perspective, personal and environmental factors may interact to influence comprehension. For example, understanding of TV content may vary as a function of individual differences in knowledge and information processing style, and variations in quality and quantity of adult mediation.

Advertising. The question of children's comprehension raises the issue: Is it ethical to direct advertising to young children? Do preschoolers recognize the 22,000 commercials they view each year for what they are? Children's ability to correctly identify TV segments as either programs or commercials improves with age (from 3 to 5 years), but at each age they showed some ability to discriminate between the two (Levin, Petros, & Petrella, 1982). More exposure to TV, however, does not necessarily mean greater comprehension of advertising and its intent and motivation. The more families view television, the *less* likely children are to understand commercials (Singer & Singer, 1983, 1986). Even children in fourth grade often do not understand the intent of commercials (Feshbach, Feshbach, & Cohen, 1982), and even when taught about commercials, children may be too trusting of premium offers (Watkins et al., 1988). Thus, children are especially vulnerable to the appeal of TV advertising. Especially insidious may be program content tied to commercial products, blurring the distinction between programming and advertising altogether (Singer & Singer, in press).

Children do remember commercial products. Furthermore, this memory goes beyond specific brands and generalizes to products that are members of the same class. Thus, advertisements have implicit, diffuse messages (Stoneman & Brody, 1983). A clear implication of this body of research is that children should be educated concerning the purpose of evaluation of commercials (Levin et al., 1982). This can be accomplished by various means, from role-playing the designing of commercials to direct instruction (Donohue, Henke, & Meyer, 1983; Watkins et al., 1988).

In conclusion, children's attention to and comprehension of TV may vary as a function of individual differences (e.g., developmental level) and characteristics of the media. Teachers and parents, however, can play an active role in mediating the impact of TV viewing through education, discussion, and monitoring.

Children's Use of Computers

Appropriateness. The term "computer" evokes cold, mechanistic images inconsistent with typical perspectives on early childhood education. For example, adults have raised concerns that computers may inhibit social and emotional development. Such concerns have not been supported by research (Clements & Nastasi, in press). We will return to this issue in a later section. There are also concerns that computers are symbolic. Much of young children's activity, however, *is* symbolic. They communicate with gestures and language, and they employ symbols in their play, song, and art. If they can use computer symbols in the same way, preschool children may benefit from using *appropriate* computer technology (Clements & Nastasi, in press). In addition, they should be used in appropriate contexts, for example, as books are used, with a caring teacher or parent.

But what is appropriate? Drawing shapes with the child-oriented Logo computer language has been criticized: "What does it mean to children to command a perfect square but still not be able to draw it themselves?" (Cuffaro, 1984, p. 561). Research indicates, however, that Logo experience encourages some children to create pictures more elaborate than those that they can draw by hand and to transfer components of this new conceptualization on to work with paper (Vaidya & Mckeeby, 1984). Computer drawing may be appropriate for children as young as 3 years, who show signs of developmental progression in the areas of drawing and geometry during such computer use (Alexander, 1983, 1984). Critics also have complained about limitations of technology, such as the limited number of colors available in drawing programs. Such criticisms overlook important issues. Newer computers can draw literally millions of colors, but this does not mean that they should replace the 16-color crayon set. Either an old technology (e.g., crayons, paint brushes) or a new may be the most appropriate medium in a given situation. The question is: What is the highest-quality environment for a particular child or group of children for a particular purpose? In addition, computers, like crayons or blocks, are tools for learning and problem solving. Teachers play a critical role in determining the manner in which these are used.

Use of Computers. Computers are being increasingly integrated into early childhood programs. Over 25% of licensed preschools had microcomputers as early as 1984; virtually all may have such access in the 1990s (Goodwin, Goodwin, & Garel, 1986). The ratio of computers to students changed from 1:125 in 1984 to 1:22 in 1990.

Young children explore these computers with comfort and confidence (Binder & Ledger, 1985). Even preschoolers can use age-appropriate software requiring only 1- or 2-character key presses. They can learn to turn the computer on and off, remove and replace disks properly, follow instructions from a picture menu, use situational and visual cues in the aid of reading, and talk meaningfully about their computer work (Hess & McGarvey, 1987; Watson, Chadwick, & Brinkley, 1986). Using the standard keyboard is not a problem for young children, and is often superior to other devices, such as a joystick. Indeed, typing appears to be a source of pride for many. For tasks that involve selecting and moving objects or drawing, a pointing device such as a "mouse" is preferable (Borgh & Dickson, 1986b; Hungate & Heller, 1984; Kumpf, 1985; Lipinski, Nida, Shade, & Watson, 1986; Muller & Perlmutter, 1985; Swigger & Campbell, 1981).

Even preschoolers can work with minimal supervision if they have adult help initially (Rosengren, Gross, Abrams, & Perlmutter, 1985; Shade, Nida, Lipinski, & Watson, 1986). However, adults continue to play a significant role; children are more interested and less frustrated when an adult is present (Binder & Ledger, 1985; Shade et al., 1986). Such findings suggest that teachers should play a facilitative role, providing guidance and support as needed; such a role is consistent with best practices in early childhood education.

Preferences Relative to Other Activities. A computer center may vary from high to moderate popularity (Clements & Nastasi, in press; Picard & Giuli, 1985). Differences may result from appeal of other activities and the computer programs used. For example, children prefer animated, problem-solving, interactive programs. These give them a feeling of control over the computer (Lewis, 1981; Shade et al., 1986; Sherman, Divine, & Johnson, 1985; Sivin, Lee, & Vollmer, 1985). Generally, 3- to 5-year-old children spend approximately the same amount of time playing in a computer interest center within the classroom as they do drawing, talking, or playing in block or art centers (Hoover & Austin, 1986; Picard & Giuli, 1985). This attraction outlives the novelty effect. Thus, the computer appears to be an interesting, but not overly engrossing, activity for young children (Lipinski et al., 1986). These studies suggest that computers can be utilized successfully as an option within early childhood classrooms without interfering with engagement in more traditional preschool activities.

Individual Differences. Preschoolers most interested in using computers tend to be older (e.g., age 4). They show higher levels of vocabulary development and more organized and abstract forms of free play behavior. They do not differ from less interested peers in creativity, estimates of social maturity, or social-cognitive ability (Hoover & Austin, 1986; Johnson, 1985). There is little evidence, however, that computers should not be introduced to younger children. Younger and older preschoolers use computers with approximately the same facility (Beeson & Williams, 1985; Essa, 1987; Lewis, 1981), although 3-year-olds take longer to become familiar with the keyboard than 5-year-olds (Sivin et al., 1985). Teachers should encourage seemingly less interested children, who might benefit from using appropriate computer programs with help.

As early as the intermediate grades, boys have more access to computers and use computers more than girls (Lieberman, 1985; Parker, 1984; Picard & Giuli, 1985). There are some indications that this is even true for 5-year-olds (Beeson & Williams, 1985; Klinzing & Hall, 1985). In addition, boys may be more interested in creative problem-solving programs, whereas girls tend to stay within the dictates of established drill-and-practice programs (Shrock, Matthias, Anastasoff, Vensel, & Shaw, 1985; Swigger, Campbell, & Swigger, 1983). Girls exhibit greater overall computer competency, variety and detail in drawings, and degree of verbalization, and boys show greater ability on robot tasks (Jones, 1987). Overall, however, there are few significant gender differences in computer use by young children (Essa, 1987; Hess & McGarvey, 1987; Hoover & Austin, 1986; Johnson, 1985; King & Perrin, n.d.; Lipinski et al., 1986; Muller & Perlmutter, 1985; Shade et al., 1986; Sherman et al., 1985; Sprigle & Schaefer, 1984; Swigger & Campbell, 1981; Swigger et al., 1983). Researchers suggest that introducing children to computers in preschool may inhibit later gender differences in computer use by establishing early that computers are used by everyone. Teachers may also wish to ensure the availability of a variety of programs appealing to both girls and boys and to encourage both to engage in a variety of activities (e.g., open-ended programs). Further, they might encourage boys and girls to work as partners at the computer and monitor these interactions to facilitate equity in participation (e.g., encouraging equal levels of participation or alternation of leadership).

Health Concerns

Early warnings of health hazards of televisions and computers have generally not been supported. While the concerns that remain pertain mostly to office workers spending full days with a computer, there are precautions that should be observed for everyone. For example, scientists do not know the long-term effects of low-level electromagnetic emissions from monitors. These emissions are greatest from the sides and back of a monitor, and weaken quickly over short distances. So, children should not sit close to the back or sides of a computer or television that is turned on. They should work about 28 inches from the computer screen, or as far as is comfortable for their vision. People typically view televisions from a greater distance, which is recommended.

Considering both these emissions and the possibility of eyestrain, long periods of use, especially when reading the screen, are not recommended. In addition, there should be no glare on the screen from room lighting and no bright light (e.g., from a window) in back of the monitor. Screen images should be clear.

COGNITION AND ACHIEVEMENT

Can educational TV make a contribution to young children's learning? What are the effects of commercial TV on children's development? Do computers play a similar or unique role in their effects on cognition and development?

Instructional TV

"Sesame Street" and "The Electric Company" can develop readiness skills in children, with younger preschoolers gaining the most (Ball & Bogatz, 1973; Bogatz & Ball, 1971; Minton, 1975). Effectiveness, however, may be limited to skills specifically programmed and to lower-level skills such as alphabet naming, matching forms, and naming numbers. Further, such programs may not narrow the achievement gap between low-income and middle-income children (Honig, 1983).

Can higher-level thinking abilities be taught? Failures of TV to teach some Piagetian tasks has lead the authors of the studies to suggest that active manipulation of concrete objects is requisite to the development of certain cognitive operations (Hoffmann & Flook, 1980). Other studies, however, have shown highly significant training effects through televised modeling of Piagetian constructs such as seriation and number conservation (Henderson, Swanson, & Zimmerman, 1975; Raeissi & Wright, 1983). In addition, stories presented on educational television, compared to those read by the teacher, were preferred by 6- and 7-year-olds and fostered greater understanding, including transfer to other domains. Benefits were only accrued when viewing was mediated by the teacher (Choat & Griffin, 1986b).

Critics have hypothesized that the production techniques of programs such as "Sesame Street" engender hyperactivity, short attention spans, and lack of interest in slower paced, less visually appealing classroom work. Initial research indicates that educational programs which use production techniques involving fast pacing and relatively high action levels do not produce hyperactivity (Wright & Huston, 1983), although the amount of viewing of *commercial* TV is significantly related to measures of impulsivity (Anderson & Maguire, 1978). In comparison, slow-paced, relatively structured programs such as "Mr. Roger's Neighborhood" may result in equal attention and more gains in cognitive and affective areas, especially for lower achievers (Singer & Singer, in press, 1983; Wright et al., 1984). Ironically, the technique of presenting quick, entertaining, brief bits of learning material in educational programs designed to secure the attention of purportedly disadvantaged preschoolers may actually decrease their comprehension (Honig, 1983).

Properly designed television, then, can positively affect young children's cognition. What about programming not so designed?

Commercial TV

Critics argue that young viewers of commercial TV will not achieve well in school. The amount infants view TV is negatively correlated with measures of their language development (Nelson, 1973); light viewers have a more sophisticated language structure, possibly due to the greater opportunities to develop speech in play (Singer & Singer, in press). Even at a young age, heavy viewers are less interested in books (Clements, 1985; Morrow, 1983). Many researchers contend that television viewing has a small negative correlation with grades in reading (Gunter, 1982; Neuman & Prowda, 1982; Ridley-Johnson, Cooper & Chance, 1983).

Other studies, however, have not found significant relationships between television viewing and achievement (Anderson & Maguire, 1978; Neuman & Prowda, 1982). Sophisticated analyses that take variables such as intelligence and educational resources into account usually report weak or nonsignificant negative relationships between hours of viewing and achievement (Reinking & Wu, 1990). Importantly, however, this effect is not consistent across the range of viewing times. The relationship is slightly positive up to about 10 hours per week of viewing, and increasingly negative until 35–40 hours per week, beyond which additional viewing time may have little effect. Females and children with high IQs may be more adversely affected by higher viewing time (Williams, Haertel, Haertel, & Walberg, 1982).

Further, Busch (1978) revealed that second- and third-grade avid TV watchers are also avid readers. It may be that TV differentially affects children in different phases of learning to read. In the intermediate grades, children are learning how to acquire new knowledge by reading. TV may displace reading and thus limit the experience children have of reading for knowledge. In contrast, younger children, in the stage of learning word recognition and decoding, may not suffer from moderate displacement of reading by TV viewing (Reinking & Wu, 1990).

TV may also be related to creativity. The less children watched TV as preschoolers and the less they viewed realistic action-adventure programming, the more likely they were to be imaginative (Singer & Singer, 1986). Thus, certain kinds of television programming may contribute to children's lack of creativity, although appropriate programs can lead to moderate gains in imaginative play, if there is mediation by an adult (Singer & Singer, in press).

These studies are based on correlations, however, so a causal connection cannot be made. For example, do large amounts of TV watching create poor readers or do poor readers prefer to watch more TV? There is some experimental evidence that restricting TV viewing can benefit children. Gadberry (1980) assigned 6-year-olds, matched on sex, age, pretest IQ, and TV viewing time, to either a restricted or unrestricted TV viewing group. Results suggest that TV restriction enhanced performance IQ, reading time, and reflective cognitive style scores.

Of course, other variables must be considered. One study suggested that the best predictor of reading comprehension emerges from a combination of many factors, including familial factors such as positive discipline techniques, the mother's self-description as resourceful, and orderly household routines with more hours of sleep; and television variables such as fewer hours of viewing during the preschool years (Singer & Singer, 1983). These researchers also found that the relationship between TV viewing and reading comprehension may differ by SES, and moderate amounts of viewing may be especially helpful for lower SES children (Reinking & Wu, 1990; Singer & Singer, 1983). The benefit may be in compensating for deficits in first-hand experiences or developing vocabulary and interests. The type of program viewed is also significant: Viewing educational programs is related to increased academic grades, whereas viewing adult comedies and action-adventure programs is associated with decreased performance (Gunter, 1982; Murray, 1980). So, this latter type of TV may indeed displace verbal activities and thus decrease creative verbal fluency and reading competence (Murray, 1980), although, again, the research is only correlational. The interaction may be cyclical.

From a different perspective, teachers' intuitive *beliefs* about the effect of TV on young children may change their approach to teaching. For example, they may believe that current students are more visual learners with shorter attention spans and thus select a videotaped rather than textbook presentation (Reinking & Wu, 1990). Such beliefs are not supported by research, but may nevertheless alter the experiences teachers provide for young children.

Instructional and Commercial TV: Conclusions

Continued governmental, private, and public support for worthwhile *educational* television programs for young children appears warranted. Just as important are efforts to educate parents in ways to use and influence TV programming. Teachers can use TV programs to promote academic goals without deleterious side effects. All those responsible for the care of young children should monitor the amount and type of commercial TV viewed, as it may have both positive and negative effects. In addition, adult mediation of TV content is just as important as mediation of learning from other media. Research is needed that posits specific hypotheses that define the relationship between TV viewing and achievement; that is, we need more fully to answer the question, "Why and how does TV viewing affect achievement?"

Comparative Media Research

Which technological medium teaches best? Decades of research reveal the answer: When everything else is held constant, there is no significant difference among media (Clements, 1984). The problem is that this type of comparison *demands* that everything be held constant, and doing so eliminates any contribution of the unique features of a medium (leading to lowest-common-denominator comparisons such as "talking head" TV programs versus lecturers not permitted to interact with students). Yet it is precisely these specific features that make an educational difference (Salomon & Gardner, 1986). As a small example, zoom shots, which specifically model the operation of relating parts-to-wholes, can help initially unskilled children to use this mental skill. So, we should be asking not what different media do to children, but what we can encourage children to do with each medium. This question is especially critical when the medium is the computer.

Computers and the Language Arts

Language Development. One thing very young children should probably not do is use computers for drill, especially when the goal is to enhance language development (Clements, 1987a; Clements & Nastasi, in press). Rather, theoretical perspectives on how children learn language and empirical evidence suggest that computers should be a catalyst for verbal communication. For example, preschoolers' language activity, measured as words spoken per minute, is almost twice as high at the computer as at such activities as Play-Doh, blocks, art, or games (Muhlstein & Croft, 1986). Computer activity is slightly more effective than toy play in stimulating vocalizations in preschoolers with disabilities (McCormick, 1987).

Computer graphics is an especially fruitful environment for encouraging language use, especially if the programs are open-ended and encourage exploration and fantasy. Children tell and write more elaborate stories about computer graphics than about static pictures (Riding & Tite, 1985; Warash, 1984). Logo programming engenders interaction and language rich with emotion, humor, and imagination (Genishi, McCollum, & Strand, 1985). Experience with Logo also can enhance perceptual-language skills of preschoolers with language impairment (Lehrer & deBernard, 1987) and first-graders' visual-motor development, vocabulary, and listening comprehension (Robinson, Gilley, & Uhlig, 1988; Robinson & Uhlig, 1988). Reports such as these help allay the fear that computers will de-emphasize play, fantasy, and the corresponding rich use of language.

If the computer program is not open-ended, however, effects may be different. Parents were observed interacting with their preschool children with alphabet books or alphabet software. Although parents and children assumed the respective roles of teacher and student with either medium, book reading elicited more interaction than using the software (Worden, Kee, & Ingle, 1987). The software was probably too slow paced; further, it probably did not constitute optimal use of the computer medium.

Early Reading Skills. To date, drill and tutorial computer programs have been the dominant approach to teaching prereading and reading skills. Most research indicates that about 10 minutes work with such CAI per day significantly benefits primary-grade children's reading skills (Fitch & Sims, 1990; Piestrup, 1981; Ragosta, Holland, & Jamison, 1981; Watkins & Abram, 1985), especially for low achievers or others at risk (Clements & Mcloughlin, 1986; Lavin & Sanders, 1983; Silfen & Howes, 1984; Teague, Wilson, & Teague, 1984). Similarly, preschoolers can develop such reading readiness abilities as visual discrimination, letter naming, and beginning word recognition (Gore, Morrison, Maas, & Anderson, 1989; Lin, Vallone, & Lepper, 1985; Moxley & Barry, 1985; Smithy-Willis, Riley, & Smith, 1982; Swigger & Campbell, 1981). Computer presentation, however, is not guaranteed to be superior to other presentations such as flash-cards (Sudia, 1985), and short sessions with simple software will probably yield minimal achievement gains (Goodwin, Goodwin, Nansel, & Helm, 1986). Further, handwriting may have an advantage over typing for improving spelling (Cunningham & Stanovich, 1990). If quality software is integrated into the curriculum, however, computer use can facilitate the acquisition of school readiness and reading readiness skills. The effect can be greater when supplemented by concurrent computing activities in the home (Hess & McGarvey, 1987).

Potentially more revolutionary are approaches that do not drill subskills of reading. Basing their work on the perspective of readers as problem solvers, several researchers have reported that children working with problem-solving computer programs actually make greater gains in reading than those working with drill software (Clements, 1987a, 1987c; Norton & Resta, 1986; Riding & Powell, 1987). These tentative findings suggest that developing children's ability to comprehend, think critically, and solve problems may be as important as developing specific reading subskills. This may depend on providing a facilitative classroom climate and a consonant, holistic approach to reading instruction. Considering such diversity of instructional approaches, it is not surprising that effects in the reading and language arts area are some of the most variable in the field (Roblyer, Castine, & King, 1988).

Computers can make a special contribution to children with special needs. After 6 weeks of reading instruction using a microcomputer, 3- to 6-year-old deaf children demonstrated a significant improvement in word recognition and identification (Prinz, Nelson & Stedt, 1982). Taking advantage of young children's cognitive readiness regardless of their primary mode of communication, the program allowed them to press a word such as "flower" and see a picture of a flower, the word, and a graphic representation of a manual sign. In this way, computers helped children communicate in new ways and interrelate different means of communication.

Composition and Word Processing. Computer word processors can provide critical support, or *scaffolding,* for young writers (Clements, 1987a; Rosegrant, 1986). In theory, scaffolding allows children to perform tasks that they could not have performed by themselves, thus allowing them to build cognitive structures that they might or could not have built in isolation (Bruner, 1986; Vygotsky, 1978). A word processor, for example, allows children to experiment with letters and words without being distracted by the fine-motor aspects of handwriting. People also provide scaffolding; a teacher might perform just those parts of a task that the children cannot perform; as children learn, the teacher encourages them to take over those parts. With these two types of scaffolding, children can use written language for its true purpose, communication.

Research supports this contention. Children using word processors write more, have fewer fine motor control problems, are less worried about making mistakes, and make fewer mechanical errors (Clements, 1987a; Daiute, 1988; Hawisher, 1989; Kurth, 1988; Phenix & Hannan, 1984; Roblyer et al., 1988). Findings regarding holistic ratings of quality are mixed, but generally positive (Bangert-Drowns, 1989; Hawisher, 1989). Computer scaffolding is especially beneficial for children who have the most difficulties in writing (Bangert-Drowns, 1989). Even those not yet capable of writing by hand are able to learn to use a keyboard to write, and those reluctant to write with a pencil seem to enjoy writing with a word processor (Cochran-Smith, Kahn, & Paris, 1988).

Furthermore, word processors can support a constructive, process approach to composition. Children begin inventing spellings at the computer at a time when they are producing only random letters with paper and pencil (Cochran-Smith et al., 1988). "Playing" with units of compositions on word processors leads preschoolers to higher sensitivity to elements of text and to thinking about the topic before writing about it (Lehrer, Levin, DeHart, & Comeaux, 1987).

Computers simplify adding, deleting, changing, and moving text. Research results are mixed, however, as to whether primary grade children revise more on computers (Bangert-Drowns, 1989; Clements, 1987a; Hawisher, 1989). At least young children, compared to older children, are more willing to plan, take risks, discuss, reread, and revise with computers than with paper and pencil (Cochran-Smith et al., 1988; Dickinson, 1986; Guddemi & Mills, 1989; Phenix & Hannan, 1984). Further, young children derive satisfaction from being able to edit easily and produce clean, printed copies of their work.

All children, from kindergarten through primary grades, have positive attitudes toward writing and word processing after working with computers (Bangert-Drowns, 1989; Bradley, 1982; Hawisher, 1989; Lehrer et al., 1987). They gain confidence in their writing (Phenix & Hannan, 1984) and are motivated to write (Casey, 1984), more so than with paper and pencil (Guddemi & Mills, 1989).

Talking Word Processors. Many age-appropriate word processors include speech synthesis; that is, the computer can pronounce what children type. This provides an extra level of scaffolding (Borgh & Dickson, 1986a; Rosegrant, 1988). Preschool to first-grade children more readily express ideas, write simple sentences, and take risks in experimenting with their writing (Rosegrant, 1988). Even when compared to those without speech, talking word processors promote early literacy (Lehrer et al., 1987). Children develop an "inner voice" for constructing and editing text subvocally and thus the ability to "hear" whether or not the text "sounds right" (Rosegrant,

1988). This fosters an awareness of the need to edit (Borgh & Dickson, 1986a), although the length and quality of the writing may not automatically increase (Borgh & Dickson, 1986a; Kurth, 1988; Kurth & Kurth, 1987; Lehrer et al., 1987). Perhaps surprisingly, talking word processors improve basic skills such as letter naming, spelling, punctuation, grammar, and phonics (Bangert-Drowns, 1989; Rosegrant, 1988). They also facilitate writing, reading, and even verbalizations in nonvocal children with severe physical impairments (Meyers, 1984) and encourage students with learning disabilities and a history of failure to write eagerly and continuously, though slowly (MacArthur & Shneiderman, 1986). Most of these studies have included substantive teacher mediation, which may be essential to realizing the educational potential of talking word processors.

Disadvantages. Research has also documented possible disadvantages of word processors. For example, the size of the screen limits the amount of text writers can see at one time. Students, especially those with learning disabilities, often use keys inefficiently, have misconceptions (e.g., they insert numerous spaces to make "room" for text instead of merely inserting the text), and in other ways erroneously equate keyboard-and-screen with pencil-and-paper (Cochran-Smith et al., 1988; MacArthur & Shneiderman, 1986). This suggests the use of "what-you-see-is-what-you-get" word processors (MacArthur & Shneiderman, 1986). Teachers should provide instruction that gives students a clear conceptual model of word processing, as well as instruction and practice on points of difficulty such as saving and loading, insertion and deletion, and proper use of returns for paragraphs and blank lines. Such instruction should be just part of the whole story, however, an issue to which we turn in closing.

Final Statements. Teachers play an important role in building a creative environment and providing scaffolding for composition. Word processors can enhance such an environment, but do not by themselves establish it (Cochran-Smith et al., 1988). Researchers and teachers in successful projects ground their learning and teaching environments in theory and research. In addition, they recognize that substantive change takes time. In one study, only after one full year and into the second year did the rich benefits emerge (Cochran-Smith et al., 1988).

In summary, word processing can be successfully integrated into a process-oriented writing program as early as kindergarten or first grade; even younger students can use computers to explore written language. If used within the context of a theoretically based educational environment, the computer becomes a language arts learning tool (Clements, 1987b).

Mathematics in Computer Environments

The computer is also an excellent mathematics learning tool. As with other subjects, drill and tutorial CAI dominates in sheer number of sales and studies. What is the effectiveness of CAI and other computer approaches to mathematics education?

CAI. This approach appears successful; the greatest gains reported in the literature are in primary-grade children's mathematics skills (Lavin & Sanders, 1983; Niemiec & Walberg, 1984; Ragosta et al., 1981). As with reading, 10 minutes per day proved sufficient for significant gains; sessions of 20 minutes per day generated treatment effects about twice as large. Such results appear to be consistent across schools, years, length of implementation, and testing instruments and have been judged to be cost feasible (Ragosta et al., 1981).

Similarly, younger children can learn counting, sorting, and other skills (Brinkley & Watson, 1987-88; Corning & Halapin, 1989; Hungate, 1982; McCollister, Burts, Wright, & Hildreth, 1986). Children should not work with such drill-and-practice programs until they understand the concepts, however; then practice may be helpful (Clements & Nastasi, in press). CAI drill may positively affect total mathematics and computational skills more than other approaches, whereas concept application skills may be improved more by regular mathematics curricula (McConnell, 1983). Thus, teachers must carefully match students and goals with appropriate approaches.

Mathematics CAI and computer/video instruction appear especially effective in remedial situations and with students from schools serving lower socioeconomic populations (Corning & Halapin, 1989; Friedman & Hofmeister, 1984; Hotard & Cortez, 1983; Lavin & Sanders, 1983; McConnell, 1983; Ragosta et al., 1981). Both achievement and attitudes are positively affected, if the system is individualized for students' specific needs (Mevarech & Rich, 1985). A potential problem is that students in special education settings have less variety in their instructional experiences than do students in the mainstream with or without disabilities (Cosden, Gerber, Semmel, Goldman, & Semmel, 1987).

Computerized Analysis of Arithmetic Errors. Programs exist that accurately and quickly diagnosis elementary students' arithmetic errors. They often can explain the reason for the underlying errors (VanLehn, 1981). Research in this area has found that most errors, or "bugs," are a result of misconceptions or idiosyncratic "repairs" of incompletely recalled standard algorithms, rather than careless mistakes. A common example is the "subtract the smaller digit from the larger" bug. In addition, bugs are not stable; they may appear during one session, but not during the next (VanLehn, 1981). One implication is that more practice at the wrong time may be detrimental, as students may commit to memory a newly invented bug. This is especially important in the primary grades, when algorithms are introduced. In another study, children exposed to a drill-and-practice CAI program in mathematics outperformed control group children. A close look, however, revealed that the former made the same type of errors (Alderman, Swinton, & Braswell, 1979). They merely omitted fewer items. So they gained speed but not necessarily concepts. This suggests that students should possess the prerequisite understandings necessary to work with the program correctly—practicing, in other words, procedures that are both correct and meaningful to them. Using error analysis software as a basis for meaningful error correction sessions before extensive practice may help achieve this goal (Drucker, Wilbur, & McBride, 1987). Teaching for understanding, rather than using drill or syntactic instruction only, is crucial.

Geometry and Spatial Sense. The graphics capability of the computer makes it a "natural" for developing geometric and spatial thinking. Computer-based programs are as effective in teaching kindergartners about shapes as teacher-directed programs (vonStein, 1982), and more effective at teaching preschoolers relational concepts such as above-below and over-under than television (Brawer, cited in Lieberman, 1985). Using the computer as a learning tool, however, is more likely to lead to substantive change in mathematics education. Certain graphics programs offer a new, dynamic way of drawing and exploring geometric concepts (Forman, 1986b). For example, children can draw rectangles by stretching an electronic "rubber band," offering a different perspective on geometric figures. They can fill closed regions with color, prompting them to reflect on the topological features of closure as the consequence of actions, rather than as a characteristic of static shapes. The power of such drawing tools lies in the possibility that children will internalize the processes, thus constructing new mental tools.

Logo provides a more powerful and extensible, if more demanding, tool. Piaget showed that children learn about geometric shapes not from their perception of objects, but from the *actions* they perform on these objects. They internalize their actions and abstract the corresponding geometric ideas. These actions are usually first physical but then can become increasingly mental (see the section "The Issues of Concreteness"). Children might walk a path and then program the Logo turtle to draw it on the screen. The programming helps children link their intuitive knowledge about moving and drawing to more explicit mathematical ideas. In constructing a series of Logo commands to draw a rectangle, for example, they analyze the visual components of this shape and make conclusions about its properties (Clements & Battista, 1989; Nastasi & Clements, 1990a). Increased awareness of the properties of shapes and the meaning of angle and angle measure has been reported in several Logo studies with primary grade children (Clements & Battista, 1989; Hughes & Macleod, 1986).

Logo and Other Areas of Mathematics. Does Logo affect general mathematics achievement? Results across all types of approaches are mixed and not particularly promising (Clements, 1986a; Robinson, Feldman, & Uhlig, 1987). Certain uses of Logo with young children, however, promote basic number sense and encourage high levels of mathematical discussion, although significant gains are not found on every skill measured (Barker, Merryman, & Bracken, 1988; Bowman, 1985; Clements, 1987c; Hines, 1983; Hughes & MacLeod, 1986; Perlman, 1976; Reimer, 1985; Robinson et al., 1988; Robinson & Uhlig, 1988). Also, benefits may take time to develop (Akdag, 1985), and preschool children's conceptual difficulties with certain aspects of Logo (e.g., left and right, defining procedures) should not be underestimated. Certain specially designed Logo environments, however, can ameliorate these problems and enhance children's learning (Clements, 1983–84; Clements & Gullo, 1984). In addition, successful teachers structure and mediate Logo work to help children form correct, complete mathematical concepts, and they help children build links between the Logo experience and their regular mathematics work (Clements, 1987c).

The Issue of Concreteness. Teachers should never forgo concrete experiences, of course. Logo experiences are supplements and extensions, not replacements. For example, one 4-year-old made the discovery that reversing the turtle's orientation and moving it backwards had the same effect as merely moving it forwards. Striking was the *significance* the child attached to this identity and his overt awareness of it. Though the child had done this previously with toy cars, Logo helped him abstract a new and exciting idea for his experience (Tan, 1985). Logo and real-world experiences differ, but both contribute to the child's development. In general, the opinion that children must reach a certain age or stage (e.g., concrete operations) before successfully using Logo appears invalid (Clements & Nastasi, in press).

Moreover, what is "concrete" to the child may have more to do with what is meaningful and manipulable than with its physical nature. Char (1989) compared a computer graphic felt board environment, in which children could freely construct "bean stick pictures" by selecting and arranging beans, sticks, and number symbols, to a real bean stick environment. The software environment actually offered equal or greater control and flexibility to young children than "concrete" bean sticks. Both computer representations and real objects were worthwhile, and one was not a prerequisite to the other. In addition, computers enrich experience with regular manipulatives. Third-grade students who used both manipulatives and software demonstrated a greater sophistication in classification and logical thinking and showed more foresight and deliberation in classification than did students who used only manipulatives (Olson, 1988).

Computers, Creativity, and Higher-Order Thinking

Creativity. Several studies have documented an increase in creativity following Logo experience, although gains in some were moderate (Clements, 1986b; Clements & Gullo, 1984; Reimer, 1985; Vaidya & Mckeeby, 1984). Logo students' graphic compositions are more fully developed in terms of completeness, originality, and drawing style (Horton & Ryba, 1986). Though most researchers have used figural measures only, a recent study reported gains in both figural and verbal creativity, suggesting the general *processes* involved in creative thinking are also enhanced (Clements, 1991a). A caution is that the creativity tasks used do not capture the broad scope of scientific and artistic creativity. Nevertheless, at least some components of creativity are amenable to development within Logo environments (Clements & Merriman, 1988; Roblyer et al., 1988).

Higher-Order Thinking. Substantial research has been conducted on the effects of Logo programming. Although some studies of Logo's effect on problem-solving performance have not been encouraging (Barker et al., 1988; Clements & Nastasi, 1985; Robinson et al., 1987), a recent meta-analysis showed a substantial and homogeneous positive effect (Roblyer et al., 1988). Interestingly, especially for young children, Logo programming is an engaging activity, fostering a high degree of problem-solving and other task-related behavior (Clements & Nastasi, 1988; Nastasi, Clements, & Battista, 1990; Strand,

1987). The result is often increased problem-solving abilities for preschool to primary-grade children (Degelman, Free, Scarlato, Blackburn, & Golden, 1986; Perlman, 1976), including preschoolers with special needs (Lehrer, Harckham, Archer, & Pruzek, 1986).

One particularly promising finding is an increase in specific higher-order thinking skills. Several studies have reported increases in both preschool and primary-grade children's ability to monitor their comprehension and problem solving processes; that is, to "realize when you don't understand" (Clements, 1986b, 1990; Clements & Gullo, 1984; Lehrer & Randle, 1986; Miller & Emihovich, 1986). This may reflect the prevalence of "debugging" in Logo programming. Other abilities that may be positively affected include understanding the nature of a problem, representing that problem, and even "learning to learn" (Clements, 1990; Lehrer & Randle, 1986).

Teachers who facilitate such growth help children to reflect on their own thinking and bring problem-solving processes to an explicit level of awareness. For example, Lehrer and Smith (1986a) found that teacher-mediation of Logo instruction was more effective in enhancing specific cognitive abilities than such instruction without the benefit of teacher scaffolding. Similarly, Clements (1990) successfully used a Logo environment in which teachers used "homunculi"—cartoon characters to represent higher-order processes—to introduce and encourage the application of these skills.

Cognition and Achievement: Final Words

Major reviews of research reveal that young children can learn from both television and computer programs (Kulik, Kulik, & Bangert-Drowns, 1984; Lieberman, 1985; Murray, 1980; Niemiec & Walberg, 1984). Television can teach almost any subject matter where one-way communication will contribute to learning. Adding the element of interaction, CAI also can contribute significantly to knowledge acquisition. There seem to be few differences between learning from these applications and learning from conventional teaching.

This does not mean, however, that the use of any program under any conditions leads to such gains. Effectiveness depends on the quality of the TV or computer program, the amount of time the program is used, and the way in which it is used. In addition, much potential is unrealized. Both the development and use of TV programs specially designed for young children are presently inadequate. Most CAI drill has yet to employ techniques of adaptive instruction that cannot be duplicated in non-computer environments. Certain adaptive techniques, such as increasing ratio review, increase students' achievement without increasing the total time they work on the task (Siegel & Misselt, 1984).

Most of the unrealized potential of computers, however, probably lies in provision of qualitatively different educational environments, from talking word processors to Logo and combined Lego™-Logo explorations, to environments yet unimagined. Even though empirical results regarding these types of applications are inconsistent at this point, recent recommendations for school reform (e.g., National Council of Teachers of Mathematics, 1989) strongly suggest that such progressive approaches be emphasized instead of drill work.

Regardless of the type of media or application, research affirms the criticality of the teaching and learning context. Both television and computer-based instruction work best when made an integral part of instruction; when they are applied to a problem for which they are appropriate; and when their use is grounded in good teaching practices. Successful uses of media are almost invariably characterized by mediation. The teacher actively encourages, questions, models, and prompts. Challenging, open-ended programs such as Logo do induce high quality instruction, even from fairly naive and inexperienced adults. However, "the importance of Logo is that it provides an unusually rich problem space within which children can confront important ideas; it does not guarantee that the confrontation will occur" (Fein, 1985, p. 22). These conclusions are valid for all types of problem-solving programs and emphasize the need to consider the classroom ecology.

SOCIAL-EMOTIONAL AND SOCIAL-COGNITIVE DEVELOPMENT

Are electronic media potentially beneficial or harmful to children's social-emotional development? The answer is complex and requires consideration of intervening variables which serve to moderate the relationship between media and child development.

Television and Social Interactions

Television and Aggression. Although researchers and policy makers may not agree that media have a significant effect on the level of societal violence, there is unequivocal support for the conclusion that excessive violence in media increases the likelihood that at least some viewers will behave more violently (Huesmann, 1986; Huesmann & Malamuth, 1986). Research has consistently documented a link between viewing media violence and subsequent aggressive behavior, with laboratory and field studies providing evidence of short-term effects and longitudinal research (e.g., time-series and naturalistic studies) confirming long-term effects (Turner, Hesse, & Peterson-Lewis, 1986).

Each research design has strengths and limitations. Correlation studies, for example, cannot confirm a causal link between media violence and aggression. It may be that violent people simply prefer to watch violence. Causal connections can be inferred from experimental studies; however, ethical considerations limit the extent to which experimental conditions can duplicate reality. Longitudinal quasi-experimental or nonexperimental studies address these limitations. With such designs, researchers collect data about early television viewing and examine subsequent social adjustment, or examine incidence of violent behavior following the broadcasting of popular portrayals of violence (e.g., prizefights). The accumulation of evidence using a variety of designs provides the basis for understanding the role of television in promoting aggression and for drawing implications regarding use of this medium.

The classic laboratory studies are those of Bandura (1978). Subjects view a segment in which an adult model displays aggressive behaviors toward an inflatable doll and are then observed in a playroom with the same doll. Those who viewed the aggressive film displayed more aggressive behavior toward the doll than the control children. Correlational studies conducted with young children have substantiated the relationship between exposure to media violence, or preference for viewing violence, and aggressive attitudes and behavior (Clements, 1985). Singer and Singer (1981), for example, found that children (especially boys) who watched a great deal of television were likely to be aggressive and uncooperative. Furthermore, early heavy television viewing by preschoolers was correlated with measures of aggressive behavior in the second and third grades (Singer & Singer, 1983).

Several theoretical views have been proposed to explain the TV violence-aggression link. For example, it has been suggested that viewing violence serves a cathartic function, by allowing the vicarious expression of aggressive impulses. This view has received little empirical support (Clements, 1985; Murray, 1980). Research used to substantiate the catharsis hypothesis (Feshbach & Singer, 1971) has been criticized on methodological grounds. There is some evidence suggesting that catharsis may occur when TV violence is stylized (and thus, unrealistic) and the victim is unseen (Clements, 1985, provides a detailed discussion; Lesser, 1977).

In contrast, viewing violence may increase emotional arousal (Rule & Ferguson, 1986). According to this view, exposure to aggressive scenes stimulates children, arousing them to aggressive acts. Such arousal has been documented during the viewing of high-salience commercials; that is, those with a high level of action, rapid change of scene and character, and frequent use of cuts and pans (Greer, Potts, Wright, & Huston, 1982). In addition, exposure to aggressive scenes may augment or maintain existing levels of arousal and aggression (Zillman, 1979; Zillman, 1982). Furthermore, viewing violence may increase tolerance for aggression such that repeated exposure may result in emotional habituation or desensitization to aggression (Drabman & Thomas, 1974; Thomas & Drabman, 1975; Thomas, Horton, Lippincott, & Drabman, 1977). Alternatively, the social learning theory of aggression (Bandura, 1978) posits that television violence teaches aggressive behavior, attenuates restraints over aggressive behavior and legitimizes violence, desensitizes and habituates individuals to violence, and shapes the images of reality upon which they base their actions (Clements, 1985). In reference to the latter influence, it has been suggested that repeated exposure to violent content can predispose viewers to expectations of danger as part of daily life; that is, a belief in a "mean and scary world" (Singer & Singer, 1986).

More recently, researchers have hypothesized a cumulative process based on social learning and information-processing theories (Huesmann, 1986; Huesmann & Malamuth, 1986). According to this perspective, scripts (mental representations of social behavior relevant to specific situations) for violent behavior are acquired during childhood through viewing of violent scenes (e.g., through the media) and are rehearsed, practiced,

and elaborated with subsequent exposure to violent scenes and opportunities to display such behavior. This cumulative learning process produces enduring mental representations for aggression that persist into adulthood (Huesmann & Malamuth, 1986, provide a more extensive discussion of this perspective). Longitudinal correlational (Eron, 1982; Eron, Huesmann, Brice, Fisher, & Mermelstein, 1983; Huesmann, Lagerspetz, & Eron, 1984) and experimental field studies (Comstock et al., 1978; Friedrich & Stein, 1973; Murray, 1980) provide support for this view. Researchers have concluded that middle childhood may be a period during which a number of factors converge and make children particularly susceptible to the effects of television (Eron, 1982; Turner et al., 1986). Although such research is suggestive of a unidirectional relationship between TV viewing of violence and later aggression, the use of cross-lagged panel correlations to support such causal hypotheses (as was done in the longitudinal research cited above) has been criticized (Rogosa, 1980) and therefore results based on this technique must be interpreted with caution.

In recognition of the complex interplay of personal and environmental factors that account for the relationship between media violence and aggression, researchers more recently have focused on the role of intervening variables. Research suggests that the following combination of factors puts a child at risk for behavior problems (particularly, aggressiveness) at early elementary school age: (a) uncontrolled-television viewing combined with minimal availability of other forms of entertainment such as books or music; (b) absence of adult mediation of TV content; (c) heavy viewing during the preschool years, especially recent heavy viewing of violent programs; (d) authoritarian parents who use physical punishment, are rejecting, whose self-descriptions do not emphasize creativity or imagination, and who themselves view "escapist" type programs; (e) poor peer popularity and intellectual ability; (f) belief that TV portrays real life (developmental differences influence the extent to which children are able to distinguish reality from fantasy portrayed on TV; Eron, 1986; Huesmann, 1986; Skeen et al., 1982); and (g) identification with aggressive characters (Clements, 1985; Desmond et al., 1987; Eron, 1982; Huesmann, 1986; Huesmann et al., 1984; Singer & Singer, 1981; Singer & Singer, 1983; Tangney, 1988). In addition, a number of immediate situational variables may influence short-term effects of violent media content on aggression: (a) the presence of co-viewers and the extent to which they indicate approval or disapproval of exhibited aggression; (b) the presence of a dominant peer or active, enthusiastic co-viewer; (c) perceived similarity to the aggressor and victim; (d) attention to aesthetic or physical aspects of the scene rather than the violent content; and (e) incidental features of the postobservation situation which function as retrieval cues (Berkowitz, 1986). These factors are believed to interact in a reciprocal, dynamic way; the interplay of multiple variables makes it difficult to establish clear causal links, although models have been proposed (e.g., see Huesmann, 1986).

The interaction of characteristics of the media and developmental differences may influence the initial learning and subsequent display of aggressive behavior patterns. Formal features of the media may influence both attention and comprehension of content which in turn influence the specific nature of the script which is encoded (Rule & Ferguson, 1986). Young child might be more likely to be influenced by an aggressive model because of attention to salient, though perhaps, irrelevant, formal features; poor memory for central plot information, especially with regard to motive; and failure to comprehend implicit information about motives and consequences (Collins, 1979; Parke & Slaby, 1983). Interpretation of motive might be particularly difficult for the young child when portrayals provide mixed messages; for example, when violence by one character (the "bad" person) is punished and violence by another (the "good" person) is rewarded (Rule & Ferguson, 1986). Information about motives has been found to moderate the likelihood that children will be affected by what they see (Collins, 1979).

Television and Prosocial Behavior. Researchers have also addressed the role of television viewing on prosocial behavior. At least in certain situations, prosocial programming can increase children's subsequent prosocial behavior (Comstock et al., 1978). The popular children's program, "Mr. Rogers' Neighborhood," has been the focus of several studies (Coates, Pusser, & Goodman, 1976; Friedrich & Stein, 1973; Sprafkin, Liebert, & Poulos, 1975), which document short-term increases in prosocial behaviors such as cooperation, empathy, helping, and sharing after viewing.

Consistent with the information-processing perspective, it has been suggested that exposure to prosocial models provides alternative "scripts" for responding to social situations (Huesmann, 1986). There is empirical support for this view (Eron, 1986). For example, in one study prosocial responding increased following the viewing of constructive solutions to conflict (Collins & Getz, 1976). Similarly, 3- to 5-year-olds showed a strong preference for play with minority children after viewing depictions of nonwhite children at play; in contrast, a control group showed no such preference (Gorn, Goldberg, & Kanungo, 1976). Eron (1986), however, cautions that exposure to prosocial models without supplementary training (e.g., role playing) may not be adequate for counteracting the effects of violent television.

Singer and Singer (1986) have suggested that heavy TV viewing pre-empts active play and use of imagination. This phenomenon might be less likely with prosocial programming. For example, viewing of "Mr. Rogers' Neighborhood" has been shown to increase creativity and imaginativeness of play (Singer & Singer, 1981).

In sum, research suggests that television has a significant and potentially long-term influence on children's social development. For example, exposure to TV violence during childhood has been linked to aggression in adulthood, up to 10 years later (for a review, see Turner et al., 1986). The viewing of aggressive or prosocial behavior provides children with models of adaptation to real-life situations. Televised models might be particularly influential for those viewers who are not provided with alternatives through other sources. Parents and educators need to be aware of the potential impact of TV on children's social development and of the role they can play in ensuring that the effects are positive. In particular, these adults can mediate the influence of TV, teach children to be knowledgeable consumers, and provide children with alternative models of social behavior. As we shall see, similar conclusions apply to computer technology.

Children's Interactions in Computer Environments

In response to dissonant views regarding the social-emotional benefits of computers, researchers have addressed the following questions: What is the nature of young children's interactions with the computer? What effects do computers have on early social and emotional development? Initially, the influx of computers into the school setting led to fears of social isolation (Barnes & Hill, 1983). Observations of children as they interact with computers, however, have supported claims that computers might serve as potential catalysts of social interaction (Papert, 1980). That is, children generally prefer not to work alone at the computer; instead, they often choose to work in dyads or small groups (Rosengren et al., 1985; Shade et al., 1986; Swigger et al., 1983; Swigger & Swigger, 1984). In addition, the computer's presence in the preschool classroom fosters a positive social climate characterized by praise and encouragement of peers (Klinzing & Hall, 1985), initiation of interaction and help-seeking behaviors (Bowman, 1985; Genishi, 1988; Genishi et al., 1985; Hungate & Heller, 1984), and spontaneous peer teaching and helping (Borgh & Dickson, 1986b; Paris & Morris, 1985; Wright & Samaras, 1986). Furthermore, the computer enhances, rather than preempts, existing patterns of social participation (Binder & Ledger, 1985; Essa, 1987; Rosengren et al., 1985; Swigger & Swigger, 1984). Both cooperative and independent play are encouraged, and children's interactions in the computer area of a preschool classroom resemble those that occur in other areas (Klinzing & Hall, 1985; Lipinski et al., 1986). Introduction of the computer into the preschool classroom provides new opportunities for forming relationships and improving sociometric status based on interest and expertise (Swigger & Swigger, 1984). Compared to more traditional school activities in preschool (e.g., puzzles, blocks) and early primary grades (paper-and-pencil writing activities), the computer has been shown to engender higher rates of collaboration (Clements & Nastasi, 1985; Daiute, 1988; Dickinson, 1986; Hawisher, 1989; Heap, 1987; Muhlstein & Croft, 1986; Muller & Perlmutter, 1985).

The nature of children's interactions within computer environments may be influenced by variables such as students' developmental levels, the teacher's instructional style, and the type of software. Results from several studies suggest a developmental progression in patterns of social interaction, from turn-taking and peer teaching during preschool (Bergin, Ford, & Meyer-Gaub, 1986; Borgh & Dickson, 1986b) to peer collaboration in the early primary grades (Clements & Nastasi, 1985; Riel, 1985). Although suggestive of a developmental trend, such results need further confirmation through cross-sectional and longitudinal research (Clements & Nastasi, in press). A similar pattern emerges as children gain experience with computers, with a shift from an egocentric to a peer-oriented focus (Bergin et al., 1986; Emihovich & Miller, 1988c; Shade et al., 1986). Paralleling this change is a shift from teacher- to peer-directed activity as children gain greater mastery and control over their learning; that is, as the amount of peer collaboration increases, teacher guidance decreases (Emihovich & Miller, 1988c; Riel, 1985).

In addition to developmental variations, other individual characteristics may influence the nature of social behavior in computer environments. For example, students of high academic ability are more likely to take a dominant role in group work (Bellows, 1987; Kurth, 1988) and to engage in competitive interactions (Hativa, Swisa, & Lesgold, 1989) than students of low academic ability. Similarly, students who are more assertive or more highly motivated are more likely to take active (collaborating, teaching) or dominant (controlling the interaction) roles in cooperative computer activities (Bergin et al., 1986; Kurth, 1988). Such factors should be considered when grouping students.

Teachers can influence the patterns of interaction. Inaccessibility of the teacher may have a positive or negative impact, fostering independence and peer teaching and helping on the one hand, but aggression and competition on the other (Bergin et al., 1986; Genishi, 1988; Genishi et al., 1985; Lipinski et al., 1986; Rosengren et al., 1985; Shade et al., 1986; Silvern, Countermine, & Williamson, 1988). In addition, the teacher might deliberately encourage certain behaviors through structuring of the learning environment; for example, by requiring that children work in pairs or establishing rules regarding turn taking and collaboration (Borgh & Dickson, 1986b; Bowman, 1985; Dickinson, 1986; Genishi 1988; Genishi et al., 1985). Altering the ratio of computers to children may alter social behaviors; for example, Lipinski et al. (1986) found that aggressive behavior was eliminated with a ratio of 1:12.

Teachers might also influence the nature of children's interactions through the choice of computer hardware and software. Thus, to encourage collaboration, one might choose hardware features and software packages that foster cooperative work and minimize the need for teacher help. For example, access to others' work through voice synthesis, the computer screen, or the printed copy may facilitate collaboration and helping on writing activities (Kurth, 1988). Open-ended, problem solving–oriented software such as Logo, graphics, or writing programs foster peer collaboration, independence from adult guidance, and successful resolution of disagreements (Clements & Nastasi, 1985, 1988; Emihovich & Miller, 1988c; Nastasi et al., 1990; Riel, 1985). In contrast, structured programs such as drill CAI elicit peer teaching, though most of it involves brief rather than elaborated responses; turn taking; and competition (Bellows, 1987; Bergin et al., 1986; Borgh & Dickson, 1986b; Hativa et al., 1989). In a similar vein, video games with aggressive content may foster aggressive behavior in much the same way as aggressive cartoons (Silvern & Williamson, 1987) and may reduce generosity (Chambers & Ascione, 1985). In contrast, a computer simulation of a Smurf playhouse attenuated the themes of territoriality and aggression that emerged with a real playhouse version of the Smurf environment (Forman, 1985; Forman, 1986a).

Thus, computer environments, like any educational environments, may influence social interaction patterns among children in preschool and primary grades. The relationship of computers to short-term behavioral changes and long-term developmental outcomes is not necessarily direct or simple. Personal characteristics of the students as well as ecological factors such as preestablished patterns of social participation, the teacher's instructional style, and computer hardware and software may individually or collectively moderate or mediate the effects of computer experiences. Most of the findings regarding the influence of ecological factors on children's interactions within computer environments are based on informal observation rather than systematic study. Whereas findings suggest the potential importance of instructional and curricular factors, further study of the connections between environmental events and child behaviors is needed. For a more elaborate discussion, see Clements and Nastasi (in press).

Effectance Motivation: Attitudes, Motivation, and Perceived Competence

Effectance motivation is defined as the degree to which an individual desires to control or effect change in his or her environment (Harter, 1978). This motive influences one's attitudes toward learning and attempts at problem solving or mastery. Successful attempts at solving problems lead to the internalization of a self-reward system and development of a sense of competence; these subsequently serve as mediators of motivational orientation. Thus, one's motivation, attitudes toward learning, and sense of competence are interrelated. The extent to which educational technology provides opportunities for exploration and mastery will influence the extent to which they contribute to the enhancement of effectance motivation and perception of the self as competent. Computer environments provide such opportunities; the impact of television on motivation, however, is less clear.

Computers foster positive attitudes toward learning. Research suggests that young children enjoy working with computers; for example, they typically display enthusiasm and positive affect (Corning & Halapin, 1989; Gélinas, 1986; Hyson & Morris, 1985; Silfen & Howes, 1984; Wright & Samaras, 1986). Preschoolers and primary-grade children prefer computers to more traditional classroom activities such as playing, drawing, and talking (Clements & Nastasi, 1985; Kurth, 1988; Picard & Giuli, 1985; Silfen & Howes, 1984). Furthermore, enjoyment is enhanced when cooperative work is encouraged (Perlmutter, Behrend, Kuo, & Muller, 1986); and certain computer environments such as Logo may be more intrinsically interesting than others such as drill CAI (Papert, 1980).

Contradicting the notion that children's initial interest in computers reflects a novelty effect, researchers have reported high levels of interest and attention following several sessions and even after several months of experience (Bergin et al., 1986; Clements & Nastasi, 1985; Lehrer, Randle, & Sancilio, 1989; Strand, 1987). The nature of that interest, however, may change over time; for example, with initial "exuberance" being replaced by "ordinary" levels of close attention (Bergin et al., 1986).

The enjoyment of educational computer experience seems to generalize to other learning activities and to school in general (Hawisher, 1989; Mevarech, 1985; Mevarech & Rich, 1985). In one study, for example, students who had received CAI mathematics instruction for two years expressed greater satisfaction with school in general, a stronger commitment to schoolwork, and more favorable attitudes toward teachers, than those receiving traditional instruction (Mevarech & Rich, 1985).

In addition to fostering positive attitudes toward learning, computer use may also engender an enhanced *sense of control,* even among preschoolers (Clements & Nastasi, 1985; Hyson & Morris, 1985; Mevarech, 1985; Shade et al., 1986; Wright & Samaras, 1986). Instructional modifications such as individualization may further enhance such effects (Mevarech, 1985).

Findings are equivocal with regard to effects on the child's sense of competence. Whereas some research suggests enhancement of self-concept (Mevarech & Rich, 1985), other findings either fail to provide evidence of positive effects (Emihovich & Miller, 1988a) or suggest a negative impact (Hativa et al., 1989). Variations in curriculum content, instructional approach, or sampling may account in part for discrepant findings. In the latter study, for example, fostering of negative self-images was associated with the use of competitive learning structures.

Research findings are not all positive. Following educational computer experiences, children in one study exhibited signs of disinterest in traditional classroom activities such as paper-and-pencil drill (Clements & Nastasi, 1985). Such effects may be specific to certain software such as CAI drill; the same effect was not observed for children working in Logo. In addition, children may exhibit individual differences in preference for the computer over the other preschool activities such as puzzles or blocks (Williams & Beeson, 1986–87).

Outcomes in attitudes, motivation, or self-perceptions are influenced by instructional and curricular aspects of computer environments such as the provision of developmentally appropriate rules, the game-like nature of software, opportunities for decision-making and self-generation of problems, provision of feedback, the frequency of successful experiences, and the presence of peers or teachers (Clements & Nastasi, in press; Gélinas, 1986; Shade et al., 1986; Strand, 1987). Positive and negative effects might need to be counterbalanced. For example, the presence of the teacher fosters greater interest but discourages self-directed activity (Shade et al., 1986).

The role of the teacher may need to change over time (Clements & Nastasi, in press; Emihovich & Miller, 1988b; Genishi, 1988; Genishi et al., 1985; Hyson & Morris, 1985). For example, the teacher might initially model problem-solving strategies, realistic goal setting, enthusiasm, and a sense of competence, for inexperienced students. As students gain expertise and begin to regulate their own learning, however, the teacher's role can become that of a facilitator who provides progressively less structure and guidance. This transition to independence might be further enhanced by peer collaboration (Emihovich & Miller, 1988b; Hyson & Morris, 1985).

Certain types of software are more likely to foster the environmental conditions described above. Computer-based

writing and Logo, in contrast to CAI drill, have been shown to foster peer collaboration and independence (Clements & Nastasi, 1985; Emihovich & Miller, 1988b; Miller & Emihovich, 1986; Riel, 1985). These and other open-ended, problem solving–oriented software have been shown to enhance personal sense of control (Burns & Hagerman, 1989; Hyson & Morris, 1985), positive attitudes toward learning (Riel, 1985), and positive self-evaluations (Strand, 1987). CAI also engenders effectance motivation and positive attitudes toward learning, although effects may vary as a function of software content, developmental level of the student, and the extent to which cooperation or competition is fostered (Clements & Nastasi, 1985, in press; Hativa et al., 1989; Lehrer et al., 1989). Similarly, the effects of Logo on self-evaluation might vary as a function of developmental level (Clements & Nastasi, in press).

In summary, research supports Papert's (1980) belief in the holding power of the computer even for children as young as 3 years of age. Although not all results have been positive (Clements & Nastasi, 1985; Goodwin, Goodwin, Nansel, & Helm, 1986), most studies have reported increases in positive attitudes after computer use, especially when children work in groups, write on the computer, or program in Logo (Clements & Nastasi, in press; Lieberman, 1985). These results are promising, especially because the motivational advantages of good computer software (i.e., challenge, curiosity, control, feedback) are consonant with the types of experiences necessary for enhancing young children's intrinsic motivation and sense of competence. In conclusion, children's work with computers may influence their attitudes toward learning, effectance motivation and sense of competence. It is critical, however, to consider the role of instruction and software in explaining such effects. It is also critical to extend this type of work to television.

Connections Between the Social and the Cognitive

We have examined the potential impact of electronic media on the social-emotional and cognitive development. However, development of these two domains is not necessarily independent. In this section, we will focus on theories and research regarding the influence of computers and television on the interaction of cognitive and social development. In designing educational programs, it is important to consider the interplay of social and cognitive growth.

Cognitive development does not occur in isolation; social interactions with adults and peers provide scaffolding as discussed previously. Children eventually become able to perform the task alone through internalization of the strategies and concepts that emerge from the interaction with teacher or peers—the interpsychological becomes the intrapsychological (Vygotsky, 1978). This perspective provides a framework for the examination of the link between social and cognitive processes.

Television, Aggression and Achievement. Research suggests that the cognitive and perceptual limitations of young children may interfere with accurate comprehension of program content; for example, they may be influenced more by extraneous features than story theme (Collins, 1979; Rule & Ferguson,

1986). Especially with young children, mediation of television viewing seems critical. One of the most reliable research findings is that a co-viewing adult significantly aids children's comprehension of, and learning from, television (Collins, Sobol, & Westby, 1981; Watkins, Calvert, Huston-Stein, & Wright, 1980; Wright & Huston, 1983). Mediation can take the form of evaluative criticism or interpretation of content, or rule-making about TV viewing (Desmond et al., 1987).

Children can be taught to become critical viewers. In one study, the critical viewing skills of kindergartners and second graders were improved through use of a classroom-based educational program (Watkins et al., 1988). Other research suggests that interventions directed at improving critical viewing skills of parents and then encouraging them to mediate the information portrayed in the media (e.g., evaluating aggression as negative and presenting alternative strategies) may help to mitigate the psychological effects of media violence on aggressive behavior (see Eron, 1986, for a review).

Co-viewers influence whether children imitate an aggressive model by verbalizing approval or disapproval of the violent behavior (Berkowitz, 1986). In addition, the co-viewer can provide examples of appropriate alternatives to the aggressive behavior, thus creating an opportunity to teach social problem-solving skills (cf. Huesmann, 1986). The presence of an enthusiastic or socially dominant co-viewer fosters imitation of modeled aggression (Berkowitz, 1986).

It is questionable whether peers or siblings are helpful co-viewers. Results from one study suggests that viewing instructional television with peers does not improve comprehension for preschoolers (Henderson & Rankin, 1986). Even when siblings who are 3 to 6 years older are able to comprehend content accurately, they fail to provide mediation that would improve comprehension for their first- and second-grade siblings (Haefner & Wartella, 1987). In the latter study, examination of the content of children's interactions indicated that their verbalizations were focused on nonessential program content such as identification of characters instead of interpretation of motives or essential plot information. Perhaps interventions to improve the critical viewing skills of children can facilitate peer mediation as well. In addition, effective peer mediation skills may need to be taught.

Research also suggests a link between TV violence, aggression and academic achievement. Children with poorer academic skills behave more aggressively, watch TV more regularly and more violent TV, and believe in the realism of TV violence (Huesmann & Eron, 1986). Longitudinal research by Huesmann and colleagues (Huesmann, Eron, & Yarmel, 1987; Lefkowitz, Eron, Walder, & Huesmann, 1977) suggests that aggression is more likely to influence intellectual achievement than vice versa; however, as previously noted, such research has been criticized on methodological grounds. In any regard, there is evidence to support a connection between TV viewing, aggressive behavior, and poor achievement. Several explanations have been proposed. For example, aggression resulting from TV viewing of violence may interfere with the social interactions with teachers and peers that are critical to achievement (Huesmann, 1986). In addition, children who fail in school may turn to TV heroes, including violent ones, for vicarious

success experiences (Turner et al., 1986). These children may be attracted to violent media heroes who are able to overcome daily hassles in seemingly simple ways and thus are viewed as competent. The aggressive solutions, however, are typically oversimplified and thus provide poor models for solving complex problems of daily life, such as those related to academics and peer interactions. Because these children are also likely to perceive TV violence as real, they are more likely to encode the violent scripts as real and subsequently use these scripts to guide their behavior, thus engaging in more aggressive behavior (Huesmann, 1986). Therefore, a cycle of aggression, poor achievement, and TV viewing is perpetuated: Frequent frustrations from academic failure cause children to both act aggressively and to seek out heroic media figures. If these heroes use violence to solve problems, they may serve as models for aggressive problem solutions. This increases the use of aggression which in turn precludes the use of adaptive school behavior and interferes with learning and achievement.

Computers, Social-Cognitive Interactions, and Cognitive Growth. Social interactions within educational computer environments can facilitate young children's achievement and cognitive growth. For example, cooperative learning within computer contexts has been associated with production of more complex stories (Goldman & Rueda, 1988), enhancement of higher-order thinking (Nastasi et al., 1990), and achievement gains (Johnson, Johnson, & Stanne, 1985; Johnson, Johnson, & Stanne, 1986). These benefits may be restricted to children beyond preschool age. Combined social and cognitive demands of collaboration may overburden the capabilities of preschoolers and thus impede effective problem solving (Perlmutter et al., 1986).

Peer collaboration engenders certain types of facilitative interactive behaviors. Children working together in computer environments, for example, are more likely to engage in cognitive conflict and metacognitive activity than those working alone (Clements & Nastasi, 1985, 1988; Lehrer & Smith, 1986b; Miller & Emihovich, 1986; Nastasi et al., 1990; Perlmutter et al., 1986). Peer-mediated problem solving and engagement in cognitive conflict and its resolution are positively related to posttreatment achievement and cognitive functioning for both preschoolers and older students (Nastasi et al., 1990; Perlmutter et al., 1986). Furthermore Logo, compared to other computer environments such as CAI, is more likely to engender collaborative problem solving, engagement in cognitive conflict and metacognitive activity, and subsequent gains in higher-order thinking (Battista & Clements, 1986; Clements, 1990; Clements & Nastasi, 1985, 1988; Miller & Emihovich, 1986; Nastasi & Clements, 1990b; Nastasi et al, 1990; Perlmutter et al., 1986).

The teacher plays an important role in amplifying the benefits of computer environments such as Logo. For example, the teacher may need to help students to shift from teacher- to peer-mediated learning for cognitive benefits to be seen (Clements & Nastasi, in press). In one study, peer-mediated problem solving was positively correlated with posttreatment achievement of preschoolers, whereas teacher-mediated learning was negatively correlated with achievement (Perlmutter et al., 1986). Such a shift has been found to characterize Logo environments (Emihovich & Miller, 1988b; Miller & Emihovich, 1986).

In conclusion, an environment in which children work together and have greater freedom to introduce topics of learning and to initiate action, and in which the teacher plays a supportive role through scaffolding is one that is more likely to facilitate mediated learning and the consequent internalization of higher-order regulatory processes (Emihovich & Miller, 1988b). Within such a sociocultural context, both student-student and teacher-student interactions are important. Cooperative learning research provides some guidelines for the design of such environments (Nastasi & Clements, 1991). Further investigation of the connections between such interactions and documented cognitive gains within computer environments is needed. Such information will help us to design computer learning environments more effectively.

Final Words: Media and Socioemotional Development

In sum, research suggests that television and computers represent important factors in the socialization of today's children. The effects are not clearly positive or negative but are influenced by individual as well as environmental factors. Educators and parents can help to ensure positive effects through controlling or mediating use of such media, educating children to be effective consumers, and providing alternative opportunities for learning.

Television. Researchers and consumers have raised concerns about the negative impact of television, particularly with regard to aggressive behavior. As suggested earlier, educators can intervene to reduce such negative effects and foster positive outcomes. Interventions aimed at mitigating negative psychological effects of TV have been successful (Eron, 1986; Eron, 1982; Eron et al., 1983; Huesmann, Eron, Klein, Brice, & Fischer, 1983). Based on the assumption that aggression is a learned approach to problem solving, this work used a combination of cognitive and behavioral techniques, focused on teaching children that aggression is undesirable, that TV characters are not real, and that there are alternatives to aggression. As a result, children altered their attitudes toward TV and became less aggressive, even though they still watched violent TV. Other approaches that involve direct teaching are those focused on teaching affection-like behaviors as alternatives to television-provoked aggression (Marton & Acker, 1981) or, drawing upon clinical literature, teaching children self-control strategies (Eron, 1986).

Furthermore, children can learn adaptive skills from TV. In one study, instructional video was used to teach kindergartners and first graders self-protective responses to potential abductors (Poche, Yoder, & Miltenberger, 1988). Pairing video presentation with behavioral rehearsal was found to be most successful; video alone was superior to standard safety program formats.

When deciding to use instructional TV, teachers need to consider potential effects on children, taking into consideration developmental differences. For example, one group of researchers (Bryant, Brown, Parks, & Zillmann, 1983) found that 4- and 6-year-olds responded differently to alternate corrective procedures portrayed in the media. The preschoolers were most responsive to commands, whereas the older children were more likely to modify modeled behavior which was followed in the portrayal by ridicule. Thus, consideration of specific features of the medium is necessary.

Computers. Research indicates that the application of computers in education may enhance social interactions, attitudes toward learning, intrinsic motivation, and perceived competence. In addition, collaborative interactions, particularly those focused on problem-solving and resolution of discrepant ideas, are more likely to facilitate cognitive development. Developmental limitations warrant consideration. For example, the combined social and cognitive demands of collaborative problem solving may overburden the capabilities of preschoolers. Similarly, the cognitive capabilities of the young child may limit the ability to engage in perspective taking and consideration of alternative ideas. Research in cooperative problem solving has typically involved children beyond the primary grades, and findings may not be generalizable (Nastasi & Clements, 1991).

EARLY CHILDHOOD AND ELECTRONIC MEDIA: SUMMARY AND IMPLICATIONS

Electronic media such as television and computers have potential advantages and disadvantages for fostering the development of young children. Research suggests that the relationship between such media and development is not necessarily simple or direct, but is influenced by intervening individual and environmental factors. Thus, efficacious use depends on consideration of these intervening variables. In this section, we provide suggestions for effective use of television and media to enhance the development of young children.

Television

Young children are heavy, but active, viewers of TV. Their development of viewing skills is facilitated by television content that is related to their existing knowledge and that demands cognitive skills just above their present level. Commentary made in an informal way by an adult also promotes this development.

Viewing TV is not necessarily related to lower school achievement; in fact, moderate amounts of viewing may be helpful, especially for children at risk for achievement problems. Of course, this does not imply that TV represents an optimal enrichment program. Above a certain threshold (from 10 to 20 hours per week), however, negative effects emerge. Many ecological factors, such as home environment and type of programs (e.g., educational vs. adult comedies or action- adventure programs), mediate these effects.

A policy recommendation is to continue governmental, private, and public support for the development of educational television programs and to lobby for an increase in the quality of commercial TV designed for young children. The extensive research guidance presently available concerning comprehensible, beneficial TV programming should be applied;

for example, moderate difficulty, intrinsic motivation, and story format with slow pacing. Also, concern about advertising directed towards young children is justified. Children should be educated concerning the purpose and evaluation of commercials. Schools are an appropriate place to educate children about television; suggestions have been offered (Doerken, 1983; Morrow, 1977; Singer, Singer, & Zuckerman, 1981; White & Collins, 1983; Winick & Wehrenberg, 1982).

Finally, television viewing will potentially play an important role in socialization of children, particularly with regard to development of social problems solving skills; for example, use of prosocial versus aggressive solutions. Instead of, or in addition to, attempting to influence the television industry, it behooves us to intervene at the child and family level in order to mediate the effects of TV. This mediation can take the form of interpreting content, teaching of alternative behaviors, or changing other aspects of the ecology which influence vulnerability (e.g., providing academic remediation). Thus, an ecologically based intervention approach seems optimal.

Several specific recommendations can be drawn from this research corpus. Teachers and parents should ensure that children have rich real-world experience and a participatory style of viewing. Adult mediation enhances every child's comprehension of every type of programming; for example, discussing program content before, during, and after viewing and giving feedback. Teachers should examine their intuitive beliefs about the effect of TV on young children; for example they should be aware that there is no empirical evidence that the "TV generations" have short attention spans or tend to learn visually. They should instead integrate TV viewing and other activities such as reading, possibly using the former to develop background for the latter. Additional implications include:

- *Consider not exposing children below 3 years of age to television.* Older children may benefit from limited viewing of programming especially designed for them, not to exceed 3 hours per day on the average.
- *View with children.* A co-viewing adult significantly aids children's comprehension of and learning from television. Evoke active participation through questioning, draw attention to important segments, and provide feedback. Emphasize interpretation and discussions and encourage children to express their own views in creative ways. Discuss formal features and how they are used. Ask older children to evaluate programs on criteria such as language, plot and character development, artistic style, and stereotyping.
- *Talk with children,* especially about TV plots and characters. Discuss grief and sorrow of hurt, disapprove of violence. Explain difficult words and ideas and build on concepts introduced (Honig, 1983). Discuss the consequences of behavior and motives of characters.
- *Counteract the effects of any TV violence that is viewed* through presentation of alternative social scripts, particularly for responding to conflict and frustration. Discuss the reality of TV portrayals and emphasize that violent heroes should not be imitated. A combination of cognitive and behavioral techniques designed to change interpretation and teach new

behaviors may be optimal. Provide alternative opportunities for learning social problem solving and developing social judgment; for example, through modeling, storytelling, literature or prosocial TV.
- *Provide activities that allow enactment and reconstruction of TV content.* This content should be consonant with children's experiences or used to design new experiences.
- *When using instructional TV, consider developmental level and provide supplementary activities.* For example, consider whether the content is comprehensible and the instructional strategies age-appropriate. Provide opportunities to practice the skills being taught through the medium of TV; for example, through role playing or guided practice of modeled behavior.
- *Provide opportunities to develop imaginative play and cognitive skills;* for example, through play and such preschool activities as block building, puzzles, drawing and storytelling.
- *Teach children critical TV viewing skills at school and home,* including advertising and the image of society it conveys. This may also help to facilitate mediation of content by peers or siblings. Have older children keep a TV log and discuss it objectively, encouraging children to make intelligent decisions about viewing. Create a classroom center that includes surveys of viewing patterns, children's critiques of shows, TV specials, and information such as maps and articles that provide context for televised shows.
- *Have children produce their own programs,* whether simple skits, cartoons, or videotape productions.
- *Overall, stress active viewing.*
- *Do not compete with or attempt to copy TV.* Develop instead self-expression, the ability to ask questions, and sense of wonder.
- *Educate parents in children's use of television.* Emphasize that parental sanctions and rules regarding the use of TV and discussions of programs counteract some of TV's negative effects. Remember, however, that the baby-sitting function of TV may be very attractive, so also provide alternatives, such as home-based development of creativity and problem solving, or at least the selection of programs, which could be facilitated by the availability of VCRs. Of course, many of the previous suggestions pertain to parents as well as teachers. Stress the importance of co-viewing; despite its value, research suggests that most viewing is done with siblings, peers, or alone (Lawrence & Wozniak, 1990; Tangney, 1988).

Computers

Appropriate computer programs can contribute to early childhood education. Young children use computers successfully and confidently, in balance with other activities. They prefer to control programs that are animated, problem solving–oriented, and interactive. Quality software also provides meaningful instructions, ways of responding, and feedback. It is open-ended, allowing children to create, revise, program, or invent new activities (Clements, in press-a). Girls and boys, when young, do not differ in computer use, leading to recommendations that preschool is a good time to introduce moderate, safe use of this technology.

CAI programs can be effective for reinforcing early literacy skills, though curricular integration must be considered. Perhaps more appropriate computer programs include open-ended, exploratory programs and word processors that foster verbal and written communications. Talking word processors in particular can support a constructive, process approach to composition. They provide scaffolding that helps children plan, write, discuss, and revise more frequently.

Similarly, CAI is effective for reinforcing mathematics skills, with a caveat that meaning should be established before such use. Here too, however, technological learning tools that extend learning opportunities, such as carefully planned Logo activities that supplement hands-on work, might be more efficacious in implementing recent recommendations for school reform (National Council of Teachers of Mathematics, 1989). Such activities also have the potential to develop creativity and higher-order thinking abilities.

Computers also have the potential to enhance development of social skills, perceived competence, and effectance motivation. Children seem to prefer social use of computers and find them intrinsically interesting. In addition, certain types of interactions such as those focused on collaborative problem solving and resolution of discrepant perspectives are likely to foster cognitive development. Use of alternative software programs and instructional approaches may produce different results. As they plan computer activities, teachers need to be cognizant of the environmental factors that moderate social-emotional and social-cognitive effects.

Effectiveness depends on additional factors, from the quality of the program to the duration of its use. Perhaps most important is the teaching and learning context. As with TV, computer programs should be integrated into ongoing instruction in appropriate ways. Initial adult supervision and continued adult mediation are critical. To develop higher-order thinking, teachers must provide scaffolding for and help children reflect on their computer activity. To foster independent work and peer collaboration, however, teachers need to encourage children to rely less on their assistance as children's skill improves. Though teacher education is needed in all areas of electronic media, it is perhaps more critical in the area of computer technologies. Several additional, specific recommendations follow (Clements, in press-a, provides detailed research-based recommendations, including organizing a computer environment for young children).

- *Select appropriate software.* Choosing quality software is critical. Children should be able to use the software independently after initial adult guidance. They should be in control of a fully manipulable environment that encourages them to invent new activities and offers multiple opportunities for success that should be offered. Actions and graphics should provide a meaningful context and feedback should be informative. Violent content such as that in certain video games should not be present. To encourage collaboration, choose software that can be used cooperatively and that perhaps engenders cooperation.

- *Use programs such as talking word processors to enrich children's experiences with written communication.* Introduce them in the context of a theoretically based environment featuring a process approach to writing. Use the computer screen to lend a public quality to writing and thus encourage sharing. Encourage children to use computer editing features so as to perceive text as flexible and malleable (Clements, in press-a, provides additional suggestions).

- *Challenge students with meaningful mathematics problems.* Combine the use of manipulatives with the use of software that does what textbooks and worksheets cannot do; for example, helping students connect multiple representations of mathematical ideas. Plan for children's progressive growth in the use of powerful tools such as Logo.

- *Facilitate children's use of higher-order thinking.* Use open-ended, creative programs. Actively elicit the desired thinking processes through questioning, prompting, and modeling. Encourage children to reflect on their own thinking behaviors and bring these processes to an explicit level of awareness. In general, emphasize cooperation, especially resolution of conflicts about ideas, and exploration; de-emphasize correct answers and competition.

- *Provide substantial support and guidance initially, then gradually encourage self-directed and cooperative learning.* Enhance sharing and peer teaching behaviors by choosing software such as Logo or writing programs that fosters cooperation, encouraging children to use computers in pairs, and structuring tasks so that collaboration is necessary. Once children are working independently, provide enough guidance so that do not become frustrated, but not more than they need to proceed.

- *Avoid quizzing or offering help before children request it.* Instead, prompt children to teach each other by physically placing one child in a teaching role or verbally reminding a child to explain his or her actions and respond to specific requests for help.

- *Monitor student interactions to ensure active participation of all.* Assign roles or encourage children to choose specific roles. Encourage individual accountability; for example, by emphasizing or rewarding individual contributions as well as the group outcome. Use intrinsically interesting software such as Logo.

- *Plan for critical whole group discussion sessions following computer work.* Remember that preparation and follow-up are as necessary for computer activities as they are for any other. These discussions should focus on task-related as well as social aspects of computer activities.

- *When necessary, teach and control the use of effective social interaction skills.* Placing children in pairs or groups will not guarantee successful collaboration.

- *To foster effectance motivation, structure activities so that success is likely.* Make sure children have prerequisite social and cognitive skills. Provide models of effective and confident use.

- *Use computers as a means, not an end.* Computer applications make a special contribution to children's learning and development.

Technologies can offer opportunities for constructive, creative learning environments. Used wisely, they promise opportunities for children to control their own learning. But they also present challenges. We need to understand the possibilities, the advantages, and the disadvantages of each technology, new and old. We need ecologically sound research based on specific hypotheses, for example, that define the relationship between specific uses of technology and young children's development. We need teacher education focusing on teaching and learning with TV, computers, and other media.

The child of today *will* learn about and learn from these ubiquitous technologies, whether or not teachers use them. They can be an essential aspect of a rich educational environment, if and only if a human teacher embraces them into a humanistic and constructivist vision of early childhood education.

References

Akdag, F. S. (1985). *The effects of computer programming on young children's learning*. Unpublished doctoral dissertation, Ohio State University.

Alderman, D. L., Swinton, S. S., & Braswell, J. S. (1979). Assessing basic arithmetic skills and understanding across curricula: Computer-assisted instruction and compensatory education. *Journal of Children's Mathematical Behavior, 2*, 3–28.

Alexander, D. (1983). *Children's computer drawings*. Medford, MA: Tufts University. (ERIC Document Reproduction Service No. ED 238 562).

Alexander, D. (1984). Mathematical, geometric and spatial reasoning, In E. Pitcher, E. Feinburg, & D. Alexander (Eds.), *Helping young children learn (4th ed.)*. Columbus, OH: Charles E. Merrill.

Anderson, C. C., & Maguire, T. O. (1978). The effect of TV viewing on the educational performance of elementary school children. *Alberta Journal of Educational Research, 24*, 156–163.

Anderson, D. R., Lorch, E. P., Field, D. E., & Sanders, J. (1981). The effects of TV program comprehensibility on preschool children's visual attention to television. *Child Development, 52*, 151–157.

Anderson, D. R., Lorch, E. P., Smith, R., Bradford, R., & Levin, S. R. (1981). Effects of peer presence on preschool children's television viewing behavior. *Developmental Psychology, 17*, 446–453.

Ball, S., & Bogatz, G. A. (1973). *Reading with television: An evaluation of The Electric Company (PR–74–15)*. Princeton, NJ: Educational Testing Service.

Bandura, A. (1978). Social learning theory of aggression. *Journal of Communication, 28*(3), 12–29.

Bangert-Drowns, R. L. (1989, March). *Research on wordprocessing and writing instruction*. Paper presented at the meeting of the American Educational Research Association, San Francisco.

Barker, W. F., Merryman, J. D., & Bracken, J. (1988, April). *Microcomputers, math CAI, Logo, and mathematics education in elementary school: A pilot study*. Paper presented at the meeting of the American Educational Research Association, New Orleans, LA.

Barnes, B. J., & Hill, S. (1983, May). Should young children work with microcomputers—Logo before Lego™? *Computing Teacher*, pp. 11–14.

Battista, M. T., & Clements, D. H. (1986). The effects of Logo and CAI problem-solving environments on problem-solving abilities and mathematics achievement. *Computers in Human Behavior, 2*, 183–193.

Beeson, B. S., & Williams, R. A. (1985). The effects of gender and age on preschool children's choice of the computer as a child-selected activity. *Journal of the American Society for Information Science, 36*, 339–341.

Bellow, B. P. (1987, April). *What makes a team? The composition of small groups of CAI*. Paper presented at the meeting of the American Educational Research Association, Washington, DC.

Bergin, D., Ford, M. E., & Meyer-Gaub, B. (1986, April). *Social and motivational consequences of microcomputer use in kindergarten*. Paper presented at the meeting of the American Educational Research Association, San Francisco.

Berkowitz, L. (1986). Situational influences on reactions to observed violence. *Journal of Social Issues, 42*, 93–106.

Binder, S., & Ledger, B. (1985). *Preschool computer project report*. Oakville, Ontario, Canada: Sheridan College.

Bogatz, G. A., & Ball, S. (1971). *The second year of Sesame Street: A continuing evaluation (PR–71–21; 2 vols.)*. Princeton, NJ: Educational Testing Service.

Borgh, K., & Dickson, W. P. (1986a). *The effects on children's writing of adding speech synthesis to a word processor*. Unpublished manuscript, University of Wisconsin, Madison, WI.

Borgh, K., & Dickson, W. P. (1986b). Two preschoolers sharing one microcomputer: Creating prosocial behavior with hardware and software. In P. F. Campbell & G. G. Fein (Eds.), *Young children and microcomputers* (pp. 37–44). Reston, VA: Reston Publishing.

Bowman, B. T. (1985, November). *Computers and young children*. Paper presented at the meeting of the National Association for the Education of Young Children, New Orleans.

Bradley, V. N. (1982). Improving students' writing with microcomputers. *Language Arts, 59*(7), 732–743.

Braithwaite, V., & Holman, J. (1981). Parent observed behaviors of preschool television viewers. *Australian Journal of Psychology, 33*, 375–382.

Brinkley, V. M., & Watson, J. A. (1987–88). Effects of microworld training experience on sorting tasks by young children. *Journal of Educational Technology Systems, 16*, 349–364.

Bronfenbenner, U. (1989). Ecological systems theory. In R. Vasta (Ed.), *Annals of Child Development, Vol. 6* (pp. 187–249). Greenwich, CT: JAI Press.

Bruner, J. (1986). *Actual minds, possible worlds*. Cambridge, MA: Harvard University Press.

Bryant, J., Brown, D., Parks, S. L., & Zillmann, D. (1983). Children's imitation of a ridiculed model. *Human Communication Research, 10*, 243–255.

Burns, B., & Hagerman, A. (1989). Computer experience, self-concept and problem-solving: The effects of Logo on children's ideas of themselves as learners. *Journal of Educational Computing Research, 5*, 199–212.

Busch, J. S. (1978). TV's effect on reading: A case study. *Phi Delta Kappan, 59*, 668–671.

Campbell, T. A., Wright, J. C., & Huston, A. C. (1987). Form cues and content difficulty as determinants of children's cognitive processing of televised educational messages. *Journal of Experimental Child Psychology, 43*, 311–327.

Casey, J. M. (1984, March). *Beginning reading instruction: using the LEA approach with and without micro-computer intervention*. Paper presented at the meeting of the Western Regional Reading Conference of the International Reading Association, Reno, NV.

Chambers, J. H., & Ascione, F. R. (1985, April). *The effects of prosocial and aggressive videogames on children's donating and helping*. Paper presented at the meeting of the Society for Research in Child Development, Toronto.

Char, C. A. (1989, March). *Computer graphic feltboards: New software approaches for young children's mathematical exploration.* Paper presented at the meeting of the American Educational Research Association, San Francisco.

Choat, E., & Griffin, H. (1986a). Young children, television & learning: Part I. The effects of children watching a continuous off-air broadcast. *Journal of Educational Television, 12,* 79–104.

Choat, E., & Griffin, H. (1986b). Young children, television & learning: Part II. Comparison of the effects of reading and story telling by the teacher and television story viewing. *Journal of Educational Television, 12,* 91–104.

Clements, D. H. (1983–84). Supporting young children's Logo programming. *Computing Teacher, 11*(5), 24–30.

Clements, D. H. (1984, November). Implications of media research for the instructional application of computers with young children. *Educational Technology,* pp. 7–16.

Clements, D. H. (1985). Technological advances and the young child: Television and computers. In C. S. Mcloughlin & D. F. Gullo (Eds.), *Young children in context: Impact of self, family and society on development* (pp. 218–253). Springfield, IL: Charles Thomas.

Clements, D. H. (1986a, September). Early studies on Logo and mathematics. *Logo Exchange,* pp. 27–29.

Clements, D. H. (1986b). Effects of Logo and CAI environments on cognition and creativity. *Journal of Educational Psychology, 78,* 309–318.

Clements, D. H. (1987a). Computers and literacy, In J. L. Vacca, R. T. Vacca, and M. Gove (Eds.), *Reading and learning to read* (pp. 338–372). Boston: Little, Brown.

Clements, D. H. (1987b). Computers and young children: A review of the research. *Young Children, 43*(1), 34–44.

Clements, D. H. (1987c). Longitudinal study of the effects of Logo programming on cognitive abilities and achievements. *Journal of Educational Computing Research, 3,* 73–94.

Clements, D. H. (1990). Metacomponential development in a Logo programming environment. *Journal of Educational Psychology, 82,* 141–149.

Clements, D. H. (1991a). Enhancement of creativity in computer environments. *American Educational Research Journal, 28,* 173–187.

Clements, D. H. (1991b). Current technology and the early childhood curriculum. In B. Spodek & O. N. Saracho (Eds.), *Issues in early childhood curriculum: Yearbook in early childhood education* (Vol. 2, pp. 106–131). Hillsdale, NJ: Teachers College Press.

Clements, D. H., & Battista, M. T. (1989). Learning of geometric concepts in a Logo environment. *Journal for Research in Mathematics Education, 20,* 450–467.

Clements, D. H., & Gullo, D. F. (1984). Effects of computer programming on young children's cognition. *Journal of Educational Psychology, 76,* 1051–1058.

Clements, D. H., & Mcloughlin, C. S. (1986). Computer-aided instruction in word identification: How much is enough? *Educational and Psychological Research, 6*(3), 191–205.

Clements, D. H., & Merriman, S. L. (1988). Componental developments in Logo programming environments. In R. Mayer (Ed.), *Teaching and learning computer programming: Multiple research perspectives* (pp. 13–54). Hillsdale, NJ: Erlbaum.

Clements, D. H., & Nastasi, B. K. (1985). Effects of computer environments on social-emotional development: Logo and computer-assisted instruction. *Computers in the Schools, 2*(2–3), 11–31.

Clements, D. H., & Nastasi, B. K. (1988). Social and cognitive interactions in educational computer environments. *American Educational Research Journal, 25,* 87–106.

Clements, D. H., & Nastasi, B. K. (in press). Computers and early childhood education. In T. Kratochwill, S. Elliott, & M. Gettinger (Eds.), *Advances in school psychology: Preschool and early childhood treatment directions.* Hillsdale, NJ: Erlbaum.

Coates, B., Pusser, H. E., & Goodman, I. (1976). The influence of "Sesame Street" and "Mister Rogers' Neighborhood" on children's social behavior in the preschool. *Child Development, 47,* 138–144.

Cochran-Smith, M., Kahn, J., & Paris, C. L. (1988). When word processors come into the classroom. In J. L. Hoot & S. B. Silvern (Eds.), *Writing with computers in the early grades* (pp. 43–74). New York: Teachers College Press.

Collins, W. A. (1979). Children's comprehension of television content. In E. Wartella (Ed.), *Children communicating: Media and development of thought, speech, understanding* (pp. 21–52). Beverly Hills, CA: Sage.

Collins, W. A., & Getz, S. K. (1976). Children's social responses following modeled reactions to provocation. Prosocial effects of a television drama. *Journal of Personality, 44,* 488–500.

Collins, W. A., Sobol, B. L., & Westby, S. (1981). Effects of adult commentary on children's comprehension and inferences about a televised aggressive portrayal. *Child Development, 52,* 158–163.

Comstock, G., Chaffee, S., Katzman, N., McCombs, M., & Roberts, D. (1978). *Television and human behavior.* New York: Columbia University Press.

Corcoran, F., & Schneider, M. J. (1985). Correlates of the interpretation of televised drama: A study of young children's abilities. *Early Child Development and Care, 20,* 301–313.

Corning, N., & Halapin, J. (1989, March). *Computer applications in an action-oriented kindergarten.* Paper presented at the meeting of the Connecticut Institute for Teaching and Learning Conference, Wallingfor, CN.

Cosden, M. A., Gerber, M. M., Semmel, D. S., Goldman, S. R., & Semmel, M. I. (1987). Microcomputer use with micro-educational environments. *Exceptional Children, 53,* 399–409.

Cuffaro, H. K. (1984). Microcomputers in education: Why is earlier better? *Teachers College Record, 85,* 559–568.

Cunningham, A. E., & Stanovich, K. E. (1990). Early spelling acquisition: Writing beats the computer. *Journal of Educational Psychology, 82,* 159–162.

Daiute, C. (1988). The early development of writing abilities: Two theoretical perspectives. In J. L. Hoot & S. B. Silvern (Eds.), *Writing with computers in the early grades* (pp. 10–22). New York: Teachers College Press.

Degelman, D., Free, J. U., Scarlato, M., Blackburn, J. M., & Golden, T. (1986). Concept learning in preschool children: Effects of a short-term Logo experience. *Journal of Educational Computing Research, 2*(2), 199–205.

Desmond, R. J., Hirsch, B., Singer, D. G., & Singer, J. L. (1987). Gender differences, mediation, and disciplinary styles in children's responses to television. *Sex Roles, 16,* 375–389.

Desmond, R. J., Singer, J. L., Singer, D. G., Calam, R., & Colimore, K. (1985). Family mediation patterns and television viewing: Young children's use and grasp of the medium. *Human Communication Research, 11,* 461–480.

Dickinson, D. K. (1986). Cooperation, collaboration, and a computer: Integrating a computer into a first-second grade writing program. *Research in the Teaching of English, 20,* 357–378.

Doerken, M. (1983). *Classroom combat: Teaching and television.* Englewood Cliffs, NJ: Educational Technology.

Donohue, T. R., Henke, L. L., & Meyer, T. P. (1983). Learning about television commercials: The impact of instructional units on children's perceptions of motive and intent. *Journal of Broadcasting, 27,* 251–261.

Drabman, R. S., & Thomas, M. H. (1974). Does media violence increase children's tolerance for real-life aggression? *Developmental Psychology, 10,* 418–421.

Drucker, H., Wilbur, C., & McBride, S. (1987). Using a computer-based error analysis approach to improve basic subtraction skills in the third grade. *Journal of Educational Research, 80,* 363–365.

Emihovich, C., & Miller, G. E. (1988a). Effects of Logo and CAI on black first graders' achievement, reflectivity, and self-esteem. *Elementary School Journal, 88,* 473–487.

Emihovich, C., & Miller, G. E. (1988b). Learning Logo: The social context of cognition. *Journal of Curriculum Studies, 20,* 57–70.

Emihovich, C., & Miller, G. E. (1988c). Talking to the turtle: A discourse analysis of Logo instruction. *Discourse Processes, 11,* 183–201.

Eron, L. (1986). Interventions to mitigate the psychological effects of media violence on behavior. *Journal of Social Issues, 42,* 155–169.

Eron, L. D. (1982). Parent-child interaction, television violence, and aggression of children. *American Psychologist, 37,* 197–211.

Eron, L. D., Huesmann, L. R., Brice, P., Fisher, P., & Mermelstein, R. (1983). Age trends in the development of aggression, sex typing, and related television habits. *Developmental Psychology, 19,* 71–77.

Essa, E. L. (1987). The effect of a computer on preschool children's activities. *Early Childhood Research Quarterly, 2,* 377–382.

Fein, G. G. (1985, April). *Logo instruction: A constructivist view.* Paper presented at the meeting of the American Educational Research Association, Chicago.

Feshbach, S., Feshbach, N. D., & Cohen, S. E. (1982). Enhancing children's discrimination in response to television advertising: The effects of psychoeducational training in two elementary school-age groups. *Developmental Review. 2,* 385–403.

Feshbach, S., & Singer, R. D. (1971). *Television and aggression: An experimental field study.* San Francisco: Jossey-Bass.

Field, D. E., & Anderson, D. R. (1985). Instruction and modality effects on children's television attention and comprehension. *Journal of Educational Psychology, 77,* 91–100.

Fitch, J. L., & Sims, J. L. (1990). The effects of computer managed cognitive/perceptual tasks on achievement of basic concept skills. *Journal of Computing in Childhood Education, 1*(4), 15–20.

Forman, G. (1985, April). *The child's understanding of record and replay in computer animated graphics.* Paper presented at the meeting of the American Educational Research Association, Chicago.

Forman, G. (1986a). Computer graphics as a medium for enhancing reflective thinking in young children. In J. Bishop, J. Lockhead, & D. N. Perkins (Eds.), *Thinking* (pp. 131–137). Hillsdale, NJ: Erlbaum.

Forman, G. (1986b). Observations of young children solving problems with computers and robots. *Journal of Research in Childhood Education, 1,* 60–74.

Friedman, S. G., & Hofmeister, A. M. (1984). Matching technology to content and learners: A case study. *Exceptional Children, 51,* 130–134.

Friedrich, L. K., & Stein, A. H. (1973). Aggressive and prosocial television programs and the natural behavior of preschool children. *Monographs for the Society for Research in Child Development, 38* (4, Serial No. 151).

Gadberry, S. (1980). Effects of restricting first graders' TV viewing on leisure time use, I.Q. change, and cognitive style. *Journal of Applied Developmental Psychology, 1,* 45–57.

Gélinas, C. (1986). *Educational computer activities and problem solving at the kindergarten level.* Quebec City, Quebec: Quebec Ministry of Education.

Genishi, C. (1988). Kindergartners and computers: A case study of six children. *Elementary School Journal, 89,* 184–201.

Genishi, C., McCollum, P., & Strand, E. B. (1985). Research currents: The interactional richness of children's computer use. *Language Arts, 62*(5), 526–532.

Goldman, S. R., & Rueda, R. (1988). Developing writing skills in bilingual exceptional children. *Exceptional Children, 54,* 543–551.

Goodwin, L. D., Goodwin, W. L., & Garel, M. B. (1986). Use of microcomputers with preschoolers: A review of the literature. *Early Childhood Research Quarterly, 1,* 269–286.

Goodwin, L. D., Goodwin, W. L., Nansel, A., & Helm, C. P. (1986). Cognitive and affective effects of various types of microcomputer use by preschoolers. *American Educational Research Journal, 23,* 348–356.

Gore, D. A., Morrison, G. N., Maas, M. L., & Anderson, E. A. (1989). A study of teaching reading skills to the young children using microcomputer assisted instruction. *Journal of Educational Computing Research, 5,* 179–185.

Gorn, G. J., Goldberg, M., & Kanungo, R. (1976). The role of educational television in changing the intergroup attitudes of children. *Child Development, 47,* 277–280.

Greer, D., Potts, R., Wright, J. C., & Huston, A. C. (1982). The effects of television commercial form and commercial placement on children's social behavior and attention. *Child Development, 53,* 611–619.

Griffin, W. H. (1983). Can educational technology have any significant impact on education? *T.H.E. Journal, 11*(3), 96–99.

Guddemi, M., & Mills, H. (1989). The impact of word processing and play training on literacy development. *Journal of Computing in Childhood Education, 1*(1), 29–38.

Gunter, B. (1982). Does television interfere with reading development? *Bulletin of The British Psychological Society, 35,* 232–235.

Haefner, M. J., & Wartella, E. A. (1987). Effects of sibling coviewing on children's interpretations of television programs. *Journal of Broadcasting & Electronic Media, 31,* 153–168.

Harter, S. (1978). Effectance motivation reconsidered: Toward a developmental model. *Human Development, 21,* 34–64.

Hativa, N., Swisa, S., & Lesgold, A. (1989, March). *Competition in individualized CAI.* Paper presented at the meeting of the American Educational Research Association, San Francisco.

Hawisher, G. E. (1989). Research and recommendations for computers and composition. In G. E. Hawisher & C. L. Selfe (Eds.), *Critical perspectives on computers and composition instruction* (pp. 44–69). New York: Teachers College Press.

Heap, J. L. (1987, April). *Organizational features of collaborative editing activities at a computer.* Paper presented at the meeting of the American Educational Research Association, Washington, DC.

Henderson, R. W., & Rankin, R. J. (1986). Preschooler's viewing of instructional television. *Journal of Educational Psychology, 78,* 44–51.

Henderson, R. W., Swanson, R., & Zimmerman, B. J. (1975). Training seriation responses in young children through televised modeling of hierarchically sequenced rule components. *American Educational Research Journal, 12,* 479–489.

Hess, R., & McGarvey, L. (1987). School-relevant effects of educational uses of microcomputers in kindergarten classrooms and homes. *Journal of Educational Computer Research, 3,* 269–287.

Hines, S. N. (1983, July–August). Computer programming abilities of five-year-old children. *Educational Computer Magazine,* pp. 10–12.

Hoffmann, R., & Flook, M. A. (1980). An experimental investigation of the role of television in facilitating shape recognition. *Journal of Genetic Psychology, 136,* 305–306.

Hollenbeck, A. R., & Slaby, R. G. (1982). Influence of a televised model's vocabulary pattern on infants. *Journal of Applied Developmental Psychology, 3,* 57–65.

Honig, A. S. (1983). Research in review: Television and young children. *Young Children, 38*(4), 63–76.

Hoover, J., & Austin, A. M. (1986, April). *A comparison of traditional preschool and computer play from a social/cognitive perspective.* Paper presented at the meeting of the American Educational Research Association, San Francisco, CA.

Horton, J., & Ryba, K. (1986). Assessing learning with Logo: a pilot study. *Computing Teacher, 14*(1), 24–28.

Hotard, S. R., & Cortez, M. J. (1983). *Computer-assisted instruction as an enhancer of remediation.* Lafayette, LA: Lafayette Parish.

Huesmann, L. R. (1986). Psychological processes promoting the relation between exposure to media violence and aggressive behavior by the viewer. *Journal of Social Issues, 42,* 125–139.

Huesmann, L. R., & Eron, L. D. (Eds.). (1986). *Television and the aggressive child: A cross-national comparison.* Hillsdale, NJ: Erlbaum.

Huesmann, L. R., Eron, L. D., Klein, R., Brice, P., & Fischer, P. (1983). Mitigating the imitation of aggressive behaviors by changing children's attitudes about media violence. *Journal of Personality and Social Psychology, 44,* 899–910.

Huesmann, L. R., Eron, L. D., & Yarmel, P. W. (1987). Intellectual functioning and aggression. *Journal of Personality and Social Psychology, 52,* 232–240.

Huesmann, L. R., Lagerspetz, K., & Eron, L. D. (1984). Intervening variables in the television violence-aggression relation: Evidence from two countries. *Developmental Psychology, 20,* 746–777.

Huesmann, L. R., & Malamuth, N. M. (1986). Media violence and antisocial behavior: An overview. *Journal of Social Issues, 42,* 1–6.

Hughes, M., & Macleod, H. (1986). Part II: Using Logo with very young children. In R. Lawler, B. du Boulay, M. Hughes, & H. Macleod (Eds.), *Cognition and computers: Studies in learning* (pp. 179–219). Chichester, England: Ellis Horwood.

Hungate, H. (1982, January). Computers in the kindergarten. *Computing Teachers,* pp. 15–18.

Hungate, H., & Heller, J. I. (1984, April). *Preschool children and microcomputers.* Paper presented at the meeting of the American Educational Research Association, New Orleans.

Hyson, M. C., & Morris, S. K. (1985). 'Computers? I love them!': Young children's concepts and attitudes about computers. *Early Child Development and Care, 23,* 17–29.

Johnson, J. E. (1985). Characteristics of preschoolers interested in microcomputers. *Journal of Educational Research, 78,* 299–305.

Johnson, R. T., Johnson, D. W., & Stanne, M. B. (1985). Effects of cooperative, competitive, and individualistic goal structures on computer-assisted instruction. *Journal of Educational Psychology, 77,* 668–677.

Johnson, R. T., Johnson, D. W., & Stanne, M. B. (1986). Comparison of computer-assisted cooperative, competitive, and individualistic learning. *American Educational Research Journal, 23,* 382–392.

Jones, E. E. (1987). *Sex differences in preschoolers' use of the computer?* Unpublished master's thesis, Tufts University.

King, M., & Perrin, M. (n.d.). *An investigation of children's use of microcomputers in an early childhood program.* Ohio University, Athens, OH.

Klinzing, D. G., & Hall, A. (1985, April). *A study of the behavior of children in a preschool equipped with computers.* Paper presented at the meeting of the American Educational Research Association, Chicago.

Kulik, C. C., Kulik, J., & Bangert-Drowns, R. L. (1984, April). *Effects of computer-based education of elementary school pupils.* Paper presented at the meeting of the American Educational Research Association, New Orleans, LA.

Kumpf, G. H. (1985, April). *Utilizing microcomputer capabilities in the classroom: A look at word processing, graphics and electronic communication experiences in four case studies at third grade level.* Paper presented at the meeting of the American Educational Research Association, Chicago.

Kurth, R. J. (1988, April). *Process variables in writing instruction using word processing, word processing with voice synthesis, and no word processing.* Paper presented at the meeting of the American Educational Research Association, New Orleans, LA.

Kurth, R. J., & Kurth, L. M. (1987, April). *A comparison of writing instruction using and word processing, word processing with voice synthesis, and no word processing in kindergarten and first grade.*

Paper presented at the meeting of the American Educational Research Association, Washington, DC.

Lavin, R., & Sanders, J. (1983). *Longitudinal evaluation of the CAI Computer Assisted Instruction Title 1 Project: 1979–82.* Chelmsford, MA: Merrimack Education Center.

Lawrence, F. C., & Wozniak, P. H. (1989). Children's television viewing with family members. *Psychological Reports, 65,* 395–400.

Lawrence, F. C., & Wozniak, P. H. (1990). Children's television viewing with family members. *Psychological Reports, 65,* 395–400.

Lefkowitz, M. M., Eron, L. D., Walder, L. O., & Huesmann, L. R. (1977). *Growing up to be violent: A longitudinal study of the development of aggression.* New York: Pergamo.

Lehrer, R., & deBernard, A. (1987). Language of learning and language of computing: The perceptual-language model. *Journal of Educational Psychology, 79,* 41–48.

Lehrer, R., Harckham, L. D., Archer, P., & Pruzek, R. M. (1986). Microcomputer-based instruction in special education. *Journal of Educational Computing Research, 2,* 337–355.

Lehrer, R., Levin, B. B., DeHart, P., & Comeaux, M. (1987). Voice-feedback as a scaffold for writing: A comparative study. *Journal of Educational Computing Research, 3,* 335–353.

Lehrer, R., & Randle, L. (1986). Problem solving, metacognition and composition: The effects of interactive software for first-grade children. *Journal of Educational Computing Research, 3,* 409–427.

Lehrer, R., Randle, L., & Sancilio, L. (1989). Learning pre-proof geometry with Logo. *Cognition and Instruction, 6,* 159–184.

Lehrer, R., & Smith, P. (1986a, April). *Logo learning: Is more better?* Paper presented at the meeting of the American Educational Research Association, San Francisco.

Lehrer, R., & Smith, P. C. (1986b, April). *Logo learning: Are two heads better than one?* Paper presented at the meeting of the American Educational Research Association, San Francisco.

Lesser, H. (1977). *Television and the preschool child.* New York: Academic Press.

Levin, S. R., Petros, T. V., & Petrella, F. W. (1982). Preschoolers' awareness of television advertising. *Child Development, 53,* 933–937.

Lewis, C. (1981). A study of preschool children's use of computer programs. In D. Harris & L. Nelson-Heern (Eds.), *Proceedings of the National Educational Computing Conference* (pp. 272–274). Iowa City, IA: National Educational Computing Conference.

Lieberman, D. (1985). Research on children and microcomputers: A review of utilization and effects studies. In M. Chen & W. Paisley (Eds.), *Children and microcomputers: Research on the newest medium* (pp. 59–83). Beverly Hills: Sage.

Lin, S., Vallone, R. P., & Lepper, M. R. (1985, April). *Teaching early reading skills: Can computers help?* Paper presented at the meeting of the Western Psychological Association, San Jose, CA.

Lipinski, J. M., Nida, R. E., Shade, D. D., & Watson, J. A. (1986). The effects of microcomputers on young children: An examination of free-play choices, sex differences, and social interactions. *Journal of Educational Computing Research, 2,* 147–168.

Lorch, E. P., Bellack, D. R., & Augsbach, H. (1987). Young children's memory for televised stories: Effects of importance. *Child Development, 58,* 453–463.

MacArthur, C. A., & Shneiderman, B. (1986). Learning disabled students' difficulties in learning to use a word processor: Implications for instructions and software evaluation. *Journal of Learning Disabilities, 19,* 248–253.

Marton, J. P., & Acker, L. E. (1981). Television provoked aggression: Effects of gentle, affection-like training prior to exposure. *Child Study Journal, 12,* 27–43.

McCollister, T. S., Burts, D. C., Wright, V. L., & Hildreth, G. J. (1986). Effects of computer-assisted instruction and teacher-assisted instruction on arithmetic task achievement scores of kindergarten children. *Journal of Educational Research, 80,* 121–125.

McConnell, B. B. (1983). *Evaluation of computer instruction in math. Pasco School District. Final Report.* Pasco, WA: Pasco School District 1.

McCormick, L. (1987). Comparison of the effects of a microcomputer activity and toy play on social and communication behaviors of young children. *Journal of the Division for Early Childhood, 11,* 195–205.

Meltzoff, A. N. (1988). Imitation of televised models by infants. *Child Development, 59,* 1221–1229.

Mevarech, Z. R. (1985). Computer-assisted instructional methods: A factorial study within mathematics disadvantaged classrooms. *Journal of Experimental Education, 54,* 22–27.

Mevarech, Z. R., & Rich, Y. (1985). Effects of computer-assisted mathematics instruction on disadvantaged pupils' cognitive and affective development. *Journal of Educational Research, 79,* 5–11.

Meyers, L. F. (1984). Unique contributions of microcomputers to language intervention with handicapped children. *Seminars in Speech and Language, 5,* 23–34.

Miller, G. E., & Emihovich, C. (1986). The effects of mediated programming instruction on preschool children's self-monitoring. *Journal of Educational Computing Research, 2*(3), 283–297.

Minton, J. H. (1975). The impact of Sesame Street on readiness. *Sociology of Education, 48*(2), 141–151.

Morrow, J. (1977). *Media & Kids: Real-world learning in the schools.* Rochelle Park, NJ: Hayden Book Co.

Morrow, L. M. (1983). Home and school correlates of early interest in literature. *Journal of Educational Research, 76,* 221–230.

Moxley, R. A., & Barry, P. A. (1985). Spelling with LEA on the microcomputer. *The Reading Teacher, 39,* 267–273.

Muhlstein, E. A., & Croft, D. J. (1986). *Using the microcomputer to enhance language experiences and the development of cooperative play among preschool children.* Cupertino, CA: De Anza College.

Muller, A. A., & Perlmutter, M. (1985). Preschool children's problem-solving interactions at computers and jigsaw puzzles. *Journal of Applied Developmental Psychology, 6,* 173–186.

Murray, J. P. (1980). *Television & youth: 25 years of research and controversy.* Boys Town, NE: The Boys Town Center for the Study of Young Development.

Nastasi, B. K., & Clements, D. H. (1990a, August). *Metacomponential functioning in young children.* Paper presented at the meeting of the American Psychological Association, Boston.

Nastasi, B. K., & Clements, D. H. (1990b). Social-cognitive behaviors and higher-order thinking in educational computer environments. Manuscript submitted for publication.

Nastasi, B. K., & Clements, D. H. (1991). Research on cooperative learning: Implications for practice. *School Psychology Review, 20,* 110–131.

Nastasi, B. K., Clements, D. H., & Battista, M. T. (1990). Social-cognitive interactions, motivation, and cognitive growth in Logo programming and CAI problem-solving environments. *Journal of Educational Psychology, 82,* 150–158.

National Council of Teachers of Mathematics. (1989). *Curriculum and evaluation standards for school mathematics.* Reston, VA: Author.

Nelson, K. (1973). Structure and strategy in learning to talk. *Monographs of the Society for Research in Child Development, 38*(1–2, Serial No. 149).

Neuman, S. B., & Prowda, P. (1982). Television viewing and reading achievement. *Journal of Reading, 25,* 666–670.

Niemiec, R. P., & Walberg, H. J. (1984). Computers and achievement in the elementary schools. *Journal of Educational Computing Research, 1,* 435–440.

Norton, P., & Resta, V. (1986). Investigating the impact of computer instruction on elementary students' reading achievement. *Educational Technology, 26*(3), 35–41.

Olson, J. K. (1988, August). *Microcomputers make manipulatives meaningful.* Paper presented at the meeting of the International Congress of Mathematics Education, Budapest, Hungary.

Papert, S. (1980). *Mindstorms: Children, computers, and powerful ideas.* New York, Basic Books.

Paris, C. L., & Morris, S. K. (1985, March). *The computer in the early childhood classroom: Peer helping and peer teaching.* Paper presented at the meeting of the Microworld for Young Children Conference, College Park, MD.

Parke, R. D., & Slaby, R. G. (1983). The development of aggression. In P. H. Mussen (Ed.), *Handbook of child psychology* (4th ed.) (pp. 547–642). New York: Wiley.

Parker, J. (1984). *Some disturbing data: Sex differences in computer use.* Paper presented at the meeting of the National Educational Computing Conference, Dayton, OH.

Perlman, R. (1976). *Using computer technology to provide a creative learning environment for preschool children. AI Memo 360.* Cambridge, MA: MIT.

Perlmutter, M., Behrend, S., Kuo, F., & Muller, A. (1986). *Social influence on children's problem solving at a computer.* Unpublished manuscript, University of Michigan, Ann Arbor.

Pezdek, K., & Hartman, E. F. (1983). Children's television viewing: Attention and comprehension of auditory versus visual information. *Child Development, 54,* 1015–1023.

Phenix, J., & Hannan, E. (1984). Word processing in the grade one classroom. *Language Arts, 61,* 804–812.

Picard, A. J., & Giuli, C. (1985). *Computers as a free-time activity in grades K–4: A two year study of attitudes and usage.* Unpublished manuscript, University of Hawaii, Honolulu, HI.

Piestrup, A. M. (1981). *Preschool children use Apple II to test reading skills program.* Portola Valley, CA: Advanced Learning Technology.

Pingree, S. (1986). Children's activity and television comprehensibility. *Communication Research, 13,* 239–256.

Poche, C., Yoder, P., & Miltenberger, R. (1988). Teaching self-protection to children using television techniques. *Journal of Applied Behavior Analysis, 21,* 253–261.

Prinz, P. M., Nelson, K., & Stedt, J. (1982). Early reading in young deaf children using microcomputer technology. *American Annals of the Deaf, 127,* 529–535.

Raeissi, P., & Wright, J. C. (1983, April). *Training and generalization of number conversation by television for preschoolers.* Paper presented at the meeting of the Society for Research in Child Development, Detroit, MI.

Ragosta, M., Holland, P., & Jamison, D. T. (1981). *Computer-assisted instruction and compensatory education: The ETS/LAUSD study.* Princeton, NJ: Educational Testing Service.

Reimer, G. (1985). Effects of a Logo computer programming experience on readiness for first grade, creativity, and self concept. "A pilot study in kindergarten". *AEDS Monitor, 23*(7-8), 8–12.

Reinking, D., & Wu, J.-H. (1990). Reexamining the research on television and reading. *Reading Research and Instruction, 29*(2), 30–43.

Reiser, R. A., Tessmer, M. A., & Phelps, P. C. (1984). Adult-child interaction in children's learning from "Sesame Street". *Educational Communication and Technology, 32,* 217–223.

Rice, M. L. (1984). The words of children's television. *Journal of Broadcasting, 28,* 445–461.

Riding, R. J., & Powell, S. D. (1987). The effect on reasoning, reading and number performance of computer-presented critical thinking activities in 5-year-old children. *Educational Psychology, 7,* 55–65.

Riding, R. J., & Tite, H. C. (1985). The use of computer graphics to facilitate story telling in young children. *Educational Studies, 11,* 203–210.

Ridley-Johnson, R., Cooper, H., & Chance, J. (1983). The relation of children's television viewing to school achievement and I.Q. *Journal of Educational Research, 76,* 294–297.

Riel, M. (1985). The Computer Chronicles Newswire: A functional learning environment for acquiring literacy skills. *Journal of Educational Computing Research, 1,* 317–337.

Robinson, M. A., Feldman, P., & Uhlig, G. E. (1987). The effects of Logo in the elementary classroom: An analysis of selected recent dissertation research. *Education, 107,* 434–442.

Robinson, M. A., Gilley, W. F., & Uhlig, G. E. (1988). The effects of guided discovery Logo on SAT performance of first grade students. *Education, 109,* 226–230.

Robinson, M. A., & Uhlig, G. E. (1988). The effects of guided discovery Logo instruction on mathematical readiness and visual motor development in first grade students. *Journal of Human Behavior and Learning, 5,* 1–13.

Roblyer, M. D., Castine, W. H., & King, F. J. (1988). *Assessing the impact of computer-based instruction: A review of recent research.* New York: Haworth Press.

Rogosa, D. (1980). A critique of cross-lagged correlation. *Psychological Bulletin, 88,* 245–258.

Rosengrant, T. J. (1986). Using the microcomputer as a scaffold for assisting beginning readers and writers. In J. Hoot (Ed.), *Computers in early childhood education: Issues and practices* (pp. 128–143). Englewood Cliffs, NJ: Prentice Hall.

Rosengrant, T. J. (1988). Talking word processors for the early grades. In J. L. Hoot & S. B. Silvern (Eds.), *Writing with computers in the early grades* (pp. 143–159). New York: Teachers College Press.

Rosengren, K. S., Gross, D., Abrams, A. F., & Perlmutter, M. (1985, September). *An observational study of preschool children's computing activity.* Paper presented at the meeting of the "Perspectives on the Young Child and the Computer" conference, University of Texas at Austin.

Rule, B. G., & Ferguson, T. J. (1986). The effects of media violence on attitudes, emotions, and cognitions. *Journal of Social Issues, 42,* 29–50.

Salomon, G., & Gardner, H. (1986). The computer as educator: Lessons from television research. *Educational Researcher, 15,* 13–19.

Shade, D. D., Nida, R. E., Lipinski, J. M., & Watson, J. A. (1986). Microcomputers and preschoolers: Working together in a classroom setting. *Computers in the Schools, 3,* 53–61.

Sherman, J., Divine, K. P., & Johnson, B. (1985, May). An analysis of computer software preferences of preschool children. *Educational Technology,* pp. 39–41.

Shrock, S. A., Matthias, M., Anastasoff, J., Vensel, C., & Shaw, S. (1985, January). *Examining the effects of the microcomputer on a real world class: A naturalistic study.* Paper presented at the meeting of the Association for Educational Communications and Technology, Anaheim, CA.

Siegel, M. A., & Misselt, A. L. (1984). Adaptive feedback and review paradigm for computer-based drills. *Journal of Educational Psychology, 76,* 310–317.

Silfen, R., & Howes, A. C., (1984). A summer reading program with CAI: An evaluation. *Computers, Reading and Language Arts, 1*(4), 20–22.

Silvern, S. B., Countermine, T. A., & Williamson, P. A. (1988). Young children's interaction with a microcomputer. *Early Childhood Development and Care, 32,* 23–35.

Silvern, S. B., & Williamson, P. A. (1987). Aggression in young children and video game play. *Applied Developmental Psychology, 8,* 453–462.

Singer, D. G., & Singer, J. L. (in press). Television and the young child. In L. R. Williams & D. P. Fromberg (Eds.), *Encyclopedia of Early Childhood Education.* New York: Garland.

Singer, D. G., Singer, J. L., & Zuckerman, D. M. (1981). *Teaching television.* New York: The Dial Press.

Singer, J. L., & Singer, D. G. (1981). *Television, imagination, and aggression: A study of preschoolers.* Hillsdale, NJ: Erlbaum.

Singer, J. L., & Singer, D. G. (1983). Psychologists look at television: Cognitive, developmental, personality, and social policy implications. *American Psychologist, 38,* 826–834.

Singer, J. L., & Singer, D. G. (1986). Family experiences and television viewing as predictors of children's imagination, restlessness, and aggression. *Journal of Social Issues, 42,* 107–124.

Sivin, J. P., Lee, P. C., & Vollmer, A. M. (1985, April). *Introductory computer experiences with commercially-available software: Differences between 3-year-olds and 5-year-olds.* Paper presented at the meeting of the American Educational Research Association, Chicago, IL.

Skeen, P., Brown, M. H., & Osborn, D. K. (1982). Young children's perception of "real" and "pretend" on television. *Perceptual and Motor Skills, 54,* 883–887.

Slavenas, R. (1987). Young children's preference for television viewing compared with other activities. *Illinois School Journal, 66,* 39–47.

Smith, R., Anderson, D. R., & Fischer, C. (1985). Young children's comprehension of montage. *Child Development, 56,* 962–971.

Smithy-Willis, D., Riley, M., & Smith, D. (1982, November/December). Visual discrimination and preschoolers. *Educational Computer Magazine,* pp. 19–20.

Sprafkin, J. N., Liebert, R. M., & Poulos, R. W. (1975). Effects of a prosocial televised example on children's helping. *Journal of Experimental Child Psychology, 20,* 119–126.

Sprigle, J. E., & Schaefer, L. (1984). Age, gender, and spatial knowledge influences on preschoolers' computer programming ability. *Early Child Development and Care, 14,* 243–250.

Stoneman, Z., & Brody, G. H. (1983). Immediate and long-term recognition and generalization of advertised products as a function of age and presentation mode. *Developmental Psychology, 19,* 56–61.

Strand, E. B. (1987, April). *Observations of preschoolers' problem-solving experiences with Logo.* Paper presented at the meeting of the American Educational Research Association, Washington, DC.

Sudia, D. (1985). *The computer's effect on the learning of new words.* Unpublished master's thesis, Kean College of New Jersey.

Swigger, K., & Campbell, J. (1981). Computers and the nursery school. In D. Harris & L. Nelson-Heern (Eds.), *Proceedings of the National Educational Computing Conference* (pp. 264–268). Iowa City, IA: National Educational Computing Conference.

Swigger, K. M., Campbell, J., & Swigger, B. K. (1983, January/February). Preschool children's preferences of different types of CAI programs. *Educational Computer Magazine,* pp. 38–40.

Swigger, K. M., & Swigger, B. K. (1984). Social patterns and computer use among preschool children. *AEDS Journal, 17,* 35–41.

Tan, L. E. (1985). Computers in pre-school education. *Early Child Development and Care, 19,* 319–336.

Tangney, J. P. (1988). Aspects of the family and children's television viewing content preferences. *Child Development, 59,* 1070–1079.

Teague, G. V., Wilson, R. M., & Teague, M. G. (1984). Use of computer assisted instruction to improve spelling proficiency of low achieving first graders. *AEDS Journal, 17,* 30–35.

Thomas, M. H., & Drabman, R. S. (1975). Toleration for real-life aggression as a function of exposure to televised violence and age of subject. *Merrill-Palmer Quarterly, 21,* 227–232.

Thomas, M. H., Horton, R. W., Lippincott, E. C., & Drabman, R. S. (1977). Desensitization to portrayal of real-life aggression as a function of exposure to television violence. *Journal of Personality and Social Psychology, 35,* 450–458.

Turner, C. W., Hesse, B. W., & Peterson-Lewis, S. (1986). Naturalistic studies of the long-term effects of television violence. *Journal of Social Issues, 42,* 51–73.

Vaidya, S., & Mckeeby, J. (1984, September). Computer turtle graphics: Do they affect children's thought processes? *Educational Technology,* pp. 46–47.

VanLehn, K. (1981). *Bugs are not enough: Empirical studies of bugs, impasses and repairs in procedural skills*. Palo Alto, CA: Xerox Palo Alto Research Center.

vonStein, J. H. (1982). An evaluation of the microcomputer as a facilitator of indirect learning for the kindergarten child. *Dissertation Abstractions International, 43*, 72A. (University Microfilms No. DA8214463).

Vygotsky, L. S. (1978). Internalization of higher psychological functions. In M. Cole, V. John-Steiner, S. Scribner, & E. Souberman (Eds.), *Mind in society*. Cambridge, MA: Harvard University Press.

Warash, B. G. (1984, April). *Computer language experience approach*. Paper presented at the meeting of the National Council of Teachers of English Spring Conference, Columbus, OH.

Wartella, E., & Reeves, B. (1983, June). Recurring issues in research on children and media. *Educational Technology*, pp. 5–9.

Watkins, B., Calvert, S., Huston-Stein, A., & Wright, J. C. (1980). Children's recall of television material: Effects of presentation mode and adult labeling. *Developmental Psychology, 16*, 672–674.

Watkins, L. T., Sprafkin, J., Gadow, K. D., & Sadetsky, I. (1988). Effects of a critical viewing skills curriculum on elementary school children's knowledge and attitudes about television. *Journal of Educational Research, 81*, 165–170.

Watkins, M. W., & Abram, S. (1985, April). Reading CAI with first grade students. *Computing Teacher*, pp. 43–45.

Watson, J. A., Chadwick, S. S., & Brinkley, V. M. (1986). Special education technologies for young children: Present and future learning scenarios with related research literature. *Journal of the Division for Early Childhood, 10*, 197–208.

White, K. B., & Collins, R. W. (1983). An experimental investigation utilizing the computer as a tool for stimulating reasoning abilities. *AEDS Journal, 16*, 234–243.

Williams, P. A., Haertel, E. H., Haertel, G. D., & Walberg, H. J. (1982). The impact of leisure-time television on school learning: A research synthesis. *American Educational Research Journal, 19*, 19–50.

Williams, R. A., & Beeson, B. S. (1986-87). The "holding power" of the computers: A study of young children's computer time. *Teacher Educator, 23*(3), 8–14.

Winick, M. P., & Wehrenberg, J. S. (1982). *Children and TV II: Mediating the medium*. Washington, DC: Association for Childhood Education International.

Worden, P. E., Kee, D. W., & Ingle, M. J. (1987). Parental teaching strategies with preschoolers: A comparison of mothers and fathers within different alphabet tasks. *Contemporary Educational Psychology, 12*, 95–109.

Wright, J. C., & Huston, A. C. (1983). A matter of form: Potentials of television for young viewers. *American Psychologist, 38*, 835–843.

Wright, J. C., Huston, A. C., Ross, R. P., Calvert, S. L., Rolandelli, D., Weeks, L. A., Raeissi, P., & Potts, R. (1984). Pace and continuity of television programs: Effects on children's attention and comprehension. *Developmental Psychology, 20*, 653–666.

Wright, J. L., & Samaras, A. S. (1986). Play worlds and microworlds. In P. F. Campbell & G. G. Fein (Eds.), *Young children and microcomputers* (pp. 73–86). Reston, VA: Reston Publishing.

Zillman, D. (1979). *Hostility and aggression*. Hillsdale, NJ: Erlbaum.

Zillman, D. (1982). Anatomy of suspense. In P. H. Tannenbaum (Ed.), *The entertainment functions of television* (pp. 133–164). Hillsdale, NJ: Erlbaum.

Part

·III·

FOUNDATIONS OF
EARLY CHILDHOOD
EDUCATIONAL POLICY

·18·

TESTING, TRACKING, AND RETAINING YOUNG CHILDREN: AN ANALYSIS OF RESEARCH AND SOCIAL POLICY

Samuel J. Meisels, Dorothy M. Steele, and Kathleen Quinn-Leering

THE UNIVERSITY OF MICHIGAN

Testing of school children has expanded dramatically during the past decade. The number of students taking the SAT has increased by more than 15 percent, and nearly every state has translated its concerns for student achievement into formalized competency testing since the 1983 publication of "Children at Risk" by the U.S. Department of Education.

The drive for accountability has had a major impact on young children as well. In many school districts 5- and 6-year-olds are expected to pass entry examinations before beginning kindergarten or first grade. Children who are judged "not ready" are retained in grade or placed in extra-year programs before kindergarten or first grade.

The rise in early childhood testing has been accompanied by changes in the curriculum, changes controlled by teachers' and administrators' perceptions of what children must learn in order to do well on the standardized tests they will encounter later in elementary school. As is the case with teachers of older students, kindergarten or first grade teachers experience pressure for their students to be successful on these tests and many of them alter their curricula to reflect the content of the tests. This situation results in a host of problems, including downward extension of academic curricula, rigidified content, homogeneous approaches to teaching, early tracking, and a reification of the concept of "readiness."

Many professionals are convinced that more testing, tracking, and retentions are taking place in the early years of school than ever before, and that developmentally inappropriate modifications to curricula are being implemented. Furthermore, the inappropriate use of standardized tests has resulted in disproportionate numbers of poor and minority children being retained or placed in extra-year programs.

The suggestion that large numbers of children entering public kindergarten may fail, or may not be prepared to benefit from the regular classroom program, is a cause for great concern. This chapter will explore this issue and others mentioned above. Recommendations will be made concerning future uses of assessment data and the development of alternatives to conventional testing practices.

TESTING, TRACKING, AND RETENTION: BACKGROUND AND ISSUES

Most educators are extremely ambivalent about standardized tests. They love them, and they hate them; they adopt them, and they reject them; they need them, and they do not understand them. However, whenever a new trend in education emerges, a national commission reports its recommendations, or a novel idea is introduced, standardized tests are usually mentioned as the preferred means of measurement, implementation, or evaluation.

Today we are witnessing an increasing commitment on the part of public schools to serve 4- and 5-year-old children. Recent reports estimate that more than half of the states have

This chapter is based in part on material published in Meisels (1986, 1987a, 1989a, 1989b). An earlier version was originally commissioned by the National Center for Education Statistics, Office of Education Research and Improvement, U.S. Department of Education.

enacted legislation providing for some form of early childhood education, and about one-quarter of the country's 15,000 school districts are offering formal instruction of some kind to 4-year-olds. Accompanying this rapid growth in early childhood programs is an inevitable controversy about testing.

It is becoming apparent that early childhood curricula are undergoing change and that standardized tests are either contributing to this change or are at least reinforcing it. Early childhood programs are focusing increasingly on narrowly construed academic objectives, behavioral compliance, abstract thinking, and one-dimensional teaching methods. Never before have we witnessed such a "downward extension" of traditional early elementary curriculum goals and methods into programs for 4- and 5-year-olds (see Shepard & Smith, 1988). While early childhood programs have become more rigid, predictable, subject-matter oriented, and linear, they have also become more amenable to standardized testing. Indeed, academically oriented early childhood curricula and group-administered standardized tests are a marriage made in heaven. Previously, when teachers and professionals were seeking to test and evaluate children in child-centered programs based on individuality goals, discovery learning, and extensive opportunities for children's initiation and activity in the classroom, standardized tests were seen as a poor fit and were criticized as irrelevant and unhelpful (see Bryk, Meisels, & Markowitz, 1979; Carini, 1975; Hein, 1979). But today testing has become much more prevalent in public schools generally and in kindergarten programs in particular. For example, a recent survey of more than 300 school districts in Michigan reported that 83 percent of the districts annually test all children who are eligible for kindergarten (Riley et al., 1988). Reports indicate that more than half of the states require pre-kindergarten screening in compliance with Public Law 94–142 (Meisels, Harbin, Modigliani, & Olson, 1988), while testing of other kinds occurs in three-fourths of the states before children enter first grade (E. Fiske, 1988; Gnezda & Bolig, 1988).

The trend toward increased use of standardized testing with kindergarten and elementary school children has been well-documented in the press. During one 4-month period in 1988 the *Boston Globe* published an article entitled, "Fears for a son going into a test-crazy world" (Yagelski, 1988), *Time* ran a story called, "Can Kids Flunk Kindergarten?" (Bowen, 1988), and the *New York Times* devoted 5 pages in their Spring Education supplement to "America's Test Mania" (E. Fiske, 1988). All of this attention is not simply a recent phenomenon. Madaus (1988) reports that, as measured by column inches in *Education Index* (a widely used index of publications relating to educational issues), "attention devoted to testing has increased ten-fold in the last fifty years, rising from only 10 to 30 column inches in the 1930s and 1940s to well over 300 inches in the 1980s" (p. 84). Shepard (1989) has also commented on the rise in testing, saying that it is "running amok" in our nation's schools.

In addition to testing, changes in early childhood curricula have also received widespread attention in the press. The *Wall Street Journal* suggests that you should "check out your neighborhood school. Reading, arithmetic and computers are fast replacing playtime in kindergarten. The four-to-six set spends more hours at desks, faces more rigorous tests and sits behind more computer screens that ever. It's even possible now to flunk kindergarten in places such as Minneapolis and Georgia" (Putka, 1988). Similar reports have been published in other newspapers, ranging from Boston ("Yesterday's kindergarten program is now considered right for kindergarten" [Coons, 1987]) to Marin County, CA ("Kindergarten isn't child's play anymore"[Cahil, 1988]), and from New York ("More than three million children are starting kindergarten this month, and for many it will be the first opportunity to fail" [Hechinger, 1988]) to Riverside, CA ("possibly a fourth of the kindergarten population is not ready for an academic push" [J. Fiske, 1988]). The notion that nearly 1 in every 4 children entering public kindergarten may fail or may not be prepared to benefit from the regular classroom program is startling. No evidence has been presented to support the large-scale policy of retention/extra-year placement. Indeed, the available data indicates without exception that retention is a policy that has negative effects on children (Bredekamp & Shepard, 1989; Charlesworth, 1989; Holmes & Matthews, 1984; Shepard & Smith, 1986, 1987; Smith & Shepard, 1987). Either we are witnessing a population shift of immense proportions, or we are experiencing a vast alteration in education policy—aided and abetted by the inappropriate use of standardized tests. This chapter presents documentation that schools have changed, not children. Further, tests have contributed heavily to the shape and rationale for this change.

Why Schools Have Changed

One of the major sources of change in contemporary education is the pressure for accountability. The series of national reports that began with the National Commission on Excellence in Education's *Nation at Risk* (1983) called for standardized tests to be administered at all levels of schooling. The purpose of the tests was both to identify the need for remedial instruction and to "certify the student's credentials" (p. 28). It is only a short step from this statement to the assumption that tests can be used to evaluate not only the student's learning but also the quality of the student's program and teacher.

In fact, an "accountability culture" has begun to emerge in our schools (Shepard & Smith, 1988). The pressure for teachers at one grade level to be held accountable, as measured by standardized tests, has resulted in an "academic trickle-down" process that has had a major impact on teachers in earlier grades (Cunningham, 1988). "As third grade teachers experience pressure for their children to perform well on standardized tests, they in turn put pressure on the second and first grade teachers to prepare their children for the 'demands of the third grade curriculum'" (*op. cit.,* pp. 24–25). Teachers' decisions about curriculum are thus influenced by a need for their students to perform well in the next grade level, a need that originates in part with the standards of accountability that are implied by standardized tests. In other words, teachers are very likely to shape their curriculum around a test's specific focus (see Darling-Hammond & Wise, 1985). This phenomenon, known as "measurement-driven instruction" (Madaus, 1988, p. 84), transforms testing programs, which should be the servants of educational programs, into masters of the educational process. This results in a narrowing of the curriculum, a concentration on those skills most amenable to testing, a constraint on the creativity and flexibility of teachers, and a demeaning of teachers' professional judgment.

Cross-National Studies

Research by Engel (1989) indicates that the controversy surrounding practices in early education are by no means limited to the United States. Engel looked at the following issues: age at school entry, measuring school readiness, ability grouping, kindergarten retention practices, and kindergarten curriculum in 8 industrialized nations (the former Soviet Union, Switzerland, the former West Germany, Sweden, England, New Zealand, Australia, and Japan). Although the study did not present a comprehensive picture of these practices in the 8 nations, the results of the research provide an interesting perspective from which to view these practices in the United States.

The age at which children enter school ranges from 4 (Britain and Australia) to 7 years (Sweden). Differences in performance between the older and younger children entering school were found in all the countries regardless of entry age, but these differences seem to disappear by about third grade. Interestingly, the entry age in the different nations has more to do with historical, political, and climatic reasons than with an educational rationale. Six of the countries studied by Engel (1989) reported that ability grouping in the early grades does not occur. Only New Zealand and England practice ability grouping, but in New Zealand the teachers form fluid groups based on observations of children, and in Britain the use of ability grouping has recently become less popular. None of the countries reported using standardized tests to group children.

Retention in kindergarten is viewed differently in the eight nations. For example, in both Japan and Russia grade promotion is automatic. The same is generally true for Australia. Germany reports a retention rate between 5% and 10% although in Switzerland the retention rate is quite high (in one canton [district] it is 33%), but this policy is being reconsidered. Further, the curriculum of the kindergarten seems to be a source of debate in some of the nations. In England, Russia, and Japan, for example, there is a growing concern that kindergarten, or entry-level classes, is becoming too academic.

The use of testing in kindergarten to measure school readiness, although not required by any of the eight governments, does take place, but the purpose varies by country. For example, Russia opposes the use of testing for any purpose but evaluating children who might be handicapped. The Swiss education laws are generally interpreted as stating that testing should be used to identify children with handicaps, but some interpret the law to mean that tests should also be used to indicate children's readiness for school, and tests are often used in this manner. In Sweden, the most widely used school readiness test, "Hostproven," which has little data supporting its validity, is used for diagnosis and curriculum planning at the beginning of the year. Switzerland, Germany, and England all have a number of tests that are often used to assess school readiness. Entry into

private and national public schools in Japan (1 percent of the elementary schools) requires that children take examinations. School readiness checklists, rather than standardized tests, are used in Japan and are also used in Australia and New Zealand. Although it is evident that tests are commonly used in these countries, general opposition to the use of standardized tests with very young children was reported in all but 2 of the countries studied.

Summary

At this point, 3 caveats must be raised about testing young children in American schools. First, the demographic changes in our society, particularly the changes in the composition of the workforce in the past generation that have resulted in more and more mothers of young children returning to work, have brought about an expansion in out-of-home care for young children. Children are entering kindergarten with two or more years of preschool or day care experience and have had exposure to school-related tasks and routines. Although this means that kindergarten-age children may "know" more and may even be somewhat more advanced developmentally, it does not follow that they are able to profit from modes and materials of instructions that are appropriate for children who are chronologically and developmentally a year or more older.

Second, schools may be pressured to adjust their curricula in order to meet standards of accountability, but these standards are typically driven by societal forces. Parents, school boards, legislatures, and governmental commissions all exert authority over the process and product of schooling. Ultimately, test manufacturers develop tests that reflect the priorities of these individuals and sociopolitical forces. But it remains the responsibility of professional educators to inform society about the best practices and most optimal objectives for children. Unfortunately, strong dissenting opinions have not stemmed the misuse of standardized tests—even when these voices have carried the imprimatur of the National Association for the Education of Young Children (1988), the National Association of Early Childhood Specialists in State Departments of Education (1987), and the National Association of State Boards of Education (1988). All 3 of these organizations have produced position statements calling for a more rational use of tests in early childhood. Related statements have been written by national organizations of school psychologists, elementary principals, and pediatricians.

Finally, not all tests are bad for kids. It is easy to be a "test basher." It is considerably more difficult to understand the complexities of psychometric research and the importance of selecting the right test for the right child at the right time. Specifically, reliable and valid developmental screening tests, when administered to individual children by trained testers, can be used to identify children who are at high risk for school failure (see Meisels, 1988, 1989a, 1989b, 1989c; Meisels & Wasik, 1990). Children so identified would move on to a more comprehensive diagnostic process to determine conclusively the nature of their problems and, subsequently, to obtain appropriate interventions. Developmental screening tests and school readiness tests differ from one another. As described later in this chapter, significant problems are introduced when their purposes and procedures are confused. The problem is not tests *per se,* but the inappropriate use of tests in specific situations by specific individuals.

HIGH-STAKES TESTING

The kinds of tests that have created a crisis in public early childhood education are readiness or achievement tests that are used for classifications, retention, or promotion. Tests used in this manner can be described as *high-stakes tests:* "those whose results are seen—rightly or wrongly—by students, teachers, administrators, parents, or the general public as being used to make important decisions that immediately and directly affect them" (Madaus, 1988, p. 87). The high-stakes decisions that flow from such tests concern retention, promotion, placement in prekindergarten or pre–first grade programs, evaluation and rewards for teachers or administrators, and allocation of resources to specific schools or school districts. Three specific characteristics of high-stakes tests that have been analyzed previously (Meisels, 1989a) will be described.

Perceptions

High-stakes tests often achieve a life of their own, in which the tests' original purposes are blurred and their results begin to assume greater importance than ever imagined by those who proposed them. The SAT is the best example of this phenomenon, in which a test that was intended to provide supplementary information to assist in decisions regarding college admission has not only become an absolute criterion for admissions decisions in many cases, but has become a barometer of the entire nation's educational progress. Similarly, when actions are taken that have an impact on the results of high-stakes testing, e.g., instituting a preparatory course designed to boost SAT scores, it is assumed that the underlying skills and abilities measured by the test have been changed, rather than that test-taking skills were improved. As Madaus (1988) puts it, "People fail to distinguish between the skill or trait itself and a secondary, fallible indicator or sign of them" (p. 90).

Instruction

The corollary to this is that high-stakes tests have a major influence on teachers' behavior and on their instructional decisions. It is virtually a maxim of American educational research and practice that a teacher's perceptions of a child can be heavily influenced by the child's race, sex, and socioeconomic status, and by quantitative measures that purport to assess the child's potential (see Brophy, 1983). If we manipulate any of these variables we are likely to alter teachers' attitudes and behavior toward their pupils. In a similar manner, teachers' instructional decisions can be affected by the tests they use. If teachers know that their pupils will be tested on certain skills or certain subject areas, and if the results of the examination are to be made public, it is very likely that the teacher's

curriculum will reflect these test-specific characteristics. This is an example of measurement-driven instruction, a concept mentioned earlier. High-stakes achievement tests invariably narrow instruction and learning, focusing the curriculum on the content that will be included on a test (see Koretz, 1988).

Decision-Making

Another characteristic of high-stakes testing is that these tests transfer control over the curriculum to the agency that sets or controls the exam (Madaus, 1988). Given the previous statements about the potential effects of using high-stakes tests, it is clear that test developers have a powerful role in shaping instructional and other educational decisions. In high schools and colleges one can assume at least some consensus about content. However, in early childhood, no such consensus exists. For example, there are many ways to learn to read. A test that focuses on children's knowledge of sight words may overlook their ability to decode, use phonic skills, or engage in activities associated with emergent literacy programs (see Teale & Sulzby, 1986). Yet, if a school district adopts a test that reflects a particular approach to reading, teachers may feel enjoined to teach that approach. Hence, educational decision-making is removed from the arena of teacher-child interaction and is supplanted by the instructional approach implicit in the high-stakes test that has been selected for the school or the district.

This situation raises the concerns of many parents, professionals, and policymakers. Yet the tide of expanded testing keeps rising, and the implications of making educational decisions based on many of these tests becomes increasingly alarming.

Examples of High-Stakes Testing in Kindergarten

Many examples of tests that have achieved high-stakes status in early childhood programs can be presented. Three specific tests and a state testing program will be reviewed briefly in order to illustrate the impact of high-stakes testing in the early childhood years.

The Gesell School Readiness Tests. Madaus (1988) suggests that the power of high-stakes testing is "a perceptual phenomenon: if students, teachers, or administrators believe that the results of an examination are important, it matters very little whether this is really true or false—the effect is produced by what individuals perceive to be the case" (p. 88). This principle is clearly embodied in the widespread adoption of the Gesell School Readiness Test (Haines, Ames, & Gillespie, 1980). The problems with the Gesell are extensive and have been described at length elsewhere (Bear & Modlin, 1987; Bradley, 1985; Kaufman, 1985; May & Campbell, 1981; May & Welch, 1984a, 1984b; Meisels, 1987a; Naglieri, 1985; Shepard & Smith, 1985, 1986, 1987; Smith & Shepard, 1987). Its principal fault lies in the discrepancies between its stated purposes and the empirical evidence available to support those statements. Clearly, the Gesell is a high-stakes test: It promises to identify children who are at high risk for school failure, and it asserts that it can be used to determine when children should begin school, which children should be promoted, and which should be retained in grade.

Unfortunately, there are no data to support these assertions. In one study that paradoxically claims to validate the Gesellian concept of developmental age, Wood, Powell, and Knight (1984) found that more than half of those kindergarten-age children who were considered "ready" by the Gesell did not have successful kindergarten experiences, as reported by their classroom teachers. A second study by May and Welch (1984b) also revealed major problems with the Gesell's accuracy, and found no support for the effectiveness of an extra-year program based on Gesell recommendations. Other studies with similar results are reviewed in the publications noted above. In short, these studies demonstrate that the claims of the Gesell theorists cannot be supported by empirical data.

Yet, the tests continue to be widely used—based, perhaps, on the unfounded perception that they are efficacious and because they provide a means for teachers to cope with the process of "academic trickle down," the inappropriate curriculum demands that they must endure and implement. In other words, if, as the Gesell theorists claim, their test measures "developmental age," which they claim is maturationally driven and genetically derived, a child who cannot cope with an academically oriented school curriculum does not necessarily represent a failure on the part of the child, teacher, or parent. Rather, the child is simply not "ready," and no amount of instruction, intervention, or effort can be expected to have an effect. But this assumes that readiness is an absolute concept, not a relative one. Bruner (1966) notes that the idea of readiness is a "mischievous half-truth. It is a half-truth largely because it turns out that one *teaches* readiness or provides opportunities for its nurture, one does not simply wait for it. Readiness, in these terms, consists of mastery of those simpler skills that permit one to reach higher skills" (p. 29). When the Gesell tests are used to define readiness, not only has the concept of readiness been reified and misrepresented, the stakes have become very high indeed.

Use of Readiness Tests for Instructional Decisions. Consistent with Bruner's perspective, the purpose of readiness tests is to evaluate a child's relative preparedness to profit from a specific curriculum (see Meisels, 1986, 1989c). Most readiness tests are described as criterion-referenced instruments—those in which a particular child's score is indicative of a specific level of concurrent performance mastery. In contrast, norm-referenced tests are interpreted on the basis of a child's standing in relationship to a larger population or group of children (See Angoff & Anderson, 1967; Barnes, 1982). Predictions about future performance can be made based on this standing. Thus, the basis purpose of criterion-referenced tests is to measure current achievement, not to predict future performance.

It follows, therefore, that the use of criterion-referenced readiness tests for high-stakes purposes of classification, retention, and promotion is unjustified. The Brigance K & 1 Screen (Brigance, 1982) exemplifies this problem. The Brigance is a brief inventory designed to provide a general picture of a young child's language development, motor ability, number skills, body awareness, and auditory and visual discrimina-

tion. Based on its content and its criterion-referenced structure, the Brigance is a readiness test, rather than a developmental screening instrument. Nevertheless, the Brigance is in wide use nationally to make predictions, that is, to "rank or group children who are high, average, or lower than their local reference group in order to contribute to readiness decisions, to make placement decisions, and to serve as an indicator for more comprehensive evaluation or referral for special services" (Boehm, 1985, p. 224). In order to fulfill these purposes, it is necessary that the test be norm-referenced and that it be accurate, so that high-stakes decisions will not be based on misleading data.

However, no reliability, validity, or standardization data are available for the Brigance. The test consists of a number of characteristic traits, skills, and behaviors that children at different ages demonstrate. To assume that this unstandardized collection of criterion-referenced items gives a definitive picture of a child's future ability is highly questionable. Furthermore, high-stakes testing carries high-stakes consequences for the tester as well as the child. As one review cautions, the lack of standardization data for the Brigance suggests that "any school system that formally and systematically uses the Brigance inventories without going through a local validation effort is placing itself at risk legally" (Robinson & Kovacevich, 1984).

Given this background, the use of the Brigance for instructional decision-making is also questionable. Indeed, most achievement/readiness tests are of limited relevance to teachers because they assess a restricted range of instructional objectives, they omit major adaptive and socioemotional behavior, or they are perceived as doing little more than confirming what the teacher knew about the child already (Durkin, 1987; Kelleghan, Madaus, & Airasian, 1982; Salmon-Cox, 1981). The missing ingredient is the match between the test and the teacher's curriculum. To the extent that the test reflects the teacher's approach and instructional goals, it is likely that it will have a positive impact on educational decision-making. When readiness tests are used for low-stakes internal testing programs, they are often not perceived as particularly efficacious because of this lack of fit with the teacher's goals, and they usually do not have a major impact on instruction. Yet, when the same tests are transformed by administrative decree into high-stakes tests, they can and do influence instruction, though clearly not for the right reasons.

The Georgia Experience. The final characteristic of high-stakes testing to be discussed concerns the subtle transfer of control over the curriculum to the test developer. Nowhere was this abrogation of instructional authority better exemplified than in the testing program implemented by the state of Georgia in 1988. In 1986 the state passed a bill known as the Quality Basic Education (QBE) Act. This bill required all children seeking to enter first and fourth grades to pass a test that would demonstrate their academic readiness. Students who did not pass such tests and, in kindergarten, whose teachers completed a locally developed checklist that confirms the results of the readiness assessment, would be required to repeat kindergarten or third grade. Because of the national outcry concerning this program, Georgia revised its testing program significantly, and is no longer following the practices it implemented in 1988. Nevertheless, there are many lessons to be learned from the original Georgia plan, because their approach has been used by many local school districts around the country.

The test selected for first-grade entry by the Georgia Department of Education was the California Achievement Test (CAT), level 10 (CTB/McGraw-Hill, 1988). In the "Georgia Edition" of the CAT, however, only 64 of the 146 items (44%) were administered. The stated purpose of the Georgia CAT was to measure achievement in the basic skills and to provide specific information about students' instructional needs. The manual states that CAT items "may be used to establish reference points for beginning instruction in kindergarten and to predict first grade reading achievement" (CTB/McGraw-Hill, 1988, p. 1). Thus, the Georgia CAT was a high-stakes test: It was designed to render decisions about student classification, retention, and promotion; it was intended to guide instructional decisions; and it was perceived as carrying out the state's mandate to establish quality education programs. Unfortunately, the test and the testing program fell far short of achieving these goals. An analysis of 9 of these shortcomings demonstrates clearly how high-stakes early childhood achievement testing can have potentially deleterious effects on a public system of education.

First, the test was modified without any published empirical validation, although it is a psychometric axiom that subsets of items do not share the psychometric properties of the core test from which the items were drawn (APA/AERA/NCME, 1985). The entire test was piloted in Georgia (the complete test takes nearly 3 hours to administer), but no specific validity data were reported about the subsample of items that were selected.

Second, the Georgia CAT represented a very narrow view of learning, as only the three subtests of visual recognition, sound recognition, and mathematical concepts are included, constituting a limited focus on literacy and numeracy. Missing was any assessments of the child's attention, motivation, expressive language, motor development, use of materials, rate of learning, preferred modality, etc.

Third, the enterprise of whole-group standardized testing in high-stakes testing is questionable. Wodtke, Harper, Schommer, and Brunelli (1989) conducted a study of teachers' group testing practices in 8 kindergartens. Their findings revealed wide variation in testing conditions, many departures from standardized testing procedures, and extensive variations in children's behavior. This study highlighted the variability, lack of objectivity, and the dependence on context of standardized testing. The Georgia CAT, which was a whole-group administered test, was subject to the same type of variability and limited reliability.

Fourth, the decision mechanism of the test was unstandardized. As originally conceived, children were administered the CAT and assessed by their teachers. If any discrepancy existed between the standardized assessment and the nonstandardized teacher report, then the child would be administered another readiness test. But all 3 of the assessment procedures were of unproven reliability and validity. Thus, an unstandardized test was to be accompanied by an idiosyncratic, nonsystematic teacher report form, which could be followed by testing with another nonstandardized instrument that may have measured different phenomena altogether!

A fifth problem concerned the establishment of cutoff points to indicate failure. Initial results indicated that 8 percent of the children who took the CAT in 1988 failed to score above the Georgia cutoff, that is, the tenth percentile. In some districts the failure ratio was as low as 1 percent; in others it was as high as 26 percent (Cunningham, 1988). No data were made available concerning the racial, ethnic, geographic, and socioeconomic composition of this group of children. It is possible that poor and minority children were overrepresented among these "failures" and that the lack of cultural sensitivity of the test may have contributed to this problem. In any event, if as many as 8 percent of the children were unable to perform above the tenth percentile on this test, it is clear that the school districts had not previously identified those children who were at high risk for school failure. Use of a validated developmental screening test at the outset of kindergarten (see Meisels, 1984) could have resulted in most of these children being identified before they experienced a year of kindergarten failure.

The sixth concern relates to the consequence for failing the CAT—retention in grade. The evidence concerning kindergarten retention does not support its use of improving academic achievement (Plummer, Lineberger, & Graziano, 1986; Shepard & Smith, 1987, 1988). Indeed, it is likely that retention under these circumstances may result in lower self-esteem and rejection by the child's peer group, issues that overshadow any short-term academic gains.

Seventh, the Georgia law has the potential for creating a highly stratified, homogenous group of children who are retained in grade. One might ask why these children should not have been mainstreamed. One must also be concerned about the potential long-term consequences of being a year or more older for grade than one's peers. According to a recent report of one large city school-sponsored task force, age/grade status is the single most sensitive indicator of dropout potential in urban school districts (Detroit Dropout Prevention Collaborative, 1987). Of those students who were at least one year overage in ninth grade, more than 45 percent dropped out of school by twelfth grade.

Eighth, the state imposed the Quality Basic Education Act, but it did not provide financial resources to support its implementation. No new funds were made available to school districts for remedial programs, new materials, or hiring staff in order to reduce class size and improve teacher-child ratios.

Finally, the Georgia plan abridged parental and children's rights that were secured nationally in the 1970s. The Georgia program did not grant parents the right of appeal or of due process; it permitted placement decisions to be made on an arbitrary and capricious basis by classifying children with a nonscientific and invalid test; and it ignored provisions for the least restrictive environment, parent participation, and the use of validated tests from multiple sources and multiple disciplines that are fundamental to Public Law 94–142 and other education and civil rights legislation (Gartner & Lipsky, 1987; Heller, Holtzman, & Messick, 1982).

The action of the Georgia legislature in promulgating this Act should serve as a warning to parents, professionals, and lawmakers throughout the nation. The Georgia plan for kindergarten testing and retention defamed the importance and value of accurate educational measurement. It was the *reductio ad absurdum* of high-stakes testing in which an entire state (and so far the only state) transferred control over its early education program to a single group-administered, paper-and-pencil test. Teachers began to alter their curriculum and their teaching styles so that children would have a better chance to do well on the test. Administrators and teachers in local school districts were told that their performance would be evaluated by the gains made by their students on the CAT in succeeding years. Private firms began to offer preparatory classes to kindergartners (called "CAT Academies") so that they would pass the test, and national companies have begun to market kindergarten beginning test-taking skills programs.

Although Georgia was the only state to institute a policy that required every child to pass a readiness test or else repeat kindergarten, and then rescinded this requirement a year after its full implementation, a recent study commissioned by the National Academy of Sciences and the National Association of State Boards of Education documented the existence of some form of kindergarten testing policies in more than 30 states (Gnezda & Bolig, 1988). The study also noted that 43 states reported that some districts use academic readiness tests prior to first grade, and 40 states reported that their local districts sponsored developmental kindergarten or transitional first grades in some of their schools.

However, as the authors of the report state, "Early in the data collection phase it became clear that in all states the majority of testing decisions are made locally with minimal, if any, input from the state level" (Gnezda & Bolig, 1988, p. 2). Thus, most of the essential data needed to analyze the impact of testing of young children can only be obtained from local education agencies.

Despite the absence of such data—or perhaps because of it—much of what we know about the extent of early childhood testing, tracking, and retention has emerged from reports in local and national newspapers and national news weeklies, as noted earlier (see, for example, Coons, 1987; Carmody, 1989; Fiske, E. B., 1988; Fiske, J. 1988; Hechinger, 1988; Ordovensky, 1989; Putka, 1988). The absence of systematic data about testing, tracking, and retentions greatly impairs the development of policy alternatives. Although a strong suspicion exists that the way in which standardized tests are being used is having a negative impact on children, schools, and teachers—and particularly on minority children—the extent, range, and intensity of these problems are unknown.

HOW SCHOOLS, TEACHERS, AND TESTS ARE FAILING MINORITY CHILDREN

School achievement is measured generally by student performance on tests and by grades given to students by teachers. But the ultimate measure of school success is whether or not a student's school experience provides the basis for leading a competent adult life, including meaningful work that can support an economically independent family. For poor and minority children, this basic criterion for school success is frequently not met. Every year, one-fourth of all students from poor families drop out of high school (Schorr, 1988, p. 300). In large central cities with large minority populations, the statistics are even worse. For instance, in Chicago, 63% of minority students drop out before graduation. Of the students who remain in high school, only a small fraction can read at or above the national average (Schorr, 1988, p. 9). What happens to poor and minority children in schools that constrains their academic achievement, and to what extent do standardized tests play a role in this national tragedy?

Teacher Perceptions

Teachers' perceptions of children's abilities seem to have an undeniable effect on children's success in school. In a longitudinal study of black children in a segregated urban school, Rist (1970) found that the kindergarten teacher he studied made evaluations of her student's expected abilities based on their appearance, language style, and family SES characteristics. Without any objective indication of these new kindergartners' academic ability this teacher placed children at one of three tables or ability groups. All of the "fast learners" were clean and neatly dressed, spoke standard English, interacted verbally with the teacher, and had families that were intact and not on welfare. The hierarchical seating placements made by the kindergarten teacher remained stable throughout the year with no child moving from one table to another. Most astonishing is that when these children were in second grade, the second-grade teacher seated them in the same hierarchical manner. The only change in placement that occurred from the first week of kindergarten until the end of second grade took place in December of the second-grade year. Two students seated at the "fast learner" table were moved down one table because "they kept their table and floor messy." Two students from this second group moved up to the "fast learner" table in their place because they kept their table and floor neat. The kindergarten teacher's perception of student ability accurately forecasted these student's future school success.

The powerful effect of negative teacher perceptions on the school achievement of poor and minority students has been described extensively (see Chunn, 1988). These students are less likely to be placed in programs for gifted and talented students; they are disproportionately enrolled in special education; they are overrepresented in vocational education programs; and they are underrepresented in academic programs. In general, teachers expect black children to do less well than white students, nonstandard English–speaking students to do less well than standard English–speaking students, and low-income students to do less well than middle-income students. These perceptions result in children being tracked into low ability groups early in their education. Research has shown that for the majority of children, heterogeneous groups are a preferable way for students to be grouped in school (Chun, 1988). The effect these teacher perceptions have on students' scores on standardized tests is, of course, an important question.

TESTS

The use of tests with minority students is controversial, reflecting a belief that tests do not measure what they are purported to measure when used with children who are not white and middle class (Hilliard, 1990). California has outlawed the use of standardized individual tests of intelligence with black students for any purpose (Dent, Mendocal, Pierce, & West, 1987). This decision resulted from a class action suit brought by parents on behalf of children who had been misclassified as educably mentally retarded in special education classes in San Francisco. School districts in California must now devise alternative methods to determine the educational needs of black students.

Another variable that influences the performance of minority children on standardized achievement tests is familiarity with the examiner. In a meta-analysis of 14 studies of examiner familiarity in primarily preschool and elementary school testing, Fuchs and Fuchs (1989) concluded that the use of familiar examiners had a significant effect on the scores of minority youths, but did not seem to have a comparable impact on white children's performance. They showed that use of a familiar examiner would raise a minority child's score on a typical standardized IQ test from 100 to 111, while having virtually no effect on a white child's score. The results of this study prompted the authors to state that "comparing minority students' suboptimal performance with unfamiliar examiners to the more maximal performance of largely Caucasian normative populations could result in spuriously low and improperly restrictive educational placements of minority children" (p. 307).

Still another factor to consider is the impact of teacher perceptions of students' ability levels on students' success on standardized tests. Alexander, Entwisle, and Thomson (1987) compared teachers' family of origin SES with the perceptions they had about their students and the schools in which they worked. High-SES teachers, regardless of their race, seem to have lower expectations for black students. The authors note that high-SES teachers "perceive such [black] youngsters are relatively lacking in the qualities of personal maturity that make for a 'good student,' hold lower expectations of them, and evaluate the school climate much less favorably when working with such students. As a result, blacks who begin first grade with test scores very similar to their white age-mates have fallen noticeably behind by year's end" (p. 679).

These studies show the futility of making important judgments about minority students' academic abilities based solely or primarily on grades and tests. They demonstrate the negative relationship between lower social-class status and performance on standardized tests and the powerful effect of teachers' SES on their judgments about student academic ability based on how children are dressed, their social-class status, and their ability to speak standard English. When children are tracked or placed in ability groups based on these nonacademic attributes, there is little hope of their ever moving out of the "low" group into another level. By examining how teachers treat children in differential ability groups in terms of amount of time spent engaging children in the teaching/learning process, giving support and help for academic work, and providing children with opportunities to demonstrate what they know by being called on and asked to participate in group projects, it is clear why "fast learners" continue to succeed in school as the gap between them and the other children continues to widen with each year in school.

Race and Achievement

Alexander and Entwisle (1988) conducted an important study that demonstrated the interaction of teacher perception, student characteristics, and test performance with school success. In this longitudinal study of the first two years of schooling, they uncovered factors regarding the effects of schooling on academic achievement. The data is notable for its account of achievement and expectancies that occurred for black children and their families from the beginning of first grade to the fall of second grade.

Over 800 first-graders were randomly selected, with their parents and teachers, to participate in this study of achievement in the first two years of school. These 800 students were administered the CAT at the beginning of their first-grade year. There were no significant differences in performance on these initial CAT scores due to race or gender. Small effects for parents' beliefs about their child's ability and for parents' expectancy about school success were found. However, initial similarities between white and black first-graders were replaced with important and significant differences by the first marking period (within the first 3 months) of first grade. For black children the CAT scores obtained as school started were not predictive of the first marks given by the teachers. Yet these first-quarter marks were strong predictors for black children of their second year CAT scores. Specifically, these first-quarter grades were twice as predictive of CAT gains in math scores for black as compared with white students at the beginning of second grade. These same first-quarter marks, not CAT scores, predicted retention for black students at the end of first grade (Cadigin, Entwisle, Alexander, & Pallas, 1988). In fact, retention at the end of first grade was predicted by the first-quarter reading marks and by the questionnaire administered to teachers about their perceptions of these students' abilities while they were in kindergarten. These teacher-based judgments resulted in 16 percent of the students being retained by the end of their first-grade year, independent of scores on the CAT. Alexander, Entwisle, and Thompson (1987) found that teacher values affected teachers' evaluations of student performance, and these values interacted with the SES of the children. High-SES teachers rated lower-SES students more negatively than other students, and first-quarter marks were dominated by negative coefficients for black children. They summarize their findings by saying that "Teachers identify some students as losers from the start" (p. 76).

Another important finding of this longitudinal study was that between the fall of first grade and the fall of second grade the focus of the black parents moved away from their childrens' abilities to a preoccupation with retention status (p. 102). Parsons, Adler, and Kaczala (1982) found that parent perceptions of children's abilities have more powerful effects on student achievement than children's "actual" abilities. Entwisle and Hayduk (1981) found that if parents believe that their children are smarter than other children, these children do better than other children. If, despite achievement scores, children are retained by the end of first grade, it seems intuitive that parents would be concerned about this status, and doubt their own beliefs about their children's abilities. It follows that if parents' positive beliefs have positive academic outcomes for children, parents' negative beliefs about ability would have negative academic outcomes.

The complex psychological web that is generated beginning in the first week of kindergarten, a web that appears to prescribe success and failure in school life, cannot be blamed solely on teachers, parents, or tests. But teachers and other school personnel must cease consigning groups of children to a poor education by making judgments of children based on anything that denies them the chance to see themselves as able and equal participants in the teaching/learning process. Tests, teacher perceptions, and retention are too powerful to be used as weapons against children.

WHY TEST YOUNG CHILDREN?

Given this background concerning the misuse of tests and other associated problems, particularly for children from minority backgrounds, one can question the value of testing young children at all—especially if the results are used for high-stakes purposes. One such purpose is that of retention. Shepard and Smith (1986) provide a thorough analysis of the relationship between readiness testing and kindergarten retention policies. In addition, they examine the research literature about the "problem of being youngest." They conclude that children should not be retained in kindergarten or placed in a two-year prekindergarten or readiness program based on the use of readiness tests alone. These tests are insufficiently accurate to be used for screening and placement. Moreover, they cite research that shows that when such tests are used to assign children to extra-year programs, these programs contribute to children's lower self-esteem, rather than their higher achievement. Finally, they note that the rationale for such programs—to give younger children time to mature— is not supported by research. "The disadvantage of the youngest first graders is small...the youngest problem will disappear by third grade unless it is cast in stone by a learning disability label or grade retention" (p. 83). Salzer (1986) also comments on the limited accuracy of readiness tests and the potential costs of labeling children. His recommendation is to focus instructional attention on children's strengths, rather than their weaknesses. He sees the "test-teach-test" model in use in many school districts as inherently limited and shortsighted.

These papers, and others like them (e.g., Bredekamp & Shepard, 1989; Charlesworth, 1989; Cunningham, 1988), make critically important points about testing young children—points that should be considered by everyone who establishes policies for young children. Chief among these points is that school readiness tests cannot be used appropriately for prediction and class placement. The data obtained by means of such tests—e.g., the Metropolitan Readiness Tests (Nurss & McGauvran, 1976), the Gesell School Readiness Test (Ilg & Ames, 1972), and the Cognitive Skills Assessment Battery (Boehm & Slater, 1977)— are intended to describe a child's current level of skill achievement or pre-academic preparedness. These entry level skills are not strongly associated with those outcomes that are measured by tests, grades, or retention practices (see Meisels, 1986). If one's goal is to predict quickly whether a child might have difficulty succeeding in school, or could profit from a specialized educational placement, then a different kind of test must be used: one with predictive validity, developmental content, and normative standardization. Tests that have these properties are known as developmental screening tests. Examples include the Early Screening Inventory (Meisels & Wiske, 1983), the McCarthy Screening Test (McCarthy, 1978), and the Minneapolis Preschool Screening Inventory (Lichtenstein, 1980).

Thus, the answer to the question, "Why test young children?" depends on the goals of the individuals who select and administer the tests. Different goals call for different kinds of tests, and some of the most common abuses of testing are attributable to the use of tests in situations for which they were not designed.

What Kinds of Tests Should We Use?

Developmental screening tests and school readiness tests represent the two most widely used kinds of tests for prekindergarten and kindergarten-age children. Neither test should ever be used to label children or assign them to diagnostic categories. But beyond this similarity these two types of tests differ from each other in purpose, content, standardization procedures, and psychometric properties. Developmental screening tests are used to identify children potentially in need of special education services. Readiness tests focus on a child's relative preparedness for benefiting from a special pre-academic program or curriculum. Developmental screening tests reflect a child's ability or potential to acquire skills, while readiness tests identify a child's current skill achievement, performance, and level of general knowledge. Screening tests are norm-referenced and must have excellent reliability and predictive validity. In contrast, readiness tests are typically criterion-referenced, and have reliability, but usually only construct validity (see Meisels [1984; 1989a] for explanations of these terms).

These differences between the two kinds of tests underlie the differences in their use. Developmental screening tests are intended to predict which children will be high-risk or handicapped—although only screening tests with well-established validity can accomplish this goal. Readiness tests should not be used for prediction or placement. They inform us about a child's current status, but give us little information about a child's potential to move to another level of skill accomplishment.

The use of readiness tests as predictors of school success is beset with problems: Children who can do well in regular classes are misidentified as "slow" or "developmentally immature," while children who could profit most from an individuality program or special education placement may be missed altogether (Meisels, 1987a, 1989c). Furthermore, issues concerning chronological versus developmental age have become almost hopelessly entangled by some advocates of readiness testing because all too often younger children who score low on readiness tests are labeled "developmentally immature" (the Gesell is a good example of this), and will be placed in "developmental readiness" classes. However, readiness test content is not in fact developmental, but is more closely related to the impact of direct instruction on skill acquisition. Thus, children who may simply need an individuality program of skill development are being erroneously labeled and/or retained in grade.

In short, two kinds of tests can be of value to educators working with young children: developmental screening tests and school readiness tests. But one cannot be substituted for the other. Screening tests provide a brief assessment of the developmental abilities highly associated with children's future school success. Readiness tests are concerned with which curriculum-related skills a child has already acquired. If a school administrator or teacher wants *both* kinds of information, then both kinds of tests should be administered.

Which Tests Should We Adopt?

After making a decision about what kind of test to administer, one of the next questions concerns which test to adopt. Descriptions of screening and readiness tests are available from many sources (e.g., Barnes, 1982; Lichtenstein & Ireton, 1984; Meisels, 1989a; Meisels & Provence, 1989). But more important than lists of tests are the criteria that should be applied to any test in order to select an appropriate instrument.

Listed in Table 18–1 are 4 criteria for the selection of developmental screening tests (see Meisels [1989a] for a complete explanation of these criteria). Criteria for the selection of school readiness tests can also be enumerated (Meisels, 1986). Table 18–2 presents these criteria.

TABLE 18–1. Criteria for the Selection of Developmental Screening Instruments

1. A brief procedure designed to identify children who may have a learning problem or handicapping condition that could affect their overall potential for success in school.
2. Primarily samples the domain of developmental tasks rather than the domain of specific accomplishments that indicate academic readiness.
3. Focuses on performance in a wide range of areas of development, including speech, language, cognition, perception, affect, and gross- and fine-motor skills.
4. Classificational data is available concerning the reliability and validity of the instrument.

From: Meisels, 1986, p. 91.

TABLE 18–2. Criteria for the Selection of School Readiness Tests

1. Designed to test briefly the relative preparedness of children to participate in a specific prekindergarten or kindergarten program.
2. Content should be consistent with the educational values and curriculum goals of the educational program the child is about to enter.
3. Should be criterion referenced, wherein a child's performance is indicative of a specific level or degree of mastery, rather than norm referenced, in which a child's performance is compared to the average performance of a standardization sample.

From: Meisels, 1986, p. 91.

SUMMARY

Testing is not an end in itself. Tests should only be used to obtain the best and most appropriate services for the greatest number of children. If the results of testing are not used—or are not used correctly—then testing should not take place. It is essential to understand how test data can be used appropriately in an educational situation to improve educational practice (see Meisels & Wasik, 1990). Whenever possible, test information should be supplemented with data derived from parents, teachers, other professionals, and first-hand observations (Meisels & Provence, 1989). The task of keeping testing in perspective includes a recognition of the following issues (see Meisels, 1989):

1. *Tests do not have magical powers.* A test does not in itself have power, nor does it automatically convey power to its users. Tests are only powerful if we transfer to them our control over decisions regarding what is to be taught, what is to be learned, who is to be promoted, or who is to be retained. Tests can assist us in making these decisions. But they need not be the masters of the educational process; they should facilitate that process (Meisels, 1989a).
2. *There are various types of tests; testing is not a monolith.* The principal types of tests that are used by early childhood educators are developmental screening tests and readiness/achievement tests (Meisels, 1986, 1987a, 1987b, 1988, 1989a). These tests differ in very significant ways from one another and should never be used interchangeably. Specifically, readiness tests should never be used to predict a child's future potential. Only a valid and reliable developmental screening test can serve this purpose, and only then under limited circumstances.
3. *It is essential that tests only be used for their intended purposes.* Both developmental screening tests and readiness/achievement tests have a role to play in early childhood programs. But they serve different purposes. Screening tests help select children who are likely to be in need of special services because of a learning program or handicapping condition. Only developmental screening tests that are reliable and valid should be used. Readiness/achievement tests can determine a child's relative preparedness to partic-

ipate in a particular classroom program, or can document a child's acquisition of skills and knowledge (Meisels, 1989b; Meisels & Provence, 1989).

4. *Tests should not be used to make high-stakes decisions in early childhood programs.* High-stakes tests are those that are directly linked to decisions regarding promotion or retention, that are used for evaluating or rewarding teachers or administrators, that affect the allocation of resources to programs, and that result in changes in the curriculum (Madaus, 1988; Meisels, 1989c). None of these decisions should be controlled solely by tests in early childhood. Rather, if such decisions are undertaken, tests should only provide supplementary information to help the teacher, parent, and other specialist arrive at the best possible decision for each child.

5. *Instructional decisions and documentation of accountability should be based on teacher-derived information, rather than on test data.* Early childhood programs should focus on the teacher's contributions to instructional decision-making and accountability rather than relying on tests to perform these functions. "Measurement-driven instruction" and "test-based accountability" distort both the test's importance and the teacher's role. For purposes of instruction and accountability more emphasis should be placed on enhancing the teacher's "kid watching" abilities, and systematic means of recording teacher's observations of children need to be devised (Cunningham, 1988; Meisels, 1989c; Shepard & Smith, 1986). All of these concerns become even more important when the situation of children from minority backgrounds is explored.

AFTER TESTING—WHAT?

Beyond the observations made in this chapter a number of questions remain in need of systematic study. For example, what alternatives to standardized testing can be developed to document student learning and to respond to needs for public accountability? How can standardized tests be modified so as to be of greater use in instructional planning? What types of inservice training, ongoing supervision, and parent and community education programs must be devised to support such innovation?

Clearly, many research questions remain to be answered. Among the most pressing are the following:

1. How widespread is standardized testing in kindergarten through grade 3?
2. Which tests are being used, and what are their psychometric properties?
3. Who selects the tests used in K–3? What is the basis for this selection?
4. What is the failure/retention rate in kindergarten and first grade, and how has it changed over the past 5 years?
5. At what rate are parents holding out their children from kindergarten?
6. How many children are enrolled in extra-year programs before first grade?
7. What is the cost and funding sources of these programs?

8. What are the demographic characteristics of those children who are retained and/or enrolled in extra-year programs in terms of race, sex, socioeconomic status, ethnic group, and family configuration?
9. How have curricula changed in relationship to the increased emphasis on testing?
10. What impact have tests had on teachers' classroom practices, sense of professional efficacy, and beliefs and expectations about student learning?

Answers to these questions are essential for the development of sound policy alternatives. Indeed, two general areas of inquiry are in need of further effort. First, as elaborated in this paper, educators today need accurate information on the extent and use of different kinds of tests, the differential effects of standardized tests by demographic characteristics, and the impact of such tests on curricula and teachers. In addition, alternative assessment procedures must be developed that can provide a richer, more valid picture of children's educational performance and that can satisfy responsibly the nation's apparently insatiable need for accountability.

The current reliance on whole-group administered, norm-referenced tests to demonstrate accountability in the early years has, as demonstrated in this paper, contributed to more problems than it has solved. An alternative model, following the administration of a valid developmental screening instrument, would involve the use of three types of procedures: (1) an ecologically valid, criterion-referenced assessment of classroom learning, (2) a portfolio approach to documenting student progress, and (3) a systematic, standardized teacher-report form to record student achievement summatively. These 3 alternative measures are designed to work together, checklists indicating students' weaknesses and strengths while informing portfolio goals, as portfolio objectives inform the teachers' year-end summative report. This system poses an alternative to product-oriented standardized tests by serving as more than a mere summary of achievement. Rather than a general snapshot of academic skills at a single point in time, the ongoing evaluation process entailed by this set of alternative assessment procedures should have a positive effect on both instructional behavior and student outcomes, and is intended to reflect more closely the actual goals and objectives of the classroom teacher.

A multidimensional assessment of children's progress such as that proposed above would have the potential for eliminating many of the problems and abuses that have accompanied early childhood testing in recent years. But such an approach, with its emphasis on encouraging teachers to take responsibility for making important high-stakes decisions, must be implemented with great care, supervision, and systematic research. Because of its focus on how children learn and on helping teachers to better understand and chart individual children's styles of learning, this approach has the potential for transforming assessment information into important learning experiences. It is time to focus on educationally and developmentally appropriate assessment— assessment that takes place in the service of the child and teacher—rather than assessment that occurs at the expense of learning and at high personal cost to children, teachers, families, and the community at large.

References

Alexander, K. L., & Entwisle, D. R. (1988). Achievement in the first 2 years of school: Patterns and processes. *Monographs of the Society for Research in Child Development, 53* (2, Serial No. 218).

Alexander, K. L., Entwisle, D. R., Cadigan, D., & Pallas, A. (1987). Getting ready for first grade: Standards of deportment in home and school. *Social Forces, 66,* 57–84.

Alexander, K., Entwisle, D., & Thomson, M. (1987). School performance, status relations, and the structure of sentiment: Bringing the teacher back in. *American Sociological Review, 52,* 665–682.

American Psychological Association, American Educational Research Association, and National Council on Measurement in Education (1985). *Standards for educational and psychological tests.* Washington, DC: American Psychological Association.

Angoff, W. H., & Anderson, S. B. (1967). The standardization of educational psychological tests. In D. A. Payne & R. F. McMorris (Eds.), *Educational and psychological measurement* (pp. 9–14). Waltham, MA: Blaisdell.

Barnes, K. E. (1982). *Preschool screening: The measurement and prediction of children at-risk.* Springfield, IL: Charles C. Thomas.

Bear, G. G., & Modlin, P. D. (1987). Gesell's developmental testing: What purpose does it serve? *Psychology in the Schools, 24,* 40–44.

Boehm, A. E. (1985). Review of Brigance K & 1 Screen. In J. Mitchell, Jr. (Ed.), *The ninth mental measurements yearbook* (vol. 1, pp. 223–225). Lincoln, NE: University of Nebraska Press.

Boehm, A. E., & Slater, B. R. (1977). Cognitive Skills Assessment Battery. New York: Teachers College Press.

Bowen, E. (1988, April 25). Can kids flunk kindergarten? Yes, sir—especially where the law mandates tests for first grade. *Time,* p. 86.

Bradley, R. H. (1985). Review of Gesell School Readiness Tests. In J. Mitchell, Jr. (Ed.), *The ninth mental measurements yearbook* (vol. 1, pp. 609–610). Lincoln, NE: University of Nebraska Press.

Bredekamp, S., & Shepard, L. (1989). How best to protect children from inappropriate school expectations, practices, and policies. *Young Children, 44,* 14–24.

Brigance, A. H. (1982). Brigance K & 1 Screen for Kindergarten and First Grade. North Billerica, MA: Curriculum Associates.

Brophy, J. E. (1983). Research on the self-fulfilling prophecy and teacher expectations. *Journal of Educational Psychology, 75,* 631–661.

Bruner, J. S. (1966). *Towards a theory of instruction.* Cambridge, MA: Harvard University Press.

Bryk, A. S., Meisels, S. J., & Markowitz, M. T. (1979). Assessing the effectiveness of open classrooms on children with special needs. In S. J. Meisels (Ed.), *Special education and development: Perspectives on young children with special needs* (pp. 257–296). Baltimore: University Park Press.

Cadigan, D., Entwisle, D. R., Alexander, K. L., & Pallas, A. M. (1988). First-grade retention among low achieving students: A search for significant predictors. *Merrill-Palmer Quarterly, 34,* 71–88.

Cahil, G. (1988, August 28). Ready or not? Kindergartens are looking for a few good kids. *Marin (CA) Independent Journal,* pp. E-1, E-10.

Carini, P. F. (1975). *Observation and description: An alternative methodology for the investigation of human phenomena.* Grand Forks, ND: University of North Dakota.

Carmody, D. (1989, May 10). Debate intensifying on screening tests before kindergarten. *The New York Times,* pp. 1, 14.

Charlesworth, R. (1989). "Behind" before they start? *Young Children, 44,* 5–13.

Chunn, E. W. (1988). Sorting black students for success and failure: The inequity of ability grouping and tracking. *Urban League Review, 11,* 93–106.

Cooper, D. H., & Farran, D. C. (1988). Behavioral risk factors in kindergarten. *Early Childhood Research Quarterly, 3,* 1–19.

Coons, P. (1987, November 29). Kindergarten: Who is ready? *Boston Sunday Globe,* pp. B-77, B-79.

CTB/McGraw-Hill. (1988). California Achievement Test, Grade K (Georgia Edition). Monterey, CA: Author.

Cunningham, A. E. (1988). *Eeny, meeny, miny, moe: Testing policy and practice in early childhood.* Berkeley, CA: National Commission on Testing and Public Policy.

Darling-Hammond, L., & Wise, A. E. (1985). Beyond standardization: State standards and school improvement. *Elementary School Journal, 85,* 315–336.

Dent, H. E., Mendocal, A. M., Pierce, W. D., & West, G. I. (1987). Court bans use of I.Q. tests for blacks for any purpose in California state schools: Press release by law offices of Public Advocates, San Francisco. *Negro Educational Review, 38,* 190–191.

Detroit Dropout Prevention Collaborative. (1987). Vested Interest Program: A program for children at-risk. Detroit, MI: Detroit Public Schools.

Durkin, D. (1987). Testing in the kindergarten. *Reading Teacher, 40,* 766–770.

Engel, P. (1989, June). Assessment of kindergarten readiness for first grade: Policies and practices of industrialized nations. Paper presented at the 1989 Annual Assessment Conference of the Educational Commission of the States, Boulder, CO.

Entwisle, D. R., & Hayduk, L. A. (1981). Academic expectations and the school attainment of young children. *Sociology of Education, 54,* 34–50.

Fiske, E. B. (1988, April 10). America's test mania. *New York Times Spring Education Supplement,* pp. 16–20.

Fiske, J. (1988, May 8). Kindergarten: The rules have changed. *Press-Enterprise* (Riverside, CA), pp. B-1, B-3.

Fuchs, D., & Fuchs, L. S. (1989). Effects of examiner familiarity on black, caucasian, and Hispanic children: A meta-analysis. *Exceptional Children, 55,* 303–308.

Gartner, A., & Lipsky, D. K. (1987). Beyond special education: Towards a quality system for all students. *Harvard Educational Review, 57,* 367–395.

Gnezda, M. T., & Bolig, R. (1988). *A national survey of public school testing of prekindergarten and kindergarten children.* Washington, DC: National Academy of Sciences.

Haines, J., Ames, L. B., & Gillespie, C. (1980). *The Gesell Preschool Test Manual.* Lumberville, PA: Modern Learning Press.

Hechinger, F. M. (1988, September 14). Repeating kindergarten: Does it hurt more than it helps? *New York Times,* p. 24.

Hein, G. E. (1979). Evaluation in open education: Emergence of a qualitative methodology. In S. J. Meisels (Ed.), *Special education and development: Perspectives on young children with special needs* (pp. 231–250). Baltimore, MD: University Park Press.

Heller, K., Holtzman, W., & Messick, S. (Eds.). (1982). *Placing children in special education: A strategy for equality.* Washington, DC: National Academy Press.

Hilliard, A. (1990). Secrecy in testing: The social costs from an equity perspective. In J. L. Schwartz & K. A. Viator (Eds.), *The prices of secrecy: The social, intellectual, and psychological costs of current assessment practice* (pp. 11–18). Cambridge, MA: Educational Technology Center, Harvard Graduate School of Education.

Holmes, C. T., & Matthews, K. M. (1984). The effects of nonpromotion on elementary and junior high school pupils: A meta-analysis. *Review of educational research, 54,* 225–236.

Ilg, F. L., & Ames, L. B. (1972). *School Readiness.* New York: Harper & Row, 1982.

Kaufman, N. L. (1985). Review of Gesell Preschool Test. In J. Mitchell, Jr. (Ed.), *The ninth mental measurements yearbook* (vol. 1, pp. 607–608). Lincoln, NE: The University of Nebraska Press.

Kelleghan, T., Madaus, G. F., & Airasian, P. W. (1982). *The effects of standardized testing.* Boston, MA: Kluwer-Nijhoff Publishing.

Koretz, D. (1988). Arriving in Lake Wobegon: Are standardized tests exaggerating achievement and distorting instruction? *American Education,* Summer, 8–15; 46–52.

Lichtenstein, R. (1980). The Minneapolis Preschool Screening Inventory. Minneapolis: Minneapolis Public Schools.

Lichtenstein, R., & Ireton, H. (1984). *Preschool screening: Identifying young children with developmental and educational problems.* Orlando, FL: Grune & Stratton.

Madaus, G. F. (1988). The influence of testing on the curriculum. In L. N. Tanner (Ed.), *Critical issues in curriculum, 87th Yearbook of the National Society for the Study of Education* (pp. 83–121). Chicago: University of Chicago Press.

May, D. C., & Campbell, R. M. (1981). Readiness for learning: Assumptions and realities. *Theory Into Practice, 20,* 130–134.

May, D. C., & Welch, E. L. (1984a). The effects of developmental placement and early retention on children's later scores on standardized tests. *Psychology in the Schools, 21,* 381–385.

May, D. C., & Welch, E. L. (1984b). Developmental placement: Does it prevent future learning problems? *Journal of Learning Disabilities, 17,* 338–341.

McCarthy, D. (1972). McCarthy Scales of Children's Abilities. New York: Psychological Corporation.

McCarthy, D. (1978). *The McCarthy Screening Tests.* New York: Psychological Corporation.

Meisels, S. J. (1984). Prediction, prevention, and developmental screening in the EPSDT program. In H. W. Stevenson & A. G. Siegel (Eds.), *Child development research and social policy* (pp. 267–317). Chicago: University of Chicago Press.

Meisels, S. J. (1986). Testing four- and five-year olds. *Educational Leadership, 44,* 90–92.

Meisels, S. J. (1987a). Uses and abuses of developmental screening and school readiness testing. *Young Children, 42,* 4–6; 68–73.

Meisels, S. J. (1987b). Using criterion-referenced assessment data to measure the progress of handicapped children in early intervention programs. In G. Gasto, S. Ascione, & M. Salehi (Eds.), *Perspectives in infancy and early childhood* (pp. 59–64). Logan, UT: DCHP Press.

Meisels, S. J. (1988). Developmental screening in early childhood: The interaction of research and social policy. In L. Breslow, J. E. Fielding, & L. B. Lave (Eds.), *Annual Review of Public Health* (vol. 9, pp. 527–550). Palo Alto, CA: Annual Reviews.

Meisels, S. J. (1989a.). *Developmental screening in early childhood: A guide.* Third edition. Washington, DC: National Association for the Education of Young Children.

Meisels, S. J. (1989b). Can developmental screening tests identify children who are developmentally at risk? *Pediatrics, 83,* 578–583.

Meisels, S. J. (1989c). High stakes testing in kindergarten. *Educational Leadership, 46,* 16–22.

Meisels, S. J., Harbin, G., Modigliani, K., & Olson, K. (1988). Formulating optimal state early childhood intervention policies. *Exceptional Children, 55,* 159–165.

Meisels, S. J., & Provence, S. (1989). *Screening and assessment: Guidelines for identifying young disabled and developmentally vulnerable children and their families.* Washington, DC: National Center for Clinical Infant Programs.

Meisels, S. J., & Wasik, B. A. (1990). Who should be served? Identifying children in need of early intervention. In S. J. Meisels &

J. P. Shonkoff (Eds.), *Handbook of early childhood intervention* (pp. 605–632). New York: Cambridge University Press.

Meisels, S. J., & Wiske, M. S. (1983). *The Early Screening Inventory* (2nd ed.). New York: Teachers College Press.

Naglieri, J. A. (1985). Review of Gesell Preschool Tests. In J. Mitchell, Jr. (Ed.), *The ninth mental measurement yearbook* (vol. 1, pp. 608–609). Lincoln, NE: University of Nebraska Press.

National Association for the Education of Young Children, (1988). *Position statement on standardized testing of young children 3 through 8 years of age. Young Children, 43,* 42–47.

National Association of Early Childhood Specialists in State Departments of Education. (1987). *Unacceptable trends in kindergarten entry and placement: A position statement.* Lincoln, NE: Author.

National Association of State Boards of Education. (1988). *Right from the start: The report of the NASBE Task Force on early childhood education.* Alexandria, VA: Author.

National Commission on Excellence in Education. (1983). *A nation at risk: The imperative for education reform.* Washington, DC: U.S. Government Printing Office.

Nurss, J. R., & McGauvran, M. E. (1976). Metropolitan Readiness Tests. New York: Harcourt, Brace, Jovanovich.

Ordovensky, P. (1989, June 14). Repeating a grade may drive kids to drop out. *USA Today,* p. D-1.

Parsons, J. E., Adler, T. F., & Kaczala, C. M. (1982). Socialization of achievement attitudes and beliefs: Parental influences. *Child Development, 53,* 310–321.

Plummer, D. L., Lineberger, M. H., & Graziano, W. G. (1986). The academic and social consequences of grade retention: A convergent analysis. In L. G. Katz (Ed.), *Current topics in early childhood education* (vol. 6, pp. 224–252). Norwood, NJ: Ablex.

Putka, G. (1988, July 6). Tense tots: Some schools press so hard kids become stressed and fearful. *Wall Street Journal,* pp. 1, 6–7.

Riley, S., Carter, P., Cummings, C., Firestone, J., Flynn, C., Javid, S., & Ruiter, D. (1988, September). Survey results: Early childhood programming. Paper presented at state kindergarten conference, Flint, MI.

Rist, R. D. (1970). Student social class and teacher expectations: The self-fulfilling prophecy in ghetto education. *Harvard Educational Review, 40,* 411–451.

Robinson, J. H., & Kovacevich, D. A. (1984). The Brigance Inventories. In D. J. Keyser & R. C. Sweetland (Eds.), *Test critiques* (Vol. 1, pp. 79–98). Kansas City, MO: Test Corporation of America.

Salmon-Cox, L. (1981). Teachers and standardized achievement tests: What's really happening? *Phi Delta Kappan, 62,* 631–633.

Salzer, R. (1986). Why not assume they're all gifted rather than handicapped? *Educational Leadership, 44,* 74–77.

Schorr, L. (1988). *Within our reach: Breaking the cycle of disadvantage.* New York: Doubleday.

Shepard, L. A. (1989). Why we need better assessments. *Educational Leadership, 46,* 35–40.

Shepard, L. A., & Smith, M. L. (1985). *Boulder Valley Kindergarten Study: Retention practices and retention effects.* Boulder, CO: Boulder Valley Public Schools.

Shepard, L. A., & Smith, M. L. (1986). Synthesis of research on school readiness and kindergarten retention. *Educational Leadership, 44,* 78–86.

Shepard, L. A., & Smith, M. L. (1987). Effects of kindergarten retention at the end of first grade. *Psychology in the Schools, 24,* 346–357.

Shepard, L. A., & Smith, M. L. (1988). Escalating academic demand in kindergarten: Counterproductive policies. *Elementary School Journal, 69,* 135–145.

Smith, M. L., & Shepard, L. A. (1987). What doesn't work: Explaining policies of retention in the early grades. *Phi Delta Kappan, 69,* 129–134.

Taylor, O. L., & Lee, D. L. (1987). Standardized tests and African-American children: Communication and language issues. *Negro Educational Review, 38,* 67–80.

Teale, W. H., & Sulzby, E. (1986). Emergent literacy as a perspective for examining how young children become writers and readers. In W. H. Teale & E. Sulzby (Eds.), *Emergent literacy: Writing and reading* (pp. vii–xxv). Norwood, NJ: Ablex.

Wodtke, K. H., Harper, F., Schommer, M., & Brunelli, P. (1989). How standardized is school testing? An exploratory observational study of standardized group testing in kindergarten. *Educational Evaluation and Policy Analysis, 11,* 223–235.

Wood, C., Powell, S., & Knight, R. C. (1984). Predicting school readiness: The validity of developmental age. *Journal of Learning Disabilities, 17,* 8–11.

Yagelski, R. P. (1988, January 17). Fears for a son going into a test-crazy world. *Boston Globe,* pp. A-44, A-48.

THE MORASS OF SCHOOL READINESS SCREENING: RESEARCH ON TEST USE AND TEST VALIDITY

Lorrie A. *Shepard*
UNIVERSITY OF COLORADO AT BOULDER

M. *Elizabeth Graue*
UNIVERSITY OF WISCONSIN, MADISON

Confusion surrounds the issue of school readiness testing. Although parents, teachers, and policymakers use the term *readiness* as if it had a common meaning, the nature and causes of readiness can be thought about from vastly different perspectives. Some believe readiness is a biological trait that unfolds within the individual, much like the developmental processes that determine when a child first learns to crawl and to walk. Others believe that readiness is strongly influenced by previous learning experiences at home or in preschool. Some hold to a threshold model of school readiness in which a child is unable to learn in formal settings until all relevant aspects of development are fully in place; others see readiness to learn as a continuum that begins when a child first "learns" to smile and continues without interruption into the school context.

According to competing definitions of readiness at least 3 distinguishable (but overlapping) populations of children may be identified as at risk for school failure: (1) those who are socially immature, (2) those who have recognized developmental delays or incipient learning handicaps, and (3) those who are "culturally disadvantaged" because their home language and learning experiences do not meet the normative expectations of the school. Different theories also imply contradictory interventions or treatments for unreadiness. Proponents of the Gesell philosophy (Gesell, 1940) hold a primarily biological perspective and take a hands-off approach, thereby allowing the "gift of time" to cure developmental immaturity (category 1

above). In contrast, intervention is the key for those working with both handicapped (category 2) and environmentally at-risk (category 3) children, even if in the former case learning difficulties are presumed to be biological in origin. From the perspective of special education and early intervention, the types of instructional interventions are the same regardless of the inferred cause of slowed development. As a result, there is conceptual blurring between the special education population and children said to be at risk for socioeconomic reasons.

It is often impossible for parents approaching schools with their 5-year-olds or for readers of journal articles to tell which theories are being invoked when children are called unready or at risk. Trying to make sense of different conceptions of readiness is complicated further because competing theories are not always formal and explicit; often they are only vaguely formed ideas. When readiness theories are implicit and unexamined they can lead to inconsistent policies. For example, legislators presumably subscribe to an environmental theory of readiness when they support Head Start and other preschool programs for the disadvantaged but implicitly endorse a biological theory when they deny school entry to children who cannot pass a readiness test.

The literature on the measurement of readiness is equally confused and confusing. Meisels (1987) has attempted to draw the distinction between *developmental screening tests,* intended to identify "children who may need early intervention or special education services," and *readiness tests,* designed to measure prerequisite skills to determine "a child's relative preparedness to benefit from a specific academic program" (p. 5). But as we see in this chapter, these two types of measures are, in practice, used almost interchangeably. Furthermore, the technical meaning of *screening,* referring to a preliminary measurement followed by in-depth assessment for those who might be at risk, is often ignored.

The purposes of this chapter are to sort out the various uses of readiness tests and to analyze the research evidence on the validity of readiness tests for their respective purposes. It would be convenient if we could say that there are 2 types of test—developmental screening measures and academic readiness measures—that correspond to two different purposes for testing—handicap identification and selection for school entry. However, in practice there are several types of tests and several different testing purposes with no clear mapping between test content and test purpose. Tests designed for one purpose are often misused for another. It is therefore necessary to treat the uses of tests separately from the kinds of readiness tests.

In the first section of this chapter, survey data are presented to describe how states and local school districts use readiness tests. In the second section, we explain current standards for validity evidence. In the third section of the chapter, we described briefly the different kinds of readiness measures. In the final section, we consider validity evidence for each of the uses of readiness tests: identification of children as handicapped, selection for school entry, placement in 2-year kindergarten programs, placement in at-risk kindergartens, and instructional planning. For each test use we present the theoretical arguments underlying both the measurement and the intended intervention. Then we consider the research evidence to support each set of theoretical claims.

USES OF SCREENING AND READINESS TESTS

Gnezda and Bolig (1988) conducted a survey of early childhood specialists or testing specialists in the departments of education in each of the 50 states. They identified 3 major purposes for administering tests to young children either before or during kindergarten: developmental screening, kindergarten or first-grade readiness testing, and program accountability.

Developmental screening may refer either to a health screening for hearing, vision, and normal physical developmental milestones or to testing of performance on cognitive, language, perceptual, and motoric tasks. Its purpose is to identify children with potential handicapping conditions. Children with a "positive" screening result, indicating that they may have learning difficulties, are referred for more in-depth developmental assessment. According to Gnezda and Bolig (1988), screening is mandated in 19 states and practiced to some extent by local districts in 20 additional states. The most frequently used instruments cited in the study were the Brigance, Battelle, Denver, DIAL-R, Early Prevention of School Failure, Gesell, and locally developed tests.

One of the most critical findings from the Gnezda and Bolig survey was that screening devices intended to signal the need

for additional diagnostic services were often used instead to deny kindergarten entry, to encourage parents to keep their children home for an extra year, or to place children in 2-year kindergarten programs.

Readiness testing is used to determine whether children possess the skills necessary to be successful in school. According to Meisels (1987), readiness tests should be used for instructional planning, not special placement decisions. Gnezda and Bolig (1988) found widespread use of readiness testing that went well beyond an instructional focus. Such testing is mandated for incoming kindergartners in 4 states and occurs locally in an additional 26 states. Six states require first-grade readiness testing and 37 more states report first-grade readiness testing at the local level. Considering both kindergarten and first-grade readiness policies jointly, only 3 states did not report the occurrence of either prekindergarten or pre–first-grade readiness testing. Instruments used most frequently before kindergarten were the DIAL-R, the Gesell, the Metropolitan, and the *Peabody Picture Vocabulary Test.* At the end of kindergarten, achievement tests such as the *California Achievement Test* (CAT), the *California Test of Basic Skills* (CTBS), and the *Iowa Test of Basic Skills* (ITBS) were cited as well as the *Missouri Kindergarten Inventory of Developmental Skills* (Gnezda & Bolig, 1988; Gnezda, Garduque, & Schultz, 1991). According to Gnezda and Bolig: "Kindergarten readiness testing was perceived to serve similar purposes as screening. In most cases, respondents suggested that readiness test results were used with other indicators for placement, denial of entry into kindergarten, identification of special needs, and as a guide to teachers for curriculum planning" (p. 3). The most common use of first-grade readiness tests was kindergarten retention and placement in special first-grade programs such as transition first grade. Note that no clear lines can be drawn between the type of test given and the type decision to be made from the test results.

A typical example of the kind of special-placement use of readiness testing found on a large scale by Gnezda and Bolig was described in a report from Chesterfield County, Virginia, by Galloway and George (1986).

Testing for appropriate placement is crucial to the success of the junior kindergarten. In Chesterfield County, the placement process begins the spring preceding school entry, when children are administered the McGraw-Hill Cooperative Preschool Inventory and the "Draw a Person" test. During the first month of school, children are given SRA's Primary Mental Abilities test and assessed for fine and gross motor development. The results of these tests and teacher observations are then used to determine which kindergarten tier is most appropriate for the child. (p. 68)

Galloway and George went on to explain that, by the end of September, children judged to be developmentally immature on the basis of these measures are placed in junior kindergarten, which means they take three years to complete kindergarten and first grade. The extra-year kindergarten with curriculum geared to the child's developmental level is "designated to prevent early failure syndrome" (p. 68).

Another highly visible example of readiness testing is the Georgia test for kindergartners, mandated by the state legislature to determine which children can be promoted to first grade. Originally, a blue-ribbon commission appointed by the governor had recommended mandatory full-day kindergartens and compulsory attendance for all 5-year-olds (Blount & Meinhardt, 1988) as key elements in educational reform. However, when this proposal ran into political obstacles, the legislature substituted the requirement that 6-year-olds pass a "school readiness assessment" to be allowed to enter first grade in public schools. The first test adopted was a shortened version of the *California Achievement Test*, based on the visual recognition, sound recognition, and mathematical concepts subtests. After 2 years, the CAT was replaced by a specially developed test involving more hands-on kinds of tasks; current practice relies on teacher judgment as well as test results to determine promotion to first grade (Georgia Department of Education, 1990). According to Georgia Department of Education personnel, the retention rate in kindergarten continues to be about what it was without the test, on the order of 10% per year.

In each of these examples of test use, we try to make clear what decisions follow from the test results. Children in these examples were retained in kindergarten or placed in 2-year kindergarten programs. We also emphasize what effect the test-based decisions are intended to have. In the first example, junior kindergarten was promised to prevent early failure syndrome; in the second example, Georgia legislators believed that retaining unready children in kindergarten would improve their chances for success in first grade. These intentions are essential to the analysis of validity evidence that we take up in later sections of the chapter.

Accountability uses of tests are not addressed in this chapter because testing for accountability purposes or to evaluate educational programs does not involve making decisions about individual children. The issues and standards for judging the validity of tests under these circumstances are different (Shepard, 1990). For example, if only group means are reported and not individual test scores, the test does not have to meet quite so stringent a standard for statistical reliability. And predictive accuracy is not a concern for accountability tests. Although omitted from discussion here, the effects of accountability testing on early grades curriculum and indirectly on the well-being of teachers and children are of great concern (see Shepard, 1991).

CURRENT STANDARDS FOR VALIDITY EVIDENCE

Standards for determining test validity have evolved over time. In the earliest days of psychological testing, there was no requirement to verify what a test measured apart from the initial logic of test development. By the 1940s, however, scientists understood that inferences based on tests had to be tested and evaluated like other elements in scientific theories. The first codification of validity standards required that empirical evidence be gathered to show the relationship between test scores and criterion performance; for complex inferences about constructs like "intelligence," a whole series of interconnected relations had to be demonstrated (American Psychological Association, 1954). Early validity standards might be thought of as "truth in labeling" requirements—that is, test developers had to show that tests measured what they claimed to measure.

The demands for validity evidence continued to grow, however, often prompted by experiences with test misuse. In order to conduct research to support test inferences, those inferences had to be articulated. It became clear that inferences, and hence validity requirements, depended on test use (Cronbach, 1971). For example, the *Peabody Picture Vocabulary Test* would have to supply different validity data depending on whether it was used as a measure of *vocabulary* or as a measure of *intelligence*. Although makers of the PPVT-R are now careful to say that it is a measure of a "subject's receptive (hearing) vocabulary for Standard American English" (Mitchell, 1985, p. 1123), the original PPVT was used as a measure of intelligence complete with deviation IQ scores (see Lyman, 1965). (As recently as the Buros's 1978 *Mental Measurements Yearbook*, the PPVT was listed as an individual intelligence test.) This is a classic example of test bias, or test invalidity. Obviously, a vocabulary test can only be used to measure intelligence if all examinees have had equal opportunity to learn; then one could infer that differences in amount learned were due to differences in ability to learn. (Today similar questions can be raised about the PPVT-R and other measures used to determine readiness.)

The 1985 *Standards for Educational and Psychological Testing* (APA) now explicitly require that tests be validated for each intended use. Decisions based on test results must be taken into account in the validation process. Of particular relevance to the issue of readiness testing is the stipulation in the standards that, "Test validation for classification decisions requires demonstrating statistical interaction between the test variable and the classification variables" (APA, 1985, p. 11). The standards go on to say that tests must do more than demonstrate a correlation with later performance when they are used to make placement or classification decisions, such as placing children in 2-year kindergarten programs, or classifying some as unready and sending them home. "It is possible for tests to be highly predictive of performance for different education programs or jobs without providing the information necessary to make a comparative judgment of the efficacy of assignment or treatment" (APA, 1985, p. 13). *Efficacy* is the key word in this statement. Tests cannot be used to assign children to different educational treatments unless it can be shown that those treatments are differentially effective; that is, children with a given test performance must be better off as the result of a special placement than they would have been in the normal or usual placement.

Messick (1989) emphasized essentially the same demand for evidence of effects in his now classic article on measurement validity.

An important type of selection or classification decision might be called *readiness diagnosis*, whereby individuals are predicted to respond favorably to the available treatment or more favorable to one among a set of alternative treatments. This is in contrast with *remedial diagnosis*, whereby current needs or disorders are identified (Snow & Lohman, 1988). Remedial diagnoses followed by prescription of treatment become readiness diagnoses. The point is that the identification of needs is separable from the prescription of treatments, and tests can be separately validated for the two purposes. (p. 71)

Not only are the 2 types of validity evidence separable, but if a test has only been validated to describe a student's status or to identify student needs, its authors cannot claim that it is valid to make prescriptive or placement decisions. Messick went even further in explicating the kinds of validity evidence required to support test use, saying that evidence must be provided to assess side effects as well as the intended effects of test-based decisions. Today, these more demanding validity standards in effect resemble the requirements for testing a new drug, rather than merely ensuring that a test is accurately named.

Contemporary validity standards create a harsh perspective for judging the literature on readiness testing. Some tests have no empirical data to support their use. For example, the Brigance cited by Gnezda and Bolig (1988) as a frequently used prekindergarten screening device has been used to deny school entry or to make 2-year kindergarten placements. Its authors claim that it can be used "to comply with mandated screening requirements" (Brigance, 1982, p. iv) as well as to plan instruction. Yet the *Brigance K and 1 Screen for Kindergarten and First Grade* has *no* norms and *no* reliability and validity data whatsoever (Boehm, 1985). Even worse, many textbooks and other reviews of instruments like the *Brigance* accept the author's assertion that normative and validity data are not needed because the *Brigance* is a "criterion-referenced" instrument. But under what circumstances are norms and validity data not needed? Instructional use within the regular classroom is very different from a referral to special education or a 2-year kindergarten placement; using the Brigance to decide what to teach next might be appropriate, but making placement decisions based on its results would certainly not be defensible. It is unusual to find a review like Boehm's (1985) where the reader is warned not to use the *Brigance* for "readiness and placement decisions" (p. 225) because of the lack of validity evidence. Thus, the uninitiated reader is often not helped by reviews to know when *not* to use a measure. Other tests have predictive correlations, but they are of the crudest *actuarial* kind. Researchers appear to be interested in maximizing the multiple or simple r but uninterested in understanding predictive relations or in examining their relevance for intervention. A correlation coefficient simply does not tell the whole story. Given sufficient cognitive load in both the predictor and criterion measure, and enough variability among subjects, any test will show a significant correlation. Comparative studies are needed to sort out the influence on predictive correlations of sample variability, choice of criterion, and substantive differences among predictor tests; yet such studies are rarely conducted.

Because of legal challenges, the field of special education has some appreciation of the need to consider both the efficacy of intended placements and possible negative side effects, and to impose more stringent psychometric requirements when making potentially serious decisions about individuals. An example of a judicious placement strategy can be found in the set of recommendations by the National Academy of Sciences Panel on Selection and Placement of Students in Programs for the Mentally Retarded (Heller, Holtzman, & Messick, 1982). However, even in special education journals, run-of-the-mill studies look for early predictors of learning disabilities, reading disorders, or other categories of school failure without any conceptual framework to connect predictor and crite-

rion. In a review of 74 studies, Tramontana, Hooper, and Selzer (1988) concluded that "with few exceptions, investigators have not been very explicit in their assumptions regarding either the normal development of academic skills or the developmental precursors of learning problems" (p. 140). The learning disorders field seems stunted at a 1950s stage of validity development, when any predictive correlation would do. In early childhood education, there is no greater technical knowledge and even less concern about the need to consider placement effects as part of measurement validity.

TYPES OF "READINESS" MEASURES

Here we consider briefly the kinds of tests—IQ tests, developmental screening tests, and academic readiness tests—that are sometimes used at the start of school to make a variety of referral, placement, and instructional decisions. As noted earlier, Meisels (1987) draws a distinction between developmental screening measures used for the identification of potential handicaps and readiness measures used to measure a child's mastery of prerequisite skills needed for success in a particular school curriculum. Although this chapter focuses on issues of readiness testing (as opposed to developmental assessment or developmental screening), we cannot entirely ignore developmental measures for several reasons. First, given that Meisels's distinction is not respected in practice, we have the problem of dealing with developmental screening devices used to make school entry and kindergarten placement decisions. Second, we dislike the connotation that, because developmental screening measures are appropriate for making referrals to special education, instruments called "readiness" tests are valid for making school entry decisions. Indeed, Meisels (1987) would agree that readiness measures are best used by classroom teachers to make "initial curriculum decisions about individual children" (p. 68). Therefore, depending on the evidence, it may be the case that neither developmental screening measures nor school readiness tests are adequate for making school entry decisions.

In what follows we review briefly the content and technical properties of 3 types of tests: individual intelligence tests, developmental screening tests, and academic readiness tests. In addition, the *Gesell School Readiness Screening Test* is considered separately because it does not fit well in any of the other categories. The Gesell test is called a readiness test and is used to deny school entry and place children in 2-year kindergartens, but its content seems similar to that of developmental screening measures.

Individual Intelligence Tests

Individual intelligence tests for young children typically are broad measures of language and social awareness, reasoning, memory, and perceptual-motor abilities. For example, the *Wechsler Preschool and Primary Scale of Intelligence-Revised* (WPPSI-R) has the following subtests (facsimile items are from Sattler, 1988):

Information (How many legs does a cat have?)
Comprehension (What makes a sailboat move?)

Similarities (In what way are a quarter and a dollar alike?)

Arithmetic (Judy had 4 books. She lost 1. How many books does she have left?)

Vocabulary (Name pictures like boot and book.)

Sentences (Repeat a sentence like, "Ted likes to eat apples.")

Picture Completion (Identify missing parts in a picture like a doll without a leg.)

Block Design (Use 3 or 4 blocks to reproduce the design presented in a picture.)

Object Assembly (Put together puzzle pieces to form a complete object.)

Animal Pegs (Children must learn an association between certain colors and animals and perform a matching task.)

Mazes and Geometric Design (Children must first pick matching shapes and then draw a circle, triangle, square, and diamond.)

Individual intelligence tests must be administered by trained clinicians and are used primarily for the identification of children at the extremes of the ability distribution, especially those whose functioning is abnormally low. When used for the purpose of handicapped identification and placement in special education, intelligence tests compose only a part of a multifaceted assessment that also examines adaptive behavior and (if important principles are followed) the adequacy of instructional modifications in the regular classroom (Heller et al., 1982). IQ tests administered to 5- and 6-year-olds typically correlate .45 to .50 with later school performance (Horn & Packard, 1985). Of all of the tests considered in this chapter, individual intelligence tests such as the Stanford-Binet and WPPSI have the most extensive psychometric evidence of reliability, predictive power, and construct validity. Intelligence tests are measures of developed ability and will therefore be strongly influenced by children's past learning experiences.

Developmental Screening Measures

Developmental screening measures are like mini-IQ tests. They are intended to address the same traits as in-depth assessments, but to do so quickly and without requiring a trained clinician for administration, so that they can be administered to mass numbers of children in schools and pediatrician offices. In addition to the content domains shared with intelligence tests, such as language, social comprehension, reasoning, memory, and perceptual-motor abilities, screening measures for preschool children typically also include gross- and fine-motor skills and personal-social skills such as self-care. If one were to do a content analysis of overlap between particular developmental screening measures and IQ tests, the extent of similarity would vary from 60% to 90% similar items. As an example of a measure with the least overlap, the screening version of the *Battelle Developmental Inventory* has 2 subtests, Cognitive and Communication, that are entirely redundant with IQ-type items. In addition, some items from each of the other 3 Battelle subtests, Personal-Social, Adaptive, and Motor, are also like tasks on IQ tests. Even when shared content is only 60% of items, however (so that as many as 40% of the items in developmental screening measures are not found on IQ tests), psychometrically the amount of redundancy is much greater because

the cognitive and language measures account for much more of the variance among individuals. (Furthermore, it should not be argued that screening decisions are based on separate interpretation of noncognitive subtests, given that screening subtests lack sufficient reliability to support separate interpretation.)

It is a psychometric truism that short tests are less reliable and therefore less valid (compared to long tests of the same content). Screening measures also have the disadvantage that they can be administered by untrained personnel. Therefore, they are vulnerable to misinterpretations such as drawing conclusions from unreliable subtest differences or interpreting performance as a sign of innate capacity. Several of the most popular screening instruments are adequate for their original purpose, which is to act as a preliminary check for problems. Notice that because the use of these tests only involves the recommendation to collect additional information, we do not hold screening measures to the requirement that they provide data on effects. Regardless of sometimes respectable predictive correlations, however, screening measures should never be used for making special education or kindergarten placement decisions.

Although some of the best-known measures are valid for screening purposes, popularity does not ensure validity. Some tests, like the Brigance, have face validity and look remarkably similar to measures that have predictive validity, but their authors have failed to report minimal data on reliability and validity. Therefore, these instruments should *not* be used. In some cases (e.g., the Battelle), test makers have conducted concurrent validity studies but have failed to provide any predictive validity data. (Given that children with "no problem" screening results are not assessed further, the predictive validity of the no-problem classification has to be established.)

The content and construct similarity of developmental screening measures and IQ tests is of particular importance given that developmental measures are so frequently misused to make school entry decisions and kindergarten placements. As noted in a policy study by Shepard (1990), the euphemistic name of developmental tests makes them publicly acceptable whereas the use of IQ tests to make the same kinds of school entry decisions would provoke immediate protest. Yet developmental tests suffer from precisely the same problem as IQ tests in that they cannot sort out (except in cases of serious deficiency) the difference between inherent problems and those caused by limited opportunities to learn or lack of familiarity with the specific content of the test. If the public were better informed about the kinds of tests being used, it is likely that they would ask more demanding questions about test validity and program benefits.

The Gesell School Readiness Screening Test

The *Gesell School Readiness Screening Test* is treated in a category of its own because, although it is called a school readiness measure, it does not measure curriculum-specific content as suggested by Meisels's definition. Instead, the Gesell covers content that makes it indistinguishable from developmental screening measures and broad measures of intelligence. This assertion that the Gesell tests are very much like IQ tests is denied by the tests' authors and therefore should be examined with some care. The test that we describe here is the screening version of the complete battery. Note that the Gesell Institute uses the term *screening* to mean screening for school entry and grade placement. They do not use *screening* to mean that testing should be followed by more in-depth assessment to determine readiness; placements are made based on screening results. The Gesell tests are not intended for handicapped screening, but a child is referred for further evaluation if suspected to have special learning needs (Gesell Institute of Human Development, 1982).

The similarities between Gesell subtests and subtests on intelligence measures can be seen as follows. The Gesell Initial Interview and the Animals and Interests subtests are verbal measures tapping the same language development and general knowledge constructs as measured by the Information and Vocabulary subtests of the WPPSI. Note that the Animals question (How many animals can you name in a minute?) is an item from the old Binet intelligence test (Ilg, Ames, Haines, & Gillespie, 1978). Although it might be argued that the verbal subtests also allow Gesell examiners to form opinions about the social and emotional maturity of children's responses, no empirical evidence has ever been gathered to corroborate these claims. The Gesell performance measures include (1) the Cube Test, which is analogous to Block Design on the WPPSI, (2) Copy Forms, which is like the WPPSI Geometric Design and the Stanford-Binet Copying Test, and (3) the Incomplete Man subtest, which is just like the Stanford-Binet Incomplete Man. The scoring rules for evaluating the copying tasks and the incomplete man are not the same for the respective tests, however; Gesell examiners attend to the process of a child's response—directions of strokes and the like—as well as to the quality of the finished product. Again, however, validity data for process scoring have never been presented. The Letters and Numbers subtests on the Gesell are measures of preschool learning as well as psychomotor development and do not have counterparts on intelligence tests.

Statistically, the Gesell, which is said to measure "developmental maturity" or "behavioral age," has not been shown to have discriminant validity from IQ tests. Kaufman (1971) found that a quantified scoring of the Gesell correlated just as highly with the Lorge-Thorndike Intelligence Tests ($r = .61$) as with a test of Piagetian developmental tasks ($r = .64$). Similarly, in a study involving only 46 subjects, Lichtenstein (1990) obtained a correlation of .62 between Gesell developmental age and a shortened version of the Kaufman Assessment Battery for Children (K-ABC). Lichtenstein did, however, find evidence suggesting that the contents of the 2 tests are not identical. Teacher rating of cognitive skills correlated with the K-ABC composite and not with the Gesell; whereas teacher ratings of maturity correlated more highly with the Gesell developmental age score than with K-ABC.

A careful reading of the Lichtenstein (1990) article reveals one of the reasons that there continues to be disagreement about the overlap between the Gesell and IQ tests. Gesell authors appear to equate IQ with a narrow definition of verbal cognitive ability. And, of course, the Gesell tests are not synonymous with this narrow construct. However, if one recognizes that intelligence tests, especially for young children, have al-

ways been broader measures of language development, social competence, verbal ability, and perceptual-motor abilities, then it is not clear what the Gesell actually measures that is different from what individual IQ tests measure. Perhaps it would be helpful to restate our conclusion about the Gesell. We do not assert that the test is precisely the same as any particular intelligence test. Rather we would say that it is no more different from IQ tests than IQ tests are different from one another—the WPPSI, the Stanford-Binet, and Kaufman, for example. Because of the lesser weight given to verbal subtests, the Gesell is especially like performance IQ tests. The claim that the Gesell measures social and emotional development as well as intelligence (Ilg et al., 1978) has never been systematically investigated. In fact, in Lichtenstein's (1990) study the Gesell did not correlate more highly with a measure of socialization than did the K-ABC.

The Gesell tests have been severely criticized in recent years (Bradley, 1985, Meisels, 1987, Shepard & Smith, 1985, Waters, 1985) because they are so widely used in kindergarten screening programs but lack adequate reliability and validity data. The technical manual for the screening test is the book *School Readiness* (Ilg et al., 1978). It contains no data on either test-retest or interjudge reliability. The only validity data are agreement rates with teacher judgments for a sample of 120 kindergarten, first- and second-graders tested in 1957; the test showed on average a 74% agreement rate with teacher judgments at the end of the same year but diminished agreements with teachers' judgments in subsequent grades. The authors did not provide breakdowns of the data to allow for a check of the unready-unready agreements; usually agreement rates look good because of the larger number of ready-ready correspondences. Thus the Gesell has been distributed for widespread use without sufficient technical evidence to meet even the old test standards (APA, 1954).

Lichtenstein's (1990) study reflects recent efforts by the Gesell Institute to provide necessary data. However, Lichtenstein's findings do not support the technical adequacy of the test for making important placement decisions:

Reliability data from this study contraindicate using the GSRST as a sole, or even primary, basis for grade placement decision.... Test-retest reliability in correlational terms ($r = .73$) falls short of the .80 figure that Sattler (1988) called generally acceptable 'for most tests of cognitive and special abilities' (p. 25) and well below the .90 level recommended by Nunnally (1978) and by Salvia and Ysseldyke (1988) for tests used in making decisions about individuals.

Interrater reliability of the GSRST is of particular concern. Although reliability coefficients above .90 would be expected for most tests, which use highly specific scoring rules and quantitative procedures for deriving overall scores, the GSRST's nonstandard scoring system leaves much room for inconsistency between examiners. As might be expected, the intraclass correlation of .71 reflected substantial examiner differences in interpreting the same test performance. (p. 374)

Oddly, if predictive data were gathered on the Gesell, it is likely that it could be useful as a developmental screening measure, that is, to refer children for follow-up evaluation of potential learning problems. Ironically, however, it is not the intention of the authors that the tests be used in this way. Instead they are interested in making school placement recommendations—such as for 2-year kindergartens or staying home a year—for children in the normal range of ability. In the last section of the chapter, we consider the research evidence bearing on these special placement uses of test results.

Academic Readiness Tests

Academic readiness tests are intended to measure skills prerequisite to school learning, especially reading. Often these tests focus exclusively on reading readiness skills; hence our focus on reading readiness here is based on the content representation of the tests in use. The well-known *Metropolitan Readiness Test,* for example, has the following subtests on the beginning-kindergarten version: Auditory Memory, Beginning Consonants, Letter Recognition, Visual Matching, and School Language and Listening. The utility of such tests is based on the assumption that mastery of particular knowledge domains, such as reading or mathematics, proceeds along a well-ordered continuum of proficiency. It is assumed further that assessments can be used to locate a child on each continuum so that teachers can know precisely where to target the next phase of instruction. Note that skills tests like the Metropolitan and the Brigance are sometimes misused to make school entry or kindergarten retention decisions (Gnezda & Bolig, 1988) but are not recommended by their authors for such purposes. Rather these tests are intended to be used to make instructional-planning decisions within regular class placements. An exception is the *California Achievement Test,* which had originally been designed for instructional and group accountability purposes but which the test publishers adapted for use in Georgia as a first-grade entry test without collecting new validity data.

Stallman and Pearson (1990) have provided a history of reading readiness research and a disconcertingly negative analysis of current academic readiness tests. Basically, the tests in use today are nearly identical to those devised in the 1930s, which means that they continue to be strongly influenced by psychological theories about learning that dominated the field 60 years ago. Traditional readiness tests derive from behaviorist psychology, which assumed that learning of complex understandings (such as reading comprehension) could be facilitated by breaking knowledge down into constituent skills and providing practice on each component skill. Unfortunately, this theory, now sharply rejected by the last 20 years of research in cognitive psychology, made no provision for how component skills were to be reassembled into complex, higher-order thinking abilities (Resnick & Resnick, 1991). As a consequence of the behaviorist decomposibility and decontextualization assumptions, children today are tested on skills in isolation without context that would make the tasks more meaningful and without opportunity to engage in reading as a constructive process. In addition, Stallman and Pearson's analysis of existing readiness measures found that tests (1) are dominated by recognition, not production, tasks, (2) involve pictures and oral stimuli, not real literacy experiences, and (3) are overwhelmed by attention to test-taking behaviors such as filling in bubbles and moving the marker. Thus, Stallman and Pearson make us realize that, even if readiness tests are not intended for more serious and per-

manent placement decisions, their use could still be harmful if the content of readiness tests misdirects instruction.

Numerous authors have recently made efforts to develop alternative early school assessment instruments based on more current research findings on emergent literacy. In this new work, assessment tasks are presented within a functional literacy activity. For example, Clay (1985) developed the *Concepts about Print Test,* which involves the teacher sitting with the child and a real book and asking questions like, "Show me where to start reading," and, "Show me a word." In some cases the actual skills assessed may not be that different from those measured on traditional tests, except that an effort is made to embed skills in normal literacy contexts. For example, Mason and Stewart (1990) ask children to spell words with magnetic letters to observe their phonetic knowledge. However, assessments developed from an emergent literacy perspective also invoke a much broader set of constructs, including an understanding of the purpose of reading and the interconnected development of reading, listening, and writing skills.

Emergent literacy research is distinct from contemporary cognitive research on the development of intelligence (see Brown, Campione, Webber, & McGilly, 1991) and the development of thinking abilities (Resnick & Resnick, 1991); but these are compatible perspectives that share in the general rejection of earlier maturationist and behaviorist learning theories, which characterize the Gesell test and traditional academic readiness tests, respectively. Note that changes in theoretical perspective about how learning occurs also imply changes in expectations about the purposes of assessment. Contemporary researchers like Clay, Mason, and Stewart are not interested in conducting assessments for the purpose of screening or placement; the goal of testing is not to sort children. Rather, the purpose of assessment is to support and guide instruction. Although it is still implied that one must have a general understanding of the normal progression in the development of reading and writing abilities, there is no longer so great a need for strict normative data and linear scaling of abilities. Assessments can be contextualized, flexible, and ongoing; tests assume the central role of the teacher working interactively with children, thus blurring the distinction between assessment and instructional tasks. This change in purpose likewise has implications, addressed in this chapter's final section, for how validity should be evaluated when measures are intended to support instruction.

VALIDITY OF READINESS TESTS FOR SPECIFIC USES

From the Gnezda and Bolig (1988) survey we see that a variety of school readiness tests and developmental screening measures are administered to prekindergartners and pre–first-graders to make a variety of decisions. Although tests are sometimes used in ways consistent with their original purposes, tests designed for one purpose are often used interchangeably for another. (Furthermore, we have seen that oftentimes we cannot rely on test authors to understand the validity evidence needed to support an intended test use.) In states without mandated programs, Gnezda and Bolig's (1988) state-level respondents reported very little control over local test use and test selection policies. Tests appear to be selected with little attention to their technical adequacy. Survey respondents perceived that other factors were more influential in test selection, namely: "familiarity with the instrument (i.e., neighboring districts use it, it has a long history of use in the district), the intensity and success of marketing strategies by test publishers (often mentioned as the major reason the Gesell is selected), and the ease and cost associated with administering the test" (p. 4).

Are the numerous readiness tests in use valid for a variety of purposes? In this section we apply for each intended test use both the old and new standards for judging test validity. Do the tests have adequate reliability and predictive validity data? What claims are made about the use of the test and the effect of the placement that follows from the test? Is there evidence to support these claims?

In the analyses that follow we are not talking about a particular type of test such as an IQ, developmental screening measure, or academic skills test. Instead we address 5 intended uses or purposes for testing: identification of children as handicapped, selection for school entry, placement in 2-year kindergarten programs, placement in at-risk kindergartens, and instructional planning within the regular classroom.

Identification of Children As Handicapped

In the case of early identification of children as handicapped, we are concerned about both screening measures and developmental assessments involved in the entire process from referral to placement in special education. Several developmental screening measures—the Denver, the Battelle, and the DIAL-R—have adequate reliability and predictive validity to be used to refer children for more complete assessments. Some traditional academic skills tests like the *Metropolitan* have adequate predictive correlations in an actuarial sense to be used for referral; however, the content of skills tests is likely to cause excessive over-referral of children who have not attended preschool.

Taken together, tests available for use in making special education placements are technically adequate at least for identifying children with moderate or severe handicaps. The necessary battery includes individual intelligence tests used in conjunction with measures of social and adaptive behavior. Early identification of mild or "potential" handicaps in preschool and kindergarten children, however, poses special problems. IQ is the best available predictor of school success; however, IQ measured before age 5 correlates only .5 with later IQ (about as good as using parents' IQ to identify children). Assessments at this age are not so accurate as at later ages, in part because measurement cannot disentangle intrinsic disorders from differences in maturational rates or from differences in opportunities to learn.

Once a child is identified as handicapped, what treatment is offered? Is there evidence that the treatment has the desired effects as now required to establish the consequential validity of the test? Special education is intended to provide extra help. By intervening early it is expected that support can reshape the course of development. From experimental studies there is certainly ample evidence to show that supported development produces greater cognitive gains than no support (Feuerstein,

Rand, Hoffman, & Miller, 1979; Brown et al., 1991). However, empirical evidence confirming the efficacy of early intervention *programs* is much more equivocal (Casto & Mastropieri, 1986). (A likely explanation for the apparent contradiction is the superficial nature of most intervention programs, which may provide 1 to 3 hours per week rather than the intensive interventions found in research studies.) Therefore, it should not be presumed that special programs are automatically beneficial.

In the past special education has been harmful to many school-age children because placements that were presumed to be beneficial actually resulted in poorer teaching, watered-down curricula, and stigmatizing labels (see reviews in Heller, Holtzman, & Messick, 1982; Shepard, 1989b). More recent studies continue to raise questions about the efficacy of pull-out programs for children with mild and ambiguously defined problems. Because it is in lieu of regular instruction (and contrary to expectations), special help does not increase instructional time. More often than not the fragmented skills that children practice on resource-room work sheets bear no relation to instruction in the regular classroom (Allington, 1991). In the absence of research evidence demonstrating benefits, our opinion is that such placements are wise only if it can be shown that children are not removed from normal class experiences and interactions with their peers, and only if it can be shown that the instruction provided is challenging and effective. Thus a special education identification resulting in participation in a before-school program is desirable because it is clearly *extra* help. But a concurrent resource-room placement that removes a child from regular kindergarten for drilling on visual memory tasks is highly questionable. In this chapter's section on readiness testing for at-risk placements, we discuss the problems with both skills-training and process-training curricula.

In sum, developmental screening measures and developmental assessments for placement of moderately and severely handicapped children have adequate psychometric validity and evidence of differential placement validity; that is, children are better off because of the placement. The same cannot be said, necessarily, for identification of children with mild and vaguely defined problems. Therefore, special precautions should be instituted for such children to ensure that special education help is in addition to normal instruction, not in lieu of it.

Selection for School Entry

Readiness "screening" programs for entering kindergartners or entering first-graders have the purpose of deciding who should come to school. Developmental screening measures, including the Gesell, as well as academic readiness tests are used by local school districts for this purpose. When children are found to be unready they are either sent home and told to wait a year or are entered into a 2-year kindergarten track. Because the research evidence on effects is different, 2-year placements are considered in the next section.

For either purpose, none of the available measures is sufficiently reliable and valid to permit its use in making important individual decisions. Typical predictive correlations range from .25 to .55 (see Meisels, 1989; Mitchell, 1985). It is particularly worrisome that the data bases for these instruments are so weak that even the tests appearing to "win" by having a high correlation in a single study might have done so because of the variability in the study sample or because of the choice of criterion measure and not because the instrument is reliably better than others. As stated previously, comparative studies are rarely conducted. The very best predictive correlations we could find were correlations of .70 and .78 for the *Metropolitan Readiness Test* with achievement test scores a year later. This test was, however, designed for instructional planning—not school entry decisions. Shepard and Smith (1985) demonstrated that even tests with moderately good correlations would lead to misidentifying many children as unready. With a correlation of .70 with a designated criterion (and a selection ratio of one-third as recommended by the Gesell), only 63% of the children scored as unready on the test are actually unsuccessful on the later criterion performance. For more typical predictive correlation, on the order of .50 for the Gesell, for example (Walker, 1992), only 50% of the children labeled as unready by the test do poorly later on the criterion measures.

There is virtually no empirical data available on the consequential validity of the decision to delay school entry. The claims that delaying school entry will make unready children more successful and content in school are based on the maturationist theory of Arnold Gesell (1925, 1940) and on data that show the correlation between school achievement in the early grades and age within grade. Gesell's work from the 1920s to the 1940s emphasized the importance of biological maturation in determining children's observed abilities (see Ilg et al., p. 3, 162, 190). The within-grade age effect literature shows a consistent advantage on first-grade outcome measures for children who are in the oldest 3 months for their grade as compared to those in the youngest 3 months. Elsewhere, Shepard and Smith (1986) have argued that the benefit of being oldest tends to be exaggerated (actual effects are only 7 to 8 percentile points) and that, averaged across studies, the benefit of being oldest disappears by third grade.

Without direct data on effects—which would require follow-up studies comparing unready children who stayed home with unready children who went to school—theoretical perspective is very important to arguments about what the effects of delayed school entry are likely to be. Advocates for the "gift of time" believe that greater biological maturation of intellectual, social, and emotional dimensions of development will occur during the intervening year (and surely they will unless the child stays in a closet) and that the child will, as a consequence, not only do better in kindergarten than he would have the year before but will also do better in subsequent years as a result of having waited. A theory that emphasizes the importance of biological influences on the development of intellectual and social abilities, however, ignores research findings on cognitive development from the last several decades. Intelligence, broadly defined, is not innately determined but grows as a result of complex social interactions between the child and her environment. From the perspective that sees development as the product of supported learning experiences (Brown et al., 1991), waiting a year might retard development rather than foster it (if in the interim a child does not have stimulating experiences supported by adult interpretations and explanations).

Although biological development continues regardless of context, the critical question for predicting long-term effects of wait-a-year decisions is whether children receive optimal learning experiences in the interim to support their development.

Given our cognitive-constructivist perspective on how learning abilities are developed interactively with the social environment, we expect that the consequences of wait-a-year decisions are likely to be very different for poor versus advantaged children. For middle-class children who spend the intervening year in a stimulating, high-priced preschool environment, we surmise that no serious negative effects result, only the opportunity cost of not being allowed to proceed with their agemates and the possibility that 6-year-olds might be bored in kindergarten if the curriculum is developmentally appropriate for 5-year-olds. Note that a prediction of no effect, positive or negative, for children in preschool settings is consistent with the research findings in the next section of no benefit for unready children placed in 2-year kindergarten programs. (Contrary to popular wisdom, it is a mistake for middle-class parents to believe that they will gain a competitive academic advantage for *chronologically young but able* children if they hold them out of school until age 6. Shepard and Smith [1985] found that the age effect was pronounced for low-ability first-graders and held true for children at the median. However, there was no age effect for children at the seventy-fifth percentile and above. The top quarter of children who entered kindergarten at age 5:0 to 5:2 did just as well as the top quarter of children who were the oldest kindergartners [5:9 to 5:11].)

We are concerned, however, that decisions to deny school entry are decidedly harmful to poor children if they spend the intervening year in warehouse day care settings. It is a fact that only 50% of eligible 4-year-olds receive Head Start services. Therefore, it is not unreasonable to speculate that many poor children denied entry to public school do not have adequate learning opportunities in the year they spend in a holding pattern. Further, it has been demonstrated that poor and minority children are overrepresented in the group of children selected as unready by a variety of readiness measures (Ellwein, Walsh, Eads, & Miller, 1991).

Our conclusion, then, is that various readiness measures are not sufficiently accurate to support making important individual decisions like denying entry to school. Furthermore, the treatment of waiting a year, although presumed to be a benefit on the basis of an outmoded theory of development, has no basis on evidence.

Placement in Two-Year Kindergarten Programs

The same tests are used to make 2-year kindergarten placements as are used to deny school entry. Staying home or attending developmental kindergarten are often 2 alternative choices when a test shows that a child is unready. In addition, achievement tests are sometimes used in testing at the end of kindergarten to decide on kindergarten retention or placement in transitional first-grade. In view of evidence from the preceding section that none of the available readiness and developmental screening measures are technically adequate for making these kinds of important placement decisions, do achievement tests seem any better? First, we should not be confused by test names. There is virtually no difference between the content of traditional readiness skills tests and the first (prereading) levels of standardized achievement test batteries. The CAT, CTBS, and ITBS are cited by Gnezda and Bolig (1988) as tests frequently used to make kindergarten retention decisions. Although they are perfectly adequate as outcome measures of what children have learned by the end of kindergarten, the CAT and CTBS technical manuals provide *no* data on predictive validity. The ITBS does provide predictive validity correlations, although not over a very long time span—that is, .67 from the beginning to the end of kindergarten and .63 from the beginning to the end of first grade. Therefore, the ITBS is roughly the same as the Metropolitan. Again, these tests may be adequate for making instructional planning decisions but not for making critically important individual decisions that divert a child from normal progress in school.

Do extra-year programs—developmental kindergarten, kindergarten retention, or transition first grade—meet the APA (1985) standards for differential prediction? In other words, are children labeled unready by tests and assigned to these treatments better off than they would have been without the special placement? Shepard (1989a) provided a review of 15 controlled studies, which we summarize here only briefly. The predominant finding across studies indicated no difference at the end of first grade or later grades between unready children who spent an extra year before first grade and unready children who went directly on to first grade. Thus, the validity requirement that evidence of treatment efficacy be provided is not met.

Because these findings from controlled studies are often disputed by advocates of 2-year placements, we should clarify several specific points.

1. The finding of "no difference" holds true even when we isolate the studies where children were selected for placement on the basis of developmental immaturity using the Gesell test rather than being at risk because of low-cognitive functioning.
2. The no-difference results also hold true if we look only at transition and readiness placements rather than kindergarten retention. Thus it cannot be said that the "gift of time" works for socially immature children but not for other at-risk populations; and it cannot be said that transition placements are more beneficial than kindergarten retention. They are each ineffective.
3. It is a failing of the literature that most studies provide only standardized achievement test scores as outcome measures, even though improving emotional adjustment is suggested by proponents as the more important goal of extra-year placements. However, Mossburg (1987), Bell (1972), and Shepard and Smith (1989) did include measures of self-concept and adjustment and found either no difference or negative effects when transition children were compared to controls. For example, in the Shepard and Smith study (1989), extra-year children had poorer attitudes toward school compared to control groups. Therefore, it cannot be said that the benefits of extra-year programs were missed by controlled studies focused primarily on achievement outcomes.

Readiness tests used to place children in 2-year kindergarten programs meet neither the old nor the new standards for validity. Although some measures have moderately strong predictive correlations, even the best tests have sufficiently high error rates that it is indefensible to use them to classify children as unready. Two-year kindergarten placements of any sort do not meet the requirement of demonstrated efficacy.

Placement in At-Risk Kindergartens

Programs developed for at-risk populations often identify children on the basis of skill deficits and result in special placements for extra services. This type of homogeneous grouping, which separates identified children from their agemates, is closely parallel to traditional tracking practices whereby children were grouped on the basis of tested ability. The negative effects of tracking or ability grouping are well known. Children in the low groups experience dumbed-down instruction and lowered expectations from teachers, themselves, and classmates (Oakes, 1985). In recent years tracking has been eliminated in many elementary schools. In many ways, however, readiness screening and extended-day kindergartens for children at risk appear to be a veiled means to reinstitute tracking.

Research studies have shown the academic benefits of extended-day compared to half-day kindergarten for at-risk student (Karweit, 1988; Olson & Zigler, 1989). These studies did not invoke the issue of tracking, however, because they examined the effects of activities that were provided beyond the regular kindergarten day; extended-day programs were originally additions to the regular program with normal, heterogeneous placements. A problem arises in practice when school districts have insufficient funds for all kindergartners to participate in extended-day programs. Readiness tests often become the basis for determining who is to receive the benefit of limited funds. There are 2 different ways, however, that this instructional "benefit" may be organized. One is to assign all children to normal half-day kindergarten classes (heterogeneous in ability) and then to regroup the "at-risk" children in the afternoon to receive extended-day enrichment activities. The other way is to assign all of the at-risk children to a separate extended-day classroom with instruction "geared to their level." The latter arrangement is clearly tracking.

Readiness tests of all sorts are used to identify children at risk of school failure, including skills tests like the Metropolitan and developmental measures like the DIAL-R. (The Gesell test is not typically used for placement in extended-day programs because the notion of intervening to remediate "unreadiness" is inconsistent with the Gesell philosophy.) Psychometric data reviewed previously are equally applicable here. Readiness tests can predict chances of school success moderately well with correlations from .25 to .70, but designations of "at-riskness" for individual children are still fallible (and the particular children identified will vary appreciably from test to test). Therefore, the critical validity question remains, as before, does the planned intervention work? If the treatment is unambiguously a benefit, then it might be legitimate to make placements on the basis of flawed tests.

Unlike the body of research on the effects of kindergarten retention, there are no well-controlled studies examining the effects of separate extended-day placements for homogeneous groups of at-risk children. (An example of a study that attempted to provide this type of comparison was the Early Prevention of School Failure [1990] evaluation. However, the lack of initial equivalence between groups and a 60% attrition rate make it impossible to draw conclusions from this study about the effectiveness of the EPSF program. In any case, the comparison in the EPSF [1990] study was between specially treated and control instructional conditions, rather than the comparison of concern here, which is heterogeneously placed children receiving extra help versus homogeneously placed children receiving extra help.)

Our concern that this type of arrangement is likely to be harmful is based on generalization from past research on tracking. In addition, we point to negative findings from remedial class placements (Allington, 1991) and to case-study findings in one district where the Early Prevention of School Failure (EPSF) assessment was used for kindergarten placement (Graue, 1990). Instruction in remedial classes and special education resource rooms is often dominated by drilling on isolated skills. Studies cited by Allington (1991) show that children spend their time working alone (hardly an indication of supported learning) on low-level skills work sheets and are thus denied experience with authentic literacy tasks. These instructional practices derive from the pervasive influence of behaviorism, which assumes that children cannot acquire conceptual knowledge until they have learned rudimentary skills by rote. Yet, given current insights from research in emergent literacy and cognitive psychology, children consigned to such instruction are clearly denied opportunities for integrated development of language and reasoning abilities (Resnick & Resnick, 1991; Stallman & Pearson, 1990).

We are especially concerned about separate at-risk kindergartens where a readiness test becomes not only the mode of selection but the designated curriculum as well. In Graue's (1990) study, the EPSF curriculum was used in the extended-day program for at-risk kindergartners. In these classrooms, instruction was oriented toward "prereading skills"—that is, visual, auditory, language, fine- and gross-motor skills—based on the results of the EPSF screening tests. Children were grouped according to modality (for example, auditory skills) and proficiency to receive direct instruction for a large portion of the kindergarten day. This skills focus of instruction was in contrast to the regular district curriculum, which was developed with a focus on content areas. An example of one of the district objectives given up as too advanced for the EPSF children was the following reading objective: "The student will demonstrate an understanding of the concept of 'reading' as a communications process" (Graue, 1990, p. 203).

One implication of arranging curriculum in this way is that the child's learning is fragmented into constituent skills. It becomes, then, very easy (1) to lose sight of more important, integrated learning goals, and (2) to forget that skills exist in the context of particular activities. Overreliance on this skills-based approach ignores the integrated manner in which children and activities are related and it waters down rather than

enriches instruction. In recent years the EPSF program has been modified to reflect new conceptions of emergent literacy and cognitive science in general with a greater emphasis on skills in context and naturally occurring language and literacy experiences (Betz, personal communication, 1991; EPSF, 1991). These newer curricular guidelines are more in line with what we know about appropriate practices, but the concern remains about the use of more dated versions of the EPSF curriculum and other at-risk programs that focus on training of prerequisite skills.

A focus on training of prerequisite skills makes the same mistake as earlier efforts in special education to train underlying psycholinguistic processes—such as auditory reception, visual reception, verbal expression, and manual expression—for children with learning difficulties. Although empirical studies have shown that children who receive process training do better on process skills per se (as measured by the *Illinois Test of Psycholinguistic Abilities* pre and post) (Kavale, 1981), there has never been any evidence that process training improves children's learning of academic subjects (Arter & Jenkins, 1979). Thus the time spent on process training might actually be a diversion from more important learning opportunities. When children are not ready to learn difficult material, decomposition into constituent skills is only one way to make the material "easier." For children who are not yet decoding, for example, reading comprehension can be modeled by listening comprehension. Remediation should not be synonymous with simplification of task.

In sum, the use of readiness tests to place children in segregated classrooms for at-risk children poses the same problem as when used for kindergarten retention or placement in special education. Given a negative history of treatments that are harmful (which includes tracking, retention, and special education for marginally identified children), the burden of proof lies with the special placement. Instructional treatments must be proven effective before it is defensible to remove children from normal placements. Therefore, providing extra help *in addition to* regular kindergarten is more defensible than a permanent segregated placement.

Instructional Planning

Making instructional decisions within the regular classroom is the safest use of readiness test information because these decisions do not have such serious consequences for students, as do separate placements. Furthermore, any misjudgments that are made about a child's level of performance can be constantly reevaluated and redressed. Tests do not have to meet stringent standards of technical accuracy under these circumstances where the test serves only as a clinical device supplying systematic information to the teacher, who draws her own professional conclusions. However, we should note that this greater latitude in technical requirements carries with it a concomitant increase in teachers' responsibility. Teachers should be aware of the limitations of the test and must not impute to the test greater scientific insight than is warranted. In particular, teachers should not rely on test results when they have contrary evidence based on instructional interactions with relevant tasks. Finally, the scientific authority of "the test" should not be invoked to win arguments with parents.

Although tests do not have to meet strict reliability and validity requirements when used for in-class purposes, concerns remain about "teaching to the test" and the influence of test content and format on what is taught. How good is the test as curriculum? Assessment information cannot guide instruction unless what it tells about a child's strengths and weaknesses has implications for what to teach next. This brings us back to Stallman and Pearson's (1990) serious criticism of the content of traditional readiness skills tests. Such tests, with their emphasis on isolated skills, are based on outmoded learning theories. Using traditional readiness tests as templates for instruction has the same deleterious effects on curriculum as does teaching to standardized tests at other grade levels (Shepard, 1991). This criticism does not imply that children should not be assessed on their knowledge of letter-sound correspondence or ability to count. Rather it means that traditional test formats are a poor way to envision instructional tasks. Assessment of skills should occur in the context of real literacy experiences and real problem-solving activities, what Stallman and Pearson call "situated assessments."

CONCLUSION

School readiness tests and developmental screening measures are widely used in response to state and local policies to make a variety of important decisions about young children: referral for special education evaluation, denial of school entry, placement in 2-year kindergarten programs, placement in at-risk kindergartens, and instructional planning. Unlike the field of special education, where controversial court decisions have led to some awareness of the need to use reliable tests and to defend special placements, the extensive use of tests in early childhood education has burgeoned with little scrutiny of the technical adequacy of tests. Even by traditional measurement standards, readiness tests currently in use are not sufficiently reliable and their predictive validity is not great enough to warrant their use in making important classification decisions. Many tests are technically adequate for instructional planning and for initial screening for handicapping conditions, given that referrals are followed by in-depth assessment; however, these distinctions in purpose are often ignored in practice.

More importantly, we stress in this chapter that validity standards have been broadened in recent years to include more than psychometric accuracy (APA, 1985). If a test is used in a context where it is claimed not only that it can distinguish between ready and unready children, but also that ready children should be assigned to treatment A and unready children to treatment B, it must be demonstrated empirically that each group is better off in their respective treatments. If not, then the test cannot be used to make these placement decisions. Given research on program effects, the use of available tests can be defended for the identification of severely and moderately handicapped children. But there is *not* evidence to support the use of tests to delay school entry, to place children in readiness rooms or transition grades, to retain children in kindergarten, or to assign children to segregated at-risk classrooms.

Instructional uses of tests within regular classroom settings do not require rigorous psychometric evidence. The use of traditional readiness skills tests to plan instruction may be ill-advised, however, given their emphasis on isolated skills, a practice out of keeping with current research on how young children learn.

References

Allington, R. L. (1991). Children who find learning to read difficult: School responses to diversity. In E. Hiebert (Ed.), *Literacy for a diverse society: Perspectives, practices, and policies* (pp. 237–252). New York: Teachers College Press.

American Psychological Association. (1954). *Technical recommendations for psychological tests and diagnostic techniques*. Washington, DC: Author.

American Psychological Association, American Educational Research Association, & National Council on Measurement in Education. (1985). *Standards for educational and psychological testing*. Washington, DC: American Psychological Association.

Arter, J. A., & Jenkins, J. R. (1979). Differential diagnosis— prescriptive teaching: A critical appraisal. *Review of Educational Research, 49,* 517–555.

Bell, M. (1972). *A Study of the readiness room program in a small school district in suburban Detroit, Michigan*. Unpublished doctoral dissertation, Wayne State University.

Blount, J. E., & Meinhardt, S. K. (1988). *First grade readiness assessment–a state perspective*. Marietta, GA: Georgia Department of Education.

Boehm, A. E. (1985). Review of Brigance K and 1 Screen for Kindergarten and First Grade. In J. V. Mitchell (Ed.), *The ninth mental measurements yearbook* (Vol. 1, pp. 223–225). Lincoln, NE: Buros Institute of Mental Measurements.

Bradley, R. H. (1985). Review of The Gesell School Readiness Test. In J. V. Mitchell, Jr. (Ed.), *The ninth mental measurements yearbook* (Vol. 1, pp. 609–610). Lincoln, NE: Buros Institute of Mental Measurements.

Brigance, A. H. (1982). *Brigance K and 1 Screen for Kindergarten and First Grade*. Billerica, MA: Curriculum.

Brown, A. L., Campione, J. C., Webber, L. S., & McGilly, K. (1991). Interactive learning environments: A new look at assessment and instruction. In B. R. Gifford & M. C. O'Connor (Eds.), *Changing assessments: Alternative views of aptitude achievement and instruction* (pp. 121–211). New York: Kluwer Academic.

Buros, O. K. (Ed.). (1978). *The eight mental measurements yearbook, Volume 1*. Highland Park, NJ: Gryphon Press.

Casto, G., & Mastropieri, M. A. (1986). The efficacy of early intervention programs: A meta-analysis. *Exceptional Children, 52,* 417–424.

Clay, M. (1985). *Emergent reading behavior*. Unpublished doctoral dissertation, University of Auckland, New Zealand.

Cronbach, L. J. (1971). Test validation. In R. L. Thorndike (Ed.), *Educational measurement* (2nd ed., pp. 443–507). Washington, DC: American Council on Education.

Early Prevention of School Failure. (1990). *On the way to success in reading and writing: A second year with Early Prevention of School Failure*. Report submitted to Program Effectiveness Panel. Peotone, IL: Author.

Early Prevention of School Failure. (1991). *Awareness Packet*. Peotone, IL: Author.

Ellwein, M. C., Walsh, D. J., Eads, G. M., & Miller, A. (1991). Using readiness tests to route kindergarten students: The snarled intersection of psychometrics, policy, and practice. *Educational Evaluation and Policy Analysis, 13*, 159–175.

Feuerstein, R., Rand, Y., Hoffman, M., & Miller, R. (1979). Cognitive modifiability in retarded adolescents: Effects on instrumental enrichment. *American Journal of Mental Deficiency, 83*, 539–550.

Galloway, J. E., & George, J. (1986). Junior kindergarten. *Educational Leadership, 33*, 68–69.

Georgia Department of Education. (1990). *Georgia kindergarten assessment program: Assessment guide*. Marietta, GA: Author.

Gesell, A. (1925). *The mental growth of the preschool child*. New York: Macmillan.

Gesell, A. (1940). *The first five years of life*. New York: Harper & Bros.

Gesell Institute of Human Development. (1982). *A gift of time: A developmental point of view*. New Haven, CT: Author.

Gnezda, M. T., & Bolig, R. (1988). *A national survey of public school testing of pre-kindergarten and kindergarten children*. Washington, DC: National Forum on the Future of Children and Families, National Research Council.

Gnezda, M. T., Garduque, L., & Schultz, T. (Eds.). (1991). *Improving instruction and assessment in early childhood education*. Washington, DC: National Academy Press.

Graue, M. E. (1990). *Socially constructed readiness for kindergarten in three communities*. Unpublished doctoral dissertation, University of Colorado at Boulder.

Heller, K. A., Holtzman, W. H., & Messick, S. (Eds.). (1982). *Placing children in special education: A strategy for equity*. Washington, DC: National Academy Press.

Horn, W. F., & Packard, T. (1985). Early identification of learning problems, *Journal of Educational Psychology, 77*, 597–607.

Ilg, F. L., Ames, L. B., Haines, J., & Gillespie, C. (1978). *School readiness*. New York: Harper & Row.

Karweit, N. (1988). Quality and quantity of learning time in preprimary programs. *Elementary School Journal, 89*(2), 119–133.

Kaufman, A. S. (1971). Piaget and Gesell: A psychometric analysis of tests built from their tasks, *Child Development, 42*, 1341–1360.

Kavale, K. (1981). Functions of the Illinois Test of Psycholinguistic Abilities (ITPA): Are they trainable? *Exceptional Children, 47*, 496–510.

Lichtenstein, R. (1990). Psychometric characteristics and appropriate use of the Gesell School Readiness Screening Test. *Early Childhood Research Quarterly, 5*, 359–378.

Lyman, H. B. (1965). Review of the Peabody Picture Vocabulary Test. In O. K. Buros (Ed.), *The sixth mental measurements yearbook* (pp. 820–823). Highland Park, NJ: Gryphon Press.

Mason, J. M., & Stewart, J. P. (1990). Emergent literacy assessment for instructional use in kindergarten. In L. M. Morrow & J. K. Smith (Eds.), *Assessment for instruction in early literacy* (pp. 155–175). Englewood Cliffs, NJ: Prentice Hall.

Meisels, S. J. (1987). Uses and abuses of developmental screening and school readiness testing, *Young Children, 42*, 4–6, 68–73.

Meisels, S. J. (1989). *Developmental screening in early childhood: A guide* (3rd ed.). Washington, DC: National Association for the Education of Young Children.

Messick, S. (1989). Validity. In R. L. Linn (Ed.), *Educational measurement* (3rd ed., pp. 13–103). New York: American Council on Education & Macmillan.

Mitchell, J. V. (Ed.). (1985). *The ninth mental measurements yearbook, Vols. I and II*. Lincoln, NE: Buros Institute of Mental Measurement of the University of Nebraska-Lincoln.

Mossburg, J. W. (1987). *The effects of transition room placement on selected achievement variables and readiness for middle school*. Unpublished doctoral dissertation, Ball State University, Muncie, IN.

Nunnally, J. S. (1978). *Psychometric theory* (2nd ed.). New York: McGraw-Hill.

Oakes, J. (1985). *Keeping track: How schools structure inequality*. New Haven, CT: Yale University Press.

Olson, D., & Zigler, E. (1989). An assessment of the all-day kindergarten movement. *Early Childhood Research Quarterly, 4*, 167–186.

Resnick, L. B., & Resnick, D. P. (1991). Assessing the thinking curriculum: New tools for educational reform. In B. R. Gifford & M. C. O'Connor (Eds.), *Changing assessments: Alternative views of aptitude, achievement and instruction* (pp. 37–75). New York: Kluwer Academic.

Salvia, J., & Ysseldyke, J. E. (1988). *Assessment in special and remedial education* (4th ed.). Boston: Houghton Mifflin.

Sattler, J. M. (1988). *Assessment of children* (3rd ed.). San Diego, CA: Author.

Shepard, L. A. (1989a). A review of research on kindergarten retention. In L. A. Shepard & M. L. Smith (Eds.), *Flunking grades: Research and policies on retention* (pp. 64–78). London: Falmer Press.

Shepard, L. A. (1989b). Identification of mild handicaps. In R. L. Linn (Ed.), *Educational measurement* (3rd ed., pp. 545– 572). New York: American Council on Education & Macmillan.

Shepard, L. A. (1990). Readiness testing in local school districts: An analysis of backdoor policies. *Journal of Educational Policy, 5*, 159–179.

Shepard, L. A. (1991). The influence of standardized tests on early childhood curriculum, teachers, and children. In B. Spodek, & O. N. Saracho (Eds.), *Yearbook in early childhood education* (pp. 166–189). New York: Teachers College Press.

Shepard, L. A., & Smith, M. L. (1985). *Boulder Valley kindergarten study: Retention practices and retention effects*. Boulder, CO: Boulder Valley Public Schools.

Shepard, L. A., & Smith, M. L. (1986). Synthesis of research on school readiness and kindergarten retention, *Educational Leadership, 44*, 78–86.

Shepard, L. A., & Smith, M. L. (1989). Academic and emotional effects of kindergarten retention in one school district. In L. A. Shepard & M. L. Smith (Eds.), *Flunking grades: Research and policies on retention* (pp. 79–107). London: Falmer Press.

Snow, R. E. & Lohman, D. F. (1988). Implications of cognitive psychology for educational measurement. In R. L. Linn (Ed.), *Educational measurement* (3rd ed., pp. 263–331). New York: Macmillan.

Stallman, A. C., & Pearson, P. D. (1990). Formal measures of early literacy. In L. M. Morrow & J. K. Smith (Eds.), *Assessment for instruction in early literacy* (pp. 7–44). Englewood Cliffs, NJ: Prentice Hall.

Tramontana, M. G., Hooper, S. R., & Selzer, S. C. (1988). Research on the preschool prediction of later academic achievement: A review. *Developmental review, 8*, 89–146.

Walker, R. N. (1992). The Gesell Developmental Assessment: Psychometric properties. *Early Childhood Research Quarterly, 7*, 21–43.

Waters, E. (1985). Review of The Gesell Readiness Test. In J. V. Mitchell, Jr. (Ed.), *The ninth mental measurements yearbook* (Vol. 1, pp. 610–611). Lincoln, NE: Buros Institute of Mental Measurements.

·20·

PLAY ENVIRONMENTS IN EARLY

CHILDHOOD EDUCATION

James D. Dempsey

UNIVERSITY OF NORTH TEXAS

Joe L. Frost

UNIVERSITY OF TEXAS AT AUSTIN

The inclusion of a chapter on children's play in educational environments in this volume reflects the phenomenal growth of interest in play and in appropriate play settings. Interest in children's play is well documented (Rubin, Fein, & Vandenberg, 1983) and is exemplified elsewhere in this volume (Pellegrini and Boyd, Chapter 8). This interest is spurred by the substantial body of research that points to the role of play in encouraging problem solving (Sylva, 1977), language (McCune-Nicolich, 1981), creative use of materials (Dansky, 1980), manipulative skills (Pepler & Ross, 1981), social skills (Eisenberg & Harris, 1984), and motor skills (Seefeldt, 1984). Because play enhances children's development educators are seeking ways to promote play in educational settings. However, there exists a "communication gap between developmentalists doing basic research in human early experience and professionals concerned with design or public policy issues involving child care" (Wachs, 1989, p. 4). It is the intent of this chapter to narrow this gap by presenting an overview of research on the effects of environmental variables on children's play and to delineate the critical issues for design of appropriate play settings in early childhood education.

For the purposes of this chapter, the term "environment" may be defined as any factor impinging on the play of the child that is not inherent in the child. To illustrate, consider the factor of age. The age of the child is inherent in the child and so is not an environmental factor. However, the age of the peer who may be playing with the child is an environmental factor. As this illustration indicates, this chapter will use a broad definition of environment, including physical, social, and temporal aspects.

An understanding of the environment in which play occurs is important for educators for 3 reasons. First, the environment signals to children what they can or should do. The beginning teacher soon learns that, if she wants children to pay attention at group time, toys must be put away. She learns that a large open room invites running, regardless of the number of times she says, "We walk inside. Running is for outside." The wise teacher uses the environment to achieve her goals. Second, the environment tells the child whether we think he is capable of success. Books and other important materials within the child's reach communicate our confidence in the child's ability to choose and to succeed at his choices. Thus, the environment that promotes success builds the child's self concept. Third, the environment in large part embodies the curriculum of early childhood education. Arranging the physical, social, and temporal aspects of the environment is a primary role of the teacher, care giver, or administrator. In a view of the learner as instrumental in learning, as interactive with the environment, and as reliant on hands-on experience (Piaget, 1963), the environment is the interface between the teacher and the child. The rise of this view of the learner and the learning process is a foundational development in the appreciation of play as instrumental in child growth and development. The teacher brings an arranged environment, then, and the child brings an inexhaustible capacity to learn through play. It is no wonder that play environments in early childhood education should be of increasing concern.

The evidence of a growing interest in environments for play is clear in certain recent events as well as in the research literature. Among these events are (1) the publication of a journal,

Children's Environments Quarterly, dedicated to environments for children; (2) the recent completion of a 4-year project by the American Association for Leisure and Recreation resulting in publication of nationwide surveys of American playgrounds in various settings—public elementary schools (Bruya & Langendorfer, 1988), public parks (Thompson & Bowers, 1989), and child care centers (Wortham & Frost, 1990); (3) the ongoing efforts of a subcommittee of the American Society for Testing and Materials (ASTM) in producing a comprehensive U.S. standard for playground equipment, layout, and surfacing; and (4) formation of the Association of Child Care Consultants International, an association of over 100 consulting firms whose clients seek professional design of comprehensive child care environments. Driving the current need to know more about environments for play in early childhood education is the increasing amount of time young children spend in school and child care settings (Children's Defense Fund, 1990; Travers, Goodson, Singer, & Connell, 1980). Indeed, recent state and federal legislation blurs the lines between "child care" and "public education" as public schools increasingly become the sites for full-day child care. It is consequently all the more important to understand the effects on play behaviors of time spent in educational environments, and to protect the young child's freedom to play during the school experience.

In addition to these events a corpus of literature is accumulating on issues related to play settings in early childhood education. The reasons for increased interest in play settings are varied, having their roots in psychodynamics (Isaacs, 1933), anthropology (Opie & Opie, 1969), and sociology (Feitelson, Weintraub, & Michaeli, 1972), but most clearly in studies of child development (Vygotsky, 1962; Erikson, 1976).

CHILD DEVELOPMENT AND THE ECOLOGY OF PLAY

Play has long been important for its implications in child development. Early writings by Parten (1932) and Buhler (1951) established a foundation for discussion of social and cognitive development in young children through play. However, it was the work of Piaget (1962) that gave children's play its theoretical underpinnings as part of an interactive process in the child's development of social, cognitive, and physical abilities. Smilansky's (1968) research on socioeconomic status and play behavior further stimulated the interest of researchers and educators. In addition to the discrete findings of these researchers, their efforts led to a categorization scheme that has been preeminent in the literature of children's play. This scheme includes 4 levels of cognitive play—functional play, constructive play, dramatic play, and games with rules—and 4 levels of social play—solitary, parallel, associative, and cooperative play. The interaction of these categories results in a "nested hierarchy," a more specific codification scheme that has been a primary research tool in the literature (Rubin, Maioni, & Hornung, 1976). More recent writers have refined or supplanted these categories, but, with only minor adaptations, this hierarchical scheme continues to dominate as a framework for the study of play (Takhvar & Smith, 1990).

Criticism has been leveled at this scheme for its use as an indicator of development—for example, suggesting that solitary play is a less mature form than parallel play (Moore, Evertson, & Brophy, 1974)—and for its failure to include certain playful behaviors (Takhvar & Smith, 1990; Dale, 1989). A key reason for increasing awareness and study of ecological, or setting, factors in children's play is embedded within these criticisms. That is, whether a particular type of play occurs at a particular point in a child's development depends in part on ecological, situational concomitants (Smith & Connolly, 1980). Similarly, whether a behavior is considered to be play is affected somewhat by the context of the activity, for example, painting during free play versus painting as part of a teacher-directed lesson. It is clear that the environment surrounding play behaviors is an integral element regardless of how one categorizes or defines play.

As previously stated, a discussion of the play environment may include those factors outside of the child himself, factors such as who and what the child plays with, and of course where the child plays. The range of factors, or variables, that are attributed to the environment of a play situation is great, but each may be categorized as either a *molecular* or a *molar* variable (Darvill, 1982). The *molecular* environment consists of "within setting" variables, whereas the *molar* environment consists of "between setting" variables. That is, variables that can be interjected into the setting are molecular (equipment, peers, or arrangement of space), whereas variables into which the subject must be interjected are molar (culture, socioeconomic status, playground type).

MOLECULAR VARIABLES IN PLAY SETTINGS

Density

One of the molecular variables commonly studied is the effect of *density,* or the amount of space in the setting, on the behavior of the child, particularly in regard to aggression (Smith & Connolly, 1976). Greater density (i.e., less space) results in greater amounts of group play, aggression, and anger (Loo & Kennelly, 1979). Children's play is also affected in that increased spatial density (less space per child) results in decreased running and increased physical contact (McGrew, 1972). Increasing space elicits rough-and-tumble play, and decreasing space inhibits running (Smith & Connolly, 1976, 1980). These findings are consistent with those of Henniger (1985), who concluded that running is more prevalent on the playground than in the smaller indoor environment. Peck and Goldman (1978) found that imaginative play and onlooker play increases with increased density. However, Campbell and Dill (1985) reported no significant differences in observed play behavior when space was reduced from 4.29 square meters per child to 2.7 square meters per child. Interview data from their study showed that both children and staff preferred the larger-area condition. Teacher quality (highly educated and experienced), failure to reach a threshold of sufficient density (Smith & Connolly, 1976, suggest this threshold is 2 square meters), and excellent space management were factors influencing their findings. One child in the study was profoundly and negatively affected by the diminished space, corroborating the argument that individual factors also determine children's responses to density (Wachs, 1989).

Space Arrangement

According to Yawkey, Melizzi, and Jones: "The major consideration of space isn't quantity but delineation and flexibility of available space. Space must be delineated so that children have places to play individually as well as in social groups" (1982). Private spaces are much sought by young children (Gramza, 1970). Infant children in this study, allowed to choose among several cubes that varied in the degree of privacy afforded, consistently preferred full enclosure over partial enclosure. Age of the child plays a role in this preference. Older infants prefer enclosure as an attribute of playground equipment, but younger infants avoid enclosures that inhibit vision (Steele & Naumann, 1985). This coincides with other findings that children prefer enclosures with a "visual connection" to other areas of the environment (Kirkby, 1989). In her study centering on "refuge" characteristics of a playground, Kirkby found that 47 percent of children's play occurs in the 10 percent of the area that provides enclosure, or refuge. The size of the enclosure also affects the type of dramatic theme in play, with domestic themes predominating in the smaller refuge areas and adventure themes occurring more often in the larger enclosures. Kirkby hypothesized that larger enclosures better accommodate the large-muscle activities associated with adventure themes. She also observed that the presence of a ceiling or canopy is important for a sense of refuge. The ability to "hide and watch" is affirmed in numerous children's comments related to favorite features on elementary school playgrounds (Moore, 1974).

The preference of children for more or less enclosure in play spaces needs further study and clarification. The authors' observations of 5- to 8-year-old children over a period of several years revealed that children chose a semiopen play structure (roof and wall on one side) over a closed play structure (roof and 4 walls with crawl space for entry) by a significant margin (5 to 1 ratio). Children appear to want to see and be seen, hear and be heard, not only by peers but by adult supervisors as well. Age and developmental levels appear to influence the types of spaces children choose.

The openness of play structures is also important for public policy regarding playground design. Discarded condoms and hypodermic needles found in increasing numbers in and around the enclosures on park playgrounds have created a health and safety concern to municipalities (Thompson, 1989). The tendency of play structures to obstruct clear vision, affecting care givers attempting to supervise children as well as law enforcement personnel attempting to keep playgrounds secure, is a legitimate issue in the design of play environments.

A driving force in the study of space arrangement was the popularizing of the open classroom. Neill (1982) reported that open classrooms lacking clear boundaries are likely to increase aggression and raise activity levels in preschool children. His findings suggest that better organization of space leads to desirable behaviors in early childhood settings. There is evidence that increased organization of space can lead to positive changes in play behavior (Teets, 1985). Among the changes are increased use of materials in appropriate areas, increased level of construction play, decreased onlooker behavior, and decreased deviant behavior. Teets suggests the following criteria for good classroom organization: (1) paths should be clear and unobstructed (Kritchevsky, Prescott, & Walling, 1969), (2) incompatible activities should not be placed in proximity, for example, language arts areas should not be contiguous with block play areas, (3) interest areas should be clearly defined with recognizable boundaries, (4) materials should be displayed in ways to facilitate children's selection and use, and (5) to avoid a perception of crowding, at least one-third to one-half of the floor space should be free of equipment.

A fundamental practice in early childhood education is the use of specific areas, or learning centers, for different types of activities, such as art, manipulatives and/or blocks, housekeeping, music, science, and language arts. Research bears out the implicit reasoning for these separate areas: Children act—and play—differently in different areas within the same classroom (Shure, 1963). Significant differences exist in the types and quality of play predominating in construction-play centers versus dramatic-play centers (Pellegrini, 1985). Children engage in constructive and solitary play in the block and the art areas, and dramatic and interactive play in the replica or dramatic area (Pellegrini & Perlmutter, 1989). In addition, the gender of the player affects play in centers, in that boys play more in the block center than do girls. Other researchers have reported differences in play types in manipulative centers versus house-play centers (Rubin, 1977) and in gross-motor areas versus manipulative areas (Vandenberg, 1981). In sum, the materials and equipment placed in these centers strongly influence the specific types and qualities of children's play behavior. The adult solicits and gets the type of play desired, not only by organizing the environment into learning centers, but also by her choices of materials and equipment.

Materials and Equipment

The effects of the amount and types of materials or equipment available in the play environment has been examined along many different lines. Among the topics considered are the effects of materials on symbolic play, the effects of materials on level of social play, the preferences for play materials at various ages, the effects of quantity of toys or equipment on play, the effects of war-theme toys, and the dynamics of play with gender-stereotyped toys. The following discussion presents an overview of the literature addressing these topics.

The Effects of Materials on Symbolic Play. A large number of researchers have examined the enhancement of symbolic or representational types of play. This concentration of effort is due in part to the prominent role of symbol manipulation in cognitive processes (Piaget, 1962; Vygotsky, 1962) and the perceived connection between symbolic play and language (Smilansky, 1968; Fein, 1981). Interaction with objects is an important indicator of the child's progress in transition from reliance on the attributes of signifiers to independence from the attributes of signifiers in play transformations (Wagner, 1985).

For example, the 2-year-old uses replicas of cars in pretending, whereas the 4-year-old feels free to use any similarly shaped object to represent a car (Fein, 1975).

The attribute of realism in play materials, sometimes considered in tandem with the *structure* of materials, has been studied in some detail. Pulaski (1973), McGhee, Ethridge, and Benz (1984), and Einsiedler (1985) found that minimal structure in toys enhances richness and variety of fantasy themes. Pepler and Ross (1981) allowed children to play with a puzzle with and without its accompanying formboard, assuming that the formboard added structure to the material. The children engaged in construction-type play (product-oriented play) in the presence of the formboard, but engaged in both construction and symbolic play (using the materials in a symbolic way) in the less-structured setting. Mann (1984) reported an inverse relationship between high-structure materials and creativity in children who retold a story using either realistic or unrealistic props. Children who used the realistic props exhibited better memory of detail but children who replayed the story with unrealistic props were more creative. In a study of 4 experimental settings varying in both realism and structure, Dodge and Frost (1986) reported that unstructured materials were conducive to a wider variety of role play, but that the absence of any connotation of theme in the materials was not stimulative of pretend play. This finding of a "floor effect" in realism was consistent with McLoyd (1983), who reported that low-structure items with no pretend connotation (metal cans, pipe cleaners) did not enhance pretend play.

The effect of object realism on children's play is highly sensitive to the age of the child. Younger children need more realistic props to encourage and sustain symbolic play than do older children (Fein & Robertson, 1975). Realistic props tend to inhibit pretend play for older preschoolers (Olszewski & Fuson, 1982). The evidence now available suggests that realistic play props can inhibit creative aspects of play among older children, but a modicum of realism in play materials is necessary to stimulate their pretend play. Whereas younger preschoolers appear to need realism in play materials to stimulate role play (Pederson, Rook-Green, and Elder, 1981), non–theme-specific raw materials such as sand, water, and building blocks are needed to support role play and to encourage creativity for all age groups.

Another attribute of play materials studied for its effect on symbolic play is novelty. The question of whether novelty elicits play or rather elicits exploration as a precursor to play is discussed in Rubin et al. (1983). A period of intense manipulation (exploration) occurs in the presence of novel play materials, and novelty gradually gives way to familiarity as children use the materials. Props designed to facilitate dramatic play in the classroom can become too familiar and thus boring. Dodge and Frost (1986) and Griffing (1983) suggest that introduction of novel and realistic props into the dramatic play area enlivens and refreshes role play. Materials and equipment that stimulate symbolic play should be highly realistic for very young children, less realistic but at least believable for older children, and moderately novel. A study by Scholtz and Ellis (1975) addresses the effect of novelty of peers (introducing new peers) in play situations on group symbolic play. There was a decrease

in use of materials by children as peer novelty decreased (as familiarity increased) through repeated exposure. Simultaneously there was an increase in play with peers as familiarity increased during the same period of exposure. In sum, whereas novelty of materials fosters exploration activity and suppresses playful activity, peers stimulate group social play as they become more familiar and less novel. The findings also suggest that complexity (peers are highly complex stimuli!) mitigates the effects of decreasing novelty.

The Effects of Materials on Social Play. Complexity of materials affects the social qualities of play. A complex climbing structure containing multiple access and egress options elicits more peer contacts than a simple climber for 3-, 4-, and 5-year-olds (Bruya, 1985). Particular levels of social play are elicited by certain materials (Rubin, 1977). Children using clay, puzzles, sand and water tubs, paints, and colors engage in solitary or parallel play a high proportion of the time. Cooperative play, which is considered more mature than solitary or parallel play, occurs more often during house play and in play with cars or vehicles.

Howes and Rubenstein (1978) have offered some insight into Rubin's findings. They compared the play of toddlers in 2 settings, 1 containing numerous small portable toys and 1 containing few portable toys but many large, nonportable toys, for example, climbing structures or rocking boats. Toddlers exhibited more cooperative play when using large toys. The researchers explained that the large equipment permitted simultaneous use by 2 children without the imposition of having to take turns or to share, and that it put children in juxtaposition to one another. Thus, equipment or physical space arrangement that focuses toddlers' attention on each other and allows them to respond to each other without physically intruding encourages more socially mature play among toddlers (Mueller & Bergstrom, 1982).

Rogers (1985) compared the play of children with small unit blocks and with large hollow blocks. Group cooperative play was more likely to occur with large hollow blocks, whereas parallel and solitary play were more likely to occur with unit blocks. Rogers hypothesized that the size of the hollow blocks forced children to work together to move them around and that the resulting space requirements fostered opportunities for social interaction.

A line of research has emerged dealing with the interaction between the use of objects and the "peer culture" of play. Elgas, Klein, Kantor, and Fernie (1988) examined the functions that objects play in the social environment of the preschool. Certain objects and places determine the membership of peers in particular groupings, termed the "core" group. In this study, a prominent example was a set of superhero capes, which were regularly and often used to permit or deny entry to the core group's play episode. They also reported, consistent with Corsaro (1985), that play centered around climbing structures, presumably for the power and control gained through elevation. Similar findings of territoriality around climbers and possession of socially empowering objects were reported by Bell and Walker (1985). Further research could provide a helpful rationale for teachers and administrators making purchases of equipment both for the indoor and the outdoor environment, especially for play props that may encourage children to play together successfully. An enlightening description of the workings of boys and girls in dramatic play is presented by Paley (1984). Nowhere are the subtleties of gender, peer culture, and pretend play in preschool settings described with more insight and charm.

Preference of Play Materials at Various Ages. There is a relative lack of research on the effects of age on the materials children select in play. Most studies of the effects of age on play have focused on the quality of play (for a review of literature on this topic, see Fein [1981] or Hughes [1991]). Children show differential preferences for play equipment according to their age, with younger infants preferring the security of well-lit, open spaces and older infants/toddlers preferring enclosure (Steele & Naumann, 1985). Children rely less on objects for symbolic play as they increase in age (Matthews, 1977; McLoyd, 1980). Tizard, Philps, and Plewis (1976a) found that 3-year-olds used play materials in "partial" fashion more than 4-year-olds. "Partial use" in this study was analogous to exploratory use or use without an apparent end in mind. Several studies have reported on children's preferred play equipment on the playground as a function of age. Frost and Strickland (1985) reported that play without equipment of any kind increased from kindergarten to first and from first to second grade. Wheeled vehicles were used by kindergartners 3 times as often as by first graders; the "fort" and housekeeping area underneath were very popular with kindergarten children, but their use dropped off rapidly with increasing age; and loose parts were popular with all 3 grade levels. The importance and popularity of manipulable loose parts has been confirmed by Moore (1985) and Allen (1968).

The Effects of Quantity of Materials on Play. The quantity of play materials available to the child is clearly correlated with children's cognitive development. A synthesis of studies found a mean correlation coefficient of .37 between quantity of play materials in the home and IQ scores at ages 3 and 4 (Gottfried, 1984). This correlation is understandable in light of studies of the effects of quantity of play materials on children's play behaviors. One early study of playground setting looked at the effect of amount of equipment and material on children's play behavior (Johnson, 1935). Among the prominent findings were that undesirable behavior increased with the reduction in play materials, and that social contacts increased and children used sand and dirt more in the absence of specific play materials. Smith and Connolly (1980) also reported that conflicts were considerably fewer when more equipment was available. The absence of small toys, leaving only "apparatuses," led to increased verbal and physical contacts, more group cooperative play, and more creative uses of available equipment. Clearly, decisions about quality of materials are linked to decisions about quantity.

Possibly the best advice to educators based on these findings would be to limit, at least on occasion, the quantity of small toys so that children are forced to focus on social possibilities and to discover novel uses of the environment. This advice in no way diminishes the need for sufficient quantity and variety of materials (Olds, 1989; Griffing, 1983), but only suggests that variety may be found not in quantity alone, but in novelty, complexity, and the child's own resourcefulness in adapting to the setting. The wise care giver provides enough materials for each child to find both age-appropriate and individually appropriate play outlets (Bredekamp, 1987).

The Effects of War-Theme Toys on Behavior. War toys present a quandary for developmentalists and educators, torn between a recognition of the child's apparent need to engage in war play, and society's increasing awareness of the link between exposure to violence through play and television viewing and later aggressive or violent behavior. Numerous studies establish empirically the deleterious effects of play with war toys. Play with weapon replicas, action figures (e.g., G.I. Joe), and victim toys (figurines displaying a range of disfigurements and injuries) increases aggressive behavior of children (Feshbach, 1956; Mallick & McCandless, 1966; Turner & Goldsmith, 1976; Potts, Huston, & Wright, 1986). Aggressive behavior also increases after play with a violent video game (Silvern, Williamson, & Countermine, 1983).

Educators and parents are particularly concerned about war toys that are associated with their own television cartoon series, for example, He-Man and G.I. Joe (Carlsson-Paige & Levin, 1988, 1990; Frost, 1986). These television cartoons are little more than extended advertisements for the toys themselves, demonstrating ways to subdue one's enemies by violence. The combination of passive viewing of these incredibly violent cartoon sequences with one-dimensional, violence-connoting toys leads to an imitative form of play devoid of any active, creative aspects that *might* allow children to deal with their concerns about violence through war-theme play.

Carlsson-Paige and Levin (1988) suggest that adults avoid 2 options for response to war play—banning all war-theme play and ignoring its occurrence—in favor of a third, "to allow war play and to intervene actively in it to affect the learning that can result from it" (p. 84). When children create their own weapons from available, flexible-connotation material, they are at least actively constructing their own ideas about coping with violence. Adults who interact with children during play can teach about the effects of violence, can regulate the presence of war toys in educational settings, and can become advocates for responsible television viewing. A remaining critical issue is the educational system's response in light of differences between home and school regarding war toys. Teachers or care givers may limit or negotiate the amount and nature of war play while parents impose no restrictions on TV viewing, toy selection, or resulting play. Consequently, the child is influenced by 2 conflicting value systems with potential negative consequences. The effects of toys in maintaining gender stereotypes represents a related issue.

Play with Sex-Stereotyped Toys. Boys and girls approach the play environment differently, both in their use of available space (Harper & Sanders, 1975) and in their use of toys (Fagot, 1978). Very early children begin to associate toys with a particular gender, showing preferences as early as 10 months (Roopnarine, 1986). The reasons for such preferences are likely to be social or cultural, and not biological (Hughes, 1991).

Eisenberg, Wolchik, Hernandez, and Pasternack (1985) found that parents did not appear to actively encourage gender-specific use of toys. However, other researchers have reported clear evidence of just such parental influence (Langlois & Downs, 1980; Caldera, Huston, & O'Brien, 1989). Such conflicting findings may result from the ages of the children, as parents may be less comfortable with older children's use of "inappropriate" toys.

Are there any benefits or disadvantages of such stereotypical behavior? Play with gender-stereotyped toys correlates with certain intellectual skills (Tracy, 1987; Serbin & Connor, 1979). Boys who exhibited frequent use of stereotyped toys were more likely to excel in math and science than boys using stereotyped toys less often, and girls who played with stereotyped toys were more likely to excel in verbal skills than girls showing a more diverse use of toys. A causal relationship is not clear, so parents and educators are left with the common sense advice that all children should have the opportunity, and be encouraged, to play with any toy that adds necessary skills and abilities.

Play equipment and materials may be more important resources than space for the child at play. Both equipment and its arrangement are static components of the environment. One other variable, which is clearly not static, must be considered. This variable—actually many variables—is the influence of other persons, both peers and adults.

Effects of Social Variables on Play

Peers. A prominent feature of the environment of play in educational settings is a player's peers. Several aspects of peer influence, including familiarity, gender, and group size, are common research topics. Concerning the effect of peers' familiarity on play behavior, Howes (1988) reported that, among a stable group of peers, children in a child care setting play in more mature ways than children not exposed to a stable group of peers. Such findings have been used by supporters of child care to argue that children are not hurt by the increased reliance of care outside the home. Rubin et al. (1983) summarized the research by saying that "children play more, and at higher cognitive levels, when in the company of an acquaintance than when alone or with an unfamiliar child," and that "there is a corresponding increase in the amount and in the complexity of pretense play" (pp. 731). A consistent finding concerning the gender of players is that the presence of opposite-sex play partners tends to increase gender-stereotyped play and inhibit nonstereotyped play (Eisenberg, Tryon, & Cameron, 1984; Lloyd & Smith, 1985). An insightful overview of these issues is presented in Hughes (1991).

A primary aspect of the peer environment is group size. Group size is related to the previously discussed topic of play space density because teachers' and administrators' decisions about the number of students in a class invariably affect density. It is also related to adult/child ratio because the group dynamics are very different between the classroom with 1 teacher and 12 children and the classroom with 2 teachers and 12 children. The National Day Care Study (Ruopp, Travers, Glantz, & Coelen, 1979) identified group size as one of the most important variables in predicting quality in child care settings. Smaller groups (12 versus 24 children) result in more cooperation and compli-

ance, less noninvolved or aimless behavior, and less adult-child interaction. Evidence suggests that relatively small increases in adult/child ratio in preschool settings lead to more verbal exchange among peers, less verbal exchange with teachers, less absorption in play activity, and more teasing among children (Russell, 1990). Fantasy play is more likely to occur in a small class of preschoolers (10) versus a large class (30) (Smith & Connolly, 1980). Consequently, recommendations for quality child care include limiting the size of groups and promoting the involvement of children in activity subgroups. It should be noted here that group size may be determined by the children themselves in response not only to available space options but also to activity options. Vandenberg (1981) found that self-selected group size in free play is related to the focus of the activity in the particular play area. For example, the large-muscle play area is used by larger groups than the fine-motor play area. Thus it appears that there are intricate interactions between group size and type of play, with the direction of influence operating in reciprocal ways. In settings that allow a range of group sizes, from very small to large groups, many more occasions are afforded to children to achieve a sense of privacy and intimacy. These occasions are provided through both grouping and space arrangement.

Adults/Teachers. A sizable body of research exists on the role of adults in the environment of play. Most of this research has examined the effects of training or tutoring of play behaviors. As Frost (1992) has noted, "play tutoring" is a contradiction of terms because play by definition is intrinsic and nondirected. However, if tutoring is understood to be encouragement in play through indirect means such as provision of time and materials or through direct means such as timely suggestions offered by the adult, and if the adult's interventions respect the child's initiatives, then discussion of play tutoring is consistent with the definition of play. Because most of the studies on play tutoring examine its effects on cognitive variables, and few examine its effects on children's play, this chapter will not discuss effects on cognitive variables at length. The reader is referred to one of several reviews of the literature (Frost, 1992; Fein, 1981; Smith, 1988).

Play tutoring, or the systematic efforts of adults to increase incidence or quality of play behavior through adult-child interaction, does affect the play of children. Generally, play tutoring for a given type of play produces increases in both the incidence and quality of that play type (Smith & Syddall, 1978). For example, "training" children in thematic fantasy play (Saltz & Johnson, 1974) results in greater quantities and higher levels of fantasy play. Both fantasy and group play are increased through training in sociodramatic play (Smith & Syddall, 1978), which is predictable in that both of these variables are defining qualities of this type of play. Solitary play was increased in the same study among children exposed to training in construction play. In addition to strict training paradigms, everyday parent and child interactions affect the play of children. Parents' presence and interaction with their children during play can increase amount of play with toys, body movements, and verbalizing during play (Cox & Campbell, 1968). Children play significantly longer when adults are present and involved than when children play alone or only with peers (Sylva, Roy, &

Painter, 1980). Children whose parents display more emotional warmth play more intently and are more absorbed in the materials or themes of play (Kooij & Neukater, 1987).

Also resulting from the research on play tutoring are increasingly well-developed recommendations for the administration of play tutoring. Christie (1985) described 4 strategies for the adult's intervention; modeling play behaviors, verbal guidance (suggestions), thematic-fantasy training (helping children act out familiar fairy tales), and imaginative play training (mental exercises in fantasizing). Tamburrini (1982) cautioned against intervention that disregards the child's own intentions in the play episode, arguing that extending the child's play is preferable to redirecting it. Both Wolfgang and Sanders (1982) and Dempsey (1985) recommended a continuum of intervention techniques, from active observation as least intrusive to direct physical intervention, such as taking a role within the pretend play episode, as most intrusive. Both these studies make clear the adult's responsibility to respect the child's initiative in setting the theme and direction of play. The adult should choose the least intrusive means necessary to encourage particular play behaviors. Peters, Neisworth, and Yawkey (1985) listed 3 major strategies for adult intervention: free discovery (no intervention), prompted discovery (indirect assistance, suggestions, encouragement—all within the role as teacher), and direct discovery (questions and prompts aimed at encouraging creative use of the materials in the play context). These authors stress the teacher's role in preparing a rich and varied environment that accommodates creative play with materials.

The literature on play tutoring addresses the child at play primarily in classroom or home settings. Descriptions of European playgrounds demonstrate the value of play *leaders* on public playgrounds. The notion of a static environment into which children are turned loose, of indestructible playgrounds that can be neither vandalized nor appropriately manipulated by children, is the prevailing design basis for most American playgrounds (Moore, 1985). In contrast, the primarily European phenomenon of adventure playgrounds, so called because of their high level of changeability *by the child himself*, affords children the opportunity to build, rearrange, experiment, and consequently, to learn. Adventure playgrounds are characterized by quantities of building materials, tools, gardens, places for children to cook on a bonfire, and the permission to use all these materials. A key element in this environment is the play leader (Frost, 1992); an adult who can supervise, guide, check out tools, provide raw materials or loose parts, and otherwise assist children in their efforts. Teachers and care givers in early childhood education settings act in much the same way as these play leaders, facilitating the exploration and independence of the child through play. Several studies have shown that teachers can be trained to provide effective play leadership (Wade, 1985; Collier, 1985; Dempsey, 1985).

Temporal Aspects of the Setting

In addition to physical and social dimensions of the setting, the amount of time provided affects children's play. One critical decision for educators is the schedule of the program. Recent trends point to decreasing amounts of free-play time in early

childhood education settings as a result of the "back-to-basics" movement (Glickman, 1984). The effects of short versus long play periods (15 versus 30 minutes) on children's play were investigated by Christie, Johnsen, and Peckover (1988). Mature levels of cognitive play types—constructive, group-constructive, and group-dramatic—are more likely to occur in the longer play period. Complex play behaviors involving planning and negotiation of social roles such as would occur in group-dramatic play require a reasonable provision of time. Indeed, one measure of the quality of dramatic play is the length of time of the play episode (Smilansky, 1968).

Although Peters et al. (1985) and Yawkey (1990) recommend 60-minute free-play periods, there is little argument that play periods in early childhood settings should be at least 30 minutes in length. Shorter periods do not allow time for children to initiate, develop, and extend play themes. Some of the richest and most creative play episodes observed by the present authors occurs as children tire of common dramatic play themes and begin to incorporate the setting into novel uses or combinations of play themes. The skillful play leader looks to the child for cues to cut short or extend the play period.

All of the variables heretofore discussed—materials, space, schedules, and social components—can be changed within a given early childhood education setting. The variables that follow either require a view across settings (e.g., indoor versus outdoor) or form the context for individual educational settings (nationality, culture, curriculum orientation).

MOLAR VARIABLES IN PLAY SETTINGS

Several lines of questioning have been pursued by researchers related to variations in play according to the molar features of the setting, features in which the setting itself is nested. These features include the player's nationality (how play differs across nations), cultural affiliation, and socioeconomic status. They also include variables such as approach to curriculum, indoor versus outdoor setting, and type of playground. These "between setting" variables have embedded in them many of the molecular components discussed earlier. For example, in comparing the indoor versus outdoor environment, researchers have noted differences in amount of space; variability of texture, lighting, and temperature; availability of equipment and materials; adult attention; and peer interaction. Because in the real world these molecular variables combine in various ways, it is important to keep the research on molecular variables in mind as we examine the play of children in the larger, molar setting.

Nationality, Culture, and Socioeconomic Status

Several researchers have noted striking similarities in the developmental sequence of play among children of various nations. Kooij (1989) compared the play maturity of children from the Netherlands, Germany, and Norway and reported no differences among the 3 populations. Much the same finding was reported in comparing the developmental sequence of play between American and Japanese children (Seagoe & Murakami,

1961). American and Senegalese children play about the same proportion of time (30%), engage in functional, constructive, exploratory, rough-and-tumble, music/art, and pretense play in similar amounts, but American children engage in more gross-motor play than Senegalese children (Bloch, 1989).

In an extensive study employing children in 6 nations, Seagoe (1971a) reported that: (1) differences between rural and suburban children's social play behaviors were negligible in all 6 nations; (2) age was positively related to level of social play in the United States, England, Norway, Spain, and Egypt but not in Greece (this could not be explained); (3) boys led girls in level of social play in all six countries; (4) each country showed similar levels of social play yet national styles were evident; and (5) the form of government (individualistic-democratic in the United States, England, and Norway; monolithic-authoritarian in Spain, Egypt, and Greece) predicted these national styles. The most significant difference in social play style occurred in the onset and incidence of adult involvement and individual-informal play (earlier onset and higher incidence in the United States, England, and Norway).

Children's games, though not entirely spontaneous, are a type of play (Piaget, 1962), and the complexity of the child's culture affects children's games (Sutton-Smith & Roberts, 1981). In hunter-gatherer cultures, games are exclusively contests of physical skills, such as races. In complex societies, though, children's games require complex strategies, whether with or without physical components (e.g., Monopoly and soccer). The competitiveness of a culture is reflected in the presence of competition in the play of children (Parker, 1984); in some cultures, competitive games of any sort are nonexistent (Hughes, 1991).

Within the classrooms of many Western societies, many cultures come into contact with each other. In one study Smilansky (1968) reported lower levels of dramatic play in children of lower socioeconomic status; however, the subjects also differed in ethnic origin (European versus North African). In a comparison of Israeli and South African children, occurrence of dramatic play was influenced more by socioeconomic status (SES) than nationality (Udwin & Shmukler, 1981). Smilansky and Shefatya (1990) have subsequently reported that the level of parent education "is the single major background variable related to the level of make-believe play across the various cultures" (p. 90).

The assumption of a deficit, as opposed to simply a difference, in the symbolic play of low-SES children has been hotly debated, with mixed results. Although the findings of differences have been widely corroborated (Rubin et al., 1976; Golomb, 1979; Udwin & Shmukler, 1981), it has been shown that low-SES children exhibit higher levels of verbal and social skills when measured in the home compared to the classroom setting (Labov, 1972; Schwartzman, 1984). The assumed explanation is that the symbolic play of low-SES children would certainly appear more mature in familiar home or neighborhood surroundings than in the perhaps unfamiliar surroundings of a middle-class nursery school. Further research is needed to determine the extent to which the differences observed among children in high-and low-SES groups are due to the context of measurement.

Feitelson, Weintraub, and Michaeli (1972) compared the social interactions of heterogeneous groupings of low- and high-SES preschoolers with those of homogeneous groupings (either low-SES only or high-SES only). They reported that both low- and high-SES children in the heterogeneous groupings interacted mainly with same-SES children. Low-SES children in the heterogeneous setting did interact more with each other than did their counterparts in the homogeneous condition. An interesting finding was that although low-SES children in the homogeneous grouping developed good peer cooperation skills, low-SES children in the heterogeneous grouping remained very dependent on adults. Perhaps children know what is best for themselves in this regard: They appear to prefer playmates similar to themselves. Black and white kindergartners in a playground setting prefer same-color playmates (Finkelstein & Haskins, 1983). Recalling that familiarity of peers is associated with mature levels of play, it may be that ethnicity and cultural homogeneity provide an increased level of familiarity, at least initially. Seagoe (1971b) reported differences in social maturity in play among Anglo American, Mexican American, and African American children when socioeconomic level was held constant. Homogeneous groupings at 3 different schools were measured for degree of socialization, and findings suggest that culture was a stronger predictor of level of social play than socioeconomic status. That is, similarity of level of play was more likely to be found among children of a similar cultural affiliation (e.g., Latino) than of a similar socioeconomic status.

The Effects of Curriculum on Play

The curriculum may be viewed as an aspect of the ecology of the setting in that various curricula differentially prescribe appropriate and necessary materials, space arrangements, group size, and social interaction, both peer/peer and adult/child. Studies have concentrated primarily on the variable of structure of the curriculum. Within the variable of structure, focus has centered on the amount of adult direction and the structure of the materials, as exemplified in Montessori programs. Greater imaginativeness in play is related to less-structured classrooms (Huston-Stein, Freidrich-Cofer, & Susman, 1977). High structure was defined as high teacher directedness, program structure, and harsh discipline. Comparing 4 types of preschool programs, Miller and Dyer (1975) reported that children in a Montessori program engaged in more manipulation with materials and less role play than did children in a less-structured traditional nursery school program. Preschoolers in a Montessori program engage often in solitary and constructive-parallel play but significantly less often in functional-cooperative and dramatic-cooperative play (Rubin & Seibel, 1979). Johnson and Ershler (1981, 1982) summarized the research on differences in high- and low-structured programs. In general they reported that high structure in curriculum elicits construction play, whereas low structure encourages symbolic and functional play. However, Griffing (1980) observed that these differences in play behavior may be in performance only and not in competence. Children moved from one setting to another showed corresponding changes in play behavior (e.g., engaging in construction-play behaviors in a high-structure setting, then symbolic play behaviors in a low-structure setting). Thus children appear to be able to adjust their play preferences quickly to changes in the structure of the environment, allaying fears that children may be unable to play in all the various play types as a result of exposure to a particular curriculum. This also suggests that play preference may not be generalizable across all settings.

Christie and Johnsen (1989) compared preschool and kindergarten classrooms differing in orientation (social versus academic). Children in the social curriculum classrooms exhibited similar levels of social play to children in an academic program. Cognitive play types, however, were different in the 2 programs, with dramatic play twice as likely to occur in the social kindergarten as opposed to the academic kindergarten. Structure of the program as well as apparent support of dramatic play through teacher attitudes and available materials were salient and predictable differences between the 2 programs. Smith and Connolly (1980) conducted a long-range study of children placed in either a free-play or a structured-activities group. More social interaction between peers and more spontaneous fantasy play occurred in the free-play group, as did higher rates of aggressive behavior among structured-activity subjects once they were allowed more free play. The researchers concluded that the benefits of free social interaction during free play resulted in better social coping skills, a conclusion supported by Seagoe (1971).

Indoor Versus Outdoor Settings

Only a few studies have contrasted the play of children in indoor versus outdoor settings. Sanders and Harper (1976) compared the play of preschoolers in the 2 settings and reported that boys engaged in more fantasy play outdoors than girls, and older children spent proportionately more of their outdoor time in fantasy play than did younger children. Differences have been reported in play indoors versus outdoors and between working-class and middle-class 3- and 4-year-old children (Tizard, Philps, & Plewis, 1976a, 1976b). In this study the play of working-class children was more mature outdoors as opposed to indoors. Solitary and parallel play were less likely to occur outdoors compared to indoors for these children, and working-class children chose to play in the outdoor environment more often than did middle-class children. Adults in these studies gave less information and made fewer suggestions to children outdoors versus indoors, and verbal initiations were fewer outdoors from both adults to children and children to adults. These findings reinforce the importance of the outdoor environment for establishing a "peer culture," and as a laboratory for studying play free of adult intervention.

Tizard et al. also reported that boys engaged in more fantasy play outdoors than did girls, and that boys' language was more complex on the playground than in the classroom. This intriguing finding suggests strongly that educational programs for young children should resist the pull toward shorter periods on the playground in the assumed interest of academic gains. It is entirely possible that the playground provides boys with a unique setting favorable to language development. Yerkes

(1982) also reported gains for children who played in the outdoor setting versus those exposed only to indoor settings during free play. Visual-motor integration was improved through exposure to the "adventure-style" playground (extensive loose manipulable materials). This increase was more pronounced for girls than for boys. Such a finding again reinforces the value of outdoor settings in encouraging skills that strengthen the particular weaknesses of each gender. The qualitative work of Paley (1984) clearly points to this propensity of the outdoor environment to lessen the rigidity of gender-stereotypes in preschoolers' play. She describes the changes in girls' dramatic play as they move from the classroom to the playground, feeling greater freedom to "try on" a superhero role instead of domestic, house-play roles. Boys were more likely to accept and play with girls in characteristically male roles in the outdoor context. Studies of these phenomena in quantifiable ways would be a valuable addition to the research literature.

An obvious advantage to play in an outdoor environment is in increased opportunities for physical or motor development. There is evidence that free play on well-developed playgrounds contains more active, physical components than does structured physical education (Myers, 1985). Other researchers have shown, however, that free-play opportunities alone do not provide sufficient cardiovascular stimulation (Hovell, Bursick, Sharkey, & McClure, 1978). Specific environmental components, for example, equipment, are necessary in addition to opportunities to increase particular motor abilities. For example, upper-body muscular endurance is enhanced among children who are exposed to overhead ladders and climbers during free play on playgrounds (Gabbard, 1979).

Henniger (1985) provides some of the rare quantitative data comparing the play of children in indoor versus outdoor environments. He compared the play behaviors of 3- and 4- year-old children using social and cognitive play categories. His findings were that each environment was important in encouraging certain types of play. The indoor environment was linked to constructive play in all children, to dramatic play in younger children and girls, and to solitary play for all children. The outdoor environment was linked to functional play and to dramatic play in older children and boys. Henniger argued that similar levels of cooperative social play in both settings implies that both should be included in teachers' planning if cooperative play is a goal of the curriculum, and that children restricted by reduced space and increased noise levels in the indoor setting would profit from use of the outdoors as an alternative learning environment. It remains then for educators to determine the best use of each setting for particular goals.

Playground Design Issues

"the school playground festival is now one of the few places where a distant and non intrusive supervision is possible.... The school playground still provides the one assured festival in the lives of children." (Sutton-Smith, 1990)

Playgrounds have been and must continue to be studied in and of themselves, for reasons beyond the comparison of their effects on children's play and development versus indoor environments. Because playgrounds in particular, and outdoor environments in general, are characterized by less direction by adults than are indoor environments, they are especially significant in the experience of childhood (Sutton-Smith, 1990). Interest in playgrounds has grown necessarily, one reason being that their effects and attributes have been lightly studied in comparison to the classroom environment. One strand of research has looked at the different types of playgrounds. Also, societal concern about children's safety has prompted study of playground equipment, design, and management. Finally, the design of outdoor play environments is in a sense the purest application of knowledge about play and play environments. Most indoor educational environments are designed to accommodate play as a secondary consideration, or as a means to an educational end. Teacher direction is woven into the fabric of the indoor environment. Perhaps the design of outdoor environments to accommodate play is itself an intrusion on the child's freedom to encounter his or her surroundings through play.

Comparisons of Playground Types. The labels or designations for playground types are essentially arbitrary, for no 2 are alike. Even within types, there are differences in space, natural features, equipment, materials, and so on. The reader must review the individual studies of types of playgrounds to determine the nature and range of play opportunities, for it is the *molecular variable* and not the designation of type that distinguishes between environments and allows meaningful comparison.

Playgrounds differ in many ways, but 3 distinct types have emerged in the literature (Naylor, 1985). These are (1) the *traditional playground* of fixed, primarily single-use, and exercise-oriented apparatuses; (2) the *contemporary playground*, which is architecturally and aesthetically more advanced than the traditional (but arguably no more developmentally advanced), characterized by fixed complex climbing structures; and (3) the *adventure playground*, characterized by children's constructions using amalgams of loose manipulable parts. The great majority of American playgrounds lie on a continuum, on which are these 3 types, and on which may be found a few components of each type. American elementary school and public playgrounds are likely to be in the traditional model (Frost, 1992; Vernon, 1976) whereas only a handful of American adventure playgrounds exists in the European model (Frost & Klein, 1983). It should be noted that at least one other type of playground has been described. The *creative playground* is characterized by both fixed and movable equipment designed to provide a variety of play options. This hybrid of contemporary and mini–adventure playgrounds has been studied, as have other, undesignated settings for play such as yards, streets, and vacant lots.

Hayward, Rothenberg, and Beasley (1974) compared traditional, contemporary, and adventure playgrounds using behavior mapping and interviews with children. They reported that children spent more time, engaged in more cognitive-play activities, and exhibited a wider range of play activities on adventure playgrounds than they did on the other types. They also noted a tendency for more adult involvement with children on the adventure playground. Hart and Sheehan (1986) found that children's play was more passive on the contemporary playground than on a traditional playground, but no differential effects were found in verbal interaction, social play, and cognitive play. Frost and Campbell (1985) found that children alternating sessions between a traditional and creative playground engaged almost exclusively in exercise play on the traditional playground, but exhibited near equal incidence of dramatic play versus exercise play on the creative playground. Similar findings were reported by Frost and Strickland (1985).

A study by Brown and Burger (1984) reported different results, finding that, compared with traditional playgrounds, contemporary designs did not necessarily promote greater amounts of social, language, or motor behaviors. A closer inspection of the 2 environments showed both settings were similar in the predominance of fixed equipment, though the contemporary playground was more aesthetically pleasing. Their conclusions affirmed the importance of certain attributes of the materials and equipment in the setting: complexity via multifunctional and linked climbers, zoning (e.g., cloistered sand-play areas sheltered from traffic), movement (wheeled toys), encapsulation or enclosure, and manipulability through such items as loose parts (Nicholson, 1971). Similar conclusions regarding complexity, zoning, and manipulability were reported by Andel (1984).

Moore (1989) used an ethnographic approach to document the differences in a public school playground before and after redevelopment into a much more natural environment. Children's interviews as to their perceptions of the predeveloped, blacktop play area and of the postdeveloped, diverse play environment suggested several dimensions of change noted by the children: greater safety owing to both the surface material and the reduction of inappropriate behavior (e.g., bottle smashing and fights); a feeling of being "at home" evoked by areas for solitary play as well as group games; a "pride of place" and a consequent "sense of belonging"; an increased environmental awareness and appreciation for beauty; and finally a sense of loss if the playground were to revert to its previous condition.

Moore (1985) reported on comparisons of adventure playgrounds versus neighborhood play settings. His findings confirm the importance of adventure playgrounds in supporting cognitive play, but stress the importance of neighborhood settings for social play and of traditional playgrounds for motor development: "What seems to be emerging is a type of complementary relationship among various settings—no one type of play setting seems to provide for all of children's play activities and developmental needs" (pp. 178–179). Indeed, data has historically suggested that when children play outdoors it is most often in settings other than designated playgrounds (Moore, 1985). However, with the increased proportion of time spent in child care and school settings, and with the increasing fear of violence against children, this data is surely under pressure to change. In addition, it is the "built" environment, not the neighborhoods, over which educators have control, or at least influence. For these reasons the playground must not be relegated to an afterthought in either the design or the funding of educational environments.

The history of playground development offers certain insights regarding the development of play environments in preschool versus primary-grade educational settings. In a comprehensive review of the history of American playgrounds, Frost (1989) described their philosophical roots. The development of American playgrounds has been characterized by parallel tracks consisting of a preschool context and a park context. The influences of Rousseau and Froebel on the kindergartens and nursery schools in the late 19th century contributed to a more developmentally appropriate view of playgrounds in preschool settings; thus, they often included gardens, dirt- and sand-play areas, and woodworking provision. Elementary school playgrounds developed along the lines of American parks, which were dominated by apparatuses for physical development, a trend that continues to the present (Bowers & Bruya, 1988; Thompson & Bowers, 1989; Vernon, 1976). This dual nature of playground development may be an extension of the very different curricular approaches typified by preschools, where an interactive learning style is assumed, and the primary grades, where didactic methods dominate. The net effect, confirmed by survey data (Bruya & Langendorfer, 1988), is that American public school playgrounds are "a national disgrace, light years apart from the compelling play environments of our most visionary thinkers" (Frost, 1989, p. 22).

Playground Safety. The safety of children using playgrounds in educational settings is of concern for several reasons, not the least of which is that the majority of accidents reported on early childhood settings occur during outdoor activity (Charlesworth, 1987). The number of injuries on all American playgrounds resulting in hospital or emergency room treatment is about 200,000 annually according to the National Electronic Injury Surveillance System, with a disproportionate number affecting children under 5 years of age (Frost, 1990). Although many of these injuries might in fact be relatively minor, in the 2 years between March 1985 and February 1987, 28 children died as a result of playground injuries (Tinsworth & Kramer, 1990). Consequently, children's attitudes and behaviors are affected by the danger of sterile playgrounds, as reported by Moore (1989). Given the clear and present danger, how do we determine what safe playgrounds should look like? First we must know what components within the environment result in children's safe use of playgrounds.

The elements that determine playground safety include the design, durability, and installation of equipment; zoning of the area; surfacing; maintenance of both equipment and surface; age/developmental appropriateness of equipment/layout; area security; supervision; and the child's preparedness/self-confidence. In addition, such concerns as liability, risk management, volunteer/community built versus commercial manufactured, and inspection/record keeping are discussed in the current literature on playground safety. Various writers have addressed these components either singly or in clusters, and the information available as a result is too voluminous to treat adequately here. The discussion that follows will first paint a clear if frightening picture of elementary school and preschool playgrounds and second present sources that will allow the interested reader to gain a foothold on the literature.

A primary factor in the dismal assessment of elementary school playgrounds is a general inattention to the well-documented and too common sources of serious injury in outdoor play settings, especially hard surfaces under equipment. In spite of decades of information (Beckwith, 1988) pointing to the part played by surfacing in causing injuries, a large percentage of American elementary schools still harbor patently unsafe surface materials under slides (57%), swings (51%), rotating and rocking equipment (52%), see-saws (74%), and climbers (55%) (Bowers & Bruya, 1988). Of the *potentially* safe materials found by this survey to exist, in relatively few instances do they exist is sufficient depth to ensure safe use (the survey did not evaluate this aspect, although experience verifies this). To underscore this issue, consider the following statistics reported by Tinsworth and Kramer (1990): "Falls to the surface accounted for about 60% of all injuries reported. Of all potentially 'serious' injuries on home playground equipment, 9 out of 10 resulted from falls to the surface, and all hospitalized victims reported were injured in this manner" (p. 17). Extensive data has been reported comparing various types of surfaces for their impact-attenuating properties (Ramsey & Preston, 1990) with data indicating that loose materials such as wood chips, sand, or small-size gravel perform best at depths from 9 to 12 inches, and that rubber-type mats vary considerably according to both thickness and construction but can provide substantial resilience. Each particular type of material has unique benefits as well as disadvantages.

Numerous other common problems on the nation's elementary school playgrounds have been reported:

1. 22% of playgrounds have equipment not easily supervised.
2. 36% have no equipment for younger children.
3. 43% do not separate equipment for older and younger children.
4. An average of 5.6 exposed concrete footings exist on each playground.
5. 80% have slides eight feet tall (40% are over ten feet tall). Many experts note that when a child stands on a platform at eight feet, his or head is 11–13 feet above ground—no resilient surface now available will provide protection sufficient to prevent concussion from these heights.
6. 31% have pipes on climbers which allow finger entry.
7. 41% of climbers have sharp edges or protrusions.
8. 63% of climbers have horizontal openings between 7 and 11 inches which constitute potential head entrapments. (Bowers & Bruya, 1988)

These are just some of the highlights, or lowlights, of the survey's findings. Certainly a coordinated effort to remedy these problems is warranted and has been advocated (Bruya, 1988). A similar survey was conducted on preschool playgrounds, and, although the picture there is somewhat brighter, many of the same problems exist in an unacceptably high percentage of preschool sites (Wortham & Frost, 1990).

To date the most comprehensive information on both the status of American playgrounds and on issues of design and use of play equipment resides in the 4 volumes of the national survey project from which many of the playground statistics are taken. This project, spearheaded by the American Association for Leisure and Recreation, surveyed over 300 playgrounds at elementary schools, public parks, and preschools. The project's findings represent a monumental contribution to both the awareness of current problems and the provision of strategies to remediate them. Another source of information on a broad range of design issues is the *Play for All Guidebook* (Moore, Goltsman, & Iacafano, 1987). Manufacturers, architects, child-development specialists, and designers produced this comprehensive guide for development of safe, appropriate, and accessible play environments.

A subcommittee of the American Society for Testing and Materials (ASTM) will soon publish a comprehensive standard for public playground equipment, design, installation, and surfacing. Each standard must have provided a rationale for inclusion, and more than 70 subcommittee members from pediatricians to designers to lawyers to manufacturers have wrestled with the final composition of the document. In addition, the Consumer Product Safety Commission will publish revised safety guidelines for playground equipment. Coming approximately 10 years after the initial CPSC guidelines (1981a, 1981b), the ASTM standards and the revised CPSC guidelines will provide much-needed direction in designing safe outdoor play environments for children.

A Model for Play Environment Design

All educational environments for young children, both indoor and outdoor, should be designed for play. These designed environments should reflect children's developmental needs regarding safety and appropriateness and should reflect their need to play without undue interference from adults. The latter need cannot be satisfied without safe and appropriate play environments, for adults must interfere more when they supervise children in unsafe or inappropriate play environments.

A developmental perspective for play environment design is shown in a call for separate playground environments for infants/toddlers, preschoolers, and school-agers (Frost & Dempsey, 1991). Play environments for infants/toddlers reflect their reliance on sensorimotor input, and their need for space to move (Olds, 1989) and for forgiving surfaces to compensate for immature balance. Play environments for preschoolers provide more challenges, complexity, diversity, and opportunities for successful independence, as preschoolers achieve autonomy and self-confidence (Erikson, 1963). School-age children need maximum opportunity to increase their abilities to plan and

succeed in individual and group efforts. The adventure playground provides a glimpse of an intensively child-directed environment where children take part in creating their own environment in preparation for increased responsibilities.

Children's needs provide another model for play environment design. In this model, the needs of children expressed in the types of play they exhibit produce several corresponding zones. The play environment can be arranged as 4 zones providing materials and space for exercise play, constructive play, dramatic play, and rule-oriented group play (Frost & Klein, 1979). Esbensen (1990) suggests the following 7 zones: manipulative/creative, projective/fantasy, focal/social, social/dramatic, physical, natural elements, and transition (which ties zones together). Designers of play environments can use these zones to ensure that all types of play are encouraged.

Children can themselves provide information to assist in the design of play environments (Parkinson, 1985). Playgrounds that are designed in cooperation with schoolchildren are more used and less abused by children (Hutslar, 1976). Adults, on the other hand, may not know what children prefer on their playgrounds (Bishop, Peterson, & Michaels, 1972). Talbot and Frost (1989) formed design principles for "magical playscapes," using reflections from child perspectives. These design principles extend the nature and scope well beyond the usual or ordinary. Designers of appropriate, interactive play environments should seek input from children, directly in the case of older children, and by observation and study of young children to ensure that play environments are indeed child appropriate.

SUMMARY

Play environments in early childhood education are affected by a multitude of variables, many of which can be set or manipulated by educators and designers. A respect for the child's own agenda in play is fundamental to the appropriate decisions educators and designers must make in providing appropriate play environments. A study of the play environment provides a rich appreciation for the tenacity of children's play as human behavior, for play is surprisingly adaptive across cultures, through curriculum fads, and in spite of adult intervention. Even as we seek to define, manipulate, and train children's play, children go on blessedly oblivious to our efforts. We would not have it any other way.

References

Allen, M. (1968). *Planning for play*. Cambridge, MA: M.I.T. Press.

Andel, J. van. (1984). *Effects of the redevelopment of an elementary school-yard*. Paper presented at the IAPS conference, Berlin.

Beckwith, J. (1988). Negligence: Safety from falls overlooked. In L. D. Bruya & S. J. Langendorfer (Eds.), *Where our children play: Elementary school playground equipment*. Reston, VA: American Alliance for Health, Physical Education, Recreation and Dance, 223–226.

Bell, M. J., & Walker, P. (1985). Interactive patterns in children's play groups. In J. L. Frost & S. Sunderlin (Eds.), *When children play,*

(pp. 139–144). Wheaton, MD: Association for Childhood Education International.

Bishop, R. L., Peterson, G. L., & Michaels, R. M. (1972, January). *Measurement of Children's Preferences for the Play Environment*. Paper presented at Environmental Design Research Association Annual Conference, Los Angeles.

Bloch, M. N. (1989). Young boys' and girls' play at home and in the community: A cultural-ecological framework. In M. N. Bloch & A. D. Pellegrini (Eds.), *The ecological context of children's play* (pp. 120–154). Norwood, NJ: Ablex.

Bowers, L., & Bruya. L. (1988) Results of the survey. In L. D. Bruya & S. J. Langendorfer (Eds.), *Where our children play: Elementary school playground equipment.* Reston, VA: American Alliance for Health, Physical Education, Recreation and Dance, 31–44.

Bredekamp, S. (Ed.). (1987). *Developmentally appropriate practice in early childhood programs serving children from birth through age 8.* Washington, DC: National Association for the Education of Young Children.

Brown, J. G., & Burger, C. (1984). Playground designs and preschool children's behaviors. *Environment and Behavior, 16*(5), 599–626.

Bruya, L. D. (1985). Design characteristics used in playgrounds for children. In J. L. Frost & S. Sunderlin (Eds.), *When children play,* (pp. 215–220). Wheaton, MD: Association for Childhood Education International.

Bruya, L. D. (1988) The new challenge: Playground upgrades. In L. D. Bruya & S. J. Langendorfer (Eds.), *Where our children play: Elementary school playground equipment.* (pp. 227–234). Reston, VA: American Alliance for Health, Physical Education, Recreation and Dance.

Bruya, L. D., & Langendorfer, S. J. (Eds.). (1988). *Where our children play: Elementary school playground equipment.* Reston, VA: American Alliance for Health, Physical Education, Recreation and Dance.

Buhler, C. (1951) *From birth to maturity.* (6th impression). London: Routledge and Kegan Paul.

Caldera, Y. M., Huston, A. C., & O'Brien, M. (1989). Social interactions and play patterns of parents and toddlers with feminine, masculine, and neutral toys. *Child Development, 60,* 70–76.

Campbell, S. D., & Dill, N. (1985). The impact of changes in spatial density on children's behaviors in a day care setting. In J. L. Frost & S. Sunderlin (Eds.), *When children play,* (pp. 255–264). Wheaton, MD: Association for Childhood Education International.

Campbell, S. D., & Frost, J. L. (1985). The effects of playground type on the cognitive and social play behaviors of grade two children. In J. L. Frost & S. Sunderlin (Eds.), *When children play,* (pp. 81–88). Wheaton, MD: Association for Childhood Education International.

Carlsson-Paige, N., & Levin, D. E. (1988). *Educational Leadership, 45*(4), 80–84.

Carlsson-Paige, N., & Levin, D. E. (1990). *Who's calling the shots? How to respond effectively to children's fascination with war play and war toys.* Philadelphia, PA: New Society.

Charlesworth, R. (1987). *Understanding child development.* Albany, NY: Delmar.

Children's Defense Fund. (1990). *Children 1990: A report card, briefing book, and action primer.* Washington, DC: Author.

Christie, J. F. (1985). Training of symbolic play. *Early Child Development and Care, 19,* 43–52.

Christie, J. F., & Johnsen, E. P. (1989). The constraints of settings on children's play. *Play and Culture, 2,* 317–327.

Christie, J. F., Johnsen, E. P., & Peckover, R. B. (1988). The effects of play period duration on children's play patterns. *Journal of Research in Childhood Education, 3*(2), 123–131.

Collier, R. G. (1985). The results of training preschool teachers to foster children's play. In J. L. Frost & S. Sunderlin (Eds.), *When children play* (305–311). Wheaton, MD: Association for Childhood Education International.

Corsaro, W. A. (1985). *Friendships and peer culture in the early years.* Norwood, NJ: Ablex.

Cox, F. N., & Campbell, D. (1968). Young children in a new situation with and without their mothers. *Child Development, 51,* 921–924.

Dale, N. (1989). Pretend play with mothers and siblings: Relations between early performance and partners. *Journal of Child Psychology and Psychiatry, 30,* 751–759.

Dansky, J. L. (1980). Make-believe: A mediator of the relationship between play and associative fluency. *Child Development, 51*(2), 576–579.

Darvill, D. (1982). Ecological influences on children's play: Issues and approaches. In D. J. Pepler & K. H. Rubin (Eds.), *The play of children: Current theory and research in Contributions to Human Development, 6,* 144–153. Buffalo, NY: S. Karger.

Dempsey, J. D. (1985). *The effects of training in play on cognitive development in preschool children.* Unpublished doctoral dissertation, University of Texas, Austin.

Dodge, M. K., & Frost, J. L. (1986). Children's dramatic play: Influence on thematic and nonthematic settings. *Childhood Education, 62*(3), 166–170.

Einsiedler, W. (1985, September). *Fantasy play of preschoolers as a function of toy structures.* Paper presented at the International Symposium of the Netherlands Organization for Postgraduate Education in The Social Sciences, Amsterdam.

Eisenberg, N., & Harris, J. D. (1984). Social competence: A developmental perspective. *School Psychology Review, 13,* 267–277.

Eisenberg, N., Tryon, K., & Cameron, E. (1984). The relation of preschoolers' peer interaction to their sex-typed toy choices. *Child Development, 55,* 45–70.

Eisenberg, N., Wolchik, S. A., Hernandez, R., & Pasternack, J. F. (1985). Parental socialization of young children's play. *Child Development, 56,* 1506–1513.

Elgas, P. M., Klein, E., Kantor, R., & Fernie, D. E. (1988). Play and the peer culture: Play styles and object use. *Journal of Research in Childhood Education, 3*(2), 142–153.

Erikson, E. (1963). *Childhood and society* (2nd ed.). New York: Norton.

Erikson, E. (1976). Play and actuality. In J. S. Bruner, A. Jolly and K. Sylva (Eds.), *Play.* (pp. 688–704). New York: Basic Books.

Esbensen, S. (1990). Play environments for young children: Design perspectives. In S. Wortham & J. L. Frost (Eds.), *Playgrounds for young children: National survey and perspectives.* (pp. 49–68). Reston, VA: American Alliance for Health, Physical Education, Recreation and Dance.

Fagot, B. I. (1978). The influences of sex of child on parental reactions to toddler children. *Child Development, 49,* 459–465.

Fein, G. G. (1975). A transformational analysis of pretending. *Developmental Psychology, 11,* 291–296.

Fein, G. G. (1981). Pretend play: An integrative review. *Child Development, 52,* 1095–1118.

Fein, G. G. & Robertson, A. R. (1975). *Cognitive and social dimensions of pretending in two-year-olds.* Detroit: Merrill-Palmer Institute. (ERIC Document Reproduction Service No. ED 119 806).

Feitelson, D., Weintraub, S., & Michaeli, O. (1972). Social interactions in heterogeneous preschools in Israel. *Child Development, 43,* 1249–1259.

Feshbach, S. (1956). The catharsis hypothesis and some consequences of interaction with aggressive and neutral play objects. *Journal of Personality, 24,* 449–462.

Finkelstein, N. W., & Haskins, R. (1983). Kindergarten children prefer same-color peers. *Child Development, 54*(2), 502–508.

Frost, J. L. (1986, August 26). *Influences of television on children's behavior: Implications for war and peace.* Paper presented at the International Association for the Child's Right to Play Seminar, Birmingham, England.

Frost, J. L. (1989). Play environments for young children in the USA: 1800–1990. *Children's Environments Quarterly, 6*(4), 17–24.

Frost, J. L. (1990). Young children and playground safety. In S. Wortham & J. L. Frost (Eds.), *Playgrounds for young children: National survey and perspectives* (pp. 29–48). Reston, VA: American Alliance for Health, Physical Education, Recreation and Dance.

Frost, J. L. (1992). *Play and playscapes*. Albany, NY: Delmar.

Frost, J. L., & Campbell, S. D. (1985). Equipment choices of primary-age children on conventional and creative playgrounds. In J. L. Frost and S. Sunderlin (Eds.) *When children play*, (pp. 89–92). Wheaton, MD: Association for Childhood Education International.

Frost, J. L., & Dempsey, J. D. (1991). Playgrounds for infants, toddlers, and preschoolers. In B. Brizzolara (Ed.), *Parenting education for school-age parents*, (pp. 55–69). Lubboch, TX: Home Economics Curriculum Center, Texas Tech University.

Frost, J. L., & Klein, B. L. (1979). *Children's play and playgrounds*. Boston: Allyn and Bacon.

Frost, J. L. & Strickland, E. (1985). Equipment choices of young children during free play. In J. L. Frost & S. Sunderlin (Eds.), *When children play, Proceeding of the International Conference on Play and Play Environments* (pp. 93–102). Wheaton, MD: Association for Childhood Education International.

Gabbard, C. (1979). Playground apparatus experience and muscular endurance among children 4–6. (ERIC Document Reproduction Service, SP 022 020; ED 228 190).

Getz, S. K., & Berndt, E. G. (1982). A test of a method for quantifying amount, complexity and arrangement of play resources in the preschool classroom. *Journal of Applied Developmental Psychology, 3*, 295–305.

Glickman, C. D. (1984). Play in public school settings: A philosophical question. In T. D. Yawkey & A. D. Pellegrini (Eds.), *Child's play: Developmental and applied.* (pp. 255–271). Hillsdale. NJ: Erlbaum.

Golomb, C. (1979). Pretense play: A cognitive perspective. In N. Smith and M. Franklin (Eds), *Symbolic functioning in childhood* (pp. 101–116). New York: Wiley.

Gottfried, A. W. (Ed.). (1984). *Home environment and early cognitive development: Longitudinal research*. New York: Academic Press.

Gramza, A. F. (1970). Preferences of preschool children for enterable play boxes. *Perceptual and Motor Skills, 31*, 177–178.

Griffing, P. (1980). The relationship between socioeconomic status and sociodramatic play among black kindergarten children. *Genetic Psychology Monographs, 101*, 3–34.

Griffing, P. (1983). Encouraging dramatic play in early childhood. *Young Children, 38*, 13–22.

Harper, L. V., & Sanders, K. M. (1975). Preschool children's use of space: Sex differences in outdoor play. *Developmental Psychology, 11*, 119.

Hart, C. R., & Sheehan, R. (1986). Preschoolers' play behavior in outdoor environments: Effects of traditional and contemporary playgrounds. *American Educational Research Journal, 23*(4), 668–678.

Hayward, D. G., Rothenberg, M., & Beasley, R. R. (1974). Children's play and urban playground environments: A comparison of traditional, contemporary, and adventure playground types. *Environment and Behavior, 6*(2), 131–168.

Henniger, M. L. (1985). Preschool children's play behaviors in an indoor and outdoor environment. In J. L. Frost & S. Sunderlin (Eds.). *When children play* (pp. 145–150). Wheaton, MD: Association for Childhood Education International.

Hovell, M., Bursick, J., Sharkey, R., & McClure, J. (1987). An evaluation of elementary students' voluntary physical activity during recess. *Research Quarterly, 49*, 460–474.

Howes, C. (1988). Peer interaction of young children. *Monographs of the Society for Research in Child Development, 53*, (Serial No. 17).

Howes, C., & Rubenstein, J. (1978, March 29–April 1). Peer play and the effect of the inanimate environment. Paper presented at the Annual Convention of the Eastern Psychological Association, Washington, DC.

Hughes, F. P. (1991). *Children's play and development*. Boston: Allyn & Bacon.

Huston-Stein, A., Friedrich-Cofer, L., & Susman, E. J. (1977). The relation of classroom structure to social behavior, imaginative play, and self-regulation of economically disadvantaged children. *Child Development, 48*, 908–916.

Hutslar, J. (1976). *A democratic approach to creative playgrounds*. (ERIC Document Reproduction Service No. ED, 150 096, 33 pp.)

Isaacs, S. (1933). *Social development in young children: A study of beginnings*. London: Routledge and Kegan Paul.

Johnson, J. E., & Ershler, J. (1981). Developmental trends in preschool play as a function of classroom program and child gender. *Child Development, 52*, 995–1004.

Johnson, J. E., & Ershler, J. (1982). Curricular effects on the play of preschoolers. In D. J. Pepler & K. H. Rubin (Eds.), *The play of children: Current theory and research* Vol. 6 (pp. 130–143). Basel, Switzerland: S.Karger.

Johnson, M. W. (1935). The effect on behavior of variation in the amount of play equipment. *Child Development, 6*, 56–68.

Kirkby, M. (1989). Nature as refuge in children's environments. *Children's Environments Quarterly, 6*(1), 7–12.

Kooij, R. van der, (1989). Research on children's play. *Play and Culture, 2*, 20–34.

Kooij, R. van der, & Neukater, H. (1987). Parental steering and play in an international comparison. In U. Haeberlin & C. Amrein (Eds.), *Forschung und Lehre fur diesonderpadagogische Praxis*. Bern, Switzerland: Paul Haupt.

Krichevsky, S., Prescott, E., & Walling, L. (1969). *Planning environments for young children: Physical space*. Washington, DC: National Association for the Education of Young Children.

Labov, W. (1972). *Language in the inner city: Studies in the black English vernacular*. Philadelphia: University of Pennsylvania Press.

Langlois, J. H., & Downs, A. C. (1980). Mothers, fathers, and peers as socialization agents of sex-typed play behaviors in young children. *Child Development, 51*, 1217–1247.

Lloyd, B., & Smith, C. (1985). The social representation of gender and young children's play. *British Journal of Developmental Psychology, 3*, 65–73.

Loo, C., & Kennelly, D. (1979). Social density: Its effects on behaviors and perceptions of preschoolers. *Environmental Psychology and Non-Verbal Behavior, 3*(3), 131–146.

Mallick, S. K., & McCandless, B. R. (1966). A study of catharsis of aggression. *Journal of Personality and Social Psychology, 4*, 591–596.

Mann, B. L. (1984). Effects of realistic and unrealistic props on symbolic play. In T. D. Yawkey & A. D. Pellegrini (Eds.), *Child's play: Developmental and applied*, (pp. 359–376). Hillsdale, NJ: Erlbaum.

Matthews, W. S. (1977). Modes of transformation in the initiation of fantasy play. *Developmental Psychology, 13*, 212–216.

McCune-Nicolich, L. (1981). Toward symbolic functioning: Structure of early pretend games and potential parallels with language. *Child Development, 52*, 785–797.

McGhee, P. E., Ethridge, L., & Benz, N. A. (1984). The effect of level of toy structure on pre-school children's pretend play. *Journal of Genetic Psychology, 144*, 209–217.

McGrew, W. C. (1972). *An ethological study of children's behavior*. London: Academic Press.

McLoyd, V. C. (1980). Verbally expressed modes of transformation in the fantasy play of black preschool children. *Child Development, 51*, 1133–1139.

McLoyd, V. C. (1983). The effects of the structure of play objects on the pretend play of low-income preschool children. *Child Development, 54*, 626–635.

Miller, L. B., & Dyer, J. L. (1975). Four preschool programs: Their dimensions and effects. *Monographs of the Society of Research in Child Development, 40* (Serial No. 162).

Moore, G. T. (1985). State of the art in play environment. In J. L. Frost & S. Sunderlin (Eds.), *When children play* (pp. 171–192). Wheaton, MD: Association for Childhood Education International.

Moore, N. V., Evertson, C. M., & Brophy, J. E. (1974). Solitary play: Some functional reconsiderations. *Developmental Psychology, 10,* 830–934.

Moore, R. C. (1974). Anarchy zone: Kids' needs and school yards. *School Review. 82*(4), 621–645.

Moore, R. C. (1989). Before and after asphalt: Diversity as an ecological measure of quality in children's outdoor environments. In M. Bloch & A. D. Pellegrini (Eds.), *The ecological context of children's play* (pp. 191–213). Norwood, NJ: Ablex.

Moore, R., Goltsman, S., & Iacafano, D. (1987). *Play for all guidelines: Planning, design, and management of outdoor play settings for all children.* Berkeley, CA: MIG Communications.

Mueller, E., & Bergstrom, J. (1982). Fostering peer relations in young normal and handicapped children. In K. M. Borman (Ed.), *The Social life of children in a changing society* (pp. 191–218). Hillsdale, NJ: Erlbaum.

Myers, G. D. (1985). Motor behavior of kindergartners during physical education and free play. In J. L. Frost & S. Sunderlin (Eds.), *When children play* (151–155). Wheaton, MD: Association for Childhood Education International.

Naylor, H. (1985). Outdoor play and play equipment. *Early Child Development and Care, 19,* 109–130.

Neill, S. R. (1982). Preschool design and child behaviour. *Journal of Child Psychology and Psychiatry and Allied Disciplines, 23,* 309–318.

Nicholson, S. (1971). How not to cheat children: The theory of loose parts. *Landscape Architecture, 62,* 30–34.

Olds, A. R. (1989). Psychological and physiological harmony in child care center design. *Children's Environments Quarterly, 6,* 8–16.

Olszewski, P., & Fuson, K. (1982). Verbally expressed fantasy play of preschoolers as a function of toy structure. *Developmental Psychology, 18,* 57–61.

Opie, I., & Opie, P. (1969). *Children's games in streets and playgrounds.* London: Clarendon Press.

Paley, V. G. (1984). *Boys and girls: Superheroes in the doll corner.* Chicago: University of Chicago Press.

Parker, S. T. (1984). Play for keeps: An evolutionary perspective on human games. In P. K. Smith (Ed.), *Play in animals and humans.* Oxford: Basic Blackwell, 271–294.

Parkinson, C. E. (1985). *Where children play: An analysis of interviews about where children aged 5–14 normally play and their preferences for out-of-school experiences.* London: Association for Children's Play and Recreation and Carrick James Market Research.

Parten, M. B. (1932). Social participation among preschool children. *Journal of Abnormal and Social Psychology, 27,* 243–269.

Peck, J., & Goldman, R. (1978, March). *The behaviors of kindergarten children under selected conditions of the physical and social environment.* Paper presented at the meeting of the American Educational Research Association, Toronto.

Pederson, D. R., Rook-Green, A., & Elder, J. L. (1981). The role of action in the development of pretend play in young children. *Developmental Psychology, 17,* 756–759.

Pellegrini, A. D. (1985). Social cognitive aspects of children's play: The effects of age, gender, and play context. *Journal of Applied Developmental Psychology, 6,* 129–140.

Pellegrini, A. D., & Perlmutter, J. C. (1989). Classroom contextual effects on children's play. *Developmental Psychology, 25*(2), 289–296.

Pepler, D. J., & Ross, H. S. (1981). The effects of play on convergent and divergent problem-solving. *Child Development, 52,* 1202–1210.

Peters, D. L., Neisworth, J. T., & Yawkey, T. D. (1985). *Early childhood education: From theory to practice.* Monterey, CA: Brooks/Cole.

Piaget, J. (1962). *Play, dreams and imitation in childhood.* New York: Norton.

Piaget, J. (1963). *The origins of intelligence in children.* New York: Norton.

Potts, R., Wright, A. C., & Huston, J. C. (1986). The effects of television form and violent content on boys' attention behavior. *Journal of Experimental Child Psychology, 41,* 1–17.

Pulaski, M. A. (1973). Toys and imaginative play. In J. L. Singer (Ed.), *The child's world of make-believe* (pp. 74–103). New York: Academic Press.

Ramsey, L. F., & Preston, J. D. (1990). *Impact attenuation performance of playground surfacing materials.* Washington, DC: U.S. Consumer Product Safety Commission.

Rogers, D. L. (1985). Relationships between block play and the social development of young children. *Early Child Development and Care, 20,* 245–261.

Roopnarine, J. L. (1986). Mothers' and fathers' behaviors toward the toy play of their infant sons and daughters. *Sex Roles, 14,* 59–68.

Rubin, K. H. (1977). The social and cognitive value of preschool toys and activities. *Canadian Journal of Behavioural Science, 9,* 382–385.

Rubin, K., Fein, G., & Vandenberg, B. (1983). Play. In E. M. Hetherington (Ed.), *Handbook of child psychology: Socialization, personality and social development,* (pp. 693–774). New York: Wiley.

Rubin, K., Maoini, T., & Hornung, M. (1976). Free play behaviors in middle and lower class preschoolers: Parten and Piaget revisited. *Child Development, 47,* 414–419.

Rubin, K., & Seibel, C. (1979). *The effects of classroom ecology on the cognitive and social play behaviors of preschoolers.* Paper presented at the 9th Annual Interdisciplinary Conference on Piagetian Theory and the Helping Professions, Los Angeles.

Ruopp, R., Travers, J., Glantz, F., & Coelen, C. (1979). *Children at the center: Final report of the National Day Care Study.* New York: Abt Books.

Russell, A. (1990). The effects of child-staff ratio on staff and child behavior in preschools: An experimental study. *Journal of Research in Childhood Education, 4*(2), 77–90.

Saltz, E., & Johnson, J. (1974). Training for thematic-fantasy play in culturally disadvantaged children: Preliminary results. *Journal of Educational Psychology, 66,* 623–630.

Sanders, K. M., & Harper, L. V. (1976). Free-play fantasy behavior in preschool children: Relations among gender, age, season, and location. *Child Development, 47,* 1182–1185.

Scholtz, G. J. L., & Ellis, M. J. (1975). Repeated exposure to objects and peers in a play setting, *Journal of Experimental Child Psychology, 19,* 448–455.

Schwartzman, H. B. (1984). Imaginative play: Deficit or difference? In T. D. Yawkey & A. D. Pellegrini (Eds.), *Child's play: Developmental and applied* (pp. 49–62). Hillsdale, NJ: Erlbaum.

Seagoe, M. V. (1971a). A comparison of children's play in six modern cultures. *Journal of School Psychology, 9,* 61–72.

Seagoe, M. V. (1971b). Children's play in three American subcultures. *Journal of School Psychology, 9,* 167–172.

Seagoe, M. V., & Murakami, K. (1961). A comparative study of children's play in America and Japan. *California Journal of Educational Research, 11,* 124–130.

Seefeldt, V. (1984). Physical fitness in preschool and elementary school-aged children. *Journal of Health, Physical Education, Recreation, and Dance, 55,* 34–40.

Serbin, L. A., & Conner, J. A. (1979). Sex-typing, children's play preferences, and patterns of cognitive performance. *Journal of Genetic Psychology, 134,* 315–316.

Shure, M. B. (1963). Psychological ecology of a nursery school. *Child Development, 34*(4), 979–992.

Silvern, S. B. (1985). Video game play and social behavior: Preliminary findings. In J. L. Frost & S. Sunderlin (Eds.), *When children play.* (pp. 279–282). Wheaton, MD: Association for Childhood Education International.

Silvern, S. B., Williamson, P. A., & Countermine, T. A. (1983). *Aggression in Young Children and Video Game Play.* Paper presented at the biennial meeting of the Society for Research in Child Development, Detroit, MI, April 22.

Smilansky, S., (1968). *The effects of sociodramatic play on disadvantaged preschool children.* New York: Wiley.

Smilansky, S. & Shefatya, L. (1990). *Facilitating play: A medium for promoting cognitive, socio-emotional and academic development in young children.* Gaithersburg, MD: Psychosocial & Educational Publications.

Smith, P. K. (1988). Children's play and its role in early development: A re-evaluation of the "play ethos". In A. D. Pellegrini (Ed.), *Psychological bases for early education* (pp. 207–226). Chichester UK: Wiley.

Smith, P. K., & Connolly, K. (1976). Social and aggressive behavior in preschool children as a function of crowding. *Social Sciences Information, 16,* 601–620.

Smith, P. K., & Connolly, K. (1980). *The ecology of preschool behavior.* Cambridge, UK: Cambridge University Press.

Smith, P. K., & Syddall, S. (1978). Play and non-play tutoring in preschool children: Is it play or tutoring which matters? *British Journal of Educational Psychology, 48,* 315–325.

Steele, C., & Naumann, M. (1985). Infants' play on outdoor play equipment. In J. L. Frost & S. Sunderlin (Eds.), *When children play* (pp. 121–128). Wheaton, MD: Association for Childhood Education International.

Sutton-Smith, B. (1990). The school playground as a festival. *Children's Environments Quarterly, 7*(1).

Sutton-Smith, B., & Roberts, J. M. (1981). Play, games, and sports. In H. C. Triandis & A. Heron (Eds.), *Handbook of cross-cultural psychology, 4, Developmental psychology* (pp. 425–471). Boston: Allyn & Bacon.

Sylva, K. (1977). Play and learning. In B. Tizard & D. Harvey (Eds.), *Biology of play* (pp. 51–73). London: Heinemann.

Sylva, K., Roy, C., & Painter, M. (1980). *Childwatching at playgroup and nursery school.* Ypsilanti, MI: High/Scope Press.

Takhvar, M., & Smith, P. K. (1990). A review and critique of Smilansky's classification scheme and the "nested hierarchy" of play categories. *Journal of Research in Childhood Education, 4,* 112–122.

Talbot, J. & Frost, J. L. (1989). Magical playscapes. *Childhood Education, 66,* 11–19.

Tamburrini, J. (1982). Play and the role of the teacher. *Early Child Development and Care, 8,* 209–217.

Teets, S. (1985). Modification of play behaviors of preschool children through manipulation of environmental variables. J. L. Frost & S. Sunderlin (Eds.) *When children play* (pp. 265–272). Wheaton, MD: Association for Childhood Education International.

Thompson, T. (1989). Children held hostage by terrorists on playgrounds. *Congressional Record,* September 6, 1989, S10668; submitted by Senator Mark Hatfield.

Thompson, D., & Bowers, L. (1989). *Where our children play: Community park playground equipment.* Reston, VA: American Alliance for Health, Physical Education, Recreation and Dance.

Tinsworth, D. K., & Kramer, J. T. (1990). *Playground equipment related injuries and deaths.* Washington, DC: U.S. Consumer Product Safety Commission.

Tizard, B., Philps, J., & Plewis, I. (1976a). Play in preschool centers—I: Play measures and their relation to age, sex and IQ. *Journal of Child Psychology and Psychiatry, 17,* 241–264.

Tizard, B., Philps, J., & Plewis, I. (1976b). Play in preschool centers—II: Effects on play of the child's social class and of the educational orientation of the center. *Journal of Child Psychology and Psychiatry, 17,* 265–274.

Tracy, D. M. (1987). Toys, spatial ability, and science and mathematics achievement: Are they related? *Sex Roles, 17,* 115–138.

Travers, J., Goodson, B. D., Singer, J. D., & Connell, D. B. (1980). *Research results of the National Day Care Study.* Cambridge, MA: Abt Books.

Turner, C. W., & Goldsmith, D. (1976). Effects of toy guns and airplanes on children's antisocial free play behavior. *Journal of Experimental Child Psychology, 21,* 303–315.

Udwin, O., & Shmukler, D. (1981). The influence of sociocultural, economic and home background factors on children's ability to engage in imaginative play. *Developmental Psychology, 17,* 66–72.

U.S. Consumer Product Safety Commission. (1981a). *A handbook for public playground safety. Volume 1: General guidelines for new and existing playgrounds.* Washington, DC: U.S. Government Printing Office.

U.S. Consumer Product Safety Commission. (1981b). *A handbook for public playground safety. Volume II: Technical guidelines for equipment and surfacing.* Washington, DC: U.S. Government Printing Office.

Vandenberg, B. (1981). Environmental and cognitive factors in social play. *Journal of Experimental Psychology, 31,* 169–175.

Vernon, E. A. (1976). *A survey of preprimary and primary outdoor learning centers/playgrounds in Texas public schools.* Unpublished doctoral dissertation, University of Texas, Austin.

Vygotsky, L. S. (1962). *Thought and Language.* Cambridge, MA: M.I.T. Press.

Vygotsky, L. S. (1976). Play and its role in the mental development of the child. In J. S. Bruner, A. Jolly & K. Sylva (Eds.), *Play* (pp. 537–554). New York: Basic Books.

Wachs, T. D. (1989). The development of effective child care environments: Contributions from the study of early experience. *Children's Environments Quarterly, 6*(4), 4–7.

Wade, C. (1985). Effects of teacher training on teachers and children in playground settings. In J. L. Frost & S. Sunderlin (Eds.), *When children play* (pp. 313–318). Wheaton, MD: Association for Childhood Education International.

Wagner, B. S. (1985). Assessing symbolic maturity through pretend play. In J. L. Frost & S. Sunderlin (Eds.), *When children play* (pp. 343–348). Wheaton, MD: Association for Childhood Education International.

Wolfgang, C. H., & Sanders, T. (1982). Teacher's role: A construct for supporting the play of young children. *Early Child Development and Care, 8,* 107–120.

Wortham, S. C., & Frost, J. L. (Eds.). (1990). *Playgrounds for young children: National survey and perspectives.* Reston, VA: American Alliance for Health, Physical Education, Recreation and Dance.

Yawkey, T. D. (1990). *Effects of Title VII Project PIAGET Academic Excellence Programs: A final report covering 1987–1990.* Office of Bilingual Education and Minority Languages Affairs, U.S. Department of Education. University Park, PA: Pennsylvania State University.

Yawkey, T. D., Melizzi, M. A., & Jones, K. C. (1982, April). *A symposium on understanding and promoting imaginative play in early childhood: Part II.* Paper presented at Study Conference of The Association for Childhood Education International, Atlanta, GA.

Yerkes, R. (1982). *A playground that extends the classroom.* ERIC Document Reproduction Service No. ED 239 802.

·21·

CHILD CARE FOR YOUNG CHILDREN

Carollee Howes and Claire E. Hamilton

UNIVERSITY OF CALIFORNIA, LOS ANGELES

Most children in the United States in the 1990s will participate in one or more extrafamilial child care arrangements before they enter formal school. Child care, in this chapter, is defined as any care-giving arrangement other than that provided by parents and supplementing parent care. Child care arrangements are extremely variable. The form of care, the amount of care, and the consistency of the care across the day can vary widely; the child is considered to be in child care regardless of these variations. For example, child care is not defined by the number of hours the child spends in the arrangement. Janice attends a Head Start program in the morning and stays with her neighbor in the afternoon. Mike attends the neighborhood nursery school 3 mornings a week and is with his mother the rest of the time. Georgia spends 12 hours a day, 5 days a week in the Busy Bees Child Care Center. All of these children are child care children.

Child care varies greatly in its form. Chrissa is enrolled full-time in the campus child care center, which also functions as a lab school. Mark stays at home and is cared for by Sylvia, an au pair who lives with the family. Jannine goes to her neighbor down the street while her mother works the night shift at the hospital. Raphael attends the early enrichment program for musically talented preschoolers in the morning and is picked up and taken home by his housekeeper, Maria. Rachel attends a parent cooperative child care center 5 days a week—her mother works there Thursday mornings. Sayeh stays with her aunt who also cares for 5 other children. Jordan goes to a licensed family day care provider, part of a network of providers set up by the community center. Molly's child care center is located in the basement of a church, although the center has no religious affiliation. All of these children are child care children.

Child care may be on the site of the parent's work and still be variable. Becky goes to work with her father and spends the day in the child care center located in his office building. Juan attends the migrant day care program that travels with the migrant workers as they follow the harvest. Tina goes to high school with her mother and stays in the on-site child care center while her mother attends classes. All of these children are child care children.

Child care is sometimes affiliated with another community agency but still functions as child care. Abraham attends a full-day day care center in the temple, where he learns Jewish culture. Marylou spends her days in the Christian Bible School Child Care Center. Marcus's child care center is at the YWCA; Mindy's is in the YMCA. Jennifer's child care center is part of the public schools and is called a state preschool. Marjorie's child care center, the Early Learning Center, is also on school grounds, but it is operated by parents. These children, too, are all child care children.

In this chapter we examine the research literature on children's development in child care. We argue that, despite the extreme variability in child care arrangements, children's outcomes in these programs are relatively independent of variation in child care forms. Instead, children's child care outcomes are influenced by the quality of relationships that the child is able to form and sustain with the adults and peers in child care. We will build the rationale for this argument through a review of research on children in child care.

The literature on child care is primarily a literature from developmental psychology, rather than education. Thus, it has been less concerned with provision of educational services than with care-giving processes and children's outcomes. This is due to theoretical and societal presuppositions. Major theoretical positions in the field, for example, attachment theory, suggest that parents, particularly mothers, are significant influences on a child's emotional and social adjustment. Child care, by definition, is other than mother care. Our society has been ambivalent about working mothers. Some segments of the population believe that working mothers neglect their children and therefore contribute to antisocial behaviors. Thus, there is a fear that child care produces aggressive children who create problems in schools and communities. Our focus will emphasize social and emotional development somewhat more than cognitive development.

WHO USES CHILD CARE?

Although child care is a way of life for most American children, there are variations in the kinds of families that use different forms of child care and that use child care for children of different ages. However, most families use child care because the parent or parents work outside the home. We begin this chapter with a discussion of the demographics of work force participation. In summarizing this material we draw heavily on the recent report on America's child care produced by the National Academy of Science (Hayes, Palmer, & Zaslow, 1990).

Work Force Demographics

The demographics of working women have undergone dramatic shifts in the last decade. Between 1970 and 1988 the proportion of women with children under 6 years old in the work force rose from 30% to 56% (Hayes et al., 1990). The largest increase in working mothers was for mothers with infants 1 year old or younger. Over half of these mothers were in the work force in 1987 (U.S. Bureau of Labor Statistics, 1988). Thus, it does not appear that mothers with preschool or older children are the only ones who need child care.

It is often assumed that single mothers are more likely to work and therefore need child care more than married mothers; however, 1988 figures suggest differently. Fifty-three percent of children under 6 with married mothers and 47.9% of children under 6 with single mothers have working mothers (U.S. Bureau of Labor Statistics, 1988). This trend holds even for infants. Slightly less than 50% of children under 1 with single mothers and slightly more than 50% of children under 1 with married mothers are in the labor force (U.S. Bureau of Labor Statistics, 1988).

Likewise, it is often assumed that poor or less-educated women are more likely to both have children and work. Census Bureau statistics suggest otherwise. Mothers with 4 or more years of college are more likely to be in the labor force than mothers with less than 12 years of schooling (U.S. Bureau of the Census, 1988).

Finally, women of color have always been in the labor force. However, recent trends suggest that the proportion of white children with working mothers is likely to exceed that of black children by the mid-1990s (Hofferth & Phillips, 1987). One reason for this change is that the jobless rate of black women with preschool age children is over twice as high as that of white women with preschoolers (U.S. Bureau of Labor Statistics, 1988). Thus, most families in the United States, not primarily poor women or single mothers or women of color, face the task of making arrangements for the extrafamilial care of children.

CHILD CARE FORMS

Child care forms fall into 3 basic categories: center based, family day care homes, and in-home care with either a relative or nonrelative. In the past 20 years we have accumulated a substantial amount of research on the first 2 forms of care. In contrast, we know relatively little about in-home care.

Briefly, center-based care includes child care provided in a setting limited in function to the care of children. Centers are usually staffed by teachers, although there is great variation in the education and training of these teachers. Family day care homes are out-of-home child care arrangements in the home of another family. The child care provider in a family day care home generally performs the dual role of teacher and housekeeper. In-home nonrelative child care providers range from nannies and au pairs, whose job descriptions usually cover only the care of children, to housekeepers, whose job descriptions are broader than care of children.

Descriptions of Center and Family Day Care

The recent National Child Care Staffing Study (NCCSS) (Whitebook, Howes, & Phillips, 1990) provides a descriptive profile of variations in center-based child care in 1988. The study was conducted in 5 representative cities in the United States and included staff interviews as well as teacher observations. Centers included in the sample provided full-day care; thus, many public school and Head Start programs were excluded. Child care centers in the NCCSS enrolled an average of 84 children (range 15 to 260) and employed an average of 15 teachers (range 6 to 68). Thirty percent of the children cared for were 2 years old or younger. Generally, children were cared for in single age groupings, such as infants, toddlers, and preschoolers. Only 36% of the centers had at least one mixed-age group.

In 1980 the federal government passed and then rescinded Federal Interagency Day Care Requirements (FIDCR) representing a consensus of experts on center-care standards. The FIDCR set standards for both group size and adult-to-child ratios in center care. In the NCCSS, infant classrooms averaged 7.1 children (range 2 to 18), toddler classrooms averaged 9.6 children (range 2 to 30) and preschool classrooms averaged 14.2 children (range 3 to 37). Almost 60% of infant classrooms, almost 30% of toddler classrooms, and almost 25% of preschool classrooms exceeded the FIDCR provisions for group size.

In the NCCSS the adult-child ratio in infant classrooms averaged 1:3.9 (range 1:1.5 to 1:9), in toddler classrooms 1:5.8 (range 1:1 to 1:14), and in preschool classrooms 1:8.4 (range 1:1.6 to 1:33). Sixty-four percent of infant classrooms, 55% of toddler classrooms, and more than one-quarter of preschool classrooms had worse ratios than the FIDCR provisions.

The child care teachers in the NCCSS were predominantly women (97%)—approximately one-third women of color—in their childbearing years (74% between 19 and 40 years old). Almost half of the teachers were married and 41% had children. Almost half of the teachers with children had children younger than school age and between half and three-quarters of the teachers with young children used their own centers for child care.

More than half of the assistant teachers and three-quarters of the head teachers in the NCCSS had attended college. Thirty percent of the head teachers had B.A. degrees. Most teachers in the NCCSS, 65% of head teachers and 57% of assistants, had some course work in early childhood education or child development. The level of the training varied greatly, from courses at the high school or vocational training school level to graduation from B.A. and M.A. degree programs.

Despite higher levels of education and training than the United States civilian labor pool, teachers in the NCCSS received low pay and few benefits. Their average hourly wage in 1988 was $5.35, which is an annual income of $9,363 for full-time employment. The 1988 poverty threshold for a family of 3 (the average family size in the sample) was $9,431 a year. Not surprisingly, the annual turnover of teachers was 41%.

There has been no comparable recent study of family day care homes. Kontos (1992) has reviewed a substantial number of smaller-scale studies sampling family day care in a number of U.S. urban and rural communities. She provides the following profile of family day care homes.

The average family day care home provider cares for between 1 and 12 children, an average of 5 to 8 children. In approximately 70% of the states a second adult must be present if the home cares for more than 6 children. The family day care provider, in almost all cases a woman, is usually married. As is true for teachers in center care, the family day care provider is most often in her childbearing years and often cares for her own children as well as those of other families. In contrast to center teachers, the majority of family day care providers have only high school or less education. Very few have college degrees. Also, unlike center-care teachers, family day care providers are unlikely to have received training in child development or early childhood education through the formal education system. However, increasing numbers of family day care providers in some regions of the country are receiving informal training through workshops or conferences. Many family day care providers believe, somewhat erroneously, that the best training for their job is previous experience as a mother; therefore training is unnecessary.

Estimates of family day care income are difficult to obtain, but all reliable data suggests that the average income is very low. It is rare for a family day care provider to earn $10,000 per year in 1988 dollars. Unlike center-care teachers, though, family day care providers are unlikely to be supporting a family. It is more likely for them to be contributing approximately one-quarter of the total household income in a low- to middle-income family. Annual turnover rates in family day care are estimated at 59%, somewhat higher than center teachers.

What Kind of Families Use What Kind of Child Care

According to the U.S. Bureau of the Census, in 1985 approximately one-third of children under 5 with working mothers received care from their parents, grandparents, or siblings (U.S. Bureau of the Census, 1987). Some mothers, employed primarily as private household or child care workers, brought their children to work with them. Some families work split or alternating shifts. For example, the father may work during the day and mother at night, so someone is always home to care for the children. Twenty-four percent of children under 5 received care from a grandmother or other relative in her home (15%) or the child's home (9%).

The other children under 5 with working mothers are enrolled in family day care (22%) or center care (24%) or are cared for at home by a nonrelative (6%). The use of center care has increased substantially since the 1970s and is expected to become the predominant form of care in the 1990s (Hofferth & Phillips, 1987).

Mothers who work full-time are more likely to use center or family day care. Their needs for care generally cannot be met by other household members or relatives who themselves have job or career commitments. Mothers who work part-time or who work other than daytime hours are more likely to use relatives, particularly the children's fathers, for child care.

Single, unmarried mothers usually cannot rely on the child's father for child care. Grandmothers are more commonly the care givers for the children of single women (16%), as opposed to married women (3%) (U.S. Bureau of the Census, 1987). About one-third of the grandmothers who provide child care are themselves working, so, even when grandmothers are used for child care, the work schedules of the mother and the alternative care giver must mesh.

In 1985 infants and toddlers were more likely to receive care from relatives or in family day care homes than in centers (14%) (U.S. Bureau of the Census, 1987). However, center-based infant care is growing rapidly (Whitebook, Howes, & Phillips, 1990). In 1985, 25% of preschoolers whose mothers worked were cared for in child care centers. Parents increasingly enroll 3- and 4-year-olds in part- or full-day preschool programs, whether or not their mothers are working (U.S. Department of Education, 1986).

African American families are more likely than Anglo-American or Latino families to enroll their child in a child care center rather than use less formal arrangements. Single mothers are also more likely to use child care centers instead of family day care if they use out-of-home facilities. Mothers with 4 or more years of college education and those working in managerial or professional positions are more likely to use child care centers than more informal arrangements. Mothers with less than a high-school education and those in service jobs are less likely to use child care centers (U.S. Bureau of the Census, 1987).

Parents do not necessarily use only one child care arrangement. Many children spend their days and weeks in a series of patchwork arrangements. Likewise, parents with more than 1 child may have a variety of child care arrangements. Approximately one-quarter of preschool-age children are cared for in more than 1 child care arrangement across the week (Kisker, Maynard, Gordon, & Strain, 1988).

The child care that parents use may not be their preferred form of care. Parents are constrained by the costs of care, the location of care, and the way that their work hours mesh with those of the child care facility. Parents who search for high-quality care may not be able to find such care, either because they are not high enough on a waiting list or because such care does not exist in a convenient location.

Paradoxically, parents generally report that they are satisfied with their child care arrangements (Kisker et al., 1988; Shinn, Phillips, Howes, Galinsky, & Whitebook, 1990). However, maternal satisfaction with child care is unrelated to the quality of the child care arrangement as measured by researchers (Shinn et al., 1990). Balancing work and family responsibilities is never easy, and finding child care is often difficult. Therefore, it is in the parents' interests to be satisfied with their child care arrangements. Parental satisfaction may be based on the child care meeting the parents' needs for low cost and convenient care rather than directly based on the child's needs.

In summary, most U.S. mothers with young children work and use child care arrangements. Increasingly, diverse segments of the population—single and married women, well educated and less-educated women, poor women and more affluent women, women of color and Anglo-American women—are working while their children are young. Relatives, particularly fathers and grandmothers, still provide a substantial portion of the other-than-mother child care. Increasingly, non-relative care and out-of-home care, particularly center-based care, is being used by American families to care for children of all ages. Child care arrangements are difficult for families. Children are often cared for in more than one arrangement and children in a family may have an assortment of child care arrangements.

QUALITY OF CHILD CARE

It is repeatedly asserted that there have been 2 waves of child care research. The first basically attempted to answer the question "Is day care good or bad for children?" The answer to that question was a resounding "maybe," leading to the second wave of child care research, which focuses on the question "How does the quality of child care influence children's development?" Defining quality has not been an easy task. First we must reference quality in terms of the goal of child care itself. As Ruopp and Travers (1982) suggest, child care can function as a service to children and parents, as a source of support for families, as an umbrella system for delivering social services, or as a general tool of social policy. Child care also functions as a workplace and profession for teachers. All of these functions are important aspects to consider in evaluating child care quality. This chapter will focus on child care as a service to children.

Having defined the function of child care, we are now faced with the difficult task of defining quality. There are various levels at which quality can be measured. At the policy level, we may be most interested in defining quality in terms of indicators that are regulatable, such as adult-child ratio, group size, and staff training and experience. As professionals in early childhood education, we might add to that definition issues such as appropriate curricula and guidelines for adult behaviors, as has been done by the National Association for the Education of Young Children (Bredekamp, 1986). As researchers, we might define quality as specific behaviors observable in the classroom, such as teacher sensitivity or involvement, or as more global ratings of overall quality that encompass adult-child interactions and physical space. Thus, research on child care has often used the Early Childhood Environmental Rating Scale (ECERS) (Harms & Clifford, 1980) or the Infant-Toddler Environmental

Rating Scale (ITERS) (Harms & Clifford, 1986) as global indicators of quality. Lastly, as parents, we might define quality in terms of the fit between our child; our values, resources, and needs; and a particular setting.

Researchers conceptualize child care quality in either structural or process terms. *Structural quality* generally refers to regulatable variables including adult-child ratio, group size, and the education and training of adult care givers. *Process quality* refers to the provision of developmentally appropriate activities and to warm, nurturing, and sensitive care giving within the child care arrangement. Structural quality is associated with process quality (Howes, Phillips, & Whitebook, 1990). Children are most likely to receive appropriate care giving in child care arrangements with better ratios, smaller groups, and well-educated and well-trained teachers (Howes, 1990a). Children's development, as we will discuss later in this chapter, is related to both structural and process quality.

Given all of these possible definitions, what research has been done on quality? Most of it has focused on regulatable indicators, observed teacher behavior, overall ratings, age of entry, and stability of child care arrangements. Child care research has yet to address all of these issues. As Clarke-Stewart (1987) has suggested, research has now entered yet a third wave, that of examining the interaction between child care quality and family characteristics.

Quality of Child Care in Center and Family Day Care Homes

It makes little sense to compare forms of child care on structural variables. For example, center groups are by definition almost always larger than family day care groups. It is more reasonable to examine relations among structural variables and children's outcomes within different forms of care to determine whether the same types of relations hold for all types of care: For example, are group size and effective care giving positively related in both family day care and in center care? Several studies suggests that, on the whole, structural variables and child-outcome variables are related in similar ways across both family day care and center care (Clarke-Stewart & Gruber, 1984; Howes, 1983; Howes & Rubenstein, 1985).

Process quality can be compared across child care forms. We begin by examining process quality of child care in different forms of care, and then we review studies that examine particular aspects of care giving.

There is currently one measure of global process quality that has both a family day care form and a center form and that has been used in several studies: the Early Childhood Environmental Rating Scale (ECERS). ECERS and the Family Day Care Rating Scale (FDCRS) were developed by Harms and Clifford (1980; 1984). ECERS has an infant and toddler version (ITERS) (Harms & Clifford, 1986). These scales comprehensively assess the day-to-day quality of care provided for children. ECERS is widely used in child development research, has acceptable reliability, and predicts optimal child development in a number of studies (Phillips, 1987). Individual items are rated in the scale from a low of 1 to a high of 7. A rating of 3 on these scales indicates minimally acceptable quality, whereas a 5 indicates good quality. Infant and toddler classrooms in the NCCSS averaged 3.4 (range 1.3 to 5.6) on the ITERS (Whitebook et al., 1990). Preschool classrooms in the NCCSS averaged 4.1 (range 2.0 to 6.7). Kontos (1992) reports in her comprehensive review that average FDCRS scores range from 2.9 to 4.3. Based on these figures, we conclude that the average child care center or family day care home in the United States in the late 1980s was merely adequate in global process quality. Center classrooms appear more likely to move into the good-quality range than family day care homes.

Critics of the FDCRS suggest that, because the scale is based on a center standard, it is easier for a center classroom to achieve high scores than a family day care home (Modigliani, 1990). The same critics argue that the most important feature of a family day care home is its unstructured, informal, home-like quality. The extension of this argument is that family day care homes with a teaching function, as opposed to a nurturing function, become cold and inappropriate. An alternative viewpoint is that developmentally appropriate activities for young children occur in informal, everyday contexts and that this type of teaching can occur as easily in either centers or homes. For example, washing dishes in a family day care home can be a developmentally appropriate or developmentally inappropriate activity, just as washing dishes in a water table at a center. We suggest that the crucial component in both settings is an adult who both (1) permits the children to actively explore and (2) verbally guides their learning experiences.

An early research study of family day care homes found that care givers rated highest in the category of child-designed space expressed the most positive and least negative affect and were least restrictive of children's behavior (Howes, 1983). Family day care homes with high ratings on child designed space were organized more similarly to a center than a home. We suspect that the underlying construct for the relation between child designed space and adult care-giving behavior is an understanding of developmental appropriate activity.

Most research studies comparing particular care-giving processes and children's development in centers and family day care homes were completed in the 1970s. The most comprehensive of the studies was completed by Clarke-Stewart and Gruber (1984; 1987). They studied 150 Chicago children ages 2 to 4 years. The children were distributed across 7 different care arrangements including family day care and center care. In this study, centers received higher ratings than family day care homes on providing opportunities for children's learning, play, education, discipline, socialization, and experiences with people of other backgrounds. Family day care homes were rated as less messy, more dangerous, and more likely to have children watching television. Children in family day care homes engaged in more one-to-one interaction with adults, whereas children in centers were more likely to interact with their care givers as part of a group.

In addition to the Chicago study there are other small-scale family day care comparison studies that examine care-giver behaviors. These studies suggest that family day care providers show higher rates of restrictions and demands toward children and lower rates of positive affect expression than center-based care givers (Cochran, 1977; Howes, 1983).

In summary, when the process of care giving is compared across family day care and center child care, it appears that family day care may provide somewhat lower-quality care. However, the overall quality of both forms of care was, in the late 1980s, far from optimal.

Differences in Children's Development in Different Forms of Child Care

Clarke-Stewart and Gruber (1984) found that as children moved along a continuum from the most at-home arrangement—at home with parents—to the most out-of-home arrangement—center care—children also advanced in social, emotional, and intellectual competence. These advances were short term. Children who entered center care a year later than the first cohort of center-based children were also advanced in development. When specific comparisons were made between children attending family day care and center care, 1 significant effect was found out of 16 outcome measures. Other comparison studies show a similar pattern of few concurrent or long-term differences between children in family- and center-based care (Cochran, 1977; Everson, Sarnat, & Ambron, 1984; Howes, 1981; Lamb, Hwang, & Bookstein, 1988; Scar, Lande, & McCarthy, 1989).

To our knowledge there is only one comparison study of in-home nonrelative care and center care. Although it is a small-scale, 1-location study, we review it in an effort to encourage more research on in-home nonrelative care. Twelve 3-year-old children and their nannies were observed during informal play groups of 4 to 6 children (Herndon, 1990). Attachment to care giver was assessed using the Waters and Deane (1985) Attachment Q-Set, and play with peers was assessed with the Howes Peer Play Scale (Howes, 1980; 1988a). The 12 children were matched by age, sex, and socioeconomic status of parents with 12 children in center care. The attachment and peer-play assessments for center-care children were made at the center in groups of 15 to 20 children. There were no differences in attachment security scores between the 2 groups of children. Center-care children engaged in more play with peers, but nanny-care children engaged in more complex play with peers. Center-care children expressed more positive affect and nanny-care children more negative affect.

In interpreting differences in children's development when they attend different forms of child care, it is important to realize that the heterogeneity of quality within each child care form is more important than differences in forms of care. For example, differences in group size between the center- and nanny-care children seems the most parsimonious explanation of the differences found in the Herndon study. Likewise, in the study (cited previously) that found lower rates of positive affect expression in family day care providers than in center care givers, differences between child care forms disappeared when quality was controlled (Howes & Rubenstein, 1985). Similarly, when both family and center child care were divided into high- and low-quality groups, the amount of total verbal interaction and restrictiveness was best predicted by quality, not form, of child care (Howes & Rubenstein, 1985).

Some of the differences in children's outcomes are attributable to differences in the parents who select the different forms of care. Goelman and Pence (1987) found that a higher proportion of married, highly educated mothers enrolled their children in center care than family day care. In this sample, single, less-educated mothers were most likely to select family day care. However, among those mothers who used family day care, the mothers most likely to use programs with better-trained care givers were married and better-educated. In the Chicago study, parents who placed the highest value on education most often enrolled their children in part-day center care (Clarke-Stewart & Gruber, 1984). Families who used part-day center care were similar in income to families who used other forms of care, but less likely to have working mothers.

Child care forms are the most apparent differences within child care arrangements. Parents and many professionals have firm beliefs about which form of care is optimal for children. However, despite their visibility, differences between forms appear to be relatively unimportant to children's development. Child care in whatever form is basically a system of relationships with others. The child develops competence within a matrix of relationships with others. A child can have wonderful or horrid adult-child interactions in any form of care. Likewise, peer play can be either expansive or stereotypical and constricted within each form of care.

Children's Development and Regulatable Quality

Adult-Child Ratio. Adult-child ratio is often assumed to be an easily quantified measure. However, in using this variable as a quality measure, it may be necessary to consider the role of the teacher in a particular setting and the ratio that the child actually experiences, rather than simply the licensed ratio or the reported ratio. For example, teachers may have responsibilities, such as food preparation, that take them out of the classroom. As a consequence, the actual ratio may differ from the stated ratio. This issue has not always been addressed in research.

Adult-child ratio is expected to have an effect on children because it is assumed that, as the number of children an adult cares for increases, there will be less opportunity for interaction between the adult and each child. Additionally, the responsibility for a larger group of children may change the management style that the adult employs. The influence of adult-child ratio seems especially important in the social realm, though some effects have also been found on cognitive development.

Infants and toddlers in centers or family day care homes with lower adult-child ratios were more compliant and self-regulated (Howes & Olenick, 1986), and exhibited more play behaviors (Howes & Rubenstein, 1985). When adults cared for more children, infants were less persistent at tasks (Howes & Olenick, 1986) and more distressed and apathetic (Ruopp, Travers, Glantz, & Coelen, 1979). Infants' and toddlers' verbal skills to some extent also seemed to be affected by ratio. Lower ratios are associated with more gestural and vocal imitation (Francis & Self, 1982) and with more overall vocalizations (Howes & Rubenstein, 1985). There was, however, no association between ratio and standardized measures of vocabulary (Ruopp et al., 1979). Similar findings have been found in preschool classrooms, though group size may be a more relevant indicator of quality for this age (Ruopp et al., 1979). A lower adult-child is associated with more elaborated play (Bruner, 1980) and higher frequencies of peer interaction and fantasy play (Field, 1980).

The effects of adult-child ratio are seen particularly in differences in teacher behavior. In infant/toddler classrooms, teachers were more restrictive and controlling when the ratios were higher (Ruopp et al., 1979, Howes & Rubenstein, 1985; Whitebook et al., 1990). In family day care homes, providers with lower ratios were more sensitive (Howes, 1983). For preschoolers, similar influences are again apparent. Teachers in classrooms with higher ratios rate their jobs as more exhausting and spend more time controlling children than those in classrooms with lower ratios (Smith & Connolly, 1981). Teachers who have less children to care for engage the children in more conversation (Bruner, 1980; Smith & Connolly, 1981).

Group Size. Group size, another regulatable indicator of quality, is often highly correlated with adult-child ratio. Infants and toddlers in smaller groups express more positive affect (Cummings & Beagles-Ross, 1983) and engage in more talk and play (Howes & Rubenstein, 1985). Those in larger groups are more apathetic and distressed (Ruopp et al., 1979). Preschool children in small groups also seem not to play more but also to engage in more fantasy and pretend play (Bruner, 1980; Smith & Connolly, 1981). They may also be more creative and cooperative than children in larger groups (Ruopp et al., 1979).

The higher amounts of play in small groups may be linked to the fact that children in smaller groups seem to know each other better than children in larger groups (Smith & Connolly, 1981), be more cooperative (Ruopp et al., 1979), be more socially competent with familiar peers, and score higher in social cognitive measures (Clarke-Stewart & Gruber, 1984). Most studies of group size have looked only at the effects of too many children. Clarke-Stewart and Gruber (1984), however, report the effects of too few as well as too many children. Their results indicate that infants and toddlers enrolled in family day care with either too few (less than 3) or too many (more than 5 children) were less socially competent than their peers.

The influence of group size on care giver outcomes is not surprising given the added demands that caring for a larger group may have on teachers. With a large group of children, the teacher may often be responsible not only for monitoring more children, but also for monitoring and supervising additional adults. These increased demands seem to lead to an increase in restrictive management techniques (Howes, 1983; Ruopp et al., 1979) and a decrease in social interaction and language stimulation in infant/toddler classrooms (Smith & Connolly, 1981). Preschool teachers may not be as sensitive to the effects of group size, perhaps because their role involves less direct care giving of children, though Ruopp et al. (1979) did find that teachers in larger groups engaged in less social interaction with the children. This decrease in social interaction may be related to the lack of gains in verbal measures of children enrolled in larger groups (Ruopp et al., 1979).

Teacher Characteristics. The characteristics of the teachers themselves are indicators of quality. These characteristics include the amount and kind of formal education the teacher has, her experience in child care, and her stability in the classroom. There has been growing concern about the turnover in child care teachers and family day care providers. Child care directors reported to the NCCSS (Whitebook et al., 1990) that, in the preceding 12 months, 41% of their teachers had left the center. Forty-six percent of the teachers themselves reported that they did not expect to remain in their present positions. Estimates of family day care turnover are even higher (Kontos, 1992).

Infants and toddlers may be particularly susceptible to the effects of care-giver stability because they are in the process of forming attachment relationships both to their parents and also presumably to their care givers. Cummings (1980) found that infants and toddlers were more positive and less negative in their interactions with stable care givers. Clarke-Stewart and Gruber (1984) found that infants and toddlers did better on cognitive tests when they retained the same care giver. Howes and Hamilton (1990) found that children who experienced a change in care giver between 18 and 24 months were less likely to have stable care-giver attachments than those who experienced changes later.

The amount of formal education, particularly at the college level, and the effects of child-related training can be difficult to untangle because teachers with more college-level formal education are also likely to have specialized training (Whitebook et al., 1990). In infant/toddler classrooms, teachers or day care providers with more child-related training provide more sensitive care giving (Whitebook et al., 1990; Stallings & Porter, 1980) and are more responsive and engaged in more social stimulation (Howes, 1983). Infants and toddlers cared for by these teachers are less apathetic (Ruopp et al., 1979). The influence of teacher training and education may be particularly important in preschool classrooms, again because of the differences in roles between infant and preschool teachers. In one study, preschoolers who had family day care providers with some formal education and a knowledge of child development were more socially and cognitively competent (Clarke-Stewart & Gruber, 1984; Stallings & Porter, 1980). In centers, children with teachers who had more child-related training were also more cognitively competent (Clarke-Stewart & Gruber, 1984; Ruopp et al., 1979). Ruopp et al. found that child-related training was associated with the children's level of social activity. However, Clarke-Stewart and Gruber found that child-related training was negatively associated with children's social competence with peers. Teachers with more training may foster these outcomes in children because they engage in more social interaction (Ruopp et al.) and have more positive and less restrictive classroom management techniques (Berk, 1985; Arnett, 1989).

The findings on teacher experience are not consistent. Howes (1983) found that teachers and family day care providers

with more years of experience were more responsive to infants and toddlers. In contrast, Ruopp et al. (1979) found that an increase in years of experience was negatively related to teachers' social interaction and language stimulation in infants and toddlers and not related to any measured outcomes in preschoolers. The NCCSS found no association between experience and effective teaching (Whitebook et al., 1990). Years of experience may be a poor index of quality given the nature of the child care profession itself. Child care teachers are poorly paid relative to their equally educated peers. The lack of benefits, pay, and status in the child care profession may force teachers into other careers. Some teachers may be able to remain in child care because they are supported by someone else. Other teachers may remain in child care because they believe that they would be unable to find other employment.

Children's Development and Process Quality

Having examined specific indicators of quality, we return to overall quality and its influence on children. Overall quality as it is defined in most studies is either a rating scale, such as ECERS, that examines various aspects of the child care center (physical space, provision materials, etc.) or a combination of specific indicators such as adult-child ratio, group size and physical space. Overall quality in infant/toddler classrooms and family day care homes is associated with high levels of object and social play (Howes & Stewart, 1987) and with an increase in attachment behaviors directed toward the care giver (Anderson, Nagle, Roberts, & Smith, 1981). Preschoolers in higher-quality centers were rated as more considerate, intelligent, task oriented, and sociable by their teachers (Phillips, McCartney, & Scarr, 1987); had higher intellectual and language test scores (McCartney, 1984); and were more socially competent (McCartney, Scarr, Phillips, Grajek, & Schwarz, 1982; Vandell, Henderson, & Wilson, 1988). Children in lower-quality programs were more likely to rate themselves lower in self-esteem (Vandell et al., 1989) and more likely to engage in solitary or unoccupied activities (Vandell & Powers, 1983).

What conclusions can be drawn from the research on child care quality? First, there appears to be a general strong relation between child care quality and children's development. Second, the specific indicators for quality may differ for different age groups. Infants and toddlers are susceptible to the effects of both group size and adult-child ratio, although group size is a more potent indicator for preschoolers. Finally, we may need to reexamine the outcome measures we choose. Early child care research based on intervention programs normally focuses on cognitive measures. The majority of children currently in child care programs are not in intervention programs per se, but they are being cared for by multiple adults in groups of same-age peers. It might be more appropriate to focus our attention on outcomes related to social competence with peers and adults.

Child care quality indicators are proxies for interactions and relationships within child care. In the following 2 sections of the chapter, we focus on the child's relationships with others in child care in order to examine what combination of variables best predicts optimal development.

TEACHER-CHILD INTERACTION AND RELATIONSHIPS

Teachers' Roles

Teachers of young children play a variety of roles, such as facilitating development, providing emotional support and guidance, managing both children and other adults, mediating peer contacts, and instructing. The emphasis a particular teacher may place on one of these roles over another and the value she associates with them may vary with the quality and goals of the program, the age of the children she cares for, and her education, personal teaching philosophy, and experience. The balance between these roles is not clear-cut, though the National Association for the Education of Young Children, the professional organization for early childhood educators, does provide, in its Guidelines for Developmentally Appropriate Practices (Brede-Kamp, 1986), exemplars of interaction strategies for teachers. It is clear from these examples that, in infancy and toddlerhood, the primary role of the teacher is to provide sensitive, individualized care giving. As children become older, teachers may also mediate peer contacts and facilitate learning through structuring the environment and modeling exploratory behavior. Thus, though not specifically stated, the role of the teacher as instructor increases and the role of the teacher as care giver decreases with the age of the children.

Program goals can also influence how the teacher evaluates her role. Early programs geared toward intervening with high-risk children emphasize the need to provide cognitive stimulation. Teachers in many of these programs for preschoolers are expected to assume the role of instructor. Though the form of instruction was not necessarily didactic, many of the early Head Start models did emphasize didactic teaching styles. In contrast, Montessori programs use self-correcting teaching materials. The role of the teacher in these programs is to observe and provide materials to children that are appropriate to their interests and skill level; instruction per se is not a major role.

Teachers may emphasize their role of cognitive instruction to the exclusion of others. In one study, family day care providers felt that one of the major differences between center care and home settings involved the activities they did with the children (Long & Garduque, 1987). Although they and the parents of the children in their care also felt that center care provided social experiences with peers, the family day care providers viewed that as a by-product rather than something directly taught.

The role of teacher as a mediator of peer contacts has not been widely studied. Certainly mothers of young children may mediate peer contacts between their children in a variety of ways (Unger, 1992). Teachers too may either facilitate or ignore peer interactions. The Guidelines for Developmentally Appropriate Practices (Bredekamp, 1986) suggest that, although mediating peer contacts is not a major consideration for teachers of infants and young toddlers, teachers do assume a role for mediating both conflict and for facilitating interaction as children become older. Considering the guidelines, it seems that the role of mediator must be particularly important in the preschool years and decrease somewhat in the elementary years. This may be because preschool is still viewed as a major time for socializing children, whereas peer contact in elementary school is managed more by the children themselves.

The quality of the child care arrangement, especially group size and adult-child ratio, may certainly influence the role that the teacher assumes. All teachers and providers must, to some extent, manage children and, perhaps, other adults. Children must be kept safe; they must be fed, given naps, and moved from one activity to another. In some cases a head teacher must also manage the other teachers in her classroom, providing a model for appropriate teaching behavior and seeing that the teachers as well as the children get through the day. Several researchers have found that larger groups and higher adult-child ratios are associated with more restrictive and controlling behavior on the part of teachers (Ruopp et al., 1979; Howes & Rubenstein, 1985). This is not surprising because, as the number of people that must be managed increases, teachers probably have to rely on more restrictive techniques despite their own or the program's emphasis on other roles. Teachers can, however, manage children in less restrictive ways. How this might be done has not been the subject of much research. Our informal observation of child care suggests that teachers may employ a variety of strategies to help children regulate their own behavior. Good teachers control their classrooms through rituals and routines rather than through controlling or restrictive management. Research could add much to our understanding of how this is accomplished and what factors influence teacher competencies in this area.

Quality may also influence the teacher's role through the level of education and experience that the teacher has. The effects of education and experience are far from clear. Experience may not have a linear relationship with child outcomes (Clarke-Stewart & Gruber, 1984), but certainly direct experience with children must to some extent influence how teachers perceive their roles. The research on teacher education is likewise not clear. In some studies the level of formal education, regardless of whether it is child related, has been associated with better child outcomes (Whitebook et al., 1990). In other instances it has been associated with an emphasis on cognitive instruction (Clarke-Stewart & Gruber, 1984). Research has also found that these effects may differ for infant/toddler and preschool teachers. The NCCSS found that infant/ toddler teachers with higher levels of specialized training were more sensitive care givers, but this effect did not hold for preschool teachers (Whitebook et al., 1990).

This influence of teacher education that has been found in the research may be especially affected by cohort effects. The education and training that day care providers receive in higher education settings (i.e., universities and community colleges) does not have a long history, especially for infants and toddlers. Well into the late 1970s and early 1980s many of the early childhood education programs trained teachers either in models drawn from nursery school programs or from the early elementary grades. Gradually, as day care itself has proliferated, so too have changes occurred, albeit more slowly, in preparation programs for teachers.

The final role of the teacher is that of providing emotional support and guidance. As more and more children spend more and more time in child care centers and family day care homes, the role of the teacher as a source for emotional support becomes even more important. This role may be particularly important for infants and toddlers as well as young preschoolers. Research examining early entry into infant child care has raised concerns that these infants may develop insecure patterns of attachment with their mothers (Belsky, 1988; Clarke-Stewart, 1989). Insecure attachment has been associated with incompetent social behaviors with both peers and adults through early childhood. If entry into child care may place children at risk for developing insecure attachments to their mothers, it may be especially important that they form positive relationships with the adults who care for them in child care.

Whether or not these relationships are in fact attachment relationships is not clear. Attachment theory suggests that, at least for infants and young toddlers, these relationships could be considered attachments. Bowlby (1982) theorized that infants form attachment relationships to their care givers over the course of the first year. The quality or patterns of attachment formed depends on the infants' experience or nonexperience of sensitive, responsive care giving (Ainsworth, Blehar, Waters, & Wall, 1978). However, all infants would be expected to form attachment relationships with adults who provide them with care and protection. Infant teachers certainly provide such care for extended periods of time.

Some research has examined whether infants do indeed form attachments to their teachers. Farran, Burchinal, Hutaff, and Ramey (1984) examined the social interactions between infants and their care givers at 6, 9, and 12 months. Using social preference as a marker of attachment behavior, there was little if any stability across time in the specific teachers that infants preferred. They concluded that infants do prefer their familiar teachers to strangers or visitors, but do not form true attachments to these teachers. They further suggested that forming such attachements in a day care environment may not be advantageous. Because several adults provide care giving and specific adults may change frequently in the child care setting, children might be better to be adaptable to a wide range of care givers.

To address the same question, a second study by Ainslie and Anderson (1984) examined child-teacher relationships using the Ainsworth Strange Situation, a standard assessment of infants' quality of maternal attachment. They found that although attachment relationships between toddlers and their teachers could be classified into the same patterns and distributions as those found in relationships between mothers and children, the actual behaviors of the children in the Strange Situation with their teachers did not vary across the classification patterns. Basically, children exhibited the same behaviors with teachers whether or not they were classified as having secure or insecure relationships with them. Based on the lack of differentiation of behaviors across patterns of secure and insecure teacher attachments, the researchers concluded that these children are not truly attached to their teachers, though they may be "familiar" with them. Contrary to Farran et al., however, they feel that it is in the best interests of the child to form a secure attachment

with the care giver. They further note that the Strange Situation, developed for the assessment of maternal attachment, may not be the ideal assessment of teacher attachment.

A similar study was conducted with children enrolled in Dutch day care centers (Goosens & van IJzendoorn, 1990). These researchers were interested not only in the differences in the distributions across classifications that might exist among teacher, maternal, and father attachments, but also in the possibility that attachment to teachers might serve in a compensatory capacity. That is, children with insecure parental attachments might be able to form secure teacher attachments. They found, contrary to their hypothesis, that the distribution of secure and insecure attachments was similar for mothers, fathers, and teachers. There was little concordance in the pattern of attachment a child had with parents and teachers. They were also able to examine the security of attachments teachers had with more than one child. These relationships were found to vary in degree of security: Teachers had secure and insecure relationships with different children. The researchers concluded that infants and teachers do form attachment relationships and that these relationships might be compensatory. However, they too cautioned that the Strange Situation might not be the ideal assessment of teacher-child attachment.

Howes and colleagues have continued this line of investigation using a newly developed measure, the Attachment Q-Set (Waters & Deane, 1985). Unlike the Strange Situation, this measure was designed as a naturalistic observational measure of attachment and is a valid assessment of attachment throughout the toddler and preschool periods. Howes has used this Q-Set to examine children's attachment relationships with care givers across a broad age range and with diverse samples. Children's attachment security with care givers is generally lower than with mothers but not significantly so (Howes & Hamilton, 1992; Howes, Galluzzo, Hamilton, Matheson, & Rodning, 1989; Howes, Rodning, Galluzzo, & Myers, 1988). Howes and Hamilton found meaningful associations between the quality of teacher attachments and teacher behaviors (1992). Just as mothers who respond sensitively to their children have children who form secure attachments to them, so too teacher behaviors that are more responsive, involved, and less detached are associated with secure attachment relationships. Additionally, children's security of attachment with teachers seems to have a strong influence on their social competence with peers, both concurrently and predictively (Howes et al., 1989). This research suggests that it is adaptive for children to form secure attachments with their teachers and that these attachment relationships may have important influences interacting with and adding to parental attachments.

What do we know from the research on child-teacher attachments? Children do not have concordant attachment relationships with their mothers and teachers (Goosens & van IJzendoorn, 1990; Howes et al., 1988). They are able to form secure or positive relationships with teachers even if they have insecure attachment relationships with their mothers. The relationship with the teacher may compensate for an insecure relationship with the parents. The troubling note is that teachers, though they are significant people in children's lives, are not stable. Children in child care are not able to maintain consistent relationships with their teachers because of the high rate of teacher turnover, state and program policies that encourage age-segregated classrooms, and changes in the child care arrangements determined by the parents. The formation of a positive relationship with the teacher, be it a "true" attachment or not, has implications for children's development. The effects of repeatedly losing significant relationships needs to be further addressed in research.

Work Environments That Permit Teachers to Enhance Optimal Adult-Child Interaction

Much of child care research has focused on the child care setting as an environment for child development. Child care settings also are work environments for adults. As with any work environment, the child care setting can influence the work behavior of its workers. Thus, some child care environments promote effective adult interactions with children, whereas some inhibit them. There is a small body of research that examines relations between child care as an adult work environment and effective teaching behaviors. The most substantial portion of this literature has focused on adult-child ratios. In both center-based and family day care, adult care givers are more sensitive and responsive when they care for fewer children (Howes, 1983; Ruopp et al., 1979; Smith & Connolly, 1981; Whitebook et al., 1990).

The National Child Care Staffing Study was the first full-scale study to examine relations between teacher salaries and the quality of care provided for children. In the NCCSS, teacher salaries were the single best predictor of both classroom environments and effective teaching (Whitebook et al., 1990). Centers that paid teachers better wages also hired sufficient teachers to create acceptable adult-child ratios and hired well-educated teachers with sufficient training in child development to provide sensitive and appropriate care giving.

The NCCSS also highlighted the importance of the legal status of center-based child care. Child care centers can be operated either for profit or not for profit. For-profit centers created worse adult work environments for their staff, paying lower salaries and creating classrooms with worse ratios than not-for-profit centers. Teachers in for-profit centers were less sensitive and appropriate than teachers in not-for-profit centers.

CHILDREN'S PEER INTERACTIONS AND FRIENDSHIPS IN CHILD CARE

Children in out-of-home child care typically experience more intense peer contact than children in in-home arrangements who usually spend their days with an adult care giver or possibly a sibling. For some child care children the peer group is a more stable and consistent part of the social environment than the adult care giver. Children in full-time center care usually have more than one care giver but only one peer group across the course of the day. With high turnover of teaching staff, a peer group may experience few changes in composition but several different teachers over a year. Even without teacher turnover, children typically "move up" in a center and,

with their peers, have new sets of teachers as they become older. Thus, the peer group as well as the adult care givers have the potential to influence the child's development.

The peer context is important for the acquisition of several important social skills. Children learn about forming, maintaining, and losing friendships with peers. Children also learn to enter social groups—to make contact and neither disrupt the ongoing activity, nor be excluded from it, but rather to find a social role and join the activity. Children also fight with peers. Through fighting, children learn to resolve conflicts. In order to successfully use materials in a child care center, children must figure out how to share and divide up resources in a reasonably equitable manner.

Social interaction and friendship formation with peers are usually considered independent and interacting aspects of social competence with peers. *Competent social interaction* is defined as social behaviors used to engage a peer and maintain a mutually satisfying encounter. *Friendships between children* are defined as stable and affective dyadic relationships. Friendships are mutual preferences. Each child in a friendship prefers the other as a partner over other children in the group, at least at some time during the contact or for some activities. Friendships are characterized by reciprocity. The children select each other as partners, rather than just one child selecting the other as a friend. Finally, friendships are marked by positive affect: The children enjoy each others' company.

It is often assumed that one of the major potential benefits of child care is socialization experiences with peers. Several studies of competence with peers suggest that social competence with peers is dependent on experiences within peer groups rather than on age, with more experienced children engaging in more complex play (Mueller & Brenner, 1977). Thus, several studies report that children who enter child care early are especially socially competent with peers as older children (Gunnarsson, 1978; Howes, 1988a; Macrae, Calhoun, & Herbert-Jackson, 1976; Schwarz, Krolick, & Strickland, 1973; Schindler, Moely, & Frank, 1987). In contrast, some studies of early child care report that children who enter center care (and thus peer groups) as infants are more aggressive with peers (Haskins, 1985), whereas other studies suggest that only children who enter low-quality child care as infants have more problematic relationships with peers (Howes, 1990b).

In general, the literature linking child care quality and children's competence in peer relations offers mixed findings. Howes and Stewart (1987) and Lamb, Hwang, Bookstein, Broberg, Holt, and Frodi (1988) found no relation between child care quality and children's play with peers. However, Vandell et al., (1988) found that children who had been in low-quality child care as preschoolers had difficulty with peers as third graders. Howes (1990b) and Holloway and Reichart-Erickson (1988) found concurrent relations between social competence with peers and child care quality. Results may differ across studies because teacher behaviors mediate between quality variables and peer behavior.

We suspect, given the previous review of teacher influences, that children in lower-quality child care are given little guidance or structure for their peer relations. Teachers can use peer contacts as contexts for helping the children to acquire social problem-solving skills; alternately, they can ignore peer contacts and punish children when they fail to maintain smooth peer relations and therefore disturb the teacher. For example, play-group entries ("She won't let me play"), sharing resources ("I had the doll with the long hair first"), and aggression ("He bit me") are frequently brought to the teacher's attention. We have observed untrained teachers "settle" these problems in harsh, adult-directed, and arbitrary ways: "In this school we are all friends, you have to let her play," "If you can't share the dolls nobody will play with them today," and "Only animals bite, stay in time out until I tell you you can get up."

Children enrolled in child care programs do form friendships as early as the infant and toddler period. If these friendships are not disrupted, children often remain friends throughout their time in child care (Howes, 1988a; Phillipsen & Howes, 1990). For infants and toddlers in particular, child care friendships appear to be an important context for learning social skills. Children who are friends engage in more developmentally advanced social interaction before children who are not friends (Phillipsen & Howes, 1990).

Child care friendships also appear to serve as social support and aid in children's school transitions. Howes (1988a) reported that children who moved between child care centers with familiar children were more socially skilled than children who made these transitions alone. Ladd and Price (1987) found that children who began kindergarten with classmates familiar from child care were more accepted by their classmates and were more positive toward school. These familiar classmates were not necessarily friends. In a second study of the transition between preschool and kindergarten, Ladd (1990) found that children who either maintained the friendships that they entered school with or formed friendships within the first 2 months of school had the easiest adjustment to school.

FAMILY CHARACTERISTICS AND CHILD CARE

Family factors may influence children's experience in child care. First, families choose whether or not their child will be in child care and, if so, what form that child care will take and what specific child care setting will be used. Second, families decide when to enroll their child in care, perhaps in early infancy or maybe not until preschool. Third, families in part influence the stability of care that a child experiences by deciding to keep the child in or remove the child from a particular child care arrangement. Finally, all of the outcome measures examined as arising from child care experience must to some extent also be related to family characteristics. Children in child care are not just in child care; they are part of a family, and the characteristics of the family interact with and may override the experience of being in child care.

The influence of family characteristics on child care selection is disturbing. Children who are perhaps most in need of high-quality, stable child care because of unstable home situations may not receive it because their families opt for lower-quality programs (Goelman & Pence, 1987; Howes & Olenick, 1986; Kontos & Fiene, 1987; Petrie, 1984; Schliecker, White, & Jacobs, 1989). Parents who are more involved and more nurturing or who have more appropriate child-rearing values

select higher-quality programs (Howes & Stewart, 1987; Howes & Olenick, 1986; Howes, 1990b; Kontos & Fiene, 1987; Phillips, McCartney, & Scarr, 1987). Children who have insecure parental attachments are also more likely to be enrolled in programs of lower quality (Howes et al., 1988). Parents who lead disorganized and perhaps more stressful lives may not have the energy to find higher-quality programs. Parents with inappropriate child-rearing values may not see the need to find such programs.

There is likely also to be a link between the levels of stress and disorganization a family experiences and their socioeconomic status; such families may not be able to afford higher-quality programs, or those programs may not even exist in their communities. NCCSS (Whitebook et al., 1990) found that children from low-income families were the least likely to be enrolled in programs accredited by the National Association for the Education of Young Children. Children from higher-income families were the most likely to be enrolled in higher-quality programs. Surprising, children from middle-income families were in the lowest-quality programs.

The stability of the care a child receives is often reflective of (1) the nature of child care itself and (2) high teacher turnover rates. However, there do seem to be some associations between parent characteristics and stability of care. Children of divorced parents are more likely to experience multiple child care arrangements (Jacobs, Guidubaldi, & Nastasi, 1986). Children with insecure maternal attachments are also more likely to experience unstable child care arrangements as infants (Suwalsky, Zaslow, Klein, & Rabinovich, 1986). It seems, then, that children who may particularly benefit from a sustained relationship with an adult through child care may not receive it.

Parental characteristics, their level of education, child-rearing values, and attitudes toward their child's enrollment in child care may all influence child outcome measures. Many studies have found that a combination of child care quality, child characteristics, and parent characteristics are better predictors of child outcome than a single variable (Kontos & Fiene, 1987; Goelman & Pence, 1987; Lamb, Hwang, Broberg, & Bookstein, 1988). Scarr et al. (1989), in contrast, found that maternal and family characteristics, rather than child care characteristics, were the best predictors of child outcome. The relation between family and child care influences may be further complicated by the age that the child enters child care. Howes (1990b) found stronger relations between family influences and child outcomes when the child entered child care after his or her first birthday than when the child entered care as an infant.

Child care may also have different influences on child outcome depending on family characteristics. The early intervention studies with high-risk populations suggest that child care may have a positive effect on children's cognitive development (e.g., Ramey & Haskins, 1981). (This effect does not, however, seem to hold for middle-class populations.) Day care may have a positive influence on children who come from less-advantaged families if they are in high-quality programs. Andersson (1987) followed up children ages 8 to 10 years who had been enrolled either early or late in child care. Children from mother-headed families who had early child care experiences did as well if not better than children from nuclear families, whereas those children from mother-headed families who did not enter child care early did the worst on social and cognitive measures. In Goelman and Pence's research (1987) the lowest language test scores were associated with children who were in unlicensed day care settings and who were from one-parent families. Robertson (1982) found that lower-class children were more socially responsive in first grade if they had not attended child care, but for middle-class children the reverse was true. The interaction of child and family characteristics are not clear; however, it seems clear that children who come from lower socioeconomic groups, single-parent families, or stressed families may benefit from high-quality child care. Unfortunately, it is most likely that such children will find themselves in low-quality settings.

The role of parent attitudes is also important in understanding child outcomes. Parents may enroll their children in child care by choice or by economic necessity. For many middle-class parents today, having a stay-at-home mom is not realistic given economic restraints. Mothers may or may not be comfortable with the decision to enroll their child in child care. Everson et al. (1984) found this to be particularly true for mothers of infants. Though there were no differences in children's social behaviors prior to entry, by 10 months after entry, toddlers whose mothers did not want them in child care but had sent them anyway were less cooperative, less compliant, less persistent, and less prosocial. The attitudes the mothers held toward the decisions regarding child care were more powerful predictors of child behavior than whether or not the children were enrolled in child care.

Finally, we can ask if child care influences the family. It is often assumed that child care provides a service to parents as well as to children and that a primary role of the teacher is parent educator—whether or not there is formal time set aside for such education. The influence of child care on families has not been well documented. The intervention literature does suggest an effect but these programs often specifically included parent education or supports, so the influence of child enrollment per se cannot be separated from these effects. Enrollment in child care should help families if it enables them to find and maintain employment or further their own education (Ramey & Haskins, 1981; Rescorla, Provence, & Naylor, 1982). It may also provide parents with a support network among teachers as well as other parents. Teachers may serve as role models to help parents better understand children. Child care may even serve as a staging area for other support services such as nutrition and health care, which may be quite helpful for families. However, we have little research in these areas.

It may also be that factors supporting parents are not those directly benefiting children. Some benefits to parents may actually be in direct conflict with what is beneficial to children. For instance, longer day care hours (for example, 7 A.M. till 7 P.M.) are a real benefit for working parents, especially those who must commute a long distance to work. However, such a long day may not be in the best interests of the child.

There have been 2 waves of child care research, the first centered on the question of whether child care is bad or good for children—the answer was maybe. This led to the second wave of child care research, which sought to determine what quality factors influence the child's development in the context of child care. The third wave, the one we are now engaged in

as researchers, asks how quality and family factors influence child outcomes. In examining the long-term consequences of child care experience, we return basically to the first wave of research. Does enrollment in child care have an effect, positive or negative, on long-term development? And more specifically, does the age of entry into childcare have an effect on development?

AGE OF ENTRY

There are both short- and long-term studies of how age of entry into child care affects children's development. The short-term studies have looked at preschoolers who either had or did not have previous child care experience. The results of these studies are mixed. There are some indications that early child care—that is, as infants—may lead to more aggressive behavior with peers (Schwarz, Strickland, & Krolick, 1974) and less cooperative behavior with adults (Rubenstein, Howes, & Boyle, 1981; Schwarz et al., 1974). This is consistent with research that finds elevated rates of insecure maternal attachment to be associated with early maternal employment (Belsky, 1988; Clarke-Stewart, 1989). However, many other researchers have found little difference in preschoolers' behavior to be dependent on their age of entry (Howes, 1990b; Roopnarine & Hempel, 1990). As with any study of child care, the outcome does seem to be associated with the quality of the child care itself. McCartney et al. (1982) found that children who were enrolled in infant programs with low verbal interaction were rated as more anxious and maladjusted than children who were enrolled into programs with rich verbal interaction. Howes (1990b) found that only those infants who entered low-quality care looked less competent as kindergartners. Infants who entered high-quality care were no different than children who entered care as older children.

Studies examining the effects of infant/toddler or preschool care in the early elementary years depict a mixed picture; some researchers find early care experiences to be linked with less-skilled social behaviors (Haskins, 1985), whereas others find no differences (Hegland & Rix, 1990) in social behaviors. There do seem to be more sustained differences in academic, school adjustment, and cognitive measures. Earlier age of entry as infants or toddlers into community centers has been linked to better school performance in the early elementary grades (Andersson, 1987; Howes, 1988b). Reviews of Head Start and other early intervention programs for disadvantaged families (Harrell, 1983; McKey et al., 1985; Lazar, Darlington, Murray, Royce, & Sniper, 1982) have found that these types of programs do continue to have positive effects on children's cognitive competence throughout the first 3 to 4 years of elementary school. Beyond elementary school there are less consistent findings, but early intervention may continue to have some positive influences on academic achievement and school performance (Beller, 1983; Gray, Ramsey, & Klaus, 1981). In the one retrospective study of patterns of early child care and social, cognitive, and academic functioning in the college years, no differences were found between whether or not children had or did not have child care experience (Ipsa, Gray, & Thornburg, 1987). In this context it is important to note that there are many intervening influences in a child's life between child care and college.

Age of entry in and of itself may not be a particularly promising area of child care research. As with child care research in general, more attention needs to be paid to the quality and the stability of child care. Howes (1988b) found that both quality and stability of care were better predictors of outcomes in first grade than age of entry. Age of entry is linked both to issues of overall quality and to stability of care. Children who enter child care earlier may experience less stability in care. This, in turn, may have more long-term implications than the age at which they began child care.

CONCLUSIONS

We have sufficient research in the area of child care to make several overarching conclusions. Child care quality appears more important than either child care form or age of entry in predicting children's development. Quality in child care is closely linked to the adult providing care. In settings where the adult can effectively perform both nurturing and teaching roles, children are able to develop more social and cognitive competence. Teacher effectiveness is linked to individual characteristics, including formal education and specialized training, and to setting characteristics, particularly salaries and adult-child ratio. Although family and child care influences are difficult to separate, most studies find that the best predictions of children's outcomes come from a combination of family and child care influences.

In essence, we now know that good child care can enhance development; we also know how to provide good child care. Despite this impressive knowledge base, child care quality in America is far from optimal. Simultaneously, we are losing our well-educated and well-trained teachers and providers because of poverty-level salaries. If we, as a nation, are to provide good quality child care for our children, efforts must be made to enhance both salaries and the supply of high-quality care.

References

Ainslie, R. C., & Anderson, C. W. (1984). Day care children's relationships to their mothers and caregivers: An inquiry into the conditions for the development of attachment. In R. C. Ainslie (Ed.), *The child and the day care setting* (pp. 98–132). New York: Praeger.

Ainsworth, M., Blehar, M. C., Waters, E., & Wall, S. (1978). *Patterns of attachment*. Hillsdale, NJ: Erlbaum.

Anderson, C., Nagle, R., Roberts, W., & Smith, J. (1981). Attachment to substitute caregivers as a function of center quality and caregiver involvement. *Child Development, 57*, 53–61.

Andersson, B. E. (1987). *The importance of public day care for preschool children's later development*. Paper presented at the biennial meeting of the Society for Research in Child Development, Baltimore, MD.

Arnett, J. (1989). Caregivers in day care centers: Does training matter. *Journal of Applied Developmental Psychology, 10*, 541–552.

Beller, E. K. (1983). The Philadelphia study: The impact of preschool on intellectual and socioemotional development. In Consortium for Longitudinal Studies, *As the twig is bent . . . Lasting effects of preschool programs* (pp. 193–217). Hillsdale, NJ: Erlbaum.

Belsky, J. (1988). The "effects" of infant day care reconsidered. *Early Childhood Research Quarterly, 3*, 235–272.

Berk, L. (1985). Relationship of educational attainment, child orientated attitudes, job satisfaction, and career commitment to caregiver behavior toward children. *Child Care Quarterly, 14*, 103–129.

Bowlby, J. (1982). *Attachment and loss. Vol. 1*. New York: Basic Books.

Bredekamp, S. (Ed.). (1986). *Developmentally appropriate practice in early childhood programs serving children from birth through age 8*. Washington, DC: National Association for the Education of Young Children.

Bruner, J. (1980). *Under five in Britain*. Ypsilanti, MI: High/Scope.

Clarke-Stewart, A. (1987). In search of consistencies in child care research. In D. A. Phillips (Ed.), *Quality in child care: What does research tell us* (pp. 105–120). Washington, DC: National Association for the Education of Young Children.

Clarke-Stewart, A. (1989). Infant day care: Maligned or malignant? *American Psychologist, 44*, 266–273.

Clarke-Stewart, A., & Gruber, C. (1984). Day care forms and features. In R. C. Ainslie (Ed.), *Quality variations in day care* (pp. 35–62). New York: Praeger.

Clarke-Stewart, A., & Gruber, C. (1987). Predicting child development from child care forms and features: The Chicago study. In D. Phillips (Ed.), *Quality in child care: What does the research tell us?* (pp. 21–42). Washington, DC: National Association for the Education of Young Children.

Cochran, M. (1977). A comparison of group day care and family child rearing patterns in Sweden. *Child Development, 48*, 702–707.

Cummings, E. (1980). Caregiver stability and day care. *Developmental Psychology, 16*, 31–37.

Cummings, M., & Beagles-Ross, J. (1983). Towards a model of infant day care: Studies of factors influencing responding to separation in day care. In R. C. Ainslie (Ed.), *Quality variations in day care* (pp. 159–182). New York: Praeger.

Everson, M. D., Sarnat, L., & Ambron, S. R. (1984). Day care and early socialization: The role of maternal attitudes. In R. C. Ainslie (Ed.), *Quality variations in day care* (pp. 63–97). New York: Praeger.

Farran, D. C., Burchinal, M., Hutaff, S. E., & Ramey, C. (1984). Allegiances or attachments: Relationships among infants and their day care teachers. In R. C. Ainslie (Ed.), *The child and the day care setting* (pp. 133–158). New York: Praeger.

Field, T. M. (1980). Preschool play: Effects of teacher:child ratio and organization of classroom space. *Child Study Journal, 10*, 191–205.

Francis, P., & Self, P. (1982). Imitative responsiveness of young children in day care and home settings: The importance of the child to the caregiver ratio. *Child Study Journal, 12*, 199–126.

Goelman, H., & Pence, A. (1987). Effects of child care, family and individual characteristics on children's language development: The Victoria Day Care Research Project. In D. Phillips (Ed.), *Quality in child care: What does the research tell us?* (pp. 89–104). Washington, DC: National Association for the Education of Young Children.

Goosens, F. A., & van IJzendoorn, M. H. (1990). Quality of infants' attachment to professional caregivers: Relation to infant-parent attachment and day care characteristics. *Child Development, 61*, 832–837.

Gray, S., Ramsey, B., & Klaus, R. (1981). *From three to twenty: The early training project*. Baltimore, MD: University Park Press.

Gunnarsson, L. (1978). *Children in day care and family day care in Sweden* (Research Bulletin No. 21). Gothenburg, Sweden: University of Gothenburg.

Harms, T., & Clifford, R. (1980). *Early childhood environmental rating scale.* New York: Teachers College Press, Columbia University.

Harms, T., & Clifford, R. (1984). *The family day care rating scale.* Unpublished document, University of North Carolina–Chapel Hill.

Harms, T., & Clifford, R. (1986). *Infant-toddler environmental rating scale.* Unpublished document, University of North Carolina–Chapel Hill.

Harrell, A. (1983). *Preliminary report: The effect of the Head Start program on children's cognitive development.* Washington, DC: U.S. Department of Health and Human Services.

Haskins, R. (1985). Public school aggression among children with varying day care experience. *Child Development, 56*, 698–703.

Hayes, C. D., Palmer, J. L., & Zaslow, M. (1990). *Who cares for America's children: Child care policy for the 1990s.* Washington, DC: National Academy Press.

Hegland, S., & Rix, M. (1990). Aggression and assertiveness in kindergarten children differing in day care experiences. *Early Childhood Research Quarterly, 5*, 105–116.

Herndon, M. (1990). *Nanny care as an alternative.* Unpublished manuscript, University of California at Los Angeles.

Hofferth, S. L., & Phillips, D. A. (1987). Child care in the United States: 1970–1995. *Journal of Marriage and the Family, 49*, 559–571.

Holloway, S., & Reichart-Erickson, M. (1988). The relationship of day care quality of children's free play behavior and social problem solving skills. *Early Childhood Research Quarterly, 3*, 39–53.

Howes, C. (1980). The peer play scale as an index of complexity of peer interaction. *Developmental Psychology, 16*, 371–372.

Howes, C. (1981). Toddler peer behaviors in two types of day care. *Infant Behavior and Development, 4*, 387–393.

Howes, C. (1983). Caregiver behavior in center and family day care. *Journal of Applied Developmental Psychology, 4*, 99–107.

Howes, C. (1988a). Peer interaction of young children. *Monographs of the Society for Research in Child Development, 53* (1, Serial No. 217).

Howes, C. (1988b). Relations between early child Cree and schooling. *Developmental Psychology, 24*, 53–57.

Howes, C. (1990a). Caregiving environments and their consequences for children: The experience in the United States. In E. Mulhuish & P. Moss (Eds.), *Day care and the young child: An international perspective.* London: Tavistock.

Howes, C. (1990b). Can the age of entry into child care and the quality of child care predict adjustment in kindergarten? *Developmental Psychology, 26*, 292–303.

Howes, C., Galluzzo, D. C., Hamilton, C. E., Matheson, C. C., & Rodning, C. (1989). *Social relationships with adults and peers within child care and families.* Paper presented at the biennial meeting of the Society for Research in Child Development, Kansas City, MO.

Howes, C., & Hamilton, C. E. (1992). Children's attachment with their child care teachers. *Child Development, 62.*

Howes, C., & Olenick, M. (1986). Family and child care influences on toddlers' compliance. *Child Development, 57*, 202–216.

Howes, C., Rodning, C., Galluzzo, D. C., & Myers, L. (1988). Attachment and child care: Relationships with mother and caregiver. *Early Childhood Research Quarterly, 3*, 403–416.

Howes, C., & Rubenstein, J. (1985). Determinants of toddlers' experience in day care: Age of entry and quality of setting. *Child Care Quality, 14*, 140–151.

Howes, C., Phillips, D., & Whitebook, M. (1992). Thresholds of quality implications for the social development of children in center based child care. *Child Development, 62,* 449–460.

Howes, C., & Stewart, P. (1987). Child's play with adults, toys and peers: An examination of family and child care influences. *Developmental Psychology, 23*(3), 423–430.

Ipsa, J., Gray, M. M., & Thornburg, K. R. (1987). *Long-term effects of day care.* Paper presented at the biennial meeting of the Society for Research in Child Development, Baltimore, MD.

Jacobs, N. L., Guidubaldi, J., & Nastasi, B. (1986). Adjustment of divorced-family day care children. *Early Childhood Research Quarterly, 1*(4), 361–378.

Kisker, E. E., Maynard, R., Gordon, A., & Strain, L. (1988). *The child care challenge: What parents need and what is available in three metropolitan areas.* Princeton, NJ: Mathematica Policy Research.

Kontos, S. (1992). *Family day care monograph.* National Association for the Education of Young Children. Washington, DC.

Kontos, S., & Fiene, R. (1987). Child care quality, compliance with regulations, and children's development: The Pennsylvania Study. In D. A. Phillips (Ed.), *Quality in child care: What does research tell us* (pp. 57–80). Washington, DC: National Association for the Education of Young Children.

Ladd, G. (1990). Having friends, keeping friends, making friends, and being liked by peers in the classroom: Predictors of children's early school adjustment. *Child Development, 61*, 1081–1100.

Ladd, G., & Price, J. (1987). Predicting children's social and school adjustment following the transition from preschool to kindergarten. *Child Development, 58*, 1168–1189.

Lamb, M. E., Hwang, C., Bookstein, F. L. Broberg, A., Hult, G., & Frodi, M. (1988). Determinants of social competence in Swedish preschoolers. *Developmental Psychology, 24*, 58–70.

Lamb, M. E., Hwang, C. P., Broberg, A., & Bookstein, F. (1988). The effects of out of home care on the development of social competence in Sweden: A longitudinal study. *Early Childhood Research Quarterly, 3*, 379–402.

Lazar, I., Darlington, R., Murray, J., Royce, J., & Sniper, A. (1982). Lasting effects of early education. *Monographs of the Society for Research in Child Development, 47* (1–2, Serial No. 194).

Long, F., & Garduque, L. (1987). Continuity between home and family day care: Caregivers' and mothers' perceptions of children's' social experience. In D. L. Peters & S. Kontos (Eds.), *Continuity and discontinuity of experience in child care* (pp. 69–90). Norwood, NJ: Ablex.

Macrae, J., Calhoun, C., & Herbert-Jackson, E. (1976). Are behavioral effects of infant care program specific? *Developmental Psychology, 12*, 269–270.

McCartney, K. (1984). Effect of quality of day care environment on children's language development. *Developmental Psychology, 20*, 244–260.

McCartney, K., Scarr, S., Phillips, D., Grajek, S., & Schwarz, C. (1982). Environmental differences among day care centers and their effects on children's levels of intellectual, language, and social development. In E. Zigler & E. Godron (Eds.), *Day care: Scientific and social policy issues* (pp. 126–151). Boston: Auburn House.

McKey, R. H., Condelli, L., Ganson, H., Barrett, B. J., McConkey, C., & Plantz, M. C. (1985). *The impact of Head Start on children, families, and communities: Final report of the Head Start evaluation, synthesis, and utilization project.* Washington, DC: CSR Incorporated for the Head Start Bureau, Administration for Children, Youth and Families, U.S. Department of Health and Human Services.

Modigliani, C. (1990). *Assessing the quality of family child care. A comparison of five instruments.* New York: Bank Street College of Education.

Mueller, E., & Brenner, J. (1977). The origins of social skills and interaction among playgroup toddlers. *Child Development, 48*, 854–861.

Petrie, P. (1984). Day care for under 2's at child minders and in day nurseries. *Early Child Development and Care, 16*, 205–216.

Phillips, D. A. (1987). *Quality in child care: What does research tell us?* Washington, DC: National Association for the Education of Young Children.

Phillips, D. A., McCartney, K., & Scarr, S. (1987). Child care quality and children's social development. *Developmental Psychology, 23,* 537–543.

Phillipsen, L., & Howes, C. (1990). *Early friendships and social skills: Is there a relationship?* Paper presented at the International Conference on Infant Studies, Montreal.

Ramey, C., & Haskins, R. (1981). The cause and treatment of school failure: Insights from the Carolina Abecedarian project. In M. J. Begab, H. C. Haywood, & H. L. Garber (Eds), *Psychosocial influences in retarded performance: Strategies for improving competence* (pp. 63–131). Baltimore, MD: University Park Press.

Rescorla, L., Provence, S., & Naylor, A. (1982). The Yale child welfare research program: Description and results. In E. Zigler & W. Gordon (Eds.), *Day care: Scientific and social policy issues* (pp. 183–199). Boston: Auburn House.

Robertson, A. (1982). Day care and children's responses to adults. In E. Zigler & E. W. Gordon (Eds.), *Day care: Scientific and social policy issues* (pp. 152–173). Boston: Auburn House.

Roopnarine, J. L., & Hempel, L. (1990). Day care and family dynamics. *Early Childhood Research Quarterly, 5,* 335–346.

Rubenstein, J., Howes, C., & Boyle, P. (1981). A two year follow-up of infants in community based day care. *Journal of Child Psychology and Psychiatry, 22,* 209–218.

Ruopp, R., & Travers, J. (1982). Janus faces day care: Perspectives on quality and cost. In E. F. Zigler & E. W. Gordon (Eds.), *Day care: Scientific and social policy issues* (pp. 72–101). Boston: Auburn House.

Ruopp, R., Travers, J., Glantz, F., & Coelen, C. (1979). *Children at the center: Final report of the national day care study.* Cambridge, MA: Associates.

Scarr, S., Lande, J., & McCarthy, K. (1989). Child care and the family. In J. Lande, S. Scarr, & N. Gunzenhauser (Eds.), *Caring for children: Challenge to America.* Hillsdale, NJ: Erlbaum.

Schindler, P. J., Moely, B. E., & Frank, A. L. (1987). Time in day care and social participation of young children. *Developmental Psychology, 23,* 255–261.

Schliecker, E., White, D. R., & Jacobs, E. (1989). *Predicting preschool language comprehension from SES, family structure, and day care quality.* Paper presented at the biennial meeting of the Society for Research in Child Development, Kansas City, MO.

Schwarz, C., Krolick, G., & Strickland, R. (1973). Effects of early day care experience on adjustment to a new environment. *American Journal of Orthopsychiatry, 43,* 340–346.

Schwarz, J., Strickland, R., & Krolick, G. (1974). Infant day care: Behavioral effects at preschool age. *Developmental Psychology, 10,* 502–506.

Shinn, M. B., Phillips, D. A., Howes, C., Galinsky, E., & Whitebook, M. (1990). *Correspondence between mothers' perception of observer ratings of quality in child care centers.* Unpublished manuscript.

Smith, P., & Connolly, K. (1981). *The behavioral ecology of the preschool.* Cambridge, UK: Cambridge University Press.

Stallings, J., & Porter, A. (1980). *National day care home study.* Palo Alto, CA: SRI International.

Suwalsky, J., Zaslow, M., Klein, R. P., & Rabinovich, B. A. (1986). *Continuity of substitute care in relation to infant-mother attachment.* Paper presented at the annual meeting of the American Psychological Association, Washington, DC.

Unger, O. A. (1992). Mothers' beliefs about mediating peer play and toddler age children's peer networks. In C. Howes (Ed.), *The collaborative construction of pretend play* (pp. 79–88). Albany, NY: SUNY Press.

U.S. Bureau of the Census. (1987). Who's minding the kids? *Current Population Reports,* Series P-70, No. 9. Washington, DC: US Department of Commerce.

U.S. Bureau of the Census. (1988). Fertility of American women: June 1987. *Current Population Reports,* Series P-20, No. 427. Washington, DC: U.S. Department of Commerce.

U.S. Bureau of Labor Statistics. (1988). *Marital and family characteristics of the labor force: March 1988.* Unpublished data. U.S. Department of Labor, Washington, DC.

U.S. Department of Education. (1986). *Preschool enrollment: Trends and implications.* Publication No. 065-000-0276-1. Washington, DC: U.S. Government Printing Office.

Vandell, D. J., Henderson, V. K., & Wilson, K. S. (1988). A longitudinal study of children with day care experiences of varying quality. *Child Development, 59,* 1286–1292.

Vandell, D. J., & Powers, C. (1983). Daycare quality and children's free play activities. *American Journal of Orthopsychiatry, 53,* 293–300.

Waters, E., & Deane, K. E. (1985). Defining and assessing individual differences in attachment relationships: Q-methodology and the organization of behavior in infancy and early childhood. In I. Bretherton & E. Waters (Eds.), Growing points of attachment theory and research. *Monographs of the Society for Research in Child Development, 50,* (1-2, Serial No. 209) 41–65.

Whitebook, M., Howes, C., & Phillips, D. A. (1990). *Who cares: Child care teachers and the quality of care in America.* Final Report of the National Child Care Staffing Study. Oakland, CA: Child Care Employee Project.

22

THE INFLUENCE OF PARENTS ON CHILDREN'S DEVELOPMENT AND EDUCATION

Joseph H. Stevens, Jr., and Ruth A. Hough

DEPARTMENT OF EARLY CHILDHOOD EDUCATION, GEORGIA STATE UNIVERSITY, ATLANTA

Joanne R. Nurss

CENTER FOR THE STUDY OF ADULT LITERACY, GEORGIA STATE UNIVERSITY, ATLANTA

Parents' interactions with their children are influenced by many overlapping factors. These include their children's behavior and characteristics; parents' judgements about socialization objectives; their beliefs, values, and internal working models of mothering or fathering; the familial and social context; and the behavior of others in that context (Holden, 1983; Holden & West, 1989). Bronfenbrenner's (1979, 1986) ecological model of human development has been particularly useful in guiding empirical studies of the complex factors that affect parent-child interactions.

In Bronfenbrenner's ecological model, the developing organism is viewed as embedded within several overarching systems that influence and are influenced by that individual: the nuclear and extended families, the neighborhood and city or town, the nation-state and country, and the international community. If we consider the parents to be the developing organism of interest, their ties to both informal systems (circles of friends, extended family members) and formal systems (community organizations, government agencies, educational institutions) exert significant influence on their behavior, and therefore on their interactions with their children. Parent education, day care, and family support programs are examples of formal systems within a family's social context that seek to and often do exert significant influence on how parents interact with their young children (Kagan, Powell, Weissbroud, & Zigler, 1987; Powell, 1989).

Recent research has also focused on informal systems that significantly influence parents' behavior. According to the ecological model, these networks include social relationships with relatives, friends, workmates, and neighbors. Research has demonstrated that the extent, intensity, and content of interchanges between parents and members of their personal social networks (i.e., their circle of intimates) influence their perceptions, resources, and behaviors. In turn, these perceptions, resources, and behaviors influence the child's development (Boukydis, 1987; Cochran & Brassard, 1979; Stevens, 1988).

PARENTS' BELIEFS AND CHILD-REARING PRACTICES

Within this systems view of development, there has been increasing interest in studying the role of cognitive processes in parenting behaviors (Goodnow, 1988). Several conclusions can be drawn from this research:

1. Parents' knowledge of children's developmental milestones influences the interpretations they make about their children's development and their ability to be responsive to children's development.
2. Parents' ideas, knowledge, and beliefs about the relationship between their own behavior and children's development, and between environmental factors and children's development, influence the type of environment they structure and how they behave with their children.
3. The transmission of information about child rearing between adults within informal support systems is an important mechanism whereby individuals learn about parenting.

Parents' Knowledge About Development

Relationships between parent knowledge and child-rearing practices are not well documented even though the knowledge-behavior link is well accepted and knowledge transmission has been the focus of most parent-involvement programs. However, a few studies of diverse populations (black and white parents at low- and middle-income levels) have shown that parents who have more accurate knowledge about children's normative development provide more responsive care, show less punitive and restrictive patterns of interaction, and provide greater stimulation of language and cognitive development (Freeland & Nair, 1985; Fry, 1985; Stevens, 1984). On the other hand, parents' late expectations for developmental milestones also affect the timing of some child-rearing practices. Ninio (1979) found that low-SES Israeli mothers were more likely than middle-SES mothers to hold late estimates for when their infants would be able to see, hear, think, and understand intonations and words, as well as identify pictured objects. These low-SES mothers were also more likely to delay appropriate stimulation such as talking to infants, telling them stories, buying them books, and talking to them about absent objects. An open question at this point of inquiry is whether acquiring more accurate information allows parents to become more sensitive and responsive in their care giving, or whether parents' already existing observation skills support both increased knowledge about children's development and a responsive interaction style.

Other researchers have examined parents' accuracy in estimating their own children's development and its relationship to actual development. Hunt and Paraskevopoulos (1980) reported that parents who more accurately estimated children's performance on the Uzgures-Hunt Scales of Mental Development had children who demonstrated higher levels of performance. Miller (1986) also found that children with higher mental test scores had parents who made more accurate estimates of ability, especially on intelligence tests using items that closely resembled everyday play activities. Thus there are some data to show that accurate judgments of developmental level allow parents to support their children by more appropriately matching environmental inputs to children's current level of functioning.

Parents' Beliefs and Home Environment

Another research question of interest has been whether parent knowledge about the factors that influence development affects the ways that parents typically support children's development. Several studies suggest that relationships between this type of knowledge and parenting measures may be stronger than those between knowledge of normative development and parenting. Luster and Rhodes (1989) found a significant relationship between scores on the Caldwell HOME scale and mothers' beliefs about spoiling the child, providing freedom for exploration, reading and talking with children, and discipline. Stevens (1984) also reported significant positive relationships between knowledge about environmental factors and parenting. Duffield (1988) found significant positive relationships among well-educated middle-income white mothers;

Parks and Smerglio (1986) reported similar results for low-income, but not middle-income, families.

Parents' perception of their own influence on their children's development, which Luster and Rhodes labeled *perceived contingency*, has not been extensively studied. However, early evidence suggests the potential impact of these beliefs. Luster and Rhodes (1989) reported that both adolescent and adult mothers who felt that their own parenting behavior could and would influence their children's development provided more supportive home environments. Relationships between parents' perceived contingency and scores on the Caldwell HOME scale were quite strong, $r = .56$ for adults and .73 for teenagers. In contrast, for parents who felt that they were incompetent parents, perceived contingency was significantly and negatively related to HOME scores for adults only ($r = -.48$). Stevens (1984) found that feelings of internal personal control were strongly related to effective parenting behaviors for adult mothers, but not for teenage mothers. Adult mothers who felt that their own efforts were significant determinants of the outcome of life events did provide more stimulating and supportive home environments. Duffield's study using a well-educated, upper-middle-class white sample found no relationship between mothers' feelings of competence as parents and their HOME scores, suggesting the possible influence of income level on this variable (1988).

Child-rearing Practices

Parents' interactions with their children vary according to their beliefs and knowledge about child development and also according to their sociocultural background. Fogel and Melson (1988) summarize the literature on the relationship between parenting styles and certain child behaviors and conclude that "consistent, involved, and firm parents have children who are less likely to be inappropriately aggressive or out of control" (p. 437). The single most important variable in child rearing is **love** (McClelland, Constantian, Regalado, & Stone, 1978). Children who are secure in their parents' love for them are more likely to be well adjusted and mature.

Research on different parenting styles and their effects on young children, initially reported 25 years ago, describes 3 parenting styles (Baumrind, 1967). Observers rated nursery-school children's behavior on 5 dimensions (self-control, exploration, self-reliance, vitality, and peer affiliation). Parents' behavior was then rated on 2 home visits, in parent interviews, and during a structured laboratory observation. Three parenting styles were described: authoritative, authoritarian, and permissive. The behavior of the parents and their children was matched. Parents who were nurturing, responsive, firm but flexible, and less punitive (authoritative parents) were more likely to have children who were self-reliant, curious, and positive with their peers. Parents who were unresponsive, inflexible, and harsh (authoritarian parents) were more likely to have children who were hostile, negative, apprehensive, and easily upset. Parents who failed to set firm limits or require appropriate behavior (permissive parents) were more likely to have children who lacked self-control and self-reliance and were impulsive. The authoritative parent exercised firm control but was flexible;

set standards but reasoned with the child; valued both self-will and self-control; and set expectations based on the child's development and individual strengths at the present time, but was future directed in behavioral goals. Other research (Maccoby & Martin, 1983; Sroufe & Cooper, 1988; Radke-Yarrow & Zahn-Waxler, 1984; Baumrind, 1977) has confirmed these findings, concluding that high social competence is related to parental warmth and nurturance; low social competence is related to excessive use of parental power for both preschool and elementary-school children. Baumrind (1978) suggests that the authoritative parent tends to foster the kind of social competence valued by the mainstream American society.

This child-rearing research, however, did not consider the effect the child's personality has on the parents' style of parenting. What are the interaction effects between the child's temperament and the parent's behaviors? Clarke-Stewart (1988) reviewed early socialization studies that consider parent-child interactions and concluded that "we can no longer make simple generalizations about one-sided effects of parents' discipline on children's behavior or development" (p. 55). The child, the parent, and their influence on one another—in both directions—must be considered. Children's temperament may allow parents to use a particular style of child rearing successfully. For example, Lewis (1981) found that some parents could be reasonable because their children were reasonable, not the reverse. Discipline efforts are affected by the child's temperament; the child's response to discipline, in turn, affects the parents' discipline efforts. Lewis suggests that the child's willingness to obey is more important than parents' firm control.

Parental behavior is most influential on intellectual development; children's competence has been shown to be positively influenced by consistent verbal interaction and stimulation. Parents who play and talk with their children, who assist them in exploring and manipulating their environment, and who provide new, interesting experiences are more likely to have creative, curious, competent children. In the area of social development, however, the child's behavior has a greater influence on parental behavior. Dimensions of temperament (e.g., active-passive, aggressive-submissive) and social responsiveness (e.g., eye contact, facial expression) affect how the parent responds to the child. Positive expressions are more likely to elicit positive responses and to yield mature, socially competent behavior in the child.

In an extensive review of research on child rearing (Clarke-Stewart, 1977), both the child's gender and the parent's gender were identified as significant variables in parent-child interaction patterns. Gender differences were less apparent in parents' interactions with infants than with preschoolers. In general, fathers were more demanding and more likely to be strict with their preschool-age children than were mothers. Social context variables such as socioeconomic status, family size, and birth order also influenced parents' child-rearing practices and their effects on children's development.

Parenting expectations and discipline have been shown to vary according to the parents' appraisal of the individual child. As children mature and are seen as more socially competent, more mature behavior is expected of them. For example, mothers of kindergarten and primary-grade children, responding to descriptions of situations involving their children, were more influenced by age- and task-specific data in making decisions about discipline than they were by a theory of discipline (Dix, Ruble, & Zambarano, 1989; Grusec & Kuczynski, 1980). Many studies are, however, of hypothetical situations in which parents respond according to their beliefs, rather than actual situations in which parents' behavioral responses are described (Goodnow, 1988; Mills & Rubin, 1990). More research on actual behavior in real situations taking account of the sociocultural context is needed to shed light on parents' child-rearing behaviors in addition to parents' beliefs about child rearing.

Much of the research on child-rearing practices has been done in middle-SES white families, thereby limiting its generalizability to the rest of the American population. Levine (1980) suggests that the child-rearing goals of middle-class, mainstream American parents are separateness, self-sufficiency, and self-confidence, designed to produce children who are socially competent and perform well in school. The goals of other American parents vary with their own cultural and economic background and may yield different child-rearing practices. Lin and Fu (1990) found that Chinese American parents' scores on the Child-Rearing Practices Report indicate they are more controlling and more likely to encourage independence and achievement in their kindergarten and primary-grade children than mainstream American parents. Studies of Japanese American families' child-rearing practices indicate that even families who are well assimilated into American culture foster calm, nonaggressive, orderly patterns of behavior in their children (Staples & Mirande, 1980). In the Native American community, child rearing is focused on the child as a member of the community rather than as a member of the individual family. This focus has been shown to influence Native American children's social-emotional development and self-concept (Burgess, 1980).

Latino parents have been described as being warm, supportive, and more permissive than African American parents, who are more likely to expect early autonomy, to be less tolerant of wasting time, and to be stricter (Bartz & Levine, 1978). Using an adaptation of the Parental Attitude Research Scale, Bartz and Levine interviewed African American, white, and Latino parents of elementary-school children in Title I programs. The Latino and African American parents favored earlier autonomy of walking, weaning, and toileting than did white parents. African American parents were significantly less tolerant of wasting time than were Latino and white parents. African American and white parents were more supportive of equality in parent-child relationships than were Latino parents. African American parents reported providing more emotional support for their children and using more controlling behaviors than did the other 2 groups. Unfortunately, this study presents self-report data only. The findings need to be verified by observational data.

Parents who are members of cultural subgroups must decide whether to adopt child-rearing practices that foster assimilation, isolation, or multiculturalism. Their decisions affect their children's competence in the mainstream culture. Survey research of Mexican American parents (Ramirez & Cox, 1980) indicates support for rearing children who are both bicultural and bilingual. These parents' child-rearing practices encouraged flexibility, allowing their children to move between the 2 cultures.

Extensive research on the interaction of parents and children in the home, family, and community is needed to more clearly describe child-rearing practices of American families. The use of ethnographic research methods for this research would place these practices within the contexts defined in Bronfenbrenner's ecological framework.

INFORMAL PARENT SUPPORT SYSTEMS

Many researchers have investigated the role of informal support systems in enhancing parenting. Support from these networks comes in 2 major ways: general emotional support from being well integrated into a supportive network, and functional or instrumental support representing specific help, guidance, or advice (Belsky, 1984; Cohen & Wills, 1985). Cohen and Wills (1985) have proposed that social integration has a beneficial effect on general well-being, but that it is instrumental or functional support that buffers individuals from the deleterious effects of stress. They argue that functional support enhances an individual's ability to cope or adapt, and therefore is more likely to affect parenting, which requires adjusting child-rearing behaviors to child characteristics and to contextual demands. The effects of social support are not universally salutary, however (Kiesler, 1985). Social support may impede optimal parenting if close friends and family members model punitive or hostile interactive patterns, or if the type of support provided is intrusive, ill-timed, or poorly matched with that needed (Parke & Lewis, 1981).

One significant type of instrumental support that may be shared among networks of friends and relatives is information about children and child rearing. It appears that these exchanges account, in part, for what parents come to know about children and what strategies for interaction they have available. Several studies have shown significant positive relationships between mother and father knowledge about development (Miller, 1986; Sigel, 1985; Stevens, 1984), and mother and grandmother knowledge about infants (Sistler & Gottfried, 1990; Stevens, 1984).

Extensive research with families has documented the importance of social-network relationships, particularly kinship ties, for family functioning (Harrison, Serafica, & McAdoo, 1984; McAdoo, 1982; Slaughter & Dilworth-Anderson, 1985; Wilson, 1984, 1986). Among African Americans, kin-help systems provide instrumental assistance in upward mobility (McAdoo, 1978), help in buffering stress (Stack, 1971; McAdoo, 1982), and assistance in caring for young family members (Furstenberg, 1976; McKinlay, 1973; Slaughter & Dilworth-Anderson, 1985; Wilson, 1984). McAdoo's (1978) extensive study of middle-income black women revealed that the kin-help system was used in several ways, especially by single women. Emergency and occasional child care was important help provided most often by family, but also by friendship networks. Mothers who moved from a working-class background into a middle-class adulthood received more financial help from family; whereas those born into middle-class families reported receiving more

emotional support. Thus, financial assistance from the extended family may be a key to upward mobility among African Americans.

Among low-income urban African Americans, Stack (1971) found that exchange systems and the swapping of resources established close-knit personal networks, primarily among the female members of various households. Friendships were established by careful testing via these material exchanges; child keeping or temporary fosterages among these various adults also appeared to cement relationships and to obligate one network member to another. Slaughter and Dilworth-Anderson's (1985) study of extended-family support to families with a sickle-cell anemic child indicated that the mother's mother most often provided instrumental help (e.g., help with child-rearing tasks, babysitting), whereas sisters were more likely to provide emotional support.

For the African American teenage mother, ties to extended-family members, especially the grandmother, appear to be critical for her educational and economic success (Furstenberg, 1976; Gray & Ramsey, 1986; Berreuta-Clement, Schweinhart, Barnett, Epstein, & Weikart, 1984), for her knowledge about parenting (Stevens, 1984; Unger & Wandersman, 1985), and for her child's development (Furstenberg, 1976; Egeland & Sroufe, 1981; Crockenberg, 1981). The African American grandmother and older women play important roles in providing emotional support, advice, parenting models, and as sounding boards for the inexperienced young mothers. In the absence of sound, instrumental help from competent older extended-family members, very young mothers are likely to be substantially less skillful as parents (Stevens & Duffield, 1986). Baltes, Reese, and Nesselroade (1977) argued that adolescence and early adulthood are developmental periods during which socialization influences from extended-family members (particularly older family members) are quite salient and likely to influence one's subsequent skills as a parent. Further, Tinsley and Parke (1984) suggested that grandparents, in particular, influence novice parents through modeling, advice, and provision of corrective feedback.

PARENT SUPPORT PROGRAMS

Transitions in the life course are periods of particular opportunity and vulnerability that require new behaviors, often heavily taxing one's resources, skills, and abilities. The transition to parenthood is one such key period that necessitates appropriate support from neighbors, friends, family, professionals, or institutions. Various types of parent support programs have attempted to provide environmental support in the form of relevant new information, assistance in learning new behaviors, affirmation of one's ability to cope, and shared perspectives of individuals with similar experiences.

Programs for Teen Mothers

Social support is particularly important when the life transition is "off-time," as nonnormative life transitions place the individual at greater risk for poor developmental outcomes (Caspi & Elder, 1988; Burton & Bengston, 1985; Parke, 1988). When the transition to parenthood occurs early in life to an individual with meager resources (e.g., poor school achievement, caste status, low income, limited opportunities, few achieving role models, restricted social ties), then a poor outcome is highly likely (Gray & Ramsey, 1986). Social-support interventions that enhance the adolescent mother's knowledge about parenting, her interactional skills with her child, and her ability to utilize professionals, friends, and family for assistance may prevent many negative outcomes. Those programs that strengthen the adolescent's literacy and numeracy skills, enable school completion, help to limit family size, and enhance occupational preparedness promote the adolescent's economic self-sufficiency and her ability to support her children.

Two major types of programs have been implemented. The first type of program is generally community based and often provides health services and parent-education services to adolescents beginning prenatally and continuing through the first months of parenthood. The second type of program is generally comprehensive, in that it provides pre- and postnatal health services, opportunities for the parent to complete school, child care, parent education, and job training.

Community-Based Health and Parent Education Services. Prenatal and well-baby care, parent education, and appropriate utilization of community services and resources were the priorities of the Prenatal/Early Infancy Project in rural New York (Olds, Henderson, Tatelbaum, & Chamberlin, 1986a, 1986b; Olds, 1982). Women selected for the program, who were each having their first child, demonstrated any of 3 risk factors for poor infant development: single parenthood, low socioeconomic status, or teen parenthood. Four hundred women, mostly white, were randomly assigned to 1 of 4 treatment groups: (1) infant developmental screening with follow-up referral; (2) screening plus transportation for prenatal and well-baby care; (3) prenatal home visitation targeted on health and nutrition and preparedness for the birth; and (4) pre- and postnatal home visitation to strengthen the quality of mother-infant interaction, to support mothers' completion of education and use of job training, and to enhance the support provided to the mother by significant others (e.g., mother's spouse and/or own parent). Treatment 4 continued until the infant's second birthday.

Positive effects on knowledge and use of relevant health services and on indices of social support were evident during pregnancy for all treatment participants. Differences between all treatment and control subjects, regardless of risk, were not found on parenting measures during infancy. However, the most intensive intervention, treatment 4, resulted in enhanced pregnancy outcomes and improved quality of care giving among the poor, unmarried teenage mothers at greatest risk. Effects of home visitation during infancy included a lowered incidence of child abuse/neglect, more positive maternal perceptions of infant temperament, fewer emergency room visits during the first year of life, less punitive and restrictive mother-infant interaction behavior, and home environments furnished with more play materials. This pattern of results suggests that early and extended consultation by a nurse/home visitor prevented the emergence of insensitive care giving and child maltreatment among this very young parent group.

Large-scale replication of this model with low-income African American mothers is underway.

The Resource Mother Program sent trained paraprofessional resource mothers to visit rural pregnant and parenting teenagers once a month (Unger & Wandersman, 1985; 1988a; 1988b). Planned activities emphasized prenatal development, nutrition, family planning, the birth process, infancy care and development, and infant stimulation. Home visits often involved fathers and grandmothers and also focused on strengthening the young mothers' ability to maintain and effectively use her available informal social ties. Participating mothers, compared to nonparticipants, were less likely to have low-birthweight infants, showed more responsive interactive behavior, were more knowledgeable about children's development, and reported more satisfaction with mothering. However, active participants received less support from a male partner or the infant's father, and relied more on the support of their family of origin. Less-active participants had more contact with the father and felt more confident about future support from the baby's father.

The Infant Stimulation/Mother Training Program for urban white and African American teen mothers used either monthly home visits or weekly mother-infant classes beginning in the infant's first month and continuing until the twelfth month (Badger, Elsass, & Sutherland, 1974; Badger & Burnes, 1980; Badger, 1981; Badger & Goldman, 1987). For the home-visit group, a nurse or social worker made visits to discuss the infant's development, stimulation, health, and nutrition, and to demonstrate the use of toys, which were then left in the homes. In the group sessions, nurse-consultants modeled, observed, and coached mothers as they played with their infants. Discussions were also held about discipline, health, safety, nutrition, family planning, and infant development. In both treatment groups the focus was on increasing mothers' awareness of the importance of their own interactions for children's subsequent development, expanding their skill in observing infant behavior, selecting activities to match and extend their infant's capacities, and teaching parents how to select materials to stimulate their children's growth.

Infants of the younger teens (15- and 16-year-olds) enrolled in the group sessions showed greater mental development in the first year of life than the babies of the younger teens in the home-visiting group. Badger speculated that the opportunities to observe other young mothers, the social feedback of other teen mothers, and the consultation strategies of coaching and confrontation proved particularly effective with the younger mothers. No significant differences were observed between the babies of the younger teens in classes, the older teens (18- and 19-year-olds) receiving home visits, and the older teens enrolled in classes. It appeared that the younger teens were more eager participants than were the older teens. Badger argued that this interest was motivated by their strivings for independence from their own mothers, with whom they shared child-rearing responsibilities.

In a longitudinal study of a community hospital's comprehensive prenatal-care program, Furstenberg (1976; Furstenberg, Brooks-Gunn, & Morgan, 1987) reported that teen mothers who completed school and delayed further child bearing were less likely to be on welfare 17 years later. Attendance at the special school for adolescent mothers and participation in the hospital-based comprehensive health program enhanced economic well-being in adulthood because subsequent child rearing was delayed and school completion increased. It appears that personal characteristics of the girls influenced their likelihood to participate in the school program; participants were more likely to be at an age-appropriate grade level and demonstrate higher educational aspirations (Hofferth, 1987; Hayes, 1987). A related finding by Gray and Ramsey (1986) indicated that adolescent mothers who returned to complete school had experienced more positive elementary- and secondary-school careers, which may have influenced their attendance in a high-quality preschool program.

Comprehensive Programs for Adolescent Mothers. Office of Adolescent Pregnancy and Parenting (OAPP) programs provide comprehensive services to reach the goals of improving maternal and infant health, enabling mothers' school completion, increasing the employability of mothers, and reducing their welfare dependency. Two evaluations of these federal programs have been conducted (Burt, Kimmich, Goldmuntz, & Sonenstein, 1984; JRB Associates, 1981). In neither study was a comparison group incorporated so that treatment effects could be clearly identified. However, some services have been linked to differential outcomes across the more than 20 programs studied. Programs that used case management, in which 1 staff person coordinated service delivery, appeared to be more successful in securing needed services for clients. Programs that provided child care for parents had greater success in reducing repeat pregnancies, enabling adolescent mothers to complete more schooling, and increasing the likelihood that they would be employed. Availability of family planning services appeared to reduce the likelihood of a repeat pregnancy during the first year after the infant's birth (Burt et al., 1984).

Project Redirection (Quint & Riccio, 1985; Polit, Quint, & Riccio, 1988) provided comprehensive services at 4 sites (New York, Boston, Phoenix, and Riverside, CA) to girls 17 years and younger who were parents or pregnant, received AFDC (Aid to Families with Dependent Children), and had not yet completed high school. The program was designed to enable young women to continue their education; delay subsequent child-bearing; gain job skills and employability; and acquire more adaptive life management skills in family planning, parenting, and nutrition. These services were provided directly or through brokerage with existing community services. Group comparisons suggested that Project Redirection participants were more likely to receive parenting classes, well-baby care, family-planning services, counseling, and employment training than comparison teens in the first year of the program. In the second year participants were much more likely to receive counseling and employment services than comparison teens.

At the end of 1 year small differences in favor of Project Redirection teens were evident in education, fertility, and employment. At the end of 2 years, few differences were found. At the 5-year follow-up, groups did not differ in school completion or in employment status; however, the group difference for those receiving welfare did approach significance. Although participating women had more children than the controls, they were somewhat more likely to work more

hours per week, receive higher weekly earnings, and be less likely to receive welfare. More striking differences were evident on parenting measures. Participating teens provided more stimulating home environments, were more likely to have a child enrolled in Project Head Start, and had children who demonstrated greater language and social competence. Dimensions of the home environment that showed important differences between participants and comparison teens were those reflective of language stimulation, maternal warmth and affection, and maternal acceptance.

INTERVENTION PROGRAMS TO TRAIN PARENTS TO EDUCATE THEIR CHILDREN

In addition to documenting the effects of parent-support projects on young mother's efforts to enhance their children's development, there has been extensive research on the effects of intervention programs designed to affect directly parents' efforts to enhance their children's education.

Programs to Train Parents as Teachers

Assessing the effects of Parent-education programs and drawing firm conclusions about their direct and indirect influence on children's development has been complicated by several related factors: (1) Parent-education programs are often service- rather than research-oriented, resulting in the lack of control groups for comparison; (2) these efforts are often a component in comprehensive programs, making it difficult to measure the independent effects of parent education; and (3) such programs are often tailored to the unique and evolving needs and characteristics of a particular parent group, limiting the generalizability of results (Clarke-Stewart & Apfel, 1978; Clarke-Stewart, 1983; Powell, 1988, 1989; Seitz, 1987; Weiss & Jacobs, 1988; Wandersman, 1987). Given these constraints, there are some tentative trends that can be drawn from a small group of studies, primarily measuring high-quality research-and-demonstration parent-education programs.

Reports from these studies suggest that programs to help parents teach their own children may have small but potentially important positive effects. Positive short-term effects for target children have been found by a number of investigators on measures of IQ (Andrews et al., 1982; Lally & Honig, 1977; Beller, 1979; Slaughter, 1983; Gray & Ruttle, 1980) and on measures of social competence, such as appropriate infant responsiveness to parent behavior (Dickie & Gerber, 1980), increased verbalization during play (Slaughter, 1983), and positive social-emotional functioning in early education settings (Honig, Lally, & Mathieson, 1982; Cochran, 1988). Although these positive results are the apparent result of parent participation in supportive programs, most of the programs studied trained parents to teach their children within a broader parent-child support system. Therefore, it is not possible to say absolutely whether these improvements are due to differences in parent-child interactions or some other aspect of the support program.

Some investigators have also measured program effects on parents as they interact with their children in teaching situations. Again short-term effects have been most commonly reported, including increases in maternal behaviors such as positive interactions and comforting (Andrews et al., 1982) and increased parent responsiveness to infant cues (Dickie & Gerber, 1980). Slaughter (1983) found that low-income African American mothers in both toy-demonstration and discussion-group interventions showed increased scores on measures of openness and flexibility relative to child-rearing attitudes and practices. Other investigators have also found increases in parental use of positive and facilitating language interactions with their children after program participation (Lambie, Bond, & Weikart, 1974).

Only a few evaluations have compared the effects of different types of interventions focused on parent-child interactions, leaving open the question of the most effective format for parent-education programs (Clarke-Stewart, 1983; Wandersman, 1987). Slaughter (1983) found that mothers participating in a discussion group differed from mothers in the toy-demonstration and control groups in maternal teaching style, more often contacting their child during play, elaborating on the child's ongoing activity, and demonstrating or telling the child how to use an object. A study of the effects of center-based, mixed-model, and home-based Head Start programs demonstrated that children in all program modes made comparable gains in intelligence, achievement, and in teacher ratings of school adjustment. However, the results indicated that parents in programs with strong home components showed greater gains in such parent-child interactions as verbal and academic stimulation, improvement of the physical environment, and the provision of toys, games, and reading materials. The investigators hypothesize that these factors are likely to lead to greater support for long-term benefits for the target children (Peters, Bollin, & Murphy, 1991).

Although most studies have reported short-term effects, a few investigators have measured effects of longer duration. A 5-year evaluation of the Parent Child Development Centers (PCDCs) found some evidence that children's enhanced cognitive, language, conceptual, and abstraction skills were still present one year after they completed the program. (Dokecki, Hargrove, & Sandler, 1983). Although there is no current evidence of IQ increases being sustained more than 1 year beyond the interventions (Bridgemen, Blumenthal, & Andrews, 1981; Levenstein, O'Hara, & Madden, 1983), there are some data to support other enduring effects of parent-education programs, such as reduced placement in special-education classes and less negative school behavior and juvenile delinquency (Lally, Mangione, & Honig, 1988; Jester & Guinagh, 1983; Seitz, Rosenbaum, & Apfel, 1985).

School-Based Parent-Involvement Programs

In recent investigations of the family-school partnerships that influence children's learning, researchers have identified a number of conflicting tensions that affect the conceptualization of parent involvement and therefore the ways it is implemented in schools. On the one hand, schools are limited in providing a full range of support services to families by resources and their primary focus on the academic achievement of students

(Powell, 1991). However, there are also trends toward broadening the concept of parent involvement, which are signaled by the various terms used in describing innovative programs. The more encompassing term "family" is often used to reflect the reality that, in addition to or instead of parents, significant adults in children's lives may be grandparents, siblings, extended kin, or neighbors who provide child care (Davies, 1991). Terms such as "partnership," "participation," and "empowerment" are sometimes used in place of "involvement" or "education" to indicate that parents are decision makers who share responsibility for educating their children, rather than the low members of an institutional hierarchy invited to schools to remediate some deficiency (Cochran & Dean, 1991; Davies, 1991; Potter, 1989).

School-based programs to involve and support families have been organized in the context of reform initiatives at the level of the individual school or school system. These efforts to promote family-school-community interaction recognize that the task of educating and socializing students requires coordination among several institutions. Some form of parent participation has been required in federal educational programs such as Project Head Start, Follow Through, Chapter I, and the Fund for the Improvement and Reform of Schools and Teaching (FIRST) grants (Epstein, 1991). These national initiatives to improve education have also recognized the critical role that families play in realizing the potential of children. Increasing numbers of states are now developing and adopting policies that link the school and family with the community. California's comprehensive program of parent involvement illustrates the new state efforts. Their policy states that programs should be designed to

1. Help parents develop parenting skills and foster conditions at home that support learning
2. Provide parents with the knowledge of techniques designed to assist children in learning at home
3. Provide access to and coordinate community and support services for children and families
4. Promote clear two-way communication between the school and the family as to the school programs and children's progress
5. Involve parents, after appropriate training, in instructional and support roles at school
6. Support parents as decision makers and develop their leadership in governance, advisory, and advocacy roles (Solomon, 1991, p. 361)

Program planners have experimented with many different activities in various combinations to achieve these objectives of supporting families of school children. Although it is clear that earlier and sustained interventions have greater impact on student outcomes, it appears that no single implementation design fits all families. The most successful programs have responded to the qualities, characteristics, and needs of the families being served. D'Angelo and Adler (1991) outline the variables that may affect communication with parents of children served by Chapter I programs: "parents' level of literacy; language preferred for reading, listening, speaking, and writing; daily commitments and responsibilities that may affect the time, energy, and attention available to devote to school; and parents' level of comfort in becoming involved in their children's education" (p. 350). Thus, they stress the importance of analysis of "the range of parent interests, energies, ideas, needs, cultures, languages, and lifestyles represented in their schools and communities in order to design activities and programs that will draw parents into the education of their children" (p. 350). Multifaceted family involvement and support systems with many different participation options and levels are more likely to match the diverse needs and interests represented in today's schools.

The success of school-based family-support programs has been measured by scores on achievement tests, but also on other outcomes likely to show more rapid improvement, such as attendance, discipline, grades, and level of parent involvement. Studies of schools including parent involvement as part of their program demonstrated that (1) parents increase home interactions with their children, feel more positive about their abilities to help their children, and perceive the school more positively; and (2) students improve their attendance, attitudes, and achievement (Becher, 1984; Cochran & Dean, 1991; Epstein, 1986; Henderson, 1987).

Some evaluations have been specific to the content goals of particular programs. For example, an inner-city elementary school with a largely Latino population proposed to improve the language and writing skills of students through a language program that included parents as guides on field trips and scribes for stories about their experiences. The success of this program was demonstrated by the improvement in writing skills and vocabulary by both children and parents, and the greater confidence and skill shown by the parents as they worked with children on academic tasks (Chapman, 1991). Analyses of the Follow Through projects indicated improvements in parents' skills as advocates and decision makers, and as teachers of their children through volunteering in the classroom and using home-learning activities (Kennedy, 1978; Olmstead, 1991). Researchers with the Institute for Responsive Education have found that key elements of successful programs include parent centers that make possible a continuing, positive parent presence in the school; home visitors to support parents' positive reinforcement of children's academic efforts; and action research teams to involve teachers directly in home-school-community partnership programs (Davies, 1991).

The common trend in all these family-support programs appears to be the effort to reach and involve all families to support the success of all students in a positive way. Serving the whole child by sharing responsibility among family, school, and community agencies is the common goal.

Literacy-Based Interventions

There is growing evidence that an important component of the home environment is the support that parents provide for early language and literacy development. Young children learn how oral and written language work as they experiment with print alone and with siblings, and watch more skilled family members use literacy materials. Studies of home environments have noted the diversity of literacy materials available that reflect the interests, needs, and abilities of particular families: picture books, adult novels, adult nonfiction and reference books, letters and other mail, the Bible and other religious works, magazines, newspapers, school bulletins, adult and children's school texts, instructions for household products, and so on (Taylor, 1983; Teale, 1986; Delgado-Gaitan, 1987; Taylor & Dorsey-Gaines, 1988).

It is through the natural-language environment of the home—functional spoken and written language—that parents contribute to their children's literacy development. A summary of studies of several homes found the following common characteristics of literacy contexts and events that support early development: activities that are meaningful to children because they are functional; instruction on details as part of a broader language context; child initiation and often child direction of these activities; and an adult-child partnership (Schickedanz et al., 1990). In a study of the home environments of low-income white, African American, and Mexican American preschoolers, Teale (1986) found differences in the number of daily literacy events (from 5 to 53) and the amount of time spent daily in literacy events (from 40 minutes to 7.5 hours). Although there was great variation in the range of literacy activities, in general they were social, taking place as components of interactions within the home (e.g., daily living, entertainment, interpersonal communication). Parents, through the natural-language context in their homes, provide literacy tuition and stimulation necessary to young children's emergent literacy development.

Many investigators of parent-child interactions point to storybook reading as a most potent factor affecting children's early literacy development (Wells, 1986; Snow & Ninio, 1986). Studies of parents reading to their preschool children in the United States, Britain, Israel, and New Zealand indicate that regular story-reading times occurring naturally in these homes were child-centered, pleasurable events for the families (Cochran-Smith, 1986; Wells, 1986; Phillips & McNaughton, 1990; Snow & Ninio, 1986; Taylor, 1983; Taylor & Dorsey-Gaines, 1988). Closer study of the parent-child interactions during reading demonstrated that, most frequently, the comments and questions of both parents and children were used to clarify or highlight the meaning of the text, not the illustrations or the print. Parents moved from clarifying meaning to anticipating events and drawing inferences—processes needed to construct meaning from text and therefore needed to succeed in school literacy instruction. In other words, home adult-child interaction around print, especially story reading, occurs as part of routine social interaction, not as a deliberate pedagogical device.

Parents engage in a variety of literacy-based interventions designed to support their children's development and education. Research on 4 types of interventions will be reviewed. These include literacy-based interventions involving parents and children with limited English proficiency, parents and children reading together, parents reading to children, and children reading to parents.

Literacy for Limited-English-Proficient Parents and Children. Involving limited-English-proficient (LEP) parents in early childhood programs has many of the same purposes and potential benefits as it does for all parents: (1) helping and encouraging parents to provide a home environment that supports children's learning needs, particularly in the areas of language and literacy; (2) maintaining open communication between parents and teachers about children's educational progress; (3) participating in school activities through parent-teacher organizations and taking on various roles in the classroom; (4) tutoring children at home; and (5) reinforcing classroom lessons with home activities (Simich-Dudgeon, 1986; Weinstein-Shr, 1990). However, differences in language and culture may be barriers for the full participation of LEP parents in school programs. The American school expectation that parents can and should be actively involved in children's schooling may be unfamiliar to some immigrant and refugee parents. Parent-involvement programs may need to break the concept that parent involvement in schools is interference and therefore to be avoided for the negative effects it may have on children's performance in school.

Programs designed to involve LEP parents have attempted to bridge language and cultural differences between home and school in a number of ways: using bilingual liaisons, facilitating intercultural communication through social and educational exchanges, developing parents' English and literacy skills, offering bilingual sessions on important school topics, and training parents to use books and other literacy and school activities with their children. Most of the studies based on these projects have been designed as program evaluations rather than empirical, quantitative research studies. Program success has been documented through a variety of informal techniques, including amount and level of program participation, parent self-reports, and other anecdotal evidence of changes in parent and child behavior and attitude.

Project FIEL (Family Initiative for English Literacy) is typical of the multiple goals embraced by parent-involvement projects with LEP parents. This project attempted to increase the number of whole-life literacy behaviors used by the Latino parents participating, and thereby enhance the ability of LEP parents to facilitate their own and their children's acquisition of English literacy (Quintero & Macias, 1990). A 5-step intergenerational curriculum focused on in-class practice of parent-child literacy activities, which could then be transferred to other appropriate settings. Class sessions provided information on literacy development and other parenting concerns and modeled ways for parents to increase self-control as they helped their children in educational activities. The program was deemed a success based on (1) the high number of classes attended (indicating enhanced literacy development of parent and child); (2) positive changes in the patterns of parent-child interactions during the in-class literacy activities; (3) parent responses on the postprogram interview indicating greater self-control in assisting children, and (4) parent self-reports of literacy use outside the program, e.g., serving as a RIF (Reading is Fundamental) volunteer.

Some programs for LEP parents support intergenerational learning patterns that can be important in becoming a fully functioning member of a new and unfamiliar culture. Many authors have cited the common occurrence of young children acting as interpreters for more isolated adult family members less proficient in English. Auerbach (1989) argues for the importance of reducing some of the pressure on young ESL

(English as a second language) learners to be their sole brokers for transactions with the English-speaking society. She suggests assistance through programs, such as Project LEIF (Learning English through Intergenerational Friendship), that offer help with English and the culture and expectations of the school. The Mothers' Reading Program (McIvor, 1990), associated with the New York Head Start program, designates only a portion of its sessions for reading interactions between parents and children. However, through parents' increased reading levels and the increased confidence that comes from sharing their own writing on personally relevant life issues, the program empowers LEP parents to regain responsibility for helping their children in school. Thus, parent-involvement programs may fill adult ESL learners' need to be able to support their children in school in appropriate ways.

Programs that involve LEP parents in some aspect of the school program provide tangible proof of the parents' support of the school and reinforce the notion that school is important. Parents may be able to provide teachers with valuable information about expectations and experiences characteristic of the home culture that can affect the child's performance in the classroom or enrich the educational opportunities for that child and others in the classroom. One university-school collaborative effort attempted to increase minority parent involvement by acknowledging the importance of the home-school partnership and the key roles that teachers play in initiating contact with parents (Bermudez & Padron, 1988). Classes were provided for 100 Latino parents across 3 school districts for 2 hours a week for 6 weeks. Each session includes an English lesson, a 45-minute session in Spanish about a selected school topic, a review, and an extension of the school topic presented in English. Comparison of questionnaire responses before and after the sessions showed a significant increase in (1) awareness of the school's instructional program and the parents' responsibility for their children's schooling; (2) amount of participation in school activities; and (3) positive attitude toward school achievement and the school's instructional program.

A program sponsored by the Marin County Library served 75 Latino LEP adults living on remote ranches by providing Latino home-school liaisons, bilingual reading materials, and story times with monthly bookmobile stops and weekly home tutoring (McIvor, 1990). Parent participants in the project reported increased attendance in back-to-school nights and other parent meetings. As a result of the program, children demonstrated more recognition of their place in their school, and their Anglo peers placed more value on Spanish. Thus, interaction of parents among themselves and with school staff can also provide opportunities for developing a cross-cultural sensitivity that is much needed in a multilingual, multicultural society.

In the specific area of language and literacy instruction, parent-involvement programs or sessions may demonstrate to parents how to use existing literacy in a new form (English) or may help parents develop literacy skills that can immediately be put to meaningful use with their children. Some nonnative English-speaking families were included in the Tizard, Schofield, and Hewison (1982) study, in which children read books to parents and discussed them; the experiences produced positive effects on the children's reading performance. Several programs have used techniques such as telling and discussing stories in both English and native languages in an effort to develop both a familiarity with book language and a love of literature—2 components that are often cited as critical to successful literacy development (Ada, 1988; Viola, Gray, & Murphy, 1986, cited in Weinstein-Shr, 1990). The Punjaro Valley project with Latino parents in rural California schools reported increased adult confidence as they discussed children's books in group meetings, with some parents taking leadership roles. In addition, parents reported increased pride in their children's school achievements and deepened family feelings as they increased their activities with books, for example, asking children to answer questions about books, reading aloud, having children bring books home from school, and obtaining and using library cards (Ada, 1988).

Parents and Children Reading Together. Involving parents and children together in literacy activities appears to be one way to break the cycle of illiteracy for native English-speaking families as well. Several different intergenerational literacy-based intervention studies have been implemented in an attempt to determine the most effective way to increase parent literacy, change the home's social-language literacy context, and encourage the children's emerging literacy (Sticht, 1983; Sticht & McDonald, 1989; Business Council for Effective Literacy, 1989).

Many of the studies reported were implemented as service-delivery programs with evaluation components, rather than empirical, quantitative research studies with control groups, adequate sample sizes, and careful attention to minimizing threats to validity and reliability. In the absence of a wealth of carefully controlled studies, these evaluations provide some direction for forming hypotheses to be tested and some guidelines for further research.

Anecdotal evidence, descriptions of participant enthusiasm and interest, and success in recruitment and retention have been used to evaluate many family literacy programs (McIvor, 1990; Nash, 1987). For example, the Mothers' Reading Program reported a 60% to 90% retention rate in their classes, which taught mothers to read children's books in order to improve their own and their child's literacy development (McIvor, 1990, p. 26). Given the high dropout rate in adult literacy programs (Boraks & Richardson, 1985), these figures are impressive. Other programs that included instruction in selection of and strategies for reading books with the children reported parents' increased enthusiasm, motivation, and interest in reading to their children as well as an improvement in their own reading (McIvor, 1990, p. 46; Handel & Goldsmith, 1989). However, these projects provide limited information on their effects on adult and child literacy achievement.

Also found to be effective in improving literacy was the use of individual tutors to assist parents in developing their reading skills and to model how they could read to their children at home (Nickse, Speicher, & Buchek, 1988). Retention was high (73%) and parents demonstrated gains in vocabulary and comprehension in proportion to the number of hours of tutoring they received. However, no control group was reported for this study, nor was the effect of the program on the children's literacy measured.

The Kenan Family Literacy Project incorporates a component for parents (literacy classes at their child's school), a component for children (a developmentally appropriate prekindergarten program at the public school for 3- and 4-year-olds), a joint component (parent-child activities in the prekindergarten room), shared school experiences (breakfast and lunch at school, riding the school bus together), and parent activities (volunteering as a classroom aide, attending parent groups discussing child development, language and literacy acquisition). The project, replicated in several sites in Kentucky and North Carolina, has demonstrated a high retention rate (80% to 90%), parent gains on literacy tests (85% of the adults increased 2 grade levels or passed the GED examination), and child gains of 67% on the High/Scope Development Scale (National Center for Family Literacy, 1989, p. 13; BCEL, 1989; Darling, 1989).

Another study of family literacy considered the effect of using computer-assisted instruction on parents' literacy attainment. Parents with initial reading levels below fourth-grade level received 20 hours of literacy instruction, at least 80% of which was computer assisted. They demonstrated significantly greater gains in oral reading and functional vocabulary than did a control group; their children's school attendance increased significantly; and both parents and children showed improved attitude changes (Maclay & Askov, 1988).

These studies suggest that intergenerational family literacy (1) has a positive effect on parents' reading levels and children's emerging literacy; (2) increases motivation, interest, and enthusiasm for reading; and (3) encourages a high adult retention rate in the literacy program.

Parents Reading to Children. Parents of young children are constantly encouraged to read to their young children; the benefits that may be expected include enjoyment, language and literacy acquisition, and cognitive development (Mavrogenes, 1990; Strickland & Morrow, 1989; Trelease, 1989). Training parents to select and read appropriate storybooks has been shown to have a positive effect on young children's development. In Missouri, parent education was begun at the child's birth by providing parents with services such as information on development, home visits by parent educators, group meetings, periodic screening of the children, and a referral network (Winter & Rouse, 1990). Parent-child activities included showing parents the kinds of books their child would enjoy and modeling how to use the books with their child. At age 3 years, children in the program were "significantly more advanced than comparison group children in language, social development, problem solving, and other cognitive abilities" (p. 383).

Edwards (1989) coached 5 mothers of Head Start children in reading stories to their children over a period of 8 weeks. Only 1 of the mothers acquired successful book-reading strategies (e.g., use of scaffolding). She was the best reader in the group and the one most willing to change. Edwards concludes that urging parents to read to their children is not sufficient; they must also be shown how to read effectively and be supported in their attempts (p. 248).

Children Reading to Parents. In a series of studies, British researchers have considered the effects of children reading to their parents on the children's literacy attainment (Hannon & Jackson, 1987; Johnston, 1989; Tizard et al., 1982). Children 5 to 8 years old took their reading books home every evening to read aloud to their parents. Parents listened to their child read and signed a card indicating completion of the reading. Parents and teachers also used the cards to make comments on reading activities and the child's progress in reading. The researchers made home visits to monitor the program and to teach parents how to "hear" reading. In the Haringey Project, Tizard et al. (1982) found that, for working-class families, participation in this program significantly increased children's reading scores and produced positive attitudes toward reading for both children and parents. In the Belfield Project, also with working-class families (Hannon & Jackson, 1987), there was no improvement in the children's reading scores, but their attitudes toward reading improved.

In a U.S. replication of this British research, first- and second-grade children demonstrated improved attitudes toward reading, increased motivation to read, increased interest in reading, and improved progress through the school's series of reading books (Nurss, Huss, & Hannon, 1992). Without engaging in a specific instructional program, parents positively affected their children's reading through daily interactions around books.

In another study, Head Start children (low-SES 4- and 5-year-olds) were given stories to share with their parents (McCormick & Mason, 1989). Children in the book recitation (treatment) group heard their teacher read short stories emphasizing the print, and they reread (recited) the stories several times. One of these books was mailed home each week for the children to read to the parents. Children in the story discussion (control) group had stories told to them and copies of the illustrations mailed to them. During kindergarten the book recitation group continued to receive storybooks at home, whereas the story discussion group was sent worksheets. At the end of kindergarten the book recitation group scored significantly higher on story-reading tasks and on reading, letter sounds, and parental assessment of literacy knowledge. At the end of first grade more of the treatment group were in the middle or high reading groups than were the control group, and none of the treatment group were retained or placed in special (transition or learning disabilities) programs, as were children in the control group. By listening to their children read aloud, parents had a beneficial effect on the children's acquisition of literacy.

SUMMARY

Parent involvement in early childhood education significantly affects both the behavior of the parents and the development and education of their children. Research discussed in this chapter suggests several conclusions about the influence of parents.

1. Parental knowledge about child development allows parents to support their child by matching the environment (e.g., activities, materials, expectations) to the child's current developmental level.
2. Parents' knowledge about factors affecting child development and their beliefs about their own influence on their children's development may be even more influential than parental knowledge about child development.
3. Child-rearing practices are influenced by the parents' style, the child's temperament, demographic variables, and the family's culture and ethnicity.
4. Parents receive important support in their parenting roles through informal family and social networks, which supply both general emotional support and specific child-rearing assistance.
5. Community-based parent-education and -support programs, especially those designed for teen mothers, are effective in decreasing negative parenting behaviors and in increasing appropriate parent-child interactions, which leads to increased competence and educational opportunities for the children.
6. Programs that train parents as teachers of their children may lead to gains in children's cognitive and social competence and to more positive parent-child interactions.
7. School-based family-support programs have been effective in increasing student attendance and performance and in positively changing both parent and child attitudes toward school.
8. Reading stories to children as well as the natural language and literacy interactions between parents and children at home support children's emergent literacy development.
9. Family literacy interventions—parents and children reading together, parents reading to children, and children reading to parents—are all effective in increasing both parent and child literacy. Family literacy interventions are especially effective for families in which English is a second language.

References

Ada, A. F. (1988). The Pajaro Valley experience: Working with Spanish-speaking parents to develop children's reading and writing skills in the home through the use of children's literature. In T. Skutnabb-Kangas & J. Cummins (Eds.), *Minority education: From shame to struggle* (pp. 223–237). Philadelphia: Multilingual Matters.

Andrews, S. R., Blumenthal, J. B., Johnson, D. L., Kahn, A. J., Ferguson, C. J., Lasater, R. M., Malone, P. E., & Wallace, D. B. (1982). The skills of mothering: A study of parent child development centers. *Mono-graphs of Society for Research in Child Development, 47* (6, Serial No. 198).

Auerbach, E. R. (1989). Toward a social-contextual approach to family literacy. *Harvard Educational Review, 59* (2), 165–181.

Badger, E. (1981). Effects of parent education on teenage mothers and their offspring. In K. G. Scott, T. Field, & E. G. Robertson (Eds.), *Teenage parents and their offspring* (pp. 283–310). New York: Grune & Stratton.

Badger, E., & Burnes, D. (1980). Impact of a parent education program on the personal development of teenage mothers. *Journal of Pediatric Psychology, 5,* 415–422.

Badger, E., Elsass, S. & Sutherland, J. M. (1974). *Mothering as a means of accelerating childhood development in a high risk population.* Paper presented at a meeting of the Society for Pediatric Research, Washington, DC. (ERIC Documentation Reproduction Service No. ED 104 522)

Badger, E., & Goldman, B. M. (1987). Program design of parent support systems as a function of population served: Some comparisons. In C. F. Z. Boukydis (Ed.), *Research on support for parents and infants in the postnatal period* (pp. 197–224). Norwood, NJ: Ablex.

Baltes, P. B., Reese, H. W., & Nesselroade, J. R. (1977). *Lifespan developmental psychology.* Monterey, CA: Brooks/Cole.

Bartz, K., & Levine, E. (1978). Childrearing by black parents: A description and comparison to Anglo and Chicano parents. *Journal of Marriage & the Family, 40* (4), 708–719.

Baumrind, D. (1967). Child care practices anteceding three patterns of preschool behavior. *Genetic Psychology Monographs, 75,* 43–88.

Baumrind, D. (1977). Some thoughts about childrearing. In S. Cohen & T. J. Comiskey (Eds.), *Child development: Contemporary perspectives* (pp. 248–258). Itasca, IL: Peacock.

Baumrind, D. (1978). Parental disciplinary patterns and social competence in children. *Youth & Society, 9* (3), 239–276.

Becher, R. M. (1984). *Parent involvement: A review of research and principles of successful practice.* Washington, DC: National Institute of Education.

Beller, E. K. (1979). Early intervention programs. In J. Osofsky (Ed.), *Handbook of Infant Development* (pp. 852–894). New York: Wiley.

Belsky, J. (1984). The determinants of parenting: A process model. *Child Development, 55,* 83–96.

Bermudez, A. B., & Padron, Y. N. (1988). University-school collaboration that increases minority parent involvement. *Educational Horizons, 66,* 83–86.

Berreuta-Clement, J. R., Schweinhart, L. J., Barnett, W. S., Epstein, A. S., & Weikart, D. P. (1984). *Changed lives: The effects of the Perry Preschool program on youths through age 19.* (Monographs of the High/Scope Educational Research Foundation, 8). Ypsilanti, MI: High/Scope Press.

Boraks, N., & Richardson, J. S. (1985). Teaching the adult beginning reader: Research based instructional strategies. *Adult Literacy and Basic Education, 9*(3), 131–143.

Boukydis, C. F. Z. (Ed.). (1987). *Research on support for parents and infants in the postnatal period.* Norwood, NJ: Ablex.

Bridgeman, B., Blumenthal, J., & Andrews, S. (1981). *Parent-child development center: Final evaluation report. Report to Department of Health and Human Services.* Princeton, NJ: Educational Testing Service.

Bronfenbrenner, U. (1979). *The ecology of human development.* Cambridge, MA: Harvard University Press.

Bronfenbrenner, U. (1986). Ecology of the family as a context for human development: Research perspectives. *Developmental Psychology, 22,* 723–742.

Burgess, B. J. (1980). Parenting in the Native-American community. In M. D. Fantini & R. Cardenas (Eds.), *Parenting in a multicultural society* (pp. 63–73). New York: Longman.

Burt, M. R., Kimmich, M. H., Goldmuntz, J., & Sonenstein, F. L. (1984). *Helping pregnant adolescents: Outcomes and cost of service delivery.* Final Report on the Evaluation of Adolescent Pregnancy Programs. Washington, DC: Urban Institute.

Burton, L. M., & Bengston, V. L. (1985). Black grandmothers: Issues of timing and continuity of roles. In V. L. Bengston & J. F. Robertson (Eds.), *Grandparenthood* (pp. 61–78). Beverly Hills, CA: Sage.

Business Council for Effective Literacy. (1989). Literacy begins at home. *BCEL Business Council for Effective Literacy Newsletter, 19,* 1, 4–6.

Caspi, A., & Elder, H., Jr. (1988). Childhood precursor of the life course: Early personality and life disorganization. In E. M. Hetherington, R. M. Lerner, & M. Perlmutter (Eds.), *Child development in life span perspective* (pp. 115–142). Hillsdale, NJ: Erlbaum.

Chapman, W. (1991). The Illinois experience: State grants to improve schools through parent involvement. *Phi Delta Kappan, 72,* 355–358.

Clarke-Stewart, A. (1977). *Child care in the family: A review of research and some propositions for policy.* New York: Academic Press.

Clarke-Stewart, K. A. (1983). Exploring the assumptions of parent education. In R. Haskins & D. Adams (Eds.), *Parent education and public policy* (pp. 257–276). Norwood, NJ: Ablex.

Clarke-Stewart, K. A. (1988). Parents' effects on children's development: A decade of progress? *Journal of Applied Developmental Psychology, 9,* 41–84.

Clarke-Stewart, K. A., & Apfel, N. (1978). Evaluating parental effects on child development. In L. S. Shulman (Ed.), *Review of research in education* (pp. 47–119). Itasca, IL: Peacock.

Cochran, M. (1988). Parental empowerment in family matters: Lessons learned from a research program. In D. R. Powell (Ed.), *Parent education as early childhood intervention,* (pp. 23–50). Norwood, NJ: Ablex.

Cochran, M., & Brassard, J. (1979). Child development and personal social networks. *Child Development, 50,* 601–616.

Cochran, M., & Dean, C. (1991). Home-school relations and the empowerment process. *Elementary School Journal, 91,* 261–269.

Cochran-Smith, M. (1986). Reading to children: A model for understanding texts. In B. Schieffelin & P. Gilmore (Eds.), *The Acquisition of literacy: Ethnographic perspectives* (pp. 35–54). Norwood, NJ: Ablex.

Cohen, S., & Wills, T. A. (1985). Stress, social support and the buffering hypothesis. *Psychological Bulletin, 98,* 310–357.

Crockenberg, S. B. (1981). Infant irritability, mother responsiveness and social support influences on the security of infant-mother attachments. *Child Development, 52,* 44–52.

D'Angelo, D. A., & Adler, C. R. (1991). Chapter I: A catalyst for improving parent involvement. *Phi Delta Kappan, 72,* 350–354.

Darling, S. (1989). *Kenan Trust family literacy project guidebook.* Louisville, KY: Kenan Trust Family Literacy Project.

Davies, D. (1991). Schools reaching out. *Phi Delta Kappan, 72,* 376–382.

Delgado-Gaitan, C. (1987). Mexican adult literacy: New directions for immigrants. In S. R. Goldman & H. Trueba (Eds.), *Becoming literate in English as a second language* (pp. 9–32). Norwood, NJ: Ablex.

Dickie, J. R., & Gerber, S. C. (1980). Training in social competence: The effect on mothers, fathers, and infants. *Child Development, 51,* 1248–1251.

Dix, T., Ruble, D. N., & Zambarano, R. J. (1989). Mothers' implicit theories of discipline: Child effects, parent effects, and the attribution process. *Child Development 60,* 1373–1391.

Dokecki, P., Hargrove, E., & Sandler, H. (1983). An overview of the Parent Child Development Center social experiment. In R. Haskins & D. Adams (Eds.), *Parent education and public policy,* (pp. 80–111). Norwood, NJ: Ablex.

Duffield, B. N. (1988). Belief systems determinants of parenting (Unpublished doctoral dissertation, Georgia State University, 1989). *Dissertation Abstracts International, 50*(2), 35 2A.

Edwards, P. A. (1989). Supporting lower SES mothers attempts to provide scaffolding for book reading. In J. B. Allen & J. M. Mason (Eds.), *Risk makers, risk takers, risk breakers: reducing the risks for young literacy learners* (pp. 222–250). Portsmouth, NH: Heinemann.

Egeland, B., & Sroufe, L. A. (1981). Attachment and early maltreatment. *Child Development, 52,* 44–52.

Epstein, J. L. (1986). Parents' reactions to teacher practices of parent involvement. *Elementary School Journal, 86,* 277–294.

Epstein, J. L. (1991). Pathways to partnership: What we can learn from federal, state, district and school initiatives. *Phi Delta Kappan, 72,* 345–349.

Fogel, A., & Melson, G. (1988). *Child development: Individual, family, and society.* St. Paul, MN: West.

Freeland, C. A. B., & Nair, P. (1985, April). *The role of parent knowledge and support in the development of parent-child relationships within very high risk families.* Paper presented at the Society for Research in Child Development, Toronto.

Fry, P. S. (1985) Relations between teenagers' knowledge, expectations, and maternal behavior. *British Journal of Developmental Psychology, 3,* 47–55.

Furstenberg, F. F., Jr. (1976). *Unplanned parenthood.* Glencoe, IL: Free Press.

Furstenberg, F. F., Brooks-Gunn, J., & Morgan, S. P. (1987). *Adolescent mothers in later life.* Cambridge, UK: Cambridge University Press.

Goodnow, J. J. (1988). Parents' ideas, actions, and feelings: Models and methods from developmental and social psychology. *Child Development, 59,* 286–320.

Gray, S. W., & Ramsey, B. K. (1986). Adolescent childbearing and high school completion. *Journal of Applied Development Psychology, 7,* 167–179.

Gray, S. W., & Ruttle, K. (1980). The family-oriented home visiting program: A longitudinal study. *Genetic Psychology Monographs, 102,* 299–316.

Grusec, J. E., & Kuczynski, L. (1980). Direction of effect in socialization: A comparison of the parent's versus the child's behavior as determinants of disciplinary techniques. *Developmental Psychology, 16* (1), 1–9.

Handel, R. D., & Goldsmith, E. (1989). Children's literature and adult literacy: Empowerment through intergenerational learning. *Lifelong Learning, 12*(6), 24–27.

Hannon, P., & Jackson, A. (1987). *The Belfield reading project. Final report.* London: National Children's Bureau.

Harrison, A., Serafica, F., & McAdoo, H. P. (1984). Ethnic families of color. In R. D. Parke, R. N. Ernde, H. P. McAdoo, & G. P. Sackett (Eds.), *Review of child development research. Vol. 7: The family* (pp. 329–371). Chicago: University of Chicago Press.

Hayes, C. D. (Ed.). (1987). *Risking the future: Adolescent sexuality, pregnancy and childbearing. Vol. I.* Washington, DC: National Academy Press.

Henderson, A. T. (1987). *The evidence continues to grow: Parent involvement improves student achievement.* Columbia, MD: National Committee for Citizens in Education.

Hofferth, S. L. (1987). The effects of programs and policies on adolescent pregnancy and childbearing. In S. L. Hofferth & C. D. Hayes (Eds.), *Risking the future: Adolescent sexuality, pregnancy and childbearing. Vol. II* (pp. 207–263). Washington, DC: National Academy Press.

Holden, G. W. (1983). Avoiding conflict: Mothers as tacticians in the supermarket. *Child Development, 54,* 233–240.

Holden, G. W., & West, M. J. (1989). Proximate regulation by mothers: A demonstration of how differing styles affect young children's behavior. *Child Development, 60,* 64–69.

Honig, A. S., Lally, J. R., & Mathieson, P. H. (1982). Personal and social adjustment of school children after five years in the Family Development Research Program. *Child Care Quarterly, 11* (2), 136–146.

Hunt, J. McV., & Paraskevopoulos, J. (1980). Children's psychological development as a function of the inaccuracy of their mothers'

knowledge of their abilities. *Journal of Genetic Psychology, 136,* 285–298.

Jester, R. E. & Guinagh, B. J. (1983). The Gordon Parent Education Infant Toddler Program. In the Consortium for Longitudinal Studies, *As the twig is bent: Lasting effects of preschool programs* (pp. 103–132). Hillsdale, NJ: Erlbaum.

Johnston, K. (1989). Parents and reading: A U. K. perspective. *Reading Teacher, 42*(6), 352–357.

JRB Associates. (1981). Final report on national study of teenage pregnancy. DHHS Contract No. 282-80-0070-LG.

Kagan, S. L., Powell, D. R., Weissbourd, B., & Zigler, E. F. (Eds.). (1987). *America's family support programs.* New Haven, CT: Yale University Press.

Kennedy, M. M. (1978). Findings from the Follow Through planned variation study. *Educational Researcher, 7,* 3–11.

Kiesler, C. A. (1985). Policy implications of research on social support and health. In S. Cohen & S. L. Syme (Eds.), *Social support and health* (pp. 347–364). Orlando: Academic Press.

Lally, J. R., & Honig, A. S. (1977). *The Family Development Research Program: A program for prenatal, infant & early childhood enrichment. Final report.* Syracuse, NY: Syracuse University Press.

Lally, J. R., Mangione, P. L., & Honig, A. S. (1988). The Syracuse University Family Development Research Program: Long- range impact of early intervention with low-income children and their families. In D. R. Powell (Ed.), *Parent education as early childhood intervention* (pp. 79–104). Norwood, NJ: Ablex.

Lambie, D. Z., Bond, J. T., & Weikart, D. P. (1974). *Home teaching with mothers and infants.* (Monographs of the High/Scope Educational Research Foundation, *2*). Ypsilanti, MI: High/Scope Press.

Levine, R. A. (1980). A cross-cultural perspective on parenting. In M. D. Fantini & R. Cardenas (Eds.), *Parenting in a multicultural society* (pp. 17–26). New York: Longman.

Levenstein, P., O'Hara, J., & Madden, J. (1983). The Mother-Child Home Program for Verbal Interaction Project. In Consortium for Longitudinal Studies, *As the twig is bent: Lasting effects of preschool programs* (pp. 237–263). Hillsdale, NJ: Erlbaum.

Lewis, C. C. (1981). The effects of parental firm control: A reinterpretation of findings. *Psychological Bulletin, 90,* 547–563.

Lin, C. C., & Fu, V. R. (1990). A comparison of child rearing practices among Chinese, immigrant Chinese, and Caucasian-American parents. *Child Development, 61,* 429–433.

Luster, T., & Rhodes, K. (1989). The relation between childrearing beliefs and the home environment in a sample of adolescent mothers. *Family Relations, 38,* 317–322.

Maccoby, E. E., & Martin, J. A. (1983). Socialization in the context of the family. In P. Mussen & E. M. Hetherington (Eds.), *Handbook of child psychology: Socialization personality and social development* (4th ed., pp. 1–101). New York: Wiley.

Maclay, C. M., & Askov, E. N. (1988). Computers and adult beginning readers: An intergenerational study. *Lifelong Learning, 11*(8), 23–28.

Mavrogenes, N. A. (1990). Helping parents help their children become literate. *Young Children 45*(4), 4–9.

McAdoo, H. P. (1978). Factors related to stability in upwardly mobile black families. *Journal of Marriage and the Family, 40* (4), 761–776.

McAdoo, H. P. (1982). Stress absorbing systems in black families. *Family Relations, 31,* 479–488.

McClelland, D., Constantian, C. A., Regalado, D., & Stone, C. (1978, June). Making it to maturity. *Psychology Today,* 42–53, 114.

McCormick, C. E., & Mason, J. M. (1989). Fostering reading for Head Start children with little books. In J. B. Allen & J. M. Mason (Eds.), *Risk makers, risk takers, risk breakers: reducing the risks for young literacy learners* (pp. 154–177). Portsmouth, NH: Heinemann.

McIvor, M. C. (Ed.). (1990). *Family literacy in action: A survey of successful programs.* Syracuse, NY: New Readers Press.

McKinlay, J. (1973). Social networks, lay consultation, and help-seeking behavior. *Social Forces, 51,* 275–292.

Miller, S. A. (1986). Parents' beliefs about their children's cognitive abilities. *Developmental Psychology, 22,* 276–284.

Mills, R. S. L., & Rubin, K. H. (1990). Parental beliefs about problematic social behaviors in early childhood. *Child Development, 61,* 138–151.

Nash, A. (1987). *English family literacy: An annotated bibliography.* Boston: University of Massachusetts.

National Center for Family Literacy. (1989). *A place to start: The Kenan Trust Family Literacy Project.* Louisville, KY: Author.

Nickse, R. S., Speicher, A. M., & Buchek, P. C. (1988). An intergenerational project: A family intervention/prevention model. *Journal of Reading, 31* (7), 634–642.

Ninio, A. (1979). The naive theory of the infant and other maternal attributes in subgroups in Israel. *Child Development, 50,* 976–980.

Nurss, J. R., Huss, R. L., & Hannon, P. (in press). Parents hearing children read: Trying a British approach. *International Journal of Early Childhood.*

Olds, D. (1982). The prenatal/early infancy project: An ecological approach to prevention of development disabilities. In J. Belsky (Ed.), *In the beginning* (pp. 270–285). New York: Columbia University Press.

Olds, D. L., Henderson, C. R., Jr., Tatelbaum, R, & Chamberlain, R. (1986a). Improving the delivery of prenatal care and outcomes of pregnancy: A randomized trial of nurse home visitation. *Pediatrics, 77,* 16–28.

Olds, D. L., Henderson, C. R., Jr., Tatelbaum, R., & Chamberlain, R. (1986b). Preventing child abuse and neglect: A randomized trial of nurse home visitation. *Pediatrics, 78,* 65–78.

Olmstead, P. P. (1991). Parent involvement in elementary education: Findings and suggestions from the Follow Through program. *Elementary School Journal, 91,* 221–231.

Parke, R. D. (1988). Families in life-span perspective: A multilevel developmental approach. In E. M. Hetherington, R. M. Lerner, & M. Perlmutter (Eds.), *Child development in life span perspective* (pp. 159–190). Hillsdale, NJ: Erlbaum.

Parke, R. D., & Lewis, N. G. (1981). The family in context: A multilevel interactional analysis of child abuse. In R. W. Henderson (Ed.), *Parent-child interaction: Theory, research and prospect* (pp. 169–204). New York: Academic Press.

Parks, P. L., & Smerglio, V. L. (1986). Relationships among parenting knowledge, quality of stimulation in the home and infant development. *Family Relations, 35,* 411–416.

Peters, D. L., Bollin, G. G., & Murphy, R. E. (1991). Head Start's influence on parental competence and child competence. *Advances in Reading/Language Research, 5,* 91–123.

Phillips, G., & McNaughton, S. (1990). The practice of storybook reading to preschool children in mainstream New Zealand families. *Reading Research Quarterly, 25*(3), 196–212.

Polit, D. F., Quint, J. C., & Riccio, J. A. (1988). *The challenge of serving teenage mothers: Lessons from Project Redirection.* New York: Manpower Demonstration Research.

Potter, G. (1989). Parent participation in the language arts program. *Language Arts, 66,* 21–28.

Powell, D. R. (1988). Emerging directions in parent-child intervention. In D. R. Powell (Ed.), *Parent education as early childhood intervention* (pp. 1–22). Norwood, NJ: Ablex.

Powell, D. R. (1989). *Families and early childhood programs.* Washington, DC: National Association for the Education of Young Children.

Powell, D. R. (1991). How schools support families: Critical policy tensions. *Elementary School Journal, 91,* 307–319.

Quint, J. C., & Riccio, J. A. (1985). *The challenge of serving pregnant and parenting teens: Lessons from Project Redirection.* New York: Manpower Demonstration Research.

Quintero, E., & Macias, A. H. (1990). *Reading Teacher, 44* (4), 306–312.

Radke-Yarrow, M., & Zahn-Waxler, C. (1984). Roots, motives, and patterns in children's pro-social behavior. In E. Staub, D. Bartal, J. Karylowski, & J. Reykowski (Eds.), *The development and maintenance of pro-social behaviors* (pp. 81– 99). New York: Plenum.

Ramirez, M., III, & Cox, B. G. (1980). Parenting for multiculturalism: A Mexican-American model. In M. D. Fantini & R. Cardenas (Eds.), *Parenting in a multicultural society* (pp. 54–62). New York: Longman.

Schickedanz, J. A., Chay, S., Gopin, P., Shang, L. L., Song, S. M., & Wild, N. (1990). Preschoolers and academics: Some thoughts. *Young Children, 46*(1), 4–13.

Seitz, V. (1987). Outcome evaluation of family support programs: Research design alternatives to true experiments. In S. L. Kagan, D. R. Powell, B. Weissbourd, & E. F. Zigler (Eds.), *America's family support programs: Perspectives and prospects* (pp. 329–344). New Haven, CT: Yale University Press.

Seitz, V., Rosenbaum, L. K., & Apfel, N. (1985). Effects of family support intervention: A ten-year follow-up. *Child Development, 56,* 376–391.

Sigel, I. E. (1985). A conceptual analysis of beliefs. In I. Sigel (Ed.), *Parental belief systems: The psychological consequences for children* (pp. 345–371). Hillsdale, NJ: Erlbaum.

Simich-Dudgeon, C. (1986). Parent involvement and the education of limited-English-proficient students. *ERIC Digest.* (ERIC Document Reproduction Service No. ED 279 205)

Sistler, A. K., & Gottfried, N. W. (1990). Shared child development knowledge between grandmother and mother. *Family Relations, 39* (1), 92–96.

Slaughter, D. T. (1983). Early intervention and its effects on maternal and child development. *Monographs of the Society for Research in Child Development, 48* (4, Serial No. 202).

Slaughter, D. T., & Dillworth-Anderson, P. (1985, April). *Child care of sickle cell anemia children.* Paper presented at the Society for Research in Child Development, Toronto.

Snow, C. E., & Ninio, A. (1986). The contracts of literacy: What children learn from learning to read books. In W. H. Teale & E. Sulzby (Eds.), *Emergent literacy: Writing and reading* (pp. 116–138). Norwood, NJ: Ablex.

Solomon, Z. P. (1991). California's policy on parent involvement. *Phi Delta Kappan, 72,* 359–362.

Sroufe, L. A., & Cooper, R. G. (1988). *Child development: Its nature and course.* New York: Knopf.

Stack, C. B. (1971). *Black kindred: Parenthood and personal kinship networks among African Americans "on aid."* Urbana, IL: University of Illinois. (ERIC Document Reproduction Service No. ED 062 449)

Staples, R., & Mirande, A. (1980). Racial and cultural variations among American families: A decennial review of the literature on minority families. *Journal of Marriage and the Family, 42*(4), 887–903.

Stevens, J. H., Jr. (1984). Black grandmothers' and black adolescent mothers' knowledge about parenting. *Developmental Psychology, 20,* 1017–1025.

Stevens, J. H., Jr. (1988). Social support, locus of control, and parenting in three low-income groups: Black adults, white adults and black teenagers. *Child Development, 59,* 635–642.

Stevens, J. H., Jr., & Duffield, B. N. (1986). Age and parenting skill among black women in poverty. *Early Childhood Research Quarterly, 1*(3), 221–225.

Sticht, T. G. (1983). *Literacy and human resources development at work: Investing in the education of adults to improve the educability of children.* Alexandria, VA: Human Resources Research Organization. (ERIC Document Reproduction Service No. ED 262 291)

Sticht, T. G., & McDonald, B. A. (1989). *Making the nation smarter: The intergenerational transfer of cognitive ability.* University Park, PA: Institute for the Study of Adult Literacy, Pennsylvania State University.

Strickland, D. S., & Morrow, L. M. (1989). Family literacy and young children. *Reading Teacher, 42* (7), 530–531.

Taylor, D. (1983). *Family literacy: Young children learning to read and write.* Portsmouth, NH: Heinemann.

Taylor, D., & Dorsey-Gaines, L. (1988). *Growing up literate: Learning from inner-city families.* Portsmouth, NH: Heinemann.

Teale, W. H. (1986). Home background and young children's literacy development. In W. H. Teale & E. Sulzby (Eds.), *Emergent literacy: Writing and reading* (pp. 173–206). Norwood, NJ: Ablex.

Tinsley, B. R., & Parke, R. D. (1984). Grandparents as support and socialization agents. In M. Lewis (Eds.), *Beyond the dyad* (pp. 161–194). New York: Plenum.

Tizard, J., Schofield, W. N., & Hewison, J. (1982). Collaboration between teachers and parents in assisting children's reading. *British Journal of Educational Psychology, 52,* 1–15.

Trelease, J. (1989). *The New Read-Aloud Handbook.* NY: Penguin.

Unger, D. G., & Wandersman, L. P. (1985). Social support and adolescent mothers: Action research contributions to theory and applications. *American Journal of Community Psychology, 11,* 291–300.

Unger, D. G., & Wandersman, L. P. (1988a). The relation of family and partner support to the adjustment of adolescent mothers. *Child Development, 59,* 1056–1060.

Unger, D. G., & Wandersman, L. P. (1988b). A support program for adolescent mothers: Predictors of participation. In D. R. Powell (Ed.), *Parent education as early childhood intervention: Emerging directions in theory, research, and practice Vol. 3: Annual advances in applied developmental psychology* (pp. 105–130). Norwood, NJ: Ablex.

Viola, M., Gray, A., & Murphy, B. (1986). *Report on the Navajo parent child reading program at the Chinle Primary School.* Chinle, AZ: Chinle School District.

Wandersman, L. P. (1987). New directions in parent education. In S. L. Kagan, D. R. Powell, B. Weissbourd, & E. F. Zigler (Eds.), *America's family support programs: Perspectives and prospects* (pp. 207–227). New Haven, CT: Yale University Press.

Weiss, H. B., & Jacobs, F. (Eds.). (1988). *Evaluating family support programs.* Hawthorne, NY: Aldine de Gruyter.

Weinstein-Shr, G. (1990). Family and intergenerational literacy in multilingual families. *NCLE Q & A* [National Clearinghouse on Literacy Education Questions & Answers]. Washington, DC: Center for Applied Linguistics.

Wells, G. (1986). *The meaning makers: Children learning language and using language to learn.* Portsmouth, NH: Heinemann.

Wilson, M. N. (1984). Mothers' and grandmothers' perceptions of parental behavior in three-generational black families. *Child Development, 55,* 1333–1339.

Wilson, M. N. (1986). The black extended family: An analytical consideration. *Developmental Psychology, 22,* 246–258.

Winter, M., & Rouse, J. (1990). Fostering intergenerational literacy: The Missouri parents as teachers program. *Reading Teacher, 43* (8), 382–387.

23

PORTRAIT OF A CHANGING FIELD:
POLICY AND PRACTICE IN EARLY
CHILDHOOD SPECIAL EDUCATION

Jeanette A. McCollum
DEPARTMENT OF SPECIAL EDUCATION, UNIVERSITY OF ILLINOIS AT URBANA-CHAMPAIGN

Susan P. Maude
ALLEGHENY–SINGER RESEARCH INSTITUTE AT PITTSBURGH, PA

The brief history of Early Childhood Special Education (ECSE) has been characterized by heterogeneity and change. Nevertheless, strengthened by a growing body of experience and research, ECSE has taken shape as a distinct new field, contributed to by, but more than the intermixture of, its various parts (Peterson, 1987; Shonkoff & Meisels, 1990). Three relatively distinct phases have been apparent in ECSE's brief but eventful history. The first was its initial emergence from within its 2 primary parent fields, special education and early childhood education. Programs for young children with special needs began to appear on a regular basis less than 3 decades ago, most grounded in one of these 2 parent fields. Programs growing from special education roots came about primarily through the efforts of parents who, as public special education for school age children became more common and was finally mandated, turned their attention to younger children. Programs growing from early childhood education roots, in contrast, evolved primarily from compensatory programs for disadvantaged children. The two movements converged with the passage in 1968 of P.L. 90-538, a law supporting the Handicapped Children's Early Education Program.

The second phase, continuing into the early 1980s, was one of evolution, definition, and solidification of ECSE as a profession and a field of study. Although there was a sometimes uneasy fit between the two bodies of knowledge in addressing the needs of children who were both *young* and *special*, the characteristics of the population necessitated continual self-examination, experimentation and development of new approaches to service delivery (Allen, Holm, &

Schiefelbusch, 1978; Garwood & Fewell, 1983; Guralnick, 1978; Hanson, 1984a; Jordan, Gallagher, Hutinger, & Karnes, 1988; Linder, 1983; Meisels, 1979; Peterson, 1987; Safford, 1989). This process greatly stimulated and strengthened the evolution of ECSE, and contributed new knowledge and new approaches to the 2 parent fields as well.

The third phase in the evolution of ECSE is still in process, and may be defined as a period of reexamination and redefinition. ECSE entered this phase as part of the events surrounding the development, passage and implementation of P.L. 99-457, the Amendments to the Education of the Handicapped Act of 1986 (Gallagher, Trohanis, & Clifford, 1989; Meisels & Shonkoff, 1990). The local, state and national activity accompanying this new law resulted in reexamination not only in ECSE (Division for Early Childhood, 1987), but in all fields serving young children with special needs and their families (Hauser-Cram, Upshur, Krauss, & Shonkoff, 1988; Meisels, 1989). Through this process, the values and practices of many fields are becoming increasingly intertwined and mutually supportive (Shonkoff & Meisels, 1990). The concentrated effort which has gone into the implementation of P.L. 99-457, reauthorized by the passage of Public Law 102-199 in 1991, has helped immeasurably to meld these elements into a new, integrated whole, undergirded by solid and increasingly clear beliefs, values and practices. ECSE has been forced not only to examine critically the values and practices of each of its 2 primary parent fields as they apply to young children with special needs, but to recognize the value of knowledge, skills and practices from many other related disciplines and fields. In many ways,

ECSE's trajectory as a field now has begun to converge with those of others, including health (Gilkerson, Gorski, & Panitz 1990; Greenspan, 1990; Shonkoff & Meisels, 1990) and social services (Garbarino, 1990; Halpern, 1990; Seitz & Provence, 1990).

Despite its eclecticism and rapid change, the values and theoretical frameworks which have framed ECSE since its inception are, if anything, becoming stronger. ECSE is firmly grounded in the knowledge that the course of development is not fixed (Hunt, 1961, 1979), even for those children with biologically-based disabilities and delays (Guralnick & Bricker, 1987). Rather, it is the interaction between biology and environment which determines developmental outcomes for all children (Sameroff & Fiese, 1990; Sameroff & Chandler, 1975). As an environmental manipulation, early intervention therefore provides the opportunity and the responsibility to optimize children's access to the best possible beginning. Given the diverse population served, the goals and purposes of ECSE also have been diverse: to facilitate, optimize, minimize, remediate, and prevent. Prevention (whether of primary or secondary disabilities or delays) consistently has been regarded as preferable to remediation (Scott & Carran, 1985). Hence the belief that earlier is better, with benefits to the child, the family, and society. What is changing is not the goals, but rather *how* these goals are approached.

The primary purpose of this chapter is to discuss the evolution and emerging status of ECSE. This will be divided into three major sections: evolution and characteristics of the field prior to the passage of Public Law 99-457; the content and policy implications of that law; and a discussion of one of the major themes characterizing this changing field as it has worked toward meeting the intent of this legislation.

LOOKING BACK: BIRTH OF A FIELD

To understand the field of ECSE, we must look first to its history. ECSE is the child of 2 major parent fields, early childhood education and special education (Bricker, 1989; Hanson & Lynch, 1989; Peterson, 1987). This section will review the legislation supporting policy in early childhood education and special education as it relates to young children with special needs; describe program models that have characterized the field; and briefly review two important themes that pervaded the literature in the period immediately prior to P.L. 99-457.

Supporting Legislation

The federal legislative history of ECSE is embedded largely within that of special education, which itself is intertwined with the legal and legislative system to a far greater extent than most other areas of education (Shonkoff & Meisels, 1990). A Bureau of Education for the Handicapped (BEH) was established in 1966 for the purpose of stimulating and supporting research, practice, and personnel training (Peterson, 1987); this office, now the Office of Special Education Programs, provides national leadership in special education. Activities at the national level have played a critical role in the development of ECSE as a field. Typically, policies and practices enacted to address the

needs of school age children and adults with disabilities eventually have been extended to include younger children, either through interpretation, new initiatives, or new legislation.

The first legislation specifically to address the developmental needs of young children, however, occurred outside of education. Title V of the Social Security Act (SSA) of 1935 authorized the establishment of 3 federal programs with implications for young children with special needs (Shonkoff & Meisels, 1990): (a) maternal and child care health services, (b) crippled children's services, and (c) child welfare services. In 1939, funding for innovative programs was provided through Title V, using Special Projects of Regional and National Significance (SPRANS) grants. Public Law 88-164, passed in 1963, was designed to support training, service, and research addressing mental retardation (Allen, 1984). It was through this legislation that University Affiliated Facilities (UAFs), now referred to as University Affiliated Programs (UAPs), were funded and developed. Because many early demonstration centers for young children with disabilities were established within these interdisciplinary centers, they played an important role in the development of ECSE. Another significant outgrowth of this same legislation occurred in 1965 with the passage of the Medicaid provisions of the SSA, providing early medical and health prevention and intervention programs for poor children. Also required through this legislation was the screening of each newborn for phenylkentonuria (PKU), as well as other potential contributors to mental retardation (Shonkoff & Meisels, 1990). A very important amendment to this law, passed in 1967 as P.L. 20-248, established the Early and Periodic Screening, Diagnosis and Treatment (EPSDT) program, mandating that early health screening and case-finding be available to children in poverty, as well as ensuring appropriate referral and treatment (Allen, 1984).

Prior to 1986, the majority of educational legislation in the United States for individuals with handicaps supported services for school-aged children (Peterson, 1987). However, many of these laws led directly or indirectly to legislation for very young children. The civil rights movement of the 1960s has been viewed as the underlying impetus for the enactment of both education and non-education legislation for individuals with handicaps (Peterson, 1987). Public Law 89-313 (1965) was one of the first laws to provide aid to states for the special education of school-aged children with handicaps; more recently, many states have used this funding source to provide services to infants and toddlers with special needs. Public Law 93-112, passed in 1973, provided another boost to federally authorized services for the young child with handicaps through Section 504 of the Rehabilitation Act. Essentially a civil rights law for the handicapped, Section 504 mandated that any state offering public school services to preschoolers without handicaps must also offer these services to preschoolers with handicaps. Another helpful law was P.L. 93-380 (1974), which extended the Elementary and Secondary Education Act (ESEA) to set in place due process procedures that later became part of P.L. 94-142.

The most significant legislation for children with handicaps, however, was signed into law by President Ford in 1975. The Education for the Handicapped Act (EHA), P.L. 94-142, and its amendment, the Education for All Handicapped Children Act of 1983, provided federal funds to states and local education agencies for the education of children and young adults (ages

3 to 21) with handicaps (Hanson & Lynch, 1989; Peterson, 1987; Shonkoff & Meisels, 1990). Public Law 94-142 contained 6 principles required of all state education agencies (SEAs) and, through them, of local education agencies (LEAs): zero-reject education; nondiscriminatory classification; free appropriate public education, including an individualized education program (IEP); least restrictive placement; due process; and parent participation (Gallagher, 1984; Turnbull, 1986; Turnbull, Strickland, & Brantley, 1978). As increasing numbers of young children are served in public school programs, the values and policies contained in these requirements have been interpreted as applying to them as well. Public Law 94-142 also contained important support for the development and funding of personnel preparation programs in special education, and, in recent years, a substantial portion of the programs funded under this Part have been designed to prepare personnel in infancy and early childhood special education and related services.

Federal legislation affecting the education of young children without disabilities also has had important implications for young children with special needs. Broad-based support by the federal government began in the 1960s with the Kennedy and Johnson administrations' war on poverty (Peterson, 1987). Policy enacted during this period, especially through the Elementary and Secondary Education Act, or ESEA (P.L. 89-10), was built upon the belief that children could break the cycle of poverty through education (Bricker, 1989; Peterson, 1987; Zigler & Valentine, 1979). In 1965, P.L. 92-924 established community-based Head Start programs sponsored by the Office of Economic Opportunity (Bricker, 1989; Halpern, 1990; Hanson & Lynch, 1989). This program was for low-income populations. In 1967, it was extended to support the development of Parent-Child Centers for families with children from birth through age 3. In 1972 and later in 1974, two amendments to the Economic Opportunity Act (P.L. 92-424 and P.L. 93-644) further impacted the availability of services to young children with handicaps, mandating Head Start to make 10% of its total enrollment in each state open to children with handicaps, and providing these children with services to meet their special needs (Allen, 1984; Bricker, 1989; Peterson, 1987). The Home Start program was funded in 1972 to provide home visitors to function as liaisons between Head Start center-based programs and families. In 1974, the Head Start/EPSDT Collaborative Program was funded to facilitate better access of Head Start families to the services of EPSDT (Shonkoff & Meisels, 1990).

Special education and early childhood education first came together legislatively in 1968 with the passage of P.L. 90-538, the Handicapped Children's Early Education Assistance Act (HCEEAA), the single most powerful force in establishing ECSE as a field. Based on findings by Kirk (1958) on the efficacy of intervention at a young age and new knowledge about the impact of early experience on development (Bloom, 1964; Hunt, 1961), this legislation was designed specifically to address the needs of young children with handicaps (Allen, 1984; DeWeerd, 1977; Harvey, 1977; Jordan, Hayden, Karnes, & Wood, 1977). Through this Act, which established the Handicapped Children's Early Education Program (HCEEP) within the Bureau of Education for the Handicapped, federal funds were authorized for the education of young children with handicaps in experimental

and demonstration preschool centers, popularly referred to as the "First Chance Network" or simply as "HCEEP." The mission of these 3-year projects was (and is) to develop and disseminate program models and best practices. Over 500 projects have been funded through HCEEP. This work has had a major influence on the development of the field of ECSE: from this point in history, ECSE developed in a parallel line with school-age special education and with early childhood education, although both continued to contribute new knowledge to the field (Peterson, 1987).

Despite these important beginnings, prior to P.L. 99-457 a relatively small proportion of children from birth through age 5 received early intervention services (Meisels, Harbin, Modigliani, & Olson, 1986). Under P.L. 94-142, services for children ages 3 through 5 and for young adults ages 18 through 21 were permissive in nature: it was up to each state to decide whether to include such programs. The law included a separate authority, Part B, that provided preschool incentive monies to states offering programs for children from the ages of 3 through 5, clearly pointing out the responsibility of the public education system for young children with special needs. Studies completed into the mid-1980s, however, indicated that not all states had taken advantage of these incentives to develop legislation and policy for this population (Carran, 1984; Cohen, Semmes, & Guralnick, 1979; Lessen & Rose, 1980; Smith, 1984; Swan, 1980). Carran's study, for example, found that mandates varied considerably across the 57 states and territories: 18% had no mandated services for the 0 to 5 age group, 35% mandated services for only 4- and 5-year-olds, 22% mandated services for 2- to 5-year-olds and an additional 21% mandated services for 0- to 5-year-olds. Furthermore, Smith (1984) reported that "while several states have enacted laws over the past twenty years mandating early intervention, an almost equal number have repealed mandates" (p. 34). In 1987, Peterson reported that only 19 states had mandated services for children under the age of 5, with the majority of mandates supporting services for children falling within the 3 to 5 age bracket.

Perhaps even more influential than this inconsistent service delivery in the subsequent passage of additional legislation specifically for young children with special needs was the growing awareness that P.L. 94-142, even where utilized in establishing public education programs for young children, did not adequately address the unique needs of these children and their families. Not only were services uncertain, but those services that were available also tended to be provided through a myriad of overlapping and often uncoordinated health, education, and social policies and mandates, each impacting the same lives, but separately from one another (Shonkoff & Meisels, 1990; Hauser-Cram, et al., 1988). Knowledge and best practice were emerging, but were constrained by the particular histories of many separate efforts. Professional literature in early childhood special education clearly stressed the key principles of family-oriented services, interdisciplinary and interagency collaboration, and noncategorical definitions of eligibility (Peterson, 1987). Although parent participation was mandated by P.L. 94-142 with regard to parental consent and procedural due process, and parent training was allowed as a service under this legislation, there was an increasing call for parents to be viewed as key decision makers with active roles in all aspects of their childrens' programs (Turnbull & Turnbull, 1986; Winton, 1986).

Coordination across agencies also was considered particularly important when working with infants, toddlers, and preschoolers with handicaps and their families, since multiple agencies provide services which address their needs (Fraas, 1986; Harbin & McNulty, 1990). Public Law 94-142 is a public school education bill, so strong linkages with other public or private agencies who may provide allied health, medical, or social support are not emphasized. Finally, to provide services under P.L. 94-142, and to allocate funds, children must fall within certain eligibility categories (e.g., trainably mentally handicapped, visually impaired). There are many issues related to using categorical labels with young children (Meisels, 1989; Meisels & Wasik, 1990). While some young children may manifest fairly easily diagnosed disabilities (e.g., Down syndrome, cerebral palsy, spina bifida), the majority are not so easily categorized. Early childhood is a period of rapid change, and behavioral indicators are often transient. Measurement techniques applied to determining eligibility with older children are less valid and reliable with younger children (Fewell & Vadasy, 1987; Meisels, 1989). Labels may not only unnecessarily stigmatize the child and family, but also may not reflect accurate information. Hence, the use of categorical eligibility criteria with young children is of questionable value.

Much attention was given in the early 1980s to the need to design new legislation more in line with current understanding of early development, family systems, and effective intervention practices. Public Law 98-199, Education of the Handicapped Act Amendments, passed in 1983, provided money for states to use in planning comprehensive service delivery systems for young children with handicaps from birth through age 5 and their families (Harbin & McNulty, 1990). Through this funding, many states already had begun to plan for this population even prior to the passage of P.L. 99-457.

The impetus behind these efforts led more quickly than expected to the development and passage of new federal legislation (Hauser-Cram, et al, 1988). In 1986 President Reagan signed into effect P.L. 99-457, Amendments to the Education of the Handicapped Act, thereby providing landmark legislation for young children and their families. This amendment to P.L. 94-142, particularly Part B (the Preschool Grant Program) and Part H (the Handicapped Infants and Toddlers' Program) addressed many of the issues discussed above. These programs provide financial incentives to states for establishing early intervention services from birth through age 5. It is this law which has and is bringing about much change in early intervention and all of its component parts, including early childhood special education. Because of its pervasive influence on current activities in the field, P.L. 99-457, now reauthorized by Public Law 102–199, will be described in more detail in a later section of this chapter.

Characteristics of ECSE Programs

ECSE services for children ages birth through 5 have been tremendously diverse in how their organizational and structural components are defined. Initially, these differences resulted from the response of each new ECSE program to the conditions, resources, and needs of individual communities and states, as well as to the practices of the parent field in which the particular program was grounded. Results of federally funded demonstration models such as those stemming from the First Chance Network supported the premise that many different service delivery alternatives could be effective for young children and their families (Peterson, 1987).

ECSE program models may be analyzed across at least 6 different organizational components: (a) types of children served; (b) administrative settings; (c) service delivery settings; (d) recipients of services; (e) curriculum goals; and (f) instructional methods (Dunst, 1986; Filler, 1983; Linder, 1983; Peterson, 1987). It is the wide range of options possible within each component that has led to such great diversity among programs (Karnes & Zehrbach, 1977; Karnes & Stayton, 1988; Peterson, 1987).

With regard to the types of children served, most ECSE programs provide services on a non-categorical basis. Hence, children enrolled in any one ECSE program typically display a wide variety of special needs such as language delays, motor impairments, and developmental delays, as well as established risk conditions such as Down syndrome or cerebral palsy. Also included may be children with biological risk factors such as medical fragility, or environmental risk factors such as poverty. Other programs may serve children of only 1 category. Differences may also occur according to age. Some programs may serve birth through 5-year-old children, whereas others may serve more restricted age ranges. Age groupings within some center-based classrooms range widely (e.g., 2 to 5), while in others same-age groups are used.

Prior to P.L. 99-457, ECSE programs also differed widely in the types of administrative structures under which they were governed, including state agencies, university programs, private or other public agencies, and clinics or hospitals. With P.L. 99-457, those programs serving 3- through 5-year-olds have become the responsibility of state education agencies, although this agency may choose to allow contracting by public schools to entities other than themselves. Programs for infants and toddlers continue to be offered under a myriad of administrative structures.

Service delivery settings also differ widely. Programs may use a home-based, center-based, or a combination mode of delivery. The actual physical settings of center-based programs include public schools, hospitals, universities, day care settings, community preschool programs, churches, and private agencies.

At the preschool level, the recipient of the services of the ECSE program is most often the child. However, many programs also offer services for significant others, including parents, siblings, extended family members, and child care providers. At the birth through age 2 level, the focal recipient varies more widely, and may be the child, the parent, a parent-child dyad, or the total family, depending on the philosophy and history of the particular program (Meisels, 1989).

ECSE programs also differ from one another on at least 5 interlocking curricular and instructional dimensions (Dunst,

1985; Peterson, 1987): (1) the degree of structure in the learning activities; (2) the degree to which activities are individualized or group focused; (3) the degree to which the curriculum includes academics, developmental areas, readiness, experiential knowledge, or functional skills; (4) the theoretical model underlying and guiding all practices (e.g., Montessori, Piagetian, developmental, or behavioral); and (5) the degree to which activities are child-directed, teacher-directed, or both.

It is on these curricular and instructional dimensions that the differences in philosophy between programs grounded in different parent fields are clearest, since practice in one field grew from work with young children, and in the other from work with older individuals with disabilities. What is unique about ECSE is that the population is both young *and* special. Recent research with young children with special needs has led to new ways of thinking about curriculum and instruction for this population (Berkeley & Ludlow, 1989; Bricker & Veltman, 1990; Warren & Kaiser, 1988). The interaction between these 2 facets of the child (young and special), and the implications of that interaction for intervention, are critical. For young children, the most powerful settings for learning and development are those which support the child's self-initiated interactions and those which map new experiences onto what the child has already mastered (Bredekamp, 1987). From this perspective, young children must be provided with environments which elicit and support these interactions. Having a disability or delay, however, may upset the naturally occurring balance between child and environment (Walker & Crawley, 1983). Young children who are also special may need to be taught basic processes such as exploration and play that are usually assumed to be present in young children. More direct approaches may be required to teach the child basic skills (e.g., imitation) to use in interaction with the environment (Bailey, 1989). Thus, the individualization of intervention approaches as derived from special education, with careful assessment and analysis, and precise planning and use of environments and adult-child interactions, is also required (Bricker & Veltman, 1990). For early childhood special educators, the basic dilemma between developmental and direct instruction approaches will arise continuously as attempts are made to provide the appropriate balance between what the child can do and the support needed to foster more advanced interaction. The more multiple needs the child has, the more delicate this balance.

Many of the same programmatic attributes apply to both birth to 3 and preschool programs (Peterson, 1987). Although not as rich in history as services for the preschool population, there have been many programs for the younger age group, and in many cases these have operated under the same auspices as the preschool programs. Characteristics of best practice include individualization, a family focus, a curriculum that is both developmental and functional, transdisciplinary teaming, and interagency collaboration (Hanson & Lynch, 1989).

Karnes & Stayton (1988) sampled a variety of birth to 3 programs supported under the HCEEP program between 1981 and 1986. Results indicated that most early intervention services for birth to 3-year-olds were located in large cities, with a majority of the programs administered by universities. Services usually were begun at or fairly soon after birth, with the majority of

services provided to those with severe handicaps. The largest recipient group were those children and families of low socioeconomic status. Service delivery options were similar to the options provided to preschoolers, including home, center, and a combination, with a majority of the programs operating from a center. There appeared to be a great deal of flexibility regarding the frequency of services, with the most typical services provided 1 to 2 days per week. Finally, the theoretical orientations identified by the programs fell into 5 categories: developmental, behavioral, combination of developmental and behavioral, medical, and parent-child.

Two Early Themes in ECSE

Of the themes dominating the early childhood special education literature prior to the mid-1980s, 2 of the most common were the efficacy of early intervention (Dunst, 1986; Guralnick, 1988; Guralnick & Bennett, 1987; Shonkoff & Hauser-Cram, 1987; White & Casto, 1985), and the use of mainstreamed environments (Guralnick, 1978, 1981; Odom & McEvoy, 1988). Determining the effectiveness of early intervention is an important question. There are implications not only for public support and funding, but also for gaining knowledge to guide practice (Guralnick, 1988).

Early studies documented benefits for children who were delayed or at risk of delay due to environmental factors (Beller, 1979; Bronfenbrenner, 1975; Lazar & Darlington, 1982), children with established disabilities such as Down syndrome (Bidder, Bryant, & Gray, 1975; Guralnick & Bricker, 1987; Hanson, 1981, 1984b; Hayden & Dmitriev, 1975; Ludlow & Allen, 1979), and children who were multiply or severely handicapped (Bricker & Dow, 1980; Fredericks, Baldwin, Moore, Templeman, & Anderson, 1980; Hanson, 1985). The results of these studies appeared to support the following conclusions: (a) there are certain vulnerable periods in a child's development, especially within the first 3 years of life, during which intervention may be particularly powerful (Guralnick, 1989); (b) intervening at an early age may remediate a primary handicap or may prevent a secondary handicap from occurring (Hanson & Lynch, 1989); and (c) outcomes of early intervention services may improve the developmental status of the child (Hunt, 1979; Lazar & Darlington, 1982; Meisels, 1985; Schweinhart & Weikart, 1985). Some data indicated that children who had been in ECSE programs were more likely to outscore their peers on later intelligence test measures (Lazar & Darlington, 1982). Moreover, individuals who received educational and support services at an early age were less likely to need special education services at an older age, and were more likely to make positive contributions to society with less delinquency than those children who did not receive early education support (Schweinhart & Weikart, 1985; Schweinhart, Berrueta-Clement, Barnett, Epstein, & Weikart, 1985). Studies also suggested that children entering preschool programs earlier were less likely to need later, more costly, special education programs than those who either started later or never received early childhood special education (Barnett & Escobar, 1990; Garland, Stone, Swanson, & Woodruff, 1981; Schweinhart, Berrueta-Clement, Barnett, Epstein, & Weikart, 1985).

While these early efficacy studies were promising, they suffered from many methodological problems (Dunst & Rheingrover, 1981; Farran, 1990; Guralnick, 1988). There are many issues inherent in conducting efficacy research with young children with handicaps. At a minimum, issues arise with regard to the population, the treatment, and the outcome measures. As previously mentioned, there is vast diversity among children in early intervention. The multicategorical nature of ECSE, including the degree of the associated disability, adds variability to the population as well as to subject reliability (Guralnick, 1988). The diversity in program factors such as intensity, location, intervention recipient, duration of services, and theoretical model also adds variety to the treatment (Guralnick, 1988; Meisels, 1985), and it therefore is difficult to compare across studies. With regard to measurement, young children with special needs present many difficulties to the use of standardized measures (Fewell & Vadasy, 1987; Walker & Crawley, 1983). Moreover, some of the most commonly used outcome measures (e.g., IQ, achievement) may not only not be appropriate with this population (Meisels & Wasik, 1990), but also may not measure the most important child outcomes (Fewell & Vadasy, 1977; Hauser-Cram, 1990). Families of children with handicaps also have many needs and concerns which are addressed by early intervention; effects on families may be even more critical to the long-term outcome of the child than those directly addressing child needs (Bronfenbrenner, 1975). Finally, research designs employed in early studies have been questioned (Casto & Mastropieri, 1986; Dunst & Rheingrover, 1981; Dunst & Snyder, 1985), with most studies using variations of a pre-post approach.

In the early 1980s, in an effort to combine the knowledge available from these different sources, the results of all earlier studies were grouped together for the purpose of conducting meta-analytic studies (Casto & Mastropieri, 1986; Casto & White, 1984). The outcomes indicated that early intervention had few effects, and challenged two of the most widely held beliefs of the field: that parent involvement makes a difference, and that earlier is better. However, these meta-analytic studies have been criticized based on their "apples and oranges" approach: less than precise definitions and less than careful control of the variables used in grouping data (Dunst & Snyder, 1985; Strain & Smith, 1985). Subsequent, better controlled meta-analyses of the same data did in fact yield different, more positive results (Shonkoff & Hauser-Cram, 1987).

Efficacy research has changed in focus as researchers have begun to ask more precise questions: what works for whom, under what conditions, and toward what goals (Guralnick, 1988; Meisels, 1985). More recent studies, controlling on different subject characteristics such as degree of handicap, have yielded clearer results (Guralnick & Bricker, 1987; Infant Health and Development Project, 1990). Summaries of research examining the efficacy of services at the infant/toddler level also indicate that it is intervention directed toward the child alone that has yielded the most equivocal results (Simeonsson & Bailey, 1990). The one factor that best differentiates successful from unsuccessful early intervention with infants and toddlers is the degree to which family needs are addressed and family members have roles as central players in the early

intervention process (Guralnick, 1989; Shonkoff & Hauser-Cram, 1987). These results corroborate Bronfenbrenner's conclusion almost 2 decades ago that it is change in families which accounts for long-term change in children (1975). As a family-centered approach is implemented, questions will of necessity be broadened to focus on outcomes for families as well as for children and new methodology will be necessary (Bickman & Weatherford, 1986; Dokecki & Heflinger, 1989; Weiss & Jacobs, 1988).

A second theme prevalent prior to the mid-1980s was the issue of mainstreaming and its benefits for young children with special needs (Guralnick, 1978; Spodek, Saracho, & Lee, 1984). A key principle of P.L. 94-142 was that children with handicaps were to be educated with their normally developing peers to the greatest extent possible for each individual. The 3 issues receiving most attention with regard to young children included how to accomplish it administratively, whether it had benefits, and how to foster it within the classroom setting (Guralnick, 1978, 1982; Odom & McEvoy, 1988). Although mandated, mainstreaming of preschoolers with special needs has been difficult to achieve. Public schools traditionally have not provided early childhood programs for normally developing children under the age of 5, so that there often are no readily available settings into which children with special needs can be mainstreamed. Where mainstreaming has been achieved, it has occurred primarily by including children without handicaps in classes or settings for children with handicaps ("reverse mainstreaming") for the primary purpose of enhancing social interaction (McLean & Odom, 1987; Odom & McEvoy, 1988; Odom & Speltz, 1983; Turnbull & Blacher-Dixon, 1981). Public Law 99-457 and its accompanying Rules and Regulations reiterated the importance of mainstreaming, and encouraged alternative community placements as a possible means of achieving it. With regard to the second issue, it is clear that even given available peers, merely placing children with handicaps in settings with children without handicaps does not promote meaningful interactions (Guralnick, 1980; O'Connell, 1984; Odom & McEvoy, 1988; Snyder, Apolloni, & Cooke, 1977). There is considerable evidence that social interaction will not occur, nor will social skills be learned, without active teacher planning and participation, especially for children with moderate or severe handicaps (Blacher-Dixon, Leonard, & Turnbull, 1981; Cooke, Ruskus, Apolloni, & Peck, 1981; Guralnick, 1990; Stainback & Stainback, 1981; Strain & Kerr, 1981). There is evidence that when positive social interactions do occur, there are benefits for the children with disabilities (Cooke, Ruskus, Apolloni, & Peck, 1981; Jenkins, Speltz, & Odom, 1985) and for normally developing children as well (Cooke et al., 1981; Strain, Hoyson, & Jamieson, 1985). Families of both groups of children also view mainstreaming in a positive light (Blacher & Turnbull, 1983; Bricker & Bricker, 1976).

A large number of studies have addressed the issue of how to foster positive social interactions between children with and without disabilities (Odom & McEvoy, 1988; Strain & Kohler, 1988). One of the most common approaches is to teach or "coach" young children without handicaps to interact socially with their peers with handicaps (Odom & McEvoy, 1988; Odom & Strain, 1984). Strategies include manipulating proximity, using prompts and reinforcement, and teaching peer initiations (Odom & McEvoy, 1988). Thus, teachers must consciously employ strategies to foster interactions between children with handicaps and their peers (Guralnick, 1990; Odom, Hoyson, Jamieson, & Strain, 1985; Strain & Odom, 1986). Another component of this literature relates to the attitudes of teachers, peers, and other parents toward a child with handicaps (Guralnick, 1981). Planning for increased awareness and understanding by all key constituents is a key ingredient in the success of the actual implementation of integration.

Two factors indicate that mainstreaming will continue to be an important area of study. The first is the extent to which it is emphasized in P.L. 99-457. The second is the increasing number of state-funded public school programs for young children who do not have disabilities or delays, but who are at high risk of developing them: These programs have greatly enhanced the opportunities that will be available for mainstreaming. Another set of issues that will need to be addressed in the future is how this principle applies to work with neonates, infants and toddlers, as well as to work with families themselves.

PUBLIC LAW 99-457: SUPPORT FOR EARLY INTERVENTION

Events leading up to and resulting from the passage of P.L. 99-457 in 1986 forced a reexamination of many issues in ECSE. As a result, ECSE has become both more heterogeneous in who is served and in the resources brought to bear, and more tightly woven into a larger tapestry of practice from an array of early intervention fields including health and social services as well as education (Shonkoff & Meisels, 1990). Better articulation is occurring among disciplines and agencies serving different populations. Much new information is available with regard to the nature of early development, including that of young children who have disabilities or whose biological, birth, or environmental histories place them at risk (Hanson, 1984). ECSE also is increasingly grounded in its own body of knowledge (Jordan, Gallagher, Hutinger & Karnes, 1988; Meisels & Shonkoff, 1990; Odom & Karnes, 1988).

For young children with special needs and their families, P.L. 99-457 is the most significant piece of legislation ever passed (Report 99-860, 1986). Under this legislation and its accompanying Rules and Regulations (Federal Register, June, 1989), all states must provide a free, appropriate, public education for children with handicaps ages 3 through 5, or risk losing other portions of federal funding related to this population; this section of the law, Part B (Preschool Grants Program), amends Title II of P.L. 94-142. Thus, all provisions of 94-142 apply. Services for preschool children became mandatory in 1991–92 and are the responsibility of each state's department of education, and part of the special education system. The majority of P.L. 99-457, however, relates to establishing new state programs for infants and toddlers with handicaps from birth through 2 years of age. This section is referred to as Title I, or Part H (Program for Infants and Toddlers). This state program is permissive in nature, and, if the state chooses to participate, it is the responsibility of

the Governor of each state to put a structure in place (National Center for Clinical Infant Programs, 1989).

Public Law 99-457 amends Part B of P.L. 94-142 in 3 significant ways. First, a new category of developmental delay may be added if the state so chooses, so that eligibility for services based upon narrow categorical classifications is no longer required at the preschool level. If this new designation is used, the state must develop a definition for this population. While existing categories used under P.L. 94-142 do not have to be used, however, the new definition of developmental delay must nevertheless be in accord with federal categorical definitions ("Response to Pennsylvania," 1990), so that counts of eligible children still come to the federal level using these definitions. Thus, it is not yet clear whether this amendment will have any benefits in terms of overcoming current barriers to defining eligibility. A second way in which the amendment changes Part B is that whenever appropriate and to the extent desired by the parents, the IEP may include "parent counseling and training" as a related service. Although parent participation was a component of P.L. 94-142, Part B regulations emphasize and support direct services for parents. Third, variations in service delivery are affirmed as viable and desirable options by this amendment. Therefore, non-traditional service options such as community preschools, home based services, or flexible scheduling, among others, may be developed as options. However, there are many barriers to implementing these alternative service delivery models for 3 to 5-year-olds with special needs and their parents. Most existing programs have focused solely on the child and have employed a primarily center-based model. Personnel also have not been trained in family-based approaches or in providing consultation to alternative community settings. Finally, variations in service delivery may be restricted by existing funding patterns.

Rather than amending an existing section, Part H (birth through 2 years) of P.L. 99-457 adds a new section to P.L. 94-142, and contains provisions that differ fundamentally from Part B. Unlike Part B, Part H is not mandatory. Rather, financial incentives are included for those states wishing to provide services to infants and toddlers with handicaps and their families. This funding is meant to be used primarily as "glue" to bind together available public and private services. In congruence with the collaborative intent of this legislation, any state agency, not just the state department of education, may be designated as the lead agency. The lead agency in each state then must establish a State Interagency Coordinating Council (ICC) to serve as a mechanism to facilitate cross-agency collaboration: its functions are to assist the designated lead agency in developing state policy and implementation guidelines, and to serve as a state framework for interagency collaboration. The ICC must be composed of parents, public or private providers of early intervention, a state legislature representative, a personnel preparation provider, and representatives from any state agency providing funding for early intervention services to infants and toddlers with handicaps and their families. In formulating the statewide system, the ICC must develop policy related to 14 specific components named in the legislation, and bring this to fruition over a 5-year period. Therefore, in any state choosing to participate under this legislation, a comprehensive, coordinated plan across agencies was in place or well on the way by 1991–92.

A second way in which Part H differs significantly from Part B and the rest of P.L. 94-142 is that services are not defined as "education plus related services," but rather as an array of services which may be brought to bear for any individual child and family unit. Services listed in the legislation include family training, counseling, and home visits; special instruction; speech pathology and audiology; occupational therapy; physical therapy; psychological services; case management services; medical services for diagnostic or evaluation purposes; and early identification, screening and assessment services as well as health services.

One of the first of the 14 Part H components to be addressed in each state has been the definition of eligibility to be used in providing services. Once eligibility is defined and accepted by the state as policy, the state must serve all eligible children. Therefore, the definition of eligibility is critical to all other aspects of state planning (Harbin, Gallagher, Lillie, & Eckland, 1990; Meisels & Wasik, 1990), influencing not only the number of children and families to be served, but also the cost of early intervention to the state (Barnett & Escobar, 1990). Eligibility estimates range considerably, depending on the criteria used (Meisels & Wasik, 1990). Infants and toddlers with established or diagnosed physical or mental conditions, or with developmental delays, must be included. However, each state may set its own criteria for defining developmental delay. Measurement issues are, if anything, even more difficult to solve with this age group than with preschoolers (Meisels, 1989). Thus, many states have chosen to include clinical judgment by a team of professionals as one criterion for determining eligibility (Harbin, Terry, & Daguio, 1989; Meisels & Wasik, 1990). At each state's discretion, it also may include populations of children who are at risk for delay or disability, based upon either biological or environmental factors. If included, appropriate definitions also must be developed for these groups. Criteria for biological risk, for example, might include low birth weight, a low Apgar score, or neonatal medical complications, whereas those for environmental risk might include child abuse, maternal age, or maternal drug addiction. Many issues related to establishing eligibility based on at-risk criteria have been identified (Meisels & Wasik, 1990).

Public Law 99-457 delineates 10 specific disciplines which may provide services: audiologists, nurses, nutritionists, occupational therapists, psychologists, physical therapists, physicians, social workers, special educators, and speech and language pathologists (P.L. 99-457: Sec. 672(2)), 1986); additional occupational categories may be added if needed. Two of the 14 components for which policy and implementation guidelines must be developed by each state relate to personnel: setting standards for early intervention personnel and proving a comprehensive system of personnel development. An important issue that each state must address in developing these components is the conflict between quality of training and a severe shortage of personnel in many of the disciplines that provide early intervention services (Bricker & Slentz, 1988; Bruder &

McLean, 1988; McCollum & Bailey, 1991; Yoder & Coleman, 1990).

Because of their pervasive importance in Part H, 2 particular aspects of the legislation have dominated the attention of early intervention professionals since the mid 1980s: professional teaming and collaboration, and a family focus for service delivery. These two themes reflect the philosophical foundations of P.L. 99-457, and are woven throughout the law and its accompanying Rules and Regulations (Meisels, 1989). In practice, they cannot be separated from one another, since families are viewed as partners on the early intervention team (Johnson, McGonigel, & Kaufmann, 1989).

The concept of collaboration pervades and undergirds the legislation. The provisions of the law supporting interprofessional collaboration are extensions of similar provisions in P.L. 94-142. However, P.L. 99-457 has gone beyond the concept of *multi*disciplinary as contained in P.L. 94-142 to stress *inter*disciplinary collaboration and case management: the clear intent of the formulators of the law was that someone be responsible for analyzing, synthesizing, and integrating information and recommendations into a single service plan (Harbin & McNulty, 1990). Collaboration is especially important when children and families have such diverse needs that no one discipline or agency has all of the resources or expertise needed to handle them (Fewell, 1983; Hanson & Lynch, 1989; Holm & McCartin, 1978; McNulty, 1986). At the agency level, P.L. 99-457 supports the development of a state system built on interagency collaboration, with the goal of coordinating, supplementing, and expanding existing services: at this level, collaboration influences the strength of decisions made about program structures and processes. At the program and family levels, interprofessional collaboration is meant to provide families with integrated rather than fragmented services (Audette, 1980; Nordyke, 1982; Rubin & Quinn-Curran, 1983), influencing decisions made about individual children and families. From the perspective of child and family, a system of collaboration among professionals not only is congruent with the natural processes of early development, but also is clearly more consumer friendly.

Two different but interrelated yardsticks, effectiveness and efficiency, support interprofessional collaboration as an essential component of early intervention systems. Interagency collaboration is intended to coordinate and integrate multiple services, with a positive effect on accessibility of services to families, as well as on elimination of duplicative services, allowing the shifting of state resources to fill gaps in the system (Harbin & McNulty, 1990). The yardsticks of efficiency and effectiveness support interdisciplinary as well as interagency collaboration. Services delivered by multiple professionals are difficult to coordinate and integrate (Golin & Ducanis, 1981; Holm & McCartin, 1978; Woodruff & McGonigel, 1988), and fragmentation may actually contribute to the stress already experienced by families. The effectiveness of each of these services also will be compromised (Harbin & McNulty, 1990), as contradictory, nonintegrated individual service plans lessen the impact of any one service.

Despite its obvious benefits, interprofessional collaboration is difficult to achieve, and, at both the interagency (McNulty,

1986) and interdisciplinary (Dyer, 1977) levels, presents a challenge to the early intervention field. Public Law 99-457 contains provisions to encourage collaboration at both levels, but it is left to practitioners and researchers to determine how it might be accomplished (Harbin & McNulty, 1990; McGonigel & Garland, 1988; United Cerebral Palsy National Collaborative Infant Project, 1976). There are several barriers. With regard to efficiency, there are significant gaps as well as duplications in services. At the agency level, 16 different programs in 7 different federal offices or agencies administer programs that affect young children with special needs and their families, and as many as 12 separate offices or agencies have been identified in states and local areas (Fraas, 1986; Meisels, et al, 1988). A 1979 study of federal agencies found the system to be so complex that neither consumers nor providers had a clear idea of how to access and make use of the resources available (Brewer & Kakalik, 1979).

Part H also differs significantly from other legislation in the emphasis given to family roles, and represents a change in perspective for federal policy related to children (Meisels, 1989; Winton & Bailey, 1990). The word "family" (or "families") appears 29 times in Part H of the legislation. This orientation was explicitly recognized in Executive Order 12606, as cited in the Rules and Regulations for Part H:

"Part H recognizes the unique and critical role that families play in the development of infant and toddlers who are eligible under this Part. It is clear, both from the statute and the legislative history of the Act, that the Congress intended for families to play an active, collaborative role in the planning and provision of early intervention services. Thus, these regulations...strengthen the authority and encourage the increased participation of parents in meeting the early intervention needs of their children." (Federal Register, 54 (119), June 22, 1989, p. 26309)

The legislation strengthens the roles of families at all levels of the early intervention system, from policy development to individual service delivery. It also stresses services that meet family needs related to supporting the child's development. The pervasiveness of the family orientation of the law is shown in Table 23–1, which summarizes provisions specifically addressing the relationships between families and the early intervention system. While unique in its explicitness, it should be noted that the family roles in this law extend concepts already contained in P.L. 94-142. Moreover, the emphasis on families in this law is but one manifestation of a larger family-centered movement within all human service fields including health (Shelton, Jeppson, & Johnson, 1987), social services (Friesen & Koroloff, 1990), and public education (Olson, 1990; Kagan & Zigler, 1987). Increased family involvement in schooling is occurring throughout the educational system, with families playing governance, management, and direct service, as well as recipient, roles.

Family involvement in early intervention is not a new idea. On the contrary, it has been a required component of projects funded since 1968 under the Handicapped Children's Early Education Program (HCEEP); it is in these settings that family involvement programs for families of young children with special needs have been most strongly advocated and most extensively

TABLE 23–1. Overview of Family Provisions in Public Law 99-457

State Early Intervention System

Parents of handicapped infants or toddlers or handicapped children aged 3 through 6...as members of the Interagency Coordinating Council (Sec. 682 (b)(1))

Procedures to ensure that (see p. 1149) (Sec. 676 (b)(9)(D))

Training provided under CSPD relates specifically to...assisting families in enhancing the development of their children, and in participating fully in the development and implementation of IFSPs (Rules & Regulations, Sec. 303.360)

Local Early Intervention System

Timely, comprehensive, multidisciplinary evaluation of...and the needs of the families to appropriately assist in the development of the handicapped infant/toddler (Sec. 676 (b)(3))

Individual family service plan including case management services...(Sec. 676 (b)(4))

Family training, counseling and home visits (Sec. 672 (2)(E)(8))

Procedural safeguards including timely resolution of complaints, right to confidentiality, opportunity to examine records, prior notice, full information

Individual Family Service Plan

Developed by a multidisciplinary team, including the parent or guardian...(Sec. 677 (a)(2))

Statement of family strengths and needs relating to enhancing the development of the family's handicapped infant or toddler (Sec. 677 (d)(2))

Outcomes expected to be achieved for...the family (Sec. 677 (d)(4))

Specific services necessary to meet the unique needs of the family (Sec. 677 (d)(4))

Name of case manager from profession most immediately relevant to...family's needs (Sec. 677 (b)(6))

Evaluated once a year and reviewed at 6-month intervals (or more often where appropriate) (Sec. 677 (b))

(Abstracted from P. L. 99-457 and from Rules and Regulations for Part H)

developed. It was only with the passage of P.L. 94-142 in 1976, however, that parents were guaranteed the right to be active participants in selecting special education and related services for their children. Although P.L. 94-142 contained provisions to guarantee this right, subsequent research indicated that participation tended to be either passive, or, at the other extreme, adversarial (Turnbull & Turnbull, 1986). Neither extreme promoted the parent-professional collaboration intended. Research on parent involvement activities indicated that participation was low, suggesting that the approaches used were not meeting families' needs (Winton, 1986). These outcomes led professionals to reassess their own approaches to providing parent involvement opportunities (Foster, Berger, & McLean, 1981; Turnbull & Turnbull, 1986). The family orientation of P.L. 99-457 offers a new set of lenses through which to view the development and delivery of services for young children with special needs. As early intervention professionals have worked toward translating the family focus on P.L. 99-457 into practice, the field has moved beyond the letter of the law to address its intent.

THE THEME OF THE 1990S: A FAMILY-CENTERED APPROACH TO EARLY INTERVENTION

Public Law 99-457 has brought a comprehensive family perspective to virtually every aspect of early intervention service delivery. In contrast to service systems in which families must fit into prescribed service patterns, they increasingly are viewed as the central figures in service delivery, selecting services to address their unique individual characteristics and needs (Turnbull & Turnbull, 1986). Intertwined with these changes is a movement within the helping professions toward an empowerment model of service delivery (Dunst & Trivette, 1988a), with the goal of supporting clients in confronting and meeting their own needs, using the help available to them from a variety of service delivery systems and informal networks (Trivette, Dunst, Deal, Hamer, & Propst, 1990). The latter work has guided the "how" of emerging definitions of best practice in relation to families and early intervention services.

For early childhood special educators, this new view of families represents the latest step in an evolutionary process describing the relationships between families and service delivery programs and professionals (Bricker, 1989; Silber, 1989; Simeonsson & Bailey, 1990; Turnbull & Turnbull, 1986), mirroring changes in basic values and knowledge with regard to families, their rights, and their roles in child development (Hanson, Lynch, & Wayman, 1990; Kaiser & Hemmeter, 1989; Turnbull & Turnbull, 1986; Winton, 1986). This evolution is characterized in Table 23–2, which clearly indicates that the trend in early childhood special education, and more broadly in all early intervention services, has turned (and is turning) from child-oriented toward family-oriented services. The terms used to describe successive stages in this process are instructive: family involvement; family-focused; family-centered. The term "family-guided" already has been suggested as the next, as yet undefined, step in this evolution (Bricker, 1989), and is totally congruent with emerging views on how programs and professionals are being encouraged to work with families. This shift in orientation calls for basic changes not only in how services are organized and delivered (Dunst & Trivette, 1988a; Johnson, McGonigel, & Kaufmann, 1989), but in the values, knowledge, and skills of professionals (Bailey, 1988, 1989; McCollum & Thorp, 1988; Trivette, Deal, & Dunst, 1986; Trivette, Dunst, Deal, Hamer, & Propst, 1990; Winton, 1988a; Winton & Bailey, 1990).

Why Focus on Families?

Families of children with special needs have needs of their own which may differ from, or be in addition to, those of parents whose children are developing normally; an increased family focus is justifiable on these grounds alone (Beckman-Bell, 1981; Mahoney, O'Sullivan, & Dennebaum, 1990). As already noted, however, emerging efficacy research also provides a strong rationale for family-based services.

A family orientation to the provision of early intervention services is firmly grounded in what is known about the nature of young children and families (Filler & Olson, 1990). Of particular relevance to a family approach is expanding knowledge of the influence of early social and physical environments on the development of young children. All aspects of early development are imbedded within social contexts (Clarke-Stewart, 1973; Goldberg, 1977; Uzgiris, 1981; Bruner, 1974). Early relationships with caregivers provide the most powerful component of the developmental environments of very young children (Sameroff & Chandler, 1975), and in a variety of ways set the stage for later development. The quality of early attachment relationships, in particular, appears to have implications for later emotional and cognitive development (Bristol & Gallagher, 1982; Silber, 1989). It is within this context that young children develop working models of themselves and others that are carried forward into later relationships (Fraiberg, Adelson, & Shapiro, 1980). Security and predictability in these earliest relationships serve as filters for the young child's encounters with the physical environment, influencing motivation and exploration as well as the breadth and types of experiences to which the child has access (Goldberg, 1977). Thus, the quality

TABLE 23–2. The Evolution of Family Roles in Early Intervention

Focus	Professional Role	Family Role	Related Terminology
Child	Develop, implement child's program	Bystander or not present	Parent involvement
Child	Explain child's needs and services to parents develop, implement child's program	Cooperate in IEP development	Parent involvement
Child	Develop, implement child's program; teach parents to conduct home activities/therapies	Cooperate in IEP development; conduct home activities/therapies	Parent involvement
Family	Develop, implement program that considers and addresses needs of family system	Share strengths and needs; participate in activites to promote strength of family unit	Family focused
Family	Collaborate with family to develop, manage, and implement program that supports and empowers family unit	Collaborate with interventionists to develop, manage, and implement identified array of services	Family centered

of early relationships may influence not only the experiences available to the young child, but the typical ways in which the child learns to engage the environment.

The importance of the family as the primary context for early development and learning, and therefore for early intervention, also is evident from research on parent-child interactions. A number of aspects of early dyadic interactions appear to influence the development of emotional and motivational systems (Belsky, Goode, & Most, 1980; Goldberg, 1977; Tronick & Gianino, 1986), communication and language (Holdgrafer & Dunst, 1986; Ratner & Bruner, 1977), and cognition (Bornstein, 1989; Bruner, 1974; Goldberg, 1977; Rogoff & Gardner, 1984). Social interactions, therefore, are important mediators of the development of competence (Field, 1983; Goldberg, 1977; Kaye, 1982). As the infant develops, the physical environment assumes an increasingly salient and independent role, making unique and specific contributions to the early development of competence (Wachs, 1985; Wachs & Gruen, 1982). The caregiver's role in mediating the child's interaction with the physical environment also is critical (Rogoff & Gardner, 1984).

Young children with special needs bring to interactions with their social and physical environments characteristics and behaviors that may interfere with their experience of these environments, and therefore with their optimal development (Walker & Crawley, 1983). As social partners, they present unique challenges to others' ability to engage them in pleasurable and developmentally supportive interaction (Als, 1982; Crawley & Spiker, 1983; Dunst, 1985; Emde, Katz, & Thorpe, 1978; Field, 1980, 1983; Fraiberg, 1974, 1975; Jones, 1977; Lockman, 1986; Richard, 1986; Rosenberg & Robinson, 1988; Walker, 1982). Mutual attachment, therefore, may be more difficult to achieve (Blacher, 1984; Cardone & Gilkerson, 1989; Spieker, 1986). Interactions with the physical environment may be affected as well (Landry & Chiapeski, 1989; Lockman, 1986; McCune & Ruff, 1985): not only may there be direct interference from the child's disability, but also direct interference from the child's greater reliance on others for access to environmental experiences (Kopp & Shaperman, 1973). Mutual enjoyment between the child and other family members, as well as opportunities for the development of competence in the physical environment, therefore may be in jeopardy.

A transactional model of early development (Sameroff & Chandler, 1975; Sameroff & Friese, 1990) has proven useful for understanding the mutual influences between conditions in the child and environment, as well as their relation to developmental outcomes (Frey, Fewell, & Vadasy, 1989). During the early childhood period, non-optimal conditions in either child or environment may have powerful effects. The relative influence of the environment may be even more powerful when the child is at biological risk due to birth circumstances (Sameroff & Chandler, 1975). In cases of established biological risk, where the environment might be expected to have less influence on ultimate outcomes, development nevertheless appears to be optimized by sensitive matching of social and physical environments by caregivers and professionals to the child's current and emerging characteristics and abilities. For example, with early intervention, the decline in developmental trajectory typical of children with Down syndrome may be slowed substantially (Guralnick, 1989). Both social and physical environments can be adapted to achieve a better match (Hunt, 1961, 1979), and facilitating this match within all of the child's everyday social and physical environments is a primary purpose of early intervention (Bromwich, 1981; McCollum, 1992).

Family systems theory is a second body of knowledge which has provided a rationale of fundamental importance for a family-focused approach to early intervention (Barber, Turnbull, Behr, & Kerns, 1988; Turnbull & Winton, 1984). All families serve basic nurturing, economic and educational functions, and progress through certain normative life events such as marriage, births of children, and school entry. As social systems, families are characterized by the presence of sub-units (e.g., husband-wife, mother-child), with linkages among sub-units such that the characteristics of each influence every other. The characteristics of each member and sub-unit also are influenced by the history of that member and unit, and by change over time. Families are imbedded within larger layers of social systems (e.g., extended family, community, cultural group) (Bronfenbrenner, 1977, 1986). Influence and interaction among these layers also influence family functioning. As systems, families achieve a dynamic balance that addresses their needs, taking into account the particular life circumstances to which they are adapting. Family functioning at any point in time will reflect this system in interaction with current role demands, as well as with stresses and supports operating both from within the family system and from without (Dunst, Trivette, & Deal, 1988).

A family systems perspective has been invaluable for understanding families in which there is an individual member with disabilities, as well as for understanding the responses of families to early intervention systems and professionals. The birth of a child with a disability is a non-normative event in the life of a family, and has implications for all components of family functioning (Beckman, 1983; Featherstone, 1981; Hanson & Hanline, 1990; Crnic, Friedrich, & Greenberg, 1983). Individual differences in systems and in the individuals who comprise them will mediate the extent and type of impact that the child with disabilities may have on the family (Dunst & Trivette, 1986; Frey, Vadasy, & Fewell, 1989; Hodapp, 1988). Typical family functions (such as employment) may be interrupted, or developmental stages prolonged (Hanson & Lynch, 1989). There may be increased financial burdens such as those due to repeated hospitalizations of the child. Extreme modifications in family roles may be necessary (Bristol & Gallagher, 1982). The child's disability also may interfere with the development of interaction and attachment, and thence with the caregiver's self-esteem and sense of efficacy as a parent (McCollum, 1992; Silber, 1989). Hence, as a component within the family system, the child's disability will affect not only the child, but other aspects of the system as well (Bernheimer, Young, & Winton, 1983). New knowledge, skills, and resources may be required to adapt to these new demands and to fulfill family functions (Hanson & Lynch, 1989). Addressing these needs within the ecological contexts of each family is an important responsibility of the early intervention system, and provides a powerful rationale for a family-focused approach.

Family-Centered Early Intervention

The content and organization of family-centered service delivery are based on the young child's being imbedded both physically and psychologically within a family. At a very basic level, early intervention must reflect an understanding of the important direct and mediating roles that families play in early development (Barber et al, 1988; Frey, Fewell, & Vadasy, 1989). Family systems theory indicates that the ecology of the family will serve as a mediator of all intervention efforts (Turnbull & Turnbull, 1986). Systems theory also informs our understanding of families' goals for their child and for themselves, and of why and how families choose to participate in early intervention efforts with their child (Trivette, Dunst, Deal, Hamer, & Propst, 1990). Further, the family environment, by definition, provides the most important context for early intervention. Children will be best served when early intervention is imbedded within the contexts of the family system and its everyday environments, as these will determine not only what is important, but also the characteristics of the intervention that are optimal for that child and family (Dunst & Trivette, 1990; McGonigel & Garland, 1988). Removing the young child from this context for the purposes of intervention may work contrary to the natural processes most supportive of early development.

Systems theory also implies that family functions other than meeting the child's early intervention needs may take priority: a knowledge of family priorities therefore will not only inform understanding, but will direct the focus of attention toward what is salient to the family at that point in its history (Bailey, 1987; Dunst & Trivette, 1988b; Winton, 1988b; Winton & Bailey, 1988). The actual focus of any individual family's program thus may be described on a continuum of proximal to distal with regard to the child with disabilities (Bailey, Winton, Rouse, & Turnbull, 1990), even though the broad purpose is to increase the probability that the child will experience social and physical environments optimally supportive of early development. Intervention may, for example, include supporting the family in meeting its basic needs for housing and employment. Families also may want access to resources such as counseling, respite care, or assertiveness training. More directly related to their child, they may want training in the use of adaptive equipment, instructions in carrying out the recommendations of a therapist, or support in modifying their interaction skills to better match those of their child (Mahoney, 1988; McCollum & Stayton, 1985). Families must have current, sound information in order to make informed decisions, including information about the disability, knowledge of relevant laws, knowledge of available community services, and information about financial resources (Ziegler, 1989).

Although there is general agreement that family needs are a critical focus for early intervention services, to date there is lack of agreement on how to determine family goals and services (Bailey et al, 1990), or which areas of family life are appropriate to include (Bailey et al, 1990; Simeonsson & Bailey, 1990). There are substantial theoretical differences among programs with regard to who is the focus of intervention and where to set the parameters for intervention aimed at family or parent-child, rather than child, goals (Stern-Bruschweiler &

Stern, 1989). Nevertheless, from these new viewpoints, early intervention that is not family centered is a contradiction in terms.

How systems and individuals go about helping families is a second component of the family-centered approach. It is the family that provides the child's most powerful environment and which must martial, coordinate, and apply resources (including those from the early intervention program) in support of the child's development. Thus, collaboration between families and professionals is essential for program effectiveness. Because families are highly individual in their priorities, concerns, characteristics, and resources, approaches to assessment and planning must be developed to match early intervention efforts to each family's individuality (Hanson & Lynch, 1989). Methods used to work with families must be carefully selected to match and support a family-centered philosophy (Bromwich, 1990).

Each child and each family manifest a unique combination of needs, characteristics, and ecological contexts. The cornerstone of the family provisions of P.L. 99-457 is the Individual Family Service Plan (IFSP), which not only explicitly acknowledges this individuality, but also provides a framework and process to guide interaction among participants (Dunst & Trivette, 1989; Johnson, McGonigel, & Kaufmann, 1989). The IFSP process embodies changes in both why and how professionals communicate with families (Winton & Bailey, 1990). The goal is to support, not supplant, the natural roles of families. The IFSP is designed to guide professionals and each family with whom they work through the process of defining their own individual relationships and purposes.

To establish this partnership, it has been necessary to define new collaborative models for professional-parent interactions (Bailey, 1987; Bailey & Simeonsson, 1988; Bailey, Winton, Rouse, & Turnbull, 1990; Trivette, Dunst, Deal, Hammer, & Propst, 1990; Winton & Bailey, 1990) and to apply these not only to the IFSP process but to all interactions. Literature on social support and helping behaviors have contributed enormously to early intervention practice within the family systems framework (Dunst, Trivette, & Deal, 1988). Dunst and his colleagues have identified two organizing principles to guide professionals in their interactions with families. The first, "enablement," refers to creating the opportunity and means by which families can display their current abilities and acquire new ones, thereby maintaining or acquiring a sense of control over their own lives. The second, "empowerment," refers to professional behaviors that allow families to attribute positive changes in their lives to their own abilities and actions. These two overriding principles have implications at a systems level in determining how professional and family roles are defined at different steps of the early intervention process, and at an individual professional level in determining the behaviors that professionals use with families.

Dunst also has provided a set of 12 guidelines to characterize helping relationships most likely to strengthen families as well as to promote the acquisition of new competencies (Dunst & Trivette, 1988a; Dunst, Trivette, & Deal, 1988). At the systems level, these guidelines suggest that families be seen as voluntary consumers of program services, choosing the level and the nature of the program's involvement in their lives

(McGonigel & Garland, 1988). They also suggest that enhancing the family's own resources and ability to access them will yield the most beneficial and longest-lasting outcomes. Familial and social networks are crucial as sources of assistance and help, influencing the extent to which the family is able to adapt to new demands and develop ways of meeting its needs and achieving its goals (Dunst, Trivette, & Cross, 1986). Informal support systems appear to be more powerful in achieving this end than are formal systems (such as early intervention programs), and therefore must be viewed as an important part of early intervention (Dunst & Trivette, 1990). To reinforce this view, Dunst (1985) defined early intervention as an aggregate of child and family support that impacts directly and indirectly on parent, family, and child functioning. Social support, including emo-

tional, psychological, informational, instrumental, and material aid, comprises a major form of intervention (Dunst, Trivette, & Deal, 1988). One important goal of the early intervention program is to facilitate the family's efforts to identify and access its own resources, with the purpose of strengthening the family system as a whole.

At the individual level, principles for interacting with families as defined by Johnson, McGonigel, and Kaufmann (1989) mirror the same perspectives: convey respect; offer assistance when requested; provide information so families can make informed choices; obtain information needed to make program planning decisions; offer an array of services so families have a choice; and match services to families' own priorities, concerns, and circumstances. Table 23–3 illustrates how one early inter-

TABLE 23–3 "We Altered Our Process": An Example from Project Dakota

Our Old Way	Our New Way
1. Each staff plans their assessment of their developmental area	1. Planning the assessment a. The facilitator asks the parents for priorities/questions they wish to be addressed in the assessment. b. The facilitator then shares this with other team members, who help plan a comprehensive assessment that focuses on issues raised by parents.
2. Each staff conducts their own assessment, if possible, at a time when a parent can be present, so that each assessment can be discussed with the parent. This usually means 3–5 assessment sessions.	2. The assessment is scheduled when parents can be present; only the facilitator and parent interact with the child while other staff on the team observe and record.
3. Each staff summarizes their assessment findings, and recommends goals and treatment settings at a meeting of staff. These staff recommendations are shared with parents at the planning conference.	3. Immediately after the assessment, the parents share what they have seen during the assessment: their child's strengths, interests, motivators, challenges, and frustrations. Staff elaborate on these observations and together with parents produce a complete and practical description of the child.
4. Parents are asked if they agree with the recommended goals or have other goals. Staff share their recommended approaches to meet each goal.	4. Next, parents draw conclusions or state what seems most important to them regarding the child and define major goals. Staff supplement as needed and accepted. (Typically there are 2 to 4 goals.)
5. To carry out the goals, a primary service setting is chosen by the team. (Generally, either home-based for infants and toddlers or center-based for preschoolers.)	5. To carry out the goals, strategies are created that draw upon adults and children encountered by the child throughout the day. Supporting contact with non-delayed peers is given priority.
6. Each staff provide direct service or consult in their area of development as needed, and plan the center-based services; parents reinforce goals in activities at home.	6. The facilitator consults with family and community resources to carry out the plan, and provides direct service when it cannot be accomplished through consultation. The other staff remain accountable for their area of expertise through active consultation with the facilitator.
7. Every few months the plan is reviewed and sometimes revised; reassessment and planning occur annually.	7. The plan is reviewed and revised monthly; reassessment and planning occur every four months.
8. Success is meassured by: • child progress	8. Success is measured by: • child progress • parent satisfaction • staff responsiveness to parents' needs and concerns • integrated versus segregated service settings and contact with non-delayed peers • parents' gains in knowledge, skill and confidence in describing their child, setting goals, and carrying out strategies.

From: Project Dakota Outreach.

vention program redefined its basic practices to better support the staff's philosophy about families. Such efforts are directed toward supporting the intent, rather than just the letter, of P.L. 99-457, and are grounded in the values and thinking that undergirded its development. All early intervention programs must engage in similar self-analysis as services are developed to reflect a family-centered perspective. As such approaches become more common, early intervention programs also must begin to develop ways of evaluating the extent to which their practices reflect this philosophy (Dokecki & Heflinger, 1989; Mahoney, O'Sullivan, & Dennebaum, 1990; McCollum, in press Weiss & Jacobs, 1988).

To date, little attention has been given to the implications of a family-centered philosophy for providing services at the preschool level. Where preschoolers with special needs are served in home-based programs, new practices being developed with infants and toddlers appear to be directly applicable. Family-oriented services may be more difficult to achieve in center-based group programs, regardless of the age of the children involved. The 2 major principles of (a) family as primary decision maker and (b) family as active participant will of necessity require different programmatic structures from those that have evolved in birth through age 3 programs, which more commonly serve parent and child together, utilizing the parent-child relationship as part of the intervention process.

LOOKING FORWARD

In all fields serving young children with special needs and their families, P.L. 99-457 has spurred rethinking of approaches and directions. Although technically an amendment to a special education law (P.L. 94-142), and therefore administered through the Department of Education's Office of Special Education Programs, this legislation and the work that has supported its development and implementation are much broader in scope. In recognition of the diverse characteristics and needs of the children and families to be served, P.L. 99-457 represents a conscious blending of principles from many areas of research and practice: education, child development, family systems theory, health and medicine, psychological and social services, and organizational theory (Simeonsson & Bailey, 1990). These converging sources of knowledge and practice have enriched the understanding of every early intervention discipline, and their combination is bringing about major changes in the way that early intervention services are delivered (Meisels & Shonkoff, 1990). A major challenge for the near future will be to merge the practice of multiple bureaucracies into a coherent system of services that can be applied with a range of young children with special needs and their families.

Thus far, most of the attention of policy makers has been given to services for infants and toddlers and their families through the implementation of Part H of the legislation. However, it is clear that the formulators of P.L. 99-457 intended that the same family and collaborative principles woven through-

out Part H also extend throughout the birth through 5 age range (Dokecki & Heflinger, 1989). Early childhood specialists increasingly are advocating a seamless delivery system in which the values and practices of Part H are filtered upward into services at the preschool level as well (Division for Early Childhood, 1990; "Response to Pennsylvania," 1990). Some states that prior to 1986 had developed policy to achieve seamlessness have reported that the differences between Parts H and B have created barriers to continuity ("Four States Respond," 1990). This may be a particular problem in states in which Part H is administered by a lead agency other than the state education agency, which has responsibility for Part B. Thus, there are many issues yet to be addressed. It is clear that this work will affect all areas of the service system (Hodgkinson, 1989).

As one part of the early intervention system, early childhood special education is changing almost daily as professionals of many disciplines work together to develop an integrated early intervention system. The developing identity of ECSE is evident from the increasing attention being given to professional certification for early childhood special educators (McCollum, McCartan, McLean, & Kaiser, 1989), universities offering personnel preparation programs in this specialization (Bricker & Slentz, 1988), and new textbooks supporting the coursework within these programs (e.g., Bailey & Simeonsson, 1988; Bailey & Wolery, 1984, 1992 Bricker, 1989; Hanson & Lynch, 1989; Safford, 1989; Thurman & Widerstrom, 1990). A number of specialized professional journals are now available (e.g., *Infants and Young Children, Journal of Early Intervention, Topics in Early Childhood Special Education*), and there is a 7,000 member professional organization (Division for Early Childhood, Council for Exceptional Children) whose sole focus is young children with special needs and their families. A great deal of attention has been given to defining personnel competencies needed to serve young children with special needs and their families (Bailey, 1989; McCollum, McCartan, McLean, & Kaiser, 1989; Thorp & McCollum, 1988), as well as to outlining characteristics of personnel preparation programs to develop these competencies (Fenichel & Eggbeer, 1990). This work is becoming increasingly important with full implementation of the legislation (McCollum & Bailey, 1991).

The next phase in the development of early childhood special education also will undoubtedly by characterized by change and diversity. The population being served is becoming increasingly heterogeneous in both child and family characteristics. As the theoretical foundations of early intervention and of early childhood special education continue to mature (Meisels & Shonkoff, 1990), and as the legislation is brought to full implementation, professionals will continue to engage in research and discussion to ensure that practice matches what is known and valued about children and families. Issues currently facing the field will continue to be of concern and new ones will arise. Within the blending among disciplines, early childhood special educators will continue to reexamine their own contributions to early intervention, and to redefine their roles as part of this larger fabric.

References

Allen, K. (1984). Federal legislation and young handicapped children. *Topics in Early Childhood Special Education, 4*(1), 9–18.

Allen, K. E., Holm, V. A., & Schiefelbusch, R. L. (Eds.) (1978). *Early intervention: A team approach*. Baltimore, MD: University Park Press.

Als, H. (1982). The unfolding of behavioral organization in the face of a biological violation. In E. Z. Tronick (Ed.), *Social interchange in infancy: Affect, cognitive and communication* (pp. 125–160). Baltimore, MD: University Park Press.

Audette, H. (1980). Interagency collaboration: The bottom line. In J. O. Elder & P. R. Magrab (Eds.), *Coordinating services to handicapped children* (pp. 25–44). Baltimore, MD: Paul H. Brookes.

Bailey, D. B. (1987). Collaborative goal-setting with families: Resolving differences in values and priorities for services. *Topics in Early Childhood Special Education, 7*(2), 59–71.

Bailey, D. B. (1988). Rationale and model for family assessment in early intervention. In D. B. Bailey & R. J. Simeonsson (Eds.), *Family assessment in early intervention* (pp. 1–26). Columbus, OH: Merrill.

Bailey, D. B. (1989). Issues and directions in preparing professionals to work with young handicapped children and their families. In J. J. Gallagher, R. M. Clifford, & P. Trohanis (Eds.), *Policy implementation for children with special needs* (pp. 97–130). Baltimore, MD: Paul Brookes.

Bailey, D., & Simeonsson, R. (1988). Assessing the needs of families with handicapped infants. *The Journal of Special Education, 22*, 117–127.

Bailey, D. B., Winton, P. J., Rouse, L. & Turnbull, A. P. (1990). Family goals in infant intervention: Analysis and issues. *Journal of Early Intervention, 14*, 5–26.

Bailey, D. B., & Wolery, M. (1984). *Teaching infants and preschoolers with handicaps*. Columbus, OH: Charles E. Merrill.

Bailey, D. B., & Wolery, M. (1992). *Teaching infants and preschoolers with disabilities*. New York: Macmillan.

Barber, P. A., Turnbull, A. P., Behr, S. K., & Kerns, G. M. (1988). A family systems perspective on early childhood special education. In S. L. Odom & M. B. Karnes (Eds.), *Early intervention for infants and children with handicaps: An empirical base* (pp. 179–198). Baltimore, MD: Paul H. Brookes.

Barnett, S. W., & Escobar, C. M. (1990). Economic costs and benefits of early intervention. In S. J. Meisels & J. P. Shonkoff (Eds.), *Handbook of early childhood intervention* (pp. 560–582). New York: Cambridge University Press.

Beckman-Bell, P. (1981). Child-related stress in families of handicapped children. *Topics in Early Childhood Special Education, 1*(3), 45–53.

Beller, E. (1979). Early intervention programs. In J. D. Osofsky (Ed.), *Handbook of infant development* (pp. 852–894). New York: Wiley.

Belsky, J., Goode, M., & Most, R. K. (1980). Maternal stimulation and infant exploratory competence: Cross-sectional, correlational and experimental analyses. *Child Development, 51*, 1168–1178.

Berkeley, T. R., & Ludlow, B. L. (1989). Toward a reconceptualization of the developmental model. *Topics in Early Childhood Special Education, 9*(3), 51–66.

Bernheimer, L. P., Young, M. S., & Winton, P. J. (1983). Stress over time: Parents with young handicapped children. *Developmental and behavioral pediatrics, 4*, 177–181.

Bickman, L., & Weatherford, D. L. (1986). *Evaluating early intervention programs for severely handicapped children and their families*. Austin, TX: Pro-Ed.

Bidder, R., Bryant, G., & Gray, O. (1975). Benefits to Down's syndrome children through training their mothers. *Archives of Disease in Childhood, 50*, 383–386.

Blacher, J. (1984). Attachment and severely handicapped children: Implications for intervention. *Developmental and Behavioral Pediatrics, 5*, 178–183.

Blacher, J., & Turnbull, A. (1983). Are parents mainstreamed? A survey of parent interactions in the mainstreamed preschool. *Education and Training of the Mentally Retarded, 18*, 10–16.

Blacher-Dixon, J., Leonard, J., & Turnbull, A. (1981). Mainstreaming at the early childhood level: Current and future perspectives. *Mental Retardation, 19*(5), 235–241.

Bloom, B. (1964). *Stability and change in human characteristics*. New York: Wiley.

Bornstein, M. C. (1989). Maternal responsiveness: Characteristics and consequences. *New Directions for Child Development, 43*. San Francisco: Jossey-Bass.

Bredekamp, S. (1987). *Developmentally appropriate practice in early childhood programs serving children birth through age 8, expanded edition*. Washington, DC: National Association for the Education of Young Children.

Brewer, G. D., & Kakalik, J. S. (1979). *Handicapped children: Strategies for improving services*. New York: McGraw-Hill.

Bricker, D. D. (1989). *Early intervention for at-risk and handicapped infants, toddlers, and preschool children*. Palo Alto, CA: VORT.

Bricker, D. D., & Dow, M. G. (1980). Early intervention with the young severely handicapped child. *Journal of the Association for the Severely Handicapped, 5*, 130–142.

Bricker, D., & Slentz, K. (1988). Personnel preparation: Handicapped infants. In M. C. Wang, M. C. Reynolds, & H. J. Walberg, (Eds.), *Handbook of special education: Research and practice* (Vol. 3, pp. 319–345). Elmsford, New York: Pergamon Press.

Bricker, D., & Veltman, M. (1990). Early intervention programs: Child-focused approaches. In S. J. Meisels & J. P. Shonkoff (Eds.), *Handbook of early childhood intervention* (pp. 373–399). New York: Cambridge University Press.

Bricker, W., & Bricker, D. (1976). The infant, toddler, and preschool research and intervention Project. In T. D. Tiossem (Ed.), *Intervention strategies for high-risk infants and young children* (pp. 545–572). Baltimore, MD: University Park Press.

Bristol, M. M., & Gallagher, J. J. (1982). A family focus for intervention. In Ramey, C. & Trohanis, P. (Eds.), *Finding and educating the high-risk and handicapped infant* (pp. 137–161). Baltimore, MD: University Park Press.

Bromwich, R. M. (1981). *Working with parents and infants: An interactional approach*. Baltimore, MD: University Park Press.

Bromwich, R. M. (1990). The interaction approach to early intervention. *Infant Mental Health Journal, 11*(1), 66–69.

Bronfenbrenner, U. (1975). Is early intervention effective? In B. Z. Friedlander, B. M. Sterritt, & G. E. Kirk (Eds.), *Exceptional Infant: Assessment and intervention* (Vol. 3, pp. 499–475). New York: Brunner/Mazel.

Bronfenbrenner, U. (1977). Toward an experimental ecology of human development. *American Psychologist, 32*, 513–531.

Bronfenbrenner, U. (1986). Ecology of the family as a context to human development: Research perspectives. *Developmental Psychology, 22*, 723–742.

Bruder, M. B., & McLean, M. (1988). Personnel preparation for infant interventionists: A review of federally funded projects. *Journal of the Division for Early Childhood, 12*(4), 299–305.

Bruner, J. (1974). The organization of early skilled action. In M. P. M. Richards (Ed.), *The integration of the child into a social world*, (pp. 167–184). New York: Cambridge University Press.

Cardone, I. A., & Gilkerson, L. (1989). Family administered neonatal activities: An innovative component of family-centered care. *Zero-to-three, 10*(1), 23–28.

Carran, N. (1984). *National directory of early childhood special education services, 1984*. Consortium of State Education Agency Early Childhood/Special Education Coordinators. Des Moines, IA: Department of Public Instruction.

Casto, G., & Mastropieri, M. (1986). The efficacy of early intervention programs: A meta-analysis. *Exceptional Children, 52*, 417–424.

Casto, G., & White, K. (1984). The efficacy of early intervention programs with environmentally at-risk infants. *Journal of Children in Contemporary Society, 17*, 37–48.

Clarke-Stewart, A. (1973). Interactions between mothers and their young children: Characteristics and consequences. *Monographs of the Society for Research in Child Development, 38* (6–7 Serial No. 153).

Cohen, S., Semmes, M., & Guralnick, M. (1979). Public Law 94-142 and the education of preschool handicapped children. *Exceptional Children, 45*, 279–285.

Cooke, L., Ruskus, J., Apolloni, T., & Peck, C. (1981). Handicapped preschool children in the mainstream: Background, outcomes, and clinical suggestions. *Topics in Early Childhood Special Education, 1*, 73–83.

Crawley, S., & Spiker, D. (1983). Mother-child interactions involving two-year-olds with Down syndrome: A look at individual differences. *Child Development, 54*, 1312–1323.

Crnic, K., Friedrich, W. N., & Greenberg, M. T. (1983). Adaptation of families with mentally retarded children: A model of stress, coping, and family ecology. *American Journal of Mental Deficiency, 88*, 125–138.

DeWeerd, J. (1977). Introduction. In J. Jordan, A. Hayden, M. Karnes, & M. Wood (Eds.), *Early childhood education for exceptional children: A handbook of ideas and exemplary practices* (pp. 1–7). Reston, VA: Council for Exceptional Children.

Division for Early Childhood. (1987). *Position statements and recommendations related to P.L. 99-457 and other federal and state early childhood policies*. Reston, VA: Council for Exceptional Children.

Division for Early Childhood. (1990). *Statement of the International Division for Early Childhood of The Council for Exceptional Children to the Congress of the United States with respect to reauthorization of Part H and amendments to Part B of the Education of the Handicapped Act regarding services to children from birth to age six years*. Reston, VA: Council for Exceptional Children.

Dokecki, P. R., & Heflinger, C. A. (1989). Strengthening families of young children with handicapping conditions: Mapping backward from the "street level." In J. J. Gallagher, P. L. Trohanis, & R. M. Clifford (Eds.), *Policy implementation and P.L. 99-457: Planning for young children with special needs* (pp. 59–84). Baltimore, MD: Paul H. Brookes.

Dunst, C. J. (1985). Communicative competence and deficits: Effects on early social interactions. In E. T. McDonald & D. L. Gallagher (Eds.), *Facilitating social-emotional development in multiply-handicapped children* (pp. 93–140). Philadelphia, PA: Michael C. Prestegord.

Dunst, C. J. (1986). Overview of the efficacy of early intervention programs. In L. Bickman & D. Weatherford (Eds.), *Evaluating early intervention programs for severely handicapped children and their families* (pp. 79–148). Austin, TX: Pro-Ed.

Dunst, C. (1986, March). *The qualities of high quality preschool programs*. Paper presented at the first annual Oregon Early Intervention Conference, Eugene, OR.

Dunst, C., & Rheingrover, R. (1981). An analysis of the efficacy of infant intervention programs with organically handicapped children. *Evaluation and Program Planning, 4*, 287–323.

Dunst, C., & Snyder, S. W. (1985). A critique of the Utah State University early intervention meta-analysis research. *Exceptional Children, 53*, 269–276.

Dunst, C. J., & Trivette, C. M. (1986). Looking beyond the parent-child dyad for the determinants of maternal styles of interaction. *Infant Mental Health Journal, 7*(1), 69–80.

Dunst, C. J., & Trivette, C. M. (1988a). A family systems model of early intervention with handicapped and developmental at-risk children. In D. R. Powell (Ed.), *Parent education as early childhood intervention: Emerging directions in theory, research and practice* (pp. 131–179). Norwood, NJ: Ablex.

Dunst, C. J., & Trivette, C. M. (1988b). Determinants of parent and child interactive behavior. In K. Marfo (Ed.), *Parent-child interaction and developmental disabilities: Theory, research and intervention* (pp. 3–31). New York: Praeger.

Dunst, C. J., & Trivette, C. M. (1989). An enablement and empowerment perspective of case management. *Topics in Early Childhood Special Education, 8*(4), 87–102.

Dunst, C., & Trivette, C. (1990). Assessment of social support in early intervention programs. In S. Meisels & J. P. Shonkoff (Eds.), *Handbook of early childhood intervention* (pp. 326–349). New York: Cambridge University Press.

Dunst, C., Trivette, C., & Cross, A. (1986). Mediating influences of social support: Personal, family and child outcomes. *American Journal of Mental Deficiency, 91*, 403–417.

Dunst, C., Trivette, C., & Deal, A. (1988). *Enabling and empowering families*. Cambridge, MA: Brookline Books.

Dyer, W. G. (1977). *Team building: Issues and alternatives*. Reading, MA: Addison-Wesley.

Education of the Handicapped (pp. 3–4). (1990 November 7) Washington, DC: Author.

Emde, R., Katz, E. & Thorpe, J. (1978). Emotional expression in infancy: II. Early deviations in Down's syndrome. In M. Lewis & L. Rosenblum (Eds.), *The development of affect* (pp. 351–360). New York: Plenum.

Farran, D. C. (1990). Effects of intervention with disadvantaged and disabled children: A decade review. In S. J. Meisels & J. P. Shonkoff (Eds.), *Handbook of early childhood intervention* (pp. 501–539). New York: Cambridge University Press.

Featherstone, H. (1981). *A difference in the family: Living with a disabled child*. New York: Penguin Books.

Federal Register. (June 22, 1989). *Early intervention programs for infants and toddlers with handicaps: Final regulations*. Vol. 54, No. 119.

Fenichel, E. S., & Eggbeer, L. (1989). Educating allies: Issues and recommendations in the training of practitioners to work with infants, toddlers and their families. *Zero to Three, 10*(1), 1–7.

Fewell, R. (1983). The team approach to infant education. In S. G. Garwood & R. Fewell (Eds.), *Educating handicapped infants: Issues in development and intervention* (pp. 299–322). Rockville, MD: Aspen.

Fewell, R. R., & Vadasy, P. F. (1987). Measurement issues in studies of efficacy. *Topics in Early Childhood Special Education, 7*(2), 885–896.

Field, T. (1980). Interactions of high-risk infants: Quantitative and qualitative differences. In S. B. Sawin, R. C. Hawkins, L. O. Walker, & J. H. Penticuff (Eds.), *Exceptional infant: Psychosocial risks in infant-environment transactions* (Vol. 4, pp. 10–143). New York: Brunner/Mazel.

Field, T. (1983). High risk infants "have less fun" during early interactions. *Topics in Early Childhood Special Education, 3*, 77–87.

Filler, J. (1983). Service models for handicapped infants. In S. G. Garwood & R. Fewell (Eds.), *Educating handicapped infants: Issues in development and intervention* (pp. 369–386). Rockville, MD: Aspen.

Filler, J., & Olson, J. (1990). Early intervention for disabled infants, toddlers and preschool age children. In R. Gaylord-Ross (Ed.), *Issues and research in special education* (Vol. 1, pp. 82–109). New York: Teachers College Press.

Foster, M., Berger, M., & McLean, M. (1981). Rethinking a good idea: A reassessment of parent involvement. *Topics in Early Childhood Special Education, 1*, 55–65.

Four States Respond to Infant, Preschool Programs (1990, November). *Education of the Handicapped, 16*(23), 3–6.

Fraas, C. J. (1986). *Preschool programs for the education of handicapped children*. Washington, DC: Senate Subcommittee on the Handicapped, and Congressional Research Service.

Fraiberg, S. (1974). Blind infants and their mothers: An examination of the sign system. In M. Bullowa (Ed.), *Before speech: The beginnings of interpersonal communication* (pp. 149–169). New York: Cambridge University Press.

Fraiberg, S. (1975). The development of human attachments in infants blind from birth. *Merrill-Palmer Quarterly, 21*, 315–334.

Fraiberg, S., Adelson, E., & Shapiro, V. (1980). Ghosts in the nursery: A psychoanalytic approach to the problem of impaired infant-mother relationships. In S. Fraiberg (Ed.), *Clinical studies in infant mental health* (pp. 146–196). New York: Basic Books.

Fredericks, H., Baldwin, V., Moore, W., Templeman, T., & Anderson, R. (1980). The teaching research data-based classroom model. *Journal of the Association for the Severely Handicapped, 5*(3), 211–223.

Frey, K., Fewell, R. R., & Vadasy, P. (1989). Parental adjustment and changes in child outcome among families of young handicapped children. *Topics in Early Childhood Special Education, 8*(4), 38–57.

Friesen, B. J., & Koroloff, N. M. (1990). Family-centered services: Implications for mental health administration and research. *Journal of Mental Health Administration, 17*(1), 13–25.

Garbarino, J. (1990). The human ecology of early risk. In S. J. Meisels & J. P. Shonkoff (Eds.), *Handbook of early childhood intervention* (pp. 78–96). New York: Cambridge University Press.

Gallagher, J. (1984). Policy analyses and program implementation. *Topics in Early Childhood Special Education, 4*(1), 43–53.

Gallagher, J., Trohanis, P., & Clifford, R. (1989). (Eds.). *Policy implementation and P.L. 99-457*. Baltimore MD: Paul Brookes.

Garland, C., Stone, N., Swanson, J., & Woodruff, G. (Eds.) (1981). *Early intervention for children with special needs and their families*. Monmouth, OR: Western States Technical Assistance Resource (WESTAR).

Garwood, S. G. & Fewell, R. (1983). *Educating handicapped infants: Issues in development and intervention*. Rockville, MD: Aspen.

Gilkerson, L., Gorski, P. & Panitz, P. (1990). Hospital-based intervention for preterm infants and their families. In S. Meisels & J. Shonkoff (Eds.), *Handbook of early childhood intervention* (pp. 78–96). New York: Cambridge University Press.

Goldberg, S. (1977). Social competence in infancy: A model of parent-infant interaction. *Merrill-Palmer Quarterly, 23*(3), 163–177.

Golin, A. K. & Ducanis, A. J. (1981). *The interdisciplinary team*. Rockville, MD: Aspen.

Greenspan, S. (1990). Comprehensive clinical approach to infants and their families. In S. Meisels & J. Shonkoff (Eds.), *Handbook of early childhood intervention* (pp. 150–172). New York: Cambridge University Press.

Guralnick, M. J. (1978). *Early intervention and the integration of handicapped and nonhandicapped children*. Baltimore, MD: University Park Press.

Guralnick, M. (1980). Social interactions among preschool children. *Exceptional Children, 46*(4), 248–253.

Guralnick, M. J. (1982). Mainstreaming young handicapped children. In B. Spodek (Ed.), *Handbook of research in early childhood education* (pp. 456–500). New York: Free Press.

Guralnick, M. J. (1988). Efficacy research in early childhood intervention programs. In S. L. Odom & M. B. Karnes (Eds.), *Early intervention for infants and children with handicaps: An empirical base* (pp. 75–88). Baltimore, MD: Paul Brookes.

Guralnick, M. J. (1989). Recent developments in early intervention efficacy research: Implications for family involvement in P.L. 99-457. *Topics in Early Childhood Special Education, 9*(3), 1–17.

Guralnick, M. J. (1990). Social competence and early intervention. *Journal of early intervention, 14*(1), 3–14.

Guralnick, M. J., & Bennett, F. C. (1987). *The effectiveness of early intervention for at-risk and handicapped children*. New York: Academic Press.

Guralnick, M. J., & Bricker, D. (1987). The effectiveness of early intervention for children with cognitive and general developmental delays. In M. Guralnick & F. Bennett (Eds.), *The effectiveness of early intervention for at-risk and handicapped children* (pp. 115–173). New York: Academic Press.

Halpern, R. (1990). Community-based early intervention. In S. Meisels & J. Shonkoff (Eds.), *Handbook of Early Childhood Intervention* (pp. 469–498). New York: Cambridge University Press.

Hanson, M. (1981). Down's syndrome children: Characteristics and intervention research. In M. Lewis & L. Rosenblum (Eds.), *The uncommon child* (pp. 83–114). New York: Plenum.

Hanson, M. J. (1984a). *Atypical infant development*. Baltimore, MD: University Park Press.

Hanson, M. J. (1984b). The effects of early intervention. In M. J. Hanson (Ed.), *Atypical infant development* (pp. 385–406). Baltimore, MD: University Park Press.

Hanson, M. (1985). An analysis of the effects of early intervention services for infants and toddlers with moderate and severe handicaps. *Topics in Early Childhood Special Education, 5*(2), 36–51.

Hanson, M. J., & Hanline, M. F. (1990). Parenting a child with a disability: A longitudinal study of parental stress and adaptation. *Journal of Early Intervention, 14*(3), 234–248.

Hanson, M. J. & Lynch, E. W. (1989). *Early intervention: Implementing child and family services for infants and toddlers who are at-risk or disabled*. Austin, TX: Pro-Ed.

Hanson, M. J., Lynch, E. W., & Wayman, K. I. (1990). Honoring the cultural diversity of families when gathering data. *Topics in Early Childhood Special Education, 10*(1), 112–131.

Harbin, G., Gallagher, J. J., Lillie, T., & Eckland, J. (1990). *Status of states' progress in implementing Part H of P.L. 99-457: Report #2*. Chapel Hill, NC: Carolina Policy Studies Program, University of North Carolina at Chapel Hill.

Harbin, G., & McNulty, B. (1990). Policy implementation: Perspectives on service coordination and interagency cooperation. In S. Meisels & J. Shonkoff (Eds.), *Handbook of early childhood intervention* (pp. 700–721). New York: Cambridge University Press.

Harbin, G. L., Terry, D., & Daguio, C. (April, 1989). *Status of the states' progress toward developing a definition for developmentally delayed as required by P.L. 99-457, Part H*. Chapel Hill, NC: Carolina Policy Studies Program, University of North Carolina.

Harvey, J. (1977). The enabling legislation: How did it all begin? In J. Jordan, A. Hayden, M. Karnes, & M. Wood (Eds.), *Early childhood education for exceptional children: A handbook of ideas and exemplary practices* (pp. 1–7). Reston, VA: Council for Exceptional Children.

Hauser-Cram, P. (1990). Designing meaningful evaluations of early childhood services. In S. Meisels & J. Shonkoff (Eds.), *Handbook of early childhood intervention* (pp. 583–602). New York: Cambridge University Press.

Hauser-Cram, P., Upshur, C. C., Krauss, M. W., & Shonkoff, J. P. (1988). Implications of Public Law 99-457 for early intervention services for infants and toddlers with disabilities. *Social Policy Report, 3*(3), 1–16.

Hayden, A., & Dmitriev, V. (1975). The multidisciplinary preschool program for Down's syndrome children at the University of Washington Model Preschool Center. In B. Z. Friedlander, B. M. Sterritt, & G. E. Kirk (Eds.), *Exceptional infant: Assessment and intervention* (Vol. 3, pp. 193–221). New York: Brunner/Mazel.

Hodapp, R. M. (1988). The role of maternal emotions and perceptions in interactions with young handicapped children. In K. Marfo (Ed.), *Parent-child interaction and developmental disabilities: Theory, research and intervention* (pp. 32–46). New York: Praeger.

Hodgkinson, H. L. (1989). *The same client: The demographics of education and the service delivery systems*. Washington, DC: Institute for Educational Leadership, Center for Demographic Policy.

Holdgrafer, G., & Dunst, C. J. (1986). Communicative competence: From research to practice. *Topics in Early Childhood Special Education, 6*(3), 1–22.

Holm, V. A., & McCartin, R. E. (1978). Interdisciplinary child development team: Team issues and training in interdisciplinariness. In K. E. Allen, V. A. Holm, & R. L. Schiefelbusch (Eds.), *Early intervention: A team approach* (pp. 97–122). Baltimore, MD: University Park Press.

Hunt, J. M. (1961). *Intelligence and experience*. New York: Ronald Press.

Hunt, J. M. (1979). Psychological development: Early experience. In M. R. Rosenzweig & L. W. Porter (Eds.), *Annual review of psychology* (Vol. 30, pp. 103–143). Palo Alto, CA: Annual Reviews.

Infant Health and Development Program. (1990). Enhancing the outcomes of low-birth-weight, premature infants. *Journal of the American Medical Association, 263*(22), 3035–3042.

Jenkins, J., Speltz, M., & Odom, S. (1985). Integrating normal and handicapped preschoolers: Effects on child development and social interaction. *Exceptional Children, 52*, 7–18.

Johnson, B., McConigel, M., & Kaufmann, R. (1989). *Guidelines and recommended practices for the individualized family service plan*. Chapel Hill, NC: NEC*TAS.

Jones, O. (1977). Mother-child communication with prelinguistic Down's Syndrome and normal infants. In H. Schaffer (Ed.), *Studies in mother-infant interactions: Proceedings of the Loch Lomond Symposium* (pp. 379–402). London: Academic Press.

Jordan, J., Gallagher, J., Hutinger, P., & Karnes, M. (1988). *Early childhood special education: Birth to three*. Reston, VA: Council for Exceptional Children.

Jordan, J., Hayden, A., Karnes, M., & Wood, M. (1977). *Early childhood education for exceptional children: A handbook of ideas and exemplary practices*. Reston, VA: Council for Exceptional Children.

Kagan, S. L., & Zigler, E. F. (Eds.). (1987). *Early schooling: The national debate*. New Haven: Yale University Press.

Kaiser, A., & Hemmeter, M. (1989). Value-based approaches to family intervention. *Topics in Early Childhood Special Education, 8*(4), 72–86.

Karnes, M. B., & Stayton, V. D. (1988). Model programs for infants and toddlers with handicaps. In J. B. Jordan, J. J. Gallagher, P. L. Hutinger, & M. B. Karnes (Eds.), *Early childhood special education: Birth to three* (pp. 67–108). Reston, VA: Council for Exceptional Children.

Karnes, M., & Zehrbach, R. (1977). Alternative models for delivering services to young handicapped children. In J. Jordan, A. Hayden, M. Karnes, & M. Wood (Eds.), *Early childhood education for exceptional children: A handbook of ideas and exemplary practices* (pp. 1–7). Reston, VA: Council for Exceptional Children.

Kaye, K. (1982). Organism, apprentice, and person. In E. Z. Tronick, (Ed.), *Social interchange in infancy: Affect, cognition and communication* (pp. 183–196). Baltimore, MD: University Park Press.

Kirk, S. (1958). *Early education of the mentally retarded: An experimental study*. Urbana, IL: University of Illinois Press.

Kopp, C. D., & Shaperman, J. (1973). Cognitive development in the absence of object manipulation during infancy. *Developmental Psychology, 9*, 430.

Landry, S. H., & Chapieski, M. L. (1989). Joint attention and infant toy exploration: Effects of Down syndrome and prematurity. *Child Development, 60*, 103–118.

Lazar, I., & Darlington, R. (Eds.). (1982). Lasting effect of early education: A report from the Consortium of Longitudinal Studies. *Monographs of the Society for Research in Child Development, 47*, (2–3, Serial No. 195).

Lessen, E., & Rose, T. (1980). State definitions of preschool handicapped populations. *Exceptional Children, 46*(6), 467–469.

Linder, T. W. (1983). *Early childhood special education: Program development and administration*. Baltimore, MD: Brookes.

Lockman, J. J. (1986). Perceptualmotor coordination in sighted infants: Implications for visually impaired children. *Topics in Early Childhood Special Education, 6*(3), 23–26.

Ludlow, J., & Allen, L. (1979). The effect of early intervention and preschool stimulus on the development of the Down's syndrome child. *Journal of Mental Deficiency Research, 23*, 19–44.

Mahoney, B. (1988). Enhancing the developmental competence of handicapped infants. In K. Marfo (Ed.), *Parent-child interaction and developmental disabilities: Theory, research, and intervention* (pp. 203–219). New York: Praeger.

Mahoney, G., O'Sullivan, P., & Dennebaum, J. (1990). Maternal perceptions of early intervention services: A scale for assessing family-focused intervention. *Topics in Early Childhood Special Education, 10*(1), 1–15.

McCollum, J. A. (1992). At the crossroad: Reviewing and rethinking interaction coaching. In K. Marfo (Ed.), *Early intervention in transition* (pp. 147–176). New York: Praeger.

McCollum, J. A. (in press). Emerging practice in teacher education in early childhood special education. In P. L. Safford (Ed.), *Planning to prepare teachers of preschool age children with handicaps in Ohio*. Columbus, OH: Ohio State Board of Education.

McCollum, J. A., & Bailey, D. B. (1991). Developing comprehensive personnel systems: Issues and alternatives. *Journal of Early Intervention, 15*(1), 57–65.

McCollum, J. A., McLean, M., McCartan, K., & Kaiser, C. (1989). Recommendations for certification of early childhood special educators. *Journal of Early Intervention, 13*(3), 195–212.

McCollum, J. A., & Stayton, V. (1985, Spring). Infant/parent interaction: Studies and intervention guidelines based on the SIAI model. *Journal of the Division for Early Childhood*, 125–135.

McCollum, J. A., & Stayton, V. (1988). Gaze patterns of mothers and infants as indicators of role integration during play and teaching with toys. In K. Marfo (Ed.), *Mental handicap and parent-child interaction: Theory, research and intervention* (pp. 47–63). New York: Praeger.

McCollum, J. A., & Thorp, E. K. (1988). Training of infant specialists: A look to the future. *Infants and Young Children, 1*(2), 55–65.

McCune, L., & Ruff, H. A. (1985). Infant special education: Interactions with objects. *Topics in early childhood special education, 5*(3), 59–68.

McGonigel, M., & Garland, C. (1988). The individualized family service plan and the early intervention team: Team and family issues and recommended practices. *Infants and Young Children, 1*(1), 10–21.

McLean, M., & Odom, S. (1987). *Least restrictive environment and social integration for young children with handicaps*. Division for Early Childhood White Paper. Reston, VA: Council for Exceptional Children.

McNulty, B. A. (1986). Leadership and policy strategies for interagency planning: Meeting the early childhood mandate. In J. J. Gallagher, P. L. Trohanis, & R. M. Clifford (Eds.), *Policy implementation (P.L. 99-457): Planning for young children with special needs* (pp. 147–167). Baltimore, MD: Paul H. Brookes.

Meisels, S. J. (Ed.). (1979). *Special education and development: Perspectives on young children with special needs*. Baltimore, MD: University Park Press.

Meisels, S. (1985). The efficacy of early intervention: Why are we still asking these questions? *Topics in Early Childhood Special Education, 5*(2), 1–12.

Meisels, S. J. (1989). Meeting the mandate of Public Law 99-457: Early childhood intervention in the nineties. *American Journal of Orthopsychiatry, 59*(3), 451–460.

Meisels, S. J., Harbin, G., Modigliani, K., & Olson, K. (1986). Formulating optimal state early childhood intervention policies. *Exceptional Children, 55*, 159–165.

Meisels, S. J., & Shonkoff, J. P. (Eds.) (1990). *Handbook of early childhood intervention*. New York: Cambridge University Press.

Meisels, S. J., & Wasik, B. A. (1990). Who should be served: Identifying children in need of early intervention services. In S. J. Meisels & J. P. Shonkoff (Eds.), *Handbook of early childhood intervention* (pp. 605–632). New York: Cambridge University Press.

National Center for Clinical Infant Programs. (1989). *The intent and spirit of P.L. 99-457: A Sourcebook*. Washington, DC: Author.

Nordyke, N. S. (1982). Improving services for young, handicapped children through local, interagency collaboration. *Topics in Early Childhood Special Education, 2*, 63–72.

O'Connell, J. (1984). Preschool integration and its effects on social interactions of handicapped and nonhandicapped children: A review. *Journal of the Division for Early Childhood, 8*, 38–48.

Odom, S., Hoyson, M., Jamieson, B., & Strain, P. (1985). Increasing handicapped preschoolers' peer social interactions: Cross-setting and component analysis. *Journal of Applied Behavior Analysis, 18*(1), 3–16.

Odom, S. L., & Karnes, M. B. (1988). *Early intervention for infants and children with handicaps: An empirical base*. Baltimore, MD: Paul H. Brookes.

Odom, S., & McEvoy, M. (1988). Integration of young children with handicaps and normally developing children. In S. Odom & M. Karnes (Eds.), *Early intervention for infants and children with handicaps: An empirical base* (pp. 241–267). Baltimore, MD: Brookes.

Odom, S., & Speltz, M. (1983). Program variations in preschools for handicapped and nonhandicapped children: Mainstreamed vs. integrated special education. *Analysis and Intervention in Developmental Disabilities, 3*, 89–104.

Odom, S., & Strain, P. (1984). Peer-mediated approaches to increasing children's social interaction: A review. *American Journal of Orthopsychiatry, 54*, 544–557.

Olson, L. (1990, April). Parents as partners: Redefining the social contract between families and schools. *Education Week, 4*, 17–24.

Peterson, N. (1987). *Early intervention for handicapped and at-risk children: An introduction to early childhood special education*. Denver, CO: Love.

Public Law 99-457: Education of the handicapped act amendments of 1986. (1986). Washington, DC: U.S. Government Printing Office.

Ratner, N. & Bruner, J. (1977). Games, social exchange and the acquisition of language. *Journal of Child Language, 5*, 391–401.

Report 99-860 (1986, September). Washington, DC: U.S. House of Representatives.

Response to Pennsylvania Questions on Implementing a Birth through Five Early Intervention Program. (1990, June). *Early Childhood Reporter, 1*(6), 11–12.

Richard, N. B. (1986). Interactions between mothers and infants with Down Syndrome: Infant characteristics. *Topics in Early Childhood Special Education, 6*(3), 54–71.

Rogoff, B., & Gardner, W. (1984). Adult guidance of cognitive development. In B. Rogoff & J. Lave (Eds.), *Everyday cognition: Its development in social context* (pp. 95–116). Cambridge, MA: Harvard University Press.

Rosenberg, S. A., & Robinson, C. C. (1988). Interactions of parents with their young handicapped children. In S. L. Odom & M. B. Karnes, (Eds.), *Early intervention for infants and children with handicaps: An empirical base* (pp. 159–178). Baltimore, MD: Paul H. Brookes.

Rubin, S., & Quinn-Curran, N. (1983). Lost, then found: Parents' journey through the community service maze. In M. Seligman (Ed.), *The family with a handicapped child* (pp. 63–94). New York: Grune & Stratton.

Safford, P. L. (1989). *Integrated teaching in early childhood: Starting in the mainstream*. White Plains, NY: Longman.

Sameroff, A. J., & Chandler, M. J. (1975). Reproductive risk and the continuum of caretaking casualty. In F. D. Horowitz (Ed.), *Review of child development research* (Vol 4, pp. 187–244). Chicago: University of Chicago Press.

Sameroff, A. J., & Fiese, B. H. (1990). Transactional regulation and early intervention. In S. J. Meisels & J. P. Shonkoff (Eds.), *Handbook of early childhood intervention* (pp. 119–149). New York: Cambridge University Press.

Schweinhart, L., Berrueta-Clement, J., Barnett, W., Epstein, A., & Weikart, D. (1985). Effects of the Perry Preschool Program on youths through age 19: A summary. *Topics in Early Childhood Special Education, 5*(2), 26–35.

Schweinhart, L., & Weikart, D. (1985, April). Evidence that good early childhood programs work. *Phi Delta Kappan*, 545–553.

Scott, K. G. & Carran, D. T. (1985). The future of early childhood special education: A perspective on prevention. In J. J. Gallagher & B. B. Weiner (Eds.), *Alternative futures in special education* (65–80). Reston, VA: Council of Exceptional Children.

Seitz, V., & Provence, S. (1990). Caregiver-focused models of early intervention. In S. Meisels & J. Shonkoff (Eds.), *Handbook of early childhood intervention* (pp. 400–427). New York: Cambridge University Press.

Shelton, T., Jeppson, E., & Johnson, B. (1987). *Family-centered care for children with special health care needs*. Washington, DC: Association for the Care of Children's Health.

Shonkoff, J. P., & Hauser-Cram, P. (1987). Early intervention for disabled infants and their families—A quantitative analysis. *Pediatrics, 80*, 650–658.

Shonkoff, J. P., & Meisels, S. J. (1990). Early childhood intervention: The evolution of a concept. In S. Meisels & J. Shonkoff (Eds.), *Handbook of early childhood intervention* (pp. 3–32). New York: Cambridge University Press.

Silber, S. (1989). Family influences on early development. *Topics in Early Childhood Special Education, 8*(4), 1–23.

Simeonsson, R. J., & Bailey, D. B. (1990). Family dimensions in early intervention. In S. J. Meisels & J. P. Shonkoff (Eds.), *Handbook of early childhood intervention* (pp. 428–444). New York: Cambridge University Press.

Smith, B. (1984). Expanding the federal role in serving young special needs children. *Topics in Early Childhood Special Education, 4*(1), 33–42.

Snyder, L., Apolloni, T., & Cooke, T. (1977). Integrated settings at the early childhood level: The role of nonretarded peers. *Exceptional Children, 43*, 262–266.

Spieker, S. J. (1986). Patterns of very insecure attachment found in samples of high-risk infants and toddlers. *Topics in Early Childhood Special Education, 6*(3), 37–53.

Spodek, B., Saracho, O. N., & Lee, R. C. (1984). *Mainstreaming young children*. Belmont, CA: Wadsworth.

Stainback, W., & Stainback, S. (1981). A review of research on interaction between severely handicapped and nonhandicapped students. *Journal of the Association for the Severely Handicapped, 6*(3), 23–29.

Stern-Bruschweiler, N., & Stern, D. N. (1989). A model for conceptualizing the role of the mother's representational world in various mother-infant therapies. *Infant Mental Health Journal, 10*(3), 142–156.

Strain, P., Hoyson, M., & Jamieson, B. (1985). Normally developing preschoolers as intervention agents for autistic-like children: Effects on class deportment and social interaction. *Journal of the Division for Early Childhood, 9*, 105–115.

Strain, P., & Kerr, M. (1981). *Mainstreaming of children in schools: Research and programmatic issues*. New York: Academic Press.

Strain, P. S., & Kohler, F. W. (1988). Social skill intervention with young children with handicaps: Some new conceptualizations and directions. In S. L. Odom & M. B. Karnes (Eds.), *Early intervention for infants and children with handicaps* (pp. 129–144). Baltimore, MD: Brookes.

Strain, P., & Odom, S. (1986). Peer social initiations: Effective intervention for social skills development of exceptional children. *Exceptional Children, 52*(6), 543–551.

Strain, P., & Smith, B. (1985). A counter-interpretation of early intervention effects: A response to Casto & Mastropieri. *Exceptional Children, 53*, 260–265.

Swan, W. (1980). The handicapped children's early education program. *Exceptional Children, 47*(1), 12–16.

Thorp, E. K. & McCollum, J. A. (1988). Defining the infancy specialization in early childhood special education. In J. B. Jordan, J. J. Gallagher, P. L. Hutinger, & M. B. Karnes (Eds.), *Early childhood special education: Birth to three* (pp. 147–161). Reston, VA: Council for Exceptional Children.

Thurman, S. K., & Widerstrom, A. H. (1990). *Infants and young children with special needs: A developmental and ecological approach*. Baltimore, MD: Brookes.

Trivette, C. M., Deal, A., & Dunst, C. J. (1986). Family needs, sources of support, and professional roles: Critical elements of family systems assessment and intervention. *Diagnostique, 11*(3–4), 246–267.

Trivette, C. M., Dunst, C. J., Deal, A. G., Hamer, A. W., & Propst, S. (1990). Assessing family strengths and family functioning style. *Topics in Early Childhood Special Education, 10*(1), 16–35.

Tronick, E. Z., & Gianino, A. F. (1986). The transmission of maternal disturbance to the infant. In E. A. Tronick & T. Field (Eds.), *Maternal depression and infant disturbance* (pp. 5–11). San Francisco: Jossey-Bass.

Turnbull, A., & Blacher-Dixon, J. (1981). Preschool mainstreaming: An empirical and conceptual review. In P. Strain & M. Kerr (Eds.), *Mainstreaming children in schools* (pp. 71–100). New York: Academic Press.

Turnbull, A., Strickland, P., & Brantley, J. (1978). *Developing and implementing individualized education programs*. Columbus, OH: Merrill.

Turnbull, A., & Turnbull, H. (1986). *Families, professionals, and exceptionality: A special partnership*. Columbus, OH: Merrill.

Turnbull, A., & Winton, P. (1984). Parent involvement policy and practice: Current research and implications for families with young,

severely handicapped children. In J. Blacher (Ed.), *Severely handicapped young children and their families: Research in review* (pp. 377–397). New York: Academic Press.

Turnbull, H. (1986). Appropriate education and Rowley. *Exceptional Children, 52*(4), 347–352.

United Cerebral Palsy National Collaborative Infant Project. (1976). *Staff development handbook: A resource for the transdisciplinary process*. New York: United Cerebral Palsy Associations of America.

Uzgiris, I. C. (1981). Experience in the social context: Imitation and play. In R. L. Schiefelbusch & D. D. Bricker (Eds.), *Early language; Acquisition and intervention* (pp. 477–515). Baltimore, MD: University Park Press.

Wachs, T. D. (1985). Toys as an aspect of the physical environment: Constraints and nature of relationship to development. *Topics in Early Childhood Special Education, 55*(3), 31–46.

Wachs, T. D., & Gruen, G. (1982). *Early experience and human development*. New York: Plenum.

Walker, J. A. (1982). Social interactions of handicapped infants. In D. Bricker (Ed.), *Intervention with handicapped and at-risk infants: From research to application* (pp. 217–232). College Park, MD: University Park Press.

Walker, J. A., & Crawley, S. (1983). Conceptual and methodological issues in studying the handicapped infant. In S. G. Garwood & R. R. Fewell (Eds.), *Educating handicapped infants: Issues in development and intervention* (25–41). Rockville, MD: Aspen.

Warren, S. F., & Kaiser, A. P. (1988). Research in early language intervention. In S. L. Odom & M. B. Karnes (Eds.), *Early intervention for infants and children with handicaps: An empirical base* (pp. 89–108). Baltimore, MD: Paul Brookes.

Weiss, H. B., & Jacobs, F. H. (Eds.). (1988). *Evaluating family programs*. New York: Aldine de Gruyter.

White, K., & Casto, G. (1985). An integrative review of early intervention efficacy studies with at-risk children: Implications for the handicapped. *Analysis and Intervention in Developmental Disabilities, 5*, 7–31.

Winton, P. (1986). Effective strategies for involving families in intervention efforts. *Focus on Exceptional Children, 19*(2), 1–12.

Winton, P. J. (1988a). Effective communication between parents and professionals. In D. B. Bailey & R. J. Simeonsson (Eds.), *Family assessment in early intervention* (pp. 207–228). Columbus, OH: Merrill.

Winton, P. J. (1988b). The family-focused interview: An assessment measure and goal setting mechanism. In D. B. Bailey & R. J. Simeonsson (Eds.), *Family assessment in early intervention* (pp. 185–206). Columbus, OH: Merrill.

Winton, P. J., & Bailey, D. B. (1988). The family-focused intervention: A collaborative mechanism for family assessment and goal-setting. *Journal of the Division for Early Childhood, 12*(3), 195–207.

Winton, P. J., & Bailey, D. B. (1990). Early intervention training related to family interviewing. *Topics in Early Childhood Special Education, 10*(1), 50–62.

Woodruff, G., & McGonigel, M. J. (1988). Early intervention team approaches: The transdisciplinary model. In J. B. Jordan, J. J. Gallagher, P. L. Hutinger, & M. B. Karnes (Eds.), *Early childhood special education, 0–3* (163–182). Reston, VA: Council for Exceptional Children.

Yoder, D. E., & Coleman, P. L. (1990). Allied health personnel: Meeting the demands of Part H, Public Law 99-457. Chapel Hill, NC: Carolina Policy Studies Program, University of North Carolina.

Ziegler, M. (1989). A parent's perspective: Implementing P.L. 99-457. In J. J. Gallagher, P. L. Trohanis, & R. M. Clifford (Eds.), *Policy implementation and P.L. 99-457: Planning for young children with special needs* (85–96). Baltimore, MD: Paul H. Brookes.

Zigler, E., & Valentine, J. (1979). *Project Head Start: A legacy of the War on Poverty*. New York: Free Press.

·24·

THE EDUCATION OF LINGUISTICALLY AND CULTURALLY DIVERSE CHILDREN

Eugene E. García

UNIVERSITY OF CALIFORNIA, SANTA CRUZ

In recent years, the U.S. population has continued in a trend of ethnic and racial population diversification, particularly among its young and school-age children. With this increasing diversification, our young children, ethnic and racial minority children in particular, continue to be placed at risk in today's social institutions.

Let's consider the 3.5 million of 1989's 4-year-olds, who will move slowly through society's institutions—family, schools, and the workplace:

- Twenty-four percent of these four-year-olds live below poverty level. They are part of the nearly 11 million children in poverty under the age of 15. (One in five of all children live in poverty).

- One-third of these 4-year-olds are nonwhite. By the turn of the century, 40% of those under 6 years of age will be nonwhite, with half of these children speaking a language other than English when they enter their first day of school. Moreover, these children continue to live in racial isolation: 56% in 1966, 72% in 1986.

- Eighteen percent of today's 4-year-olds were born out of wedlock. (Twenty-one percent of today's four-year-old girls will become pregnant during their teens.)

- More than 45% will be raised by a single parent before they reach the age of 18; half will experience 1 or more family breakups.

- Fifty-five percent have mothers who work outside the home. By 1995, 70% of their mothers will work outside the home, most full time. (Hodgkinson, 1989).

Our future lies in understanding how a diverse population placed in contexts of vulnerability can achieve social, educational, and employment competence. It is in the best inter-ests of all of us for these vulnerable populations to succeed. Of course, this challenge begins directly for society within the framework of early childhood education.

This portrait of vulnerability has been a historic reality for children in the linguistic and cultural minority in the United States. Although the term "linguistic/cultural minority" is an educationally related identifier with little appreciation for the diverse groups it entails, it is quite evident that such identified populations—Hispanics (Mexican Americans, Puerto Ricans, Cubans, and other Latinos), Asians (Southeast Asians, Chinese, Filipinos), and so on—have been perceived by the majority society as linguistically/cognitively, socially, and educationally vulnerable because of their "Mexicanness," "Puerto Ricanness," or "minority-ness." Such a perception has led to a variety of reactive social and educational programs aimed at ridding this population of these "at-risk" characteristics. Table 24–1 attempts to summarize present data relevant to the Hispanic population in the United States by focusing on general demographic indicators, as well as the specific educational character and social indexes that mark this population as particularly vulnerable to U.S. institutions. It is quite evident, both independently and comparatively, that the plight of Hispanics and other such linguistic and cultural minorities in the United States is highly problematic and that attention must be directed to answering the following questions:

1. Why does this deplorable state of affairs exist?
2. What can be directly accomplished, educationally, to resolve this situation?

Recent theoretical and empirical contributions have redefined the nature of the Hispanic population's vulnerability, destroying both stereotypes and myths, and laying a foundation

TABLE 24–1. Hispanic Demographic Synthesis

I. General Demographic Character
A. Of the 18.8 million Hispanics in the continental United States, the following characterizes the population's ethnic diversity:

Country/Area of Origin	Number	Percent
Mexico	11.8 million	62.8
Puerto Rico	2.3 million	12.2
Central/South America	2.1 million	11.2
Cuba	1.0 million	5.3
Other	1.6 million	8.5

B. 82% of this Hispanic population is found in 8 states: Arizona (3%), California (31%), Colorado (3 %), Florida (6%), Illinois (4%), New Mexico (3 %), New York (11%), and Texas (20%).
C. Average age of this population is 25.1 years (compared to 32.6 years for the general population).
D. 200,000 Hispanics immigrate legally to the U.S. yearly—40% of all legal immigrants. (An estimated 200,000 Hispanics immigrate illegally.)
E. The Hispanic population grew by 61% from 1970 to 1980 compared to an 11% growth in the general population.
F. 11 million Hispanics report speaking Spanish in the home.
G. 7% of Hispanics live in metropolitan areas; 50% in central cities.

II. Education
A. 40% of Hispanics leave school prior to graduation (40% of these leaving do so by grade 10).
B. 35% of Hispanics are held back at least 1 grade.
C. 47% of Hispanics are over-aged at grade 12.
D. 85% of Hispanic students are in urban districts.
E. 70% of Hispanic students attend segregated schools (up 56% in 1956).
F. Hispanics are significantly below national norms on academic achievement tests or reading, math, science, social science and writing at grades 3, 7, and 11, generally averaging 1 to 2 grade levels below the norm. At grade 11, Hispanics average a grade 8 achievement level on these tests.

III. Indexes of "Vulnerability"
A. Median family income has fluctuated for Hispanics (1972—$18,880; 1982—$16,227; 1986—$19,995), remaining below non-Hispanics (1972—$26,261; 1982—$23,907; 1986—$30,321).
B. 29% of Hispanic families live below the poverty line, up from 21% in 1979. (10.2% of while families live below the poverty line.)
C. 905,000 (23%) of Hispanic families are maintained by a female head-of-household (up from 17% in 1970). 53% of these households live below the poverty line.
D. 50% of Hispanic women are in the labor force.
E. Hispanics are twice as likely to be born to an unmarried, teen mother compared to whites.
F. 56% of Hispanics are functionally illiterate compared to 46% for blacks and 16% for Whites.
G. 65% of Hispanics hold unskilled and semiskilled jobs compared to 35% of non-Hispanics.

Compiled from: Bureau of U.S. Census, 1984, 1987; *Change* (1988); Appleby, Langer, & Mullis (1988).

upon which new initiatives for this population can be an enhancing educational enterprise.

The following discussion is an attempt to provide an overview of these new contributions and understandings, with particular attention to linguistic/cognitive, social, and educational issues concerning the growing number of linguistic and cultural minority families and children in the United States. Particular emphasis will be placed on significant instructional issues and how an instructionally responsive and proactive stance with regard to these populations can lead to a more productive educational future.

Before addressing the above questions directly, it seems appropriate to frame this discussion in a broad theoretical continuum. At one end of this continuum, it is argued that addressing linguistic and culturally diverse populations calls for a deeper understanding of the interaction of a students' home culture and the prevailing school culture (Tharp, 1989). This "cultural difference" position, supported by a rich contribution of mostly ethnographic research, suggests that the educational failures of "diverse" student populations are related to the culture clash between home and school. Evidence for such a position comes from Boykin (1986) for African American students: Heath (1983) for poor white students; Wiesner, Gallimore, and Jordan (1988) for Hawaiian students; Vogt, Jordan, and Tharp (1987) for Navaho students; García (1988) for Mexican American students; and Rivera-Medina (1984) for Puerto

Rican students. In essence, these researchers have suggested that, without attending to the distinction between home and school culture, educational endeavors for these culturally distinct students is likely to fail. Theoretically, students do not succeed because the difference between school culture and home culture lead to an educationally harmful dissonance. Sue and Padilla (1986), directly enunciating this position, argue: "The challenge for educators is to identify critical differences between and within ethnic minority groups and to incorporate this information into classrooms practice" (p. 62).

On a large scale, the implementation of bilingual-bicultural education in the United States is an example of a widely implemented educational treatment in concert with this educational position. This education intervention is based on the notion that utilizing the student's home language coupled with cultural support in school will produce a positive academic difference (August and García, 1988). Whether such programs do produce accordingly has been the subject of an ongoing research debate during the last decade (Willig, 1986; Baker, 1990).

At the other extreme of this theoretical continuum lies the position that instructional programs must ensure the appropriate general principles of teaching and learning. The academic failure of any student rests on the failure of instructional personnel to implement what we know "works." Using the now-common research tool known as meta-analysis, Walberg (1986) has found robust indicators of instructional conditions that have academically significant effects across various conditions and student groups. Other reviews (Baden & Maehr, 1986; Bloom, 1984; Slavin, 1989) have articulated this same position. In this vein, a number of specific instructional strategies—including direct instruction (Rosenshine, 1986), tutoring (Bloom, 1984), frequent evaluation of academic progress (Slavin, Karweit, & Madden, 1989) and cooperative learning (Slavin, 1989)—have been particular candidates for the "what works with everyone" category. Implied in this "general principle" position is that the educational failure of "diverse" populations can be eradicated by the systemic and effective implementation of these general principles of instruction.

Clearly, these extreme positions are somewhat exaggerated. The "cultural compatibility" and "general principles" positions need not be incompatible in any attempt to address the educational circumstances of linguistically and culturally diverse students. But, at the base of any "new" discussion of instructional alternatives that may enhance the educational success of this historically unsuccessful student population, these distinctions prove useful as the following discussion of theoretical perspectives and empirical data indicates. Directly, the discussions point to a concern for a culturally compatible approach to the education of diverse populations.

LANGUAGE AND COGNITION

Bilingualism/Multilingualism as a "No-No"

Early, as well as more recent, literature addressing issues related to linguistically and culturally diverse children primar-

ily addresses their dual linguistic character. The exploration into this population's bilingual or multilingualism, however, has shifted dramatically in its theme. The early identification and study of bilingualism, particularly in young children, was aimed at uncovering how and why bilingualism might best be envisioned as a linguistic, intellectual, and academic liability. Much early work near the turn of the century concerning issues of immigration and intelligence indicated that bilingualism was a mental burden leading to decreased intellectual and linguistic functioning and, in turn, to low academic achievement (García, 1983; Hakuta, 1986; Smith, 1923). Bilingualism was even more recently perceived as a negative attribute to be at a minimum discouraged and, when possible, institutionally eliminated: "There can be no doubt that the child reared in a bilingual environment is handicapped in his language and intellectual growth. One can debate the issue as to whether speech facility in two languages is worth the consequent retardation," (Thompson, 1952, p. 367).

As Diaz (1983) documents, this early research—with its emphasis on exploring the relationship between bilingualism, intelligence, and school achievement—included subjects meeting only the criterion of "foreign" surnames; that is, such research often did not recognize the effects of immigrant status and linguistic ability, or psychoeducational test validity and reliability. The measures of intelligence and school achievement did not consider the constraints regarding the use of such measures on these linguistically and culturally different populations. Yet, as a result of such studies, conclusions constantly pointed to the negative relationship between bilingualism and intelligence, mobilizing a reactive educational establishment determined to rid all immigrants (and many native southwestern Hispanics) of this malady. Such efforts reached beyond the schooling context and into the homes of many Hispanics. For example, the Southwest Family Improvement Project, a cooperative venture between the federal, state, and private sectors, sent English-speaking civic volunteers into Spanish-speaking homes to instruct family members, particularly females, in how they might help their children learn English and eliminate use of Spanish (Gonzalez, in press).

Bilingualism/Multilingualism Revisited

Research in the last 2 decades has more clearly explored the relationship between bilingualism and specific aspects of linguistic and cognitive development. This more sophisticated research has concerned itself with distinct measures of language proficiency in each language, along with the utilization of more reliable and valuable psychometric measures of intelligence and cognition. What has emerged is a relatively consistent picture of linguistic and cognitive development quite opposite to the view held previously. Instead of concluding that bilingualism is a detriment, this new set of data suggests that, within the United States' linguistically diverse populations, bilingualism is not a linguistic liability. Rather, higher degrees of bilingualism are associated with higher levels of cognitive functioning (Cummins, 1979, 1981; Galambos & Hakuta, 1988; García, 1983; Hakuta, 1986; Hakuta & García, 1989; Ramirez, 1985).

Other evidence directly supports the conclusion that degrees of bilingualism are associated with higher levels of cognitive attainment (Diaz, 1983; Hakuta, 1986). Measures have included cognitive flexibility, metalinguistic awareness, concept formation, and creativity. These findings are based primarily on research with children in additive bilingual settings — that is, where the second language is added as an enrichment to the native language, and not at the expense of the native language. Specific causal relationships have been difficult to establish; however, positive outcomes have been noted, particularly in situations where bilingualism is not a socially stigmatized trait, but a symbol of membership in a social elite (Hakuta, 1986).

There is also considerable research support for the more recent view that bilingualism is not a linguistic liability. For example, in the process of second-language acquisition, the native language does not interfere in any significant way with the development of the second language. Second-language acquisition and first-language acquisition are apparently guided by common principles across languages and are part of the human cognitive system (McLaughlin, 1990). From this structural point of view, the learning of a second language is not hampered by the first. Furthermore, the rate of acquisition of a second language is highly related to proficiency level in the native language, suggesting that the 2 capacities share and build upon a common underlying base, rather than competing for limited resources (Cummins, 1984).

Just as recent work in intelligence has moved away from regarding it as a single unitary construct (Sternberg, 1985), recent work on language proficiency has revealed a rich and multifaceted phenomenon. Research has extended our understanding that language is highly situational, varying by social and physical context and relating to the functions that language plays in these contexts (Cazden, 1989; Snow, 1987). The diversification of language proficiency into different task domains complicates our understanding of bilingual ability. The measurement of bilingualism has always been complex; the maintenance of bilingualism in communities has been regarded by sociolinguists as best understood with respect to situational and functional constraints imposed on language use (Fishman, Cooper & Ma, 1966; Pedraza, 1987). What is important is that language ability does not develop or atrophy "across the board," that is, across the various domains of application.

Research on children's use of multiple languages (Zentella, 1981) suggests that they are adept at shifting from one language to the other depending on the conversational situation (a process known as *codeswitching*) and that this behavior is not the result of the confusion of the 2 languages. Rather, multilinguals code-switch with each other to take advantage of the richness of the communicative situation. From the viewpoint of ethnographers, one function of such code alternation is to establish and regulate social boundaries (Gumperz, 1982; Pedraza, 1987). Such studies are important because they remind anyone studying children's multilingualism (and language use in general) that language is a social phenomenon taking place between 2 or more parties, and that questions of language use are really questions about social context, not about linguistic structure.

Summary

The research on bilingual children from Mexican, Puerto Rican, Cuban and Asian backgrounds in the United States has destroyed the myth that bilingualism is a handicap to young children and that English language development should be the primary goal of social institutions serving this population. This research concludes that multilingualism is not a linguistic or cognitive liability; rather, it may serve as linguistic enrichment with possible cognitive advantages. The implications from such conclusions should mobilize our social institutions to sustain and enhance multilingualism as once those institutions mobilized to eliminate it.

SOCIAL/CULTURAL ISSUES

Just as the linguistic character of linguistic and cultural minority children has been seen as a limitation, so have the social attributes of these children been viewed as detrimental to their educational and economic success in this country. This negative view of minorities seems again to be precipitated by prevailing confrontations between second- and third-generation immigrants and more recent immigrants during the early part of this century. Even today it is common in dealing with ethnic minorities to emphasize a holistic view toward Americanizing such populations. For linguistic minorities this has meant more than ridding them of their native languages. However, recent recognition of cultural differences, particularly by the educational establishment and by researchers interested in understanding such differences (Mead, 1937), has led to a growing body of literature regarding socialization. In particular, that literature has attempted to relate familial characteristics to the emergence of particular social organizations that distinguish minority populations from other populations (Tharp, 1989). These co-occurring trends — the threat of Americanization (and therefore cultural homogeneity) in contrast with the thrust to understand ethnic differences — will be discussed in this section.

Americanization

In the past, "Americanization" was the prime objective for educating linguistic and cultural minority children (Elam, 1972; Gonzalez, in press). Schooling practices were reorganized whenever such populations rose to significant numbers in a community and children were increasingly visible on the school registers. This reorganization established special programs, and was applied to both children and adults in urban and rural schools and communities. The desired effect of "Americanizing" students was to socialize the minority community. In essence, if only schools could serve as the social institution that taught their students English and succeeded in instilling "American" values, the problem of educational failure would be solved. Ironically, social economists have argued that this effort was coupled with systematic societal efforts to maintain disparate conditions existing between Anglos and ethnic minorities. Indeed, more than anything else, past attempts at addressing the "minority educational problem" have tended to preserve the political and economic subordination of the minority community (Spencer, 1988).

"Americanization" was a key ingredient and was the particular form that the general sociological theory of assimilation recognized as a solution to the problem of immigrants and ethnicity in the modern industrialized United States. "Americanization" was to lead to the merging and the eventual disappearance of small ethnic and linguistically diverse communities. These communities, initially scattered and separate, would merge into a single dominant national institutional structure and culture. Ethnic culture, and therefore the consciousness it spawned, allegedly corresponded to a traditional, or folk, society that was justifiable and necessary only in a premodern context—a context incompatible with the modern industrial setting.

Thomas and Park (1921) argued that European immigrants' Old World consciousness would eventually be overcome by "modern" American values. However, there are important distinctions between European and many modern minority experiences regarding assimilation, according to Gonzalez (in press). First, the Americanization of today's minority community has been attempted in a segregated society. Second, it has been both rural and urban, as contrasted with the European experience, which was overwhelmingly urban. Third, it has been heavily influenced by the regional agricultural economy, which retarded a "natural" assimilation process. Finally, immigrants from Mexico, Puerto Rico and other Spanish-speaking countries have not been able to escape the effects of the economic and political relationship between an advanced industrialized nation, the United States, and semiindustrialized, semifeudal nations and territories, the latter increasingly under the political and economic sway of the United States. None of the contributory European nations had such a relationship with the United States; thus, their national cultures tended to be judged more on an equal footing with nations/territories struggling to realize their interests against the nationalism of a rising world power. This factor alone should make for a significant modification in the objectives and manner in which "Americanization" is applied to the present-day minority community.

It continues to be evident that Americanization is the goal of many programs aimed at linguistic and cultural minorities. Americanization for Hispanics, as an example, means the elimination not only of linguistic and cultural differences but of an undesirable culture. Americanization programs assume a single homogeneous ethnic culture in contact with a single homogeneous modern one; the relationship between the 2 cultures is not viewed as one of equals. The dominant community, enjoying greater wealth and privileges, claims its position by virtue of cultural superiority. In one way or another, nearly every Hispanic child, whether born in the United States or elsewhere, is likely to be treated as a foreigner, an alien, or an intruder. In 1923 the Los Angeles school superintendent voiced a common complaint in an address to district principals: "We have the [Mexican] immigrants to live with, and if we Americanize them, we can live with them" (Gonzales, 1989). Unfortunately, the objective today continues to be to transform the Hispanic community into an English-speaking and American-thinking community. This attitude was recently articulated by Dr. Ken Hill, a California superintendent in a district serving a large number of Mexican American students and who has received national and state distinction for his efforts: "We've got to attend to the idea of assimilation and to make sure that we teach English as quickly as we can so these kids can get in the mainstream of American life" (Walsh, 1990, p. B4). The dropout rate for Hispanics in this school districts was recently reported as over 40% (Matute-Bianchi, 1990).

Cultural Difference

Even as the Americanization mentality has predominated, research during the last 2 decades has begun to perceive ethnic culture as more than a target of elimination. On foundations established by the noted anthropologist Margaret Mead (1937), researchers such as McClintock (1974), Kagan (1983) Gallimore and Tharp (1989), and Nieto (1979) have begun to explore socialization as a means by which cultural differences can be understood rather than eliminated.

One of the most significant functions of socialization is the transmission of values. By socialization, Mead (1937) and McClintock (1972) refer to the process through which prescriptions and prohibitions are transmitted to members of the social group. Thus the family organization creates opportunities for the child to learn values just as other agents such as the media may communicate value-based information that also influences socialization. Cooperative, competitive, and individualistic reward distribution patterns are considered products of socialization.

The traditional socialization view generally presented in the literature has focused upon the family (including siblings and the extended family) as important socialization agents. More recent conceptualizations (e.g., Hetherington & Parks, 1988) have considered socialization agents outside the family as well as the reciprocal roles of the socialization agents and the child. The familial socialization agents include parents, siblings, and the extended family. The nonfamilial socialization agents include teachers, peers, the media (especially television), and other persons with whom the child regularly comes into contact.

A central assumption of the socialization model most recently proposed for many U.S. linguistic and cultural minorities (Kagan, 1983; Knight, Bernal, & Carlos, in press) is that the preference for the equal sharing of rewards is based upon a value system linked to the "culture" and is transmitted through socialization experiences. A substantial body of research has yielded the consistent finding that cooperative (equal) reward distributions occur more often among Mexican American, Puerto Rican, poor White, African American and other minority children than middle-class Anglo American children (e.g., Knight & Kagan, 1977a; McClintock, 1974; Nieto, 1979; Knight, Bernal, & Carlos, in press). Such findings support the assumption that these children prefer equal sharing of rewards, and, therefore, that such preference reflects cultural value.

In particular, investigations of theoretically relevant subsets of the Mexican American and Mexican populations also support this assumption. For example, Knight and Kagan (1977b) compared the reward distribution behaviors of second-generation Mexican American children (one or both parents born in

Mexico), third-generation Mexican American children (one or more grandparents born in Mexico, but both parents born in the United States), and Anglo American children. This study revealed significant linear trends indicating that, at least for second- and third-generation Mexican American children, there is an apparent loss of cooperative values in favor of competitive values through successive generations. The preference for equal sharing of rewards has been related to self-evaluations in a manner consistent with the assumption that these preferences reflect an ethnic value (Kagan & Knight, 1979): among second-generation Mexican American children, high self-esteem was associated with a preference for equal reward distributions; in contrast, among third-generation Mexican American and Anglo American children, high self-esteem was associated with a preference for unequal and competitive reward distributions. These patterns are precisely what one would expect if the equal sharing of rewards were a Mexican American ethnic value transmitted through socialization experiences that are changing in response to the extended interaction with an Anglo American environment.

Although these reward distribution preferences and group differences have been clearly demonstrated in an experimental paradigm, research has not isolated the specific naturalistic behavioral referents or values for such experimentally elicited behaviors. However, a likely candidate is demonstrated in the often frequent reminders to Hispanic children to behave in a manner consistent with the term *pórtate bien*, which refers to general good behavior, with cooperative values implied. The value of *pórtate bien* includes politeness and respectful behavior toward others. A child *que se porta bien* knows how to behave under many social contexts because many different situational behaviors are regulated by this generalized value. If one accepts that a number of behaviors such as the aforementioned are subsumed under the rubric of the generalized value, then the preference for equal reward distributions might best be likened to sharing with others, and understood as a value-based behavior resulting from the child's socialization experience.

Several authors (Keefe & Padilla, 1987; McClintock, Bayard, & McClintock, 1983; Knight, Bernal, & Carlos, in press) have discussed the variables associated with the family background, the family structure, and the broader social ecology that influence the socialization experiences of minority children. In considering the processes through which these types of variables may lead to specific socialization experiences, it is important to note that these variables probably do not function independently. The family structure variables related to the parents' socialization goals include strength of familial interdependence, pattern of status in relationships within the family, and family size (see McClintock et al., 1983, for more details). Strength of familial interdependence consists of feelings of family solidarity as well as attachment and commitment to the family. There is some empirical evidence regarding the presence of close family ties among Mexican American families (Keefe, 1979; Keefe, Padilla, & Carlos, 1979). For example, in studies comparing Mexican American families to Anglo American families, the results suggest that Mexican American families provide closer relations and greater loyalty among members, more frequent visitation

of relatives, parental encouragement of family-centered orientations in their children, fewer opportunities for children to bring friends over to the house, less freedom for children to play away from home, greater disapproval for children contradicting authority, and fewer decision-making opportunities for the children. Similarly, Johnson, Teigen, and Davila (1983) found parents with Mexican backgrounds to be relatively demanding and restrictive of their children compared to Anglo parents. Caution is advocated regarding the generalizing of results that suggest stronger interdependence among Hispanic families; however, McClintock et al. (1983) have speculated about the implications of these characteristics for the Hispanic child's exposure to nonfamilial peers, and in turn for their reward distribution preferences. Thus, less exposure and, therefore, opportunities for social comparisons with nonfamilial peers may make Anglo peers less relevant referents for Hispanic children, thereby reducing the value of competitive (superiority) reward distributions for these children.

The broader social ecology has also been suggested as an important determinant of the socialization of minority children (Kagan, 1984; Keefe & Padilla, 1987). This broader social ecology includes environmental characteristics such as the urbanization level of the community in which the child lives, the socioeconomic status of the family and the community, the nature of the minority status of other minorities in the community, and the prevailing views of the broader society regarding minorities. In many ways a relatively rural or a relatively low socioeconomic environment may lead to socialization experiences that foster interdependency, respect for others, and greater sharing of resources. In contrast, a more urban environment may lead to socialization experiences that foster independence, competitiveness, and more reliance upon social supports that are external to the family. There has been some empirical demonstration of a relation between the social behaviors of children and urbanization level (e.g., Kagan, Knight, Martinez, & Espinoza-Santana, 1981) and socioeconomic status (Knight & Kagan, 1977a). Minority status may lead to considerable variability in socialization experiences simply because the minority child generally has direct contacts with the minority group as well as the dominant Anglo American group. Therefore, the linguistic and cultural minority child may also encounter unique socialization experiences because he or she is a minority (Ogbu, 1982; 1987).

Summary

The socialization model suggests that characteristics of the family background, the family structure, and the broader social ecology are important determinants of the socialization content provided by numerous socialization agents, and to a great degree the socialization practices to which minority children are exposed. Although this understanding of minority cultural differences is far from complete, such conceptual rethinking of the minority child, the family, and the development of social motives within particular social and family organizations is a far cry from the general conceptualizations that being a minority is a negative social attribute. Enlightened understanding of children in the linguistic and cultural minority cannot be founded on the "Americanization" prescription: that is, take all who are not "American" and make then "American." The future for Hispanics in this country is best understood if "Americanization" issues are set aside and the nature of social variables, with their relationship to "cultural differences" as well as educational practices and outcomes, are more closely examined.

CARING FOR LINGUISTICALLY AND CULTURALLY DIVERSE INFANTS AND TODDLERS

In relation to the socialization of infants, caring for young children continues to be perceived as one of the most important activities in our society. The early years are the foundation for all the years that follow. This is particularly true for the social communication skills we call language. Understood in its broadest sense, language is an important and complex social repertoire that allow young children to understand and influence their environment. Care givers and infants enter into an important social enterprise that depends on the emerging communicative skills of the infant and the "expert" communicative ability of the care giver.

Infants and toddlers need a rich linguistic environment in order to thrive and develop their language and communication competence. When a child is first learning language, it is best to provide a rich linguistic environment—both at home and in the child-care setting—that is the same as and supports the native language and culture of the infant's family. This is true regardless of the family's language or cultural group. In essence, preserving a family's home language and cultural heritage is very important to the identity and sense of well-being for the entire family. For young children, cultural and linguistic identity provides an important sense of self and family belonging, which in turn supports a wide range of learning capability, not the least of which is learning a second language. Another important consideration is the relationship of language development and learning about one's culture. Language learning for the young child is closely tied to cultural learning.

The optimal situation for "good" care assumes that the care giver's language matches that of the infant and infant's family. Providing the native language in the care-giving situation supports and reinforces the many rich encounters with language that the infant has within the family. As children begin speaking, it is very important for them to be exposed to and use their native language in a wide variety of ways. Because language and cognitive development are so closely related, when young children hear their native language spoken in familial settings as well as in the wider community, they are exposed to more words, more complex grammar, and more complex ideas, thoughts, and concepts. This broad range of linguistic and cognitive experiences in natural situations enriches the development of both languages and intellectual functioning in the older infant and preschool child (Heath, 1986).

Infants develop and thrive linguistically in rich but natural communication interactions. They do not require any special "teaching" (Ervin-Tripp, 1974). In other words, care givers

should not formally "teach" any language. What care givers naturally do is what supports native-language learning.

It is important for the care giver who speaks the child's home language to communicate in a variety of ways, especially with the older infant toddler. In one-to-one interactions with the young and mobile infant the care giver should speak very intimately with the child, using informal language forms, and simple, familiar words. As the infant gets older, the care giver's communication about objects and activities in the environment, as well as use of words and language forms, naturally becomes more diverse and varied. As the child hears the care giver speak to her or his parents and other care givers, yet another form and context of language is modeled. In all of these different conversations, the child receives exposure to language and communications in his or her native language. This exposure to vocabulary and grammar in a natural setting provides the child with a firm foundation in his or her native language. It is this foundation that supports and enables the child to learn a second language more easily.

But what if it is impossible to provide native language or bilingual care givers? Won't this harm the linguistic development of these infants? Certainly, if the care giver refuses to interact with the infant by ignoring the child's natural communicative attempts, the infant will soon stop communicating. Over 60 percent of any communicative act is nonverbal. Infants communicate initially by pointing, crying, wiggling, nodding, grimacing, and such. The best approach to handling a language mismatch in a care-giving situation is for the care giver to attend to all of the infant's communicative signals and to respond naturally with understanding and a visible willingness to communicate.

Regardless of the language environment, all infants can be expected to attempt communication. Young children have not yet learned to be afraid of making mistakes; they "risk" communicating with care givers regardless of the language they speak. Care givers should do the same. The child will not be "mixed up" or "confused" by the use of an unfamiliar language by the care giver as long as that communication is authentic.

Care givers can help with the language mismatch by playing tapes of stories, rhymes, and songs in the child's native language. Toys, photos, pictures, and books that show the child's home culture give the child things to point out, name, and talk about in his or her native language.

Still, it is important to find someone who can speak the infant's native language (a parent, relative, or community volunteer), even if that person cannot be the child's principal care giver. The infant must feel welcome in this nonhome environment. The presence of his or her language can assist greatly. However, care givers whose native language is different from the child should never fear that their language is "bad" for the child and should not hesitate to speak to the child just as they would to infants from their own language background. The language mismatch is simply not optimal for the child's overall language and cognitive development.

An unfortunate social circumstance often reported in caregiving situations with bilingual and non-English speaking children is the care giver's tendency to perceive these children and their families as foreigners. Because these children and their families usually do not speak English, they are marked as "different;" this observed difference sometimes leads to negative feelings and treatment, perhaps out of defensiveness or suspicion. This uncomfortable social situation often leads to the desire to change this "difference" by ridding children and their families of those attributes that make them different. Unfortunately, such attempts only develop suspicion and negative reactions from infants and their families. Rather than attempting to minimize diversity, appreciating and respecting diversity can enrich all of our lives.

Appreciating the significance and validity of the family's language and culture is a challenge in itself. But today, when such a large number of children from diverse language and cultural groups experiences early child care, this appreciation must be transformed into challenging actions that go beyond acknowledging diversity. Moreover, this challenge is quite formidable, considering that only a few care givers come from these varied language and cultural groups. Therefore, through no fault of their own, they lack personal experience with other language and cultures. It is important to have care givers from the cultural and linguistic backgrounds of the families needing child care.

Meeting this diversity challenge creates conflict—some of it inevitable and some of it unnecessary. "Majority" attitudes of condescension can be viewed as a signal to children and their parents to abandon their language and culture in favor of the "mainstream" culture and English. Care givers who emphasize these "mainstream" values pull children away from the important linguistic and social resources available in the family and community. As a result, some parents may become wary of placing their children in care-giving situations that do not emphasize and practice their own values, traditions, and language. Other parents may come to believe that only if they abandon their language and culture will their children succeed in American society. A family's rich culture heritage need not be robbed from them because of insensitive attitudes and incorrect understanding about language development.

SCHOOLING OF THE YOUNG LINGUISTIC AND CULTURAL MINORITY CHILD

For linguistic and cultural minority students, availability of educational data is no problem. Unfortunately, that data continues to paint a picture of academic underachievement. Analysis of standardized measures of academic achievement at the local, state, regional, and national levels continues to confirm the educational system's failure to "deliver" (see Table 24–1 for an example of Hispanic student circumstances). The following discussion will explore the persistent educational debate regarding the major educational reform for linguistic and cultural minority students: bilingual education. Even this reform has suffered from the overriding perspective of bilingualism as a negative, wherein the goal is, instead, to teach English as soon as possible and generally to "Americanize." Let us now

consider a more informed perspective regarding education of these students—a responsive educational approach based on the recent empirical and theoretical understandings discussed earlier.

Education

The education of linguistic and cultural minority students has been characterized by an overriding debate regarding the instructional use of the 2 languages of this student population. Programs for these students have been developed on a broad scale. These programs are a result of local, state, and federal educational policy as well as important court-related policy organized around the linguistic character of the language minority student (August & García, 1988). Such myopic treatment of the student population's academic situation ignores the complexity of the student's linguistic context as it interacts with the myriad of variables that we know affect the schooling process. Unfortunately, the debate continues.

At one end of this debate are supporters of native-language instruction. Proponents of this specially designed instructional strategy (transitional bilingual education) recommend the utilization of the student's native language and mastery of that language prior to the introduction of an English curriculum. This approach suggests that the competencies in the native language, particularly as related to academic learning, provide important cognitive and social foundations for second-language learning and academic learning in general—"you really only learn to read once" (Hudelson, 1987). At the other end of this debate, introduction to the English curriculum is recommended at the onset of the students' schooling experience with minimal use of the native language. This specially designed approach (*immersion*) calls for English language "leveling" by instructional staff (to facilitate the understanding on behalf of the limited-English-proficient student) combined with an English-as-a-second-language component. In essence, the earlier the student confronts English and the more times it is confronted, the greater the English linguistic advantage (Baker & deKanter, 1983).

Each of these approaches argues that the results of its implementation would be short-term linguistic advantages leading to more long-term psychological, linguistic, and educational advantages and, in turn, to direct social and economic advancement (Cardenas, 1986; Rossel & Ross, 1986). Simply put, each of these approaches suggests that a simple change in the language component of the educational curriculum, particularly in the early years, can fix the problem. Thus, policy and practice have been driven by this debate and its related assumptions regarding the importance of the language character of the linguistically diverse student.

Such policy and practice have ignored the contributions of Cummins (1986), Heath (1986), Ogbu (1986) and Trueba (1987), who have suggested that the schooling vulnerability of such students (particularly Hispanic students) must be understood within the broader contexts of this society's treatment of minorities in and out of schools. That is, no quick fix is likely under social and schooling conditions that mark the language minority student for special treatment of his/her language difference without consideration for the psychological and social circumstances in which that student resides. This is not to suggest that the linguistic character of this student is insignificant. Instead, it warns us against the isolation of this single attribute as the only variable of importance. This more comprehensive view of schooling includes an understanding of the sociocultural incongruities between home and school, and the resulting effects on learning and achievement (Tharp, 1989).

Based on the notion that schools function as transmitters of culture (Spindler, 1955), the development of academic competence is seen as related to academic socialization, instruction, the schooling enterprise, and student learning (Au & Jordan, 1981; Duran, 1983; Diaz, Moll, & Mehan, 1986; Erickson, 1986; Trueba, 1987). Recent ethnographic studies (Au & Jordan, 1981; Diaz, Moll, & Mehan, 1986; Duran, 1983; Erickson, 1986), have reported a significant relationship between cultural congruency in instruction and children's control of academic literacy (Trueba, 1988). Other sociolinguistic studies have shown that the language of the classroom, academic discourse, is a highly specialized code that students need to learn, and "is not simply a transparent medium through which the academic curriculum is transmitted" (Mehan, 1987, p. 124). From this perspective, schooling is not only about cognitive development and the acquisition of knowledge; it is also a process of socialization (Spindler, 1974; 1982).

Imbedded in this perspective are the understandings (1) that language, culture, and their accompanying values are acquired in the home and community environment (Cummins, 1986; Goldman & Trueba, 1987; Heath, 1981), (2) that children come to school with some knowledge about what language is, how it works, and what it is used for (Hall, 1987; Goodman, 1980; Smith, 1971), (3) that children learn higher-level metacognitive and metalinguistic skills as they engage in socially meaningful activities (Duran, 1987), and (4) that children's development and learning is best understood as the interaction of linguistic, sociocultural, and cognitive knowledge and experiences (Trueba, 1988). For linguistically and culturally diverse students, however, their attributes and experiences are not those that are celebrated and acknowledged by the schooling enterprise, nor are they those upon which school learning and academic socialization are based (Ogbu, 1982; Trueba, 1987). Such a standing serves to foster an inappropriate and negative perception of self as a learner, reader, writer, and speaker. The resulting vulnerability of the linguistic and cultural minority child is not generally accounted for when learning and schooling are considered within the larger sociocultural context of the student's role and value in the classroom and in the larger society (Guttierez & García, 1989).

A more appropriate perspective of learning, then, is one recognizing that learning is enhanced when it occurs in contexts both socioculturally and linguistically meaningful for the learner (Diaz, Moll, & Mehan, 1986; Heath, 1986; Scribner & Cole, 1981; Wertsch, 1985). Such meaningful events, however, are not generally accessible to linguistic and cultural minority children. Those schooling practices that contribute to the academic vulnerability of this student population and that tend to dramatize the lack of fit between the student and the school

experience are reflected in the monolithic culture transmitted by the schools in the forms of pedagogy, curricula, instruction, classroom configuration, and language (Walker, 1987). Such practices include (1) systematic exclusion of the students' histories, language, experience, and values from classroom curricula and activities (Giroux & McLaren, 1986; Ogbu, 1982); (2) limited access to academic courses and learning environments that do not foster either academic development and socialization (Duran, 1986; Eder, 1982) or perception of self as a competent learner and language user; and (3) limited opportunities to engage in developmentally and culturally appropriate learning outside of teacher-led instruction (García, 1988).

A Responsive Pedagogy

The previous discussion has profound implications for the teaching/learning enterprise related to linguistically and culturally diverse students (August & García, 1988; García, 1988). This new pedagogy is one that redefines the classroom as a community of learners where speakers, readers, and writers come together to define and redefine the meaning of the academic experience. It might be described by some as a pedagogy of empowerment (Cummins, 1986) and by others as cultural learning (Heath, 1986; Trueba, 1987). In any case, it argues for the respect and integration of the students' values, beliefs, histories, and experiences and recognizes the active role that students must play in the learning process. This responsive pedagogy expands students' knowledge beyond their own immediate experiences, while using those experiences as a sound foundation for appropriating new knowledge. For many minority students, this involves using the native language or bilingual abilities that are a substantive part of a well-functioning social network in which knowledge is embedded.

Furthermore, a responsive pedagogy for academic learning requires a redefinition of the instructor's role. Instructors must become familiar with the cognitive, social, and cultural dimensions of learning. They need to recognize the ways in which diversity of instruction, assessment, and evaluation affect learning. They should become more aware of the classroom curriculum, its intended purpose, and the degree of its implementation. Of significance is the configuration of the classroom environment and the nature of interaction of students with teacher and students. Further, instructors must recognize that the acquisition of academic content requires helping students display their knowledge in ways that suggest their competence as learners and language users. Analysis of these dimensions will underscore the potential for equipping the classroom for the particularly sensitive task of ensuring success with linguistically and culturally diverse students.

Finally, teachers must destroy preconceived myths about learning processes and the potentially underprepared student and, in particular, myths about those who come from lower-SES households and/or who come from homes in which English is not the primary language. For those embracing this new concept of responsive pedagogy, new educational horizons for themselves and their students are not only possible but inevitable.

The above conclusions can be supported by recent research documenting educationally effective practices with linguistic minority students in Carpenteria, California (Cummins, 1986), San Diego, California (Carter & Chatfield, 1986; Diaz, Moll, & Mehan, 1986), and Phoenix, Arizona (García, 1988; Moll, 1988). This recent research provides some answers regarding effective academic environments for these students:

1. *What role did native language instruction play?* These "effective" schools considered native-language instruction key in the early grades (K–3).
2. *Was there one best curriculum?* No common curriculum was identified. However, a well-trained instructional staff implementing an integrated "student-centered" curriculum with literacy pervasive in all aspects of instruction was consistently observed across grade levels. Basals were utilized sparingly and usually as resource material.
3. *What instructional strategies were effective?* Consistently, teachers organized so as to ensure small collaborative academic activities requiring a high degree of heterogeneous grouped student-to-student social (and particularly linguistic) interaction. Individual instructional activity such as work sheets and workbooks was limited, as was individual competition as a classroom motivational ingredient.
4. *Who were the key players in this effective schooling drama?* School administrators and parents played important roles. However, teachers were the key players. They achieved the educational confidence of their peers and supervisors. They worked to organize instruction, create new instructional environments, assess effectiveness, and advocate for their students. They were proud of their students—academically reassuring but consistently demanding. They rejected any notion of academic, linguistic, cultural, or intellectual inferiority regarding their students.

In summary, a responsive curriculum necessarily recognizes that academic learning has its roots in language experiences and processes of communication. This type of curriculum provides abundant and diverse opportunities for speaking, listening, reading, and writing, along with the scaffolding to help guide students through the learning process. A focus on process, both social and cognitive, encourages students to take risks, to construct meaning, and to seek reinterpretations of knowledge. Such an approach recognizes that errors are necessary in experimenting with new ideas, forms, and structures. Within this knowledge-driven curriculum (i.e., academic and cultural knowledge), skills are tools for acquiring knowledge, not a fundamental target of teaching events (Gallimore & Tharp, 1989; García, 1988).

CONCLUSION

Several key issues are of importance regarding the linguistic/cognitive, sociocultural, and education plight of linguistic and cultural minority children and families as they interact with several key U.S. institutions, particularly the schools. This population has been viewed as foreign, culturally inferior and has been characterized by its academic underachievement and low socioeconomic liability. Historically, these characteristics have been attributed to this population's disadvantaged language and culture. Recently, a more informed analysis suggests that such attributions are both incorrect and unproductive in understanding why significant educational underachievement exists for these populations. Specifically, this new view suggests that

1. The bilingual/multilingual character of many children is not a linguistic, cognitive, or educational liability but may actually serve as a cognitive advantage. Therefore, bilingualism should not be feared or exterminated, but instead assisted and promoted (August & García, 1988; García, 1983; Hakuta, 1986).
2. "Americanization" for minorities has failed; continued attempts at assimilation will not serve this population educationally, socially, or economically (Gonzalez, 1990; Spencer, 1988).
3. The "culture" of the minority family and child are better understood with regard to socialization variables and processes that produce potential differences when compared to Anglo families and children. These differences seem to reflect distinct social motives, favoring cooperative as opposed to competitive social orientations (Kagan, 1983; Knight, Bernal, & Carlos, 1989; McClintock, 1974).
4. The educational strategies for linguistic and cultural minority students must be rethought. The doctrine of "Americanization," as well as English-language and skill-oriented education programs, must be abandoned in favor of a responsive curriculum and pedagogy that recognizes academic learning within a schooling context capable of respecting and integrating students' values, beliefs, history, and experiences within a community of learners in where new knowledge is appropriated (Cummins, 1986; García, 1988; Heath, 1986; Trueba, 1987).

If the above can be perceived as a new set of "understandings," then the following are specific principles that need to be addressed for the growing linguistically and culturally diverse population and the increasing number of classrooms where cultural and linguistic diversity is the norm:

- Any curriculum, especially one for "diverse" children, must address all categories of learning goals.
- The more "diverse" the children are linguistically and culturally, the more content must be related to the child's own environment and experience.
- The more "diverse" the children are, the more important it is for content, knowledge, and skills to have horizontal relevance.
  - Vertical relevance is preparation for the next stage of life.
  - Horizontal relevance means that the knowledge and skills are relevant to the child's everyday life.
- The more "diverse" the children are, the more the curriculum should address learning through active endeavors rather than passive ones.

- The more "diverse" the children are, the more important it is for the curriculum to offer opportunities to apply what they are learning in a meaningful context (work sheets are not meaningful).
- The more "diverse" the children are, the more likely it is that excessive "skill" practice and drills will endanger the dispositions to use them.
- In general, the more the curriculum emphasizes performance goals, the more likely it is that children will distance themselves from the school.
  - Performance goals mean the pressure to get the right answer, as opposed to learning goals that emphasize how much one can learn.
- The more "diverse" the children are, the larger the proportion of time that should be spent on informal activities, particularly group work on projects.
- The more "diverse" the children are, the more content integrated the curriculum should be. Children should have opportunities to study a topic in depth, to apply all kinds of skills they have acquired.
- The more "diverse" the children are, the larger the variety of instructional strategies should be used.
  - In a unidimensional classroom with one method of teaching, children are at greater risk of having to deal with low self-esteem.
  - In a multidimensional system children find a place for themselves and can enhance their self-esteem.

Educational reform must take this new set of assumptions into consideration if it is to enhance the minority educational experience in the United States. As in the "Sputnik," "New Frontier," or "War on Poverty" eras, we must grasp the significance of these new understandings and challenges. General principles of teaching and learning must be accommodated to the linguistic and cultural diversity of a growing student population.

References

Appleby, A. N., Langer, J., & Mullis, I. J. S. (1988). *The Nation's Report Card: NAEP.* Princeton, NJ: Educational Testing Service.

Au, K., & Jordan, C. (1981). Teaching reading to Hawaiian children: Finding a culturally appropriate solution. In H. Trueba, G. Guthrie, & K. Au (Eds.), *Culture and the bilingual classroom: Studies in classroom ethnography* (pp. 139–152). Rowley, MA: Newbury House.

August, D., & García, E. (1988). *Language minority education in the U.S.: research policy and practice.* Springfield, IL: Charles L. Thomas.

Baden, B., & Maehr, M. (1986). Conforming culture with culture: A perspective for designing schools for children of diverse sociocultural backgrounds. In R. Feldman (Ed.), *The social psychology of education* (pp. 289–309). New York: Cambridge University Press.

Baker, K. A. (1990). Language Minority Education: Two Decades of Research. In A. Barena & E. Garcia (Eds.), *Students "At-Risk"* (pp. 3–41). Washington, D.C.: National Association of School Psychologists.

Baker, K. A., & deKanter, A. A. (1983). An answer from research on bilingual education. *American Education, 48,* 88.

Bloom, B. (1984). The search for methods of group instruction as effective as one-to-one tutoring. *Educational Leadership, 41*(8), 4–17.

Boykin, A. (1986). The triple quandary and the schooling of Afro-American children. In U. Neisser (Ed.), *The school achievement of minority children* (pp. 57–92). New York: New Perspectives.

Bureau of the U.S. Census. (1984). *Conditions of Hispanics in America Today.* Washington DC: U.S. Government Printing Office.

Bureau of the U.S. Census. (1987). *The Hispanic Population in the United States: March 1986 and 1987.* Washington DC: U.S. Government Printing Office.

Cardenas, J. (1986). The role of native-language instruction in bilingual education. *Phi Delta Kappan, 67,* 359–363.

Carter, T. P. & Chatfield, M. L. (1986). Effective bilingual schools: Implications for policy and practice. *American Journal of Education, 5*(1), 200–234.

Cazden, C. (1989). *Classroom discourse.* Cambridge, MA: Harvard University Press.

Change. (1988, May/June). Washington, DC: American Association of Higher Education.

Cummins, J. (1979). Linguistic interdependence and the educational development of bilingual children. *Review of Educational Research, 19,* 222–251.

Cummins, J. (1981). The role of primary language development in promoting educational success for language minority students. In California State Department of Education (Ed.), *Schooling and language minority students: A theoretical framework* (pp. 3–50). Los Angeles, CA: Evaluation, Dissemination, and Assessment Center.

Cummins, J. (1984). *Bilingualism and special education.* San Diego, CA: College Hill Press.

Cummins, J. (1986). Empowering minority students: A framework for intervention. *Harvard Educational Review, 56*(1), 18–35.

Diaz, R. M. (1983). The impact of bilingualism on cognitive development. In E. W. Gordon (Ed.), *Review of research in education* (pp. 23–54). Washington, DC: American Educational Research Association.

Diaz, S., Moll, L., & Mehan, H. (1986). Sociocultural resources in instruction: A context-specific approach. In Bilingual Education Office, California State Department of Education (Ed.), *Beyond Language: Social and cultural factors in schooling language minority students* (pp. 197–230). Sacramento, CA: Bilingual Education Office, California State Department of Education.

Duran, R. (1983). *Hispanics' education and background: Predictors of college achievement.* New York: College Entrance Examination Board.

Duran, R. (1986). *Improving Hispanics' educational outcomes: Learning and instruction.* Unpublished manuscript. Graduate School of Education, University of California, Santa Barbara.

Duran, R. (1987). Metacognition in second language behavior. In J. A. Langer (Ed.), *Language, literacy, and culture: Issues of society and schooling* (pp. 49–63). Norwood, NJ: Ablex.

Eder, D. (1982). Differences in communicative styles across ability groups. In L. C. Wilkinson (Ed.), *Communicating in the classroom* (pp. 167–184). Orlando, FL: Academic Press.

Elam, S. (1972). Acculturation and learning problems of Puerto Rican children. In F. Corrdasco & E. Bucchini (Eds.), *The Puerto Rican Community and its Children on the Mainland* (pp. 65–74). Metuchen, NJ: Scarecrow Press.

Erickson, F. (1986). Qualitative methods in research on teaching. In M. C. Wittrock (Ed.), *Handbook of research on teaching* (pp. 119–158). New York: Macmillan.

Ervin-Tripp, S. M. (1974). Is second language learning like the first? *TESOL Quarterly, 8*(2), 111–127.

Fishman, J. A., Cooper, R. L., & Ma, R. (1966). *Bilingualism in the barrio.* Bloomington, IN: Indiana University Press.

Galambos, S. J., & Hakuta, K. (1988). Subject-specific and task-specific characteristics of metalinguistic awareness in bilingual children. *Applied Psycholinguistics, 9,* 141–162.

Gallimore, R., & Tharp, R. G. (1989). *Challenging cultural minds.* London: Cambridge University Press.

García, E. (1983). *Bilingualism in early childhood.* Albuquerque, NM: University of New Mexico Press.

García, E. (1988). *Effective schooling for language minority students.* Arlington, VA: National Clearing House for Bilingual Education.

Giroux, H. A., & McLaren, P. (1986). Teacher education and the politics of engagement: The case for democratic schooling. *Harvard Educational Review, 56,* 213–238.

Goldman, S., & Trueba, H. (Eds.). (1987). *Becoming literate in English as a second language: Advances in research and theory.* Norwood, NJ: Ablex.

Gonzales, G. (1990). *The education of Mexican students during the era of segregation.* Tucson, AZ: University of Arizona Press.

Goodman, Y. (1980). The roots of literacy. In M. P. Douglass (Ed.), *Reading: A humanizing experience* (pp. 286–301). Claremont, CA: Claremont Graduate School.

Gumperz, J. (1982). *Discourse strategies.* New York: Cambridge University Press.

Gutierrez, K. & García, E. (1989). Academic literacy in linguistic minority children: the connections between language, cognition and culture. *Early Child Development and Care, 51,* 109–126.

Hakuta, K. (1986). *Mirror of Language: The debate on bilingualism.* New York: Basic Books.

Hakuta, K., & García, E. (1989). *Bilingualism and bilingual education.* American Psychologist, *44*(2), 374–379.

Hall, N. (1987). *The emergence of literacy.* Portsmouth, NH: Heineman.

Heath, S. B. (1981). Toward an ethnohistory of writing in American education. In M. Farr-Whitman (Ed.), *Variation in writing functional and linguistic-cultural differences. Vol. 1. of Writing: The nature, development, and teaching of written communication* (pp. 225–246). Hillsdale, NJ: Erlbaum.

Heath, S. B. (1983). *Ways with words: Language, life, and work in communities and classrooms.* Cambridge, England: Cambridge University Press.

Heath, S. B. (1986). *Sociocultural contexts of language development. In Beyond language: Social and cultural factors in schooling language minority children* (pp. 143–186). Sacramento, CA: Bilingual Education Office, California State Department of Education.

Hetherington, E. M., & Parks, R. D. (Eds.). (1988). *Contemporary reading in child psychology* (3rd ed.). New York: McGraw-Hill.

Hodgkinson, H. (1989). Reform? Higher Education? Don't be absurd! *Higher Education, 18,* 271–274.

Hudelson, S. (1987). The role of native language literacy in the education of language minority children. *Language Arts, 64*(8), 827–841.

Johnson, D. L., Teigen, K., & Davila, R. (1983). Anxiety and social restriction: A study of children in Mexico, Norway, and the United States. *Journal of Cross-Cultural Psychology, 14,* 439–454.

Kagan, S. (1983). Social orientation among Mexican-American children: A challenge to traditional classroom structures. In E. Garcia (Ed.), *The Mexican-American child: Language, cognition and social development* (pp. 163–182). Tempe: Center for Bilingual Education, Arizona State University.

Kagan, S. (1984). Interpreting Chicano cooperativeness: Methodological and Theoretical considerations. In J. L. Martinez & R. H. Mendoza (Eds.), *Chicano Psychology* (2nd ed., pp. 289–333). Orlando, FL: Academic Press.

Kagan, S., & Knight, G. P. (1979). Cooperation-competition and self-esteem: A case of cultural relativism. *Journal of Cross-Cultural Psychology, 10,* 457–467.

Kagan, S., Knight, G. P., Martinez, S., & Espinoza-Santana, P. (1981). Conflict resolution style among Mexican children: Examination, urbanization and ecology effects. *Journal of Cross-Cultural Psychology, 12,* 222–232.

Kagan, S., & Zahn, G. L. (1983). Cultural differences in individualism? Just Artifact. *Hispanic Journal of Behavioral Sciences, 5,* 219–232.

Keefe, S. E. (1979). Urbanization, acculturation, and extended family ties: Mexican Americans in cities. *American Ethnologist,* Summer, 349–362.

Keefe, S. E., & Padilla, A. M. (1987). *Chicano Ethnicity.* Albuquerque, NM: New Mexico Press.

Keefe, S. E., Padilla, A. M. & Carlos, M. L. (1979). The Mexican American extended family as an emotional support system. *Human Organization, 38,* 144–152.

Knight, G. P., Bernal, M. E., & Carlos, G. (1991). Socialization and the development of cooperative, competitive, and individualistic behaviors among Mexican American children. In E. Garcia, L. Moll, & A. Borano (Eds.), *The Mexican American child: Language, cognition, and socialization.* Tempe, AZ: Arizona State University.

Knight, G. P., & Kagan, S. (1977a). Development of prosocial and competitive behaviors in Anglo American and Mexican American children. *Child Development, 48,* 1385–1394.

Knight, G. P., & Kagan, S. (1977b). Acculturation of prosocial and competitive behaviors among second and third-generation Mexican American children. *Journal of Cross-Cultural Psychology, 8,* 273–284.

Matute-Bianchi, E. (1990). *A report to the Santa Clara County School District: Hispanics in the schools.* Santa Clara, CA: Santa Clara County School District.

McClintock, C. G. (1972). Social motivation: A set of propositions. *Behavioral Science, 17,* 438–454.

McClintock, C. G. (1974). Development of social motives in Anglo-American and Mexican-American children. *Journal of Personality and Social Psychology, 29,* 348–354.

McClintock, E., Bayard, M. P., & McClintock, C. G. (1983). The socialization of prosocial orientations in Mexican American families. In E. Garcia (Ed.), *The Mexican American child: Language, cognition and social development* (pp. 143–162). Tempe, AZ: Center for Bilingual Education.

McLaughlin, B. (1990). Development of bilingualism: Myth and reality. In A. Barona and E. Garcia (Eds.), *Children at risk: Poverty, minority status and other issues in educational equality* (pp. 65–76). Washington, DC: National Association of Psychologists.

Mead, M. (1937). *Cooperation and competition among primitive peoples.* New York: McGraw.

Mehan, H. (1987). Language and schooling. In G. Spindler & Spindler (Eds.), *Interpretive ethnography of education at home and abroad* (pp. 109–136). Hillsdale, NJ: Erlbaum.

Moll, L. (1988). Educating Latino students. *Language Arts, 64* (10), 315–324.

Nieto, S. (1979). *Curriculum decision-making: The Puerto Rican family and the bilingual child.* Unpublished doctoral dissertation, University of Massachusetts, Amherst.

Ogbu, J. U. (1982). Cultural discontinuities and schooling. *Anthropology and Education Quarterly, 13*(4), 168–190.

Ogbu, J. U. (1986). The consequences of the American caste system. In Ulric Neisser (Ed.), *The school achievement of minority children: New perspectives.* Hillsdale, NJ: Erlbaum.

Ogbu, J. U. (1987). Variability in minority school performance: A problem in search of an explanation. *Anthropology and Education Quarterly, 18,* 312–334.

Ogbu, J. U., & Matute-Bianchi, M. E. (1986). Understanding sociocultural factors: Knowledge, identity, and school adjustment. In California State Department of Education (Ed.), *Beyond language: Social and cultural factors in schooling language minority students* (pp. 73–142). Los Angeles: Evaluation, Dissemination, and Assessment Center, California State University Los Angeles.

Pedraza, P. (1987). *Language in context: Puerto Ricans in New York.* Doctoral dissertation, Columbia University, New York.

Ramirez, A. (1985). *Bilingualism through schooling.* Albany, NY: State University of New York Press.

Rivera-Medina, E. J. (1984). The Puerto Rican return migrant student: A challenge to educators. *Educational Research Quarterly, 8,* 82–91.

Rosenshine, B. (1986). Synthesis of Research on Explicit Teaching. *Educational Leadership, 43,* 60–69.

Rossell, C., & Ross, J. M. (1986). *The social evidence on bilingual education.* Boston: Boston University.

Scribner, S., & Cole, M. (1981). Unpackaging literacy. In M. Farr-Whiteman (Ed.), *Variation in writing: functional and linguistic-cultural differences. Vol. 1. Writing: the nature, development, and teaching of written communications* (pp. 71–88). Hillsdale, NJ: Erlbaum.

Slavin, R. E. (1989). The pet and the pendulum. Fadism in education and how to stop it. *Phi Delta Kappan, 70,* 252–278.

Slavin, R., Karweit, N., & Madden, N. (1989). *Effective programs for students at risk.* Needham Heights, MA: Allyn & Bacon.

Smith, F. (1923). Bilingualism and mental development. *British Journal of Psychology, 13,* 271–282.

Smith, F. (1971). *Understanding reading.* New York: Holt, Rinehart & Winston.

Snow, C. E. (1987). Beyond conversation: second language learners' acquisition of description and explanation. In J. P. Lantolf & A. Labarca (Eds.), *Research in second language learning: Focus on the classroom* (pp. 3–16). Norwood, NJ: Ablex.

Spencer, D. (1988). Transitional bilingual education and the socialization of immigrants. *Harvard Educational Review, 58*(2), 133–153.

Spindler, G. (1955). *Anthropology and education.* Stanford, CA: Stanford University Press.

Spindler, G. (1974). *Education and cultural process: Toward an anthropology of education.* New York: Holt, Rinehart & Winston.

Sternberg, R. (1985). *Beyond IQ: A triarchic theory of human intelligence.* New York: Cambridge University Press.

Sue, S., & Padilla, A. (1986). Ethnic minority issues in the United States: Challenges for the educational system. In California State Department of Education (Ed.), *Beyond language: social and cultural factors in schooling language minority students* (pp. 35–72). Los Angeles: Evaluation, Dissemination, and Assessment Center, California State University, Los Angeles.

Tharp, R. G. (1989). Psychocultural variables and k constants: Effects on teaching and learning in schools. *American Psychologist, 44,* 349–359.

Thomas, S. V., & Park, B. (1921). *Culture of immigrants.* Cambridge, MA: Newcome Press.

Thompson, G. G. (1952). *Child Psychology.* Boston: Houghton-Mifflin.

Trueba, H. (1987). *Success or failure? Learning and the language minority student.* Scranton, PA: Harper & Row.

Trueba, H. (1988). *Rethinking learning disabilities: Cultural knowledge in literacy acquisition.* Unpublished manuscript, Office for Research on Educational Equity, Graduate School of Education, University of California, Santa Barbara.

Vogt, L. A., Jordan, C. J., & Tharp, R. G. (1987). Explaining school failure, producing school success: Two cases. *Anthropology and Education Quarterly, 18,* 276–286.

Walberg, H. (1986). Synthesis of research on teaching. In M. Wittrock (Ed.), *Handbook of research on teaching* (3rd ed., pp. 214–229). New York: Macmillan.

Walker, C. L. (1987). Hispanic achievements: Old views and new perspectives. In H. Trueba (Ed.), *Success or failure? Learning and the language minority student* (pp. 15–32). Scranton, PA: Harper and Row.

Walsh, D. (1990, January 21). Californian new students speaking in many languages. *San Francisco Examiner,* B1–B4.

Wiesner, T. S., Gallimore, R., & Jordan, C. (1988). Unpackaging cultural effects on classroom learning: Native Hawaiian peer assistance and child-generated activity. *Anthropology and Education Quarterly, 19,* 327–353.

Wertsch, J. (1985). *Vygotsky and the social formation of the mind.* Cambridge, MA: Harvard University Press.

Willig, A. (1986). Effectiveness of bilingual education. *Review of Educational Research, 55,* 269–317.

Zentella, A. C. (1981). Ta bien you could answer me en cualquier idioma: Puerto Rican code-switching in bilingual classrooms. In R. Duran (Ed.), *Latino language and communicative behavior* (pp. 109–132). Norwood, NJ: Ablex.

·25·

EFFECTIVE PRESCHOOL AND KINDERGARTEN PROGRAMS FOR STUDENTS AT RISK

Nancy Karweit

CENTER FOR RESEARCH ON EFFECTIVE SCHOOLING FOR DISADVANTAGED STUDENTS

THE JOHNS HOPKINS UNIVERSITY

Early childhood education has traditionally been aligned with social and educational reform efforts (Lazar & Darlington, 1982). From the first pioneers who championed early intervention for the poor (e.g., Comenius, Pestalozia, and Montessori) to present-day advocates of quality preschool programs for students "at risk," the connection between early schooling and social intervention has clearly been made. For example, in the United States the early efforts of the Peabody sisters in Massachusetts to provide early education for children of poverty were motivated by the desire to better the future lives of these children. More recently, the establishment of the Head Start program as a part of President Johnson's War on Poverty provides evidence of the connection between early education and social reform.

Despite the existence of this long-term connection between education of young children and social reform, actual support for preschool and kindergarten has been intermittent, being picked up and abandoned as a function of economic, social, and political forces. For example, during the depression and World War II, the federal government sponsored nursery schools, but had little other involvement until the mid-1960s. This spotty history is in part due to the fact that preschools are operated by multiple sponsors, including churches, public schools, private schools, and profit and not-for-profit day care centers. Given the different auspices, regulations and governing agencies vary widely. Consequently, no regularized, institutionalized system guarantees preschool for the disadvantaged or for any other group. Head Start, and programs run under Chapter 1 funds, have existed for more than 20 years, but are constantly in jeopardy and have never served a large proportion of the eligible students. At present, early programs have little legal, pro-visional, or guaranteed financial foundation. Part of the issue surrounding the future direction of prekindergarten and kindergarten programs is the question of legal and financial status within the education system. Although such questions are inherently political and social, issues of educational benefit are clearly relevant in this debate.

It is therefore important and especially timely for a discussion of the evidence regarding the short-term and long-term effects of early education. What does research indicate about the effectiveness of preschool and kindergarten as an intervention strategy? What is the evidence about the effects of particular programs for students at risk? Finally, what are some of the larger issues that need to be considered as states and locales incorporate preschools and kindergartens into their elementary schools?

This chapter reviews the major literature on the effects of preschool and kindergarten for disadvantaged students. Particular attention is given to the question of the effects of specific curricular models and programs, including programs that have been certified as effective by the U.S. Department of Education's Joint Dissemination Review Panel (JDRP). We first focus on programs for 4-year-olds (preschool) and then consider programs and practices for 5-year-olds (kindergarten).

RECENT PRESCHOOL TRENDS

The term *preschool* covers a wide variety of early educational experiences. It may mean a half-day nursery school program that emphasizes play and socialization, or it may mean a full-day academic program where the intention is to teach reading and math readiness skills. It may mean programs for 4-year-olds, 3-year-olds, or even earlier intervention efforts. Here, we focus primarily on prekindergarten programs for 4-year-olds.

The first important change in preschool programs is the very rapid rate of growth over the last 20 years. Whereas only 15% of all 4-year-olds were enrolled in 1964, almost half of all 4-year-olds are presently enrolled in preschool (Center for Education Statistics, 1989, fig. 1).

A second important change is the auspices for preschool. There is a growing involvement of public schools in the provision of preschool programs. State education agencies in 31 states and the District of Columbia currently fund prekindergarten programs for 4-year-olds (Mitchell, 1989). State-funded programs are operated either by permissive language in the state's school code or by special legislative provision for programs.

A third area of change is the singular view of the significance of early childhood experiences for later development. The early 1960s saw an increased focus on early childhood as a prime time for intervention. Part of the reasoning was that because infancy is a period of unusually rapid maturation and sensitivity, intervention at this point was particularly critical. Bloom (1964) states the prevailing beliefs about early development and intervention were as follows:

In terms of intelligence measured at age 17, about 50% of the development takes place between conception and age 4, 30% between 4 and 8, 20% between 8 and 17.... The evidence so far available suggests that marked changes in environment in the early years can produce greater changes in intelligence than will equally marked changes in the environment at later periods of development.

Thus the prevailing belief in the mid-1960s was that a single, restricted, and essentially modest intervention could have lifelong consequences. As Elkind (1986) states, "Great expectations and promises were based on the view that the young child was plastic material to be molded quickly and permanently by the proper school environment." The early childhood intervention programs of this era were conceived in a period of great optimism and equally great naïveté about the possibility of the strength of early intervention.

Some of the enthusiasm was diminished by early evaluations of Head Start and by conclusions that compensatory education was tried and failed (Jensen, 1969). Yet, of the interventions born in this era, the long-term positive effects recently documented are altering this gloomy picture (Berrueta-Clement, Schweinhart, Barnett, Epstein, and Weikart, 1984).

Accompanying this shift in the view of environment on development was an important redefinition of the role of early cognitive experiences. Prior to the 1960s, there was actually very little concern with the issue of early intellectual functioning. Instead, the concern was with the development of the healthy personality of the child, which if properly taken care of would automatically include intellectual maturity as well. There was little interest or concern over providing appropriate learning environments, since satisfactory intellectual development was seen as primarily maturational, not environmental. After the late 1960s and into the present, this view of childhood has

given way to what Elkind (1986) calls the 'competent infant' point of view.

The competent infant movement has two important assumptions: (1) malleability of traits such as IQ, and (2) singular importance of early intervention to prevent later impoverishment in intellectual functioning. The latter issue points directly to the need for appropriate early childhood education programs both as an intervention strategy for the disadvantaged and as an appropriate educational step for advantaged students as well.

With these changes in the views of children and with ever increasing numbers of women in the labor force, it is not surprising that the area of early education became an area of great interest in the 1980s. Many states and local districts are continuing to buy into the idea, but there are some concerns being voiced. For example, some black citizens note that the school system has failed them already and question why the public schools should have any better a record in early education than they do in elementary and secondary education. Others note the difficulty in funding programs at a sufficiently high level to duplicate the quality programs that served as an impetus for implementing preschool programs in the first place (Grubb, 1987). Still others are concerned that the preschools are being implemented to help alleviate the need for child care and question why the public schools should foot the bill for these services. Therefore, many social, political, and educational issues are involved in present discussions about preschool. Nonetheless, the educational benefits of preschool programs should be a primary consideration and understanding the short- and long-term educational benefits of such programs is central to the current debate. The discussion here focuses first on those studies that have examined the effects on students of attendance at preschool in comparison to students who did not attend preschool. Next, the discussion considers the results of participation in particular types of preschool curricula.

PARTICIPATION IN PRESCHOOL PROGRAMS

The first set of studies we consider addresses the issue of the effects of participation in preschool programs. An important body of studies, collectively known as The Consortium for Longitudinal Studies (1982), provides critical evidence of the long- and short-term effects of early intervention efforts. The Consortium came about in response to the finding of an influential Westinghouse (1969) evaluation of Head Start, which concluded that the program was not having long-term effects on success in school. Lazar and Grotberg proposed in 1974 finding well-designed earlier studies that could be used as a base for follow-up efforts. Fifteen such studies, authored by 12 developers, were located. The studies differed in many respects— sample size, age of student, approach to intervention—but they all had in common the intention to assist the future chances of low-income children, primarily from minority homes. The Consortium then examined the long- and short-term benefits of enrollment in these programs.

For our purposes, we are primarily interested in programs whose effectiveness was determined by an adequate experimental design and which focused on programs for 4-year-olds.

We focus on 4-year-olds because most programs being implemented today are specific to this age child.

From the 15 projects in the Consortium studies, 6 projects were located that focused on 4-year-olds (those developed by Bellar, Deutsch, Gray, Karnes, and Weikart). From this list of 6, 2 studies (Gray and Weikart) randomly assigned students to treatment and control groups. Following Slavin's (1986) best-evidence synthesis methodology, these 2 studies are therefore given the greatest attention here.

Gray (Early Training Project)

Gray's Early Training Project (Gray, Ramsey, & Klaus, 1982) consisted of a 10-week summer program in which students met for 4 hours daily, 5 days per week. Students participated in a class of 20, served by 1 teacher and 4 assistants. During the school year, home visitors also worked with each family once a week for a period of 1 hour.

The Early Training Project focused on perceptual/cognitive and language development using a traditional nursery school format, but with activities sequenced to become increasingly complex and carefully focused on increasing language use. The first entry in Table 25–1 summarizes the major features and effects of Gray's study.

Sixty-one students were randomly assigned to 1 of 3 conditions: 2 groups that entered the program just described at different ages, and an untreated control group. An additional control group in another city was also used. The 2 treatment conditions differed only in the age at which they started the program.

The pretest IQ scores for the treatment and control groups were 89.4 and 87.3, respectively. At age 5, after participation in the program, the IQ scores were 96.05 and 86.3. By age 17, the IQs were once again very similar: 78.7 and 76.4.

Gray determined that 2.4% of the program children were placed in special education and 23.8% of the control children were so placed. The program children also showed a greater likelihood of not being retained in grade. Nearly 56% of the program children were retained in grade, whereas the figure was closer to 69% for the control children. About 22% of the program children dropped out of high school prior to completion; the corresponding figure for control children was about 43%. Thus the program had significant effects on important variables of grade repetition, special education status, and high school completion. The effect sizes are in the range of 0.14 to 1.09 (see Table 25–1, far right-hand column).

Concerning the effects on reading and mathematics achievement in elementary schools, the Gray study provides little reason to expect continued effects of program participation. The performance of students in the program was not significantly different from that of control students in math or reading at grades 4 and 6. Thus the study does not lend support to long-term effects of this type of early intervention effort on achievement.

When the effects are analyzed separately by sex, a somewhat different picture emerges. There are pronounced sex differences. In particular, the Gray program appears to have been beneficial for girls, but not for boys. It is not clear what factors or processes created these sex differences in the Gray study.

Weikart (Perry Preschool)

The other study included in the longitudinal follow-up that focused on 4-year-olds and used random assignment in its design is the Perry Preschool Project (Berrueta-Clement et al., 1984). There are 2 parts to the Perry Preschool data that will be discussed. The first considers the effect of participation in preschool versus no preschool. The second considers the effect of participation in a particular preschool curricula.

The sample consisted of 123 disadvantaged, low-IQ children from Ypsilanti, Michigan. The subjects were recruited by locating all families with 3-year-old children and interviewing the parents to determine their occupation, education, and household density. Children from low-SES families were administered an IQ test and those who scored in the 70–85 range were selected. Students were randomly assigned to treatment and control groups.

There were 5 waves of this study, beginning in 1962 and continuing through 1967. Across the 5 waves, 58 students were assigned to the preschool condition and 65 to the no preschool condition.

In contrast to the Gray project, the Perry Preschool Project took place during the academic year as a regular school program. The curricular approach was based on the theories of development of Piaget. "[The] theoretical framework emphasized the interplay of content (e.g., classification and spatial relationship), 3 levels of representation (e.g., index, symbol, and sign), and 2 levels of operation (motor and verbal)" (Lazar and Darlington, 1982). The approach emphasized developmentally appropriate activities and stressed the role of students' planning and initiation in their own learning.

Children entered the program at age 3 and attended the program for 2 years, mid-October to May. The sessions were half-day, 5 days per week. In addition, the teachers visited the home of the students for 90 minutes weekly.

The short-term benefit of the Perry Preschool program is evident in the 11-point differences in IQ scores between program and control students. The percent enrolled in special education is also appreciably lower for the preschool enrollees (45% vs 31%). The differences between those repeating and not repeating a grade were 2%. The largest differences were in the percent who graduated from high school, with 67% of the experimental students completing high school and only 49% of the students in control classes. Similar differences in the percent employed and arrested were found, favoring the Perry Preschool Program.

The differences in the percent correct on the CAT, taken at ages 7, 8, 9, 10, 11, and 14, favored the Perry preschool children but were not statistically significant and ranged from only 2% to 8%. The second entry in Table 25–1 summarizes the findings from the Perry Preschool.

Both the Gray and the Perry Preschool programs support the conclusion that preschool programs can have strong immediate effects on cognitive functioning, as measured by IQ tests. These effects are apparent at the onset of treatment and continue several years afterward. In the case of Perry Preschool, the experimental group is 44% of a standard deviation above the control at age 7. In the case of Gray's study, the effects are still detectable 6 years after the initial treatment (effect size = .51).

TABLE 25–1. Effects of Preschool Attendance on Achievement and Other Outcomes

Project	Program/Focus	Strategy/Treatment	Population	Study Design	IQ	Measure/Effects TRT	CTL	ES
Early Training Project (Gray)	Intervention program to change attitudes/aptitudes needed for school success.	Morning (4 hours) summer session for 10 weeks and weekly 1-hour home visits with parent and child to emphasize parental role in education of child. Small staff ratio (5:1).	88 African American children in Murfreesboro, TN, ages 3½–4½ in 1962; group A=61 children in same town; group B=27 children in similar town.	Group A (67 students) randomly assigned to T1 (3-year treatment), T2 (2-year) or T3 (no treatment). Group B was second control group (T4).	end of yr.	89.4	87.3	.15
					+1 yr.	96.1	86.3	.81
					+2 yr.	94.9	81.9	1.09
					+3 yr.	97.7	89.6	.63
					+4 yr.	93.6	86.1	.51
					+6 yr.	88.4	81.2	.54
					Spec. ed.	2.4	23.8	.50
					Repeat	47.5	55.6	.16
					Drop out	22.0	43.0	.14

Project	Program/Focus	Strategy/Treatment	Population	Study Design	Age	PS	No PS	ES
Perry Preschool (Berreuta-Clement et al., 1983)	Examination of effect of preschool on disadvantaged children. Longitudinal study that followed students up through age 19.	Curricular approach based on developmentally appropriate activities, stressing role of planning and active learning of child.	123 disadvantaged 3- to 4-year-olds from Ypsilanti, MI with IQs between 60 and 90, not otherwise handicapped.	5 waves, 1962–67. Students in each wave randomly assigned to experimental control or condition.	Pre	79.6	78.6	.17
					5	94.1	83.2	1.01
					6	91.3	86.3	.45
					7	91.7	87.1	.44
					8	88.1	86.9	.11
				Wave/PS/NoPS	10	84.9	84.6	.03
				0 13 15	14	82.3	82.0	.04
				1 8 9			Cat (percent correct)	
				2 12 14	Age	PS	No PS	ES
				3 13 14	7	37%	32%	.17
				4 <u>12 13</u>	8	53	47	.12
				Tot 58 65	9	46	38	.14
					10	60	54	.12
					11	67	65	.05
					14	36	28	.17

(continued)

TABLE 25–1. (*continued*)

Project	Program/Focus	Strategy/Treatment	Population	Study Design
NY State Experimental PreK Program (Levine)	Individualized program emphasizing total environment and student choice.	Parent involvement; Health service; Social service.	Longitudinal PreK–3, 5000 disadvantaged in program, selected into program on low economic status. Control group was "waiting-list control group" eligibles without space; and other district control group, similar but not operating PreK.	2 waves: 1975, 1976.

Measure/Effects

School Success

Age	PS	No PS	ES
HS Grad	67%	49%	+.72
Retain	15	13	–.22
Social	31	45	+.27

Social/Behavioral

	PS	No PS	ES
Arrest	22	43	+.85
Employ	48	29	.92
Wave:		I	II
Walker	WL/CTL		WL/CTL
Readiness PK		+	+
Start K		+	+
End K		0	0
1		0	0
2		0	0
3		0	0
Peabody PK			+
Start K		+	0
End K		+	+
1		+	0
(Longitudinal analysis) 2		+	0
3		+	0
Grade repetition	+		
Special education	+		

Both studies also showed similar patterns of effects on reduced referral to special education and lower rates of dropping out of high school. In the case of the Perry Preschool Program, the effect size was 0.72 for high school graduation. In the case of Gray, the effect size was 0.80 for females and 0.10 for males.

Both studies showed minimal long-term effects on achievement as measured by standardized tests. Gray's study measured achievement at grades 4 and 6 and showed no significant effect on achievement scores at either grade. Weikart's study also shows only modest achievement effects (effect sizes of 0.05 to 0.17).

Head Start Evaluations

Head Start programs were begun in 1965 as a national effort to "improve children's intellectual skills, to foster their social and emotional growth, and to help meet their health and nutritional needs." The importance of early intervention was based on the belief that infancy was an especially critical time for intervention. It was believed that intervention of a short duration during this critical time could provide a life-long developmental boost.

Perhaps the most publicized evaluation of Head Start was the Westinghouse Evaluation (1969), which concluded that Head Start was not satisfactorily meeting its objectives. However, many methodological and philosophical issues were leveled against the report and its conclusions.

The study used a posttest-only research design, comparing the achievement of Head Start attendees with a sample of students matched on age and sex. The Head Start sample included children who attended summer school only and children who attended full-year Head Start programs.

The posttest-only comparisons indicated no measurable advantage of Head Start children in summer programs over comparison children. The full-year program was more effective than the summer program but the lack of robust effects led the authors to conclude that "the benefits cannot be described as satisfactory."

A major criticism of the report was the expectation that success would be measured as positive effects not only immediately after the program, but also several years later. Other criticisms of the report cited the insensitivity of the research design to differences in programs and the nonequivalence of the control and experimental groups.

More recent and methodologically rigorous evaluations (McKey, Condelli, Ganson, Barrett, McConkey, and Plantz, 1985) have emphasized that Head Start was apparently successful in meeting many of its objectives. Studies using random assignment or matched control groups in the McKey review provide very strong evidence of the immediate effects of Head Start on cognitive functioning (average effect sizes = 0.52), but little evidence for long-term effects (effect size = 0.10 after first year, 0.08 after second year, and 0.02 after 3+ years). A more positive picture of the long-term effects emerges if grade retention and special education placement are used as the criteria. Here, the three studies of the long-term effects indicate median effect sizes of 0.31 for retention and 0.29 for special education placement (McKey et al., 1985, p. 19).

Irvine (New York Experimental Prekindergarten Study)

New York state began an experimental prekindergarten program in 1966, designed to serve children from low-economic homes (Irvine, 1982). The prekindergarten program had 4 components: classroom experience, health services, social services, and parent involvement.

The effects of the program were assessed by comparison of the prekindergarten group with two control groups. One group was comprised of students who were on a waiting list for the program. The other group was comprised of eligible but not participating students.

The effects of the program were assessed by a comparison of these groups at the end of the prekindergarten year and at the beginning and end of kindergarten and at the end of grades 1, 2, 3, and 6.

The comparisons suggest that the prekindergarten program had immediate effects and some sustained effects in terms of achievement, grade retention, and rates of referral to special education. With the available technical and published reports, it was not possible to compute effect sizes for all relevant comparisons. Thus Table 25–1 indicates only the direction of the effect without its magnitude.

These 4 studies collectively suggest that there is an immediate and sizeable cognitive effect for participation in preschool that is diminished but still detectable in the elementary grades. The effect sizes diminish from a range of around 1.00 standard deviation at the end of the prekindergarten year, to around 0.20 by the end of the third grade.

PARTICIPATION IN PARTICULAR PRESCHOOL PROGRAMS

We now consider studies that have examined the effect of participation in particular preschool curricula. Two types of studies are considered—those that make direct comparisons among particular curricular models (Table 25–2), and those that provide evidence of effectiveness of a particular model, in particular JDRP programs (Table 25–3).

Curriculum Comparison Studies

The first study contrasted the immediate and long-term effects of 3 different preschool curricula. The 3 models were a language training approach based on the work of Bereiter and Engelman (1966), a cognitively oriented approach based on the Perry Preschool model, and a unit-based approach which followed a traditional nursery school model. These models represent a wide range of approaches to preschool education.

The structural features of the programs were identical. The programs met for half days and had a low adult/child ratio. Home visits of $1\frac{1}{2}$ hours were made every 2 weeks with an emphasis on training the parents as teachers in a method consistent with the model.

Students were randomly assigned to treatment groups. Eligible students lived within the Ypsilanti public school attendance area, were from low-SES homes, were 3 years old, and were below average in IQ. (The average IQ range was 62–90.)

Four waves of children participated in the CD project from 1967–1970. These waves were called waves 5 through 8, following waves 0 through 4 in the original study.

Wave 5 (n = 27) contained children who had been in the Perry Preschool program the previous year either as controls or as program participants, as well as new enrollees. Control group children went to the language program, new enrollees to the unit-based, and Perry Preschool program continued in the cognitively oriented group. In the original report of the CD project, these 27 children were not included. Because children in Wave 5 experienced different educational programs as three year olds and were not enrolled for 2 consecutive years in 1 of the 3 CD project programs, they were not included in the longitudinal sample. However, we note that these students were included in later reports and analyses.

Siblings were assigned to the same programs. Some reassignment of children was necessary to maintain equivalence along IQ lines. Of the various background features, the only one that was significantly different across the three groups was "years of mother's education" (the language group had 9.7, the cognitively oriented curriculum group had 9.3, and the nursery school had 10.9).

Cognitive measures of the 3 different preschool groups were taken at ages 3 through 8 and 10. The most striking pattern is the large jump in IQ for all 3 groups after entry into the program and a steady decline after the initial jump. However, many factors influence the validity of these results. First, the predictive validity of IQ scores before age 5 is minimal (McCall, Applebaum, and Hogarty, 1973). Second, students were selected on the basis of low IQ scores, ensuring that the means would tend to rise over time due to statistical regression. These difficulties and the fact that the means are based on a small number of cases suggest a great deal of caution in interpreting these results. We do note that, in most cases, the mean IQ for students in the language group exceeded that of the cognitively oriented group, by as much as nearly half of a standard deviation (at age 5) and by a third of a standard deviations (ages 7 and 10). These results are not statistically significant given the small sample size, but are suggestive that the language program did have more positive impact on means of IQ measures than did the cognitive curriculum.

The recent major finding from this study, which has received a great deal of attention, is the claim that there is a connection between type of preschool experience and delinquency at age 15. Schweinhart and Weikart (1986) followed 54 of the original 68 children in the study at age 15 and obtained self-reports of delinquent acts for these groups. They found that the cognitively oriented and nursery groups reported engaging in half as many delinquent acts as the direct instruction group—5 for the High/Scope, 7 for the nursery school, and 13 for the direct instruction group. From this finding, the authors (Schweinhart, Weikart, and Larner, 1986) have suggested that enrollment in academic preschool programs is linked to delinquency. In particular, the lack of autonomy and self-direction in direct instruction models is suggested to be related to the emergence of different rates of juvenile delinquency.

How credible are these claims of different effects by preschool program type? Bereiter (1986) and Gersten (1986) point out several difficulties with the study design and methodology.

First, there is the problem that sample attrition from the original sample of 15-year-olds resulted in an uneven distribution of females across the 3 groups. In the original sample (n = 68), the female proportion was 59, 52, and 59 for direct instruction, cognitively oriented curriculum, and nursery school; in the sample of 15-year-olds, the respective female proportion was 44, 61 and 55. These differences, although not statistically significant, are important because the differences between self-reported incidents of juvenile delinquency vary by sex, with males reporting far more and more serious delinquent behaviors than females (Gottfredson, 1987). As Bereiter (1986) points out, this difference in the sex composition of the sample could account for the difference between the treatments. Schweinhart and Weikart, however, replied that the "delinquency scale showed no gender bias, with study males reporting an average of 9 offenses and study females an average of 8." They go on to note that direct instruction males averaged 12 offenses whereas females averaged 14 offenses. Unfortunately, separate results by sex are not presented to assess the role that differential attrition by sex may have contributed, although the authors report that a series of 2-way analyses of variance that controlled for sex, race, and mother's education found the same pattern of results.

Second, some of the children in the nursery and direct instruction models had only one year of preschool experience, but all the cognitively oriented children were enrolled 2 years. Again, it is not clear that extent to which these duration differences is of consequence.

A third concern is that observational data collected at the time of the study (Seifert, 1969) do not suggest that the operating environments in the classrooms were in fact all that different in terms of the major intervening theoretical variable—opportunities for self-direction and child-initiated activities.

Finally, the conclusions of this study seem to be at odds with the conclusions of other longitudinal studies of the effects of different curricula. Two other longitudinal studies that have made curricular comparisons similar to the ones made by the Curriculum Demonstration project (Karnes, Shwedel, & Williams, 1983; and Miller & Bizzel, 1983) do not find differences by curricula. The results of these 2 studies are summarized in Table 25–2. The Karnes studies contrasted 5 treatments: traditional nursery school, community/integrated, Montessori, GOAL (Karnes), and direct verbal (Bereiter-Engelman). The authors conclude that no one method demonstrated superiority over the others. They also conclude that the effects of preschool fade out after about the middle of the elementary years. It does appear that the initial scores for students in the GOAL and the direct verbal treatment were greater than the other treatments, although these results do not appear to be long lasting.

Miller and Bizell (1983) found an interesting pattern of treatment by sex interaction effects in their comparison of the short- and long-term effects of participation in 4 distinct preschool curricula. The 4 treatments were Bereiter-Engelman, Gray, Montessori, and a traditional nursery school. They found minimal evidence of effects until the results were analyzed

TABLE 25-2. Comparison of the Effectiveness of Particular Curricular Approaches

Project	Program/Focus	Treatment	Population	Study Design
Perry Preschool CD Project	Comparison of effects of 3 distinct preschool curricular approaches on short- and long-term factors.	Half-day preschool sessions and home visits 1½ hr/wk. T1 = Academic preschool program (N = 23); T2 = Cognitively oriented curriculum (N = 22); T3 = Traditional nursery school (N = 23). N = 68 Perry N = 65 Control group	Disadvantaged black 3-year-olds in Ypsilanti, MI, who scored between 62-90 on Stanford Binet test.	4 waves of children entered the project from 1967–70. Students randomly assigned to 1 of 3 treatment conditions and then reassigned to balance on IQ. (Control group was Perry preschool group from wave 0–4 in previous study)
Louisville (Miller & Bizzel, 1983)	To compare the effects of 4 distinct preschool curricular approaches. Longitudinal study K–10. Program had demonstrated effectiveness and represented different philosophies.	All 4 treatments attended preK classes 6.5 hours/day for 1 academic year. T1 = B-E (Bereiter-Engelman); T2 = Darcee (Gray); T3 = Montessori; T4 = Traditional; C = Regular	14 preK classes in Louisville, KY. Students assigned to T1 = 64 T2 = 64 T3 = 33 T4 = 53 N = 214	Random assignment to T/C.
	Followup sample in 9th and 10th grade. Random assignment to groups	Head Start. B-E—Academic preschool carefully structured, highly verbal, patterned drill and practice in small groups. Darcee-Gray's program focused on language development and motivation in teacher-directed format.	Students in program for 1 year. Kindergarten year they were in different program.	

Effects

Cognitive Effects-IQ

Age	DSTR	H/S	NS	CTL	DSTR (HS)	NR (HS)
3	79	77	79	79	HS	HS
4	107	106	102	83	+.06	-.26
5	104	97	92	84	+.46	-.35
6	99	97	93	87	+.13	-.26
7	97	92	95	87	+.35	-.33
8	91	92	90	87	-.06	-.13
10	97	92	90	85	+.35	-.13

School Achievement (CAT + APL)

Age	DSTR	H/S	NS	D/HS	NS/HS
7	100	102	106	-.05	+.10
8	160	167	154	-.14	-.14
15	15.1	17.7	18.4	-.29	+.07

School Success

	DSTR	H/S	NS
Repeat grade	20%	18%	20%

Social/Behavior (age15)

	DSTR	H/S	NS	C
Delinquent	12.8%	5.4%	5.4%	6.9%

IQ	T1 BE	T2 DAR	T3 MONT	T4 TRAD	C CTL
PPK	94.7	96.7	90.9	91.8	89.0
EPK	99.8	96.4	96.8	98.2	90.8
K	94.7	93.2	93.3	95.0	95.0
1	91.4	93.4	93.8	93.4	93.0
2	86.6	89.3	92.5	90.8	92.8
7	82.9	84.8	87.4	86.0	ND
8	86.7	85.3	88.9	86.6	ND

Males

IQ	T1	T2	T3	T4
PPK	97.1	94.3	89.1	91.3
EPK	100.5	95.8	91.7	96.0
K	93.2	93.8	91.3	97.9
1	93.1	94.2	92.8	97.5
2	90.2	89.4	96.6	94.3
8	90.0	83.5	92.7	88.1
10	84.5	78.0	93.3	83.9

(continued)

TABLE 25–2. (*continued*)

Project	Program/Focus	Treatment	Population	Study Design	Effects					

Effects (first project — Montessori/Traditional):

IQ				Females	
PreK	92.9	100.0	92.4	92.1	
EndK	99.2	97.5	101.1	99.4	
K	95.8	92.2	94.8	93.4	
1	90.1	92.2	94.6	91.1	
2	83.8	89.1	89.2	88.8	
8	84.1	88.3	85.7	85.7	
10	82.1	88.5	77.4	87.1	

Treatment (first project):

Montessori—Emphasis on use of self-corrected materials and discovery; focus on relation, development of mind and senses. Structured curriculum in which sequence of activities controlled.

Traditional—Traditional nursery school program focusing on social and emotional development.

Karnes (comparison of 5 approaches)

Program/Focus:

Comparative evaluation of 5 preschool programs for children from low-income families.

Programs varied on extent of structure and program emphasis.

Differential program effectiveness favored T4 and T5 on immediate cognitive effects, but T3 on long-term effects.

No IQ effects by age 16.

Treatment:

T1 = Traditional nursery; T2 = Community/Integrated; T3 = Montessori; T4 = GOAL (Karnes); T5 = Direct verbal (B-E).

T4 = emphasis on sensory motor with concurrent emphases on exp. language.

T5 = direct instruction in preskills.

Low parental involvement in these projects.

Half-day program for 1 year.

Second year: T1, T2, T3 attended regular K; T4 attended regular K + 1 hr. session; T5 attended intensive language, not regular, K.

Population:

Low-income families from Champaign/Urbana, IL. 123 students in original sample, 45 in post hoc comparison group.

Age 4 at entry. Duration 1 hr. and some treatment in second year.

Study Design:

Random assignment to treatment, no control group at the time, post hoc group constructed later, 15-yr study.

Effects:

	T1	T2	T3	T4	T5	
IQ	94.5	93.3	94.1	96.0	93.5	
	102.6	98.4	99.6	110.3	109.2	.39

T4 and T5 > T1, T2, T3

Comparison post hoc control group

		Percent
Referred spec. ed.	21.6	33.3
Retained	12.9	35.7

separately by sex. The Montessori males had achievement and IQ scores in the range of 0.25 to 0.50 of a standard deviation higher than the other treatments. The Montessori males also had higher achievement at kindergarten and through the eighth grade.

Taken together, the 3 studies do not present a consistent picture of the greater effectiveness of a particular preschool model. On the basis of these data, it would be difficult to justify or condemn a particular approach. This suggests that many competing programs may be worthwhile and not injurious to children and that other considerations may therefore be more important in deciding how to organize and deliver prekindergarten instruction. This finding is also consistent with evidence for the kindergarten year, considered also in this chapter.

JDRP Studies

In addition to these 3 studies that contrast specific programs, evidence of program effectiveness is provided by evaluations submitted to the U.S. Department of Education's Joint Dissemination Review Panel (JDRP), from the Compensatory Education Source Book and from other published literature. We wrote to the developers of the programs listed by the JDRP and by the Compensatory Education Source Book for details of program design, operation, and evaluation. Many of the evaluations provide only a limited description of the evaluation or did not use a strong evaluation design. Virtually none of the studies in the 2 compilations used random assignment to treatment or control or used a matched control group. Therefore, many of these studies should be viewed as illustrative of possible effective strategies and be candidates for a more thorough evaluation.

The studies listed in Table 25–3 are illustrative of the programs found in these sourcebooks. They cover a wide range of approaches to early childhood education. There are parent involvement programs centered in the home (Levenstein and Compensatory Early Education Home Based Program) and in the school (Child Parent Centers and Seton Hall), diagnostic prescriptive programs (Reading Improvement and Preschool, Early Prevention of School Failure), supplemental programs (Communication Program), general curricular models (Cognitively Oriented Preprimary Experience/COPE and Cognitively Oriented Curriculum), and language enrichment (Peabody Language Development Kit/PLDK evaluations).

We list these studies to give a flavor of the variety of approaches and to make a plea for evaluations with adequate control groups so that effectiveness might be better judged. Of the studies listed here, typical of the ones listed by JDRP and the other sourcebook, effectiveness was judged primarily by comparing pre-post gains with expected pre-post score gains. But such an approach does not control for the operation of other factors that influence the growth as well. The 2 exceptions to this are the evaluations by Levenstein and the evaluations of the Peabody Language Development Kit. In Levenstein's case (1970), individuals were randomly assigned to a treatment and control group for comparisons on maternal interactive behavior (the major intervening variable) and to a matched control group on cognitive and school success measures. In the case of the PLDK, although the findings of various meta-analyses have

been disputed, the original evaluation of the pilot materials (Dunn, Horton, and Smith, 1981) does provide evidence of its effectiveness.

Summary Prekindergarten

These studies suggest that there are short-term and long-term benefits for children from participation in preschool programs. The benefits are most pronounced immediately after participation and exhibit the familiar washout effect as students progress through elementary school.

The examination of program effectiveness does not suggest the superiority of one particular approach. However, this conclusion does not imply that schools can therefore open up their doors to 4-year-olds and automatically expect the same types of effects as demonstrated by the curriculum studies. The curriculum studies all used well-conceptualized highly integrated, very structured, and coherent approaches to preschool education. They were quality versions of a particular philosophical approach. We actually know very little about the effectiveness of programs as they are currently being implemented, which often fall far short of the quality programs discussed here. We do not know, for example, how far programs can deviate from the conditions in these studies in terms of class size, teacher training, and physical environment before the effects disappear. It is important to learn if programs, as implemented, are indeed as effective as the research on which they are based indicates they might be.

KINDERGARTEN TRENDS

At present there are no precise national data on kindergarten attendance. The National Center for Educational Statistics has conducted a household survey which will provide such estimates in late 1991. Estimates from different states suggest that, 87–93% of all first graders attended kindergarten. Most estimates provide statistics on the number of 5-year-olds enrolled in school, which can differ from those attending kindergarten. The kindergarten experience itself is not uniform. Kindergartens may be operated by public or private schools, may be academic or developmental in focus, may be in session for a full day every day, a half day every day, or, more rarely, for a full day part week. As the first introduction to the formal apparatus of schooling for many children, kindergarten is an important experience, but one that clearly takes on different meaning for different children.

It is especially important to understand how these different kindergarten experiences affect students at risk of future academic difficulty. Do these students enter first grade adequately prepared to succeed in elementary school or do they enter already behind and on their way to failure? What alternatives are there for students who are not successful in the kindergarten year? And finally, what arrangements of kindergarten seem most likely to increase the chance of academic success for these students?

The purpose of this part of the chapter is to describe effective kindergarten programs and practices for students at

TABLE 25–3. Description of Evaluated Preschool Programs

Name	Program Description	Staffing/Components	Study Design
Verbal Interact Project (Levenstein)	Home-based early intervention program for ages 2–4 based on view that conceptual growth is built on language of mother/child in home.	Toy demonstrator (High school education) Half-hour home sessions twice/week for 7 months over 2 years.	Comparison with randomly assigned control group.
Compensatory Early Education Home-Based Program	Identification of students who are significantly deficient in language development, gross- and fine-motor and readiness skills. Treatment to provide instructional activities; instruct parents in home in $1\frac{1}{2}$ hr./wk. training session.		Pre-post gains over 10-month period.
Parent Child Early Education (PCEE) Ferguson, MO	Primary focus on early identification and treatment of educationally disadvantaged child; focus on improving parent competencies. Identification— Comprehensive diagnosis includes initial evaluation by parents and teachers and diagnosis by staff specialist as needed. Treatment— (1) home teaching visits to provide individualized instruction Saturday school, and (2) home activity guides.	Saturday school and parent. Home visits/teaching carried out by specialist in learning disabilities.	Comparison of PreK participants with control with no PreK at entry to kindergarten; no evidence of initial equivalence groups.
Portage Project Portage, WI	Home teaching program for multicategorically handicapped birth to 6 and for nonhandicapped with developmental delays. Individualized curriculum; parents as teachers; weekly data collection on progress in home.	Individual assessment Individual planning Home teaching/visits Monitoring progress	Comparison of Portage Project with local preschool program for disadvantaged. Original certification by JDRP on basis of pre-post growth scores of 1.3 to 2.3 months in areas of physical, cognitive, language.
Child Parent Centers (CPC)	Individualized, highly structured half-day program; parent participation emphasized; general readiness objectives.	Support services by nurse, social worker, speech therapist and curriculum specialist. 17:1 staff	Comparisons with control group of children living in comparable conditions.
Seton Hall	Parent-child visit, school weekly; 2-hour session for structured learning; activities/parent discussion group: home activities to take away.	Parent educator	Pre-post design
Reading Improvement and Preschool	Students selected to participate on basis of developmental delays, using Denver Developmental Screening Test, program consisted of balance of activities taken from guidebook. Children attended 3 hours/day 4 days/ wk. for 160 days/yr. Training session with parents on fifth day.	One teacher, one aide, and volunteers to make ratio 5:1.	Pre-post design; NCE gain.
Communication Program	Supplemental 30-minute period/week in which teaching focuses primarily on communication.	Speech/language clinician works with classroom teacher.	Pre-post design; monthly gain.
COPE Cognitively Oriented Pre-Primary Experience	General and academic curriculum for preschool children, focuses on provision of cognitively appropriate curriculum.		Pre-post design; monthly gain.
Cognitively Oriented Preschool Curriculum	Open framework curriculum based on Piaget, plan-do-review sequence.	Teaching team; 2 adults/classroom.	Pre-post design

risk of future academic failure. Program is defined as a set of procedures intended to be implemented as a total package (including curriculum materials, inservice training, and strong evidence of effectiveness) and capable of being replicated by others. In order to be included in this review, evaluations had to present convincing evidence of effectiveness based on rigorous methodology. Alterable features of kindergarten, such as class size, length of day, and staffing patterns, are also highlighted.

What students are at risk of later failure? Is there a single diagnostic procedure or a series of procedures to identify such students? The definition and assessment of "at risk" is both a political and methodological issue that cannot be addressed in detail here. Instead, we leave the definition of "at risk" purposely vague. Students may be at risk because they enter school with specific auditory, visual, or other developmental lags. Students may be at risk because the linguistic opportunities in their daily lives are very limited and they lack the necessary background and experience in receptive and expressive language. Students may be at risk because they lack the necessary social/emotional skills to function semi-independently in a group setting such as a kindergarten classroom. Lastly, students may be at risk because the school program is inappropriate for them either in its approach or in its difficulty level.

The kindergarten year is pivotal for students who may encounter later academic difficulties—it provides the basis for their success in the elementary curriculum that follows. Once viewed primarily as a year of transition and outside the realm of the elementary program, today the kindergarten year is primarily viewed as an academic/preparatory year (Educational Resource Services, 1986) with clear connections to the elementary curriculum. Most of the programs in the public schools are focused either directly on academics (22%) or on academic preparation (63%).

These changes in the focus of kindergarten have gone along with changes in enrollment patterns and governance structure of kindergartens. Kindergarten enrollment has soared from about 5% of 5-year-olds in 1901 to the present 93% enrollment. At the same time, more and more of the kindergarten programs (84%) are provided by public schools. There is also increasing activity by states to make the kindergarten year mandatory. Finally, kindergarten programs, which started as full-day programs but were reduced to half-day programs during the baby boom era, are moving to full-day programs again.

These changes in enrollment, provision, and length of the kindergarten day are occurring concurrently with great pressures to increase the academic standards of schools, and a renewed optimism about the efficacy of early programs for disadvantaged youths. Also, the movement against social promotions has had a general effect on escalation of the curriculum for those who are promoted (Shepard and Smith, 1985), and this has produced increasing demands for accountability for the performance of kindergarten students. In the past, when kindergartens were mainly in private schools, were attended by only some students, and were mainly focused on socialization and adjustment, questions of program effectiveness and accountability were of little interest.

Today, kindergarten teachers need to send the first-grade teacher "prepared students." If children need to be ready to read in the first grade, then the kindergarten is held responsible for that preparation. If children need to be ready to add and subtract in first grade, then the kindergarten needs to teach them the necessary prerequisite number skills and concepts.

Some commentators are concerned that the push to early academics is harmful rather than beneficial to children (Elkind, 1986). The stress created by the demands of the formal learning situation, rather than benefitting students, may well place them at risk of future academic failure. Despite these concerns, the pressures for an academic kindergarten continue. In a recent survey, 61% of public school principals and about the same number of kindergarten teachers said the primary focus of their kindergarten program was "academic and social preparation" for first grade. About 22% of the principals said the primary focus was on academics. The kindergartens in urban areas were most likely to focus on academics.

Kindergarten Focus

If the major task of the kindergarten is to get students ready to read and compute, we need to know what readiness in these areas means. Many school districts are specific about the intended outcomes of the kindergarten year. For example, Table 25–4 shows the 23 objectives given by one school district. The kindergarten report card for this district indicates that kindergarten students are formally evaluated on these stated objectives.

Another way to examine the academic requirements for kindergarten is to look at the typical readiness tests given children in the kindergarten year. For example, consider the Metropolitan Readiness Test, a widely used test whose valida-

TABLE 25–4. Expected Student Outcomes: Kindergarten

1. Recognize and print name.
2. Name colors and letters.
3. Distinguish beginning sounds.
4. Tell a picture story in sequence.
5. Name 6 shapes.
6. Name and count objects 0–10.
7. Sequence numerals 0–10.
8. Match numerals with objects 0–10.
9. Color within boundaries.
10. Know personal data.
11. Fasten and tie shoes and coat.
12. Use scissors with ease.
13. Express ideas and take part in group discussion.
14. Listen attentively.
15. Recognize likenesses and differences.
16. Practice self-control.
17. Work and play cooperatively.
18. Follow directions.
19. Complete projects promptly.
20. Obey safety rules.
21. Practice good health habits.
22. Work independently.
23. Participate in organized activities.

tion centers on an analysis of the beginning reading process. Level I (early kindergarten) and Level II (late kindergarten) assess the following areas:

Level I	Level II
Auditory skill area	Auditory skill area
1. Auditory memory	1. Beginning consonants
2. Rhyming	2. Sound-letter correspondence
Visual skill area	Visual skill area
3. Letter recognition	3. Visual matching
4. Visual matching	4. Finding patterns
Language skill area	Language skill area
5. School language and listening	5. School language
6. Quantitative language	6. Listening
	Quantitative skill area
	7. Quantitative concepts
	8. Quantitative operations

Some of the skills, such as auditory memory and rhyming, may not seem directly related to reading. But learning to read requires calling upon a complex combination of visual, auditory, and kinesthetic skills. Visual perception is required in order to differentiate different letters, such as *w* versus *m* and *b* versus *d*. Auditory discrimination of similar sounds, such as *t* versus *d*, is needed to link the visual to the language known orally. The sound-sight correspondence of letters (phonemes) must also be mastered. The child needs to understand the concept of a word and syllable and how blending of phonemes creates words. Short-term memory is important—children need to be able to recall accurately the syllables they have blended, such as an-i-mal, not am-i-nal, a common confusion. Thus the kindergarten goal of preparing children for reading and arithmetic instruction in the first grade involves activities and tasks that may have little obvious resemblance to first-grade activities. Prerequisite skills are not necessarily the same skills in smaller dosages or of less difficulty. Mastering prerequisite skills does not mean working on smaller ditto sheets. Instead, readiness for reading and math involves conquering many visual, auditory, and fine and gross motor skills that are necessary in the process of reading, but may not seem to be obviously connected to reading.

Alternative approaches to beginning reading which focus on a more holistic and less fragmented view of literary acquisition and are currently challenging the skills-driven kindergarten. Whole language and other approaches focusing on the integration of writing and reading are dramatically changing the focus, content and process of kindergarten education. Stahl and Miller (1989) report on the positive effects of language experience/whole language for beginning reading. However, the effectiveness for disadvantaged and at risk students is not clear, or at least not demonstrated by the studies reviewed by Stahl and Miller.

Kindergarten Schedule and Activities

In the recent ERS (1986) study of public kindergartens, about three-fifths of all teachers stated that they followed "definite time allotments and sequence for each activity." A fairly typical half-day kindergarten schedule might be:

8:30–8:35	Arrival/get together
8:35–9:25	Reading
9:25–9:45	Exploration (free time)
9:45–10:10	Math
10:10–10:25	Movement/music
10:25–10:55	Social living/art
10:55–11:00	Dismissal

Reading or reading readiness instruction is typically based on a commercial reading readiness series (75% of all teachers in the ERS survey said they used the readiness series), and the teacher typically provides formal structured instruction during reading and math periods.

Objectives for the kindergarten year may be explicitly stated. For instance, detailed objectives for minimum, average, and above-average students may be formulated for comprehension skills (e.g., noting details, main idea, sequence, drawing conclusions), and vocabulary (e.g., phonetic analyses, short vowel, word meaning, final consonant, and consonant blends). As an example, the kindergarten objectives for the Baltimore City Public Schools covering phonetic analyses of initial consonant sounds states that "given a picture of an object or an action and several words, one with the same beginning sound as the pictured object, the student will select the word that begins the same as the pictured object or action."

KINDERGARTEN PRACTICES

One of the major problems facing the transition from kindergarten to first grade is how to assess readiness for first grade and what to do with and for students who are deemed not ready to go on to first grade. There are varied practices for assessing student readiness for first-grade work. These include teacher recommendation and judgment, results of standardized screening and assessment devices, and evaluations by specialized personnel. Bases for nonpromotion include student immaturity, low attention span, small size for kindergarten, inability to sit still, and retarded large/fine motor or language development. Concerning who is most likely to experience difficulty in kindergarten, we know that males far outnumber females, and that low-SES and minority students also outnumber their advantaged peers. The specific reasons for these referrals are quite different, however. For example, the males may be retained more often because of immaturity, whereas low-SES or disadvantaged students are more often retained because of language or other developmental lags.

Actions taken as a result of the failure to thrive in kindergarten generally fall into 3 categories: repetition of the kindergarten program, additional time within the kindergarten year, and alternative programs. The most common practice is an additional year either by repeating kindergarten or by pre-first transition, or junior first-grade placements. This approach is based on the belief that children who fail to prosper in the kindergarten year are simply "young" for their age, and by letting them mature, they will be able to perform adequately and even blossom. However, the evidence on student grade repetition (discussed later) offers no support for this view.

A second approach has been to provide more time within the same year for kindergarten students, usually by extending the kindergarten day. There are several variations on this approach. One is to screen children and give only some students additional remedial or enrichment instruction. Another way is to add time for an entire school system that has a high percentage of at-risk students. Finally, many school systems that do not have a high percentage of at-risk students are extending the school day for kindergarten students anyway. We discuss the effectiveness of the increased time approach in the next section.

The third approach involves screening and assessment of children for learning problems prior to entry to kindergarten and the delivery of a specialized curriculum to suit their needs. This approach differs from the other two in its assumption about learners and the role of the school and the personnel needed. It assumes that children learn in different ways and through different modalities and styles and that intervention strategies are needed to address these distinct areas of strength and weakness. This is not just individualizing instruction according to the level of difficulty of the material or rate of learning, but according to the learning avenues best suited for a particular child (e.g., visual, auditory, kinesthetic).

We will now examine the effects of these approaches.

Retention

One of the outgrowths of the 1983 reform movement has been a renewed focus on standards and a renewed interest in nonpromotion as a way to achieve these standards. However, nonpromotion has not been supported as an effective policy (Holmes and Matthews, 1984; Jackson, 1975; Niklason, 1984; Shepard and Smith, 1985). Gredler (1984), after examining the effects of transition rooms for students deemed unready for first grade, concludes:

Analysis of the research studies of transition rooms raises questions about the degree of educational payoff obtained with such programs. Research indicates that transition room children either do not perform as well or at most are equal in achievement levels to transition room eligible children placed in regular classrooms (p. 469).

Research findings notwithstanding, schools continue to retain students as a remediation strategy, especially at the early grades. Part of the reason for continuation of the practice may be that schools cannot locate other alternatives. Also, teachers may view the practice as effective—retained students do make some gain during the retained year, and teachers are unable to

compare this gain during the retained year to gains the students would have made had they been promoted.

Shepard and Smith (1985) took advantage of the existing variation in school kindergarten retention rates to address this issue. They noted that many previous studies were flawed methodologically because the comparisons were not of equivalent students under different policies, so they sampled same-sex students with similar birthdates, family backgrounds, and entering test score data from schools with contrasting retention rates. They compared retained students with nonretained students. The results were striking. Students who had spent an additional year in kindergarten were basically identical to those control students who had been promoted. The only notable difference was that the repeaters scored one month higher (1.9 versus 1.8) on the CTBS reading comprehension test taken at the end of the first grade. One month gain for one year does not seem like a very economical practice. (See also *Flunking Grades* Shepard & Smith, 1989.)

Full-Day Kindergarten

Karweit (1987) examines the effects of full-day versus half-day kindergarten in detail. Table 25–5 summarizes the individual studies reviewed in that paper. Table 25–6 provides an indication of the direction of effects by the adequacy of the study design and the population served.

Table 25–6 suggests where the effects of full-day kindergarten programs are located. Disadvantaged students who receive additional instruction are the primary source of the positive effects. Nine studies focused on the effect of full-day kindergarten for underachieving and disadvantaged students. Of the two strongest studies (using random assignment), one showed significant effects for the full-day kindergarten treatment. The other 7 studies fell into the less methodologically rigorous category, and all of these found positive effects for full-day kindergarten.

There are no long-term effects demonstrated for attendance at full-day kindergarten. Only one study (Nieman & Gastright, 1981) found significant long-term effects, but limitations of this study limit the credibility of the results. First, the study compared students who had preschool and all-day kindergarten to those in half-day programs, a somewhat different comparison than in the other studies. Second, their test for equivalence of the 2 groups at entry into kindergarten was of unknown validity and reliability. Finally, the long-term results in grades 4 and 8 included only 70 and 50% of their initial samples. Sample attrition may have been differentially important.

Other studies focusing on the effects of compensatory efforts (Lazar, Hubbell, Murray, Rosche, & Royce, 1977; McKey, et al., 1985) have found that the results of the extended day/year are primarily immediate and not long-term, and our findings support this conclusion concerning the effects of full-day kindergarten.

The finding that full-day kindergarten programs seem most effective on short-term measures for disadvantaged populations raises many new questions. To what extent is this finding due to differences in the sheer amount of time in school or due

TABLE 25–5. Summary of Effects of Full-Day and Half-Day Kindergarten Programs

Study	Sample	Treatment	Effects	Effect Size	Notes

Johnson (1974)
 	
Pre-post; Random assignment; Replicated longitudinal effects.
	Princess Anne, MD, 20 students matched on age, race, SES, gender, and ability assigned to treatment (full day) or control (half day). 3 experiments 1970, 1971, 1972.	EXP = full day (5'15")
		CTL = half day (2'30") same curriculum enrichment given full day.
		
		Measures:
		Walker Readiness
		Stanford Achievement
		Reading group grade 1
			Fall/Spring Walker Readiness K
			Cohort 1 posttest
			    2
			    3
			
			Spring Stanford Achievement
			Cohort 1 posttest only
			    2
			    3
			Reading Group Placement 1st
			Cohort 1
			    2
			    3
				.66 $p<.05$
				.58 ns
				.08 ns
				
				.13 ns
				.28 ns
				.59 ns
				
				.00 ns
				.06 ns
				.57 ns	

Winter and Klein (1970) Screened; then random assignment to treatment/control.	2 studies: (1) Disadvanaged—Treatment and control selected from lowest 10% of K class. TRT: n = 6 CTL: n = 7 (2) Advantaged—Selected Treatment and control from those most able to benefit. TRT: n = 26 CTL: n = 29	CTRL = attendance AM/PM TRT = regular+90 minutes academic program No pre-test difference. CTL = attendance regular TRT = regular+90 minutes academic program Significant pre-test differences favoring TRT.	Metropolitan at end of K Stanford at end of K Stanford at end of 1st Pretest Peabody Picture Metropolitan at end of K (adj post) Stanford at end of K (adj post) Stanford at end of 1st (adj post)	+3.01 $p<.005$ .62 ns .62 ns 1.28 $p<.05$ – ns – ns 1.03 $p<.05$	
Oliver (1980) Pre-post; ANCOVA; no pretest differences; comparable program.	61 students in 4 classes half day. 98 students in 6 classes full day. Cambridge, MA	EXP = full day with structured curriculum. 117 minutes/day CTL = half day with same structured curriculum 83.8 minutes per day.	Clymer-Barrett Prereading Inventory Murphy-Durell Prereading	2.84 $p<.05$ 1.16 $p<.05$	Effect size inflated by use of class means
Carapella and Loveridge (1978) ANCOVA; both groups eligible; control group of nonparticipants who were eligible.	St. Louis public schools 507 students who scored below 50th percentile on CPI who were eligible for attendance at extended day kindergarten: 273 enrolled; 234 control.	Supplementary instruction for kindergarten pupils using small group and individual instruction in extended day.	Comprehensive Test of Basic Skills Mathematics Reading	.43 $p<.001$ .32 $p<.001$	

(continued)

TABLE 25–5. (continued)

Study	Sample	Treatment	Effects	Effect Size	Notes
Neiman and Gastright (1981) Existing sample. Longitudinal; post only with evidence of initial equivalence.	551 kindergarten students in 16 Cincinnati schools receiving Title I. Full-day students had preschool experience, half-day did not.	EXP = full day K (n = 410) CTL = half day K (n = 141) EXP also had preschool	Pretest (Sept Kinder "Goal card") Boehm (December Kinder) Metropolitan (April Kinder) Metropolitan (4th grade—70% sample) Metropolitan (8th grade—50% sample) Grade retention Special education	NS .35 p<.001 .35 p<.001 .25 p<.01 .25 p<.01 .13 p<.01 .25 p<.001	
Hatcher (1980) ANCOVA; adhoc sample.	4 school districts in Texas, 2 having half-day K and 2 having full-day K. 60 students selected at random.	Half day vs full day. No information on curriculum or on differences in treatments.	Metropolitan Readiness California Test of Personality Valett Developmental Survey Basic	ns ns ns	
Adock (1980) ANOVA; adhoc sample.	189 urban and rural kindergarten children in 5 Maryland local education agencies. Comparison of existing full-day and half-day Ks.	EXP = full day (n = 131) CTL = half day (n = 58) Measures: Metropolitan (pre and post)	Results ANCOVA Post = pre + K type	.56 p<.001	Estimated setting t = 3.09; minimum value for p<.001.
Jarvis and Molnar (1986) ANOVA; half day sample; schools in process of going full day.	New York City. 1807 full-day K; 223 half-day K. Citywide conversion to full-day K. Half day were ones unable to convert.	Contrasts: Half day/language Full day/language Measures: Brigance Pre/Post LAB Pre/Post	Results ANCOVA Brigance English speakers Non-English speakers LAB	.09 ns .45 p<.05 .38 p<.05	
Evans and Marken (1984) Pre-post; ANCOVA; students at different points beyond K.	Metropolitan schools district in Washington state, mostly white, middle-class. 174 first-, second- and third-graders in 2 elementary schools, who had different kindergarten programs.	Contrasts: Full Day (n-87) Half Day (n-87) Measures: Ability test (kinder) CAT (1, 2, or 3) Early Chd School Sentiment Teacher ratings Reading attitude	Results ANCOVA CAT Reading attitudes Referral special education	– ns + –.26 p<.05	
Derosia (1980) Pre-post; ANCOVA; students at different points beyond K.	384 students in kindergarten, 1st and 2nd grades having full or half-day kindergarten. Jefferson City, Colorado	Full day (n = 67) Half day (n = 93)	Boehm (adjusted for pretest, SES, age) CTBS (Grade 1) CTBS (Grade 2)	.36 p<.05 ns ns	

(continued)

TABLE 25–5. (*continued*)

Study	Sample	Treatment	Effects	Effect Size	Notes
Warjanka (1982)	30 students who scored < 65 on Metropolitan Readiness Test and 40 students who were in same K classes with scores > 65.	6-month treatment, regular kindergarten + extended day curriculum based on participant's ability.	At pre-test, FDK group 1 standard deviation lower than other group (37.8 vs 20.5) on Metropolitan Readiness Test. After 6 months of treatment, EKD group and regular group were same (54.3).	(+)	
Slaughter (1983)	96 students who were identified as at risk and 191 other K students.	Additional instruction (119 to 242 hours); smaller classes (15:1); curricular change—whole-language approach.	Pre-post design. At pretest FDK group significantly lower than regular group on CAT listening skills subtest. (In NCEs, 24 vs 45). At posttest FDK made significant gains, while regular group declined. (35 NCE to 42 NCE)	(+)	
Lysiak and Evans (1976) Convenience sample; replicated 2 years.	916 students in 111 K classes in Fort Worth, TX.	Comparison of 6 curricular models, for students of differing SES, ethnicity and for full day and half day.	Full day > half day for low SES and for high SES.	(+)	
Alper and Wright (1979)	98 students in Phoenix, AZ, kindergartens in extended day and regular.	Full day had longer day (5 vs 2½) and smaller classes (12–25). Teacher visits to homes; 3-month study.	Metropolitan Readiness Test Extended day > regular No report of significance level.	(+)?	No significant levels computed.
Humphrey (1983)	Evansville-Vanderburg School District	Contrasts: 2 cohorts 78–79 full = 81 half + 108 79–80 full + 115 half = 114	Reading Gates MacGintie 78–79 79–80 CTBS 78–79 Grade retention 78–79 19% Half 9% Full	(+) (+) (+) (+) (+)	Not reported
McClinton and Topping (1984) Post only with no evidence of initial equalvance.	80 1st-graders in 10 public schools, randomly selected. EXP = enrolled EKD CTL = enrolled reg	EXP = 4'15" CTL = 2'40" Major difference was amount of time, not curriculum.	CAT at end of K CAT at end of 1st Teacher ratings academic ability EXP>CTL F(1,9)=5.15 p<.05	− ns − ns 1.45 p<.05	
Harman (1982) Convenience sample	55 half day 66 full day in K classes in same school and matched on ethnicity, mobility, and SES.	Posttest only; design comparison of CAT reading and math at end of year.	CAT reading CAT math .40 p<.05	+.27	
Chicago's Govt-Funded Kindergarten Programs Convenience sample	Comparison of 110 schools; existing programs.	Contrasts: Funding source: Chapter 1 Chapter 2 OEEO Board Funded Format: All Day Full Day No pretests	Percent scoring in first quartile ITBS HDK, Chpt 1, size 16 = 26% ADK, Chpt 2, size 23 = 39 ADK, size 26 = 46 OEEO, size 28 = 51 board HDK, size 28 = 73		

TABLE 25–6. Summary of Effects for Full-Day Kindergarten by Quality of Study, Immediacy of Effect, and Population Studied

	Regular or Advantaged Students				Disadvantaged Students			
	Kindergarten		Long term		Kindergarten		Long term	
Random Assign or Matched	Johnson	+	Johnson	0	Johnson	0	Johnson	0
	Oliver	+	Winter	0	Winter	+	Winter	0
	Winter	0						
Nonmatched	Hatcher	0	Evans	0	Carapella	+	Niemann	+
	Adcock	+	Derosia	0	Niemann	+		
	Jarvis	0			Jarvis	+		
	Derosia	+			Warjanka	+		
					Slaughter	+		
					Lysiak	+		
					Entwisle	+		

to differences in program emphasis and focus? It seems possible that a combination of more time and greater emphasis on academic preparation is important. Studies linking the allocation of time to differences in achievement results typically find only modest results (Karweit, 1983). One primary reason is that the same allocated time can have quite varied actual usages in different classrooms, depending on the grouping patterns, the curriculum, the teacher, and the students.

An observational study of kindergarten instruction in 3 school districts by Meyer (1985) illustrates this point. Contrasting the use of time in districts that have half-day and full-day programs, Meyer showed that the actual amount of time on academic matters was not all that different in full- and half-day programs observed. The total minutes allocated to instruction in the half-day classes (150-minute sessions) was 78 minutes, whereas in the full-day classes (330 minutes) the total instructional time allocated was 130 minutes. In general, the students in the full-day programs had more total minutes allocated to instruction, but some teachers in the half-day schedule actually exceeded the allocated time of some teachers in the full-day schedule. Again, individual teacher practices and curricula seemed to be important elements in determining how the school day was spent.

This suggests the importance of understanding more than the effects of the length of the kindergarten day. What instructional programs are effective for kindergarten students? What difficulties are there in operating these programs in a full-day or half-day setting? Is it possible to have effective half-day programs and thus save the considerable expense in expanding the kindergarten? And if districts decide to extend their kindergarten day, what programs have been demonstrated to be effective? Do they require a full day for successful implementation?

The major conclusion from examining the effects of full-day kindergarten is that attendance at full-day programs appears to be beneficial for disadvantaged students. The source of this effect—whether it is simply more time in school or a change in the focus of the kindergarten program that accompanied a full day—is not clear. In the next section, we focus on the nature of the programs that seem to be effective for disadvantaged kindergarten students.

Effects of Programs of Instruction

There are 2 major sources for the programs reviewed here: programs approved by the U.S. Department of Education's Joint Dissemination Review Panel (JDRP), and programs listed in the Office of Educational Research and Improvement's Effective Compensatory Education Sourcebook (Griswold, Cotton, & Hansen, 1986). The studies/programs are classified and presented (see Table 25–7) by the adequacy of the research design. Programs that used random assignment to treatment and control groups were weighted most heavily, followed by studies that used a matched/experimental control group design. Cohort, or before and after implementation designs, are discussed next. Given the least weight are studies that base their evidence of effectiveness on comparisons of expected fall-to-spring growth, or on posttest-only effects.

Assessments of effective early childhood programs not only suffer from all the methodological difficulties discussed for elementary studies (see Madden & Slavin, 1987), but include a few of their own. One, it is much less clear what the goals of kindergarten programs may be, and there are fewer reliable measures of the goals. Measures are often homegrown tests of unknown reliability. When tests of known reliability are used, there is little consensus about which to use. For example, the 20 JDRP-approved programs for kindergarten used 12 different standardized tests.

Furthermore, the test selected may not match the objectives of the program. For example, in a school with an outstanding prekindergarten program, the principal was asked her primary goal for the prekindergarten students. She was very quick to respond, "To make them articulate." Yet no test or measure of the children's language was used in evaluating the program's effectiveness. Instead, the program effects were measured using standard paper and pencil instruments.

Also, the evaluations can render false positive effects if they measure skills that improve test-taking performance on narrow educational goals, but not skills that lay the foundation for future learning. For example, children can be taught to recognize numbers and count to fifty without having the necessary skills to master addition. Or children can learn at an early age to recognize letters, but still not possess the necessary language skills to learn how to read. An evaluation that shows mastery of discrete components related to reading and the separate skills related to math comprehension does not show competency in reading and math. There needs to be integration of the skills and the necessary linguistic and numeric background for the skills to be applied.

Finally, kindergarten programs may have very different goals, so that comparison of treatment and control groups can be misleading. Comparing an academic kindergarten program to a traditional control group that is basically nonacademic in orientation, one should not be surprised to find large effects on readiness activities for the academic program, since the traditional program did not intend to teach these objectives. This problem of program goal is particularly at issue for kindergarten programs because the purpose of kindergarten has been changing over time and evaluations indicate very little about the curriculum for the control group.

Table 25–6 provides a synopsis of the kindergarten programs for which we have evaluation data. As noted, these programs are presented by the adequacy of the research design in the following order:

1. Random assignment
2. Matched control group
3. Cohort comparison
4. Spring-to-spring growth (no control)
5. Fall-to-spring growth (no control)

We consider studies that used random assignment, matched control groups, or cohort comparison groups to be methodologically adequate studies. Effect sizes are presented for these more adequate studies. The less rigorous methodological studies/programs are presented along with the general direction of effect.

Alphaphonics/Astra's Magic Math. Alphaphonics and Astra's Magic Math are 2 widely used and successful beginning readiness programs. Combining systematic, sequenced lessons into a game-like format, both programs are motivating and fun yet still provide abundant practice and repetition of presentation. Friendly visitors from outer space (Astro for reading; Astra for math) leave a bag of lesson materials daily for the teacher and children. The suspense and anticipation derived from the magic bag appear to sustain student interest and motivation.

In the Alphaphonics program, the letters of the alphabet are introduced sequentially one at a time, in a 26-week sequence. Astro's bag contains items that start with the letter the class is studying, such as apple, (plastic) alligator, alarm clock, and an abacus for the letter A. Badges, stickers, and letters to parents are also in the bag.

There are 6 lessons for each letter of the alphabet. The student learns to name a letter, then to write it, and then to locate the upper- and lower-case example of the letter. Astro manages to create and keep a fantasy and fun-like atmosphere for the children while getting them to practice and review. Astro also brings ditto sheets or other tools for independent practice.

Astra's Magic Math uses a similar outer space theme for the introduction of 22 math concepts in a sequenced manner. The units are introduced to the whole class. The 22 units cover shapes, matching, size comparison, counting and recognition of the numbers 0 to 30, number sequences, addition and subtraction of the numerals 0 to 5, and time in hours.

The Alphaphonics program takes about an hour each day. A typical schedule would be:

1. Sing alphabet song
2. Sing poem song (for particular letter group)
3. Class discussion
4. Individual work
5. Sing poem song

The evaluation of the program used a posttest-only analysis of variance. The treatment classrooms were compared with twelve control schools in the same district, which did not differ with respect to entering IQ or SES. The achievements of treatment classes and control classes were measured at the end of kindergarten, first, second, and third grade using the Metropolitan Achievement Test. The effect sizes were 0.89, 1.14, 0.90 and 1.1 respectively for these grades. Data for the equivalence of control/experimental classes and method of assignment to treatment were not detailed.

The evaluation of Astra's Magic Math used random assignment to treatment and control classes. The effectiveness of the program was gauged by performance on the CTBS. The effect size computed here was 0.45 at the end of kindergarten.

The evaluations do not indicate very much about the goals and practices of the comparison group. It is likely that the comparison classrooms may have been traditional kindergarten programs that include readiness activities, but not in a systematic fashion that assures coverage, practice of skills, and teacher feedback.

There is no evidence supplied that the program is equally effective for all students or, on the other hand, that it is not effective for students at risk of failure. The general orientation of the program is that of a whole class, direct instruction model with individual assistance and remediation provided as can be accommodated. That is, remediation efforts are not structured in any specific way in these programs.

MECCA. Make Every Child Capable of Achieving (MECCA) is a diagnostic/prescriptive program that provides daily observation, assessment, and planning for specialized teaching depending on children's needs. Additional instruction within the classroom is provided based on students' learning profiles. The additional activities are based on a task analysis of the learning activity with which the student is having difficulty. Task analysis is the process of breaking down a learning activity into the steps necessary for its successful completion, such as breaking down the activity into its auditory, visual, and gross and fine motor components. Specialized instruction prescribed by a team composed of classroom aide, learning disabilities specialist, and classroom teacher, is provided either individually or in small groups in the classroom.

The target group of children is identified by a preschool screening with the school psychologist and a speech and language clinician. High-risk children are those who do not attain age appropriate scores on 3 out of 4 areas on the DIAL

TABLE 25–7. Programs Evaluated with Random Assignment or Matched Control Group Design

JDRP #	Name	Developer	Grade	Content	Instructional Strategy	Evaluation Design	Measures	Effects	Cost/Training	Adoptions/Activity
74–15	Alpha Phonics	So. San Francisco U.S.D.	K	Rdg. Readiness	Readiness phonics program focusing on sequential learning, immediate correction, feedback & game-like presentation for about 1 hr/day.	Post ANOVA treatment sch. & remaining 12 in district. Stated that IQ & background of T & C equivalent. All students there for K-3.	Metropolitan ach. readiness ach. G1 ach. G2 ach. G3	 .89 1.14 .90 1.07	$135 for materials classroom. 1-day training; pay trainer, honorarium, travel.	6000 cities 50 states
83–54	Astra Math	So. San Francisco U.S.D.	K	Math Readiness	Comprehensive, structured, and sequenced curriculum with 22 self-contained units. Uses multisensory approach, behavior modification, and high-interest materials.	Pre-post random assignment to treatment—control 3 classes each.	CTBS fall-spring	.45<1> (adj) .30 (not adj)	$112 for materials classroom; 1-day training.	4000 cities 30 states
77–111	MECCA	Trumbull Public Schools (CT)	K	Development & implementation of early identification procedures & prescriptive educational programs for children entering K with specific potential handicaps.	Pre-post random assignment to treatment and control.	JANSKY Metropol. Monroe	.67 .88	.57 .96	no data	no data
78–189	TALK	Rockford, IL school system	K–3	Language	Lang. specialist in class instruction in listening skills for 4 wk ½ hour for 6 mos then classroom tchr continues lessons.	Pre-post ANCOVA on treatment and matched control. Original study—(75–6); replication—(76–77).	PPVT WISC PPVT (K)	75 .25 76 .42 75 .38 76 .46 75 .26 (K) 76 .74 75 .38 (K) 76 .55	$50 manual for teacher and sub time for teacher to attend ½-day training.	572 dists. 33 states 6 int'l currently active

(continued)

TABLE 25–7. (continued)

IDRP #	Name	Developer	Grade	Content	Instructional Strategy	Evaluation Design	Measures	Effects		Cost/Training	Adoptions/Activity
79–7	MARC	Walkulla City and Crawfordville, FL	K–1	Reading	Continuous progress using multisensory activities and systematic instruction. Diagnostic and record-keeping instrument, skill sheets provied.	Post ANOVA on treatment and matched local control at end of K and end of 1st. Pre ANOVA to ensure equivalence.	SESAT (II) letters word rdg. sent rdg. BOEHM KUHLMAN ANDERSON SESAT (I)	#1 1.12 .88 .25 ns ns ns	#2 .55 na na	$\frac{3}{5}$-day training or self-training manual	no exact data (FL&SC) not active at present
79–7	INSTRUCT	Lincoln Public Schools	K–3	Reading	Individual placement & progress through multi-unit model.	ANCOVA comparison of treatment and comparable schools chosen on similar SES, school organization, and number of compensatory students.	Metropolitan word know. reading spelling	.35** .25* < 2 > ns		5 days training; materials $100/class.	no data
79–38	PLAY	Bristol, VA	K–1 and $3\frac{3}{4}$ years	Motor/ cognitive	Diagnostic/prescriptive direct instruction in perceptual/motor skills; monthly home reinforcement and activities.	ANOVA on treatment and control. Control were eligibles (score below cut off) not enrolled because positions filled.	BOEHM 75–76 76–77 77–78	1.77 .23 1.33		na	not active
81–44	CLIMB	Middlesex, NJ	K–12	Reading and math	Diagnostic/prescription approach in acquisition of reading and math skills, providing a management design for coordinating & integrating classroom and support personnel.	Spring-to-spring achievement compared to nat'l norms and compensatory growth.	CTBS	+			781 (1982–6) from sponsor
76–87	STAMM	Lakewood, CO	K–8	Math	Continuous progress math with management system.	Pre-post implementation scores for district and adoption site.	CAT	+		Number of students × 7, avg. startup; number of student × c if workbooks used as consumables.	41 states 1500 adoptions
78–184	Education Assessmt. & Inst. for the Educationally Deprived	Kenosha, WI	K–10	Language	Extended day K 2–3 hrs in afternoon, additional time for remedial instruction.	Pre-post design.	PPVT	+			

405

(continued)

TABLE 25–7. (*continued*)

IDRP #	Name	Developer	Grade	Content	Instructional Strategy	Evaluation Design	Measures	Effects	Cost/ Training	Adoptions/ Activity
78–198	Every Student Every Day	St. Mary Parish	K–4 K–6	Math and reading	Daily diagnosis, evaluation, and prescription, computer scoring for coordination. Pullout design using 40 min. each day.	Pre-post design; changing percentile; fall to spring. 7 52 (76) 7 59 (77) 7 32 (82) 2 40 (83)	TOBE (preschool & K)	+		
74–102	Baptist Hill K	Baptist Hill K, Greenville, AL	K	Reading and math	Full-day K, learning centers, diagnose individual learning needs on continuous basis with appropriate learning activities.	Pre-post design; fall to spring. 3rd stanine 6th stanine		TOBE	+	no data
74–46R	Early Prevention of School Failure	Peotone District, IL	4-, 5-, 6-year-olds		Early identification of developmental needs and learning styles of 4-, 5-, and 6-yr-olds. Screening, planning and pull-out; 20–30 minute instruction in different modalities at learning centers.	Improvement per month on different scales—no comparison data either w/ a control group or pre-implementation.	getting data	+	2-day training $127/classroom teacher materials.	6000 (from sponsor)
84–1	First Level Math	PRIMAK Educational Foundation	K or 1	Math	Sequential curriculum and management system that is diagnostic/prescriptive. Instructional groups formed on basis of pretests. Instruction in 3–4 groups for about 20–30 minutes.	Pre- post design; fall to spring.	CIRCUS	+ not possible to compute	$35/kit	
74–71	New Adventure in Learning	Moore Elem. School, Tallahassee, FL	K		Individually determined instruction with positive behavior management.	Pre-post; nat'l norm comparison using expected growth.	PPVT—mean improvmt 1.67/math. Gilmore oral reading test—10% on grade level at pre, 57% at post.	no current data	no current data	

406

(*continued*)

TABLE 25–7. (*continued*)

IDRP #	Name	Developer	Grade	Content	Instructional Strategy	Evaluation Design	Measures	Effects	Cost/ Training	Adoptions/ Activity
74–75	Strategies in Early Childhood Education	Waupun, WI	preK and K	Screening	Developmental and screening model. Self instructional, individually paced, learning centers, developmentally sequenced materials.	Ad hoc comparison of treatment children with another group. No evidence of prior comparability.			10 sessions inservice	
74–93	Right to Read	Glassboro, NJ	K–3	Reading	Diagnostic, prescriptive, individual progress model. Ungraded.	No control; 325 children; pre-post.	CRI Classroom Reading Inventory	Avg. gain 1.52 yr.	20 hr. in service + 1 hr/wk.	no data
	Project Catch Up	Newport Mesa, CA	K–6	Reading and math	Remedial instruction in reading & math to underachieving students using diagnoses, prescription. Positive contacts with family.	Mean gain by grade on CTBS from fall to spring. No data on K	CTBS fall-spring			
	Amphitheater School District KIP	Tuscon, AZ	K		Parent involvement: once a week training of parents in game or activity that gives practice in basic skills with followup practice with students who need practice in that skill and monitoring of student progress.	Comparison to comparable school on percent scoring above 50 percentile 1 year after.	CAT	66% vs. 38%	ND	ND
VIP	Spokane, WA	K		Develop skills	Develop friendly, feeling parents and school, provide training for parents in how to help children at home, to send home games that reinforce skills learned at school.	Santa Clara Inventory gain of 2.32 mo. in developmental age/month; no control group.	Santa Clara Inventory (note problem with fall-spring)			

Pretest effect size = −.15 was added to posttest effect size .30 to arrive at the adjusted effect size.

Effect sizes were computed by determining the t value to generate p<.01 and .05 respectively.

taken in the spring. In September, further assessment is done on marginal and high-risk students and an individual programming survey is administered to identify particular strengths and weaknesses. From this profile, an educational plan is devised.

For example, a child who has a very limited use of expressive language—such as single-word responses to questions or no usage of pronouns or adverbs—might be placed in a speech and language program. In the beginning of the program, the child would be rewarded continuously with praise or with tokens. The basic structure of each lesson is:

1. *Auditory reception:* The instructor gives verbal directions to which the student responds with a gross motor or fine motor action ("Pick up the tomato").
2. *Verbalization:* The child uses the language she or he has responded to in step I ("Here is the tomato").
3. Reading readiness activities are combined with a lesson using the words and sounds from the first two parts.

The lessons are structured to give the child practice in increasingly more difficult auditory reception, memory, and other readiness skills.

Eligible students were randomly assigned to the MECCA treatment or a control group. The Jansky Predictive Screening Index, an individually administered 20-minute test, was used as the pretest and one of the posttest measures. There are five predicting tests: letter naming, picture naming, Gates word matching, Bender motor Gestalt, and Binet Sentence Memory. The posttests used were the Jansky and the Metropolitan Readiness Test.

The comparisons found no significant differences in pretest scores between the 37 students in the MECCA program and the 33 in the control classes. At the posttest, the MECCA group outperformed the comparison group by about 7 points (effect size = +.67). Similar effects were found on the Metropolitan Readiness Posttest, where the effect size was 0.88.

Another comparison between students randomly assigned to MECCA and a "multidisciplinary" comparison group shows similar results (Jansky effect size = .57, Monroe Reading Aptitude Test effect size = .96). In the comparison classrooms, the children were taught by a learning disabilities teacher and three other specialists.

The replication of effects under the multidisciplinary comparison is significant for it suggests that the power of MECCA arises from more than its use of specialized personnel. It suggests that the curriculum, materials, and approach are important factors in MECCA's effectiveness. Screening, diagnoses and task analysis of learning activities target the time and resources within the school in a productive way, especially for students very much at risk of future failure.

TALK. The focus of Project TALK is to improve expressive and receptive language skills in children in grade K–3. This is accomplished by structured activities that foster language growth. A language specialist teaches specific expressive and receptive language lessons to the class twice a week for half an hour over a six-month period. The classroom teacher watches and then participates in the demonstration lessons, and conducts followup lessons twice each week.

The following sample indicates the type of lesson used in TALK.

Lesson 92

TITLE:
Describe all.

PURPOSE:
To encourage use of descriptive words of color, size, shape, and quantity.

MATERIALS:
List of simple descriptive words—descriptive word list.

PROCEDURE:
The teacher walks through the class, stopping here and there by a child. The teacher describes the child with one word. For instance, "Blond John," "Listening Susan," "Tired Billy," and so on. The teacher may build from this by continuing and adding more descriptive words like "Pretty, blonde Sherry," "Clever, old Johnny," and so on.

Now the teacher asks the class what has been happening. A short discussion of descriptions and descriptive words should follow. How do you describe things? What kinds of words do you use to describe things? You use words that tell size, shape, color, smell, taste, feelings, and so on.

The teacher will begin by standing and telling one word about herself or himself such as: *tall, big, teacher, woman,* and so on. Now each child must stand one at a time and think of one word or a phrase to tell about him or her, such as: *little, red hair, freckles, braids,* and so on. When everyone has had a chance to tell a word then everyone can have another turn and think of still another word that tells about him or her. When a child gives a self-descriptive word that might fit another child in the room, stop and discuss it—How many people fit Mark's word?—this will broaden the lesson.

Younger children may want to pick a favorite self-descriptive word. The teacher can make a card for the child to wear pinned on all day that describes him or her. This will give the child a chance to explain his or her word to people who ask about it.

MORE IDEAS:
The teacher picks a simple descriptive word, such as *hard.* Each child in the class must find an object in the room that fits the descriptive word, such as "hard floor," "hard desk," "hard pencil," "hard window pane," and so on. The teacher chooses one word from a box of slips with simple descriptive words written on them. Each student finds an item in the classroom that fits the descriptive word. Now the children take turns drawing a descriptive word and finding objects that fit on his or her own. For a more difficult twist, especially in the upper grades, have children draw 2 or 3 descriptive words and place them in the proper sentence order, such as big, red _____ and not a red, big _____, or two small _____, and not small two _____ .

Three experimental and control schools were compared. Target groups of 26 students were randomly selected for pretesting from each grade level (K–3). In Table 25–2, we provide 2 sets of results: for overall (K–3) and for kindergarten alone.

The Peabody Picture Vocabulary Test (PPVT) was used to measure receptive oral vocabulary. The expressive measure used was the vocabulary subtest of the Wechsler Intelligence Scale (WISC).

Results for the original experiment and a replication the following year gave effect sizes (across all grades) around 0.38. Results presented for the separate grades indicate that the program was as effective or more effective for kindergarten students as for first- through third-grade students.

The amount of actual time spent on the Project TALK activities is small compared to the results obtained. Only 2 hours per week are actually spent on the program. If the results are generally replicable, this program seems to be particularly powerful in its effects. Additional evaluations need to be conducted to learn if these effect sizes are generalizable.

Early Prevention of School Failure (EPSF). This program provides developmental screening, diagnosis, and training based on identified learning styles and modalities. Screening of 4-, 5- and 6-year-olds is carried out in fine and gross motor auditory, visual, and language areas using a variety of instruments: the Preschool Language Scale (PLS, developed in conjunction with the program), the Peabody Picture Vocabulary Test (PPVT), and the Developmental Test of Visual Motor Integration. On the basis of these tests, a profile is created for each child which identifies his or her strengths and weaknesses. Students who are 2 years or more below expectancy on 2 modalities are classified as high risk; 1 year or more below are classified as medium risk.

Students are given additional instruction in their weak areas in a pullout setting. The program presents guides for direct modality instruction in the areas of language, auditory, visual, and fine and gross motor. Student profiles indicate their performance in these areas on a scale from 1 to 5.

Guides for modality instruction include correlation with major texts and breaking down a specific skill into a sequenced set of prerequisite skills. For example, if the skill is to tell stories in sequence with/without the aid of pictures, 9 distinct skill performance areas are checked:

1. Child arranges picture stories in sequence.
2. Child tells story using sequence cards.
3. Child tells story in parts before retelling entire story.
4. Child uses felt pieces or fingerplay to tell story.
5. Child uses pictures to tell story.
6. Child uses assorted toys and objects to tell story.
7. Child unscrambles story.
8. Child gives a narrative to the series of drawn pictures.
9. Child uses puppet to help tell a story.

The outcome data that is presented pertained to growth per month and based its evidence of effectiveness on exceeding expected growth. No data on growth for a comparable control group was presented.

Summary Kindergarten

The JDRP evaluations do not in general address the issue of a program's effectiveness for special populations. Data are not routinely presented that detail the progress of students by race, sex, SES, or entering ability/achievement level. Thus these JDRP data are not ideally suited for addressing the question with which we began this chapter.

However, as a basis for improving practices for students at risk in the kindergarten years, this data base is a worthwhile place to start. It seems likely that sound instructional programs,

with demonstrated effectiveness across several sites, will be effective for most students. Analyses of aptitude-by-treatment interactions from studies of later grades do not find many interaction effects; programs effective for one subgroup tend to be effective for others (see Slavin & Madden, 1987). On the other hand, it may be that the nature of differences between the backgrounds of disadvantaged and advantaged children as they enter school would make programs differentially effective for different subgroups at the kindergarten level.

There is some evidence (Lysiak & Evans, 1976) of interaction effects for program and SES background. In this examination of the effectiveness of different kindergarten programs, they found that the lower SES students benefitted in particular from a structured curricular approach. This finding is consistent with the common wisdom about the need for structure for disadvantaged students, although it is really not clear what *structure* means. On one hand, structure is conceived of as the opposite of the open classroom, itself an ill-defined intervention. On the other hand, structure is thought of as rigid and heavily prescribed. Semantics aside, structure in the sense of a systematic approach to instructional delivery is a vital ingredient for any effective program. What is striking about the kindergarten approaches here—which encompass a wide variety of philosophies—is the extent of the specificity of activities, planning, and goals. Effective programs are ones that are detailed and specific.

The systematic aspects of programs may be more important in effectiveness than are the philosophical aspects. Is this a program that can be implemented on a day-to-day basis by a regular teacher teaching 30 students? We do find successful systematic approaches that encompass quite different philosophies. For example, with respect to the degree of individualization and attention to individual differences, there are effective programs that focus basically on providing whole-class instruction (that is, that do not differentiate instructional pace, delivery, or content), and there are effective programs that have as their basic premise the need to focus on individual strengths and weaknesses.

This contrast is seen in the approaches taken by Early Prevention of School Failure and MARC. Early Prevention of School Failure diagnoses modality strengths and weaknesses and tailors instruction to these modalities. MARC underscores the significance of different avenues of learning but does not differentiate instruction for students based on their modality profiles. Both programs assume that an appropriate kindergarten program is multisensory in its approach: EPSF customizes instruction or provides modality training for those below a certain cutoff point; MARC structures every lesson to include linkages among the different avenues of learning. Not only are these programs quite different in their philosophical approach to learning style differences, they require quite different staff and support personnel as well. A team of specialists including psychologist and speech clinician is required to evaluate and screen all students in the EPSF model. Instruction is then provided in a pullout format to address modality weaknesses, such as practice in fine motor coordination.

Thus, although different approaches may be effective, effective kindergarten practices incorporate specific materials, management plans, activities, and structures. The teachers have an instructional plan that they follow and specific activities that make sense in the context of that plan. For example, MARC contains detailed lesson plans and activities across various reading levels. The programs are not overly rigid, nor do they reduce teachers to automatons—but they are specific. It is possible to tell that teachers are implementing the program. Such specificity is needed to ensure a faithful implementation of a program.

CONCLUSION AND DISCUSSION

Our knowledge base on which we can form decisions about early childhood programs is limited in 4 important regards. First, we are lacking empirical studies of the relative costs/merits of alternative ways of combining preschool and other services for young children. There are pressing child care needs for young children that are only partially addressed by the availability of preschool. We need studies of the costs and the effects of alternative arrangements to meet the child care, educational, and emotional needs of young children and their families. What workable combinations of day care, before and after school care, and preschool education might there be? Under what conditions is preschool a good investment? For everyone? In what type of program? Would home-based models, which are considerably cheaper to operate, have the same type of effectiveness?

Second, we lack sufficient empirical studies of the effects of major approaches to preschool curricula. The review conducted here of this issue was based on *3 studies!* As important a topic as the curriculum of the preschool is certainly deserving of more intense research scrutiny.

A third limitation is the nature of the methodology used in many of the evaluations of program effectiveness. By and large these evaluations based their judgment of effectiveness on pre-post gain scores. Of course, this procedure does not control for other factors, beside the program, which may have contributed to the gain. More rigorous evaluations are needed to inform the question of the usefulness of most of the curriculum used today.

A fourth limitation in the available studies is that they often fail to consider how preschool is connected to the kindergarten and elementary grades. Given that resources for education are constrained, it is important to assess whether placing resources into preschool is more effective than adding these same resources into kindergarten or elementary grades. Would a student benefit more from attending a preschool program or from attending an all-day kindergarten and tutorial program in the first grade? Simply distributing a small amount of resources around to provide more services is probably not going to benefit very many children—at risk or otherwise. The critical question is how the demand for preschool can be balanced against the urgent need for so many other educational services for at-risk students.

We have evaluations of reasonable adequacy that compare programs to control classes. However, we do not have data about the relative effectiveness of these different approaches or their effectiveness for different students. What are the relative costs and implementation difficulties of the different approaches? These basic data are needed to make intelligent decisions about approaches to early childhood instruction. Otherwise, the present practice of individual districts building their individual curriculum without benefitting from the successes and failures of other locations seems likely to continue. Improving educational practice can be a cumulative effort, but it requires sustained and systematic evaluations. As the kindergarten and prekindergarten have become the first schooling experience for many students, the need to locate effective practices for this start of school remains great.

To address this issue fairly, we need more than rhetoric or a handful of studies. We need to carry our experimental contrasts of interesting combinations of services to provide an empirical base for future decisions among educational alternatives for young children.

References

Bereiter, C. (1986). Does direct instruction cause delinquency? *Early Childhood Research Quarterly, 1*(3), 289–292.

Bereiter, C., & Engelman, S. (1966). *Teaching disadvantaged children in the preschool*. Englewood, Cliffs, NJ: Prentice Hall.

Berrueta-Clement. J. R., Schweinhart, L. J., Barnett, W. S., Epstein, A. S., & Weikart, D. P. (1984). Changed lives: The effects of the Perry Preschool program on youths through age 19. *Monographs of the High/Scope Educational Research Foundation, 8.*

Bloom, B. (1964). *Stability and change in human characteristics*. New York: Wiley.

Center for Education Statistics. (1986). *Pre-School Enrollment Trends and Implications Issue Paper.*

Dunn, L. M., Horton, K., & Smith, J. (1981). *Peabody Language Development Kits—Revised Teachers Guide Level P.* American Guidance Service, Circle Pines, MN 56014.

Educational Research Service Report. (1986). *Kindergarten programs and practices in public schools*. Study conducted and reported by Randolyn Gardner.

Elkind, D. (1986, May). Formal education and early childhood education: An essential difference. *Phi Delta Kappan, 67*, 631–636.

Gersten, R. (1986). Response to consequences of three preschool curriculum models through age 15. *Early Childhood Research Quarterly, 1*(3), 303–312.

Gottfredson, G. (1987). *American education—American delinquency*. (Report No. 22). Baltimore, MD: The Johns Hopkins University, Center for Research on Elementary and Middle Schools.

Gray, S., Ramsey, B., & Klaus, R. (1982). *From 3 to 20: The Early Training Project*. Baltimore: The University Park Press.

Gredler, C. (1984). Transition rooms: A viable alternative for the at-risk child? *Psychology in the Schools, 21*, 463–470.

Griswold, P. A., Cotton, K. J., & Hansen, J. B. (1986). *Effective education sourcebook*. Washington, DC: U.S. Government Printing Office.

Grubb, N. (1987). *Young children face the states: Issues and options for early childhood programs*. New Brunswick, NJ: Rutgers University, Eagleton Institute of Politics, Center for Policy Research in Education.

Holmes, C. T., & Matthews, K. M. (1984). The effects of nonpromotion on elementary and junior high school pupils: A meta-analysis. *Review of Educational Research, 54*(2), 225–236.

Holmes, C. T., & McConnell, B. M. (1990). *Full-day versus half-day kindergarten: An experimental study.* Paper presented at the annual meeting of the American Educational Research Association, Boston, MA.

Irvine, D. J. (1982). *Evaluation of the New York State Experimental Prekindergarten Program.* Paper presented at the annual meeting of the American Educational Research Association, New York.

Jackson, G. B. (1975). The research evidence on the effect of grade retention. *Review of Educational Research, 45,* 438–460.

Jensen, A. R. (1969). How much can we boost IQ and scholastic achievement? *Harvard Educational Review, 39,* 1–23.

Karnes, M. B., Shwedel, A. M., & Williams, M. B. (1983). A comparison of five approaches for educating young children from low-income homes. In Consortium for Longitudinal Studies (Authors), *As the twig is bent...lasting effects of preschool programs* (pp. 133–169). Hillsdale, NJ: Erlbaum.

Karweit, N. (1983). *Time-on-task: A research review* (Report No. 322). Baltimore, MD: The Johns Hopkins University, Center for Social Organization of Schools.

Karweit, N. (1987). *Full day or half day kindergarten: Does it matter?* (Report No. 11). Baltimore, MD: The Johns Hopkins University, Center for Research on Elementary and Middle Schools.

Kirk, S. (1958). *Early education of the mentally retarded.* Urbana, IL: University of Illinois Press.

Lazar, I., Hubbell, V., Murray, H., Rosche, M., & Royce, J. (1977). *The resistance of preschool effects* (DHEW Publication NO. OHDS 78–30129).

Lazar, I., & Darlington, R. (1982). Lasting effects of early education. *Monographs of the Society for Research in Child Development, 47* (2–3, Serial No. 195).

Levenstein, P. (1970). Cognitive growth in preschoolers through verbal interaction with mothers. *American Journal of Orthopsychiatry, 40*(3), 426–432.

Lysiak, F., & Evans, C. (1976). *Kindergarten-Fun and games or readiness for first grade: A comparison of seven kindergarten curricula.* Paper presented at the annual meeting of the American Educational Research Association, San Francisco. (ERIC Document Reproduction Service No. ED 121 803)

Madden, N., & Slavin, R. (1987). *Effective programs for students at risk of academic failure.* Paper presented at the annual meeting of the American Educational Research Association, Washington, DC.

McCall, R. B., Applebaum, M. I., & Hogarty, P. S. (1973). Developmental changes in mental performance. *Monographs of the Society for Research in Child Development, 38,* (3).

McKey, R., Condelli, L., Ganson, H., Barrett, B., McConkey, C., & Plantz, M. (1985). *The impact of Head Start on children, families, and communities.* (DHHS Publication No. OHDS 85–31193). Washington, DC.

Meyer, L. (1985). *A look at instruction in kindergarten: Observations of interactions in three school districts.* (ERIC Documentation Reproduction No. ED 268 489)

Miller, L. B. & Bizzel, R. P. (1983). The Louisville experiment: A comparison of four programs. In Consortium for Longitudinal Studies (Authors), *As the twig is bent...lasting effects of preschool programs* (pp. 171–199). Hillsdale, NJ: Erlbaum.

Morado, C. (1985). *Pre-kindergarten programs for four year olds.* State Education Agency Initiatives. Washington, DC: National Association for the Education of Young Children.

Nieman, R., & Gastright, J. (1981, November). The long-term effects of Title I preschool and all-day kindergarten. *Phi Delta Kappan, 63,* 184–185.

Niklason, L. B. (1984). Nonpromotion: A pseudoscientific solution. *Psychology in the Schools, 21,* 485–499.

Schweinhart, L. J. (1986). *Early childhood development programs in the eighties: The national picture.* High/Scope Educational Research Foundation, 600 N. River Street, Ypsilanti, MI 48197.

Schweinhart, L. J., Weikart, D. P., & Larner. M. B. (1986). Consequences of the preschool curriculum models through age 15. *Early Childhood Research Quarterly, 1,* 15–45.

Seifert, K. (1969). Comparison of verbal interaction in two preschool programs. *Young Children, 24,* 350–355.

Shepard, L. A. & Smith, M. L. (1985). *Boulder Valley kindergarten study: Retention practices and retention effects.* Boulder, CO: University of Colorado and Boulder Valley Public Schools, Laboratory of Educational Research.

Shepard, L. A. & Smith, M. L. (Eds.), (1989). *Flunking grades: research and policies on retention.* New York: Falmer.

Skeels, H. (1966). Some preliminary findings of three follow-up studies of the effects of adoption of children from institutions. *Young Children, 12,* 33–34.

Slavin, R. (1986). Best evidence synthesis: An alternative to meta-analytic and traditional reviews. *Educational Researcher, 15*(9), 5–11.

Slavin, R., & Madden, N. (1987). *Effective classroom programs for students at risk* (Report No. 19). Baltimore, MD: The Johns Hopkins University. Center for Research on Elementary and Middle Schools.

Smith, M. L., & Shepard, L. A. (1987, October). What doesn't work: Explaining policies of retention in the early grades. *Phi Delta Kappan, 69,* 129–134.

Stahl, S. A., & Miller, P. D. (1989). Whole language and language experience approaches for beginning reading: A quantitative research synthesis. *Review of Educational Research, 59*(1), 87–116.

Westinghouse Learning Corporation (1969). *The impact of Head Start: An evaluation of the effects of Head Start on children's cognitive and affective development.* (ERIC Document Reproduction Service No. ED 036 321)

26

PREPARING TEACHERS FOR EARLY CHILDHOOD PROGRAMS IN THE UNITED STATES

Olivia N. Saracho

UNIVERSITY OF MARYLAND

The number of early childhood education programs in the United States has increased significantly over the last few years. Along with this increase has come an increase in the number of people who staff them, including teachers, assistants, and aides. These early childhood personnel are prepared in 2 types of programs. Teachers who are hired in public school prekindergartens, kindergartens, and primary classes are prepared in 4- and 5-year programs in colleges and universities. Teachers in child care programs along with assistants and aides are prepared in 1- and 2-year programs in community colleges, and in vocational programs in high schools. 4-year institutions also support the continued professional development of teachers by offering graduate degree and in-service programs.

There is a great deal of research on teacher education in 4-year institutions. Much less research has been done on the preparation of educational personnel in 1- and 2-year programs. Unfortunately, the research related to early childhood teacher education has not grown in response to the growth of activity in the field. This may be due to the fact that teacher education research has concerned itself more with issues and processes that are central to the entire process of teacher education or because researchers have traditionally looked at the preparation of elementary and/or secondary teachers. The number of early childhood teachers being prepared is, in comparison, rather small and, therefore, may not have been viewed as worthy of increased attention. Whatever the case, the result is that, in order to understand the early childhood teacher education programs and processes, we are forced to extrapolate from work related to other areas. Although much of the research should be applicable, there is always a danger that we have gone beyond the generalizability of available studies. With this warning in mind, we present what knowledge is available to the field.

Teacher education programs plan experiences designed to allow teacher candidates to acquire the knowledge, skills, and attitudes needed to teach. These experiences are founded on research, theory, and practice. Ethical considerations also influence these programs. In order to codify the characteristics of early childhood teacher education in the United States the preparation of early childhood teachers is described here using a framework developed by Saracho and Spodek (1983). The framework includes the 6 components of an early childhood teacher education program: *recruitment and selection, general education, professional foundations, instructional knowledge, practice,* and *program modification* as described below.

RECRUITMENT AND SELECTION

Recruiting and selecting teacher candidates requires procedures to attract and judge appropriate teacher education applicants. The need to improve the quality of America's teachers is not just limited to early childhood education, but applies to all levels of education. A number of scholars (e.g., Goodlad, 1983; Schlechty & Vance, 1983; Sizer, 1984; Adler, 1982), commissions (e.g., National Commission on Excellence in Education, 1983; Education Commission of the States, 1983; Boyer for the Carnegie Foundation for the Advancement of Teaching, 1983), and organizations (e.g., American Associations of Colleges for Teacher Education, 1985; Holmes Group, 1986; National Education Association, 1982) have reported that the preparation and retention of high-quality teachers are essential to improve

The author wishes to thank Renee Clift for her thoughtful comments to an earlier version of this manuscript.

American education at all levels. Much of the reform of teacher education has focuses on recruiting and selecting teacher education candidates that have the attributes necessary for becoming outstanding teachers. A great deal of attention has been directed toward identifying these characteristics in candidates.

As early as 1960, Ryans identified essential qualities for teachers, including warmth, enthusiasm, and a businesslike attitude. Other essential characteristics have been identified for early childhood teachers since, including flexibility, warmth, and an ability to enjoy and encourage children (Katz, 1969); and patience, maturity, energy, encouragement of individual responsibility, and ingenuity in providing teaching and play materials (Almy, 1975). Prospective teachers should also be motivated to teach and hold appropriate attitudes, including an openness to new ideas, some tolerance for ambiguity, and interest in unraveling cause-effect relationships, and an ability to think and organize information in multidimensional categories (Almy 1975).

Turner (1975) also recommends using motivation as a selection criterion. Those who select teaching as their first career choice and have had prior experiences with young children should be the first to be selected. Individuals who are already working with young children, for example, could be recruited into teacher education programs. Head Start programs, child-care centers, and nursery schools employ many people from diverse socioeconomic and cultural backgrounds. Some of these people may have little formal teacher preparation but have demonstrated success in working with young children and their parents. These individuals are generally well motivated and would be prime candidates for teacher education programs.

One may question whether the criteria presented here can actually serve as a valid basis for selection of candidates for early childhood teacher education programs. The criteria presented by Katz (1969) and Almy (1975) do not have an empirical base. They represent a "common sense" view of what is needed for early childhood education and are accepted by many in the field, even though it has not been shown that these characteristics do, indeed, make a difference in early childhood teachers. Neither the work of Ryans and Turner (1975) is specific to early childhood teachers. In addition, Ryans's work, though empirical in nature, was not related to actual classroom practice.

Early childhood teachers in the public schools are generally prepared in institutions that also prepare elementary and secondary school teachers. The recruitment and selection practices of these teacher education programs range from open admissions to rigorous selection procedures designed to limit those who enter the program. When rigorous selection procedures are used, they most often take the form of judging academic achievement as measured by high school grades and achievement tests (Lewin and Associates, 1977). These criteria, though widely used, may only remotely relate to success in teaching, although certain basic requirements such as adequate reading ability and verbal communication skills are seen as essential to effective teaching.

Sporadic modifications in the selection process for teacher preparation and employment in the profession has occurred over the past decades. Although entrance to the teaching profession should be carefully screened, there is great variability in the procedures used. When there is a great need for teachers, the assessment of teacher candidates tends to be done less rigorously. Teacher shortages force the lowering of standards for those entering the teaching profession (Applegate, 1987). To meet these shortages, alternative approaches to teacher certification are often established that waive many of the requirements for teachers. Applegate (1987) broadly reviewed 4 issues on the selection of teacher candidates: (1) purpose of selection, (2) standards and criteria, (3) professional judgment, and (4) legal and ethical considerations. Each of these issues must be given serious consideration in the selection of teacher candidates.

Issue 1: The Purpose of Selection

The main purpose of selection is to determine an individual's ability to succeed in teaching. Since a teacher preparation involves a lengthy and complex process, selection criteria should attend to developmental considerations. Each phase of a teacher preparation program serves a different purpose, which should be reflected in the selection criteria. For example, the characteristics essential to succeed in college course work may not be the same as those essential to succeed in student teaching. Selection criteria should anticipate later stages and consider the demands of all elements. Sometimes this is done through a continued review which selects students for each stage of the program. Thus, on the basis of performance at prior stages, students are admitted to more advanced stages of the program.

Issue 2: Standards and Criteria

Different selection criteria are used for different teacher education institutions. Lagan and Reeves (1983) surveyed 121 institutions holding membership in the American Association of Colleges for Teacher Education (AACTE) concerning admission to their teacher education program. The standards ranged from applying several demanding and explicit criteria to using only one criterion: graduation from high school. Some institutions do not go beyond the general university or college admissions requirements. Grade point average is the most widely used criterion. This standard has risen over the last decade. In 1972 the required GPA for admission was usually 2.0 on a scale of 4, while in 1982 the GPA was frequently reported to be 2.5. Other selection criteria included a formal application, written recommendations, speech tests, informal written language tests (writing samples), physical examinations, psychological examinations, and standardized tests to determine proficiency in basic skills.

Dejnozka and Smiley (1983) studied criteria for admission to graduate teacher education programs. They found a common, but limited set of graduate admissions criteria, including grade point average, professional or related experience, letters of recommendation, scores on standardized tests (e.g., Graduate Record Examination, Miller Analogies Test), a personal interview, and a writing sample.

Standardized tests are also used in selecting candidates. A study of 356 institutions showed that standardized tests were used at some point in the teacher preparation or certification process, mainly to judge competence in basic skills. The Pre-Professional Skills Test, the American College Test, the Scholastic Aptitude Test, and the National Teachers Examination are some of the tests used (American Association of Colleges for Teacher Education, 1984). Many states have mandated that institutions with approved programs require standardized tests and have explicit admissions standards policies or require a certification examination. The Carnegie Forum on Education and the Economy (1986) has recommended a national licensure examination to be used for admission to the teaching profession.

The studies reported here used institutional self-report data to illustrate the effort made in the development of selection criteria. There is also a lack of true criteria identification. The focus seems to be on the assessment (e.g., written recommendations) rather than on the criteria themselves. Admissions criteria must be understood through clear instructions that indicate the real purpose of the index applied. A few validation studies have explored the relationship between selection variables and student outcomes.

Since little effort is made to relate explicit program outcomes to selection criteria, it is difficult to determine the effects that programs have on teacher candidates or the relationship among specific characteristics of teacher candidates and the effects of their competence on learning to teach. Howey and Strom (1987) have suggested how students, faculty, and institutional variables (contingency factors) might relate to environmental factors. For instance, program, classroom, and educational environment variables, and *criterion factors* or *outcomes* (e.g., teaching performance, personality development, attitude toward self, others and work, leadership traits) can be used to study and evaluate these areas.

Issue 3: Professional Judgment

In applying selection criteria, colleges make judgments about candidates. Entry into teacher preparation is also based upon the candidates' self-selection. Several factors (including interest, attitudes toward professors, time, efforts, and cost) determine a person's desire to become a teacher. A person's background, personal qualities, individual traits, perceived occupational status, and incentive all contribute. Robertson, Keith, and Page (1983) found that among high school seniors, mainly white females select teaching as a profession. They prefer to work with friendly people and are less concerned with earning a high income. They are also less academically proficient than their college classmates. Book and Freeman (1986) studied the attributes of college students desiring to enter the teaching profession. They found that elementary teacher candidates had a child-centered orientation whereas secondary teacher candidates had a subject-centered orientation. Their results also showed that while elementary teacher candidates had weaker academic backgrounds than their secondary counterparts, secondary teacher candidates lacked experiences with school-aged youth.

Teacher educators also exercise professional judgment as members of committees reviewing the candidates' credentials. The collective wisdom of shared decision-making is a strength of this approach. Involvement in decision-making requires that faculty get to know the candidates, a time consuming task (Raths, 1984).

The degree to which faculty members participate in discussions concerning the selection of the candidates is unclear. They may manifest greater control over this process than is recognized. One form of external control on teacher selection is the dependence upon standardized tests as evidence of prospective teachers' qualities. Test scores usually become the basis for professional judgment. Educators believe that their results "guarantee" the accuracy of their judgment. It is easier and less time-consuming to trust test results than to appraise a cluster of characteristics for which standard measures are not available.

Increasingly, teacher candidate selection reflects social policy. State legislators have mandated higher selective standards and more criteria for admission into teacher education. Howsam, Corrigan, and Denemark (1985) have noted the increased imposition of external or "mediated" control: "External control of a profession has the effect of placing the authority of public policy and government ahead of the authority of knowledge and expertise" (p. 198). If teachers, teacher educators, school personnel, and policy makers conjointly make decisions, appropriate selection practices can be enhanced. Unfortunately, each group makes independent decisions without consulting others who are involved.

Issue 4: Legal and Ethical Considerations

Admission to a teacher education program is not a student's right. Regardless of that fact, the purposes, standards, and criteria used in selection must be made clear and be justified to those applying to enter the teaching profession. Since judgments about a student's right to seek a professional education have been challenged in many institutions, university attorneys and campus personnel are becoming more informed about the Uniform Guidelines on Employee Selection Procedures of the Equal Employment Opportunity Commission, which require that criteria for admission and retention in programs of study be clearly stated. Teacher educators should solicit guidance from local officials concerning the legal aspects of specific selection criteria.

The social impact of the selection process must also be inspected. Building greater ethnic diversity within the teaching profession, including members of high-risk populations, and recruiting individuals from low socioeconomic backgrounds is seen as desirable. Yet these individuals are typically not recruited, and less likely to be selected in the conventional way. Those entering the teaching profession continue to be predominately white, monolingual, and parochial. American teachers continue to be selected from the majority population, while a shortage of minority teachers keeps increasing. The selection criteria presently in use may need to be redefined to select and recruit more diverse candidates who are more representative of the society.

The studies reviewed above suggest that most teacher education programs use 1 or more criteria to select applicants into teacher education, that selection criteria are minimal in most cases, and that selection criteria often fail to consider preparation program outcomes or teaching competence. Evidence fails to show that institutions take their selection policies seriously enough to study the effects their policies have on subsequent practice.

The changes in teacher supply and demand of the past decades and the economics and politics of teacher education are probably most responsible for the lack of validation studies on teacher selection criteria along with conceptual and methodological limitations. The high demand for teachers in the 1950s and 1960s forced the market to disregard stringent selection criteria. The low demand for teachers in the 1970s compelled enrollments in teacher preparation programs to decline and restricted the allocation of resources for research in teacher education. The present teacher shortage and the growth in interest in professional teaching may stimulate a new research agenda on the selection and recruitment of teacher candidates.

Applegate (1987) recommends that, in order to better understand the selection and recruitment process, research on teacher education address the following questions:

1. What constitutes aptitude for teaching?
2. What implicit beliefs, understandings, or dispositions undergird current admission into teacher preparation?
3. What organizational or procedural dimensions exist to enhance or inhibit selective admission?
4. What lessons might be learned from other professions that employ selective admissions strategies?
5. What relationships exist among entry criteria, program goals, and exit criteria?

Research can help teacher educators recognize the complexity of teacher candidate selection and improve existing procedures. Knowledge of the institutional, programmatic, and personal variables which contribute to the success of teacher candidates requires comprehensive preparation models and complex research designs in order to understand this phase of teacher preparation. The recruitment and selection of teacher candidates should be done cautiously. National reports criticizing the level of public school education in America have prompted several individuals to investigate teacher education programs. Their reports concentrate on poor public school student performance and the poor quality of applicants accessible to teacher education programs (Benner, George, & Cage, 1987). Improvement in the recruitment and selection of teacher candidates will certainly help to reform teacher education.

The selection of students into early childhood teacher preparation programs is not much different from the selection of students of other programs of teacher education. Yet one might argue that teaching young children is considerably different from teaching older children and that, therefore, different selection criteria should apply. Some of Applegate's (1987) questions might be modified in addressing the issues in selecting early childhood teacher education candidates: (1) If the task of teaching young children is different than that of teaching older children (e.g., more caring, more concerned with nurturance, requiring different communications skills, encompassing a broader range of tasks related to children, parents, community agencies and others), should not the aptitudes required of candidates be broader? and (2) Are there different beliefs or dispositions that should be considered for early childhood teachers than for teachers of older children? While many

of the same selection procedures and criteria might apply to early childhood teacher education, there is probably a need to either add criteria or modify criteria applied to other levels of teacher education.

GENERAL EDUCATION

General education is basic to all teacher education since teachers should be well-educated individuals. Early childhood education is drawn from various disciplines such as language, social studies, mathematics, science, aesthetics, and humanities. Thus, the content of early childhood education is drawn from general education. Simply providing a range of separate subject courses is not an adequate general education for early childhood teachers. Knowledge must be integrated and understood to create a broad perspective and should be made relevant to the general conditions of human life. The American Association of Colleges for Teacher Education (1977), in their standards for accreditation of teacher education programs, suggests that "general education should include the studies most widely generalizable. The general studies component is taught with emphasis upon generalization rather than academic specialization as a primary objective" (p. 4).

Some time ago, in *Realms of Meaning*, Phenix (1964) developed an organization of knowledge that can be used to identify the appropriate scope, content, and organization of the general education curriculum related to human nature and knowledge. The first realm, *symbolics*, includes both spoken and written communication. Unique to language is a knowledge of specific sounds, concepts, and grammatical patterns. Language provides a means of understanding and expressing different kinds of experiences and representing the profundity and complexity of the world.

Knowledge and understanding of *aesthetics*, another realm according to Phenix, provides access to particular perceptions. Each work has its own meaning and speaks for itself. Students can learn to appreciate manufactured and natural objects as well as to express themselves aesthetically through their own work. Scientific knowledge, Phenix's realm of *empirics*, relates to laws and theories based upon consistent observations which lead to prediction and verification. Science helps in the formulation of valid general descriptions of factual matters by providing information of the world as experienced through measurement. Measurement is used in physical science to develop and test generalizations, laws, and theories.

The social sciences relate to both empirics and the realm of *synnoetics*, and include history, sociology, psychology, and anthropology. History deals with civilization and government and is related to personal and moral knowledge. Events are temporally organized to show the results of decisions which were made during those times studied. Students are encouraged to make predictions and verifications of the historical events by employing different kinds of empirical knowledge as well as personal understanding and ethical insight. Physical education, another area of general education, is composed of intentional activities whose desired effects are communicated through body movement. Health, physical education, and recreation invigorate the human organism and foster neuromuscular skills, good emotional balance and control, and sound judgment. While the play of young children is usually considered universal, different cultures include different forms of play and games that teachers should know.

General education can firmly ground teacher candidates in the culture of the community and the basic structure of the scholarly disciplines. Each community's culture must be known if the teacher candidate is to become a part of it and feel comfortable within it. Each discipline provides a unique point of view, style of thinking, and organization of ideas that contribute to the preparation of teachers. During the last 2 decades the importance of the arts and science was drastically decreased. The humanities, subjects Boyer (1983) refers to as our collective memory, have been hurt the most. In 1984–1985, students in 3 out of 4 American colleges received a bachelor's degree without any study in European history and they may have graduated without a course in American history or literature. The proportion of institutions requiring a foreign language for graduation dropped from 89% to 47% between 1963 and 1983. In addition, increased certification requirements squeezed out most of the academic studies for students in teacher education programs.

Some scholars have suggested that general education has been distorted into a vocational orientation. Hirsch (1983) reports an historical tension between cultural unity and curricular diversity. He recommends that general education offer a common body of content in order for acculturation to occur, but he is unsure as to how and whether it is possible. Bennett (1984) blames the problem on the failure of those responsible for teaching the humanities. The curriculum has become disjointed, compartmentalized, and incoherent. He also suggests that, during the 1960s, university faculty members disregarded standards and abdicated control of education to the students.

The relationship between general education and "professional role expectations" has been disputed based on the referents for the term "professional role expectations," which may be demonstrably antithetical. The need to "anticipate and adapt to changes in society and technology" may indicate a narrow intellectual conformity and a dependence of thought traditionally identified with general education (Gore, 1987).

It is generally agreed that the general education part of teacher education should be shared by all and should be taught by faculty who are the experts in this area. There is also general agreement that the curriculum for general education must be different from that of a conventional academic major. However, there continues to be disagreement about what the nature of general education should be for all students, as well as for teacher education students. The inclusion of non-western studies and women's and minority studies has been advocated and adopted in many institutions of higher education and has been the source of controversy and even conflict in others. In addition, there is no unified view of the various scholarly disciplines which constitute the general education of college students, let alone in general education as a whole. Attempts were made in the curriculum reform movement of the 1950s and 1960s to identify the structure of the scholarly disciplines. Many different structures were identified for each. Similarly, over the years there have been attempts to arrive at a comprehensive view of the liberal arts and sciences or general education, without any acceptable view being agreed upon by university educators.

The situation is more problematic for early childhood teachers. In general, the field has not addressed the issue of what should be taught in the early childhood classroom. More often, the field is simply admonished to present whatever it is that should be taught in a manner that is consistent with the children's level of development (e.g., Bredekamp, 1987). Spodek (1989), however, has suggested that the early childhood teacher is a teacher of general education. Since the general education component provides teachers of young children with a great deal of the content of what is to be taught, albeit in an indirect fashion, the issue of the content of the general education component of the early childhood teacher education program takes on added significance in these teachers' preparation.

PROFESSIONAL FOUNDATIONS

In the past, teachers have learned to teach through working with experienced practitioners on the job rather than through the study of educational theory (Peters, 1977). Their teaching has been based on mastering skilled techniques rather than on knowledge and understanding. Today, theory is presented through foundation courses, which are often eclectic in orientation. These foundation courses should broaden the base of teachers' decisions and actions.

Professional foundations are concerned with those aspects of anthropology, economics, history, philosophy, psychology, politics, and sociology that inform decision-making in education. Linguistics might also be considered a foundation for early childhood education. Professional foundations are concerned with a search for knowledge *about* education rather than with professional techniques (Laska, 1973: Peters, 1977).

Foundation courses present the world differently from its practical reality (March, 1973). Through these courses, teacher candidates learn to restructure their views of children, school, and subjects to analyze American educational patterns in relation to democratic ideals, and to have a more humanized vision of the education of society (Gillett & Laska, 1973). They can help students become more sensitive to how children from different cultural backgrounds have been treated in school, and help students examine and appreciate the aims, ideas, values, influences and assumptions of a practical education system (Skinner, 1968).

Teachers in early childhood education need a broad range of educational foundations. They need to become aware of the history and traditions of their field. They need to know principles of child growth and development and learning theory, as well as the cultural, social, and political contents in which they will be working. This knowledge goes beyond general education since it is applied in a professional context.

The foundations component should lead to a basic understanding of regional, social, and developmental differences in children's language and how culture is reflected in thinking styles, learning styles, and language development. Teacher candidates learn to understand and judge various alternative educational theories and methods.

The purpose of professional education should be to prepare competent teacher candidates and to reinforce the improvement of general practice. This process requires that theory and practice be integrated. A separate program should be responsible for attaining the purpose of professional education, whereas the purposes of general education for teachers should be similar to the other students.

INSTRUCTIONAL KNOWLEDGE

Instructional knowledge refers to the knowledge that teachers use in planning, implementing, and evaluating classroom practice. Teachers must demonstrate knowledge of the subject matter they teach as well as knowledge of teaching methods. Shulman (1986) has suggested that decisions about teaching should be rooted in knowledge about:

1. Organization in preparing and presenting instructional plans
2. Evaluation
3. Recognition of individual differences
4. Cultural awareness
5. Understanding youth
6. Management
7. Educational policies and procedures

Shulman (1986) suggests that these be embedded in different forms of knowledge. *Content knowledge* is the degree and order of knowledge per se in the teachers' mind. Content knowledge can be represented using Bloom's cognitive taxonomy, or Gagne's varieties of learning. *Pedagogical content knowledge* includes knowledge about teaching subject matter. It is composed of important topics in the teacher's subject area which are integrated with teaching strategies to present representation of important concepts, the most powerful analogies, illustrations, examples, explanations, and demonstrations. Pedagogical content knowledge also includes strategies to individualize the instruction from easy to difficult topics. For example, it must consider students of different abilities, ages, and backgrounds. Thus, teachers must possess knowledge of the effective strategies which promote learning, which is an important area. *Curricular knowledge* is knowledge of the education program, which includes instruction in specific subjects and topics at a specific level as well as the use of a special curriculum or program materials in particular circumstances.

Teacher education programs help teacher candidates acquire knowledge and skills to plan and implement educational programs for young children. Saracho (1984) identified 6 roles of the teacher that could provide another way of determining the professional knowledge component of the program:

1. *Diagnostician.* Teachers need to assess children's strengths and needs in order to plan the proper match of successful learning experiences for children.
2. *Curriculum designer.* Teachers develop curricula for young children within their capabilities based upon theories and practices of early childhood education as well as the learnings which the community considers important.
3. *Organizer of instruction.* Teachers use their outcomes from long-range and short-range planning to organize the classroom activities to achieve the educational goals. Teachers

inquire about appropriate available resources and make these resources to their best use of them.
4. *Manager of learning.* Teachers facilitate learning by creating a learning environment and offering learning experiences which are relevant and of interest to the children.
5. *Counselor/advisor.* Teachers continuously interact with children and provide them with care, emotional support and guidance as well as instruction. Teachers also help children to learn socialization skills.
6. *Decision maker.* Constantly, teachers make a range of decisions about children, materials, activities and goals. Some are instantaneous decisions, while others reflect decisions as teachers plan, select and implement from among alternatives.

These roles, which are summarized in Table 26–1, are directly related to the teacher's performance within the classroom. If the role of the teacher is conceptualized beyond classroom responsibilities, other roles (e.g., child advocate, adult educator, or supervisor) can be added.

The identification of roles indicates that successful performance of each role requires that teachers of young children acquire a range of knowledge, skills, and attitudes. As teachers acquire knowledge and understanding, they can apply the principles and practices of early childhood education to practical situations. Saracho (1987, 1988a, 1988b, 1988c, 1988d) tested this analysis through a series of observational studies. She found an equal balance in the teacher's roles as a curriculum designer, organizer of instruction, and counselor/advisor; however, the role of decision maker was integrated within these roles. As a result, the roles were modified in several ways: (1) organizer of instruction and manager of learning were integrated; (2) unsophisticated tasks, like cleaning, were identified as the teacher's responsibility even if the teacher delegates these tasks.

Teacher education programs emphasize knowledge that is expected to be taught in schools. There are a number of ways to gain this knowledge. One model of teacher education provides an apprenticeship structure, where teacher candidates learn the primary curriculum in the public schools and the methods of teaching that curriculum as apprentices in teachers' classrooms (Zeichner & Tabachnick, 1981). Both the curriculum and pedagogical methods are inclined to resemble the teacher candidates' educational backgrounds.

Evidence shows that teacher candidates learn new theories and pedagogical methods that complement the conventional curriculum (Guskey, 1986; Hollingsworth, 1986; Joyce & Showers, 1982) and that some teacher candidates execute these in field-based programs (Hollingsworth, 1988; Shefelbine & Hollingsworth, 1987). Teacher candidates who learn both managerial and subject matter practices possess a metacognitive competence, which permits them to use that knowledge in a flexible manner when the context changes and when their supervisors direct them. A related consideration is that of program content for teacher candidates. An explicit knowledge base for teaching has not been acknowledged (Richardson-Koehler, 1987; Shulman, 1986), but Hollingsworth (1989) has identified 3 overlapping areas containing teaching knowledge bases: (1) subject matter—both content and subject pedagogy, (2) general

TABLE 26–1 Summary of the Different Roles of the Teacher

Roles	Knowledge	Skills	Attitudes
Decision maker	Curriculum of early childhood education Content and methods of different subject areas	Organizing the classroom Planning the curriculum Matching materials and methods to children	Community's values
	Child development	Meeting individual needs	Behavioral style
		Obtaining techniques to work with children	Teaching style
		Obtaining information about children	
	Theories of play	Knowing how to use play as a tool of learning	Play as educational
	Recent research, development, and practice in early childhood education	Acquiring research skills	Objectives
	Role of the teacher	Teaching duties, responsibilities, obligations, functions	Ethics, attitudes, ideological position, self-image, membership and reference group, commitment to the profession
Organizer of Instruction	Child development—Process of development and learning	Knowing how certain procedures affect children and teachers Integrating information within some structure to give meaning	Behavioral style Teaching style
		Developing materials Operating equipment Locating resources for a variety of materials Working with other adults in the classroom	
	Evaluation methods	Evaluating materials, resources, and equipment Knowing self-evaluation Knowing evaluation of teaching and programs	
Curriculum Designer	Curriculum theory	Selecting scope, sequence, and balance	Community's values
		Adapting content to individual differences	Cultural values
		Knowing different methods of teaching	Teacher's ideology of early childhood education
		Selecting materials and equipment without demeaning individuals	Ethnic groups
		Planning long-range and short-range goals	Teacher's values
		Establishing goals, content, and teaching techniques	Teaching style
		Matching goals, methods, and experiences	
	Child development theory	Knowing developmental norms to group children for appropriate experiences	

(continued)

TABLE 26–1 (*continued*)

Roles	Knowledge	Skills	Attitudes
	Knowledge of curriculum areas (language, reading, mathematics, social studies, etc.)	Selecting concepts from a mixture of different forms of knowledge	
		Integrating knowledge with understanding	
		Integrating curriculum areas and teaching practice	
	Philosophy	Integrating activities with the different disciplines	
Diagnostician	Child development	Judging children's maturation stages, achievement of prior learnings, behavior, and so on	Concern for individual differences
		Collecting, analyzing, and interpreting data	
		Becoming aware of individual skills, abilities, interests, and behavior	
	Assessment techniques	Using:	
		Sociometric scales Observation techniques Interviews	
		Selecting appropriate experiences, materials, and equipment	
	Curriculum and methods	Selecting activities	
Manager of Learning	Psychology of learning	Creating an attractive educational environment	Awareness of individual differences such as cognitive styles, interests, and needs
	Curriculum theory	Planning and implementing learning activities	
	Child development	Guiding children's behavior in performing educational tasks	
		Establishing work routines	
		Presenting subject matter	
		Providing educational tools and classroom displays	
		Offering a wide range of learning alternatives	
		Scheduling and implementing transitions	
Counselor/Advisor	Child psychology	Knowing different methods of interacting	Teacher's values and priorities
	Child development	Creating an environment that motivates the child's exploration and discovery	Accept individual differences
	Sociology	Helping children make decisions	Provide warmth and emotional support
	Anthropology	Promoting children's creative growth and self-actualization	Present a sense of trust and security
	Philosophy		Society's values
	Psychology of learning	Manifesting their personality in an authentic way	
		Searching their educational and teaching values	

Source: Saracho, O. N. (1984). Perception of the Teaching Process in Early Childhood Education Through Role Analysis. *Journal of the Association for the Study of Perception, International*, 19(1), 35–38.

pedagogy or management and instruction, and (3) the ecology of learning in classrooms.

Subject Pedagogy. Teachers need to know both the content of the subjects and the strategies for instruction. Shulman and his associates (Shulman, 1986; Wilson, Shulman, & Richert, 1987) emphasize the importance of pedagogical content in learning to teach. However, they do not identify the content and pedagogy subject area the teacher candidates must know, nor how and when that content should be taught to teacher candidates in their programs in order that they effectively learn to individualize instruction for students with different learning abilities and backgrounds.

Management Instruction. Teacher candidates should possess general management knowledge that can be applied across subject areas. Management absorbs much of the teachers' time; it directs instruction and adapts organizational routines to the content and contexts that are necessary to successfully teach the academic content in classrooms (Rosenshine, 1987; Wilson, Shulman, & Richert, 1987). Successful ways for teacher candidates to learn pedagogical routines in teacher education programs have not been established.

Ecology of Learning in Classrooms. In addition to content knowledge and pedagogical knowledge, teacher candidates must know ways students learn in the classroom. That is, teachers should know both theories of knowledge acquisition and the social learning in classrooms to describe and explain the roles they will assume as teachers. In addition, teacher candidates must know techniques to integrate knowledge of human learning, subject, and pedagogy into precise academic tasks. The convergence of these areas in academic tasks indicates the complexity of teaching and learning in classrooms and must be explained.

An *academic task* is a hypothetical association "defined by the answers students are required to produce and the routes that can be used to obtain those answers" (Doyle, 1983, p. 161). Tasks determine conditional organizations guiding both thought and action in the classroom. Goals of the task, cognitive operations, and obtainable resources are identified (Doyle, 1983; Doyle & Carter, 1984). The power of the academic task depends on the teacher's approach in sequencing the subject matter content into a system that can be easily managed. Social and curricular facets of the academic task must be integrated to promote the students' knowledge in different subjects and classroom contexts.

In Hollingsworth's (1989) study, the ultimate level of learning to teach reading was *task awareness* or understanding students' learning from text-related tasks. Teacher candidates achieve that level by arranging their thinking in a precise manner to subdue the complexities of managing a classroom. For example, a teacher candidate becomes an apprentice and decreases classroom complexities by default (imitating the cooperating teacher's approach). While imitating the cooperating teacher decreases the complexity, it also restricts the candidate's learning. Teacher candidates learn more as they encounter inapplicable beliefs and use competent direction to sort, schematize, organize, and integrate teaching. The teacher candidates who recognize the academic task can integrate subjects with instructional techniques that focus on the students' learning. Hollingsworth (1989) also found that teacher candidates tested their new knowledge as they worked with cooperating teachers who may differ from them but would permit them to test their knowledge in different contexts (i.e., students from various backgrounds and abilities) and provide them with support and content-specific feedback. Obviously, the divergence in points of view assisted teacher candidates to disentangle complex aspects of the classroom and cultivated comprehensive learning when testing their own ideas. The academic task is based on the idea that students learn what teachers want them to learn. In Hollingsworth's (1989) study, the tasks consisted of concepts that students learn best. Thus, more accountable assignments could have been provided to illustrate what students accurately learned in these teaching situations. Assignments might also show the teacher candidates' learning progress, especially in individualizing instruction. It is important to concentrate on the depth of the teacher candidates' learning of those concepts instead of their conformity for concurrence.

Teacher education programs must be flexible in their preparation approach to assist teacher candidates meet their individual differences (e.g., incoming beliefs, methods, management, content) and those of children from different schools and backgrounds. A standard approach to teacher education can reinforce existing instructional patterns and superficial learning (Hollingsworth, 1989). Saracho's (1984) list of early childhood teachers' roles can provide guidelines for selecting appropriate content for early childhood teacher education programs.

PRACTICE

According to Dearden (1968), there are 3 kinds of learned concepts:

1. Perceptual concepts about physical objects and properties;
2. Practical concepts about how people use the objects in their culture; and
3. Theoretical concepts which are the intellectual concepts transmitted in the process of gaining knowledge and understanding.

Teacher candidates learn practical concepts as they apply theory in a practice situation with help and guidance from cooperating teachers and college supervisors (Tibble, 1971).

Field experiences are used to integrate previous learning with emerging experiences and transform theoretical instruction into reality (Borrowman, 1965). The practice component should use intellectual methods to understand the nature of good practice as well as provide opportunities to improve practice. An overemphasis on field experiences to the exclusion of other program components may move teacher education toward a nonintellectual apprenticeship program. If only the practical is emphasized, basic theories and a merging of ideas with practice may be overlooked or undervalued (Gillett, 1973).

The practice component of the teacher education program could include a range of field experiences including workshops, observations, simulations, practica, and student teaching. Workshops allow students to present and practice teaching techniques with different types of materials and to study the effects of these techniques on children. A workshop may consist of constructing children's equipment, presenting a movement and dance session, painting or sculpting, experimenting with science materials, designing and using puppets, or exploring new materials (Almy, 1975).

Classroom observation allows students to see teachers in action and relate observations of practice to theory. Sensitive observing allows a student or teacher to recognize the significant clues that lead to an understanding of the event and allows inferences to be made and responses to be planned based on something more than intuition.

In simulation, students play a hypothetical role in a simple, controlled situation. In microteaching, a form of simulation, the teacher candidate presents a short activity to a small group of children which is later viewed, analyzed, and evaluated. Field experiences can be integrated with foundations courses through activities such as visits to school board meetings, conferences with officials or teacher's unions, and meetings with parents and members of child advocacy groups. Early experiences with children can also allow student teachers to develop greater responsibility and self-confidence (Borrowman, 1965).

Field experiences can improve teacher candidates' performances as they learn about the importance of teacher-pupil relationships and observe children in a variety of circumstances (Borrowman 1965). Field experiences, unfortunately, may also negatively affect attitudes and behaviors of teacher candidates who may become more authoritarian, rigid, controlling, restrictive, impersonal, and custodial; and less student centered, accepting, and humanistic if this is what they experience in the field (Hull, Baker, Kyle, & Good, 1982; Peck & Tucker 1973; Zeichner, 1980). Thus, it is essential that teacher candidates be exposed from the beginning to high-quality field placements.

Student teaching is considered the most important element in the preparation of teachers (Brimfield & Leonard, 1983). It can offer teacher candidates both negative and positive results as a result of this experience (Hull, Baker, Kyle, & Good, 1982; Zeichner, 1980). Research has identified several problems intrinsic to student teaching and related field experiences. The university supervisor and cooperating teacher's responsibilities are unclear and often overlap (Grimmett & Ratzlaff, 1986; Applegate & Lasley, 1982, 1984). Cooperating teachers have the most influence in the student teaching experience. However, they are more practice-oriented and do not depend on research and theory to make generalizations about practice. In feedback sessions by cooperating teachers, Griffin, Barnes, Defino, Edwards, Hukill, and O'Neal (1983) observed that student teachers receive very little evaluation of behavior or statements of reasons to justify their practice. Discussions were focused on one individual child or problem in the classroom. Feiman-Nemser and Buchmann (1985), in their case study of a student teacher who failed to learn ways to develop and extend the content side

of instruction, also found that the cooperating teacher failed to give appropriate feedback on this topic.

The university supervisor can assume the responsibility of increasing the level of discourse in the feedback session. Unfortunately, O'Neal (1983) found that the university supervisors' feedback was similar to that of the cooperating teachers. In addition, university supervisors do not seem especially effective in contributing to the teacher candidates' classroom experiences (Koehler, 1984).

Several factors may detract from the university supervisors' ability to affect the process. The university supervisor may be reluctant to present a rigorous evaluation of teaching since the student teacher is placed within the context of an environment where the cooperating teacher establishes the processes and routines. Discussion between student teachers and cooperating teachers focused on activities for the next day and coming weeks. Cooperating teachers explain classroom actions in a specific way disregarding principles of practice. For example, groups of children to teach a specific topic usually change regularly. The student teachers do not know their cooperating teachers' implicit theories. Discussions on the day's activities between cooperating teachers and teacher candidates generally focus on issues of classroom management.

Role of the Cooperating Teacher

Richardson-Koehler (1988) reports that student teachers usually assume full responsibility for the classroom for some period during the semester. Full responsibility consists of planning and implementing the full day's activities, assessing student progress, and having discussions with parents. Student teachers are constrained to work within the cooperating teachers' classroom structures and routines, which impacts on their performance. Routines include the overall organization of the school day, and the timing, task demands, and method of presentation of opening-of-the day segments and other lessons. Scheduling is an example of a critical factor in the cooperating teachers' routines. Student teachers experience pressure to cover content overage in a short period of time.

Cooperating teachers tend not to discuss routines. Their discussions emphasize socializing goals: "getting the kids to work with each other in centers," but not the broader outlines of the organization of their lessons and day. They depend on the student teachers' observations to infer the basis for establishing routines. One student teacher expressed his disorientation because he did not understand the nature of the routines and also the routines were not explained to him. He did not understand the relationship to the goals of the cooperating teacher's classroom organization. As a result the student teacher parroted the cooperating teacher's language and behavior. Although he did not understand the routines, he functioned within the classroom and manipulated the classroom routines as he had observed them.

In a 3-way discussion between the cooperating teacher, student teacher, and university supervisor, the university supervisor described a routine and asked the cooperating teacher to talk about it. Cooperating teachers assess routines as being "good" or "okay" based on management and efficiency concerns: the students' degree of participation and completing a task quickly. Cooperating teachers also believe that student teachers need to experiment and create their own routines.

Role of the University Supervisor

The university supervisors' role is vague concerning their expectations for the cooperating teachers (Grimmett & Ratzlaff, 1986). The university supervisors' influence in the student teachers' classroom practices and their experiences is unknown. Koehler (1984) found the university supervisors' impact on the student teachers' classroom practices to be low in comparison to the cooperating teachers'. Cooperating teachers clearly feel the need to protect their student teachers in their final assessment. Although cooperating teachers are aware of the student teachers' problems, they praise their student teachers during final assessment and try to excuse problems that the supervisors present.

The ambiguity of the university supervisor's role may be due to a lack of consensus in relation to the classroom practices. Bird (1984) found that cooperating teachers felt that the university supervisors had a university perspective which disregarded the schools; university supervisors always rushed in and out of the school with little opportunity to learn about the school or classroom. Little (1981) found that student teachers and cooperating teachers did not see the university supervisors' efforts as equal; nor would an exchange of benefits appear to be taking place. Thus, a combination of equality of effort, an exchange of benefits, and a particular way in the discussions of the student teachers' performance was missing in the university supervisor's involvement. It can be concluded that a number of obstacles are found in the student teaching experience:

1. Student teachers are not exposed in schools to a model of learning to teach that uses rigorous analysis of teaching and collegiality.
2. The cooperating teachers' lack of ability or willingness to participate in reflection on their classroom practices reinforces the poor quality of feedback received by the student teachers.
3. The university supervisors cannot change the norms or affect the feedback process by working with individual dyads (cooperating teacher and student teacher) because they do not spend the time in the schools necessary to build trust.

A number of teacher education programs have been developed to deal with these problems. According to Zeichner and Liston (1987), Korthagen (1985), and Adler and Roth (1985), some teacher education programs have worked on developing reflective habits in their student teachers by focusing on the student teachers and the university supervisors instead of the cooperating teachers. Carter (1987) feels that cooperating teachers could be trained to analyze their teaching and supervision techniques. Bird (1984) suggests considering supervising student teaching within a larger school improvement context where reflection and critical analysis of teaching are

recompensed. Little (1987) proposes that schools should make provisions for student teachers to have access to shared understandings. Schools must accept their role as a reflective and self-renewing institution where student teachers become socialized into their settings. Ideal places for student teaching are needed to accomplish the goal of helping to empower the teaching profession through well educated and socialized new teachers.

Student teaching is a culminating experience and should be as nearly like teaching as possible. Student teachers should attend regular seminars which allow them to share their experiences and work out their problems in a group. These seminars should be designed to promote intellectual growth and professional socialization. The university supervisor can also have individual conferences with the student teacher and cooperating teacher to provide additional opportunities beyond the seminar.

Student teaching is very important in a teacher education program. Student teaching tests the teacher candidates' decision to enter the profession. It requires them to transfer theoretical knowledge into practice. Ideal images are challenged by their demands of reality. The novice is challenged to confirm the scientific basis of the art of teaching under the scrutiny of both a cooperating and a supervising teacher's ability to successfully handle the students' classroom. Beginning teachers, particularly student teachers, are interested in classroom management and their own competence as teachers. Solving the dilemmas about control, motivation, and personal competence is a vital element in the student teachers' socialization (Hoy & Woolfolk, 1990).

In applying the knowledge available on practice to early childhood teacher education programs, one must determine, as in other areas, what of this knowledge is valid for early childhood education. Field experiences and student teaching seem to have a universal quality to them. Simulations, however, have been used primarily in the preparation of secondary school teachers, possibly because it is easier for college students to take on the roles of high school students than to act in a realistic manner like young children. The roles of college supervisor and cooperating teacher are found in early childhood teacher preparation programs as in other teacher education program and may be generic to college based teacher education programs that depend on schools to provide and supervise a variety of field experiences, including student teaching. Similarly, the problems in the nature and structure of student teaching are inherent in the institutional structure and processes of teacher education, rather in the level of teacher preparation. Thus knowledge from these areas should be applicable to early childhood teacher education.

PROGRAM MODIFICATION

Program modification is an essential component for any teacher education program because it provides a vehicle for program improvement. Planning an evaluation is an art. Each attribute of the evaluation provides advantages and incorporates specific sacrifices. A broad validity and utility theory is needed as a basis for appraising the satisfactory evaluation plans (Cronbach, 1982).

Program evaluation tries to facilitate decisions. Stake (1971) identifies 3 goals of educational evaluation: (1) to foster an understanding of the current status of the educational system; (2) to provide data for the correction of shortcomings; and (3) to move the never-ending evolution of the curriculum toward a better balance among the rational, the intuitive, and the humane.

Evaluation incorporates elements of inquiry, valuing, and social change. According to Smith (1981), evaluation, as currently conceived, is based on *inquiry* procedures; it shares with the sciences a preoccupation with the question "What is true?" and is aimed at increasing understanding. Evaluation is also concerned with value and shares with the arts an attempt to answer the question "What is beautiful and good?" Evaluations are conducted to facilitate change and share with the world of practical affairs a concern with the question, "What is viable and fair?" (p. 30) aiming to improve the human condition.

Spodek (1975) specifies several ways to evaluate teacher education programs:

- Programs of education and teacher education are based upon specific ideals and values, whether or not these ideals and values are made explicit. These determine the judgment of what treatments are considered worthy and what outcomes are considered worthy for each program.
- Program treatments can be portrayed to determine whether treatment elements are consistent with values and expected outcomes.
- Program outcomes can be assessed in terms of their consistency with program ideals and values as well as with the context in which the teacher is operating. Indicators of outcomes may vary for different types of programs.
- Programs of teacher education can be compared on common dimensions.

Program evaluation requires information on its worth, practicality, and effectiveness. The worth of a program relates to both the underlying values of the program and the evaluator's values. The program's practical aspects can be assessed by observing the degree to which activities are generated that are consistent with the program's intentions. The program's effectiveness is supported with evidence about outcomes (Spodek, 1983).

There are different ways to evaluate programs. Most programs use preordinate evaluations that depend on prespecification of goals, tests of student performance, and a research-type report. Responsive evaluation can be used in place of preordinate evaluation. In responsive evaluation the concerns and issues of stake holding audiences are used (Guba & Lincoln, 1981). It uses program experiences instead of program intents and assesses what people do naturally. Observations and reactions are the major means of collecting data. The evaluator observes the perceptions and values of individuals, examines records, and presents a report formally or informally, orally or in writing, and in different forms such as brief narratives, portrayals, product displays, or graphs, depending upon the needs

of the audience. The evaluator's major responsibility is to provide sufficient information about the program in order that others have a basis for making decisions. It is not the role of the evaluator to make a judgment about changing a program. If the evaluator assumes the role of judge, the availability of data might decrease (Stake 1974, 1976). Responsive evaluation uses cues from issues that local audiences identify as interesting or relevant to local needs. The evaluator gathers and presents the information. In the final analysis audiences will use the information that they have identified as important (Guba & Lincoln, 1981).

Teacher education programs should include both internal and external evaluation. Internally, information about what is actually happening in the program could be collected through group sessions, conferences, observations, and a monitoring of program elements. The purpose of this evaluation would be to broaden the staff's perception of the program and to clarify the staff's perception of the program and the staff's concerns regarding issues and values.

Staff members are often too involved in a program to be objective (Scriven 1973). An external evaluator, a trusted person with broader perspective could be used to provide this objectivity. Program documents such as samples of students' work, inventories, curriculum guides, syllabus, and staff meeting reports could be examined. Group sessions, student conferences, classes, practicum sites, and staff meetings could be observed. Student files could be reviewed to provide evidence to be verified by other procedures such as observation. Guba and Lincoln (1981) also suggest using running notes, field experience logs, chronologs, context maps, taxonomies or category systems, observation schedules, sociometries, panels, and debriefing questionnaires. Although many methods have been mentioned here, the observer should feel free to generate other ways of recording the information necessary to complete the evaluation.

Evaluation could also make use of participants' perceptions of the program. This measure of program effectiveness can be assessed directly or indirectly. Interviews or questionnaires could be used to collect data, but should not be trusted blindly (Cronbach, 1972). Although Guba and Lincoln (1981) suggest that any respondent might lead the interviewer down the primrose path, most individuals will offer reasonably honest answers. Structured interviews rarely probe deeply enough to cause a respondent to lie to the interviewer. In contrast, the unstructured interview (intensive, key, investigative, elite, specialized, nonstandardized, or depth) is less abrupt, remote, and arbitrary. It is used in situations where the evaluator is looking for nonstandardized information.

The demand for improved teacher quality requires that evaluation focus on teachers. Behavioral observation systems are used to assess their competence. Some educational reformers urge the assessment of teachers as reflective or thoughtful professionals (e.g., Carnegie Forum on Education and Economy, 1986; Futrell, 1986; Holmes Group, 1986; Shanker, 1985). Thus, several educational researchers are generating assessment systems to measure teachers' classroom behaviors as well as their thinking and decision-making skills (Peterson & Comeaux, 1989; Shulman & Sykes, 1986).

CONCLUSION

Teachers can have a long-lasting influence on the young children in their classes. Teacher competence must be rooted in an understanding of children and culture and in a set of values that determines appropriate influences on young children. Thus, all aspects of a teacher education program must be considered in designing a program to prepare teachers of young children.

While our knowledge of the nature and consequences of various elements of early childhood teacher education programs is limited, there is a great deal that we do know. Much of this knowledge is derived from studies of programs preparing teachers for other levels of education. While such knowledge is useful, especially in the absence of knowledge specific to early childhood teacher education programs, caution must be advised in its use. There is always the danger that we have overgeneralized in such applications. Similarly, we must caution in applying knowledge of baccalaureate level teacher education programs to nonbaccalaureate programs. Powell and Dunn (1990) have provided a useful review of research and practice at this level that should be referred to understand the nature of this kind of personnel preparation and the limitations of our knowledge in this area.

Finally, we need to make a plea for developing increased research about early childhood teacher education programs. As more resources are provided to increase the preparation of early childhood teachers, increased research activities in this area also need to be supported. Only with increased scholarly activity will we develop a more reliable base of knowledge about the preparation of early kithed teachers.

References

Adler, M. J. (1982). *The Paideia proposal.* New York: Macmillan.

Adler, S., & Roth, R. (1985, April). *Critical inquiry in teacher preparation.* Paper presented at the annual meeting of the American Association for Teacher Education, Chicago.

Almy, M. (1975). *The early childhood educator at work.* New York: McGraw-Hill.

American Association of Colleges for Teacher Education. (1977). *Standards and evaluative criteria for the accreditation of teacher education: A draft of the proposed new standards with study guide.* Washington, DC: AACTE.

American Association of Colleges for Teacher Education. (1984). *AACTE Briefs, 5*(5), 8.

American Association of Colleges for Teacher Education. (1985). *A call for change in teacher education.* Washington, DC: Author.

Applegate, J. H. (1987). Teacher candidate selection: An overview. *Journal of Teacher Education, 38*(2), 2–6.

Applegate, J. H., & Lasley, T. J. (1982). Cooperating teachers' problems with preservice field experience students. *Journal of Teacher Education, 33*(2), 15–18.

Applegate, J. H., & Lasley, T. J. (1984). What cooperating teachers expect from preservice field experience students. *Teacher Education, 24,* 70–82.

Benner, S., George, T., & Cage, L. (1987). Admission boards: The contribution of professional judgment to the admission process. *Journal of Teacher Education, 38*(2), 7–11.

Bennett, W. J. (1984). *To reclaim a legacy: A report on the humanities in higher education.* Washington, DC: National Endowment for the Humanities.

Bird, T. (1984, July). *Propositions regarding the analysis and supervision of teaching.* Paper presented to the Loveland, Colorado School Administrators Workshop, Vail, CO.

Book, C. L., & Freeman, D. J. (1986). Differences in entry characteristics of elementary and secondary teacher candidates. *Journal of Teacher Education, 37*(2), 47–51.

Borrowman, M. L. (1965). *Teacher education in America.* New York: Teachers College Press.

Boyer, E. L. (1983). *High school: A report of secondary education in America.* New York: Harper & Row.

Bredekamp, S. (1987). *Developmentally appropriate practice in early childhood programs serving children from birth through age 8.* Washington, DC: National Association for the Education of Young Children.

Brimfield, R., & Leonard, R. (1983). The student teaching experience: A time to consolidate one's perceptions. *College Student Journal, 17,* 401–406.

Carnegie Forum on Education and the Economy (1986). *A nation prepared: Teachers for the 21st century.* (A report of the Task Force on Teaching as a Profession). New York: Carnegie Foundation.

Carnegie Foundation for the Advancement of Teaching. (1988). *Condition of teaching: A state-by-state analysis.* Princeton, NJ: Princeton University Press.

Carter, K. (1987). *University of Arizona cooperative teacher project: An interim report to OERI, Department of Education.* Tucson, AZ: University of Arizona.

Cronbach, L. J. (1972). Course improvement through evaluation. In P. A. Taylor and D. M. Cowley (Eds.), *Readings in curriculum evaluation,* (pp. 11–19). Dubuque, IA: Brown.

Cronbach, L. J. (1982). *Designing evaluations of educational and social programs.* San Francisco: Jossey-Bass.

Dearden, R. F. (1968). *The philosophy of primary education.* London: Routledge & Kegan Paul.

Dejnozka, E. L., & Smiley, L. R. (1983). Selective admissions criteria in graduate teacher education programs. *Journal of Teacher Education, 34*(1), 24–27.

Doyle, W. (1983). Academic work. *Review of Educational Research, 53,* 159–199.

Doyle, W., & Carter, K. (1984). Academic tasks in classrooms. *Curriculum Inquiry, 14,* 129–149.

Education Commission of the States. (1983). *Action for excellence: A comprehensive plan to improve our schools.* Washington, DC: Author.

Feiman-Nemser, S., & Buchmann, M. (1985, February). *On what is learned in student teaching: Appraising the experience.* Paper presented at the annual meeting of the American Association for Teacher Education, Chicago.

Futrell, M. (1986). Restructuring teaching: A call for research. *Educational Researcher, 15*(10), 5–8.

Gillett, M. (1973). Introduction to new directions. In J. A. Laska & M. Gillett (Eds.), *Foundation Studies in Education: Justifications and New Directions.* Metuchen, NJ: Scarecrow Press.

Goodlad, J. (1983). *A place called school: Prospects for the future.* New York: McGraw-Hill.

Guba, E. G., & Lincoln, Y. S. (1981). *Effective evaluation.* San Francisco: Jossey-Bass.

Guskey, T. R. (1986). Staff development and the process of teacher change. *Educational Researcher, 15*(5), 5–12.

Haberman, M. (1986). Alternative teacher education programs. *Action in Teacher Education, 8*(2), 13–18.

Hermanowicz, H. J. (1986). *Key concepts and past developments contribution to a new model of teacher education.* Unpublished discussion paper for ACSESULGC/APU.

Hirsh, E. D., Jr. (1983). Cultural literacy. *American Scholar, 52*(5), 159–169.

Hollingsworth, S. (1989). Prior beliefs and cognitive change in learning to teach. *American Educational Research Journal, 26*(2), 160–189.

Hollingsworth, S. (1988). Making field-based programs work: A three-level approach to reading education. *Journal of Teacher Education, 39*(4), 28–36.

Hollingsworth, S. (1986). *Learning to teach reading.* Unpublished doctoral dissertation, University of Texas at Austin.

Holmes Group, Inc. (1986). *Tomorrow's teachers: A report of the Holmes Group.* East Lansing, MI: Author.

Howey, K. R., & Strom, S. M. (1987). Teacher selection reconsidered. In M. Haberman & J. Backus (Eds.), *Advances in teacher education III,* (pp. 1–34). Norwood, NJ: Ablex.

Howsam, R. B., Corrigan, D. C., & Denemark, G. W. (1985). *Educating a profession: Reprint with postscript.* Washington, DC: American Association of Colleges for Teacher Education.

Hoy, W. K., & Woolfolk, A. E. (1990). Socialization of student teachers. *American Educational Research Journal, 27*(2), 279–300.

Hull, R., Baker, R., Kyle, J., & Good, R. (Eds.) (1982). *Research on student teaching: A question of transfer.* Eugene, OR: University of Oregon, Division of Teacher Education. (ERIC Document Reproduction Service No. ED 223 561).

Joyce, B. R., & Showers, B. (1982). The coaching of teaching. *Educational Leadership, 40,* 4–10.

Katz, L. G. (1969). *Teaching in Preschools: Roles and Goals.* Urbana, IL: ERIC Clearinghouse on Early Childhood Education.

Korthagen, F. (1985, April). *Reflective thinking as a basis for teacher education.* Paper presented at the annual meeting of the American Association for Teacher Education.

Laman, A. E., & Reeves, D. E. (1983). Admission to teacher education programs: The status and trends. *Journal of Teacher Education, 34*(1), 2–4.

Laska, J. A. (1973). Introduction to Perspectives on Foundation Studies. In J. A. Laska & M. Gillett (Eds.), *Foundation Studies in Education: Justifications and New Directions.* Metuchen, NJ: Scarecrow Press.

Lewin and Associates. (n.d.) *The state of teacher education, 1977.* Washington, DC: U.S. Department of Health, Education and Welfare.

Little, J. W. (1987). Teachers as colleagues. In V. Richardson-Koehler (Ed.), *Educators handbook* (pp. 491–518). New York: Longman.

March, L. (1973). Generic and Specific Contributions of Sociology to Teacher Education. In J. A. Laska & M. Gillett (Eds.), *Foundation studies in education: Justifications and new directions.* Mituchen, NJ: Scarecrow Press.

McLaughlin, M. W., & Pfeifer, R. S. (1988). *Teacher evaluation: Improvement, accountability, and effective learning.* New York: Teachers College Press.

Mortimer, K. P. and Associates (1984). *Involvement in learning: Realizing the potential of American higher education.* Washington, DC: National Institute of Education.

National Commission on Excellence in Education (1983). *A Nation at risk: The imperative for educational reform.* Washington DC: U.S. Department of Education.

National Education Association. (1982). *Excellence in our schools: Teacher education.* Washington, DC.

O'Neal, S. (1983). *Supervision of student teachers: Feedback and evaluation.* Austin, TX: University of Texas, Research and Development Center for Teacher Education.

Peck, R. F., & Tucker, J. A. (1973). Research on teacher education. In R. M. W. Travers (Ed.), *Second handbook of research on teaching.* Chicago: Rand McNally.

Peters, R. (1977). *Education and the education of teachers.* Boston: Routledge & Kegan Paul.

Peterson, P. L., & Comeaux, M. A. (1989). Assessing the teacher as a reflective professional: New perspectives on teacher evaluation. In A. E. Woolfolk (Ed.), *The graduate preparation of teachers* (pp. 132–152). Englewood Cliffs, NJ: Prentice Hall.

Peterson, P. L., & Comeaux, M. A. (1990). Evaluating the systems: Teachers' perspectives on teacher evaluation. *Educational Evaluation and Policy Analysis, 12*(1), 3–24.

Phenix, P. H. (1964). *Realms of meaning.* New York: McGraw-Hill.

Powell, D. R., & Dunn, L. (1990). Nonbaccalaureate Teacher education in early childhood education. In B. Spodek & O. N. Saracho (Eds.), *Early childhood teacher preparation. Yearbook in early childhood education, Vol. 1* (pp. 45–66). New York: Teachers College Press.

Raths, J. (1984). [Commentary]. In E. Asburn & R. Fisher (Eds.). *Methods of assessing teacher education students.* Conference proceedings of the American Association of Colleges for Teacher Education. Washington, DC: American Association of Colleges for Teacher Education.

Robertson, S. D., Keith, T. Z., & Page, E. B. (1983). Now who aspires to teach? *Educational Researcher, 12*(6), 13–21.

Rosenshine, B. V. (1987). Explicit teaching and teacher training. *Journal of Teacher Education, 38*(3), 34–36.

Roth, R. A. (1986). Emergency certificates, mis-assignment of teachers and other "dirty little secrets." *Phi Delta Kappan, 67*(10), 725–727.

Ryans, D. G. (1976). *Characteristics of teachers.* Washington, DC: American Council on Education.

Saracho, O. N. (1984). Perception of the teaching process in early childhood education through role analysis. *Journal of the Association for the Study of Perception, International, 19*(1), 26–29.

Saracho, O. N. (1987). An instructional evaluation study in early childhood education. *Studies in Educational Evaluation, 13,* 163–174.

Saracho, O. N. (1988a). An evaluation of an early childhood teacher education curriculum for preservice teachers. *Early Child Development and Care, 38,* 81–101.

Saracho, O. N. (1988b). A study of the roles of early childhood teachers. *Early Child Development and Care, 38,* 43–56.

Saracho, O. N. (1988c). Using observation to study the roles of the teacher. *College Student Journal, 22*(4), 396–400.

Saracho, O. N. (1988d). Assessing instructional materials in an early childhood teacher education curriculum: The search for impact. *Reading Improvement, 25*(1), 10–27.

Saracho, O. N., & Spodek, B. (1983). The preparation of teachers for bilingual bicultural early childhood classes. In O. N. Saracho & B. Spodek (Eds.), *Understanding the multicultural experience in early childhood education* (pp. 125–146). Washington, DC: National Association for the Education of Young Children.

Schlechty, P. C., & Vance, V. S. (1983). Recruitment, selection and retention: The shape of the teaching force. *Elementary School Journal, 83*(4), 469–487.

Schwab, J. J. (1978). *Science, curriculum, and liberal education.* Chicago: University of Chicago Press.

Scriven, M. (1973). Goal-Free Evaluation. In E. T. House (Ed.), *School evaluation: The politics and process* (pp. 319–328). Berkeley, CA: McCutchan.

Shanker, A. (1985). *The making of a profession*. Washington, DC: American Federation of Teachers.

Shefelbine, J. L., & Hollingsworth, S. (1987). The instructional decisions of pre-service teachers during a reading practicum. *Journal of Teacher Education, 38*(1), 36–42.

Shulman, L.S. (1986). Those who understand: Knowledge growth in teaching. *Educational Researcher, 15*(2), 4–14.

Shulman, L. S., & Sykes, F. (1986, May). *A national board for teaching: In search of a bold new standard*. (Paper prepared for the Task Force on Teaching as a Profession, Carnegie Forum on Education and the Economy). Stanford, CA: Stanford University.

Sizer, T. R. (1984). *Horace's compromise: The dilemma of the American high school*. Boston: Houghton Mifflin.

Skinner, B. F. (1968). Teacher-training and the foundational studies. *Teacher Education, 19*(1), 26–38.

Smith, N. L. (1981). Developing evaluation methods. In N. L. Smith (Ed.), *Metaphors for evaluation: Sources of new methods* (pp. 17–49). Beverly Hills, CA: Sage.

Spodek, B. (1975). Early childhood education and teacher education: A search for consistency. *Young Children, 30*(3), 168–173.

Spodek, B. (1983). Early childhood education and evaluation: An overview. *Studies in Educational Evaluation, 8,* 203–207.

Spodek, B. (1988). Conceptualizing today's kindergarten curriculum. *Elementary School Journal, 89*(2), 203–211.

Stake, R. E. (1971). *The evaluation of college teaching: A position paper*. Urbana, IL: University of Illinois.

Stake, R. E. (1974). *SAFARI project: Safari, innovation, evaluation, research and the problem of control: Some interim papers*. Norwich, England: Center for Applied Research in Education, University of East Anglia.

Stake, R. E. (1976). *Evaluating educational programmes: The need and the response*. Paris: Organisation for Economic Cooperation and Development.

Tibble, J. W. (1971). The organization and supervision of school practice. In J. W. Tibble (Ed.), *The future of Teacher Education*. London: Routledge & Kegan Paul.

Turner, R. L. (1975). An Overview of Research in Teacher Education. In K. Ryan (Ed.), *Teacher Education, 74th Yearbook of the National Society for the Study of Education*. Chicago: University of Chicago Press.

Wehlage, G. (1981). Can teachers be more reflective about their work? A commentary on some research about teachers. In B. R. Tabachnick, T. S. Popkewitz, & B. B. Szekely (Eds.), *Studying teaching and learning* (pp. 101–113). New York: Praeger.

Zeichner, K. M. (1980). Myths and realities: Field-based experiences in pre-service teacher education. *Journal of Teacher Education, 31*(6), 45–55.

Zeichner, K. M., & Liston, D. P. (1987). Teaching student teachers to reflect. *Harvard Educational Review, 57*(1), 23–48.

Zeichner, K. M., & Tabachnick, B. (1981). Are the effects of university teacher education washed out by school experience? *Journal of Teacher Education, 32,* 7–11.

27

EARLY CHILDHOOD CARE AND DEVELOPMENT: ISSUES FROM THE DEVELOPING COUNTRY PERSPECTIVE

Judith A. Evans

SENIOR ADVISOR, AGA KAHN FOUNDATION

Despite rituals that guard and glorify the child, children across [India] live robbed of childhood, a period seen as a time to grow, learn and play. Responsibility descends on them even as they grow. . . . As they come in singly, holding hands, carrying a bag, a slate or a tiffin the teacher separates them. . . . The boys fall into lines on the right and the girls on the left. I wonder if this is where it begins—the barriers that separate men from women. . . . I see two little girls walk in an hour late. The older girl, who is four, clutches the hand of the younger one who is two. . . . As they squat together, the elder one holds the younger one's pencil and helps her draw. . . . The four year old, it seems, has already assumed the role of a mother.

Anees Jung, 1987, pp. 78–79

Society's view of young children, what they are like and what we want them to become, determines how we provide for their needs. It has changed over time and differs across societies. It is influenced by a blending of scientific knowledge with a philosophical definition of the value of human life and a vision of what the future will demand. In situations where there is a high rate of infant mortality, survival is of primary concern. Little thought is given to the child's intellectual and social development. When the infant mortality rate changes, attention can be shifted to the intellectual and psychological development of the child. The situation is changing; more and more infants are surviving.

The child survival crusade undertaken in the early 1980s has led to a marked decline in infant mortality rates for developing countries from an average of 150 per 1000 live births in 1960, to 84 per 1000 in 1985 (Goldstone, 1986). What this means is that 11 out of 12 children in developing countries survive; by the mid-1990s 12 out of 13 will survive. While it is important to continue efforts to lower the infant mortality rate, it is also

time to pay attention to what happens to those who survive, the majority of whom live in circumstances that put them at risk of arrested or delayed development.

In recent years, the persuasive humanitarian and social equity arguments traditionally put forward in support of early childhood provision have been buttressed by scientific and economic data that compel us to look more closely at what happens for young children once they "survive" infancy. Internationally, within Third World (developing) countries, this has meant an increased awareness of and commitment to meeting the needs of young children and their families on the part of nongovernmental organizations (NGOs), at the governmental level and within the donor community.

In this chapter some of what has been accomplished as a result of the increased interest in programming for young children will be described, followed by a delineation of some of the questions that have yet to be answered, and a highlighting of some of the challenges for the future. Although this chapter focuses on a selected range of global significant issues, project examples derive primarily from India and East Africa, countries served by the Aga Khan Foundation, and from South America, which provides the richest source of relevant research data.

AN OVERVIEW

A summary of accomplishments within the last decade, derived from an analysis of recent donor agency and project reports, reviews of related literature, and experience, leads to the following set of conclusions.

1. The international community has come to value the importance of early childhood provision.
2. Evidence for this comes from increased governmental commitment to early childhood programming and donor agency willingness to fund such initiatives.
3. Throughout the developing world there are models for how early childhood programming could be done once there is political will to put them into place.
4. It is quite clear that the best models for provision are those that provide integrated or multifocal services.
5. There are data to suggest that interventions for very young children (0–3 years) might, in fact, be even more effective than for those from 3–6.
6. Another conclusion that is being reached is that, because of the important relationship between women and children, programs developed with women are likely to have very positive benefits for children.
7. It is clear from experience to date that it is possible to develop effective training systems to put into place whatever model of provision is chosen for implementation.
8. And last but not least, there is recognition of the need for small-scale experimental models to be created in a way that they can be realistically adopted for implementation on a wider scale.

A WORKING DEFINITION

Before describing each of these accomplishments in more detail, it is important to come to some understanding of terms. Until recently, the phrase *early childhood education* has been used to characterize programs for young children. As Myers (1991) aptly noted, for too many people early childhood education immediately brings to mind the image of a group of small children, ages 3 to 6 years, playing with toys and blocks, fitting shapes into brightly colored puzzle boards, and supervised by a professional teacher in a preschool classroom. Associating early childhood provision with this preschool model is unfortunate because it focuses narrowly on a child's mental development, is relatively expensive, and begins late in terms of the child's basic development. It also involves a direct, institutional approach, relying on the creation of centers that compensate for missing elements in the family and community environment while too often leaving parents and community members out of the program. As has become evident over the past decade, this image seldom provides the most appropriate guide to programming for child care and development in the Third World.

A literature review, as well as experience working in early childhood programs, quickly reveals that there is much more to the child than educational needs. For that reason it is more appropriate to refer to a child's development. The word *develop* means "to expand or realize the potentialities of; bring gradually to a fuller, greater, or better state" (American Heritage Dictionary). The implication is that all aspects of an individual are involved as one develops: the physical, the mental or cognitive (the ability to think, reason and engage in problem solving), the social, the emotional, and the spiritual. While the term *development* encompasses all these domains, there is recognition of the fact that they are not discrete. Changes in one domain necessarily impact all the others. Alterations in a child's health, nutritional status, and intellectual, social or psychological well-being necessarily affect all the other aspects of a child's life.

Of equal significance is the fact that children are both influenced by and influence their wider environment. Children do not exist in a vacuum; they are part of a family and community. In particular, children's development is linked with what happens for women in the family. When women are unhealthy and lack economic resources, children feel the impact. However, the reverse is also true. When women have income at their disposal, children are the first to benefit. Thus the lives of women and children are inextricably entwined.

Any intervention program for young children must consider its consequences in all domains of the child's development and in terms of the context within which the child lives. To try to convey this broader conceptualization of programming, a phrase found more and more commonly in the field is *early childhood care and development* (ECCD). The phrase helps to focus on the importance of a child's basic needs (care) as well as the role of education in supporting the child's overall development. When programming also includes a focus on the interaction between parents and children, particularly the mother, early childhood programs may well be included under the rubric *young children and the family*.

ACCOMPLISHMENTS AND THEIR ATTENDANT CHALLENGES

The broadening of the concept of early childhood provision is one of the spinoffs of the many accomplishments of the past decade, some examples of which are expanded below.

A. *Many people have been sold on the importance of early childhood care and development (ECCD), based on data from longitudinal studies that demonstrate the value of investment in early childhood programming.*

Early childhood programming has been actively promoted by practitioners for decades. Educational psychologists have also advocated attending to children's developmental needs during the early years. But neither practitioners nor theorists have been able to command national or international attention. What finally has made a difference is that the hypothesized importance of investment in the early years has been largely substantiated through longitudinal studies that have included an examination of social as well as academic outcomes. Economic analyses of quality early childhood programs demonstrate that there are long-term benefits for society of investment in the early years. Policy makers now pay attention to discussions of the benefits of quality early childhood programming because they are being discussed in terms of increased productivity, cost savings, and rate of return on investment.

The most impressive data have been generated in long-term studies conducted in the United States (Berrueta-Clement et al., 1985). A number of medium-term (3–5 year) studies have been carried out in the Third World. While not available from all developing countries, the results would appear to be generalizable (Halpern & Myers, 1985). From a review of several studies from Latin America and Asia, several conclusions can be drawn.

1. In relation to primary school performance, early intervention programs can have a positive effect on the probability of enrollment, on initial adjustment (as represented by repetition and drop-out rates), and on achievement in the early years of primary school. These positive effects result from some combination of earlier age of enrollment, improved school readiness (as indicated by tests of mental and social development), and improved health and energy levels (Halpern & Myers, 1985). Further, parental education and changes in parental expectations can play an important role in aiding improvement in primary school. It is important to note that supporting parental confidence and self-esteem may be at least as important in the process of working with parents as the provision of specific information about parenting (Myers, 1988).

2. In terms of social equity issues, there is a growing body of evidence to validate earlier arguments that early childhood provision helps address social equity issues (Myers, 1988). The argument speaks specifically to the fact that the social and economic circumstances that inhibit healthy psychosocial development affect the poor more than the rich. Therefore poor children enter school significantly behind their more affluent peers, and the academic and social distance between the two groups increases over time. Further, discrimination occurs between the sexes as well as across social class. The importance of early childhood programs for girls, in particular, has been demonstrated in a number of studies. One example comes from an evaluation of the Integrated Child Development Services (ICDS) program in India, which demonstrated that the benefits of participating in an early childhood program are highest for girls and unscheduled castes. Those who attended an ICDS center were more likely to enroll in school and less likely to drop out than those who did not attend an ICDS center. (Lal & Wati, 1986).

3. In terms of parent and community development, in a review of programs that (1) serve low-income families, (2) attempt to incorporate health, nutrition, and education, (3) have some form of community participation, and (4) are nonformal (outside the public school system), the clear message is that if one were to focus only on the young child, much of the value of intervention would be missed (Myers & Hertenberg, 1987, p. 35). Benefits were demonstrated across programs for the providers (teachers, care givers) and the community. Through their involvement in early childhood programs, providers (generally paraprofessionals from the local communities) have increased job opportunities, express a high level of job satisfaction, evidence high self-esteem, are ascribed higher social status, and have increased mobility. Further, when community involvement has been one of the desired outcomes, there appears to be an increase in participation and mobilization of community members in response to a range of community problems. Thus, to focus only on the education of the young child greatly limits the potential of investment in early childhood programming.

The research reviews cited above suggest that early childhood programs help prepare children for primary schools, address social equity issues, and suggest that there is a rationale for focusing on the development and implementation of integrated programming, given the range of outcomes that have been demonstrated.

Questions that Arise. There are at least 2 specific questions that have arisen in relation to the successful promotion of early childhood programming. One has to do with the relationship of the early childhood investment to investment in primary education. The second has to do with the relationship between quality and cost.

First, what is the value of the investment in early childhood programming when children subsequently enter a low-quality primary school? While it is known that investment in children before they arrive at school helps maximize the primary school experience, the issue of whether the primary school is prepared to continue support of the child's learning is only beginning to be addressed. The question has been raised as those offering high-quality ECCD programs have watched their graduates enter poor-quality primary schools. In many developing countries the conditions in primary schools are less than optimal: Classrooms contain 40 to 60 children; there are no teaching aids; teachers, poorly paid and little motivated, drill students on what it is perceived they should know. Such an environment is not conducive to learning. These conditions lead to repetition of grades and high dropout rates.

The impact on the children of the differences in the 2 settings is currently being examined in 2 tracer studies funded by the Aga Khan Foundation, one conducted in India by the Center for Research and Development in Bombay (Zaveri, 1992) and the other on the coast in Kenya (Wamahiu, 1992). Preliminary results are not encouraging, particularly when the preschool children do not all enter the same primary school but are scattered so that no more than 5 or 6 children enter the same primary school (Wamahiu, 1992). It would appear that, in order to sustain the gains made in preschool, the educational experience of children in the primary grades needs to be examined and resources allocated to their improvement.

In sum, in instances where there is a high degree of success in promoting early childhood education, programs developed may be out of step with subsequent educational provisions. The question is whether it is worth making a contextually disproportionate investment in early childhood provision if gains are quickly lost as a result of children's subsequent educational experiences.

While not going to the extreme of arguing that investments should not be made in preschool if the primary school is not adequately prepared to receive the children, Myers' (1988) review of the research on the relationship between preschools and primary school performance concludes:

Enrollment, progress, and performance in school are influenced both by the cognitive and social characteristics a child brings to the school and by the availability and quality of schooling. Either or both of these sets of variables can favor or present obstacles to successful school enrollment, adjustment, progress, and achievement...Program decisions about early childhood intervention and about improvements in primary schooling should be considered together, not separately. (pp. 2–3)

Thus, there is an emerging awareness that those involved in early childhood provision must be concerned not only with preparing the child for the primary school, but they must also be able to assess the readiness of the primary school to accept children who have had a quality early childhood experience. Given the interdependency between what happens in the preschool and what happens at the primary level, it is clear that programming for the needs of children before they enter the formal school system cannot be done in isolation.

Second, what is the real value of our investment when low-cost models of preschool provision are actively promoted and implemented? It is clear that there is still a lot to learn about the economics of early childhood education. On the one hand, there are data to suggest that increased investment in quality early childhood interventions is economically valid; that is, the rate of return for investment in the early years is higher than rates of return at other points in the education system. Thus it is argued that governments should increase their spending for such programs. On the other hand, aware of the increasing burden on government to provide even basic primary education and fearing they will not be heard, early childhood advocates promote the adoption of low-cost early childhood models. What this generally means is that the program is implemented by paraprofessionals (hopefully with some, but generally only minimal, training) who are paid less than minimal wages or expected to provide volunteer service, use locally made materials almost exclusively, and operate in makeshift space.

Can it really be expected that these low-cost efforts will generate the same yield on investment as high-quality programming? Although one would not argue that high dollar investment is sufficient or necessary to guarantee quality, it is important to ascertain what minimum level of investment is necessary to yield positive results. The data on this are not in, nor are they being collected, but they should be.

The Challenges. Even as increased attention to the development of early intervention programs is promoted, the challenge is to be cognizant of the context within which early childhood programs are created and to plan accordingly. Further challenges are to understand the economics of early childhood programming better and to be bolder in statements about what investment is needed if that investment is going to pay off.

B. *Government and donor agencies have increased their support for early childhood care and development programs, as evidenced by policy documents and to some extent the allocation of resources.*

During the last decade, developing-country governments have created policy guidelines in support of ECCD and have even included programming for young children and their families as a national priority. A leader on this front is India, which as early as 1972 created a blueprint for a national program, ICDS (Integrated Child Development Services), of integrated care for young children and pregnant and lactating women. The program was put into place in the mid-1970s, and was projected to reach 130 million children by 1990 (Central

Advisory Board of Education Committee Report, 1989, p. 10). Although ICDS is fraught with the difficulties any large system encounters, there is strong political will to reach those most in need and to provide them with a range of services to support the health, nutrition, and education of children from birth to 6 years of age, as well as attend to the needs of child-bearing women.

Early childhood care and education is also beginning to find its place on the agenda of major donor agencies. When the Child Survival Development Revolution was adopted by the UNICEF Board in 1983, those involved in child development saw the title as an indication of policy makers' awareness of the interrelationship of survival and development. In actuality, however, development was only part of the title; the focus of the effort has been on the promotion "of a group of interventions aimed specifically at the significant improvement of child health, with the consequent reduction in infant and child deaths" (UNICEF, 1987, p. 3). And while there have been significant strides in terms of ensuring children's survival, attention has yet to be focused on issues related to the quality of a child's life once survival is accomplished.

However, multilateral donors are beginning to give attention to children's overall development. The most recent UNICEF publications indicate that child development may yet get on the agenda.

Stimulation of the pre-school-age child through health, nutrition, psycho-motor and cognitive development activities has a significant impact on the child's educational attainment and overall development... Investment in such schemes has yielded such high benefits in health, nutrition, and education that early childhood development is emerging as the precursor to all other development. A major effort in this area should be a priority goal for the 1990's. (UNICEF, 1989, p. 14)

Other international and bilateral governmental agencies beginning to invest in early childhood provision include the World Bank, which is currently in the process of developing a program with the government of India to strengthen the ICDS system in 4 districts and has undertaken to support major child care initiatives in Colombia and Brazil. Discussions of appropriate ways to support early childhood programs are also already underway in Venezuela, Chile, Ecuador, and Mexico.

An even broader avenue for early childhood programs is available through *women (gender) in development* initiatives. As women have been increasingly involved in development activities, they have become concerned about meeting the needs of their young children. In recognition of the importance of children in women's lives, and the impact of the family on all development programming, donors that have focused on women's development issues (e.g., USAID, IDRC, UNESCO, NORAD) are seeing more clearly the importance of addressing the needs of the family. Many times this leads to the creation of programs for young children.

Questions that Arise. The primary question has to do with how to move from policy to practice. Where governments have made a commitment to address the needs of young children, they are to be applauded. The problem comes in terms of allocating resources to implement the policy. The challenge in

India in implementing the ICDS program is enormous, given the numbers involved. Countries with fewer children to reach still face enormous problems if they lack financial resources, but there are even more problems when there are few human resources available to implement policy. An example comes from Tanzania, where in 1986 the government assessed the situation for young children in the country and took responsibility for the development and management of preschools. Their analysis of the situation revealed a number of problems: (1) While the government had developed a policy in 1975 related to the establishment and running of preschools, the policy manual was never printed or distributed to the authorities concerned with its implementation; (2) 50% of the preschools lacked trained teachers and had no curriculum; and (3) only 75% of the classes were held in permanent structures (Government of Tanzania, 1987, pp. 3–4). The Ministry of Education has now been charged with promoting preschool education and providing support to communities so that each primary school can have a preschool by the year 2000. A major question is, how can this be done? There is no early childhood degree-granting institution in the country, and no more than a handful of Tanzanians within the government are capable of providing appropriate training. Unfortunately, this situation is not unique among developing countries.

The Challenges. Where government policy is in place to support early childhood provision, the challenge is in bringing to bear the appropriate resources to implement the policy. As will be noted later, one of the ways of doing this is by developing and supporting linkages between the private and public sectors and to involve international donor agencies. Where national policy is lacking, the challenge remains to make policy makers aware of the importance of the early years.

C. *An abundance of strategies have been created for the provision of preschool education for children 3 to 6 years of age, a subset within early childhood care and development programming.*

In all corners of the world one can find preschool programs for the 3–6 year age group. Some of these have strong theoretical foundations; others are based on the model for primary schooling that prevails in that country. Some are well known, documented, and promoted; others are known only to those whom they serve. Many include high levels of parent involvement or are community based. Almost all attempt to be culturally appropriate, particularly in terms of curriculum and materials used by and with children. Some have even successfully integrated traditional religious and cultural activities with more secular learning. Because of the variety of options currently available to a group or community that wants to create a preschool program, it is hard to imagine that someone could come up with a truly innovative approach, at least within the limits of our current beliefs, values, and assumptions about learning and the purpose of education.

Questions that Arise. Despite the availability of a variety of ECCD strategies, funders continue to support the development of new approaches. The question is, why is this so? One of the reasons the donor community and governments continue to fund new approaches is that it is unclear what can be achieved by the strategies that already exist. This problem is not unique to the field of early childhood programming. Writing about the work of nongovernmental organizations (NGOs) involved with income generation projects, Tendler (1987) described what she saw as a common phenomenon among them.

Programs have difficulty achieving impact partly because they are plagued...with the syndrome of "reinventing the wheel." NGOs claim they are pioneering with a new approach when, indeed, they are not. Project proposers allege that past efforts have not worked when, indeed, there is not enough of a record to know whether or not this is true...There is a lack of comparative knowledge about what has worked and what has not. (p. vi)

The same can certainly be argued for NGOs involved in innovative curriculum development for the preschool age group. Attention might more profitably be focused on testing the efficacy of various strategies and identifying those that might be combined to create an integrated program, creating new, or at least more clearly defined, models that can usefully be disseminated.

That raises the question, what is a model? The American Heritage Dictionary defines the word as "a preliminary pattern representing an item not yet constructed and serving as the plan from which the finished work, usually larger, will be produced, or, a tentative ideational structure used as a testing device." From that definition, an early childhood intervention model can be seen as a framework (plan) that provides the theoretical underpinnings for the creation of a program that is built locally and tested for appropriateness.

If this definition is applied to the various early childhood initiatives available, it is soon evident that most are not models. Rather, they are sets of strategies that may or may not be part of a larger whole that could be called a model. For example, in Karnataka state in India, the Cognitively Oriented Preschool Program for Children (COPPC) has been developed. It is seen by some as a preschool curriculum. In fact, it consists of a set of games and activities teachers can use to engage children in the learning process. During COPPC training, teachers are actively engaged in learning as they construct games and activities to be used with the children. Having experienced active learning themselves, the teachers are better able to understand its value, and that is the primary learning they take into the classroom. Even though the COPPC approach is neither a model or a total curriculum, it is valuable in that it is able to stimulate a teacher's thinking and behavior, which in turn makes a difference how the teacher works with children and therefore how the children learn.

While it is possible to observe the difference that the COPPC training makes in terms of teacher behavior, it is difficult to know what impact this relatively short-term training has on the teacher's ongoing skills and children's development. An evaluation was conducted 3 years into the program that in fact suggested it made quite a difference in terms of children's development of language skills and over a range of cognitive tasks (Srivastava, 1986). But this effort, like so many others, lacks a rigorous ongoing research component that could help clarify the relative value of such small-scale investment.

The Challenges. One challenge is to make sense of the different approaches, techniques, and methodologies and to determine what could be disseminated with confidence. A further challenge becomes evident as the different strategies and methodologies that have been created are analyzed in terms of their audience. It is immediately apparent that the majority have been created for the 3–6-year-old child. Little programming beyond custodial care has been done for the child from the point of infant survival to the age of three. Children within this age group are relatively invisible. Yet, as research to be discussed later indicates, it is a critical period in a child's development, particularly in terms of health, nutrition, and cognitive stimulation.

D. *It has been demonstrated that the most effective programs are those which integrate health, educational, nutritional, social, and economic development.*

The basic premise of integrated (multifocal) programming is that one-dimensional (monofocal) interventions are not likely to have significant or lasting effects. The reason that integrated programs are more effective is that they are based on a premise that the child is a whole organism and needs to be treated as such in any intervention effort. The child's nutritional status and basic health are being established prenatally. If there are problems, a cycle is set into motion that leads to an increasingly deteriorating situation. A child who enters the world at a low birth weight or is unresponsive to its environment will elicit few adult responses. These children are less likely to be fed or involved in social interactions with adults and other care givers. Over time their nutritional status worsens, making them even less responsive. On the other hand, children who enter the world in a healthy condition are fed and played with more frequently. This makes the child more alert and increases the probability that there will be continued positive interactions.

The impact of the interactive nature of health, nutrition, and psychosocial development during the early years is felt during the school years. In a review of research looking at nutrition and educational achievement, Pollitt (1984) concludes that "malnutrition in infants and children is a potent contributor to school wastage" (p. 7). Given this finding, Pollitt reviewed research on projects that have attempted to improve children's later academic performance by providing nutritional supplementation during the early years. The results of these studies were disappointing. Pollitt concludes, "the remedial or preventive effects of monofocal nutrition supplementation intervention programmes during early life on the intellectual deficits associated with early chronic malnutrition are questionable" (p. 31).

If that conclusion is valid, what kind of intervention is appropriate? Again Pollitt's review of the research suggests that an integrated approach is the most effective. One study reviewed was an elaborate intervention research project conducted in Cali, Colombia, in the early 1970s. Children's experience in the program varied in relation to the ages at which they entered the program and the components of the intervention they received. The components consisted of things such as supplementary foods for the family, regular health monitoring, a full-day child care and education program, and some parent education. Those who received the full complement of services evidenced positive results in terms of health and nutritional status as well as higher academic achievement. From his review of the Cali project and other similar efforts, Pollitt concludes, "It is apparent...that nutrition interventions per se, as monofocal programmes, are not as successful as those multifocal interventions which add educational and health services to a good diet." (p. 26)

Questions that Arise. The research cited (Pollitt, 1984) is but one example of the range of studies currently suggesting the efficacy of integrated programming. Today there are few that would argue for a monofocal program, but what does it mean to provide integrated programming? For many professionals, integrated services is seen as a panacea. Commonly heard phrases include, we could use day care centers as a vehicle for offering integrated services to the family; programs would be more cost-effective if they could provide integrated health and education services; children are already getting an education, why can't we add a health component; we should develop a child care program in conjunction with the women's income-generating activities. In various ways people have been attempting to stimulate cross-sectoral discussion with the goal of creating integrated service programs.

One of the problems has been that no one has defined what *integration* means. According to *The Concise Oxford Dictionary*, the word *integrate* has 2 meanings: (1) Complete by addition of parts; combine parts into a whole. (2) Bring or come into equal membership. Using the first definition, integrated programming might be accomplished with relative ease. What tends to happen, however, is that people assume that the second definition obtains; there is the implication of *equal* partnership, and no one sector—be it health, education, or social services—is quite willing to be equal with another. In the final analysis, it comes down to who will really be in charge, be responsible, have decision-making power, be held accountable. Perhaps a less threatening term should be used—the word, *co-ordinate*, for example, which means to bring parts into proper relation, cause to function together. Perhaps co-ordination is more easily accomplished.

However, rather than struggling for a definition of integration or looking for a word to replace it, it makes more sense to look at the nature of the relationships that actually occur as 2 or more sectors attempt to work together. It is evident that a variety of words are needed to describe those relationships. For example, *liaison* (connection) could be used when groups are at least meeting together to learn more about what the other can provide. *Cooperation* (working together toward the same end, mutual reinforcement of messages and practices) would describe instances where sectors work together to reduce duplication of services, perhaps jointly identifying gaps in services that need to be filled and deciding who might best address the gap. *Coalition* (temporary combination of parties that retain distinctive principles), a stronger word, could be used when 2 or more sectors actually work together toward some common goal, where the coming together is goal specific or time limited. A *federation* (forming a unity but remaining independent in internal affairs) suggests that separate sectors actually accept each others' goals and together focus on the best way to meet community needs. In a federation the approach is consciously planned rather than ad hoc, even to the point of agreement on budgeting and organization of services. Federation appears to be necessary to formulate national policy or guidelines. The ultimate in integration is *unification* (reduce to unity or uniformity), which occurs when there is a single administrative system for the delivery of all services.

At this point there are some guidelines as to how child care and education programs might cooperate with the health sector to introduce maternal and child health components (Evans, 1985b), and questions have been raised about how a federation can be created to link the intersecting needs of women and children (Evans, 1985a). There are also examples of unification where child care is used as an entry point for community development (Macy, 1985). However, it is quite evident that the mechanisms for integrated programming and its potential have only begun to be explored.

The Challenges. It is unrealistic to expect that there is going to be one model of integration; in different situations integration is going to mean different things. Thus, in looking toward the creation of integrated projects, the challenge is for all actors involved in any one project to agree on a definition of the term as it is to be used in that context. Perhaps clusters of programs can be created over time that exemplify the various ways sectors can work together. From an analysis of these experiences there will then be a clearer understanding of the impact of different models of linkage.

E. It is a reasonable hypothesis that because of the plasticity of the child during the early years, programs designed to support growth and development are most effective during this time period.

One of the early rationales for the development of early childhood programs was provided by Hunt (1961), who put forth evidence that the rate of learning during the first 3 years of life is greater than at any other time in the life span, and who, along with Bloom (1964), argued that the early years provide the necessary base for later learning. These seminal works provided the base for much continuing research on the relationship between early experiences and later development. While there is some debate on specifics of the relationship, most researchers would agree that opportunities missed within the early years have a negative effect on one's later intellectual abilities. Another possible corollary is that the earlier the intervention the more effective it is likely to be. For example, in multifocal interventions (addressing nutritional, health, and education needs) younger children in developing countries are likely to reap greater benefits from the program than those who are older (Pollitt, 1984). This would clearly suggest that there is a need to develop programs for younger children, particularly since more and more children are surviving infancy.

Questions that Arise. What is the optimal age at which to introduce integrated interventions? As cited above, Pollitt noted that in the studies he reviewed, children receiving services from a younger age benefitted more from them than older children involved in the same program. However, the younger children in the studies he reviewed were 3 years of age. One of the problems is that little longitudinal research has been undertaken to look at the impact of integrated programs for children ages 0 to 3 years. Thus questions remain: Should services be offered earlier than age 3? Would there be an even greater impact if they were? What is the appropriate way to intervene? Should provision be made through center-based efforts or through home interventions? What are the relative costs and benefits of such programs?

The Challenges. The challenge is to address the potential and nature of interventions appropriate for young children below the age of 3 years, in terms of the hypothesized benefits, the sectors that should be involved, and the range of provision that can and should be provided by familial and nonfamilial agents. One of the primary challenges derives from the fact that an analysis of appropriate interventions for the youngest children frequently begins with the assumption that the family environment is lacking or deficient and that outside intervention is required. Today, more and more emphasis is given to trying to build programs from family strengths, rather than removing the child from the family in order to provide appropriate care and education. This requires more creativity in developing interventions that can provide support to young children within the context of the family.

F. There is increasing evidence that given the intersecting needs of women and young children, programming for one should not be done in isolation of programming for the other.

In the mid-1960s the development world began to do direct programming for women, based on a preliminary assessment of how women might be more explicitly involved in development initiatives. Early efforts were disappointing largely because there was little understanding of the world of women's work. While programs were designed to increase women's participation in economically productive roles, there was little acknowledgement of their reproductive/domestic roles. Today there is an increased appreciation for women's involvement in economically productive as well as reproductive work within the family and community, and a recognition that the dual roles place enormous demands on a woman's time and energy. There is also an increasing understanding that women need support for their current child care and household responsibilities in order for them to participate more fully in development efforts.

Traditionally women have been able to turn to members of the extended family to help with child care. However, modifications in traditional family patterns, brought about as a result of migration and changing work patterns, have decreased the likelihood that extended family members are not available for child care. Another traditional source of child care has been older siblings. But with increased primary school attendance, particularly for girls, there is a decrease in older children's availability to care for younger children. These changes in social patterns require an examination of child care arrangements.

An analysis of the impact of women's increased participation in development efforts would suggest that children "have a stake in their mother's human development that frequently supersedes their interest in enjoying her personal care" (Anderson, 1988, p. 5). This proposition is particularly thought provoking. It suggests that direct programming for women may be one of the most effective ways to have a positive impact on the child's development. A series of studies indicates that this might indeed be true. In a research review conducted by Engle (1986), she discovered that variables such as a mother's positive self-image, knowledge of her culture, and general savvy contributed to the child's well-being. Other research indicates that a woman's level of education (Levine, 1980) and her capacity to earn income that she controls (Leslie and Paolisso, 1990) also have a positive effect on the child's health and educational status. In sum, by attending to the mother's needs, there are multiple benefits for the child.

Questions that Arise. First, it is clear that alternative forms of care need to be developed. One question is, where should child care be provided—in the neighborhood in the form of family day care, at the place of employment, in center-based facilities? Different options require different training and support systems and different levels of resource allocation. The challenge is to match the kind of care with the needs of the families who would use the care.

Child care can be developed at the work place. The Mobile Creche program in India is an example of a quality work place child care program. In this instance, creches for children from 6 weeks to 12 years of age are established at building sites for families involved in all aspects of the construction industry. The program includes health, nutrition, education, and parent-education components. As women move from one construction site to another, their children move from creche to creche. While the creches are run by an NGO, funding for the site and materials comes from the contractor.

Other appropriate forms of care for children 1 to 6 years of age include neighborhood women providing day care in their homes or cooperatives being created where the care of young children is rotated among the women in a given village. There are drop-in centers where women not involved in full-time work outside the home are able to bring their children to be cared for in the off hours. In all these instances, child care had been developed with a clear understanding of the intersecting needs of women and children. No one model of care has been imposed.

One of the primary difficulties in providing child care for women entering the wage economy is the fact that their wages are so low that they cannot afford to pay for the care. Privately operated child care with fees paid by parents is thus available to only a small minority of families. The question then arises, who should pay for child care? In some instances the burden has been put on employers. In other instances, cooperatives have been established, but again this only meets the needs of a small minority of families.

An experiment designed to develop alternative sources of support for child care was begun in India by SEWA (Self-Employed Women's Association), an NGO created to help women from the lowest economic strata come together and create cooperatives to raise the status, security, and pay of their work. As women have become more systematically involved in work, it has become evident that they need access to child care in order for them to be most productive. Thus, in 1988 SEWA helped form a child care cooperative within which women have developed several income-generating activities to help subsidize child care services. To date, however, the activities of the cooperative have not been able to cover the full costs of child care. While alternatives are being explored, the question continually being asked is, what is the larger society's responsibility in these instances?

Another question raised as a result of looking at the relationship between women's and children's development is, what kinds of programs for women are likely to have the greatest impact on children's development? Experience and research to date would indicate that a range of different types of interventions could be created, but at the core of what they do, programs that enhance women's education, skills development, and sense of self, as well as those that lead to increased income controlled by the woman, are likely to have a positive impact on the child.

The Challenges. One challenge includes creating appropriate models of care for young children, models that include health, nutritional, psychosocial, and educational inputs, in addition to providing a safe place for the child, and that also meet the needs of the family as well as the child. Another challenge is to create models of care that are affordable to the client group. If the child care is not affordable, then appropriate resources need to be identified to ensure that children are properly cared for. Yet another challenge is to increase awareness about ways in which accommodating women's needs positively impacts children's growth and development.

G. *A range of training and dissemination systems have been created in order to make early childhood programming available to a wider audience.*

For every intervention strategy developed, there is an accompanying training system. The multitude of training schemes can be compared by placing them on a grid, as in Figure 27–1.

On the horizontal axis is pre- versus in-service training. The left end represents preservice training only; at the other end is the type of on-the-job training generally created for untrained teachers who continue their work while undergoing training. In between is every imaginable combination. The vertical axis represents theory versus practice. The predominant model in most developed countries is preservice training, with a highly theoretical focus (quadrant I). But this does not begin to meet the needs or realities in most Third World countries. In recent years, the movement in developing countries has been to quadrant III, where there is greater focus on the learning of practical skills provided through a predominantly in-service training model.

Quadrant III training is illustrated by the District Centers for Early Childhood Education (DICECEs), developed by the Kenya Institute of Education (KIE). Within the last 15 years there has been a boom in the creation of community-based preschools in Kenya. The pressures of rapid population growth have meant that there are not enough places in primary school for all the

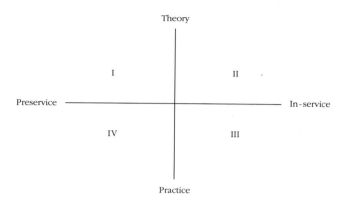

FIGURE 27–1. Mapping of Training Schemes

children who are age eligible. Recognizing that preschool education would give children a better chance of obtaining scarce places, parents have created their own preschools. Within the *harambee* tradition, these schools are built by the community, staffed by untrained parent-paid teachers, and operated with sparse equipment and materials.

In the late 1970s, KIE began to address the issue of how to provide training to the teachers in these community-based preschools. Rather than expanding the existing 2-year preservice model that catered to only a small, elite population, the Kenya Institute of Education opted to create district training-centers where locally employed teachers receive intensive training over a 2-year period. While coming together for group instruction over school holidays, during the school year they receive on-the-job training through periodic visits by training-center staff. At the end of the course, teachers receive a certificate in early childhood education. In essence, KIE designed a training system to meet a very specific set of needs, and the system is solidly in place. After having been involved in the district training-process since the early 1980s, KIE is experiencing 2 demands. One is for a course for teachers unable to attend the 2-year course because of lack of space or lack of minimum academic requirements. And from those who have completed the course, there is a demand for additional theoretical input.

While the development of the DICECE training system in Kenya quite consciously took into consideration the academic level of most untrained teachers, the local cultural variations, the need for a balance of theory and practice, the need for ongoing supervision, and the availability of resources, some training programs have been developed in response to external factors rather than the needs of those being trained. Again we turn to the COPPC program in India, where the contents and process of a supervisor's training course was determined primarily by administrative constraints.

After teachers had been trained in the COPPC methodology, it was determined that the 650 supervisors within the state ICDS system should be trained in the approach in order for them to train teachers and provide ongoing support to those already trained. Given staffing, time constraints, and the basic framework of the model—which calls for intensive group training with follow-up training in the field—the administration decided that there could be only 8 days of training for

supervisors, and 8 days there has been. Over time the actual training content, the balance of theory, and practice within, was worked out. While there has been no evaluation of the effort, observation would suggest that it is less than ideal to create a training scheme based primarily on administrative constraints.

Questions that Arise. From the Kenya Institute of Education and related training experiences, it is clear that when training systems are designed to meet the needs of those to be trained and the systems they will serve, it is possible to create highly effective training programs. However, when there are too many constraints (personnel, geography, time, lack of opportunities for reinforcement of learning), the effectiveness of the training is more questionable.

Still other experiences have stimulated questions about the limits of in-service training if teachers lack minimal skills. For example, the Aga Khan Foundation has sponsored what is known as the Field-Based Teacher Development (FBTD) Project in northern Pakistan. Within the project, untrained teachers from local schools are provided basic training through resource centers established in regional schools, making it possible for the teachers to receive training while continuing their teaching. An evaluation of the project indicated that while the teachers are able to gain pedagogical skills through the FBTD approach, there are difficulties when teachers take the national exams because their basic level of knowledge is so low (Bude, 1989). Thus, to be most effective, the FBTD effort has to spend considerable time providing teachers with rudimentary knowledge that should have been gained as they progressed through secondary school.

The Challenges. One challenge is to continue to experiment with the more flexible in-service training models, the substance and form of which should be developed from needs and sound educational practice. The bigger challenge is to try to establish the threshold between theory and practice that gives teachers the practical skills they need to get children actively involved in the learning process, while at the same time giving teachers a solid enough theoretical base for them to invent new activities that support children's learning.

Training for untrained teachers with minimal levels of basic education tends to focus on the acquisition of practical skills, exemplified by providing teachers with a set of activities that can be undertaken to teach a given topic. It is relatively easy for teachers to set up the activities and carry them through appropriately. The problem comes when teachers are asked to generalize, that is, to create activities in relation to another topic. This is frequently very difficult. Without a basic understanding of the theory that provides the *why*, teachers are unable to create new activities. An evaluation of the FBTD program found that teachers could apply the activities they were taught, but that subjects not addressed through the training effort were taught using traditional methods. The concept of student-centered learning used for the teaching of one specific subject had not been internalized and incorporated into the teacher's basic approach to teaching. The problem, once again, is the lack of a solid educational base that encourages conceptualization and problem-solving skills, the kind of skills required for an understanding of theory and how to translate that into practice. The challenge, as Bude notes, is to "turn teachers from passive recipients of other people's ideas into professionals who are interested in the achievements of their pupils" (Bude, 1989, p. 137). This does not happen through a one-time teacher training effort.

H. *Greater collaboration is occurring among nongovernmental organizations (NGOs), governments, and national and international donor agencies in order to achieve development goals.*

Within developing countries there are 3 primary actors involved in the creation, implementation, and dissemination of new approaches within the various sectors (health, education, social services, and economic development). The first set of actors includes nongovernmental organizations (NGOs), which are generally created by people responding to needs at the grassroots level. The second set of actors are the national and international donor agencies that provide funding to NGOs to assist them in the creation of an experimental project designed to meet local needs. Some of the international donor agencies also provide direct funding to governments, the third set of actors, who define national policy and generally provide basic services within a given country.

Within recent years there has been a move toward greater collaboration among these three groups. This has come about for a multitude of reasons, among which are an awareness that (1) nongovernmental organizations are most in touch with what is going on at the grassroots level and thus have a wealth of insight and experience that would be helpful for national programming, (2) NGOs have greater administrative flexibility and can implement new initiatives more rapidly than governmental agencies, and (3) governments, given limited resources, cannot deliver all the services required. As noted earlier, Tanzania is a case in point. The government has determined that preschool provision should be made available to all children of appropriate age, yet the government does not have the resources necessary to make this happen. Thus they are developing relationships with national and international NGOs that have developed early childhood curriculum, materials, and teacher training processes in order to get the assistance necessary to implement policy.

Collaboration between the public and private sector can occur in several ways. It can begin with the government creating a national initiative and then inviting NGOs to work with the government to implement that initiative at the local level, as in the Tanzanian case. Alternatively, collaboration occurs when an experimental project developed by an NGO is determined to be successful and then adopted by the government to be implemented on a wider scale. An example of this comes from India, where an AKF-funded health education project (the curriculum, materials, teaching methodology, and teacher-training systems), developed by the Municipal Corporation of Delhi schools has been adopted as a part of a large, national health education effort.

Another approach is to provide greater support to a successful NGO so that it can expand its scope of work. In this instance the work of the NGO is not being taken over by the government, but the NGO is being strengthened to continue to provide services complementary to those provided by the government. A good example comes from Bangladesh, home of one of the world's best-known and largest NGOs, BRAC (Bangladesh Rural Advancement Committee). For years BRAC has been receiving funds from international donor agencies to implement a full range of rural economic development and education programs. For each agency, BRAC has had to generate proposals and write reports (all with different formats and timelines). To facilitate its work, BRAC, with government approval, has organized a consortium of donors with whom it will work as a group rather than as individual agencies, greatly simplifying administrative responsibilities while ensuring results for donors.

Questions that Arise. The primary question concerns the nature of the relationship that can and should be established between the 3 groups. Answers to the question come partly from a better understanding of NGOs. While the general belief has been that the more NGOs the better, the validity of that assumption is currently under review. Significant questions about the proliferation of, need for, appropriate size of, and role of NGOs have been raised. For example, while some have questioned whether sizeable funds should be committed to a single NGO, as in the case of BRAC, others have argued that, given the proliferation of groups already, it is more valuable to provide adequate backing to those that are working well than to support numerous small, untried NGOs (Smillie, 1988).

Questions about how to create appropriate collaborative models are not restricted to the early childhood sector; they are being asked in all sectors. For example, a recent review of income-generating projects by Tendler (1987) indicates that similar questions about the nature of NGOs and their relationship to government are being raised within the economic development sector. Smillie's and Tendler's work together suggests that common questions are appropriate across sectors. For example, to what extent does NGO strength, often derived from its smallness and homogeneity, get lost when the NGO tries to expand to reach a larger number of people?

Among the projects funded by the Aga Khan Foundation, there are examples of creative people who have needed to become NGOs (to incorporate) in order to receive funding. This often necessitates their transformation from creative workers and trainers to administrators of organizations. This has not always been a successful transformation. Unless these individuals are willing to give up some measure of control (i.e., let someone else run the organization while they continue to do what they do best), there is likely to be a struggle between further developing the ideas that were funded and devoting time to the maintenance of an organization, which may, in fact, get in the way of the message. The challenge is knowing when people should be supported in what they are currently doing best, and when they are ready to take on new challenges. It is not always obvious.

Another question derives from the fact that, although NGO projects may have small budgets in comparison to the public sector, their costs per beneficiary are often high. Does this mean that successful small-scale projects are not necessarily feasible as models for serving large populations? Some of the issues are addressed by looking at the experience of the Center for Learning Resources in Pune, India, which has produced excellent curriculum materials for use by preschool teachers. The materials have a strong theoretical base underpinning the curriculum, and appropriate techniques and materials have been developed for use by teachers. A complete set of materials, adequate for a teacher's use for one year with only minimal replacement needed in subsequent years, was mass produced at what appeared to be a relatively low cost ($16/set). While all who reviewed the materials agreed on their high quality, it was clear that if the materials were to be adopted on a large scale, (i.e., within the ICDS system serving 130 million children in 1990), the costs to the government would be prohibitive. So a compromise was made. The Center for Learning Resources produced another set of materials at about half the original cost. This brought the costs within a manageable range, and the teaching materials have now been made available to government training centers. However, even that compromise does not get the materials directly to teachers.

The COPPC project, described earlier, also includes a set of materials known as the COPPC kit. Made from locally available materials, the kit is created by teachers or supervisors during their training. The basic cost of the kit is about $3. This is about as low-cost a kit as can be produced. Once costs get to this level there is a real question about the durability of the materials. Games made from newspaper, cardboard, and scrap material do not last long if they are used as teachers are trained to use them.

One of the real dilemmas facing any NGO is the fact that even though cost is taken into account as materials are being created, there is a minimum that must be invested. A legitimate question is, how low can the cost per beneficiary be and still keep the project worthwhile?

A related issue is that of scale. While the ability of a group to create a small-scale experimental project is of importance to the group served by the model, given the scarcity of resources allocated to development programs, there is ultimately pressure for the group to address the issue of how the model they have created can be utilized on a larger scale. In selecting projects to be funded, donor agencies ask the question, is there the potential for the model being developed to be adopted for wider implementation? Not all projects have to be adopted nationally, particularly in a country like India. We might better ask, what is the appropriate *scale* to which a project can legitimately be taken?

The Challenges. As noted, the primary challenge is to determine an appropriate mix of NGO, government, and donor support for an effort, both in its inception and in terms of long-term investment. For the government, the challenge is to maximize what the private sector has to offer, providing scarce government resources only when it is clear that efforts developed by NGOs can be implemented appropriately and economically to meet national objectives. For the NGO, the challenge is to respond to local needs while taking into account the larger context within which the model they are creating might be implemented. For an international donor agency, the challenge is to identify NGOs that are viable, not only in terms of the ideas they are currently developing, but in terms of their longer-term

capacity for management and self-sustainability. The challenge is to examine current efforts to determine their real value, now and in terms of future growth. Further, the challenge is to be aware of some of the limitations of working with NGOs and to seek ways to work with both public and private enterprises to achieve desired outcomes.

CONCLUSIONS

In sum, during the 1980s there has been tremendous growth in understanding the needs of young children and their families. Persuasive arguments on the economic benefits of early childhood programming have convinced many policy makers of the importance and necessity of early childhood provision. There are a variety of program models available to meet the needs of the 3–6-year age group, yet few for the 0–3-year-olds. Further, there is an increased understanding of the interrelationship of children's health, socio-emotional, and cognitive needs, and appropriate programming is being done to meet those needs. As in many other aspects of our lives, the more we achieve and learn, the more we see the need for greater achievement and learning. The challenges ahead are abundant:

1. Given the economic benefits of quality early childhood programs, there is a need to understand better what resources are required to produce the desired results, and to be bolder advocates for those resources.

2. Given the ability to develop and implement quality preschool programs, there is an opportunity to apply lessons learned at the preschool level to improve the quality of education provided at the primary level, thereby capitalizing on investments.

3. Given the relationship between early and later learning, there is a need to be aware of the context within which programs are being developed and to develop them so there is a continuity for children from one educational level to another.

4. Given the interests of government and donor agencies in developing policy to support increased investment in early childhood provision, there is a need to provide them with the kinds of technical support that will assist them in turning policy into high-quality, viable programs.

5. Given the widespread availability of strategies for preschool provision, there is a need to more systematically analyze their validity and then to build on what is good and discard what is inappropriate.

6. Given the value of integrated efforts, there is a need to support the development of different models of integrated programming for young children and their families, and to evaluate the effectiveness of each approach.

7. Given the importance of the earliest years in terms of later development, there is a need to support the development and evaluation of flexible and appropriate models of care for 0–3-year-olds.

8. Given the interdependence of women and children, there is a need to support the creation of program models that meet their intersecting needs.

9. Given the diversity of knowledge and skills that trainees bring to a learning situation, there is a need to create pre- and in-service training models that provide trainees with a theoretical understanding and a range of practical skills built on current knowledge and abilities.

10. Given the scarcity of resources and the range of resources that different groups can bring to a situation, there is a need to promote greater private- and public-sector cooperation in the creation and dissemination of innovative models of care and provision.

References

Anderson, J. (1988). *Child care and the advancement of women.* Paper prepared for the meeting on Social Support Measures for the Advancement of Women. Vienna, Austria: Center for Social Development and Humanitarian Affairs, United Nations Office.

Berrueta-Clement, J., Schweinhart, L., Barnett, W., Epstein, A., & Weikart, D. P. (1985). *Changed lives: The effects of the Perry Preschool Program on youths through age 18.* Ypsilanti, MI: High/Scope Press.

Bloom, B. (1964). *Stability and change in human characteristics.* New York: Wiley.

Bude, U. (1989). *Improving primary school teaching: An evaluation of the Field-Based Teacher Development Programme in the northern areas of Pakistan.* (DOK 1597 C/a). Bonn, Germany: Education, Science and Documentation Center.

Central Advisory Board of Education Committee on early Childhood Education. (1989). *Linkage between early childhood care and education and primary education.* New Delhi, India: Ministry of Education.

Engle, P. (1986). *The intersecting needs of working mothers and their young children: 1980–1985.* Paper presented to the meeting on Women, Work and Child Care in the Third World. International Center for Research on Women/Consultative Group on Early Childhood Care and Development. Washington DC.

Evans, J. L. (1985a). *Improving program actions to meet the intersecting needs of women and children in developing countries: A policy and program review.* Paper prepared for the Consultative Group on Early Childhood Care and Development. New York.

Evans, J. L. (1985b). *The utilization of early childhood care and education programmes for delivery of maternal and child health/primary health care components: A framework for decision-making.* Paper commissioned by the World Health Organization. Geneva, Switzerland: WHO.

Goldstone, L. (1986). *Statistical review of the situation of children in the world with possible public statements.* New York: UNICEF.

Government of Tanzania. (1987). *Pre-school education policy.* Dar es Salaam, Tanzania: Cabinet Report.

Halpern, R., & Myers, R. (1985). *Effects of early childhood intervention on primary school progress and performance in developing countries.* Ypsilanti, MI: The High/Scope Educational Research Foundation.

Hunt, J. McV. (1961). *Intelligence and experience.* New York: Ronald Press.

Jung, A. (1987). *Unveiling India: A woman's journey.* Calcutta, India: Penguin Books.

Lal, S., & Wati, R. (1986, February). *Non-formal preschool education—An effort to enhance school enrollment.* A paper prepared for the National Conference on Research on the Integrated Child Development Services programme. New Delhi, India: National Institute for Public Cooperation on Child Development.

Leslie, J., & Paolisso, M., (Eds.). (1990). *Women's work and child welfare in the third world.* Washington DC: American Association for the Advancement of Science and Westview Press.

Levin, R. (1980, June). Influences of women's schooling on maternal behavior in the Third World. *Comparative Education Review,* 24:2, S78–S105.

Macy. (1985). *Dharma and development: Religion as resource in the Sarvodaya self-help movement.* Hartford, CT: Kumarian Press.

Morris, W. (Ed.). (1980). *The American heritage dictionary of the English language.* New York: Houghton Mifflin.

Myers, R. G. (1991). *The twelve who survive: Strengthening programmes of early childhood development in the third world.* London: Routledge and Kegan Paul.

Myers, R. G. (1988, April). *Effects of early childhood intervention on primary school progress and performance in the developing countries: An update.* Paper presented at a seminar on the Importance of Nutrition and Early Stimulation for the Education of Children in the Third World. Stockholm, Sweden.

Myers, R. G., & Hertenberg, R. (1987). *The eleven who survive: Toward a re-examination of early childhood development program options and costs.* (Report No. EDT69) Discussion Paper, Education and Training Series. Washington DC: World Bank.

Pollitt, E. (1984). *Nutrition and educational achievement.* Nutrition Education Series Issue 9. Paris: UNESCO.

Smillie, I. (1988). *BRAC at the turning point: The donor challenge.* (Unpublished paper).

Srivastava, S. (1986). *Cognitively oriented programme for preschool education: Evaluation report.* Bangalore, India: Karnataka State Council for Child Welfare.

Tendler, J. (1987). *What ever happened to poverty alleviation?* Unpublished report prepared for the mid-decade review of the Ford Foundation's programs on livelihood, employment and income generation, New York.

UNICEF. (1987). *Progress review of the child survival and development revolution 1983–1986.* New York: Author.

UNICEF. (1989). *Strategies for children in the 1990's* (E/ICEF/1989L.5.) New York: Author.

Wamahiu, S. (1992). *Impact of one pre-school intervention programme on later school success of Muslim children in Mombasa: A tracer study.* Research report submitted to the Aga Kahn Foundation, Nairabi, Kenya.

Zaveri, S. (1992). *India village preschool study: First interim report.* Pune, India: Centre for Research and Development.

Part

• IV •

RESEARCH STRATEGIES FOR EARLY CHILDHOOD EDUCATION

·28·

YOUNG CHILDREN AND MEASUREMENT: STANDARDIZED AND NONSTANDARDIZED INSTRUMENTS IN EARLY CHILDHOOD EDUCATION

William L. Goodwin and Laura D. Goodwin
UNIVERSITY OF COLORADO AT DENVER

Measurement is defined here as the process of determining, through observation, testing, or other means, an individual's traits or behaviors, a program's characteristics, or the properties of some other entity, and then assigning a number, rating, score, or label to that determination. It usually involves numbers, scales, constructs, reliability, and validity. This definition includes many measuring devices other than paper-and-pencil tests, such as observation systems and nonreactive measures. Measurement is pervasive in education and in society, and has been for some decades. Early in this century, Thorndike (1918) proposed that anything that exists exists in some amount, and therefore can be measured. The galaxy of available measuring instruments and methods has dramatically grown since Thorndike's time, with no apparent diminution in sight.

We begin this chapter by looking at the "why" of measuring young children. We then examine "how" young children should be measured. Standards for measures are explicated and types of measure are presented. The last major section considers "what" aspects of young children and their behavior are measured by existing instruments. The related questions of "when," "where," and "by whom" tend to be quite specific to particular settings and programs. Note, however, that the "when" question extends to even before birth and potentially

occurs continuously from then on; further, the concepts of formative and summative evaluation, discussed subsequently, also relate to the "when" of measurement. The chapter concludes with ideas based on all of the foregoing.

WHY MEASURE YOUNG CHILDREN?

A significant functional role is played by measurement in the educational enterprise. For example, Mehrens and Lehmann (1991) described 4 related purposes of measurement and evaluation related to decision making. Measurement related to *instructional* decisions concern promoting effective student learning by providing feedback to students and assisting teachers in curriculum planning; this purpose is centrally important to early childhood educators. Decisions involving *guidance* encompass instruments focused on making educational and vocational choices or increased self-understanding. The *administrative* purpose incorporates decisions involving measures used for selection, classification, and placement. The fourth purpose, *research/program evaluation* decisions, in part spans the previous 3 categories and represents an important emphasis in this *Handbook*. Although the guidance function is unusual in an early childhood context, the other 3 functions are evident, particularly in programs for special needs children.

There are any number of issues surrounding the use of measurement and evaluation in early childhood education (Goodwin & Driscoll, 1980). The 4 issues selected for examination here are pivotal and timely.

Issue One: What Is the Overall Value of Measurement in American Society?

Most recently, the arenas of public policy and employment opportunities, both of which overlap with education, have been concerned with measurement questions (Gifford, 1989a, 1989b). Within education itself, it is clear that the use of standardized tests is increasing (Chachkin, 1989; Fremer, 1989; Haney, 1989; Neill & Medina, 1989), with estimates of a 10% to 20% *annual* increase over the past 4 decades (Haney & Madaus, 1989). The National Center for Fair and Open Testing placed the usage of standardized tests in the 1986–87 academic year at 105 million tests for 40 million students, an average of over 2.5 tests per student that year (Neill & Medina, 1989). Test publishing has become a big business (Fremer, 1989). The pace of standardized test use is doubly noteworthy as it has occurred amid many calls for reform (e.g., Cannell, 1988a, 1988b; Haney, 1984, 1989; Owen, 1985), and some litigation focused on fairness (Chachkin, 1989). Cannell (1988a, 1988b), for example, studied how states and school districts reported standardized achievement test results, and found that most of them claimed to be "above average."

Positions currently being taken by national professional organizations and individuals make apparent considerable dissatisfaction with available instruments. Concerns such as these are not new, nor are they specific to American society (e.g., Satterly, 1989). So, why are tests still a prominent feature on the American landscape? One obvious reason is that they represent "truth" for a large constituency. Resnick (1981) traced the societal support for testing to values related to efficiency, equality of opportunity, and visible national standards. Baker (1989) noted that test scores serve as an attractive operationalized dependent or outcome variable for policy makers, conveying that they "mean business." Similarly, Kamii (1990) described the vote-getting game—legislators at all levels and school board members can embrace accountability by directing that tests be given. Shanker (1990) visualized tests as necessary for the American public to discern what it is getting for its huge educational outlays. Frechtling (1989) observed that test scores are increasingly being used as the primary indicator of how well an educational program or institution is functioning. Numerous other reasons for the entrenchment of tests in American society exist.

At the same time, several quests for different and better forms of student assessment seem well underway. Examples include transdisciplinary assessment, play-based assessment, judgment-based assessment, authentic assessment, and ecological assessment; later in this chapter, we consider some of these emphases. While it is relevant to study the new and evolving approaches, we should also examine *how* any alternative assessments are used (Haney & Madaus, 1989).

Issue Two: Are Instruments Used with Young Children Fair?

This issue is most often presented in terms of test bias, the "differential validity of a given interpretation of a test score for any definable, relevant subgroup of test takers" (Cole & Moss, 1989, p. 205). The determination of bias is extremely complex; Cole and Moss (1989) proposed 5 considerations: the constructs, examined in lieu of the context or purpose; the content and format of the measure; the test's administration and scoring procedures; the internal test structure; and the external test relationships. Two central questions about any test's use are whether it is a good measure of the characteristic it is supposed to assess, and whether the test should be used for the proposed purpose (Messick, 1975).

Concerns related to bias are widespread (Chachkin, 1989; First & Cardenas, 1986; Hilliard, 1990, 1991; Jencks, 1989; O'Connor, 1989; Rosser, 1988). Most concerns have centered on language and cultural, ethnic, and gender bias; others, however, have extended to socioeconomic status and age. Often the bias concerns interaction between factors. For example, O'Connor (1989) expressed concerns about differential performance by minorities on standardized tests and queried about links to language and social factors. Duran (1989) focused on potentials for test bias with linguistic minorities and raised concerns about culture, language, thought, and even the context of the assessment itself (also see Laosa, 1977, and Miller-Jones, 1989). Some accusations of test bias have led to court cases.

Certainly the fairness of tests is an important question for children who are school-disadvantaged (Goodwin & Klausmeier, 1975; Jencks, 1989; Neill & Medina, 1989; Oakland, 1977). [At the same time, Anastasi (1988) documented well the many problems inherent in making decisions without test data.] Any number of early childhood programs have as their audience children from school-disadvantaged backgrounds; from racial, ethnic, and linguistic minority groups; and from low-SES homes. The possibility of bias exists, too, in measures being used with infants, toddlers, and preschoolers. In effect, bias potentially becomes an issue whenever one attempts to select or develop measures to use with young children. For example, Harmon (1990) questioned the fairness of reading tests used with less advantaged children. Another illustration involved trying to develop a new battery of measures for Head Start (Taub, Love, Wilkerson, Washington, & Wolf, 1980). Attempting to avoid bias, this project solicited desired outcome behaviors for children from a representative group of Head Start parents, behaviors subsequently reviewed by an advisory panel of measurement experts from numerous ethnic groups. Measures then were developed for the behaviors that survived the various reviews. However, due to several reasons, only portions of the original project (primarily the cognitive components) were completed by a new contractor (Raver & Zigler, 1991). The resultant Head Start measures were criticized by an original advisory panel member for departing greatly from their initially intended form and for appearing to be merely a warmed-over achievement test approach (Cordes, 1985).

Issue Three: Is Measurement Influential with Early Childhood Educators?

In general, the limited influence perceived by us (Goodwin & Goodwin, 1982) and by others (e.g., LaCrosse, 1970) continues to be the case. However, particularly because of the efforts of the National Association for the Education of Young Children (NAEYC), the issue is better defined than ever before. In effect, some qualifications to the "limited influence" stance are relevant. Importantly, there are some valid reasons why early childhood educators resist features of measurement which are perceived as unwelcome intrusions into their world. For example, such educators are committed to appreciating and knowing the full context of children's lives, including many aspects not addressed or adequately captured by existing measures.

Numerous studies have portrayed the increasingly shaky status and checkered reputation among educational practitioners of standardized (particularly achievement) tests for children (e.g., Salmon-Cox, 1981; Sproull & Zubrow, 1981; Stetz & Beck, 1981; Wolf, Bixby, Glenn, & Gardner, 1991). Many types of measure for young children have been heavily criticized. Readiness tests reflect skill acquisition and should be used for curriculum planning and placement within a class; if they are used to delay school entrance or to retain children in grade, it is inappropriate (Bredekamp & Shepard, 1989; Kagan, 1990; Meisels, 1989b). For example, Meisels (1989b) began with the concept of high-stakes tests—those whose outcomes were viewed, correctly or not, by students, educators, parents, or the public at large, as being utilized to reach important decisions that directly affected them (Madaus, 1988). Meisels then traced his concerns about the use of readiness measures, in or even before kindergarten, as high-stakes tests to make inappropriate retention and classification decisions (also see Durkin, 1987).

Relatedly, achievement tests for the early grades often are considered unsuitable, and even counterproductive (Kamii & Kamii, 1990a, 1990b; Harman, 1990; Perrone, 1990). Kamii and Kamii (1990b) objected to achievement tests for not measuring true learning (as they overlook the child's internal thinking, construction of knowledge, and developing autonomy) and for fostering developmentally harmful practices, such as sliding curriculum and its accompanying expectations for students to lower and lower grade levels (also see Shepard & Smith, 1988). In general, such writers wish to avoid measurement-driven instruction—whereby the content of the achievement tests dictates curricular and instructional practices (Airasian, 1988; Haertel, 1989; Shepard, 1989). A related phenomenon, "hothousing," was defined as "the process of inducing infants to acquire knowledge that is typically acquired at a later developmental level" (Sigel, 1987, p. 212). Societal conditions that have spawned the hothousing trend, with its significant pressures on young children, have been widely lamented (e.g., Elkind, 1981, 1987; Gallagher & Coche, 1987; Hills, 1987; Postman, 1982; Sigel, 1987).

Similarly, teachers at all levels have experienced pressure to teach the test (Amspaugh, 1990; Chaille & Barber, 1990; Cohen & Hyman, 1991; Durkin, 1987; Grover, 1990; Mehrens & Kaminski, 1989; Morgan-Worsham, 1990; Shepard, 1990; Thompson,

1990). Such pressure appears very intense when average test scores are published by local media, broken down by school, grade, or even teacher. To amplify, Chaille and Barber (1990) decried achievement-like tests that pressured teachers to use test-aligned practices, such as extensive paper-and-pencil work, drill-and-practice activities, convergent problem solving, and insufficient sensitivity to individual differences. Perceiving deleterious effects on both teacher and child motivation, they believed that such test mania precipitated a serious reduction in teachers' attention to the child's own construction of knowledge.

NAEYC (1988) went on record endorsing the Standards for Educational and Psychological Testing (American Educational Research Association, American Psychological Association, & National Council on Measurement in Education, 1985) discussed later. They also added an important qualifier to their support: measures should meet a "utility criterion," to be used with young children only in situations where it is clear that such use will benefit the children involved. More recently (Bredekamp & Shepard, 1989), NAEYC emphasized that its stance was not antistandardized tests, and cited, for example, the beneficial aspects that should accrue from the use of standardized tests for early and periodic screening of children for developmental, health, and learning problems. Interestingly, that use of tests at times has been challenged as poorly done (e.g., Lehr, Ysseldyke, & Thurlow, 1987; Meisels, 1989a). Lehr and her associates, for instance, examined the tests used in 54 demonstration projects funded by the Handicapped Children's Early Education Program. While many tests were used, only 19 were common to 5 or more of the programs; only 3 of the 19 were deemed technically adequate in terms of validity, reliability, and norms. Another indication that the influence of measurement with early childhood educators is undergoing change is the active search for alternatives to standardized tests (e.g., Chittenden & Courtney, 1989; Engel, 1990; Grover, 1990; Kamii & Kamii, 1990a, 1990b; Morgan-Worsham, 1990; Morrow & Smith, 1990b: Schultz, 1989; Thompson, 1990).

Issue Four: Are the Measurement Needs of Practitioners and Researchers Synonymous?

For a quarter of a century, writers have argued for a closer linkage between researchers and practitioners, between theory and practice (e.g., Casanova, 1989; Klausmeier, Goodwin, Prasch, & Goodson, 1966). This linkage has never been forged, to our knowledge, in a lasting fashion. Thus, the measurement needs of the 2 types of professionals continue to be somewhat separate.

While most early childhood practitioners would agree that instruction should not be measurement-driven as defined earlier, they do want measures used to link directly to their role of nurturing children's development. As noted, Mehrens and Lehmann (1991) identified *instructional* decisions as an important function of measurement and evaluation. Airasian and Madaus (1972) had previously denoted 4 types of classroom decisions, in which practitioners are involved, that serve to elaborate the instructional role. These were: (1) *placement* decisions to match the child initially and appropriately with the curriculum experiences; (2) *formative* decisions to provide on-going feedback to both teacher and child; (3) *diagnostic* decisions to meet special, recurring needs of the child; and (4) *summative* decisions to evaluate the child's overall progress and development at specified, important junctures. For the most part, these instructional decision categories have not been of central importance to researchers. In a related study, Cole (1988) distinguished between measurement that served instructional needs and measurement for accountability and policy issues; the former tended to be characterized by informality and minimal pressure, while the latter connoted formality and substantial pressure.

Another factor affecting this issue (and, to some extent, the previous one) is a fast-growing body of practitioners—early childhood special educators—increasingly in evidence in diverse settings, such as integrated preschools, Child Find teams, county or community center boards, hospitals, and infant intervention programs. Eligibility for services in such settings is determined by special handicapping needs and/or "at-risk" performance on 1 or more measures. Most often, such qualifying assessment is required by legislators or others establishing the program. Thus, early childhood special educators need to be well-versed in measurement issues and procedures; how their preparation and orientation may influence other professionals working with young children remains to be seen.

Measurement is, of course, a critical component of all research endeavors—whether the research is quantitative, qualitative, or a collage of these 2 general approaches. In qualitative research, the data ultimately assessed and interpreted typically includes fieldnotes, interviews, photographs, and documents (Bogdan & Biklen, 1992). In general, researchers seek measures and data that will accurately and directly address the phenomena under investigation. Researchers often adapt existing measures or develop new ones (Bonjean, Hill, & McLemore, 1970). A greater congruence between the measures embraced by practitioners and by researchers might lead to a stronger bond between research generated and its perceived utility in the field.

HOW SHOULD YOUNG CHILDREN BE MEASURED?

Important advantages accrue through the systematic use of measurement and evaluation. Still, many early childhood programs approach such topics casually or sporadically. Be that as it may, some general principles to guide measurement with young children can be specified, extending ideas from several sources (Decker & Decker, 1988; Feeney, Christensen, & Moravcik, 1987; Seefeldt & Barbour, 1986; Wortham, 1990).

1. Whenever possible, use multiple measures and types of measure that match well the major objectives of the program.
2. Employ measures with appropriate levels of difficulty and include measures of higher-order thinking skills.

3. Establish an informal, relaxed atmosphere to ensure that children are comfortable and not anxious during assessment.
4. When possible, utilize skilled examiners who are familiar with the children and are sensitive to their developmental needs.
5. Present tasks to children in a standard way; uniform procedures increase the meaning of the data obtained.
6. Record accurately the measurement data and products, and store them in a well-organized, easily retrievable, and readily comprehendable form.
7. Plan any formal measurement sessions on a reasonable, timely basis; seek a balance between extremes of an annual evaluation (usually too little) and "continuous" assessment (usually not feasible), assessing principally when the data obtained can affect instructional planning.
8. Avoid the "getting-better-and-better" syndrome; when measuring a child several times across the year, a bias may operate to see the child's behavior or performance as improved with each assessment when, in reality, this may not be the case.
9. Handle data secured about children confidentially, professionally, and for the stated purpose of the assessment.
10. Communicate candidly with parents on their child's progress, using interpretation guidelines for any measures used and providing work samples and descriptions of skills performed.

Many ideas on how to measure behaviors and characteristics of young children and how to evaluate programs for them exist (e.g., Bloom, Madaus, & Hastings, 1981; Goodwin & Driscoll, 1980; Hambleton, Swaminathan, & Cook, 1982; Wortham, 1990; Worthen & Sanders, 1987). Some practical ideas on conducting assessments with individual preschoolers were provided by Paget (1991) on both the child's and examiner's behavior, the assessment surroundings, and specific adaptations required if the child had a handicapping condition (e.g., hearing, visual, neurological).

Most sources above noted Scriven's (1967, 1991) concepts of formative and summative evaluation—2 major roles that judgment-based evaluation can take. Formative evaluation involves frequent judgments focused on the improvement of an ongoing activity or a developing product; summative evaluation concerns judgments made of the overall value of an activity or product, normally at a critical or concluding decision point. While these concepts initially were applied to program evaluation, they have been widely adapted. In terms of student learning, formative evaluation provides necessary data to facilitate student progress toward set objectives. Summative evaluation ascertains the degree of student attainment of more general objectives at the end of a meaningful period of time. Additional purposes of summative evaluation are reporting to parents, program sponsors, or others.

Standards for Educational and Psychological Tests

Persons constructing or selecting a measuring instrument need to ensure that it will actually measure what it purports to measure, result in accurate scores, and be "user friendly," that is, straightforward to administer, score, and interpret. Respectively, these characteristics refer to validity, reliability, and usability. A full description of validity and reliability and, to a lesser extent, usability, is available in the *Standards for Educational and Psychological Testing* (AERA-APA-NCME, 1985), hereafter referred to as the *Standards*.

Our treatment of the *Standards*' validity and reliability recommendations is brief. More elaborate interpretations of them exist (e.g., Cole & Moss, 1989; Feldt & Brennan, 1989; Goodwin & Goodwin, 1991; Hopkins, Stanley, & Hopkins, 1990; Mehrens & Lehmann, 1991; Messick, 1989; Traub & Rowley, 1991). Also relevant, the "Code of Fair Testing Practices in Education" (Diamond & Fremer, 1989) extends the *Standards* in a sense, examining issues on proper test use. Responsibilities for both test developers and users are described in terms of developing/selecting appropriate tests, interpreting scores, seeking fairness, and informing test-takers. The "NAEYC Position Statement on Standardized Testing of Young Children 3 Through 8 Years of Age" (NAEYC, 1988) also endorses and builds on the *Standards*. It added the utility criterion for tests involving young children (previously noted) and developed the following points:

- Decisions involving young children should not be based on a single test score.
- Administrators and teachers should use tests only for the purposes for which they were intended.
- Administrators and teachers should be knowledgeable, accurate, and cautious when interpreting test results.
- Tests selected to assess achievement or evaluate program progress should match locally determined program philosophy and objectives.
- Young children should be tested by individuals sensitive to children's developmental needs and well-trained in test administration.
- All testing of young children should involve recognition of, and sensitivity to, individual diversity.

Validity. The validity of a measure is the extent to which it fulfills its stated purpose.

Validity is the most important consideration in test evaluation. The concept refers to the appropriateness, meaningfulness, and usefulness of the specific inferences made from test scores. Test validation is the process of accumulating evidence to support such inferences (AERA-APA-NCME, 1985, p. 9).

Thus, a measure may be valid for 1 purpose, but not for others; the validity question always pertains to particular uses. The focal question is not, "Is this measure valid?," but rather, "Is this measure valid for this particular purpose?" In estimating validity, more sources of evidence, especially of high quality, are better than fewer.

Three types of validity evidence have been categorized in the *Standards*—content-related, criterion-related, and construct-related—and primarily correspond to the types of inference that can be made from the test scores. *Content-related validity*

is the degree to which the test items, tasks, or questions represent the content or processes of a defined curricular domain. It makes possible inferences about how well a student would do on the larger set of items or tasks that the test purportedly represents. Usually associated with achievement tests, either standardized or teacher-made, content-related validity is ascertained primarily through logical analysis of a test's content by subject-matter experts and potential users. *Criterion-related validity* denotes the correspondence between test scores and present or future performance as measured in some other way (the criterion). At issue is how accurately the criterion performance can be predicted from the test scores. The inference examined is the student's present or future probable standing on some other relevant test or task. Two types of criterion-related validity are: concurrent validity, which usually applies when the purpose is to substitute the measure for another, already available measure of the same behavior, trait, or ability; and predictive validity, which occurs when the purpose is to predict future performance (such as giving a readiness test to kindergartners to predict reading performance at the end of first grade). Criterion-related validity typically is reported in the form of correlation coefficients. *Construct validity* conveys how well a test measures a theoretical, psychological construct. It provides the basis for inferences about the student's relative standing on a theoretical construct presumed to be the principal determinant of that test performance. While the 3 types of validity require different types of evidence, the categories do overlap. Thus, validation of a measure often involves information of all 3 types. Some psychometricians have questioned separating validity into distinct types. For example, Cronbach (1988) offered the term "validity argument," and proposed that, "The 30-year-old idea of three types of validity, separate but maybe equal, is an idea whose time has gone. Most validity theorists have been saying that content and criterion validities are no more than strands within a cable of a validity argument" (p. 4).

Reliability. The reliability of a measure concerns the accuracy or consistency of the scores it yields.

Reliability refers to the degree to which test scores are free from errors of measurement.... Measurement errors reduce the reliability (and therefore the generalizability) of the score obtained for a person from a single measurement (AERA-APA-NCME, 1985, p. 19).

A measure must correlate with itself to be reliable; if it does not, it cannot correlate well with any external criterion. Evidence on reliability is relatively easy to obtain, compared with validity. At the same time, reliability is secondary in importance to validity; reliability is a necessary, but not sufficient, condition for validity.

Four types of operational reliability coefficient are described in the *Standards* and elsewhere. The *coefficient of stability* (or test-retest reliability coefficient) estimates the consistency of scores over time. The same measure is given twice to a single group of subjects and the 2 sets of resultant scores are correlated. Generally, the longer the time interval between testings, the lower the stability reliability. The *coefficient of equivalence* (or alternate-forms or equivalent-forms reliability coefficient) expresses the equivalence between 2 forms of the same test. Two forms of a test are administered at about the same time to a single group of subjects and the 2 sets of scores are correlated. The *coefficient of stability and equivalence,* essentially a combination of the first 2 types, results when 2 forms of the same test are administered at different times to a single group of subjects and the resulting sets of scores are correlated. Frequently, the construction of alternate forms of a test is not feasible due to the cost and time required. To estimate the reliability of a single-form measure administered only once, several procedures, known as *coefficients of internal consistency* or internal analysis, are available to examine the degree of consistency of content within the single-test form. Another type of reliability, alluded to in the *Standards* and distinct from the 4 operational types, is termed *interobserver, interscorer,* or *interjudge reliability.* It assesses the extent of agreement between different observers in their independent recordings of the same behaviors or events.

Usability. When selecting measuring instruments for use with young children or others, greatest weight first must be given to validity and reliability. Then, practical elements can be examined under the general rubric of usability—the degree to which a test can be used. Matters reviewed are technical quality data, format, cost, administration, scoring, interpretation, and sources of irrelevant difficulty (also see Wortham, 1990).

Technical quality data convey specific information on the validity and reliability of a measure, on the nature of groups used in determining them, and should be clearly reported in the test manual. Amazingly, given the ready accessibility of the *Standards,* many manuals fail to fully provide such information. Manuals of measures for young children often exhibit this deficiency. If only partial data are provided, the potential user is unsure about the psychometric quality of the instrument; if no data are presented, one must wonder if they exist.

Test format should be examined along multiple dimensions. Appropriateness for the intended examinees is critical. Obvious features are the suitability of instructions (their clarity, brevity, and vocabulary level), the number and quality of available practice items, the clarity and visual appeal of the actual items, the organization of the content, and the type of response demanded. Instructions, typically read aloud to young children, need to be clear, concise, and complete. Instructions given by adults are easily misunderstood by young children (Gelman, 1978); preschoolers when questioned, are disinclined to state the obvious (Blank, 1975). Numerous practice items increase children's understanding of directions. On paper-and-pencil tests, each page should feature distinct pictures and large, clear print. Well-spaced items, or even a single item per page, reduce examinee confusion. Ordering items by increasing difficulty keeps children from becoming discouraged early in the test. Finally, the type of response called for is important. If oral responses are required, a child's command of English emerges as crucial, no matter what is being measured. More subtle, item difficulty in a paper-and-pencil response format may vary for some children when the same items are recast in a slightly modified format, such as paper-and-crayon or even sand-and-stick (Laboratory of Comparative Human Cognition, 1979).

The *cost* of tests should not be a major factor affecting their selection and use. However, in testing programs with many children, even small per-test costs quickly add up. Some savings occur via resuable test booklets with separate answer sheets, though such sheets confuse some children (Cashen & Ramseyer, 1969); relevant practice might permit their appropriate use. Other costs include training administrators and scoring tests.

Administration features—stimulus standardization, administrator training, group size, and time—directly influence a test's usability. The manual should be detailed enough to allow each child measured to receive an equivalent standard stimulus. The preparation needed to learn proper administration procedures is also significant. Convenience and practicality result if measures require only limited special training and if they can be given by teachers and aides. Individually administered intelligence tests, many personality tests, and some observational measures are less feasible due to the extensive examiner or observer training required.

The "developmentally sensitive" requirement for test administrators (NAEYC, 1988), also could increase training time and costs. Size of test group also affects usability. Too large a test group can hinder performance, especially with young children. Testing smaller groups initially seems to be a simple and good solution, although this means more groups to test and, thus, an increase in total testing time. Regrettably, manuals of tests for young children often are silent on proper group size.

Testing time required is another usability feature. Meisels suggested that "it is important that the test items be enjoyable, easily understood, and interesting enough so that a child's best performance can be quickly elicited" (1989a, p. 14). Some test tasks may not hold a child's attention, and possibly young children have not mastered test etiquette (Ambron, 1978). Consequently, test reliability may be adversely affected. In theory, reliability can be enhanced by adding comparable items to an existing measure, unless the new, longer test causes examinees to become inattentive or bored. If they are so affected (and the very young are likely to be), reliability will not necessarily improve and new sources of error, such as guessing and neighbor-poking, may surface. Thus, tests for the very young should be designed to be given in several short sessions with hours or even days between sessions.

Scoring provisions, such as degree of objectivity, affect a test's usability. On objective tests, the same score results regardless who marks the test (assuming the scoring instructions are followed and no careless errors are made). The provision of detailed scoring instructions, keys, and masks permit rapid and accurate scoring. While costly, scoring services of test publishers, often computerized, allow a marked saving of teacher or aide time and normally result in accurate scoring; however, results must be returned on a timely basis. Subjective measures, on the other hand, exhibit special scoring difficulties. Less reliable scoring is the rule even with extensive scorer training.

Test interpretation also is a usability concern. The time and training necessitated are important; for many measures, skillful interpretation is much more demanding than satisfactory administration and scoring practices. Interpretation is also affected by the types of score and how they are reported. Transformed scores of several types—percentile equivalents, stanines, or other standard scores—should be described in the manual. Although still common, age- or grade-equivalent scores have such serious statistical and interpretation problems that a ban on their use has been called for by several professional organizations (see Bennett, 1982). Interpretability of norm-referenced tests is greatly affected by the samples used, which should be fully described. Norm tables aid proper interpretation if presented by sex, age, geographic region, ethnicity, socioeconomic status, and other demographic variables. Regrettably, few norm-referenced measures present their norms broken down by *any* such variables, although some give norms separately for boys and for girls.

Sources of irrelevant difficulty refer to test features unrelated to the behaviors, traits, or abilities being measured that nonetheless affect the difficulty level of the test for some examinees. Such sources reduce test accuracy and often spring from inadequate attention to usability elements already noted, such as test content and format, testing conditions, and test-wiseness (Messick & Anderson, 1970). Content represents irrelevant difficulty if items favor one sex over another or one racial group over another due to reasons unrelated to what is being measured. Irrelevant difficulty due to test format may occur if children have to read the directions for a test of listening skills; other sources of irrelevant difficulty are implied in the discussion of format, above. If children vary in their familiarity and comfort with taking tests, this could bias scores in favor of the more experienced. These sources of irrelevant difficulty can be reduced by selecting tests carefully in the first place and by using test practice materials.

Usability's limited importance relative to validity and reliability must be kept in mind. (At the same time, some usability considerations—particularly problems of sex or racial bias—directly affect validity.) Unjustifiable weighting of factors such as cost, administration time, or scoring ease occurs too often in test selection. Wise test consumers focus first on the validity of measures under consideration and then their reliability.

Particular Uses and Applications. Particular uses and applied areas were addressed in the *Standards* document, some of them of special relevance to early childhood education. In terms of *program evaluation,* the *Standards* particularly examined the role of tests in evaluations that were in inform policy decision makers. Noted was the problem of interpretation when the test scores reflected *both* the effects of particular programs *and* the individual's developmental and learning histories. Appropriately, the *Standards* indicated that the evaluation of service providers in a program, such as teachers, should not depend exclusively upon the test scores of those whom they serve.

The presentation on *educational and psychological testing in the schools* looked at several applications. Germane here were the discussions of school testing programs and special education; the latter extended even further in another section on *testing persons with handicapped conditions.* Taken together, the sections addressed concerns when assessing children with disabilities via legislator-mandated testing, as well as modifications potentially needed in both the way a test is administered and the manner in which the examinee responds. Given these modifications, validity concerns were addressed. (Also

see Hayes, 1990; Niesworth & Bagnato, 1988; and Willingham, 1986.)

In addition, the *Standards* gave attention to *testing linguistic minorities.* Presented were background concerns and ideas related to tests in other languages, language proficiency tests, testing children in schools, and relevant standards.

Types of Measure

Selecting a specific type of measure revolves about the purpose of the measurement; different types have varying strengths and weaknesses. Once a type of measure has been selected, the particular instrument will be chosen on the basis of its validity, reliability, and usability. Numerous measures, likely thousands, have been developed for use with children from birth on. A significant proportion of the instruments are available commercially, while many others are found in research project offices, universities, and schools.

Several common schemes exist for categorizing measures. One typical method is to separate them in terms of the child characteristic they assess—cognitive, affective, or psychomotor. Other differentiation schemes involve format, purpose, scope, and reactivity. Here, we first distinguish between norm-referenced and criterion-referenced tests, and then examine basic types of standardized test, authentic assessment devices (which we believe overlap substantially with both performance tests and teacher-made measures), and nonreactive measures. (The reader interested in teacher-made measures will want to review our chapter in the first *Handbook* [Goodwin & Goodwin, 1982]; Gronlund & Linn, 1990; Hopkins, Stanley, & Hopkins, 1990; or Mehrens & Lehmann, 1991.) Observational measures, interviews, and questionnaires are omitted given the substantive *Handbook* chapter on qualitative methodology. (Also note Bracken, 1991, and Kerlinger, 1986.)

Norm-Referenced and Criterion-Referenced Measures. The manner in which performance on a measure takes on meaning or is interpreted, that is, how it is referenced, is important. With *norm-referenced* measures, frequently standardized, interpretation occurs by comparing an individual's score with those of others, for example, showing how a student performs compared with external norm groups. With *criterion-referenced* measures, more often nonstandardized, interpretation involves comparing an individual's performance with preestablished criteria, for instance, noting whether or not a student can perform a certain behavior. Special demands accompany the establishment of both norms and any criteria used for referencing test performance.

Rather than a distinct dichotomy, Gronlund and Linn (1990) envisioned an interpretation continuum, with norm-referenced tests on one end concerned more with discrimination among individuals and criterion-referenced tests on the other end involved more with description of performance. They also noted that objective-referenced tests were criterion-referenced, but narrow in scope, interpreting performance in terms of a specific instructional objective.

Norms are numerical descriptions of the test performance of a specified group; they are not goals or standards to be met. A diverse sample of students is often used as the basis for the national standardization of a measure via which norms are determined; norms can also be developed on a local basis. Norm tables are prepared to convert an individual's raw score into one or more derived scores; the meaning of the person's score is deduced by comparing it with those of others on the same measure. The utility of norms depends mainly on their recency and the representativeness of the norm group. When developing norm-referenced measures in education, the intent is to maximize variability of student performances. Examples of norm-referenced measures are the Wechsler Preschool and Primary Scale of Intelligence-Revised or WPPSI-R (Wechsler, 1989), the Metropolitan Readiness Tests or MRT (Nurss & McGauvan, 1986), and the Peabody Picture Vocabulary Test, Revised or PPVT-R (Dunn & Dunn, 1981).

Criterion-referenced measures avoid distinctions between individuals' performances by usually separating students into 2 groups—those who have mastered the criterion and those who have not. "Passing" implies meeting or achieving a minimum criterion, an absolute level of performance or standard. Examples of criterion-referenced tests for young children include the Learning Accomplishment Profile or LAP (Sanford, 1974), in part, the Denver Developmental Screening Test or DDST (Frankenburg, Dodds, Fandal, Kazuk, & Kohrs, 1975), and the Early Screening Inventory or ESI (Meisels & Wiske, 1983). Many measures combine both norm- and criterion-referencing; norms are available for such measures, and there also is some preset "cut-off" score for making decisions like "pass versus no pass." A controversial aspect of criterion-referenced measures is setting the standards or criteria, a process with no one agreed-upon procedure that is usually quite arbitrary (Hopkins, Stanley, & Hopkins, 1990).

Standardized Measures. Educational measures usually are developed to provide systematic procedures for describing behaviors in numerical or categorical form. Standardized tests also carefully define the content of the measure, set explicit administration directions, fix scoring procedures, and derive tables of norms (Hopkins, Stanley, & Hopkins, 1990). In general, standardized measures are published commercially, developed over several years, and are intended for widespread use. When constructing standardized tests, the representativeness of the norming samples is crucial, more so than their absolute size.

Numerous types of standardized tests exist. *Intelligence* tests, or tests of general mental aptitude, are designed to assess an individual's mental capacity, use several types of items in so doing, and often provide a single IQ score (although subtest scores, such as verbal, performance, or quantitative, sometimes are available). Though just a century old, intelligence testing has experienced a volatile history. Typical intelligence tests for young children include the WPPSI-R (Wechsler, 1989) and the Stanford Binet Intelligence Scale: Fourth Edition or Binet IV (Thorndike, Hagen, & Sattler, 1986).

Aptitude tests examine elements thought to be pertinent to later performance, achievement, or learning in a given area. The popular Differential Aptitude Tests or DAT (Bennett, Seashore, & Wesman, 1990) yield high-school students' (and now adults') aptitude scores in several areas. Analogous aptitude tests for young children are not evident, although individual testing for intelligence and related constructs occurs with some frequency.

Achievement measures determine a student's current level of knowledge or skill, whereas aptitude tests aim at predicting future achievement. Thus, achievement tests are past- or present-oriented and link to completed instruction, while aptitude tests are future-oriented and purportedly assess the cumulative effect of learning experiences. On a global-specific continuum, the content of intelligence tests would ordinarily lie at the global end, aptitude tests in the middle, and achievement measures at the specific end (as they depend on specific learning experiences). While most people accept that both genetic and environmental influences affect intelligence test performance, the environment is usually deemed more influential on achievement test performance. Of importance for any achievement test is the correspondence between its content and the local curriculum. Measures termed "achievement tests," per se, are not commonly in evidence until the primary and later grades.

"*Readiness* tests focus on a child's current skill achievement and performance rather than on a child's developmental potential" (Meisels, 1989a, p. 7). They are "used to predict who is, or who is not, ready for instruction (an aptitude test)" (Mehrens & Lehmann, 1991, p. 363). Thus, such tests have features of both achievement and aptitude tests. The field's tendency to use readiness instruments to measure current skill achievement *and* to predict future instructional success is a major element in their controversial use (Bredekamp & Shepard, 1989; Kagan, 1990; Meisels, 1989b). Representative of readiness tests is the Boehm Test of Basic Concepts-Revised (Boehm, 1986b). The Boehm-R uses a picture format with children in kindergarten through grade two and provides norms for their comprehension of 50 basic concepts (e.g., size, sequence, direction, and quantity). A preschool version of the Boehm (1986a) for 3- to 5-year-olds assesses 26 simpler concepts.

Screening tests have become increasingly evident in the past 2 decades. Meisels viewed developmental screening measures as "designed to identify children who may have a learning problem or handicapping condition that could affect their *potential* for learning" (1989a, p. 8). While performance on screening tests depends in part on a child's knowledge and experience, the instruments themselves are not restricted to items that assess particular achievements and experiences. Developmental screening measures often include items in three domains: language and cognition, visual-motor/adaptive, and gross motor/body awareness. While having some reservations, Meisels (1989a) identified 4 screening instruments which he labeled "valid"—the Denver Developmental Screening Test (Frankenburg et al., 1975), the Early Screening Inventory (Meisels & Wiske, 1983), the McCarthy Screening Test (McCarthy, 1978), and the Minneapolis Preschool Screening Instrument (Lichtenstein, 1982). We pointed out (Goodwin & Driscoll, 1980) that legislatively mandated screening often was not operating as intended; the purpose of screening at times was vague, and screening and diagnostic operations were sometimes commingled and confused. Such concerns persist (e.g., Lichtenstein & Ireton, 1991; Meisels, 1989a; Wolery, 1989).

Diagnostic measures differ from screening, as well as achievement, tests in purpose and in the specificity of the information yielded. Most often with young children, a screening instrument is used to identify those who *may* have a problem or delay; then a diagnostic assessment is conducted with such children to determine the specific strengths and weaknesses involved. Such an assessment likely would be done by a multidisciplinary or transdisciplinary team, using 1 or more diagnostic instruments or procedures. Given their purpose, diagnostic measures are high in specificity, and require considerable time to administer and, especially, to score and interpret; norms obviously are important. Results frequently are used to plan interventions. In addition to the Binet IV and WPPSI-R, Meisels (1989a) identified other measures often used diagnostically, such as the Kaufman Assessment Battery for Children or K-ABC (Kaufman & Kaufman, 1983) and the McCarthy Scales of Children's Abilities or MSCA (McCarthy, 1972).

Personality and attitude measures, frequently standardized, examine affective characteristics rather than cognitive capabilities (the central focus of the standardized measures already noted). They complement more subjective assessments of children's noncognitive behaviors.

Personality typically refers to a diverse array of characteristics and traits. Not all personality measures are standardized; both observational and sociometric measures frequently target personality variables. Standardized personality instruments for school-age children often are structured self-report inventories (such as problem checklists and needs surveys). Distinct items on them are intended to be interpreted uniformly by all respondents. Administration and scoring of such instruments usually is straightforward, but their interpretation often requires special training. Projective tests, a special case, have standard but ambiguous stimuli (e.g., photos, sketches, or inkblots), whereby respondents reveal their personalities while interpreting them. Their relatively unstructured administration, scoring, and interpretation require extensive examiner training. While vulnerable to many criticisms involving validity and reliability, projective tests (as compared with self-report measures) are richer as examinees reveal more than when answering a standard set of questions, less susceptible to faking, less prone to response sets (tendencies to respond in a given direction regardless of the question asked), and better matched with young children in that some tests de-emphasize verbal abilities and can be game-like (for instance, doll play and finger painting). Early childhood educators should insist on expert help in interpreting personality test outcomes (particularly of projective measures) prior to making decisions affecting children. For very young children, personality and socioemotional characteristics are typically assessed via rating scales completed by parents and teachers, sometimes accompanied by a psychologist's observations (Martin, 1991).

While one element of the global construct of personality, *attitudes* are less stable than personality (especially with young children as they daily learn and modify attitudes). Similar to personality inventories, standardized attitude measures are self-report, paper-and-pencil instruments and thus are subject to faking and response sets. Still, they are easy to administer and score. Available are measures of attitudes toward school, study

and work habits, and self; unfortunately, the technical quality of many of them is poor. At the same time, carefully developed attitude measures can help a teacher's understanding of children, especially if local norms are also established.

There are significant concerns about standardized measures related to bias, age-appropriateness, misuse, and use of tests to determine curriculum. Mehrens and Kaminski (1989) attempted to place on a 7-point continuum activities that educators might engage in while preparing students to take a test— from general instruction on objectives not derived by looking at standardized tests (the innocuous end of the continuum) to instruction on objectives that specifically match the test (the midpoint) to practice on the actual test to be given (the cheating end of the continuum). Their views were challenged by Cohen and Hyman (1991) who assailed the "child-sorting" function of standardized achievement tests and defended a very close match between the curriculum experienced by students and the assessment procedures used, "instructional alignment," in their terms. For our purposes here, the central point is the undermining of the standardization feature. If educators and schools prepare differently for a test (and variability in preparation is likely), then the standardization process underlying the measure is seriously compromised.

Such concerns are not new. Nearly a century ago, Rice (1897) suggested that indirect hints given by teachers when administering a standardized spelling test might substantially aid students to obtain higher scores; Lowell (1919) and Traxler (1951) reached similar positions. Goodwin (1966) found higher class means on a standardized arithmetic achievement test for those classes whose regular teacher administered the test as compared with "outside" administrators. Wodtke, Harper, Schommer, and Brunelli (1989) observed standardized group testing in 10 kindergartens on readiness measures. They found a large number of "violations" of the standardization procedures in terms of environmental and general features (e.g., using a poorly illuminated cloakroom, providing no or insufficient breaks between subtests, and being interrupted after failing to post "Do Not Disturb" signs), teacher behaviors (e.g., departing from the instructions, repeating items, cuing correct answers, and encouraging/rewarding high performance), and child behaviors (e.g., calling out answers, helping one another, copying, and being disruptive or inattentive). Significant departures from standardization occurred in 7 of the 10 classrooms. Wodtke and his colleagues appropriately questioned the meaning of scores generated under such conditions. They also opined that very young children may not be up to the substantial demands inherent in many standardized tests, analogous to Orne (1962) who documented the demands placed on subjects in research studies. With standardized tests, implicit assumptions are that test-takers have sufficient maturity and experience to undertake the task and that they will try to do their best. Wodtke and his associates (1989) wondered whether kindergartners had such prerequisites and, accordingly, also challenged the use of such measures in a high-stakes context (Madaus, 1988).

Authentic Measures. A number of organizations and authors in America have challenged our society's allegiance to standardized tests and have initiated quests for alternate assessment procedures of varying types. Perhaps most in evidence is a procedure dubbed "authentic assessment" using, of course, "authentic tests" (Wiggins, 1989a, 1989b). Unimpressed by secondary school level grading and testing practices and seeking a quantum leap forward in the demands placed on students for deep intellectual thought, Wiggins (1987, 1988) targeted standardized tests as a major culprit in education. Using a medical metaphor, he noted that using standardized tests to determine the effectiveness of education was like using pulse rate alone to ascertain the effect of a healthful regimen (Wiggins, 1989a). In place thereof, he recommended authentic tests.

If tests determine what teachers actually teach and what students will study for—and they do—then test those capacities and habits we think are essential, and test them in context. Make them replicate, within reason, the challenges at the heart of each academic discipline. Let them be—authentic (Wiggins, 1989b, p. 41).

Viewing teachers as coaches and students as performers, Wiggins championed the notion of teachers operating in ways that prepared students to exhibit mastery and intellectual prowess via exemplary tasks such as debates, recitals, plays, and contests. Criteria and standards to assess and judge their accomplishments would be determined by educators. Emphasis would be on student constructivism, production, and performance, rather than student passivism, reception, and recognition (e.g., recognizing the correct response on a multiple-choice item). Examples of authentic tests included an oral history project for high school freshmen and a course-ending simulation "exam" in economics. Ideas similar to Wiggins' were sketched for: assessing secondary students in England on mathematics, language, and foreign language (Burstall, 1986); determining thinking capabilities at most grade levels via written essays (Resnick & Resnick, 1990); assessing older children's progress in numerous subjects, such as the arts and humanities, using student work samples maintained in portfolios (Paulson, Paulson, & Meyer, 1991; Wolf, 1989); and evaluating intermediate grade students in the social studies "experienced curriculum" (Rogers, 1989). Newmann (1991) linked the effective restructuring of schools to establishing authentic achievement which challenged students to produce, rather than reproduce, knowledge.

In our view, a movement comparable to authentic assessment is underway involving young children. It takes several forms, but each of them appears developmentally appropriate for young children, is less rather than more formal, is considered useful to teachers for instructional planning, and is often promoted as a better alternative than standardized measures. Common and interrelated forms include: documentation of progress in numerous ways, such as performance samples and observation (e.g., Chittenden & Courtney, 1989); "keeping track" of developmental progression in subject areas (Engel, 1990; Kamii & Rosenblum, 1990); and portfolio assessment for young children, whereby their products are systematically collected, dated, analyzed, and stored (Elkind, 1991; Heublein & Edmiaston, 1989; Newmann, 1991).

In part, this new activity is quite reminiscent of low-structure assessment methods that early childhood and other educators

have used for decades, such as informal observation, work samples, checklists, and rating scales (e.g., Goodwin & Driscoll, 1980; Goodwin & Goodwin, 1982; Wortham, 1990). Teacher-constructed checklists and rating scales, for instance, have been popular for they are easily developed, versatile in the range of student behaviors they assess, and readily can be designed to match local instructional objectives. But in other regards, the authentic measure effort in early childhood is different—more detailed, more complex, and more integrated with considerable and recent research on development.

This shift to a "more prescribed informality" is most apparent with respect to the assessment of emergent or early literacy. In contrast to the construct of reading readiness, emergent literacy in children is viewed as both a cultural and developmental process which begins long before formal school instruction, like oral language acquisition (Strickland & Morrow, 1989; Teale, 1988; Teale & Sulzby, 1986). In fact, literacy is conceptualized as the interrelated and concurrent development of oral language, reading, and writing, a generalized-stage process stimulated through social interactions with peers and literate older children and adults in everyday contexts where there is a need to read, write, or otherwise communicate (International Reading Association, 1985). Thus, the process of developing literacy is continuous and begins in infancy via exposure to oral and written language, stories, and books (Morrow & Smith, 1990b).

Substantive ideas and concrete illustrations on how to assess developmental progress toward literacy have emerged (e.g., Morrow & Smith, 1990a; Teale, 1988). We view them as "authentic" in the world of the young child. For the most part, the assessments proposed are consistent with a Piagetian cognitive-developmental, constructivist theoretical framework (Wadsworth, 1989), buttressed with ideas from a meaningful learning perspective, such as generative learning (Wittrock, 1974). Examples of such assessments include: emergent writing as well as knowledge of the functions of writing (Sulzby, 1990; Teale, 1988); emergent reading of storybooks (Teale, 1988) and understanding of story via both constructing meaning during storytelling and retelling the story subsequently (Morrow, 1990); stages of learning to decode and encode words (Juel, 1990); and knowledge of letter-sound correspondences (Teale, 1988). Other authors demonstrated how such assessments can be linked to activities and "instruction" for young children (e.g., Athey, 1990; Mason & Stewart, 1990; Schickedanz, 1989). Relatedly, Engel (1990) and Kamii and Rosenblum (1990) provided 3-level documentation systems—primary data, summaries of individual children's progress, and quantitative information about groups—for tracking progress in early literacy and constructivist mathematics, respectively. In similar fashion, Chittenden and Courtney (1989) advanced documentation as an alternative to testing in assessing young children's reading. (Also see Guerin & Maier, 1983.)

We are excited by this attention to assessment with young children and applaud the imaginative new techniques and revitalized former procedures that are under development. Over a decade ago (Goodwin & Driscoll, 1980), we wished for a greater focus on some middle ground between informal and formal measurement in early childhood education; authentic measures seem to us to address that desire. Still, we do not share the optimism of others that a new age of psychometrics is dawning. Like Smith (1990), we are waiting hopefully that these more informal procedures can assemble adequate evidence of validity, reliability, objectivity, and freedom from bias. Important feasibility questions must be answered. Many of the proposed alternatives to standardized measures for young children appear to us to share the massive work and time requirements foreseen by Wiggins (1989a). Further, extensive training on how to conduct such assessments would be needed; such preparation heretofore, relevant to more typical measures, has been deemed inadequate (e.g., Schafer, 1991; Stiggins, 1991a, 1991b). Other feasibility questions concern the cost of such a measurement system (e.g., Terrazas, 1990) and, crucially, whether an informal, yet authentic approach to assessment can be legitimized in the eyes of the public and policy makers (Teale, 1990).

Nonreactive Measures. Initially dubbed unobtrusive measures (Webb, Campbell, Schwartz, & Sechrest, 1966), *nonreactive measures* are procedures for obtaining data that neither contaminate the response themselves nor require the cooperation of the respondent (Webb, Campbell, Schwartz, Sechrest, & Grove, 1981). Subjects are not asked to take a test, to tell about themselves, or to perform in some specified manner; the measuring process does not intrude upon or alter the person or event being measured. Webb and his colleagues (1966, 1981) denoted the hazards to research and decision making of relying on a sole measurement strategy, and especially were concerned about over dependence on questionnaires and interviews. Nonreactive measures were advanced as a supplement to, not a replacement for, such overt measures. Used with more typical measures, nonreactive measures help effect a triangulation of measurement methods on a given variable; one's confidence would increase if compatible data emerged from diverse types of measure.

Four types of nonreactive measure were suggested by Webb and his associates (1966, 1981). *Physical traces* involve tangible evidence of past use and behaviors, available data that were not originally produced for comparison or inference. Erosion indicators note selective measurable wear on some material, while accretion indices concern the accumulation of material. *Archival records* consist of existing documents and records, either continuing over time and often public (e.g., birth records, newspapers) or episodic and more likely private (e.g., diaries, letters, hospitals records). *Simple observation* occurs when the observer has no control over the behavior being noted, takes a passive, nonintrusive role in the situation, and can assume the observee is unaware of the measurement effort underway. *Contrived observation* connotes a calculated, proactive measurement stance, either by using mechanical observational devices rather than humans or by varying the setting on purpose.

Educational and care environments for young children offer numerous opportunities to use nonreactive measures. The relative wear and tear of various pieces of playground equipment reveal play patterns and preferences. Over time, nonreactive observation of children's social interactions with peers can help identify the social leaders or "stars," those of moderate popularity, and the loners or "isolates." The frequency with which books are taken from the library can help a teacher ascertain her students' favored types of book, while smudged and dog-eared pages signal favorite passages. Variations in the types of toy brought to the center or school or displayed at "show and tell" might mark a shift from war-oriented toys to space-oriented ones. The type and amount of food brought for lunch—and that thrown away after lunch—indicates children's eating patterns and food preferences (Rathje, 1979). The activity level of children could be measured, at least partially, by charting the rate at which shoes are worn out.

Certain threats to validity associated with self-report procedures are circumvented with nonreactive measures since respondents do not provide direct answers and are unaware they are being assessed. Reactivity (changes in behavior by subjects knowing they are being measured or studied) is avoided. Social desirability is also prevented. For example, when a teacher asks children what type of book or television show they like (in typical self-report fashion), they may reply what they think she wants to hear rather than their true choice; a nonreactive measure of book or television show escapes this problem. Also avoided are some response sets, like the tendency to acquiesce (agreeing more often to positively phrased statements than disagreeing with the same statements when negatively stated).

Many sources have presented examples of nonreactive measures (e.g., Bouchard, 1976; Brandt, 1972; Sechrest, 1969; Webb, 1978; Webb et al., 1966; Webb et al., 1981). Extending such work, Goodwin and Goodwin (1989) listed examples focused on young children and their worlds. Suggestive rather than prescriptive or exhaustive, the list provides a starting base for those interested in such measures.

The simplicity and ingenuity of nonreactive measures can precipitate a false sense of security about their use. Depending on a single nonreactive measure—and excluding more typical measures from use—is myopic. Nonreactive measures should supplement, rather than supplant, more usual measures by adding either confirming or refuting evidence. Using several nonreactive measures, well-balanced with more traditional instrumentation, can improve most measurement or research endeavors. Our reluctance to endorse nonreactive measures for exclusive use is based on both their subtle complexity and their unknown quality (in terms of properties such as validity and reliability). Still, used judiciously, nonreactive measures can contribute substantially to measurement and research in early childhood education.

WHAT CHARACTERISTICS OF YOUNG CHILDREN SHOULD BE MEASURED?

In this final major section, we review measures in 3 separate domains—cognitive, affective, and psychomotor—a typical but not fully defensible practice. Human behavior does not partition itself tidily into 3 domains; instead, interaction between the domains is substantive and continuous. While arbitrary, the classification scheme based on the 3 domains aids organization and permits 3 generalizations (White, Day, Freeman, Hantman, & Messenger, 1973). First, the psychometric respectability of the domains' instruments can be ordered from cognitive to psychomotor to affective; the strongest validity and reliability is generally found in cognitive measures, the weakest in affective. Second, the psychometric strength of most measures in all 3 domains increases with the age of the child measured; measurement is more difficult with younger children. Third, the "supply" or availability of instruments for young children is greatest in the cognitive domain and least in the psychomotor, although the actual usage pattern can vary markedly depending on the purpose and site of measurement. Thus, a preschool concentrating on social development and skills might focus primarily on affective assessment, while an academically oriented one might use mostly cognitive measures. While all the generalizations require qualification, they do sketch an approximate gestalt of the landscape of measures available for young children. Certain types of measure are not addressed systematically by us given the substantial scope of this *Handbook*. Rather, we define the general nature of the 3 domains and identify selected measurement emphases within each relevant to young children and early childhood education.

Cognitive Measures

Cognition is the intellectual process by which knowledge is gained and utilized; important cognitive processes include perceiving, knowing, learning, thinking, assigning meaning, and intellectualizing. Bloom (1956) provided a cognitive domain taxonomy with 2 principal categories: (1) knowledge; and (2) intellectual abilities and skills. The second category was further ordered (from simple to more complex mental operations) into comprehension, application, analysis, synthesis, and evaluation. While the taxonomy has been criticized (e.g., Madaus, Woods, & Nuttall, 1973; Sedden, 1978), it has been quite influential in research, measurement, and instruction (Slavin, 1991). We consider 3 types of measure in the cognitive domain—intelligence, instruction-related, and creativity.

Intelligence Measures. Over the past century, intelligence testing has been heralded as a major achievement of psychology, as well as a shameful endeavor (Scarr, 1981). For certain, intelligence has been defined variously, and IQ tests designed to measure it have also varied (Bouchard, 1968; Kelley & Surbeck, 1991; Scarr-Salapatek, 1975; Salvia & Ysseldyke, 1991). Young children have frequently been involved with intelligence tests.

Several matters involving intelligence and IQ tests are significant and should be kept in mind:

1. Intelligence as a construct is societally defined; its meaning changes from culture to culture and, within a culture, changes occur for various subgroups and for all groups over time.
2. Elements constituting intelligent behavior vary with age (McCall, Hogarty & Hurlburt, 1972); for preschoolers, defining and measuring intelligence is complicated by the limited pool of common experiences on which to base test items (Anastasi, 1988).
3. IQ test scores obtained after formal school entrance display relative stability, but more so for groups than for individuals (Honzik, 1973; Moriarty, 1966); for individual children, the

change in IQ scores over time is more often in the direction of the child's family's socioeconomic status (Anastasi, 1988).
4. IQ tests have significant and numerous limitations (Sattler, 1988), such as their uncertain fairness for particular children.
5. IQ test scores describe, but do not explain, a child's performance; predictions of intellectual competence in school settings will likely be enhanced if measures of motivation and adjustment are given equal weight with IQ scores (Scarr, 1981).
6. IQ test scores are merely scores on a test and, thus, are far from synonymous with intelligence; in other words, they simply sample behaviors (Salvia & Ysseldyke, 1991).

Sensitivity to these 6 points will help control the abuses too frequently associated with IQ tests, such as permanently labeling children and making inappropriate interpretations.

There are a number of well-known individually administered IQ measures for young children. A set of them dubbed "the big 4" (Schakel, 1986) includes: (1) the Stanford-Binet Intelligence Scale: Fourth Edition or Binet IV (Thorndike, Hagen, & Sattler, 1986) used with children as young as 2 years and now based on a 3-factor theoretical model of intelligence, crystallized ability, fluid/analytic ability, and short-term memory; (2) the Wechsler Preschool Primary Scale of Intelligence-Revised or WPPSI-R (Wechsler, 1989) now designed for a wider age range of children (ages 3 to 7 years, 3 months) and which retains the Verbal IQ, Performance IQ, and Full Scale IQ format; (3) the McCarthy Scales of Children's Abilities (McCarthy, 1972) normed for ages $2\frac{1}{2}$ years to $8\frac{1}{2}$ years and which provides a General Cognitive Index (among other scores) that comes closest to IQ; and (4) the Kaufman Assessment Battery for Children or K-ABC (Kaufman & Kaufman, 1983) designed for children $2\frac{1}{2}$ years to $12\frac{1}{2}$ years and which yields measures of both intelligence and achievement.

Schakel's (1986) "big 4" are among the most commonly used intelligence measures for young children, and the McCarthy and K-ABC provide other cognitive indices besides intelligence. These tests are cited/used often, especially the Binet and the Wechsler, as can be seen in 3 recent *Mental Measurements Yearbooks* or *MMY* (Buros, 1978; Conoley & Kramer, 1989; Mitchell, 1985). Two other measures deserve mention here because of their frequent *MMY* citations and common use in research. First, the Peabody Picture Vocabulary Test-Revised or PPVT-R (Dunn & Dunn, 1981) uses a multiple-choice picture format for ages $2\frac{1}{2}$ to adult; in effect, the PPVT-R is a test of receptive vocabulary often used to estimate verbal ability or scholastic aptitude. Second, the Goodenough-Harris Drawing Test (Harris, 1963) assesses intellectual maturity based on the drawings of a man and a woman by children ages 3 years to 15 years. All the intelligence measures just noted are individually administered; for school-age children, several group-administered IQ tests are available (although most publishers have "expunged" the word *intelligence* from the titles of such tests).

For infants, the best known and most used intelligence measure likely is the Bayley Scales of Infant Development (Bayley, 1969; Rhodes, Bayley, & Yow, 1983). The Neonatal Behavioral Assessment Scale (Brazelton, 1973, 1984) is given to infants 3 days to 4 weeks of age. In general, assessing infants from birth to 2 years old is difficult and such measures typically are poor predictors of later IQ scores (Anastasi, 1988; Yang & Bell, 1975). (O'Donnell & Oehler, 1989, reviewed measures used with newborn infants; also see Langley, 1989.)

Scales of intellectual development based on Piagetian theory also exist. For infants, typical instruments include the Piagetian Infant Scales (Honig & Lally, 1970) and the Ordinal Scales of Psychological Development, also known as the Infant Psychological Development Scales (Uzgiris & Hunt, 1975, 1987). The latter, probably the most frequently used scale of its type (Simeonsson, 1986), is used to assess a fully cooperative infant on six scales, such as object permanence and imitation. For preschoolers and children, sample Piagetian measures include the Cartoon Conservation Scales (De Avila & Havassy, 1975) and the Laurendeau and Pinard (1970) scales. While such measures yield results that correlate substantially with more traditional measures of intelligence (e.g., Gottfried & Brody, 1975; Wachs, 1975), they do paint a richer picture of what the child can do, and how it is done (Anastasi, 1988).

Appropriate to note here are Gelman's views. "We should study preschoolers in their own right and give up treating them as foils against which to describe the accomplishments of middle childhood. We have made some progress in recent years, but there is still plenty of room for those who are willing to take on the mind of the young child" (Gelman, 1979, p. 904). Reorienting to what preschoolers can do rather than what they cannot seems most appropriate to us, given their amazing accomplishments.

Instruction-Related Measures. This second category of cognitive measures for young children, intended in a general sense to include readiness and achievement tests, was difficult to form for a number of reasons; let us note 3. First, some measures have misleading titles. Second, a number of tests have vague purposes or claim multiple purposes, without substantive validity evidence for each purpose. Third, and more important in our view, are the issues already discussed pertaining to the misuse of readiness tests and to the condemnation by many of typical standardized achievement tests for young children. Nevertheless, we have attempted to negotiate this definitional and issue-tangled jungle by including in the category those measures that have in common some relationship to learning and instruction, at least more so than intelligence measures.

Numerous measures, both group and individual, appear to be *readiness-oriented* or to seek the assessment of "mastery of readiness concepts" (Langhorst, 1989). Typical group tests include: the Boehm Test of Basic Concepts-Revised or Boehm-R (Boehm, 1986b); Circus (Anderson & Bogatz, 1974, 1976, 1979); and the Metropolitan Readiness Test (Nurss & McGauvran, 1986). Individually administered measures are: the Boehm Test of Basic Concepts-Preschool Version or Boehm-PV (Boehm, 1986a); the Bracken Basic Concept Scale or BBCS (Bracken, 1984); the Test of Language Development 2, Primary or TOLD-2 Primary (Newcomer & Hammill, 1988); and the Tests of Early Language Development or TELD (Hresko, Reid, & Hammill, 1991), Mathematics Ability-2 or TEMA-2 (Ginsburg & Baroody, 1990), Reading Ability-2 or TERA-2 (Reid, Hresko, &

Hammill, 1989), and Written Language or TEWL (Hresko, 1988). The individually administered tests generally are normed to younger ages, often 3 or 4 years.

Typical *achievement* measures for young children include: the California Achievement Test (CTB/McGraw-Hill, 1985); the Iowa Tests of Basic Skills (Hieronymus, Hoover, & Lindquist, 1986); and the Peabody Individual Achievement Test-Revised or PIAT-R (Markwardt, 1989). These achievement measures all are available for kindergartners and older school children, and all are given to groups (except the PIAT-R). Most of these instruction-related measures are examined in the Mental Measurements Yearbook series and elsewhere (e.g., Boehm, 1991; Langhorst, 1989; Stallman & Pearson, 1990).

Conceivably, the nature of instruction-related measures in early childhood education might change appreciably by the 21st century. One contributory factor could be the current interest in authentic measures. New teacher-friendly measures that link assessment more directly to instruction might result, and dependence on the currently embattled standardized achievement and readiness tests concomitantly could be reduced. A second factor could be the addition of cognitive-style instruments, measuring such variables as attentiveness, risk-taking or cautiousness, field dependence or independence, and reflection-impulsivity (Banta, 1970; Goldstein & Blackman, 1977; Kogan, 1976; Messick, 1984). Measures of such constructs have gradually been appearing, but typically for use in research; in time, they may have important educational applications (Messick, 1984).

Creativity Measures. Research on creativity in this country has been substantial since mid-century, and a limited amount of it has involved young children. A historical review of such research and of educational programs established to nurture creativity reveals the roller coaster ride that such efforts have been on (often due to perceived pressures on this society to develop creativity in its children so that as adults they can compete well internationally). Attempts to measure creative potential have shared this ride and also have been buffeted by the far-ranging definitions proposed for creativity (e.g., Carroll & Laming, 1974; Getzels & Dillon, 1973; Guilford, 1986; Khatena, 1982; Sternberg, 1986; Torrance & Caropreso, 1991; Wallach, 1970).

For the past 15 years or so, a moderate reaffirmation has occurred of schools' responsibilities to gifted, talented, and creative children (variously defined), leading to new programs for identified students and concomitant needs for suitable measures. Such programs, and attempts to measure creativity or potential therefore, have extended to even preschoolers. While many early childhood educators delight in children's creative behavior such as inventiveness, independence, original thinking, and artistic individuality, they question formal instruments to measure such behavior.

Only a limited number of standardized creativity tests for very young children exist. Quite likely the best known and most comprehensive battery available for kindergarten and primary grade children, the Torrance Tests of Creative Thinking (Torrance, 1974) consist of separate verbal and figural tests, each with subtests. The tests, used extensively in research studies since their initial development in 1958, purport to measure potential for creative thinking. The verbal tests yield scores for fluency (the number of responses), flexibility (the number of categories of responses), and originality. These same 3 scores can be derived from the figural tests, as well as elaboration (the extent to which detail is added) and, via a new scoring procedure, additional measures such as resistance to premature closure, richness of imagery, and humor. In a different approach considered more developmentally appropriate for preschoolers, Torrance examined the movement of children as young as 3 years, and also their related verbalizations, via Thinking Creatively with Action and Movement (Torrance, 1981).

Other instruments to assess young children's creativity include Make-a-Tree in Circus (Anderson & Bogatz, 1979), the S. O. I. Learning Abilities Test (Meeker & Meeker, 1979), and the Multidimensional Stimulus Fluency Measures (Moran, Milgram, Sawyers, & Fu, 1983; Tegano, Moran, & Godwin, 1986). Our impression is that none of the measures of creativity have yet demonstrated sufficient validity and reliability to permit score-based decisions about individual children. Still, sustained attention to creativity measures might one day result in instruments adequate to help understand children and nurture their development, although such assessment of creativity in very young children is complex (Torrance & Caropreso, 1991).

Affective Measures

The affective domain spans the social, emotional, and feeling aspects of behavior, including intuitions, emotions, preferences, interests, attitudes, values, morals, and life philosophies. The *Taxonomy of Educational Objectives in the Affective Domain* (Krathwohl, Bloom, & Masia, 1964) categorizes such behavior on a continuum of increasing internalization: receiving, responding, valuing, organizing, and characterizing. In all, the taxonomy has assisted the effort to develop affective objectives and measures.

Affective behavior and outcomes—children's self-concepts, social competencies, attitudes—have long been important to many early childhood educators (Hartup, 1968; Zigler, 1970). Their importance, and ways to measure them, is especially crucial if a program has established affective goals, as many have (Evans, 1974; Zimiles, 1987). For example, 98 percent of the agencies involved in the California Preschool Project ranked self-concept development as either first or second in program importance (Hoepfner & Fink, 1975).

Martin (1991) noted 2 recent phenomena that may have amplified the pressures for affective assessment of very young children. First, the "continuing explosion" of knowledge related to psychological development has revealed important information about emotional and social skill development, as well as developmental psychopathology. This knowledge increasingly is available to professionals with responsibilities for applications in the field. Second, and likely more influential in our view, is the growing exodus of children—infants to age 5 years—from their homes for many of their waking hours. Note too the fast-changing demographics of the American "family" (Halpern, 1987; Morrison, 1986). This increase in out-of-home experiences for child care, education, or what have you, signals a shift from the home/family as the sole (or even primary) socialization agent to other institutions, groups, and individuals. Few families would conduct assessments of their own child's social development, but such measurement is more common in the new environments in which young children find themselves, and often is practiced in the name of identification (e.g., for interventions) or accountability (e.g., for the child's proper social development). Overall, then, there is a growing need for good affective measures for young children.

Unfortunately, as noted earlier, measuring affect is difficult in general and particularly so as age decreases. Ball (1971) discerned problems when measuring young children's attitudes: their limited test-taking skills; their mecurial attitudes; their eagerness to please the test administrators (giving the edge to socially desirable responses); and their susceptibility to response sets, such as answering "yes" regardless of the question asked. Others (e.g., Martin, 1991; Walker, 1973) remarked on children's motor activity "deprivation" and short attention span during formal measurement situations. Additionally, with very young children, measurement options are constrained. Thus, Martin (1991) displayed little enthusiasm for self-report, interview, and projective measures with preschoolers or younger children, noting instead the assessor's usual restriction to parent or teacher rating scales. Odom and McConnell (1989) believed that measuring children's social skills and interactions would most often occur via observation in natural settings—either recorded by an observer or reported by a parent.

Sociometric techniques exist for very young children, but they are both applauded and challenged (e.g., Asher, Singleton, Tinsley, & Hymel, 1979; McConnell & Odom, 1986; Musun-Miller, 1990; Poteat, Ironsmith, & Bullock, 1986). While self-report inventories are available, they often involve pictures or photographs that allow the young child to respond by pointing and/or they involve a single or simple preference ranking (e.g., Goodwin, Goodwin, Nansel, & Helm, 1986). Most affective instruments for young children are rating scales and observational; norm-referenced measures are in short supply. Walker (1973) concluded that nonverbal, observational techniques (often costly to conduct properly) held a psychometric advantage for measuring affective variables involving young children.

In general, the technical data provided for affective measures for young children tends to reflect a paucity of meaningful evidence related to validity. Content validity is claimed by some developers based on item-construction procedures, but few provide data pertinent to criterion-related or construct validity. Affective instruments more often provide reliability data, sometimes approaching respectability. Too frequently, though, the estimates are based on small nonrepresentative samples of children, result in only low to moderate coefficients, and represent internal consistency when stability or interrater coefficients would have been suitable. Another shortcoming of many such measures is their inadequate norms.

Representative *personality* measures for young children include Animal Crackers: A Test of Motivation to Achieve (Adkins & Ballif, 1973), the Martin Temperament Assessment Battery (Martin, 1988), and the Personality Inventory for Children (Wirt, Lachar, Klinedinst, & Seat, 1984). Illustrative *self-concept* instruments are the Behavioral Academic Self-Esteem scale

(Coopersmith & Gilberts, 1979, 1982), and the Preschool Self-Concept Picture Test (Woolner, 1966, 1968). Instruments for children's *attitudes and preferences* include Circus, namely, 2 subtests on reactions to school-related activities (Anderson & Bogatz, 1974, 1976, 1979), the Preschool Racial Attitude Measure II and the Color Meaning Test II (Williams, Best, & Associates, 1975), and the Sex Stereotype Measure II and Sex Attitude Measure (Williams, Best, & Associates, 1976). Typical instruments of *social skills and competencies* are the California Preschool Social Competency Scale (Levine, Elzey, & Lewis, 1969), the Scale of Social Development (Venn, Serwatka, & Anthony, 1987), the Social Skills Rating System (Gresham & Elliott, 1990), the Test of Early Socioemotional Development (Hresko & Brown, 1984), and the Vineland Adaptive Behavior Scales (Sparrow, Balla, & Cicchetti, 1984, 1985).

Psychomotor Measures

The third collection of measures relevant to the "what" question resides in the psychomotor domain for which there is no preeminent taxonomic scheme, although several exist (Harrow, 1972; Simpson, 1966; and Singer, 1972). Movement has significant status in early childhood. Piaget's first stage of cognitive development was sensorimotor, with motor elements prominent. Young children's daily activities often are dominated by movement (Ellis, 1973; Herron & Sutton-Smith, 1971; Wolery & Bailey, 1989). From birth to age 8, the increases in motor control and physical skills are phenomenal, and early childhood programs often have psychomotor and health objectives. Most texts dealing with activities and "curriculum" for very young children address movement, play, and physical development (e.g., Day, 1988; Hendrick, 1988; Spodek, Saracho, & Davis, 1987), and some exclusively so (e.g., Flinchum, 1975; Sinclair, 1973). Notwithstanding this prominence, the psychomotor domain plays an impoverished role in that few education-relevant measures are available and such measures are infrequently used in federally sponsored research on children and adolescents (Heyneman & Mintz, 1977). As society serves more preschoolers this decade, especially those with disabilities, more attention to psychomotor measure development may occur.

Categorization of psychomotor behaviors commonly uses one of 3 schemes. One scheme is simply to list motor tasks or activities, often by age (e.g., Hendrick, 1988; Sinclair, 1973). A second method is in terms of typical performance measures, such as amount of response, rate of response, latency of response, errors, trials, reminiscence, and retention (Drowatzky, 1975). A third, and likely most common classification scheme, is to differentiate behaviors as either fine motor (those employing small or manipulative muscles) or gross motor (those involving large muscle groups). Cratty (1973) considered such a distinction as misleadingly simple and suggested adding an intermediate point. Still, the differentiation has had utility in specifying psychomotor objectives for young children and in designing measures. For example, most developmental screening measures contain fine and gross motor sections, and systematic writings about psychomotor instruments often follow such a scheme (e.g., Weeks & Ewer-Jones, 1991; Williams, 1991).

Puzzling to us is the relative absence of measures of handwriting, given its substantial relevance in education; we located essentially no measures for preschoolers and only 4 for somewhat older children (Ayres, 1940; Larsen & Hammill, 1989; Levine, Fineman, & Donlon, 1973; Zaner-Bloser, 1979). Note also the expanded conception of what to assess about children's writing provided by Sulzby (1990).

Illustrative psychomotor measures in early childhood education include the Bruininks-Oseretsky Test of Motor Proficiency (Bruininks, 1978), the Developmental Test of Visual-Motor Integration (Beery, 1982, 1989), the Frostig Movement Skills Test Battery (Orpet, 1972), and the Southern California Sensory Integration Tests (Ayres, 1980). Additionally, certain developmental screening instruments, such as the Miller Assessment for Preschoolers (Miller, 1982), give substantial attention to motor areas. Any number of informal psychomotor measures also exist (e.g., Guerin & Maier, 1983; Wortham, 1990). Early childhood educators could establish relevant psychomotor tests for their own use; over time, local norms could also be determined. Finally, psychomotor performance also can be and is measured through observational means; mechanical recording via videotape is widespread.

SOME CONCLUDING THOUGHTS

We conclude with 3 somewhat interconnected points. *First,* this clearly will be an exciting decade for measurement as it relates to early childhood education. Several conditions likely to produce significant change are already in evidence and have been alluded to—exactly how these conditions will interact with each other and with future societal trends remains unknown.

To recap some of these conditions, increasing numbers of young children are spending considerable time outside their homes and/or family units—in preschools, child care centers, special programs, and the like. Another undeniable condition is the considerable dissatisfaction of many persons with the nature and use of standardized tests in society in general, and with young children in particular; these concerns are often accompanied by pleas for developmentally appropriate practice and authentic assessment. Yet another influential factor, the mandating of educational services for 4-year-olds with disabilities by Public Law 99-457, will almost certainly change substantively the nature, scope, and perceptions of early childhood education by the end of the century. These elements and others have direct implications for assessment procedures with young children. For example, Lidz (1991) opined that assessment is justified if the purpose is to identify at-risk children in order to remediate problems early *and* if the intervention planned for children so identified has been *proven effective.* Thus, there is a double-barreled measurement requirement—the measures must be valid and reliable for identifying such children *and* they or other measures also must have established, likely through evaluation, that the intervention planned is indeed effective.

It is very hard to predict what eventually will result. While change is in the air, it would be foolish to underestimate the status quo and particularly Resnick's (1981) observation that tests are viewed by the general public as relating to efficiency, equal opportunity, and setting visible national standards. To take the position that standardized tests are as American as apple pie, motherhood, and the Fourth of July is obviously an overstatement, but likely not by much in the eyes of a large proportion of the American public (quite possibly a majority). The National Education Goals Panel (1991a, 1991b), empowered by President Bush and the nation's governors, has drafted a statement for discussion on how to measure progress toward the 6 national education goals "adopted" in Fall 1990. Combining these documents with an April 1991 Presidential address makes it appear probable that a "voluntary" national test yet to be developed for 4th, 8th, and 12th graders would be a cornerstone of the plan to assess progress toward Goals 3 (student achievement and citizenship, that is, competency in challenging subject matter) and 4 (first in the world in science and math). Although Goal 4 may particularly target the "early grades," Goal 1 likely is most pertinent to early childhood education: "By the year 2000, all children in America will start school ready to learn." Measures presently proposed for Goal 1 are broad in both scope and philosophical base. For example, for a national *sample* of kindergarten children, they range from performance portfolios of student work samples to an individually administered developmental profile aimed at producing valid and reliable assessment of student readiness in terms of physical well-being, emotional maturity, social confidence, language richness, and general knowledge. Observing the implementation of this national process will be interesting; the implications for measurement in early childhood education are enormous.

Second, although the development of standardized tests and other measures has accelerated, the types of measure now available have not broadened appreciably (authentic tests may constitute an exception) nor has their psychometric quality advanced dramatically. In terms of the types of measure available, certainly the richly diverse collection proposed for development some time ago (Anderson & Messick, 1974)—in all, 29 measures spread across the 3 domains we have discussed above as well as the areas of motivational competence and personal care—remains little more developed than it was then. Turning to psychometric quality, note the comprehensive guide published 2 decades ago rating 120 early childhood measures comprised of 630 subtests (Hoepfner, Stern, & Nummedal, 1971). Only 7 of the 630 were rated as providing *good* validity, and

the ratings for normed technical excellence (essentially reliability) were typically *fair* or *poor* (Kelley & Surbeck, 1991). More recently, Langhorst (1989) similarly rated 58 early childhood measures primarily published since 1980 that provided technical information and that required only limited professional training for administration. While her ratings were higher overall (about 35% received a *good* in validity and about 35% a rating of *good* in reliability), almost two-thirds were rated *fair* or *poor* or, surprisingly, provided no information on that particular characteristic. Extensive room for improvement obviously exists.

Third, little direct attention has been paid to the psychometric literacy of those thousands of professionals who use and interpret the results of measures and assessments in early childhood education. How qualified are they to be skilled and wise in such matters? To what extent have their preparation programs addressed psychometric literacy? Given the many rotten apples in our measures' barrel, how adept are they at avoiding flawed instruments in the first place? Our concerns extend to most professionals in education. We have heard of countless examples of misuse or misinterpretation of a child's performance on a measure. This should not happen. We also hear or read frequently about young children's interpretations of the "testing experience." Such views range from the comic to the tragic. To illustrate, Seefeldt and Barbour (1986) wrote about the little girl who excitedly informed her mother that she knew she had done well on the reading readiness test because she finished marking every answer before the teacher even completed handing out the test booklets. At the other end of the range, Morgan-Worsham (1990) reported asking a second-grade boy why he was crying during "test week" in the spring; he replied that he had not filled-in all the circles and thus could not go on to third grade. Psychometric literate professionals should help to reduce such tragedies, misuses, and misinterpretations.

Our hope, of course, is that the winds of change will blow in the direction of better lives for young children, as children and later as adults. Better measures, more links between the children's daily activities and the measures used (by teachers, policy makers, and researchers), and more appropriate and sound assessment procedures should help address such a goal, as should a corps of early childhood professionals with ever increasing psychometric literacy. We are encouraged that the field is pointed in the right direction—or is it direction*s*—but realistically know that the journey is long indeed.

References

Adkins, D. C., & Ballif, B. L. (1973). *Animal Crackers: A Test of Motivation to Achieve: Examiner's manual.* Monterey, CA: CTB/McGraw-Hill.

Airasian, P. W. (1988). Measurement driven instruction: A closer look. *Educational Measurement: Issues and Practice, 7*(4), 6–11.

Airasian, P. W., & Madaus, G. J. (1972). Functional types of student evaluation. *Measurement and Evaluation in Guidance, 4,* 221–233.

Ambron, S. R. (1978). Review of Circus. In O. K. Buros (Ed.), *The eighth mental measurements yearbook* (Vol. 1, pp. 20–21). Highland Park, NJ: Gryphon Press.

American Educational Research Association, American Psychological Association, & National Council on Measurement in Education. (1985). *Standards for educational and psychological testing.* Washington, DC: American Psychological Association.

Amspaugh, L. B. (1990). How I learned to hate standardized testing. *Principal, 69*(5), 28–31.

Anastasi, A. (1988). *Psychological testing* (6th ed.). New York: Macmillan.

Anderson, S. B., & Messick, S. (1974). Social competency in young children. *Developmental Psychology, 10,* 282–293.

Anderson, S. B., & Bogatz, G. A. (1974, 1976, 1979). *Circus manual and technical report*. Monterey, CA: CTB/McGraw-Hill.

Asher, S. R., Singleton, L. C., Tinsley, B. R., & Hymel, S. (1979). A reliable sociometric measure for preschool children. *Developmental Psychology, 15,* 443–444.

Athey, I. (1990). The construct of emergent literacy: Putting it all together. In L. M. Morrow & J. K. Smith (Eds.), *Assessment for instruction in early literacy* (pp. 176–183). Englewood Cliffs, NJ: Prentice Hall.

Ayres, A. J. (1980). *Southern California Sensory Integration Tests: Manual* (rev. ed.). Los Angeles: Western Psychological Services.

Ayres, L. P. (1940). *Ayres Measuring Scale for Handwriting.* Iowa City: University of Iowa, Bureau of Educational Research & Service.

Baker, E. L. (1989). Mandated tests: Educational reform or quality indicator? In B. R. Gifford (Ed.), *Test policy and test performance: Education, language, and culture* (pp. 3–23). Boston: Kluwer.

Ball, S. (1971). *Assessing the attitudes of young children toward school.* Princeton, NJ: Educational Testing Service.

Banta, T. J. (1970). Tests for the evaluation of early childhood education: The Cincinnati Autonomy Test Battery (CATB). In J. Hellmuth (Ed.), *Cognitive studies* (Vol. 1, pp. 424–490). New York: Brunner/Mazel.

Bayley, N. (1969). *Bayley scales of infant development.* San Antonio, TX: The Psychological Corporation.

Beery, K. E. (1982, 1989). *Revised administration, scoring, and teaching manual for the Developmental Test of Visual-Motor Integration.* Cleveland: Modern Curriculum Press.

Bennett, G. K., Seashore, H. G., & Wesman, A. G. (1990). *Manual for Differential Aptitude Tests, Form C* (5th ed.). San Antonio, TX: Psychological Corporation.

Bennett, R. E. (1982). The use of grade and age equivalent scores in educational assessment. *Diagnostique, 7,* 139–146.

Blank, M. (1975). Eliciting verbalization from young children in experimental tasks: A methodological note. *Child Development, 46,* 254–257.

Bloom, B. S. (Ed.). (1956). *Taxonomy of educational objectives. Handbook I: Cognitive domain.* New York: McKay.

Bloom, B. S., Madaus, G. F., & Hastings, J. T. (1981). *Evaluation to improve learning.* New York: McGraw-Hill.

Boehm, A. E. (1986a). *Manual for the Boehm Test of Basic Concepts—Preschool Version.* San Antonio, TX: Psychological Corporation.

Boehm, A. E. (1986b). *Manual for the Boehm Test of Basic Concepts—Revised.* San Antonio, TX: Psychological Corporation.

Boehm, A. E. (1991). Assessment of basic relational concepts. In B. A. Bracken (Ed.), *The psychoeducational assessment of preschool children* (2nd ed., pp. 241–258). Boston: Allyn & Bacon.

Bogdan, R. C., & Biklen, S. K. (1992). *Qualitative research in education* (2nd ed.). Boston: Allyn & Bacon.

Bonjean, C. M., Hill, R. J., & McLemore, S. D. (1970). Continuities in sociological measurement. In N. K. Denzin (Ed.), *Sociological methods: A sourcebook* (pp. 144–150). Chicago: Aldine.

Bouchard, T. J., Jr. (1968). Current conceptions of intelligence and their implications for assessment. In P. McReynolds (Ed.), *Advances in psychological assessment* (Vol. 1, pp. 14–33). Palo Alto, CA: Science & Behavior Books.

Bouchard, T. J., Jr. (1976). Unobtrusive measures: An inventory of uses. *Sociological Methods and Research, 4,* 267–300.

Bracken, B. A. (1984). *Bracken Basic Concept Scale: Examiner's manual.* San Antonio, TX: Psychological Corporation.

Bracken, B. A. (1991). The clinical observation of preschool assessment behavior. In B. A. Bracken (Ed.), *The psychoeducational assessment of preschool children* (2nd ed., pp. 40–52). Boston: Allyn & Bacon.

Brandt, R. M. (1972). *Studying behavior in natural settings.* Fort Worth, TX: Holt, Rinehart, & Winston.

Brazelton, T. B. (1973). *Neonatal Behavior Assessment Scale.* Philadelphia: Lippincott.

Brazelton, T. B. (1984). *Neonatal Behavior Assessment Scale* (2nd ed.). Philadelphia: Lippincott.

Bredekamp, S., & Shepard, L. (1989). How best to protect children from inappropriate school expectations, practices, and policies. *Young Children, 44*(3), 14–24.

Bruininks, R. H. (1978). *Bruininks-Oseretsky Test of Motor Proficiency.* Circle Pines, MN: American Guidance Service.

Buros, O. K. (Ed.). (1978). *The eighth mental measurements yearbook.* Highland Park, NJ: Gryphon Press.

Burstall, C. (1986). Innovative forms of assessment: A United Kingdom perspective. *Educational Measurement: Issues and Practice, 5*(1), 17–22.

Cannell, J. J. (1988a). Nationally normed elementary achievement testing in America's public schools: How all 50 states are above the national average. *Educational Measurement: Issues and Practice, 7*(2), 5–9.

Cannell, J. J. (1988b). The Lake Wobegon effect revisited. *Educational Measurement: Issues and Practice, 7*(4), 12–15.

Carroll, J. L., & Laming, L. R. (1974). Giftedness and creativity: A literature review. *Gifted Child Quarterly, 18,* 85–96.

Casanova, U. (1989). Research and practice: We can integrate them. *NEA Today, 7*(6), 44–49.

Cashen, V. M., & Ramseyer, G. C. (1969). The use of separate answer sheets by primary age children. *Journal of Educational Measurement, 6,* 155–157.

Chachkin, N. J. (1989). Testing in elementary and secondary schools: Can misuses be avoided? In B. R. Gifford (Ed.), *Test policy and the politics of opportunity allocation: The workplace and the law* (pp. 163–187). Boston: Kluwer.

Chaille, C., & Barber, L. (1990). The dilemma for teachers. In C. Kamii (Ed.), *Achievement testing in the early grades: The games grown-ups play* (pp. 71–80). Washington, DC: National Association for the Education of Young Children.

Chittenden, E., & Courtney, R. (1989). Assessment of young children's reading: Documentation as an alternative to testing. In D. S. Strickland & L. M. Morrow (Eds.), *Emerging literacy: Young children learn to read and write* (pp. 107–120). Newark, DE: International Reading Association.

Cohen, S. A., & Hyman, J. S. (1991). Can fantasies become facts? *Educational Measurement: Issues and Practice, 10*(1), 20–23.

Cole, N. S. (1988). A realist's appraisal of the prospects of unifying instruction and assessment. In *Assessment in the service of learning: Proceedings of the 1987 Forty-eighth ETS Invitational Conference.* Princeton, NJ: Educational Testing Service.

Cole, N. S., & Moss, P. A. (1989). Bias in test use. In R. L. Linn (Ed.), *Educational measurement* (3rd ed., pp. 201–219). New York: Macmillan.

Conoley, J. C., & Kramer, J. J. (Eds.). (1989). *The tenth mental measurements yearbook.* Lincoln: University of Nebraska Press.

Coopersmith, S., & Gilberts, R. (1979, 1982). *Behavioral Academic Self-Esteem* (exper. ed.). Monterey, CA: CTB/McGraw-Hill.

Cordes, C. (1985, December). New Head Start battery criticized. *APA Monitor,* p. 33.

Cratty, B. J. (1973). *Teaching motor skills.* Englewood Cliffs, NJ: Prentice Hall.

Cronbach, L. J. (1988). Five perspectives on validity argument. In H. Wainer & H. I. Braun (Eds.), *Test validity* (pp. 3–17). Hillsdale, NJ: Erlbaum.

CTB/McGraw-Hill (1985). *California Achievement Test.* Monterey, CA: Author.

Day, B. (1988). *Early childhood education: Creative learning activities* (3rd ed.). New York: Macmillan.

DeAvila, E. A., & Havassy, B. E. (1975). Piagetian alternative to IQ: Mexican American study. In N. Hobbs, M. H. Matheny, L. Odum, W. Molleil, D. A. Bartlett, & J. R. Black (Eds.), *Issues in the classification of children: A sourcebook on categories, labels, and their consequences* (Vol. 2, pp. 246–265). San Francisco: Jossey-Bass.

Decker, C. A., & Decker, J. R. (1988). *Planning and administering early childhood programs* (4th ed.). Columbus, OH: Merrill.

Diamond, E. E. & Fremer, J. (1989). The Joint Committee on Testing Practices and the Code of Fair Testing Practices in Education. *Educational Measurement: Issues and Practice, 8*(1), 23–24.

Drowatsky, J. N. (1975). *Motor learning: Principles and practice.* Minneapolis, MN: Burgess.

Dunn, L. M., & Dunn, L. M. (1981). *Manual for Peabody Picture Vocabulary Test—Revised.* Circle Pines, MN: American Guidance Service.

Duran, R. P. (1989). Testing of linguistic minorities. In R. L. Linn (Ed.), *Educational measurement* (3rd ed., pp. 573–587). New York: Macmillan.

Durkin, R. (1987). Testing in the kindergarten. *The Reading Teacher, 40,* 766–770.

Elkind, D. (1981). *The hurried child: Growing up too fast, too soon.* Reading, MA: Addison-Wesley.

Elkind, D. (1987). *Miseducation: Preschoolers at risk.* New York: Knopf.

Elkind, D. (1991). Developmentally appropriate practice: A case study in educational inertia. In S. L. Kagan (Ed.), *The care and education of America's young children: Obstacles and opportunities. Part I of the Ninetieth Yearbook of the National Society for the Study of Education* (pp. 1–16). Chicago: University of Chicago Press.

Ellis, M. J. (1973). *Why people play.* Englewood Cliffs, NJ: Prentice Hall.

Engel, B. (1990). An approach to assessment in early literacy. In C. Kamii (Ed.), *Achievement testing in the early grades: The games grown-ups play* (pp. 119–134). Washington, DC: National Association for the Education of Young Children.

Evans, E. D. (1974). Measurement practices in early childhood education. In R. W. Colvin & E. M. Zaffiro (Eds.), *Preschool education: A handbook for the training of early childhood educators* (pp. 283–341). New York: Springer-Verlag.

Feeney, S., Christensen, D., & Moravcik, E. (1987). *Who am I in the lives of children? An introduction to teaching young children* (3rd ed.). Columbus, OH: Merrill.

Feldt, L. S., & Brennan, R. L. (1989). Reliability. In R. L. Linn (Ed.), *Educational measurement* (3rd ed., pp. 105–146). New York: Macmillan.

First, J. M., & Cardenas, J. (1986). A minority view on testing. *Educational Measurement: Issues and Practice, 5*(1), 6–11.

Flinchum, B. M. (1975). *Motor development in early childhood: A guide for movement education with ages 2 to 6.* St. Louis, MO: Mosby.

Frankenburg, W. K., Dodds, J. B., Fandal, A. W., Kazuk, E., & Cohrs, M. (1975). *Denver Developmental Screening Test: Revised reference manual.* Denver: LADOCA Foundation.

Frechtling, J. A. (1989). Administrative uses of school testing programs. In R. L. Linn (Ed.), *Educational measurement* (3rd ed., pp. 475–483). New York: Macmillan.

Fremer, J. J. (1989). Testing companies, trends, and policy issues: A current view from the testing industry. In B. R. Gifford (Ed.), *Test policy and the politics of opportunity allocation: The workplace and the law* (pp. 61–80). Boston: Kluwer.

Gallagher, J. M., & Coche, J. (1987). Hothousing: The clinical and educational concerns over pressuring young children. *Early Childhood Research Quarterly, 2,* 203–210.

Gelman, R. (1978). Cognitive development. In M. R. Rosenzweig & L. W. Porter (Eds.), *Annual Review of Psychology, 29,* 297–332.

Gelman, R. (1979). Preschool thought. *American Psychologist, 34,* 900–905.

Getzels, J. W., & Dillon, J. T. (1973). The nature of giftedness and the education of the gifted. In R. M. W. Travers (Ed.), *Second handbook of research on teaching.* Skokie, IL: Rand McNally.

Gifford, B. R. (Ed.). (1989a). *Test policy and test performance: Education, language, and culture.* Boston: Kluwer.

Gifford, B. R. (Ed.). (1989b). *Test policy and the politics of opportunity allocation: The workplace and the law.* Boston: Kluwer.

Ginsburg, H. P., & Baroody, A. J. (1990). *Test of Early Mathematics Ability-2.* Austin, TX: Pro-Ed.

Goldstein, K. M., & Blackman, S. (1977). Assessment of cognitive style. In P. McReynolds (Ed.), *Advances in psychological assessment* (Vol. 4, pp. 462–525). San Francisco: Jossey-Bass.

Goodwin, L. D., & Goodwin, W. L. (1991). Estimating construct validity. *Research in Nursing and Health, 14,* 235–243.

Goodwin, L. D., Goodwin, W. L., Nansel, A., & Helm, C. P. (1986). Cognitive and affective effects of various types of micro-computer use by preschoolers. *American Educational Research Journal, 23,* 348–356.

Goodwin, W. L. (1966). Effect of selected methodological conditions on dependent measures taken after classroom experimentation. *Journal of Educational Psychology, 57,* 350–358.

Goodwin, W. L., & Driscoll, L. A. (1980). *Handbook for measurement and evaluation in early childhood education: Issues, measures, and methods.* San Francisco: Jossey-Bass.

Goodwin, W. L., & Goodwin, L. D. (1982). Measuring young children. In B. Spodek (Ed.), *Handbook of research in early childhood education* (pp. 523–563). New York: Free Press.

Goodwin, W. L., & Goodwin, L. D. (1989). The use of nonreactive measures with preschoolers. *Early Child Development and Care, 41,* 173–194.

Goodwin, W. L., & Klausmeier, H. J. (1975). *Facilitating student learning: An introduction to educational psychology.* New York: Harper & Row.

Gottfried, A. W., & Brody, N. (1975). Interrelationships between and correlates of psychometric and Piagetian scales of sensorimotor intelligence. *Developmental Psychology, 11,* 379–387.

Gresham, F. M., & Elliott, S. N. (1990). *Social Skills Rating System.* Circle Pines, MN: American Guidance Service.

Gronlund, N. E., & Linn, R. L. (1990). *Measurement and evaluation in teaching* (6th ed.). New York: Macmillan.

Grover, S. P. (1990). The approach of a school system. In C. Kamii (Ed.), *Achievement testing in the early grades: The games grown-ups play* (pp. 49–59). Washington, DC: National Association for the Education of Young Children.

Guerin, G. R., & Maier, A. S. (1983). *Informal assessment in education.* Palo Alto, CA: Mayfield.

Guilford, J. P. (1986). *Creative talents: Their nature, use, and development.* Buffalo, NY: Bearly Limited.

Haertel, E. (1989). Student achievement tests as tools of educational policy: Practices and consequences. In B. R. Gifford (Ed.), *Test policy and test performance: Education, language, and culture* (pp. 25–50). Boston: Kluwer.

Halpern, R. (1987). Major social and demographic trends affecting young families: Implications for early childhood care and education. *Young Children, 42*(6), 34–40.

Hambleton, R. K., Swaminathan, H., & Cook, L. (1982). Evaluation methods for early childhood program personnel. In D. T. Streets (Ed.), *Administering day care and preschool programs* (pp. 291–346). Boston: Allyn & Bacon.

Haney, W. (1984). Testing reasoning and reasoning about testing. *Review of Educational Research, 54,* 597–654.

Haney, W. M. (1989). Making sense of school testing. In B. R. Gifford (Ed.), *Test policy and test performance: Education, language, and culture* (pp. 51–62). Boston: Kluwer.

Haney, W., & Madaus, G. (1989). Searching for alternatives to standardized tests: Whys, whats, and whithers. *Phi Delta Kappan, 70,* 683–687.

Harman, S. (1990). Negative effects of achievement testing in literacy development. In C. Kamii (Ed.), *Achievement testing in the early grades: The games grown-ups play* (pp. 111–118). Washington, DC: National Association for the Education of Young Children.

Harris, D. B. (1963). *Children's drawings as measures of intellectual maturity.* San Antonio, TX: Psychological Corporation.

Harrow, A. J. (1972). *A taxonomy of the psychomotor domain: A guide for developing behavioral objectives.* New York: McKay.

Hartup, W. W. (1968). Early education and childhood socialization. *Journal of Research and Development in Education, 1,* 16–29.

Hayes, A. (1990). The content and future of judgment-based assessment. *Topics in Early Childhood Special Education, 10*(3), 1–12.

Hendrick, J. (1988). *The whole child: Developmental education for the early years* (4th ed.). Columbus, OH: Merrill.

Herron, R. E., & Sutton-Smith, B. (Eds.) (1971). *Child's play.* New York: Wiley.

Heublein, E., & Edmiaston, R. (1989). *Evaluation plan for Colorado Preschool Project.* Unpublished manuscript, University of Colorado, INREAL Outreach Education Center, Boulder.

Heyneman, S. P., & Mintz, P. C. (1977). The frequency and quality of measures utilized in federally sponsored research on children and adolescents. *American Educational Research Journal, 14,* 99–113.

Hieronymus, A. N., Hoover, H. C., & Lindquist, E. F. (1986). *Iowa Tests of Basic Skills.* Chicago: Riverside.

Hilliard, A. G., III. (1990). Discussion on "What is test misuse?" In *The uses of standardized tests in American education: Proceedings of the 1989 Fiftieth ETS Invitational Conference* (pp. 27–35). Princeton, NJ: Educational Testing Service.

Hilliard, A. G., III (1991). Equity, access, and segregation. In S. L. Kagan (Ed.), *The care and education of America's young children: Obstacles and opportunities: Part I of the Ninetieth Yearbook of the National Society for the Study of Education* (pp. 199–213). Chicago: University of Chicago Press.

Hills, T. W. (1987). Children in the fast lane: Implications for early childhood policy and practice. *Early Childhood Research Quarterly, 2,* 265–273.

Hoepfner, R., & Fink, A. (1975). *Evaluation study of the California State Preschool Program.* Los Angeles: University of California at Los Angeles, Center for the Study of Evaluation.

Hoepfner, R., Stern, C., & Nummedal, S. G. (1971). *CSE-ECRC preschool/kindergarten test evaluations.* Los Angeles: University of California at Los Angeles, Center for the Study of Evaluation and Early Childhood Research Center.

Honig, A. S., & Lally, J. R. (1970). *Piagetian Infant Scales.* Syracuse, NY: Syracuse University, Children's Center.

Honzik, M. P. (1973). The development of intelligence. In B. B. Wolman (Ed.), *Handbook of general psychology* (pp. 644–655). Englewood Cliffs, NJ: Prentice Hall.

Hopkins, K. D., Stanley, J. C., & Hopkins, B. R. (1990). *Educational and psychological measurement & evaluation* (7th ed.). Englewood Cliffs, NJ: Prentice Hall.

Hresko, W. P. (1988). *Test of Early Written Language.* Austin, TX: Pro-Ed.

Hresko, W. P., & Brown, L. (1984). *Test of Early Socioemotional Development—manual.* Austin, TX: Pro-Ed.

Hresko, W. P., Reid, D. K., & Hammill, D. D. (1991). *Test of Early Language Development* (2nd ed.). Austin, TX: Pro-Ed.

International Reading Association (1985). *Literacy development and pre-first grade.* Newark, DE: Author.

Jencks, C. (1989). If not tests, then what? Conference remarks. In B. R. Gifford (Ed.), *Test policy and test performance: Education, language, and culture* (pp. 115–121). Boston: Kluwer.

Juel, C. (1990). The role of decoding in early literacy instruction and assessment. In L. M. Morrow & J. K. Smith (Eds.), *Assessment for instruction in early literacy* (pp. 135–154). Englewood Cliffs, NJ: Prentice Hall.

Kagan, S. L. (1990). Readiness 2000: Rethinking rhetoric and responsibility. *Phi Delta Kappan, 72,* 272–279.

Kamii, C. (Ed.). (1990). *Achievement testing in the early grades: The games grown-ups play.* Washington, DC: National Association for the Education of Young Children.

Kamii, C., & Kamii, M. (1990a). Negative effects of achievement testing in mathematics. In C. Kamii (Ed.), *Achievement testing in the early grades: The games grown-ups play* (pp. 135–145). Washington, DC: National Association for the Education of Young Children.

Kamii, C., & Kamii, M. (1990b). Why achievement testing should stop. In C. Kamii (Ed.), *Achievement testing in the early grades: The games grown-ups play* (pp. 15–38). Washington, DC: National Association for the Education of Young Children.

Kamii, C., & Rosenblum, V., (1990). An approach to assessment in mathematics. In C. Kamii (Ed.), *Achievement testing in the early grades: The games grown-ups play* (pp. 147–162). Washington, DC: National Association for the Education of Young Children.

Kaufman, A. S., & Kaufman, N. L. (1983). *Interpretive manual for the Kaufman Assessment Battery for Children.* Circle Pines, MN: American Guidance Service.

Kelley, M. F., & Surbeck, E. (1991). History of preschool assessment. In B. A. Bracken, Jr. (Ed.), *The psychoeducational assessment of preschool children* (2nd ed., pp. 1–17). Boston: Allyn & Bacon.

Kerlinger, F. N. (1986). *Foundations of behavioral research* (3rd ed.). Fort Worth, TX: Holt, Rinehart & Winston.

Khatena, J. (1982). *The educational psychology of the gifted.* New York: Wiley.

Klausmeier, H. J., Goodwin, W. L., Prasch, J., & Goodson, M. R. (1966). *Maximizing opportunities for development and experimentation in learning in the schools* (Occasional Paper No. 3). Madison: University of Wisconsin, Wisconsin Center for Education Research.

Kogan, N. (1976). *Cognitive styles in infancy and early childhood education.* Hillsdale, NJ: Erlbaum.

Krathwohl, D. R., Bloom, B. S., & Masia, B. B. (1964). *Taxonomy of educational objectives: The classification of educational goals. Handbook II: Affective domain.* New York: McKay.

Laboratory of Comparative Human Cognition (1979). Cross-cultural psychology's challenges to our ideas of children and development. *American Psychologist, 34,* 827–833.

LaCrosse, E. R., Jr. (1970). Psychologist and teacher: Cooperation or conflict? *Young Children, 25,* 223–229.

Langhorst, B. H. (1989). *Assessment in early childhood education: A consumer's guide.* Portland, OR: Northwest Regional Educational Laboratory.

Langley, M. B. (1989). Assessing infant cognitive development. In D. B. Bailey, Jr., & M. Wolery (Eds.), *Assessing infants and preschoolers with handicaps* (pp. 249–274). Columbus, OH: Merrill.

Laosa, L. M. (1977). Nonbiased assessment of children's abilities: Historical antecedents and current issues. In T. Oakland (Ed.), *Psychological and educational assessment of minority children* (pp. 1–20). New York: Brunnel/Mazel.

Larsen, S. C., & Hammill, D. D. (1989). *Test of Legible Handwriting.* Austin, TX: Pro-Ed.

Laurendeau, M., & Pinard, A. (1970). *The development of the concept of space in the child.* New York: International Universities Press.

Lehr, C. A., Ysseldyke, J. E., & Thurlow, M. L. (1987). Assessment practices in model early childhood special education programs. *Psychology in the Schools, 24,* 390–399.

Levine, E. L., Fineman, C. A., & Donlon, G. McG. (1973). *Prescriptive profile procedures for children with learning disabilities.* Miami, FL:

Dade County Public Schools. (ERIC Document Reproduction Service No. ED 074 673.)

Levine, S., Elzey, E. F., & Lewis, M. (1969). *California Preschool Social Competency Scale manual.* Palo Alto, CA: Consulting Psychologists Press.

Lichtenstein, R. (1982). New instrument, old problem for early identification. *Exceptional Children, 49,* 70–72.

Lichtenstein, R., & Ireton, H. (1991). Preschool screening for developmental and educational problems. In B. A. Bracken (Ed.), *The psychoeducational assessment of preschool children* (2nd ed., pp. 486–513). Boston: Allyn & Bacon.

Lidz, C. S. (1991). Issues in the assessment of preschool children. In B. A. Bracken (Ed.), *The psychoeducational assessment of preschool children* (2nd ed., pp. 18–31). Boston: Allyn & Bacon.

Lowell, F. (1919). A preliminary report of some group tests of general intelligence. *Journal of Educational Psychology, 10,* 323–344.

Madaus, G. F. (1988). The influence of testing on the curriculum. In L. N. Tanner (Ed.), *Critical issues in curriculum: Part I of the Eighty-seventh Yearbook of the National Society for the Study of Education* (pp. 83–121). Chicago: University of Chicago Press.

Madaus, G. F., Woods, E. M., & Nuttal, R. L. (1973). A causal model of Bloom's taxonomy. *American Educational Research Journal, 10,* 253–262.

Markwardt, F. C., Jr. (1989). *Peabody Individual Achievement Test — Revised.* Circle Pines, MN: American Guidance Service.

Martin, R. P. (1988). *The Temperament Assessment Battery for Children — Manual.* Brandon, VT: Clinical Psychology Publishing.

Martin, R. P. (1991). Assessment of social and emotional behavior. In B. A. Bracken (Ed.), *The psychoeducational assessment of preschool children* (2nd ed., pp. 450–464). Boston: Allyn & Bacon.

Mason, J. M., & Stewart, J. P. (1990). Emergent literacy assessment for instructional use in kindergarten. In L. M. Morrow & J. K. Smith (Eds.), *Assessment for instruction in early literacy* (pp. 155–175). Englewood Cliffs, NJ: Prentice Hall.

McCall, R. B., Hogarty, P. S., & Hurlburt, N. (1972). Transitions in infant sensorimotor development and the prediction of childhood IQ. *American Psychologist, 27,* 728–748.

McCarthy, D. (1972). *Manual for the McCarthy Scales of Children's Abilities.* San Antonio, TX: Psychological Corporation.

McCarthy, D. (1978). *Manual for the McCarthy Screening Test.* San Antonio, TX: Psychological Corporation.

McConnell, S. R., & Odom, S. L. (1986). Sociometrics: Peer-referenced measures and the assessment of social competence. In P. Strain, M. Guralnick, & H. Walker (Eds.), *Children's social behavior: Development, assessment, and modification* (pp. 215–286). New York: Academic Press.

Meeker, M., & Meeker, R. (1979). *S.O.I. Learning Abilities Test: Examiner's manual* (rev. ed.). El Segundo, CA: S.O.I. Institute.

Mehrens, W. A., & Kaminski, J. (1989). Methods for improving standardized test scores: Fruitful, fruitless, or fraudulent? *Educational Measurement: Issues and Practice, 8*(1), 14–22.

Mehrens, W. A., & Lehmann, I. J. (1991). *Measurement and evaluation in education and psychology* (4th ed.). Fort Worth, TX: Holt, Rinehart & Winston.

Meisels, S. J. (1989a). *Developmental screening in early childhood: A guide* (3rd ed.). Washington, DC: National Association for the Education of Young Children.

Meisels, S. J. (1989b). High-stakes testing. *Educational Leadership, 46*(7), 16–22.

Meisels, S. J., & Wiske, M. S. (1983). *Early Screening Inventory.* New York: Teachers College Press.

Messick, S. (1975). The standard problem: Meaning and values in measurement and evaluation. *American Psychologist, 30,* 955–966.

Messick, S. (1984). The nature of cognitive styles: Problems and promise in educational practice. *Educational Psychologist, 19,* 59–74.

Messick, S. (1989). Validity. In R. L. Linn (Ed.), *Educational measurement* (3rd ed., pp. 13–103). New York: Macmillan.

Messick, S., & Anderson, S. (1970). Educational testing, individual development, and social responsibility. *The Counseling Psychologist, 2,* 80–88.

Miller, L. J. (1982). *Miller Assessment for Preschoolers—Manual.* San Antonio, TX: Psychological Corporation.

Miller-Jones, D. (1989). Culture and testing. *American Psychologist, 44,* 360–366.

Mitchell, J. A. (Ed.). (1985). *The ninth mental measurements yearbook.* Lincoln: University of Nebraska Press.

Moran, J. D., III, Milgram, R. M., Sawyers, J. K., & Fu, V. R. (1983). Original thinking in preschool children. *Child Development, 54,* 921–926.

Morgan-Worsham, D. (1990). The dilemma for principals. In C. Kamii (Ed.), *Achievement testing in the early grades: The games grown-ups play* (pp. 61–69). Washington, DC: National Association for the Education of Young Children.

Moriarty, A. E. (1966). *Constancy and IQ change: A clinical view of relationships between tested intelligence and personality.* Springfield, IL: Thomas.

Morrison, P. A. (1986). *Changing family structure: Who cares for America's dependents?* Washington, DC: National Institute of Child Health and Human Development.

Morrow, L. M. (1990). Assessing children's understanding of story through their construction and reconstruction of narrative. In L. M. Morrow & J. K. Smith (Eds.), *Assessment for instruction in early literacy* (pp. 110–134). Englewood Cliffs, NJ: Prentice Hall.

Morrow, L. M., & Smith, J. K. (Eds.) (1990a). *Assessment for instruction in early literacy.* Englewood Cliffs, NJ: Prentice Hall.

Morrow, L. M., & Smith, J. K. (1990b). Introduction. In L. M. Morrow & J. K. Smith (Eds.), *Assessment for instruction in early literacy* (pp. 1–6). Englewood Cliffs, NJ: Prentice Hall.

Musun-Miller, L. (1990). Sociometrics with preschool children: Agreement between different strategies. *Journal of Applied Developmental Psychology, 11,* 195–207.

National Association for the Education of Young Children (1988). NAEYC position statement on standardized testing of young children 3 through 8 years of age. *Young Children, 43*(3), 42–47.

National Education Goals Panel (1991a). *Measuring progress toward the national education goals: Potential indicators and measurement strategies: Compendium of interim resources group reports.* Washington, DC: Author.

National Education Goals Panel (1991b). *Measuring progress toward the national education goals: Potential indicators and measurement strategies: Discussion document.* Washington, DC: Author.

Neill, D. M., & Medina, N. J. (1989). Standardized testing: Harmful to educational health. *Phi Delta Kappan, 70,* 688–697.

Newcomer, P. L., & Hammill, D. D. (1988). *Test of Language Development—2, Primary.* Austin, TX: Pro-Ed.

Newmann, F. M. (1991). Linking restructuring to authentic student achievement. *Phi Delta Kappan, 72,* 458–463.

Niesworth, J. T., & Bagnato, S. J. (1988). Assessment in early childhood special education: A typology of dependent measures. In S. L. Odom & M. B Karnes (Eds.), *Early intervention for infants and children with handicaps* (pp. 23–49). Baltimore: Brookes.

Nurss, J. R., & McGauvran, M. E. (1986). *Metropolitan Readiness Test* (5th ed.). San Antonio, TX: Psychological Corporation.

Oakland, T. (Ed.). (1977). *Psychological and educational assessment of minority children.* New York: Brunner/Mazel.

O'Connor, M. C. (1989). Aspects of differential performance by minorities on standardized tests: Linguistic and sociocultural factors. In

B. R. Gifford (Ed.), *Test policy and test performance: Education, language, and culture* (pp. 129–181). Boston: Kluwer.

O'Donnell, K. J., & Oehler, J. M. (1989). Neurobehavioral assessment of the newborn infant. In D. B. Bailey, Jr., & M. Wolery (Eds.), *Assessing infants and preschoolers with handicaps* (pp. 166–201). Columbus, OH: Merrill.

Odom, S. L., & McConnell, S. R. (1989). Assessing social interaction skills. In D. B. Bailey, Jr., & M. Wolery (Eds.), *Assessing infants and preschoolers with handicaps* (pp. 390–427). Columbus, OH: Merrill.

Orne, M. T. (1962). On the social psychology of the psychological experiment: With particular reference to demand characteristics and their implications. *American Psychologist, 17,* 776–783.

Orpet, R. E. (1972). *Examiners manual: Frostig Movement Test Battery.* Palo Alto, CA: Consulting Psychologists Press.

Paget, K. D. (1991). The individual assessment situation: Basic considerations for preschool-age children. In B. A. Bracken (Ed.), *The psychoeducational assessment of preschool children* (2nd ed., pp. 22–29). Boston: Allyn & Bacon.

Paulson, F., Paulson, P., & Meyer, C. (1991). What makes a portfolio a portfolio? *Educational Leadership, 48*(5), 60–63.

Perrone, V. (1990). How did we get here? In C. Kamii (Ed.), *Achievement testing in the early grades: The games grown-ups play* (pp. 1–13). Washington, DC: National Association for the Education of Young Children.

Postman, N. (1982). *The disappearance of childhood.* New York: Delacorte.

Poteat, G. M., Ironsmith, M., & Bullock, J. (1986). The classification of preschool children's sociometric status. *Early Childhood Research Quarterly, 1,* 349–360.

Rathje, W. L. (1979). Trace measures. In L. Sechrest (Ed.), *Unobtrusive measurement today* (pp. 75–91). San Francisco: Jossey-Bass.

Raver, C. C., & Zigler, E. F. (1991). Three steps forward, two steps back: Head Start and the measurement of social competence. *Young Children, 46*(4), 3–8.

Reid, D. K., Hresko, W. P., & Hammill, D. D. (1989). *Test of Early Reading Ability—2.* Austin, TX: Pro-Ed.

Resnick, D. P. (1981). Testing in America: A supportive environment. *Phi Delta Kappan, 62,* 625–628.

Resnick, L. B., & Resnick, D. P. (1990). Tests as standards of achievement in schools. In *The uses of standardized tests in American education: Proceedings of the 1989 Fiftieth ETS Invitational Conference* (pp. 63–80). Princeton, NJ: Educational Testing Service.

Rhodes, L., Bayley, N., & Yow, B. (1983). *Manual supplement: Bayley Scales of Infant Development.* San Antonio, TX: Psychological Corporation.

Rice, J. M. (1897). The futility of the spelling grind. *Forum, 23,* 163–172.

Rogers, V. (1989). Assessing the curriculum experienced by children. *Phi Delta Kappan, 70,* 714–717.

Rosser, P. (1988). Girls, boys, and the SAT: Can we even the score? *NEA Today: Issues '88, 6*(6), 48–53.

Salmon-Cox, L. (1981). Teachers and standardized achievement tests: What's really happening? *Phi Delta Kappan, 62, 631–634.*

Salvia, J., & Ysseldyke, J. E. (1991). *Assessment* (5th ed.). Boston: Houghton Mifflin.

Sanford, A. R. (1974). *A manual for use of the Learning Accomplishment Profile.* Winston-Salem, NC: Kaplan School Supply.

Satterly, D. (1989). *Assessment in schools* (2nd ed.). Oxford, England: Basil Blackwell.

Sattler, J. M. (1988). *Assessment of children* (3rd ed.). San Diego, CA: Jerome M. Sattler.

Scarr, S. (1981). Testing for children: Assessment and the many determinants of intellectual competence. *American Psychologist, 36,* 1159–1166.

Scarr-Salapatek, S. (1975). Genetics and the development of intelligence. In F. D. Horowitz (Ed.), *Review of child development research* (Vol. 4, pp. 1–57). Chicago: University of Chicago Press.

Schafer, W. D. (1991). Essential assessment skills in the professional education of teachers. *Educational Measurement: Issues and Practice, 10*(1), 3–6, 12.

Schakel, J. A. (1986). Cognitive assessment of preschool children. *School Psychology Review, 15,* 200–215.

Schickedanz, J. A. (1989). The place of specific skills in preschool and kindergarten. In D. S. Strickland & L. M. Morrow (Eds.), *Emerging literacy: Young children learn to read and write* (pp. 96–106). Newark, DE: International Reading Association.

Schultz, T. (1989). Testing and retention of young children: Moving from controversy to reform. *Phi Delta Kappan, 71,* 125–129.

Scriven, M. (1967). The methodology of evaluation. In R. E. Stake (Ed.), *Perspectives of curriculum evaluation* (AERA Monograph Series on Curriculum Evaluation, No. 1, pp. 39–83). Skokie, IL: Rand McNally.

Scriven, M. (1991). Beyond formative and summative evaluation. In M. W. McLaughlin & D. C. Phillips (Eds.), *Evaluation and education: At quarter century: Part II of the Ninetieth Yearbook of the National Society for the Study of Education* (pp. 19–64). Chicago: University of Chicago Press.

Sechrest, L. (1969). Nonreactive assessment of attitudes. In E. P. Willems & H. L. Raush (Eds.), *Naturalistic viewpoints in psychological research* (pp. 147–161). New York: Holt, Rinehart, & Winston.

Seddon, G. M. (1978). The properties of Bloom's taxonomy of educational objectives for the cognitive domain. *Review of Educational Research, 48,* 303–323.

Seefeldt, C., & Barbour, N. (1986). *Early childhood education: An introduction.* Columbus, OH: Merrill.

Shanker, A. (1990). The social and educational dilemmas of test use. In *The uses of standardized tests in American education: Proceedings of the 1989 Fiftieth ETS Invitational Conference* (pp. 1–13). Princeton, NJ: Educational Testing Service.

Shepard, L. A. (1989). Why we need better assessment. *Educational Leadership, 46*(7), 4–9.

Shepard, L. A. (1990). Inflated test score gains: Is the problem old norms or teaching the test? *Educational Measurement: Issues and Practice, 9*(3), 15–22.

Shepard, L. A., & Smith, M. L. (1988). Escalating academic demand in kindergarten: Counterproductive policies. *The Elementary School Journal, 89,* 135–145.

Sigel, I. E. (1987). Does hothousing rob children of their childhood? *Early Childhood Research Quarterly, 2,* 211–225.

Simeonsson, R. J. (Ed.). (1986). *Psychological and developmental assessment of special education.* Boston: Allyn & Bacon.

Simpson, E. J. (1966). *The classification of educational objectives: Psychomotor domain.* Urbana, IL: University of Illinois Press.

Sinclair, C. B. (1973). *Movement of the young child: Ages two to six.* Columbus, OH: Merrill.

Singer, R. N. (Ed.). (1972). *Readings in motor learning.* Philadelphia, PA: Lea & Febiger.

Slavin, R. E. (1991). *Educational psychology: Theory into practice* (3rd ed.). Englewood Cliffs, NJ: Prentice Hall.

Smith, J. K. (1990). Measurement issues in early literacy assessment. In L. M. Morrow & J. K. Smith (Eds.), *Assessment for instruction in early literacy* (pp. 62–74). Englewood Cliffs, NJ: Prentice Hall.

Sparrow, S. S., Balla, D. A., & Cicchetti, D. V. (1984, 1985). *Vineland Adaptive Behavior Scales.* Circle Pines, MN: American Guidance Service.

Spodek, B., Saracho, O. N., & Davis, M. B. (1987). *Foundations of early childhood education: Teaching three-, four-, and five-year-old children.* Englewood Cliffs, NJ: Prentice Hall.

Sproull, L., & Zurbrow, D. (1981). Standardized testing from the administrative perspective. *Phi Delta Kappan, 62,* 628–631.

Stallman, A. C., & Pearson, P. D. (1990). Formal measures of early literacy. In L. M. Morrow & J. K. Smith (Eds.), *Assessment for instruction in early literacy* (pp. 7–44). Englewood Cliffs, NJ: Prentice Hall.

Sternberg, R. J. (1986). Intelligence, wisdom, and creativity: Three is better than one. *Educational Psychologist, 21,* 175–190.

Stetz, F. P., & Beck, M.D. (1981). Attitudes toward standardized tests: Students, teachers, and measurement specialists. *NCME Measurement in Education, 12,* 1–10.

Stiggins, R. J. (1991a). Assessment literacy. *Phi Delta Kappan, 72,* 534–539.

Stiggins, R. J. (1991b). Relevant classroom assessment training for teachers. *Educational Measurement: Issues and Practice, 10*(1), 7–12.

Strickland, D. S., & Morrow, L. M. (Eds.). (1989). *Emerging literacy: Young children learn to read and write.* Newark, DE: International Reading Association.

Sulzby, E. (1990). Assessment of writing and children's language while writing. In L. M. Morrow & J. K. Smith (Eds.), *Assessment for instruction in early literacy* (pp. 83–109). Englewood Cliffs, NJ: Prentice Hall.

Taub, H. P., Love, J., Wilkerson, D. A., Washington, E. D., & Wolf, J. M. (1980). *Accept my profile: Perspectives for Head Start profiles of program effects on children.* Black Rock, CT: Mediax Interactive Technologies.

Teale, W. H. (1988). Developmentally appropriate assessment of reading and writing in the early childhood classroom. *The Elementary School Journal, 89,* 173–183.

Teale, W. H. (1990). The promise and challenge of informal assessment in early literacy. In L. M. Morrow & J. K. Smith (Eds.), *Assessment for instruction in early literacy* (pp. 45–61). Englewood Cliffs, NJ: Prentice Hall.

Teale, W. H., & Sulzby, E. (Eds.). (1986). *Emergent literacy: Writing and reading.* Norwood, NJ: Ablex.

Tegano, D. W., Moran, J. D., III, & Godwin, L. J. (1986). Cross-validation of two creativity tests designed for preschool children. *Early Childhood Research Quarterly, 1,* 387–396.

Terrazas, C. M. (1990). Discussion on "Tests as standards of achievement in schools." In *The uses of standardized tests in American education: Proceedings of the 1989 Fiftieth ETS Invitational Conference* (pp. 81–86). Princeton, NJ: Educational Testing Service.

Thompson, E. W. (1990). Dilemma for superintendents. In C. Kamii (Ed.), *Achievement testing in the early grades: The games grown-ups play* (pp. 39–47). Washington, DC: National Association for the Education of Young Children.

Thorndike, E. L. (1918). The nature, purposes, and general methods of measurements of educational products. In G. M. Whipple (Ed.), *The measurement of educational products* (17th Yearbook, Part 2, National Society for the Study of Education, pp. 16–24). Chicago: University of Chicago Press.

Thorndike, R. L., Hagen, E. P., & Sattler, J. M. (1986). *Technical manual: The Stanford Binet Intelligence Scale* (4th ed.). Chicago: Riverside Publishing.

Torrance, E. P. (1974). *Norms-technical manual: The Torrance Tests of Creative Thinking.* Bensenville, IL: Scholastic Testing Service.

Torrance, E. P. (1981). *Thinking Creatively with Action and Movement.* Bensenville, IL: Scholastic Testing Service.

Torrance, E. P., & Caropreso, E. J. (1991). Assessment of preschool giftedness: Intelligence and creativity. In B. A. Bracken (Ed.), *The psychoeducational assessment of preschool children* (2nd ed., pp. 430–449). Boston: Allyn & Bacon.

Traub, R. E., & Rowley, G. L. (1991). Understanding reliability. *Educational Measurement: Issues and Practice, 10*(1), 37–45.

Traxler, A. E. (1951). Administering and scoring the objective test. In E. F. Lundquist (Ed.), *Educational measurement* (pp. 329–416). Washington, DC: American Council on Education.

Uzgiris, I. C., & Hunt, J. McV. (1975). *Assessment in infancy: Ordinal Scales of Psychological Development.* Urbana: University of Illinois Press.

Uzgiris, I. C., & Hunt, J. McV. (Eds.). (1987). *Infant performance and experience: New findings with the ordinal scales.* Urbana: University of Illinois Press.

Venn, J. J., Serwatka, T. S., & Anthony, R. A. (1987). *Scale of Social Development.* Austin, TX: Pro-Ed.

Wachs, T. D. (1975). Relation of infants' performance on Piaget scales between twelve and twenty-four months and their Stanford-Binet performance at thirty-one months. *Child Development, 46,* 929–935.

Wadsworth, B. (1989). *Piaget's theory of cognitive and affective development* (4th ed.). New York: Longman.

Walker, D. K. (1973). *Socioemotional measures for preschool and kindergarten children.* San Francisco: Jossey-Bass.

Wallach, M. A. (1970). Creativity. In P. H. Mussen (Ed.), *Carmichael's manual of child psychology* (3rd ed., Vol. 1, pp. 1211–1272). New York: Wiley.

Webb, E. J. (1978). Unconventionality, triangulation, and inference. In N. K. Denzin (Ed.), *Sociological methods: A sourcebook* (2nd ed., pp. 322–328). New York: McGraw-Hill.

Webb, E. J., Campbell, D. T., Schwartz, R. D., & Sechrest, L. (1966). *Unobtrusive measures: Nonreactive research in the social sciences.* Skokie, IL: Rand McNally.

Webb, E. J., Campbell, D. T., Schwartz, R. D., Sechrest, L., & Grove, J. B. (1981). *Nonreactive measures in the social sciences* (2nd ed.). Boston: Houghton Mifflin.

Wechsler, D. (1989). *Manual for the Wechsler Preschool and Primary Scale of Intelligence—Revised.* San Antonio, TX: Psychological Corporation.

Weeks, Z. R., & Ewer-Jones, B. (1991). Assessment of perceptual-motor and fine motor functioning. In B. A. Bracken (Ed.), *The psychoeducational assessment of preschool children* (2nd ed., pp. 259–283). Boston: Allyn & Bacon.

White, S. H., Day, M. C., Freeman, P. K., Hantman, S. A., & Messenger, K. P. (1973). *Federal programs for young children: Review and recommendations* (Vols. 1–4). Washington, DC: Department of Health, Education, & Welfare.

Wiggins, G. (1987). Creating a thought-provoking curriculum: Lessons from whodunits and others. *American Educator, 11*(4), 10–17.

Wiggins, G. (1988). Rational numbers: Toward grading and scoring that help rather than harm learning. *American Educator, 12*(4), 20–25, 45–48.

Wiggins, G. (1989a). A true test: Toward more authentic and equitable assessment. *Phi Delta Kappan, 70,* 703–713.

Wiggins, G. (1989b). Teaching to the (authentic) test. *Educational Leadership, 46*(7), 41–47.

Williams, H. G. (1991). Assessment of gross motor functioning. In B. A. Bracken (Ed.), *The psychoeducational assessment of preschool children* (2nd ed., pp. 284–316). Boston: Allyn & Bacon.

Williams, J. E., Best, D. L., & Associates. (1975). *Preschool Racial Attitude Measure II and Color Meaning Test II: General information and manual of directions.* Winston-Salem, NC: Wake Forest University, Department of Psychology.

Williams, J. E., Best, D. L., & Associates. (1976). *Sex Stereotype Measure II and Sex Attitude Measure: General information and manual of directions.* Winston-Salem, NC: Wake Forest University, Department of Psychology.

Willingham, W. W. (1986). *Testing handicapped people—the validity issue* (Research Rep. No. 86–26). Princeton, NJ: Educational Testing Service.

Wirt, R. D., Lachar, D., Klinedinst, J. K., & Seat, P. D. (1984). *Multidimensional description of child personality: A manual for the Personality Inventory for Children* (rev. ed.). Los Angeles: Western Psychological Services.

Wittrock, M. C. (1974). Learning as a generative process. *Educational Psychologist, 11,* 87–95.

Wodtke, K. H., Harper, F., Schommer, M., & Brunelli, P. (1989). How standardized is school testing? An exploratory observational study of standardized group testing in kindergarten. *Educational Evaluation and Policy Analysis, 11,* 223–235.

Wolery, M. (1989). Child find and screening issues. In D. B. Bailey, Jr., & M. Wolery (Eds.), *Assessing infants and preschoolers with handicaps* (pp. 119–143). Columbus, OH: Merrill.

Wolery, M., & Bailey, D. B., Jr. (1989). Assessing play skills. In D. B. Bailey, Jr., & M. Wolery (Eds.), *Assessing infants and preschoolers with handicaps* (pp. 428–446). Columbus, OH: Merrill.

Wolf, D. P. (1989). Portfolio assessment: Sampling student work. *Educational Leadership, 46*(7), 35–39.

Wolf, D., Bixby, J., Glenn, J., III, & Gardner, H. (1991). To use their minds well: Investigating new forms of student assessment. In G. Grant (Ed.), *Review of research in education* (Vol. 17, pp. 31–74). Washington, DC: American Educational Research Association.

Woolner, R. B. (1966, 1968). *Preschool Self-Concept Picture Test.* Memphis, TN: Memphis State University, Department of Curriculum and Instruction.

Wortham, S. C. (1990). *Tests and measurement in early childhood education.* Columbus, OH: Merrill.

Worthen, B. R., & Sanders, J. R. (1987). *Educational evaluation: Alternative approaches and practical guidelines.* New York: Longman.

Yang, R. K., & Bell, R. Q. (1975). Assessment of infants. In P. McReynolds (Ed.), *Advances in psychological assessment* (Vol. 3, pp. 137–185). San Francisco: Jossey-Bass.

Zaner-Bloser. (1979). *Evaluation Scales for Handwriting.* Columbus, OH: Author.

Zigler, E. F. (1970). Raising the quality of children's lives. *Children, 17,* 166–170.

Zimiles, H. (1987). The Bank Street approach. In J. L. Roopnarine & J. E. Johnson (Eds.), *Approaches to early childhood education* (pp. 163–178). Columbus, OH: Merrill.

THE INTERPRETIVE VOICE: QUALITATIVE RESEARCH IN EARLY CHILDHOOD EDUCATION

Daniel J. Walsh
UNIVERSITY OF ILLINOIS AT URBANA-CHAMPAIGN

Joseph J. Tobin
UNIVERSITY OF HAWAI'I

M. Elizabeth Graue
UNIVERSITY OF WISCONSIN-MADISON

Qualitative research is very diverse, drawing on many theoretical and methodological traditions. Erickson, in an attempt to encapsulate the diversity, described a body of research "alternatively called ethnographic, qualitative, participant observational, case study, symbolic interactionist, phenomenological, constructivist, or interpretive." He continued, "These approaches are all slightly different, but each bears strong family resemblance to the others" (1986, p. 119).

The qualitative approaches to research in early childhood education that we see as most useful and exciting differ from quantitative work in research ethics, notions of knowledge, and the relationship of the researcher to the researched. The qualitative approaches we discuss are as closely tied to the humanities as to the social sciences. They borrow usefully from linguistics, literary studies, philosophy, psychology, and, especially, anthropology.

Following Erickson, we will opt for the term *interpretive*. As Erickson argued, "interpretive" is more inclusive, avoids the nonquantitative connotations that "qualitative" has acquired, and points to the common interest across approaches in "human meaning in social life and in its elucidation and exposition by the researcher" (p. 119). In using the term *interpretive*, we draw on an extended family of traditions rather than on a single tradition.

This strong family resemblance is best seen in the day-to-day practices of interpretive researchers, who despite "differences in methodology and breadth of research focus . . . share a commitment to understanding the complexity of the phenomenon of interest to them" (Peshkin, 1988, p. 416). Jacob (1988) listed 3 attributes: the research is conducted in a natural setting; stress is placed on the importance of understanding participants' perspectives; and questions and methods emerge in the process of fieldwork. To these, the Spindlers (1982) added 2 attributes: observations are contextualized, both in the immediate setting and in the larger contexts within which the immediate setting is framed; and observation is prolonged and repetitive. This latter point is crucial. Good interpretive inquiry is very labor intensive, requiring long periods in the field, typically a year or more. Gaining access to meanings constructed by others is a slow process.

To these we will add the centrality of the relationship between the researcher and the researched to the research process. The meaning sought in inquiry is understood only through dialogue and negotiation between the researcher and the researched. Further, researchers have the responsibility to be sensitive to the inequities of power that exist between them and those with whom they are working, for example, between university scholar and school district practitioner, or between adult and child.

We have divided the chapter into 4 sections and a conclusion. In the first, we argue for the importance of interpretive inquiry in research in early childhood education. In the second, we review a range of interpretive studies in the field. Third, we discuss issues peculiar to studying children. Fourth, we examine the problem of judging interpretive work. Finally, we address the politics of doing qualitative inquiry.

THE IMPORTANCE OF INTERPRETIVE RESEARCH FOR EARLY CHILDHOOD EDUCATION

We have as a field too often restricted ourselves to questions that can be best answered using a narrow range of quantitative methods—questions concerning educational outcomes, as measured by tests, and measures of individual and group differences. Those aspects of life that cannot be readily measured have been dismissed as unimportant, or worse, they have been operationalized in most questionable fashion. As the political scientist Achen remarked, "To replace the unmeasurable with the unmeaningful is not progress" (1977, p. 806).

Many important questions have been unanswered or, worse yet, unasked. One crucial question that has been systematically ignored concerns the quest for meaning in what Bruner called "the ordinary conduct of life" (1990, p. 19). How do children make sense of their lives in day care settings and classrooms? How do teachers make sense of their lives as teachers?

As researchers, we have measured people, but we have not listened well to them. We have gone into classrooms and come out with little but numbers, as though the day-to-day interactions of human beings who spend large portions of their waking hours in classrooms could be reduced to computations. One wonders what happens when those who have been researched look at the studies done of them and fail to see themselves in those studies. As Rich put it, "When someone with . . . authority . . . describes the world and you are not in it, there is a moment of psychic disequilibrium, as if you looked into a mirror and saw nothing" (1989, p. ix).

Interpretive inquiry compels both researcher and researched to see themselves in a new way. At the heart of interpretive inquiry is a passion to understand the meaning that people are constructing in their everyday *situated actions,* that is, actions "situated in a cultural setting, and in the mutually interacting intentional states of the participants" (Bruner, 1990, p. 19). We emphasize here the notion of *action* and the distinction between action and *behavior,* which is action stripped of actors' intentions and meanings. This distinction is critical to understanding the difference between interpretive and computational approaches to research. The reductionist predilection to compress all human phenomena into behaviors has permeated educational research in general and early childhood education in particular. Interpretive researchers do not study behaviors. Behaviors are, by definition, meaningless.

Researchers from various fields, particularly anthropology and sociology, have contributed substantially to our understanding of the meaning constructed by young children and those adults who work with them. The richness of their work, however, has served to highlight how little interpretive work has been done by researchers whose primary identification is with the field of early childhood education. Recently, however, a cadre of interpretive researchers has emerged whose primary identification is with the field of early childhood education. A significant moment in this movement was the 1989 conference at the University of Tennessee on qualitative studies in early childhood education. This conference yielded a 1990 special issue of *Qualitative Studies in Education* edited by Hatch and Wisniewski.

Two final points. First, interpretive research has often been relegated to pilot study status, as though interpretive researchers were merely doing advanced scout work for their positivist colleagues. We argue to the contrary that interpretive inquiry has the potential to allow access to the contextual issues that give meaning to research findings and, in so doing, can provide understandings that allow us to make sense of existing positivist work.

Second, and most important, interpretive work is accessible to the practitioner. Teachers have little use for much of the research literature. What do tables of means, standard deviations, *t*'s, *F*'s, and *p*'s less-than-or-equal-to have to do with the decisions that must be made day-in and day-out in a classroom? This is not a matter of understanding, it is a matter of utility. Interpretive inquiry is accessible not simply because it is written in nonarcane language, but also because, instead of viewing teachers as research subjects, it privileges teachers' interpretations. Consider the description by Bolster, both a public school teacher and a university researcher:

The more I became aware of and experienced with this methodology [interpretive research], the more I became convinced that of all the models of research I know, this model has the greatest potential for generating knowledge that is both useful and interesting to teachers . . . this approach focuses on situated meanings which incorporate the various reactions and perspectives of students. In common with the teacher's perspective, it assumes the multiple causation of events; the classroom is viewed as a complex social system in which both direct and indirect influences operate. Unanticipated contingencies potentially illuminate rather than confound understanding since reaction to the unexpected often highlights the salient meanings assigned to what is normal. (1983, pp. 305–306)

Bolster here spoke of one type of interpretive inquiry, symbolic interactionism. Likewise Hymes, in the paragraph below, referred specifically to ethnography. We interpret both as applying to the larger interpretive research endeavor.

Erickson (1986) emphasized the similarities between the actions and purposes of interpretive researchers and teachers. "Teachers too are concerned with specifics of local meaning and local action; that is the stuff of life in daily classroom practice" (p. 156). Interpretive researchers make sense of children and classrooms not by turning to obscure, and often forbidding, methods of data collection and analysis but instead by systematically using the same sensibilities and sensitivities that make for good teachers, friends, lovers, parents, and people— listening, conversing, interpreting, reflecting, describing, and narrating. Hymes (1982) argued forcefully that the interpretive researcher is engaged in an endeavor that is "most compatible with a democratic way of life, the least likely to produce a world in which experts control knowledge at the expense of those who are studied" (p. 57).

INTERPRETIVE STUDIES

As with all paradigm shifts, there is a danger that interpretive research will result in a new elite in control of knowledge. Guided by this concern, we selected for this review studies by authors sensitive to issues of power and accessibility in the way they frame their questions, their research methods, and their research presentations.

We review 3 categories of interpretive studies of early education: ethnographic, case study, and constructivist. Although some studies do not fit comfortably into only 1 category, these categories give a useful structure to our review. This review is not designed to be comprehensive but rather to present a representative range of work. We have attempted to limit the review to studies that focus on the lives of children and the adults who work with them in preschool through third grade. We apologize to the many researchers whose worthy efforts we have overlooked.

Ethnography

Anthropology is currently enjoying considerable influence in educational research. The central research methodology of the anthropologist has been ethnography. The ethnographer works to recreate the shared lives of a group of people through description of their beliefs, knowledge, behaviors, and tools. The term *ethnography* is an important, if overused one, and vehement arguments have raged within the field over its appropriate use (e.g., Wolcott, 1980).

In educational research, there are 2 distinct types of ethnography: studies of children, teachers, and schools in cultures other than the researcher's (including cultural and ethnic groups within the United States), and studies conducted within the researcher's culture. These 2 types of educational research present very different practical and epistemological problems (Erickson, 1973; Ogbu, 1981; Watson-Gegeo, 1988).

Cross-Cultural Studies. Much of the cross-cultural work that holds implications for early childhood education has been conducted by anthropologists studying socialization, family relations, and cognitive development outside of school settings. Following in the "culture and personality" tradition of Mead, Benedict, and the Whitings, researchers including LeVine, B. Whiting and Edwards, and Super and Harkness have looked at early childhood in societies where young children typically do not attend preschool. LeVine and White's *Human Conditions* (1986) is an ambitious attempt to relate child rearing and early childhood experience to family size and modernization. Drawing on studies conducted in Japan, China, and Mexico, Levine and White contrast parental investment and child rearing practices in agricultural settings where infant mortality is high and family size is large with urban and urbanizing settings where the birth rate is decreasing and traditional ways of relating and making a living are disappearing. Whiting and Edwards' *Children of Different Worlds* (1988) mixes quantitative and qualitative descriptions to present pictures of childhood in societies unlike our own where children are cared for largely by other children or by adults in settings other than the nuclear family home. Super and Harkness' ethnographic work on parenting and childhood in Africa led them to develop the idea of "ecological niche" (1986), which suggests that child development needs to be understood in terms of specific biological, social, and culturally contextual pressures.

A number of researchers trained in the Benedict-Mead-Whiting-LeVine culture-and-personality tradition have recently turned their attention to early childhood in cultures like Japan and Italy, which have nearly universal preschool education for 4- and 5-year-olds. Important cross-cultural early childhood research tends to occur when there is a felicitous concentration of several researchers writing on the same culture and reacting to each others' work. In 1984, Lewis wrote a provocative piece on "Cooperation and control in the Japanese nursery school," in which she found that children most effectively internalize social rules when they are given great latitude to misbehave. Lewis' contribution was followed by ethnographic papers by Peak on the Suzuki method and the Japanese mother's role in early childhood education (1986); White and LeVine on "What is an *ii ko?*" (good child) (1986); Tobin, Davidson, and Wu on why Japanese preschools have such large student-teacher ratios (1987); Fujita and Sano on the group orientation of Japanese day care (1988); Singleton on the importance of *gambaru* (perseverance) as a central value in Japanese early education (1989); and DeCoker on the balance of academics and play in the Japanese preschool curriculum (1989). Full-scale ethnographies of Japanese early childhood include White's *The Japanese Educational Challenge* (1987), Hendry's *Becoming Japanese* (1986), and Tobin, Wu, and Davidson's *Preschool in Three Cultures* (1989). These ethnographic studies of Japanese early childhood education deepened the debate on educational achievement by showing that, although Japanese students outperform Americans on school achievement tests, there is little explicit academic emphasis in Japanese early education. These studies of a culture that is outstripping our own educationally and economically have challenged American educators and theorists to rethink culture-bound assumptions about classroom management, ability grouping, teacher-student ratios, and self-expression.

As we write, a similar concurrence of ethnographic work on early education in Italy is emerging. New (1988, 1989; New & Benigni, 1987) is conducting longitudinal studies of Italian child development, family relations, and early schooling. Corsaro and Rizzo (1988) have written on language and social relations in the *scuola materna,* showing that even in early childhood, *discussione* differs in interesting ways from middle-class conversation in the United States. Edwards and Gandini (1989; Edwards, Forman, & Gandini, in press) and New (1990) have formed research alliances with Italian colleagues in the town of Reggio Emilia. Their work is introducing the highly innovative Reggio Emilia preschool integrated-arts curriculum to non-Italian readers.

Important ethnographic studies are also being conducted on marginalized groups within the researchers' home country. For more than a decade the Kamehameha Early Education Project (KEEP) has provided an important model for applied educational research. KEEP researchers have published important ethnographic work on Hawaiian early childhood (D'Amato, 1986); on incongruities between the worlds of home and school (Boggs, 1985; D'Amato, 1988; Jordan, 1977); on cultural differences in learning and techniques for helping children make a bridge from home to school (Jordan, 1978, 1984, 1985), and on culturally appropriate curriculum and instruction for young children (Au, 1979, 1980; Au & Jordan, 1981). A hallmark of the KEEP approach has been collaborative research by a multidisciplinary team matching ethnographers, developmental psychologists, and educators (for an overview of KEEP research see Tharp and Gallimore, 1988). In the past few years, the KEEP program has been embroiled in political controversy, and there has been a diaspora of KEEP researchers from the Kamehameha Schools.

Taylor and Dorsey-Gaines (1988) used interpretive approaches to explore the speech and (pre)literacy of African American children. Heath (1983) compared African American children and working- and middle-class children's "ways with words." Cazden (1988) left Harvard for a year to become a first-grade teacher in a classroom of African American and Mexican American children and there studied the "language of teaching and learning." Delpit (1986, 1988), an African American researcher and educator, challenged researchers and reading and writing specialists to examine the culture-bound (i.e., white middle-class) assumptions that underlie the whole-language approach to literacy instruction. Lubeck (1985) compared an African American working-class Head Start classroom with a white middle-class preschool, using these 2 classrooms as "'windows' through which to observe the child rearing practices of two sets of women" (p. 133). Lubeck concluded that, in contrast to the white middle-class preschool's "adult-individualistic" orientation, the African American Head Start program was "adult-collective."

Other work in this tradition would include Bennett's studies of Appalachian children (1991) and Yup'ik Eskimo girls (Bennett, Nelson, & Baker, 1992); Goldenberg's (1987, 1989) and Gallimore and Goldenberg's (in press) literacy studies of low-income Hispanic parents and children; Delgado-Gaitan's ethnography of school and home of second- and third-grade Spanish-speaking Mexican children (1990); Fishman's research on Amish literacy (1988); Swadener's study of a Friend's school (1988); Miller's (1982) study of language learning in a white ethnic working class neighborhood (1982); and Zinnser's investigation of literacy teaching in a fundamentalist church (1986). (For a review of studies of minority school failure see the Spring, 1987, special issue of *Anthropology and Education Quarterly*.)

At the core of these anthropologically inspired studies of children and schooling is the tension produced by the "otherness" of the researcher and the researched. When researchers study groups other than their own, there is a fundamental, irreducible difference in world view and experience between ethnographers and informants that requires a negotiation of meaning—how can an exotic or strange world view be presented in familiar terms? In choosing what to describe, whom to interview, and how to interpret what they see and hear in the field, ethnographers enjoy a great deal of power over the people they write about, a power some argue is analogous to

colonial political domination (Clifford, 1988; Said, 1989). But the "otherness" of researchers can also be seen as a methodological advantage, allowing them to ask naive questions that insiders would never think to ask and to see meanings in responses that insiders would consider self-evident or mundane. When well done, cross-cultural ethnographic studies of early childhood provide a corrective to our ethnocentric tendency to build notions of child development and good teaching on research conducted only within our culture. Ethnography serves as a form of cultural critique (Marcus & Fisher, 1986), challenging our taken-for-granted assumptions and offering perspectives and ideas that widen the scope of our research, theory, and practice.

In contemporary anthropology, comparative studies like Mead's 3-culture study (1963) and the Whiting's 6-culture study (1975) have fallen out of fashion. It is thus noteworthy that anthropologists of early childhood and early schooling are bucking that trend and continuing to do comparative work. Recent examples include Tobin, Wu, and Davidson's comparison of Japanese, Chinese, and American preschools (1989); Whiting and Edward's (1989) *Children of Different Worlds*, which follows up the original 6-culture study; Edwards and Gandini's (1989) and Corsaro's (1988) Italy-United States comparisons; the Spindlers' Germany-United States comparisons (1987); and the 5-culture Comparative Human Infant Project (CHIP) coordinated by LeVine at the Harvard Graduate School of Education (Richman et al., 1988). The challenge in conducting comparative ethnography is to be systematic without reducing discrete, unique cultural features to homogenizing codes and categories.

Within-Cultural Studies. Within mainstream educational research the term "ethnography" is currently being used as a synonym for interpretive, contextually rich studies of classrooms within the researcher's culture. In these studies the tension between inside and outside meaning is not so explicit as in the cross-cultural encounter. The interpretive and ethical problem in classroom ethnography centers on differences in world view, concerns, language, and power in our society between academicians and the people they study: children, teachers, and, occasionally, parents.

In early childhood classrooms, where practitioners are particularly disempowered, these differences can be acute. How can classroom teachers be transformed from subjects to authors of the research carried out in their classrooms? Once or twice a generation a Paley comes along, who tells a rich, ongoing story of what it means to be a young child in school and, in the process, what it means to be a teacher of young children (1979, 1981, 1984, 1986, 1990). For those of us, however, who are unable to excel, like Paley, as classroom teacher, researcher, and author simultaneously, the solution lies in developing new types of research collaborations. The work of Walsh and his colleagues (1989, 1991) is an example of an attempt to deal constructively with this tension by experimenting with ways researchers and teachers can jointly narrate, interpret, and even author research.

In recent years a number of interesting and informative classroom studies have appeared. Examples of preschool studies would include work by Fernie (1988; Fernie, Kantor, Klein,

Meyer, & Elgas, 1988), Kantor (1988; Kantor, Elgas, & Fernie, 1989), and Corsaro (1979, 1985), as well as Hatch and Freeman's study of kindergarten philosophies and practice (1988) and Genishi's (1988) study of the computer curriculum in a kindergarten classroom. Foundational work on classroom discourse has broadened our understandings of the conversational rules that frame teacher-student interactions in the classroom. Through the use of microethnography, that is, the detailed analysis of short segments of face-to-face interaction, Mehan (1979), Cazden (1988), and Shultz and Florio (1979), among others, have teased apart the complex nature of classroom participatory structures, that is, the etiquette of interaction.

Within-culture ethnographers share with their cross-cultural colleagues a concern with culture. Although culture is being continually defined and redefined, for this discussion Goodenough's definition is useful: "The culture of any society is made up of the concepts, beliefs, and principles of action and organization that an ethnographer has found could be attributed successfully to the members of that society in the context of dealing with them" (1976, p. 5). An ethnographic approach sees the meanings of children's and teachers' thoughts and actions as embedded in culturally defined contexts, where the "same" words or behaviors have different meanings in different settings. Cross-cultural ethnographers attempt to link what they see and hear in homes and schools with larger cultural processes, seeing, for example, the children's conversations in the *scuola materna* as an embryonic version of a dialogical and interpersonal style characteristic of Italian adults, or the aggressive approach to dealing with "spoiled" children in a Chinese day care center as a response to the national, single-child family policy. Within-culture classroom ethnographers view classrooms, playgrounds, and schools as "mini-cultures," each of which must be understood in terms of rules and systems of meaning which are both peculiar to the setting and reflective of the larger culture. Paley, for example, used classroom narratives to show how "Spiderman," "Transformers," and other super heroes have specific and, in some cases, unexpected local meanings in a particular classroom in a particular year.

The relationship of cross-cultural to within-cultural inquiry is complex. While sharing many features, they present very different interpretive and rhetorical challenges. Cross-cultural studies, by presenting Western readers with sympathetic explanations of alien beliefs and practice, work best when they succeed in making the exotic familiar. In contrast, researchers who study classrooms within their own culture must choose between making the familiar exotic or exemplary. In the former case, teachers being studied may well feel used or resentful. In the latter, readers are likely to find the account lacking in verisimilitude or tension (Tobin & Davidson, 1990; Newkirk, in press).

In the past few years technological developments have led to changes in the ways both groups are conducting their research. In addition to the traditional ethnographic methods of interviewing and observing, many educational ethnographers are using videotape as a tool for producing culturally rich interpretation. The Spindlers made pioneering contributions to this use of visual images as "evocative stimuli" and "reflective interviewing tools" in their comparative study of German and American views of elementary education (1987). Their students, Fujita and Sano, have used videotape in a similar way in their comparisons of Japanese and American nursery schools (1988). Tobin, Wu, and Davidson showed videotapes of typical days in Chinese, Japanese, and American preschools to children, staff, and parents in each culture to stimulate a cross-cultural, "multivocal" ethnographic text (Tobin, 1989). McDermott's "Rosa tapes" were part of a fascinating study of a first-grade reading group (1976). A powerful medium for early childhood research, videotape also presents troubling ethical issues. It produces a record that is not easily disguised by assigning fictitious names to people and places. It also produces a record that is problematic in other ways:

Contemporary social science's ravenous appetite to see in and through people, our insatiable "panopticism" (Foucault, 1978) produces in the objects of our gaze a self-awareness and self-consciousness that inevitably changes notions of who they are and how they should behave. Videotaping focuses, magnifies, distorts, and prolongs this effect. (Tobin & Davidson, 1990).

Case Studies

No other issue so clearly distinguishes interpretive researchers from others than their confidence in the worth of case studies, here defined as the in-depth description of a single individual, event, or site (see Yin, 1989). Interpretive researchers find the well done case study both interesting and persuasive.

In *Actual minds, possible worlds* (1986), Bruner contrasts arguing and story telling and suggests that the paradigmatic (scientific) and the narrative (imaginative) are 2 fundamentally different ways of describing and interpreting the world. Quantitative researchers make sense of the world by counting and classifying; interpretive researchers make sense of the world by thick description and narrative (true, of course, of all types of interpretive studies, not just the case study). As Donmoyer (1990) pointed out, case studies have the virtues of being accessible (most readers find narratives more interesting and intelligible than statistical studies) and interpersonally meaningful: when reading a good case study, we get a chance to experience the world through the eyes of the author as well as the subject of the study.

The case study in early childhood education draws on a variety of narrative traditions, combining the ordered observation of the medical case study (e.g., Freud or Sacks) with the power of the mythic tale, and the quotidian specificity of the journal or the diary (Newkirk, in press). To write an effective case study requires a combination of the skills of the ethnologist and the novelist.

Case studies of early childhood were once written primarily by child psychologists and psychiatrists. Freud, Piaget, Erikson, and Bettelheim wrote case studies of young children's emotional and cognitive development that have strongly influenced educators. The past decade or so has seen the rise of nonclinical case studies, including some very sensitive and well documented case studies of young children as writers and meaning-makers, for example, Bissex's *Gnys at Wrk* (1980), Newkirk's *More than Stories* (1989), Paley's *Molly is Three*

(1986), and Hubbard's *Author of Pictures, Draughtsman of Words* (1989).

Another important form of the case study has as its subject the teacher. Examples of this genre include Ayers *The Good Preschool Teacher* (1989) and Walsh, Baturka, Colter, and Smith's "Changing One's Mind—Maintaining One's Identity: A First-Grade Teacher's Story" (1991).

Constructivist/Social Critique

At the cutting edge of interpretive work in early childhood education are approaches concerned with destabilizing widely accepted assumptions and constructing social change. This evolving body of work includes neo-Marxist critiques, feminist explorations of the origins of gender inequity in early childhood, and constructivist analyses of the deeper meanings and larger ramifications of seemingly innocent early educational policies, such as ability grouping, developmentally appropriate practice, and readiness. (For interesting examples of new directions in research in early childhood education see Kessler & Swadener, 1991.)

Davies, who draws on both poststructuralist and feminist theory, has done seminal work on preschool children and gender. She succinctly addressed the issue of effecting change in the introduction to *Frogs and Snails and Feminist Tales:*

...I have set out to analyze the way in which the dualistic gender order is experienced by preschool children. To the extent that I have successfully mapped out what is going on in the processes whereby children are constituted as male or female, then I have opened up the possibility for programs of change that may genuinely work. (1989, pp. x–xi)

Suranksy's *Erosion of Childhood* (1982) juxtaposes mini-ethnographies of 5 preschools to make telling critiques of what is usually viewed as "good practice." Suranksy's neo-Marxist and feminist concerns with social justice and social change are central to her project. Leavitt (1991; Leavitt & Power, 1989) draws on an even wider range of theoretical frameworks including hermeneutic, phenomenological, interactionist, critical, postmodern, and feminist perspectives. In so doing, she serves as an exemplar of the wide multi-theoretical underpinnings of much of the best interpretive work. She wrote of her research on the lived experience of infants and toddlers in day care:

Young children's daily experiences are as important as the outcomes of these experiences, thus the necessity of looking at their experiences *as it is lived*. Infants and toddlers have few means and little power to make their "voices" heard, therefore a great deal of attention and interpretive effort is involved in understanding their experience. (in press)

Leavitt's colleague Power, working from a similar perspective, has studied the ritualization and socialization of emotions in early childhood in both day cares and homes (1985, 1986).

Nelson's *Negotiated Care: The Experience of Family Day Care Providers* (1991) is an exemplary interpretive study, political and critical in the best sense of each term. Nelson brings attention to the least empowered and least studied of all early childhood practitioners. Working from interviews with providers and clients, she revealed the complex and ambiguous workings of gender and class as one group of ambivalent and economically struggling working women hire the services of another similarly struggling group.

Taylor's landmark studies of literacy (1983, 1991) grew out of a basic concern of interpretive inquiry—the need to study people in everyday life. What began as an attempt to find "systematic ways of looking at reading and writing as activities that have consequences in and are affected by family life" grew out of her disenchantment with reading and writing "presented as decontextualized language skills largely unconnected to reading and writing in everyday life" (1983, preface). Cox chose to study one of the most commonplace of kindergarten activities—the teacher reading storybooks to a large group of children. Drawing on the sociohistorical approaches of Bakhtin and Vygotsky, she showed how the children were daily engaged in a struggle to socially construct literary meaning (1990a, 1990b).

Carlsson-Paige and Levin have authored a series of books and articles reporting their research on controversial issues in early childhood education, including war-play, gendered toys, and media-influenced violence (e.g., 1987). A hallmark of their work is a combination of earnest concern and a balanced presentation of the issues, inviting the readers to enter the debate.

The world of kindergarten has been the focus of much interpretive work, from Gracey's (1975) and LeCompte's (1980) studies of how kindergarten children learn to become students and Shultz and Florio's (1979) microethnography of developing social competence to Apple and King's (1977) study of the hidden curriculum in kindergarten.

The increase in the use of screening tests for children entering kindergarten and the growing rates of retention in kindergarten has drawn the attention of a number of interpretive researchers. Taylor (1991) explored the tangled system of standardized testing that obscured school officials' view of one child, Patrick. She showed how school officials doggedly pursued a diagnosis of Patrick that explained away their own failures. This work exposes the prevailing assessment paradigm that reduces learning to scores on a test. Smith and Shepard (1989; Shepard & Smith, 1989) looked at the attitudes of parents and teachers and found, despite widespread public support for retention in the early grades, that parents gave equivocal evidence of its effects and that teachers varied practices of retention according to their tacit theories of child development, teacher role, and school structure.

Byrnes interviewed children and found that they feared retention as an unpredictable punishment (1989). Baturka and Walsh (1991), following up on Byrnes, conducted in-depth interviews with children who had either been retained or placed in transition grades during the kindergarten/first grade sequence. They found, despite assurances by adults that such children "felt good about themselves," that these children were very concerned about themselves and their experience.

Graue (1992) questioned the pervasive idea of readiness for kindergarten. Working from a social-constructivist perspective, she described readiness as varying from community to community. The concept of the ready child, rather than being universal or psychological, was negotiated by adults working with children and used to influence decisions about kindergarten enrollment and instruction. This work is also interesting for its use of Vygotsky's notion of the "activity setting" (explicated in Eisenhart & Graue, 1990).

Walsh and colleagues' work (1989, 1991, 1992, in press) has focused mainly on prekindergarten, kindergarten, and first-grade teachers, attempting to give voice and visibility to a group that for the most part labors in isolation and silence. Ott (1991) listened carefully to a group of teachers, whose isolation and silence were intensified first because they were kindergarten teachers and thus perceived as marginal to the elementary school and also because they worked in small rural districts. Anderson-Levitt's (1987) fascinating study of a first grade teacher in France looked at the relationship between her cultural knowledge and her work in the classroom.

Work focusing on parents has examined the link between the home and formal settings such as day care or school. The socialization process by which parents learn their responsibilities as the parent of a school-age child was addressed by Graue (1991). She found that expectations for good parenting were not universal and that they had practical implications for the interactions between families and schools. This theme was also addressed in Lareau's (1989) study of the nature of class differences in parental involvement in elementary school. Her investigation utilized the concept of cultural capital to explain the degree of fit between middle and working class families and their schools. Bloch and Tabachnick (in press) examined the rhetoric of parent involvement and the reality of its enactment in 3 schools working with families of color. They concluded that reform efforts did not necessarily transform relationships or empower parents.

ISSUES IN STUDYING YOUNG CHILDREN

Researchers interested in adults who work with young children have many resources to turn to. For example, if one is interested in studying teachers, Erickson's (1986) "Qualitative methods in research on teaching" is readily available. The resources available for those interested in doing interpretive work with children are more scarce.

Studying children is a most important endeavor. Unfortunately it seems that much of the research in early childhood education has lost sight of its focus in its emphasis on developmental change and treatment differences. Fine and Sandstrom (1988) begin *Knowing Children: Participant Observation with Children*, their excellent introduction to observing and interviewing children, by noting:

Perhaps the most obvious goal of qualitative research with children is to get to know them and better see the world through their eyes. On a deeper level, this style of research additionally assumes that minors are knowledgeable about their worlds, that these worlds are special and noteworthy, and that we as adults can benefit by viewing the world through their hearts and minds (p. 12).

Studying children is a different and more problematic endeavor than studying adults. Studying young children is even more different and problematic. Both interviewing and observing are much more difficult with young children than with older children or adults because of the distance between the researcher and the subject. Physical, social, cognitive, and political distances between the adult and child make their relationship very different from the relationship between adults. In doing participant observation with children, one can never become a child. One remains a very definite and readily identifiable "other."

Researchers, unless working "under cover"—which raises serious ethical issues—remain "others" in whatever group studied. How much of an other, however, is relative, depending on cultural, gender, and other distances. In most cases, adults working with other adults are able to decrease the distance between researcher and subject by finding some salient area of commonality. For example, many people doing research on teachers were once or are teachers themselves. Although the distance between adult and child is less absolute than gender (generally), as we were all once children ourselves, the distance is also ambiguous, for children are often *physically* close but *socially* distant.

While there is some disagreement among scholars as to how easy it is for adults to gain access to the world of children (Wacksler, 1986), the assumptions and values of these two social categories [adults and children] inevitably differ.... Like the white researcher in black society, the male researcher studying women, or the ethnologist observing a distant tribal culture, the adult participant observer who attempts to understand a children's culture cannot pass unnoticed as a member of that group (Fine & Sandstrom, 1988, pp. 10–13).

Despite the difficulties, some researchers have been able to, in Corsaro's words, "enter the child's world." Corsaro initially struggled in his efforts to gain entry. His field notes described an early and unsuccessful initial attempt:

Two 4-year-old girls (Betty and Jenny) and adult researcher (Bill) in the nursery school:
Betty: You can't play with us!
   Bill: Why?
Betty: Cause you're too big.
   Bill: I'll sit down. (Sits down)
Jenny: You're still too big.
Betty: Yeah, you're "Big Bill!"
   Bill: Can I just watch?
Jenny: OK, but don't touch nuthin'!
   Bill: OK.
Jenny: OK, Big Bill?
   Bill: OK.
   (Later Big Bill got to play.) (1985, p. 1)

Corsaro eventually developed a strategy for entering the child's world that he termed *reactive*. Looking for ways not to act like an adult, he noticed that "adults primarily initiate contacts with children: that is, they were primarily *active* rather than *reactive*" (p. 28). For example, adults began conversations with children without expecting to become engaged in extended interaction. Adults also tended to stay in certain areas while avoiding others, where they rarely interacted with children. "Adults seldom entered the playhouses, outside sand-piles, climbing bars, or climbing house" (p. 28). His strategy became one, then, of waiting:

For the first week in school, I continually made myself available in peer-dominant areas and waited for children to react to me. For the first few days, the results were not encouraging. I would enter the school shortly after the children arrived and sit down in the peer area...without any overt response from the children beyond several smiles and a few puzzled stares. Of all the many hours observing in this setting, these were the most difficult for me. I wanted to say something ("anything") to the children, but I stuck with my strategy and remained silent (p. 28).

Eventually, on the fourth day, children did approach Corsaro and permitted him to enter into their activities.

Sue then handed me a shovel. "You wanna dig?" "Sure," I said, and we shoveled sand into buckets. Later we were joined by Christopher and Antoinette. This activity ended when one of the TAs announced "clean-up time," whereupon we put away our shovels and went inside for meeting time. (p. 30)

In contrast, Mandell took an extreme and, we feel, theoretically and ethically weaker position on participant observation with young children. "While acknowledging adult-child differences, the researcher suspends all adult-like characteristics except physical size.... I argue that even physical differences can be so minimized when participating with children as to be inconsequential in interaction" (1988, p. 435). Quite simply, we do not believe that these differences can be minimized, or, more importantly, that they should be. Implicit in Mandell's assertion is the belief that one can lose one's otherness as a researcher and become, as it were, a native. This is neither possible nor desirable. What Geertz said of adults is particularly true of children:

We cannot live other people's lives, and it is a piece of bad faith to try. We can but listen to what...they say about their lives.... Whatever sense we have of how things stand with someone else's inner life, we gain through their expressions, not through some magical intrusion into their consciousness. It's all a matter of scratching surfaces (1986, p. 373).

If participant observation with young children is problematic, formal interviewing is even more so. The younger the child, the more difficult interviewing can be. Fine and Sandstrom as well as Corsaro deal with interviewing young children. Hatch's (1990) discussion of interviewing children in classrooms is quite useful, although we feel his stress on a Piagetian view of egocentrism needs to be tempered (for post-Piagetian treatments of children's ability to decenter see Donaldson, 1978, or Bruner & Haste, 1987). Also helpful are Tammivaara and Enright (1986) and Parker (1984).

An extremely useful strategy, which was first suggested to us by D'Amato, is to interview children in pairs or small groups. D'Amato (1986) and Baturka and Walsh (1991) have used this strategy most effectively with kindergarten, first-, and second-grade children. Children are more relaxed when with a friend. They tend to keep each other both on track and truthful. D'Amato described how when one child would begin to embellish a tale, the other child would respond, "You lie! You lie!" (personal communication). Baturka found that the richest parts of the interviews came from the discussion between the children as they responded to her questions, rather than from their direct answers, which often appeared to be attempts to give the "right" answer. In their discussions, the children would change the question to one that was more to their liking and then answer that one. As Spradley has stated, "In ethnographic interviewing, *both the questions and answers must be discovered from informants*" (italics in original) (1979, p. 84). Interviewing children in pairs may well give children the opportunity to indirectly let researchers know what questions they should be asking.

There are also the more mundane problems peculiar to doing research with young children. One must be willing to work with children on one's lap and hanging over one's shoulders, to let children draw in one's notebook, to type on one's laptop computer. One must be willing to deal with runny noses and grimy hands, to brave the school lunch room and fingers covered with ketchup and mashed potatoes if one is to gain access to young children. And one must be ready for the unexpected.

On one occasion they used me in a game of "all after that man there" and for fifty seconds I was mobbed, pulled, and kicked by a bevy of five-year-olds. Happily the noise was more alarming than the blows (Sluckin, 1981, pp. 6–7).

JUDGING INTERPRETIVE RESEARCH

Many excellent texts and articles have been written on the process of doing interpretive work. A short list of important texts describing the interpretive endeavor would include Bernard (1988), Bogdan and Biklan (1982), Denzin (1989), Dobbert (1982), Fetterman (1989), Goetz and LeCompte (1984), Lincoln and Guba (1985), Wolcott (1990b). There have been too many important overview articles and chapters to even attempt a comprehensive list, but we find the following of particular interest: Peshkin's (1988) "Understanding Complexity: A Gift of Qualitative Inquiry"; Wolcott's (1988), "Ethnographic Research in Education"; and Erickson's (1986) "Qualitative Methods in Research on Teaching." Books and articles treating specific topics include Spradley (1979) and Mishler (1986) on interviewing, Spradley (1980) on observation, Grimshaw (1982) on filming and videotaping, and Jackson (1987) on "mechanical matters," including cameras, audio recorders, and video recorders.

We will not attempt to describe interpretive work in detail. Instead we will give short descriptions of *fieldwork* and *interpretation* and then proceed to the more problematic issue of judging interpretive work, which is the focus of this section. Our purpose in including these very brief descriptions is to make more accessible to the reader the ensuing discussion.

Fieldwork

The interpretive researcher has basically 3 ways to gather information about activities in naturally occurring settings: observation, interviewing, and document analysis. Observation gives a running account of the life in a context. Observational techniques vary from the detached observer who becomes part of the wallpaper taking notes, to full participant observation, in which the researcher becomes as much as possible a member of the group under study. Interviews provide a directed data collection opportunity in which the researcher asks questions of informants. Interviews are often used to provide in depth discussion of events and relationships that come up in observations. Document analysis addresses the information about a group that resides in the various written records found in a setting, which in classroom interpretive research might include report cards, home-school communications, plan books, and student records.

Interpretation

The interpretation portion of interpretive research has a special nature that differentiates it from positivist work. Interpretation occurs while work is still ongoing in the field. Part of the process includes negotiation with informants on the adequacy of interpretations and representations. The importance of the relationship between the researcher and the researched cannot be understated here; it is hard to get the story right unless one has the informed and patient cooperation of the people who know the setting.

Judging the Results

Traditionally the adequacy of research has been evaluated in terms of validity, reliability, and generalizability. This approach has been used to judge the evidence provided in experimental, quasi-experimental, and correlational work that examines individual and group differences and the aggregation of information on educational products. Key in this tradition is an enforced distance between researcher and researched; good positivist research assumes that the researcher does not influence the behavior of those studied in any way.

The usefulness of these norms in judging interpretive research is limited. How are rules and standards developed in a hands-off tradition to be applied to work that relies on the interaction between researcher and researched, that conceives of knowledge in a completely different way? Attempts to answer this question have ranged from efforts to adapt standards of evidence to interpretive work (Goetz & LeCompte, 1984), discussion of transformation of norms given the basic epistemological and ontological distinctions between the 2 world views (Howe & Eisenhart, 1990), to assertions that the norms should be rejected altogether (Lincoln & Guba, 1985).

How, then, does one judge interpretive research? If interpretive research must begin with the *immediate and local meanings of actions* as defined from the actors point of view..." (Erickson, 1986, p. 119), then so must any judgment of it. The actors may not agree with the eventual analysis, "but

they must recognize the building blocks of that analysis" (McDermott, 1982, p. 322). The researcher's responsibility is to show the reader that her interpretations get at and are informed by these meanings, and that her interpretation is better than alternative ones. McDermott, Gospodinoff, and Arons argue that,

...description of behavior and its context [must] be presented in a way that readers can decide for themselves whether or not to believe or not to believe the ethnographer's account of what it is that a particular group of people are doing at any given time. (1978, p. 245)

The narrative that is produced and presented to the reader must have what Dewey (1929) and Geertz (1973) described as "assertability," Campbell (1978) termed "plausibility," Denzin (1989) labeled "verisimilitude," Erickson (1989) called "trustability," and what Wolcott (1990a) simply calls "understanding." It also must reveal to the reader the disciplinary traditions, theoretical frameworks, and foundational assumptions that inform the study.

How does the researcher produce such a narrative? Erickson (1989) argued that there are 3 criteria for trustability. The first is interpretive: Did the actors' meanings get into the narrative? The second is adequacy of evidence: How well is the evidence presented and marshaled? Are discrepant cases looked at systematically? Has the researcher been able to "triangulate" the evidence, that is, is there evidence from more than one epistemological source? Has it been made "clear to the reader what is meant by the various assertions, and to display the evidentiary warrant for the assertions" (Erickson, 1986, p. 149)? And the final is critical: Does the researcher address issues of power and advantage? Has fear and pressure been examined? Has the researcher addressed issues of belief, ideology, and voice?

Although we agree that the interpretive researcher must struggle with each of these questions and issues, we believe that, in the end, the meaning and worth of interpretive studies lies less with authors than with readers. Ultimately, however we position ourselves in our studies, however we argue for the reasonableness of our interpretations and the consequences of our findings, our readers will decide whether they find our studies interesting, meaningful, and useful (Tobin & Davidson, 1990). They will do this not because we let them, but because we are powerless to stop them. Good interpretive work invites readers to enter into a critical dialogue with the researcher and the researched. The meaning and worth of the research emerge in the interaction of reader and text. It is for that reason that interpretive researchers see writing not just as a means of communicating their findings, but as the soul of the interpretive enterprise.

CONCLUSION: THE POLITICS OF INTERPRETIVE RESEARCH

To treat a broad topic in a relatively few pages, one must be selective. Our selectivity has been due to more than space constraints. We have stressed the more radical and critical perspectives within which we work. The new interpretive work presented here is more than a counterpart to traditional computational research, it is more critical, less reverent, and more concerned with issues of power. As such it does more than simply present a complementary picture to computational research, it presents a very different and richer picture.

Some readers might welcome a conciliatory conclusion in which we stress the compatibility and communality between quantitative and interpretive research and in which we call for collaboration between the computationalists and the interpretivists. Certainly there are interesting ways to combine quantitative and qualitative data and analyses in the same study. And certainly there is room in research in early childhood education for researchers from both perspectives. Some of our best friends do quantitative work. As a matter of fact, the 3 of us have.

But we have intentionally made an argument for interpretive research on the education of young children that emphasizes rather than smoothes over the differences between paradigms. We do so because interpretive researchers are still at something of a disadvantage in the field, and this disadvantage should not be glossed over. Before we conclude, we will make 2 points in this regard. First, interpretive work is very labor intensive and time-consuming. Conducting and writing up a study can easily take 2 years or more, a disadvantage in an environment where sheer numbers of refereed-journal articles are seen as a necessary, even if not sufficient, measure of productivity. In addition, the dissemination of interpretive research takes many forms beyond the expected articles, such as technical reports and contributions to edited books.

Second, interpretive research is often not easily situated in the training of graduate students in early childhood education. Too often interested graduate students may add qualitative methodology to their research tool kit, but only after mastering the statistics sequence. This makes it difficult to locate trained research assistants from within the program. It also makes it unlikely that well-trained interpretive researchers will emerge from doctoral programs in early childhood education. Perhaps, ideally, researchers should be conversant in both paradigms. If so, the expectation should hold for both interpretivists and computationalists.

In conclusion, we will restate the central argument of this chapter: Interpretive research has an important place in research on the education of young children. It has the potential, in the negotiated, collaborative relationship between the researcher and the researched, to give voice and visibility to those groups, children and practitioners, who historically have been silenced and isolated. When those children and practitioners stand in front of the mirror that research provides them, the image they see should be their own.

References

Achen, C. H. (1977). Measuring representation: Perils of the correlation coefficient. *American Journal of Political Science, 21,* 805–815.

Anderson-Levitt, K. (1987). Cultural knowledge for teaching first grade: An example from France. In G. Spindler & L. Spindler (Eds.), *Interpretive ethnography of education: At home and abroad.* Hillsdale, NJ: Erlbaum.

Apple, M. W., & King, N. (1977). What do schools teach? *Curriculum Inquiry, 6,* 341–358.

Au, K. H. (1979). Using the experience-text-relationship method with minority children. *Reading Teacher, 32,* 677–679.

Au, K. H. (1980). Participation structures in reading lessons with Hawaiian children. *Anthropology and Education Quarterly, 11,* 91–115.

Au, K. H., & Jordan, C. (1981). Teaching reading to Hawaiian children: Finding a culturally appropriate solution. In H. Trueba, G. P. Guthrie, & D. H. Au (Eds.), *Culture and the bilingual classroom: Studies in classroom ethnography* (pp. 139–152). Rowley, MA: Newbury House.

Ayers, W. (1989). *The good preschool teacher.* New York: Teachers College Press.

Baturka, N. L., & Walsh, D. J. (1991, April). *"In the Guiness Book of World Records it says that a girl stayed in kindergarten until she was 13": First graders who have been retained make sense of their world.* Paper presented at the Annual Meeting of the American Educational Research Association, Chicago.

Bennett, K. P. (1991). Doing school in an urban Appalachian first grade. In C. Sleeter (Ed.), *Empowerment through multicultural education* (pp. 27–46). Albany: SUNY Press.

Bennett de Marrais, K. P., Nelson, P., & Baker, J. (1992). Meaning in mud: Yup'ik Eskimo girls at play. *Anthropology and Education Quarterly, 23,* 120–144.

Bernard, H. R. (1988). *Research methods in cultural anthropology.* Newbury Park, CA: Sage.

Bissex, G. (1980). *Gnys at wrk: A child learns to write and read.* Cambridge, MA: Harvard University Press.

Bloch, M. N., & Tabachnick, B. R. (in press). Improving parent involvement as school reform: Rhetoric or reality? In N. P. Greenman & K. Borman (Eds.), *Changing schools: Recapturing the past or inventing the future?* Norwood, NJ: Ablex.

Bogdan, R. C., & Biklen, S. K. (1982). *Qualitative research for education: An introduction to theory and methods.* Boston: Allyn & Bacon.

Boggs, S. T. (1985). *Speaking, relating, and learning: A study of Hawaiian children at home and at school.* Norwood, NJ: Ablex.

Bolster, A. S. (1983). Toward a more effective model of research as teaching. *Harvard Educational Review, 53,* 294–308.

Bruner, J. (1986). *Actual minds, possible worlds.* Cambridge, MA: Harvard University Press.

Bruner, J. (1990). *Acts of meaning.* Cambridge, MA: Harvard University Press.

Bruner, J., & Haste, H. (1987). *Making sense: The child's construction of reality.* New York: Methuen.

Byrnes, D. (1989). Attitudes of students, parents, and educators toward repeating a grade. In L. A. Shepard & M. L. Smith (Eds.), *Flunking grades: Research and policies on retention* (pp. 108–131). New York: Falmer.

Campbell, D. T. (1978). Qualitative knowing in action research. In M. Brenner, P. Marsh, & M. Brenner (Eds.), *The social context of method* (pp. 184–209). New York: St. Martin's.

Carlsson-Paige, N., & Levin, D. (1987). *The war play dilemma.* New York: Teachers College Press.

Cazden, C. (1988). *Classroom discourse: The language of teaching and learning.* Portsmouth, NH: Heinemann.

Clifford, J. (1988). *The predicament of culture: Twentieth-century ethnography, literature, and art.* Cambridge, MA: Harvard University Press.

Corsaro, W. A. (1979). "We're friends, right?": Children's use of access rituals in a nursery school. *Language in Society, 8,* 315–336.

Corsaro, W. A. (1985). *Friendship and peer culture in the early years.* Norwood, NJ: Ablex.

Corsaro, W. A. (1988). Routines in the peer culture of American and Italian nursery school children. *Sociology of Education, 61,* 1–14.

Corsaro, W. A., & Rizzo, T. (1988). *Discussione* and friendship: Socialization processes in the peer culture of Italian nursery school children. *American Sociological Review, 53,* 879–874.

Cox, S. T. (1990a). "Who the boss?": Dynamic tensions in oral storybook reading. *International Journal of Qualitative Studies in Education, 3,* 231–252.

Cox, S. T. (1990b). Reconciling theory and data: In situ analysis in a study of oral storybook reading. In M. J. McGee-Brown (Ed.), *Processes, applications, and ethics in qualitative research* (pp. 358–367). Athens, GA: University of Georgia.

D'Amato, J. (1986). *"We cool, tha's why": A study of personhood and place in Hawaiian second graders.* Unpublished doctoral dissertation: University of Hawaii.

D'Amato, J. (1988). "Acting": Hawaiian children's resistance to teachers. *The Elementary School Journal, 88,* 529–544.

Davies, B. (1989). *Frogs and snails and feminist tales: Preschool children and gender.* Sydney: Allyn & Unwin.

DeCoker, G. (1989). Japanese preschools: Academic or nonacademic? In J. Shields (Ed.), *Japanese schooling: Patterns of socialization, equality, and political control* (pp. 45–58). University Park, PA: Pennsylvania State University.

Delgado-Gaitan, C. (1990). *Literacy for empowerment: The role of parents in children's education.* New York: Falmer.

Delpit, L. (1986). Skills and other dilemmas of a progressive Black educator. *Harvard Educational Review, 56,* 379–385.

Delpit, L. (1988). The silenced dialogue: Power and pedagogy in educating other people's children. *Harvard Educational Review, 58,* 280–297.

Denzin, N. K. (1989). *Interpretive interactionism.* Newbury Park, CA: Sage.

Dewey, J. (1929). *The quest for certainty.* New York: Minton, Balch.

Dobbert, M. L. (1982). *Ethnographic research: Theory and application for modern schools and societies.* New York: Praeger.

Donaldson, M. (1978). *Children's minds.* New York: Norton.

Donmoyer, R. (1990). Generalizability and the single case study. In E. Eisner & A. Peshkin (Eds.), *Qualitative inquiry in education: The continuing debate* (pp. 175–200). New York: Teachers College Press.

Edwards, C., & Gandini, L. (1989). Teachers' expectations about the timing of developmental skills: A cross-cultural study. *Young Children, 44*(4), 15–19.

Edwards, C., Forman, G., & Gandini, L. (1992). *Education for all the children: The symbolic languages approach to early education in Reggio Emilia, Italy.* Norwood, NJ: Ablex.

Eisenhart, M. A., & Graue, M. E. (1990). Socially constructed readiness for school. *International Journal of Qualitative Studies in Education, 3,* 253–269.

Erickson, F. (1973). What makes school ethnography "ethnographic"? *Council on Anthropology and Education Quarterly, 4*(2), 10–19.

Erickson, F. (1986). Qualitative methods in research on teaching. In M. C. Wittrock (Ed.), *Handbook of research on teaching* (3rd ed., pp. 119–161). New York: Macmillan.

Erickson, F. (1989). *The meaning of validity in qualitative research.* Paper presented at the Annual Meeting of the American Educational Research Association, San Francisco.

Fernie, D. (1988). Becoming a student: Messages from first settings. *Theory into Practice, 27,* 3–10.

Fernie, D., Kantor, R., Klein, E., Meyer, C., & Elgas, P. (1988). Becoming students and becoming ethnographers in a preschool. *Journal of Research in Childhood Education, 3,* 132–141.

Fetterman, D. M. (1989). *Ethnography: Step by step.* Newbury Park, CA: Sage.

Fine, G. A., & Sandstrom, K. L. (1988). *Knowing children: Participant observation with children.* Newbury Park, CA: Sage.

Fishman, A. (1988). *Amish literacy: What and how it means.* Portsmouth, NH: Heinemann.

Foucault, M. (1978). *Discipline and punish: The birth of the prison.* New York: Pantheon.

Fujita, M., & Sano, T. (1988). Children at American and Japanese day care centers: Ethnography and reflective cross-cultural interviewing. In H. Trueba & C. Delgado-Gaitan (Eds.), *School and society: Learning content through culture* (pp. 73–97). New York: Praeger.

Gallimore, R., & Goldenberg, C. (in press). Activity settings of early literacy: Home and school factors in children's emergent literacy. In E. Forman, N. Minick, & C. A. Stone (Eds.), *Contexts for learning: Socialcultural dynamics in children's development.* Oxford: Oxford University Press.

Geertz, C. (1973). *The interpretation of cultures.* New York: Basic Books.

Geertz, C. (1986). Making experience, authoring selves. In V. W. Turner & E. M. Bruner (Eds.), *The anthropology of experience* (pp. 373–380). Urbana, IL: University of Illinois.

Genishi, C. (1988). Kindergartens and computers: A case study of six children. *Elementary School Journal, 89,* 185–201.

Goetz, J. P., & LeCompte, M. D. (1984). *Ethnography and qualitative design in educational research.* Orlando, FL: Academic Press.

Goldenberg, C. (1987). Low-income Hispanic parents' contributions to their first-grade children's word-recognition skills. *Anthropology and Education Quarterly, 18,* 149–179.

Goldenberg, C. (1989). Parents' effects on academic grouping for reading: Three case studies. *American Educational Research Journal, 26,* 329–352.

Goodenough, W. (1976). Multiculturalism as the normal human experience. *Anthropology and Education Quarterly, 7*(4), 4–7.

Gracey, H. L. (1975). Learning the student role: Kindergarten as academic bootcamp. In H. R. Stub (Ed.), *The sociology of education: A sourcebook* (pp. 82–85). Homewood, IL: Dorsey.

Grimshaw, A. (Ed.). (1982). *Sound-image records in social interaction research.* Special issue of *Journal of Sociological Methods and Research, 11*(2).

Graue, M. E. (1992). *Ready for what? Constructing meanings of readiness for kindergarten.* Albany, NY: SUNY Press.

Graue, M. E. (1991, April). Construction of community and the meaning of being a parent. Paper presented at the Annual Meeting of the American Educational Research Association, Chicago.

Hatch, J. A. (1990). Young children as informants in classroom studies. *Early Childhood Research Quarterly, 5,* 251–264.

Hatch, J. A., & Freeman, E. B. (1988). Kindergarten philosophies and practices: Perspectives of teachers, principals, and supervisors. *Early Childhood Research Quarterly, 3,* 151–166.

Heath, S. B. (1983). *Ways with words: Language, life, and work in communities and classrooms.* Cambridge, UK: Cambridge University Press.

Hendry, J. (1986). *Becoming Japanese.* Honolulu, HI: University of Hawaii.

Howe, K., & Eisenhart, M. (1990). Standards for qualitative (and quantitative) research: A prolegomenon. *Educational Researcher, 19*(4), 2–9.

Hubbard, R. (1989). *Author of pictures, draughtsman of words.* Portsmouth, NJ: Heinemann.

Hymes, D. (1982). Ethnographic monitoring. In H. Trueba, G. P. Guthrie, & D. H. Au (Eds.), *Culture in the bilingual classroom: Studies in classroom ethnography* (pp. 56–68). Rowley, MA: Newbury House.

Jackson, B. (1987). *Fieldwork.* Urbana, IL: University of Illinois.

Jacob, E. (1988). Clarifying qualitative research: A focus on traditions. *Educational Researcher, 17,* 16–24.

Jordan, C. (1977). *Maternal teaching modes and school adaptations in an urban Hawaiian population* (Technical report no. 67). Honolulu, HI: Kamehameha Schools/Bishop Estate, Kamehameha Educational Research Institute.

Jordan C. (1978). Teaching/learning interactions and school adaptations: The Hawaiian case. In *A multidisciplinary approach to research in education: The Kamehameha Early Education Program* (Technical report no. 81) (pp. 31–38). Honolulu, HI: Kamehameha Schools/Bishop Estate, Kamehameha Educational Research Institute.

Jordan, C. (1984). Cultural compatibility and the education of ethnic minority children. *Educational Research Quarterly, 8*(4), 59–71.

Jordan, C. (1985). Translating culture: From ethnographic information to educational program. *Anthropology and Education Quarterly, 16,* 106–123.

Kantor, R. (1988). Creating school meaning in preschool curriculum. *Theory into Practice, 27,* 25–35.

Kantor, R., Elgas, P., & Fernie, D. (1989). First the look and then the sound: Creating conversations at circle time. *Early Childhood Research Quarterly, 4,* 433–440.

Kessler, S., & Swadener, E. B. (1991). *Reconceptualizing Early Childhood Education.* Special issue of *Early Education and Development, 2*(2).

Lareau, A. (1989). *Home advantage.* London: Falmer.

Leavitt, R. L. (1991). Power and resistance in infant-toddler day care centers. In S. E. Cahill (Ed.), *Sociological studies of child development* (Vol; 4 pp. 91–112). Greenwich, CT: JAI.

Leavitt, R. L., & Power, M. B. (1989). Emotional socialization in the postmodern era: Children in day care. *Social Psychology Quarterly, 52,* 35–43.

LeCompte, M. D. (1980). The civilizing of children: How young children learn to become students. *The Journal of Thought, 15*(3), 105–127.

LeVine, R., & White, M. (1986). *Human conditions: The cultural basis of educational development.* London: Routledge & Kegan Paul.

Lewis, C. (1984). Cooperation and control in the Japanese nursery school. *Comparative Education Review, 28,* 69–84.

Lincoln, Y. S., & Guba, E. G. (1985). *Naturalistic Inquiry.* Newbury Park, CA: Sage.

Lubeck, S. (1985). *Sandbox society.* Philadelphia: Falmer.

Mandell, N. (1988). The least-adult role in studying children. *Journal of Contemporary Ethnography, 16,* 433–467.

Marcus, G., & Fisher, M. (1986). *Anthropology as cultural critique.* Chicago: University of Chicago Press.

McDermott, R. P. (1976). *Kids make sense: An ethnographic account of interactional management of success and failure in one first grade classroom.* Unpublished doctoral dissertation, Stanford University, Stanford, CA.

McDermott, R. P. (1982). Rigor and respect as standards in ethnographic description. *Harvard Educational Review, 52,* 321–328.

McDermott, R. P., Gospodinoff, K., & Aron, J. (1978). Criteria for ethnographically adequate description of concerted activities and their contexts. *Semiotics, 24,* 245–275.

Mead, M. (1963). *Sex and temperament in three primitive societies.* New York: Morrow.

Mehan, H. (1979). *Learning lessons: Social organization in the classroom.* Cambridge, MA: Harvard University Press.

Miller, P. (1982). *Amy, Wendy, and Beth: Learning language in South Baltimore.* Austin, TX: University of Texas.

Mishler, E. G. (1986). *Research interviewing: Context and narrative.* Cambridge, MA: Harvard University Press.

Nelson, M. (1986). *Negotiated care: The experience of family day care providers.* Philadelphia: Temple.

New, R. (1988). Parental goals and Italian infant care. In R. A. LeVine, R. Miller, & M. West (Eds.), *Parental behavior in diverse societies* (New Directions for Child Development number 40) (pp. 51–63). San Francisco: Jossey-Bass.

New, R. (1989). The family context of Italian child care. *Early Child Development and Care, 50,* 99–108.

New, R. (1990). Excellent early education: A city in Italy has it. *Young Children, 45*(6), 4–10.

New, R., & Benigni, L. (1987). Italian fathers and infants: Cultural constraints on paternal behavior. In M. Lamb (Ed.), *The father's role: Cross-cultural perspectives* (pp. 139–168). Hillsdale, NJ: Erlbaum.

Newkirk, T. (1989). *More than stories.* Portsmouth, NH: Heinemann.

Newkirk, T. (in press). Case studies in research in composition. In P. Sullivan (Ed.), *Approaches to composition research.* Portsmouth, NH: Heinemann.

Ogbu, John (1981). School ethnography: A multilevel approach. *Anthropology and Education Quarterly, 12,* 3–29.

Ott, D. (1991). *An analysis of kindergarten teachers' concerns.* Unpublished doctoral dissertation, University of Wisconsin-Madison.

Paley, V. G. (1979). *White teacher.* Cambridge, MA: Harvard University Press.

Paley, V. G. (1981). *Wally's stories.* Cambridge, MA: Harvard University Press.

Paley, V. G. (1984). *Boys and girls: Superheroes in the doll corner.* Chicago: University of Chicago Press.

Paley, V. G. (1986). *Molly is three.* Chicago: University of Chicago Press.

Paley, V. G. (1990). *The boy who would be a helicopter: The uses of storytelling in the classroom.* Cambridge, MA: Harvard University Press.

Parker, W. C. (1984). Interviewing children: Problems and promise. *Journal of Negro Education, 53,* 18–28.

Peak, L. (1986). Training learning skills and attitudes in Japanese early educational settings. In W. Fowler (Ed.), *Early experience and the development of competence* (pp. 111–123). San Francisco: Jossey-Bass.

Peshkin, A. (1988) Understanding complexity: A gift of qualitative inquiry. *Anthropology and Education Quarterly, 19,* 416–424.

Power, M. B. (1985). The ritualization of emotional conduct in early childhood. In N. K. Denzin (Ed.), *Studies in symbolic interaction* (Vol. 6, pp. 213–217). Greenwich, CT: JAI.

Power, M. B. (1986). Socializing of emotionality in early childhood: The influence of emotional associates. In P. Adler and P. Adler (Eds.), *Sociological studies of child development* (Vol. 1, pp. 259–282). Greenwich, CT: JAI.

Rich, A. (1989). Invisibility in academe. Quoted in R. Rosaldo, *Culture and truth: The remaking of social analysis.* Boston: Beacon Press.

Richman, A., LeVine, R., New, R., Howrigan, G., Welles-Nystrom, B., & LeVine, S. (1988). Maternal behavior to infants in five cultures. In R. LeVine, P. Miller, & M. West (Eds.), *Parental behavior in diverse societies* (pp. 81–97). San Francisco: Jossey-Bass.

Said, E. (1989). Representing the colonized: Anthropology's interlocutors. *Critical Inquiry, 15,* 205–225.

Shepard, L. A., & Smith, M. L. (1989). Academic and emotional effects of kindergarten retention in one school district. In L. A. Shepard & M. L. Smith (Eds.), *Flunking grades: Research and policies on retention* (pp. 79–107). New York: Falmer.

Shultz, J. & Florio, S. (1979). Stop and freeze: The negotiation of social and physical space in a kindergarten/first grade classroom. *Anthropology and Education Quarterly, 10,* 166–181.

Singelton, J. (1989). *Gambaru:* Perseverance in Japanese early education. In J. Shields (Ed.), *Japanese schooling: Patterns of socialization, equality, and political control* (pp. 8–15). University Park, PA: Pennsylvania State University.

Sluckin, A. (1981). *Growing up in the playground.* London: Routledge & Kegan Paul.

Smith, M. L., & Shepard, L. A. (1989). Kindergarten readiness and retention: A qualitative study of teachers' beliefs and practices. *American Educational Research Journal, 25,* 307–333.

Spindler, G. D. (Ed.). (1982). *Doing the ethnography of schooling: Educational anthropology in action*. New York: Holt, Rinehart & Winston.

Spindler, G. D., & Spindler, L. (1987). *Interpretive ethnography of education: At home and abroad*. New York: Holt, Rinehart & Winston.

Spradley, J. P. (1979). *The ethnographic interview*. New York: Holt, Rinehart & Winston.

Spradley, J. P. (1980). *Participant observation*. New York: Holt, Rinehart & Winston.

Super, C., & Harkness, S. (1986). The developmental niche: A conceptualization at the interface of child and culture. *International journal of behavioral development, 9*, 545–569.

Suransky, V. P. (1982). *The erosion of childhood*. Chicago: University of Chicago Press.

Swadener, E. B. (1988). *Toward teaching peace and social responsibility in the early elementary years: A Friends school case study* (Scholarly Report Series No. 27). University Park, PA: Center for the Study of Child and Adolescent Development, Pennsylvania State University.

Tammivaara, J., & Enright, D. S. (1986). On eliciting information: Dialogues with child informants. *Anthropology and Education Quarterly, 17*, 218–238.

Taylor, D. (1983). *Family literacy: Young children learning to read and write*. Exeter, NH: Heinemann.

Taylor, D. (1991). *Learning denied*. Portsmouth, NJ: Heinemann.

Taylor, D., & Dorsey-Gaines, Catherine (1988). *Growing up literate: Learning from inner city families*. Portsmouth, NJ: Heinemann.

Tharp, R. G., & Gallimore, R. (1988). *Rousing minds to life*. New York: Cambridge University Press.

Tobin, J. (1989). Visual anthropology and multivocal ethnography: A dialogical approach to Japanese preschool class size. *Dialectical Anthropology, 13*, 173–187.

Tobin, J., & Davidson, D. (1990). The ethics of polyvocal ethnography: Empowering versus textualizing children and teachers. *International Journal of Qualitative Studies in Education, 3*, 271–283.

Tobin, J., Davidson, D., & Wu, D. (1987). Class size and student-teacher ratios in the Japanese preschool. *Comparative Education Review, 31*, 533–549.

Tobin, J., Wu, D., & Davidson, D. (1989). *Preschool in three cultures: Japan, China, and the United States*. New Haven, CT: Yale University Press.

Wacksler, F. C. (1986). Studying children: Phenomenological insights. *Human Studies, 9*, 71–92.

Walsh, D. J., Baturka, N. L., Colter, N., & Smith, M. E. (1991). Changing one's mind—maintaining one's identity: A first grade teacher's story. *Teachers College Record, 93*, 73–86.

Walsh, D. J., Smith, M. E., Alexander, M., & Ellwein, M. C. (in press). The Curriculum as Mysterious and Constraining: Teachers' Negotiations of the First Year of a Pilot Program for At-Risk 4-Year-Olds. *Journal of Curriculum Studies*.

Walsh, D. J., Smith, M. E., & Baturka, N. L. (1992). The two-year route to first grade: Administrative decisions and children's lives. *Educational Foundations, 6*, 67–84.

Walsh, D. J., Smith, M. S., Eiden, J., Endahl, J., Lear, C., Czerwinski, B., Dwier, A., White, P., Asti, M., Clement, L., & Baturka, N. L. (1989, October). *Conversations: "How do we know what we're thinking until we hear what we say?"* Paper presented at the annual Bergamo Conference on Curriculum Theory, Dayton, OH.

Watson-Gegeo, K. (1988). Ethnography in ESL: Defining the essential. *TESOL Quarterly, 22*, 575–592.

White, M. (1987). *The Japanese educational challenge: A commitment to children*. New York: Free Press.

White, M., & LeVine, R. (1986). What is an *Ii ko?* In R. Stevenson, H. Azuma, & K. Hakuta (Eds.), *Child development in Japan* (pp. 55–62). New York: Freeman.

Whiting, B. B., & Edwards, C. (1988). *Children of different worlds*. Cambridge, MA: Harvard University Press.

Whiting, B. B., & Whiting, J. W. M. (1975). *Children of six cultures: A psychocultural analysis*. Cambridge, MA: Harvard University Press.

Wolcott, H. F. (1980). *How to look like an anthropologist without really being one*. Paper presented at the Annual Meeting of the American Educational Research Association, Boston.

Wolcott, H. F. (1988). Ethnographic research in education. In Richard Jaeger (Ed.), *Complementary methods for research in education*. Washington, DC: American Educational Research Association.

Wolcott, H. F. (1990a). On seeking—and rejecting—validity in qualitative research. In E. W. Eisner & A. Peshkin (Eds.), *Qualitative inquiry in education: The continuing debate* (pp. 121–152). New York: Teachers College Press.

Wolcott, H. F. (1990b). *Writing up qualitative research*. Newbury Park, CA: Sage.

Yin, R. K. (1989). *Case study research*. Newbury Park, CA: Sage.

Zinsser, C. (1986). For the Bible tells me so: Teaching children in a fundamentalist church. In B. B. Schieffelin & P. Gilmore (Eds.), *The acquisition of literacy: Ethnographic perspectives* (pp. 55–71). Norwood, NJ: Ablex.

· 30 ·

STUDYING EDUCATIONAL SETTINGS

Thelma Harms and Richard M. Clifford

FRANK PORTER GRAHAM CHILD DEVELOPMENT CENTER,

UNIVERSITY OF NORTH CAROLINA AT CHAPEL HILL

Beginning sometime between the age of 4 years 8 months and 5 years 11 months most children enter either public or private kindergarten. The National Household Education Survey found that among children in first and second grade in early 1991, only 2% had not attended some form of kindergarten (West, Hausken, Chandler, & Collins, 1991). However, kindergarten is by no means the first early educational setting for a majority of American children. Increasingly over the past 40 years, children have been exposed to educational experiences outside their home prior to school entry. In a recent study (Clifford, Wenger, Lubeck, Gallagher, & Harms, 1988; Garrett, Wenger, Lubeck, & Clifford, 1989), three quarters of the children registering for public school kindergarten were reported by their parents to have been in some type of nonparental child care or educational setting during the year before entering school. The preliminary findings of the National Household Education Survey appear to confirm this high level of use of nonparental care prior to school entry for the country as a whole (West et al., 1991).

For the past 3 decades much attention has been focused on the potential effects of these nonparental settings on children. Studies of the effects of early childhood care and education on child development from the mid-1960s to the late 1970s tended largely to view all out-of-home care settings as a common treatment. Maternal attachment and intellectual development were used as the major outcome measures in order to detect any harmful effects of out-of-home care, but relatively little was done to document and evaluate the practices of the early childhood settings. In the late 1970s studies comparing the effects of different types of out-of-home settings, such as the New York City Infant Day Care Study (Golden, Rosenbluth, Grossi, Policare, Freeman, and Brownlees, 1979) started to focus more attention on the nature of the setting itself. During the 1980s quality of setting became an important dimension of studies looking at child outcomes. The level of quality in both family child care and center-based care was shown to be associated with process variables, such as adult-child interaction, and child outcomes, such as language and social behavior (McCartney, Scarr, Phillips, Grajek, & Schwarz, 1982; Howes & Rubenstein, 1985; Howes & Stewart, 1987; Kontos & Fiene, 1987; McCartney, 1984; Goelman & Pence, 1988; Phillips, McCartney, & Scarr, 1987; Phillips & Howes, 1987; Doherty, 1991). In addition to studying the effect of quality of the educational setting on children, studies in the late 1980s sometimes addressed public policy issues by studying contextual factors outside the classroom that influence the quality of settings (Whitebook, Howes, & Phillips, 1989).

In this chapter we will examine some of the important issues that inform the study of educational settings. We will explore the diversity of early childhood programs through a taxonomy, consider the implication of a theoretical framework that links contextual with intraprogram dynamics, and examine a number of global quality-assessment instruments for early childhood settings.

DIVERSITY OF EARLY CHILDHOOD SETTINGS

At no other time in their lives are students exposed to such a wide variety of educational settings as they are during the preschool years. If we are to deal effectively with this diversity, a taxonomy is a good place to begin a study of educational settings. Table 30–1 depicts the range of settings children are potentially exposed to for major portions of their lives before entry into the traditional pattern of school attendance.

The first major distinction in the taxonomy is between home and center settings. These 2 settings are quite different physically. Homes are generally designed for adults, as illustrated by the necessity to child proof a home when infants begin to crawl and walk. Parents, for example, put safety gates on stairwells to protect their children from falls, and they provide steps and a toilet seat adapter to permit independence in toileting. The

TABLE 30–1. Taxonomy of Early Childhood
Educational Settings

I. Home settings
  A. Child's own home
    1. Parent care primarily
    2. Nonparental care
      a. Relative care
      b. Nonrelative care
  B. Family day-care home
    1. Licensed or registered home
    2. Unregulated home
II. Center-based settings
  A. Part-day programs
    1. Private part-day or part-week preschool
    2. Head Start
    3. School-based prekindergarten
  B. Full-day child-care centers
    1. Church-related centers
    2. Other nonprofit centers
    3. Interstate chain proprietary centers
    4. Independent proprietary centers
    5. Unregulated centers

need for modification is even greater in a home setting used for family child care. In a Canadian study of 300 informal family day care providers, Johnson and Dineen (1981) found that care givers seriously restricted the activity of the children because of concern with "protecting their home from the children and with protecting the children from potential hazards in the home" (p. 142). Johnson and Dineen express concern about the restrictions placed on children in home day care settings that are contrary to the developmental need for active play and exploration.

Modifying homes to meet the needs of young children takes conscious effort. In a study of 25 homes that had achieved a good balance of use by both adults and children (about half private residences and half family child care homes), Johnson, Shack, and Oster (1980) found that 80% had renovated their homes to be more suitable for children. These homes allowed children considerably more freedom to use various parts of the home, family furnishings, and equipment for play. The authors point out that incorporating children to this degree in a home setting requires not only physical renovations, but also a belief in the value of children's activities and a flexible attitude toward the use of the home itself.

Prescott (1987) presents a picture of child-centered home-based settings in her comparison of family child care homes and centers. She characterizes home-care settings as having a greater variety of furnishings and objects for play, more provisions for privacy, fewer interruptions, a cozier, softer, and more relaxing atmosphere, and more opportunities for personalized play. In contrast, she characterizes the child care centers she studied as more institutionalized settings with standardized furnishings that are "woefully simple compared to naturally occurring environments such as homes and neighborhoods" (Prescott, 1987, p. 86). Prescott also reports that centers imposed more time constraints, were more schedule conscious,

and offered less softness and privacy. The family settings were associated with richer play and longer, more involved conversations. Her characterizations of home and center settings contradict somewhat the findings of the New York City Infant Day Care Study (Golden et al., 1979), where centers were found to be more stimulating.

Given the differences between center and home child care settings, it is not surprising that separate instruments for assessing the quality of family child care homes and child care centers have been developed (Harms & Clifford, 1980, 1989; Abbott-Shim & Sibley, 1987a, b, c). It should be clear that results from research on one type of setting may be generalized to the other only with great caution, if at all.

Within home settings, the taxonomy presented here differentiates between the child's own home and that of a family day care home. Further, within the child's own home, settings where children are cared for primarily by their parents are differentiated from those with a nonparental care giver such as a nanny, relative, or other adult. Little work has been done to illuminate the differences in the home settings with and without a nonparental care giver. The importance of understanding the impact of these home situations is, however, highlighted by the recent report that 28 percent of all children now receive home-based care by a relative and 27 percent by a nonrelative prior to school entry (West et al., 1991).

Data from the National Child Care Survey revealed that family day care (defined as care in another person's home) was used almost exclusively by employed mothers. Use of this type of care decreased from 27% for employed mothers of infants and toddlers to 16% of employed mothers of 3- and 4-year-olds. Such care was used by only 3% of unemployed mothers of infants and toddlers and 1% of unemployed mothers of preschoolers (Willer, Hofferth, Kisker, Divine-Hawkins, Farquhar, & Glantz, 1990).

Family day care homes are categorized into regulated and unregulated settings. While little work has been done to examine unregulated child care in general, the National Family Day Care Home study (Fosburg, 1981) documented significant differences in regulated and unregulated homes in the United States. Similarly, Stuart and Pepper (1988) found in Canada that regulated family day care homes were consistently rated higher in overall child care quality than unregulated settings. While the lack of consistent definitions of licensing and registration across the United States makes any distinction between the two types of homes meaningless in a practical sense, the variation in regulation from state to state may be significant (Morgan, 1987).

The actual number of family day care homes in the United States is not clear. The National Child Care Survey (Hofferth, Brayfield, Deich, & Holcomb, 1991) estimates that there were between 550,000 and 1.1 million unregulated homes in 1990. A comparison study, the Profile of Child Care Settings (Kisker, Hofferth, Phillips, & Farquhar, 1991) estimates only about 118,000 regulated family day care homes.

Center-based settings are grouped into two categories, part day and full day. As with family day care, there is little research comparing part- and full-day programs. However, there is some evidence that programs of different length of day have differential impact on children. For example, for very young children there is some increase in the chances of infection in programs that operate for longer periods of time per day.

Part-day center-based programs are further subdivided into private programs, Head Start programs, and school-based prekindergarten programs. While there is a substantial research base on Head Start programs, little is known about how they compare with other part-day programs. Furthermore, current efforts to wrap child care services around Head Start part-day and part-year programs will have unknown consequences on the effect of Head Start programs on the children served. While Head Start and public school programs both serve primarily disadvantaged children, the public school programs have grown to be a substantial effort only in the very recent past. Private part-day programs tend to serve a more affluent population and were originally begun to provide a socializing function in contrast to the aim of both Head Start and Chapter 1 programs to prepare children cognitively for school. Thus one would expect to find differences among these settings.

The final category of early childhood settings in the taxonomy is full-day child care centers. A growing percentage of care is being provided to children in full-day centers in the United States (Hayes, Palmer, & Zaslow, 1990). However, there are significant variations in full-day child care that necessitate dividing this category into a number of subgroups. One such subgroup is church-operated programs. In a National Council of Churches survey of some 25,000 parishes in 1982, nearly one third reported some form of child care offered on their premises (Linder, Mattis, & Rogers, 1983). The more recent Profile of Child Care Settings study (Kisker et al., 1991) estimated that 14.9% of all centers were religious-sponsored programs. Thus a significant portion of child care centers are church-operated programs, and we have included them as a separate category.

Another distinction that exists among child care centers is between nonprofit and for-profit centers. As indicated in the National Council of Churches survey, a substantial group of church-housed programs are not operated by the churches and are usually operated by another nonprofit group. Research indicates that these nonprofit centers are in many ways different from the for-profit sector. The National Child Care Staffing Study (Whitebook et al., 1989) and other smaller studies (Russell, Clifford, & Warlick, 1990) indicate that for-profit programs are more likely to pay lower wages to employees, employ staff with less training, and provide care rated lower in overall quality than their nonprofit counterparts. It therefore seems prudent to consider nonprofit centers separately from the proprietary sector.

Little is currently known about differences between the small operators of child care centers and the large interstate chains. It is hoped that a current study of centers that includes a large number of proprietary settings will provide much needed insight into the nature of the settings available in this rapidly growing segment of the child care industry (Scarr, 1991). In the taxonomy, we have chosen to place the small and large operators into separate categories.

Finally, we have created a category for unregulated centers. Church-operated centers are exempt from licensing in a number of states. However, they typically have some supervision for basic health and safety, or at least some oversight by church officials, and would be categorized also in the church-operated category already described. Most state regulators consider this group to be negligible in number, but in a few states there are relatively large numbers of unregulated programs of this type.

A number of other program characteristics could be used to identify an even more finely grained taxonomy. Variables such as size of program, ages of children served, urban versus rural location, and focus on children with special needs are all thought to have some relation to setting characteristics. While we do not advocate further divisions in the taxonomy, careful reporting of all program features when presenting research results is essential for accurate interpretation and as a safeguard against overgeneralization of results.

There has been a tendency to generalize the findings of studies of one type of setting to all early childhood settings. Perhaps the most significant example of this type of overgeneralization in recent years has been the extrapolation of the findings of the Perry Preschool Project (Berrueta-Clement, Schweinhart, Barnett, Epstein, & Weikart, 1984) to apply to a broad range of early childhood settings, from Head Start programs to day care centers (132 Congressional Record, 1986; Committee for Economic Development, 1987; Blinder, 1987). The effects of a particular part-day program for children at risk for school failure have been used to justify a broad range of early childhood programs. While these generalizations have typically been made by advocates or others not associated with the research projects, it is clear that research must clarify the relationship between program characteristics and child outcomes (Haskins, 1989).

STUDYING SETTINGS IN CONTEXT

The diversity of educational setting types exists within a larger contextual framework. The importance of contextual influences on child care and other educational settings is recognized in the formulations of Bronfenbrenner (1977, 1979), Moos (1980), Whitebook, Howes, and Phillips (1989), and Doherty (1991). Bronfenbrenner conceptualized the environment as a nested set of spheres of influence on children. His work initiated a rethinking of the way in which early childhood professionals view learning settings for young children.

At the heart of Bronfenbrenner's model is the immediate setting containing the developing individual—the microsystem. Factors outside the microsystem may also have a significant, direct impact on the individual. This set of factors is referred to as the mesosystem. A third level of influence on the development of the individual, the exosystem, includes events that occur where the individual is not even present but nevertheless indirectly influence what is happening to the individual and thus influence that individual's development. Bronfenbrenner argues that there is still a fourth level of influence on the development of individuals. This fourth level includes influences of the culture and subculture within which the individual develops and is referred to as the macrosystem (Bronfenbrenner, 1979).

As we apply this framework to the study of educational settings, we are concerned primarily with the influences on the child in the immediate setting itself and, to a lesser extent, on the direct and indirect influences on that setting from the outside. That is, we are concerned with the microsystem and somewhat with the mesosystem and exosystem. We do not try to include the larger cultural influences in the model, but we recognize that many of the components of the microsystem, mesosystem, and exosystem are in fact expressions of the larger culture.

Figure 30–1 shows the educational setting influenced directly by a number of external forces, depicted in the model in the ring of forces immediately surrounding the central circle.

The outer ring of forces represents the exosystem—forces that indirectly influence the development of the child, most typically through their impact on the teacher or care giver responsible for the child and also on the physical environment of the immediate educational system. We have indicated some of the major influences; however, there are certainly others that may be quite important in a given educational setting.

At the center of the model is the immediate educational setting in which the child is situated. Often that setting includes a group of children along with the adults responsible for the group. We will return to discuss this immediate setting in detail, but for the moment we will focus on the set of factors in the mesosystem and exosystem that impact the child

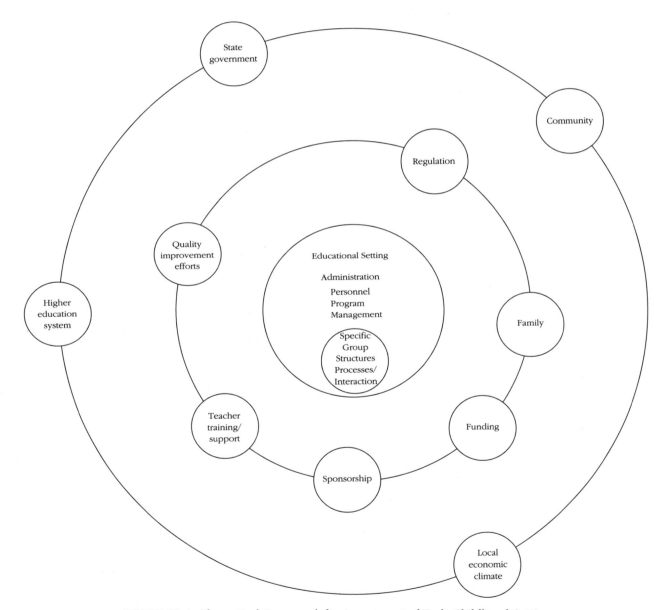

FIGURE 30–1. Theoretical Framework for Assessment of Early Childhood Settings

and the setting. *Regulation* of family day care homes, child-care centers, or schools by the community and state has obvious and profound consequences on the operation of the setting. Whitebook, Howes, and Phillips (1989) in their study of child care centers in 5 U.S. metropolitan areas documented the impact of various regulations in these areas on the quality of care observed. In family day care homes in Canada, Pepper and Stuart (1985) found that regulated homes scored significantly higher on measures of quality of environment than unregulated homes, especially on those aspects that were covered in the regulations. *Quality improvement efforts* in communities are designed to influence the environments available to children. These efforts may be referred to as school reform, as child care quality improvement, or as parent education, but in each case they target the improvement of the settings available to young children. These efforts are frequently linked to *teacher training and support* programs of provider organizations, resource and referral agencies, school systems, community and technical colleges, and other institutions of higher education.

Settings under the *sponsorship* of some larger organizations, such as child care food program umbrella agencies, school systems, or Head Start agencies, are often required to adhere to the regulations or guidelines of the sponsoring agency. In addition, teachers often receive training and other forms of support from their sponsors. Funding for the programs also has an obvious impact on the ability of the teacher or care giver to equip and operate the program. While little has been done to examine the impact of funding on the quality of programs, 2 studies illustrate the connection. In child care centers in the Los Angeles area, Olenick (1986) found that the expenditure per child was directly related to the quality of care provided and, further, that the proportion of the total budget of a program devoted to staff compensation was also correlated with quality. Similar connections between cost and quality were found in the National Child Care Staffing Study (Whitebook et al., 1989). Funding of programs is profoundly affected by the *economic climate* in the community. While the economic climate is not seen as directly impacting the child in the educational setting, its indirect influence is substantial. Thus the economic influences are shown in the outer circle of the model, the exosystem.

The close tie between early educational settings and the families whose children are in those settings is a hallmark of high-quality programs. In fact, the relationship is often one in which the families and the care giver are both members of the same, close-knit *community*. Here we show the *family* as more directly influencing the child in the educational setting and thus a part of the mesosystem. The influences of the community are seen as more indirect and thus a part of the exosystem. It is surprising that so little research has been done to document and understand the impact of the nature and strength of the community relationships on the development of children in early educational settings.

It is in the context of these and other influences that educational settings have their impact on young children. Our assessment procedures do not ordinarily address these mesosystem and exosystem factors directly. But it is imperative that the study of educational settings take these external factors into account when decisions are made about what should be assessed, how the assessment should be conducted, and how the findings should be interpreted. For example, family day care homes are often not subject to regulation by public health authorities. Thus assessment instruments for family day care must be more specific about the health and safety concerns of children than instruments for day care centers that are typically inspected by health inspectors as part of the licensing procedure.

The primary focus of measurement is on the educational settings themselves. Figures 30–2 and 30–3 (on pages 482 and 483) give a more detailed view of key aspects of all settings in the major types of early childhood settings. Figure 30–2 depicts the family day care home. The most striking feature of the model is the overlapping responsibilities of the family-based care giver for the child care group and for the care giver's personal family. These 2 spheres of the care giver's life each are further divided into 2 dimensions, *structure* and *processes/interactions*. Goelman and Pence (1987a, 1987b) have pointed out the importance of considering both structural and process dimensions of home-based care and center-based care for young children. As our model shows, both dimensions are important in determining the ultimate quality of the family child care experience for children in that setting. The structural or frame conditions in both the child care and personal family spheres include components related to *people, space-materials,* and *recurring patterns.* The particulars of each of these components of the structure and process dimensions in the child care and personal family domains sometimes overlap.

In addition to the child care group and personal family responsibility spheres, there is an administrative function that does not involve the children directly but nevertheless has significant impact on them. The *personnel, program,* and *management* features of administration are shown in Figure 30–2 only for the child care portion of the total operation of the home. It is important to recognize that family day care givers have administrative concerns paralleling those of other forms of nonparental care and education settings in our society. Family child care home administration includes *personnel* concerns, such as hiring and training of substitute providers; *program concerns,* such as providing appropriate toys, books, and other resources for play; and *management* concerns, such as meeting regulatory requirements.

The family day care home is a complex microsystem constantly influenced by its external environment and, in turn, exerting influence on those environments. Assessment systems must be designed to deal with the complexity and fluidity of the setting. A particular difficulty from a measurement point of view is that these various aspects of the family child care setting are not independent of one another.

Figure 30–3 shows the model expressed for a center-based program. The basic dimensions of the setting are the same as those described for the family day care home. The most obvious difference is that there are multiple groups of children within a single facility, each group forming its own microsystem. The management functions, here referred to as administration, increase in magnitude as the size of the program increases, but

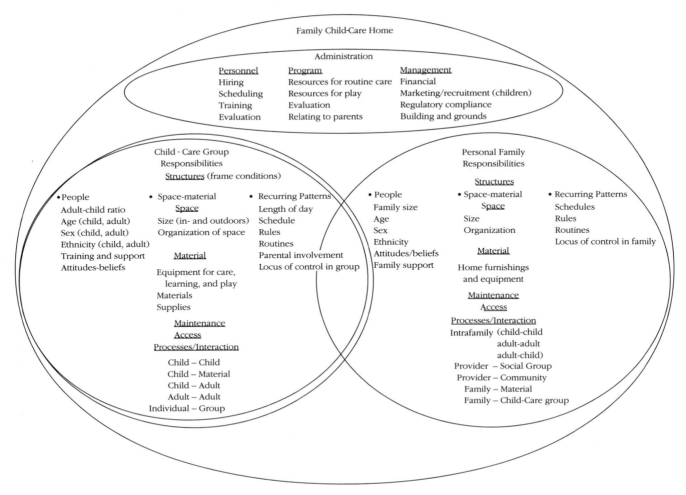

FIGURE 30–2. Family Child Care Home

again the same basic categories of administration are present—personnel, program, and management. For each of the groups or classes the structures and processes/interactions dimensions would contain the same categories of concern presented in Figure 30–2 for the family day care setting.

This theoretical framework suggests that key dimensions of structure and process operate across the various early educational settings listed in the taxonomy. We turn next to the real world to see whether there is empirical validation of these theoretical constructs and to note the degree to which assessment instruments address these constructs in the various types of settings.

IDENTIFYING THE KEY COMPONENTS OF EDUCATIONAL SETTINGS

Despite the extensive variation in early childhood programs, there have been important advances in identifying the key components common to all early educational settings. In 1974

the Child Development Associate (CDA) competency goals and functional areas were developed for staff in early childhood center-based group programs, and in 1983 they were applied to family child care homes. The 7 CDA functional areas focus on teacher competence including (1) maintaining a safe, healthy, learning environment; (2) enhancing children's physical and intellectual competence; (3) supporting social-emotional development; (4) using positive guidance methods; (5) establishing productive relationships with families; (6) establishing effective program management; and (7) maintaining a commitment to professionalism (Council for Early Childhood Professional Recognition, 1985).

In 1984 the National Association for the Education of Young Children (NAEYC) published *Accreditation Criteria and Procedures* for quality early childhood programs and launched its accreditation procedure for centers and schools. All types of center-based programs are eligible, including child care, preschool and kindergarten, public and private, and full or part day. In contrast to the CDA, which is awarded to the teacher, the NAEYC accreditation is awarded to the program. The quality

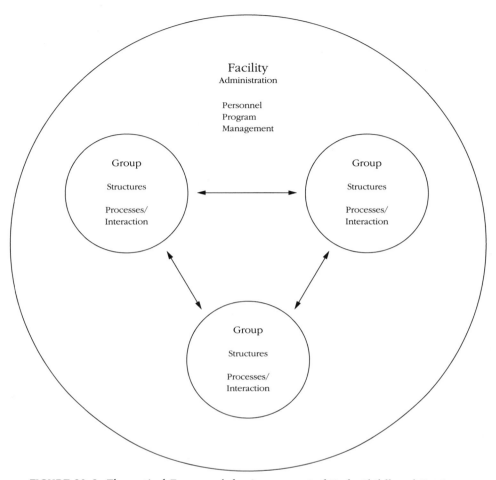

FIGURE 30–3. Theoretical Framework for Assessment of Early Childhood Settings

criteria cover interactions among staff and children, curriculum, staff-parent interaction, staff qualifications and development, staffing patterns, physical environment, health and safety, and nutrition and food service.

In 1988 the National Association for Family Day Care (NAFDC) began its accreditation process for family day care providers. Included in the NAFDC quality criteria are indoor safety, health, nutrition, play environment, interaction, outdoor play, and professional responsibility.

Although targeting different settings, all three accreditation/credentialing systems have common components: interaction, environment (including health and safety), curriculum activities, relating to parents, and professional development. In addition, the NAEYC center accreditation and the NAFDC day care home accreditation include a management/administration component.

An insight into which of the quality criteria are considered of greater importance comes from a survey conducted by NAEYC during the development of their accreditation process. The survey was sent to 250 early childhood specialists and had a return rate of 78%. Each one of the accreditation criteria was rated on

a 4-point scale: 4 = essential, 3 = important, 2 = somewhat important, and 1 = unimportant. All criteria obtained mean scores between 3 and 4, which attests to the validity of the entire system. Table 30–2 lists the 14 criteria with mean scores of 3.8 and above that Bredekamp (1989) calls the "live or die" criteria, those that determine success or failure in accreditation decisions.

While the 3 recognition programs—CDA, NAEYC, and NAFDC—give the current professional view of key components of quality early childhood programs, several recent factor analyses of preschool/kindergarten classroom ratings also help us gain insight into empirically based key components. A factor analysis of assessments of 3- to 6-year-olds in child care, preschool, and kindergarten groups using the *Early Childhood Environment Rating Scale (ECERS)*, a recognized global quality-assessment instrument, yielded 4 factors (Rossbach, Clifford, & Harms, 1991). These factors were teacher stimulation, which taps the teacher's stimulation of child development and includes items such as language stimulation, tone of interaction, and supervision; space and materials, which focuses on the availability of materials and arrangement of space as

TABLE 30–2. Accreditation Criteria Rated Most Important by Early Childhood Specialists

Component	Criterion	Mean
Health and safety	The center is licensed.	3.874
	Written health records are maintained.	3.802
	Children are under adult supervision at all times.	3.889
	Staff wash hands before feeding, after diapering.	3.837
	Dangerous chemicals, medicines are safely stored.	3.912
Interactions	Staff interact frequently with children, showing affection and respect.	3.933
	Staff are responsive to children, listen.	3.905
	Staff speak with individual children in a friendly, positive manner.	3.855
	Staff use positive techniques of guidance.	3.917
Curriculum	Staff plan developmentally appropriate activities.	3.827
	Schedule provides a balance of child-initiated/teacher-initiated, quiet/active, indoor/outdoor activities.	3.793
Staffing	Group size is limited.	3.794
	Staff-child ratio is appropriate.	3.874
Staff qualifications	Staff are trained in child development or early childhood education.	3.803

prerequisites for learning, including blocks, art, free play, group time, and room arrangement; routine care, which includes activities to meet the physical-care needs of the child, such as meals, toileting and grooming; and provisions for motor development, which includes gross and fine motor space and equipment.

A factor analysis of the Early Childhood Classroom Observation, the instrument used in the NAEYC accreditation process (Bredekamp, 1989) yielded 3 factors: preschool curriculum, which includes a number of activities to encourage language and physical development; positive interactions, which includes staff responsiveness, positive behavior guidance, and encouragement of prosocial behavior; and balanced schedule of activity, which includes items related to scheduling of indoor/outdoor, quiet/active, and individual/group. Despite the difference in instruments, there is a basic similarity between these 2 factor analyses (see Table 30–3 on page 485). Both sets of empirically derived factors underscore the importance of structure and process variables in quality child care. They also support the importance of 3 key areas in the classroom—interaction, activities, and routines—identified in the theoretical framework as people/interaction, space/material, and recurring patterns. Additional factor and cluster analyses of other quality-assessment instruments are needed to further specify the basic components of quality care.

SOURCES OF INFORMATION ABOUT SETTING COMPONENTS

There are a number of different ways to study the various setting components. Inspection of documents and records is an appropriate way to check on operating policies, regulatory compliance, and various administrative functions. Reports from staff about aspects of the program that are not observed can give additional information, and questionnaire responses from parents and staff can provide insights into how well the program is meeting their needs. But it is only through observation of children and staff as they function in a setting that we can judge the implementation of the curriculum, the tone of the interpersonal interactions, and the responsiveness of the physical environment.

Using the NAEYC accreditation procedure as an example of incorporating observation, documentation, and reporting as sources of information about programs, we can identify the areas best-suited to each information source. Observation in the classroom is a primary source for information about staff/child interaction, curriculum activities, physical environment, and to a lesser extent health and safety provisions and staff-to-child ratio. An interview with the director and questionnaire responses from parents and staff provide information about curriculum planning, staff/parent communication, parent conferences, staff inservice, staff understanding of administrative policies, and evaluation procedures. Documents are inspected to gain information about program philosophy, curriculum planning, administrative policies, administrative procedures, staff qualification, staffing, licensing, and health and safety inspections.

Another important issue in assessment brought to the fore by the various accreditation processes is the value of self-assessment by teachers and directors. Both the NAEYC center accreditation and the NAFDC family day care home accreditation have the candidate do a self-assessment using the same instrument that is used by the validator. The use of self-assessment is an effective means for stimulating self-improvement.

In addition to considering different sources of information we must also consider two different orientations toward the study of settings, namely quantitative and qualitative approaches. Quantitative methods typically structure the research instruments beforehand, deciding on the most pertinent categories and questions based on previous knowledge of the subject. Questions are predetermined for interviews and questionnaires, categories set for recording observations, and scales devised to focus on key components. Quantitative methods try to ensure objectivity and lead to data suitable for statistical analysis. Qualitative methods, on the other hand, are more open ended, consisting of detailed descriptions of ongoing situations and interactions, including direct quotations, without attempting to fit the data into predetermined categories at the outset. Qualitative methods use the subjective experiences of the observer, who is allowed to become identified with the object of the observation and thereby to extract a depth of meaning.

Educators and psychologists are generally more familiar with quantitative methods. Qualitative methods, commonly

TABLE 30–3. Comparison of 2 Factor Analyses

Interaction

ECERS		NAEYC Classroom Observation	
Factor 1: Teacher Stimulation	Loadings	**Factor 2: Positive Interactions**	Loadings
14. Informal language	.74	1. Staff interact frequently with children.	.75
12. Using language	.73	2. Staff are responsive to children.	.67
13. Reasoning	.63	3. Staff speak in a friendly, courteous way.	.67
32. Tone	.63	74. Staff are flexible.	.57
11. Understanding language	.62	75. Routines are individualized.	.57
16. Supervision (fine motor)	.62	12. Staff encourage prosocial behaviors.	.53
27. Supervision (creative)	.55	7. Staff use positive guidance.	.51
26. Schedule (creative)	.48	10. Children are comfortable, relaxed, involved.	.49
10. Child related display	.47	8. Staff do not use physical punishment.	.44
29. Free play	.46	11. Staff help children deal with anger, sadness, frustrations.	.43
30. Group time	.45	9. Sound of group is pleasant.	.41
21. Art	.43		
15. Fine motor	.41		

Space/Materials

ECERS		NAEYC Classroom Observation	
Factor 2: Space/Material		**Factor 1: Preschool Curriculum**	
23. Blocks	.66	64. Develop social skills.	.94
30. Group time	.59	66. Encourage language development.	.94
9. Room Arrangement	.56	67. Enhance physical development.	.92
29. Free play	.54	69. Encourage creative expression.	92
7. Learning furnishings	.54	65. Encourage children to think, reason, question, experiment.	.91
21. Art	.53	68. Encourage health, safety, nutrition.	.86
24. Sand/water	.48	63. Foster positive self-concept.	.78
8. Relaxation furnishings	.45	59. Appropriate materials for preschoolers.	.76
28. Space (alone)	.40	70. Respect cultural diversity.	.74
Factor 4: Motor Activity			
17. Gross-motor space	.60		
18. Gross-motor equipment	.48		
15. Fine motor	.42		

Recurring Patterns

ECERS		NAEYC Classroom Observation	
Factor 3: Routine Care		**Factor 3: Balanced Schedule of Activity**	
2. Meals	.53	51. Balance of quiet/active play.	.87
4. Toilet	.52	53. Balance of large/small-muscle activity.	.82
5. Grooming	.49	52. Balance of individual/small-group/large-group activities.	.81
7. Learning furnishing	.49	54. Balance of child/staff-initiated activities.	.78
24. Sand/water	.44		

used in anthropology, are also used for case studies in various social service fields. Lubeck (1985) reports a comprehensive definition of the qualitative approach by Bauman as "the process of constructing through direct personal observations of social behavior, a theory of the workings of a particular culture in terms as close as possible to the way members of that culture view the universe and organize their behavior within it" (p. 182).

Increasingly it is being recognized that educational programs are complex social systems that require a combination of quantitative and qualitative methods of study. For example, the Comprehensive Child Development Program, funded in 24 different sites throughout the United States by the Administration on Children, Youth and Families, employs an ethnographer at each site to provide qualitative data, in addition to collecting extensive quantitative data. These programs are working comprehensively with the economically stressed families of infants and toddlers, providing health services and job training as well as parenting education and child care in an effort to support family functioning and establish self-sufficiency.

The ethnographers are documenting the process of program implementation, including institutional and community change, while the quantitative researchers are collecting data on services provided, parent and child participation, and outcomes in parents and children.

In an award-winning book based on an ethnographic study, Lubeck (1985) compares 2 preschool programs in the same community, one a black Head Start program, the other a white preschool. The author selected two programs similar in size and equipment but differing in social class and race because she was interested in studying the cultural patterning that children experience before they enter school. The study was conducted over a period of a year. The investigator was a participant observer in both preschools, working alongside staff and writing comprehensive observation notes after the school day, which were checked for validity by the staff. The children's use of space, time, and materials was charted as well. Lubeck points out that ethnographic studies, and other types of qualitative studies as well, are likely to be weak regarding issues of reliability, but strong regarding validity. A carefully done ethnographic study conducted over time can move back and forth between description and analysis to reveal people's attitudes and beliefs.

INSTRUMENTS TO ASSESS QUALITY OF EARLY EDUCATION SETTINGS

In addition to observation and interview, which is basic to qualitative studies, a number of global quality-assessment instruments have been developed. The instruments reviewed below were selected because they are widely used measures of quality based on observation. The first 4 instruments were designed for and are used in quality ensurance for credentialing, accreditation, or purchase of care with state funds. The other 4 instruments were designed as quality-assessment instruments for general use.

Early Childhood Classroom Observation (National Academy of Early Childhood Programs, 1985).

The Early Childhood Classroom Observation was developed as part of NAEYC's National Academy of Early Childhood Program's center-accreditation system. The instrument has 68 items, each presented as a statement with examples and indicators. The indicators must be observed; the examples are given for clarification. Rating is done on a 3-point scale: 1 = not met, 2 = partially met, 3 = fully met. The items are linked to the Criteria for Quality Early Childhood Programs (NAEYC, 1984), and are organized under 5 categories: interaction among staff and children, curriculum, physical environment, health and safety, and nutrition. This instrument is meant to be used across all age groups from birth through school age in early childhood center or school settings.

Interrater reliability of .89 is reported based on data from only 5 classrooms in a study by Holloway and Reichhart-Erickson, 1988 (cited in a personal communication by S. Bredekamp, July 12, 1991). Internal consistency was verified with a coefficient Alpha of .70 and standardized-item Alpha of .86 (Bredekamp, 1989). A factor analysis produced 3 factors accounting for about 48 percent of the variance in the scores. The factors, discussed earlier, are preschool curriculum, positive interaction, and balanced schedule of activity (see Table 30–3).

The Criteria for Quality Early Childhood Programs (NAEYC, 1984) on which this scale is based has become the accepted definition of early childhood program quality both in the United States and increasingly in foreign countries as well. The NAEYC observation instrument is closely tied to these criteria and derives its validity thereby. As mentioned previously, validity of the instrument was also established by having 250 early childhood specialists rate the importance of each of the criteria on a 4-point scale. Based on a 78% return, all the criteria obtained mean scores between 3 and 4, that is, between "important" and "essential" (Bredekamp, 1986).

CDA Advisor's Report Form (Council for Early Childhood Professional Recognition, 1991).

The CDA Advisor's Report form was developed for use in the Child Development Associate credentialing process. The CDA is awarded to an individual, not to a program. The instrument consists of 43 items, each presented as a 3-point scale: 1 = rarely, 2 = sometimes, 3 = mostly. The observer uses the instrument on 3 occasions and all items must be rated by the end of the third visit. It is meant to be used in all types of settings, including family child care, child care centers, Head Start, and other preschool programs, and by people working with all age groups. This inclusive approach differs from the other instruments presented here.

No reliability studies have been undertaken as yet (personal communication, C. Phillips, 1991). Validity of the scale derives from its close ties to the CDA competency goals and functional areas, a widely accepted set of quality criteria for care giver competence. Each of the items is linked to one of the observable functional areas.

Assessment Profile for Family Day Care (Abbott-Shim & Sibley, 1987c).

This instrument was designed for the National Association for Family Day Care (NAFDC) and is used exclusively in their accreditation process. It is to be used only for family child care, that is, a setting where a group of children is cared for in the care giver's home. The Profile includes 194 items that are scored either "yes" or "no." The items are grouped under 7 dimensions of child care: indoor safety, health, nutrition, indoor play environment, outdoor play environment, interacting, and professional responsibility. Three sources are used in obtaining information to assess the items on the scale—observation, response, and documentation. The source of the information (O, R, or D) is indicated in a column near each statement.

The Profile is completed by the provider and validated by a parent whose child is not in the provider's care, as well as by a NAFDC representative, all using the same scale. The family day-care provider must be judged positively on at least 85% of the items on the Profile, with at least 75% on each dimension, in order for the home to be accredited (personal communication, K. Hollestelle, July 1991).

No information on reliability or validity is available at this time. The NAFDC accreditation process is currently undergoing revision.

Infant and Toddler Program Quality Review Instrument (California State Department of Education, 1988). California requires an hour of observation as part of its monitoring procedure for child care purchased with state funds. Presented here is 1 of the 4 observation instruments used in the monitoring of subsidized child care. Separate but similar instruments are used for monitoring family child care homes, preschool, and school-age care settings.

The Infant and Toddler Program Quality Review (PQR) was developed for use in the evaluation of infant and toddler center-based state-subsidized child care in California, serving children from birth through 33 months of age. The instrument is designed for 3 purposes: to be used in an annual self-assessment by the staff, to teach the administration and support staff about assessing the quality and needs of the program, and to be used by the Child Development Division to monitor and evaluate program quality. The program review is done by 2 peer reviewers who are program directors or head teachers practicing in the field, and the review takes a full day. Sources of information used in completing the PQR are observation, review of documents, and interviews.

The PQR is organized under 7 categories: philosophies/goals/objectives, administration, developmental profiles for children, developmental program, parent education and involvement, community resources, and evaluation. Observation is used for only the developmental program category; the other categories are assessed through review of documents or through interviews. Each reviewer must spend at least 60 minutes observing the children's program and answering "yes" or "no" on 62 items covering the areas of learning environment, care giver influence on environment, health, nutrition, language and communication, emotional development, social development, physical development, and cognitive development.

The function of the PQR is to stimulate program improvement. Compliance with state regulation is achieved through a separate contract monitoring visit. At the end of the PQR assessment the peer reviewers meet with the staff and share their findings. Together they set goals for improvement, which are sent to the Child Development Division along with the complete report (personal communication, K. Witcher, July 19, 1991).

No information is available on the reliability of this instrument. As to validity, the instrument is based on a statement of goals developed by the California Child Development Section with the collaboration of a major educational research laboratory and under the guidance of state and national advisory groups. The goals are available in a booklet called *Visions for Infant/Toddler Care* (Center for Child & Family Studies, 1988). These goals are compatible with the developmentally appropriate practices outlined by NAEYC (Bredekamp, 1987).

Assessment Profile for Preschool, Infant, and School Age (Abbott-Shim & Sibley, 1987a & b). The Profile consists of 2 booklets. One contains the assessments for preschool, infant, and school-age programs. The other contains the manual and the assessment for the program's administration. The purpose of the Profile as stated in the manual is to guide "in-depth self evaluation."

The format is the same in each of the 3 age-specific assessments and the administration section. Each indicator is presented as a statement to be rated "yes" or "no". Three sources of information are used—observation, report, and documentation. The source of the information is noted near each indicator (O, R, or D).

The items are grouped under categories appropriate for the content of each section. Thus the Preschool Profile uses the headings safety and health, learning environment, scheduling, curriculum, interacting and individualizing. For infants the headings are safety and health, nutrition, learning environment, and interacting. For school-age programs the headings are safety and health, learning environment, curriculum, interacting, and scheduling. The administration section includes physical facility, food service, program management, personnel, and program development.

Interrater reliabilities ranging from .85 to .95 are reported by the authors. Measures of internal consistency (Cronbach's Alpha) resulted in .90 on the infant scale (127 items, 39 centers), .97 on the toddler scale (151 items, 28 centers), .96 on the preschool scale (142 items, 46 centers), and .90 on the administration scale (134 items, 44 centers).

The content of the Assessment Profile has been cross-referenced with the NAEYC Accreditation Criteria, the Early Childhood Environment Rating Scale (ECERS), and the Child Development Associate (CDA) competencies to establish content validity. The consistency among these 3 references is reported to be extensive.

The Early Childhood Environment Rating Scale [ECERS] (Harms & Clifford, 1980). The ECERS is a 37-item scale organized under 7 categories: personal care routines, furnishings and display for children, language-reasoning experience, fine and gross motor activities, creative activities, social development, and adult needs. It is designed to be used with 1 group or in 1 room at a time and is best used for groups of preschool/kindergarten children, 2 through 6 years of age. Although there are 4 alternate items for infants and toddlers in the ECERS, the *Infant/Toddler Environment Rating Scale* (Harms, Cryer, & Clifford, 1990) is preferable for this age group. Following publication of the scale, 5 additional items for use with the scale in groups that include children with special needs were developed. Each of the 37 items is presented as a 7-point scale with quality descriptors under 1 = inadequate, 3 = minimal, 5 = good, and 7 = excellent. Scoring is based on observation and answers to questions about aspects of the program not observed.

In an interrater reliability study conducted in 25 classrooms, 2 independent ratings were obtained and compared, giving a rank-order correlation of total-scale scores of .88 (Harms & Clifford, 1983). Comparable interrater reliabilities have since been reported in other studies (McCartney et al., 1982; Whitebook et al., 1989). A test/retest reliability of .96 with a 2-week interval between first and second testing resulted from a study of 31 rooms. In the interval between the 2 ratings, other classrooms were rated to prevent raters from remembering previous ratings. The internal consistency of the scale as a whole is quite acceptable, with alphas ranging from .81 to .91 in 4 studies (Harms & Clifford, 1980, 1983).

The validity of the ECERS has been substantiated in several ways: First, ratings of all the scale items by 7 nationally recognized experts resulted in 78% of the items being rated as of high importance and only 1% as low importance on a 3-point scale. Second, a comparison of expert opinions with scale scores resulted in a correlation of .74 (Harms & Clifford, 1983). Finally, considerable evidence from studies documenting the relationship of ECERS scores to child-outcome measures and teacher-process variables attests to its validity (Harms & Clifford, 1983; McCartney et al., 1982; Goelman & Pence, 1988; Whitebook et al., 1989).

Family Day Care Rating Scale [FDCRS] (Harms & Clifford, 1989). The FDCRS is a rating scale especially developed to assess the quality of care in family child care settings, that is, group care provided in the care giver's home. The scale is composed of 32 basic items organized under 6 categories: space and furnishings for care and learning, basic care, language and reasoning, learning activities, social development, and adult needs. A seventh category called "supplementary items: provisions for exceptional children" contains 8 items to be used in addition to the scale in programs that include children with handicapping conditions.

The format of the FDCRS is the same as the ECERS. Each of the 40 items of the FDCRS is presented as a 7-point scale with descriptors under 1 = inadequate, 3 = minimal, 5 = good, and 7 = excellent. Ratings are based on observation and answers to questions about aspects of the program not observed.

Evidence of interrater reliability and validity are reported in the scale (Harms & Clifford, 1989, pp. 1–3). An interrater reliability of .86 was obtained in a study of 19 family day care homes in North Carolina on the basic 32 items of the scale. (The items for exceptional children have been widely field tested but no reliability studies have yet been conducted on these items.) The 8 items that had interrater reliability levels of under .5 in this study were clarified and revised prior to publication. Several subsequent studies have reported interrater reliabilities for the basic 32 items with coefficients of approximately .90 (personal communication, C. Howes, 1987; Howes & Stewart, 1987). Howes and Stewart also calculated the internal consistency of the FDCRS subscales with resulting alphas ranging from .70 on adult needs to .93 for learning activities. Howes reports confidence in use of the subscale scores in her studies. Similarly high alphas are reported by Stuart and Pepper (1985) in their study of family day care homes in Canada. Since the FDCRS is an adaptation of the ECERS, a scale with established validity, this provides face evidence that the FDCRS is also a valid measure of environmental quality. In addition, the FDCRS covers the nationally recognized CDA competencies (Harms & Clifford, 1980, p. 1). Beyond that, a number of studies using the FDCRS (and an earlier version, the DCERS) report correlations with child behavior (Howes & Stewart, 1987), child language development, and care-giver language stimulation behaviors (Goelman & Pence, 1987a and b, 1988). Stuart and Pepper (1985) compared professional judgments of quality with FDCRS scores in 2 studies in Ontario with correlation coefficients of .64 and .75.

Infant/Toddler Environment Rating Scale (Harms, Cryer, & Clifford, 1990). The ITERS is a scale designed to give a global assessment of quality for center-based group care of children under 30 months of age. Infants are defined in the scale as children from birth through 11 months; toddlers are 12 through 30 months of age. The scale consists of 35 items under 7 categories: furnishings and display for children, personal care routines, listening and talking, learning activities, interaction, program structure, and adult needs. As in the ECERS and FDCRS, the ITERS presents each of the 35 items as a 7-point scale with descriptors under 1 = inadequate, 3 = minimal, 5 = good, and 7 = excellent. Scoring is based on observation and answers to questions.

Reliability and validity data are reported in the scale and also more extensively in a reliability and validity study report (Harms et al., 1990, p. 2; Clifford, Russell, Fleming, Peisner, Harms, & Cryer, 1989). Three studies of reliability were carried out with the findings that the Spearman correlation coefficient for interrater reliability in 30 day care center rooms was .84; test/retest reliability after 3 to 4 weeks in 18 rooms was .79 for the overall scale; internal consistency measured by Cronbach's Alpha was .83 for the overall scale.

Three validity studies were also conducted. Expert ratings of 12 rooms as "high" or "low" by 2 experts were compared with ITERS scores with an agreement of 83 percent. An item-by-item comparison of the ITERS with 7 other comparable instruments showed that 82% of the ITERS items were covered on the other scales and 75% of the items on the other scales were covered on the ITERS. In another study of validity, 5 nationally recognized experts rated the importance of each item on the ITERS using a scale from 1 (low) to 5 (high). The scores on 86% of the items were 4 or 5. Minor revisions were made for clarification on a few items following the reliability and validity studies. In addition, a content analysis of the ITERS found it compatible with the CDA competencies.

PURPOSES FOR STUDYING EDUCATIONAL SETTINGS

The measurement of educational settings serves several purposes, including compliance with state regulations, voluntary accreditation or credentialing, evaluation to document changes in programs or to explain outcomes, and research on a range of topics including teacher, family, and child variables. State regulations vary greatly and 1 issue that has aroused attention in the study of settings is the relationship of regulation to quality.

Most states regulate what we might call a base or floor level of quality by establishing staff-child ratios, maximum group size, and protective health and safety regulations. Monitoring for regulatory compliance usually requires inspecting documents and records, counting children and staff, measuring space, and documenting successful inspections by health and safety officials. In very few states is an observation of the ongoing program required during a monitoring visit. A study in North Carolina (Cryer, Clifford, & Harms, 1988) comparing the level of regulatory compliance to scores on a global quality-assessment measure, the ECERS, (Harms & Clifford, 1980) in

116 child care groups showed no correlation between degree of regulatory compliance and quality. This was due in part to the fact that monitoring for compliance in North Carolina relied completely on the inspection of documents, records, and plans. No observation was required, thus bypassing completely the interaction and curriculum aspects, which are key in professional definitions of quality (Bredekamp, 1989). In contrast, a similar study in Pennsylvania, a state that includes an observation period during the regulatory visit (Kontos & Fiene, 1987), found correlations between regulatory compliance scores and the same quality measure that was used in the North Carolina study. The correlation was particularly strong between the 20-minute observation mandated during the monitoring visit and the total score on the quality-assessment instrument.

This discussion does not mean to imply that regulation is not an important foundation on which to build quality. In fact, both of the accreditation systems—the NAEYC Center Accreditation and the NAFDC Family Day Care accreditation—require compliance, with state regulation as a prerequisite for initiating the voluntary accreditation process. The National Child Care Staffing Study (Whitebook et al., 1989), which examined the quality of care in 227 licensed child care centers, gives us insight into how the level of regulation fits into a constellation of work, environment, and teacher-qualification factors to produce quality. This study was conducted in 5 states that have widely varying regulations. Centers that met the relatively high Federal Interagency Day Care Requirements paid their teachers better wages and employed teachers with more formal education. These teachers were observed to be more sensitive and less harsh, and they engaged in more appropriate caregiving activities. Higher standards were correlated with higher levels of quality, but it was not regulation alone that achieved this effect. A combination of factors, including wages, benefits, teacher preparation, and regulation, was responsible.

In the absence of high national standards for early childhood educational settings, the major professional early childhood organizations have developed voluntary credentialing for teaching staff (CDA), for center-based preschool, child care and kindergarten programs (NAEYC center accreditation), and, more recently, for family day care homes (NAFDC accreditation). Typically, accreditation programs require a comprehensive self-study conducted with quantitative instruments, which is later validated in an on-site visit. Since accreditation instruments reflect widely held professional views of best practice in early childhood settings, the accreditation process serves as a catalyst for change.

The issue of how best to define and assess quality for research purposes has long been an issue. In order to assess quality in the more exacting studies of the 1980s and 1990s, which seek to link level of quality with teacher behavior and child outcomes, 2 main approaches have been used. In some studies a global construct of inputs to early childhood programs is formed by combining discreet indicators associated with positive child outcomes such as staff/child ratio, group size, and teacher qualification (Ruopp, Travers, Glantz, & Coelen, 1979; Divine-Hawkins, 1981), and more recently including cost, job satisfaction, and teacher turnover as well (Howes & Olenick, 1986; Whitebook et al., 1989). The limitation of this approach is that input variables do not capture important aspects of the processes/interactions in the setting that can be measured only through observation (McCartney et al., 1982). Many studies, therefore, use a global quality-assessment instrument based on ratings of observation such as the Early Childhood Environment Rating Scale (Harms & Clifford, 1980) or the Assessment Profile (Abbott-Shim & Sibley, 1987b). Current studies often combine the input-variable and observational-rating-scale approaches in order to be able to specify correlations between quality of care and structural features of the environment, such as staff/child ratio and group size. Some studies use more detailed observational recording of key components, such as verbal interaction, as well (McCartney et al., 1982).

In a careful review of studies relating child outcomes with quality of center and family day care settings, Doherty (1991) finds evidence that quality is correlated with higher levels of language development; parental and care-giver ratings of the child as considerate, socially adept, and able to focus on a task (Phillips, McCartney, & Scarr, 1987); higher scores on a social competence test (Kontos & Fiene, 1987); more compliance with adult requests and greater ability to refrain from touching a forbidden object in toddlers (Howes & Olenick, 1986); more positive behavior with and toward adults (Vandall & Powers, 1983); better language development in children enrolled in quality family day care homes (Goelman & Pence, 1988); more competent level of play with peers, care givers, and objects in quality family day care homes (Howes & Stewart, 1987); and quality of child care center–predicted teacher ratings of school skills and presence or absence of behavior problems at the end of grade 1 (Howes, 1983). To summarize, programs with a high global assessment of quality are associated with a number of positive outcomes in children: greater social competence, higher levels of language development, higher developmental levels of play, better ability to self-regulate, greater compliance, and fewer problems in grade school.

Most global assessment instruments include some coverage of the physical setting and interpersonal interactions, but not in as much detail as in approaches designed to focus solely on these dimensions. Below we examine a framework for assessing the physical setting and a widely used observation system for assessing interpersonal interaction.

The physical environment is considered important by early childhood educators but is rarely studied directly. Gary Moore, an architect and educator, identifies 10 critical dimensions of spatial organization in child care centers that influence both program and behavior: (1) visual connection between spaces, (2) closure of spaces, (3) distance between different activity areas, (4) mixture of larger open areas and smaller enclosed areas, (5) separation of staff areas from children's areas, (6) separation of functional areas from activity areas, (7) separation of age groups, (8) separation of circulation pathways from activity spaces, (9) visibility of activity areas from entry, and (10) connection between outdoors and indoors. Moore used this framework in a study of children's engagement in cognitively oriented behavior in classrooms with 3 spatial organizations: the totally open plan, modified open plan, and closed plan (Moore, 1987). He found that children in the modified open plan used significantly more activity centers, worked in small groupings, and engaged in more cognitively oriented behavior. In the open plan, children engaged in more random or unsustained activity, and in the closed plan, there was more moving between activities and more staring into space. Both the open plan and modified open plan afford easy access to a variety of different activity centers, but the modified open plan provides acoustic separation and a greater feeling of containment and privacy for each area. This combination of privacy and access stimulates engagement.

In studies of educational settings, interaction is often observed in greater detail in addition to a global measure. An elaborate coding system used for recording classroom interaction is the SRI (Stallings, 1977). The SRI Classroom Observation Five Minute Interaction records the who, to whom, what, and how of interactions. Codes in the "what" column cover a variety of verbal interactions, including command or request, directing questions, open-ended questions, response, instruction and explanation, general comments/action, task-related comments, acknowledgement, praise, and corrective feedback.

CONCLUSION

Educational settings for preschool children encompass a wider variety than is found in schooling at any other age. Therefore, as we study early educational settings, it is important to take into consideration the characteristics of the different types of settings as well as the level of quality of the programs within the specific setting type. Studies relating child development outcomes to preschool educational experience should be careful not to overgeneralize in a misleading way to nonrelated settings. A taxonomy of early childhood educational settings is useful to provide a context within which programs can be placed.

Not only do we need a structure to deal with diversity, but also a framework that ties programs together by revealing the underlying elements that cut across all programs. The theoretical framework described in this chapter is based on an ecological model, with the child care group representing the microsystem. Within each individual group we have both structural and process variables. This framework applies equally well to home- and center-based settings. The framework is also supported by empirical evidence from 2 factor analyses of scores from different classroom-quality assessment instruments, and by the categories included in the 3 major credentialing/accreditation systems. The 3 key components of the children's program are adult-child interaction, space/materials/curriculum, and recurring patterns or routines. In addition, there is a management component that applies to both center and home settings.

When we study settings, we need to focus on the particular area of interest related to our purpose without losing track of the total framework. Since educational settings are complex social systems, it may be necessary to use several different assessment approaches simultaneously. Global assessment instruments can give an overall quality measure of one group or room, relating the various program components to one another. More finely focused observations, such as those recording interaction, can show the details of program implementation in a specific area. Qualitative methods can also add insight into the dynamics of the setting and help interpret the larger cultural issues involved.

At the very heart of our interest in the quality of educational settings for young children is the notion that the behavior of children evolves from the interaction between the child and the total environment, including the people in the environment in which that child develops. Thus we see the study of these early educational settings as critical for furthering the optimal developmental progress of the next generation.

References

Abbott-Shim, M., & Sibley, A. (1987a). *Assessment profile for early childhood programs: Manual administration*. Atlanta, GA: Quality Assist.

Abbott-Shim, M., & Sibley, A. (1987b). *Assessment profile for early childhood programs: Preschool, infant and school age*. Atlanta, GA: Quality Assist.

Abbott-Shim, M., & Sibley, A. (1987c). *Assessment profile for family day care*. Atlanta, GA: Quality Assist.

Berrueta-Clement, J. R., Schweinhart, L. J., Barnett, W. S., Epstein, A. S., & Weikart, D. P. (1984). *Changed lives: The effect of the Perry preschool program on youths through age 19*. (Monograph of the High/Scope Educational Research Foundation, No. 8). Ypsilanti, MI: High/Scope Press.

Blinder, A. S. (1987, December 14). Improving the chances of our weakest underdogs—poor children. *Business Week*, p. 20.

Bredekamp, S. (1986). The reliability and validity of the early childhood classroom observation scale for accrediting early childhood programs. *Early Childhood Research Quarterly, 1*, 103–118.

Bredekamp. S. (Ed.). (1987). *Developmentally appropriate practice in early childhood programs serving children from birth through age 8*.

Washington, DC: National Association for the Education of Young Children.

Bredekamp, S. (Ed.). (1989, March). *Measuring quality through a national accreditation system for early childhood programs*. Paper presented at the Annual Meeting of the American Educational Research Association, Washington, DC.

Bronfenbrenner, U. (1977). Toward an experimental ecology of human development. *American Psychologist, 32*, 513–531.

Bronfenbrenner, U. (Ed.) (1979). *The ecology of human development: Experiments by nature and design*. Cambridge, MA: Harvard University Press.

California State Department of Education. (1988). *Infant and toddler program quality review instrument*. Sacramento, CA: California State Department of Education, Child Development Division.

Center for Child and Family Studies. (1988). *Visions for infant/toddler care: Guidelines for professional caregiving*. Sacramento, CA: California State Department of Education.

Clifford, R. M., Russell, S. D., Flemming, J., Peisner, E. S., Harms, T., & Cryer, D. (1989). *Infant/toddler environmental rating scale:*

Reliability and validity study, final report. Chapel Hill: University of North Carolina.

Clifford, R. M., Wenger, M., Lubeck, S., Gallagher, J. J., & Harms, T. (1988). *Family needs for child care and early education* (Working Paper 88.4). Chapel Hill: University of North Carolina, Carolina Institute for Child and Family Policy.

Committee for Economic Development. (1987). *Children in need: Investment strategies for the educationally disadvantaged*. New York.

132 Congressional Record H2221-H2223 (April 29, 1986).

Council for Early Childhood Professional Recognition. (1985). *Child Development Associate assessment system and competency standards*. Washington, DC: Child Development Associate National Credentialing Program.

Council for Early Childhood Professional Recognition. (1991). *Advisor's Report Form*. Washington, DC: Child Development Associate National Credentialing Program.

Cryer, D., Clifford, R. M., & Harms, T. (1988). *Day care center compliance and evaluation project: Final report*. Unpublished manuscript, University of North Carolina, Frank Porter Graham Child Development Center, Chapel Hill.

Divine-Hawkins, P. (1981). *Final Report of the National Day Care Home Study, Family day care in the United States: Executive Summary*. Washington, DC: Center for Systems and Program Development.

Doherty, G. (1991). *Factors related to quality in child care: Annotated bibliography* (Document prepared for the Child Care Branch; Ontario Ministry of Community and Social Services). Toronto: Queen's Printer for Ontario.

Fosburg, S. (1981). *Final report of the national day care home study: Vol. 1. Family day care in the United States: Summary of findings*. Washington, DC: Department of Health and Human Services.

Garrett, P., Wenger, M., Lubeck, S., & Clifford, R. M. (1989). *Child care arrangements for 4-year-olds: A state-level view*. Chapel Hill: University of North Carolina, Frank Porter Graham Child Development Center.

Goelman, H., & Pence, A. R. (1987a). Effects of child care, family and individual characteristics on children's language development: The Victoria Day Care Research Project. In D. A. Phillips (Ed.), *Quality in child care: What does the research tell us?* (pp. 89–104). Washington, DC: National Association for the Education of Young Children.

Goelman, H., & Pence, A. R. (1987b). Some aspects of the relationships between family structure and child language development in three types of day care. In D. L. Peters & S. Kontos (Eds.), *Annual advances in applied developmental psychology: Vol. 2. Continuity and discontinuity of experience in child care* (pp. 129–146). Norwood, NJ: Ablex.

Goelman, H., & Pence, A. R. (1988). Children in three types of day care: Daily experiences, quality of care and developmental outcomes. *Early Child Development and Care, 33*, 67–76.

Golden, M., Rosenbluth, L., Grossi, M., Policare, H., Freeman, H., & Brownlees, E. (1979). *The New York City infant day care study*. New York: Medical and Health Research Association of New York City, Inc.

Harms, T., & Clifford, R. M. (1980). *The early childhood environment rating scale*. New York: Teachers College Press.

Harms, T., & Clifford, R. M. (1983). Assessing preschool environments with the early childhood environment rating scale. *Studies in Educational Evaluation, 8*, 261–269.

Harms, T., & Clifford, R. M. (1989). *Family day care rating scale*. New York: Teachers College Press.

Harms, T., Cryer, D., & Clifford, R. M. (1990). *Infant/toddler environment rating scale*. New York: Teachers College Press.

Haskins, R. (1989). Beyond metaphor: The efficacy of early childhood education. *American Psychologist, 44*(2), 274–282.

Hayes, C. D., Palmer, J. L., & Zaslow, M. J. (1990). *Who cares for America's children? Child care policy for the 1990's*. Washington, DC: National Academy Press.

Hofferth, S.L., Brayfield, Deich, S., & Holcomb, P. (1991). *National child care survey, 1991*. Washington, DC: The Urban Institute Press.

Howes, C. (1983). Caregiver behaviour in center and in family day care. *Journal of Applied Psychology, 4*, 99–107.

Howes, C., & Olenick, M. (1986). Family and child care influences on toddler's compliance. *Child Development, 57*, 202–216.

Howes, C., & Rubenstein, J. (1985). Determinant of toddlers' experiences in day care: Age of entry and quality of setting. *Child Care Quarterly, 14*(2), 140–151.

Howes, C., & Stewart, P. (1987). Child's play with adults, toys, and peers: An examination of family and child care influences. *Developmental Psychology, 23*, 423–430.

Johnson, L., & Dineen, J. (1981). *The kin trade*. Toronto: McGraw-Hill Ryerson.

Johnson, L., Shack, J., & Oster, K. (1980). *Out of the cellar and into the parlour*. Ottawa, Ontario: Canada Mortgage and Housing Corporation.

Kisker, E., Hofferth, S., Phillips, D., & Farquhar, E. (1991). *A profile of child care settings: Early education and care in 1990*. Princeton, N.J.: Mathematica Policy Research, Inc.

Kontos, S., & Fiene, R. (1987). Child care quality, compliance with regulations and children's development: The Pennsylvania study. In D. Phillips (Ed.), *Quality in child care: What does the research tell us?* (pp. 57–79). Washington, DC: National Association for the Education of Young Children.

Linder, E. W., Mattis, M. C., & Rogers, J. R. (1983). *When churches mind the children: A study of day care in local parishes*. Ypsilanti, MI: High/Scope Press.

Lubeck, S. (1985). *Sandbox society. Early education in black and white America*. Philadelphia: Falmer Press.

McCartney, K. (1984). Effect of quality of day care environment on children's language development. *Developmental Psychology, 20*(2), 244–260.

McCartney, K., Scarr, S., Phillips, D., Grajek, S., & Schwarz, C. (1982). Environmental differences among day care centers and their effects on children's development. In E. F. Zigler & E. W. Gordon (Eds.), *Day care: Scientific and social policy issues* (pp. 126–151). Boston: Auburn House.

Moore, G. (1987). The physical environment and cognitive development in child care centers. In C. S. Weinstein & T. G. David (Eds.), *Spaces for children: The built environment and child development* (pp. 41–72). New York: Plenum.

Moos, R. H. (1980). Evaluating classroom learning environments. *Studies in educational evaluation, 6*, 239–252.

Morgan, G. (1987). *The national state of child care regulation*. Watertown, MA: Work/Family Directions.

National Academy of Early Childhood Programs. (1985). *Early childhood classroom observation* (NAEYC No. 90021). Washington, DC: National Association for the Education of Young Children.

National Association for the Education of Young Children (NAEYC). (1984). *Accreditation criteria and procedures*. Washington, DC.

Olenick, M. (1986). The relationship between quality and cost in child care programs. *Child and Family Policy Renewal*. Los Angeles: University of California, School of Social Welfare.

Pepper, S., & Stuart, B. (1985). *Informal family day care: A study of caregivers*. Unpublished manuscript, Department of Psychology, The University of Western Ontario, London, Ontario.

Phillips, D., & Howes, C. (1987). Indicators of quality in child care: Review of the research. In D. Phillips (Ed.), *Quality in Child Care: What does the research tell us?* (pp. 1–19). Washington, DC: National Association for the Education of Young Children.

Phillips, D., McCartney, K., & Scarr, S. (1987). Child care quality and children's social development. *Developmental Psychology, 23,* 537–543.

Prescott, E. (1987). The environments as organizer of intent in child care settings. In C. S. Weinstein & T. G. David (Eds.), *Spaces for children: The built environment and child development* (pp. 72–83). New York: Plenum.

Rossbach, H. G., Clifford, R. M., & Harms, T. (1991, April). *Dimensions of learning environments: Cross-national validation of the Early Childhood Environment Rating Scale.* Paper presented at the AERA Annual Conference, Chicago.

Ruopp, R., Travers, J., Glantz, F., & Coelen, C. (1979). *Children at the center: Final report of the National Day Care Study.* Cambridge, MA: Abt Associates.

Russell, S. D., Clifford, R. M., & Warlick, M. T. (1990). *Working in child care in North Carolina.* Carrboro, NC: Day Care Services Association.

Scarr, S. (1991, June). *Variations in quality in child care centers and effects on children's development.* Paper presented at "New directions in child and family research: Shaping Head Start in the 90's" (Conference of the Administration for Children, Youth and Families, June 24–26, Arlington, VA).

Stallings, J. (1977). *Learning to look: A handbook on classroom observation and teaching models.* Belmont, CA: Wadsworth.

Stuart, B., & Pepper, S. (1985). *Private home day care providers in Ontario: A study of their personal and psychological characteristics.* Unpublished manuscript, Department of Family Studies, University of Guelph, Guelph, Ontario.

Stuart, B., & Pepper, S. (1988). The contribution of the caregivers' personality and vocational interests to quality in licensed family daycare. *Canadian Journal of Research in Early Childhood Education, 2,* 99–109.

Vandall, D. L., & Powers, C. P. (1983). Day care quality and children's free play activities. *American Journal of Orthopsychiatry, 53,* 493–500.

West, J., Hausken, E. G., Chandler, K. A., & Collins, M. (1991). *Experiences in child care and early childhood programs of first and second graders prior to entering first grade: Findings from the 1991 national household education survey.* Washington, DC: National Center for Education Statistics, U.S. Department of Education.

Whitebook, M., Howes, C., & Phillips, D. (1989). *Who cares? Child care teachers and the quality of care in America.* Final report of the National Child Care Staffing Study, Oakland, CA.

Willer, B., Hofferth, S. L., Kisker, E. E., Divine-Hawkins, P., Farquhar, E., & Glantz, F.B. (1991). *The demand and supply of child care in 1991.* Washington, DC: National Association for the Education of Young Children.

· 31 ·

TRENDS IN DEMOGRAPHIC AND BEHAVIORAL RESEARCH ON TEACHING IN EARLY CHILDHOOD SETTINGS

Donald L. Peters

UNIVERSITY OF DELAWARE

It is generally agreed that the central factor in quality early education and child care programming is the staff (Costley, Morgan, & Genser, 1991; Jorde-Bloom, in press), and pleas for addressing issues of training and professionalism have been frequently and ever more urgently sounded (Spodek, Saracho, & Peters, 1988; Jorde-Bloom, in press).

Despite the high priority awarded early childhood personnel issues, there are few empirical studies in the literature, when compared to studies done on other levels of education, that directly address theoretical and practical questions about teachers and teaching within early childhood classrooms. It is the purpose of this chapter to review some of the chief methodological and substantive issues, direct attention to the research that remains to be done, and discuss several key methodological challenges confronting the field. This chapter addresses the evolving paradigms and models for research on teachers and teaching in early childhood education and the questions the models are designed to illuminate. Attention is given to examples of specific empirical methodologies culled from recent and classical research. Finally, suggestions are offered for future research.

The term teacher is used here with broad intent, including child care providers in child care settings and family day care providers, as well as teachers in early childhood classrooms, kindergartens, and early intervention group settings. A conscious effort has been made to include examples in this chapter of research covering nursery schools, kindergarten, early special education, day care centers, and family day care. The early primary grades have been little addressed.

In the research cited, the emphasis is on teachers of preschool age children. Less attention is given to teachers or care givers for infants or to teachers of children in the early elementary grades. Though both were intentional decisions, they were prompted by somewhat different reasons. The literature about training teachers for formal infant and toddler programs falls primarily within the domain of early intervention or special education and focuses on the need for pedagogical adaptations to meet the specialized needs of the children involved. The research concerning early primary teachers is embedded in the larger body of research focused on elementary education. In both cases their inclusion would have taken this review beyond the scope possible in the space available.

Finally, the emphasis of this chapter is on demographic and behavioral research. While the contributions of qualitative or interpretive methods of inquiry to the understanding of teachers and the teaching process are acknowledged, they are touched on only briefly here.

HISTORICAL PERSPECTIVES ON RESEARCH QUESTIONS

Expansion of our knowledge through empirical research always involves an active interplay between more precise conceptual understanding and the development of the methodological capabilities needed to answer the theoretical, practical, and policy questions of the day. Each era of research expands our knowledge, clarifies our thinking, and generates a new line of inquiry. Each new line of inquiry is increasingly complex.

The notion that a more complex model is needed for research in early education is not new. It has been the conclusion of every thoughtful review of the field for at least the last quarter century. For example, after reviewing the research from 1920 to 1960 dealing with nursery-school teaching, Sears and Dowley (1963) concluded that

When gathered together, the literature constitutes a considerable body of knowledge bearing on the problems of teaching. A number of variables have been isolated, defined, and tested for their effects. Relationships between certain events have been shown to appear with some predictable regularity. Yet, the body of knowledge is spotty and difficult to organize and integrate. (p. 858)

Sears and Dowley suggested that the "shadowy and blurred" picture of teaching in early childhood was attributable to (1) a lack of theory for the teaching process, (2) the reluctance of researchers to replicate even in modified form the work of others (either in the variables studied or the ways of measuring them), and (3) the difficulty of abstracting "method" from the social context defined by the characteristics of the teachers and children involved. They also bemoaned the lack of longitudinal research that would test the validity of conclusions over time. These concerns have been addressed in more recent research but they remain persistent shortcomings.

A decade later, Beller (1973) described the studies in early childhood education conducted during the era of civil rights and the war on poverty. His review included a lengthy analysis of the teaching process. He defined "process" research as clear attempts to determine the patterns of teaching and their relationship to child outcome variables. Beller distinguished teaching techniques—the strategies and methods employed by the teacher to accomplish her objectives and teacher style—from the system of beliefs, attitudes, and other personality characteristics that are not planned components of the teacher's functioning but still influence the pattern of teacher/child interactions (Beller, 1973). Beller also acknowledged the research of Prescott, Jones, and Kritchevsky, (1967) and the influence of environmental context factors (such as physical and spatial organization of the classroom) on teacher functioning. Beller stated,

I have tried to present a multivaried approach to the study of teacher-child interactions. Such an approach leads to a preference for the question, "Who benefits from what?" or "How does a given technique of teaching affect child A differently from child B?" (p. 583)

He concluded that

The new evidence points to a more complex yet more meaningful relationship between teacher and child variables because it takes into account not only how, but also what and who is being taught. (p. 595)

The *Second Handbook of Research on Teaching*, in which Beller's chapter appears, also devotes a full chapter to "Techniques of Observing Teaching in Early Childhood" (Gordon & Jester, 1973), a considerable rarity in the literature.

The third edition of the *Handbook of Research on Teaching* (Wittrock, 1986) reviews the results of longitudinal studies on the effects of early education intervention programs but does little to unravel the complexity of the issues involved in teaching (Stallings & Stipek, 1986). The chapter, "Teacher Behavior and Student Achievements," intentionally excluded preprimary research (Brophy & Good, 1986). We shall come back to the relation issue between teacher behavior and learning outcomes later.

A clarification of similar areas for further study can be traced in the research on day care. (The distinction between day care and early education intervention has continued to diminish.) In their seminal paper "The Present Status and Future Needs in Day Care Research," Grotberg, Chapman, and Lazar (1971) reviewed a range of critical research topics in need of work. They concluded that the one issue on which there is unanimous agreement by all researchers is that the staff of the child care center or service is the single most important determinant of the quality of the care provided. They suggested that research is most needed in the areas of (1) staff characteristics, including staff qualifications and selection, staff training, and the causes and solutions to staff turnover and (2) staff context variables, including staff/child ratios, cross-age helping relationships, gender and ethnic mix (both staff and child), and staff supervision. As the authors pointed out, the implication is that these variable clusters affect child outcomes of the day care experience, but little research has been available to guide policy or practice.

More recently, Belsky (1984, 1990) and others (Peters & Kontos, 1987) have called for a second and third wave of day care research with more complex designs to address the more complex and relevant questions of the relationships between children's experiences outside and within child care, as well as the outcomes associated with those experiences. As Belsky noted, social structure (social-economic context) influences experience and experience influences development.

This notion has been further elaborated by those who advocate a contextual-systems approach for understanding early child care experience (Peters & Kontos, 1987; Long, Peters, & Garduque, 1985; Pence & Goelman, 1987). These researchers have stressed the view that what is important in understanding the experiences of children within day care and other early childhood settings involves not only looking at the teacher/child interaction, but understanding how that set or pattern of interactions matches or conflicts with the child's other adult/child interactions, particularly in the home. These researchers viewed compound variables such as consistency, congruity, stability, and continuity as critically important for child outcomes (Peters & Kontos, 1987).

Interestingly, recent concerns about the "pressures of early childhood education" (Elkind, 1987) have prompted research into early childhood education experience of middle-class children. This research directs attention to the role parents play in the selection of that experience for their children (Hirsh-Pasek, Hyson, & Rescorla, 1990).

The direction of research on early childhood teaching has shifted from studies of the effects specific teacher behaviors have on specific child outcomes of middle-class children (in the

1920s, 1930s, 1940s, and 1950s) through an increasingly complex view of the patterns of teacher/child interactions within specially designed programs for low-income children (in the 1960s and 1970s), to the development of multivariate, context-acknowledging models for research on day care and early education in the 1980s. Researchers now generally realize what teachers have long known: The process of teaching within the early childhood classroom involves antecedents (what children, parents, and teachers bring to the situation) coming together in a context (definable and important at several levels), and yielding certain patterns of interaction that have certain consequences for all parties concerned (Pence & Goelman, 1987).

QUESTION DOMAINS

It seems useful to view the questions implied in this model of the early childhood teaching process as falling into 5 domains: demographic questions, status/characteristic questions, historical/contextual questions, process questions, and developmental questions. Each domain deals with a different set of applied and theoretical issues, and each has relied principally on different survey and behavioral research methodologies. Briefly, the question domains may be described as follows.

Demographic Questions

Demographic studies are designed to help us assess the parameters of the populations under scrutiny. They define the universe with which we deal. While some data are available on an international level, most practical policy decisions are made at the national or subnational level, so the most useful demographics involve national studies, state studies, or local studies. Data need to be aggregated at the level relevant for the decisions that will be made (Peters & Hodges, 1980; Peters & Sibbison, 1980). In essence, demographic studies seek to establish how many persons are involved in the early childhood education enterprise. The intent is to count or project how many persons fall within each category of some useful classification scheme or taxonomy.

Demographic questions include, "How many children, of what ages, gender, or ethnic background, need or participate in early childhood programs?" "How many of what type of family units are involved in what type of early childhood programs?" "How many persons are in the early childhood education work force?" "How is this work force organized or structured?" "How do these population parameters vary geographically or over time?"

Status/Characteristic Questions

Status/characteristic questions logically follow concerns of demography, and studies often overlap the two. However, the interpretation and generalizability of findings about characteristic/status depend on the adequacy of our understanding of the population parameters established through demographic studies.

Questions within this domain seek to provide a view of who early education personnel are in a more specific sense by delineating specific stable characteristics across which individuals may differ in systematic ways. Typical concerns are, "What is the education and experience level of early childhood personnel?" "Where do they work and what job titles do they hold?" "What are their salaries and working conditions?" "What professional licenses or certificates do they hold?"

Questions concerning the patterns of relationships between and among various status and characteristic variables also fall within this category of research. These include such questions as, "What is the relationship between educational background and job satisfaction? or among age, experience, and turnover in the work force?"

Historical/Contextual Questions

The meaning of events derive from and are colored by their historical and cultural contexts as well as by their more immediate temporal and physical contexts. Questions in this domain attempt to establish an understanding of how context influences behavior patterns in ways that may occur with some regularity over time or within different situations. Questions such as, "What are the effects of group size, age mixes of children, teacher/child ratios, staffing, or supervisory patterns on teacher behavior or child outcomes?" fall into this domain. So, too, do questions such as, "Do kindergarten teachers of different ethnic backgrounds use different disciplinary techniques?" "Have teaching methods changed over the past several decades?" "Are there cross-national differences in teacher education or training?" and "Have societal attitudes changed toward the teacher/child relationship (or parent/teacher relationship) in the last century?" Such variables also are explored for their relationship to child outcomes.

Process Questions

Process questions, following Beller (1973), are concerned with the interactive patterns of behavior that occur within the early childhood setting and their relationship to outcomes of the experiences. Questions are directed toward the analysis of stable individual differences in early childhood personnel beliefs, attitudes, and behaviors toward children, parents, co-workers and the profession as well as the reciprocal attitudes, beliefs, and behaviors that early childhood personnel engender. These variables are often clustered under concepts such as teacher roles, teaching style, or teaching method (Beller 1973). More recently, interest has been directed toward teacher cognition (Saracho, 1988). Generally speaking, the intent within this domain of questions is to understand the inter- and intrapersonal dynamics of the early childhood education experience, either in some objective sense or from the perspective of the participants themselves.

Developmental Questions

Developmental questions are usually construed as concerned with change over time of intraindividual characteristics (individual development) and/or changes in interindividual differences across time (eg., cohort effects), though they do not have to be restricted to individuals. It is equally appropriate to speak of organizational development (intraorganizational change over time), family development (intrafamily change over time), national development, and the like. Of particular importance to this extension of the term is the notion that relationships of two or more individuals are involved and that these relationships form a unit with its own characteristics that may mature or develop in systematic ways. Questions here include, "Do teacher/child interactions change during the course of the school year?" "Is there a pattern to changes of teacher behavior from beginning teacher to experienced teacher?" "Are there changes in the care-giver/parent/child triad over time in family day care?"

It is important to note that not all change is developmental change. There are important reasons for being interested in the changing demographics of day care in the United States during the past two decades, but these reasons are not developmental. Developmental change implies a directionality and a structural or conceptual reorganization that has stability if not irreversibility. The analysis of developmental change requires an articulation of the assumptions underlying the concept of development.

THE ROLE OF THEORY

Viewing the 5 broad domains of questions about teachers and teaching in early childhood suggests that some levels of questions are important because the variables are considered practically important by program and policy decisionmakers. Others are important because they derive from or contribute to theory. In essence, as we descend the list of question domains a theoretical perspective, either implicit or explicit, becomes increasingly important for defining what variables are important and for organizing research findings into plausible explanations. For example, the potential number of status variables, or individual-difference characteristics by which people (including teachers or other early childhood personnel) may be classified is extremely large. Yet we have some reason for believing that the level and type of training persons receive in preparation for the teaching role is more important to educational outcomes than the make of automobile that they own or their hair style. We list both the inherent and acquired characteristics we consider important when we seek to describe the essential qualities for teachers (Almy, 1975; Peters, 1984). These range from personality characteristics such as warmth, patience, and ingenuity to listings of specific educational accomplishments or certificates. All are based on a theoretical or empirically established relationship to some desired set of teaching transactions, which in turn relate to some subjectively valued child outcomes. These assumed and/or tested relationships provide the driving theory for empirical research.

Although the field of early childhood education has not been strongly "theory driven," in recent years clearer articulations of theoretical relations have been forthcoming. These have generally incorporated the importance of context and a systems perspective (Bronfenbrenner, 1979 and 1989; Peters & Kontos, 1987), a developmental perspective on change within all persons involved (Vander Ven, 1988; Peters & Sutton, 1984), and recognition of interactional processes that reflect the reciprocity rather than the linearity of relationships (Goelman & Pence, 1987; Pence & Goelman, 1987). Each of these expansions of our theoretical understanding add complications that test our ingenuity in research design, measurement, and statistical analysis, but each is increasingly seen as essential for the adequacy of our understanding for policy formulation.

QUALITATIVE AND QUANTITATIVE METHODOLOGIES

There has been a long-standing debate within the social and behavioral sciences between those who espouse quantitative methodologies based on positivistic philosophies and those who espouse qualitative or interpretive methodologies based on phenomenological or structuralist philosophies in order to gain, inductively, a more dynamic and subjective view of human understanding and social life. The debates, their origins, and their histories have been well presented elsewhere and will not be repeated here (Porter & Potenza, 1983; Erikson, 1986). It is generally, though not universally, accepted that the origins of these methodologies represent opposing or at least incompatible sets of presuppositions or world views (Erikson, 1986). Yet both have the potential for extending our knowledge of teaching in early childhood education. Still, they do have different concerns and seek to answer somewhat different questions. For example, qualitative methods seek to gain a *local* understanding of early childhood classrooms as socially and culturally organized environments for learning and to establish a sense of the meaning-perspectives of the teacher and learner engaged in the educational process (Erikson, 1986). To gain such an understanding of local and immediate meanings, the methodology stresses the need for extensive documentation of concrete details and the meaning of these details for the participants. The idiosyncratic is as important or more important than the general or common.

The interpretive point of view asks questions such as, "What are the conditions of meaning that children and teachers create together as some children appear to learn and others do not?" "Are there differences in the meaning-perspectives of teachers and children in settings characterized by higher achievement or senses of self-worth?" "How are these meaning systems created and sustained in daily interactions?" and "How does the social ecology of teaching work through the simultaneously operating formal and informal social systems of the early childhood setting?" In each case, the focus of interpretive methodologies is on *particularizability* rather than *generalizability* (Erikson, 1986). Universals come only from the comparative analysis of detailed, particular cases.

The questions addressed by qualitative methods gain in importance as one descends the list of research questions that form the organization of this chapter, and paradigm choices can and should be made (Patton, 1990). It is important to remember, however, that one's world view and its presuppositions influence the way one asks the questions, the theories one feels comfortable or satisfied with, and the ways in which the reliability and validity of data are determined.

It is also important to distinguish between paradigm choices and data-gathering techniques. Quantitative and qualitative methods often overlap in the data-gathering techniques they employ (Reichardt & Cook, 1979; Erikson, 1986). Detailed observations and interviews, as well as the content analysis of existing documents or records are often used by both schools of researcher. How they are used and how they are interpreted differs. Using combinations of techniques and methodologies may yield results that are enlightening if the researcher doesn't lose sight of the underlying assumptions of his or her position.

THE DEMOGRAPHY OF TEACHING IN EARLY CHILDHOOD SETTINGS.

Understanding the demography of early childhood education would seem very basic for practical and policy decision-making. It also would seem to be a very easy task. Indeed, the U.S. Bureau of the Census and the U.S. Bureau of Labor Statistics keep records and make regular updates and projections of things such as the number of mothers with children under the age of 18 who are in the labor force, the number of 3–4 year-olds who are enrolled in school or preschool programs, and how many persons are in the early childhood work force nationwide. Yet we are constantly reminded of the limitations of these data sources. In discussing issues of supply and demand for child care in the United States, for example, Hofferth (1989) used data from the Census and the Bureau of Labor Statistics, as well as other studies, to point out that each data source is based on different questions. The result is that the two major national data sources do not present a very clear picture of the demand side of child care and early education. There are also major limits on our understanding of the supply side of the question, both because of definitional issues and because "We don't know the total number of family day care homes in operation, since it has been estimated that anywhere from 50% to 90% are not licensed (depending on how family day care is defined)" (Hofferth, 1989, p. 31). In discussing the child care work force, Phillips and Whitebook (1986) come to the same conclusion. We are reminded that the Bureau of the Census collects data from households while the Bureau of Labor Statistics collects data from employers—two very different sources.

Fortunately, more accurate information is available from a series of national surveys. Three principal sources of data are available. They are The National Child Care Survey, 1990 (NCCS); the Profile of Child Care Settings (CCS) study, and the National Child Care Staffing Study. Each of these studies had multiple purposes, but each also provides a demographic profile and indications of demographic trends through comparisons with similar studies conducted a decade or more before.

The NCCS data is based on a random sample of households located in 100 counties and groups of counties representative of the U.S. population. A total of 4,392 parents (primarily mothers) were telephone interviewed about their early education and care arrangements and about their activities, employ-

ment, and demographic characteristics. In addition, 162 family day care providers identified by the sampling process and 250 providers who were identified by the interviewed parents as providing care for their children were interviewed (Hofferth & Kisker, in press; Kisker, Hofferth, & Phillips, 1991).

The CCS study selected its sample by randomly selecting center-based programs and regulated family day care homes from state and county licensing and registration lists in the same nationally representative counties and county groups used by the NCCS. The final sample included telephone interviews with 2,089 center directors and 583 regulated family day care providers. (Hofferth & Kisker, in press; Kisker, Hofferth & Phillips, 1991; Willer, et al., 1991).

Since both the NCCS and the CCS used the same first-stage sample of counties and county groups and were conducted at the same time, these 2 studies together represent the supply and demand for child care in the same nationally representative U.S. communities in 1990.

These surveys are extraordinarily helpful for understanding the extent of early childhood education in the United States today and the characteristics of those involved. They represent our best estimates for policy making. They are, however, not without their limitations due to sampling biases resulting from (a) the use of listings of "regulated" providers, (b) telephone survey methods, and (c) the limitations on cross-validation inherent in survey methods more generally. The National Child Care Staffing Study (Whitebook, Howes, Phillips, & Pemberton, 1989) explored how teachers and their working conditions affect the caliber of center-based child care available in the United States. While the purposes of the study go well beyond demographics, the sampling procedure provides a means of cross-validating other sources of information about the child care work force. Its comparison with the 1977 National Day Care Supply Study (Coelen, Glantz, & Calore, 1978) permits looking at trends. The study sample included 227 child care centers in 5 metropolitan areas—Atlanta, Boston, Detroit, Phoenix, and Seattle—stratified by income level of census tract. There were 107 for-profit and 120 nonprofit centers. Importantly, the research teams, consisting of trained interviewers and observers, spent 3 days in each center.

Whether these demographic studies are supposedly comprehensive, as in the census, or based on various sampling techniques, the major research issue here is that they have a dual importance. Aside from the data they provide for informing policy—particularly when they can provide trend information—they also provide researchers with estimates of the universe for designing sampling procedures for subsequent studies, as well as a basis for judging the generalizability of other research findings where the sample is adequately described. It must be remembered, however, that they tell us little about local variations in conditions.

STATUS/CHARACTERISTIC STUDIES

Status and characteristic variables of children, parents, and teachers have been used as antecedent or independent variables and as dependent or consequence variables in early childhood research. Parent and child variables have repeatedly been found to be important and powerful predictors of child outcomes from the early childhood education experience (Peters, 1988b; Peters, Bollin, & Murphy, 1991; Pence & Goelman, 1987; Silvern, 1991). They also determine to a large degree the kinds of experiences the child receives, since there is in early childhood education a wider range of discretionary choice than in elementary education (Hirsh-Pasek, Hyson, & Rescorla, 1990; Rescorla, Hyson, Hirsh-Pasek & Cone, 1990). Similarly, a wide variety of characteristics of early childhood personnel may affect the type and/or quality of teacher/child interactions and children's outcomes from the experience. Variables studied the most include teacher age, general education level, the presence or absence of specific training in child development or early education, and years or types of experience (Vondra, 1984; Feeney & Chun, 1985; Whitebook, et al., 1989). Within research on day care, where variability on the education-related variables is greatest, the results are reassuring. The level of education and specific training have been repeatedly found to predict the quality of teacher/child interactions and, to a lesser degree, child outcomes (Roupp, Travers, Glantz, & Coelen, 1979; Whitebook et al., 1989; Berk, 1985). Teacher's age and years of experience are also cited as positively related to child outcomes in some studies (Feeney & Chun, 1985) but not in others (Jambor, 1975). We have less information about other early childhood settings. In public school situations where the variance on educational level and focus is constrained at the beginning levels by credentialing, these variables are less potent predictors. Similarly, in much of the research, situational context variables such as group size, staff/child ratio and staff overall age, and educational level and training mix of multiple care-givers are confounded, producing ambiguous results (Vondra, 1984; Berk, 1985). Indeed, Jorde-Bloom (1989) has emphasized the need to recognize the differing roles of early childhood personnel and the differing structural characteristics of the employment setting in any analysis of professional orientation (see also Powell & Stremmel, 1987).

The vast majority of status/characteristic studies address what we would call the relationship between status variables (age, experience, education and training level) and dynamic characteristics of the work force. They are correlational analyses of certain relatively stable individual-difference variables and other less-stable individual-difference variables within the early childhood personnel population. Variables such as child care worker "burnout" (Townley, Thornburg, & Crompton, 1991), organizational commitment, (Krueger, Lauerman, Graham, & Powell, 1986), job satisfaction (Stremmel, 1990; McClelland, 1986; Jorde-Bloom, 1986), professional orientation (Jorde-Bloom, 1989), tenure or separation rate (Whitebook & Granger, 1989), and turnover (Whitebook et al., 1989) have been extensively studied. Russell, Clifford, and Warlick (1991), as cited in Jorde-Bloom (1992), provide a useful model for viewing the interrelation of these individual status/characteristic relationships within the context of the opportunities for and constraints on individual behavior set by the broader community and work environment.

The National Child Care Staffing Study goes considerably further. In this study it was possible to analyze separately the impact on staff outcome variables by teacher characteristics (formal education, specialized early childhood education training, work experience), general work environment characteristics (wages, benefits, auspices, accreditation), and classroom environment characteristics (teacher/child ratio, group size). Staff outcome variables included job satisfaction and turnover, the quality of the early childhood program provided (developmentally appropriate activity and appropriate caregiving), and the nature of teacher/child interactions (sensitivity, harshness, detachment). These staff variables were in turn related to child outcome variables such as attachment security, sociability, communication skills, Peabody Picture Vocabulary Test scores, time with peers, and aimless wandering. This study is particularly noteworthy because it goes beyond simple survey data.

Even within straightforward surveys, however, studies have become increasingly sophisticated in their methodology and more precise in measuring their variables. For example, Townley, Thornburg, and Crompton (1991), used factor-analytic and multiple-regression techniques to assess the relation of clusters of personal characteristics and job-setting characteristics to burnout and feelings of competency in early childhood personnel. Their sample consisted of 353 early childhood teachers working in child care centers in large metropolitan areas in 5 midwestern states. Briefly, their findings suggest that teachers who had more education, more negative-relations with parents of the children enrolled, and more work hours reported higher levels of burnout. Teachers who were married and who had more education reported feeling more competent. The strangely conflicting result that teachers with higher education levels feel more competent and also experience more burnout is difficult to assess, since insufficient information (e.g., group means) is provided in the published report.

Even if the results presented a clearer picture, however, their generalization would have been impossible. First, this survey lacked a conceptual framework or theoretical base for predicting relationships, particularly those that may be multiply determined or nonlinear. Second, the sampling procedure has several typical problems: (1) It was self-selected, based on the center director's willingness to cooperate and to encourage staff to cooperate with the researchers; (2) the sample was further constrained by the fact that only 353 questionnaires of 775 sent (46%) were returned; and (3) there is no way of knowing if any differences existed between respondents and nonrespondents or between volunteering centers and nonvolunteering centers. Further, without reference to demographic surveys there is no way of determining whether the intended sample (775) was representative of the early childhood teachers of the geographic area represented by the study.

Such issues of generalizability are not unusual, but they need to be clearly recognized. To quote from the report of NAEYC's Survey of Child Care Salaries and Working Conditions, a self-report survey of NAEYC members (43,000 at the time plus others yielding a potential sample of 48,000—but only 3,818 usable responses), "Hundreds of thousands of individuals are employed in early childhood programs....because of the small number of responses compared with the (potential) sample and the population of early childhood employees, and because of the limitations inherent in all surveys, no attempt is made in this report to draw conclusions about the significance or generalizability of the results. Readers are encouraged to resist the temptation to generalize these results to specific programs or to the entire population of early childhood employees." (NAEYC, 1984, p. 10).

When the purposes of surveys are limited (Kontos & Dunn, 1989), their limitations need to be acknowledged. When testing a set of relationships (hypothesized model), the test, within an opportunity sample, may provide additional support for the modeled relationships and their generalizability by replicating the results of prior studies. However, such studies yield little information about the generalizability of specific variables themselves. For example the relationship between salary and job satisfaction has been replicated many times, but this tells us little about job satisfaction in the early childhood work force as a whole, or about salaries or wages in general. Indeed the relationship between salary and job satisfaction may have nothing to do with absolute values of the salary variable but rather with its perceived reasonableness or appropriateness within a particular economic context.

Some research has shown that despite dissatisfaction with low pay, lack of benefits, and inadequate working conditions, there is a rather high level of organizational commitment among those who are employed in child care and early education (Jorde-Bloom, 1989; Stremmel, 1990). This suggests that a more complex theory of motivation is required to explain the behavior and that more precise measurement of the satisfaction variable is needed (Jorde-Bloom, 1986). Indeed, recent research in the area of family day care shows some of the greatest advances in the development of theory. Bollin (1990), for example, has studied the relation of care-giver characteristics, that is, factors in the care giver's family and home situation, to turnover rate or stability in child care provision. Adopting a family-systems theoretical perspective and defining such variables as "boundaries," Bollin conducted a discriminant analysis of the responses of 317 currently registered family day care providers and 67 formerly registered (dropout) providers. Her findings indicate that stable providers (those providing care for more than 2 years) were more likely to express job satisfaction, work longer hours, and have established clearer boundaries between their nuclear family and their family day care clients. Nonstable providers were more likely to have their own infants or toddlers at home and hence often had difficulty setting boundaries between their business and their family life. As Bollin points out, the issues of nurturance and control become complex when both related and nonrelated children are present, and the mixed role relations may cause circular negative-interaction patterns that increase both work and family stress. This line of research looks particularly promising in providing theory-based connections between key provider-status variables (derived from the family life cycle) and characteristic variables thought to be important to the quality of child care (eg., care-giver role acceptance, job satisfaction, stability) (Powell & Bollin, in press).

Bollin's studies also involved creative sampling procedures that permitted a more detailed view of the relationships between status variables and turnover rates in family day care. By comparing the results within a primarily white sample to those within a primarily black sample, she was able to uncover important racial and ethnic differences, and by developing a sample that permitted a prospective view (rather than the usual retrospective view) she was able to gain insights into the role of external market forces in turnover rates. Her prospective sampling involved engaging applicants and newly registered family day care providers into her sample and following them longitudinally, permitting a comparison of those who were successful with those who never opened or who dropped out of the system early on. In this manner she was able to assess the impact of market forces and the use of community support systems (I & R systems and state agency support and training) on stability of care at a particular time.

HISTORICAL/CONTEXTUAL QUESTIONS

Bollin's research (Bollin, 1989, 1990; Powell & Bollin, in press) clearly indicates that family day care providers do not operate in a vacuum. Indeed, understanding their home and family contexts is important for understanding how they carry out their roles and functions. Similarly, recent reviews of Head Start research (Raver & Zigler, 1991) reiterate the importance of understanding the historical context of research and the ways in which changing political, economic, and social pressures influence the directions of early childhood research and the kinds of questions that are addressed (Peters, 1980; Zigler & Rescorla, 1985). Research on the contexts of early childhood teaching may be viewed as dealing with the temporal, structural, or functional (process) characteristics of the environment, (Peters & Kontos, 1987)—each definable at a variety of proximal or distal system levels.

The historical or temporal dimension has often been debated (Swadener & Kessler, 1991; Walsh, 1991) at a level of discussing the predominant theories of development or practice (usually the dominant psychological theories of the day). Empirical research has been less often available. Historical research studies on teacher's attitudes, beliefs, and behaviors studied across historical time and derived from original sources are rare to nonexistent in the literature, whereas historical reviews of pedagological views about what these teacher attitudes, beliefs, and behaviors ought to abound (Braun & Edwards, 1972; Cleverley & Phillips, 1986; Hewes, 1990).

There has been a recent rise in interest in the study of the economics of child care and the ways in which historical social change has affected the opportunity costs associated with home rearing of children as compared to other forms of child care (Barnett, 1990; Barnett, in press). These broader views have provided interesting data for policy formation (Hill-Scott, 1987). Such views are particularly informative when combined with international and cross-cultural comparisons (Chavarria, 1987).

PROCESS QUESTIONS

Studying teachers and the teaching/learning process within early childhood education requires coming to grips with a dynamic, ongoing system of interactions among numerous players. Research in this area has ranged from attempts to describe what teachers do on a daily basis (job analysis—Zaccaria & Hollomon, 1976; Alciatore, 1976), through attempting to describe what teachers think they do and why they do it (teachers' role concepts and their beliefs about child development and learning—Verma & Peters, 1975; Porter & Potenza, 1983), to detailed observational analyses of teacher's interactions with children, parents, or other participants (e.g., aides, supervisors). The focus here will be on the narrower domain of observational studies of adult/child interactions within early childhood settings. This focus was chosen because it is considered essential to understanding the teaching/learning process and because, though previously neglected, it has been an exciting growth area in early education research. As Bredekamp (1986) points out, the importance of adult/child interaction is supported by several studies (Howes & Rubenstein, 1985; McCartney, 1984; McCartney, Scarr, Phillips, Grajek, & Schwarz, 1982; Roupp, et al., 1979) with the most salient determinant of the quality of children's experiences being the amount and quality of adult/child verbal interaction (McCartney, 1984; Stallings, 1975; Miller, Bugbee, & Hybertson 1985). Gordon & Jester (1973) stated in their review: "Our search of the research literature revealed few attempts to observe and describe in quantifiable fashion both teacher and pupil behavior and even fewer attempts to relate observed behavior in a teaching setting to pupil performance in other settings" (p. 184).

As a result they called for more comprehensive observational studies utilizing standardized methods. Feeney & Chun (1985) reiterated the plea. Within recent years researchers have begun to respond effectively.

Recent efforts in this area have been prompted in part by dramatic changes in the field, including the publication of NAEYC's Guidelines for Developmentally Appropriate Practice and the national, voluntary accreditation system for early childhood centers and schools, increased interest in Child Development Associate (CDA) training, and a significant increase in efforts to assess the quality of children's child care arrangements. These influences have provided a means for standardizing the focus of observation and the motivation for more observational research.

NAEYC Guidelines for Practice

Bredekamp (1986), provides data on the reliability and validity of the observation scheme used within the NAEYC accreditation process, the Early Childhood Classroom Observation (ECCO). Of particular interest here are the items dealing with interactions among staff and children. Twelve of 14 items of the ECCO were found to correlate reasonably well with each other and with the total score. Factor analysis indicated that many of these same items load on a single factor, positive interactions, that accounted for approximately 15% of the variance across the broad array of the 131 voluntarily participating classrooms observed. Included were items such as:

Staff interact frequently with children.
Staff are responsive to children.
Staff speak in a friendly courteous way.
Staff use positive guidance.

Staff do not use physical punishment.
Staff help children deal with anger, sadness, frustrations.
Staff encourage prosocial behaviors.

The content validity of this measure derives from the fact that the accreditation system was developed over $3\frac{1}{2}$ years and was reviewed by 186 early childhood specialists as well as by the NAEYC membership (Bredekamp, 1986). The construct validity is supported by the factor structure Bredekamp found.

Similarly, other researchers have focused on the use of NAEYC's criteria for developmentally appropriate teaching practices for 4- and 5-year-old children (Bredekamp, 1986) as a source of items or categories for observing teaching. The assumption here, again made with some reasonableness, is that the source work itself has content validity because of its derivation from within the expertise of the field and its rapid adoption as a standard of practice. For example, Hyson and others (Hyson, Hirsh-Pasek, & Rescorla, 1990; Hirsh-Pasek, Hyson, & Rescorla, 1990) developed the Classroom Practices Inventory; a 26-item Likert-type scale for use by observers. Each item permits observers to rate the observed classroom and teachers on a 5-point scale from not at all like this classroom (1) to very much like this classroom (5). Hyson's research supports the reliability and construct validity of the measure and the potential importance of these classroom practices for child outcomes. Over half the measure's variance was accounted for by a factor tapping encouragement of curiosity, creativity, and provision of concrete materials (Hyson et al., 1990).

Oakes & Caruso (1990) used the developmentally appropriate guidelines as the basis for a time-sampled checklist for observing the behavior of kindergarten teachers. Their 7 categories of behavior included:

Child-initiated versus teacher-directed activities.
Controlled responses versus noncontrolled responses.
Active versus passive child behaviors.
Small-group versus total-group activity.
Use of manipulative versus abstract materials.
Encouraging divergent versus convergent thinking.
Open-ended versus teacher-directed activities.

Again, their research supports the ability of trained observers to observe such behaviors reliably and their study findings are consistent with the construct that there is a cluster of "developmentally appropriate" teaching practices. Their findings also reaffirm the often-found lack of a clear relationship between teachers' espoused beliefs and their classroom practices. (Verma & Peters, 1975). The gap between ground beliefs and practices points to one of the problems of implementing desired practices on a day-to-day basis within nonexperimental classrooms.

Child Development Associate

The Child Development Associate (CDA) credential, administered through the Council for Early Childhood Professional Recognition, is recognized throughout the United States, principally within the national Head Start Program and for purposes of licensing day care providers. To receive a CDA credential an applicant must demonstrate competence in each of the 13 functional areas, including safety, health, development, communication, creativity, self-esteem and independence, social relationships, guidance (or discipline), family relationships, program management, and professionalism.

The CDS Observation Instrument provides broadly stated goals for each of the functional areas and 3 to 5 subgoals organized as numbered items, each accompanied by behavioral exemplars illustrating how the care giver or teacher might achieve these subgoals. The observer summarizes the person's performance as observed over 3 visits by rating whether the subgoal expressed in each item was achieved "rarely," "sometimes," or "mostly."

Briggs (1987) provides an example of how competency areas for CDA training and assessment have been utilized to develop an observation instrument for research purposes. Briggs' Early Childhood Teacher Behavior Checklist is a sign system composed of 63 teaching behaviors shown to affect child development and learning outcomes and to promote effective classroom management and communications. The 63 behaviors are grouped into 5 clusters: enhancing cognitive development; enhancing emotional health and self-concept; enhancing social competence; enhancing physical competence, health, and safety; and management and communication skills. Briggs' preliminary data on the reliability and validity are very promising, suggesting that this instrument may be a measure to develop an overall competency score for individual teachers, based on the definition of competency provided by CDA.

Quality Program Assessment

The Early Childhood Environment Rating Scale (ECERS) (Harms & Clifford, 1980) has been used extensively in recent research as a means of assessing overall quality of early childhood programs (Whitebook et al., 1989; Goelman & Pence, 1987). This research has supported the reliability, content validity, and the construct validity of the measure (Harms & Clifford, 1983). Interestingly, the Whitebook et al. (1989) factor analysis of the measure yielded 2 subscales: developmentally appropriate activity (e.g., materials, schedule, and activities), and appropriate care giving (e.g., supervision, adult/child interactions, and discipline).

An adaptation was made of the ECERS for assessment of the family day care environment, the Family Day Care Rating Scale (FDCRS) (Harms & Clifford, 1989). The FDCRS consists of 32 items organized into 6 subscales covering space and furnishings for care and learning, basic care, language and reasoning, learning activities, social development, and adult needs. The range of items is compatible with the CDA functional areas (See Clifford, Harms, Pepper, & Stuart, in press, for a detailed comparison.) Each item is scored on a 7-point scale anchored at 4 points with observable behavioral and environmental descriptors (Harms & Clifford, 1989). The FDCRS and an earlier version have been used as research instruments in several major studies (Goelman & Pence, 1987; Stuart & Pepper, 1988; Fiene & Melnick, 1990; Howes & Stewart, 1987; Jones & Meisels, 1987; Deiner, in press). These studies provide solid evidence of the

internal consistency and interrater reliability for this measure (Clifford, et al., in press). Importantly, there is a growing body of research, including factor analyses and studies of concurrent validity, to support the validity of this instrument for assessing the interpersonal relations within family day care (adult/child interactions) and the ability of the teacher for organizing the learning environment.

While there is and will continue to be development of interesting and important specialized procedures for observing adult/child interactions within classroom settings (see Flemming, Wolery, Venn, & Schroeder, 1991, for observing teachers' roles in mainstreamed classrooms; Durkin, 1987, for observing reading instruction in kindergarten), these special-purpose tools are of more limited interest. The ones discussed above provide an exciting development in the field because of the commonality and content validity of their origins and the confluence that appears to be developing in their findings. The results suggest that the field has made considerable strides toward the development of general-purpose observational measures, potentially interpretable across studies and across time, for use in research and evaluation of the early childhood teaching process.

DEVELOPMENTAL QUESTIONS

Within early childhood education we readily acknowledge the importance of understanding the development of children and endorse the notion that teachers should adapt their methods to the developmental level of the child. Less often do we acknowledge that teachers, and indeed all early childhood personnel, are developing as well. The fields of adult and career development provide an important supporting context for understanding teachers and the teaching process.

The concept of adult development, as exemplified by the well-known formulations of persons such as Erikson (1950) and Levinson (1978, 1986), purports that growth in affect, cognition, and overall breadth of understanding and competence can take place throughout the lifetime, and may often be described in stages. Within the field of education generally, and early education specifically, formulations of stages of career development have been proposed (Katz, 1977; Vander Ven, 1988) for early childhood personnel and for preservice and beginning teachers (Caruso, 1977; Caruso, & Fawcett 1986). Vander Ven's formulation includes 5 stages of teaching: novice, initial practice, informed practice, complex practice, and influential practice. She describes for each stage the level of professionalism, the roles and functions performed, teachers' levels of cognition and affect, and the levels of supervision they may require or provide to others.

These formulations, while provocative, are backed by little data to support specific stages or developmental progressions. However, a developmental approach does not have to be restrictive in its developmental assumptions. According to lifespan theorists, change does not have to be qualitative, irreversible, and end-state oriented (Baltes, Reese, & Nesselroade, 1977). It does, however, have to be systematic and stable change within the individual (intraindividual change).

Within the life-span framework, the determinants of development are believed to be pluralistic, generally falling within 3 broad types of influence: normative age graded, normative history graded, and nonnormative. Normative age-graded influences are biological and environmental determinants that, in terms of their onset and duration, are highly correlated with chronological age. For teachers, normative age-graded events would be college entry, student teaching, and the like. Normative history-graded influences are biological and environmental determinants associated with historical time and historical contexts related to cohort. They are normative if they occur to most members of a generation (or cohorts) in similar ways. For teachers, examples would include widespread changes in philosophy, regulation, law, or economic and social climate, such as desegregation, mainstreaming of individuals with disabilities, or a great migration. Nonnormative life events are biological and environmental determinants for which there is no general homogeneity of pattern among individuals (e.g., medical trauma, divorce, unemployment, career changes). Examples for teachers may be a loss of job through workforce reduction due to redistricting or demographic changes in the community, or changes in responsibility because of rapid staff turnover.

These 3 types of influence are sometimes called life events. Research has suggested a typology or categorization of life events (Brim & Ryff, 1980; Danish, Smyer, & Nowak, 1980) and they have been applied to our understanding of the personal and professional development of early childhood personnel (Peters, Sutton, & Yenchko, 1981). This work assumes that life events are multidimensional but that there are orderly ways of classifying them. It further assumes that professional development of early childhood personnel does not occur in a vacuum, but in a complex changing world over which the individual has some control. Implied is the notion that changes can occur in many contexts of individuals' lives and that an individual's development may proceed differently in different contexts. For research on teachers, these contexts can be divided for simplicity purposes into 2 categories: the professional or work setting and all other settings (e.g., community, home). The research has, then, addressed issues of development of teachers as teachers (Fuller, 1969; Fuller & Brown, 1975; Peters & Sutton, 1984) and teachers as persons in relation to other contexts. This crude distinction permits recognition of the fact that individuals in early childhood education experience (at least) 2 concurrent developmental patterns that may interact and influence each other. For example, the personal development of teachers may influence their professional development (Glassberg & Sprinthall, 1980; Sprinthall & Theis-Sprinthall, 1983). Alternatively, the development of the teacher as professional may impinge on the personal development of the teacher as person (Sutton, 1983; Peters, 1988a). This developmental perspective has proven useful in studying the training and professionalization of individuals who do not fall into the usual pattern of life events of typical preservice and beginning teachers. Peters' work with CDA trainees in Head Start and Bollin and others' work with family day care providers give good examples of how a more thorough understanding of personal life events can assist in predicting professional developmental outcomes. They also make it clear that the current zeitgeist about what constitutes appropriate teaching practice produces specific cohort effects as groups of teachers move through the teacher development process. Such cohort effects can produce intrainstitutional conflict as well as intrainstitutional change, as, for example, when a group of new early childhood teachers, trained under the zeitgeist of NAEYC's Guidelines for Developmentally Appropriate Practice are brought into public schools and confront elementary teachers and principals trained when different beliefs about development and methods were in favor (Oakes & Caruso, 1990).

Parents, too, are developing and there are interindividual differences in their development as people and in their family-life cycle as parents. The literature on parent/teacher and parent/care-giver relations suggests that assessment of matches and mismatches here may be important to understanding both parental and teacher satisfaction (Kontos, 1987; Powell & Stremmel, 1987; Peters & Benn, 1980; Kontos & Wells, 1986; Long & Garduque, 1987; Pence & Goelman, 1987) and child outcomes (Peters, Bollin, & Murphy, 1991). While research on this aspect of teachers and teaching has been limited to date, it does hold promise for the future as longitudinal and other developmentally sensitive research designs are incorporated into the repertoire of the early childhood education research.

FUTURE DIRECTIONS

This review began with 4 concerns expressed by Sears & Dowley 30 years ago: a lack of theory for the teaching process, the reluctance of researchers to replicate the work of others, the difficulty of abstracting teaching method from social context, and the lack of longitudinal research. It is clear that in the intervening 30 years some progress has been made, but much remains to be done.

The progress has been both general and specific. At the specific level there has been some progress in the development of theories to guide the study of teachers and the teaching process. These theories have been adapted from the theoretical positions of other research domains more often than they have been self-generated within the field of early childhood education itself. As these theories are brought together and incorporated in the thinking and research of early childhood education, in some ways they have begun to cohere into a unique formulation that has heuristic value. However, much theoretical work needs to be done.

Similarly, although agreement has not gone unquestioned, there is increased consensus concerning teaching practices that are appropriate and effective. This agreement has fostered far more commonality in the variables studied and in the ways they are assessed. As a result, many of the studies cited in this chapter provide the opportunity for partial replication and the incremental building of our understanding. The studies are far more interpretable as parts of a whole than they were in 1963.

At a more general level, what has changed is both our conception of the breadth of the early childhood field and our understanding of the complexities that need to be incorporated into that research. So, for example, we have seen a burgeoning of the research on day care, including family day care, and we are about to experience an even more rapid increase in the area of research on early intervention and early childhood special education. These socially and economically driven research interests will no doubt propel the field through the turn of the century.

Our increased awareness of the complexities of teachers and the teaching process presents us with the greatest challenge. The confounding of variables cited by Sears & Dowley and others (Miller, Bugbee, & Hybertson, 1985) as problems with current research is perhaps more appropriately seen as a realistic portrayal of a complex, continuously evolving system at work. Our recognition that the process of teaching within early childhood classrooms comprises reciprocal effects of ever-changing and developing children, parents, and historical context, interacting to bring about changes in each other, as well as in society more generally, will force us to develop new research designs and statistical methods to capture and analyze this complexity better.

As we move from univariate causal models to more complex systemic ones, the range of questions that need to be asked and answered, even within the 5 domains of questions suggested in this chapter, increases markedly. However, a clear start has been made.

References

Alciatore, R. T. (1976). *Texas Day Care Study: Job descriptions, career progression and individual training record.* San Antonio: University of Texas.

Almy, M. (1975). *The early childhood educator at work.* New York: McGraw-Hill.

Baltes, P. B., Reese, H., & Nesselroade, J. (1977). *Life-span developmental psychology: Introduction to research methods.* Monterey, CA: Brooks/Cole.

Barnett, S. (1990). Developing preschool education policy: An economic perspective. *Educational Policy,* 4(3), 245–265.

Barnett, S. (in press). The economics of family day care and the child care market. In D. Peters & A. Pence (Eds.) *Family day care: Current research for informed public policy.* New York: Teachers College Press.

Beller, E. K. (1973). Research on organized programs of early education. In R. M. Travers, (Ed.), *Second handbook of research on teaching.* (pp. 530–600). Chicago: Rand McNally.

Belsky, J. (1984). Two waves of day care research: Developmental effects and conditions of quality. In R. C. Ainselie (Ed.), *The child and the day care setting* (pp. 1–34). New York: Praeger.

Belsky, J. (1990) Parental and nonparental child care and children's socioemotional development: A decade in review. *Journal of Marriage & the Family, 52*(4), 885–903.

Berk, L. E., (1985). Relationship of caregiver education to child-oriented attitudes, job satisfaction, and behaviors toward children. *Child Care Quarterly, 14*(2). 103–129.

Bollin, G. (1989). *To be or not to be a family day care provider?: An investigation of turnover among family day care providers.* Dissertation Abstracts International, *49,* 9007A (University Microfilms No. ADG90-10393.)

Bollin, G. (1990, April). *An investigation of turnover in family day care providers.* Paper presented at the annual meeting of the American Educational Research Association, Boston.

Bredekamp, S. (1986). The reliability and validity of the early childhood classroom observation scale for accrediting early childhood programs. *Early Childhood Research Quarterly, 1*(2), 103–118.

Braun, S., & Edwards, E. (1972). *History and theory of early childhood education.* Worthington, OH: Charles Jones.

Briggs, B. A. (1987). Measuring effective early childhood teaching behavior. *Child and Youth Care Quarterly, 16*(3), 196–209

Brim, O., & Ryff, C. D. (1980). On the properties of life events. In P. Baltes & O. Brim (Eds.), *Life-span development and behavior* (Vol. 3, pp. 120–122). New York: Academic Press.

Bronfenbrenner, J. (1979). *The ecology of human development.* Cambridge, MA: Harvard University Press.

Bronfenbrenner, J. (1989). Ecological systems theory. *Annuals of Child Development,* Vol. 6, 187–249.

Brophy, J. E., & Good, T. L. (1986). Teacher behavior and student achievement. In M. C. Whittrock (Ed.) *Handbook of Research on Teaching* (3rd ed.) (pp. 328–375). New York: Macmillan.

Caruso, J. J. (1977). Phases in student teaching. *Young Children. 33* (1), 57–63.

Caruso, J. J., & Fawcett, M. T. (1986). *Supervision in early childhood education.* New York: Teachers College Press.

Chavarria, M. (1987). Macrosystem continuity, congruity and stability: Costa Rica as a case example. In D. Peters & S. Kontos (Eds.), *Continuity and discontinuity of experience in child care* (pp. 189–200). Norwood, NJ: Ablex.

Cleverley, J., & Phillips, D. C. (1986). *Visions of childhood: Influential models from Locke to Spock.* New York: Teachers College Press.

Clifford, R. M., Harms, T., Pepper, S., & Stuart, B. (in press). Assessing quality in family day care. In D. L. Peters & A. Pence (Eds.), *Family day care: current research for informed public policy.* New York: Teachers College Press.

Coelen, C., Glantz, R., & Calore, D. (1978). *Day care centers in the U.S.: A national profile, 1976–1977.* Cambridge, MA: Abt Associates.

Costley, J. B., Morgan, G. G., & Genser, A. (1991, May). Climbing the ladder: Professionalizing the field of child care. *Wheelock Magazine,* pp. 23–26.

Danish, S., Smyer, M., & Nowak, C. (1980). Developmental intervention: Enhancing life-event processes. In P. Baltes & O. Brim (Eds.), *Life-span development and behavior* (Vol. 3, pp. 132–140). New York: Academic Press.

Deiner, P. L. (in press). Family day care and children with disabilities. In D. Peters & A. Pence (Eds.), *Family day care: Current research for informed public policy.* New York: Teachers College Press.

Durkin, D. (1987). A classroom-observation study of reading instruction in kindergarten. *Early Childhood Research Quarterly, 2*(3), 275–300.

Elkind, D. (1987). *The miseducation of children: Superkids at risk.* New York: Knopf.

Erikson, E. (1950). *Childhood and society.* New York: W. W. Norton.

Erikson, F. (1986). Quantitative methods in research on teaching. In M. Whittrock (Ed.). *Handbook of research on teaching* (3rd. ed., pp. 119–162) New York: MacMillan.

Feeney, S., & Chun, R. (1985). Effective teachers of young children. *Young Children, 40*(4) 19–23.

Fiene, B. J., & Melnick, S. A. (1990). Licensure and program quality in early childhood and child care programs. Paper presented at the annual meeting of the American Educational Research Association, Boston.

Flemming, L., Wolery, M., Weizierl, C., Venn, M., & Schroeder, C. (1991). Model for assessing and adapting teacher's roles in mainstreamed preschool settings. *Topics in Early Childhood Special Education. 11*(1), 85–98.

Fuller, F. F. (1969). Concerns of teachers: A developmental conceptualization. *American Educational Research Journal, 6*, 207–226.

Fuller, F. F., & Brown, D. (1975). On becoming a teacher. In K. Ryan (Ed.), *Teacher education* (pp. 66–75), Chicago: University of Chicago Press.

Glassberg, S., & Sprinthall, N. A. (1980). Student teaching: A developmental approach. *Journal of Teacher Education, 31*(20), 31–38.

Goelman, H., & Pence, A. (1987). Some aspects of the relationship between family structure and child language development in three types of day care. In D. L. Peters & S. Kontos (Eds.), *Continuity and discontinuity of experience in child care* (pp. 129–146). Norwood, NJ: Ablex.

Gordon, I. J., & Jester, R. E. (1973). Techniques of observing teaching in early childhood and outcomes of particular procedures. In R. M. Travers (Ed.), *Second handbook of research on teaching* (pp. 194–217). Chicago: Rand McNally.

Grotberg, E., Chapman, J., & Lazar, J., (1971). *The present status and future needs in day care research.* Washington, DC: Office of Child Development.

Harms, T., & Clifford, R. M. (1980). *The Early Childhood Environment Rating Scale.* New York: Teachers College Press.

Harms, T., & Clifford, R. M. (1983). Assessing preschool environments with the early childhood environment rating scale. *Studies in Educational Evaluation, 8*, 261–269.

Harms, T., & Clifford, R. M. (1989). *Family day care rating scale.* New York: Teachers College Press.

Hewes, D. W. (1990). Historical foundations of early childhood teacher training: The evolution of kindergarten teacher preparation. In B. Spodek & O. Saracho (Eds.), *Early childhood teacher preparation: Yearbook in early childhood education; Vol. 1.* (pp. 1–22). New York: Teachers College Press.

Hill-Scott, K. (1987). The effects of subsidized, private, and unregulated child care on family functions. In D. Peters & S. Kontos (Eds.), *Continuity and discontinuity of experience in child care,* (pp. 147–168). Norwood, NJ: Ablex.

Hirsh-Pasek, K., Hyson, M. C., & Rescorla, L. (1990). Academic environments in preschool: Do they pressure or challenge young children? *Early Education and Development, 1*(6), 401–423.

Hofferth, S. L. (1989). What is the demand for supply of child care in the United States? *Young Children, 44*(5), 26–33.

Hofferth, S. L., & Kisker, E. E. (in press). The changing demographics of family day care in the United States. In D. Peters & A. Pence (Eds.), *Family day care: Current research for informed public policy.* New York: Teachers College Press.

Howes, C. & Rubenstein, J. (1985). Determinants of toddlers' experience in day care: Age of entry and quality of setting. *Child Care Quarterly, 14*, 140–151.

Howes, C., & Stewart, P. (1987). Child's play with adults, toys, and peers: An examination of family and child care influences. *Developmental Psychology, 23*, 423–430.

Hyson, M. C., Hirsh-Pasek, K., & Rescorla, L. (1990). The Classroom Practices Inventory: An observation instrument based on NAEYC's Guidelines for Developmentally Appropriate Practices for 4- and 5-year-old children. *Early Childhood Research Quarterly, 5*, 475–494.

Jambor, T. W. (1975). Teacher role behavior: Day care versus nursery school. *Child Care Quarterly, 4*(2), 93–100.

Jones, S. N., & Meisels, S. J. (1987). Training family day care providers to work with special needs children. *Topics in Early Childhood Special Education, 7*(1), 1–12.

Jorde-Bloom, P. (1986). Teacher job satisfaction: A framework for analysis. *Early Childhood Research Quarterly, 1*(2), 167–184.

Jorde-Bloom, P. (1989). Professional orientation: Individual and organizational perspectives. *Child & Youth Care Quarterly, 18*(4), 227–242.

Jorde-Bloom, P. (1992). Staffing issues in child care. In B. Spodek & O. Saracho (Eds.), *Yearbook of early childhood education, Vol. 3: Issues in Child Care.* New York: Teachers College Press.

Katz, L. (1977). *Talks with teachers.* Washington, DC: National Association for the Education of Young Children.

Kisker, E., Hofferth, S., & Phillips, D. (1991). *A profile of child care settings: Early education and care in 1990.* Princeton, NJ: Mathematics Policy Research.

Kontos, S. (1987). The attitudinal context of family-day care relationships. In D. Peters & S. Kontos (Eds.), *Continuity and discontinuity of experience in child care* (pp. 91–113). Norwood, NJ: Ablex.

Kontos, S., & Dunn, L. (1989). Characteristics of the early intervention workforce: An Indiana perspective. *Early Education and Development, 1*(2), 141–157.

Kontos, S., & Wells, W. (1986). Attitudes of caregivers and the day care experiences of families. *Early Childhood Research Quarterly, 1*(1), 47–68.

Krueger, M., Lauerman, R., Graham, M., & Powell, N. (1986). Characteristics and organizational commitment of child and youth care workers. *Child Care Quarterly, 15*(1), 60–72.

Levinson, D. (1978). *The seasons of man's life.* New York: Alfred A. Knopf.

Levinson, D. (1986). A completion of adult development. *American Psychologist, 41*(1), 3–13.

Long, F., & Garduque, L. (1987). Continuity between home and family day care: Caregivers' and mothers' perceptions and children's social experience. In D. L. Peters & S. Kontos (Eds.), *Continuity and discontinuity of experience in child care* (pp. 69–90). Norwood, NJ: Ablex.

Long, F., Peters, D. L., & Garduque, L. (1985). Continuity between home and day care: A model for defining relevant dimensions of child care. In I. E. Sigel (Ed.), *Advances in applied developmental psychology* (pp. 131–170). Norwood, NJ: Ablex.

McCartney, K. (1984). Effect of quality of day care environment on children's language development. *Developmental Psychology, 20*, 244–260.

McCartney, K., Scarr, S., Phillips, D., Grajek, S., & Schwarz, C. (1982). Environmental differences among day care centers and their effects on children's development. In E. F. Zigler & E. W. Gordon (Eds.), *Day care: Scientific and social policy issues* (pp. 126–151). Boston: Auburn House.

McClelland, J. (1986). Job satisfaction of child care workers: A review. *Child Care Quarterly, 15*(2), 82–89.

Miller, L. B., Bugbee, M., & Hybertson, D. (1985). Dimensions of preschool: The effects of individual experience. In I. Sigel (Ed.). *Advances in applied developmental psychology, Vol. 1* (pp. 25–90). Norwood, NJ: Ablex.

National Association for the Education of Young Children (NAEYC). (1984). Results of the NAEYC Survey of Child Care Salaries and Working Conditions. *Young Children, 39*(5), 14–22.

Oakes, P., & Caruso, D. (1990). Kindergarten teachers' use of developmentally appropriate practices and attitudes about authority. *Early Education and Development. 1*(6), 445–457.

Patton, M. Q. (1990). *Qualitative evaluation and research methods.* Newbury Park, CA: Sage.

Pence, A. R., & Goelman, H. (1987). Who cares for the child in day care? An examination of caregivers from three types of care. *Early Childhood Research Quarterly. 2*(4), 315–334.

Peters, D. L. (1980). Social science and social policy and the care of young children: Head Start and after. *Journal of Applied Developmental Psychology, 1*(1), 7–27.

Peters, D. L. (1984). *What does research tell us about CDA training?* Paper presented at the annual meeting of the National Association for the Education of Young Children, Los Angeles, November 8. (ERIC/ECE PSO 14806).

Peters, D. L., (1988a). The Child Development Associate credential and the educationally disenfranchised. In B. Spodek, O. Saracho, & D. Peters (Eds.), *Professionalism and the early childhood practitioner* (pp. 93–104). New York: Teachers College Press.

Peters, D. L. (1988b). Head Start's influence on parental and child competence. In S. Steinmetz (Ed.), *Family and support systems across the life span* (pp. 73–98). New York: Plenum.

Peters, D. & Benn, J. (1980). Day Care: Support for the family. *Dimensions,* 78–82.

Peters, D. L., & Hodges, W. (1980). Evaluation of day care at the state level. *Young Children, 35*(3), 3–13.

Peters, D. L., & Kontos, S. (1987). Continuity and discontinuity of experience: An intervention perspective. In D. L. Peters & S. Kontos (Eds.), *Continuity and Discontinuity of experience in child care* (pp. 1–16). Norwood, NJ: Ablex.

Peters, D. L., & Sibbison, V. (1980). Considerations in the assessment of community child care needs. *Residential & Community Child Care Administration, 1*(40) 407–419.

Peters, D. L., Bollin, G., & Murphy, R. E. (1991). Head Start's influence on parental competence and child competence. In S. Silvern (Ed.), *Literacy through family, community, and school interaction.* (pp. 91–124) Greenwich, CN: JAI.

Peters, D. L. & Sutton, R., (1984). The effects of CDA training on Head Start personnel beliefs, attitudes and behaviors. *Child Care Quarterly, 13*(4), 13–17.

Peters, D. L., Sutton, R., & Yenchko (1981). *The preschool teacher as an adult learner.* Paper presented at the annual meeting of the American Psychological Association, Los Angeles, August 24–28. (ERIC Document Reproduction Service No. ED 214 656).

Phillips, D., & Whitebook, M. (1986). Who are child care workers? *Young Children, 41*(4), 14–22.

Porter, C., & Potenza, A. (1983). Alternative methodologies for early childhood research. In S. Kilmer (Ed.). *Advances in early education and day care.* (Vol. 3, pp. 155–186). JAI.

Powell, D. R., & Bollin, G. (in press). Dimensions of parent-provider relationships in family day care. In D. Peters & A. Pence (Eds.), *Family day care: Current research for informed policy.* New York: Teachers College Press.

Powell, D. R., & Stremmel, A. J. (1987). Managing relations with parents: Research notes on the teacher's role. In D. L. Peters & S. Kontos (Eds.), *Continuity and discontinuity of experience in child care.* (pp. 129–146). Norwood, NJ: Ablex.

Prescott, E., Jones, E., & Kritchevsky, S. (1967). *Group day care as a child rearing environment.* Pasadena, CA: Pacific Oaks.

Raver, C. C., & Zigler, E. G. (1991). Three steps forward, two steps back: Head Start and the measurement of social competence. *Young Children, 46*(4), 3–9.

Reichardt, C. S., & Cook, T. D. (1979). Beyond qualitative versus quantitative methods. In T. D. Cook & C. S. Reichardt (Eds.), *Qualitative and quantitative methods in evaluation research.* Beverly Hills, CA: Sage.

Rescorla, L., Hyson, M., Hirsch-Pasek, K., & Cone, J. (1990). Academic expectations in mothers of preschool children. *Early Education and Development, 1*(3), 165–184.

Roupp, R., Travers, J., Glantz, F., & Coelen, C. (1979). *Children at the center.* Cambridge, MA: Abt Associates.

Saracho, O. N. (1988). Cognitive style and early childhood practice. In B. Spodek, O. Saracho, & D. Peters (Eds.), *Professionalism and the early childhood practitioner* (pp. 173–183), New York: Teachers College Press.

Sears, P. S., & Dowley, E. M. (1963). Research on teaching in the nursery school. In N. L. Gage (Ed.), *Handbook of research on teaching* (pp. 814–864). Chicago: Rand McNally.

Silvern, S. (1991). *Literacy through family, community, and school interaction.* Greenwich, CN: JAI.

Spodek, B., Saracho, O. N., & Peters, D. L. (Eds.). (1988). *Professionalism and the early childhood practitioner.* New York: Teachers College Press.

Sprinthall, N. A., & Theis-Sprinthall, L. (1983). The teacher as adult learner: a cognitive development view. In G. Griffin (Ed.), *Staff development, 82nd Yearbook of the National Society of the Study of Education, Part II* (pp. 13–35). Chicago; University of Chicago Press.

Stallings, J. (1975). Implementation and child effects of teaching practices in follow through classrooms. *Monographs of the Society for Research in Child Development, 40*(7-8) Serial No. 163.

Stallings, J. A., & Stipek, D. (1986). Research on early childhood and elementary school programs. In M. C. Whittrock (Ed.), *Handbook of research on teaching,* (3rd ed., pp. 727–753). New York: Macmillan.

Stremmel, A. J. (1990, April). *Predictors of intention to leave child care work.* Paper presented at the annual meeting of the American Educational Research Association, Boston.

Stuart, B., & Pepper, S. (1988). The contribution of caregivers personality and vocational interests quality in licensed family day care. *Canadian Journal of Research in Early Childhood Education, 2,* 99–109.

Sutton, R. E. (1983). *The development of a measure to assess dimensions of inservice training programs.* Unpublished doctoral dissertation, Pennsylvania State University, University Park, PA.

Swadener, B. B., & Kessler, S. (Eds.). (1991), Reconceptualizing early childhood education. [Special Issue] *Early Education and Child Development, 2*(20).

Townley, K., Thornburg, K., & Crompton, D. (1991). Burnout in teachers of young children. *Early Education and Development, 2*(3), 197–204.

Vander Ven, K. (1988). Pathways to professional effectiveness for early childhood educators. In B. Spodek, O. Saracho, & D. Peters (Eds.), *Professionalism and the early childhood practitioner* (pp. 137–160). New York: Teachers College Press.

Verma, S., & Peters, D. (1975). Day care teachers' practices and beliefs. *Alberta Journal of Educational Research, 21*(1), 46–55.

Vondra, J. I. (1984). A consideration of caregiver age variables in day care settings. *Child Care Quarterly, 13*(2), 102–113.

Walsh, D. J. (1991). Extending the discourse on developmental appropriateness: A developmental perspective. *Early Education and Development, 2*(2), 109–119.

Whitebook M., & Granger, R. C. (1989). Assessing teacher turnover. *Young Children, 44*(4), 11–14.

Whitebook M., Howes, C., Phillips, D., & Pemberton, C. (1989). Who Cares? Child care teachers and the quality of care in America. *Young Children, 45*(1) 41–45.

Whittrock, M. C. (1986). *Handbook of research on teaching,* (3rd. ed.) New York: Macmillan.

Willer, B., Hofferth, S., Kisker, E., Divine-Hawkins, P., Farquhar, E., & Glantz, F. (1991). *The demand and supply of child care in 1990.* Washington, DC: National Association for the Education of Young Children.

Zaccaria, M., & Hollomon, J. W. (1976). *Texas Day Care Study: Occupational analysis of day care personnel.* San Antonio, TX: University of Texas.

Zigler, E. F., & Rescorla, L. (1985). Social science and social policy: The case of social competence as a goal of intervention programs. In R. Kasschau, L. Rehm, & L. Ullmann (Eds.), *Psychology research, public policy and practice: Towards a productive partnership* (pp. 62–94). New York: Praeger.

· 32 ·

THE RESEARCH–POLICY CONNECTION:
MOVING BEYOND INCREMENTALISM

Sharon L. Kagan

YALE UNIVERSITY

The late 1980s and early 1990s have witnessed the most remarkable policy advancements for children and families in American history. Yet, despite these accomplishments, countless documents still lament the plight of America's education system, our national labor pool, and the status of the country's children and families (Children's Defense Fund, 1991; Committee for Economic Development, 1991; Klerman, 1991; National Governors' Association, 1990). The purpose of this chapter is to explore this schism, focusing on the role that child development and early education research has played in moving the child and family agenda, and the role that it will need to play if America is to craft the kinds of policies and programs to which its children and families are rightfully entitled.

This chapter suggests that the once tenuous research-to-policy connection as it relates to young children and families has been strengthened (Horowitz & O'Brien, 1989). Rather than being characterized by disaffection, such relationships are now commonly hallmarked by a more thoughtful search for definitions, mechanisms, and strategies that will maximize the synergy of research and policy interactions. For the most effective research-to-policy connection to occur, we must first take stock of persistent challenges that have impeded the research-to-policy link. Second, to move beyond the incrementalism that has characterized past applications of research to policy, a new research-policy synergy must be recontextualized within a vision of what all children are rightfully entitled to and the role of American government in meeting that entitlement. Third, within this broad vision, specific domains of inquiry must be addressed as we help shape a more integrated, equitable early care and education system.

THE RESEARCH AND POLICY
SCHISM: REALITY OR RHETORIC?

Writing in *The Care and Education of Young Children In America*, Irving Lazar (1980) indicated that he recalled "only three studies that directly changed policies and actions in major program areas in our field" (p. 61). He cites Spitz's (1945) work on the short- and long-term effects of institutional care on infant development, Clark and Clark's work (1952) on racial differentiation in preschool children, and the work of the Consortium for Longitudinal Studies (1977) on the long-term effects of preschool programs. Lazar is not alone in questioning the successful application of social science for policy-making. Others, writing before that time, were even more skeptical. For example, Cohen and Garet (1975) note that "there is little evidence to indicate that government planning offices have succeeded in linking social research and decision making" (p. 19). Wholey, Scanlon, Dugfy, Fikumotos, and Vogt (1971) more vehemently conclude that "the recent literature is unanimous in announcing the general failure of evaluation to affect decision making in a significant way" (p. 46). Weidman, Horst, Taher, and Wholey (1973) note that what "little use that has occurred [has been] fortuitous rather than planned." Weiss (1972) summarizes the thinking of the time by suggesting that the results of evaluation research have exerted little, if any, significant influence on program decisions.

Despite the prevailing concern at the time that social science—broadly construed—had limited effect on program and policy, many researchers, believing that such a link would advance child and family well-being and that such a link was indeed possible, explicitly called for more collaboration between research and policy (Bronfenbrenner, 1974; National Research Council, 1978; Phillips, 1984; Takanishi, DeLeon, & Pallak, 1983). Indeed, Caldwell and Ricciuti (1973) note in the introduction to their volume on child development and social policy, "It is our conviction that there should be a symbiotic relationship between social policy and social action on the one hand and child development research and its underlying theory on the other" (p. viii).

During the 1980s, efforts to link research to policy gained currency. Centers devoted to this endeavor proliferated (Policy Studies Organization, 1978), foundation support grew, and professional organizations began to more seriously consider, if not fully legitimize, social policy as an important component of their efforts. Scientists, concerned about having their findings applied to policy, sought nontraditional outlets for their work and devoted more energy to dissemination and popularization of their research findings. Collectively, these efforts yielded increased success. Certainly, Lazar's own work, coupled with that of the Perry Preschool (Berrueta-Clement, Schweinhart, Barnett, Epstein, & Weikart, 1984), was instrumental in cementing current policy commitments to early care and education.

Despite these encouraging advancements and an emerging receptivity to social science research in general, the challenges inherent in applying child development and early childhood research to child and family policy remain abundant. Sadly, important accomplishments do not alleviate the difficulties. Rather, they make us more sensitive to their pervasiveness and complexity. Four challenges in particular hallmark the difficulty of applying research to policy in early care and education. These include (1) challenges associated with differing values, (2) challenges associated with the lack of definitional clarity, (3) challenges associated with process and context, and (4) challenges associated with measuring policy-relevant outcomes. As a prelude to forging new research-to-policy connections in the field, these challenges must be fully understood.

Challenges Related to Differing Values

Although there are numerous value considerations that have impeded the effectiveness of the research-to-policy link, two in particular stand out. One is generic, unearthing value differences regarding the role of scientists in policy formation. The other is more specifically related to children and families and questions the appropriate role of government in child and family life.

The former, which has come to be understood as the "philosopher-king" issue, suggests that the purported role of scientists as bearers of truth and ultimate knowledge may be overexalted in the policy domain. Reflecting dissatisfaction with the preeminence of social scientists as foremost policy influencers, Rossi and Wright (1985) note that "a society in which social scientists play crucial policy roles through their research is a society in which human values have been subordinated to technocratic considerations, a world in which social scientists have become philosopher-kings. In a truly democratic society, social science must be content with an advisory but not dom-

inating role" (p. 331). Amplified by realistic appraisals that assail the neutrality of science, such positions have gained currency (Cronbach et al., 1980; Lindblom & Cohen, 1979; Mark & Shotland, 1985). The philosopher-king has been dethroned, and in so doing, other kinds of knowledge and knowledge-makers have ascended in the policy hierarchy. Current thinking suggests that social science evidence is just one influence on policy, one that is mediated by multiple factors including the media, funding agencies, and the receptiveness of the policy-making body (Pettigrew, 1985). Clearly, values regarding the role of science and social scientists in the policy game have been challenged.

But perhaps nowhere is the role of values in the policy process more controversial than in the child and family domain. Nested in a historical ethos that accords primacy and privacy of nurturing children to the family, public America is ambivalent about how much it values children and about how much responsibility it should accord government for their care and development. On the one hand, Americans have embraced the notion of *parens patriae*, which condones government intervention for needy populations; on the other hand, we continue to wrestle with day care and other services as a legitimate social provision for all children. Noting the controversial ideology that surrounds child care issues, Woolsey (1977) suggests that day care policy positions tend to serve as proxies for deeply held beliefs about the relationship between family and government, making day care a politically explosive issue. Because we have failed to resolve fundamental value differences, early care and education continues to be debated in the ideological, rather than the empirical, domain. The nation debates *whether* children should be in care, not *what* kind of care they should receive. Indeed, the most elegant and socially relevant child development research is often forced to withstand ideological litmus tests, litmus tests that derail the debate.

This value conflict is exacerbated because, historically, services to young children have been considered ancillary to broader social needs; they are often a policy means to a greater social end—welfare reform, tax equity, or defense policy. Woodhead (1988) notes that many children's programs have emerged in response to somewhat ephemeral social goals that are quite removed from the immediate priorities of young children. Whether the goals are ephemeral or not, the consequence of being a by-product of a broader social effort is that the real needs of children—equitable access to high-quality early care and education—are never accorded priority. Even when policy value is accorded children's issues, the primary goal for healthy and appropriate child development has been subordinated to other, more pervasive national needs and value conflicts.

Challenges Related to the Lack of Definitional Clarity

Fostering the research-policy connection is further hindered because the field lacks agreed-upon definitions of policy research, policy-related research, basic research, applied research, and evaluation research. Moreover, distinctions between such research and policy analysis, although the subject of many volumes, remain ambiguous. One school of thought suggests that many of the terms can be used interchangeably.

For example, Nagel (1990) suggests that this is the case with program evaluation, policy evaluation, policy analysis, and policy research. Echoing this general sentiment, Maccoby, Kahn, and Everett (1983) contend that policy research cannot be described as a distinct category at all because much research used by policymakers was not intended for that purpose at all.

Conversely, another school of thought suggests that policy analysis is a distinct domain of inquiry. Moroney (1981) indicates that policy analysis is distinguished from conventional research by the way in which questions are formulated as well as by the specific purposes of the analysis. Policy analysis sets out to produce something that legislators or administrators can easily translate into action, whereas traditional research attempts to provide a better understanding of social phenomena. Distinguishing policy analysis from policy evaluation, Greenberger, Crenson, and Crissey (1976) suggest that policy evaluation is used to discern how well an existing program is achieving its intended outcomes, whereas policy analysis detects whether there are conceivable combinations of programs that might achieve desired ends. For the most part, policy analysis draws on secondary data analysis, rarely depends on experimental design, and has a short turnaround time (Gallagher, 1981), distinguishing it from other research forms.

Reflecting the distinctions between conventional and policy research, though framing them differently, Weiss's work (1977) is helpful in that it suggests three approaches: the decision-driven model, the knowledge-driven model, and the interactive model. The decision-driven model includes problem definition, identification of missing knowledge, data generation and interpretation, and policy choice. The knowledge-driven model includes basic and applied research and acknowledges that the mere existence of knowledge presses its use, despite the reality that social science knowledge may not automatically lend itself for such use. Weiss's interactive model, one that has gained broad acceptance, suggests that social science research is only one part of a complicated policy process that builds upon experience, political insight, social technologies, and judgment.

Consistently, as efforts are made to refine definitions of policy research, the issue of what constitutes "utility" reemerges as a core element of the discussion. Must research be useful to be policy relevant? Is utility *the* distinguishing definitional element? In addressing these issues, Nagel (1990) responds by conceptualizing usefulness as a continuum, ranging from non-utilization to conversion of decision makers' perspectives on any given issue. The continuum construct is particularly helpful because it suggests that an array of research strategies are necessary to meet different needs.

Using this construct, we may envision a four-tiered research-to-policy continuum, moving from basic, through applied, through policy-relevant, to policy-dominant research. Classified by intention, basic research (at one end) would have limited immediate relevance to policy, whereas policy-dominant research (at the other end) would include studies specifically designed to address questions amenable to policy alteration. Using this definition, an explicit example of policy-dominant research is the National Day Care Study, whose mandate was "to examine the impact of variations in the major *regulatable characteristics of federally subsidized* [italics added] center-based

day care on the quality and cost of care received by preschool children" (Ruopp, Travers, Glantz, & Coelen, 1979, p. 12). The study focused on policy variables; its major research questions were designed to yield policy responses. Using this definition, a subcategory of policy-dominant research would be evaluation research, which is designed to produce results that will be used to reshape a particular intervention. Much of the Head Start evaluation research, as well as policy analyses designed to answer specific policy questions, would fall in this category.

In contrast to policy-dominated research, many studies, although not primarily designed to yield policy results, do produce "policy-relevant" findings. Consequently, such work is placed on the continuum just before policy-dominant research. Using this definition, policy-relevant research includes an array of applied research that serves multiple purposes, one of which is policy generation or reformation. In this category, for example, I include studies that are not commissioned to affect policy but by virtue of their content and findings may do so. Examples of such policy-relevant research may include studies of different caring-taking situations (family day care, school-age care) and their impacts on child and family outcomes, along with studies that examine the conditions and experiences of adults employed in those settings. Between policy-relevant and basic research is applied research, which has more limited policy relevance. In this category, I include research that may have indirect policy ramifications, but whose direct focus is less policy amenable (e.g., sex-role acquisition, fatherhood, and children of divorce). Such a research continuum—basic, applied, policy relevant, policy dominant—yields a bell-shaped distribution, with the vast majority of child development and early education research falling in the two middle categories—applied and policy relevant—with less being lodged at the ends of the continuum—basic and policy dominant.

Challenges Associated with Process and Context

Such a continuum suggests that the process of linking research and policy might be quite tidy. This is not the case. Creating policy-relevant and policy-dominant research and then fostering its utilization involves complex strategies that necessitate perspective-shifting and collaboration. The policymaker is interested in direct, crisp, and well-timed information. Researchers understand that the knowledge-building process, by contrast, is often indirect, murky, and slow. Realigning mindsets so that policymakers gain appreciation for research nuances while researchers grow in their ability to conceptualize issues so they are germane to pressing policy concerns is an ongoing challenge.

The challenge is further complicated because to be optimally relevant to the policymaker, social science research must be broadly contextualized. Its settings must transcend pristine laboratories and must take into consideration the realities of real-life environments. Children do not exist in isolation from their families, child care environments, and communities. Whereas policymakers are always interested in the direct impact of interventions on child outcome, researchers must broaden the conceptualization—and the frame of reference for policymakers—to include synergistic effects on children, families, and community. Echoing this sentiment, the report of the Advisory Panel for the Head Start Evaluation Design Project (1990) recommends, "Evaluation research must explicitly address diverse outcome indices related to children, families, communities and institutions" (p. 7). Despite pleas for such ecologically valid research in the field, Phillips (1984), drawing on Bronfenbrenner's (1979) ecological model of human development, points out that such efforts often falter because of the difficulties inherent in moving from research that focuses on the "familiar microsystem to the relatively uncharted exo- and macrosystems, which encompass most of the outcomes of interest to policymakers" (p. 92).

To appropriately contextualize research means that issues must be reframed and questions that have been ignored must be addressed. For example, research that has focused exclusively on the relationship between child care environments and narrow child outcomes must be reset within a broadened economic, political, and institutional context (Gormley, 1991; Grubb, 1991; Morgan, 1991; Young & Nelson, 1973). How are gains sustained over time as children and families traverse institutions? How do family support and child care interventions synergistically interact? How do maternal self-sufficiency, family stability, and program stability interact to affect child outcome? What is the relationship between regulations, costs, and quality? Further, we need to better understand how multiple, rather than isolated, treatment variables influence outcome. How do group size, child-adult ratios, and care-giver training and education interact to affect outcome?

Despite the need to improve understanding of differences in treatment variables and in treatment interactions, the challenge is difficult and has often been dubbed the black box phenomenon. McLaughlin (1985) notes that "idiosyncratic content defied systematic attention from analysts" (p. 97). This phenomenon, coupled with mounting concern about quality variation across early care and education sites (Riddle, 1988; Zigler & Valentine, 1979), led the Advisory Panel for Head Start (1990) to recommend exploration of program variation as a key component to help explain differential program outcomes. What the panel and others recognize is that factors affecting outcome interact in unique ways in different settings, demanding that policy-relevant and policy-dominant research acknowledge the importance of such programmatic and institutional relativism.

Such an approach may necessitate new research strategies. Exploring nested treatment variables may require, for example, a combination of holistic research strategies that may include qualitative and quantitative approaches (e.g., unstructured observations, case studies, open-ended interviews, observational checklists). Indeed, such combined strategies have been codified as multiplism, an approach to social science research that takes as its premise that no single research methodology, measure, or manipulation is perfect (Cook, 1985).

Challenges Associated with Measuring Policy-Relevant Outcomes

Clearly, by better understanding the array of treatment variables and their interactions, research will be better prepared to respond to policy-relevant issues. Unanswered questions will become part of the research agenda, fulfilling the queries of heretofore disquieted policymakers. A different situation exists regarding outcome data. Anxious for results that are crisp and simple to understand, policymakers have been more than content to use IQ results as a solitary expression of program efficacy. Such acceptance was fueled by an American infatuation with IQ and by acceptance of what Zigler (1970) termed the "environmental mystique," a sense that children's development was so malleable that even minimal interventions in the early years would have lasting effects on IQ. Dependence on IQ as a suitable index of effects was also accelerated because measures of IQ meet psychometric properties, avoid measurement complexities associated with other outcomes, and are widely applicable. Though widely discounted by academics (Zigler & Trickett, 1978; Zigler, 1991), policymakers have become accustomed to using IQ as the primary index of program success. Expanding horizons to embrace additional dimensions—including cognitive, physical, and socioemotional development—is a challenge that is being undertaken (National Educational Goals Panel Report, 1991) but that needs much more intensive work if the broad payoffs of child care and early intervention are to be acknowledged.

Beyond broadening the domains of impact, researchers will also need to be inventive in creating outcome categories that have salience for policymakers. Real-life measures—for example, employment, delinquency, welfare dependence, referral to special education, and attendance—seem to be most effective because they are concrete and easily understood by the media, the public, and policymakers.

Such efforts, both to broaden the range of outcomes and to make them more tangible, might also be beneficial in derailing mounting concerns regarding the nongeneralizability of research findings. To date, much of the policy-relevant research in early care and education has been conducted in high-quality child care or early education settings. Typically functioning in university-based or other favorable settings, such programs often have well-trained and highly experienced staff, low turnover, ample budgets, and they often capture considerable support (Besharov, 1987; Datta, 1983; Haskins, 1989; National Academy of Sciences, 1990). Although there are important lessons to be learned regarding the effects of optimal care, the lessons may not be generalizable to ordinary Head Start, child care, and other preschool programs. Moreover, when policy is advanced based on successful models, particular emphasis must be placed on maintaining cost comparability between the "successful" and the proposed efforts. Currently, policy expectations for results remain high while policy funding for new efforts is often lower than that of the successful efforts upon which the policy is based. Indeed, findings generated in a few exalted programs have left the nation "with the impression that preschool programs for poor children have been proved effective and that they produce large benefits that in the long run will more than repay the public's investment" (Haskins, 1989, p. 280). In the long run, more research on typical programs using broader outcome indices should produce information that will be more appropriate for policymakers as they establish new policies.

The Implications of the Challenges

Taken together, the above challenges help clarify why effective links between research and policy are not more plentiful. They suggest important strategies to be considered in the next decade if the field is to maximize the application of its knowledge to improve the quality of life for children and families. Moving beyond the incrementalism that has characterized this linkage to date demands that we span conventional boundaries and recognize that the dilemma has deep roots and demands new strategies. First, we need to seriously examine America's fundamental commitment to children. As we have seen, despite the elegance or perceived relevance of research, its utility in the policy context is bound by considerations of moral and economic imperatives. Couched within the context of a highly politicized legislative process and a faltering economy, universal children's issues—never seen as imperatives—are sifted from serious consideration. To create a context fertile for serious and sustained consideration of child development and early education research, America must come to grips with the priority it accords children and families, and with what that accord means in terms of child and family rights. What is right for children? And to what are children entitled?

Second, it is imperative that the research-to-policy link be conceptualized as dyadic, where the two processes are visioned as interactive. While research fuels policy, policy fuels and mediates research. Embedding research questions and study hypotheses in operational concerns about, for example, the quality, continuity, costs, and regulations of early care and education is critical to creating an effective and durable research-to-policy link. Any attempt to move the research-to-policy link beyond incrementalism must recontextualize the issues on precisely these two dimensions: It must establish a research-to-policy agenda within the context of a vision of the rights of children, and it must honor the demands of the policy context by creating functional child and family research. The need for vision and for functional research are posited as twin cornerstones of a revised approach to fortifying the research-to-policy link.

THE FIRST CORNERSTONE: VISION—A QUESTION OF CHILDREN'S RIGHTS

It has often been said that to have a dream come true, one must first dream. To realize a goal, one must first have one. America has no dream and no goal regarding its visions of optimal policy for children. Consequently, research regarding children is created in an abyss of what might be. It is inherently disjointed and only marginally cumulative. To optimize our research-to-policy journey, a collective sense of America's vision—what America deems is right—for children is needed.

In testimony before the Head Start Silver Ribbon Panel, Hector DeLeon cogently stated his vision in terms of rights: "It is right that we as nation offer and provide services for our children. It is right that the whole family be involved in that child's future. It is not only right but it is the family's right to expect it" (October 24, 1989). As affirmed by DeLeon's testimony, a vision is framed by two conceptions of "right." The first, predicated on empirical knowledge, asks, "What is right for young children and families in order to ensure optimal development?" Building on several of the Random House Dictionary (1975) definitions of the word *right*, it addresses (1) what is good, proper, or just; (2) what is in conformity with fact, reason, or some standard or principle; or (3) what is correct in judgment, opinion, or action. In other words, what do we know from research that is pedagogically and developmentally correct for young children? A second, more policy-related conception asks, "To what are children rightfully entitled?" This question is centered on *right* as a just claim or title and focuses on (1) that which is morally, legally, or ethically proper; (2) that which is due anyone by just claim, legal guarantees, or moral principles; and (3) that which certifies privilege. Each is discussed below to clarify a future vision for children and families toward which research and policy should be directed.

Ensuring Children's Optimal Development: What Do We Know Is Right?

Because conceptions of what is right for children vary over time and across cultures, there is no single universal definition of children's rights. Yet most agree that young children, irrespective of country of origin, culture, religion, or socioeconomic class, are vulnerable and deserve special protections. Moreover, although no codified list of rights exists, recent research has produced a generalized vision of what is right based on empirical knowledge and developmental principles that have evolved over time (Zigler & Kagan, 1982). Most experts would agree that optimal development is hastened when children are ensured the following rights:

1. Physical health, and healthy and safe environments
2. Enduring love and support from parents and family
3. Support from other individuals and institutions
4. Continuity between and among individuals nurturing children
5. Developmentally appropriate care and education

Physical Health and a Healthy, Safe Environment. We know that throughout the world each day, more than 38,000 children (ages 0–18) die from a lack of food, shelter, or primary health care; more than 100 million children live or work under hazardous or fatal conditions; and more than 80 million children live on the streets of the world's cities (Castelle, 1988). In America, in 1989 our black infant mortality rate was 32nd worldwide; then, 1 in 5 black children and 3 in 10 Latino children had no health insurance (Children's Defense Fund, 1991). Nine percent of children ages 1–5 living below 150 % of the poverty limit did not have up-to-date immunizations (Klerman, 1991). Such figures seem even more astonishing because the data consistently indicates that impressive health gains can be made through intervention. For example, the Head Start Synthesis Report indicated that children in the program had a lower incidence of pediatric problems than non–Head Start children and a level of health comparable to more advantaged children (McKey, Condelli, Ganson, Barrett, McConkey, & Plantz, 1985).

Beyond meeting children's individual health needs, environments where children live and play must not fall below a minimal level of quality or children may be damaged by such environments. This concern is especially pronounced with respect to nonfamilial facilities where children may spend much of their time and bespeaks the need for minimal health and safety standards, which recent analyses indicate are terribly insufficient (Morgan, 1987; Young & Zigler, 1986).

Enduring Love and Support from Parents and Family.
There is no question that parents and family are the most important influence on the developing child (Leichter, 1977). Consequently, enabling parents to carry out their parenting function effectively must be accorded societal priority. This means making parent education and family support services available to those who desire them; it means loosening corporate policies to allow more time and less stress for family life; and it means respecting differences in attitudes toward parenting so long as child health and development are not compromised.

Recognizing the importance of the family to optimal child development, a variety of programs have emerged over the years. Documented elsewhere (Kagan, Powell, Weissbourd, & Zigler, 1987; Powell, 1989), such programs have emerged with federal impetus (e.g., Parent Child Development Centers, Home Start) and with voluntary, foundation, state, and local support (e.g., Avance, Minnesota Early Learning Design [MELD]). Not all have evaluations and, of those that do, many are not experimental in design. Where design criteria have been met, there is evidence that such interventions can impact children's short-term IQ gains, but there is little evidence that such gains are sustained more than one year after the end of participation in the program (Epstein & Weikart, 1979; Levenstein, O'Hara, & Madden, 1983). However, we also know that when parents are involved in long-term parenting education, children are less likely to be enrolled in special education (Jester & Guinagh, 1983; Seitz, Rosenbaum & Apfel, 1985).

Support from Other Individuals and Institutions.
Although parents have the primary responsibility for nurturing their young children, many other institutions, including the school (Henderson, 1987), the church (Lindner, Mattis, & Rogers, 1983), the community, and the media, affect children's growth. This principle implies that in addition to the family's lead role, societal institutions have a critically supportive and collective role in nurturing children.

Next to the home, children spend the greatest amount of time in child care centers and schools. These institutions must acknowledge the important roles parent play in the education of their children and must create meaningful opportunities for parent-school links (Hymes, 1974; Seeley, 1981). Additionally, schools must consider taking on broader missions and work to meet the social, emotional, and caretaking needs of children. For example, while Seligson and Fink (1989) report wide ranges in the percentages of schools offering school-age child care programs (from 0% in Idaho and Montana to 84% in Florida), concerns about latchkey children are being voiced by parents, teachers, and school administrators.

A powerful influencer, the media in general and television in particular exert tremendous influence on children's development. Television programming must be sensitive to developmental needs of children, limiting the amount of advertis-

ing, and eliminating violence from the air (Huston, Watkins, & Kunkel, 1989).

Continuity for Young Children.
An agreed-upon principle of child development is that children benefit if they experience a sense of continuity between (1) the time periods of their lives and (2) the spheres of their lives (Caldwell, 1991; Zigler & Kagan, 1982). Yet, given increasingly complex care-taking and social support arrangements, such continuity is becoming more difficult to achieve (Love, 1988). Maintaining continuity between the periods of children's lives implies linking the experiences children encounter from year to year. But as children and families move from one locale to another, and from one school district to another, such continuity is difficult, if not impossible, to maintain.

The need for continuity between the spheres of a child's life is equally complex. As children enter institutional services for the first time, the transition from home to program is a difficult one for which parents and providers must be well prepared. Some school districts, recognizing the magnitude of the event, have created special programs and schedules to ease the adjustment (Glicksman & Hills, 1981). Once enrolled in a non-home-based program, children, particularly low-income youngsters, are likely to encounter a myriad of institutions such as health and social services, and after-school care. Sometimes the services rendered overlap, creating redundancy and duplication; conversely, sometimes services are delivered with no knowledge about the other services being received by the child, fostering uncertainty, if not costly and contradictory treatment plans and strategies (Kagan, 1989). Linking institutions that serve children and families more effectively is a necessary but challenging social service task of the next decade and century.

Developmentally Appropriate Care and Education.
The large, though still imperfect, body of developmental theory and pedagogy amassed over the decades can provide a guide for the delivery of care and education services. We know that children and families are extremely heterogeneous and vary on every measurable characteristic. Because of this variation, children and families have diverse needs. Such diversity, coupled with normal "spurts and starts" patterns of development in young children, creates the need to individualize services. Group activities, more appropriate for older children, belie sound pedagogy in early care and education and demand that staff be well trained. Often considered the most important variable in the quality of the early childhood programs, child-staff interactions must be finely attuned to meet children's individual developmental needs and to allow appropriate opportunities for child-initiated learning. Teachers have the all-important tasks of facilitating self-esteem (Stone, 1978) and self-control (Honig, 1985; Yarrow & Waxler, 1976).

Effective pedagogical strategies for young children must also recognize the importance of children's individual learning styles, languages, and cultures (Soto, 1991). When the language, culture, and learning styles used in the institution vary considerably from what has been previously familiar, children are made uneasy and often suffer serious sequelae (Fillmore, 1990). A growing recognition of the need for cultural saliency, sensitivity to home culture language, and learning style is taking root (Hilliard, 1985). However, a vigil must be established to ensure that such commitment is not simply met by a "foods-festivals-fashions" approach to cultural diversity. These strategies fall short of the pervasive need to realign institutional cultures to build upon the richness afforded by diversity (Hakuta & Garcia, 1989).

Although programs must accommodate and nourish individual diversity, they must also adhere to common principles. For example, from research we know that full human development involves more than cognition: It integrates intellectual, social, emotional, and physical domains and has led us to consider multiple intelligences (Gardner & Hatch, 1989; Sternberg, 1985). Yet developmentalists acknowledge that implementing a "whole child" approach is difficult (Almy, 1975; Biber, 1984; Elkind, 1986; Kline, 1985). To fully incorporate social, emotional, physical, and intellectual domains, curricula and activities must be created to reflect this comprehensive approach. A more holistic approach to curriculum suggests the integration of subjects around specific activities or themes (Katz, 1987).

Further, because young children's learning is highly episodic and dynamic, a single test (with whatever content) administered at any point in time has limited applicability to overall school performance. The educational press for accountability has accelerated the use of standardized tests and, many contend, caused tests to be used for purposes for which they were not intended—program assignment and determining school readiness (Meisels, 1989; National Association for the Education Of Young Children, 1988; National Association of Early Childhood Specialists in State Departments of Education, 1987; National Association of State Boards of Education, 1988). Such overuse and misuse of testing has had spiraling curricular effects, most notably the promotion of more highly didactic and pressured learning with less emphasis on exploratory and problem-solving behaviors.

Such direction is particularly disappointing in light of the fact that pedagogical strategies for young children have been clearly articulated by the profession. Culling information from scores of documents and reviews by hundreds of child development and early education experts, The National Association for the Education of Young Children published *Developmentally Appropriate Practices (DAP)* (Bredekamp, 1987). This volume delineates pedagogical practices for children ages 0–8. Adopted by foreign countries, states, and municipalities for programs for young children irrespective of auspices, DAP has served as an operational benchmark for high-quality early care and education.

What Is Right for Children?

Taken together, we have a good body of empirical knowledge that guides the formation of developmental principles and the implementation of sound developmental practices. Although refinements will continue to be made, a general vision of what is right for children is not a mystery. It is right that children have access to good medical, dental, and nutritional care. It is right that children grow up in healthy and safe environments. It is right that their intellectual and spiritual quests be met. It is right that children experience the security afforded by loving parents, family, adults, and nurturing institutions. It is right that child-serving institutions and policies be coordinated to ensure maximum service access and effectiveness. It is right that programs and services for children be well-designed, comprehensive, and staffed by competent, caring adults. We know what is good, proper, and just; what is in conformity with fact, reason, and principle; and what is correct in opinion and judgment. In short, what is right is clear.

To What Are Young Children Rightfully Entitled?

On the surface, it would appear that if, as a society, we understand what is right for children, then the question of rightful entitlement should follow quite easily. Idealists would claim that what is right is synonymous with what is a rightful entitlement. Unfortunately, in most societies, and certainly in the United States, what is discerned as right for children is a question quite separate from that of rightful entitlements.

In our nation, we have adopted essentially a legalistic approach to our conceptions of entitlement. We view an entitlement as the right to lay claim to something, as a rule (Hook, 1980). But such entitlements are not without burden. If one is "entitled," one is given "title" to something: a possession, a privilege, a mode of treatment (Oxford English Dictionary, 1989). In our nation, such entitlements are accompanied by the burden of meeting means-tested criteria. Entitlements, in policy terms, give "title" to some to be labeled poor and vulnerable.

Moving beyond the accepted legal interpretations of entitlement to more psychologically-based interpretations shifts the focus from the practical to the possible, from *what is* to *what might be*. Psychologically-driven interpretations of entitlement suggest that an individual is empowered "to do, to have, to enjoy" (McCloskey, 1965). Coles (1977) affirms the potency of an attitudinal orientation toward entitlement for children. He suggests that children with feelings of entitlement possess a psychological approach to the world and its possibilities. Even 5- and 6-year-old "entitled" children are confident about the future and have a sense of their place in it. Such entitlement attitudes coexist with a sense of mastery and confidence. Not coincidentally, this psychological sense of entitlement is found among affluent children, whereas legal entitlements are found among poor youngsters. Coles's work suggests that for entitlement to work for all, it must not only offer dollars, but it must afford the empowerment and hope that accompanies money. To entitle from the psychological perspective is to render a sense of the possible. Although the legal definition of entitlement has framed the extant policy ethos, I suggest that a new vision of entitlement, one that incorporates the psychological perspective, is needed if we are to ensure young children equitable rights and have a clear direction for our research and policy over generations.

Entitlement Past: Entitlement Future

It would be erroneous to suggest that broadening the construct of entitlement or fostering children's rights is new.

Indeed, throughout U.S. history, attempts have been launched to define the rights of children. Hoover, in 1930, drafted a Children's Charter that was adopted by the President's White House Conferences on Child Health and Protection. Sadly, though well-crafted and well-intentioned, the rights as envisioned were never realized. More recently, a national task force on the Constitutional Rights of the Child has considered drafting an amendment to the U.S. Constitution that would grant full rights of citizenship to children from birth to 17. In addition, the United Nations Convention on the Rights of the Child has developed a charter that was adopted by the United Nations General Assembly on November 20, 1989, but not fully accepted by the United States.

Despite these laudable efforts, to date there is no comprehensive entitlement package that exists in our nation, much less one that embraces both children's legal and psychological rights. Combining psychological and legal rights is a difficult leap conceptually and strategically. It suggests that rather than beginning with piecemeal programs, policies, and research, we begin with a vision—a goal—rooted in what we feel all young children are legitimately entitled to, and design research to inform programs and policy that will lead toward the fulfillment of that goal. Until such vision is achieved and until more universal child and family services are socially sanctioned, research legitimacy and utility will be subjugated to vacillating ideological tides.

THE SECOND CORNERSTONE: THE NEW FUNCTIONALISM OF POLICY RESEARCH

Even if realized conceptually, such a vision or goal would not be sufficient: It needs to be supported by research and policy strategies that work to meet that goal. But this is doubly difficult. First, as we have seen, designing research that is policy relevant and that advances theory is laden with challenges. Second, designing it in the absence of an overarching vision and uncertain commitments to children and families complicates the task considerably. Given these realities, we need to work on two tracks simultaneously. We need to encourage those who are working to craft a comprehensive vision of child and family rights, understanding that this is both a long-term task and an essential cornerstone for the next century's policy. We also need to expand research domains and support researchers who will concentrate their work on policy-related and policy-dominated research issues.

Inherent in framing policy-relevant or policy-dominant research is a basic understanding of what those who construct and implement policy need to know. What kind of information makes a difference? In what detail? Related to whom? At what critical junctures? Ideally, in addition to understanding the policy process and considering these issues at the onset and throughout the analysis, the vigilant policy scholar will also assess potential policy uses of the research. Is the research being generated, as Weiss (1977) suggests, for political ammunition? That is, is it intended to support a program? To discredit a failing project or effort? To delay or hasten action? To neutralize an ideological contention? To legitimate a decision already made? Is the research being generated to advance a theory or a "conceptualization" (Weiss, 1977)? Is it intention to redefine the policy questions? To sensitize policymakers to a new issue? To broaden the domain of inquiry? To lead to uncharted program inventions?

The incrementalist perspective on policy, which is widely held in the field, is that few single studies have dramatic policy effects in isolation (Woodhead, 1988). Rather, the effects of research—like knowledge itself—are cumulative. The asset of such incrementalism is that multiple perspectives, data sets, and researchers combine to influence policy. Conversely, this is sometimes problematic because multiple researchers, with their inherent value differences and competing theoretical and methodological frameworks, often produce contradictory results. Such conflicting findings leave policymakers not only confused about content, but convinced of their skepticism for social science research. Wishfully, one might argue that more and better research conducted over time would eliminate such confusion. Cohen and Weiss (1977), who have followed the research on school and race, suggest that such cohesion is unlikely.

Although humbling, this evidence need not deter us in our quest to make research functional. It means that the research community will need to move beyond conventional frameworks to explore new domains of research, new research settings and methods, and more complex interacting variables that mediate effects. Contextual issues that address the interaction between home and child care environments need special attention as do systemic challenges that emerge in times of rapid changes. Moreover, all such inquiries will have to be framed in ways that reveal the economic, political, and social costs of policy. Building on Head Start research, which has served as a mainstay of the field's empirical base for decades, policy-related and policy-dominant research will be needed in the following domains: quality, cost, and cost effectiveness of early care and education; access, affordability, collaboration, and integration of services; the context for child and family development; and training and capacity building of early care and education staff.

Quality of Early Care and Education Services

It has been suggested that garnering a better understanding of the correlates of quality child care services and their impact on child development should be a primary research goal. Over the past two decades, our knowledge has grown and researchers and policymakers have refined the questions, making them more precise. Now, inquiry needs to address which precise quality variables (e.g., ratios, group size, care-giver training and experience) affect which children in which ways. To what extent are these individual quality variables interrelated? With what effects on which youngsters? More specifically, the National Academy of Sciences (1990) has recommended that studies be conducted to examine if "manipulation of one variable (or clusters of variables) have ramifications for others" (p. 278). To what might such variations be attributed? The Panel was also concerned that a number of features of centers have not been investigated, including center size, parental involvement, stability of peer groups and, for family day care, the age and mix within the groups. To this list, we might add center auspices, duration of existence, exemption from regulation, and degree of linkage with other early care and education programs, schools, and resource and referral programs.

Given the burgeoning number of children in new programs and the growth of non-center-based programs, particular attention must be accorded the content and process of quality programming in all settings for children of all ages. Family day care (licensed, regulated, and underground), relative care, and multiple forms of care must ascend on the research agenda. Past neglect of these areas leaves us with the clear possibility "that we have not sampled programs that represent the poorest quality care offered in this country" (Scarr, Phillips, & McCartney, 1990, p. 33).

Cost and Cost Effectiveness

Limited data on comparative costs of early care and education programs is emerging (U.S. General Accounting Office, 1990), yet this domain of inquiry—perhaps the most important to policy—has not been sufficiently investigated. Unanswered questions related to cost-benefits, differential investments, and investment alternatives need sustained explorations (Hall, 1978; Kahn & Kamerman, 1987; Robins & Weiner, 1978). Further, considerably more investigation must focus on the impact of different funding streams and mechanisms on early care and education utilization and the effects of differential expenditures on quality and on child and family outcomes. New national studies funded through the Departments of Education and Health and Human Services will yield important one-time data. Provisions must be made to collect cost data more systematically through ongoing national data bases. Alternative financing mechanisms—including provider subsidies, tax benefits to consumers, and vouchers—must be explored with regard to discerning whether they foster or discourage different types of programs under different auspices (National Academy of Sciences, 1990). Given the advent of the Family Support Act, exploration should be devoted to the impact of differential fiscal and programmatic supports to families and their impact on child outcomes. The Expanded Child Care Options (ECCO) project will be helpful in this endeavor, but data from more than one state is necessary. Furthermore, a more detailed understanding is needed of the interrelationships between family income, employment, types of child care utilization and outcome, and between increases in public subsidization and the expansion of the child care market. Finally, analyses of the relationships between expenditures and quality across auspices must be discerned.

Access and Affordability

Patterns of access to child care and early education have changed and will continue to change with the implementation of new federal legislation. How will new efforts affect access and what will be the impact of rapid expansion of services on access? What is the market interplay of expanding involvement of the corporate sector and the for-profit sector? How will increased access interact with new affordability demands? What is the impact of the unavailability of early care and education services? Of the lack of choice in selecting such services? What are the cultural norms and values that influence child care choice? What will the impact of child allowances be on child care utilization and affordability? Given the grave discrepancies in the percentage of income devoted to child care between low- and upper-income families (Hofferth, 1988), will new subsidizations alleviate inequity of access? Because lack of affordable care is one of the key policy issues, especially for low-income families and families with infants and/or disabled children, survey and empirical data are badly needed in this domain.

Coordination, Collaboration, and Integration of Services

The burgeoning of early childhood policy has brought with it new realizations regarding the interconnectedness of the early care and education field (Head Start Silver Ribbon Panel, 1990; Scarr & Weinberg, 1986). Previously conceptualized as an array of separate program interventions, a fresh approach—sometimes dubbed the "ecosystem" (Mitchell, Seligson, & Marx, 1989)—suggests that early care and education must be regarded holistically. Such an approach will hopefully foster more equity and integrated services for children and the alleviation of acrimony that is fueled as separate programs routinely compete for children, space, and staff (Goodman & Brady, 1988).

Research efforts must reconceptualize early care and education interactively, stressing that what occurs in one sector or program will have systematic impact on other efforts. New research must focus on understanding the nature of interactions among such programs and the effects that such coordination has on the continuity of services for children, the cost efficiency for programs, and the heightened quality of services afforded. Research is needed to discern the impact of current and predicted growth of public school programs for 3- and 4-year-old children on supply and demand. Research on the role of resource and referral programs in the delivery system is needed, as is far closer scrutiny of the role of business and industry in meeting child and family needs. Although a growing body of literature exists regarding these efforts (Galinsky, 1991; National Council of Jewish Women, 1987), more empirical work is needed to discern impact on employers and employees, and how the provision of such services alters child care supply, access, and quality. Finally, with "integrated service," "one-stop shopping," and "service co-location" being today's buzzwords, an understanding of their efficacy in light of history and in light of child and family effects is warranted (Gage, 1976; Kagan, 1991).

The Context for Child and Family Development

As a result of theoretical advances, largely due to Bronfenbrenner's seminal works (1974; 1979), a family and community systems approach to intervention has taken place. Child outcomes are more commonly being investigated within the context of family, center, and community. New research efforts need to expand this work, ensuring that the reciprocity of impact is investigated. For example, recognizing that only a few such studies examined the impact of Head Start on communities (Kirschner, 1970), the Advisory Panel for the Head Start Evaluation Design Project (1990) recommended additional investigation. With the surge of 2-generation programs, such research will be necessitated. More information is needed regarding early care and education efforts as family supports.

The relationship between child care, family employment patterns, and income, though increasingly discussed and researched (Burghardt & Gordon, 1990), has been studied within the context of welfare dependency and income maintenance strategies, not within the context of differences in child care quality, stability, and cost, and their influences on child and family outcomes over time. Moreover, such investigations need to focus on the entire population, given dramatic changes in women's labor force participation across income levels. Variations in patterns of work force participation, including part-time, flex-time, and home-based employment, need to be examined in light of their economic costs for employers and employees, and their impacts on child and family functioning and outcomes.

Further, more empirical attention needs to be accorded intra- and inter-familial situations such as family stress, social support, marital discord, marital status, and motivation for parenting. Moving well beyond socioeconomic variables, such studies should investigate the association between quality of care and family characteristics as they affect child and family outcomes. The National Academy of Sciences (1990) suggests that such variables should be explored longitudinally so that patterns of mutual influence—child and family on the child care environment, and child care environment on child and family characteristics—over time could be investigated.

Capacity Building

As has been suggested earlier, knowledge about child development has been translated into operational practices for the field. Despite this advancement, quality in child care and early education remains disturbingly low. Although many rationales are posited for low quality (lack of regulation, inadequate funds, poor ratios and group sizes), research also points to the quality, and more recently the instability and poor wages (Whitebook, Howes, & Phillips, 1990), of the work force. Indeed, care-giver education and training, and the nature of the interaction between the child and care giver, account, in no small measure, for quality variability. To that end, additional investments in practice and research related to care-giver recruitment, training, job satisfaction, career advancement opportunities, and compensation are critical.

Although the content of training for early childhood personnel is receiving increasing attention (Spodek & Saracho, 1990a) and the need for teachers with different abilities to work in different settings is becoming clear (Spodek & Saracho, 1990b), research on these issues is needed. What kinds of training best yield the differential qualities and competencies to work in different early care and education settings? How do we maximize training investments? What is the impact of effective training subsidies and career ladders on work force stability and quality?

Moreover, research must examine pedagogical and systemic issues that inhibit the effective delivery of training. Is the knowledge base regarding *how* to work with young children sufficient? Are the institutions imparting such knowledge sufficient in number and quality? Is the training received cumulative and individually tailored to meet the needs of a widely diverse training cadre? Are institutional linkages supportive of cumulative experiences? What is the impact of differential training experiences on teacher competence? Finally, given the expansion of the field, research is needed to test whether and how underutilized training pools, the elderly and the welfare dependent, can be trained or retrained to render quality services to young children and families. This suggests that research has a critical role to play in capacity building, a task that may prove to be the key challenge of the next decade.

This chapter has been premised on the reality that the links between research and policy have been tenuous historically, leaving a legacy of challenges that must be addressed if the social science–social policy relationship is to be optimized. Overcoming challenges, though, must be coupled with both a broad vision of what we as a society want for children and a revitalized commitment to functional policy-relevant and policy-dominant research. Given mounting concern regarding the faltering social infrastructure generally and renewed interest in children and families specifically, the time to fortify scientific and policy bonds is upon us. Capitalizing upon 1980s momentum, the task of the next decade is to envision broadly and move strategically beyond the incrementalism that has characterized the research-to-policy connection.

References

Advisory Panel for the Head Start Evaluation Design Project. (1990). *Head Start research and evaluation: A blueprint for the future.* Washington, DC: U.S. Government Printing Office.

Almy, M. (1975). *The early childhood educator at work.* New York: McGraw-Hill.

Berrueta-Clement, J. R., Schweinhart, L. J., Barnett, W. S., Epstein, A. S., & Weikart, D. P. (1984). *Changed lives: The effects of the Perry Preschool on youths through age 19.* Ypsilanti, MI: The High/Scope Press.

Besharov, D. (1987). Giving the juvenile court a preschool education. In J. Q. Wilson & G. C. Loury (Eds.), *From children to citizens* (Vol. 3, pp. 207–238). New York: Springer-Verlag.

Biber, B. (1984). *Early education and psychological development.* New Haven, CT: Yale University Press.

Bredekamp, S. (Ed.). (1987). *Developmentally appropriate practices in early childhood programs serving children from birth through age 8.* Washington, DC: National Association for the Education of Young Children.

Bronfenbrenner, U. (1974). Developmental research, public policy and the ecology of childhood. *Child Development, 45,* 1–5.

Bronfenbrenner, U. (1979). *The ecology of human development: Experiments by nature and design.* Cambridge, MA: Harvard University Press.

Burghardt, J., & Gordon, A. (1990). *More jobs and higher pay: The minority female single parent demonstration.* New York: The Rockefeller Foundation.

Caldwell, B. (1991). Continuity in the early years: Transitions between grades and systems. In S. L. Kagan (Ed.), *The care and education of*

America's young children: Obstacles and opportunities. The Nineti-eth Yearbook of the National Society for the Study of Education (pp. 69–90). Chicago, IL: The University of Chicago Press.

Caldwell, B., & Ricciuti, H. (Eds.). (1973). *Child development and social policy: Review of child development research.* Chicago: University of Chicago Press.

Castelle, K. (1988). *In the child's best interest: A primer on the U.N. Conventions on the Rights of the Child.* East Greenwich, RI: Foster Parents Plan International, Inc.

Children's Defense Fund. (1991). *The state of America's children 1991.* Washington, DC: Author.

Clark, K. B., & Clark, M. P. (1952). Racial identification and preference in Negro children. In G. E. Swanson, T. M Newcomb, & E. R. Hartley (Eds.), *Readings in Social Psychology* (2nd ed., pp. 551–560). New York: Holt.

Cohen, D. K., & Garet, M. S. (1975). Reforming educational policy with applied social research. *Harvard Educational Review, 45*(1), 17–41.

Cohen, D. K., & Weiss, J. A. (1977). Social science and social policy: Schools and race. In C. H. Weiss (Ed.), *Using social research in public policymaking* (pp. 67–83). Lexington, MA: Lexington Books.

Coles, R. (1977). *Privileged ones: The well-off and the rich in America.* Boston: Little Brown & Co.

Committee for Economic Development. (1991). *The unfinished agenda: A new vision for child development and education.* New York: Author.

Consortium for Longitudinal Studies. (1977). *The persistence of preschool effects: A long-term follow-up of fourteen infant and preschool experiments* (Final Report for ACYF Grant No 18-76-07843). Ithaca, NY: Cornell University, Community Services Laboratory.

Cook, T. (1985). Postpositivist critical multiplism. In R. L. Shotland & M. M. Mark (Eds.), *Social science and social policy* (pp. 21–62). Beverly Hills, CA: Sage Publications.

Cronbach, L. J., Ambron, S. R., Dornbush, S. M., Hess, R. D., Hornik, R. C., Phillips, D. C., Walker, D. F., & Weiner, S. S. (1980). *Toward reform of program evaluation.* San Francisco: Jossey-Bass.

Datta, L. (1983). Epilogue: We never promised you a rose garden, but one may have grown anyhow. In Consortium for Longitudinal Studies (Ed.), *As the twig is bent: Lasting effects of preschool programs* (pp. 467–479). Hillsdale, NJ: Earlbaum.

DeLeon, H. (1989, October 24). Testimony presented before the Head Start Silver Ribbon Panel. Washington, DC.

Elkind, D. (1986, May). Formal education and early childhood education: An essential difference. *Phi Delta Kappan,* 631–636.

Epstein, A. S., & Weikart, D. (1979). *The Ypsilanti-Carnegie Infant Education Project: Longitudinal follow-up. (Monographs of the High/Scope Educational Research Foundation No. 6).* Ypsilanti, MI: High/Scope Press.

Fillmore, L. W. (1990). Now or later? Issues related to the early education of minority-group children. *Early childhood and family education: Analysis and recommendations of the Council of Chief State School Officers.* Orlando, FL: Harcourt Brace Jovanovich.

Gage, R. W. (1976). Integration of human services delivery systems. *Public Welfare, 34*(1), 27–32.

Galinsky, E. (1991). The private sector as a partner in early care and education. In S. L. Kagan (Ed.), *The care and education of America's young children: Obstacles and opportunities [Ninetieth Yearbook of the National Society for the Study of Education]* (pp. 131–153). Chicago, IL: University of Chicago Press.

Gallagher, J. (1981). Models for policy analysis: Child and family policy. In R. Haskins & J. Gallagher (Eds.), *Models for analysis of social policy: An introduction* (pp. 37–77). Norwood, NJ: Ablex Publishing Company.

Gardner, H., & Hatch, T. (1989). Multiple intelligences go to school: Educational implications of the theory of multiple intelligences. *Educational Researcher, 18*(8), 4–10.

Glicksman, K., & Hills, T. (1981). *Easing the child's transition between home, child care center & school: A guide for early childhood educators.* Trenton, NJ: New Jersey Department of Education.

Goodman, I. F., & Brady, J. P. (1988). *The challenge of coordination: Head Start's relationships to state-funded preschool initiatives.* Newton, MA: Educational Development Center.

Gormley, W. T. (1991). State regulations and the availability of child care services. *Journal of Policy Analysis and Management, 10*(1).

Greenberger, M., Crenson, M. A., & Crissey, B. L. (1976). *Models in the policy process.* New York: Russell Sage Foundation.

Grubb, N. (1991). Choosing wisely for children: Policy options for early childhood programs. In S. L. Kagan (Ed.), *The care and education of America's young children: Obstacles and opportunities [Ninetieth Yearbook of the National Society for the Study of Education]* (pp. 214–236). Chicago, IL: University of Chicago Press.

Hakuta, K., & Garcia, G. (1989). Bilingualism and education. *American Psychologist, 44*(2), 374–379.

Hall, A. (1978). Estimating cost equating for day care. In P. K. Robins & S. Weiner (Eds.), *Child care and public policy: Studies of economic issues* (pp. 157–185). Lexington, MA: Lexington Books.

Haskins, R. (1989). Beyond metaphor: The efficacy of early childhood education. *American Psychologist, 44*(2), 274–282.

Head Start Silver Ribbon Panel. (1990). *Head Start: The nation's pride—A nation's challenge.* Washington, DC: National Head Start Association.

Henderson, A. (1987). *The evidence continues to grow: Parent involvement improves student achievement.* Columbia, MD: National Committee for Citizens in Education.

Hilliard, A. (1985). *What is quality care?* Washington, DC: National Association for the Education of Young Children.

Hofferth, S. (1988). *The current child care debate in context.* Paper prepared for the 1987 meeting of the American Sociological Association (revised). Washington, DC: The Urban Institute.

Honig, A. (1985). Research in review: Compliance, control and discipline (Parts 1 and 2). *Young Children, 40*(2), 50–58: *40*(3), 47–52.

Hook, S. (1980). *Philosophy and public policy.* Carbondale, IL: Southern Illinois Press.

Horowitz, F. D., & O'Brien, M. (1989). In the interest of the nation: A reflective essay on the state of our knowledge and the challenges before us. *American Psychologist, 44*(2), 441–445.

Huston, A. C., Watkins, B. A., & Kunkel, D. (1989). Public policy and children's television. *American Psychologist, 44*(2), 424–433.

Hymes, J. (1974). *Effective home-school relations.* Sierra Madre, CA: Southern Association for the Education of Young Children.

Jester, R. E., & Guinagh, B. J. (1983). The Gordon Parent Education Infant and Toddler Program. In the Consortium for Longitudinal Studies, *As the twig is bent: Lasting effects of preschool programs* (pp. 103–132). Hillsdale, NJ: Erlbaum.

Kagan, S. L. (1989). Early care and education: Tackling the tough issues. *Phi Delta Kappan, 70*(6), 433–439.

Kagan, S. L. (1991). *United we stand: Collaboration for child care and early education services.* New York: Teachers College Press.

Kagan, S. L., Powell, D. R., Weissbourd, B., & Zigler, E. (Eds.). (1987). *America's family support programs: Perspectives and prospects.* New Haven, CT: Yale University Press.

Kahn, A. J., & Kamerman, S. B. (1987). *Child care: Facing the hard choices.* Auburn, MA: Dover House Publishing Company.

Katz, L. (1987). Early education: What should young children be doing? In S. L. Kagan & E. Zigler (Eds.), *Early schooling: The national debate* (pp. 157–168). New Haven, CT: Yale University Press.

Kirschner & Associates. (1970). *A national survey of the impacts of Head Start centers on community institutions.* Albuquerque, NM.

Klerman, L. (1991). *Alive and well? A research and policy review of health programs for poor young children.* New York: National Center for Children in Poverty.

Kline, L. W. (1985). *Learning to read: Teaching to read.* Newark, DE: LWK Enterprises.

Lazar, I. (1980). Social research and social policy: Reflections on relationships. In R. Haskins & J. J. Gallagher, *Care and education of young children in America: Policy, politics, and social science* (pp. 59–71). Norwood, NJ: Ablex.

Leichter, H. J. (Ed.). (1977). *The family as educator.* New York: Teachers College Press.

Levenstein, P., O'Hara, J., & Madden, J. (1983). The Mother- Child Home Program of the Verbal Interaction Project. In Consortium for Longitudinal Studies, *As the twig is bent: Lasting effects of preschool programs* (pp. 237–263). Hillsdale, NJ: Erlbaum.

Lindblom, C. E., & Cohen, D. K. (1979). *Usable knowledge.* New Haven, CT: Yale University Press.

Lindner, E. W., Mattis, M. C., & Rogers, J. R. (1983). *When churches mind the children.* Ypsilanti, MI: High/Scope Press.

Love, J. M. (1988). *Study of public school programs designed to ease the transition of children from preschool to kindergarten: Study overview and conceptual framework.* Hampton, NH: RMC Research Corporation.

Maccoby, E., Kahn, A., & Everett, B. A. (1983). The role of psychological research in the formation of policies affecting children. *American Psychologist, 38*(1), 85–90.

Mark, M. M., & Shotland, R. L. (1985). Toward more useful social science. In R. L. Shotland & M. M. Mark (Eds.), *Social science and social policy* (pp. 335–370). Beverly Hills, CA: Sage Publications.

McCloskey, H. J. (1965). Rights. *Philosophical Quarterly, 15*(59), 115–127.

McKey, R. H., Condelli, L., Ganson H., Barrett, B. J., McConkey, C., & Plantz, M. C. (1985). *Executive summary: The impact of Head Start on children, families and communities.* Washington, DC: CSR, Inc.

McLaughlin, M. (1985). Implementation realities and evaluation design. In R. L. Shotland & M. M. Mark (Eds.), *Social science and social policy* (pp. 96–120). Beverly Hills, CA: Sage Publications.

Meisels, S. J. (1989, April). High-stakes testing in kindergarten. *Educational Leadership, 46*(7), 16–22.

Mitchell, A., Seligson, M., & Marx, F. (1989). *Early childhood programs and the public schools: Between promise and practice.* Dover, MA: Auburn House.

Morgan, G. (1987). *The national state of child care regulations.* Watertown, MA: Work/Family Directions.

Morgan, G. (1991). Regulating early childhood programs: Five policy issues. In S. L. Kagan (Ed.), *The care and education of America's young children: Obstacles and opportunities [Ninetieth Yearbook of the National Society for the Study of Education]* (pp. 173–198). Chicago, IL: University of Chicago Press.

Moroney, R. M. (1981). Policy analysis within a value theoretical framework. In R. Haskins & J. Gallagher (Eds.), *Models for analysis of social policy: An introduction* (pp. 78–101). Norwood, NJ: Ablex Publishing Company.

Nagel, S. S. (1990). Introduction: Bridging theory and practice in policy/program evaluation. In S. S. Nagel (Ed.), *Policy theory and policy evaluation* (pp. ix–xxiv). New York: Greenwood Press.

National Academy of Sciences. (1990). *Who cares for America's children: Child care policy for the 1990s.* Washington, DC: National Academy Press.

National Association for the Education of Young Children. (1988). Position statement on standardized testing of young children 3 through 8 years of age. *Young Children, 43*(3), 42–47.

National Association of Early Childhood Specialists in State Departments of Education. (1987). *Unacceptable trends in kindergarten entry and placement: A position statement.* Lincoln, NE.

National Association of State Boards of Education. (1988). *Right from the start: The report of the NASBE task force on early childhood education.* Alexandria, VA.

National Council of Jewish Women, Center for the Child. (1987). *Mothers in the workplace.* New York.

National Education Goals Panel. (1991). *Measuring progress toward the national education goals: Potential indicators and measurement strategies.* Washington, DC.

National Governors' Association. (1990). *Results in education: 1987, 1988, 1989, 1990.* Washington, DC.

National Research Council. (1978). *The federal investment in knowledge of social problems (Vol. 1).* Washington, DC: National Academy Press.

Oxford English Dictionary, 2nd ed. (1989). Oxford: Clarendon Press.

Pettigrew, T. (1985). Can social scientists be effective actors in the policy arena? In R. L. Shotland & M. M. Mark (Eds.), *Social science and social policy* (pp. 121–134). Beverly Hills, CA: Sage Publications.

Phillips, D. (1984). Day Care: Collaboration between research and policymaking. *Journal of Applied Developmental Psychology, 5,* 91–113.

Policy Studies Organization. (1978). *Policy research centers directory.* Urbana, IL.

Powell, D. R. (1989). *Families and early childhood programs.* Washington, DC: National Association for the Education of Young Children.

Random House College Dictionary, revised ed. (1975). New York: Random House.

Riddle, W. (1988). *Early childhood education and development: Federal policy issues* (IB88048). Washington, DC: Congressional Research Service.

Robins, P. K., & Weiner, S. (1978). *Child care and public policy: Studies of economic issues.* Lexington, MA: Lexington Books.

Rossi, P. H., & Wright, J. D. (1985). Social science research and the politics of gun control. In R. L. Shotland & M. M. Mark (Eds.), *Social science and social policy* (pp. 311–332). Beverly Hills, CA: Sage Publications.

Ruopp, R., Travers, J., Glantz, F., & Coelen, C. (1979). *Children at the center.* Cambridge, MA: Abt Books.

Scarr, S., Phillips, D., & McCartney, K. (1990). Facts, fantasies and the future of child care in the United States. *Psychological Science, 1*(1), 26–35.

Scarr, S., & Weinberg, R. (1986, October). The early childhood enterprise: Care and education of the young. *American Psychologist, 41*(10), 1140–1146.

Seeley, D. (1981). *Education through partnership: Mediating structures and education.* Cambridge, MA: Ballinger.

Seitz, V., Rosenbaum, L., & Apfel, N. (1985). Effects of family support intervention: A ten-year follow-up. *Child Development, 56,* 376–391.

Seligson, M., & Fink, D. B. (1989). *No time to waste.* Wellesley, MA: Wellesley College Center for Research on Women, School-Age Child Care Project.

Soto, L. D. (1991). Understanding bilingual/bicultural young children. *Young Children, 46*(2), 30–36.

Spitz, R. A. (1945). Hospitalization. *Psychoanalytic Study of the Child, 1,* 53–74.

Spodek, B., & Saracho, O. (Eds.). (1990a). *Early childhood teacher preparation.* New York: Teachers College Press.

Spodek, B., & Saracho, O. (1990b). Preparing early childhood teachers for the twenty-first century. In B. Spodek & O. Saracho (Eds.), *Early childhood teacher preparation* (pp. 209–221). New York: Teachers College Press.

Sternberg, R. (1985). *Beyond IQ: A triarchic theory of human intelligence.* Cambridge, England: Cambridge University Press.

Stone, J. G. (1978). *A guide to discipline* (rev. ed.). Washington, DC: National Association for the Education of Young Children.

Takanishi, R., DeLeon, P. H., & Pallak, M. S. (1983). Psychology and public policy: Affecting children, youth, and families. *American Psychologist, 38,* 67–69.

U.S. General Accounting Office. (1990). *Early childhood education: What are the costs of high-quality programs?* Washington, DC: Author.

Weidman, D. R., Horst, P., Taher, G. M., & Wholey, J. S. (1973). *Design of an evaluation system for NIMH* Contract Report 962-7. Washington, DC: The Urban Institute.

Weiss, C. H. (1972). *Evaluation research: Methods of assessing program effectiveness.* Englewood Cliffs, NJ: Prentice-Hall.

Weiss, C. H. (1977). Introduction. In C. H. Weiss (Ed.), *Using social research in public policy making* (pp. 1–22). Lexington, MA: Lexington Books.

Whitebook, M., Howes, C., & Phillips, D. (1990). *National child care staffing study.* Oakland, CA: Child Care Employee Project.

Wholey, J. S., Scanlon, J. W., Dugfy, H. G., Fikumotos, J. S., & Vogt, E. M. (1971). *Federal evaluation policy.* Washington, DC: The Urban Institute.

Woodhead, M. (1988). When psychology informs public policy. The case of early childhood intervention. *American Psychology, 43*(6), 443–454.

Woolsey, S. (1977). Piedpiper politics and the child care debate. *Daedalus, 106,* 127–145.

Yarrow, M. R. & Waxler, C. Z. (1976). Dimensions and correlates of prosocial behavior in young children. *Child Development, 47,* 118–125.

Young, D. R., & Nelson, R. R. (1973). *Public policy for day care of young children.* Lexington, MA: Lexington Books.

Young, K. T., & Zigler, E. (1986). Infant and toddler day care: Regulations and policy implications. *American Journal of Orthopsychiatry, 56,* 43–54.

Zigler, E. (1970). The environmental mystique: Training the intellect versus development of the child. *Childhood Education, 46,* 402–412.

Zigler, E. (1991). Using research to inform policy: The case of early intervention. In S. L. Kagan (Ed.), *The care and education of America's young children: Obstacles and opportunities [Ninetieth Yearbook of the National Society for the Study of Education]* (pp. 154–172). Chicago, IL: University of Chicago Press.

Zigler, E., & Kagan, S. L. (1982). Child development knowledge and educational practice: Using what we know. In A. Lieberman & M. McLaughlin (Eds.), *Policy making in education. Eighty-first yearbook of the National Society for the Study of Education* (pp. 80–104). Chicago: University of Chicago Press.

Zigler, E., & Trickett, P. (1978). IQ, social competence, and evaluation of early childhood intervention programs. *American Psychologist, 33,* 789–798.

Zigler, E., & Valentine J. (Eds.). (1979). *Project Head Start: A legacy of the war on poverty.* New York: Free Press.

CHINESE AND JAPANESE KINDERGARTENS:
CASE STUDY IN COMPARATIVE RESEARCH

Harold W. Stevenson, Shinying Lee, and Theresa Graham
THE UNIVERSITY OF MICHIGAN

A discussion of the kindergarten experiences of children in Japan, China, and Taiwan is particularly timely in view of the noteworthy later academic accomplishments of Japanese and Chinese children. As early as first grade, Chinese children read more effectively than American children and both Chinese and Japanese children surpass American children in their knowledge of mathematics (Stevenson, 1990; Stevenson, Lee, Chen, Stigler, Hsu, & Kitamura, 1990; Stevenson, Lee, Chen, Lummis, Stigler, Liu, & Fang, 1990). It is logical, during a time when Western countries face pervasive problems in their educational systems, to ask whether we might find cues for improvement by examining practices in Asia.

For shorthand purposes we refer throughout this chapter to Japan, China, and Taiwan as Asia, although we are aware of the fact that they encompass only a small number of the Asian cultures. Similarly, we use the term *Western* as a shorthand reference to North America and Western Europe.

Our purpose in this chapter is to familiarize the reader with kindergartens in China, Japan, and Taiwan and to illustrate how comparative studies of kindergarten education not only instruct us about other cultures, but also force us into new ways of examining our own.

In the first section of the chapter we describe kindergarten programs as they exist in China, Japan, and Taiwan. To do this we rely upon two sources of information: (1) the personal experiences we and others have had in visiting Asian kindergartens and in talking with teachers and parents, and (2) published reports, typically governmental reports, describing demographic features of the kindergartens in each of the three locations.

In the second section of the chapter we describe a large study of kindergarten children we have conducted in Japan, Taiwan, and the United States. We use this study as an example of how comparative research can be conducted, the problems that are faced in carrying out such research, and ways they can be solved. A formal report of this large project will be forthcoming; in the present chapter we present some of the findings as illustrative examples of the outcome of various research procedures.

We do not present a review of research literature for the simple reason that there are few formal, quantitative studies that bear directly upon the issues we discuss in this chapter. Although several comparative studies deal with topics such as the play of Japanese and American children (e.g., Seagoe & Murakami, 1961), these studies do not form a substantial, coherent body of information. The recent appearance of comparative studies such as those of Tobin, Wu, and Davidson (1989) and of Sano (1989), where common materials and systematic methods were used to assess some aspect of early childhood education, may anticipate growth of the research literature in coming years.

ASIAN EARLY CHILDHOOD EDUCATION

Historical Background and Philosophy

Kindergartens in Asia were not the result of indigenous movements but owe their early existence to the ideas of European philosophers and educators such as Froebel and Pestalozzi (Bettleheim & Takanishi, 1976; Spodek, 1989). Leading citizens in Japan and China advanced the kindergarten movement, but their major contribution was in adapting Western ideas for use in their own countries rather than in initiating new approaches to the education of young children.

Kindergartens spread rapidly in Asia because of the same factors that led to their early popularity in the West: They were effective in providing care for children of working mothers, offering early social experience, preparing children for elementary school, compensating for life in urban environments, and (in China) providing child care during wartime.

Early childhood teachers in all countries stress the importance of social and emotional development. Asians go even further. They believe that socioemotional development is not only of fundamental importance itself but is also a necessary precursor of intellectual development (Meng, July 1991, unpublished talk, University of Michigan). They do not emphasize the direct teaching of academic skills until the child's emotional development has reached a certain stage—one that is usually attained around the age of 6, when the child begins elementary school.

Asian parents and teachers consider kindergartens to be agencies for providing children with opportunities to develop good social relations with peers and adults, to experience the joy of learning, to acquire good habits of hygiene, and to help families that are not able to provide children with what society deems to be appropriate nurturance and stimulation (Mao & Bourgeault, 1991). The kindergarten is judged to be successful if children appear to adjust well to group life, enjoy their friends, and become interested in learning more about the world. In China and Taiwan some emphasis is also placed on the development of academic skills, such as being able to write one's name and count, and on performance skills, such as being able to sing, dance, and recite.

Organization

The organization of Asian programs in early childhood education differs markedly from what is found in the West, where nursery schools and kindergartens typically are separate institutions. In Asia, the two are combined into single units serving 3- to 6-year-olds. Unlike most Western kindergartens, Asian kindergartens generally are not attached to elementary schools, and in Japan and Taiwan they are mostly privately owned.

To avoid confusion with their Western counterparts, we refer to the institutions by their Chinese and Japanese names. The following terms are used:

China: Kindergartens serving 3- to 6-year-olds are referred to as *youeryuan*; nurseries for children under 3 years of age are called *tuoersuo*.
Taiwan: *Yozhiyuan* are kindergartens that enroll 3- to 6-year-olds. In contrast to China, *tuoersuo* are day care centers serving children from the time they are young infants until they enter elementary school.
Japan: *Yochien* correspond to the *youeryuan* and *yozhiyuan* of China and Taiwan. Most *yochien* have 4- and 5-year-old groups, although some may enroll children as young as 3. Day care centers in Japan (*hoikuen*) parallel the *yochien* in terms of the ages of children served but commonly accept 3-year-olds as well as 4- and 5-year-olds.

Kindergartens in Japan

Japan's first kindergarten opened in 1876 at Tokyo Women's Normal School (now Ochanomizu University). As in the West,

the early *yochien* were established for well-to-do families in large cities.

Types. Nearly all *yochien* in Japan are privately owned. Public kindergartens exist, such as central government kindergartens and prefectural kindergartens, but they are very rare—only 2% of kindergartens are sponsored by the national or prefectural governments. More commonly, the kindergartens are privately owned, or are sponsored by Buddhist temples or Christian missions.

Hoikuen have a somewhat shorter history than *yochien*. The first *hoikuen* opened in 1890, but major development occurred after World War II. *Hoikuen* were established for children of the poor in an effort to counter the rapid urbanization and industrialization of Japan. All receive some subsidy from the local, prefectural, and national government.

Kindergartens and day care centers are open 6 days a week. The major differences between the two types of facility are in their supervisory agency and hours of operation. *Hoikuen* are supervised by the Ministry of Health and Welfare, rather than by the Ministry of Education, Science, and Culture, which administers the curriculum and operation of *yochien*. Children remain at the *hoikuen* throughout the day, rather than returning home after lunch, as is the case for children in *yochien* (Boocock, 1989). The two institutions are becoming more and more alike in terms of program and clientele. In fact, *hoikuen* are now expected to use the *yochien* manuals written for teachers of children 3 years of age and older.

Although some *yochien* enroll children as young as 3 years of age, attendance among 3-year-olds is not common: No more than 15% to 20% of 3-year-olds are enrolled in *yochien*. By the age of 5 or 6, nearly all Japanese children attend either *yochien* or *hoikuen*. Enrollment in *yochien* is a matter of parental decision, but a certificate of need from the Office of Social Service is necessary before a child can be enrolled in *hoikuen*. As might be expected, mothers of children enrolled in *hoikuen* are much more likely to be employed than are mothers of children in *yochien*. We found in our research that 98% of the mothers of children enrolled in *hoikuen* were employed, compared to only 21% of the mothers of children in *yochien*.

Although there are complicated patterns of governmental support, the operation of *yochien* is strongly dependent upon fees. The declining birthrate in Japan (and Taiwan) has recently resulted in competition in attracting children.

In addition to *yochien* and *hoikuen*, several other types of child care institutions exist in Japan: *hoikusho, takujisho,* and *bebi hoteru* (baby hotels). These institutions offer day care—or even hourly care—to children from infancy to school age. The qualifications of the caretakers in these institutions are not so high as those in *yochien* and *hoikuen*, the size of the enterprises is smaller, the cost is lower, access is informal, and the programs are less structured. Furthermore, most operate without the approval of either the Ministry of Health or Education. *Hoikusho*, once popular as agencies for short-term care, have been displaced for the most part by the other agencies.

Schedule. A typical schedule for a Japanese *yochien* is as follows:

9:00	Arrival at school, free play
9:30	Free play
9:50	Clean-up time
10:00	Calisthenics, opening ceremony, group play
10:30	Group activities
11:30	Lunch preparation, eating, and clean-up time
12:40	Play
2:00	Departure

Hoikuen follow a similar schedule, except that the children nap and have additional time for play before returning home at 5:30.

Tuition. All children in *yochien* pay tuition. Tuition for children who attend elite kindergartens is high, but the tuition for ordinary *yochien* is within the reach of most families. Depending upon the family's resources, tuition at *hoikuen* may vary from a very small percentage of the total tuition to full payment. The difference is paid by funds from the city, prefecture, and central governments.

Teachers. Teachers in Japanese kindergartens are predominantly young women who remain in their positions until the time of marriage. Each school has a principal, usually a retired public school administrator, and a head teacher, typically one of the few women who remain in the profession for more than a few years. The head teacher actually runs the kindergarten, manages the finances, and supervises and counsels the other teachers. The role of the principal is more ceremonial than functional in the kindergarten's day-to-day operation.

Salaries for staff members at *hoikuen* are generally lower than those at *yochien*, where nearly all teachers are graduates of a 2-year junior college course in early childhood education. The small percentage of *yochien* teachers who have graduated from a 4-year college receive salaries similar to those of elementary school teachers.

Teaching in Japanese *yochien* is a demanding job. There are no assistants, and the teacher is solely responsible for all aspects of the program. Western observers are astounded to find a single young woman in charge of a class containing 30 to 40 preschool children. Class size in *hoikuen* is somewhat smaller, but the teacher is solely responsible for the children throughout the whole day.

Teacher Preparation. It is difficult to find an explicit statement of the philosophy guiding the preparation of teachers in Asian schools. Nevertheless, as Peak has pointed out, teaching procedures are consistent throughout Japan and reflect "a highly elaborated indigenous cultural structuring of the learning process" (Peak, 1986). The procedures are consistent, but if they are described inexplicitly, how are budding teachers taught? Typically through *minarai kikan*, the experience of learning through observing—a method that characterizes not only Japanese training of teachers but also teacher training throughout Asia. Good examples of what works are given more emphasis than are highly articulated theories of child development and early childhood education. By observing and listening, and then by attempting to model what has been observed,

teachers come to share techniques, attitudes, and beliefs that provide a distinctive Asian perspective on early childhood education.

Curriculum. The curriculum of Japanese kindergartens is divided into six domains: health, society, nature, language, drawing, and music and rhythm. Notable is the omission of academic subjects. No time is allocated for teaching mathematics or reading, and no Japanese characters (*kanji*) are taught. In fact, any teaching of academic subjects is counter to the policies of the Ministry of Education.

Whatever is introduced about mathematical concepts of quantity, time, and space is aimed at increasing children's interest in and general knowledge about mathematics, rather than at teaching formal mathematical operations. When asked what they mean by teaching language, Japanese teachers reply that they teach children to communicate with others, to speak loudly and clearly, and to develop an interest in and awareness of the components of the writing system.

One reason that formal teaching of academic subjects is not introduced in kindergarten arises from the belief that the children are too young to benefit from this training. Another argument is that teaching academic subjects leads to unequal opportunities; some children would enter elementary school at a more advanced level than those who had not had the advantage of this type of instruction. Most important, perhaps, is the fact that Japanese parents send their children to kindergarten to learn about group life and group activities.

When Japanese mothers are asked why they sent their child to kindergarten, they make frequent allusions to their child's social development. They have told us, for example, "I send my child to kindergarten to experience with friends the kinds of things that parents have a hard time teaching them," or "I send my child to kindergarten to adjust to group activities; to develop her individual characteristics in a natural way and in a relaxed setting." Few parents described anything related to academic achievement or cognitive functioning. Those who do seek more training for their children may also enroll them in private schools (*juku*), where they may learn the rudiments of mathematics, reading, or English, or how to play the violin or piano.

When Japanese teachers in *yochien* are asked about the values they foster in children, they suggest that they want children to become good human beings and individuals who have harmonious human relationships, who persevere, and who are able to concentrate (Shiragaki, 1983). They define these values more explicitly by describing children who are sympathetic, gentle, socially conscious, kind, cooperative, patient, creative, studious, and thoughtful—values with which early childhood educators throughout the world would probably agree. Above all, teachers seek to structure the kindergarten experience so that children learn to enjoy being with the group.

Kindergarten education in Japan is not considered to be a preparatory course for elementary education, but to have meaning in itself by fostering the early development of a "desirable person" (Sakamoto, 1968). The portrayal of Asian kindergarten teachers often contained in Western media as intense, demanding adults who push children relentlessly so that they will do well on entrance examinations to elementary school is far from describing the typical kindergarten teacher. In fact, Japanese kindergarten teachers not only minimize formal teaching, they also pay little attention to preparing children for entrance examinations. There are test-conscious kindergartens in Tokyo and other large cities, but less than 5% of Japanese children attend academically oriented kindergartens and less than 1% apply to elementary schools that require an entrance examination (Peak, 1991).

The Japanese kindergarten curriculum does include practice in certain rituals. For example, children are taught to bow and greet their teacher each morning and to say thanks for their food. Rituals such as these are considered to be necessary in Japanese society, and children's participation in them is mandatory. In other activities, such as free play and story time, children are free to participate or not.

Uchi and Soto. It is difficult to understand the goals and purposes of Japanese kindergartens without brief mention of the two terms, *uchi* and *soto*. *Uchi* refers to the home, the "inside" world; *soto* refers to the world outside the home. These two worlds are separate from each other, and each fosters and tolerates different kinds of behaviors (Peak, 1991).

Japanese kindergartens seek to aid the child in adapting to the outside world—a task that parents believe cannot be accomplished at home. Parents realize that the process of adapting to group life places many demands upon their children. In order to help their child make a healthy adaptation, they attempt to maintain the home as a place where children can relax and express their feelings, and where they can receive unconditional nurturance and support. Regressive behavior, aggression, and noncooperativeness are tolerated at home because parents assume that such outlets reduce children's need to express these behaviors at school (Peak, 1991). Expression of antisocial or even destructive forms of behavior is not interpreted as an indication that something is wrong with their child. Rather, parents assume that children need to express their feelings, and that with further experience and improved social skills this need will decrease.

It must be remembered, too, says the well-known Japanese phrase, that "until the age of seven, children are with the gods." According to this belief, there are no bad children, only children who do not understand what is expected of them or who have not been taught properly. Young children must therefore be given great freedom during early childhood; otherwise they may choose to stay with the gods and not join human society!

Kindergartens in China

Chinese kindergartens were established as part of the education reform movement that began in the late Ching Dynasty. Teachers were recruited from Japan and the first kindergartens were opened in 1903 in Wuchang and Beijing. The purpose of these kindergartens was to supplement the education provided by families, but the philosophy and learning materials were heavily influenced by the Japanese. Although Western missionaries had organized other early kindergartens in China, these kindergartens were not well accepted by the Chinese government.

Imitation of Japanese kindergartens declined after the May Fourth Movement in 1919, which signaled an effort to Westernize many practices. Western philosophers such as Dewey and Russell were invited to China, and Chinese educators studied abroad. Practices rapidly became similar to those popular in the West, especially those in the United States. A great change occurred in early childhood education, however, when China underwent a mid-century transformation from a capitalist to a socialist economy, and changes are taking place again in the 1990s with the resurgence of free-market activities.

Types. As in all countries, Chinese kindergartens vary in their programs, quality, and size, depending upon the community being served, the educational and financial level of the parents, and other factors. Kindergartens are separate physically and administratively from elementary schools.

Three types of *youeryuan* exist in China: public, lane, and institutionally affiliated. The most popular are public (government-sponsored) kindergartens that are under the control of the division of kindergarten education of city or county bureaus of education. Lane (neighborhood) kindergartens are organized by the community and are collectively managed by representatives from the community. Institutions or organizations, including factories, army units, farms, scientific academies, and universities may organize their own kindergartens. The financing and management of the institutionally affiliated type of kindergarten are primarily the responsibility of the organizing unit. More recently, a new type of kindergarten for 5-year-olds has appeared in China: "before-school" kindergartens (*xueqianban*), which are attached to elementary schools in large cities and are administered by the elementary school staff. These kindergartens are distinguished from other Chinese kindergartens by their focus on the academic preparation of children for elementary school.

Because nearly all mothers and fathers work in China, children typically remain at the kindergarten all day, 6 days a week. Boarding kindergartens exist, but there has been a strong reaction against them by parents and educators. As a result, children are enrolled in boarding kindergartens only when it is literally impossible for the child to return home each evening.

Children typically enter kindergarten at the age of 3 and are divided into groups of 3- to 4-, 4- to 5-, and 5- to 6-year-olds. Prior to entering kindergarten, some children are enrolled in nurseries (*tuoersuo*) from the time they are a few months old until they reach the age for entering kindergarten. *Tuoersuo* are parallel in their sponsorship to kindergartens; there are public, lane, and institutional nurseries. The most common are institutionally affiliated *tuoersuo*, established for the benefit of the institution's staff. *Youeryuan* are under the supervision of the Ministry of Education; *tuoersuo* are under the Ministry of Public Health.

According to statistics published in the 1991 Statistical Yearbook on Education of the Ministry of Education in China, 19,720,000 3- to 6-year-olds were enrolled in 172,000 kindergartens staffed by 740,000 teachers and staff members (*Renminribao*, 1991). Between 20 to 30% of 3- to 6-year-olds were enrolled in kindergarten (Zhong, 1989). Enrollment varies, however, according to location. For example, over 90% of Shanghai's 5-year-olds attend *youeryuan*, but the percentage is quite low in some areas of the countryside.

Teachers. The typical kindergarten class consists of approximately 30 children and is managed by three persons: the person responsible for teaching and child care, an assistant, and a housekeeper who assists children during routine activities, such as lunch, nap time, and toileting. Although the Chinese term for teacher (*laoshi*) is often used for the principal person, the official title is *jiaoyangyuan*, which is translated as a person who combines teaching (*jiao*) and rearing (*yang*) children—what we might call a teacher/child care worker. Staffing is variable, however, and lane kindergartens may have only the teacher and an assistant in each classroom.

Teacher Preparation. Staff members of the *tuoersuo* seldom have training in preschool education or early childhood development. They are primarily women who have learned to care for infants and young children through practical experience in their own homes or neighborhoods. Recently, home day care has been initiated by women who are willing to care for a small number of infants and young children in their own apartments for a fee (Huang, 1991).

The quality of kindergarten teachers has varied over the past decades. The whole educational establishment has only gradually recovered from the chaos that existed during the decade of the Cultural Revolution (1966–1976), when training of teachers stopped and ideology was the primary criterion for selecting a teacher. Even today, staff members at many kindergartens have had no formal training in kindergarten education. Love of children and the ability to sing, play an organ, dance, and draw may be the only qualifications necessary for employment. Lane and institutional kindergartens attempt to upgrade their staffs by hiring older teachers from public kindergartens who have passed the age of 50, the usual retirement age for women in China.

Currently, approximately half of China's kindergarten teachers are graduates of senior middle schools—what we would consider high-school graduates. However, less than one-third of all kindergarten teachers possess a kindergarten teacher's certificate, reflecting special coursework and practical experience (*Renminribao*, 1991; Huang, 1991).

To improve their skills, teachers attend in-service training programs conducted by experienced teachers from other kindergartens or by experts from middle schools and colleges. Teachers with only a middle-school education may be sent to special 1-year training programs (*xunlianban*). Others attend middle schools that specialize in preschool education. These middle-school graduates, along with graduates of other senior middle schools and experienced kindergarten teachers, may attend 2-year preschool education colleges for further professional training. Finally, special programs leading to the bachelor's degree in preschool education exist at teachers' colleges and normal universities. Graduates of these special programs may become teachers, but more often become administrators or researchers in preschool education (Huang, 1991).

Curriculum. Chinese kindergartens stress the all-around development of the child. Eight domains of concern are defined in the official curriculum. These include personal hygiene, physical exercise, moral education, language, common knowledge, mathematics, music, and art (*Youeryuan jiaoyu gangyao*, 1981).

Most Chinese parents and teachers do not consider academic work to be a critical component of kindergarten. In fact, they suggest that children would be more likely to receive academic training from their families if they stayed at home. Teachers in *youeryuan* place primary emphasis on play, but some academic work is gradually introduced. By the time the child is in the oldest group, up to 2 hours a week may be devoted to academic subjects. The schedule varies from day to day, and on some days it includes 20 minutes for mathematics and 20 minutes for learning Chinese characters. In addition, eight 25- to 30-minute periods each week are devoted to music, drawing, common knowledge, and group exercise. A typical day in a Chinese kindergarten would be something like the following:

8:00	Arrival at kindergarten; free play
9:00	Teaching and learning activities
9:20	Playing games
10:00	Music or art
11:00	Outdoor play
11:30	Lunch
12:00	Outdoor play
12:30	Nap
3:00	Snack
3:30	Story
4:00	Dinner
5:00	Departure for home

Mode of Teaching. Chinese teachers believe that instruction through direct guidance is critical and that allowing children to explore by themselves is an inefficient avenue to learning. It is more productive and more enjoyable, they propose, if children are allowed freedom to experiment and to explore *after* they have received proper instruction. They do not believe that they should control children through commands, but that they should guide them through each step in the process of learning. The remarkable theatrical performances that impress so many visitors to Chinese kindergartens are a result of this careful instruction. Similarly, the sophistication of Chinese kindergarten children's drawings and clay and paper figures that often astonish foreign visitors are also the result of careful step-by-step instruction.

On the other hand, teachers must exercise ingenuity in keeping children involved in activities when few toys, books, and other materials are available. In compensating for limited supplies and equipment, teachers must rely heavily on group activities as teaching devices.

Physical Facilities. The facilities for kindergartens in China range from pleasant buildings that once housed private schools in large cities to near-sheds in the countryside with dirt floors and cinderblocks as chairs and desks. Most kindergartens have little or no heat in the wintertime, and children arrive at school with layer upon layer of cotton-padded clothing to protect them from the cold.

Equipment that Westerners would consider essential is usually in very short supply. Blocks, sandboxes, miniature household furniture, doll corners, and reading nooks are seldom to be found. Even the supplies of crayons, paper, and scissors are limited. Toys are scarce. For example, wind-up cars, toys with which Western children frequently play, serve as objects to be observed when the teacher demonstrates their operation, rather than to be manipulated by the children.

Teachers use many everyday objects in their teaching and often construct teaching materials out of such things as colored cardboard and crepe paper. Manipulatives are likely to be balls, buttons, wax fruit, or leaves, rather than the more elaborate materials that Westerners often use to capture and maintain children's attention. Posters and drawings serve in place of expensive audio-visual equipment.

The One-Child Family Policy. It is hard to imagine what it must be like for a nation to be faced with the task of rearing and educating a cohort of approximately 17,000,000 children born each year. Down from an earlier 20,000,000 annual birthrate, this number remains an enormous burden for a developing country like China.

The drop in the 1980s in the size of the cohort has been a result of the nation's one-child family policy whereby couples are allowed to have only one child. The policy has been more successful in large cities than in the countryside, where enforcement is more difficult. As a result, children in the cities of China tend to be reared in households where they are surrounded by doting parents and grandparents but where there are seldom other playmates.

Kindergartens have become the major locus for social interaction among young Chinese children. Only children, sometimes lonely at home without siblings and with few children among the neighboring families, are eager to spend time with their peers at kindergarten. Parents, too, are enthusiastic about kindergarten. The opportunity for children to interact with each other is considered a healthy antidote to the possibility that their child will become spoiled by parents and grandparents. Furthermore, mothers and fathers are employed full-time in nearly all Chinese families, and unless grandparents are available to care for the children during the day, the only feasible arrangement for most families is for the child to attend kindergarten.

Kindergartens in Taiwan

The history of the kindergarten movement in Taiwan is closely linked with those of both China and Japan. Taiwan was a Japanese colony for 50 years earlier in this century, and its educational system was very similar to that found in Japan. Following the defeat of the Kuomintang government in 1949, Taiwan became the new home of over 1,500,000 mainland Chinese who brought with them the Chinese conception of an educational system and specific guidelines for its operation. Because

early childhood educators were among this group of immigrants, Taiwan's kindergartens were strongly influenced by the early philosophy and practices of Chinese kindergartens.

Types. Approximately 80% of the preschools are *yuozhiyuan,* and only 20% are *tuoersuo* (Xin Yi Foundation, 1985). Attendance is not obligatory, and relatively small percentages of children are enrolled: 20.3% of 3- to 6-year-olds attend *yuozhiyuan* and 19.9% attend *tuoersuo* (Chen, 1977). Enrollment in *yuozhiyuan* is much higher in large urban areas than in the countryside.

At present, nearly 75% of the kindergartens in Taiwan are privately owned. The remaining kindergartens are attached to public elementary schools (Republic of China Department of Education, 1991). *Tuoersuo,* on the other hand, are mostly public. Only 23% are privately owned, and even these are subsidized by the government (Su, 1984).

The distinction between *yuozhiyuan* and *tuoersuo* is similar to that between kindergartens and day care centers in Japan. *Tuoersuo* are open for 8 or more hours 6 days a week and enroll children from the time they are 1 month old. *Yuozhiyuan* typically offer both half-day and all-day programs for 3- to 6-year-olds. Tuition for both *yuozhiyuan* or *tuoersuo* is paid by the child's parents.

Classes in *yuozhiyuan* are large: The average enrollment is 35 children. Teachers do have some help, however; several uncertified teachers, a housekeeper, and a janitor are often employed to assist in the four or five classes included in the typical kindergarten.

Yuozhiyuan are supervised by the Ministry of Education; *tuoersuo,* by the Bureau of Social Services. Both types are supposed to be licensed by one of these agencies, but many are not. As a result, there is great variability in physical facilities, ranging from true "children's gardens" with ponds and beds of flowers to cramped classrooms occupying what originally were the basements or small rooms of private homes.

Curriculum. The goals of preschool education in Taiwan are defined by the Early Childhood Education Law of 1981. Kindergartens are expected to maintain the physical and mental health of children, to develop good personal habits, to enrich children's daily experience, to promote children's ethical concepts, and to develop their prosocial and group behavior. Emphasis is placed on the development of appropriate attitudes and personal habits rather than on learning specific information and knowledge. In brief, children are expected to benefit from the kindergarten experience by being stimulated and trained in social, emotional, intellectual, and motor development, and in self-care and independence (Liao, 1984).

Teachers. Since 1983, teachers of *yuozhiyuan* have been required to be graduates of a 2-year teachers' training program in which they enroll after graduating from high school. However, most teachers have acquired their teacher certificate through a 2-year continuing education summer program or an evening program. Even so, 40% of the teachers are uncertified (Tsai, 1988). The majority of teachers in *tuoersuo* are high school or vocational school graduates who have had at least 3 months of special in-service training in child care (Su, 1984). In general, staff members of both *yuozhiyuan* and *tuoersuo* are not well paid and must work long hours. Perhaps because of this, teachers seldom continue working past their late twenties.

Summary

Preschool education in Japan, China, and Taiwan differs greatly in conception and practice from that currently found in the West. Despite the common early influence of Europeans, adaptations have occurred that have drawn early childhood education in the East and West apart. Western kindergartens attached to elementary schools attempt to provide experiences that will help children in their academic subjects in elementary school. Asian programs for children of kindergarten age are more like those provided in the West for children in nursery schools, which focus on socioemotional development, self-care, and habit training.

In sum, Asian kindergartens continue to embody the original philosophy of kindergarten education. Froebel, much like contemporary Chinese and Japanese educators, considered young children to be innocents; the goal of early education was to nurture the spirit of God within them (Ross, 1976). There was nothing to be gained from teaching reading and writing in classrooms; rather, the children should be taught manual dexterity, good manners, cleanliness, and industry—goals similar to those currently held in Asia. Furthermore, children were considered to be best able to acquire the skills necessary for the next stage of education through play and structured activities rather than through direct instruction. The adult's role, above all, was to cultivate children: to provide activities that would lead children to enjoy learning.

DOING CROSS-CULTURAL RESEARCH ON KINDERGARTEN EDUCATION

To our knowledge, the only major, systematic quantitative study of Chinese and Japanese kindergartens is that of Tobin, Wu, and Davidson (1989). They investigated the practices and philosophies of preschool education in China, Japan, and the United States by obtaining reactions of parents and teachers to filmed episodes of children's behavior at preschool. Other investigators have reported ethnographic studies in which they have spent long hours observing in Asian preschools (Boocock, 1989; Fujita, 1989; Hendry, 1986; Kessen, 1976; Lewis, 1984; Peak, 1991). These descriptive ethnographic studies have advanced our understanding of early education in Asia. But learning about other cultures through personal observations or observations of others is not always completely satisfying. What if strong biases entered into the observations? What if they were made under atypical conditions? What if the individuals or kindergartens being observed were not representative of the cultures? How can one be confident that the conclusions are in accord with what would be found through systematic observation or under more controlled conditions? The answer to these questions is obvious: Organize a research project that ensures, to the greatest degree possible, that the samples are represen-

tative, the research instruments are reliable and appropriate for the cultures being studied, and the research is conducted by well-trained, sensitive interviewers and observers.

Meeting the conditions required of a formal quantitative study is not easy, especially when different cultures and different languages are involved. More often than not, cross-cultural studies have been initiated by investigators with no long-term acquaintance with the cultures and little or no facility with the languages involved. Rather than being true collaborative projects, they have often been planned by representatives of one culture and then adapted to other cultures. Such practices force the investigator to rely on members of the other cultures as translators, informants, and, ultimately, implementers of the research. These methodological problems do not need to be encountered if there is close interaction among persons from each of the cultures involved in the project—a commitment that requires the investment of a great deal of time and effort.

Comparative Data for Kindergartens in Japan, Taiwan, and the United States

The remarkable levels of academic achievement attained by Asian elementary school children led us at the University of Michigan to ask whether we could discover events and experiences during the preschool years that would help to explain the later differences in performance of Asian and American children in elementary school. In embarking upon a study designed to answer this question, we sought to avoid methodological pitfalls of the types we have described.

Selecting the Research Sites

Among the early, important decisions in any research project are those involved in choosing where to conduct the study and how to select the subjects who will be studied. This is a difficult problem in cross-cultural research, because the sampling procedure must be applicable to each of the cultures and must yield representative samples of subjects from each culture. Ideally, national samples would be selected; unfortunately, this is rarely feasible because of logistical difficulties in establishing a large number of research sites and the great financial cost that this would entail. As a result, it is usually necessary to select a small number of locations within each culture—very frequently a single site in an urban area. In order to be comparable, the different sites must have a cultural and socioeconomic status within each culture that is comparable to that of the sites in the other cultures being studied.

The selection of research sites for our study of kindergarten children was dictated in part by the selections we had made in an earlier study of elementary school children. We had collected data for first- and fifth-graders in Minneapolis, Sendai (Japan), and Taipei (Taiwan) in a prior study (Stevenson, Lee, Chen, Stigler, Hsu, & Kitamura, 1990). It seemed reasonable to conduct the study of kindergartens in these same cities so that samples of children at each age level could be compared.

Minneapolis was the site of our research in the United States. Minneapolis residents tend to come from native-born, English-speaking families. Many factors were considered in our choice of Minneapolis; among the most important was its ethnic and racial composition. Selecting a city with a diverse ethnic population would require inclusion of ethnic status as a variable in all our analyses. This would have made it necessary to reduce the number of subjects in each ethnic group below what we believed to be desirable.

We chose Sendai as the Japanese city in which to conduct our study because, from our own observations and from the opinions of individuals who know both Japan and the United States, it is the city in Japan that has a cultural and economic status most similar to that of Minneapolis in the United States.

The choice of a Chinese city for our research was limited to Taipei and Hong Kong. (It did not appear likely at the time we began planning our study that we would be able to undertake this type of project in mainland China.) We believed that Hong Kong was inappropriate because it has been so strongly influenced by Western culture, and that Taipei was a more typical Chinese city.

Selecting the Subjects

Once the site is selected it is necessary to decide how subjects will be sampled within the site. The ideal solution is random sampling, but this is seldom possible because of the great expense of locating and testing or interviewing each individual subject.

To ensure that we were studying unbiased samples of children, we selected the research subjects from among children attending 24 kindergartens in Minneapolis, 24 5- to 6-year-old groups in *yuozhiyuan* in Taipei, and 24 5- to 6-year-old groups in *yochien* and *hoikuen* in Sendai. The kindergartens were chosen in consultation with educational authorities in each city to form representative samples of the full range of kindergartens, including those judged to be average, above average, and below average. The numbers of *yochien* and *hoikuen* chosen for the Sendai sample were proportional to their numbers in the city.

By selecting this number and range of kindergartens, we believed that we would be justified in making statements that would generalize to all 5- to 6-year olds in each city. There is one minor exception. Although attendance at kindergarten is nearly universal in Minneapolis and Sendai, only around 85% of the eligible children in Taipei attend *yuozhiyuan*. Locating and testing children in Taipei who were not attending kindergarten was beyond our range of possibilities.

Because the number of children attending 72 kindergarten classes was so large, it was necessary to select a sample of target subjects for intensive study. We did this by randomly choosing six boys and six girls from one randomly selected classroom in each kindergarten. The target children were given achievement and intelligence tests; they were observed in their classrooms; and their mothers were interviewed.

Constructing the Tests

Colleagues from each culture participated in all phases of the project. Our team of bilingual and trilingual researchers constructed all of the research instruments used in the study.

Working as a group has many advantages. The instruments were not biased in favor of one culture, because members of each culture were responsible for their content. Moreover, by working together as a group it was possible to immediately scrutinize the relevance and wording of the materials proposed and to decide whether or not they were potentially usable before we had devoted a large amount of time to their refinement.

Reading Test. It would be unfair to translate a reading test from one culture for use in another. The words, stories, and grammatical structures that are appropriate for one language and one culture may not be satisfactory for another. The only solution seems to be to construct new tests that are deemed to be relevant and fair for all of the cultures involved in the study.

We constructed our reading test after reviewing workbooks and textbooks used in the kindergartens and elementary schools in each city. To be sure that we included items that were appropriate for each culture, we undertook the arduous task of entering each word in the elementary school readers used in each city into the computer and noting its English equivalent and the semester the word was first introduced. (Both Chinese and Japanese words can be written in romanized form.) We knew, therefore, all of the words to which the children were potentially exposed in their readers and the semester in which this occurred. With this information, along with synopses of the content of each reader and a notation of the grade at which various grammatical structures were introduced, we were able to construct a reliable test that was judged to be culturally fair by educators and psychologists in each culture. (See Stevenson, Lee, Chen, Stigler, Hsu, & Kitamura, 1990, for further details about this approach to constructing achievement tests.)

The reading test began with simple items and continued through ones appropriate for third-graders. It tapped knowledge of letters (or their counterparts: Japanese *kana* and Chinese *zhuyin fuhao*), decoding words and short phrases, and, if the children were capable, reading simple text. Children were not only required to read the items, but also to indicate their comprehension of what they read by pointing to appropriate drawings or answering questions.

Mathematics Test. The mathematics test was constructed in a similar fashion. We compiled a list of the concepts introduced in kindergarten workbooks and elementary school textbooks from each city. From this list we were able to construct a test that contained items that children from each culture seemed likely to encounter. The items ranged from identifying numerals, counting, and ordering, through adding and subtracting in simple computation and word problems.

Intelligence Tests. We also sought to evaluate the children's intellectual abilities. Standard intelligence tests, such as the Stanford-Binet and the Wechsler Preschool Intelligence Scale for Children, have been translated and adapted in Chinese and Japanese versions. After reviewing these tests we decided that too many items were idiosyncratic to each version to allow us to use these tests for our research. We proceeded, therefore, to construct our own tests and selected several of the most common types of subtests in the standardized tests as prototypes.

A vocabulary test required kindergarten children to define such words as orange, bicycle, and yawn. In addition, a picture vocabulary test and a short test of understanding of spatial words, such as above and below, were also used. A general information test included questions about the relative size of an elephant and a horse, the color of the sky during the daytime, and what to do when one feels cold. In a test of the ability to follow instructions about spatial relations, children were asked, for example, to point to an item on their left, to select from among three pictures the one including a circle under a triangle, and to select a picture with a line above an X.

Academic Achievement and Cognitive Ability

The achievement and cognitive tests were given by local professionals and by undergraduate and graduate students in psychology, education, and social work who had been trained in their administration. Except in unusual cases, the tests required a total of approximately 20 to 30 minutes, a period that seems appropriate for children of kindergarten age.

Academic Achievement. The first question is whether children in the three cultures differed in their academic achievement during kindergarten, or whether this is a phenomenon that occurs only after they enter elementary school. To answer this question, we administered the reading and mathematics tests to all 1,975 children enrolled in the kindergarten classrooms visited.

Cross-cultural differences in academic achievement appeared as early as kindergarten (see Figure 33–1). The degrees of difference in reading vocabulary (word decoding) and comprehension were relatively constant from kindergarten through fifth grade: Chinese children consistently surpassed both Japanese and American children. (The data for first- and fifth-graders were collected in a prior study (Stevenson, Lee, & Stigler, 1986). These children attended elementary schools that many of the kindergarten children would later attend.)

Cross-cultural differences in mathematics achievement were even more significant than were those for reading (see Figure 33–1). Japanese children demonstrated high levels of understanding of mathematics at all three grade levels and the

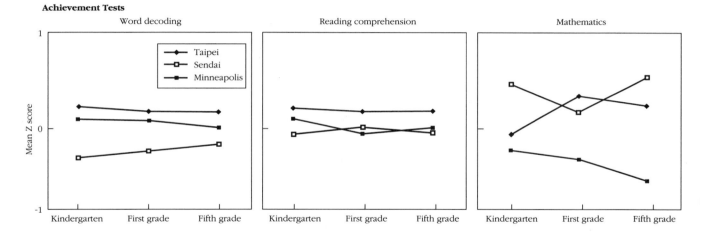

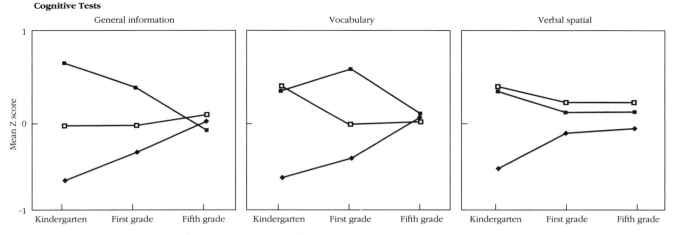

FIGURE 33–1. Performance of Taipei (Taiwan), Sendai (Japan), and Minneapolis Children on Tests of Academic Achievement and Cognitive Abilities. Scores Are in Terms of Standard Deviation Units; a Mean Score of +1 Represents the 84th Percentile; a Mean Score of −1 Represents the 16th Percentile.

performance of Chinese children improved from kindergarten through fifth grade. American kindergartners received low scores, and their scores decreased through the elementary school years relative to those of children in Taiwan and Japan.

Cognitive Ability. An explanation sometimes advanced to explain the differences in academic achievement is that Asian children are simply smarter than American children (Lynn, 1982). The results of several cognitive tests developed for this study gave no support to this proposal. In contrast to their low scores on the achievement tests, American kindergarten children received high scores on the tests of vocabulary, general information, and ability to follow instructions. However, the American children's status relative to the Chinese and Japanese children declined after kindergarten. By the fifth grade, children from all three cultures received approximately the same scores on the cognitive tests (see Figure 33–1).

On the basis of these results and other data we have collected (i.e., Stevenson, Stigler, Lee, Lucker, Kitamura, & Hsu, 1985), we can find no reason to accept the proposal that academic success of Asian children is due to superior cognitive endowment. We must look elsewhere for possible explanations. The two most obvious places are in the classroom and in the home.

Devising the Observational Method

Two methods commonly used for observing groups or classrooms are time-sampling and narrative observations. In time-sampling observations, observers are trained to observe and record clearly specified categories of behavior within short periods of time. The reliability of each observer can be determined relatively easily and training can be continued until a satisfactory level of reliability is achieved. In narrative observations, the observer is instructed to write a comprehensive account of the behavior observed during a particular period of time, such as an activity period. The observations are later coded according to a predefined scheme. Persons who have had experience in making narrative observations may produce rich, detailed descriptions, but what is recorded may—without extensive training and experience—be excessively dependent upon the interests and concerns of the particular observer. We chose a time-sampling method for our study because we thought the procedure could be conveyed more readily to members of the three cultures than that for narrative observations.

What Was Observed. We constructed a time-sampling procedure based upon frequent visits to kindergartens in each of the cities selected as research sites. Observations were made during successive 10-second periods (with appropriate rest periods) for 4 hours on preassigned days of the week and periods of the day at each kindergarten. The schedule of observations was generated so that each hour and each day were sampled with equal frequency. (No observations were made during rest periods.) An earphone and tape recorder cued the observer about whom to observe and when it was time to observe and record. Observers were trained until they were able to reach a level of agreement with the trainer of 80% or higher before they were allowed to make observations for the study. As a result of this procedure, we obtained 288 hours of observations (4 hours in each of 24 kindergartens in each of the three locations).

Observers recorded the organizational structure, content, and types of behavior of teachers and students. The observational system consisted of nine major categories: class subject, type of activity, class organization, leader, teacher-student interactions, on-task and appropriate behaviors, out-of-seat behaviors, off-task or inappropriate behaviors, and evaluative feedback.

Observation sheets were divided into these nine categories, and each category was divided into subcategories. For example, there were three types of classroom organization: The teacher worked with the whole class, separated children into small groups, or allowed children to pursue their own individual activities. For each 10-second interval, the observer was required to check one of these subcategories. Other categories were checked only when the relevant behavior occurred. For example, evaluative feedback was coded only when the child being observed was given feedback about the correctness or quality of his or her academic work or feedback about his or her behavior. Feedback was subdivided into academic feedback and behavioral or procedural feedback. In the former, the teacher might offer praise, indicate that the response was correct, provide no feedback, indicate that the response was incorrect, or criticize the child. All of the categories and subcategories cannot be reviewed here, but we can give an indication of the types of results obtained with such an observational procedure.

Type of Activity. Chinese and American children spent most of their time in organized kindergarten activities. Japanese children, in contrast, were allowed much more free time and spent less time in the regular program than the other children (see Figure 33–2). The children spent a large amount of time in transitional activities, apparently reflecting the fact that they were still learning how to move from one activity to another.

Classroom Organization. The most frequent type of class organization in all three cities was as a whole class, but this occurred somewhat more frequently in Taipei (93% of the time) than in Sendai (85%) or Minneapolis (84%). Classes were organized into small groups more often in Sendai (13%) and Minneapolis (14%) than in Taipei (6%). Very little time was spent in individually directed activities in any of the locations.

Kindergarten Program. The regular program consisted of activities in four areas: academic subjects, academic readiness, general information, and music, art, and physical education. American teachers spent more time than Chinese or Japanese teachers in teaching academic subjects and in efforts to increase children's funds of general information (see Table 33–1). Japanese teachers allocated most of their time to readiness skills: teaching children, for example, how to follow directions, pay attention, draw lines and geometric shapes, speak clearly, and work with printed materials of the types found in "readiness" books. In short, American teachers were more

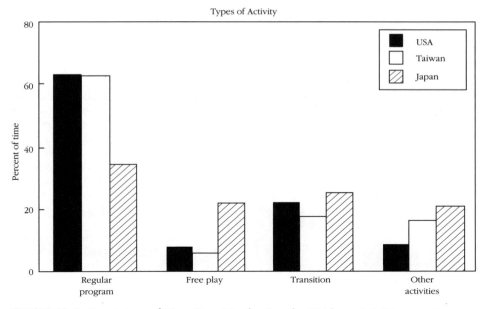

FIGURE 33–2. Percentage of Time Spent in the Regular Kindergarten Program, Free Play, Transition Activities, and Other Activities that Are Not Part of the Regular Program.

likely to teach content; Japanese teachers were more likely to teach behaviors and skills that would later be important for smooth adaptation to elementary school. Chinese teachers emphasized nonacademic skills, such as music and art.

Language arts and mathematics were the two academic subjects most frequently taught in kindergartens, but the way teachers chose to distribute their time between these two subjects differed greatly among the three cities. Minneapolis teachers spent over four times as long on language arts as on mathematics (26% versus 6% of the total time spent in the regular kindergarten program). Taipei teachers distributed their time more equally between the two subjects (12% versus 8%), and Japanese teachers spent little or no time on either subject (2% versus 0%).

It is paradoxical that there was little relation between the amount of time spent in direct teaching of a subject and children's scores on the achievement tests given late in the kindergarten year. Japanese children, who received little instruction in mathematics, received the highest scores in mathematics; Chinese children, who received less instruction in language arts than American children, outperformed them in reading.

Form of Teaching. We interpret the preceding data to indicate that the kinds of academic information and skills taught in kindergarten may be conveyed more effectively by indirect than by direct forms of teaching and by informal example than by formal instruction. The typical 5-year-old may find it easier, for example, to understand addition in the context of a story about a family of mice than through mathematical symbols, and to learn more about words by seeing labels on classroom materials than by rote learning of the alphabet.

In line with this interpretation is the Asian teachers' preference for indirect forms of teaching. We distinguished between two types of instruction. Indirect teaching was coded whenever the teacher prearranged the setting, equipment, or materials so that a particular sequence of activities would take place. An example of indirect teaching is the following: The teacher passes out leaves to the children. She then leads a simple discussion of their color, size, and shape, but does not attempt to teach the names of the trees or why leaves change color in the autumn.

In direct teaching, the teacher teaches content matter and attempts to impart information and skills. She may lead children in exercises related to prereading or premathematics skills, or she may teach them what to do in an earthquake or how to plant seeds.

When instruction occurred in Asian classrooms, it was of an indirect form 85% of the time in Japan, 77% in Taiwan, and 56% in the United States. In contrast, American teachers used direct forms of teaching 26% of the time, whereas Chinese and Japanese teachers used it 19% and 13% of the time, respectively.

On-Task Behavior. Children in a kindergarten setting engage in various irrelevant, off-task types of behavior. We considered off-task behavior to occur when they were distracted or engaged in behavior that was different from what the teacher defined. It occurred 14% of the time in Taipei, 9% in Sendai, and a low 6% in the Minneapolis classrooms.

TABLE 33–1. Percentage of Time Devoted to Areas of Kindergarten Program

	United States	Taiwan	Japan
Academic subjects	41	28	2
General information	24	7	9
Academic readiness	21	6	72
Music, art, gym	34	49	15

The converse of off-task behavior—on-task behavior—was of two types, which we termed *attending* and *involvement*. In the first type, children attended appropriately to the teachers' instructions; in the second, children carried out the activity described by the teacher.

Attending, which is often a more passive form of response, was more common in the American than in the Chinese or Japanese classrooms. During the time they were on-task, American children were attending 53% of the time, and Chinese and Japanese children were attending 30% and 37%, respectively. Active involvement was less common in the American than in the Chinese and Japanese classrooms (47% the time versus 62% and 66%). Thus American kindergarten teachers, rather than Chinese or Japanese teachers, were more likely to structure their teaching so that children assumed the role of passive listener rather than active participant in the activity at hand.

Noncompliance. American children exhibited the least amount of noncompliance to their teacher's requests or commands. They failed to respond appropriately only 8% of the time; Japanese children exhibited noncompliance 16% of the time, and Chinese children, 29%. This result is surprising in terms of the Western image of Asian children as obedient conformists to the wishes of adults.

Even more unexpected from the Western perspective were the teachers' responses to children's noncompliance. American teachers were more than twice as likely as Chinese and Japanese teachers to respond to children's noncompliance by repeating the request, modifying it, or withdrawing it. Teachers demonstrated these types of follow-up in 82% of the instances of the Minneapolis children's noncompliance, compared to only 32% in Taipei, and 44% in Sendai.

The seemingly lax response by Asian teachers may be explained in two ways. First, they believe that 5-year-olds are too young to comply readily with adults' wishes. Asian teachers are more likely to be tolerant of noncompliance and to assume that it is unrealistic to expect that young children should be required to adhere to the teachers' requests and demands. They may be less likely than American teachers, therefore, to expect that consistent follow-up is necessary or productive.

A second, closely related explanation is that Asian teachers believe that children need to learn to regulate their own behavior. Consistent follow-up by adults limits children's opportunities to learn how to do this on their own. From the teachers' point of view, experiencing the consequences of their own behavior, but certainly not punishment or repetition of the prohibition, would be more likely to have a lasting effect.

A second example of Asian teachers' failure to follow through was evident in their relatively infrequent use of feedback for children's behavior. Feedback of any type was observed in 42% of the observational periods during the regular program of the American kindergartens, but in only 29% of the periods in the Chinese and Japanese kindergartens. The explanation for Asian teachers providing less frequent feedback is the same as that for their inconsistency in following through: Frequent feedback casts the teacher in the role of arbiter of what is appropriate and inappropriate, thereby depriving children of opportunities to find out for themselves and to be motivated by the inherent interest of the activity or topic. American teachers, more strongly influenced by behaviorist psychology, generally believe that the most efficient means of modifying children's behavior is through direct feedback.

Summary. Our findings reaffirm and amplify what has been described in ethnographic studies. It is in American kindergartens, not Japanese or Chinese, where there is greater emphasis on academic topics, the daily schedule is highly organized, more time is devoted to direct teaching, children are more passively attentive, and the teacher assumes a more directive role as arbiter of what is a correct and incorrect response.

Kindergarten Teachers' Beliefs

We did not attempt to construct an interview for teachers in one language and then translate it into the other two. Instead, Chinese, Japanese, and American members of the research team met regularly as a group and constructed the interview simultaneously in all three languages. Each person in the group knew at least two of the languages.

Having members of each culture participate in constructing an interview has many advantages. Rather than relying on members of one culture to devise the interview, items were suggested by members of all three cultures. In addition, members of each culture were able to evaluate whether items proposed by others could be expressed satisfactorily in their language and whether the content of the item was relevant for their culture. At times we found it was impossible to express certain concepts effectively in all three languages. For example, there is no clear English equivalent for the Japanese word *amae*, which conveys a particular kind of dependent relation between child and adult. Similarly, it is difficult to express in Chinese and Japanese what is meant by such English words as learning disability or tension patterns, terms that have no direct counterparts in the Chinese or Japanese vocabulary. Rather than attempting to approximate the meaning of such terms, we either decided not to include questions involving such terms or to describe situations that did not require their use.

In preparing the interview, we held informal discussions with kindergarten teachers from each culture. This gave us the opportunity to obtain their reactions to the items we devised and to seek their suggestions for additional items. As a final step, the interview was submitted to colleagues in each of the cultures to obtain their criticisms and reactions.

The interview that resulted from this procedure contained both open-ended and objective types of questions. Responses to objective types of questions pose no problems for coding. In order to represent the teachers' responses to the open-ended items, however, it was necessary to construct a coding scheme for each question. We did this by randomly selecting a small sample of responses to each item from each culture and then devising categories that would represent these responses as effectively as possible. A detailed coding manual contained definitions and examples of the types of responses that should be coded under each category. Each interview was coded by two independent coders who were native speakers of the teacher's language. Discrepancies in coding usually could be resolved quite readily by discussions between the two coders, but when serious disagreements arose, the final decision was made at a meeting involving all of the coders. All teachers from the 24 kindergarten classrooms in each location were interviewed individually about a wide variety of topics by a native speaker. Among these were questions about the teacher's perception of a good child, goals for children, and her ideas about homework.

A Good Kindergarten Child. We told the teachers to "think of two or three children you had in recent years who were among the best children in your group. With these children in mind, describe what you think a good kindergarten child should be like." Nearly 70% of the Japanese teachers, 20% of the Chinese teachers, but only 10% of the American teachers spontaneously mentioned prosocial characteristics. However, over 45% of the American teachers, but fewer than 5% of the Japanese and Chinese teachers mentioned something related to learning. Cross-cultural differences in the percentages of teachers who mentioned other characteristics, such as personality, intelligence, and verbal ability, seldom exceeded 10 percent.

Goals for Kindergarten Children. Dramatic cross-cultural differences emerged in teachers' responses to a question about their goals for kindergarten children. Responses to this open-ended question fell primarily into the six major categories depicted in Figure 33–3. American teachers were more likely than Chinese or Japanese teachers to mention cognitive development; Japanese teachers were much more likely than American teachers to mention socialization.

There were other striking differences in the goals teachers held for the children. No Chinese or Japanese kindergarten teacher, but approximately a fifth of the American teachers, mentioned the child's development of a positive self-image and positive attitudes about life. In contrast, no American teacher, but over a third of the Chinese and Japanese teachers, mentioned the child's development of good personal habits.

Homework. In line with their attitudes about cognitive development, 79% of the American teachers, 59% of the Chinese teachers, and 25% of the Japanese teachers indicated that they assigned homework to their students.

From these and other responses of the children's teachers, we are able to construct a picture of the teachers' backgrounds, what they consider to be important in being a good teacher, the problems they face, and the ways they go about preparing for and conducting their classes.

Mothers' Attitudes and Beliefs

The interview for mothers was constructed in the same manner as the interview for teachers. Items came from two sources. Members of the research group devised most of the questions, but we also held informal discussions with mothers from each culture to obtain additional ideas. Again, all items were reviewed by professionals from each culture before any mothers were interviewed.

Mothers of the 288 target children in each location were interviewed about many aspects of their children's lives. Open-ended questions dealt with topics such as expectations about their child's kindergarten experiences, problems their child might have in elementary school, and their child's future education. In addition to open-ended questions, mothers were asked to make ratings of various characteristics of their children. Because most mothers had not had experience in making such

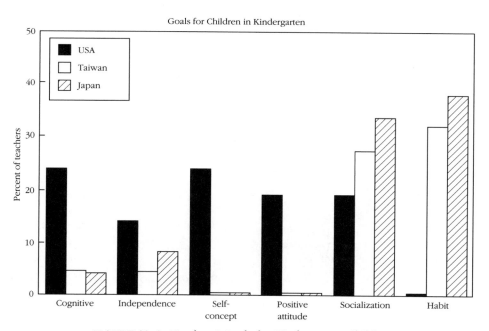

FIGURE 33–3. Teachers' Goals for Kindergarten Children.

ratings, they were carefully instructed about the use of rating scales when the first scale was introduced.

Kindergarten Experiences. Institutions such as kindergartens reflect beliefs and attitudes prevalent in a society. It is no surprise, therefore, that the mothers' attitudes were in accord with kindergarten practices. When asked specifically about the kindergarten experiences they expected their child to receive, the first thing mentioned by 91% of the Japanese mothers was some aspect of social development. The same initial response was expressed by 55% of the Chinese mothers and by 56% of the American mothers.

In contrast, the first thing mentioned by 39% of the American mothers and 35% of the Chinese mothers was that they would like their child to receive some sort of educational preparation, such as learning the basics, having general learning experiences, receiving cognitive stimulation, or getting more information. Among Japanese mothers, only 4% mentioned these types of instruction and 65% specifically said that they did not expect their children to have cognitive learning experiences during kindergarten. The percentages of American and Chinese mothers who failed to mention such cognitive experiences were 24% and 14%, respectively.

Later Problems. Would their child have problems during elementary school? American and Chinese mothers were relatively optimistic; only 29% of the American and 28% of the Chinese mothers anticipated that their child would have problems. Japanese mothers were more pessimistic: 58% said they thought their child would have problems.

The problems mothers anticipated were spread across many domains. Relatively few thought that their child would have difficulty in school because of inadequate preparation or slowness in learning: 11% of the Chinese mothers and even fewer of the American and Japanese mothers (4% and 2%, respectively).

The more frequently anticipated problems were psychological, social, and behavioral. For example, 14% of American and Japanese mothers and 11% of Chinese others believed their child would have a psychological problem such as shyness, anxiety, not being able to sit still, and being easily upset. Social problems, mentioned by 8% of American mothers, 11% of Chinese mothers, and 22% of Japanese mothers, included ability to make friends, aggressiveness, and fighting. Behavioral problems, such as not finishing tasks, not eating lunch, and being messy were mentioned by 6% of American mothers, 7% of Chinese mothers, and 13% of Japanese mothers.

The Japanese mothers' concern about social development and habit training is in accord with the goals expressed by their children's teachers. It is hard to understand, however, why American mothers placed such strong emphasis on academic training when they gave so little evidence of being worried that their children might have difficulties in elementary school.

Future Education. Mothers had high hopes for their children's ultimate educational attainments. Sixty percent of the Japanese, 87% of the Chinese, and 82% of the American mothers said they would like their child to have at least a college education. Far fewer mothers said they would like their child to attend only high school: 22% in Japan, 10% in Taiwan, and 11% in the United States.

In all three cultures, the mothers' aspirations exceeded current rates of actual college attendance. Chinese and Japanese mothers seemed to realize this. When asked if they thought it would be possible for their child to go as far as they hoped, only 54% and 63% of Chinese and Japanese mothers, respectively, agreed that it would be possible. American mothers were more confident: 92% believed their child could achieve their hoped-for level of education.

Why did the mothers think their child would be able to go as far as they hoped? The dominant explanation given by American mothers was in terms of their child's cognitive ability (see Table 33–2). Japanese mothers said that the child's motivation and the social norm would be the deciding factor. Chinese mothers' responses fell between those of the American and Japanese mothers. American mothers also mentioned money and parental involvement more frequently than Asian mothers as reasons their child could attain this level of education.

The data indicate the relative emphasis placed on cognitive ability and motivation as explanations of children's academic achievement in these cultures. From the American perspective, the route to success seems to be that of developing cognitive abilities. For Japanese, success is more dependent on proper motivation. For Chinese, it is both cognitive abilities and motivation.

These explanations help to clarify why American parents and teachers emphasize cognitive experience as the most important component of kindergarten education, whereas Japanese, and to some degree Chinese, parents and teachers, are more likely to view kindergartens as places for pleasant social interaction and play. For Americans, kindergarten is to make their children smart enough and knowledgeable enough to succeed in elementary school. For Asians, kindergarten is to prepare and motivate children for school by providing pleasant experiences that will lead them to think positively about school and learning.

Ratings of Academic and Cognitive Abilities. When the mothers were asked to rate their child's abilities, the average child was rated as above average (see Figure 33–4). Most mothers seemed satisfied that their children were progressing well in reading and arithmetic and that their children had high potential for future academic success. Japanese mothers were the

TABLE 33–2. Mothers' Explanation of Why It Is Possible for Their Child to Go as Far in School as the Mothers Would Like

	United States	Taiwan	Japan
Cognitive	64.5	54.4	17.5
Motivation	31.8	36.8	39.4
Parental involvement	27.3	21.6	15.6
Enough money	28.5	5.6	1.3
Social norm	5.8	4.8	22.5

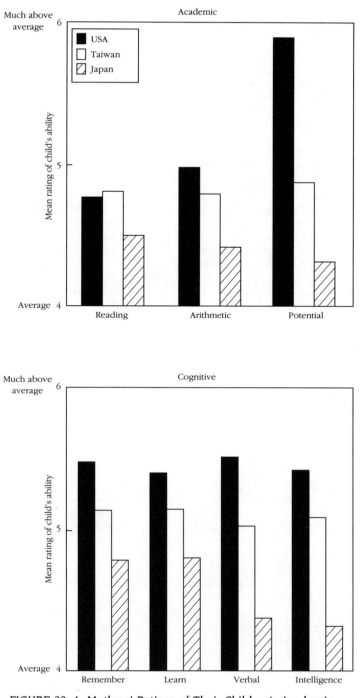

FIGURE 33–4. Mothers' Ratings of Their Children's Academic and Cognitive Abilities.

most modest in making their ratings and American mothers were the least constrained, especially in rating their children's potential for doing well in elementary school.

The ratings of academic achievement are in line with the mothers' positive attitudes when they were asked to rate their children's cognitive abilities. The average child was rated as being above average in ability to learn and remember, and in verbal ability and intelligence. Again, American mothers exceeded the Japanese and Chinese mothers in their enthusiasm about their children's abilities.

CONCLUSIONS

Quantitative Studies of Cross-Cultural Phenomena

The preceding examples from the classroom observations and the interviews with the teachers and mothers suggest that we have much to gain from further studies of the successes and problems in early education in other countries. Surveys, demographic data, and ethnographic studies are valuable sources of ideas, but formal cross-cultural studies have many additional advantages. By using common procedures and by selecting comparable, representative samples of children in all of the cultures being studied, we gain confidence in the reliability of the phenomena revealed and discover new avenues for exploring the social and psychological processes underlying these phenomena.

Subtle differences among cultures and interrelations within a culture may be more readily evident when data can be quantified and subject to statistical analyses. It is possible through such analyses to isolate variables and interactions among variables that might be missed in informal, qualitative studies. Ideally, qualitative and quantitative studies can be complementary, each informing the other about productive new avenues for exploration.

Cross-Cultural Comparison

The observations and interviews project a clear and coherent picture of the profound differences between Asian and Western conceptions of what should be accomplished during the kindergarten year. Asian and Western ideas about educating children of nursery school age are likely to be much more similar than those about educating children of kindergarten age. By the time children reach the age of 5, the cultures have distinctively different conceptions of how group experiences should be structured. Whether revealed by classroom behavior, or by statements of teachers' goals, or by mothers' desires and attitudes, Asian 5- to 6-year-olds are assumed to need continued opportunities for social development and exploration of the world around them, rather than academic training. Adjustment to the group and enjoyment of learning are prized more highly for 5-year-olds than are skills in reading and mathematics. These findings pose an interesting paradox: Asian children, for whom formal learning at kindergarten is deemphasized, obtain higher scores in tests of achievement in reading and mathematics than do American kindergarten children, for whom academic achievement and academic preparation for elementary school are more highly prized.

These and other results we have discussed contradict several commonly held explanations of Asian children's academic superiority. We cannot attribute the higher scores of Asian kindergarten children in reading and mathematics to being taught these subjects in a didactic fashion, to higher intellectual abilities, to being more attentive in class, or to being more familiar with the materials included in the tests. The more likely explanation is that they are offered opportunities to discover, in organized settings, the fundamental operations and properties that underlie the academic subjects they will be studying when they enter elementary school. These experiences, supplemented by parental support and involvement, set the stage for the following year, when formal academic instruction begins.

Implications

We realize that the direct transfer of practices across cultures is unwarranted. Practices develop within cultures over long periods of time, and it is impractical to expect that the same practices will meet the needs of widely divergent societies. Nevertheless, results from cross-cultural studies do lead all of us to examine our own practices in new ways. Just as we depend upon information about other individuals in order to make accurate self-evaluations, information about the practices that exist in other cultures helps us to gain a new perspective about the strengths and weaknesses in the ways we rear and educate children in our own cultures.

Looking at the course kindergarten education has taken during this century makes us ask whether attaching kindergartens to elementary schools in the West has not had the unanticipated effect of reducing their emphasis on social development and heightening the perception that the kindergarten is the logical place for beginning formal education. Western kindergarten teachers appear to adopt many of the practices of elementary school teachers, concentrating more strongly on children's cognitive and academic progress than would be likely if they remained in closer contact with teachers of younger children.

After studying Asian kindergartens, we are forced to ask whether Western educators who advocate early schooling are not suggesting an activity that is inappropriate for children as young as 5 — or even 4, as some have proposed (Kagan & Zigler, 1987). Additional evidence to support or reject this possibility will emerge as we begin further examinations of the practices and correlates of early childhood education in different cultures.

References

Bettleheim, R., & Takanishi, R. (1976). *Early schooling in Asia*. New York: McGraw-Hill.

Boocock, S. S. (1989). Controlled diversity: An overview of the Japanese preschool system. *Journal of Japanese Studies, 15*, 41–65.

Chen, H. C. (1977). *Woguo youer jiaoyu fazhan zhi tujin*. (The pathway of early childhood education in Taiwan.) *Jiaoyu Zhiliao Jikan, 13*, 215–235.

Fujita, M. (1989). Childcare and the socialization of working mothers in Japan. *Journal of Japanese Studies, 15*, 67–92.

Hendry, J. (1986). *Becoming Japanese: The world of the preschool child*. Honolulu: University of Hawaii Press.

Huang, R. S. (1991). *Preschool education in P.R.C. and some comparisons with preschool education in U.S.A.* Unpublished paper, Western Michigan University.

Kagan, S. L., & Zigler, E. F. (1987) *Early schooling: The national debate.* New Haven, CT: Yale University Press.

Kessen, W. (Ed.) (1976). *Childhood in China.* New Haven, CT: Yale University Press.

Lewis, C. C. (1984). Cooperation and control in Japanese nursery schools. *Comparative Education Review, 2,* 69–84.

Liao, G. (1984). *Woguo youzhiyuan zhi jiaoyu xiankuang diaoca yanjiu.* (A survey of the present condition of kindergarten education in our country.) Taipei: Department of Education.

Lynn, R. (1982). IQ in Japan and the United States shows a growing disparity. *Nature, 297,* 222–223.

Mao, L., & Bourgeault, S. E. (1991). Early childhood education and elementary education in Taiwan. In D. C. Smith (Ed.), *The Confucian continuum: Educational modernization in Taiwan* (pp. 65–97). New York: Praeger.

Peak, L. (1986). Training learning skills and attitudes in Japanese early educational settings. In W. Fowler (Ed.), *New directions for child development: No. 32. Early experience and the development of competence* (pp. 111–123). San Francisco: Jossey-Bass.

Peak, L. (1991). *Learning to go to school in Japan.* Berkeley: University of California Press.

Renminribao (People's Daily), 1991, May 28.

Republic of China Department of Education. (1991). *The educational statistics of the Republic of China.* Taipei: Department of Education.

Ross, E. D. (1976). *The kindergarten crusade: The establishment of preschool education in the United States.* Athens: Ohio University Press.

Sakamoto, H. (1968). *Explanation of kindergarten: Education outline.* Tokyo: Fureberukai.

Sano, T. (1989). Methods of social control and socialization in Japanese day care centers. *Journal of Japanese Studies, 15,* 125–138.

Seagoe, M. Y., & Murakami, K. A. (1961). A comparative study of children's play in America and Japan. *California Journal of Education Research, 11,* 124–130.

Shiragaki, I. S. (1983). Child care practices in Japan and the United States: How do they reflect cultural values of young children? *Young Children, 38,* 13–24.

Spodek, B. (1989). Chinese kindergarten education and its reform. *Early Childhood Research Quarterly, 4,* 31–50.

Stevenson, H. W. (1990). Adapting to school: Children in Beijing and Chicago. *Annual Report, Center for Advanced Study in the Behavioral Sciences.* Stanford, CA: Center for Advanced Study in the Behavioral Sciences.

Stevenson, H. W., Lee, S. Y., Chen, C., Lummis, M., Stigler, J., Liu, F., & Fang, G. (1990). Mathematics achievement of children in China and the United States. *Child Development, 61,* 1053–1066.

Stevenson, H. W., Lee, S. Y., Chen, C., Stigler, J. W., Hsu, C. C., & Kitamura, S. (1990). Contexts of achievement. *Monographs of the Society for Research in Child Development, 55,* (1–2, Serial No. 221).

Stevenson, H. W., Lee, S. Y., & Stigler, J. W. (1986). Mathematics achievement in Chinese, Japanese, and American children. *Science, 231,* 693–699.

Stevenson, H. W., Stigler, J. W., Lee, S. Y., Lucker, G. W., Kitamura, S., & Hsu, C. C. (1985). Cognitive performance and academic achievement of Japanese, Chinese, and American children. *Child Development, 56,* 718–734.

Su, C. W. (1984). *Taiwan sheng tuoersuo xiankuang diaocha baogao.* (A survey of the present condition of nursery schools in Taiwan.) Taipei: Taiwan Provincial Government.

Tsai, C. M. (1988). *Jin sishi nian lai woguo youer jiaoyu shizhi zhi peiyang.* (The training of the preschool teachers of our country in the recent forty years.) *Jiaoyu Zhiliao Jikan, 13,* 41–61.

Tobin, J. J., Wu, D. Y. H., & Davidson, D. H. (1989). *Preschool in three cultures: Japan, China, and the United States.* New Haven, CT: Yale University Press.

Xin Yi Foundation. (1985). *Taibei Shi youzhiyuan tuoersuo xiankuang fangwen diaoca zhi fenxi baogao.* (A report of the investigation of the present condition of kindergarten and nursery schools in Taipei.) Taipei: Xin Yi Foundation.

Youeryuan jiaoyu gangyao. (Keypoints of kindergarten education.) (1981). Beijing: Department of Education.

Zhong, S. H. (1989). Young children's care and education in the People's Republic of China. In P. P. Olmsted & D. P. Weikart (Eds.), *How nations serve young children: Profiles of childcare and education in 14 countries* (pp. 241–254). Ypsilanti, MI: High/Scope Press.

NAME INDEX

SUBJECT INDEX